MILEAGE CHART

10 = Distance in miles
10 = Distance in kilometers

	New York City	Washington, DC	Chicago	Miami	New Orleans	Dallas	Denver	Seattle	San Francisco
WASHINGTON, DC	**233** 375								
CHICAGO	**779** 1253	**688** 1107							
MIAMI	**1286** 2069	**1050** 1689	**1371** 2206						
NEW ORLEANS	**1300** 2092	**1073** 1726	**922** 1483	**856** 1377					
DALLAS	**1541** 2479	**1315** 2116	**921** 1482	**1349** 2171	**515** 829				
DENVER	**1793** 2885	**1669** 2685	**994** 1599	**2079** 3345	**1390** 2237	**878** 1413			
SEATTLE	**2816** 4531	**2725** 4385	**2030** 3266	**3329** 5356	**2690** 4328	**2178** 3504	**1306** 2101		
SAN FRANCISCO	**2873** 4623	**2782** 4476	**2106** 3389	**3106** 4998	**2272** 3656	**1729** 2782	**1248** 2008	**801** 1289	
LOS ANGELES	**2763** 4444	**2640** 4248	**1989** 3200	**2736** 4402	**1902** 3060	**1445** 2325	**998** 1606	**1131** 1820	**38** 61

EYEWITNESS TRAVEL

USA

EYEWITNESS TRAVEL

USA

DK

LONDON, NEW YORK,
MELBOURNE, MUNICH AND DELHI
www.dk.com

MANAGING EDITOR Aruna Ghose
ART EDITOR Benu Joshi
PROJECT EDITOR Vandana Mohindra
EDITORS Kajori Aikat, Rimli Borooah,
Nandini Mehta, Manjari Rathi
DESIGNERS Pallavi Narain, Supriya Sahai, Priyanka Thakur
SENIOR CARTOGRAPHER Uma Bhattacharya
CARTOGRAPHER Alok Pathak
PICTURE RESEARCHER Taiyaba Khatoon
ADDITIONAL PICTURE RESEARCH Kiran K. Mohan
DTP COORDINATOR Shailesh Sharma
DTP DESIGNER Vinod Harish
US EDITOR Mary Sutherland

MAIN CONTRIBUTORS
Jackie Finch, Andrew Hempstead, Jamie Jensen, Nancy Mikula, Joanne Miller, Eric Peterson, Kevin Roe, Kap Stann

MAIN PHOTOGRAPHERS
Andy Holligan, Jon Spaull, Peter Wilson

MAIN ILLUSTRATORS
Arun P, Gautam Trivedi

Reproduced by Colourscan (Singapore)
Printed and bound by South China Printing Co. Ltd. (China)

First published in Great Britain in 2004
by Dorling Kindersley Limited
80 Strand, London WC2R 0RL

Reprinted with revisions 2006, 2008, 2010

A CIP CATALOGUE RECORD IS AVAILABLE FROM THE BRITISH LIBRARY.

ISBN 978 1 40534 839 3

FLOORS ARE REFERRED TO THROUGHOUT IN ACCORDANCE WITH AMERICAN USAGE; IE THE "FIRST FLOOR" IS THE FLOOR AT GROUND LEVEL.

Front cover main image: View of the Golden Gate Bridge, California

MIX
Paper from responsible sources
FSC www.fsc.org FSC™ C018179

The information in this
DK Eyewitness Travel Guide is checked regularly.

Every effort has been made to ensure that this book is as up-to-date as possible at the time of going to press. Some details, however, such as telephone numbers, opening hours, prices, gallery hanging arrangements and travel information are liable to change. The publishers cannot accept responsibility for any consequences arising from the use of this book, nor for any material on third party websites, and cannot guarantee that any website address in this book will be a suitable source of travel information. We value the views and suggestions of our readers very highly. Please write to: Publisher, DK Eyewitness Travel Guides, Dorling Kindersley, 80 Strand, London, WC2R 0RL, Great Britain.

Statuary, Grand Central Terminal, New York City

CONTENTS

HOW TO USE THIS GUIDE **6**

VISITING THE USA

PUTTING THE USA ON THE MAP **10**

PRACTICAL & TRAVEL INFORMATION **12**

USA AT A GLANCE

USA THROUGH THE YEAR **28**

NATIONAL PARKS **34**

GREAT AMERICAN CITIES **38**

BEST SCENIC ROUTES **40**

THE HISTORY OF THE USA **42**

NYC & THE MID-ATLANTIC REGION

NEW YORK CITY **64**

NEW YORK STATE **90**

NEW JERSEY **96**

PHILADELPHIA, PA **98**

PENNSYLVANIA, **106**

NEW ENGLAND

BOSTON **132**

MASSACHUSETTS **150**

◁ **Utah's Bryce Canyon, with its series of deep amphitheaters filled with flame-colored rock formations**

RHODE ISLAND 154
CONNECTICUT 158
VERMONT 162
NEW HAMPSHIRE 166
MAINE 170

Nighttime view of the US Capitol in Washington, DC

WASHINGTON, DC & THE CAPITAL REGION

WASHINGTON, DC 194
VIRGINIA 212
WEST VIRGINIA 220
MARYLAND 222
DELAWARE 226

THE SOUTHEAST

NORTH CAROLINA 248
SOUTH CAROLINA 252
GEORGIA 256
TENNESSEE 262
KENTUCKY 268

FLORIDA

MIAMI 290

THE DEEP SOUTH

NEW ORLEANS 344
LOUISIANA 354
ARKANSAS 358
MISSISSIPPI 360
ALABAMA 364

THE GREAT LAKES

CHICAGO 386
ILLINOIS 398
INDIANA 400
OHIO 404
MICHIGAN 408
WISCONSIN 412
MINNESOTA 416

THE GREAT PLAINS

NORTH DAKOTA 442
SOUTH DAKOTA 444
NEBRASKA 448
IOWA 452
MISSOURI 454
KANSAS 458
OKLAHOMA 460

TEXAS

TEXAS 474

THE SOUTHWEST

NEVADA 510
UTAH 518
ARIZONA 528
NEW MEXICO 544

THE ROCKIES

IDAHO 574
MONTANA 578
WYOMING 582
COLORADO 588

THE PACIFIC NORTHWEST

WASHINGTON 616
OREGON 630

CALIFORNIA

LOS ANGELES 658
SAN FRANCISCO 694

ALASKA & HAWAI'I

ALASKA 732
HAWAI'I 744
GENERAL INDEX 764
ACKNOWLEDGMENTS 794

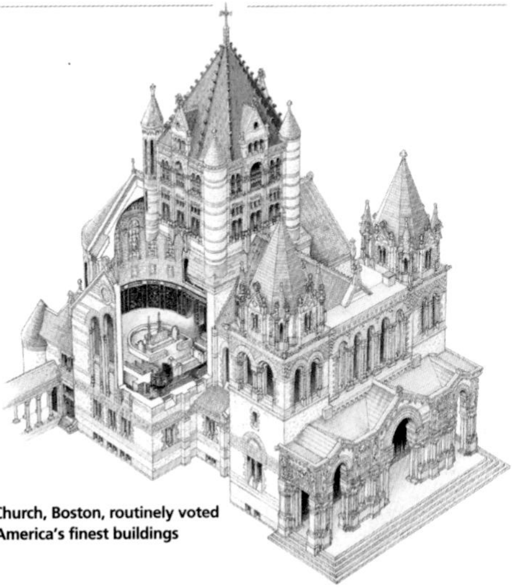

Trinity Church, Boston, routinely voted one of America's finest buildings

HOW TO USE THIS GUIDE

This guide helps you to get the most from your visit to the United States. *Visiting the USA* maps the country and gives tips on practical considerations and travel. *USA at a Glance* gives an overview of some of the main attractions and a brief history of the country. The book is divided into 14 regional sections, each covering from one to seven states. The chapter on each region starts with a historical portrait and a map of the area. The main sightseeing section then follows and includes maps of the major cities. For each region there is a section of practical and travel information, followed by listings of recommended hotels and restaurants.

USA MAP
The colored areas shown on the map on the inside front cover indicate the 14 regional chapters in this guide.

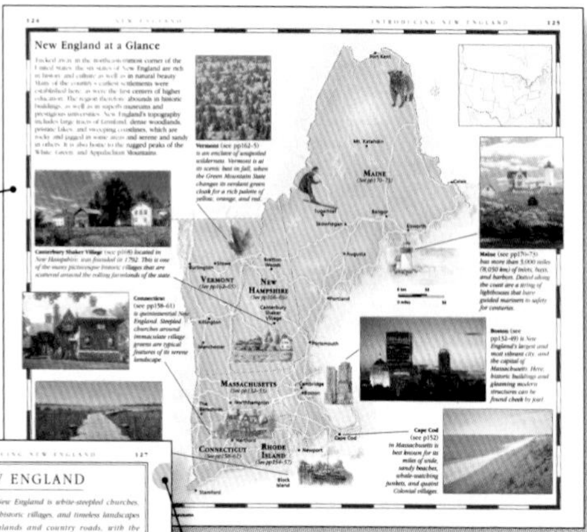

1 At a Glance
The map here highlights the different states in each section as well as the most interesting cities, towns, and regions.

Each region chapter has color-coded thumb tabs.

2 Introduction to a Region
This section gives the reader an insight into the region's geography, historical background, politics, and the character of the people. A chart lists the key dates and events in the region's history.

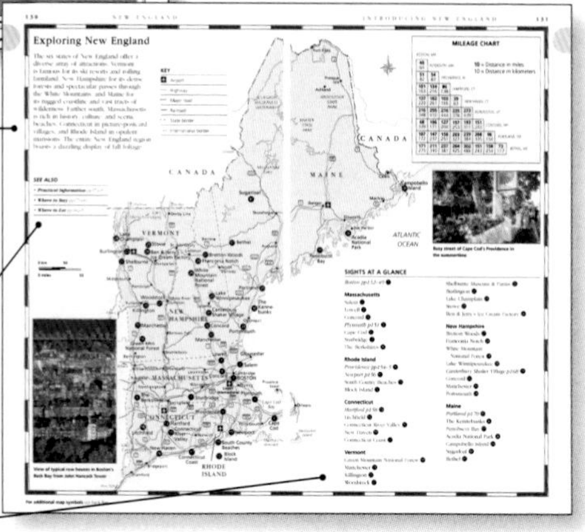

3 Regional Map
For easy reference, sights in each region are numbered and plotted on a map. The black bullet numbers (eg. ❸) also indicate the order in which the sights are covered in the chapter.

For each region there is an index of the practical and listings pages at the end of the chapter.

Sights at a Glance lists the numbered sights in sequential order.

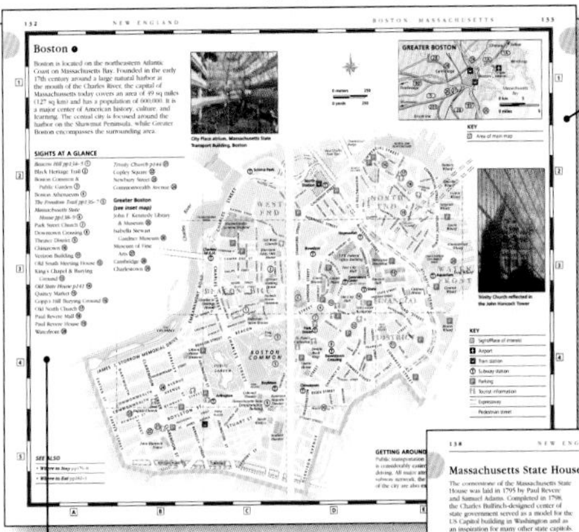

4 City Map

This plots individual sights within the most important cities. The sights within a city such as Boston are indicated with clear bullet numbers (eg. ③), in contrast to the black bullets used on the regional maps.

Visitors' Checklist gives all the practical information needed to plan your visit.

Sights at a Glance lists the numbered sights within the city.

5 Major Sights

Historic buildings are dissected to reveal their interiors, while museums and galleries have color-coded floor plans to help you find the most important exhibits.

Stars indicate the features that no visitor should miss.

6 Detailed Information

Cities, towns, and other sights are described individually. Their entries appear in the same order as the numbering on the regional map at the beginning of the section.

Each entry begins with essential practical information, including the address and telephone number of the local tourist information office. Opening times are given for major sights and museums.

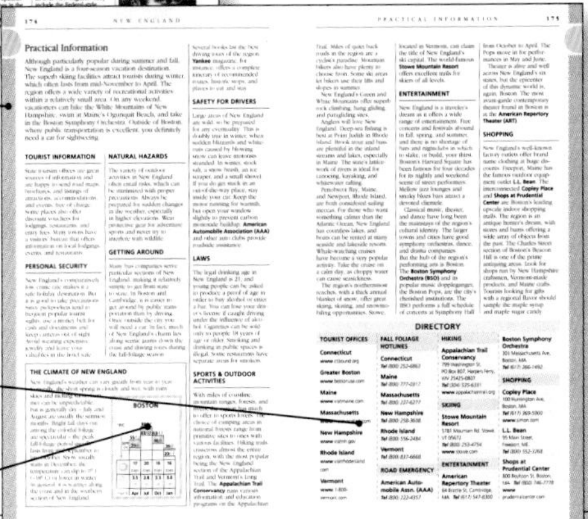

7 Practical Information

This section covers subjects such as travel, security, shopping, and entertainment. Some cities, such as New York, are covered separately.

Directory boxes give contact information for the services and venues mentioned in the text.

Climate charts are also provided for each region.

GUSTAFSON'S
MOTEL
RESTAURANT
SELF SERVE
IT'S LIKE MONEY IN THE TANK

VISITING THE USA

PUTTING THE USA ON THE MAP 10–11
PRACTICAL INFORMATION 12–19
TRAVEL INFORMATION 20–25

Putting the USA on the Map

Spreading over 3,000 miles (4,800 km) east to west between the Atlantic and Pacific Oceans, the United States covers the heart of the North American continent and has a population of 304 million people. Bordered by Mexico to the south and Canada to the north, it extends for over 1,500 miles (2,414 km), covering more than 3.5 million sq miles (9 million sq km), and includes climates from the tropics to the Arctic Circle. The continental US is divided into 48 states. These, together with the two states, Alaska in the extreme northwest, and the islands of Hawai'i in the Pacific Ocean, compose the 50 United States of America. The national capital is Washington, DC, a small federal district located between the states of Maryland and Virginia.

◁ **Gustafson's Motel in Brevort in Michigan's Upper Peninsula**

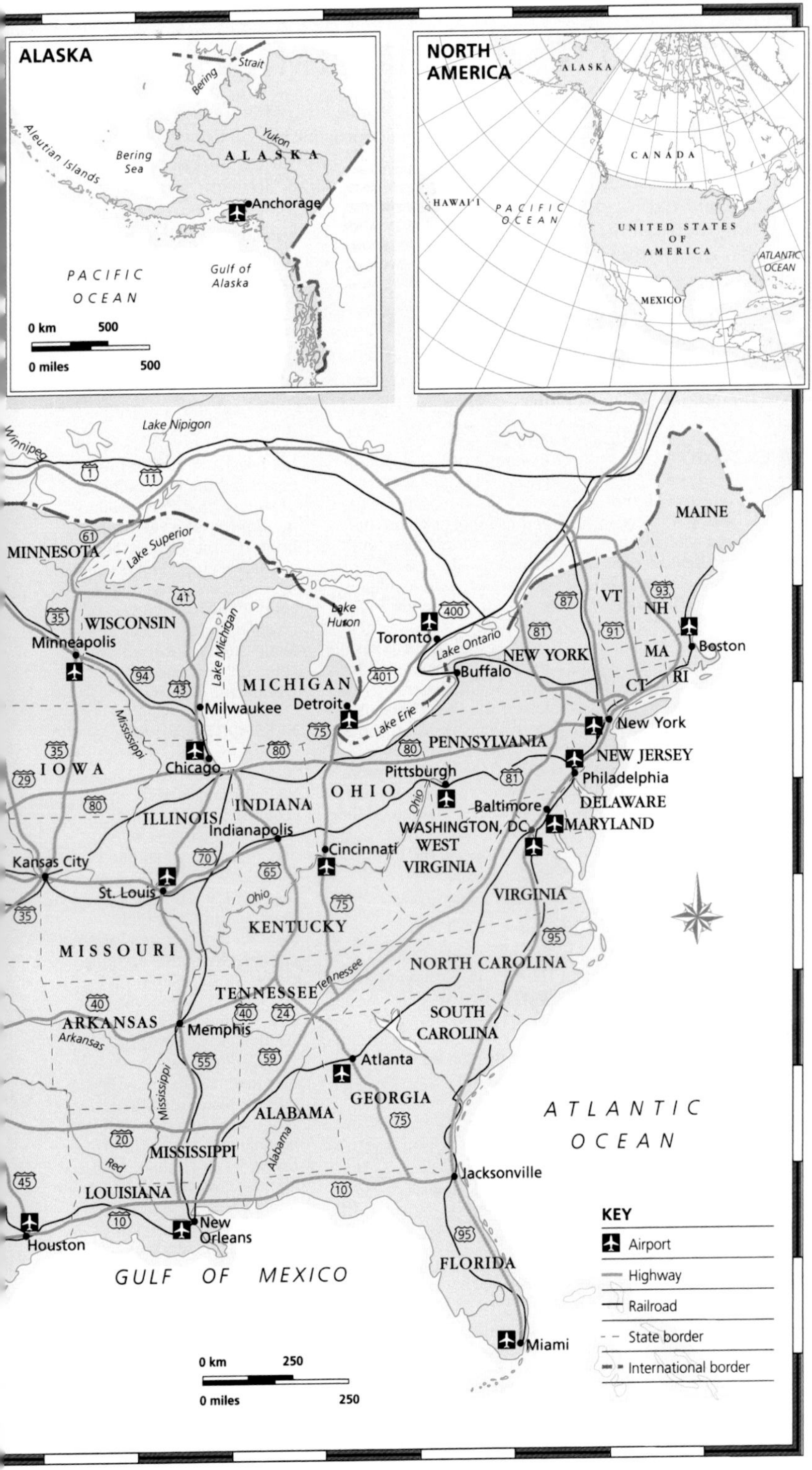
ALASKA
Bering Strait
Aleutian Islands
Bering Sea
Yukon
ALASKA
Anchorage
PACIFIC OCEAN
Gulf of Alaska
0 km 500
0 miles 500
NORTH AMERICA
ALASKA
CANADA
HAWAI'I
PACIFIC OCEAN
UNITED STATES OF AMERICA
ATLANTIC OCEAN
MEXICO
Lake Nipigon
Winnipeg
Lake Superior
MINNESOTA
WISCONSIN
Minneapolis
Lake Michigan
Lake Huron
MICHIGAN
Milwaukee
Detroit
Toronto
Lake Ontario
Lake Erie
Buffalo
NEW YORK
MAINE
VT
NH
MA
CT
RI
Boston
New York
IOWA
Chicago
PENNSYLVANIA
NEW JERSEY
Pittsburgh
Philadelphia
ILLINOIS
INDIANA
OHIO
Baltimore
DELAWARE
Indianapolis
WASHINGTON, DC
MARYLAND
Kansas City
Cincinnati
WEST VIRGINIA
St. Louis
Ohio
VIRGINIA
KENTUCKY
MISSOURI
NORTH CAROLINA
TENNESSEE
Tennessee
ARKANSAS
Arkansas
Memphis
SOUTH CAROLINA
Atlanta
Mississippi
GEORGIA
ALABAMA
Alabama
ATLANTIC OCEAN
MISSISSIPPI
Red
Jacksonville
LOUISIANA
Houston
New Orleans
GULF OF MEXICO
FLORIDA
Miami
0 km 250
0 miles 250
KEY
Airport
Highway
Railroad
State border
International border

PRACTICAL INFORMATION

Millions of visitors travel to the US from around the world every year, and millions of Americans also spend their leisure time exploring and enjoying their country. The nation's richly diverse history, culture, art, and landscape, as well as its tradition of hospitality and service, makes traveling in the US both enjoyable and stress-free. In all parts of the country, tourist facilities are generally of a very high standard. This section gives some basic information on the various transportation and accommodation options available. It deals with issues such as passport and visa formalities, travel insurance, banking, communications, and health care. This section covers the country as a whole, but more specific information is provided in subsequent *Practical Information* sections at the end of each regional chapter.

Flag of the United States of America

WHEN TO GO

The best time to visit the US depends on a visitor's interests and itinerary. It is important to time your visit carefully, because the country's geography and weather patterns vary greatly from region to region, even at the same time of the year. Summer is generally the warmest and most popular time to travel, especially to the northern areas. Summer in the southern parts, especially in the deserts of the Southwest, can be unbearably hot, while in New England they are generally cool and pleasant. All over the country, the summer months are when children are out of school and on vacation, so most resort areas and national parks are full to capacity during these times. Summer is also the time when numerous outdoor cultural events, fairs, and festivals take place.

Spring can be the best time to visit the Rockies and the Deep South; the crowds are fewer, and discounts are often available. April and May in particular are ideal times to experience the wildflowers and gardens of the southern US. Fall is another good time to travel, since the leaves on the trees in the mountain forests, particularly in the northeast, are at their peak of color, and the high humidity of summer has decreased to more pleasant levels. Winter brings on the greatest diversity of weather, ranging from heavy snows in the winter sports capitals of New England and the Rocky Moun- tains, to tropical sunshine on the beaches of Florida and Hawai'i.

THE CLIMATE OF THE USA

Given the sheer vastness of its size, the United States is characterized by a diversity of climates. In addition to the many regional variations, the country also experiences dramatically shifting weather patterns, produced mostly by the Pacific westerlies that sweep across the entire continent. The *Practical Information* section for each region contains a panel like the one below.

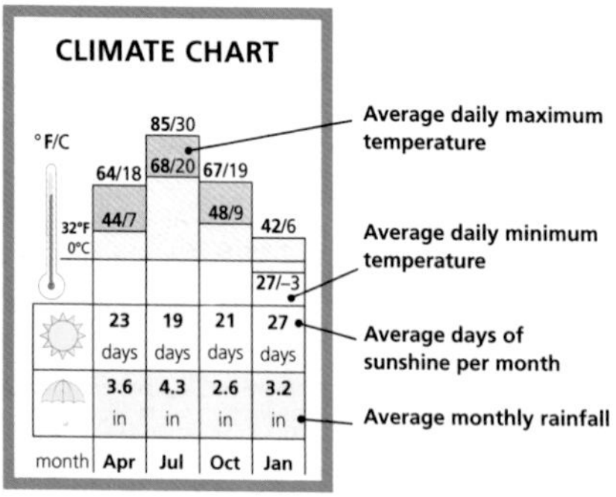

PASSPORT & VISAS

All travelers to the US, including returning Americans, are required to hold a valid passport, regardless of their age. Passports should be valid for at least six months longer than the last date you expect to remain in the country. Visas are not required for citizens of Canada, Australia, or the UK if the visit is for less than 90 days. Some form of government-issued photo ID, though, is required.

Citizens of many countries may take part in the "visa waiver" plan, using the ESTA form, which must be completed online at least 72 hours before travel at https://esta.chp.dhs.gov. However, due to increased security measures, it is wise to confirm visa requirements with the US embassy before traveling. Check with a travel agent for the latest requirements.

Travelers interested in studying, working, or staying for a longer period than the stated 90 days should request special visas from the nearest US embassy. If you are in the US and need to extend your stay, you should contact the nearest office of the **Bureau of Citizenship and Immigration Services** *(see p17)* in the US, and apply for an extension. Failure to do so may result in a fine or deportation.

CUSTOMS ALLOWANCES & DUTY-FREE

All visitors to the US are required to complete a Customs Declaration before entering the country. On this form, which is available from airlines and customs officials upon arrival, you must state the value of any goods being brought into the US, and you may be charged duty on especially valuable items. Travelers are allowed to bring small quantities of tobacco and alcohol along with them, but certain goods are forbidden. These include meat products, plants or seeds, Cuban cigars, and ancient cultural artifacts. When you leave the US, make sure that you are aware of the duty-free allowances for tobacco products (200 cigarettes for each person over 18 years old), and for alcoholic beverages (0.2 gallons or one liter of spirits for each person over 21). No meat products, plants, seeds, fruits, or firearms may be taken out of the US.

PLANNING THE TRIP

Since the country is so large and diverse, it is essential to plan ahead in order to make the most of your time in the US. Following a logical, efficient itinerary, and allowing enough time to get between places to enjoy them are two of the most important concerns. Also, bear in mind that the US is divided into six time zones *(see p20)*. All of the states and major cities offer a variety of information which can be ordered in advance over the telephone or accessed via web sites. A particularly useful web site is **www.discoveramerica.com**. Local bookstores are also a valuable source of travel information, as are municipal libraries, travel agencies, and local and regional tourism bureaus across the country.

PUBLIC HOLIDAYS

New Year's Day (Jan 1)
Martin Luther King Jr. Day (3rd Mon in Jan)
Presidents' Day (3rd Mon in Feb)
Memorial Day (last weekend in May)
Independence Day (Jul 4)
Labor Day (1st Mon in Sep)
Columbus Day (2nd weekend in Oct)
Veterans' Day (Nov 11)
Thanksgiving (4th Thu in Nov)
Christmas Day (Dec 25)

CHILDREN

Children are welcomed everywhere, and an amazing number of attractions exist primarily for the enjoyment of young people. From amusement parks and aquariums to national parks and children's museums, their enjoyment is catered to all over the US.

Most restaurants have special children's menus, with simple foods, smaller portions, and lower prices. For a small charge, most lodgings will provide an extra bed or crib *(see p19)*, and many hotels or motels have adjoining or connecting rooms available especially for families. The main exceptions to kid-friendly status are some bed-and-breakfast accommodations, certain gourmet restaurants in the larger cities, as well as those deluxe resorts that focus on providing relaxing escapes or luxurious spa-like pampering to their guests. Restaurants and lodgings that welcome children are marked in the chapter-by-chapter listings.

SENIOR CITIZENS

Older travelers, or "seniors," make up a fairly large proportion of the traveling public, and most hotels and other establishments offer discounts and special services to attract them. Visitors over the age of 50 can contact the **American Association of Retired Persons** or AARP *(see p17)* to request a membership, which costs about $13 per year. ElderHostel and a few other organizations cater to seniors who enjoy traveling both in and outside the US.

CONVERSION CHART

US Standard to Metric
1 inch = 2.54 centimeters
1 foot = 30 centimeters
1 mile = 1.6 kilometers
1 ounce = 28 grams
1 pound = 454 grams
1 US pint = 0.5 liter
1 US quart = 0.947 liter
1 US gallon = 3.8 liters

Metric to US Standard
1 centimeter = 0.4 inch
1 meter = 3 feet 3 inches
1 kilometer = 0.6 miles
1 gram = 0.04 ounce
1 kilogram = 2.2 pounds
1 liter = 1.1 US quarts

DISABLED TRAVELERS

Disabled travelers will find traveling easy in the US, because the country has initiatives aimed at providing "barrier-free" access throughout. The Americans with Disabilities Act (ADA) requires most public buildings, including museums, hotels, and restaurants, to make their services and facilities accessible to all people, including those using wheelchairs. However, it is mostly only the newer hotels that have handicap-accessible bathrooms *(see p19)*. Two of the many organizations in the country that will help disabled visitors plan and enjoy their trips are **The Guided Tour Inc** (215-782-1370/ www.guidedtour.com) and **Care Vacations** (780-986-6404/www.carevacations.com). Hotels that offer facilities for disabled tourists are marked in the "Where to Stay" listings at the end of each regional section. For restaurants that offer similar facilities, look at the restaurant listings for the wheelchair access symbol.

Communications & Banking

Any bank in the US can accept transfer of funds from foreign banks. Many travelers already use credit cards or "automated teller" (ATM) cash/debit cards, so getting money from a bank or ATM should be relatively simple. It's best to buy traveler's checks in US dollar amounts before entering the country in order to avoid delays and extra charges. The country offers excellent telephone and mail services; cell phones and public Internet cafés have made keeping in touch easier and less expensive than ever, and most hotels also offer Internet hookups.

TELEPHONES

Many companies offer telephone services in the US at varying rates. Most public pay phones accept coins, but calls can also be charged to a credit card. Local calls cost between 25 cents and $1, with additional charges for longer calls. Some hotels offer guests free local calls, but some levy hefty charges per call, so check ahead. Making international calls is very expensive. Consider using a prepaid calling card for lowest rates on overseas calls. Tri-band and quad-band cell phones may work in the US, with best rates available by buying a SIM chip for a US carrier. Prepaid cell phones are also an option. Many car rental companies also rent cell phones for customers.

REACHING THE RIGHT NUMBER

- The international code for the US is 1.
- For long distance calls within the US or to Canada: dial 1, the 3-digit area code, and the 7-digit local number.
- For local calls: dial the 7- or 10-digit local number.
- International direct-dial call: dial **011** followed by country code (UK: **44**; Australia: **61**; New Zealand: **64**; South Africa: **27**) then the city or area code (omit the first 0) and then the local number.
- International call via the operator: dial **01**, followed by country code, then city code (without the first 0), and then the local number.
- For operator assistance: dial **0**.
- An **800, 888, 877**, or **866** prefix indicates a free call.
- Directory inquiries: dial **411**.
- **For emergencies: dial 911**.

POSTAL SERVICES

Post offices are open from 9am to 5pm (weekdays) with some open on Saturday mornings. Postcards and letters can be dropped into big blue mailboxes on street corners. Domestic mail should include the five-digit zip code. Rates for international mail vary, so buy stamps from a local post office. To receive mail, General Delivery service is available, whereby letters are held for you at a specific post office for 30 days. Mail forwarding services also exist for a fee.

INTERNET ACCESS

Local libraries, shopping malls, hotels, and university hangouts are perhaps the least expensive and easiest places to access the Internet. Most library computers will let you send e-mail and surf the web. Many large cities have designated stores that offer Internet access for a small fee.

BANKING

Banks can be found in all US cities and towns, and many have service centers in supermarkets and malls. Other financial institutions such as savings-and-loans and credit unions also offer banking services. Traveler's checks can be cashed as long as you have your passport. Banks also give cash advances against credit cards, but card companies charge a high fee for this service. Most banks will not exchange foreign currency. Banking hours are 9am to 4pm, weekdays, but some banks remain open till 6pm on Fridays, and some open on Saturday mornings as well.

DIRECTORY

FINANCIAL SERVICES

Travelex
Tel (800) 287-7362.

Thomas Cook Refund Assistance
Tel (800) 223-7373.

American Express Travel Service
Tel (415) 536-2600.

American Express Helpline
Tel (800) 221-7282.

Cirrus/Mastercard
Tel (800) 424-7787.

Visa Plus
Tel (800) 843-7587.

AUTOMATED TELLER MACHINES

Almost all banks have 24-hour ATMs, as do most train stations, airports, and malls. ATMs are connected to a number of bank-card networks and can dispense cash from accounts held in other states or countries. The primary US bank-card networks are **Visa Plus, Cirrus/Mastercard**, **Star**, and **Interlink**. Be sure that your bank permits international cash withdrawals, and that your card and personal identification number (PIN) are compatible with US machines. Many ATMs charge a fee of $1 to $2.50 per transaction. Exchange rates, however, are better than those for traveler's checks or foreign currency.

CREDIT CARDS

The most commonly accepted credit cards are VISA, MasterCard, American Express, Japanese Credit Bureau (JCB),

Discover, and Diners Club (DC). Credit cards can be used in hotels, restaurants, stores, and to pay for such services as medical care or car rental. Having a credit card will make your stay much easier, and the exchange rates on cards are often better than those for traveler's checks or currency.

TRAVELER'S CHECKS

The most widely accepted traveler's checks are those issued by American Express and Thomas Cook in US dollars. It is easier to pay for purchases with traveler's checks and get cash as change, than go to the trouble of cashing the checks at a bank. Buy checks in a variety of denominations, with $10, $20, and $50 bills. It can be difficult to cash $100 bills except at a bank. Foreign currency checks are not accepted, and out-of-state checks are difficult to cash. Contact **Thomas Cook Refund Assistance** or **American Express Helpline** for lost, stolen, or destroyed traveler's checks.

FOREIGN EXCHANGE

Try to change your money into US denominations before traveling to the US. You may find it difficult to exchange foreign currency except in international airport terminals in major cities. The main foreign exchange companies in the US are American Express and Travelex. If you are in the need of ready cash, you can always visit a duty-free shop and buy something so that you can cash a traveler's check.

10-cent coin (a dime)

5-cent coin (a nickel)

1-dollar coin

25-cent coin (a quarter)

Coins
American coins come in 1-dollar, and 50-, 25-, 10-, 5-, and 1-cent pieces. 1-cent pieces are popularly called pennies, 5-cent are nickels, 10-cent are dimes, and 25-cent pieces are quarters.

Bank Notes
Units of currency are dollars and cents; 100 cents make a dollar. Notes (bills) come in $1, $5, $10, $20, $50, and $100s. All bills were once green, which made it hard to differentiate between them, now only the $1 bill is completely green.

Health & Security

The United States does not have a national health service, and health care, though excellent, is operated for the most part by the private sector, making it extremely expensive. Medical travel insurance is highly recommended in order to defer some of the costs related to an accident or sudden illness. In terms of safety, some of the larger urban areas have a higher crime rate than rural locations, so a few basic precautions are necessary for a trouble-free visit. Be sure to check with friends or hotel staff about which parts of town are best avoided.

PERSONAL SAFETY

While most places on the tourist trail are reasonably safe to travel, visitors should nonetheless take safety precautions to avoid being a victim of crime. Generally speaking, most crimes occur in neighborhoods or areas not frequented by travelers. It is always a good idea to steer clear of neighborhoods that are off the beaten track. Avoid wearing expensive jewelry, carry only small amounts of cash, wear a money belt under clothing, and always carry cameras or camcorders securely.

MONEY

Carry only small amounts of cash, and keep credit cards in a money belt rather than a backpack or trouser pocket. The safest way of carrying money is in the form of traveler's checks, which allow you to keep your hard cash to a minimum. Always use ATM machines during the day or on busy, well-lit streets.

HOTEL SAFETY

Theft from hotel rooms is uncommon, but it is best not to leave valuables out when you leave the room. Consider placing them, and any large amounts of cash, in the hotel safe, a service that is usually free of charge. While in your room, use the deadbolt lock for additional safety, and take time to familiarize yourself with the nearest emergency exits and fire escape routes. Never allow strangers into your hotel room or give them details of where you are staying.

SECURITY IN YOUR CAR

A rental car can serve as a convenient place to store your new purchases. However, it is also a magnet for criminals, especially in parking areas at major sites or hiking trails. Always lock your car when you leave it, and place suitcases and valuables in the trunk. Expensive items such as cameras left out in the open or in an unlocked car are easy targets for smash-and-grab thieves. Use hotel parking garages for overnight.

KEEPING VALUABLES & DOCUMENTS SAFE

Before you leave home, make photocopies of important documents such as passport and visa, and bring one copy with you and leave another in a safe place or with a friend. Do the same for the serial numbers of your traveler's checks and credit cards, in the event they are stolen or lost. All important documents and wallet should be kept in a money belt.

OUTDOOR SAFETY

Participating in outdoor recreational activities can entail certain risks, which can be minimized by taking proper precautions. For activities such as mountain biking, rock-climbing, white-water river-rafting, or motorcycling, wearing helmets and other protective devices are essential. Always wear a life-jacket when canoeing or sailing. Desert and high altitude travelers should wear hats and sunscreen, and drink plenty of water to avoid dehydration. In desert areas, be sure to take a first-aid kit, extra gasoline, and a tool kit for your vehicle, and always carry a cell phone.

Hikers should always be prepared for sudden weather changes, especially at higher elevations. Stay on marked trails, and if camping or hiking alone, it's best to notify someone of your plans, destination, and estimated time of arrival. Many trails have sign-in sheets where you mark the start and completion of your hike or campout. In forested areas, hikers should wear bright-colored clothes and avoid off-trail forests and fields during hunting season.

INSECTS & ANIMALS

Outdoor enthusiasts should be wary of dangerous animals in wilderness areas. Be especially careful in bear country, as attacks have become more frequent. A wise precaution is never to feed animals, or interfere with any wildlife. Insect stings and bites are an annoyance but are not usually life-threatening. Black flies, mosquitos, and deer flies are a nuisance, so be sure to carry insect repellant. Also, carry a snakebite or first aid kit if going into snake country. If bitten by a snake or scorpion, seek medical help immediately.

Try to avoid contact with allergenic plants such as poison ivy or poison oak. In the wild drinking water should always be treated or boiled to combat water-borne bacteria.

SAFETY IN WATER

If possible, surfers and ocean swimmers should stay in areas with lifeguards on duty. If you are not used to dangerous currents, avoid unguarded beaches. Whether or not you are an experienced swimmer, pay attention to the lifeguards and the overall condition of the lake or ocean water. Never swim alone, and watch out for surfers, waterskiers, motorboats, and jet skis. Keep an especially close eye on children at all times.

PREVENTING FOREST FIRES

While hiking in wilderness areas, be very careful lighting campfires. Since firewood is scarce, and forest fires start very quickly, always check whether campfires are allowed where you are camping. Make sure to extinguish all fires carefully and completely. A fire that still smokes is not out.

REPORTING LOST & STOLEN PROPERTY

Although the chances of recovering lost or stolen property are very slim, it is a good idea to report all missing items (including your car) to the police. Most public transportation companies, such as taxi firms, buses, subways, and airlines, operate Lost and Found departments, which can be reached by phoning their general access number. It is useful to have a record of your valuables' serial numbers and a receipt of purchase. Be sure to ask for a copy of the police report for your insurance claim. For lost or stolen credit cards or traveler's checks, contact **American Express** *(see also p15)*.

POLICE

Most law enforcement in the US is handled at the state and local government level. State troopers and the State Highway Patrol deal with traffic accidents and offenses outside city boundaries. County police and sheriffs patrol rural areas, small towns, and villages.

Law enforcement officers carry handguns and other weapons, and should always be treated with respect and courtesy. The officers are usually friendly, helpful, and interested in your safety. In the wake of the 2001 terrorist attacks, National Transportation Security Administration officials are stationed in all US airports, train stations, bus terminals, and large, crowded venues. They provide passenger screening, crowd control, and other services.

On federal lands, including national parks and forests, park rangers are there to protect the visitors. Wilderness areas are, for the most part, free of crime.

LEGAL ASSISTANCE

Travelers from outside the US who are in need of legal assistance should contact their nearest consulate or the embassy in Washington, DC. If arrested, you have the right to remain silent, to have legal counsel, and to make at least one phone call. The police will provide you with any necessary phone numbers, and should treat you with respect and courtesy.

INSURANCE & MEDICAL TREATMENT

Comprehensive travel insurance is highly recommended to anyone intending to visit the US. Any emergency medical or dental care can be very expensive, so having proof of insurance coverage is essential to help defray some of the costs related to an unscheduled hospital visit. Bring a back-up prescription if you take any medication.

A good insurance policy will also pay for the replacement of stolen or damaged property. If you need to cancel or change your travel plans, many policies will refund your costs.

EMERGENCIES

If you need emergency help from the fire, police, or medical services then dial 911. The call is free from any public phone, and emergency phone boxes are located along major highways and Interstates. All US medical facilities will provide emergency care to injured people, regardless of means. The **Travelers' Aid Society** specializes in giving assistance to those travelers who find themselves stranded or in need of emergency help.

DIRECTORY

EMERGENCIES

All Emergencies
Tel *911 for police, fire, or medical emergency.*

Travelers' Aid Society
www.travelersaid.org

HOSPITALS & MEDICAL FACILITIES

Tel *411 for directory assistance.*

LOST/STOLEN CREDIT CARDS & TRAVELER'S CHECKS

American Express
Tel *(800) 528-4800 (credit cards).*
Tel *(800) 221-7282 (checks).*
www.americanexpress.com

Mastercard
Tel *(800) 826-2181.*
www.mastercard.com

VISA
Tel *(800) 336-8472.*
www.visa.com

EMBASSIES

Australia
www.austemb.org

Canada
www.canadianembassy.org

New Zealand
www.nzembassy.com

South Africa
www.saembassy.org

United Kingdom
www.britainusa.com

US Embassy
www.travel.state.gov

US Immigration & Customs Enforcement
www.ice.gov

SENIOR CITIZENS

American Association of Retired Persons
601 E St NW
Washington D.C., 20049
Tel *(888) 687-2277.*
www.aarp.org

Accommodations

The US offers a wide variety of accommodations to suit all tastes and budgets. At the high end of the comfort scale, visitors can choose from luxury hotels and resorts, found in most major cities. Country inns and bed-and-breakfasts (B&Bs), usually located in large, refurbished historic houses, offer a more personal and hospitable atmosphere. If you're traveling on a budget, there are thousands of convenient inexpensive motels all along the highways. Generally, hotels, motels, and inns offer impeccably clean surroundings. For those who wish to experience the country's wide open spaces, there are more than enough campgrounds in parks and forests.

HOTELS & RESORTS

There is no better place to experience the comfort of the US than to stay in one of the country's many chain hotels, such as the **Hilton, Marriott**, and **Starwood** groups. Historic and ultramodern hotels and resorts are usually located in downtown areas, at the heart of the city. The best hotels, in major cities, often have the finest restaurants and cocktail bars. These hotels offer a full range of guest services, including swimming pools and health clubs, and their concierge can provide shopping and tourist information, as well as preferential seating at restaurants and theaters.

There are also a number of classic older hotels located in traditional vacation spots, notably the early 20th-century rustic lodges found in state and national parks. Some of the national parks' famous hotels, such as Yellowstone's Old Faithful Inn *(see p602)*, are also located in unforgettably scenic locations. Most large resort hotels focus on relaxation and offer spa facilities or access to golf courses, tennis, and other outdoor activities.

An alternative to the large chain or resort hotels are the growing boutique hotels. These small, unique places all have their own personalities and stress service over amenities. These hotels are often quite expensive, so always ask for rates. For a complete listing of accommodations, see Where to Stay in each regional section.

BUSINESS TRAVELERS

Many downtown hotels cater mainly to business people, and some offer special "club-level" accommodations with extra-large rooms for long stays or occasional meetings. These club-level suites often provide breakfast, snacks, and evening cocktails, and on weekends they are great for the whole family.

MOTELS

Most overnight accommodations are provided by motels. Generally located along the main highways, they offer parking for your car right next to your room. Motels usually have fewer amenities than hotels, but they are less expensive and often include swimming pools and children's play areas as well as a restaurant. Motel rooms usually have one large or two smaller beds, a bathroom, a TV, and a phone.

Many motels are run as part of national franchises, but many of the more pleasant ones are locally owned. Some of the most popular chain motels include **Motel 6**, **Rodeway Inn**, **Fairfield Inn**, **Holiday Inn**, and the well-known **Best Western**.

BED-AND-BREAKFAST & HISTORIC INNS

Most historic inns offer a much more luxurious experience. Generally located in beautifully restored historic homes or mansions, they are often decorated with heirlooms and antiques. B&Bs, on the other hand, offer a wider choice, from rooms in private homes, where you may have to share a bathroom, to luxurious private accomodations that differ from historic inns in name only.

Most inns and B&Bs rent rooms on a nightly basis, though some offer discounts for week-long stays. Most are run as full-time businesses by professional staff. B&Bs also offer a fully cooked breakfast, often served communally so guests can get to know each other. Breakfasts are usually fairly lavish, multi-course affairs, with eggs, pancakes, and pastries. Some B&Bs, especially in rural areas near popular tourist areas, may also serve gourmet dinners with regional specialties with advance notice.

HOSTELS

For solo travelers, one of the best ways to meet others and save money is to take advantage of the clean hostels run by **Hostelling International (HI)**, the American affiliate of the International Youth Hostels Association (IYHA). Hostels can be found in the centers of most major cities and near popular destinations. They offer inexpensive beds in dormitory-style shared rooms, segregated by sex, and many also have a few private rooms for couples or families. Some hostels are housed in unique buildings, such as lighthouses or renovated army barracks.

All hostels have kitchen facilities, bathrooms, and common rooms. HI Hostels have several rules, including no alcohol and sometimes a curfew, and guests are expected to bring their own bed linen. HI Hostels are open to travelers of all ages, although nonmembers are asked to pay a nominal surcharge in addition to nightly rates, which is usually $15–20 for a dormitory room. In many urban areas, there are also a number of privately run hostels that offer basic rooms or dormitory beds. Check the listings in the Yellow Pages.

CAMPGROUNDS

Most local, state, and national parks, national forests, and other public lands provide parking and a single or double campsite for tents, along with a picnic table, a campfire pit, toilet facilities, and sometimes hot showers. Some are fancier, with electrical and water "hook-ups" for self-contained recreational vehicles (RVs). Overnight fees vary with location, facilities, and season but generally run from $8 to $20 a night. Many campgrounds accept advance reservations, but some operate on a "first-come, first-served" basis. **Campgrounds Woodalls** and **Trailer Life** carry listings of campsites.

Privately operated campgrounds, such as those run by **Kampgrounds of America** (KOA) offer several features, including game rooms, swimming pools, and small grocery stores. Some also feature log cabins, suitable for families with children. The most popular campgrounds fill up early during vacation weekends and in the summer. It is also a good idea to set up camp well before sunset. Overnight camping in highway rest areas or along public roads is not only illegal but dangerous as well.

RUSTIC OR BASIC ACCOMMODATIONS

There are several very basic "walk-in" primitive campgrounds in forest areas, used primarily by backpackers. These are generally free, but check with park rangers about wilderness permits and other regulations you might need. Vast portions of the West have such areas, managed by US government departments such as the **National Park Service**, the **US Forest Service**, and the **Bureau of Land Management** *(see p37)*.

PRICES

Room rates for overnight accommodations vary tremendously, from under $20 a night for a campground or hostel, to well over $500 a night in a deluxe downtown hotel. Most places quote the rate per room, but in some places, such as Las Vegas and New England, rates are often quoted per person, should two people share one room.

Room rates at all levels of comfort vary with demand. It is, therefore, worthwhile to ask for discounts or special packages, especially on the weekends in urban areas, weekdays in rural areas, or almost anywhere in the off-season.

RESERVATIONS

Some lodgings offer discounts for internet and advance bookings. It is also worth checking for last-minute booking discounts. Many hotels offer package deals in conjunction with a special event, such as theater or concert tickets with overnight accommodations.

Most lodgings will request a credit card number when you make a reservation. If you choose to cancel, you may be charged for a night's stay, depending on the time. For example, if you don't cancel by 6pm or earlier, you may be charged for one night. At the most popular places in peak season, many hotels and resorts may insist on a two-night minimum stay.

Most of the large lodging companies operate toll-free telephone lines for reservations, which can be useful if you are heading to a new city. These lines give up-to-date information about room rates, availability, and are also a good way to compare prices. Most companies publish free directories of all their properties, with maps and full details of rates and facilities.

CHILDREN

Most hotels welcome children and provide extra supplies, such as cots, for families. Babysitting services may also be available. In some family-oriented spots, hotels offer activities for kids and other fun programs. Children up to the age of 12, and sometimes up to 16 or 18, can stay free of charge in their parents' room. Rooms often have sofas that unfold into beds; or extra beds may be set up for an additional fee. For more information see p13.

DISABLED TRAVELERS

US law requires that all businesses provide facilities for the disabled *(see p13)*. However, lodgings do their best to accommodate all customers. If you have specific needs, give advance notice. Most places have wheelchair accessibility, wide doorways, handicap-accessible bathrooms, and support bars near toilets and showers.

DIRECTORY

HOTELS

Hilton
Tel (800) 445-8667.
www.hilton.com

Marriott
Tel (800) 228-9290.
www.marriott.com

Starwood
Tel (888) 625-5144.
www.starwoodhotels.com

MOTELS

Holiday Inn
Tel (800) 465-4329.
www.ichotelsgroup.com

Motel 6
Tel (800) 466-8356.
www.motel6.com

Rodeway Inn
Tel (877) 424-6423.
www.rodewayinn.com

HOSTELS

Hostelling International
Tel (301) 495-1240.
www.hiusa.org

CAMPGROUNDS

Campgrounds Woodalls
www.woodalls.com

Kampgrounds of America
www.koa.com

Trailer Life
www.trailerlifedirectory.com

Travel by Air

The United States is a nation on the move, with a huge number of airlines that fly both within the country and all around the world. While international travel is offered by US airlines as well as by hundreds of airlines in other countries, domestic travel is limited to airlines based in the United States. Because the country is so enormous, and recent competition has reduced prices considerably, air travel has become an integral part of life. Today, most long-distance and medium-distance domestic travel is by plane.

FLYING TO THE US

Most large foreign cities have several daily flights to a number of US cities, especially primary gateways to the East Coast, the West Coast, and throughout the Midwest. The main East Coast cities include New York, Boston, Washington, DC, Atlanta, and Miami; Chicago, St. Louis, Houston, Dallas, and Denver serve as main cities in the central region; and the West Coast is served by Los Angeles, San Francisco, and Seattle.

Most international flights from Europe travel across the Atlantic to New York, Washington, DC, Miami, Boston, and Chicago, taking roughly seven hours. Flights from Asia arrive at the West Coast airports, often stopping in Hawai'i on the way. These flights, as well as flights from Australia, take between 11 and 12 hours.

KEEPING COSTS DOWN

Air fares fluctuate in the US depending on the season, sometimes doubling during the peak holiday periods, especially in summer, and around Thanksgiving and Christmas. Fares are usually less expensive between February and March, when round-trip transatlantic flights can cost significantly less. You often get a better deal, too, by flying mid-week.

The least expensive fares are the APEX (Advance Purchase Excursion) tickets for scheduled airlines. These must be bought 21 days in advance and are valid for a seven- to 30-day period. However, any changes that need to be made can cost an additional fee. Some airlines also offer cheaper fares if you limit your stay to a certain period of time. Senior citizens and children may also receive discounts on certain flights.

These tickets are not always available, though. Another option is the short-term Internet fares advertised by airlines if there are any available seats. These are valid within a few days of the announcement (fares may be announced on a Wednesday for traveling that weekend and returning the next weekend).

TIME ZONES ACROSS THE UNITED STATES

The United States covers six different times zones – the "Lower 48" states are divided into Eastern, Central, Mountain, and Pacific time, while Alaska and Hawai'i have their own zones. The zones are divided into one-hour increments. For instance, when it is 8pm in New York, it is 7pm in Chicago, 6pm in Denver, 5pm in Los Angeles, 4pm in Anchorage, and 3pm in Honolulu.

Eastern Time is five hours behind Greenwich Mean Time, and Hawai'i is 11 hours behind Greenwich Mean Time. With a few variations, the United States observes Daylight Savings Time between mid-March and early November.

ARRIVAL AT THE AIRPORT

All international visitors must go through customs and immigration when they arrive in the US *(see p13)*. All major airports have multilingual information booths to answer your questions and give details on transportation into the city.

Most international airports are well connected to the nearest city either by public transportation or the vast array of rental car facilities. Many rentals supply shuttle buses to car pick-up points, usually located just outside the airport. Major airlines are connected to countless domestic airline services, and all have facilities for disabled passengers. Still, it is a good idea to prearrange any necessary services through your airline or agent.

SECURITY

After the September 11, 2001 terrorist attacks, airport authorities tightened their pre-flight security checks (especially for domestic flights). International visitors should expect to be frisked thoroughly and have their hand luggage examined. Items such as battery cells, scissors, nail files, knitting needles, sharp objects, and containers holding more than 3 oz (100 ml) of liquid are prohibited. Signs throughout the Customs areas explain which items are prohibited in checked luggage.

Visitors with visas are photographed and fingerprinted on arrival, for details to be checked against a national security database. In light of increased security, expect a long wait to check in.

FLYING WITHIN THE UNITED STATES

Visitors interested in seeing the entire country may want to take advantage of domestic flights. These are operated by more than a dozen different major airlines, many of which fly internationally as well. An extensive domestic flight network serves most cities, making it easy to fly within the US.

The major US airlines operate a "hub-and-spoke" network, meaning that long-distance flights travel between regional airports, from where shorter flights continue on to your destination. Most **Delta Airlines** flights converge on their hubs in Atlanta and Minneapolis; **United Airlines** flights converge in Chicago and Denver; while **American Airlines** usually flies first to Dallas or Chicago.

BOOKING A DOMESTIC FLIGHT

For foreign visitors, the easiest way to book a domestic flight is to have it agree with your itinerary. This way you have to buy only one set of tickets and often get a better deal. Another money-saving option is to take advantage of "Visit USA" (VUSA) coupons, which are good for numerous domestic flights (between three and ten flights), for a pre-paid fee. However, these coupons must be bought before you arrive and can be redeemed only with the same airline on which you flew internationally.

The Internet and the deregulation of the airline industry have made planning trips and purchasing tickets much easier. The best prices now are on airlines' websites.

DOMESTIC AIRLINES

Most international airlines have formed alliances with domestic flights, for instance, **British Airways** is partnered with American Airlines, and **Air France/KLM** with Delta Airlines, making flight networks effectively interlinked. Beside the major international US airlines, there are a large number of domestic airlines that offer inexpensive flights. The most popular of these are **Southwest Airlines** and **Jet Blue** which connect to and from smaller airports rather than from major ones. These airlines are a less expensive and reliable means of travel. They offer basic snacks, and do not transfer to or from other carriers, which can make connecting flights a hassle, but their fares are low, and there are fewer restrictions.

FLY-DRIVE

Many airlines, in addition to travel companies and agents, offer fly-drive packages for tourists, which combine air fares and car rentals. These deals are well worth considering, since they give you flexibility and usually save you more money than if you were to book plane and car travel separately.

DIRECTORY

AIRLINE CARRIERS

American Airlines
Tel *(800) 433-7300.*
www.aa.com

British Airways
Tel *(800) 247-9297.*
www.britishairways.com

Continental
Tel *(800) 231-0856.*
www.continental.com

Delta Airlines
Tel *(800) 241-4141.*
www.delta.com

United Airlines
Tel *(800) 241-6522.*
www.united.com

AIRPORT	INFORMATION	DISTANCE FROM CITY	TAXI FARE TO CITY	AVERAGE TRAVEL TIME
Chicago (O'Hare)	*(800) 832-6352*	17 miles (27 km) from downtown	$35–40 to downtown	Road: 30 mins to downtown
Dallas–Fort Worth (International)	*(972) 574-8888*	18 miles (29 km) from Dallas	$40 to downtown Dallas	Road: 25 mins to downtown Dallas
Los Angeles (LAX)	*(310) 646-5252*	15 miles (24 km) from downtown	$30–40 to downtown	Road: 30 mins to downtown
Miami (International)	*(305) 876-7000*	10 miles (16 km) from Miami Beach	$32 to Miami Beach	Road: 20 mins to Miami Beach
New York City (JFK)	*(718) 244-4444*	15 miles (24 km) from Manhattan	$45 to downtown Manhattan	Road: 1 hr to downtown Manhattan
San Francisco (SFO)	*(650) 821-8211*	14 miles (22 km) from downtown	$37–45 to downtown	Road: 25 mins to downtown
Seattle (Sea-Tac)	*(206) 431-4444*	14 miles (22 km) from downtown	$30–40 to downtown	Road: 25 mins to downtown
Washington, DC (Dulles International)	*(703) 572-2700*	26 miles (42 km) from downtown	$51–58 to downtown	Road: 40 mins to downtown

Travel by Road

Away from major cities, where traffic can be frustrating, driving in the United States is a delightful experience. Driving is a favorite American pastime, and to see the country in all its glory, you have to drive a car. Major roads and most highways are rarely crowded, and drivers are generally courteous and safe. Gasoline in the US is comparatively inexpensive, and car rental rates are also reasonable. You can get by without a car in a few larger towns, and in cities like New York, Boston, or San Francisco you will probably be better off without one. However, in most of the country, if you want to explore the wide open spaces of the western US, you will need a car since public transportation there is limited.

TYPES OF ROAD

The us has an excellent network of roads, with over 4 million miles (6 million km) of paved roads open to the public. For long distance travelers, the fastest and most convenient part of the US highway system is the Interstate Highway, a high-speed, limited-access highway. Some have between six and 12 lanes running both directions, while rural areas generally have two or three lanes.

Stretching all across the country in an east-to-west and north-to-south grid, Interstate Highways are abbreviated on signs with a capital "I," followed by a number. The main Interstates start with I-5 on the West Coast and end with I-95, the busy main route along the East Coast. Transcontinental Interstates run east-to-west and range from I-10 between Florida and California to I-90 between Boston and Seattle.

In and around cities, a complicated system of ring roads, link roads, and spur roads are also part of the Interstate system. These roads are often better known by name than number, for instance I-405 in Southern California is referred to as the "San Diego Freeway."

Most Interstates are free, but some states charge tolls. These sections, known as "turnpikes," have the same numbers as sections without toll booths.

Before the Interstate Highway System came into use, the primary long-distance highways were federal ones. Today, these are the main routes in rural areas and are officially signed as "US" and a number, ranging from US-1 along the East Coast to US-101 along the West Coast.

RULES OF THE ROAD

- All traffic drives on the right.
- All distances are measured in miles.
- Seat belts are compulsory, and children under the age of 4 are required to have special car seats.
- At traffic signals, green lights mean you can proceed safely; amber lights mean prepare to stop; and red lights mean stop. A flashing red light means stop before proceeding; and a flashing yellow light means proceed with caution.
- At a red octagonal stop sign, traffic must come to a complete halt before proceeding. When two or more cars reach a stop sign simultaneously from different sides of the intersection, drivers must yield to traffic on the right.
- A yellow triangular yield sign directs you to give way to other traffic.
- In towns and cities, roads are usually divided by a painted center line (usually white). Smaller streets may have no dividing line.
- On all roads, a double yellow line means do not pass or cross the lines.
- Some roads have a central lane, protected by painted single lines; this is a designated turning area for making left-hand turns.
- "U" turns are legal only where posted.
- On multi-lane highways, the fastest traffic travels in the left-hand lanes; slower traffic occupies the right-hand lane.
- Cargo-carrying heavy trucks generally stay in the slow lane. Keep your distance from these vehicles, because they have poor visibility and enormous weight and size.
- On multi-lane highways traffic can pass only on the left-hand side. On smaller roads safe passing places are indicated with a broken yellow line on your side of the double yellow line.
- Speed limits vary from state to state, but range from 25mph (40 km/h) in residential areas to 65–75mph (105–120 km/h) on highways.
- There is a minimum speed of 45mph (72 km/h) on highways and Interstate Highways. Farm traffic and pedestrians are not permitted on Interstates.
- Parking is allowed on most streets, subject to posted rules, but any restrictions are posted at the site. Park only in the direction of travel. If you receive a ticket, pay it immediately or it will be charged (with a penalty) to the rental car company, who will collect it from your credit card.
- Visitors should be aware of regional exceptions to the standard US driving laws. Some of these are pointed out in the "Practical Information" section of each chapter.
- Most foreign licenses are valid, but if your license is not in English, or does not have a photo ID, you must get an International Driver's License.
- Drunk driving is a serious offense and can result in a heavy fine or jail term.

Lined by neon-lit motels, and other classic landmarks of roadside America, these roads are slower but more enjoyable, and along with many other state and country roads, provide the country's most scenic routes *(see pp40–41)*.

Road names vary from state to state. In the northeast, for example, highways are called "routes" while in Texas, roads are labeled "FM," farm to market or "RM," ranch to market.

TIPS FOR RENTING A CAR

Most rental cars are relatively new and low on mileage, and rates are as low as $150 a week. The best rates are generally offered for cars rented for full week time periods, and for returning cars to the same location they were rented from. A more economical option is the fly-drive *(see p21)*.

Small economy or subcompact cars have the lowest rates. Many companies also offer upgrades to larger or more luxurious vehicles for very modest rates. Most rental cars have automatic transmissions, power steering, and air-conditioning, but you should confirm this in advance. Also, check for any pre-existing damage to the car and note this on your contract.

To rent a car, you must be at least 25 years old, have a valid driving license, a clean driving record, and a major credit card. The car company will "authorize" an amount ranging between $250–1,000, to assure payment and return of the vehicle. Depending on your existing car insurance policy, you may want to accept the "damage waiver" and liability insurance that the rental company will offer you, and this will add $10–20 per day to the rental cost.

DRIVEAWAYS

An inexpensive option for a long-distance road trip is a driveaway car. Driveaways let you take a private car to a predetermined place in a specified amount of time. Most driveaways are offered to private members, but some ads may appear in magazines or newspapers.

Flexiblity is essential for a driveaway deal since the destination is beyond your control. You have to choose an efficient route and average about 400 miles (644 km) a day. However, since you have to pay only for the gas, the price is quite good. To use a driveaway car, you must have a clean driving record, and most companies require a minimum deposit to cover the insurance deductible.

One of the biggest driveaway companies, **Auto Driveaway**, has offices all over the US. Other firms are listed in phone books under "Automobile Transporters."

RV RENTALS

Recreational vehicles (RVs) or mobile homes, are great for families or groups, as they are equipped with beds, kitchens, and bathroom facilities. Costs run between $900–1,400 for seven nights plus a per-mile charge, but lodging is free and you have some flexibility, despite the vehicles' slow, stocky designs. Although rental RVs are usually older, conditions are similar to those for cars.

It is illegal in most places to pull over to the side of the road and camp. Many chain retail outlets, notably Wal-Mart, allow one night's free stay in their parking lots, with approval of the manager or front desk. Even with an RV, it costs about $20 a night to park in a campground *(see p19)*. For more details contact **Recreational Vehicle Association of America or Cruise America**.

INSURANCE

It is extremely important that you have adequate insurance if you plan on driving around in the US. Rental agencies generally include insurance in the cost, but if you bring a car into the country, you must make absolutely sure that you are adequately covered by car and life insurance.

DIRECTORY

CAR RENTAL AGENCIES

Alamo
Tel *(800) 354-2322.*
www.alamo.com

Avis
Tel *(800) 331-1212.*
www.avis.com

Budget
Tel *(800) 527-0700.*
www.budget.com

Hertz
Tel *(800) 654-3131.*
www.hertz.com

DRIVEAWAYS

Custom Auto Delivery
Tel *(800) 647-7992.*
www.driveaway.com

RV RENTALS

Cruise America
Tel *(800) 671-8042.*
www.cruiseamerica.com

Recreational Vehicle Association of America
Tel *(888) 467-8464.*
www.gorving.com

ROAD CONDITIONS INFORMATION

American Automobile Association (AAA)
Tel *(800) 222-4357.*
www.aaa.com

GAS STATIONS

Except in the most remote areas, gas stations are easy to find and conveniently located. Many stations require advance payment, either by cash or credit/debit card. Most gas stations also have attached convenience stores, where you can buy food, beverages, and newspapers.

REST AREAS

Conveniently located immediately adjacent to Interstates and major highways, rest areas are easily accessible and provide restrooms, telephones, picnic tables, dog-walking areas, and sometimes free coffee. Some even allow overnight stays, but be wary of strangers. It is a good idea to take a rest when driving long distances.

Travel by Motorcycle or Bike

For visitors with time on their hands as well as a sense of adventure, touring the United States by motorcycle or bicycle can be a rewarding experience. Ride the open road with a Harley-Davidson, or mountain bike throughout the beautiful and peaceful American wilderness for the adventure of a lifetime. Good planning, familiarizing yourself with the rules and regulations, and using the right equipment can make this an enjoyable way of seeing the country.

MOTORCYCLES

Fans of Marlon Brando's famous movie *The Wild One* (1954) or Jack Nicholson's classic *Easy Rider* (1969) may dream of exploring the United States on a motorcycle. Today, there are several motorcycle rental companies, especially in bike-friendly areas, where licensed riders drive classic motorcycles such as Harley-Davidsons or BMWs.

An American motorcycle license or an International Driving Permit for motorcycles is necessary. Also, the law in most states requires that you wear a helmet.

MOTORCYCLE RENTALS & TOURS

Renting is expensive, since the rates and liability insurance can add up to well over $100 a day. Moreover, you have to pay extra for collision insurance. Most companies allow short-term rentals in a single location, but larger firms such as **Eagle Rider** have branches or affiliates all over the country. If you plan to stay for a longer period, it might be less expensive to buy a bike for a few months, then resell it.

For long-distance motorcycle trips, Eagle Rider offers guided tours along selected routes. **Blue Sky Motorcycle Tours** also offers a wide range of tours.

Riders may be interested in taking part in one of the many motorcycle rallies, when thousands of riders get together for annual gatherings held in places like Daytona Beach, Florida (early March); Laconia, New Hampshire (mid June); or Sturgis, South Dakota (August).

BICYCLES

Bicycles are another great way to see the country. Unlike motorcycles, bicycles can be brought on most airplanes as luggage. Check the requirements first with your airline – many carriers require that you disassemble and pack the bike into a special box, which is available in most good bike shops.

In a great many cities, there are extensive networks of bike paths, which are often separated from car traffic. In some larger cities, bikes can be strapped onto the outside of local buses or carried on the subway.

For serious long-distance biking, it's important to equip yourself with a good bike, tools and spares, maps, and preferably a helmet. Cyclists must obey all traffic laws and should be careful to lock up their bikes and gear.

In the US, bikes are not as common as they are in many other countries. Car and truck drivers are not used to sharing the road with bikes, which can make cycling hazardous. Be aware of RV drivers in particular, because it is easy for them to misjudge the sizes of their vehicles. Bikes are prohibited on restricted-access highways and freeways.

BICYCLE RENTALS & TOURS

Bikes are available for rent in all major US cities for around $25 a day, or you can buy used bikes from flea markets or garage sales. Notices of second-hand sales appear in newspaper ads or hostel notices. Look in the Yellow Pages for local bike rental companies.

Backroads organizes a variety of guided bike tours, following some of the most spectacular scenic routes, with overnight stays in country inns or national park campsites. If interested in long-distance cycling, be sure to contact the **Adventure Cycling Association**, which has developed a network of bike-friendly routes following quieter and more scenic federal and state highways.

RECREATIONAL BIKING

In country areas, many bike paths have been reclaimed from unused railroad lines. Known as "rail trails," these are some of the best long-distance bicycling and walking routes in the country, often running alongside rivers and having moderate grades. In addition, there are miles and miles of country roads everywhere you go. Areas such as California's Wine Country and New England's river valleys are among the most popular.

The more athletic or daredevil travelers may also want to try off-road mountain biking, which is encouraged in many recreational areas such as downhill ski resorts in summer.

DIRECTORY

MOTORCYCLE RENTALS & TOURS

Eagle Rider Motorcycles
Tel (310) 536-6777.
www.eaglerider.com

Blue Sky Motorcycle Tours
Tel (800) 717-7970.
www.blueskymotorcyclerentals.com

BICYCLE TOURS

Backroads
Tel (800) 462-2848.
www.backroads.com

Adventure Cycling Association
150 E Pine St, Missoula, MT 59802. (800) 755-2453.
www.adventurecycling.org

Travel by Bus or Train

Although more time-consuming than flying, you can enjoy long-distance bus and train trips that let you see the beauty of the US. Greyhound – the major long-distance buses – offers clean, modern travel conditions with on-board movies and restroom facilities. Amtrak trains are spacious and comfortable. Amtrak provides restaurant cars, observation cars, and great social atmospheres. If you want to meet fellow travelers, buses and trains are the transportation options for you.

TRAVELING BY BUS

The nation-wide carrier **Greyhound Lines** serves all the major cities that airlines do, plus many smaller-towns along the way, but the travel times are much longer. On long journeys, be sure to take something to eat and drink as meals are determined by where the bus stops.

Buses are also a good option for urban or suburban transportation, but because service can be limited in rural areas, you should plan your route carefully when visiting the countryside. Greyhound buses also provide links with major airports as well as Amtrak services.

TICKETS & RESERVATIONS

Many bus stations are located in low-rent parts of town, so it is usually a good idea to take a taxi home from the station at night.

Ask about discounts and special fares including online booking discounts. Most major bus lines offer discounts for children under 12, students, and senior citizens (with proper ID), as well as unlimited travel within a set period. Tickets can be bought on the day of travel, although fares are less expensive if they are bought in advance. For advance tickets, contact Greyhound directly or ask a travel agent.

International visitors should know that Greyhound tickets are cheaper if bought from an agent outside the US. If you plan to interrupt your trip to explore on your own, or tour the US on an extended trip, there may be a travel package just for you.

BUS TOURS

In most states, bus companies offer short package trips in deluxe air-conditioned buses that tour major attractions. These guided tours provide a comfortable way of seeing the sights, without having to worry about time schedules, admission tickets, and opening hours.

For passengers with more time to spare, you may want to try certain bus companies, such as **Green Tortoise**, that offer leisurely trips between major cities. Passengers on these buses can take breaks to camp out, prepare meals, and explore the countryside. Unlike other buses, there are foam mattresses for sleeping. These tours are not for everyone, nevertheless they can provide an enjoyable, relaxed, and memorable tour of the country.

TRAVELING BY TRAIN

The use of railroads in the US is dwindling. Still, there is a small and enjoyable network of long-distance passenger train routes, operated by **Amtrak**, the national rail system. In spite of its limited network and sometimes inconvenient schedules, a scenic train ride can be an unforgettable experience.

TRAIN TICKETS & RESERVATIONS

To make the most of an Amtrak trip, consider paying the extra money to get a sleeping compartment, which costs around $150 a night on a twin-sharing basis. Meal service is included in the price. Amtrak travel is an especially good value for international visitors, who can take advantage of a number of rail tickets for 15, 30, or 45 days of train travel for a fee of $390–750, depending on the dates and regions of travel.

HISTORIC RAILROADS

Many pioneer railroads that braved the Wild West frontier are now back in business as tourist attractions, running short trips (often under coal-fired steam) through some spectacular scenery. Many trains, running along narrow-gauge tracks, were constructed by mining or logging companies over a century ago.

Among the most popular railroads are the **Durango and Silverton Narrow Gauge** in southwestern Colorado *(see p591)*, the **Cumbres and Toltec** line in New Mexico, and the **Grand Canyon Railroad** in Williams, Arizona, which goes to the rim of the Grand Canyon.

DIRECTORY

LONG-DISTANCE BUSES

Greyhound Lines
Tel *(800) 231-2222 (24 hrs).*
www.greyhound.com

BUS TOURS

Green Tortoise
Tel *(800) 867-8647.*
www.greentortoise.com

RAILROADS

Amtrak
Tel *(800) 872-7245.*
www.amtrak.com

Durango & Silverton Narrow Gauge
Tel *(970) 247-2733.*
www.durangotrain.com

Cumbres & Toltec Railroad
Tel *(888) 286-2737.*
www.cumbrestoltec.com

Grand Canyon Railroad
Tel *(800) 843-8724.*
www.thetrain.com

USA AT A GLANCE

USA THROUGH THE YEAR 28–33

NATIONAL PARKS 34–37

GREAT AMERICAN CITIES 38–39

BEST SCENIC ROUTES 40–41

HISTORY OF THE USA 42–53

USA THROUGH THE YEAR

The size and scope of the United States means that at almost any time of year you can find the right weather to suit any activity. In the middle of winter, for example, while skiers are enjoying the deep snows of the Rockies and New England, sun-seekers flock to Florida or the Arizona deserts. Both the weather and the calendar of events heat up in the summer with a proliferation of county fairs, arts and music festivals, and other events, many celebrating the nation's diverse history and culture. October and November are prime time for harvest festivals, especially near Thanksgiving. The year ends with a variety of religious holidays, including Christmas, Hannukah, Ramadan, and the African-American celebration Kwanzaa, while the college and professional football seasons climax with a series of New Year's Day championship games and the Super Bowl finale.

Jazz Festival musician, New Orleans

SPRING

Spring inspires a definite sense of renewal all over the country. Wildflowers carpet the deserts, the magnolias and cherry trees burst into bloom, and melting snows fill streams and waterfalls to their annual peak. Among the events that celebrate the season, the most symbolic are the first games of the baseball season, which begins in April.

MARCH

Academy Awards *(late Feb–mid-Mar)*, Hollywood, CA. The movie industry honors its stars with golden Oscars.

Lahaina Ocean Arts Festival *(early Mar)*, Lahaina, HI. Lectures, dives, and whale-watching celebrating the humpback whale that winters off the Hawaiian coast.

Bike Week *(early Mar)*, Daytona, FL. Motorcycle racers and enthusiasts congregate in one of the US's largest gatherings of bikers.

St. Patrick's Day Parade *(Sun nearest Mar 17)*, Boston, MA; New York City, NY; Chicago, IL; San Francisco, CA. Parades celebrating Irish heritage are held in these major cities. Towns such as Butte, MT, and Savannah, GA, also hold parties.

South by Southwest Festival *(mid-Mar)*, Austin, TX. An independent pop-music festival.

APRIL

Easter *(date varies)*. This spring holiday is a study in contrasts. Early morning outdoor "Easter Sunrise" services are held all over the country, while in New York City, outrageously dressed characters join in the Easter Parade down Fifth Avenue. At this time, college kids flock to warm climes in Florida, Texas, and California for their annual "Spring Break."

National Cherry Blossom Festival *(early Apr)*, Washington, DC. A number of events, such as exhibitions, walks, and concerts, celebrate the blossoming of the city's famous cherry trees.

Patriot's Day *(Mon nearest Apr 18)*, Lexington and Concord, MA. Early morning re-enactments of the first battles of the American Revolution are followed by the country's most famous race, the Boston Marathon.

New Orleans Jazz & Heritage Festival *(late Apr)*, New Orleans, LA. Performances by top and emerging talents.

MAY

Cinco de Mayo *(May 5)*. Celebrations of Mexican culture featuring folk dancing and mariachi music, take place all over the US to mark the anniversary of the Battle of Puebla.

Kentucky Derby *(first Sat in May)*, Louisville, KY. The country's biggest horse race and the start of the "Triple Crown" championship takes place at the end of a two-week-long public party.

Wright Plus *(mid- or late May)*, Chicago, IL. You can tour architect Frank Lloyd Wright's buildings and residences during this annual housewalk at Oak Park.

Spoleto Festival USA *(late May-early Jun)*, Charleston, SC. The largest arts festival in the United States.

Jockeys at Churchill Downs for the Kentucky Derby, Louisville

◁ Silhouettes of tall saguaro cacti, unique to the Sonoran Desert, Arizona

Indianapolis 500 *(Sun before Memorial Day)*, Indianapolis, IN. The most famous auto race in the US draws over 100,000 fans.
Kinetic Sculpture Race *(Memorial Day weekend)*, Arcata, CA. Northern California's good-natured culture is evident at this three-day event, in which human-powered sculptures are raced over land and sea.

SUMMER

The Memorial Day holiday, at the end of May, marks the unofficial beginning of summertime. This is prime vacation and travel time for students and families. It is also a good time to enjoy music festivals, usually held in idyllic rural locations. The weather is hot and frequently humid, with afternoon storms in much of the country.

The flamboyant Lesbian and Gay Pride Parade, New York City

JUNE

Harvard-Yale Regatta *(early Jun)*, New London, CT. This series of collegiate rowing races offers visitors a chance to observe the Ivy League elite at play.
B.B. King Homecoming Festival *(late May/early June)*, Indianola, MS. One of the oldest and most popular of the many Deep South summer blues festivals.
Red Earth Native American Festival *(first weekend)*, Oklahoma City, OK. One of the largest gatherings of Native American dancers and musicians is held at

Independence Day fireworks light up the sky in Houston, Texas

what was the last vestige of "Indian Territory."
Lesbian and Gay Pride Day *(Sun in late Jun)*, New York City, NY; San Francisco, California. Major parades and festivities fill the streets of both these cities.
Taste of Chicago, *(late Jun–early Jul)*, Chicago, IL. The city's best food and music can be experienced at an open-air party, held on the Lake Michigan waterfront.

JULY

Independence Day *(Jul 4)*, Bristol, RI; Boston, MA; Independence, MO; Stone Mountain near Atlanta, GA. Although the entire country celebrates the Fourth of July with parades and fireworks displays, these cities put on particularly good shows.
Ernest Hemingway Days *(mid-Jul)*, Key West, FL. The city where the famous writer lived offers a week of theatrical productions, short story contests, and a Hemingway look-alike competition.
Tanglewood Music Festival *(Jul–Aug)*, Lenox, MA. The Boston Symphony and Boston Pops give outdoor concerts in a beautiful Berkshire Mountains estate.
Hawaiian International Billfish Tournament *(late Jul–early Aug)*, Kailua-Kona, HI. This international fishing tournament draws people in search of record-sized marlin.

AUGUST

Sunflower River Blues Festival *(early-Aug)*, Clarksdale, MS. One of the country's most enjoyable blues festivals takes place in the home of the blues, the Mississippi Delta.
Elvis International Tribute Week *(mid-Aug)*, Memphis, TN. Also called "Deathweek," a series of events are held to celebrate the life and times of Elvis Presley, leading up to the anniversary of his death on August 16.
Newport Jazz Festival *(mid-Aug)*, Newport, RI. Sponsored by electronics firm JVC, this popular festival draws the very best jazz musicians from all over the country and the world.
Alaska State Fair *(late Aug–Sep)*, Palmer, AK. This fair is especially famous for its super-sized vegetables, with pumpkins and cabbages grown to world-record sizes due to the state's 24-hour summer sunshine.
US Open Tennis Championships *(Aug–Sep)*, New York City, NY. Professional tennis players from the world over compete in this Grand Slam tournament.

Opening ceremony of the annual US Open Tennis Championships

The famous fiery colors of New England's fall foliage

FALL

During fall in New England, the leaves of the hardwood trees turn stunning shades of red and gold, drawing appreciative tourists from all over the world. In the West, wine-growing regions celebrate the annual harvest, and in the Great Lakes and Midwest, beer lovers join the Oktoberfest celebrations in the nation's many German enclaves. The approach of winter and the start of the Christmas shopping season is kicked off by the nationally televised Macy's Thanksgiving Day parade down Broadway in New York City.

SEPTEMBER

Mississippi Delta Blues and Heritage Festival *(mid-Sep)*, Greenville, MS. A blues and African-American culture festival in the heart of the Mississippi Delta.
Norwalk Seaport Oyster Festival *(mid-Sep)*, Norwalk, CT. Fireworks, antique boats, and lots of local oysters to sample.
Northeast Kingdom Fall Foliage Festival *(mid-Sep–early Oct)*, VT. Celebrating the change of seasons, as well as the brilliantly colored fall foliage, several tours and events are held in small towns all over northern Vermont.
Major League Baseball Championships *(Sep–Oct)*. The nation's top professional teams face off, with the winners competing in October's World Series.
Texas State Fair *(late Sep–early Oct)*, Dallas, TX. One of the country's largest state fairs, with a focus on Texas.
Fall Pilgrimage *(late Sep–mid-Oct)*, Natchez, MS. A three-week-long series of events celebrate antebellum architecture and culture.

OCTOBER

Arkansas Blues and Heritage Festival *(early Oct)*, Helena, AR. Once sponsored by the King Biscuit flour company, the small Mississippi River town of Helena has been celebrating the blues since the 1920s.
Festivals Acadiens *(early Oct)*, Lafayette, LA. Over 100,000 people flock to this Cajun Country capital to enjoy the unique sights, sounds, and tastes of Louisiana life.
Ironman Triathlon *(Sat nearest to full moon)*, Kailua-Kona, HI. More than 1,000 of the world's fittest athletes take part in a highly challenging series of trials, combining a 2.4-mile (3.8-km) swim, a 112-mile (180-km) bike ride, and a 26-mile (42-km) marathon run.
American Royal Rodeo *(date varies, mid-Oct to early Nov)*, Kansas City, MO. One of the country's largest and most prominent professional rodeo competitions.
Italian Heritage Parade *(mid-Oct)*, San Francisco, CA. Columbus Avenue, winding through the city's Italian-American North Beach district, comes alive with a parade celebrating Italian pride. Other such parades are held throughout the country.
Oktoberfest *(late Oct)*. Modeled on the famous one in Munich, beer-flavored festivals are held in German neighborhoods of most large cities in the US, as well as small German towns like New Braunfels TX, Hermann MO, and Leavenworth, WA.
Haunted Happenings *(late Oct)*, Salem, MA. Leading up to Halloween, the historic home of the Salem Witch Trials stages a series of supernatural-themed events and activities.
Halloween *(Oct 31)*. While children dress up in scary costumes and beg for candy, many adults flock to raucous public parties in places like Key West, FL, and New York's Greenwich Village.

Giant cowboy balloon at the Texas State Fair in Dallas

NOVEMBER

Dia de los Muertos (Day of the Dead) *(Nov 1)*, San Francisco, CA. Festivities in San Francisco's Mission District highlight this Catholic festival, when the souls of the dead are said to visit the living. Similar festivities take place in Mexican neighborhoods across the country.
Thanksgiving *(4th Thu in Nov)*. Celebrating the survival of the pilgrims who landed at Plymouth, MA, in 1620, this holiday sees families coming together

Turkey Float in Macy's Thanksgiving Day Parade, New York City

from all over the country to share in a massive meal of roast turkey, stuffing, cranberry sauce, and pumpkin pie. Many restaurants serve special Thanksgiving meals, and the town of Plymouth, MA recreates a pilgrim Thanksgiving worship service.
Macy's Thanksgiving Day Parade *(Thanksgiving Day)*, New York City, NY. Giant inflatable figures march down New York's Broadway to celebrate Thanksgiving and the start of the Christmas holiday season.

WINTER

Perhaps best known for the shopping mania that leads up to Christmas, winter in American cities is a time of twinkling lights, ringing cash registers, and occasional snowstorms. Department stores along New York's Fifth Avenue, Chicago's State Street, and other shopping districts attract shoppers with exuberant displays in their store windows. Many ski resorts stage special winter activities, such as sleigh rides and visits from Santa Claus. Winter is also the best time to watch the gray whale migration along the Pacific Ocean, or to observe the humpback whales on the way to their winter breeding grounds in Hawai'i. February also sees a number of public parades and parties, which range from the Chinese New Year celebrations to the wild fun and festivity of Mardi Gras in New Orleans.

DECEMBER

Triple Crown of Surfing *(late Nov to mid-Dec)*, North Shore O'ahu, HI. The world's most prestigious surfing competition usually spans three weeks, waves and weather permitting.
Boston Tea Party Re-enactment *(mid-Dec)*, Boston, MA. Costumed performers and interpreters bring to life the famous Boston Tea Party, a protest that played an important role in precipitating the famous American Revolution.
New Year's Eve *(Dec 31)*, New York City, NY. The country's foremost New Year celebration starts with the countdown in New York's Times Square, which is televised live across Eastern US and repeated (on tape) for viewers elsewhere in the country. Major New Year's Eve parties occur in most major cities, with great public celebrations in Las Vegas and San Francisco.

JANUARY

New Year's Day *(Jan 1)*. Parades and festivities are held all around the country and are often connected with a championship college football game such as the Orange Bowl in Miami, the Cotton Bowl in Dallas, the Sugar Bowl in New Orleans, and the Rose Bowl in Pasadena, CA, which is usually preceded by a nationally televised parade.
Martin Luther King Jr. Day *(Mon nearest Jan 15)*. Events are held around the country to honor the birth and life of the Civil Rights leader.
Riverwalk Mud Festival *(mid-Jan)*, San Antonio, TX. While workers drain the water to clear out downtown's River Walk, musicians and artists celebrate.
Cowboy Poetry Gathering *(late Jan)*, Elko, NV. Cowboys come to this town to tell tales, quote their very own poems, and sing songs about the heroic American West.

FEBRUARY

Groundhog Day *(Feb 2)*, Punxsutawney, PA. The star of this festival is a small rodent who forecasts the beginning of spring.
Mardi Gras *(date varies, mid-Feb)*, New Orleans, LA. Colorful parades, lavish parties, and masked balls are held. Many smaller cities hold similar celebrations.

Lion dance during Chinese New Year, Chinatown, San Francisco

Chinese New Year *(date varies, late Jan to mid-Feb)*, San Francisco, CA. To celebrate Chinese New Year, colorful parades are held here, in New York City, and several other cities.
Iditarod Trail Sled Dog Race *(late Feb–early Mar)*, Anchorage, AK. This test of endurance takes packs of dogs and their drivers two grueling weeks.

Climate of the USA

Much of the US enjoys temperate weather, but the country is so vast that many regions experience climatic extremes. Alaska has the harshest winter, while the warmest temperatures are in Hawai'i and Florida. Even within the "Lower 48" states, the weather varies tremendously, from the heavy snows of the Rocky Mountains to the intense heat of Death Valley in the California desert. Besides the four main seasons, the US also sees some unusual weather, including destructive tornadoes that may form in spring and summer across the Great Plains; thunderstorms that burst over the South during summer; and powerful hurricanes that strike coastal areas in the Southeast in autumn.

Subarctic (Alaska)
Though temperatures drop well below freezing for most of the year, the warm summers are extended by the non-stop daylight of the "midnight sun."

Temperate (California)
The West Coast's mild climate is much like that of the Mediterranean regions, with mild winters and long, sunny summers.

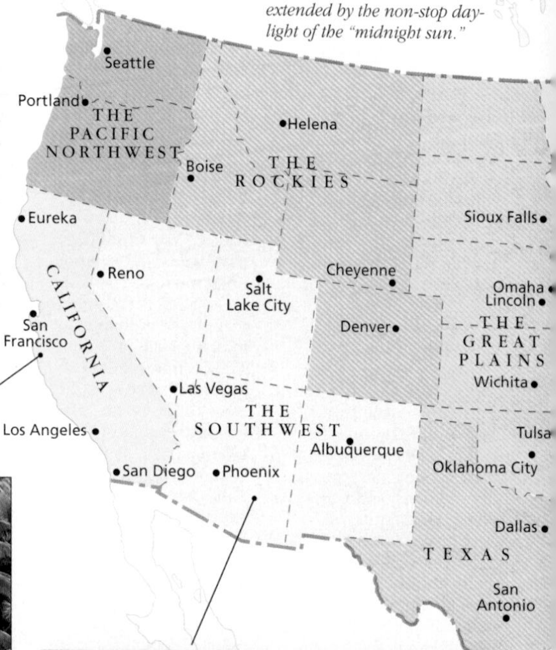

Tropical (Hawai'i)
This island paradise is warm and pleasant year-round. Significant rain falls in winter, usually on the northeastern or windward coasts.

Arid (Southwest)
The hot, dry climate of the Southwestern desert draws millions of visitors. Winter snows can fall at higher elevations, but sunshine is guaranteed throughout the year.

Cool Continental (Great Lakes)
The Great Lakes states are famous for their frigid winters, when the region receives the country's heaviest snowfall.

Cool Temperate (New England)
Bright, sunny days followed by frosty nights cause the most intense color in New England's famous autumn foliage. The region experiences warm summers and cold winters with high snowfalls in certain areas.

Cool Temperate (Great Plains)
Chilled by arctic winds in winter, and hit by fierce tornadoes in spring, the Midwest states usually enjoy long, hot summers.

Warm Tropical (Florida)
The sultry climate of Florida and the Gulf of Mexico is usually warm and frequently very humid. Hurricanes can hit the coast between June and late November, making December to April the most popular time to visit the region.

National Parks

For many visitors, the highlight of a visit to the US is to experience the country's sublime scenery and abundant wildlife. Some 84 million acres (34 million hectares) of pristine splendor have been preserved as national parks, found in 49 of the 50 states. From Acadia National Park on the rugged coast of Maine to the deserts of Death Valley in California, the parks encompass a variety of terrain, as well as the habitats of several endangered species. Most have a full range of facilities, including delightful rustic lodges, and offer a variety of outdoor activities.

Yellowstone National Park (see pp584–5) *in Wyoming is the country's first and oldest national park. Highlights include geysers and the country's largest bison herd.*

Grand Teton National Park's *(see p583)* peaks make it one of Wyoming's top sights.

Badlands National Park *(see p444)*, South Dakota's most important park, combines craggy sandstone formations with mixed grass prairie.

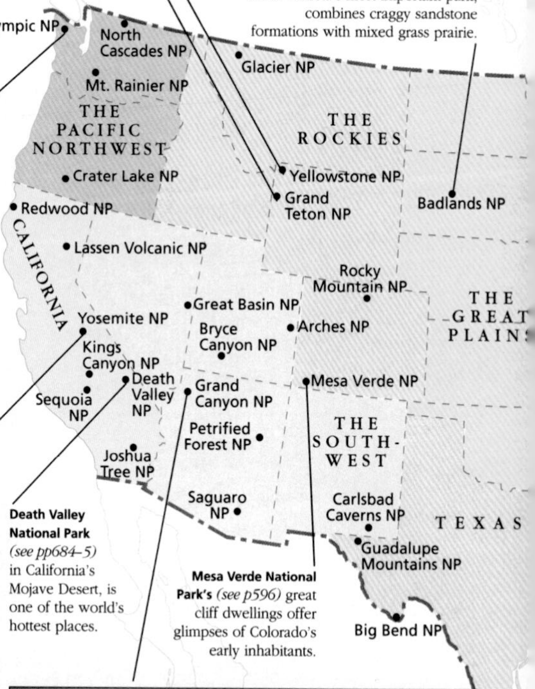

Olympic National Park (see p620), *a UNESCO biosphere reserve, preserves Washington's lush forests.*

Death Valley National Park *(see pp684–5)* in California's Mojave Desert, is one of the world's hottest places.

Mesa Verde National Park's *(see p596)* great cliff dwellings offer glimpses of Colorado's early inhabitants.

Yosemite National Park (see p718), *a wilderness of forests, meadows, and granite rocks, is California's prime destination.*

Grand Canyon National Park (see pp536–9), *perhaps the most-visited park in both Arizona and the US, is an awe-inspiring spectacle of magnificent rock formations.*

Voyageurs National Park (see p421), *an area of staggering natural beauty, was named after French-Canadian fur trappers. Although most visitors traverse the park's network of lakes and streams by boat, there are numerous hiking trails as well.*

Caribou in Denali National Park, Alaska

ALASKA

Kobuk Valley NP
Gates of the Arctic NP
Denali NP *(see pp742–3)*
Wrangell St. Elias NP
Lake Clark NP
Glacier Bay NP
Katmai NP
Kenai Fjords NP
(see p739)

HAWAI'I

Haleakalā NP
Hawai'i Volcanoes NP
(see pp752–3)

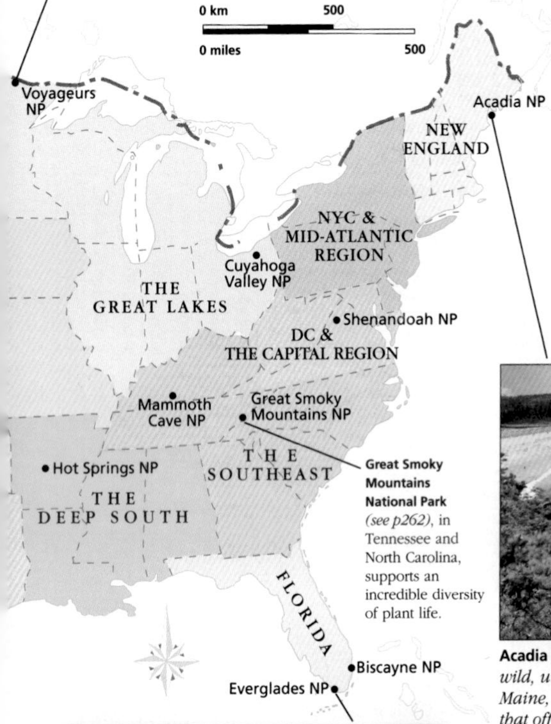

Great Smoky Mountains National Park *(see p262)*, in Tennessee and North Carolina, supports an incredible diversity of plant life.

Acadia National Park (see p172), *a wild, unspoiled island paradise in Maine, is crisscrossed by hiking trails that offer breathtaking coastal views. Its main attraction, however, is the scenic 27-mile (43-km) Loop Road.*

Everglades National Park (see p321) *covers a vast expanse of low-lying wetlands at the southern tip of Florida. This unique ecosystem is characterized by tree islands or hammocks that support a fantastic variety of flora and fauna. Alligators are the park's best-known and most-feared residents.*

Exploring the National Parks

A National Park ranger

It is no exaggeration to claim that one could spend a lifetime exploring the sprawling expanses of national parks such as the Grand Canyon or Yosemite. Most people visit parks simply because they happen to be near one, or to see specific sights such as the geysers of Yellowstone. To make their trip more worthwhile and enjoyable, visitors should restrict the number of parks they intend to visit, and instead explore a couple of the most appealing ones at leisure. Plan for a minimum of one full day per park.

BACKGROUND

The world's first national park was established in 1872 to protect the geothermal wonders and wild creatures of Yellowstone, on the crest of the Rocky Mountains. In the years since, a staggering 391 places of scenic or historical interest in the US have been given federal protection, including 58 parks within the National Park system.

America's national parks offer visitors some of the most unforgettable wilderness experiences anywhere in the world, from stunning glacial lakes and lush forests to arid expanses of desert.

The **National Park Service**, a unit of the US Department of the Interior, also manages national seashores, battlefields, and national historic sites (such as Independence Hall in Philadelphia, Pennsylvania) and national memorials (such as Mount Rushmore in South Dakota).

PLANNING YOUR VISIT

The national parks draw millions of visitors each year. In fact, the immensely popular Great Smoky Mountains National Park sees over 10 million visitors, while more than 3 million people visit comparatively remote parks such as Yellowstone and Yosemite. To avoid the crowds, aim to visit the parks outside the peak summer season (June–August), when they are full to capacity.

While the most popular parks are the jewels in the crown of US public lands, there are many quieter parks where you can enjoy nature without the crowds. Also try to take advantage of the many well-maintained trails to enable you to get away from the crowds and the traffic, and to really enjoy the parks at close range.

PASSPORTS, FEES & PERMITS

To help maintain their facilities, most parks charge admission fees, valid for seven days, which range from nominal amounts ($1–5) at the smaller sites to upwards of $20 at prime attractions. Some parks don't charge a fee but do collect charges for specific activities.

If planning to visit more than two or three parks, visitors should consider an **America the Beautiful – National Parks and Federal Recreational Lands Pass**. Valid for one year, these cost approximately $80, and give

TOP NATIONAL PARKS

Listed below, are some of the most popular national parks in the United States (in alphabetical order), including the top parks featured on the previous pages. This chart depicts the various types of landscape and geological formations that are found within each park.

	Volcanic/Geothermal	Mountainous	Glaciers	Climatic Extremes	Dramatic Erosion	Coral Reefs & Islands	Coastal Marshlands
Acadia NP, ME *(see p172)*			●				
Arches NP, UT *(see pp520–21)*					●		
Badlands NP, SD *(see p444)*					●		
Biscayne NP, FL *(see p322)*						●	
Bryce Canyon NP, UT *(see pp526–7)*					●		
Canyonlands NP, UT *(see p522)*					●		
Death Valley NP, CA *(see pp684–5)*				●			
Denali NP, AK *(see pp742–3)*		●					
Everglades NP, FL *(see p321)*							●
Glacier NP, MT *(see p579)*			●				
Glen Canyon & Lake Powell, AZ *(see p523)*					●		
Grand Canyon NP, AZ *(see p536–9)*					●		
Grand Teton NP, WY *(see p583)*		●					
Great Smoky Mts. NP, TN, NC *(see p262)*		●					
Hawai'i Volcanoes NP, HI *(see p752)*	●						
Mesa Verde NP, CO *(see p596)*				●			
Mount Rainier NP, WA *(see pp626–7)*	●						
Olympic NP, WA *(see p620)*				●			
Rocky Mountain NP, CO *(see p591)*		●					
Sequoia & Kings Canyon NP, CA *(see p719)*				●			
Shenandoah NP, VA *(see p219)*		●					
Voyageurs NP, MN *(see p421)*			●				
Yellowstone NP, WY *(see pp584–5)*	●						
Yosemite NP, CA *(see p718)*			●				
Zion NP, UT *(see p525)*					●		

Visitors overlooking Thunder Hole, Acadia National Park, Maine

admission to the bearer and passengers in the same private vehicle to all national parks and federal recreational lands, including national forests **Bureau of Land Management** properties. In parks where a per-person fee is charged, the pass admits the pass holder and three adults (children under 16 are free). This pass can be bought at any park entrance, or in advance via the Internet (www.store.usgs.gov/pass). US citizens or permanent residents over the age of 62 are eligible for the **Senior Pass** (for a one-time $10 fee), a lifetime pass to national parks, monuments, historic sites, recreation areas, and wildlife refuges. It admits the pass holder and accompanying passengers in a private vehicle (if there is a per-vehicle fee), or up to four adults (at sites with per-person fees). It also provides a 50 percent discount on federal fees charged for various facilities and must be obtained in person from a federal area, such as a national park or monument. The **Access Pass**, which has the same lifetime privileges as the Senior Pass, is issued free to US citizens or permanent residents with permanent disabilities. Documentation of disability is required.

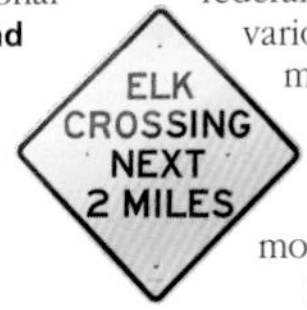

Wildlife warning sign

TYPES OF ACCOMMODATION

Visitor facilities vary from park to park. Some provide very basic amenities, while others, especially the popular ones, have deluxe hotels close by. It is advisable to make reservations for overnight accommodation well in advance. Some parks make reservations on a first-come-first-served basis only, so the sooner you arrive at your destination, the better.

Most parks have campsites for both tents and RVs but these are often "unserviced," with no RV hookups for electricity, water, or sewage. Campsites usually cost about $20 a night. The US Forest Service and **Bureau of Land Management** (BLM) campsites are less expensive and more readily available.

DIRECTORY

National Park Services
www.nps.gov
www.ohranger.com

National Park Campground Reservations
Tel (800) 365-2267.
www.recreation.gov

National Parks Pass
www.nps.gov/fee_passes.htm

US Forest Service
Tel (800) 832-1355.
www.fs.fed.us

Bureau of Land Management
Tel (202) 208-3801.
www.blm.gov

PRACTICAL TIPS FOR VISITING THE PARKS

- Wear appropriate clothing – sturdy boots, a protective hat, plus waterproof or warm clothing, depending on the conditions.
- Carry drinking water, a pair of binoculars, a first-aid kit, sun screen, and insect repellant.
- Do not litter. Use the litter bins provided, or carry your waste out of the park.
- Do not play loud music or blow car horns within park limits, as this disturbs everyone.
- Do not interfere, provoke, or try to feed any wildlife.
- Hunting is prohibited and visitors found in violation will face heavy penalties.
- Do not approach bears or other wild animals; they can be extremely dangerous.
- Talk softly when on park trails to improve your chances of spotting wildlife.
- Do not wander off on your own, and do not venture off marked park trails; it is not only hazardous if you encounter dangerous animals but is also easy to get lost in the wilderness.
- Be sure to tell a friend or fellow traveler your itinerary; in case you don't return on time they can inform the park ranger.
- Observe and obey all signs throughout the individual park regarding speed limits, food, animals, water, and all other safety precautions. Following these rules and regulations will enhance your enjoyment of the park and keep both you and the wildlife safe.

Great American Cities

One of the main attractions of visiting the US is the chance of enjoying its many great cities. They vary from Colonial-era, pedestrian-friendly places such as Boston, with its distinctly European ambience, to the frenzied modern metropolis of Los Angeles, where no one walks, except to and from the car. In between, there is a wide range of cities, each with its own history and culture. Washington, DC, the capital, is known for its political focus and national galleries; Miami offers a spicy taste of Latin America; New Orleans is packed with multicultural music, food, and fun; and New York and Chicago are famous for their architecture and exciting nightlife. On the West Coast, San Francisco and Seattle have picturesque settings and vibrant arts scenes. All in all, cities here have something for everyone.

Seattle (see pp616–19) *has risen from the ashes of the Great Fire of 1889 to become a prosperous city of gleaming skyscrapers, upscale shops, and sophisticated hotels.*

San Francisco's (see pp694–711) *many hills, ocean views, and rich ethnic mix give it a distinctive character, in keeping with its status as the West Coast's cultural capital.*

Dallas *(see pp478–9)* in many ways is synonymous with the wealth of Texan oil fields and cattle. Today, it is both the state's financial and entertainment center.

Los Angeles (see pp658–77) *is often associated with movies, the glamor of Hollywood, the luxury of residential Beverly Hills, and the excitement of Sunset Boulevard. Yet, this vibrant city is also home to some of the country's finest museums and galleries as well as the most popular beaches along the Pacific Ocean.*

Chicago (see pp386–97), *located on the southwestern edge of Lake Michigan, is famous throughout the world for its magnificent, innovative architecture. New building techniques were perfected here, and it was here too that architects, such as Frank Llyod Wright and others, created masterpieces of modern design.*

Boston (see pp132–49) *is justly proud of its past. While its Colonial heritage is reflected in its buildings, the city also includes numerous important sites directly related to America's fight for freedom.*

Philadelphia *(see pp98–105)*, where the Declaration of Independence was signed on July 4, 1776, is the birthplace of America. Today, this "City of Brotherly Love" is one of the country's most popular destinations.

New York (see pp64–89), *the "Big Apple," is one of the world's great cities. One aspect of its character lies in its striking modern architecture. Others revolve around its many outstanding museums, its ethnic neighborhoods, and the choice of entertainment.*

New Orleans *(see pp344–53)* is a fun city of bars, restaurants, and the always lively Mardi Gras celebrations.

Miami's *(see pp290–99)* focus of action concentrates on South Beach, with its Art Deco hotels and trendy shops.

Washington, DC (see pp196–211), *the nation's capital, is an impressive city of classical architecture and grand, tree-lined avenues. Beside its political focus, the city also has a cultural heart, with museums located along the Mall.*

Best Scenic Routes

One of the great pleasures of traveling in the US is the chance to explore its many scenic highways and byways. From quiet rural lanes to breathtaking coastal drives, they offer glimpses of the land's abundant natural beauty, and provide an opportunity to get to know its many inviting small towns. Many of the best-known routes are also historic and follow in the footsteps of the pioneer wagon trains, the Pony Express, or along trails taken by Civil War soldiers. For additional information on scenic routes, visit www.byways.org.

Going-to-the-Sun Road (see p579) *cuts across Glacier National Park, following the steep Rocky Mountain cliffs. The route offers breathtaking mountain views.*

Historic Columbia River Highway *(see p632)* offers incomparable views of Oregon's diverse landscape, including Mount Hood's snowcapped summit. It also passes several waterfalls and lush orchards.

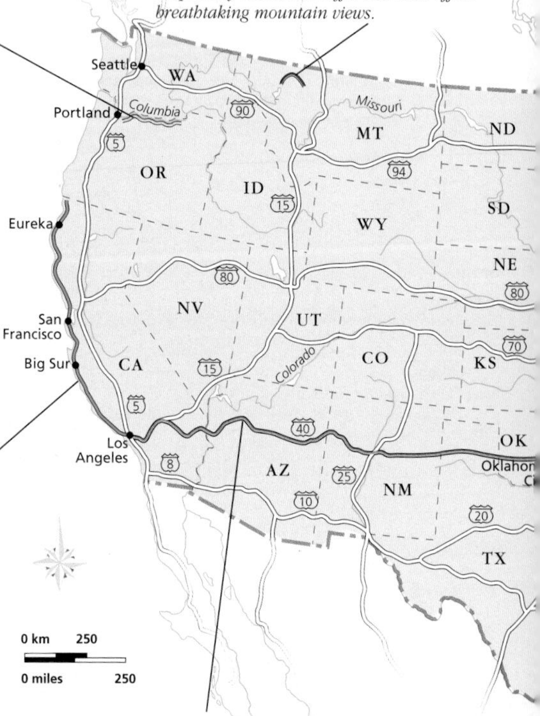

Pacific Coast Highway *(Highway 1) was named California's first scenic highway in 1966. One of the world's most stunning drives, its most beautiful stretch is through Big Sur.*

Route 66 (see p461), *from Chicago to Los Angeles, is perhaps America's best-loved highway. Much of the original route remains intact, offering a nostalgic cruise across the country's heartland.*

Route 100 *winds from north to south along the crest of the densely wooded Green Mountains in Vermont. This country road attracts "leaf peepers," who come here to enjoy the state's famous fall foliage.*

KEY

- Columbia River Scenic Highway *70 miles (113 km), 3–5 hours*
- Blue Ridge Parkway *469 miles (755 km), 2 days*
- Natchez Trace Parkway *425 miles (684 km), 2 days*
- Going-to-the-Sun Road *50 miles (80 km), 2–3 hours*
- Pacific Coast Highway *930 miles (1,497 km), 4 days*
- Route 66 *2,400 miles (3,864 km), 11 days*
- Great River Road *2,069 miles (3,331 km), 10 days*
- Route 100 *200 miles (322 km), 1 day*

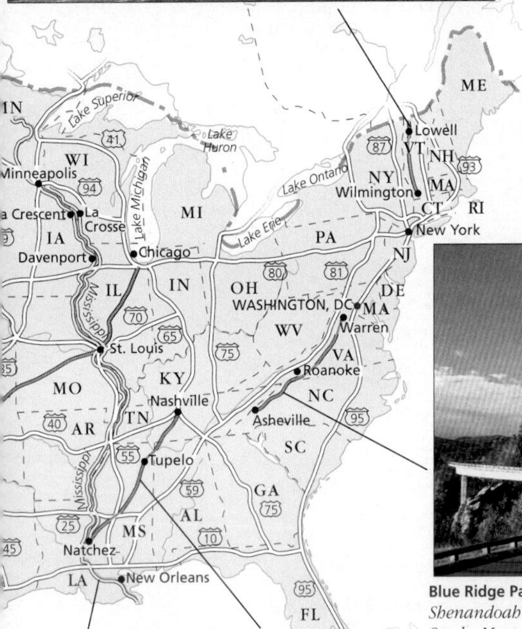

Blue Ridge Parkway (see pp218 & 249) *links Shenandoah National Park, VA and the Great Smoky Mountains National Park, NC. Over 20 million visitors travel along the road as it traverses the crest of the southern Appalachians.*

Natchez Trace Parkway (see p362), between Nashville, TN and Natchez, MS, cuts across the densely wooded trail taken by frontier traders more than a century earlier.

Great River Road *follows most of the course of the Mississippi, from its source in Minnesota to the Gulf of Mexico. Running along both banks of the river, the route takes in areas of great scenic beauty and many historic sites as well as large towns, such as St. Louis and New Orleans.*

HISTORY OF THE USA

Man first entered North America from Siberia some 13,000 and 30,000 years ago, migrating over the Bering Strait land bridge to Alaska. As the ice receded, they moved south into the rich gamelands of the Great Plains. Isolated from Eurasia by melting ice and rising sea levels, those early settlers were mainly hunter-gatherers, as agricultural life evolved sporadically.

During this period of isolation, unique ecological, genetic, and social patterns emerged that proved disastrously fragile when confronted by the first Europeans in the late 15th century.

EARLY EUROPEAN EXPLORERS

European exploration began in earnest when improvements in shipping made the longer voyages of Columbus (1492) and Cabot (1497) viable. Early explorers were astonished by the quantity of natural resources they encountered here. Fur-bearing animals such as beavers were quickly exploited for their pelts. Once Europeans began to investigate further, they were able to draw heavily on the indigenous peoples' detailed knowledge, and use their pre-existing trails to explore the continent. An early map of 1507 displays the name "America," taken from one of the New World's early explorers, Amerigo Vespucci.

COMPETING COLONIES

The long rivalry between Spain, France, and Great Britain continued with the discovery of the New World in 1492. Spain founded the first successful North American colonies, in Florida in 1565 and New Mexico in 1598, combining commercial and religious interests. France's first permanent settlement was at Quebec (1608), while the Dutch set up a trading post (1624) at the mouth of the Hudson River. However, it was the English who gained control, with colonies in Virginia (1607), New England (1620), and Pennsylvania (1681). Many early colonists died of disease and malnutrition. Virginia eventually became the most lucrative New World colony, thanks to the production of tobacco. By 1700, these English colonies' population was 250,000, excluding Native Americans, while only some 1,000 non-Natives lived in Spanish or French regions.

Christopher Columbus sets foot in the New World on October 12, 1492

◁ George Washington before Yorktown, painted by Rembrandt Peale between 1824 and 1825

John Trumbull's 1786 painting of the Battle of Bunker Hill

THE AMERICAN REVOLUTION

The 18th century was a period of significant change throughout the world, and this was especially true in the New World. Colonists expanded their domain, displacing or killing the native tribes through a combination of land purchases, warfare, and disease. In the southern colonies of Virginia and Carolina, where the lack of available land discouraged new immigrants, African slaves were imported in great numbers, reaching a total of 150,000, 40 percent of the population, by 1750.

The American Revolution began swiftly, and transformed the face of the world in a few short years. The removal of a potential French threat, following Britain's conquest of Canada in the Seven Years' War, led to American complaints about British abuse, epitomized by the phrase "No Taxation without Representation." In 1770, British troops opened fire on a group of unruly workers, killing five in what became known as the Boston Massacre. In 1773, some colonial merchants disguised as Indians dumped a boatload of tea into Boston Harbor, to protest Britain's monopoly of the tea trade.

War broke out in April 1775, when British "Redcoats" marched on the town of Concord in an attempt to seize a stockpile of weapons from the American "Minutemen." As the British fought their way back to Boston, more than 75 Redcoats and over 90 Americans were killed. The British occupied New York City and Philadelphia, while the ill-equipped Americans struggled through a harsh winter. The war moved south, and frontier fighters under Daniel Boone and George Rogers Clark captured British outposts in Kentucky and Illinois. The Americans eventually succeeded, largely due to French support, and the war officially ended in 1783.

Patriots disguised as Indians dumping tea into Boston Harbor, Boston Tea Party

KEY DATES IN HISTORY

1763 The Seven Years' War ends, France surrenders its Great Lakes lands to Great Britain

1773 Boston Tea Party

April 19, 1775 The Revolutionary War begins

1776 The Declaration of Independence is adopted in Philadelphia

1783 Treaty of Paris puts an end to the Revolutionary War

1790 A 100-mile square on the Maryland/Virginia border, Washington, the District of Columbia, is set aside as the new capital

1793 Samuel Slater's water-powered mill at Pawtucket, Rhode Island, brings the Industrial Revolution to the US

1803 Ohio is the first of the Northwest Territories to become a state

1803 The Louisiana Purchase

1814 Francis Scott Key composes "The Star-Spangled Banner"

1824 The Bureau of Indian Affairs, a division of the US War Department, is formed to handle relations with Indian tribes

1832 Resisting attempts to remove his people from their traditional homelands, Chief Black Hawk leads a militant band of 1,000 Fox-Sauk Indians but is destroyed by the US Army

George Washington holding a copy of the US Constitution, surrounded by Founding Fathers, 1787

BIRTH OF A NATION

By 1783, the newly formed United States of America had a draft constitution and a border that extended as far west as the Mississippi River. The new Constitution was officially adopted in 1788, and in 1791 the ten amendments of the "Bill of Rights" were added, enumerating each citizen's freedom of speech, press, religion, and public assembly. In 1800, the capital moved from Philadelphia to the newly created city of Washington, DC, which by now had a population of 3,200 people.

MANIFEST DESTINY

America expanded greatly in its early years, first opening the "Northwest Territory" lands along the Great Lakes in 1787. The Louisiana Purchase of 1803 added a huge area of western lands formerly controlled by France. This rapid expansion created the need to survey the new territories. Lewis and Clark's famed cross-continental expedition between 1803 and 1806, was funded by Congress at the express request of President Thomas Jefferson.

The first test of strength for this new independent country came in 1812, when the US found itself caught in the middle of an ongoing war between France and Great Britain. Though both countries agreed to stop interfering with American ships, US forces attacked British interests in Canada, and in retaliation the British burned the Capitol and White House in Washington, DC. Ironically, the war was ended by a peace treaty that was signed two weeks before its biggest skirmish – the Battle of New Orleans – took place in January 1815.

After the War of 1812, the US abandoned hopes of annexing Canada, and so began its great push westward. Settlers poured into the Great Plains, Oregon, and eventually the northern periphery of the Republic of Mexico, including Texas and California. The Santa Fe Trail, open for trade by 1823, brought New Mexico under US influence. By 1850, there was an extensive communications network. Steamboat traffic dominated the rivers, augmented by canals and cross-country railroads.

The consolidation of western lands encouraged millions of pioneers to migrate west and forge new lives for themselves. By the mid-19th century, people had grown accustomed to the idea that the country would stretch undivided across the continent, from ocean to ocean. This idea, in the words of populist journalist John L. O'Sullivan, was the country's "Manifest Destiny." Orderly settlement was made possible by the official survey and division of these lands into rectangular sections, each one square mile in area. Overland trails were opened leading west to the gold fields of California, which itself became a state in 1850. By 1860, more than half the population lived west of the Appalachian Mountains, compared to less than 10 percent in 1800.

An 1891 illustration depicting Indians fighting US soldiers

TERRITORIAL CONFLICT

Although involved in conflicts with Britain over Canada, the US managed to resolve these issues peacefully. However, this was not so with Mexico, which feared US territorial ambitions, especially after President Andrew Jackson offered to purchase Texas. The crisis accelerated after Texas declared independence from Mexico in 1835. Turning a blind eye to Native American tribes (and the legal ownership of much of the land by Spain), the United States took over Texas in 1845, a move that set off war with Mexico. This war in turn led to the US confiscation of California and much of the Southwest. In 1848, Mexico yielded nearly half of its territory; the cession of the northern Oregon territory by Britain in 1846, and James Gadsden's 1853 purchase of 30,000 square miles in the Southwest completed the westward expansion. Thus, in less than 50 years, the country had more than tripled in size.

KEY DATES IN HISTORY

1838 US Government forcibly expels native Cherokee Indians westward along the "Trail of Tears"

1846–1848 Mexican War. US acquires Arizona, California, Utah, Nevada, and New Mexico

1859 Abolitionist John Brown raids the Federal Armory at Harpers Ferry

1861 Confederates attack Fort Sumter in South Carolina

1861 The Battle of Bull Run (Manassas), the first major land battle of the Civil War

Jan 1, 1863 President Abraham Lincoln issues the Emancipation Proclamation, freeing slaves in areas controlled by the Confederate army

July, 1863 Union forces defeat General Robert E. Lee and the Confederacy at Gettysburg

April 9, 1865 Robert E. Lee surrenders to Union General Ulysses Grant at Appomattox Court House, Virginia

April 14, 1865 President Lincoln assassinated by a Confederate sympathizer, John Wilkes Booth, in Washington, DC

Dec 18, 1865 The 13th amendment to the US Constitution is adopted, effectively putting an end to slavery in the US

1870 African-Americans granted full citizenship

THE DESTRUCTION OF THE INDIANS

Since the 1500s, diseases such as small pox and syphilis had wiped out almost 90 percent of some tribes. As European settlement increased, forced relocation of tribes became frequent. It reached its peak with the forced march of most of the Cherokee Nation from the southeast to Oklahoma along the "Trail of Tears." As Europeans spread westward, tribes were forced onto reservations, often the poorest and most desolate lands, where many remain even today.

The building of the transcontinental railroads in the late 19th century opened the West to hunters who eventually killed millions of buffalo. Within a few hundred years, North America's indigenous cultures had been destroyed or marginalized by Europeans, who transformed the continent into a world economic, industrial, and political power.

CIVIL WAR

Between independence in 1783 and 1860, two very different societies developed within the US. In the North, there emerged an industrialized society, committed to liberal banking and credit systems, and protective tariffs, whereas the South was a less populous, agrarian society opposed to the sale of public land in the Midwest, high duties, and restrictions on slavery.

The causes of the Civil War are still up for debate. Though slavery was clearly the divisive issue, the war was not fought to free the slaves. Instead, the battle lines were drawn over the question of extending slavery into the newly forming western states. The South, resisting the federal government's growing power, wanted each new state to decide this question independently. The northern states wanted to keep slavery within its current limits, in part to protect their own manual labor. The federal government left the decision to the new states, and riots between pro- and anti-slave campaigners raged across the west. In 1856, pro-slave guerillas burned the city of Lawrence, Kansas, and 200 people were killed in retaliation. Three years later, 22 abolitionists led by John Brown attacked the Federal Armory at Harpers Ferry, Virginia, hoping to incite a slave rebellion. He and his forces were killed, but his efforts further polarized the already divided nation. By 1860, the country was composed of 18 "free states" – mainly in the North, and 15 "slave states" – mainly in the South. When Abraham Lincoln was elected president in 1860, South Carolina seceded from the Union, followed by six other southern states, which joined together to form the Confederate States of America.

The first shots of the Civil War were fired in April, 1861, when the Confederates attacked Fort Sumter in South Carolina. President Lincoln mobilized US soldiers to quell the rebellion, and soon four other slaveholding states, including Virginia, seceded from the Union. Richmond became the new Confederate capital, and Virginia provided most of the Confederate military leadership. Four slave states remained in the Union, and the western counties of Virginia separated to form West Virginia, which joined the Union in 1863.

The Confederates won the first major land battle at Manassas, Virginia, in July 1861, and for the next two years battles raged across Virginia and Maryland. With their defeat at Gettysburg in 1863, the Confederates were finally turned back. In the same year, Union forces gained control of the Mississippi River. Union forces destroyed Atlanta in 1864 and marched across Georgia, cutting off supply lines and virtually encircling the remaining Confederate army. By April 1865, the Civil War was over.

The destruction caused by the war was immense. Nearly three million soldiers (some 10 percent of the total population at the time) fought in the war, and 620,000 of them died. Entire cities lay in ruins, and it would be years before the nation recovered from the ravages of war.

Confederate forces occupy Fort Sumter, South Carolina, on April 15, 1861

THE WILD WEST

The end of the 19th century was a time of radical change across the country. The conquered South and the newly freed slaves suffered the ravages of the Reconstruction, while in the West, Native Americans saw their lands taken away and their lifestyles destroyed. Their culture's death knell was sounded in 1862, when the Homestead Act granted 160 acres of land to any white settler, freed slave, or single woman. The Army battled Indian tribes across the Great Plains in the 1870s and 1880s, and Indian resistance in the Southwest desert came to an end with the surrender of Apache chief Geronimo in 1886.

Buffalo Bill's Wild West poster, 1900

In the East and Midwest, massive mills and factories replaced local producers, as the population shifted from self-sufficient farms to the chaotic city life. In a relatively brief period, the pace of life was altered by the growth of railroads, the telegraph, the telephone, the airplane, and the automobile. Railroads brought the once-distant West within reach of eastern markets, and the frontier towns that appeared along the railroads were often lawless places. During this post-Civil War period, the US became an international power, buying Alaska from Russia in 1867, then taking over Hawai'i in 1893, the Philippines in 1899, and Panama in 1903.

KEY DATES IN HISTORY

1867 Russia sells Alaska for $7.2 million

1869 First transcontinental railroad is completed when the Union Pacific and Central Pacific meet at Promontory, Utah

1876 The Battle of Little Big Horn, Montana

1876 The US Supreme Court legalizes "separate but equal" facilities for whites and non-whites, sanctioning racial segregation

1884 New York and Boston telephone link

1886 The Statue of Liberty erected in New York

1898 USS *Maine* explodes in Havana, sparking Spanish-American War

1915 The Lincoln Highway from New York City to San Francisco is the first transcontinental highway

1915 The "Great Migration" of African-Americans to northern cities begins

April 6, 1917 US declares war on Germany

1925 Fundamentalist Christians ban the teaching of the theory of evolution in many states

1929 The US stock market crash

1934 Benny Goodman's orchestra popularizes "Swing" jazz

1939 The first regular commercial TV broadcasts begins

IMMIGRATION, URBANIZATION, & INDUSTRIALIZATION

While stories of the Wild West captivated people's imagination, the most significant development was the increasing importance of industrialization. The rapid demographic shift from small towns and farms to big cities and factories was inevitable. This change was made possible in part by waves of immigration that doubled the population in a few decades.

In the 1880s, over six million immigrants arrived, and by the first decade of the 20th century a million people were arriving every year. By World War I, the population reached 100 million, 15 percent of whom were foreign born. The majority settled in East Coast cities, and for the first time in US history the population was predominantly urban.

The consolidation of the population was mirrored by a consolidation in industry and business. By 1882, John D. Rockefeller's Standard Oil Company had a monopoly in the petroleum industry, followed by other effective monopolies, legally organized as "trusts," in tobacco products, banking, and steel. These corporations' abuse of monopoly power was exposed by such writers as Upton Sinclair and Frank Norris. Political movements too resisted the rise of corporations, finding an ally in "trust-busting" President Theodore Roosevelt, who also made significant steps toward protecting the natural environment from the ravages of unrestrained industrial development.

Cartoon of Uncle Sam welcoming immigrants into the "US Ark of Refuge"

The early 20th century also saw the growth of labor unions, which staged successful and sometimes violent strikes to improve pay and conditions, and helped protect children from working in factories.

BOOM & BUST

Involvement in World War I confirmed America's position as a world power, drawing the nation away from its long-cherished isolationism. But, after the war, soldiers returned home from Europe to severe unrest, with labor strikes and race riots. This economic depression caused enormous suffering and changed the domestic role of the government forever.

The 1920s, known as the "Jazz Age," saw an explosion of artistic creativity, especially in popular music. Architectural and engineering landmarks were constructed, and the rising popularity of the automobile encouraged the building of the first transcontinental highways, which linked the nation and gave rise to the first suburbs.

This creativity coincided with Prohibition, when the sale of alcohol was made illegal. Ironically, it was Prohibition itself that led to the freewheeling, drug-and alcohol-fuelled lifestyles of the Roaring Twenties.

Duke Ellington, celebrated icon of the Jazz Age

THE GREAT DEPRESSION & THE "NEW DEAL"

The Wall Street Crash of 1929 shattered millions of dreams and left many Americans destitute. Farmers and black people in cities and rural areas were particularly hard hit, as banks withdrew funding. Unemployment and the gross domestic product dropped to half of what it was in the 1920s. Extended drought and sustained winds caused such destruction that the Great Plains was dubbed the "Dust Bowl," forcing some 200,000 Great Plains farmers to migrate west to California.

The Republican government, which had promoted the boom and was blamed for the crash, was rejected by the electorate, leading to the 1932 election of Democrat Franklin Delano Roosevelt. In his first 100 days in office, Roosevelt established federal government relief programs (the "New Deal") to revitalize the economy, provide jobs, and aid those who were hurt by the economic downturn. Roosevelt also set up regulatory bodies to help prevent economic turmoil in the future. Although millions of dollars of federal funding were spent on relief, 20 percent of Americans still continued to be unemployed in 1939.

The battleships USS *West Virginia* and *Tennessee* burning after the Japanese attack on Pearl Harbor

THE COLD WAR

The Japanese attack on Pearl Harbor in 1941 and the subsequent US entry into World War II marked the beginning of America's new role in international politics. With the onset of the Cold War, the numerous US military bases, established during World War II, gained renewed importance. The Cold War also encouraged alliances with other nations. America's powerful influence, and investment overseas was seen as a way to bind other nations to the capitalist sphere. The Marshall Plan of 1948 provided $13 billion to aid reconstruction of postwar western Europe and reduce Communist influence.

Economic and social developments were often overshadowed by the specter of nuclear war. The Korean War was the first of many fought to stop the spread of Communism. Fear on the domestic front inspired years of anti-Communist "Witch Trials," such as those conducted by Senator Joseph McCarthy. Cold War fears also led to numerous military operations around the world, including the takeover of Guatemala in 1954, an ill-fated invasion of Cuba in 1961, and the Vietnam War of the 1960s and 1970s, the longest and most costly of attempts to contain the perceived Communist threat.

After Vietnam, the US retreated from an active international role. The Soviet invasion of Afghanistan in 1979 revived the Cold War for another decade. With the collapse of the Soviet Union in 1991, the United States became the world's only superpower.

KEY DATES IN HISTORY

Dec 7, 1941 Japanese attack on Pearl Harbor

1945 The UN established in San Francisco

Aug 14, 1945 After US bombing of Hiroshima and Nagasaki, Japan surrenders, ending WW II

1950 The Korean War begins

1961 Alan Shepard is the first American in outer space; the Soviets erect the Berlin Wall

1962 Naval blockade against Soviet missile bases in Cuba

1963 Assassination of John F. Kennedy, Dallas

1968 Martin Luther King Jr. assassinated

1969 Neil Armstrong walks on the moon

1970 The Environmental Protection Agency (EPA) is established

1974 Richard Nixon resigns after Watergate

1989 Fall of Berlin Wall; end of Cold War

1990–1 The Gulf War

Sept 11, 2001 Terrorist attacks on NYC & DC

2003 Space shuttle *Columbia* explodes, killing all on board

2003 George W. Bush declares war on Iraq

2005 Hurricane Katrina wreaks havoc in New Orleans and other cities of Louisiana and Mississippi, displacing more than 500,000 people

2008 Banking collapse triggers recession

POSTWAR PROSPERITY

Unlike much of the rest of the world, this was one of the most prosperous periods in US history. The economy, stimulated by mobilization of industry during World War II, and the arms race with the Soviet Union were key factors in creating unprecedented affluence. As manufacturing switched to a peacetime mode, consumer durables flowed into the marketplace. America's position at the hub of the international trading system gave her access to crucial foreign markets. Home ownership was

Vietnam veterans marching toward the Democratic National Convention, Miami Beach

brought within reach of middle-class Americans, thanks to government supports and mass-production construction techniques. Most adults owned a car, and consumer products, such as refrigerators, washers, dryers, and dishwashers, multiplied within the home.

CIVIL RIGHTS MOVEMENT

As black Americans migrated from the rural south to urban centers in the 1940s and 1950s, whites abandoned city life for the suburbs, taking their tax dollars with them. The financial crisis was made worse by the decline of traditional industries, and many cities during the 1960s and 1970s suffered as well. Housing deteriorated, roads went unrepaired, and poverty, crime, and racial tension were common features of many urban areas. Poverty was not confined to the inner cities; people in rural areas in the Deep South and the Appalachians were some of the most deprived in the country.

The new postwar opportunities were denied to many African-Americans, particularly in the still-segregated South. Aided by a 1954 Supreme Court judgment that ruled segregation unconstitutional, African Americans fought for an end to discrimination. In 1955, a bus boycott in Montgomery, Alabama, forced the company to end segregation. The success inspired similar protests throughout the South. In 1964 and 1965, Congress passed legislation banning racial discrimination.

The 1960s also saw a rise in political consciousness among other groups; protests against the Vietnam War grew in number, as did the movement for women's rights. In the 1970s, the women's movement narrowly failed to achieve an end to sexual discrimination. During the AIDS crisis of the late 1980s, homosexuality became an increasingly accepted aspect of life, with gay and lesbian couples earning greater legal protections.

THE MODERN ERA

The postwar boom ended in the early 1970s, with the Vietnam War and the energy crisis producing prolonged inflation and recession. American firms tried to secure access to valuable raw materials, particularly oil in the Middle East, and companies found ways to exploit cheap foreign labor by establishing factories overseas.

Reverend Martin Luther King Jr. delivering a sermon at the Ebenezer Baptist Church, Atlanta

In the 1980s, computers and other digital devices began to change the way Americans communicated. The Internet opened new ways of working and generated large amounts of wealth. By the turn of the millennium, the Internet-fuelled boom went bust, causing the economy to fall into recession. The controversial appointment of George W. Bush dominated the news and showed that the American public was deeply divided over crucial issues.

The terrorist attacks on New York and Washington, DC in September 2001, instigated President Bush to launch a war against terrorism. This resulted in a war against the Taliban in Afghanistan in 2002 and another one to oust Saddam Hussain in Iraq in 2003. Economic stress from five years of warfare combined with deregulation of the financial sector resulted in crisis for the economy in late 2008. The presidential election campaigns of 2008 spelled a new direction in US politics, with greater representation of women and minorities. African-American Barack Obama won, becoming the 44th president.

The American Presidents

The presidents of the United States have come from all walks of life; at least two were born in a log cabin – Abraham Lincoln and Andrew Jackson. Others, such as Franklin D. Roosevelt and John F. Kennedy, came from privileged backgrounds. Millard Fillmore attended a one-room schoolroom, and Jimmy Carter raised peanuts. Many, including Ulysses S. Grant and Dwight D. Eisenhower, were military men, who won public popularity for their great achievements in battle.

KEY TO TIMELINE

- Federalist
- Democratic Republican
- Whig
- Republican
- Democrat

George Washington (1789–97) was a Revolutionary War general. He was unanimously chosen to be the first president of the United States.

James Madison (1809–17), known as the Father of the Constitution, was co-author of the Federalist Papers.

W.H. Harrison (1841)

James K. Polk (1845–49)

Zachary Taylor (1849–50)

Millard Fillmore (1850–53)

Franklin Pierce (1853–57)

Andrew Johnson (1865–69)

Rutherford B. Hayes (1877–81)

Chester A. Arthur (1881–85)

Benjamin Harrison (1889–93)

William McKinley (1897–1901)

1775 1800 1825 1850 1875

1775 1800 1825 1850 1875

John Adams (1797–1801), a lawyer and historian, was the first president to live in the White House.

Thomas Jefferson (1801–1809), architect, inventor, landscape designer, diplomat, and historian, was the quintessential Renaissance man.

James Monroe (1817–25)

John Quincy Adams (1825–29)

Andrew Jackson (1829–37) defeated the British at the Battle of New Orleans in the War of 1812.

Martin Van Buren (1837-41)

John Tyler (1841–45)

James Buchanan (1857–61)

Abraham Lincoln (1861–65) won the epithet, the Great Emancipator, for his role in the abolition of slavery. He led the Union through the Civil War.

Ulysses S. Grant (1869–77)

James A. Garfield (1881)

Grover Cleveland (1885–89)

Grover Cleveland (1893–97)

Woodrow Wilson (1913–21) led the country through World War I and paved the way for the League of Nations.

Harry S. Truman (1945–53) made the decision to drop the atomic bombs on Hiroshima and Nagasaki in 1945.

John F. Kennedy (1961–63) was one of the most popular presidents. He sent the first astronaut into space, started the Peace Corps, and created the Arms Control and Disarmament Agency. His assassination rocked the nation.

Richard Nixon (1969–74) opened up China and sent the first men to the moon. He resigned after the Watergate scandal.

Franklin D. Roosevelt (1933–45) started the "New Deal", a reform and relief program, during the Great Depression. He was elected to four terms.

Jimmy Carter (1977–81), who brokered the peace accord between Israel and Egypt, won the 2002 Nobel Peace prize.

Barack Obama (2009–) becomes the first African-American president.

George Bush (1989–93)

1900 | 1925 | 1950 | 1975 | 2000 | 2025

1900 | 1925 | 1950 | 1975 | 2000 | 2025

William H. Taft (1909–13)

Dwight D. Eisenhower (1953–61)

Gerald Ford (1974–77)

George W. Bush (2001–09)

Herbert Hoover (1929–33)

Warren Harding (1921–23)

Calvin Coolidge (1923–29)

Lyndon B. Johnson (1963–69) escalated the Vietnam conflict, resulting in widespread protests.

Ronald Reagan (1981–89), a one-time movie actor and popular president, cut taxes, increased military spending, and reduced government programs.

William J. Clinton's (1993–2001) two-term presidency saw unprecedented prosperity.

Theodore Roosevelt (1901–9) created many national parks and oversaw the construction of the Panama Canal.

THE ROLE OF THE FIRST LADY

First Lady & Senator Hillary Clinton in New York, 1999

In the 19th century, the First Lady acted primarily as hostess and "behind-the-scenes" adviser. Dolley Madison was known as the "Toast of Washington." Later, when Eleanor Roosevelt held her own press conferences, the role of First Lady changed greatly. Jackie Kennedy gave unprecedented support to the arts, Rosalynn Carter attended Cabinet meetings, Nancy Reagan told the world to "Just Say No" to drugs, Barbara Bush promoted literacy, and Hillary Clinton ran her own political campaign.

NYC & THE MID-ATLANTIC REGION

INTRODUCING NEW YORK CITY & THE MID-ATLANTIC REGION 56–63

NEW YORK CITY 64–89

NEW YORK STATE 90–95

NEW JERSEY 96–97

PHILADELPHIA, PA 98–105

PENNSYLVANIA 106–109

NYC & the Mid-Atlantic Region at a Glance

The three-state region surrounding New York City is one of the most fascinating areas in the US. New Jersey, the region's smallest but most densely populated state, extends between New York and Philadelphia. To its west, the idyllic pastoral landscape of Pennsylvania stretches almost all the way to the Great Lakes, with towns, green farm valleys, and the rolling folds of the Allegheney Mountains. Farther north, New York State has cities, towns, and rural hamlets spreading between the Hudson River Valley and Niagara Falls. Of the two main cities, New York City is a vibrant, cosmopolitan city and the financial capital of the world, while Philadelphia is more historic, in keeping with its status as the capital of Colonial America.

Niagara Falls (see p95), *located on the border between Canada and the US, is one of New York State's prime attractions, drawing more than 10 million visitors a year.*

Pittsburgh (see p108), *in Pennsylvania, has rebuilt itself from the ashes of an industrial past to become one of the country's most attractive cities. The Andy Warhol Museum and the Carnegie Institute are popular tourist attractions here.*

Gettysburg (see p106) *is one of Pennsylvania's most significant historic sites. In July 1863, this peaceful town was the scene of a devastating Civil War battle. It was here, four months later, that President Abraham Lincoln delivered his moving Gettysburg Address.*

◁ **A view of New York City's glittering skyscrapers as seen from Brooklyn Bridge**

New York State (see p90–95) *offers a diversity of landscapes, from the beauty of the Hudson Valley, to the craggy Adirondack Mountains and the lush wine country of the Finger Lakes. Other highlights include Albany, the state capital, and the awesome Niagara Falls.*

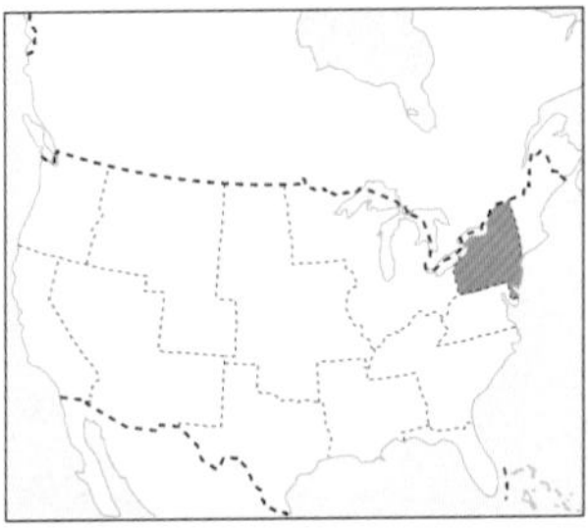

LOCATOR MAP

New York City (see pp64–89), *with its world-class museums and wide variety of shopping, dining, and entertainment options, is one of the most frequently visited cities in the United States. Its most distinctive sight is the Statue of Liberty, the symbol of freedom for millions who have now made this city their home.*

Philadelphia (see pp98–105), *the "City of Brotherly Love," was the focus of the revolutionary movement for American independence. Its historic Independence National Historic Park preserves structures and artifacts relating to those stirring times.*

Cape May (see p97), *at the southern tip of New Jersey, is a Victorian-period resort that draws many visitors. The state's other attractions include the opulent casinos of Atlantic City and the picturesque wilds of the Delaware Gap.*

NEW YORK CITY & THE MID-ATLANTIC REGION

The tri-state region around New York City truly embodies American diversity and dynamism. The vitality of New York City and Philadelphia is balanced by a surprisingly calm, almost pastoral hinterland. The Mid-Atlantic landscape is spectacular and ranges from dramatic mountain scenery, superb river valleys, and forests, interspersed with rolling farmlands.

New York City, or the "Big Apple," dominates northeastern US, and to a large extent controls the country's economy and culture. It is, without exaggeration, one of the world's great cities, and it is hard to imagine visiting the region without spending some time here. Philadelphia, the other major city, was the nation's leading city during Colonial times, and its wealth of history offers unforgettable insights into early American ideals.

Fascinating as these cities are, the broader region around them paints a much fuller picture of the nation. New Jersey, despite its reputation for heavy industry and sprawling suburbia, has much to offer, from the Victorian-era coastal resort of Cape May to Ivy League Princeton University. Pennsylvania, to the west, juxtaposes peaceful scenes of rural farmland in the "Pennsylvania Dutch" country where Amish and Mennonite communities still speak German (Deutsch), with the industrial cities of Pittsburg and Reading. Farther north, the state of New York has majestic mountains, picturesque lakes, and the scenic Hudson River Valley.

HISTORY

The Mid-Atlantic Region's natural wealth supported some of early America's most powerful and accomplished Native peoples. The first main groups were the Algonquian tribes, including the Lenni Lenape who lived in what is now New Jersey and Pennsylvania. In the early 16th century, the Algonquian Indians were ousted by incoming tribes of Iroquois Indians. Settling in the Finger Lakes area in central New York State, the

Amish farmers harvesting corn in Lancaster County, Pennsylvania

◁ Swirling mists surround the Niagara Falls, New York State's most famous natural wonder

Iroquois, one of North America's most socially sophisticated tribes, formed a powerful alliance among their five constituent tribes – the Senecas, Cayugas, Oneidas, Mohawks, and Onondagas.

Around this time, the first Europeans were making efforts to forge trade relations. Although Giovanni da Verrazano visited New York as early as 1524, it was not until 1609, when the Dutch West India Company sent Henry Hudson to explore the river that now bears his name, that the first settlements were established. In the same year, a French explorer, Samuel de Champlain, laid claim to northeastern New York State, having ventured there by way of Quebec.

Giovanni da Verrazano

In 1624 the Dutch founded the region's first colony, Fort Orange, at present-day Albany, began another at New Amsterdam (later New York) the following year, and later expanded to make footholds in New Jersey and

KEY DATES IN HISTORY

1524 Italian sailor Giovanni da Verrazano sails into New York harbor

1609 Henry Hudson explores and maps the Hudson River and New Jersey shore

1624 The Dutch establish Fort Orange

1664 England takes over New Netherland. The city of New Amsterdam is renamed New York

1731 Benjamin Franklin establishes the nation's first public library in Philadelphia

1776 The Declaration of Independence is adopted in Philadelphia

1825 The 363-mile (588-km) Erie Canal opens

1863 Union forces defeat Robert E. Lee and the Confederacy at Gettysburg

1929 Stock Market crash triggers the Great Depression

1933 New York Governor Franklin Delano Roosevelt is elected president

1978 Gambling legalized in Atlantic City

1987 Stock Market crash

1994 Rudolph Giuliani becomes mayor of New York City

2001 World Trade Center (WTC) destroyed in terrorist attack

2004 Cornerstone laid for new tower at WTC site

Detail from Benjamin West's monumental *Penn's Treaty with the Indians*, circa 1770

Pennsylvania. Relations between the Dutch and the Indians were mutually beneficial, in that the Dutch supplied guns and other metal products to the Indians, who paid for them with valuable beaver and other pelts. However, contact with foreigners led to the spread of diseases, including smallpox and measles, which soon decimated Native populations.

From the 1660s onward, as England wrestled for power in the New World, upstate New York evolved into a battleground for distant European wars. To consolidate their control over trans-Atlantic trade, the English first acquired the Dutch colonies and established a new one of their own – Pennsylvania. This colony, which developed on land granted by King Charles II to wealthy Quaker William Penn in 1680, thrived, thanks to fertile soil, a healthy climate, and a group of comparatively wealthy and industrious colonists. Its capital, Philadelphia, flourished and became the key center of the nascent movement for American independence.

INDEPENDENCE & INDUSTRY

Throughout the first half of the 18th century, the English and their American colonists fought a series of frontier battles against the French and their Indian allies. The cost of these wars in loss of life and property was high, and to pay for them the English crown raised a series of taxes, many of which were especially onerous for the merchants of New York and Philadelphia. In 1774, and again in 1776, delegates to Philadelphia's Continental Congress debated the issues and eventually declared independence from

England. Soon after, the English military occupied New York and Philadelphia and held them until the end of the Revolutionary War in 1783.

Perhaps the most significant early battle took place in the summer of 1777 at Saratoga Springs, where patriots defeated the English under General John Burgoyne. Although this success earned the Americans the vital support of France, the revolutionary forces, organized into the Continental Army under George Washington, still suffered tremendous hardships. More than 3,000 soldiers died of disease at Valley Forge, outside Philadelphia, in the winter of 1777–78. After the British abandoned their American colonies in 1783, New York City served as the capital of the new nation until 1790, followed by Philadelphia from 1790 to 1800.

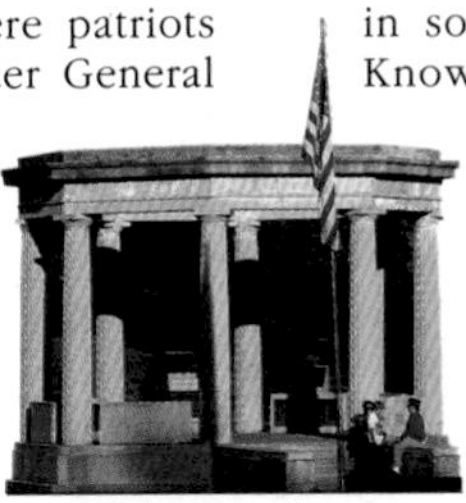

War memorial in Congress Park, Saratoga Springs

Although the battle for independence was fought and won by farmers and tradesmen, the following century saw the region emerge as a major industrial powerhouse. The Erie Canal was cut across upstate New York between 1817 and 1825, and Pennsylvania became the nation's biggest producer of coal and steel. Railroads crisscrossed the region by the mid-19th century, and it was this industrial might that enabled the North to withstand the divisive Civil War. The region sent more than 600,000 men to fight for the Union, but the main battle fought here was in July 1863, at the small town of Gettysburg in southeastern Pennsylvania. Known as the "high tide" of the war, this battle was the northern limit of Confederate success, the only time southern forces crossed the Mason-Dixon Line, the Pennsylvania–Maryland border that marked the divide between free and slave states.

San Gennaro Festival in Manhattan's Little Italy

PEOPLE & CULTURE

For nearly a century after the Civil War, the mines, mills, and factories of New York, New Jersey, and Pennsylvania attracted a huge influx of European immigrants. Between 1880 and 1910, some 12 million immigrants passed through New York City's port. During the World War years more people, including African Americans from the Deep South, came here to work in the several arms-related factories. Today, as much as one-third of the present population counts itself as ethnic minorities, and in many cities these "minorities" often comprise a large majority of the residents. Thus some neighborhoods are identified by their ethnic makeup – Chinatown or Little Italy in New York City, the Italian Market in South Philadelphia, or the Polish areas of Pittsburgh's South Side.

Years of labor strife, and many economic upheavals led to many industries closing down in the 1960s and 70s. New York City, the financial center of world capitalism, flirted with bankruptcy in the 1970s.

Today, however, things are different. "Heritage tourism" of battlefields, former industrial sites, historic canals, and railroads is a significant business, drawing almost as many millions of visitors as the natural wonders of Niagara Falls.

Exploring New York City & the Mid-Atlantic Region

The two major cities of New York and Philadelphia naturally dominate travel in the Mid-Atlantic Region. However, the region's other attractions include the exclusive summer retreats of the Hamptons, the collegian environs of Princeton, and industrial Pittsburg, today a vibrant cultural center. Equally attractive are its scenic wonders, ranging from the broad beaches of New Jersey and the tranquil beauty of Pennsylvannia's Amish Country to the wilderness of New York State's Adirondacks. A car is essential to explore the region's vast interior. All roads tend to lead through both New York City and Philadelphia, especially the New Jersey Turnpike (I-95), the main north–south artery. Heading west from the coast, the two main roads are I-80 across Pennsylvania and I-90, the New York Thruway. Many state and country roads connect the rural areas, while the major cities have good Amtrak and commuter train services.

Taughannock Falls surrounded by trees in fall foliage, Taughannock Falls State Park

SIGHTS AT A GLANCE

New York City pp64–89 1

New York State
Jones Beach State Park 2
The Hamptons & Montauk 3
Hudson River Valley 4
Albany 5
Saratoga Springs 6
Adirondack Mountains 7
Cooperstown 8
Finger Lakes 9
Syracuse 10
Rochester 11
Chautauqua 12
Buffalo 13
Niagara Falls 14

New Jersey
Princeton 15
Atlantic City 16
Cape May 17

Pennsylvania
Philadelphia pp98–105 18
Gettysburg 19
Lancaster 20
Hershey 21
York 22
Reading 23
Longwood Gardens 24
Pittsburgh 25
Laurel Highlands 26
Western Amish Country 27

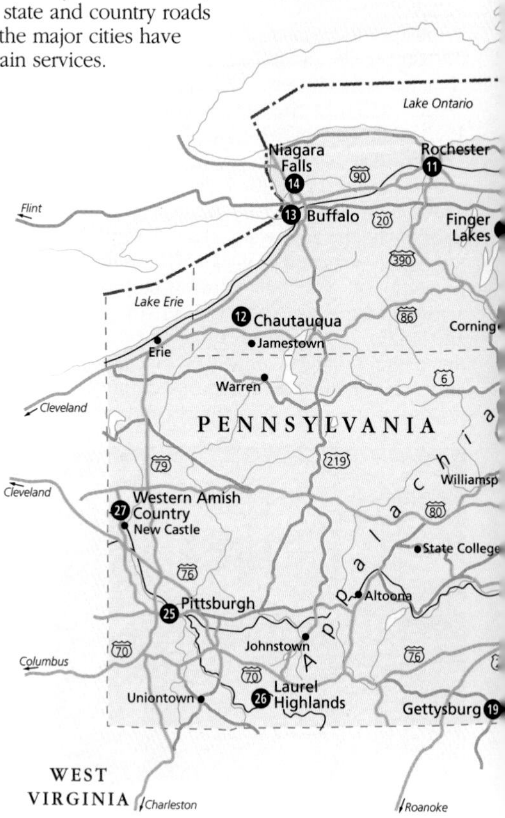

SEE ALSO

- ***Practical Information*** pp110–11
- ***Where to Stay*** pp112–17
- ***Where to Eat*** pp118–21

MILEAGE CHART

NEW YORK CITY, NY

150 241	*ALBANY, NY*					
396 634	**292** 470	*BUFFALO, NY*				
126 203	**284** 454	**475** 764	*ATLANTIC CITY, NJ*			
100 160	**251** 404	**414** 666	**62** 100	*PHILADELPHIA, PA*		
179 288	**304** 489	**420** 675	**164** 264	**102** 164	*YORK, PA*	
366 589	**499** 803	**215** 346	**366** 589	**304** 489	**220** 354	*PITTSBURGH, PA*

10 = Distance in miles
10 = Distance in kilometers

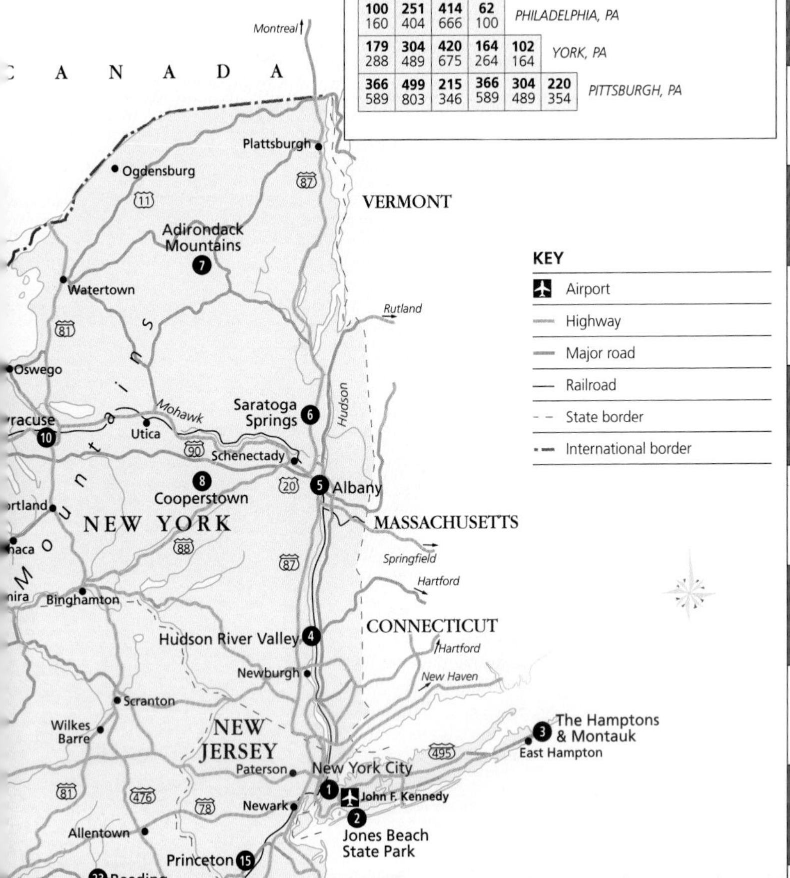

A view of Philadelphia's impressive modern architecture

New York City ❶

With its skyscrapers and bright lights, this is a city of superlatives. It covers an area of 301 sq miles (780 sq km), and comprises the five distinct boroughs of Manhattan, the Bronx, Queens, Brooklyn, and Staten Island. Most of the major sights lie within Manhattan, the southern tip of which was the target of the September 11, 2001 terrorist attack. Glittering shops, museums, and theaters are in Midtown and along Central Park.

KEY TO STREET FINDER

- Place of interest
- Airport
- Ferry terminal
- Subway station
- Main railroad station
- Bus terminal
- Tourist information
- Church
- Synagogue
- Highway

SIGHTS AT A GLANCE

Wall Street ①
World Trade Center Site ②
Battery Park City ③
Statue of Liberty ④
Ellis Island ⑤
South Street Seaport ⑥
Brooklyn Bridge p68 ⑦
Civic Center ⑧
Eldridge Street Synagogue ⑨
Chinatown ⑩
Little Italy ⑪
TriBeCa ⑫
SoHo Historic District ⑬
Washington Square ⑭
Greenwich Village ⑮
East Village ⑯
Union Square ⑰
Flatiron Building ⑱
Madison Square ⑲
Empire State Building p73 ⑳
Herald Square ㉑
Times Square ㉒
The New York Public Library ㉓
Morgan Library & Museum ㉔
Grand Central Terminal ㉕
United Nations ㉖
Rockefeller Center ㉗
St. Patrick's Cathedral p77 ㉘
Museum of Modern Art ㉙
Fifth Avenue ㉚
A Tour of Central Park pp78–9 ㉛
Whitney Museum of American Art ㉜
Frick Collection ㉝
Metropolitan Museum of Art ㉞
The Solomon R. Guggenheim Museum p82 ㉟
American Museum of Natural History ㊱
Lincoln Center ㊲

Greater New York
(see inset map)

Columbia University ㊳
Riverside Church ㊴
St. Nicholas Historic District ㊵
Studio Museum in Harlem ㊶
The Cloisters p86 ㊷
The Bronx ㊸
Brooklyn ㊹

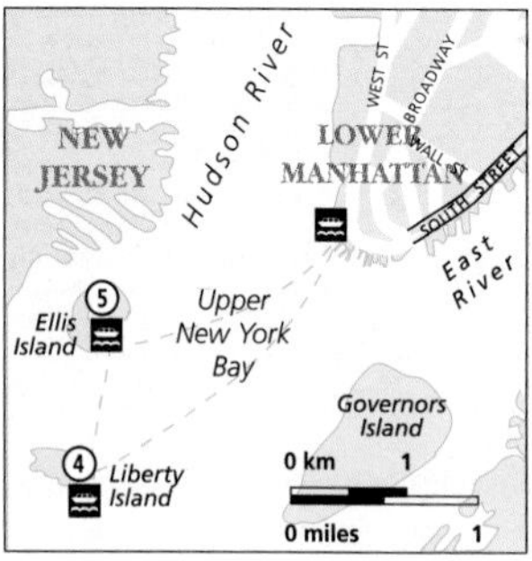

A B C

GETTING AROUND

With over 6,000 miles (9,600 km) of streets, walking around New York can be very strenuous. The city's taxis are convenient, except during rush hour. Other options are buses or the subway; the public transportation system is safe and an excellent way to get around the city.

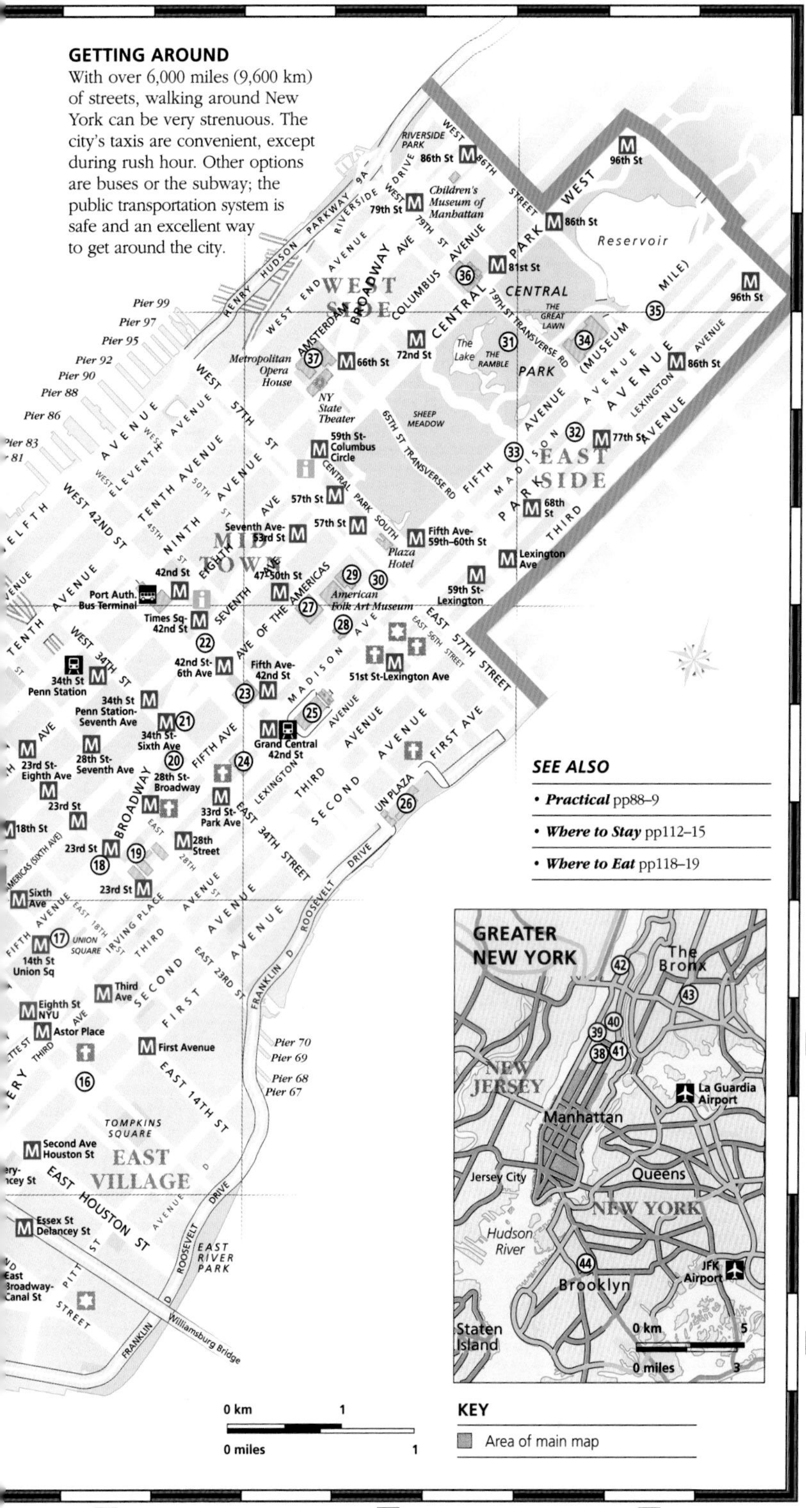

SEE ALSO

- ***Practical*** pp88–9
- ***Where to Stay*** pp112–15
- ***Where to Eat*** pp118–19

0 km 1
0 miles 1

KEY

Area of main map

Trinity Church at the foot of Wall Street

Wall Street ①

Map B5. *2, 3, 4, 5 to Wall St, I, R, W to Rector St.* *M1, M6, M15.*

Named for the wall that kept enemies and warring Indians out of Manhattan, Wall Street is now the heart of the city's financial district. One of the prominent sites here is the **Federal Reserve Bank** on Liberty Street. Inspired by the Italian Renaissance, this is a government bank for banks, where US currency is issued. Five-stories below ground is a large storehouse for international gold. Each nation's hoard is stored in its own compartment within the subterranean vault, guarded by 90-ton doors.

Farther away is the **Federal Hall National Monument**, where a bronze statue of George Washington on the steps marks the site where the nation's first president took his oath of office in 1789 *(see p61)*. The imposing structure was built between 1834 and 1842 as the US Custom House, and is one of the finest Classical designs in the city.

At the head of Wall Street is **Trinity Church**. Built in 1846, this square-towered Episcopal church is the third one on this site in one of America's oldest Anglican parishes, founded in 1697. Designed by Richard Upjohn, it was one of the grandest churches of its day, marking the beginning of the best period of Gothic Revival architecture in America. The sculpted brass doors were inspired by Ghiberti's *Doors of Paradise* in Florence. Its 280-ft (85-m) steeple was New York's tallest structure until the 1860s. Many famous New Yorkers are buried here.

The hub of the world's financial markets, the **New York Stock Exchange** (NYSE) is housed in a 17-story building built in 1903. Initially, trading in stocks and shares took place haphazardly in the area, but 24 brokers signed an agreement in 1792 to deal only with one another. This formed the basis of the NYSE. Membership was strictly limited and a "seat" that cost $25 in 1817 had climbed to $3–4 million in recent times. The NYSE became a for-profit public company in 2006. The NYSE has weathered slumps ("bear markets") and booms ("bull markets") and has seen advances in technology, from tickertape to electronic trading, turn a local market into a global one.

Bronze bull, symbol of Wall Street, near Custom House

Trinity Church
Broadway at Wall St. ***Tel*** *(212) 602-0800.* *7am–6pm Mon–Fri; 8am– 4pm Sat, 7am–4pm Sun.* *12:05pm Mon–Fri; 9am, 11:15am Sun.* **Concerts** *1pm Thu.*
www.trinitywallstreet.org

New York Stock Exchange
20 Broad St. ***Tel*** *(212) 656-3000.*
Visitors' gallery closed for security reasons.
www.nyse.com

World Trade Center Site ②

Map B5. Viewing wall on Church St. *Cortlandt St, Rector St, WTC Station.* **www**.panynj.gov/wtcprogress

Immortalized by countless filmmakers and photographers, the twin towers of the World Trade Center dominated the Manhattan skyline for 27 years, until the September 2001 terrorist attack. The enormous weight of each building was supported by an inner wire cage, which melted from the heat of the fire caused by the two aircraft that were flown into the towers. These towers were part of a buildings complex consisting of six office blocks and a hotel, connected by a vast underground concourse lined with shops and restaurants. A bridge linked the complex to the World Financial Center, which survived the attack.

The "Ground Zero" perimeter continues to shrink as buildings around the site are reoccupied. Things are moving slowly due to various disputes, but the centrepoint, Freedom Tower, is scheduled to be completed by 2011. In addition to rebuilding part of the site as business and office space, several memorials and a museum are also planned.

Battery Park City's World Financial Center from the Hudson River

Battery Park City ③

Map B5. *1 to Rector St.* **www**.batteryparkcity.org
World Financial Center West St. ***Tel*** *(212) 945-2600. 1, 2, 3, A, C, & J, M, Z to Chambers St; 4, 5, 6 to Brooklyn Bridge/City Hall Station; E to WTC Station; W, R to City Hall.* **www**.worldfinancialcenter.com; **www**.skyscraper.org

New York's newest neighborhood is an ambitious development on 92 reclaimed acres (37 ha) along the Hudson River. This huge commercial and residential complex can house more than 25,000 people, at an estimated cost of $4 billion. A 2-mile (3-km) esplanade offers grand views of the Statue of Liberty.

The most visible part is the **World Financial Center**. A model of urban design by Cesar Pelli & Associates, this development is a vital part of the revival of Lower Manhattan, and its damage in the World Trade Center attack was attended to as a matter of urgency. At the heart of the complex lies the dazzling Winter Garden, a vast glass-and-steel public space often used for concerts and arts events. It is flanked by restaurants and shops, and opens onto a lively piazza and marina on the Hudson River.

The Skyscraper Museum is located at 39 Battery Park at the Ritz Carlton hotel.

Statue of Liberty ④

Map A5. Liberty Island. *(212) 363-3200. 1, W, R to S Ferry, 4, 5 to Bowling Green. M6, M15 to S Ferry, then Circle Line–Statue of Liberty Ferry from the Battery every 30–45 mins, 9:30am–3:30pm summer (winter hours vary). Time pass required to enter monument.* ***Tel.*** *(866) STATUE 4 for reservation (recommended) or book online www.statuereservations.com Jul–Aug: 9am–6pm daily; Sep–Jun: 9:30am–5pm daily. Dec 25. Ferry fare includes entry to Ellis & Liberty Is. elevator to observation deck only.* **www**.nps.gov/stli; **www**.circlelinedowntown.com

The figure presiding over New York harbor, titled "Liberty Enlightening the World," has been the symbol of freedom for millions since her inauguration by President Grover Cleveland in 1886. A gift from the French to the American people to mark the US centennial in 1876, the statue was the brainchild of sculptor Frédéric-Auguste Bartholdi. In Emma Lazarus's poem, which is engraved on the base, Lady Liberty says: "Give me your tired, your poor, / Your huddled masses yearning to breathe free."

The 305-ft (93-m) high statue stands on a pedestal set within the walls of an old army fort. In one hand Liberty holds the new torch, with a 24-carat gold-leaf flame, while in the other is a book inscribed July 4, 1776, in Latin. The rays of her crown represent the seven seas and seven continents. The crown was closed to the public following the September 11 attacks, but reopened in 2009. Groups of 10 people at a time can now climb up to this level.

After a $100 million restoration in time for its bicentennial, the statue was unveiled on July 3, 1986.

Statue of Liberty, an enduring symbol of New York

Ellis Island ⑤

Map A5. *(212) 363-3200. 4, 5 to Bowling Green; 1, W, R to Whitehall/South Ferry, then Circle Line/Statue of Liberty Ferry from the Battery.* **Departures** *every 30–45 mins 9:30am–3:30pm summer (winter hours vary).* ***Tel*** *(212) 269-5755. Jul–Aug: 9am–6pm daily; Sep–Jun: 9:30am–5:15pm daily. Dec 25. Ferry fare incl entry to Ellis and Liberty Is.* **www**.nps.gov/elis; **www**.circlelinedowntown.com

More than half of America's population can trace its roots to Ellis Island, which served as the country's immigration depot from 1892 until 1954. Nearly 17 million people passed through its gates in the greatest wave of immigration the world has ever known. First- and second-class passengers were processed on board, but steerage passengers were ferried from arrival vessels and taken to the crowded island for medical and legal examinations. Immigrants with contagious diseases could be sent back. Ellis Island lay in ruins until 1990, when a $189 million project by the Statue of Liberty–Ellis Island Foundation, Inc., renewed the buildings.

Centered on the Great Hall or Registry Room, the site today houses the three-story **Ellis Island Immigration Museum** with permanent exhibits. Much of its story is told with photos and the voices of immigrants, and an electronic database traces ancestors. Outside, the American Immigrant Wall of Honor is the largest wall of names in the world. No other place explains so well the "melting pot" that formed the character of the nation.

A view of the main building, Ellis Island

South Street Seaport ⑥

Map C5. Fulton St.
Tel *(212) 732-7678.* *Fulton St.*
Nov–Mar: 10am–7pm Mon–Sat, 11am–6pm Sun; Apr–Oct: 10am–9pm Mon–Sat, 11am–8pm Sun.
Concerts.
www.southstreetseaport.com
South Street Seaport Museum
12 Fulton St. *(212) 748-8600.*
Apr–Dec: 10am–5pm Tue–Sun; Jan–Mar: 10am–5pm Fri–Sun.
Tue; Jan 1, Thanksg., Dec 25.
Exhibits, films.
www.southstreetseaport museum.org

Called the "street of sails" in the 19th-century, the heart of New York's port has now been imaginatively restored as a tourist center. Glitzy stores and restaurants sit harmoniously beside seafaring craft, historic buildings, and museum exhibits, with spectacular views of Brooklyn Bridge and the East River from the cobblestone streets. The historic ships docked here range from the little tugboat *W.O. Decker* to the grand four-masted bark *Peking*, the second-largest sailing ship in existence. Mini-trips on the schooner *Pioneer* are a great way to see the river.

The Ambrose lightship at a South Street Seaport pier on the East River

South Street Seaport Museum covers the 12 blocks of what was America's leading port. In addition to the six historic ships, it has more than 10,000 artifacts, artworks, and documents from the 19th- and early 20th-century maritime world. In the **Maritime Crafts Center**, at Pier 15, see ornate objects such as ships' figureheads being made using traditional woodcarving and model making skills. **Schermerhorn Row**, on Fulton and South Streets, was built as warehouses in 1813. The Row has been restored and now houses a visitor center, shops, restaurants, and an ice-skating rink.

Brooklyn Bridge ⑦

Map C5. *J, M, Z to Chambers St, 4, 5, 6 to Brooklyn Bridge–City Hall (Manhattan side); A, C to High St, Brooklyn Bridge (Brooklyn side).*
M9, M15, M22, M103.

An engineering wonder when it was built in 1883, the Brooklyn Bridge linked Manhattan and Brooklyn, then two separate cities. At that time it was the world's largest suspension bridge and the first to be constructed of steel. The German-born engineer John A. Roebling conceived of a bridge spanning the East River while ice-bound on a ferry to Brooklyn. The bridge took 16 years to build, required 600 workers, and claimed over 20 lives, including Roebling's. Most died of caisson disease (known as "the bends") after coming up from the underwater excavation chambers. From the pedestrian walkway there are fabulous views of the city towers, seen through the artistic cablework.

Brooklyn Bridge, the first ever steel suspension bridge

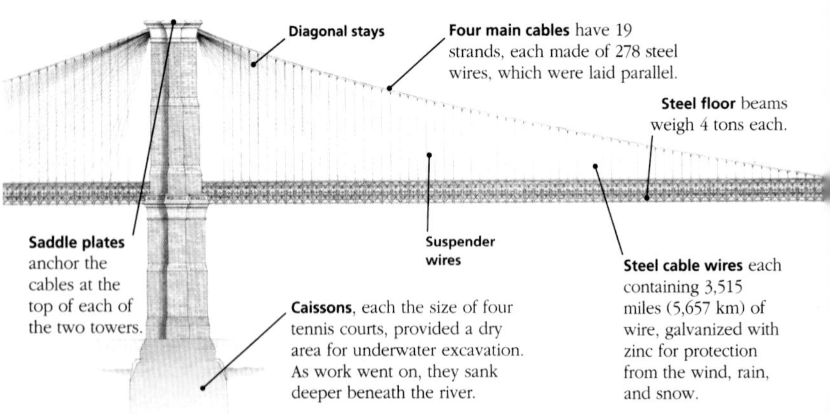

For hotels and restaurants in this region see pp112–15 and pp118–19

City Hall's imposing early 19th-century façade

Civic Center ⑧

Map C5. *2 & 3 to Park Pl; A, C to Chambers St; W, R to City Hall.* **Woolworth Building** 233 Broadway. *City Hall, Park Place.* *office hours.* **City Hall** City Hall Park. ***Tel*** *(212) 331.* *Brooklyn Br–City Hall.* *for prearranged tours only.* **Municipal Building** 1 Center St. *Brooklyn Br–City Hall.*

Manhattan's busy Civic Center is the hub of the city, state, and federal government court systems and the city's police department. The 1926 New York County Courthouse is adjacent to the 31-story pyramid-topped 1933 US Courthouse. The Tweed Courthouse, constructed by the infamous Boss Tweed, a corrupt politician, is being restored to house the Museum of the City of New York.

The monumental buildings here include the 1913 Gothic **Woolworth Building**, headquarters of Five-and-Dime mogul Frank W. Woolworth. Designed by architect Cass Gilbert, it was the city's tallest building until 1930 and set the standard for future skyscrapers. In contrast is the historic **City Hall**, the seat of government since 1812. This Georgian building with French Renaissance influences is considered one of the finest examples of early 19th-century American architecture. The City Hall Park was New York's village green 250 years ago. To its northeast, the **Municipal Building** is a wedding-cake fantasy of towers and spires, topped by the statue *Civic Fame*.

Eldridge Street Synagogue ⑨

Map C5. 12 Eldridge St. ***Tel*** *(212) 219-0888.* *E Broadway.* *11am–4pm Tue–Thu, Sun.* *Fri at sundown, Sat 10am onward.* *half hourly 10am–3pm.* **www**.eldridgestreet.org

This Moorish-style house of worship was the first large temple built in the US by Jewish immigrants from Eastern Europe, from where 80 percent of American Jews came. At the turn of the century, it was the most flamboyant temple in the neighborhood, and as many as 1,000 people attended services here. As congregants left the area, attendance waned and the temple closed in the 1950s.

Three decades later a group of citizens raised funds to restore the magnificent sanctuary. The synagogue is now a National Historic Landmark.

Chinatown ⑩

Map C5. Streets around Mott St. *Canal St.* **Eastern States Buddhist Temple** 64b Mott St. *9am–6pm daily.*

New York's largest and most colorful ethnic neighborhood is Chinatown. In the early 20th century this was primarily a male community, made up of immigrant workers. Wages were sent to families back in China who were prevented from joining them by strict immigration laws. Today, more than 200,000 Chinese Americans live here. The shops and sidewalks overflow with exotic foods and herbs, and gifts ranging from backscratchers to fine antiques. Most people, however, visit Chinatown to eat in one of the more than 200 restaurants or shop for Asian delicacies.

Other sights here include the **Eastern States Buddhist Temple**, with its incense-scented interior and more than 100 golden Buddhas; and tiny, crooked Doyers Street, called "Bloody Angle," reminiscent of the Tong wars between the 1920s and 40s. The Tongs were social clubs or rival criminal fraternities who gave the old locale its dangerous reputation.

Little Italy ⑪

Map C4. Streets around Mulberry St. *Canal St.* **www**.littleitalynyc.com

The Lower East Side's other ethnic neighborhood is Little Italy, home to southern Italian immigrants in the late 19th century. The immigrants preserved their language, customs, and food, making Mulberry Street lively with the colors, flavors, and atmosphere of Italy. Today, although Little Italy has shrunk to a few blocks, the 10-day Feast of San Gennaro in September draws crowds of joyful celebrants. Also on Mulberry Street is **Old St. Patrick's Cathedral**. It became a local parish church when the cathedral moved uptown *(see p77)*.

NoLita, north of Little Italy, is filled with boutiques, and the city's fashionable flock here for the coolest small labels.

Little Italy, once home to thousands of immigrants

TriBeCa ⑫

Map C4. S of Houston St, N of Chambers St, & W of Lafayette St to Hudson River. **M** *Spring St, Canal St, Franklin St, Chambers St.*

The neighborhood named for its geographic shape, TRIangle BElow CAnal, once consisted mostly of abandoned warehouses. Then Robert de Niro set up his TriBeCa Film Center in a converted coffee warehouse, and TriBeCa became the center of the city's movie industry. Known as Hollywood East, many screenings and events take place here. The annual TriBeCa Film Festival in the spring draws celebrities and crowds, and features a superb range of films, from foreign flicks to blockbusters. There are also musical concerts, street fairs, and premiere parties.

TriBeCa is now one of New York's most elite neighborhoods, with stylish restaurants, art galleries, and big lofts occupied by celebrity residents.

SoHo Historic District ⑬

Map C4. S of Houston St. **Greene Street** **M** *Canal St, Spring St, Prince St.*

The largest concentration of cast-iron architecture in the world survives in SoHo (south of Houston), a former industrial district. Its heart is **Greene Street**; 50 cast-iron buildings are stretched out over a five-block area. The finest are those at 72–76, the "King" and 28 –30, the "Queen." A 19th-century American innovation, cast iron was cheaper than either stone or brick and allowed decorative elements to be prefabricated in foundries from molds and used as building façades. The area was threatened with demolition in the 1960s, but was saved by the protests of the many artists living and working in its then low-rent former warehouses.

The **Singer Building** on Broadway was built by Ernest Flagg in 1904, at a time when steel-framed brick and terracotta were replacing cast iron. This ornate 12-story building, adorned with wrought-iron balconies and graceful arches painted in striking dark green, was an office and warehouse for the Singer sewing machine company. The original Singer name is cast in iron above the entrance to the store on Prince Street.

Nearby was the **Museum for African Art**, one of only two American museums devoted to African art. The museum is temporarily based in Long Island City, but moves to a permanent location at the top of Museum Mile on Fifth Avenue in late 2010. Besides museums, galleries, and cast-iron architecture, SoHo's streets are lined with trendy cafés, restaurants, shops, and chic designer boutiques. It is also the city's favorite Sunday brunch-and-browse neighborhood.

The "Queen," SoHo Historic District

Museum for African Art
Temporary location: 36–01 43rd Ave, Long Island City. ***Tel*** *(718) 784-7700.*
New location from late 2010: 5th Ave & E 110th St.
Museum Store
10am–6pm Mon–Fri.
www.africanart.org

Window on the corner of West 4th Street and Washington Square

Washington Square ⑭

Greenwich Vil. **Map** C4. **M** *W 4th St.*

Now one of the city's most vibrant open spaces, Washington Square was once a marshland that was filled to form a park. Stanford White's magnificent marble arch, completed in 1895, replaced a wooden version that marked the centenary of George Washington's inauguration. In 1916, a group of artists led by John Sloan and Marcel Duchamp broke in, climbed atop the arch, and declared the "free and independent republic of Washington Square, the state of New Bohemia." Decades later, Bob Dylan sang his first folk songs near the fountain in the small park's center.

Greenwich Village ⑮

Map C4. N of Houston St & S of 14th St. **M** *W 4th St-Washington Square, Christopher St-Sheridan Square, 8th St.*

Simply known as "the Village," this crazy-quilt pattern of streets is a natural enclave that has been a bohemian haven and home to many celebrated writers, artists, and jazz musicians. Later, it became a popular gay district, and the spirited gay Halloween Parade held here is a fantastic event. The Village comes alive at night, when cafés, theaters, and clubs beckon at every turn, particularly in the ultra-trendy Meatpacking District, south of 14th St and west of 9th Ave. A stroll through its narrow old-fashioned lanes reveal charming row houses, hidden alleys, and leafy courtyards. The 15 Italianate row houses, lining the north side of **St. Luke's Place**, date from the 1850s. Poet Marianne Moore lived here, and Theodore Dreiser wrote his *An American Tragedy* at No. 16.

The heart of the Village is **Sheridan Square**, where seven streets meet in a maze once known as "the mouse-trap." The Stonewall Inn, a gay bar on Christopher Street, was where a riot took place against police harassment on June 27, 1969. A landmark in the Gay Rights Movement.

Jefferson Market Courthouse, "Old Jeff," is perhaps the area's most treasured landmark. It was built as a courthouse in 1877 and voted the fifth most beautiful building in the US. After remaining empty for over 20 years it was restored and turned into a public library in 1967. Opposite is Patchin Place, a group of 19th-century houses where playwright Eugene O'Neill and poets John Masefield and e e cummings lived.

Jefferson Market Courthouse
425 Ave of the Americas. M *W 4th St–Washington Sq.* ***Tel** (212) 243-4334.* *noon–8pm Mon & Wed, 10am–6pm Tue, noon–6pm Thu, 1–6pm Fri, 10am–5pm Sat.* *public hols.* **www**.nypl.org

Original furnishings in East Village's Merchant's House Museum

East Village ⑯

Map D4. 14th St to Houston St.
M *Astor Place.*

Prominent New Yorkers, such as Peter Stuyvesant, the Astors, and the Vanderbilts, lived in this fomer Dutch enclave until 1900, when they moved uptown. Thereafter, it was home to German, Jewish, Irish, and Ukrainian immigrants. In the 1960s the East Village became a haven for hippies, and this is the place where punk rock was born.

The six-story **Cooper Union** was set up in 1859 by Peter Cooper, a wealthy industrialist who built the first US steam locomotive and founded New York's first free, non-sectarian and coeducational college. Its Great Hall was inaugurated in 1859 by Mark Twain, and Abraham Lincoln delivered his "Right Makes Might" speech there in 1860. Cooper Union still provides free education.

The 1832 **Merchant's House Museum**, a remarkable Greek Revival brick town house, is a time capsule of a vanished way of life. It was bought by Seabury Tredwell, a wealthy merchant, and remained in the family until 1933. It still has its original fixtures and displays authentic Federal, American Empire, and Victorian furniture.

One of New York's oldest churches, the 1799 **St. Mark's-in-the-Bowery** is located on East 10th Street. Governor Peter Stuyvesant and his descendants are buried here.

The English-style **Tompkin Square** was the site of America's first organized labor demonstration in 1874, the main gathering place during the neighborhood's hippie era and, in 1991, an arena for violent riots when the police tried to evict the homeless who had occupied the grounds. A small statue of a boy and a girl looking at a steamboat commemorates the more than 1,000 local residents who died in the *General Slocum* steamer disaster on June 15, 1904.

Pointed tower of "Old Jeff," Greenwich Village

Merchant's House Museum
29 E 4th St. ***Tel** (212) 777-1089.*
noon–5pm Thu–Mon & by appt.
(no flashes).
www.merchantshouse.com

Union Square ⑰

Map D4. M *14th St-Union Square.*
Greenmarket *8am–6pm Mon, Wed, Fri, Sat.*

Opened in 1839, this park was once the hangout for drug dealers and soapbox orators. Renovations have transformed this area into a flourishing section of Manhattan. A greenmarket fills the square where more than 200 farmers from all over New York State sell fresh produce, including herbs, berries, vegetables, flowers, home-baked pastries, honey, and woven yarns. The square is also ringed by a wide variety of shops, from discount department stores to gourmet supermarkets.

Flatiron Building ⑱

Map D3. 175 5th Ave. M *23rd St.* ☐ *office hours.*

This unusual building, its shape conforming to a triangular plot of land, has intrigued New Yorkers since it was built by Chicago architect David Burnham in 1902. One of the first buildings to use a steel frame, it heralded the era of the skyscrapers.

It soon became known as the Flatiron for its triangular shape, but some called it "Burnham's folly," predicting that the winds created by the building's shape would knock it down. It has, however, withstood the test of time.

Flatiron Building, New York's most famous early skyscraper

The stretch of Fifth Avenue to the south of the building was once rather run down, but has come to life with chic shops such as Emporio Armani and Paul Smith, giving the area new cachet and a new name, "the Flatiron District."

Appellate Court, said to be the world's busiest courthouse, Madison Square

Madison Square ⑲

Map D3. M *23rd St.*

Quiet Madison Square opened in 1847 at the center of a fashionable residential district where politican Theodore Roosevelt and writer Edith Wharton were born. It was bordered by the elegant Fifth Avenue Hotel, the Madison Square Theater, and Stanford White's Madison Square Garden. The torch-bearing arm of the Statue of Liberty was exhibited here in 1884. Nicely landscaped, this statue-filled park borders some of the city's hottest restaurants. Area residents stroll and walk their dogs at all hours.

Just off Madison Square is the spectacular **New York Life Insurance Company** building, designed in 1928 by Cass Gilbert of Woolworth Building fame *(see p69)*. The building has Gilbert's trademark pyramid-shaped tower, modeled on the Giralda in Seville. Its interior is adorned with hanging lamps, bronze doors and paneling, and a grand staircase leading to a subway station.

One block south is the **Appellate Division of the Supreme Court of the State of New York**, a small marble palace designed by James Brown Lord in 1900. Considered to be the busiest courthouse in the world, appeals relating to civil and criminal cases for New York and the Bronx are heard here. During the week, the public can admire the fine interior, designed by the Herter brothers, including the courtroom when it is not in session. Displays in the lobby often feature some of the court's more famous and infamous cases. Among the celebrities whose appeals were settled here are Babe Ruth, Charlie Chaplin, Fred Astaire, Harry Houdini, Theodore Dreiser, and Edgar Allan Poe.

Also on the east side of Madison Square is the 54-story **Metropolitan Life Tower**. Built in 1909, this was the world's tallest building at that time, an appropriate corporate symbol for the largest insurance company in the world. The huge four-sided clock has minute hands said to weigh 1,000 lb (454 kg) each. A series of historical murals by N.C. Wyeth, the famed illustrator of such classics as *Robin Hood*, *Treasure Island*, and *Robinson Crusoe* (and the father of painter Andrew Wyeth), are now on display in the lobby.

Appellate Division of the Supreme Court of the State of New York
E 25th St at Madison Ave. ☐ *9am–5pm Mon–Fri.* ● *public hols.*

Empire State Building ⓴

Map D3. 350 5th Ave. ***Tel*** *(212) 736-3100.* *M B, D, F, N, Q, R, W, 1, 2, 3 to 34th St; 6 to 33rd St.* *Q32, M1–M5, M16, M34.* **Observatories** *8am–last adm: 1:15am; 11am–7pm Jan 1; 9am–5pm Dec 24; 11am–7pm Dec 25, Jan 1.* **www**.esbnyc.com

The Empire State Building is New York's tallest and most impressive skyscraper. Construction began in March 1930 not long after the stock market crash, and by the time it opened in 1931, space was so difficult to rent that it was nicknamed "the Empty State Building." Only the immediate popularity of the observatories saved the building from bankruptcy – to date, they have attracted more than 120 million visitors – but the building soon became a symbol of the city the world over. It only took 410 days to build this 102-story limestone and brick skyscraper, with an average of four and a half stories added every week. The 102nd floor can be visited for an additional fee. Each February, the annual Empire State Run-Up is held, when 150 runners race up the 1,576 steps from the lobby to the 86th floor (known for its outdoor observation decks), in 10 minutes.

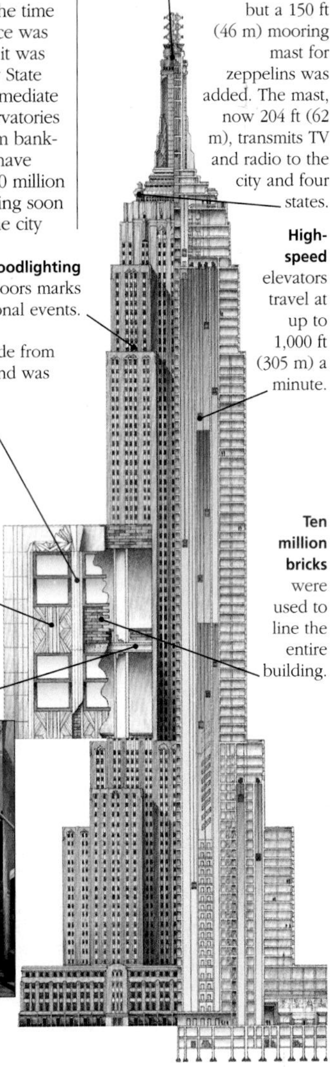

Fifth Avenue Entrance Lobby, Empire State Building

Macy's 34th Street entrance

Herald Square ㉑

Map D3. 6th Ave. *M 34th St-Penn Station.*

Named after the New York *Herald,* which had its offices here from 1893 to 1921, the square was the hub of the rowdy, mid-19th century theater district known as the Tenderloin District. Theaters, dance halls, hotels, and restaurants kept the area humming with life until reformers clamped down on sleaze in the 1890s. The ornamental clock, on an island where Broadway meets 6th Avenue, is all that survives of the Herald Building.

Herald Square became a mecca for shoppers after the Manhattan Opera House was razed in 1901 to make way for **Macy's**. The "world's largest store" began modestly. It was founded by former whaler Rowland Hussey Macy in 1857; the red star logo was from his tattoo, a souvenir of his sailing days. The store was sold in 1888 and moved to its present premises in 1902. The 34th Street façade still has its original clock, canopy, and lettering.

Macy's sponsors New York's famous Thanksgiving Day parade *(see p31)* and the Fourth of July fireworks. Its annual Spring Flower Show draws thousands of visitors.

Macy's
151 W 34th St. ***Tel*** *(212) 695-4400.* *10am–9:30pm Mon–Sat; 11am–8:30pm Sun.* *public hols.*
www.macys.com

Times Square ㉒

Map D3. 42nd St-Times Square. *1560 Broadway (46th St), 8am–8pm daily.* *noon Fri.* **www**.timessquarenyc.org

Named for the New York Times Tower, Times Square is the city's most famous intersection. Although the *New York Times* has moved from its original headquarters at the square's southern end, the crystal ball still drops at midnight on New Year's Eve, as it has since the building opened with fanfare in 1906.

Since 1899, when Oscar Hammerstein built the Victoria and Republic theaters, this has also been the heart of the city's theater district. The district's transformation in the 1990s led to the renovation of many theaters, such as the New Victory and the New Amsterdam. Their new productions, as well as the area's bars and restaurants, attract theatergoers each evening.

Old-world Broadway glamor rubs shoulders with modern entertainment in Times Square *(see p88)*. MTV has its studios here, and E Walk is a vast entertainment and retail complex. Exciting new buildings, such as the Bertlesmann building and the fashionably minimalist Condé Nast offices, sit alongside the classic establishments, such as Sardi's, the Paramount Hotel, and the Baroque Lyceum Theater.

The New York Public Library's Main Reading Room

The New York Public Library ㉓

Map E3. 5th Ave & 42nd St. ***Tel*** *(212) 930-0830.* *42nd St-Grand Central.* *daily, hours vary.* *public hols.* ***Lectures, workshops, readings.*** **www**.nypl.org

Architects Carrère and Hastings won the coveted job of designing New York's main public library in 1897. The white marble Beaux Arts edifice they designed fulfilled the library's first director's vision of a light, quiet, airy place, where millions of books could be stored and yet be available to readers as promptly as possible. Built on the site of the former Croton Reservoir, it opened in 1911 to immediate acclaim, despite having cost the city $9 million. The architects' genius is best seen in the Main Reading Room, a vast paneled space as majestic as a cathedral, extending almost two city blocks. Below it are 88 miles (140 km) of shelves, holding over seven million volumes. It takes only minutes for the staff or a computerized dumbwaiter to supply any book. The Periodicals Room holds 10,000 current periodicals from 128 countries. On its walls are murals by Richard Haas, honoring New York's great publishing houses. The original library combined the collections of John Jacob Astor and James Lenox. Its collections today range from Thomas Jefferson's handwritten copy of the Declaration of Independence to T.S. Eliot's typed copy of "The Waste Land." More than 1,000 queries are answered daily, using the vast database of the CATNYP and LEO computer catalogs.

This library is the hub of a network of 82 branches, with nearly seven million users. Other well-known branches include the New York Public Library for the Performing Arts at the Lincoln Center *(see p83)* and the Schomburg Center in Harlem.

MIDTOWN MANHATTAN

Elevator door at the Chrysler Building

Midtown Manhattan's skyline is graced with some of the city's most spectacular towers and spires – from the familiar beauty of the Empire State Building's Art Deco pinnacle to the dramatic wedge shape of Citigroup's modern headquarters. As the shoreline progresses uptown, so the architecture becomes more varied; the United Nations complex dominates a long stretch, and then Beekman Place begins a strand of exclusive residential enclaves that offer the rich and famous some seclusion.

United Nations, founded in 1945, has its impressive headquaters on an 18-acre (7-ha) site on the East River *(see p76)*.

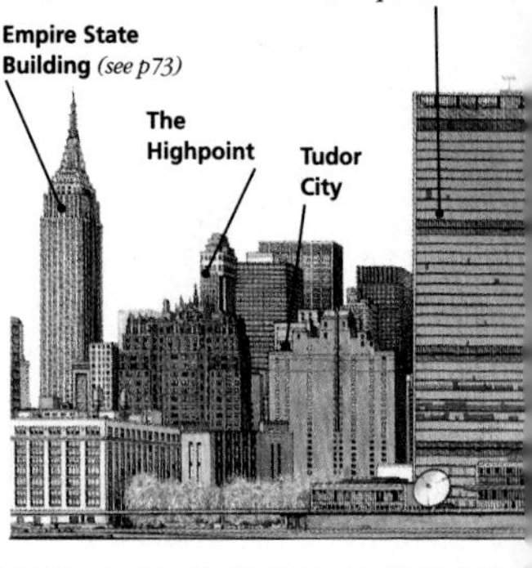

The skylit Garden Court, Morgan Library & Museum

Morgan Library & Museum ㉔

Map E3. 225 Madison Ave. ***Tel*** *(212) 685-0008. 6 to 33rd St, 7 to 5th Ave, 4, 5, 6, 7, S to Grand Central Terminal & Museum. 10:30am–5pm Tue–Thu, 10:30am–9pm Fri, 10am–6pm Sat, 11am–6pm Sun. Mon, Thanksgiving, Dec 25, Jan 1.*
www.themorgan.org

This magnificent palazzo-style building was designed in 1902 to house the private collection of banker Pierpont Morgan (1837–1913), one of the great collectors of his time. Established in 1924 as a public institution by Morgan's son, J.P. Morgan Jr, it has a splendid collection of rare manuscripts, prints, books, and bindings.

The complex includes the original library and J.P. Morgan Jr.'s home. Pierpont Morgan's opulent study and his original library contain some of his favorite paintings, objets d'art, and a wide variety of cultural artifacts. Prominent among the exhibits are one of the 11 surviving copies of the Gutenburg Bible (1455), printed on vellum, and six surviving leaves of the score for Mozart's Horn Concerto in E-flat Major, written in different colored inks.

The Garden Court, a three-story skylit garden area, links the library with the house. Exhibits are changed regularly.

Grand Central Terminal ㉕

Map E3. E 42nd St at Park Ave. ***Tel*** *(212) 532-4900. 4, 5, 6, 7, S to Grand Central. M101–104, M42. 5:30–1:30am daily. Wed 12:30pm (free), call (212) 935-3960 & Fri 12:30pm (free), call (212) 883-2420.* ***Baggage check; lost & found*** *(212) 340-2555.* **www**. grandcentralterminal.com

One of the world's great train terminals, this outstanding Beaux Arts building is New York's most visited, with 500,000 people passing through it daily. The present building, dating from 1913, remains an impressive sight. Its glory is the main concourse, dominated by three great arched windows that fill the space with natural light. The high vaulted ceiling of this vast pedestrian area is decorated with twinkling constellations. The information booth here is surmounted by a wonderful four-faced clock. The Grand Staircase, styled after the staircase in Paris' Opera House, is a reminder of the glamorous days of early rail travel. Adjacent to the main concourse is the Vanderbilt Hall.

Today, Grand Central is no longer limited to the city's commuters. It has become an attraction in its own right, with a museum, over 40 shops, and an extensive food court, including the famed Oyster Bar *(see p118)*. Also worth visiting is the bar The Campbell Apartment, which is in a beautiful space formerly the private office of tycoon John W. Campbell (smart attire must be worn here).

A fine clock on the Grand Central Terminal building

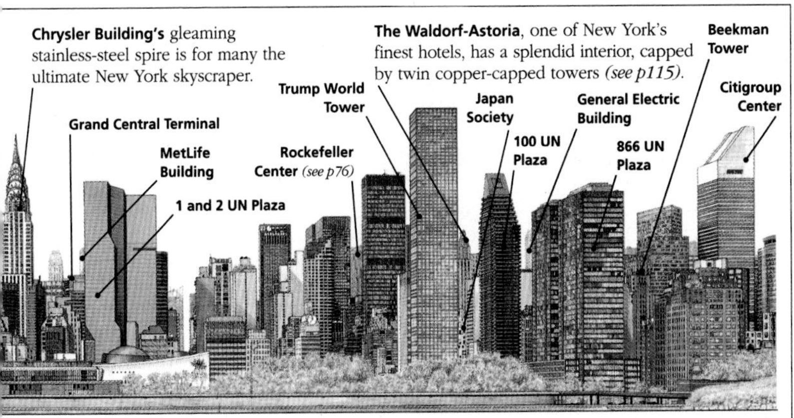

The UN Buildings seen from the garden

United Nations ㉖

Map E3. 1st Ave at 46th St. ***Tel*** *(212) 963-8687.* *4, 5, 6, 7, S to 42nd St-Grand Central Station.* *M15, M27, M42, M50, M104.* *Mar–Dec: 9:30am–4:45pm daily; Jan–Feb: Mon–Fri only.* *Jan 1, Presidents' Day, Memorial Day, Jul 4, Labor Day, Eid, Thanksgiving, Dec 25, (limited schedule during year-end hols).* *for tours.* *in 20 languages.* ***Lectures, films.*** **www**.un.org

When New York was chosen as the UN headquarters, philanthropist and multimillionaire John D. Rockefeller Jr. donated $8.5 million for the purchase of the East River site. This complex was the creation of American architect Wallace Harrison and a team of international consultants.

The United Nations was formed near the end of World War II to preserve world peace, promote self-determination, and to aid economic and social well-being around the globe. Currently 189 members meet regularly each year from mid-September to mid-December in the General Assembly, the closest thing to a world parliament.

The most powerful body is the Security Council, housed in the Conference Building. Here, delegates and their assistants meet to confer on issues related to international peace and security. In 1988, the UN was awarded the Nobel Peace Prize. The Trusteeship Council and the Economic and Social Council are in the same building.

Daily guided tours show visitors the various council chambers and General Assembly hall. A major renovation is underway (until 2014), so visitors should check access.

Rockefeller Center ㉗

Map E3. 630 5th Ave between 49th & 52nd Sts. *(212) 332-6868.* *47th-50th Sts.* *(212) 664-7174 (reservations advised).* **Top of the Rock observatory** ***Tel*** *877-NYC-ROCK.* *8am–11pm daily.* **www**.rockefellercenter.com

A city within a city, and a National Historic Landmark, this urban wonder is the world's largest privately owned complex. Begun in the 1930s, it was built on a site leased by John D. Rockefeller Jr. for a new opera house he had planned. When the 1929 Depression scuttled the plans, Rockefeller, stuck with a long-term lease, went ahead with his own development. This was the first commercial project to integrate gardens, dining, and shopping with office space. The number of buildings has now grown to 19, though the newer structures do not match the Art Deco elegance of the original 14. The center's Channel Gardens, named after the English Channel because they separate the French and British buildings, change with the calendar.

The centerpiece of the center is the 70-story G.E. Building, headquarters of NBC studios. Backstage tours of the network's studios are a popular attraction. The TV show *Today* can also be viewed live every weekday morning from the sidewalk in front of the studio. A new attraction is the **Top of the Rock** observatory on the 67th–70th floors. Another attraction is the 1932 Radio City Music Hall. Once a movie palace, it now hosts dazzling events, including the annual Christmas and Easter shows. The center also houses a skating rink.

A view of Rockefeller Center

WORKS OF ART AT THE UN

The UN Building has acquired numerous works of art and reproductions by major artists; many have been gifts from member nations. Most of them have either a peace or international friendship theme. The legend on Norman Rockwell's *The Golden Rule* reads "Do unto others as you would have them do unto you." Marc Chagall designed a large stained-glass window as a memorial to former Secretary General Dag Hammarskjöld, who was accidentally killed while on a peace mission in 1961. A Henry Moore sculpture, *Reclining Figure: Hand* (1979), graces the grounds. There are many other sculptures and paintings by the artists of many nations.

Reclining Figure: Hand **(1979), a gift from the Henry Moore Foundation**

The Great Bronze Doors in Saint Patrick's Church

Saint Patrick's Cathedral ㉘

Map E3. 5th Ave & 50th St. ***Tel*** *(212) 753-2261.* *6 to 51st St; E, V to Fifth Ave.* *M1, M2, M3, M4, M27, M50.* *7:30am–8:30pm daily.* *frequent Mon–Sat; 7, 8, 9, 10:15am & noon, 1, 4 (Spanish), 5:30pm Sun.* *8:30am–8pm* ***Concerts & lectures.***

New York's finest Gothic Revival building was designed by James Renwick Jr. and completed in 1878. This is also the largest Catholic cathedral in the United States and seats more than 2,500 people every Sunday. When Archbishop John Hughes decided to build a cathedral here in 1850, many criticized his choice of a site so far from the city's center at the time. Today, the church has one of the best locations in midtown Manhattan.

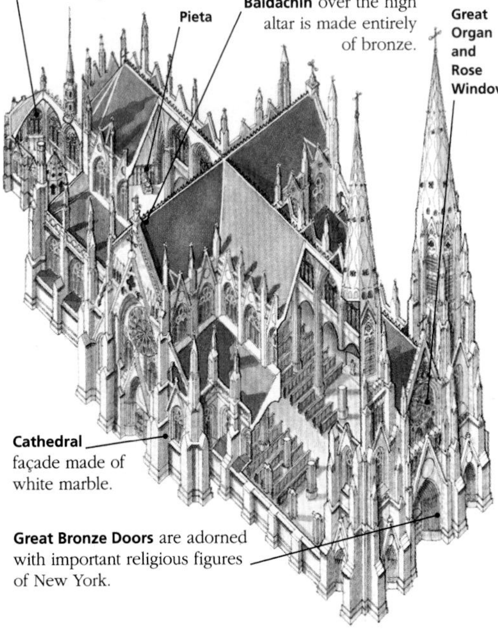

Museum of Modern Art ㉙

Map E2. 11 W 53rd St. ***Tel*** *(212) 708-9400.* *5th Ave–53rd St.* *M1, M2, M3, M4, M27, M50.* *10:30am–5:30pm Wed–Mon, 10:30am–8pm Fri.* *Tue, Thanksg., Dec 25.* *groups.* **www**.moma.org

One of the world's most comprehensive collections of modern art is on view at the Museum of Modern Art (MoMA). Founded in 1929, it set the standard for other museums of its kind. It was also the first art museum to include utilitarian objects in its collection, from ball bearings and silicon chips to household appliances.

Following a $650 million expansion project, MoMA re-opened in 2004. The building provides gallery space over six floors, almost twice that of the old museum. Expanses of glass allow abundant natural light into the building. MoMA's collection includes more than 150,000 works of art, ranging from Impressionist classics to an unrivaled collection of modern and contemporary art, including paintings, sculptures, prints, drawings, photographs and graphic designs. Some of the highlights of the collection include well-known works, such as Picasso's *Les Demoiselles d'Avigon* (1907), Van Gogh's *Starry Night* (1889), and Monet's *Water Lillies* (c.1920).

Fifth Avenue ㉚

Map E2. *5th Ave–53rd St, 5th Ave–59th St.*

From its inception in the early 1800s, Fifth Avenue has been the territory of New York's rich and famous. Then, it was lined with palatial mansions built by the Astors, Vanderbilts, Belmonts, and Goulds, giving it the sobriquet Millionaires' Row. But as retail and commercial ventures set up outlets here in the 1900s, society moved farther north.

Today, the heart of New York's best-known avenue extends from the Empire State Building *(see p73)* to the Grand Army Plaza, presided over by the 1907 Plaza Hotel. Along this stretch are a range of famous stores that have made Fifth Avenue synonymous with luxury goods throughout the world.

The Cartier store, at 52nd Street, is housed in a 1905 Beaux Arts mansion, originally the home of banker Morton F. Plant, who supposedly traded it for a perfectly matched string of pearls. Other well-known jewelry and accessory stores include Tiffany's, made famous by Truman Capote's 1958 *Breakfast at Tiffany's*, Harry Winston, and Henri Bendel. Among the high-quality department stores are Saks Fifth Avenue, Bergdorf Goodman, and the wonderful F.A.O. Schwarz toy store.

A Tour of Central Park ㉛

New York's "backyard," an 843-acre (340-ha) swath of green, provides recreation and beauty for residents and visitors. Designed by Frederick Law Olmsted and Calvert Vaux in 1858, the park took 16 years to create and involved the planting of over 500,000 trees and shrubs. A short walking tour from 59th to 79th Streets takes in some of Central Park's most picturesque features, from the dense wooded Ramble to the open formal spaces of Bethesda Terrace.

★ Strawberry Fields
This peaceful area was created by Yoko Ono in memory of John Lennon, who lived in the nearby Dakota apartments.

★ Bethesda Fountain
The richly ornamented formal terrace overlooks the Lake and the wooded shores of the Ramble.

Wollman Rink
Tycoon Donald Trump restored this rink in the 1980s for future generations of skaters.

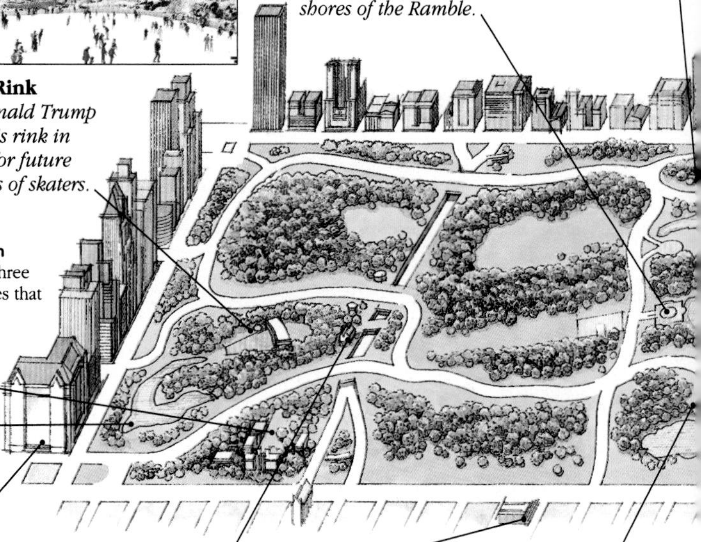

Wildlife Conservation Center has three climate zones that are home to over 130 species of animals.

The Pond

Plaza Hotel

Frick Collection
(see p80)

★ The Dairy
This Victorian Gothic building houses the visitor center. Make it your first stop and pick up a calendar of park events.

Hans Christian Andersen's Statue
A favorite Central Park landmark for children, this is a popular site for storytelling in summer.

Bow Bridge
This cast-iron bridge links the Ramble with Cherry Hill by a graceful arch, 60 ft (18 m) above the Lake.

LOCATOR MAP
See Map pp64–5

STAR SIGHTS

- ★ Belvedere Castle
- ★ Bethesda Fountain
- ★ Conservatory Water
- ★ Strawberry Fields
- ★ The Dairy

San Remo Apartments
This is one of the five twin-towered apartments on Central Park West, famed for their grace and architectural detail.

Alice in Wonderland is immortalized in bronze at the northern end of Conservatory Water, along with the Cheshire Cat, the Mad Hatter, and the Dormouse.

American Museum of Natural History *(see p83)*

The Dakota Apartment Building

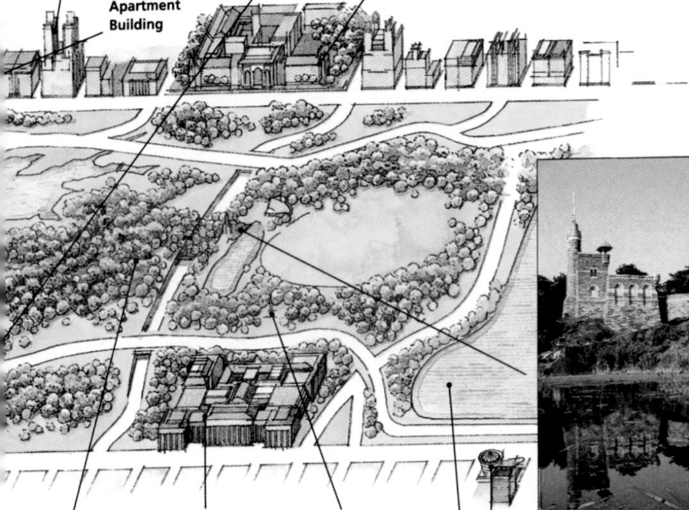

Metropolitan Museum *(see p80)*

Obelisk

Reservoir

Guggenheim Museum *(see p82)*

The Ramble is a wooded area of 37 acres (15 ha), crisscrossed by paths and streams. It is a paradise for bird-watchers – over 250 species have been spotted in the park, which is on the Atlantic migration flyway.

★ Belvedere Castle
From the terraces there are unequaled views of the city and surrounding park. Within the stone walls is the Central Park Learning Center.

★ Conservatory Water
From March to November this is the scene of model boat races each Saturday. Many of the tiny craft are stored in the boathouse that adjoins the Lake.

Whitney Museum of American Art ㉜

Map F2. 945 Madison Ave. ***Tel*** *(212) 570-3600, (800) WHITNEY.* M *6 to 77th St.* *M1, M2, M3, M4, 30, 72.* *11am–6pm Wed–Thu, Sat–Sun, 1–9pm Fri.* *public hols.* *(by donation 6–9pm Fri).* ***Lectures, film/video presentations.*** **www**.whitney.org

An entire range of 20th- and 21st-century American art is showcased in the Whitney Museum. Sculptor Gertrude Vanderbilt Whitney founded the museum in 1930 after the Metropolitan Museum of Art rejected her personal collection of works by living artists, such as George Bellows and Edward Hopper. Initially, the museum was set up behind Whitney's studio in Greenwich Village *(see pp70–71)* and moved to its present inverted pyramid building designed by Marcel Breuer in 1966. A midtown branch is now housed in the Philip Morris Building. The Leonard and Evelyn Lauder galleries on the fifth floor have permanent collections, showing works by Calder, O'Keeffe, and Hopper. Changing exhibitions occupy the lobby, and the second, third, and fourth floors. Highlights include Alexander Calder's fanciful sculpture *Circus* (1926–31), and works by Edward Hopper, whose *Early Sunday Morning* (1930) depicts the emptiness of American city life. Other artists represented here include Roy Lichtenstein. The Whitney Biennial takes place in even-numbered years and is the most significant survey of new trends in American art.

James Whistler's second portrait of *Lady Meux* (1881), Frick Collection

The grand entrance of the Metropolitan Museum of Art

Frick Collection ㉝

Map F2. 1 E 70th St. ***Tel*** *(212) 288-0700.* M *6 to 68th St.* *M1, M2, M3, M4, 30, M72, M79.* *10am–6pm Tue–Sat, 1–6pm Sun.* *most public hols.* *(children under 10 not admitted).* ***Concerts, lectures, film & video.*** **www**.frick.org

The priceless art collection of steel magnate Henry Clay Frick (1849–1919) is exhibited in a residential setting amid the furnishings of his opulent mansion, providing a rare glimpse of how the extremely wealthy lived in New York's gilded age. Frick intended the collection to be a memorial to himself and bequeathed the entire house to the nation on his death.

The collection includes a suberb display of Old Master paintings, French furniture, and Limoges enamel. Of special interest is the skylit West Gallery offering oils by Hals, Rembrandt, and Vermeer, whose *Officer and the Laughing Girl* (1655–60) is a fine example of the Dutch painter's use of light and shadow. The Oval Room features Whistler, while the Library and Dining Room are devoted to English works. In the Living Hall are works by Titian, Bellini, and Holbein.

Metropolitan Museum of Art ㉞

Map F2. 1000 Fifth Ave. *(212) 535-7710.* M *4, 5, 6 to 86th St.* *M1, M2, M3, M4.* *9:30am–5:15pm Sun & Tue–Thu, 9:30am–8:45pm Fri, Sat.* *Jan 1, Thanksgiving, Dec 25.* ***Concerts, lectures, film & video presentations.*** **www**.metmuseum.org

One of the world's great museums, the Metropolitan houses treasures that span 5,000 years of culture from all over the world. Founded in 1870 by a group of artists and philanthropists who visualized an American art institution to rival those of Europe, it began with three private European collections and 174 paintings. Today, its holdings number over two million, and the original 1880 Gothic Revival building by Calvert Vaux and Jacob Wrey has been expanded many times. Recent additions are inviting courts with huge windows overlooking Central Park, and the breathtaking **Byzantine Galleries**, located under the Grand Staircase.

Most of the collections are housed on the two main floors. On the first floor are the **Costume Institute**, and part of the **Robert Lehman Collection**. This extraordinary private collection, acquired in 1969, includes Old Masters, Dutch, Spanish, and French artists, Post-Impressionists, and Fauvists, as well as ceramics and furniture. The state-of-the-art Costume Institute covers fashion trends from the 17th century to the present day. On view are Napoleonic and Victorian ballgowns, Elsa

Cypresses (1889), painting by Vincent Van Gogh

Schiaparelli's shocking pink evening dresses, creations by Worth and Quant, and the costumes of the Ballets Russes.

The second floor includes the **American Wing**, European Sculpture and Decorative Arts, **Egyptian Art**, and the **Michael C. Rockefeller Wing**. Built by Nelson Rockefeller in memory of his son, who lost his life on an art-finding expedition in New Guinea, the wing showcases a superb collection of over 1,600 primitive artworks from Africa, the islands of the Pacific, and the Americas. Among the African works are outstanding ivory and bronze sculptures from the royal kingdom of Benin (Nigeria). Also on view are pre-Columbian gold, ceramics, and stonework from Mexico and Central and South America. The American Wing has one of the world's finest collections of American paintings, including several by Edward Hopper. Prize exhibits include Gilbert Stuart's first portrait of George Washington, John Singer Sargent's notorious portrait of *Madame X*, and the monumental *Washington Crossing the Delaware* by Emanuel Leutze. There are also period rooms, including one designed by Frank Lloyd Wright, and Tiffany glass.

The Metropolitan has one of the largest collections of Egyptian art outside Cairo. Objects range from the fragmented jasper lips of a 15th-century BC queen to the massive Temple of Dendur. Many of the objects were discovered during museum-sponsored expeditions during the early 20th century.

The **Lila Wallace Wing** holds the museum's growing contemporary art collection. Some great works include Picasso's portrait of *Gertrude Stein* (1905) and Jackson Pollock's *Autumn Rhythm*.

The heart of the museum, however, is its awe-inspiring collection of 3,000 **European Paintings**. Its highlights are masterpieces by Dutch and Flemish painters, specifically Brueghel's *The Harvesters* (1551) and Rembrandt's *Self-portrait* (1660), painted when he was 54. Among the finest Impressionist and Post-Impressionist paintings is *Cypresses* (1889), painted by Vincent Van Gogh the year before he died.

The third floor has a comprehensive collection of **Asian Art**, featuring textiles, sculpture, and ceramics from China, Japan, Korea, Southeast Asia, and India. The full-size Ming-style Chinese scholar's garden in the Astor Court was built by craftspeople from Souzhou. The **Cantor Roof Garden** has superb annual shows of 20th-century sculpture, displayed against the dramatic backdrop of the city's skyline. Guests can also visit the museum shops, located on the main floor and mezzanine.

FLOOR PLAN OF THE METROPOLITAN MUSEUM OF ART

1. Byzantine Galleries
2. Costume Institute
3. Robert Lehman Collection
4. American Wing
5. European Sculpture and Decorative Arts
6. Egyptian Art
7. Michael C. Rockefeller Wing
8. Lila Wallace Wing
9. European Paintings
10. Asian Art
11. Access to Cantor Roof Garden

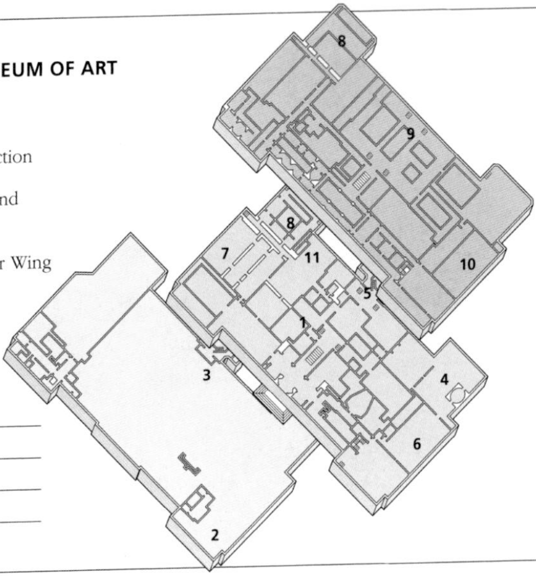

KEY TO FLOOR PLAN

- First Floor
- Second Floor
- Third Floor

The Solomon R. Guggenheim Museum ㉟

1071 5th Ave at 89th St.
Tel *(212) 423-3500.* M *4, 5, 6 to 86th St.* *M1, M2, M3, M4.*
10am–5:45pm Sat–Wed, 10am–7:45pm Fri. *Jan 1, Dec 25.*
Concerts, lectures, performing art series.
www.guggenheim.org

One of the world's finest collections of modern and contemporary art is housed in a building that is considered one of the great architectural achievements of the 20th century. The only New York building to be designed by the celebrated American architect Frank Lloyd Wright *(see p396)*, it was completed after his death in 1959. Its shell-like façade is a New York landmark, while the interior is dominated by a spiral ramp that curves down and inward from the dome, passing works by major 19th- and 20th-century artists.

Over the years, Solomon Guggenheim's core collection of Abstract Expressionist art has been added to by donations of several important collections, from William de Kooning to Jackson Pollock and Robert Motherwell. The museum now owns a large body of work by famous artists such as Kandinsky, and major holdings of Brancusi, Calder, Klee, Chagall, Miró, Léger, Mondrian, Picasso, Oldenberg, and Rauschenberg.

Not all of the permanent collection is on display at any one time. Only a small portion is on view because the main gallery, the Great Rotunda, usually features special exhibitions. The Small Rotunda shows some of the museum's famous Impressionist and Post-Impressionist holdings. The Tower galleries feature exhibitions of work from the permanent collection and contemporary pieces. A fifth-floor sculpture terrace overlooks the scenic Central Park. Two important acquisitions by the museum are the Justin Thannhauser collection and more than 100 photographs from the Robert Mapplethorpe Foundation.

An extensive renovation of the building's exterior was completed in time for the museum's 50th birthday in 2009.

Cézanne's *Man With Arms Crossed* (1895–1900), Guggenheim Museum

THE SOLOMON R. GUGGENHEIM MUSEUM

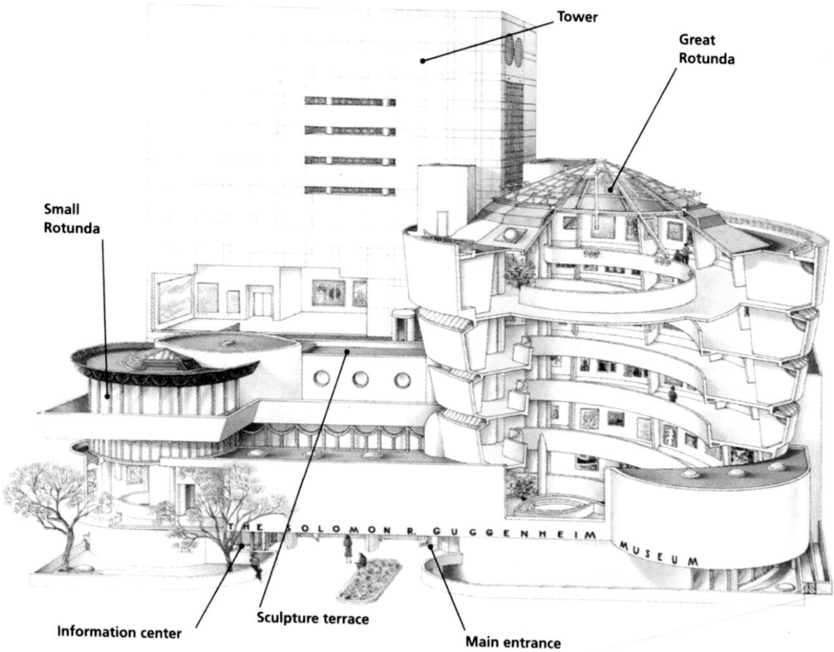

American Museum of Natural History ㊱

Central Park West at 79th St. **Tel** *(212) 769-5100.* M *B, C to 81st St.* *M7, M10, M11, M79.* *10am–5:45pm daily. Donation.* **Rose Center** *until 8:45pm 1st Fri of month.* **www**.amnh.org

This is one of the largest natural history museums in the world, attracting more than 4.5 million visitors each year. Since the original building opened in 1877, the complex has grown to cover four city blocks, and today holds more than 30 million specimens and artifacts. The most popular areas are the dinosaurs, and the Milstein Family Hall of Ocean Life.

Enter at Central Park West onto the second floor to view the Barosaurus exhibit, African, Asian, Central and South American peoples, and animals. First floor exhibits include ocean life, meteors, minerals and gems, and the Hall of Biodiversity. North American Indians, birds, and reptiles occupy the third floor. Dinosaurs, fossil fishes, and early mammals are on the fourth floor.

The **Rose Center** for Earth and Space has as its centerpiece the Hayden Planetarium. The planetarium contains a technologically advanced Space Theater, the famous Cosmic Pathway, and a Big Bang Theater.

Barosaurus, American Museum of Natural History

The Lincoln Center for the Performing Arts complex

Lincoln Center ㊲

Broadway between W 62nd & W 65th Sts. M *1 to 66th St.* *M5, M7, M10, M11, M66, M104.*

A giant cultural complex, built in the 1950s, Lincoln Center was conceived when both the Metropolitan Opera House and the New York Philharmonic needed homes. At that time, the notion of a single complex where different performing arts could exist side by side, was considered both daring and risky. Today, the Lincoln Center draws audiences of over five million each year.

The **Lincoln Center for the Performing Arts** was born in May 1959, when President Eisenhower traveled to New York to turn a shovelful of earth, composer Leonard Bernstein lifted his baton, and the New York Philharmonic and the Juilliard Choir broke into the *Hallelujah Chorus*. The center soon covered 15 acres (6 ha) on the site of the slums that had once been the setting for Bernstein's classic musical *West Side Story*.

Lincoln Center includes the **New York State Theater**, home to the highly acclaimed New York City Ballet and the New York City Opera, a troupe devoted to presenting opera at popular prices; and the **Metropolitan Opera House**, the focal point of the plaza. This fine building has five great arched windows, which offer views of the opulent foyer and two radiant murals by Marc Chagall. All the greats have sung here, including Maria Callas, Jessye Norman, and Luciano Pavarotti. The other two significant institutions here are the Lincoln Center Theater and Avery Fisher Hall, home to the New York Philharmonic, America's oldest orchestra. The best way to see the complex is by guided tour.

Although the **American Folk Art Museum** is now housed in a dramatic state-of-the-art building on West 53rd Street, the museum continues to operate the **Eva and Morris Feld Gallery** at the Lincoln Center. The gallery provides additional exhibition space for the museum, for displaying artwork from the museum's permanent collection, such as quilts, carvings, and paintings. The museum itself is well worth a visit to see its extensive collection of folk art.

The **Hotel des Artistes**, nearby at 1 West 67th Street, was built in 1918 as working artists' studios. Interesting residents have included Alexander Woollcott, Isadora Duncan, Noël Coward, Rudolf Valentino, and Norman Rockwell. The Café des Artistes is well known for its misty, romantic Howard Chandler Christy murals and fine cuisine.

Lincoln Center for the Performing Arts
Tel *(212) 546-2656.* *(212) 875-5350.* **www**.lincolncenter.org

American Folk Art Museum
45 West 53rd Street. **Tel** *(212) 265-1040.* *10:30am–5:30pm Tue–Thu & Sat–Sun; 10:30am–7:30pm Fri.* **www**.folkartmuseum.org

Eva and Morris Feld Gallery
2 Lincoln Square. **Tel** *(212) 595-9533.* *noon–7:30pm Tue–Sat; noon–6pm Sun.* **www**.folkartmuseum.org

Greater New York

Though officially part of New York City, upper Manhattan and the boroughs outside Manhattan are very different in feel and spirit. Away from the bustle of the inner city, they are residential and do not have the famous skyscrapers of New York. The difference is evident even in the way residents describe a trip to Manhattan as "going into the city." Yet these areas feature such attractions as Columbia University, the city's largest zoo, botanical gardens, museums, churches, beaches, and huge sports arenas.

View across Columbia University's quadrangle toward Butler Library

Columbia University (38)

Map F4. Main entrance at W 116th St & Broadway. ***Tel*** *(212) 854-1754.* *1 to 116th St-Columbia University.* **Visitors' Center *Tel*** *(212) 854-4900.* *9am–5pm Mon–Fri.* *1pm Mon–Fri.* **www**.columbia.edu

One of America's oldest and finest universities, Columbia was founded as King's College under a charter granted by King George II of Great Britain, in 1754. Originally situated in lower Manhattan, the present campus was built in Morningside Heights. Architects McKim, Mead & White, who designed its first buildings around a central quadrangle, placed the university on a terrace, serenely above street level. A Classical, columned building, the **Low Library**, dominates the quadrangle. Daniel Chester French's statue *Alma Mater*, in front of it, became familiar as the backdrop to the 1968 anti-Vietnam War student demonstrations. The building now houses offices, and the rotunda is used for a variety of academic and ceremonial purposes. Its books were moved to Butler Library, across the quadrangle, in 1932. To the right, the 1904 **St. Paul's Chapel** is known for its fine woodwork and vaulted interior, and has fine acoustics.

Columbia, part of the Ivy League, is noted for its law, medicine, and journalism schools. Founded in 1912 by publisher Joseph Pulitzer, the School of Journalism is the home of the Pulitzer Prize awarded for the best in letters and music. Columbia's distinguished faculty and alumni, past and present, include over 50 Nobel laureates. Famous alumni include Isaac Asimov, J.D. Salinger, and James Cagney.

Visitors to the campus can stroll along the central quadrangle, where jeans-clad future leaders of America meet and mingle between classes. Across from the campus are the cafés where students engage in lengthy philosophical arguments, debate in the topics of the day, or simply unwind.

Also across the campus to the east on Amsterdam Avenue lies the **Cathedral of St. John the Divine**. Begun in 1892 and only two-thirds finished, with its 600 ft (180 m) long and 146 ft (45 m) wide interior, this Neo-Gothic cathedral, with its hand-carved gargoyles, is slated to be the largest in the world. Medieval construction methods, such as stone on stone with supporting buttresses, continue to be used to complete the structure.

St. Paul's Chapel
Columbia University. ***Tel*** *(212) 854-1487 concert info.* *116th St-Columbia Univ.* *10am–11pm Mon–Sat (term time), 10am–4pm (breaks).* *Sun.*

Cathedral of St. John the Divine
Amsterdam Ave at W 112th St. ***Tel*** *(212) 316-7490.* *1 to Cathedral Pkwy (110th St).* *M4, M5, M7, M11, M104.* *7am–6pm Mon–Sat, 7am–7pm Sun.* *Vespers 6pm Sun. Donations.* *11am Tue–Sat, 1pm Sun.* ***Concerts, plays, lectures, exhibitions, gardens.*** **www**.stjohndivine.org

Riverside Church (39)

Map F4. 490 Riverside Dr at 122nd St. ***Tel*** *(212) 870-6700.* *116th St-Columbia Univ.* *10:30am–5pm Tue–Sun.* *10:45am Sun.* *with prior permission.* **Carillon Bell Concerts *Tel*** *(212) 870-6784. 12:30pm, 3pm Sun.* **Theater *Tel*** *(212) 870-6784.* **www**.theriversidechurchny.org

The design of Riverside Church was inspired by the cathedral at Chartres in France. This Gothic church with a 21-story steel frame was lavishly funded by John D. Rockefeller Jr, in 1930.

The Laura Spelman Rockefeller Memorial Carillon (in honor of Rockefeller's mother) is the largest in the world, with 74 bells. The 20-ton Bourdon, or hour bell, is the largest and heaviest tuned carillon bell ever cast. The organ, with its 22,000 pipes, is among the world's largest. The second gallery features a figure by Jacob Epstein, *Christ in Majesty*, cast in plaster and covered in gold leaf. Another Epstein

Carved stonework at the Cathedral of St. John the Divine

For hotels and restaurants in this region see pp112–15 and pp118–19

The 21-story Riverside Church, from the north

statue, *Madonna and Child*, stands in the court next to the cloister. The screen panels honor eight men and women including Socrates, Michelangelo, Florence Nightingale, and Booker T. Washington, whose lives exemplified the teachings of Christ.

For quiet reflection, enter the small, secluded Christ Chapel, patterned after an 11th-century Romanesque church in France. It was possible for visitors to take the elevator to the 20th floor and then walk the 140 steps to the top of the 392-ft (120-m) bell tower, but the observation deck has been closed indefinitely. There is no access to the bell tower during carillon concerts.

St. Nicholas Historic District ⑩

Map F4. 202–250 W 138th & W 139th St. Ⓜ *135th St (B, C).*

A startling contrast to the run-down surroundings, the two blocks here, known as the King Model Houses, were built in 1891 when Harlem was considered a neighborhood for New York's gentry. They still comprise one of the city's most distinctive examples of row townhouses. A distinct feature of these houses is the provision of a central service alley that can be accessed from the avenue ends and at different points along the block. The alley serves a very useful feature in concealing garbage cans and service deliveries.

The developer, David King, chose three leading architects, who succeeded in blending their different styles to create a harmonious whole. The most famous of these was the firm of McKim, Mead & White, who were responsible for the northernmost row of solid brick Renaissance palaces. Their homes featured ground floor entrances rather than the typical New York brownstone stoops. The parlor floors have ornate wrought-iron balconies below, as well as carved decorative medallions above their windows.

The Georgian buildings designed by Price and Luce are built of buff brick with white stone trim. James Brown Lord's Georgian-style buildings feel much closer to Victorian, with outstanding red-brick façades and brownstone foundations.

Over the years, many distinguished professional and civic leaders made their homes here. Among them were celebrated musicians W.C. Handy and Eubie Blake, and one of the founders of the American Negro Theater, Abram Hill. He collaborated in the production of a play set in the historic district and called it "On Striver's Row," a name by which the district is now commonly known.

Studio Museum in Harlem ㊶

Map F4. 144 W 125th St. ***Tel*** *(212) 864-4500.* Ⓜ *125th St (2, 3).* *noon–6pm Wed, Fri & Sun, 10am–6pm Sat.* *public hols.* ***Donation*** ***Lectures, children's programs, films.*** **www**.studiomuseum.org

The museum was founded in 1967 in a loft on upper Fifth Avenue with the mission of becoming the premier center for the collection and exhibition of the art and artifacts of African Americans.

The present premises, a five-story building on Harlem's main commercial street, was donated to the museum by the New York Bank for Savings in 1979. There are galleries on two levels for changing exhibitions featuring artists and cultural themes, and three galleries are devoted to the permanent collection of works by major black artists, such as Romare Bearden and Elizabeth Catlett.

The photographic archives comprise one of the most complete records in existence of Harlem in its heyday. From the main floor a side door opens onto a small sculpture garden. In addition to its excellent exhibitions, the museum also maintains a national artist-in-residence program and offers regular lectures, a variety of children's programs, and film festivals. A range of books and African crafts are available in the small shop.

Exhibition space at the Studio Museum in Harlem

The Cloisters ㊷

Map F4. Fort Tryon Park. ***Tel*** *(212) 923-3700.* M *A to 190th St (exit via elevator).* *M4.* *Mar–Oct: 9:30am–5:15pm Tue–Sun; Nov–Feb: 9:30am–4:45pm Tue–Sun.* *Jan 1, Thanksg., Dec 25.* *donations. No videos.* *book in advance.*
Concerts, lectures.
www.metmuseum.org/cloisters

Vaulted ceiling of the Pontaut Chapter House at the Cloisters

This world-famous branch of the Metropolitan Museum *(see pp80–81)*, devoted to medieval art, resides in a building that incorporates medieval cloisters, chapels, and halls. The museum, organized in chronological order, starts with the Romanesque period (AD 1000) and moves to the Gothic (1150 to 1520). It is noted for its exquisite illuminated manuscripts, stained glass, metalwork, enamels, ivories, and beautifully preserved tapestries. Perhaps the most interesting exhibits in the Cloisters are the gardens, planted according to horticultural information found in medieval treatises and poetry. Early music concerts are performed regularly here and are extremely popular. Call in advance for tickets.

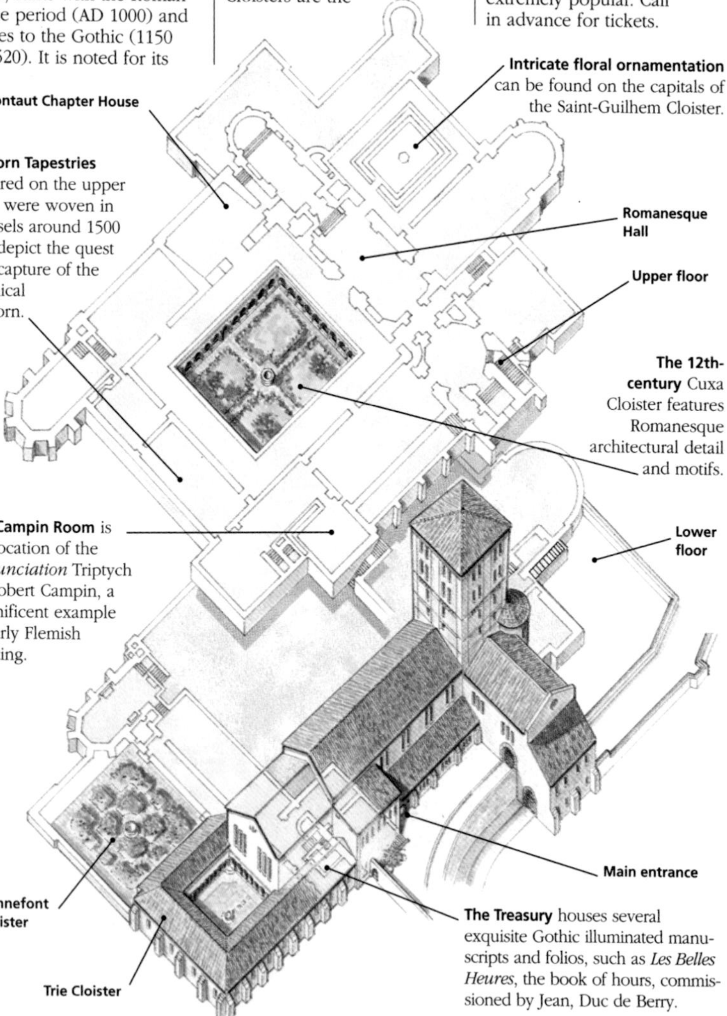

Jungle World, a climate-controlled tropical rainforest at the Bronx Zoo

The Bronx ㊸

Map F4. Ⓜ *B, D, 4 to 161st St (Yankee Std); 2, 5 to Tremont Ave (Bronx Zoo); 4, B, D to Bedford Park Blvd (NY Bot. Garden).*

Once a prosperous suburb with a famous Grand Concourse lined with apartment buildings for the wealthy, parts of the Bronx have now become a symbol of urban decay. However, visitors still frequent the area to escape the overwhelming city concrete for some beauty and quiet, while New Yorkers flock to the 1923 **Yankee Stadium**, home of the New York Yankees baseball team. Don't miss a sidetrip to one of the city's wealthiest and most beautiful parts – Riverdale – located between W 242 and Broadway.

But the most outstanding attraction of the Bronx is the **Bronx Zoo**. Opened in 1899, this is the largest urban zoo in the US, home to more than 4,000 animals of 500 species, living in realistic representations of their natural habitats. The Park is a leader in the perpetuation of endangered species, such as the Indian rhinoceros and the snow leopard. Its 265 acres (107 ha) of woods, streams, and parklands include a children's zoo, camel safaris, a seasonal SkyFari cable car, and a shuttle train that takes visitors around the sprawling park.

Across the road from the Zoo's main entrance, visitors can experience 250 acres (101 ha) of beauty and hands-on enjoyment at the **New York Botanical Garden**. One of the oldest and largest botanical gardens in the world, it has 48 specialty gardens and plant collections, 50 acres (20 ha) of virgin forest, and a vast Children's Adventure Garden. The Enid A. Haupt conservatory with 11 interconnected glass galleries has been wonderfully restored as "A World of Plants."

Bronx Zoo
Fordham Rd /Bronx River Pkwy.
Tel *(718) 367-1010.* *Nov–Mar: 10am–4:30pm daily; Apr–Oct: 10am–5pm daily (5:30pm Sat & Sun).* *by donation.* ***Children's zoo.*** **www**.bronxzoo.com; **www**.nybg.org

Brooklyn ㊹

Map F5. Ⓜ *Prospect Pk (Brooklyn Bot. Gardens); 2, 3 to Eastern Pkwy (Brooklyn Mus); C, 3 to Kingston (Brooklyn Children's Mus); D, F, N, Q to Stillwell Ave (Coney Is).*

One of the most ethnically diverse boroughs in New York, Brooklyn, if it were a separate city, would be the country's fourth largest. Many entertainment greats, such as Mel Brooks, Phil Silvers, Woody Allen, and Neil Simon, celebrate their birthplace with great affection and humor. Among the diverse neighborhoods are the historic residential districts of Park Slope and Brooklyn Heights, beautiful tree-lined enclaves that offer a wonderful stroll past Victorian houses and cafés. An oval gateway in the Grand Army Plaza, designed by Frederick Law Olmsted and Calvert Vaux, leads to the lush, green Prospect Park.

Ibis Coffin (332–330 BC) in gold leaf and silver, Brooklyn Museum of Art

The adjacent **Brooklyn Botanic Gardens** feature a traditional Elizabethan-style "knot" herb garden, one of the largest bonsai and rose collections in the country, and some rare rainforest trees.

To its southeast, lies the 1897 **Brooklyn Museum of Art**, designed by McKim, Mead & White. Though only one-fifth completed, the museum is one of the most impressive cultural institutions in the US, with a permanent collection of some 1 million objects, housed in a grand five-story structure spanning 560,000 sq ft (41,805 sq m). Highlights include African, Oceanic, and New World art; a collection of classic Egyptian and ancient Middle Eastern artifacts, and some works of American and European contemporary art.

To the north on Brooklyn Avenue lies the imaginative **Brooklyn Children's Museum**, the world's first designed especially for young people. Programs and displays are based on a remarkable collection of 20,000 cultural artifacts and natural history specimens, plants and animals, and interactive exhibits.

Brooklyn poet Walt Whitman composed many of his works on the borough's farthest point, **Coney Island**. It was billed as the "World's Largest Playground" in the 1920s, with its combination of rides and lovely beaches. Today, Coney Island is a bit run down but holds historical memorabilia. A short trip to the **New York Aquarium** is a must.

Brooklyn Museum of Art
200 Eastern Pkwy, Brooklyn. ***Tel*** *(718) 638-5000.* *10am–5pm Wed–Fri, 11am–6pm Sat, 11am–11pm first Sat in month, 11am–6pm Sun.* *Jan 1, Thanksgiving, Dec 25. Donation expected.* ***Concerts, lectures.*** **www**.brooklynmuseum.org

New York City Practical Information

Visitors to New York are treated very much the same as anyone else. While you may not be given special treatment, as long as you follow a few guidelines on personal security you'll be able to explore the city as freely as any native New Yorker. Buses and subway trains are reliable and inexpensive. Beside, the wide range of prices offered by the many hotels, restaurants, and entertainment venues means your New York trip can be both fun and affordable.

TOURIST INFORMATION

Advice on any aspect of life in New York City is available from the **New York Convention and Visitors' Bureau (NYC & Co.)**. Their 24-hour touch-tone phone service offers help outside office hours. Brochures and information kiosks are also found at the walk-in office of the **Times Square Visitors Bureau**.

PERSONAL SECURITY

Though New York is rated among the safest large US cities with around-the-clock foot, horse, bike, and car patrols by the police in tourist areas, it is always good to be cautious. At night, if you can't afford a taxi, try to travel with a group. Walk as if you know where you're going. Avoid making eye contact and getting into confrontations with down-and-outs. If someone asks you for money, do not get drawn into conversation. Always keep change handy for phone calls or bus fares; carry your Metrocard in your pocket. Never carry too much cash, and lock your valuables in the hotel safe. Do not allow anyone except hotel or airport personnel to carry your luggage.

Public toilets in bus stations should be avoided at all times of the day. It is best to find a hotel or store if you want to use a restroom. Since parks are sometimes used for drug dealing, they are safest when there is a crowd, for example, for a rally or concert. If you want to go for a jog in a park, always make sure you avoid lonely areas and pathways, and follow a map that shows safe routes.

GETTING AROUND

New York's rush hours extend from 8 to 10am, 11:30am to 1:30pm and 4:30 to 6:30pm, Mon–Fri. During these times, most forms of public transportation are crowded.

Buses are a comfortable way to get around, but they often tend to be slow. Subways are quick, reliable, and inexpensive, and make stops throughout central Manhattan. The vast system extends over 233 miles (375 km) and most routes operate throughout the year. You can buy a Metrocard for the $2 subway and bus fares. Cards come in $4 to $80 amounts depending on the number of trips you intend to take. If $7 or more is put on the card, you get a 15 per cent bonus. Other options are a $7.50 one-day unlimited fun pass and a $25 unlimited 7-day pass. Taxis are best for door-to-door service, but can be held up in traffic jams. You should hail only yellow taxis, as they are the only ones with licences. If their roof numbers are lit up, they are available.

Heavy traffic and expensive rentals make driving in New York a frustrating experience. The speed limit is 30 mph (48 km/h). Parking in Manhattan is difficult and costly. Many hotels include parking charges in their room rates. New York's tow-away crews are active, and one-third of cars towed suffer damage. If you cannot find your car at its parking place, first call the traffic department's tow-away office. For specific details call the **Department of Transportation** (Tel: 311). If you receive a parking ticket, you have seven days to pay the hefty fine. If the car is not at the pound, contact the police.

ETIQUETTE

It is illegal to smoke in *any* public place or building in New York. Bars all over the city also ban smoking.

Tipping is part of New York life. In general, 10 to 15 percent of your bill is enough – 20 percent for outstanding service. For bartenders and coat check, $1–$2 is typical.

ENTERTAINMENT

New York City is a non-stop entertainment extravaganza, every day, all year round. Whatever your taste, you can be sure the city will satisfy it on both a grand and an intimate scale.

New York is famous for its extravagant musicals and its ferocious critics. The Times Square area hosts the "power productions" of Broadway – the big, highly publicized dramas, musicals, and revivals starring many Hollywood luminaries in sure-fire money earners, in theaters such as the **Ambassador** and the **Lyceum** (1903), the oldest theater still in operation. Off-Broadway and Off-Off-Broadway stages such as **Actors' Playhouse**, host experimental shows, ranging from the well-appointed to the improvised, in lofts, churches, or even outside at the open-air **Delacorte Theater** in Central Park.

The city is also a great center of traditional ballet and modern dance. The New York City Ballet, founded by the legendary choreographer George Balanchine, performs in the **New York State Theater**. The **Dance Theater of Harlem** is world famous for its modern, and ethnic productions.

There's every imaginable form of music in New York, from international stadium rock to the sounds of the 1960s, from Dixieland jazz or country blues, soul, and world music to street musicians. The city's music scene changes at a dizzying pace, with many new arrivals, so there's no way to predict what you may find when you arrive. The top performers such as Elton John, Bruce Springsteen, and the Stones perform in the huge arenas at Shea Stadium and **Madison Square Garden**. The **Knitting Factory** has live jazz and new music.

New York's nightlife and club scene is legendary. Whatever your preference – noisy disco, stand-up comedy, or the soothing melodies of a Harry Connick Jr. – you'll be amazed at the choice. New Yorkers thrive on dancing. Dance floors available all over the city range from the ever-popular **SOB's** – for jungle, reggae, soul, jazz, and salsa – to huge basketball-court-sized places, such as **Roseland**. The historic **Copacabana** alternates live bands with a popular disco. **Cielo** is a popular, strobe-lit bar and nightclub.

The city is also a film buff's paradise. Apart from new US releases, which show months in advance of other countries, many classic and foreign films are screened in this hotbed for new and innovative talent.

New Yorkers are sports crazy, and there are activities to suit every taste. Visitors can choose from health clubs and horseback riding to playing tennis or jogging. Spectator sports are provided by professional baseball (**Yankee Stadium**), ice hockey and basketball (**Madison Square Garden**), and football (Giants Stadium), while for tennis fans there is the US Open and Virginia Slims tournaments.

SHOPPING

New York is the consumer capital of the world: a shopper's paradise, with dazzling displays and a staggering variety of goods for sale. Everything is available here, from high fashion to rare books, state-of-the-art electronics, and an array of exotic food. Keep in mind that the city's sales tax is a hefty 8.625 percent.

Known as the fashion capital of America, New York boasts such names as **Polo/Ralph Lauren** and Calvin Klein. There are fashion stores such as **Brooks Brothers** (menswear) and **Ann Taylor** (women's wear), and shops of international names such as **Yves St. Laurent** and **Giorgio Armani**. Manhattan is also known for its world-class jewelry shops including **Cartier** and **Tiffany's**. The city is a bargain hunter's dream, with huge discounts on anything from household goods to designer clothes.

As the publishing capital of the US, New York has the country's best bookstores. Don't miss the **Barnes & Noble** stores, the **Strand** for rare and used books, and Shakespeare & Co.

Dozens of tiny shops around the city specialize in unusual merchandise, from butterflies and bones to toy firefighting equipment and occult potions. Don't miss a trip to the legendary **FAO Schwarz** for toys of all kinds. Some of New York's best souvenirs can be found in the city's many museum shops, including the **Museum of Arts & Design** and the **American Museum of Natural History**.

DIRECTORY

TOURIST OFFICES

NYC & Co.
www.nycvisit.com
www.ci.nyc.ny.us

Times Square Visitors' Bureau
www.timessquarenyc.org

TRANSPORTATION

Department of Transportation
Staten Island Ferry, S Ferry.
Tel (212) 487-5761 or 66.

BARS & CLUBS

Cielo
18 Little W 12th St.
Tel (212) 645-5700.

Copacabana
560 W 34th St.
Tel (212) 239-2672.

Roseland
239 W 52nd St.
Tel (212) 247-0200.

SOB's
204 Varick St.
Tel (212) 243-4940.

ENTERTAINMENT

Actors' Playhouse
100 Seventh Ave S.
Tel (212) 463-0060.

Ambassador
219 W 49th St.
Tel (212) 239-6200.

Dance Theater of Harlem
466 W 152nd St.
Tel (212) 690-2800.

Delacorte Theater
Central Park, 81st St.
Tel (212) 535-4284 (summer time only).

Knitting Factory
74 Leonard St, New York City.
Tel (212) 219-3132.

Lyceum
149 W 45th St, New York City.
Tel (212) 239-6200.

Madison Sq. Garden
7th Ave at 33rd St.
Tel (212) 465-6741.
www.thegarden.com

New York State Theater
Lincoln Center, Broadway at 65th St.
Tel (212) 870-5570.

Yankee Stadium
River Ave at 161st St, Bronx.
Tel (718) 293-4300.

SHOPPING

American Museum of Natural History
W 79th St, Central Park W.
Tel (212) 769-5100.

Ann Taylor
645 Madison Ave.
Tel (212) 832-2010.

Barnes & Noble
105 5th Ave.
Tel (212) 807-0099.

Brooks Brothers
346 Madison Ave.
Tel (212) 682-8800.

Cartier
653 5th Ave.
Tel (212) 753-0111.

FAO Schwarz
767 5th Ave.
Tel (212) 644-9400.

Giorgio Armani
760 Madison Ave.
Tel (212) 988-9191.

Museum of Arts & Design
40 W 53rd St.
Tel (212) 956-3535.

Polo/Ralph Lauren
Madison Ave at 72nd St.
Tel (212) 606-2100.

Strand Book Store
828 Broadway.
Tel (212) 473-1452.

Tiffany & Co
5th Ave at 57th St.
Tel (212) 755-8000.

Yves St. Laurent Rive Gauche
859 Madison Ave.
Tel (212) 517-7400.

New York State

Stretching north for over 200 miles (322 km) to the Canadian border, and 400 miles (644 km) west to the Great Lakes, the "Empire State" is a world away from New York City. Due east of Manhattan, Long Island is the largest island adjoining the continental US, with miles and miles of suburbs, farmland, and beaches jutting out into the Atlantic Ocean. To the north, the Hudson River is an area of opulent mansions and small towns. The state capital, Albany, marks the start of the vast Upstate area, comprising the Adirondacks, rural farmland, and vibrant cities.

The octagonal Montauk Point Lighthouse, completed in 1796

Jones Beach State Park ❷

Wantagh. *Long Island Railroad from Penn Station to Jones Beach. Operates Jun–Labor Day, (718) 217-5477.* *(516) 785-1600.*
Jun–Labor Day: sunrise–midnight.
Jones Beach Theater
www.jonesbeach.com

Located on Long Island, Jones Beach State Park is only 33 miles (53 km) from Midtown Manhattan. A popular destination since it was created in 1929, this barrier island resort features more than 2,400 acres (972 ha) of parkland, beaches, and a wide variety of outdoor and cultural activities.

The park's oceanside beaches are complemented by a stillwater bayside beach and several swimming, diving, and wading pools, and surf facilities. The park's other recreational options include golf courses, restaurants, fishing docks, and a 2-mile (3-km) boardwalk.

The 11,200-seat **Jones Beach Theater** is a popular venue for rock and pop concerts in summer. Another landmark, the 200-ft (61-m), brick-and-stone structure, the **Jones Beach Tower**, is modeled on the campanile of St. Mark's Cathedral in Venice.

The Hamptons & Montauk ❸

15,000.
(877) 386-6654.
www.hamptonstravelguide.com

At Riverhead, Long Island splits into two peninsulas – the mostly pastoral North Fork and the more urban South Fork. Most of South Fork's beaches and cultural attractions are concentrated in the expensive and trendy summer retreats of The Hamptons and Montauk.

Most New Yorkers tend to associate The Hamptons (from west to east, Westhampton Beach, Hampton Bays, Southampton, Bridgehampton, East Hampton, and Amagansett) with its celebrity residents and fashionistas who migrate here from Manhattan during the summer. However, the area also has a rich historical heritage. In the 19th-century whaling community of Sag Harbor, to the north of Bridgehampton, the **Old Custom House**, built in 1789, commemorates the town's post-Revolutionary War heyday as one of the first official ports of entry into the US. On the Village Green in East Hampton, the **Home Sweet Home Museum** houses a variety of early Colonial, rough-shingled structures, including a classic saltbox house built in 1750, and the still-operational Old Hook Mill, constructed in 1806.

The easternmost Long Island community, Montauk is a busy summer resort, serving as a jumping-off point for the area's nature trails and beaches. Other activities are golf, horseback riding, and fishing. Montauk State Park contains the **Montauk Point Lighthouse**, commissioned by George Washington in 1792. Still in operation, the octagonal stone structure is an important landmark for oceangoing vessels.

One of the many swimming pools at Jones Beach State Park

Custom House
Main St. & Garden Sq, Sag Harbor.
Tel *(631) 692-4664.* *Memorial Day weekend–Columbus Day weekend: 1–5pm Sat–Sun.* *public hols.* **www**.splia.org/hist_custom.htm

Home Sweet Home Museum
14 James Lane, East Hampton.
Tel *(631) 324-0713.* *May–Sep: 10am–4pm Mon–Sat, 2–4pm Sun; Oct–Nov: 2–4pm Fri–Sun.* *public hols.*
www.easthampton.com/homesweethome

For hotels and restaurants in this region see pp115–16 and p120

Hudson River Valley ❹

3 Neptune Rd, Poughkeepsie. **Tel** (845) 463-4000. **www**.dutchesstourism.com

From its source high in the Adirondack Mountains, the Hudson courses past bustling riverport towns and the dramatic Catskill and Taconic mountain ranges for nearly 315 miles (507 km) to its mouth at New York harbor. Strikingly beautiful and strategically located, the valley has played a pivotal role in North American military, economic, and cultural history.

Settled by the Dutch in the 1620s *(see p43)*, it was soon dotted with trading posts that grew up around the thriving fur trade with local Iroquois tribes. The area's Dutch heritage survives in names of places such as Catskill, Kinderhook, and Claverack, as well as in the early 19th-century fictional writings of Washington Irving (1783– 1859), whose tales of *Rip Van Winkle* and *The Legend of Sleepy Hollow* made him America's first internationally recognized author. Irving's modest but whimsically eclectic Hudson River home, **Sunnyside**, is now a tourist attraction.

The Hudson's economic and transportation advantages also made it a key strategic objective of both British and American forces during the Revolutionary War, resulting in many pitched battles. Fort Putnam, one of the forts built along the river in 1778 to defend the colonies from British attacks, has been restored and is now part of the **United States Military Academy** at West Point. Established in 1802, the academy has trained the nation's leading military officers, including opposing Civil War generals Ulysses S. Grant and Robert E. Lee, and World War II commanders Douglas MacArthur and Dwight D. Eisenhower. The Military Academy Museum provides a comprehensive introduction to a tour of the fortress-like grounds.

In the 19th century, many of New York's emerging elite constructed seasonal retreats along the Hudson. The largest of these is the **Vanderbilt Mansion** in Hyde Park. Completed in 1899, this Italian-Renaissance style palace was built by the architecture firm of McKim, Mead & White, for railroad baron Frederick W. Vanderbilt. The magnificent home offers a spectacular view of the river, and is laden with French furniture, art, tapestries, and architectural details taken from a Parisian château once occupied by Napoleon. An older and less ostentatious mansion is Springwood, the home of Franklin D. Roosevelt (FDR), America's 32nd president *(see p49)*. Roosevelt was born here in 1882, and it was used as a summer White House during his 1933–45 term. The house is now part of the **Home of Franklin D. Roosevelt National Historic Site**, which also includes an extensive museum and library detailing Roosevelt's leadership during the Great Depression and World War II. Both FDR and Eleanor are buried here. The nearby Eleanor Roosevelt National Historic Site preserves Val-Kill, the First Lady's weekend and holiday cottage retreat.

The imposing exterior of the lavishly furnished Vanderbilt Mansion

Statue of George Washington at the US Military Academy

Sunnyside, Washington Irving's home

Sunnyside
W Sunnyside Lane, off Rte 9, Tarrytown. **Tel** (914) 591-8763. Apr–Oct: 10am–5pm Wed–Mon; Nov–Dec: 10am–4pm Wed–Mon; Mar: 10am–4pm Sat–Sun. Thanksg., Dec 25. **www**.hudsonvalley.org

US Military Academy
W Sunnyside Lane, Rte 9 W, West Point. **Tel** (845) 938-2638. by tour only. Mon–Sat: 9:45am–3:30pm every half hr, photo IDs required; Dec–Feb: only 2 tours per day. (for tours only). Jan 1, Thanksg., Dec 25. **www**.usma.edu

Home of Franklin D. Roosevelt National Historic Site
4097 Albany Post Rd, Rte 9, Hyde Park. 9am– 5pm daily. (grounds free) **www**.nps.gov/hofr **Library & Museum Tel** (845) 229-5320. **Museum** Apr–Dec: 9am–5pm; Jan–Mar: limited hours so call first. Jan 1, Thanksg., Dec 25. **Library** 8:45am–5pm Mon–Fri. **www**.fdrlibrary.marist.edu

New York State Capitol in Albany, a blend of architectural styles

Albany ❺

101,000. 25 Quackenbush Square, (518) 434-1217. **www**.albany.org

Albany has been a central force in New York State since 1614, when the explorer Henry Hudson *(see p60)* established a fur-trading post, Fort Orange, at the northernmost navigable point on the Hudson River. When the British took over the settlement in 1664, they changed its name to Albany. In 1797 Albany was selected as the New York State capital, and the town's political future was secured. The city expanded dramatically in the 1830s with the completion of the Erie Canal, which linked the Hudson River to the Great Lakes. When canal traffic declined in the 1850s, Albany retained its commercial dominance, rapidly evolving into a New York Central railroad terminus and manufacturing center.

While transportation and industry are still important components of the local economy, government is the main concern in today's Albany. The majestic **New York State Capitol**, built over 30 years and completed in 1898, occupies a central location near the city's downtown. The massive stone building is a curious amalgam of Italian and French Renaissance and Romanesque, replete with ornamented stairways, soaring arches, and an ornate Senate chamber embellished with red granite, yellow and pink marble, stained glass, onyx, and mahogany.

The **New York State Museum** chronicles the state's rich heritage, beginning with its first Native American occupants and incorporating the stories of New York's many immigrants, early settlers, and business elite. A reconstructed Iroquois longhouse and a restored 1940s subway car from New York City's legendary A-train are highlights here.

Saratoga Race Track

New York State Capitol
Empire State Plaza. ***Tel*** *(518) 474-2418.* *tours Mon–Sat; call ahead for times.* *Jan 1, Easter, Thanksgiving, Dec 25, public hols.*

New York State Museum
Empire State Plaza. ***Tel*** *(518) 474-5877.* *9:30am–5pm daily.* *Jan 1, Thanksgiving, Dec 25.* **www**.nysm.nysed.gov

Saratoga Springs ❻

25,000. 297 Broadway, *(518) 587-3241.* **www**.saratoga.org

This town has been known for its horseracing, gambling, and high society since it emerged as a resort in the 19th century. The therapeutic waters from the town springs at **Saratoga Spa State Park** sparked an annual influx of wealthy tourists seeking relief from various ailments. Other more enjoyable distractions were offered by the lavish casinos and horseracing facilities. One of Saratoga's original gambling establishments, the elegant Canfield Casino, is now part of **Congress Park**. The gabled grandstand of the Saratoga Race Track, built during the Civil War, is still in use, attracting large crowds during the racing season in August. For a glimpse of the area's more tempestuous Revolutionary War past, **Saratoga National Historical Park**, 15 miles (24 km) southeast, was the site of the 1777 Battle of Saratoga. Here, American commander Horatio Gates led Colonial forces to a decisive victory over 9,000 British regulars, Hessians, and Native Americans commanded by General John Burgoyne. The victory ensured American control of the Hudson River shipping corridor, and prompted the French King Louis XVI to send troops to the colonists' aid later that year.

Sprawling Saratoga National Historical Park

Saratoga Spa State Park
I-87, exit 13N. ***Tel*** *(518) 584-2535.* *8am–sunset daily.* **www**.saratogaspastatepark.org

Saratoga National Historical Park
Rte 4, 8 miles (13 km) S of Schuylerville. ***Tel*** *(518) 664-9821.* *9am–5pm daily.* *Jan 1, Thanksgiving, Dec 25.* **www**.nps.gov/sara

For hotels and restaurants in this region see pp115–16 and p120

The tranquil waters of Otsego Lake, Cooperstown

Adirondack Mountains 7

216 Main St, Lake Placid
Tel (518) 523-2445.

Spanning almost one-fourth of the state, the Adirondack Mountains encompass various ecosystems and hundreds of lakes and rivers, with only 1,100 miles (1,770 km) of road. Rugged peaks such as the 5,344-ft (1,629-m) Mount Marcy are some of the scenic highlights. Two visitor centers serve as gateways to **Adirondack Park** and provide information about the conservation movement that led to the park's creation in 1894 as part of the nation's first forest preserve.

The picturesque village of **Lake Placid** straddles Mirror Lake and Lake Placid in the north-central section of the park. Home to the 1932 and 1980 Winter Olympic Games, it is both a summer resort and winter sports training and competitive center.

Adirondack Park
1 mile N of Rte 86/Rte 30,& 14 miles (22km) E of Long Lake, Rte 28N.
Tel (518) 327-3000. 9am–5pm daily. Thanksgiving, Dec 25.

BASEBALL

"America's Pastime," the country's first nationwide spectator sport, evolved from the British games of cricket and rounders, as well as town ball, a New England variant. The first recorded amateur game took place in 1845 in New York City. Since the 1870s, when professional play matured, baseball has seen many superstars such as Babe Ruth, Ty Cobb, and Ted Williams.

Babe Ruth

Cooperstown 8

2,200. 31 Chestnut St.
Tel (607) 547-9983.

Overlooking Otsego Lake, this neat little village is the legendary birthplace of baseball and home of the **National Baseball Hall of Fame**. This engaging shrine and museum pays homage to baseball greats from the last 150 years, with a colorful array of gear, uniforms, audio-video features, and special exhibits. Founded in 1786, Cooperstown also has a superb collection of Native American artifacts, folk art, and Hudson River School paintings in the **Fenimore Art Museum**. The adjacent Farmer's Museum features exhibits on 19th-century rural life. Glimmerglass Opera, on the shores of Lake Ostego, is nationally renowned.

National Baseball Hall of Fame
25 Main St. *Tel (888) 425-5633.*
Memorial Day–Labor Day: 9am–9pm daily; Labor Day–Memorial Day: 9am–5pm daily. Jan 1, Thanksgiving, Dec 25.
www.baseballhalloffame.org

Finger Lakes 9

904 E Shore Dr, Ithaca. Tel (607) 272-1313.
www.visitithaca.com

According to the Iroquois tribes of west-central New York, the Finger Lakes were created when the Great Spirit placed his hand on the region, leaving behind a series of slender lakes. Seneca Lake is the deepest of these water bodies, at 630 ft (192 m), while Cayuga Lake is the longest, stretching 40 miles (64 km) between the lively town of **Ithaca** – containing the picturesque Cornell University campus – and historic **Seneca Falls**.

Downtown Ithaca, which has a diverse array of art galleries, bookstores, and excellent restaurants, is a pleasant place to start a tour of the Finger Lakes region. **Taughannock Falls State Park**, north of Ithaca, is a wooded oasis, with the 215-ft (65-m) falls tumbling gracefully into a cool, green pool, where swimming is permitted in season. At the top of Cayuga Lake, the quiet Seneca Falls is the spot where 19th-century feminists Elizabeth Cady Stanton and Susan B. Anthony held the first American women's rights convention in 1848, laying the foundation for the Suffrage Movement some 70 years later.

Taughannock Falls State Park
10 miles (16 km) N of Ithaca, Rte 89.
Tel (607) 387-6739. 8am–sunset daily (some trails closed in winter).
www.nysparks.state.ny.us/parks

Taughannock Falls State Park in the Finger Lakes region

Syracuse ⑩

163,900. 572 S Salina St, (315) 470-1910. www.visitsyracuse.org

Like many upstate New York cities, Syracuse prospered after the arrival of the Erie Canal in the 1820s. The **Erie Canal Museum**, housed in a restored canal-side building just east of downtown, has a full-size canal boat replica and a multimedia overview of the canal's important role in the city's history. The down-town Armory Square historic and entertainment district preserves many brick and cast-iron commercial and warehouse buildings from Syracuse's late 19th-century boom period, as well as the 3,000-seat **Landmark Theatre**, built in 1928.

A downtown surprise is the **Everson Museum of Arts**, which has a remarkable collection that ranges from Ming dynasty porcelains to works by American painters from Gilbert Stuart to Jackson Pollock and Andrew Wyeth. The museum building is the first designed by architect I.M. Pei.

Erie Canal Museum
318 Erie Blvd E. ***Tel*** *(315) 471-0593.* *10am–5pm Mon–Sat, 10am–3pm Sun.* *public hols.* www.eriecanalmuseum.org

Everson Museum of Arts
401 Harrison St. ***Tel*** *(315) 474-6064.* *noon–5pm Tue–Fri & Sun, 10am–5pm Sat.* www.everson.org

Old lithograph showing the inauguration of Erie Canal

The Kodak Company's office building in Rochester

Rochester ⑪

231,600. 45 East Ave, (800) 677-7282. www.visitrochester.com

This lovely city, with its abundant parkland and fine museums, evolved out of an industrial past, rooted in the milling industries that developed around the Genesee River's High Falls. The Center for High Falls includes a pedestrian bridge with scenic views of the still-roaring falls, an art gallery, a local history display, and a tour of an 1816 factory that lies three stories below street level. One of the city's most popular attractions is the **Strong National Museum of Play**, a hands-on, interactive center dedicated to the study of play, particularly in relation to American culture. **George Eastman House** is where the eccentric founder of the city's Eastman Kodak Company lived until his death in 1932. It is now the superb International Museum of Photography, containing massive still, film, and video holdings, and cameras and books on photography.

Strong National Museum of Play
1 Manhattan Square. ***Tel*** *(585) 263-2700.* *10am–5pm Mon– Thu & Sat, 10am–8pm Fri, noon– 5pm Sun.* *Jan 1, Thanksgiving, Dec 25.* www.strongmuseum.org

George Eastman House
900 East Ave. ***Tel*** *(585) 271-3361.* *10am–5pm Tue–Sat (to 8pm Thu), 1–5pm Sun.* *Mon, Jan 1, Thanksgiving, Dec 25.* www.eastmanhouse.org

Chautauqua ⑫

4,600. Chautauqua Institution, Chautauqua, (800) 836-2787.

A secluded community located on Chautauqua Lake in western New York State, this town doubles in population in summer, when its Victorian cottages and tree-lined streets are crowded with people attending the town's famous **Chautauqua Institution**. Founded in 1874 as an instructional center for Methodist Sunday-school teachers, it spawned the Chautauqua Movement, sponsoring correspondence courses and lecture tours in an effort to make the liberal arts more accessible. The town is now one of the nation's premier venues for theater, classical music, and opera. The shady, open-air amphitheater on the timeless Chautauqua campus holds lectures, performances, and religious services from late June to late August.

Renoir's *Little Blue Nude*, Albright-Knox Art Gallery, Buffalo

Buffalo ⑬

328,100. 617 Main St, (800) 283-3256. www.buffalocvb.org

Burned by the British during the War of 1812, the fortunes of the frontier outpost of Buffalo revived some 13 years later, when it became the western terminus of the Erie Canal. This secured its economic future as the gateway to the prosperous Great Lakes trade.

For hotels and restaurants in this region see pp115–16 and p120

Buffalo's skyline on a sunny morning from the city harbor

The **Buffalo and Erie County Historical Society** is housed in what was originally the New York State Pavilion, the only building to survive from the 1901 Pan-American Exposition. Its numerous exhibits focus on the town's rich ethnic and industrial heritage.

The nearby **Albright-Knox Art Gallery** overlooks bucolic Delaware Park, designed by Frederick Law Olmsted *(see p78)*. On display are works by Picasso and de Kooning, and a large collection of North American paintings by Jackson Pollock, Frida Kahlo, and others. Also worth a sidetrip to LeRoy is the **Jell-O Museum**, on Main Street, containing displays and trivia relating to "America's favorite dessert."

Albright-Knox Art Gallery
Elmwood Ave, Off Rte 198. ***Tel*** *(716) 882-8700.* *10am–5pm Wed, Sat & Sun, 10am–10pm Thu–Fri.* *Jan 1, Thanksgiving, Dec 25.*
www.albrightknox.org

Niagara Falls 14

61,800.
Prospect St, (716) 282-8992.
www.niagara-usa.com

Louis Hennepin, the French priest who was one of the first Europeans to gaze upon Niagara Falls in 1678, wrote that "the Universe does not afford its parallel." Even today the three Niagara Falls waterfalls, which plunge nearly 200 ft (61 m) into a rocky gorge, are as awe-inspiring as they were over 300 years ago. Despite the rampant development on both the US and Canadian sides of the Niagara River (which separates the Canadian province of Ontario from New York State), the spectacle still provides enough drama, mist, and romance to lure more than 10 million tourists a year.

Visitors on the American side often start their exploration with a visit to **Niagara Falls State Park**, where the 240-ft (73-m) Prospect Point Observation Tower provides a scenic overview of the falls. For a closer exploration, there are a number of paid excursions, such as the **Cave of the Winds** elevator ride to the base of the falls, and the **Maid of the Mist** boat ride, which departs from Prospect Park and passes directly in front of the falls and into the river's Horseshoe Basin, for a view of the more dramatic Canadian Falls.

The pedestrian-friendly Rainbow Bridge provides quick passage from downtown Niagara Falls to the Canadian side, where most of the area's commercial attractions are located. At night, the falls are dramatically illuminated by electricity generated by the **Niagara Power Project**. Its visitor center traces the development of hydroelectricity in the area and features an operating model of a hydropower turbine.

Niagara Falls State Park
Prospect St. ***Tel*** *(716) 278-1796.* *sunrise–sunset daily.* **Visitor Center** 8am–10pm summer; 8am–6pm winter.
www.niagarafallsstatepark.com
Cave of the Winds Goat Island. *mid-May–Labor Day: 9am–10pm Sun–Thu, 9am–11pm Fri–Sat; post Labor Day–Oct: 9am–8:30pm Sun–Thu, 9am–10pm Fri–Sat.*
Maid of the Mist Ride Prospect Park. *Seasonal, 10am–8pm in season. Check at office for details.*

The majestic Niagara Falls, one of the most dramatic spectacles the country offers

New Jersey

Despite the industrial image earned by New Jersey's manufacturing and railroad towns such as Newark and Hoboken, the "Garden State" really does live up to its moniker. Outside the urban, industrial corridor that lies across the Hudson River from New York City and extends all the way into Philadelphia, New Jersey is a gentle country of green and orderly small towns, dairy farms, rolling hills, pine forests, and miles and miles of white sandy beaches along the Atlantic Ocean.

Strolling on the peaceful campus of Princeton University

Princeton ⓯

12,000. *Princeton Chamber of Commerce, 216 Rockingham Row, Princeton Forrestal Village, (609) 924-1776.* **www**.visitprinceton.org

The central New Jersey village of Princeton witnessed considerable activity during the Revolutionary War period, changing hands between British forces under General Charles Cornwallis and the Continental Army, led by General George Washington. The once-sleepy agricultural village is now a pleasant tree-lined town, combining sophisticated shops, lodgings, and a variety of restaurants, with one of America's most prestigious universities.

The center of Princeton's shopping and dining area is Nassau Street. Located here is Bainbridge House, built in 1766, which now accommodates **The Historical Society of Princeton**. The Society offers local history exhibits and free walking tours, highlighting the town's fine 18th-century architecture. The popular Palmer Square, on Nassau Street, is home to Nassau Inn, Princetown's premier hotel since 1756.

The College of New Jersey, one of the 14 original Colonial colleges, moved to Princeton in 1756 and was renamed **Princeton University** in 1896. Nassau Hall, a landmark building on campus, was the site of the initial meeting of the New Jersey State Legislature in 1776. Renowned physicist Albert Einstein spent his final years here at the Institute for Advanced Study. Today, the campus covers 1,600 acres (647 ha), and the university enrolls 6,000 students annually. The grounds include sculptures by Picasso, Henry Moore, Louise Nevelson, and Alexander Calder. The Art Museum in McCormick Hall displays paintings and sculptures that range from ancient pre-Columbian, Asian, and African art to modern works.

Princeton's tiger mascot

The University Chapel is one. of the world's largest – of special interest are the Gothic architecture, stained-glass windows, and the superb 16th-century French pulpit and lectern. About 30 gargoyles in different styles decorate buildings on the campus, including the Firestone Library. Inside the Library, the Cotsen Children's Library features a small museum focused on the works of C.S. Lewis, Lewis Carroll, and E.B. White.

Princeton University Visitors' Center
Welcome Desk, First Campus Center. ***Tel*** *(609) 258-1766.* *daily.* *11:15am, 1pm, 3:30pm Mon–Sat, 1pm, 3:30pm Sun.* *mid-Dec–early Jan, public hols.* **www**.princeton.edu

Atlantic City ⓰

38,000. *Greater Atlantic City Convention & Visitors Bureau, 2314 Pacific Ave, (609) 449-7130.* **www**.atlanticcitynj.com

Called the "Queen of the Coast" by generations of beachgoers, Atlantic City has been a favored vacation spot since the mid-1800s. The first casino opened on the boardwalk in 1978, and since then the town has become one of the most popular destinations on the eastern seaboard.

All gambling – euphemistically referred to as "gaming"– takes place in the large, ostentatious, casino-hotels that lie within a block of the

Tourists in a rolling chair on the boardwalk at Atlantic City

For hotels and restaurants in this region see p116 and p121

Lucy, the Margate Elephant, near Atlantic City

boardwalk and beach. Although the casinos are justly famous for their nightlife, families will find plenty of other entertainment during the day. Atlantic City's boardwalk, lined with shops and amusement arcades, is always busy with people enjoying a stroll at any time of day or night. Another way to see the boardwalk is in a "**Rolling Chair**," a rickshaw-like wicker chair on wheels that seats up to three people. Beyond the boardwalk, white-sand beaches beckon sunbathers and swimmers.

Until 2006, Atlantic City hosted the prestigious Miss America Pageant, which had been held here since 1928. In nearby Margate City, **Lucy, the Margate Elephant** stands tall in celebration of American marketing ingenuity. Built by a real estate developer in 1881 to draw prospects to his holdings, "Lucy" has served as a residence and a tavern over the years. Today, guided tours take visitors into the 90-ton (90,000-kg) structure that has become instantly recognizable as part of the Jersey Shore and Atlantic City.

Rolling Chair
Atlantic City Famous Rolling Chair Co, 1605 Boardwalk.
Tel *(609) 347-7148.*

Lucy, the Margate Elephant
9200 Atlantic Ave, Margate City.
Tel *(609) 823-6473. mid-Jun–Labor Day: 10am–8pm Mon–Sat, 10am-5pm Sun; Apr–mid-Jun & after Labor Day–last weekend in Oct: 10am–4pm Mon–Fri, 10am–5pm weekends; Nov–Mar: hours vary.*

Cape May ⓱

4,400. Cape May Welcome Center, Lafayette & Elmira Sts, Cape May, (609) 884-9562.
www.capemaychamber.com

First explored by Cornelius Mey for the Dutch West India Company in 1621, Cape May is one of the oldest seashore resorts on the Atlantic Coast. Visited by a number of US presidents including James Buchanan, Ulysses S. Grant, Benjamin Harrison, and Franklin Pierce, it was popular with socialites from New York and Philadelphia during the late 1800s. Since then, this resort at the southernmost point of New Jersey, has continued to enjoy a fine reputation among beach lovers. A small boardwalk and sandy beach afford a lovely view of sunrise over the Atlantic Ocean.

Today, the area is characterized by the great Victorian building boom that took place in the 19th century. The central district is made up of so-called "cottages," two- and three-story buildings intended as summer homes for large families. They have been built in styles popular at the turn of the 20th century, ranging from lacy Queen Anne to Italianate. Most of the historic homes have been lovingly restored to period condition, and some are open to the public. Many others have been converted into B&B (bed-and-breakfast) lodgings. There are several tours of the Victorian homes, including a special trolley tour.

The **Historic Cold Spring Village** is a living history museum consisting of 25 authentically restored buildings set on a 20-acre (8-ha) site. Costumed interpreters portray 19th-century lifestyles that would have been common in a southern New Jersey rural community. Trades and crafts such as pottery making, book binding, and blacksmithing are also demonstrated.

Nearby, the **Cape May County Park and Zoo** is home to 200 species of animals; some, such as Brazilian golden lion tamarins, are rare or endangered. The park, which is free, also features a 35-acre (14-ha) African savanna habitat accessed by an 800-ft (244-m) long boardwalk.

Historic Cold Spring Village
720 US 9, Cape May. ***Tel*** *(609) 898-2300. late Jun–Labor Day: 10am–4:30pm Tue–Sun; after Labor Day–Sep 30 & Memorial Day–late Jun: 10am–4:30pm Sat–Sun.*
www.hcsv.org

One of Cape May's charming bed & breakfast lodgings

Philadelphia 18

William Penn's statue on Philadelphia City Hall

Pennsylvania's largest city, Philadelphia or the "City of Brotherly Love," is also the birthplace of the nation. In 1776, representatives from the 13 British colonies signed the Declaration of Independence here, and the city served as an early capital of the fledgling United States. Since its founding by English Quaker William Penn in the late 17th century, Philadelphia's port on the Delaware River has welcomed thousands of immigrants from all over the world. Their labor strengthened the expanding city through two centuries of industrial growth, wars, and economic reversals. Even today, the city's neighborhoods and restaurants reflect this ethnic mix. Philadelphia's rich history, world-class art collections, special-interest museums, fine restaurants and hotels, and the nation's largest landscaped public park combine to make the city one of America's most popular destinations.

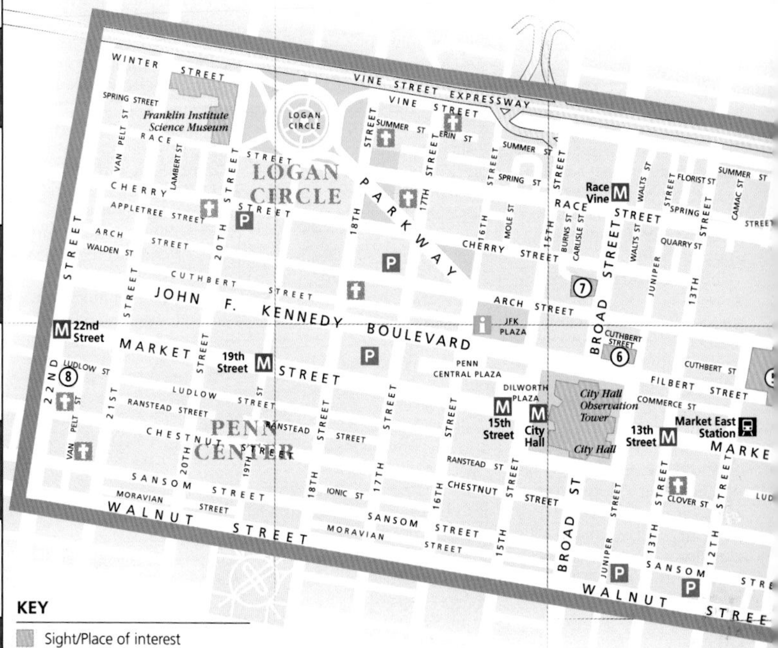

KEY

- Sight/Place of interest
- Metro station
- Train station
- Bus station
- Tourist information
- Parking
- Church
- Expressway

GETTING AROUND

Philadelphia's excellent local transit system, SEPTA, operates buses throughout Greater Philadelphia in addition to two subway lines: the Market-Frankford line (east–west, under Market St) and the Broadway Street line (north–south). Purple-painted, tourist-oriented "Philly Phlash" shuttles travel in a loop through downtown to all major attractions (late May to the end of October). Taxis are plentiful and moderately priced.

SIGHTS AT A GLANCE

Independence Hall ①
Second Bank of the United States ②
US Mint ③
Independence Seaport Museum ④
Reading Terminal Market ⑤
Masonic Temple ⑥
Pennsylvania Academy of Fine Arts ⑦
College of Physicians of Philadelphia/ Mutter Museum ⑧

Greater Philadelphia
(see inset map)

Eastern State Penitentiary ⑨
Philadelphia Zoo ⑩
Fairmount Park ⑪
Philadelphia Museum of Art ⑫
The Barnes Foundation ⑬

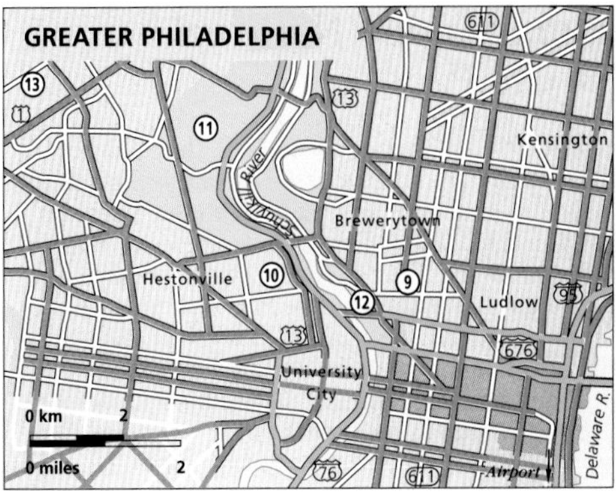

KEY

Area of main map

SEE ALSO

• ***Where to Stay*** p117

• ***Where to Eat*** p121

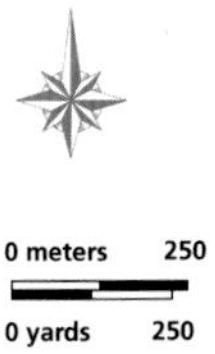

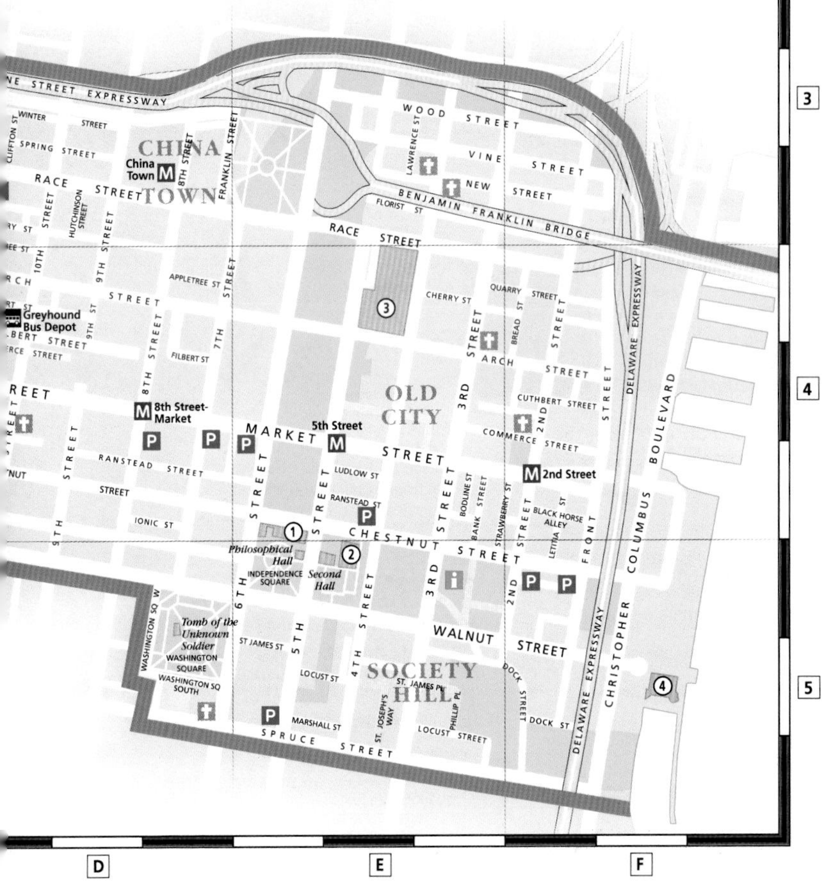

Independence National Historic Park

Known locally as Independence Mall, this 45-acre (18-ha) urban park encompasses several well-preserved 18th-century structures associated with the American Revolution. The Declaration of Independence that heralded the birth of a new nation was signed in this historic area. Dominated by the tall brick tower of Independence Hall, the park includes the oldest street in Philadelphia, the US Mint, and several special-interest museums exploring Philadelphia's Colonial and seafaring past as well as its ethnic heritage. Around 20 of the buildings are now open to the public.

Plaque commemorating Independence Hall

African American Museum
Inspirational stories of Philadelphia's famous African-American citizens are displayed alongside exhibits of contemporary works.

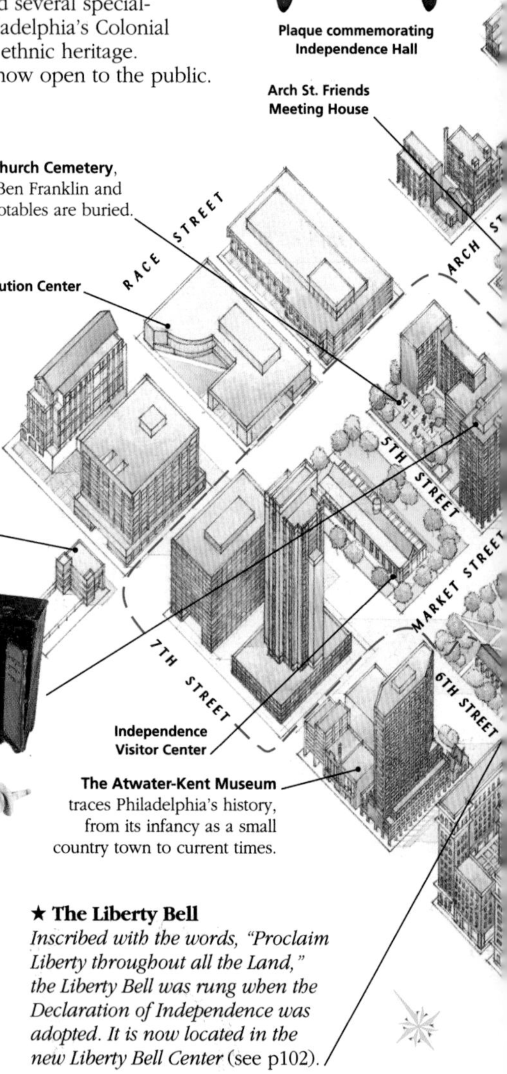

Arch St. Friends Meeting House

Christ Church Cemetery, where Ben Franklin and other notables are buried.

Constitution Center

★ National Museum of American Jewish History
This unique museum celebrates the history of Jews in America through artifacts such as this Torah scroll and ark (mid-1700s) from the collection of Congregation Mikveh Israel.

Independence Visitor Center

The Atwater-Kent Museum traces Philadelphia's history, from its infancy as a small country town to current times.

STAR SIGHTS

- ★ Independence Hall
- ★ The Liberty Bell
- ★ National Museum of American Jewish History
- ★ Second Bank of the US

★ The Liberty Bell
Inscribed with the words, "Proclaim Liberty throughout all the Land," the Liberty Bell was rung when the Declaration of Independence was adopted. It is now located in the new Liberty Bell Center (see p102).

KEY

— — — Suggested route

0 meter 200
0 yards 200

Elfreth's Alley
The city's oldest residential street is lined with 18th-century houses, many of which are now shops.

VISITORS' CHECKLIST

6th & Market Sts, (800) 537-7676. 8:30am–5pm daily. **Independence Hall, Liberty Bell** *9am–5pm daily.* **National Museum of American Jewish History** ***Tel*** *(215) 923-3811. 10am–5pm Mon–Thu, 10am–3pm Fri, noon–5pm Sun. Sat, Jewish hols.* **www**.nmajh.org **Second Bank of the US** *9am–5pm daily.* **African American Museum** ***Tel*** *(215) 574-0380. 10am–5pm Tue–Sat, noon–5pm Sun.* **www**.aampmuseum.org

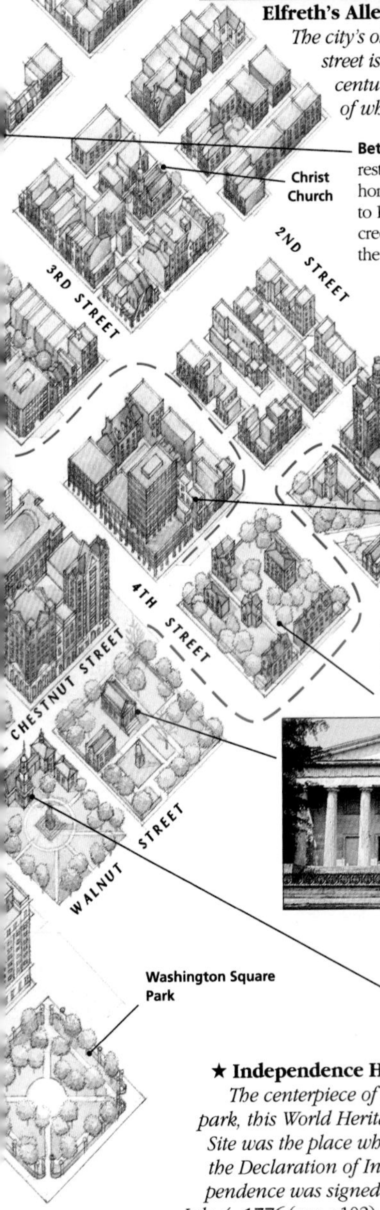

Betsy Ross House, a restored 18th-century home, is a memorial to Betsy Ross, who is credited with stitching the first American flag.

City Tavern was the venue of frequent debates during Colonial times. It still serves food and drink today.

Franklin Court
Benjamin Franklin lived and worked in these buildings, which include the B. Free Franklin post office and museum.

18th-Century Garden, created by the Pennsylvania Horticultural Society (1827), was the first of its kind in the US.

★ Second Bank of the US
An extensive collection of portraits of luminaries involved in the military, diplomatic, and political events of 1776 is on display at this Grecian style building (see p102). ②

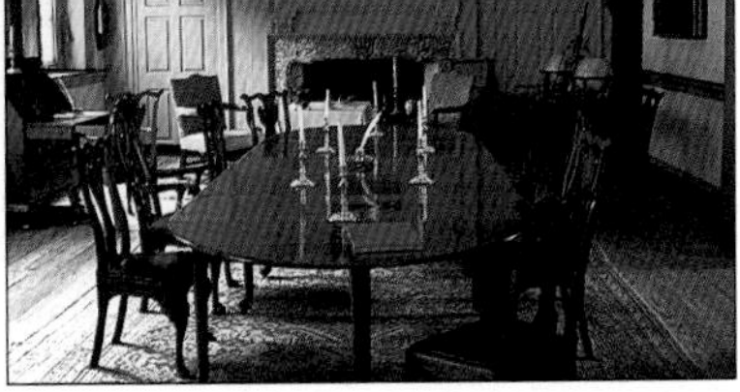

★ Independence Hall
The centerpiece of the park, this World Heritage Site was the place where the Declaration of Independence was signed on July 4, 1776 (see p102). ①

Independence Hall ①

Chestnut St between 5th & 6th Sts. **Tel** *(800) 967-2283 for timed tickets in Mar–Dec.* *5th St.* *Philly Phlash.* *9am–5pm daily, longer hours in summer.*
www.nps.gov/inde

Just west of the Delaware River, this unadorned brick building is the most important structure in the Independence Hall National Park. Previously designated the State House of Pennsylvania, it is the site of the drafting of the Declaration of Independence, the document that declared America's freedom from the British Empire.

Independence Hall, completed in 1748, was designed by master carpenter Edmund Woolley and lawyer Andrew Hamilton. The chambers of the meeting rooms are furnished simply, as they were during the late 1700s. Today, park personnel re-create history by pointing out the Windsor-style chairs from which Colonial leaders debated the contents of the Declaration. Although the Continental Congress rejected two passages in the first draft – an ill-tempered reference to the English people, and a bitter denunciation of the slave trade – the document was adopted without significant change and approved by Congress on July 4, 1776. The US Constitution was drafted in the same room in 1787.

The large, brass **Liberty Bell** that once hung in the tower has now been placed in the new Liberty Bell Center near Independence Hall. In 1846, a small crack developed and the bell could no longer be sounded. However, it remains the best-known symbol of the Colonial struggle for self-governance. The center incorporates displays that highlight Liberty Bell's importance to the story of America's independence.

The Liberty Bell on display near Independence Hall

Second Bank of the United States ②

420 Chestnut St. **Tel** *(215) 965-2305.* *call for times.* **www**.nps.gov/inde/second-bank.htm

Built between the years 1819 and 1824, this is one of America's finest examples of Greek Revival architecture. Once a repository that provided credit for federal government and private businesses, it now houses a collection of late 18th- and early 19th-century portraits. On view are 185 paintings of Colonial and federal leaders, military officers, explorers, and scientists.

Many of the portraits are by Charles Willson Peale (1741–1827), his brother James, and their respective sons and daughters, who together form America's most distinguished family of artists. After the Revolutionary War, Peale began collecting portraits, and today, 94 of his original paintings, including likenesses of the American founding fathers George Washington and Alexander Hamilton, and the Continental Army's French ally, the Marquis de Lafayette, are on display along with the portraiture of other artists.

Aerial view of Independence Hall

US Mint ③

5th & Arch Sts. **Tel** *(215) 408-0114.* *5th St.* *9am–3pm Mon–Fri.* *public hols.*
www.usmint.gov

The Philadelphia mint, the oldest in the US, makes most of the coins that Americans use every day, and also produces gold bullion coins and national medals. The first US coins, minted in 1793, were copper pennies and half pennies intended solely for local commerce in the colonies. Today, 24 hours a day, five days a week, hundreds of machines and operators in a room the size of a football field blank, anneal, count, and bag millions of dollars worth of quarters, dimes, and pennies. Commemorative coins and numismatic collectables are available in the gift shop.

Independence Seaport Museum ④

211 S Columbus Blvd. **Tel** *(215) 925-5439.* *2nd St.* *Philly Phlash.* *10am–5pm daily.* *Jan 1, Thnksg., Dec 25.* *free 10am–noon Sun.*
www.phillyseaport.org

Quartered in a stunning modern building on the waterfront, this 100,000-sq-ft (9,290-sq-m) museum's mandate is to preserve US maritime history and traditions, with special focus on the Chesapeake Bay, and the Delaware River and its tributaries. Displays combine art and artifacts with hands-on computer games, large-scale

For hotels and restaurants in this region see p117 and p121

models, and audio-visuals. The Ben Franklin Bridge, which connects Pennsylvania with New Jersey, is re-created in the museum as a three-and-a-half story replica that straddles a working model of the Delaware River.

Other highlights include "Divers of the Deep," featuring underwater technology through the ages, and "Workshop on the Water," an active boat shop and gallery where visitors can watch boat building in progress as artisans craft traditional wooden 19th-century boats. The World War II submarine USS *Becuna*, commissioned in 1943, and the USS *Olympia*, Admiral George Dewey's flagship in the Battle of Manila (1898), are berthed next to the museum.

Coffee shop in Philadelphia's Reading Terminal Market

Reading Terminal Market ⑤

12th & Filbert Sts. ***Tel*** *(215) 922-2317.* *City Hall, 13th St, Juniper St.* *Philly Phlash, SPREE bus.* *8am–6pm Mon–Sat, 9am–4pm Sun.* *Jan 1, Dec 25.*
www.readingterminalmarket.org

This market was created underneath a train shed after two farmers' markets were leveled to make space for a new terminal in 1892. So modern was the market that people came from as far as the New Jersey shore to buy fresh Lancaster County produce. Reading Terminal Market declined over the years and was nearly destroyed in the 1970s. Today, however, it has been revitalized, and fishmongers, butchers, bakers, florists, and greengrocers vie for space with quick-breakfast stands run by Amish women.

Equestrian statue in the Masonic Temple courtyard

Masonic Temple ⑥

1 N Broad St. ***Tel*** *(215) 988-1917.* *City Hall.* *Philly Phlash.* *tours at 11am, 2pm, 3pm Tue–Fri; 10am, 11am Sat.* *Jul–Aug: Sat, Jan 1, Easter, Thnksg., Dec 25.*
www.pagrandlodge.org

An architectural jewel dedicated in 1873 as the Grand Lodge of Free and Accepted Masons of Pennsylvania, this remarkable building contains a number of meeting halls in various decorative styles. Among them, the Oriental Hall's (1896) coloring and ornamentation has been copied from the Alhambra in Granada, Spain, the Renaissance Hall (1908) follows an Italian Renaissance motif, while the Egyptian Hall (1889) takes its inspiration from the Temples of Luxor, Karnak, and Philae. High arches, pinnacles, and spires form the Gothic Hall, and the cross-and-crown emblem of Sir Knights – "Under this sign you will conquer" – hangs over a replica of the Archbishop's throne in Canterbury Cathedral. The halls, still in use, were created to honor the building trades, and much of the stone and tilework are imperceptibly faux finished – an attestation to the skill of the men who made them. President George Washington wore his Masonic apron when he laid the cornerstone of the Capitol building in Washington, DC. The apron is on display in the museum on the first floor.

Pennsylvania Academy of Fine Arts ⑦

118 N Broad S at Cherry St. ***Tel*** *(215) 972-7600.* *15th St, Rocelvine.* *Philly Phlash.* *10am– 5pm Tue–Sat, 11am–5pm Sun.* *public hols.*
www.pafa.org

The collection of this museum and school, founded in 1805, spans the history of American painting. Galleries display works by some of the art world's best-known denizens. One of them, the classical stylist Benjamin West (1738–1820), a Quaker from Philadelphia, helped organize the British Royal Academy in 1768, and four years later was named Historical Painter to the King. Impressionist and former Academy of Fine Arts student, Mary Cassatt (1824–1926), and modern abstractionist Richard Diebenkorn (1922–93) among others, share wall space. This distinctive building is considered one of the finest examples of Victorian-Gothic architecture in America.

The Foxhunt **by Winslow Homer, Pennsylvania Academy of Fine Arts**

The well-lit display of medical curiosities at Mutter Museum

College of Physicians of Philadelphia/ Mutter Museum ⑧

19 S 22nd St. ***Tel*** *(215) 563-3737.* Ⓜ *22nd St.* 🚌 *17, 21.* ◯ *10am–5pm daily (9pm Fri).* ● *Jan 1, Thanksgiving, Dec 25.*
www.collphyphil.org

Founded in 1787 for the "advancement of the science of medicine," the still-active college is a major source of health information. This is provided by the institute's C. Everett Koop Community Health Information Center, through the library, video-tapes, and searchable computer system.

Mutter Museum, on the first floor of one of the buildings, is a fascinating collection of preserved specimens, skeletal constructions, and wax figures. These were originally used for educational purposes in the mid-19th century, when diseases and genetic defects were identifiable only by their physical manifestations. Some afflictions are quite grotesque, and may not be suitable for small children or those who are queasy.

The museum also contains medical instruments, exhibits on the history of medicine over the last 100 years, a re-creation of an early 20th-century doctor's office, and a medicinal plant garden. Special exhibits on medical phenomena, such as Siamese (conjoined) Twins, are an additional feature.

Eastern State Penitentiary ⑨

Fairmount Ave at 22nd St. ***Tel*** *(215) 236-3300.* 🚌 *7, 32, 33, 43, 48.* ◯ *Apr–Nov: 10am–5pm daily (last adm 4pm); Jun–Aug: to 8pm Wed.* ● *Dec–Mar, Easter, Thnksg.*
www.easternstate.org

Named the "house" by inmates and guards, the Eastern State Penitentiary, established in 1829, was a revolutionary concept in criminal justice. Prior to this, criminals were thrown together in despicable conditions and punished by physical brutality. The Philadelphia Quakers proposed an alternative – a place where a criminal could be alone to ponder and become penitent for his actions. During incarceration, with sentences seldom less than five years in length, prisoners literally never heard or saw another human being for the entire duration of their stay. The prison had a single entrance and 30-ft (9-m) high boundary walls. Each solitary cell had a private outdoor exercise yard contained by a 10-ft (3-m) wall. Eastern State's many "guests" included bootlegger and crime lord Al Capone. The prison was officially closed in 1971.

Long corridor inside the Eastern State Penitentiary

Philadelphia Zoo ⑩

3400 W Girard Ave. ***Tel*** *(215) 243-1100.* 🚌 *Philly Phlash.* ◯ *9:30am–4pm daily.* ● *Jan 1, 2nd Thu in Jun, Thnksg., Dec 24, 25 & 31.*
www.philadelphiazoo.org

This zoo, the oldest in America, was founded in 1859. Set within verdant grounds, interspersed with statuary, the zoo is home to over 2,000 animals, including rare species such as naked mole rats and bamboo-eating lemurs. A walk-through giant otter habitat shows the animals at their playful best. The big cats – lions, clouded leopards, tigers (including rare white tigers), and jaguars – are kept in near-natural habitats or inside the Carnivora House, in weather-protected cages that provide close-up views. Other features are an open bird-house with uncaged finches and hummingbirds, a reptile house, where alligators bask in a tropical paradise, and a 3-acre (1-ha) reserve for 11 primate species, including the nation's only blue-eyed lemurs. A large zoo balloon offers a panoramic view of the city.

Fairmount Park ⑪

John F. Kennedy Blvd & N 16th St, (215) 683-0200. 🚌 *Philly Phlash.* Ⓜ *Market-Frankford line.* ◯ *daily.*
www.fairmontpark.org

Designed by Frederick Law Olmsted (1822–1903), America's pre-eminent land-scape architect who also designed Central Park, Fair-mount Park is an 8,900-acre (3,601-ha) greenway. It encompasses seven historic

For hotels and restaurants in this region see p117 and p121

Downtown Philadelphia rising above Fairmount Park

manor houses decorated in period style, dozens of sculptures, a horticultural center, and Japanese house and gardens among other features. A waterworks, innovative in 1840, was designed and built to pump water from the Schuylkill River, which divides the park into east and west. The grounds are interspered with roads, hiking, biking, and bridle trails. Visitors can also rent rowboats and canoes.

A handful of rowing clubs occupy Victorian boathouses along the river. The boathouses are turreted, gabled, and decorated with coats-of-arms. At night, when viewed from the West Fairmount Park shore, the houses are outlined with tiny lights.

In 1894, wealthy manufacturer Richard Smith donated Smith Playground to the children of Philadelphia in memory of his son. Among the attractions are merry-go-rounds, a giant slide, and a mansion and playhouse. Also in Fairmount Park is the 99-acre (40-ha) **Laurel Hill Cemetery**. This vast "park within a park" is dotted with obelisks, statuary, and classic Greek mausoleums. It was such a popular picnic and walking area during the late Victorian period that admission was by ticket only.

Philadelphia Museum of Art ⑫

26th St & Benjamin Franklin Pkwy. ***Tel*** *(215) 763-8100. Philly Phlash, 7, 32, 38, 43, 48. 10am–5pm Tue–Sun; (to 8:45pm Fri). Mon, legal hols. Sun donation.*
www.philamuseum.org

This museum attracts major exhibitions to supplement its superlative permanent collection ranging from 15th-century illuminated manuscripts to modern sculpture by Constantin Brancusi. The full-scale medieval cloister courtyard and fountain on the second floor is a favorite, as are the French Gothic chapel and a pillared temple from Madurai, India. Throughout the museum are computerized stations with information on the exhibits. A collection of Pennsylvania Dutch and American decorative arts adjoins galleries that feature paintings by American artists.

Medieval diptych, Philadelphia Museum of Art

The Barnes Foundation ⑬

300 N Latch's Lane, Merion. ***Tel*** *(610) 667-0290. 44. reservation only: Sep–Jun: 9:30am–5pm Fri–Sun; Jul–Aug: 9:30am–5pm Wed–Fri. public hols.*
www.barnesfoundation.org

Established in the year 1922 to share the private collection of pharmaceutical magnate Albert C. Barnes with "people of all socio-economic levels," this museum has one of the world's premier displays of French modern and Post-Impressionist paintings. Among the more than 800 works on view, there are 180 by August Renoir, 69 by Paul Cézanne, 60 by Henri Matisse, and more by Picasso, Seurat, Modigliani, Van Gogh, Rousseau, and almost every other noteworthy artist of that era. Other exhibits include ancient Greek and Egyptian art, medieval manuscripts, African sculpture, American furniture, ceramics, and handwrought ironwork. The art is displayed to highlight artistic affinities between diverse works. For instance, the Barnes Collection is displayed in accordance with Dr. Barnes' unique specifications – paintings, sculpture, and craft pieces are grouped into 96 distinct ensembles, without labels and with very little regard to chronology.

The glittering silhouettes of Victorian boathouses along Schuylkill River, Fairmount Park

Pennsylvania

Pennsylvania has it all – American history, beautiful scenery, varied recreation, lodging, and dining, ranging from the refined to the simple. Of its two main cities, Philadelphia *(see pp98–105)*, the birthplace of America, is a complex, stunning city, while Pittsburgh re-created itself from a grimy, industrial center to a sparkling gem on the forks of the Ohio River. Most of the state, however, is rural and bucolic, a green patchwork of dairy and produce farms, embroidered with forests and waterways, trim fields and small towns.

Memorial at Gettysburg National Military Park

Gettysburg ⓳

7,000.
102 Carlisle St, (800) 337-5015.
www.gettysburg.org

A pivotal confrontation of the Civil War *(see p47)* took place near the small farming community of Gettysburg in early July 1863. Nearly 100,000 Union soldiers fought 75,000 Confederates led by Robert E. Lee. After three days of fighting, a staggering 50,000 soldiers lay dead or wounded, and the Confederates were turned back.

Though the war raged for another two years, Gettysburg was recognized as a turning point. To commemorate the site, a burial ground was purchased, and President Lincoln dedicated the **Gettysburg National Cemetery** with his Gettysburg Address. Several impressive monuments have been placed throughout the fields and forests of the battlefield, now the **Gettysburg National Military Park**. The Cyclorama, a giant circular mural painted in 1884, dramatizes a crucial battle scene – Picket's Charge, where over 6,000 Confederate soldiers were killed or wounded.

Gettysburg National Military Park
Tel *(717) 334-1124.*
Park *Nov–Mar: 6am–7pm daily; Apr–Oct: 6am–10pm daily.* **Visitor Center** *8am–5pm daily (to 6pm summer).* *Jan 1, Thanksgiving, Dec 25.*
www.nps.gov/gett

Lancaster ⓴

55,600. *501 Greenfield Rd, Lancaster, (800) 723-8824.* **www**.padutch.com

This market town at the heart of the Pennsylvania Dutch Country *(see p59)* is surrounded by almost 5,000 small farms. The region is famous for the German-immigrant "Old Order Amish" Christians, who live and work without modern conveniences like electricity. The **Landis Valley Museum's** large outdoor collection focuses on the state's German rural heritage. Among the exhibits are a crossroads village and an adjoining farmstead with traditional breeds of animals and heirloom plants. Visitors can see demonstrations of skills such as sheep-shearing.

Ephrata Cloister, northeast of town in the village of Ephrata, is a collection of medieval-style buildings, founded in 1732. It was home to one of America's earliest communal societies, semi-monastics who practiced an austere lifestyle emphasizing spirituality, and the artistic use of music and the written word. In 1745, the colony set up one of the country's earliest printing presses. This tradition continues today; Ephrata is the home of the world-famous Rodale Press.

Landis Valley Museum
2451 Kissel Hill Rd. ***Tel*** *(717) 569-0401.* *9am–5pm Mon–Sat, noon–5pm Sun.*
www.landisvalleymuseum.org

Hershey ㉑

7,400. *1255A Harrisburg Pike, Harrisburg, (800) 995-0969.* **www**.hersheypa.com

This factory town, now a popular tourist destination, revolves around chocolate, so much so that even its streetlights are shaped like silver-foil-wrapped Hershey Kisses. The town's main attraction is **Chocolate World**, which features a 15-minute ride through a series of animated tableaux revealing Hershey's chocolate-making process. A free sample awaits at the end of the tour, while a series of shops sell souvenirs and every Hershey product made. Nearby is **Hershey Park**, a 90-acre (36-ha) amusement park. Hershey Park offers 80 rides including

"Sisters House" and "Meeting House" in Ephrata Cloister

five water slides, four roller coasters, and one of the finest Philadelphia Toboggan Company four-row carousels in existence today.

Chocolate World
SR 743 & US 422, Hershey. ***Tel*** *(717) 534-4900. 9am–5pm daily, hours may vary so call for details.*
www.hersheyschocolateworld.com

York ㉒

42,200. 1425 Eden Rd, York, (717) 852-9675.
www.yorkpa.org

The first Pennsylvania settlement west of the Susquehanna River, York was laid out in 1741. At that time, its inhabitants were mainly tavernkeepers and craftspeople, catering to pioneers heading west. Since then, manufacturing has become the prime economic force. York's many covered public markets include the 1888 **Central Market**, the best place in town for local fresh produce, flowers, meats, baked goods, and inexpensive restaurants.

Last checks at the Harley-Davidson Vehicle Operations Plant in York

East of historic York, at the **Harley-Davidson Vehicle Operations Plant**, giant presses form steel sheets into fenders while gleaming motorcycles fly overhead. A small museum shows Harley-Davidson's history from its days as a motorized bike company in 1903 to the present.

Harley-Davidson Final Assembly Plant
1425 Eden Rd. ***Tel*** *(877) 883-1450. schedule varies, so phone ahead (children under 12 not allowed on factory floor). public hols. hourly 9am–2pm Mon–Fri.*
www.harley-davidson.com

A lush greenhouse in Longwood Gardens

Reading ㉓

78,400. 352 Penn St, Reading, (800) 443-6610.
www.readingberkspa.com

Once a center of industry, Reading has reinvented itself as a discount-outlet capital, with clusters of buildings housing more than 80 name-brand stores from Brooks Brothers to Mikasa and Wedgewood. The **Reading Pagoda**, on the town's outskirts, is modeled after a Shogun dynasty castle that was built as part of an early 1900s resort. Today, cherry trees encircle the building, and there are walking trails throughout the adjacent park.

Longwood Gardens ㉔

US 1, Kennett Square. ***Tel*** *(610) 388-1000. 9am–5pm daily; longer hrs in summer & at Christmas.*
www.longwoodgardens.org

Pierre du Pont, millionaire financier and industrialist, acquired the 1,000-acre (405-ha) Longwood Gardens in the beautiful, wooded Brandywine Valley in 1906. His aim was to preserve the property's unusual trees, and to provide a place of entertainment for his family and friends.

More than 11,000 varieties of plants including spectacular year-round seasonal displays, whimsical topiaries, and a children's garden are open to the public. The massive main greenhouse and conservatory are engineering marvels. But the real star of Longwood are the fabulous fountains whose choreographed eruptions rise above the treetops and are highlighted at night by colored lights, creating dazzling displays that are often the backdrop for musical events. Shows and festivals range from the annual Wine & Jazz Festival, which takes place in May, to classical music concerts of Vivaldi's *The Four Seasons*. The gardens are also the setting for many kid-friendly events, including colorful kite-flying weekends, summer camp programs, storytelling sessions, and lively explorations of treehouses.

HARLEY-DAVIDSON

15th Anniversary Fat Boy

What began as a tinkering project for 21-year-old William Harley and 20-year-old Arthur Davidson, grew into a company that has dominated racing since 1914. After World War I, the first American entered Germany astride a Harley-Davidson. In 1956, Elvis Presley posed on a model KH. Today, Harley Owners Group (HOG) has more than 900,000 members.

Pittsburgh's Golden Triangle, with its downtown skyscrapers

Pittsburgh ㉕

369,900. *425 6th Ave, 30th Floor, (800) 359-0758.* **www**.visitpittsburgh.com

Located at the point where the Allegheny and Monongahela rivers come together to form the Ohio River, Pittsburgh is an American success story. It grew from a frontier outpost to become an industrial giant, home to the huge mills of the US Steel conglomerate as well as the food-processing company Heinz and the Westinghouse electric company. From the Civil War through World War II, Pittsburgh was a thriving metropolis, but in the 1950s and 60s its fortunes faded.

Endowed by steel magnate Andrew Carnegie, the **Carnegie Museum of Art** offers a brilliantly lit suite of galleries with collections ranging from ancient Egyptian sculpture to Impressionist, Post-Impressionist, and modern American art by Roy Lichtenstein and Alexander Calder. The Hall of Sculpture is a two-storied columned hall that replicates the interior of the Temple of Athena in Athens. It is adorned with casts from the Greek classical era. Next door, the Hall of Architecture is filled with reproductions of some of the best examples of classical, medieval, and Renaissance architectural details. The Carnegie Museum of Natural History, in the same complex, opens out on a central gallery and relies on filtered natural light as a part of its architectural charm. Exhibits change from time to time, but most of the displays in this museum consist of dioramas that feature taxidermy specimens.

At the **Carnegie Science Center** on Allegheny Avenue, the idea is to make science accessible through play. More than 40,000 sq ft (3,716 sq m) of the 186,000-sq-ft (17,280-sq-m) center is devoted to numerous interactive exhibits. The Miniature Railroad and Village displays the rich historical, architectural, and cultural heritage of western Pennsylvania. In the four-story Rangos Omnimax® Theater – one of 13 in the country – audience members recline while images are projected onto a 79-ft (24-m) domed ceiling.

Students relaxing at Pittsburgh University

Hall of Sculpture at Carnegie Museum of Art, Pittsburgh

The 42-story **Cathedral of Learning** houses the University of Pittsburgh's Nationality Classrooms, which seek to reflect the different ethnic groups that contribute to the city's heritage. Started in the 1930s, each of the 26 rooms, the last of which were completed in 2000, has authentic decor and furnishings depicting a unique time and place from 5th-century BC Greece to 16th-century Poland.

In the city's north side, the tile-clad exterior of the **Andy Warhol Museum** reflects the workaday character of the neighborhood. Appearances are deceptive here, and this former warehouse conceals a brightly illuminated, ultra-modern interior. The museum celebrates the Pittsburgh-born founder of American Pop Art, Andy Warhol (1928–87) through selections of works from its archives. These include paintings, and video and film clips. Works of related artists are also on display. Located 5 miles (8 km) southeast of Pittsburgh is **Kennywood Amusement Park**. It was built in 1905 as a Luna Park, a popular name for amusement parks that showcased the new electric light bulb. The park offers thrill rides, a stunt show, and a 1926 carousel made by the Dentzel Company – premier hand-carvers of carousel animals.

Carnegie Museum of Art
4,400 Forbes Ave. ***Tel*** *(412) 622-3131.* *Jul–Aug: 10am–5pm Mon– Sat; noon–5pm Sun; Sep–Jun: 10am– 5pm Tue–Sat; noon–5pm Sun.* *public hols.*
www.cmoa.org;
www.carnegiemnh.org

Andy Warhol Museum
117 Sandusky St. ***Tel*** *(412) 237-8300.* *10am–5pm Tue–Thu, Sat–Sun 10am–10pm Fri.* *public hols.*
www.warhol.org

For hotels and restaurants in this region see p117 and p121

Laurel Highlands 26

120 E Main St Ligonier, (800) 333-5661. www.laurelhighlands.org

To the south of Pittsburgh, ridges gather together, valleys become canyons, and mountain laurel covers the slopes, giving the region its name. The splendid 1,700-ft (518-m) deep Youghiogheny Gorge cuts through the scenic Laurel Ridge Mountains, where an area of nearly 19,000 acres (7,689 ha) forms the **Ohiopyle State Park**. The park includes more than 28 miles (45 km) of the Youghiogheny River. White-water rafting is popular here, as are hiking, jogging, biking, and cross-country skiing on the 43-mile (69-km) Youghiogheny River Trail.

Fallingwater, an architectural tour de force by renowned architect Frank Lloyd Wright, lies north of the park. Built in 1936, the house reflects Wright's interest in structures that were an integral part of the landscape.

Laurel Ridge State Park stretches from the village of Ohiopyle in the west to the Conemaugh River in the east. The 70-mile (113-km) long Laurel Highlands Hiking Trail is open all year round. The Johnstown Flood Museum chronicles the Conemaugh River disaster that killed more than 2,000 people and destroyed Johnstown in 1889.

Ohiopyle State Park
7 Sheridan St, Ohiopyle. *Tel (724) 329-8591.* *daily.*

THE AMISH

All Amish trace their roots to the Swiss Anabaptist ("New Birth") movement of 1525, an offshoot of the Protestant Reformation, whose creed rejected the formality of established churches. Today's Old Order Amish are the most conservative of the sect, disdaining any device that would connect them to the larger world, including electricity, phones, and cars. Conspicuous because of their plain, dark attire – with white prayer caps for the women and straw hats for the men – and their horse-and-buggy mode of transportation, the Amish in America are little changed from their 17th-century ancestors who came seeking religious freedom.

Amish buggy on a rural highway

Fallingwater
SR 381, Mill Run. *Tel (724) 329-8501.* *mid-Mar–mid-Nov: 10am–4pm Tue–Sun; Dec–mid-Jan: 10am–4pm Sat–Sun.* *mid-Jan–mid-Mar, Jan 1, Easter, Thanksgiving, Dec 25.* www.paconserve.org

Western Amish Country 27

229 S Jefferson St, New Castle, (888) 284-7599.

The scenic territory around the town of New Castle, 56 miles (145 km) from Pittsburgh, is a hand-stitched quilt of agricultural acreage, parks. and villages. Like the residents of the Pennsylvania Dutch Country near Lancaster *(see p106)*, a large population of Old Order Amish and Mennonites have plowed and planted farms in the Enon Valley, near New Castle. **Montgomery Locks and Dam**, completed in 1936, is one of 20 huge locks and dams on the Ohio River from Pittsburgh to Cairo, Illinois. The dam creates a pool more than 18 miles (29 km) long for recreational and commercial use. **McConnell's Mill State Park** follows the path of Slippery Rock Creek and contains a former water-driven gristmill, now a museum. The untamed beauty of Slippery Rock Gorge is very popular with rock climbers and rappellers. **Moraine State Park**, which is about 5 miles (8 km) east of McConnell's Park, is a small paradise reborn from an industrial wasteland where underground and strip mining flourished until the 1950s. Mines were then sealed, gas and oil wells plugged, and the 3,225-acre (1,305-ha) Lake Arthur was constructed.

McConnell's Mill State Park
Portersville. *Tel (724) 368-8091.* *sunrise–sunset daily.*

The Youghiogheny River looping through Ohiopyle State Park, Laurel Highlands

Practical Information

Successful traveling around New York, New Jersey, and Pennsylvania benefits from advance planning, simply because there is so much to see and do in such a concentrated area. The major cities are packed with attractions, hotels, and restaurants, while the expansive and diverse areas in between often double as resort areas, catering to city-dwellers in need of a change of pace. Depending upon the time, you can explore significant historical sights, appreciate stunning scenery, take in a local celebration, or simply relax along the coast.

TOURIST INFORMATION

New York, New Jersey, and Pennsylvania each publishes a wide variety of informative, richly illustrated travel guides. All of this information can be ordered by telephone or accessed via web sites, and further information is available from the multitude of local and regional tourism bureaus across the three states. The wealth of available information covers climate, transportation, attractions, accommodations, restaurants, recreation, festivals, regional history, and much more.

NATURAL HAZARDS

Thunderstorms occur frequently across the Mid-Atlantic Region. A basic precaution that visitors should take if they find themselves in the middle of a sudden storm, is to never stand under a tree, as they are perfect targets for lightning strikes. Also, there is danger of the tree toppling due to strong winds. Western New York State and Pennsylvania experience extreme winter conditions; the Adirondacks face severe winter storms and sub-zero temperatures, while sudden heavy snowfalls often cause chaos in New York City. Visitors should listen for weather warnings and broadcasts on the radio and TV.

GETTING AROUND

Unlike much of the US, the Mid-Atlantic is a region where you can get around without a car. Some of the most modern, and fast Amtrak train services in the US link New York and Washington, DC with Philadelphia, bringing the two cities within an hour of each other. Other lines run across Pennsylvania, up the Hudson Valley between New York City and Albany then across to Buffalo and Niagara Falls, and between Philadelphia and Atlantic City. Seat belts are required for drivers and front seat passengers in the entire Mid-Atlantic Region. Most states also require seat belts for back seat passengers, and child seats are required for all automobile occupants age four and under. Speed limits vary but are usually 70 to 75 mph (113 to 121 km/h) on Interstate Highways outside of densely populated urban areas, weather permitting. Talking on a cell phone while driving is dangerous and against the law.

EVENTS & FESTIVALS

New York City and the Mid-Atlantic states stage a diverse range of annual community, regional, and national festivals. One of the nation's most unusual annual events takes place in central Pennsylvania on February 2, when a chubby rodent named "Punxsutawney Phil" wakes up from his winter hibernation on **Groundhog Day**. "Phil" forecasts the advent of spring, which in US folklore is related to whether he can see his shadow. In March, as an expression of New York City's strong Irish heritage, the city politicians and other characters march through the city as part of a boisterous **St. Patrick's Day** celebration. Summer brings a deluge of outdoor events, and fireworks, concerts in city parks, and street festivals are the norm for community celebrations of the July 4 Independence Day holiday. County and state fairs crop up in the Mid-Atlantic countryside in July and August, as do music festivals like the **Glimmerglass Opera Festival** in Cooperstown. The Christmas shopping season kicks off with the annual extravaganza of massive inflatable figures in the **Macy's Thanksgiving Day** parade in New York City.

SPORTS

With high-quality professional teams in every major sport, the New York and Mid-Atlantic Region is a great place to watch some of the world's greatest athletes perform. The cities here host a

THE CLIMATE OF THE MID-ATLANTIC REGION

Weather across the vast Mid-Atlantic Region can be as varied as the scenery. New York's Adirondack Mountains are famed for the extremities of climate, while in Long Island and the coastal areas of New Jersey, the climate is milder. Western New York and Pennsylvania see some of the nation's heaviest snowfalls in winter. By late spring, the snows melt and the foliage returns to the gardens. Summer brings warm weather and high humidity, and thunderstorms that can put a sudden end to a pleasant day. Late summer and fall have comparatively stable weather.

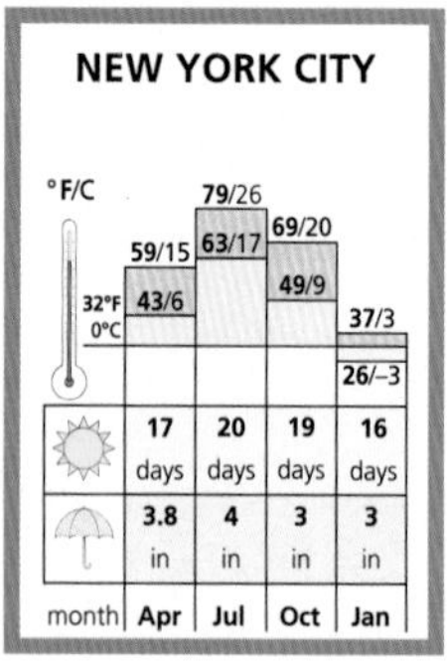

wide array of professional and amateur sports teams, with major pro baseball, football, and basketball franchises operating in New Jersey, New York City, Philadelphia, and Pittsburgh. Another extremely popular spectator sport is ice hockey.

There are also many "minor league" teams in smaller cities, and hundreds of high-quality sports teams fielded by the various public and private universities across the region.

The baseball season lasts from April to September, football from September through January, and basketball from winter through mid-Spring.

However, an extremely popular sports event is the **US Open Tennis Championships**, held annually outside New York City in August. Horseracing's **Belmont Stakes** in early June is the last leg of the "Triple Crown" championship, while throughout the months of July and August racing continues at historic Saratoga Springs. Participant sports are also prominent, with the New York Marathon in November being one of the more popular events.

OUTDOOR ACTIVITIES

New York State is also home to one of the country's prime winter sports resorts – Lake Placid in the Adirondack Mountains, where the 1932 and 1980 Winter Olympics were held. There are also ski areas in the Pocono Mountains of Pennsylvania and New Jersey, as well as Camelback Mountain and Hidden Valley in Western Pennsylvania, and Hunter Mountain and Catamount in Catskills, in New York State. For the best skiing, however, the most avid skiers head to the resorts of Vermont and New Hampshire.

ENTERTAINMENT

The world capital of the entertainment industry, New York City is a showcase for just about any form of performance. A quick read of the many local newspapers, like the *New York Times* or the *Village Voice*, and magazines such as *Time Out New York* and the *New Yorker* will point you toward hundreds of events and activities. **Lincoln Center** is home to many ballet, opera, and orchestral performances, as is legendary **Carnegie Hall**. The region's other large cities, Philadelphia, Pittsburgh, and Newark, also host numerous cultural and entertainment events. The newest venue is the **New Jersey Performing Arts Center** in Newark.

SHOPPING

New York City is without a doubt one of the world's greatest marketplaces, and it is safe to say that if you cannot buy a certain thing here, it probably does not exist at all. Everything ranging from fashionable boutiques to cut-price computers can be found in Manhattan, and some neighborhoods of New York City cater especially to the interest of shoppers and bargain hunters. Don't miss the opportunity to take a trip to at least one of the city's exceptional and world-famous department stores, such as **Bloomingdale's**, **Macy's**, or **Barney's**.

DIRECTORY

TOURIST INFORMATION

New Jersey
Tel (800) 847-4865.
www.visitnj.org

New York City
Tel (212) 484-1200.
www.nycvisit.com

New York State
Tel (518) 474-4116.
www.iloveny.com

Pennsylvania
Tel (800) 847-4872.
www.visitpa.com

FESTIVALS

Bach Festival
Bethlehem, Pennsylvania.
Tel (610) 866-4382.

Glimmerglass Opera Festival
Cooperstown, New York.
Tel (607) 547-2255.
www.glimmerglass.org

NJ Performing Arts Center
Newark, NJ.
Tel (888) 466-5722.
www.njpac.org

BASEBALL

New York Mets
Tel (718) 507-8499.
www.mets.mlb.com

New York Yankees
Tel (718) 293-4300.
www.yankees.mlb.com

Philadelphia Phillies
Tel (215) 463-1000.
www.phillies.mlb.com

BASKETBALL

New York Knicks
Tel (212) 465-6000.

Philadelphia 76ers
Tel (215) 339-7600.

FOOTBALL

Buffalo Bills
Tel (716) 649-0015.
www.buffalobills.com

New York Giants
Tel (201) 935-8222.
www.giants.com

Pittsburgh Steelers
Tel (412) 323-1200.
www.steelers.com

OTHER SPORTS

Belmont Stakes
Tel (718) 641-4700.
www.nyra.com/belmont

Skiing
www.goski.com

ENTERTAINMENT

Carnegie Hall
Tel (212) 247-7800.
www.carnegiehall.org

Lincoln Center
Tel (212) 875-5030.
www.lincolncenter.org

SHOPPING

Barney's
660 Madison Ave NYC.
Tel (212) 826-8900.

Bloomingdale's
Lexington & 59th St NYC.
Tel (212) 705-2000.

Macy's
Broadway & 34th NYC.
Tel (212) 695-4400.

Choosing a Hotel

New York City and the Mid-Atlantic region offers a wide choice of accommodation. Travelers can find budget hotels, bed-and-breakfasts, furnished apartments, and studios as well as top luxury hotels. The hotels listed here have been selected across a wide price range for their good value, excellent facilities, and location.

PRICE CATEGORIES
For a standard double room per night, including breakfast, service charges, and any additional taxes.

$ Under $150
$$ $150–$250
$$$ $250–$350
$$$$ $350–$450
$$$$$ Over $450

NEW YORK CITY

CHELSEA AND THE GARMENT DISTRICT Americana Inn $

69 W 38th St, 10018 ***Tel*** *(212) 840-6700, (888) 468-3558* ***Fax*** *(212) 840-1830* ***Rooms*** *50*

This is the place for the budget-minded traveler looking for the bare minimum essentials. Rooms have private sinks and the baths are spotless. The central location and friendly staff make a winning combination. Just be aware that the area is always busy and can get hectic and loud. **www.theamericanainn.com**

CHELSEA AND THE GARMENT DISTRICT Hotel Chelsea $$

222 W 23rd St, 10011 ***Tel*** *(212) 243-3700* ***Fax*** *(212) 675-5531* ***Rooms*** *400*

Music history was made when punk legend Sid Vicious killed girlfriend Nancy Spungen here. Since then, famous personalities such as Sandra Bernhardt and Ethan Hawke have stayed here. Some claim the large rooms and privacy are the draw, while others enjoy the bohemian, if somewhat dusty, furnishings. **www.hotelchelsea.com**

CHELSEA AND THE GARMENT DISTRICT Radisson/Martinique on Broadway $$$$

49 W 32nd St, 10001 ***Tel*** *(212) 736-3800* ***Fax*** *(212) 277-2702* ***Rooms*** *532*

The landmark French-Renaissance building houses this outpost of the reliable Radisson chain. Past the ornate lobby, the rooms have been restored to an elegant finish. Affordable Asian dining lines the blocks around the hotel, which is literally steps away from some of the best tourist sites on the island. **www.radisson.com**

EAST VILLAGE Union Square Inn $

209 E 14th St, 10003 ***Tel*** *(212) 614-0500* ***Fax*** *(212) 614-0512* ***Rooms*** *40*

All the standard comforts come at reasonable prices here. Rooms have no views and are nothing to write home about, but the beds are comfortable and bathrooms clean. European breakfast is on offer at the in-house café, which keeps limited hours. Union Square nearby is great for peoplewatching and shopping. **www.unionsquareinn.com**

EAST VILLAGE The Bowery Hotel $$$$

335 Bowery, 10003 ***Tel*** *(212) 505-9100* ***Rooms*** *135*

From the same duo who developed the Maritime in Chelsea comes this luxury lodging. An opulent 17-story hotel, it features lobby fireplaces and wood-paneled elevators, floor-to-ceiling windows in every room, and seven rooms with private terraces, hot tubs, and outdoor showers. The bar attracts a VIP scene. **www.theboweryhotel.com**

GRAMERCY AND THE FLATIRON DISTRICT Hotel 17 $

225 E 17th St, 10003 ***Tel*** *(212) 475-2845* ***Fax*** *(212) 677-8178* ***Rooms*** *120*

Young travelers love the location of this very basic budget option. Rooms are tiny with not much flair and some share baths. Woody Allen popularized this hotel in *Manhattan Murder Mystery* and supposedly Madonna stayed here as a young singer. Some cheap eats are nearby, as is good mainstream shopping. **www.hotel17ny.com**

GRAMERCY AND THE FLATIRON DISTRICT Gershwin Hotel $$

7 E 27th St, 10016 ***Tel*** *(212) 545-8000* ***Fax*** *(212) 684-5546* ***Rooms*** *150*

An original Andy Warhol *Campbell's Soup Can* in the lobby sets the tone of this pop art-inspired hotel. More art can be found on every floor. Rooms are bright and stylishly decorated. A tourist bargain as it's just steps to the Empire State Building. Many reasonable restaurants nearby. **www.gershwinhotel.com**

GRAMERCY AND THE FLATIRON DISTRICT Hotel Giraffe $$$$

365 Park Ave S, 10016 ***Tel*** *(212) 685-7700, (877) 296-0009* ***Fax*** *(212) 685-7771* ***Rooms*** *73*

Perhaps the Flatiron District's finest full-service luxury hotel, the rooms are decorated with custom furnishings invoking the Moderne style. Suites have French doors opening onto a Juliet-style balcony. The restaurant downstairs offers superb cuisine and potent cocktails with a lounge scene. **www.hotelgiraffe.com**

GREENWICH VILLAGE Washington Square Hotel $$

103 Waverly Pl, 10011 ***Tel*** *(212) 777-9515, (800) 222-0418* ***Fax*** *(212) 979-8373* ***Rooms*** *170*

Just steps away from NYU, this hotel faces Washington Square Park. The marble lobby leads to fresh, boutique-like rooms. The central location means higher than average rates, but great bars and restaurants are just around the corner. The on-site restaurant delivers good meals. **www.wshotel.com**

Key to Symbols *see back cover flap*

GREENWICH VILLAGE Abingdon Guest House $$$

21 Eighth Ave, 10014 ***Tel*** *(212) 243-5384* ***Fax*** *(212) 807-7473* ***Rooms*** *9*

This lovely guesthouse is located on one of the West Village's most beautiful brownstone- and boutique-lined streets. Each room has unique decor and is fitted with classic comforts. No on-site full-time staff means this gem is best suited to independent travelers. No breakfast, but there are coffee facilities. **www.abingdonguesthouse.com**

LOWER EAST SIDE Off SoHo Suites Hotel $$

11 Rivington St, 10002 ***Tel*** *(212) 979-9808, (800) 633-7646* ***Fax*** *(212) 979-9801* ***Rooms*** *38*

Trendy downtown neighborhoods have enveloped this budget spot making it a good choice for those wanting to be near SoHo or the Lower East Side. Small suites share facilities, while the larger ones come with private bathrooms and full kitchens, making it a good choice for bigger groups or families. **www.offsoho.com**

LOWER EAST SIDE Howard Johnson Express Inn $$$

135 E Houston St, 10002 ***Tel*** *(212) 358-8844* ***Fax*** *(212) 473-3500* ***Rooms*** *46*

This hotel offers small yet clean budget rooms, handy for checking out the trendy cafés and boutiques just outside. Steps away from the subway line and cheap eats, this location for young hipsters is hard to beat. Some rooms have microwaves and small fridges. The famous Katz's Deli is just a block away. **www.hojo.com**

LOWER MANHATTAN Best Western Seaport Inn Downtown $$

33 Peck Slip, 10038 ***Tel*** *(212) 766-6600* ***Fax*** *(212) 766-6615* ***Rooms*** *72*

You'll feel like you're stepping into a 19th-century sailor's haunt at this property with views of Brooklyn Bridge. Families enjoy the deluxe breakfast, afternoon cookies, and lounge with coffee and tea. The 24-hour fitness center is large. Upgrade to a room with a terrace if you can. **www.seaportinn.com**

LOWER MANHATTAN Gild Hall $$$

15 Gold St, 10038 ***Tel*** *(212) 232-7700* ***Fax*** *(212) 425-0330* ***Rooms*** *126*

This luxury hotel has been refurbished and boasts, among other features, a private library bar, an elegant Champagne bar, a modern English tavern run by famed chef Todd English, and uber-sleek rooms. The mini bars are stocked by gourmet food store Dean & DeLuca, and the king suites have chandeliers. **www.thompsonhotels.com**

LOWER MANHATTAN Ritz Carlton Battery Park $$$$

2 West St, 10004 ***Tel*** *(212) 344-0800* ***Fax*** *(212) 344-3801* ***Rooms*** *298*

Telescopes in the elegantly modern rooms offer spectacular close-up views of the Statue of Liberty and New York Harbor. Bathrooms are large and sleek, while business travelers are well catered for with numerous programs and amenities. Afternoon tea is served in the bar. **www.ritzcarlton.com**

LOWER MIDTOWN Courtyard New York $$

3 E 40th St, 10016 ***Tel*** *(212) 447-1500* ***Fax*** *(212) 683-7839* ***Rooms*** *185*

This neighborhood location can be pricey, but this hotel offers good value for its price range. It is now part of the Marriott chain. Families appreciate the location since it is close to the New York Public Library and the Theater District but without the noise. **www.courtyard.com**

LOWER MIDTOWN Courtyard by Marriott Midtown East $$$

866 Third Ave, 10022 ***Tel*** *(212) 644-1300* ***Fax*** *(212) 317-7940* ***Rooms*** *308*

The spacious rooms make this a good choice for families who want to be in this neighborhood. Rooms are modern and have in-room coffee makers and free high-speed Internet access. Free Wi-Fi is available in a special lounge. The neighborhood can be much quieter at night. **www.marriott.com**

LOWER MIDTOWN Kitano $$$$$

66 Park Ave, 10016 ***Tel*** *(212) 885-7000, (800) 548-2666* ***Fax*** *(212) 885-7100* ***Rooms*** *149*

Buttoned-up Japanese-style service is the name of the game at this elegant midtown hotel, which caters primarily to a business crowd. Hotel rooms are havens of serenity with complimentary Japanese green tea. The restaurant also draws a crowd. This part of Park Avenue can seem amazingly serene. **www.kitano.com**

MORNINGSIDE HEIGHTS AND HARLEM Morningside Inn Hotel $

235 W 107th St, 10025 ***Tel*** *(212) 316-0055* ***Fax*** *(212) 864-9155* ***Rooms*** *96*

Sister property to the Riverside Inn, this hotel is newer and fresher, although it still retains an air of dormitory. Best for students or single travelers. Try and score a double deluxe, which will assure you a private bath and air conditioning. All rooms are clean and well cared for. **www.morningsideinn-ny.com**

MORNINGSIDE HEIGHTS AND HARLEM Astor on the Park $$

465 Central Park W, 10025 ***Tel*** *(212) 866-1880, (800) 804-6835* ***Fax*** *(212) 316-9555* ***Rooms*** *112*

On Central Park West at 106th street, the convenient location of this hotel more than makes up for the small, basic rooms. It is an ideal choice for visitors on a budget who plan to be out for most of the day (and night!). The bathrooms are clean and the staff friendly. **www.hotels.com**

SOHO AND TRIBECA Cosmopolitan Hotel $$

95 W Broadway, 10007 ***Tel*** *(212) 566-1900, (888) 895-9400* ***Fax*** *(212) 566-6909* ***Rooms*** *125*

This budget gem is located in the heart of trendy TriBeCa. While rooms are small, they are well maintained with equally tiny but clean bathrooms. The many top restaurants nearby and easy access to public transport make this a top budget recommendation. Also great for shopping. **www.cosmohotel.com**

SOHO AND TRIBECA Tribeca Grand Hotel $$$

2 Ave of the Americas, 10013 ***Tel*** *(212) 519-6600* ***Fax*** *(212) 519-6700* ***Rooms*** *203*

The atrium lobby gives this hotel a grand look, and the private screening room downstairs has long made this a favorite of celebrities. Rooms are sleekly designed and the bathroom amenities first-rate. Score a corner room or studio suite for the most space, and make sure to sip a drink in the lounge to maximize star sightings. **www.tribecagrand.com**

SOHO AND TRIBECA 60 Thompson $$$$

60 Thompson St, 10012 ***Tel*** *(212) 431-0400* ***Fax*** *(212) 431-0200* ***Rooms*** *100*

This chic boutique hotel has an excellent restaurant and a rooftop lounge/deck available only to guests and certain trendsetters. Rooms are minimalist yet comfortable with a pleasing palette tone, and have all the latest high-tech gadgets. Location is the star here. **www.60thompson.com**

THEATER DISTRICT Big Apple Hostel $

119 W 45th St, 10036 ***Tel*** *(212) 302-2603* ***Fax*** *(212) 302-2605* ***Rooms*** *39*

For prime location and clean accommodations, this hostel is perfect for young travelers. While most beds are dormitory style, a few private rooms with queen-size beds are available. Full kitchen facilities and the backyard garden provide a respite from the harried streets of Manhattan. Book well in advance. **www.bigapplehostel.com**

THEATER DISTRICT Algonquin $$$

59 W 44th St, 10036 ***Tel*** *(212) 840-6800* ***Fax*** *(212) 944-1419* ***Rooms*** *174*

The home of Dorothy Parker's literary "Round Table" of the 1920s still draws literati to its doors. The comfortable rooms are small so, if possible, splurge on a literary-themed suite. The well-preserved mahogany-paneled lobby provides access to the legendary Oak Room cabaret. **www.algonquinhotel.com**

THEATER DISTRICT Ritz-Carlton, New York, Central Park $$$$$

50 Central Park S, 10019 ***Tel*** *(212) 308-9100* ***Fax*** *(212) 207-8831* ***Rooms*** *260*

Fans rave that this is the best hotel for service in the entire Ritz-Carlton chain. Traditional in style, the large rooms are extremely comfortable and filled with the latest technology. The full-service spa and location across from Central Park make it a true winner. **www.ritzcarlton.com**

UPPER EAST SIDE Franklin $$$

164 E 87th St, 10128 ***Tel*** *(212) 369-1000, (800) 607-4009* ***Fax*** *(212) 369-8000* ***Rooms*** *48*

Rooms may be tiny at this modern hotel, but they are well appointed with romantic canopied beds, flatscreen TVs, complimentary Wi-Fi, and the like. The limited space makes it the choice for short-term travelers or light packers. Continental breakfast included. Check for seasonal rates. **www.franklinhotel.com**

UPPER EAST SIDE Surrey Hotel $$$$

20 E 76th St, 10021 ***Tel*** *(212) 288-3700* ***Fax*** *(212) 628-1549* ***Rooms*** *130*

This all-suite hotel is a lovely choice for those willing to spend extra on dramatically more space. Each suite has a fully-equipped kitchen, but the reason to stay here is the in-suite dining from the famous Café Boulud downstairs. Cheaper diners and pizzerias are all around the area. **www.affinia.com**

UPPER EAST SIDE Carlyle $$$$$

35 E 76th St, 10021 ***Tel*** *(212) 744-1600, (888) 767-3966* ***Fax*** *(212) 717-4682* ***Rooms*** *180*

You'll feel like a true Upper Eastsider in a room at this legendary hotel with its world-class dining and entertainment. The elegant rooms and phenomenal service have drawn heads of state and movie stars alike. Afternoon tea attracts the who's who of New York socialites. **www.thecarlyle.com**

UPPER MIDTOWN Hotel 57 $

130 E 57th St, 10022 ***Tel*** *(212) 753-8841, (866) 273-2869* ***Fax*** *(212) 869-9605* ***Rooms*** *220*

The hotel lives up to the label "cheap chic," effortlessly combining high design with low prices. While the rooms can be narrow and small and often share baths in the hallway, it's hard to beat the price with such a great midtown location, close to all major shopping. Great views from the 17th-floor bar. **www.hotel57.com**

UPPER MIDTOWN Kimberly Hotel $$$

145 E 50th St, 10022 ***Tel*** *(212) 702-1600* ***Fax*** *(212) 486-6915* ***Rooms*** *185*

For large space and great value, this low-profile establishment is perhaps the best choice. The one- and two-bedroom suites feel like apartments with full-size kitchens and well-appointed furniture. The location is wonderful for a little peace and quiet, yet close to good shopping. **www.kimberlyhotel.com**

UPPER MIDTOWN Waldorf Astoria / Waldorf Towers $$$$

301 Park Ave, 10022 ***Tel*** *(212) 355-3000, (800) 925-3673* ***Fax*** *(212) 872-7272* ***Rooms*** *1242*

This New York legend is still kicking, despite complaints about indifferent service. Rates can be reasonable because the hotel is enormous, but it does have a historical feel about it. Rooms are large. If you score a room in the exclusive Towers, expect 24-hour butler service. **www.waldorfastoria.com**

UPPER WEST SIDE Jazz on the Park $

36 W 106th St, 10025 ***Tel*** *(212) 932-1600* ***Fax*** *(212) 932-1700* ***Rooms*** *220*

This arty hostel is extremely popular and brings a downtown feel to the sometimes staid Upper West Side. Don't miss the coffeehouse with live music that can be a little rowdy. Dorm rooms are very basic and so are the bathrooms. Very international crowd. The area keeps getting better and better. **www.jazzhostels.com**

Key to Price Guide *see p112* **Key to Symbols** *see back cover flap*

UPPER WEST SIDE Hotel Beacon $$

2130 Broadway, 10023 ***Tel*** *(212) 787-1100* ***Fax*** *(212) 724-0839* ***Rooms*** *236*

Families enjoy the extra-large rooms and laundry facilities on offer at this great-value hotel. The rooms are not the best in town, but they have kitchenettes and some can accommodate four people. Larger groups should ask about the two-bedroom/two-bath suites. **www.beaconhotel.com**

UPPER WEST SIDE Trump International Hotel & Tower $$$$$

1 Central Park W, 10023 ***Tel*** *(212) 299-1000, (800) 448-7867* ***Fax*** *(212) 299-1150* ***Rooms*** *167*

This modern luxury hotel tower prides itself on its exclusivity, discretion, and style. Rooms are decorated in soothing tones and offer the latest technology. The unobstructed views of Central Park are the real draw, as is the Jean George restaurant downstairs. **www.trumpintl.com**

NEW YORK STATE

ALBANY Crowne Plaza $

State and Lodge Sts, 12207 ***Tel*** *(518) 462-6611, (800) 227-6963* ***Fax*** *(518) 462-2901* ***Rooms*** *384*

Crowne Plaza is a 15-story hotel centrally located near the Pepsi Arena, the Capitol Building, and the Empire State Plaza. The hotel has two restaurants and two bars as well as a health club complete with indoor pool. Airport transportation is available. **www.cpalbany.com**

BINGHAMTON The Grand Royale Clarion Collection Hotel $

80 State St, 13901 ***Tel*** *(607) 722-0000, (888) 242-0323* ***Fax*** *(607) 722-7912* ***Rooms*** *61*

Stay in Binghamton's historic former city hall (1897). The Grand Royale Clarion Collection Hotel provides guests with free use of the fitness facilities at the YMCA, just one block away. Located in downtown Binghamton, entertainment, shopping, and dining are close by. Complimentary full breakfast. Pets accepted. **www.grandroyalehotel.com**

BUFFALO Adam's Mark $$

120 Church St, 14202 ***Tel*** *(716) 845-5100, (800) 444-2326* ***Fax*** *(716) 845-5377* ***Rooms*** *486*

Adam's Mark welcomes travelers with a 486-room, 9-story comfortably modern establishment. The hotel offers its guests an indoor pool and fitness center. There is also a business center complete with Wi-Fi. A bar and restaurants are also provided. **www.adamsmark.com**

COOPERSTOWN Otesaga Hotel $$$$$

60 Lake St, 13326 ***Tel*** *(607) 547-9931, (800) 348-6222* ***Fax*** *(607) 547-9675* ***Rooms*** *136*

One of the finest hotels in Cooperstown, Otesaga Hotel has been restored to the historic decor of the 1900s. The perfect place to stay while visiting the National Baseball Hall of Fame & Museum, facilities include a full-service gym and 18 holes of golf. The hotel is closed in winter. **www.otesaga.com**

EAST HAMPTON The Hedges Inn $$$$

74 James Lane, 11937 ***Tel*** *(631) 324-7101* ***Fax*** *(631) 324-7118* ***Rooms*** *12*

Less than a mile from Main Beach and East Hampton Village sits The Hedges Inn. Each of the comfortable rooms comes with a private bath. After enjoying the day, visitors can view the beautiful sunset from the relaxing front porch and dream of the delicious breakfast buffet awaiting them in the morning. **www.thehedgesinn.com**

EAST HAMPTON Maidstone Arms $$$$$

207 Main St, 11937 ***Tel*** *(631) 324-5006* ***Fax*** *(631) 324-5037* ***Rooms*** *19*

Built in the 1750s to be used as the Osborne family's private residence, Maidstone Arms opened its doors to guests in the 1870s and visitors can now enjoy the excitement of the Hamptons year-round. A complimentary full breakfast is included. **www.maidstonearms.com**

LAKE GEORGE VILLAGE The Georgian $$

384 Canada St, 12845 ***Tel*** *(518) 668-5401, (800) 525-3426* ***Rooms*** *164*

Though the rooms at The Georgian hotel beckon with comfort, it is the relaxing beach that is the real draw. The hotel also offers guests a restaurant, outdoor pool, and two bars. Airport transportation is available. **www.georgianresort.com**

LAKE PLACID Adirondack Inn by the Lake $$

2625 Main St, 12946 ***Tel*** *(518) 523-2424, (800) 556-2424* ***Fax*** *(518) 523-2425* ***Rooms*** *49*

The Adirondack Inn by the Lake is so named because it is located in Lake Placid. Opposite the Olympic Arena and Convention Hall, this inn has something for the whole family. Although there is a children's activity center, a fitness room for adults, and a whirlpool, the beach is the main attraction. **www.adirondack-inn.com**

NIAGARA FALLS Comfort Inn The Pointe $$

1 Prospect Pointe, 14303 ***Tel*** *(716) 284-6835* ***Fax*** *(716) 284-5177* ***Rooms*** *120*

This Comfort Inn is located near America's most spectacular natural wonder. Stay in this historic inn and be just 1,200 feet (366m) from Niagara Falls. Listen to the rushing water just outside your room. Complimentary continental breakfast. **www.comfortinn.com**

NIAGARA FALLS The Red Coach Inn $$

2 Buffalo Ave, 14303 ***Tel*** *(716) 282-1459, (866) 719-2070* ***Fax*** *(716) 282-2650* ***Rooms*** *19*

Just 1,500 feet from the overwhelming natural beauty of the Niagara Falls, the Red Coach Inn has been in operation since 1923. Built in the English Tudor style, this inn supplies guests with spectacular views, antique furniture, and a welcome with champagne, cheese, and fruit. **www.redcoach.com**

POUGHKEEPSIE Inn at the Falls $$

50 Red Oaks Mill Rd, 12603 ***Tel*** *(845) 462-5770, (800) 344-1466* ***Fax*** *(845) 462-5943* ***Rooms*** *36*

The Inn at the Falls is a romantically charming place to stay. The decor in each of the 36 rooms is inspired by different periods and styles, with furnishings to match. Complimentary continental breakfast is also provided. **www.innatthefalls.com**

ROCHESTER Strathallan Hotel $$

550 East Ave, 14607 ***Tel*** *(585) 461-5010, (800) 678-7284* ***Fax*** *(585) 461-3387* ***Rooms*** *156*

This 156-suite hotel welcomes guests into a charming European-style decor. The Strathallan Hotel is perfect for families and business people alike. A country-club style restaurant is provided for guests who would prefer to remain in rather than enjoy any of the numerous nearby attractions. Airport transportation is available. **www.strathallan.com**

SCOTIA Glen Sanders Mansion Inn $$

1 Glen Ave, 12302 ***Tel*** *(518) 374-7262* ***Fax*** *(518) 374-7391* ***Rooms*** *22*

The clientele varies at the Glen Sanders Mansion Inn, nestled along the Mohawk River. Built in 1995 to compliment the restaurant that is housed in the original residence, the inn is a mix of 20th-century comforts and historic ambience. Complimentary continental breakfast. **www.glensandersmansion.com**

SKANEATELES Hobbit Hollow Farm $$

3061 W Lake Rd, 13152 ***Tel*** *(315) 685-2791, (800) 743-7663* ***Fax*** *(315) 685-3426* ***Rooms*** *5*

Located in the Finger Lakes area, Hobbit Hollow Farm is nestled within over 300 acres of lush fields overlooking Skaneateles Lake. This welcoming country bed and breakfast has five rooms furnished with antiques and a private bath. Take a tour of the different wineries in the area. Children under 18 not permitted. **www.hobbithollow.com**

SOUTHAMPTON The Village Latch Inn $$$$

101 Hill St, 13152 ***Tel*** *(631) 283-2160, (800) 545-2824* ***Fax*** *(631) 283-3236* ***Rooms*** *67*

Sophisticated, elegant, and romantic, The Village Latch Inn is the place to stay when in Southampton. The inn, part of a five-acre estate, is within walking distance of "everything". Previous guests at this celebrity hideaway include former Vice President Al Gore and the actor Michael J. Fox. **www.villagelatch.com**

NEW JERSEY

ATLANTIC CITY Bally's Atlantic City $$

Boardwalk & Park Pl, 08401 ***Tel*** *(609) 340-2000* ***Fax*** *(609) 340-4713* ***Rooms*** *1246*

One of the few remnants of historic Atlantic City, the 1860s Dennis Hotel has been restored as part of this mega-resort complex, which also includes a modern 45-story tower. Fans of the board game Monopoly will know that the hotel stands on the city's most valuable corner. The hotel's casino features a Wild West theme. **www.ballys.com**

ATLANTIC CITY Holiday Inn Boardwalk $$

Chelsea Ave & Boardwalk, 08401 ***Tel*** *(609) 348-2200* ***Fax*** *(609) 348-0168* ***Rooms*** *220*

This modern chain hotel sits along the popular Boardwalk overlooking the beach, amidst casino properties, shopping destinations, and cosmopolitan restaurants. Each room comes with free wireless high-speed Internet access. **www.atlanticcity.holiday-inn.com**

CAPE MAY Chalfonte Hotel $

301 Howard St, 08204 ***Tel*** *(609) 884-8409, (888) 411-1998* ***Fax*** *(609) 884-4588* ***Rooms*** *70*

This whitewashed Victorian-era hotel was built in 1874 and offers old-fashioned charm, with rocking chairs on the wrap-around front porch. Chalfonte has always been unconventional – rooms have no televisions or phones, and the hotel is just two blocks from the beach. **www.chalfonte.com**

CAPE MAY Queen Victoria Bed and Breakfast $$

102 Ocean St, 08204 ***Tel*** *(609) 884-8702* ***Rooms*** *32*

Built in the 1870s and fully restored, this mansard-roofed Victorian inn is located in the heart of Cape May, just a block from the beach, antiques shops, gourmet dining, and historic tours. Bicycles to tour the area are available for free, and the hotel provides a complimentary European breakfast buffet. **www.queenvictoria.com**

CHERRY HILL Clarion Hotel & Conference Center $

1450 Rt 70 E and I-295, 08034 ***Tel*** *(856) 428-2300* ***Fax*** *(856) 354-7662* ***Rooms*** *204*

Across the Delaware River, this hotel and conference center is ideal for both the business and leisure traveler. An in-house café serves breakfast, entrées, and pastries, and a neighborhood-like pub and restaurant is situated next door. The hotel is a short drive from the Camden Waterfront and central Philadelphia. **www.clarionofcherryhill.com**

Key to Price Guide *see p112* **Key to Symbols** *see back cover flap*

PENNSYLVANIA

BIRD-IN-HAND Bird-In-Hand Village Inn and Suites $$

2695 Old Philadelphia Pike, 17505 ***Tel*** *(717) 768-1535, (800) 665-8780* ***Fax*** *(717) 768-1117* ***Rooms*** *24*

This 1734 inn is responsible for the unique naming of this small town. Four well-preserved historic buildings house rooms and suites. The complimentary continental breakfast includes local freshly-baked treats. Guests can take a two-hour complimentary bus tour of the area. **www.bird-in-hand.com/villageinn**

GETTYSBURG The Herr Tavern and Publick House $$

900 Chambersburg Rd, 17325 ***Tel*** *(717) 334-4332, (800) 362-9849* ***Fax*** *(717) 334-3332* ***Rooms*** *16*

Built in 1815, The Herr Tavern and Publick House once served as a confederate hospital. This historic house welcomes travelers with 16 different rooms. Along with a complimentary continental breakfast, the Herr Tavern also provides a restaurant and bar. Children over 12 years of age only. **www.herrtavern.com**

HERSHEY The Hotel Hershey $$$$

100 Hotel Rd, 17033 ***Tel*** *(717) 533-2171, (800) 437-7439* ***Fax*** *(717) 535-8887* ***Rooms*** *234*

Chocolate founder Milton Hershey built this delicious retreat located on 300 acres with reflecting pools, fountains, and formal gardens. The hotel's signature touch is to leave a chocolate kiss on your pillow. Indulge in a creamy dreamy chocolate bath at the Spa. Recreational facilities include golf, basketball, volleyball, and tennis. **www.hersheyPA.com**

LITITZ General Sutter Inn $

14 E Main St, 17543 ***Tel*** *(717) 626-2115* ***Fax*** *(717) 626-0992* ***Rooms*** *95*

The General Sutter Inn is one of the oldest in Pennsylvania, dating back to 1764. Spacious rooms and suites are decorated with antiques in Victorian style. It is home to two fine restaurants and a lively bar, and has a delightful courtyard that is used for outdoor dining and cocktails. **www.generalsutterinn.com**

PHILADELPHIA Chestnut Hill Hotel $

8229 Germantown Ave, 19118 ***Tel*** *(215) 242-5905, (800) 628-9744* ***Fax*** *(215) 242-8778* ***Rooms*** *36*

Built in 1891, this historic hotel is situated along the cobblestones of Germantown Avenue. Although furnished with 18th-century decor, it offers all modern amenities. Within walking distance of Fairmount Park's Wissahickon Gorge and a short drive from historic Germantown. **www.chestnuthillhotel.com**

PHILADELPHIA Renaissance Hotel Philadelphia Airport $$

500 Stevens Dr, 19113 ***Tel*** *(610) 521-5900* ***Fax*** *(610) 521-4362* ***Rooms*** *349*

This four-diamond, modern, and upscale chain hotel is on I-95, close to the airport. It is tastefully decorated with the Renaissance's signature European flair. There is an expansive lobby atrium and the rooms have high-speed internet access. It is in a convenient location for a quick drive into the city on the interstate. **www.renaissancehotels.com**

PITTSBURGH Hilton Pittsburgh $

600 Commonwealth Pl, 15222 ***Tel*** *(412) 391-4600* ***Fax*** *(412) 594-5161* ***Rooms*** *713*

With breathtaking views of Three Rivers, the Hilton Pittsburgh is the place to stay in downtown Pittsburgh. One of the city's largest and well-known hotels, the Hilton offers excellent service and comfortable surroundings. A business center is provided for the working guests. Pets are allowed; a fee will be assessed. **www.hilton.com**

PITTSBURGH Inn on Negley $$

703 Negley Ave, 15232 ***Tel*** *(414) 661-0631* ***Fax*** *(412) 661-7525* ***Rooms*** *8*

A great getaway place, The Inn on Negley was once a private residence, now renovated and restored back to its former Victorian elegance. With 8 different suites, guests can choose from rooms with canopy beds and floor-to-ceiling bay windows, or fireplaces and Jacuzzi-jetted bathtubs. The first floor is handicap accessible. **www.innonnegley.com**

PITTSBURGH The Priory $$

614 Pressley St, 15212 ***Tel*** *(412) 231-3338, (866) 337-7679* ***Fax*** *(412) 231-4838* ***Rooms*** *25*

The Priory, considered one of the city's most charming places to stay, used to be a haven for Benedictine monks in the late-19th century. This European-style bed and breakfast provides guests with plush rooms and complimentary wine in the pretty courtyard. Complimentary continental breakfast. **www.thepriory.com**

READING Best Western Dutch Colony Inn & Suites $

4635 Perkiomen Ave, 19606 ***Tel*** *(610) 779-2345, (800) 828-2830* ***Fax*** *(610) 779-8348* ***Rooms*** *62*

Beautifully landscaped grounds invite travelers to Dutch Colony Inn & Suites. Just minutes from downtown Reading, the inn is centrally located near outlet stores, the Maple Grove Raceway, and Hershey Park. The world-famous Antique Airplane restaurant resides here, serving up enticing food and great service. **www.bestwestern.com**

STRASBURG Strasburg Village Inn $

1 W Main St, 17579 ***Tel*** *(717) 687-0900* ***Fax*** *(717) 687-3650* ***Rooms*** *10*

Dating back to the late 1780s, this historic inn is situated on one corner of Strasburg's central square. Ten rooms in "Williamsburg" style are warmly furnished in Victorian decor with canopy beds and antiques. The inn sits next door to the old-style Strasburg Creamery, an ice cream and sandwich shop. **www.strasburg.com**

Choosing a Restaurant

A varied dining experience is offered across much of the Mid-Atlantic Region. New York City, especially, has more than 25,000 restaurants catering to every taste, and fashionable places change often while some favorites remain popular. The restaurants listed here have been chosen for their good value and exceptional food.

PRICE CATEGORIES
For a three-course meal for one, including a glass of house wine (where served), and all other unavoidable charges such as sales tax.
$ Under $25
$$ $25–$40
$$$ $40–$60
$$$$ $60–$80
$$$$$ Over $80

NEW YORK CITY

EAST VILLAGE Great Jones Café $$

54 Great Jones St, 10012 ***Tel*** *(212) 674-9304*

Get your fix of New Orleans cooking in this inexpensive, family-friendly, jukebox-equipped hole-in-the-wall. Staples include fried shrimp po-boys, andouille sausages, and jambalaya. The walls are lined with an array of hot sauces from all over the world, so feel free to dab on your entrées. Definitely down it all with a beer.

GRAMERCY AND THE FLATIRON DISTRICT Chat 'n' Chew $$

10 E 16th St, 10003 ***Tel*** *(212) 243-1616*

Kitschy comfort food destination in the Union Square area that fills the spot and is gentle on the wallet. Staples include mac 'n' cheese, a year-round Thanksgiving roast-turkey dinner, and mama's meatloaf. Don't forget the mashed potatoes, and a changing selection of cakes and pies for dessert. Good brunch spot.

GRAMERCY AND THE FLATIRON DISTRICT Union Square Café $$$$

21 E 16th St, 10003 ***Tel*** *(212) 243-4020*

Among the most popular of New York City restaurants, this Danny Meyer flagship serves modern American cuisine in comfortable surroundings, drawing ingredients from the greenmarket in Union Square, although the prices are anything but market level. Courteous service.

GREENWICH VILLAGE Pearl Oyster Bar $$

18 Cornelia St, 10014 ***Tel*** *(212) 691-8211*

Very succesful raw bar in the Village with top-of-the-line fresh ingredients and bold flavors. The lobster roll is a smash hit as are the Prince Edward Island mussels. Unlike other places that use quality ingredients, service is amicable too, but be prepared for long lines at rush hours.

GREENWICH VILLAGE Babbo $$$$

110 Waverly Pl, 10011 ***Tel*** *(212) 777-0303*

Chef Mario Batali's flagship restaurant is housed in this beautiful Village duplex – paradise for high-quality pasta and offal lovers alike. Hard to get reservations and service could see some improvement given the prices. A winning wine list and trendy crowd add the magic touch to a great dining experience.

LOWER EAST SIDE Grand Sichuan $

125 Canal St at Bowery, 10002 ***Tel*** *(212) 625-9212*

A never-ending menu with all kinds of Sichuan, Hunang, and "Chinese-food American style," as well as all types of hot (including spicy) and cold noodles and fried rice. It also offers a wide variety of vegetarian dishes. Sketchy service and limited decor may be the reason for the quite affordable prices.

LOWER EAST SIDE Il Palazzo $$

151 Mulberry St, 10013 ***Tel*** *(212) 343-7000*

This is among Little Italy's few good Italian restaurants, especially when it comes to service. A new glassed-in garden has boosted its charm. Homemade pastas and risotti are always a good and inexpensive choice – try the simple but well-done homemade spaghetti a la chitarra. Standard homemade desserts include cannoli and tiramisu.

LOWER MANHATTAN Battery Gardens $$$

17 State St, Battery Park, 10004 ***Tel*** *(212) 809-5508*

It is worth a trip to the tip of Manhattan for the fantastic vistas of the harbor and the Statue of Liberty from this haven on Battery Park. The American-Continental menu is standard, but the view is the lure here. On a balmy day when you can sit on the terrace, there is no place like it.

LOWER MANHATTAN Fraunces Tavern $$$

54 Pearl St, corner of Broad St, 10004 ***Tel*** *(212) 968-1776*

This historic tavern has been in operation since 1762 and was where George Washington bid a fond farewell to his officers on the eve of his retirement in 1783. Classic American steak and fish dishes are on offer, along with wholesome pot roasts and soups. In winter warm up in the snug lounge.

Key to Symbols *see back cover flap*

LOWER MIDTOWN Grand Central Oyster Bar $$$

Grand Central, Lower Level, 42nd St, 10017 ***Tel*** *(212) 490-6650*

Cavernous space inside Grand Central Station where you'll be transported to the past. The very fresh seafood in simple preparations is not too pricey, and the menu features a long list of over a dozen kinds of oysters. The setting and decor is casual, so leave the fur coats at home and bring your appetite. Waiter service included.

LOWER MIDTOWN Pampano $$$$$

209 E 49th St, 10017 ***Tel*** *(212) 751-4545*

A lovely, modern Mexican restaurant from Chef Richard Sandoval and opera legend co-owner Placido Domingo. Inventive and fresh creations in a chic dining room will make you want to sing an aria or two. Don't miss the smoked swordfish appetizer or the halibut Pampano. A beautiful terrace is also available.

MORNINGSIDE HEIGHTS AND HARLEM Sylvia's $$

328 Lenox Ave, 10027 ***Tel*** *(212) 996-0660*

A New York tradition since 1962, serving good old soul food in a kitschy dining room with occasional live music. Its success brings along plenty of tourists and locals alike to enjoy the inexpensive menu of staples such as fried chicken, collard greens, and black-eyed peas. Extremely busy on Sundays after church.

SOHO AND TRIBECA Lombardi's $$

32 Spring St, 10012 ***Tel*** *(212) 941-7994*

Among the top pizzerias of the city, the brick-oven baked pies come thin, charred, and oozing a delectable mozzarella. The offerings are limited, stick with pizza and don't expect dessert. A very welcome expansion now allows you and your friends to share the joy faster.

SOHO AND TRIBECA Kittichai $$$$

60 Thompson St, 10012 ***Tel*** *(212) 219-2000*

A high-end Thai restaurant in a beautifully designed space within the 60 Thompson hotel. A definite place to be seen. The menu offers an expensive selection of dishes including "Thai tapas", curries, and seafood options such as monkfish with ginger.

THEATER DISTRICT Virgil's Real Barbecue $$

152 W 44th St, 10036 ***Tel*** *(212) 921-9494*

Hopping BBQ joint in the heart of Times Square with an always bustling clientele and fast service. Ideal for pre-theater dining, provided that the heavy meal doesn't make you sleepy. Staples include over 10 different meat platters from around America, and tasty sidedishes such as biscuits, collard greens, grits, and mac 'n' cheese.

THEATER DISTRICT Le Bernardin $$$$$

155 W 51st St, 10019 ***Tel*** *(212) 554-1515*

A dream-come-true for seafood- and fish-lovers. This superb and elegant longstanding restaurant offers an outstanding dining experience with French haute cuisine from chef Eric Ripert. Service is flawless including the sommelier advice. It's the place to propose.

UPPER EAST SIDE Shanghai Pavilion $$

1378 Third Ave, 10021 ***Tel*** *(212) 585-3388*

Newcomer offering Shanghai cuisine, as authentic as you can get outside of Chinatown. The menu has plenty of options at reasonable prices, making it good value in this neighborhood. The service is friendly. Great dim sums, noodle dishes, and specialties such as velvet sea bass and lobster tropicana.

UPPER EAST SIDE Daniel $$$$$

60 East 65th St, 10021 ***Tel*** *(212) 288-0033*

Chef Daniel Boulud's flagship restaurant features a Venetian Renaissance-inspired dining room, one of the most luscious settings in town. His highly acclaimed creations celebrate the seasons. It is a fine place for special occasions, but beware of the sky-high prices.

UPPER MIDTOWN Dawat $$$

210 E 58th St, 10022 ***Tel*** *(212) 355-7555*

An attractive Indian restaurant with recipes from none other than famous Indian chef Madhur Jaffrey. Signature dishes include salmon rubbed with a coriander chutney and baked in a banana leaf. The clever touch is a snack car that parades to your table. If you're not an Indian food expert, ask the helpful staff for advice.

UPPER WEST SIDE Pasha $$$

70 W 71st St, 10023 ***Tel*** *(212) 579-8751*

A serene and spacious, skylit, Turkish restaurant with friendly service ideal for a good conversation amid well-executed food. The lamb dumpling appetizers are delicious as well as all of the eggplant dishes, in particular the smoky patlican salatasi, mashed with garlic, olive oil, and lemon.

UPPER WEST SIDE Picholine $$$$$

35 W 64th St, 10023 ***Tel*** *(212) 724-8585*

Terrance Brennan's elegant French-Mediterranean restaurant a few steps away from the Lincoln Center. Several prix-fixe, a la carte, and even tasting menus available, with dishes such as John Dory with grapes, chanterelles, and truffle vinaigrette. Save room for their famous artisan cheeses.

NEW YORK STATE

ALBANY Scrimshaw $$$

660 Albany Shaker Rd, 12211 ***Tel*** *(518) 869-8100*

For those with a hankering for great seafood, the Scrimshaw, located in the Desmond Hotel, offers a broad selection with surf 'n' turf options also available. Don't leave without trying their signature "scrimshaw potato" – whipped potatoes inside a puff pastry shell. Reservations are recommended.

BINGHAMTON Number Five $$$

33 S Washington St, 13903 ***Tel*** *(607) 723-0555*

The Number Five restaurant occupies an antique-filled fire station built in 1897. This steak and seafood house offers the perfect setting for an intimate dinner or a give-mom-the-evening-off family dinner. With entrees like stuffed lobster tails or filet mignon, you can't go wrong.

BUFFALO Salvatore's Italian Gardens $$

6461 Transit Rd, 14043 ***Tel*** *(716) 683-7990, (800) 999-8082*

Voted one of America's top 100 restaurants of the 20th century, the artistic presentation and savory menu at Salvatore's Italian Gardens offer the explanation. The award-lined walls attest to Salvatore's excellence in fine dining. Stuffed lobster and Veal Oscar are just two of their specialty items.

COOPERSTOWN Hoffman Lane Bistro $$$

2 Hoffman Lane, 13326 ***Tel*** *(607) 547-7055*

Located near the Baseball Hall of Fame, this restaurant is considered to be one of Cooperstown's finest. The airy and open atmosphere provides an enjoyable dining experience. The American fare consists of pork loin, steaks, hearty meatloaf, and grilled salmon. Pots of crayons and paper tablecloths are provided for your entertainment.

EAST AURORA Roycroft Inn $$

40 S Grove St, 14052 ***Tel*** *(716) 652-5552*

Housed in a landmark Arts and Crafts-style hotel, Roycroft Inn's menu features American cuisine along with a seasonal signature menu. A favorite item is the St. Andres Brie with slivered almonds, honey, toasted crostini, and cranberry coulis. Grab a fireside table and try one of the hand-crafted beers or enjoy a glass of wine on the veranda.

EAST HAMPTON The 1770 House Restaurant & Inn $$$$$

143 Main St, 11937 ***Tel*** *(631) 324-1770*

Step back in time and enjoy antique furnishings and historical items at The 1770 House (actually built in 1663). Savor entrees from a Contemporary/American menu. A standout dish is the duck breast with a truffle jus. Also, enjoy a glass of wine from one of the top vineyards of France, California, or Italy.

ITHACA Moosewood $$

215 N Cayuga St, 14850 ***Tel*** *(607) 273-9610*

One of the USA's most famous vegetarian restaurants, based in a historic school building, the Moosewood has been offering vegetarian/organic fare since 1973. Moosewood has published numerous best-selling cookbooks and has been named one of the thirteen most influential restaurants of the 20th century by *Bon Appetit* magazine.

LAKE GEORGE Log Jam $$$

1484 Ste Rte 9, Site 1, 12845 ***Tel*** *(518) 798-1155*

Residing in an authentic log cabin, the Log Jam welcomes guests with enticing meals and a breathtaking view of the Adirondacks. Inside you will find an old pot-belly stove and three stone fireplaces. Expertly prepared seafood, prime rib, and lamb chops are a few of the items offered.

MONTAUK Gosman's Dock $$$

484 West Lake Dr, 11954 ***Tel*** *(631) 668-5330*

Gosman's Dock has been serving fresh fish for over 50 years. This very popular restaurant overlooks the harbor and features a well-stocked bar. Fish entrees can be served fried, steamed, or broiled. A children's menu is available for the little ones.

ROCHESTER The Olive Tree $$$

165 Monroe Ave, 14607 ***Tel*** *(585) 454-3510*

Nestled in a restored 1864 dry goods store, The Olive Tree serves what critics have branded "Nouvelle Greek Cuisine". The restaurant is named for its use of pure olive oil and fresh ingredients to provide tasty and heart-healthy fare. The wine list consists of Greek wines only.

SKANEATELES Doug's Fish Fry $$

8 Jordan St, 13152 ***Tel*** *(315) 685-3288*

In operation since 1982, this Finger Lakes eatery offers truly fresh fish purchased five days a week. The menu also includes fresh breaded chicken tenders for the non-fish lover. Doug's has a kids counter where they can eat while Mom and Dad are nearby. Closed the first two weeks of January.

Key to Price Guide *see p118* **Key to Symbols** *see back cover flap*

NEW JERSEY

ATLANTIC CITY Atlantic City Bar and Grill $$

1219 Pacific Ave, 08401 ***Tel*** *(609) 348-8080, (609) 449-1991*

This family-owned restaurant opened more than 25 years ago and has become a favorite among locals, tourists, and even visiting celebrities and sports figures. Steaks, crabs, shrimp cocktail, lobsters, mussels, home-made pastas, pizzas, and sandwiches all feature on the menu. The spacious dining room has sports programming and is open until 4:30am.

CAPE MAY Cabanas on the Beach $$

429 Beach Ave, 08204 ***Tel*** *(609) 884-4800*

Enjoy great sandwiches, seafood, and more at this casual and easy-going beach bar that serves good food. Other attractions include a children's menu, open-air dining, and live blues and reggae entertainment acts. Oysters, shrimps, lots of shellfish specialties, crab, chicken, and prime ribs are all on the menu.

PENNSYLVANIA

GETTYSBURG Dobbin House Tavern/Alexander Dobbin Dining Room $$$

89 Steinwehr Ave, 17325 ***Tel*** *(717) 334-2100*

The Dobbin House, built in 1776 for Reverend Alexander Dobbin, is listed on the National Register of Historic Places. Savor Colonial/Continental dishes such as roast duck and cherry-stuffed pork tenderloin while enjoying traditional 18th-century stone walls and fireplaces. Reservations are suggested.

LANCASTER Olde Greenfield Inn $$$

595 Greenfield Rd, 17601 ***Tel*** *(717) 393-0668*

Located in a restored stone farmhouse, Olde Greenfield Inn has much to offer. You can enjoy dinner from an American menu with customer favorites such as lamb chops, filet mignon, or their "signature dish" seafood pasta. You can also enjoy a drink in the wine cellar or visit the Trellis Lounge and listen to live piano music.

PHILADELPHIA Jim's Steaks $

400 South St, 19147 ***Tel*** *(215) 928-1911*

With its distinctive Art Deco storefront, Jim's is undoubtedly one of Philadelphia's busiest and most popular eateries. Long lines often stretch onto hip South Street as visitors and locals alike flock here for authentic Philly cheesesteaks with mounds of onions and dripping hot cheese. It also serves excellent hoagies.

PHILADELPHIA Serrano $$

20 South Second St, 19106 ***Tel*** *(215) 928-0770*

Dine on robust international fare, from paella heaped with seafood to caramelized salmon or braised short-rib sandwich, at this colorful Old City restaurant. Afterwards, catch folk, blues, and acoustic tunes at the lively Tin Angel café-style bar upstairs.

PHILADELPHIA City Tavern $$$

138 South Second St, 19106 ***Tel*** *(215) 413-1443*

Authentic colonial-style cuisine, such as medallions of venison and braised rabbit, is served at this historically accurate reconstruction of the original 1773 tavern. Colonial ales brewed according to George Washington's and Thomas Jefferson's original recipes are also served. Three floors with colonial decor and staff in period costume.

PHILADELPHIA Susanna Foo Chinese Cuisine $$$$

1512 Walnut St, 19102 ***Tel*** *(215) 545-2666*

Not traditional Chinese by any means, this is one of the city's most popular fine-dining restaurants along ritzy Rittenhouse Row. Owner and chef Susanna Foo adds a French influence to classical Chinese dishes, creating flavorful sauces. No lunch service on the weekend. Reservations advised.

PITTSBURGH Grand Concourse $$

100 W Station Square Dr, 15219 ***Tel*** *(412) 261-1717*

Dining in this converted railroad station is a must-do event. Grand Concourse's main dining room is graced with an impressive staircase and a striking stained glass ceiling. The River Room provides breathtaking riverfront views. The inventive International/Fusion cuisine menu provides a selection of beef, chicken, seafood, and pasta entrées.

PITTSBURGH Primanti Brothers $$

46 18th St, 15222 ***Tel*** *(412) 263-2142*

An excellent place to grab a bite. Open 24 hours a day, Primanti Brothers is a beloved fixture in the Pittsburgh area with many locations around the city. The infamous "cheesesteak", a sandwich stuffed with meat, cheese, tomatoes, coleslaw, and french fries, graces the menu along with many other delicious selections.

NEW ENGLAND

INTRODUCING NEW ENGLAND 124–131

BOSTON, MASSACHUSETTS 132–149

MASSACHUSETTS 150–153

RHODE ISLAND 154–157

CONNECTICUT 158–161

VERMONT 162–165

NEW HAMPSHIRE 166–169

MAINE 170–173

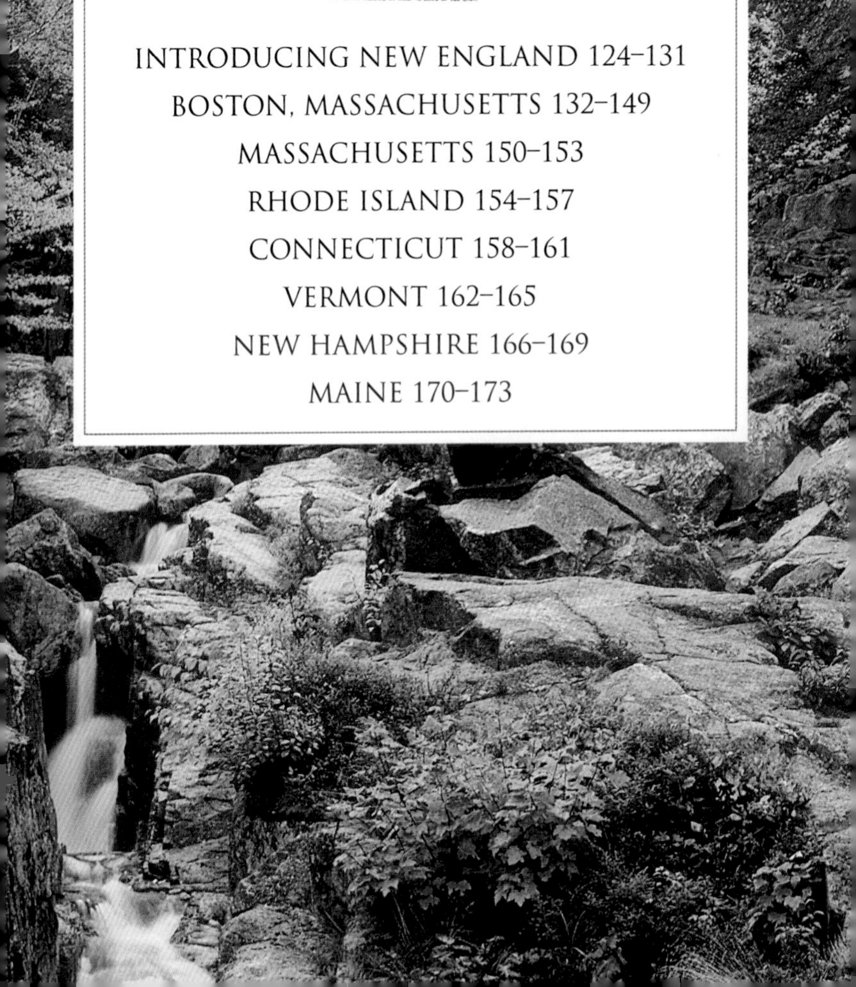

New England at a Glance

Tucked away in the northeasternmost corner of the United States, the six states of New England are rich in history and culture as well as in natural beauty. Many of the country's earliest settlements were established here, as were the first centers of higher education. The region therefore abounds in historic buildings, as well as in superb museums and prestigious universities. New England's topography includes large tracts of farmland, dense woodlands, pristine lakes, and sweeping coastlines, which are rocky and jagged in some areas and serene and sandy in others. It is also home to the rugged peaks of the White, Green, and Appalachian Mountains.

Vermont (see pp162–5) *is an enclave of unspoiled wilderness. Vermont is at its scenic best in fall, when the Green Mountain State changes its verdant green cloak for a rich palette of yellow, orange, and red.*

Canterbury Shaker Village (see p168) *located in New Hampshire, was founded in 1792. This is one of the many picturesque historic villages that are scattered around the rolling farmlands of the state.*

Connecticut (see pp158–61) *is quintessential New England. Steepled churches around immaculate village greens are typical features of its serene landscape.*

Block Island (see p157) *in Rhode Island is one of the many tranquil havens situated along the pristine shoreline of this tiny state. Great Salt Pond has three marinas and is an excellent spot for kayaking and fishing.*

◁ **Silver Cascades, Crawford Notch State Park, New Hampshire, in the autumn**

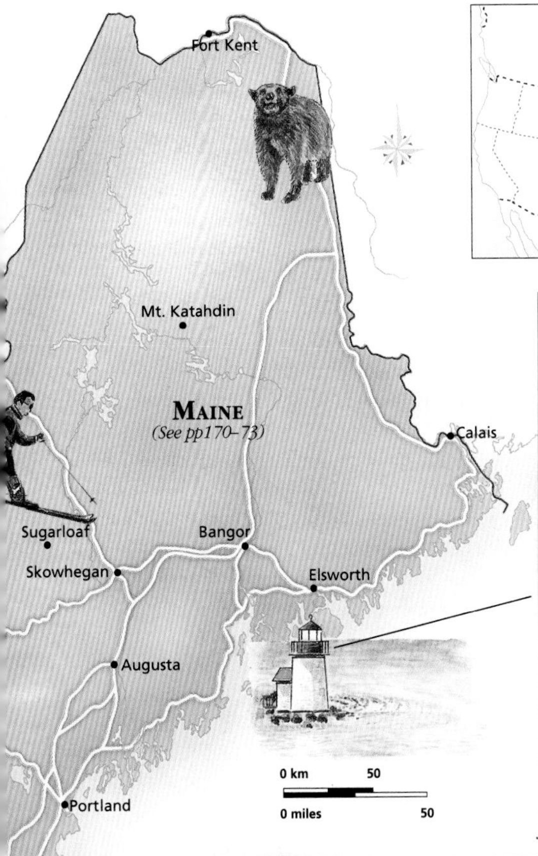

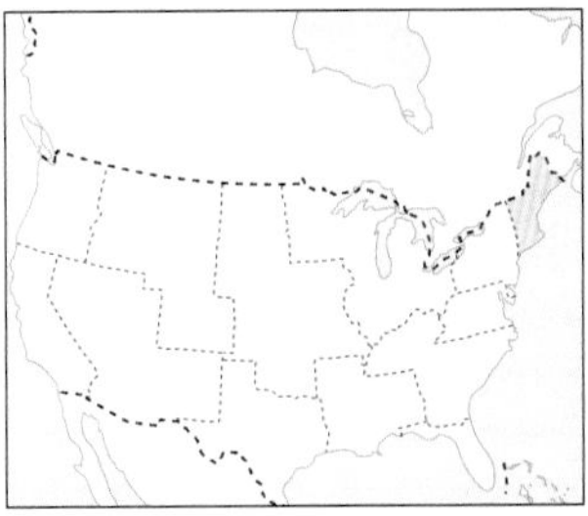

Maine (see pp170–73) *has more than 5,000 miles (8,050 km) of inlets, bays, and harbors. Dotted along the coast are a string of lighthouses that have guided mariners to safety for centuries.*

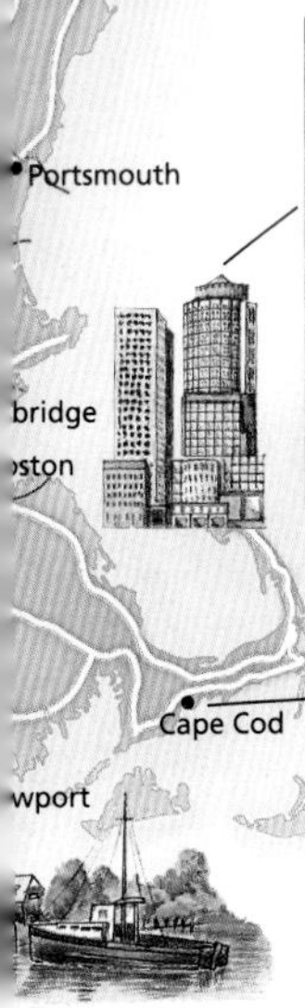

Boston (see pp132–49) *is New England's largest and most vibrant city, and the capital of Massachusetts. Here, historic buildings and gleaming modern structures can be found cheek by jowl.*

Cape Cod (see p152) *in Massachusetts is best known for its miles of wide, sandy beaches, whale-watching junkets, and quaint Colonial villages.*

NEW ENGLAND

For many people, New England is white-steepled churches, craggy coastlines, historic villages, and timeless landscapes of tranquil farmlands and country roads, with the sophisticated city of Boston as its cultural and commercial hub. Many also regard it as the cradle of American civilization, for New England's early history is the history of the United States itself.

From the beginning, the region has been shaped by both geography and climate. Early explorers charted its coastline, and communities soon sprang up by the coast, where goods and people could be ferried more easily from the Old World to the New. Early commerce depended heavily on the ocean, from shipping and whaling to fishing and boat-building.

The harsh, unpredictable climate, poor soil, hilly terrain, and dense virgin forests also helped shape the character of its people. To survive in this area required toughness, ingenuity, and a spirit of independence – all traits that became ingrained in the New England psyche. The slogan "Live free or die" on New Hampshire license plates is a reminder that the same spirit lives on. Indeed, New England today is as much a state of mind as it is a physical space. Despite this, New England is also home to the opulence of Newport, Rhode Island, the beautiful surburban communities of Connecticut, and the self-assured sophistication of Boston.

HISTORY

New England's historical connections are far richer than any other area in America, for it was here that much of the drama of forming a new country was played out. In 1614, the English explorer John Smith sailed along the coast of Massachusetts, named it New England, and declared that it was the best place to set up a new colony. On December 26, 1620, a group of 102 Puritans, who had left England to escape religious persecution, landed at Plymouth Rock after a grueling 66-day voyage on the *Mayflower* and established one of America's first permanent English settlements. Soon,

Stonington, a scenic town on Deer Isle, Penobscot Bay, Maine

◁ **Craggy Bass Harbor Head, a picturesque spot in Acadia National Park, Maine** large settlements had also grown up in Boston, Rhode Island, Connecticut, New Hampshire, and Maine.

As the colonists became more prosperous and self-sufficient, their resentment of British control and British taxes increased. The turning point came with the "Boston Tea Party" in 1773, when three British ships arrived at Boston Harbor laden with tea. About 60 local leaders, disguised as Indians, boarded the ships and dumped 342 tea chests, valued at £18,000, into the harbor as an act of defiance against an oppressive regime.

Minute Man statue in Concord

Meanwhile, locals had begun stockpiling arms in the countryside. In 1775, when British soldiers were sent to Concord to destroy these caches, American patriots (known as "Minutemen" for their ability to muster at a moment's notice) repelled them at Concord and nearby Lexington. They had been tipped off by a dramatic "midnight" horseback ride from Boston by Paul Revere. The American Revolution had begun, with the first major battle at Bunker Hill in Boston on June 17, 1775. The Declaration of Independence, signed by Colonial leaders in Philadephia on July 4, 1776, announced the birth of a new nation.

In the 19th century, New England's maritime trade grew more lucrative, as ships plied between the region's harbors and the West Indies, Europe, and the Far East. The whaling industry reached its zenith at this time, and cotton and wool manufacturing also flourished. New England's role in 19th-century America was not merely one of economic powerhouse. It was the cultural heart of the nation as well. Boston was the center of a strong protest against slavery. Instigated by a newspaper called *The Liberator*, the so-called abolitionist movement set up what came to be known as the Underground Railroad which provided escape routes for fleeing slaves.

KEY DATES IN HISTORY

1614 John Smith explores the Northeast coast

1620 The Pilgrims land at Plymouth

1630 Group of Puritans settle in Boston

1636 Harvard, America's first college, founded

1692 Salem witch trials begin

1770 British soldiers kill 5 in Boston Massacre

1773 New taxes spur Boston Tea Party

1774 British close Boston Harbor

1775 Battles at Concord and Lexington mark beginning of Revolutionary War

1776 Continental Congress ratifies Declaration of Independence

1783 Treaty of Paris ends Revolutionary War

1820 Maine breaks away from Massachusetts and becomes 20th state

1831 Abolitionist William Lloyd Garrison publishes first edition of anti-slavery newspaper

1851 Herman Melville publishes *Moby Dick*

1884 Mark Twain publishes *The Adventures of Huckleberry Finn*

1897 Country's first subway opens in Boston

1961 John F. Kennedy becomes president

1999 John F. Kennedy Jr. dies in plane crash off Martha's Vineyard

2004 Massachusetts becomes first US state to legally recognize gay marriage

PEOPLE & CULTURE

New England has continued to play an important role in the life of the nation. It was this region that produced the first flowering of American culture, with influential 19th-century literary giants such as Henry David Thoreau, Herman Melville, Nathaniel Hawthorne, and Mark Twain. All these writers won international recognition and acclaim. The literary tradition still lives on in New England, led by such outstanding

Harvard University's Widener Library, the third largest library in the United States

The New England shoreline, a haven for water sports

contemporary talents as John Updike, John Irving, and Stephen King, who are all residents of this region. The beauty and majesty of the landscape, which inspired some of America's best-known creative spirits, such as the poet Robert Frost and the painters Winslow Homer and Grandma Moses, still continues to exert its charm on contemporary artists, such as Sabra Field and photographer Frank Gohlke.

In 1636, Harvard College was founded in Boston, making it the birthplace of higher education in America. Today, the region's concentration of educational institutions, including famous Ivy League universities such as Yale, and Brown, is a magnet for some of America's best and brightest.

By the mid-19th century, New England's population, which had earlier been quite homogenous, changed dramatically as waves of Irish immigrants arrived, driven from their homeland by the potato famines in the 1840s. Immigrants from Italy, Portugal, and Eastern Europe also arrived, flocking to the textile mills which had boomed in New England just after the Industrial Revolution. They have left a lasting impact on the region's social life and politics, many of them ascending to the top of New England's social hierarchy – a fact that became evident to the country with the election of the Boston-born Democrat John F. Kennedy (1917–63) in 1960 as the very first Roman Catholic president of the US Nevertheless, even today there is a special cachet in New England's society for people known as "Boston Brahmins" popularly called WASPS (White Anglo-Saxon Protestants) – descendants of the earliest British settlers.

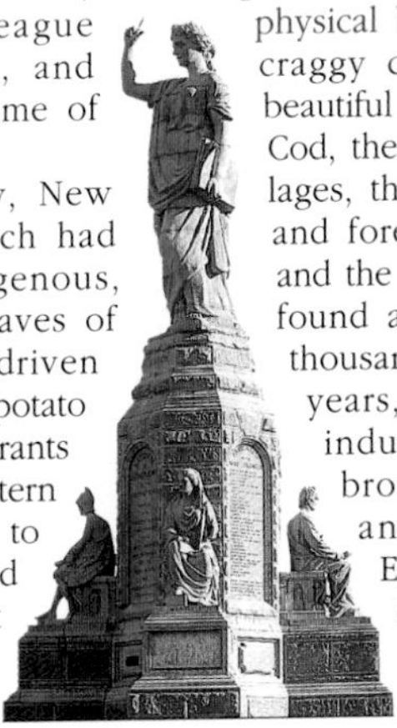

National Monument of Forefathers, Plymouth

While industrialization and urbanization have left their stamp on the region, New England's stunning physical beauty still remains. The craggy coastline of Maine, the beautiful beaches located in Cape Cod, the picturesque Vermont villages, the magnificent mountains and forests of New Hampshire, and the places of historic interest found across the region attract thousands of visitors. In recent years, the growth of hi-tech industries in the area has brought a new dynamism and prosperity to New England. This seems fitting, since it was the area's natural beauty that convinced the early settlers of New England's viable future.

Exploring New England

The six states of New England offer a diverse array of attractions. Vermont is famous for its ski resorts and rolling farmland, New Hampshire for its dense forests and spectacular passes through the White Mountains, and Maine for its rugged coastline and vast tracts of wilderness. Farther south, Massachusetts is rich in history, culture, and scenic beaches, Connecticut in picture-postcard villages, and Rhode Island in opulent mansions. The entire New England region boasts a dazzling display of fall foliage.

KEY

- Airport
- Highway
- Major road
- Railroad
- State border
- International border

SEE ALSO

- ***Practical Information*** pp174–5
- ***Where to Stay*** pp176–81
- ***Where to Eat*** pp182–5

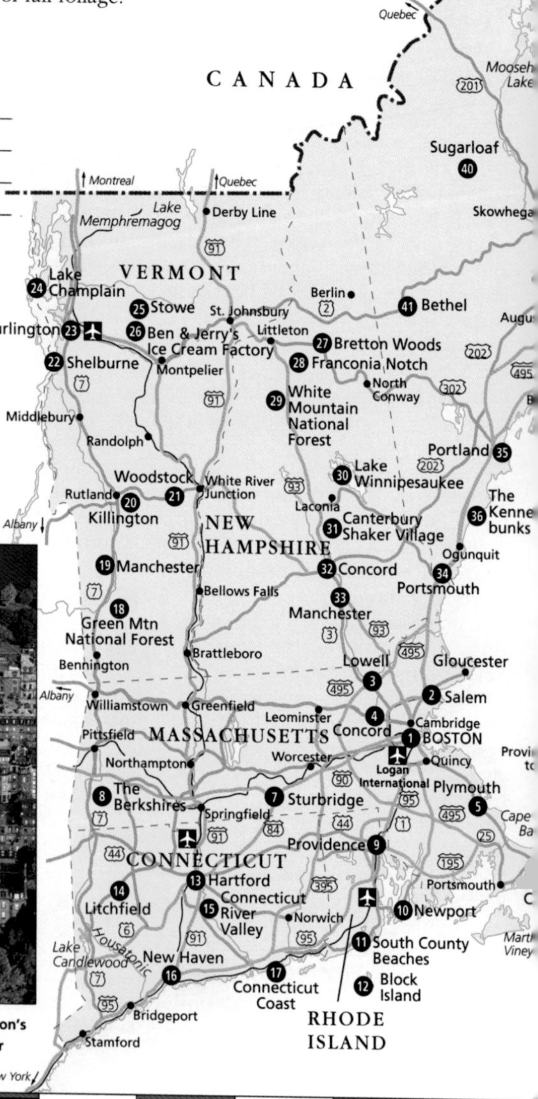

0 km 50

0 miles 50

View of typical row houses in Boston's Back Bay from John Hancock Tower

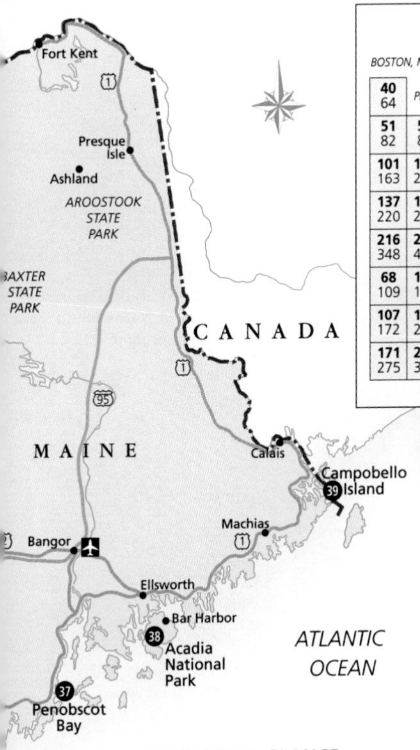

MILEAGE CHART

10 = Distance in miles
10 = Distance in kilometers

	Boston, MA	Plymouth, MA	Providence, RI	Hartford, CT	New Haven, CT	Burlington, VT	Concord, NH	Portland, ME
PLYMOUTH, MA	40 / 64							
PROVIDENCE, RI	51 / 82	54 / 87						
HARTFORD, CT	101 / 163	134 / 216	86 / 138					
NEW HAVEN, CT	137 / 220	162 / 261	103 / 166	39 / 63				
BURLINGTON, VT	216 / 348	255 / 410	276 / 444	235 / 378	273 / 439			
CONCORD, NH	68 / 109	106 / 171	127 / 204	157 / 253	193 / 311	151 / 243		
PORTLAND, ME	107 / 172	147 / 237	156 / 251	203 / 327	239 / 384	208 / 335	96 / 154	
BETHEL, ME	171 / 275	211 / 340	237 / 381	264 / 425	302 / 486	151 / 243	158 / 254	73 / 117

Busy street of Cape Cod's Providence in the summertime

SIGHTS AT A GLANCE

Boston pp132–49 1

Massachusetts
Salem 2
Lowell 3
Concord 4
Plymouth p151 5
Cape Cod 6
Sturbridge 7
The Berkshires 8

Rhode Island
Providence pp154–5 9
Newport p156 10
South County Beaches 11
Block Island 12

Connecticut
Hartford p158 13
Litchfield 14
Connecticut River Valley 15
New Haven 16
Connecticut Coast 17

Vermont
Green Mountain National Forest 18
Manchester 19
Killington 20
Woodstock 21
Shelburne Museum & Farms 22
Burlington 23
Lake Champlain 24
Stowe 25
Ben & Jerry's Ice Cream Factory 26

New Hampshire
Bretton Woods 27
Franconia Notch 28
White Mountain National Forest 29
Lake Winnipesaukee 30
Canterbury Shaker Village p168 31
Concord 32
Manchester 33
Portsmouth 34

Maine
Portland p170 35
The Kennebunks 36
Penobscot Bay 37
Acadia National Park 38
Campobello Island 39
Sugarloaf 40
Bethel 41

Boston ❶

Boston is located on the northeastern Atlantic Coast on Massachusetts Bay. Founded in the early 17th century around a large natural harbor at the mouth of the Charles River, the capital of Massachussetts today covers an area of 49 sq miles (127 sq km) and has a population of 600,000. It is a major center of American history, culture, and learning. The central city is focused around the harbor on the Shawmut Peninsula, while Greater Boston encompasses the surrounding area.

City Place atrium, Massachusetts State Transport Building, Boston

SIGHTS AT A GLANCE

Beacon Hill pp134–5 ①
Black Heritage Trail ②
Boston Common & Public Garden ③
Boston Athenaeum ④
The Freedom Trail pp136–7 ⑤
Massachusetts State House pp138–9 ⑥
Park Street Church ⑦
Downtown Crossing ⑧
Theater District ⑨
Chinatown ⑩
Post Office Square ⑪
Old South Meeting House ⑫
King's Chapel & Burying Ground ⑬
Old State House p141 ⑭
Quincy Market ⑮
Copp's Hill Burying Ground ⑯
Old North Church ⑰
Paul Revere Mall ⑱
Paul Revere House ⑲
Waterfront ⑳
Trinity Church p144 ㉑
Copley Square ㉒
Newbury Street ㉓
Commonwealth Avenue ㉔

Greater Boston
(see inset map)
John F. Kennedy Library & Museum ㉕
Isabella Stewart Gardner Museum ㉖
Museum of Fine Arts ㉗
Cambridge ㉘
Charlestown ㉙

SEE ALSO

• ***Where to Stay*** pp176–8

• ***Where to Eat*** pp182–3

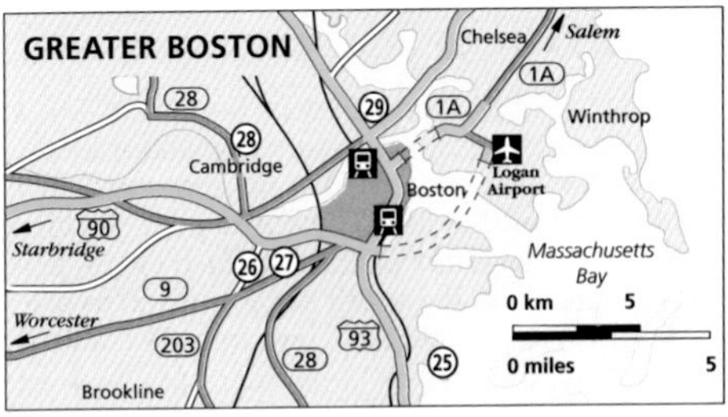

KEY

Area of main map

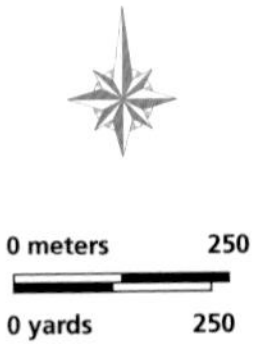

Trinity Church reflected in the John Hancock Tower

KEY

- Sight/Place of interest
- Airport
- Train station
- Subway station
- Parking
- Tourist information
- Expressway
- Pedestrian street

GETTING AROUND

Public transportation in Boston and Cambridge is very good. In fact, it is considerably easier to get around by public transportation than by driving. All major attractions in the city are accessible on its modern subway network, the T, or by bus or taxi. The historic central sections of the city are also extremely easy to navigate on foot.

Beacon Hill ①

The south slope of Beacon Hill was, from the 1790s to the 1870s, Boston's most sought-after neighborhood, until its wealthy elite decamped to the more exclusive Back Bay. Many of the district's houses were designed by the influential architect Charles Bulfinch (1763–1844) and his disciples, and the south slope evolved as a textbook example of Federal architecture. The finest houses are either on Boston Common or perched on top of the hill, offering fine views. Though the earlier houses were set well back from the street, the economic depression of 1807–12 resulted in row houses being built right out to the street.

Beacon Street
The fine Federal-style mansions here, some with ornate reliefs, overlook the beautiful green expanse of Boston Common.

Louisburg Square
The crowning glory of the Beacon Hill district, this square was developed in the 1830s. Today, it is still Boston's most desirable address.

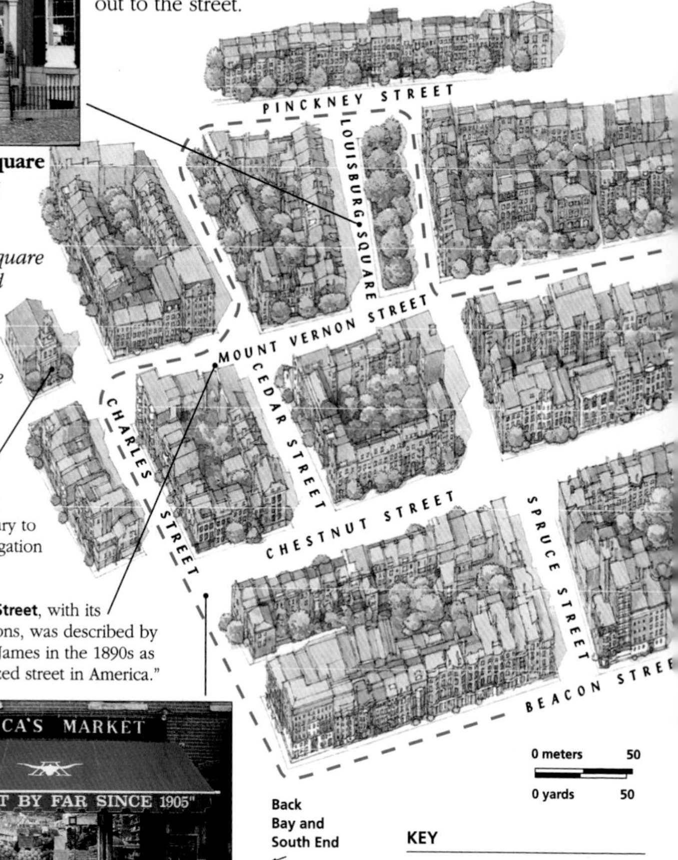

Charles Street Meeting House was built in the early 19th century to house a congregation of Baptists.

Mount Vernon Street, with its gracious mansions, was described by novelist Henry James in the 1890s as "the most civilized street in America."

KEY

- - - - Suggested route

★ Charles Street
This elegant street is lined with antique stores, fine restaurants, and gourmet groceries. At its top end are two groups of striking Greek Revival row houses.

STAR SIGHTS

★ Charles Street

★ Nichols House Museum

For hotels and restaurants in this region see pp176–8 and pp182–3

★ Nichols House Museum
This small museum offers an insight into the life and times of Beacon Hill resident Rose Nichols, who lived here from 1885 to 1960.

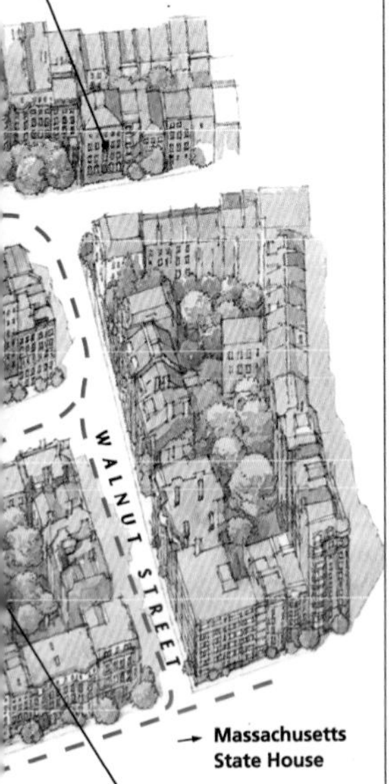

Hepzibah Swan Houses
Bulfinch designed these three elegant houses for the daughters of a wealthy Beacon Hill proprietress.

Black Heritage Trail ②

Map C3. *tours by National Park Service Rangers, (617) 742-5415.*

In the first US census in 1790, Massachusetts was the only state to record no slaves. During the 1800s, Boston's large free African-American community lived principally on the north slope of Beacon Hill and in the adjacent West End. Free walking tours of the Black Heritage Trail are led by the National Park Service Rangers in the summer, departing from the Robert Gould Shaw Memorial on Boston Common. The sights include safe houses for escaped slaves, and the **Museum of African American History** which traces Boston's black history and preserves the African Meeting House, the country's oldest black church. Dedicated in 1806, the building's simple interior once rang with the passionate oratory of abolitionists. Access to the church may be limited during ongoing renovation.

Museum of African American History
46 Joy St. ***Tel*** *(617) 725-0022.* *10am–4pm Mon–Sat.* *public hols.* **www**.afroammuseum.org

Boston Common & Public Garden ❸

Map C4. Ⓣ Park St, Boylston St, Arlington. *24 hrs.* **Visitor Center** *148 Tremont St, (617) 426-3115.* *8:30am–5pm Mon–Fri, 9am–5pm Sat–Sun (times vary in winter).* **www**.bostonusa.com

The city's most beautiful green space, the 48-acre (19-ha) Boston Common was established in 1634. For two centuries it served as a common pasture, gallows site, and a military camp and drill ground. By the 19th century, it had become a center for open-air civic activity and remains so to this day. At the northeastern edge of the Common is the **Robert Shaw Memorial**, with a magnificent relief depicting the first free black regiment in the Union Army during the Civil War, and their white colonel, Robert Shaw. In the southeastern corner is the Central Burying Ground, dating from 1756, with graves of British and American casualties from the historic Battle of Bunker Hill in 1775 *(see p149)*.

Southwest of the Common is the more formal 24-acre (10-ha) Public Garden, designed in English style in 1869. Amid its beautifully tended lawns and flowerbeds is a superb bronze equestrian statue of George Washington. A path leads from the statue to a serene lagoon, spanned by the miniature, ornamental Lagoon Bridge. Visitors can explore the lagoon on the delightful Swan Boats.

Bronze statue of George Washington in the Public Garden

Boston Athenaeum ❹

Map D3. 10½ Beacon St. ***Tel*** *(617) 227-0270.* Ⓣ *Park St.* *8:30am–8pm Mon, 8:30am–5:30pm Tue–Fri; Sep–May: 9am–4pm Sat.* **www**.bostonathenaeum.org

Housed in an elegant Palladian-style building, this library's treasures include George Washington's personal library and the theological library given by King William III of England to the King's Chapel *(see p140)*. The Athenaeum's collection, first organized in 1807, originally included many fine paintings. These were later donated to the Museum of Fine Arts *(see p146)* when that was set up.

The Freedom Trail ⑤

Boston has more sites directly related to the American Revolution than any other city. The most important of these sites, as well as some associated with the city's history, have been linked together as "The Freedom Trail." This 2.5-mile (4-km) walking route, marked in red on the sidewalks, starts at Boston Common, weaves through the central city and Old Boston, and ends at Bunker Hill in Charlestown.

Faneuil Hall, popularly known as the " Cradle of Liberty "

Central City

The Freedom Trail starts at the Visitor Information Center on Boston Common ① *(see p135)*. This is where angry colonials rallied against their British masters and where the British forces were encamped during the 1775–76 military occupation. Political speakers still expound from their soap-boxes here. Walking toward the northwest corner of the Common provides a wonderful view of the Massachusetts State House ② *(see pp138–9)*, located on Beacon Street. It was built as the new center of state governance after the Revolution. Along Park Street, at the end of the Common, is Park Street Church ③ *(see p139)*, built in 1810 and a bulwark of the anti-slavery movement. Adjacent to it, the Old Granary Burying Ground ④, is the final resting place of patriots John Hancock and Paul Revere. Continuing along Tremont Street you will come to King's Chapel and Burying Ground ⑤ *(see p140)*. The tiny cemetery is Boston's oldest, while King's Chapel was the principal Anglican church in Puritan Boston. The box pew on the right, just inside the front entrance, was reserved for condemned prisoners to hear their last sermons before going to the gallows on Boston Common.

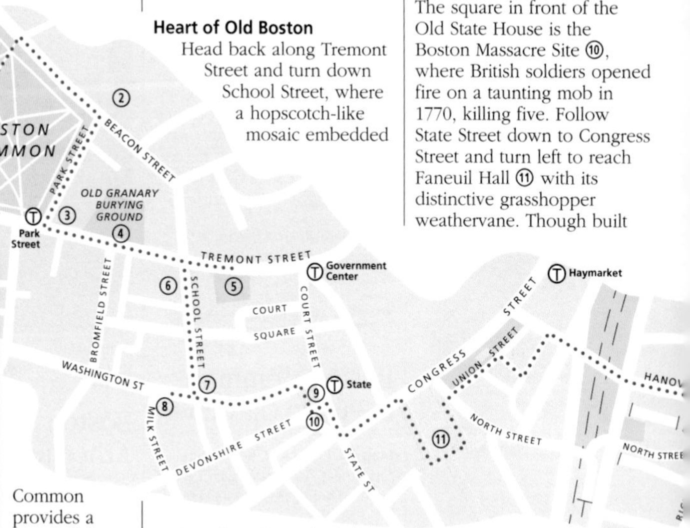

Steeple of Park Street Church

Heart of Old Boston

Head back along Tremont Street and turn down School Street, where a hopscotch-like mosaic embedded in the sidewalk marks the site of the First Public School ⑥, established in 1635. At the bottom of the street is the Old Corner Bookstore ⑦, a landmark which is more associated with Boston's literary flowering than with the Revolution. To its south on Washington Street is the Old South Meeting House ⑧ *(see p140)*, a graceful, white-spired brick church, modeled on Sir Christopher Wren's English country churches. A few blocks along, the Old State House ⑨ *(see p141)* presides over the head of State Street. The Colonial government building, it also served as the first state legislature, and the merchants' exchange in the basement was where Boston's Colonial shipping fortunes were made. The square in front of the Old State House is the Boston Massacre Site ⑩, where British soldiers opened fire on a taunting mob in 1770, killing five. Follow State Street down to Congress Street and turn left to reach Faneuil Hall ⑪ with its distinctive grasshopper weathervane. Though built primarily as Boston's first central marketplace, it was also known as "Cradle of Liberty." The red stripe of the Freedom Trail points the way to the North End and the Paul Revere House ⑫. This is Boston's oldest house, home to the man known for his "midnight ride" *(see p142)*.

The North End

Following the Freedom Trail through the North End, allow time to try some of the Italian cafés and bakeries along Hanover Street. Cross through the Paul Revere Mall to reach

Old North Church ⑬ *(see p142)*, whose spire is instantly visible over the shoulder of the equestrian statue of Paul Revere. In 1775, two lanterns hung in the belfry signaled the advance of British troops on Lexington and Concord. The crest of Copp's Hill lies close by on Hull Street. Some of Boston's earliest gallows were here, and people would gather below to watch the hangings of heretics and pirates. Much of the hilltop is covered by Copp's Hill Burying Ground ⑭, established in 1660 *(see p142)*.

Charlestown

Cross the iron bridge over the Charles River, which links the North End in Boston with City Square in Charlestown, and turn right, following the Freedom Trail along Water Street to the Charlestown Navy Yard ⑮. Berthed alongside Pier 1 is the USS *Constitution (see p149)*. In the War of 1812, she earned the nickname "Old Ironsides" for the resilience of her live oak hull against cannon fire. The granite obelisk that towers above the Charlestown waterfront is Bunker Hill Monument ⑯ *(see p149)*. This landmark commemorates the battle of June 17, 1775, which ended with a costly victory for British forces. As a monument to the first large-scale battle of the Revolution, the obelisk, based on those of ancient Egypt, remains a prototype for others across the US.

KEY

.... Walk route

Ⓣ Subway station

Tourist information

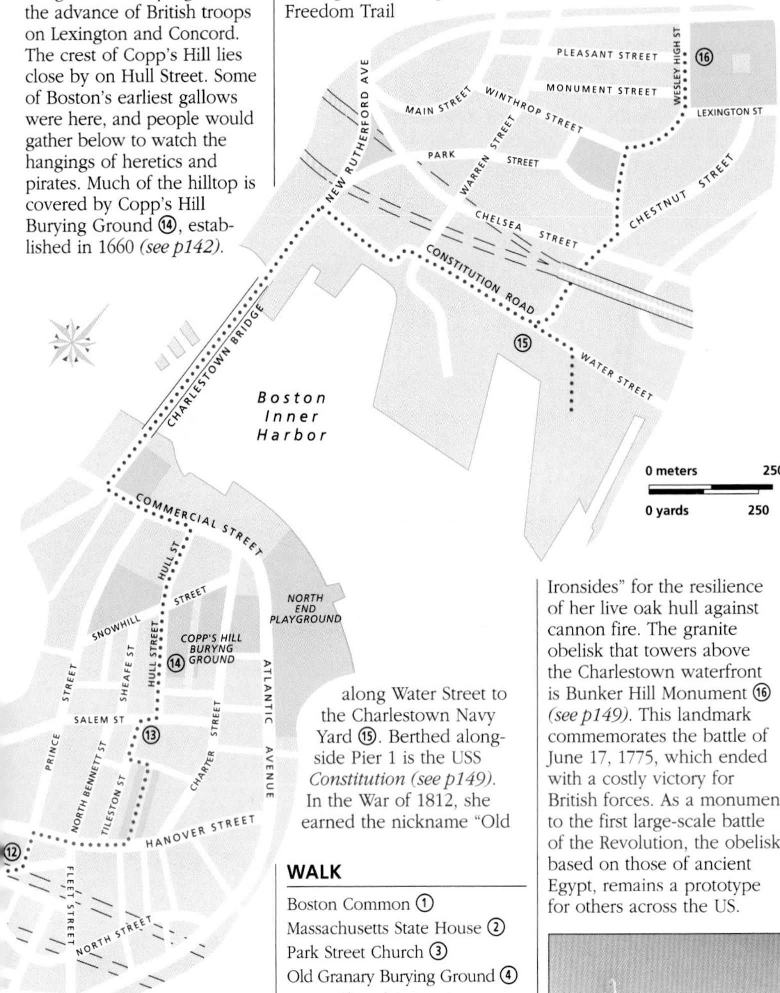

TIPS FOR WALKERS

Map C4. ***Starting point:*** *Boston Common Visitor Center. Free Park Ranger tours leave from Faneuil Hall.* ***Length:*** *2.5 miles (4 km).* ***Getting there:*** *Park Street Station (Ⓣ Green and Red lines) to start. State (Orange and Blue lines) and Haymarket (Orange and Green lines). Ⓣ stations can be found on route. Visitors should follow red stripe on sidewalk for the full route.*

WALK

- Boston Common ①
- Massachusetts State House ②
- Park Street Church ③
- Old Granary Burying Ground ④
- King's Chapel & Burying Ground ⑤
- First Public School ⑥
- Old Corner Bookstore ⑦
- Old South Meeting House ⑧
- Old State House ⑨
- Boston Massacre Site ⑩
- Faneuil Hall ⑪
- Paul Revere House ⑫
- Old North Church ⑬
- Copp's Hill Burying Ground ⑭
- Charlestown Navy Yard & the USS *Constitution* ⑮
- Bunker Hill Monument ⑯

View of Bunker Hill Monument from Charlestown harbor

Massachusetts State House ⑥

The cornerstone of the Massachusetts State House was laid in 1795 by Paul Revere and Samuel Adams. Completed in 1798, the Charles Bulfinch-designed center of state government served as a model for the US Capitol building in Washington and as an inspiration for many other state capitols. Later additions were made, but the original building remains the archetype of American government buildings. Its gilded dome serves as the zero-mile marker for Massachusetts.

★ Nurses Hall
The statue of the army nurse here was erected in honor of all the nurses who took part in the Civil War. The marble hall is lined with murals depicting important events leading up to the American Revolution.

The Great Hall, built in 1990, is used for state functions and is topped by a glass dome.

Hall of Flags

Senate Chamber

Main Staircase
Beautiful stained-glass windows, with the early state seals of Massachusetts, decorate the main staircase.

★ House of Representatives
This elegant oval chamber was built in 1895, but the "Sacred Cod" that now hangs over the gallery came to the State House when it first opened in 1798.

The dome was gilded in 23-carat gold in 1872.

Entrance

STAR SIGHTS

★ House of Representatives

★ Nurses Hall

For hotels and restaurants in this region see pp176–8 and pp182–3

VISITORS' CHECKLIST

Map D3. Beacon Hill. ***Tel*** *(617) 722-2000.* Ⓣ *Park St.* *10am–3:30pm Mon–Fri. Booking advised.* **www**.sec.state.ma.us/trs

Senate Chamber
Situated directly beneath the dome, this chamber features a beautiful sunburst ceiling.

The Wings, added in 1917, are thought by many to sit incongruously with the rest of the structure.

Hall of Flags
Flags carried into battle by regiments from the state of Massachusetts are displayed here beneath a stained-glass skylight, depicting seals of the original 13 colonies.

Park Street Church ⑦

Map D4. 1 Park St. ***Tel*** *(617) 523-3383.* Ⓣ *Park St.* *Jul–Aug: 9am–3:30pm Tue–Sat; Sep–Jun: call for hours.* **www**.parkstreet.org

Since its dedication in 1810, the Park Street Church has been one of Boston's most influential pulpits. In 1829, the firebrand crusader for the abolition of slavery, William Lloyd Garrison, gave his first abolition speech here; and in 1893 the anthem *America the Beautiful* debuted at Sunday service in this church. The church, with its 217-ft (65-m) steeple was designed by the English architect Peter Banner, who actually adapted a design by the earlier English architect, Christopher Wren.

Adjacent to the church, on Tremont Street, is the mid-17th century **Old Granary Burying Ground**, which was once the site of a grain storage facility. Among those buried in this historic cemetery are three important signatories to the Declaration of Independence – Samuel Adams, John Hancock, and Robert Paine, as well as one of the city's most famous sons, the patriot Paul Revere.

Old Granary Burying Ground
Tremont St. *9am–5pm daily.*

Downtown Crossing ⑧

Map D4. Washington, Winter, & Summer Sts. Ⓣ *Downtown Crossing.*

This lively pedestrian shopping district, crowded with sidewalk stalls and vendors' carts, is dominated by the beaux arts building that was formerly Filene's and by more modernist Macy's, a nationwide chain. Another well-known store in the area is Brattle Book Shop, founded in 1825. This bibliophiles' treasure house stocks more than 250,000 rare, used, and out-of-print books and magazines.

Theater District ⑨

Map C4. Ⓣ *Boylston, New England Medical Center.*

Boston's first theater opened in 1793 on Federal Street. Fifty years later, with patronage from the city's elite, Boston had become a major tryout town and boasted several lavish theaters. Many major US premieres were held here, among them Handel's *Messiah*, and Tennessee Williams' *A Streetcar Named Desire*. Among the grandest theaters are the opulent **Colonial Theater**, decorated with frescos and friezes; the 1,650-seat **Shubert Theater**, with its imposing Neo-Classical façade; and the **Wang Theater**, with a glittering seven-story auditorium.

Colonial Theater
106 Boylston St.
Tel *(617) 426-9366.*
phone to check.
www.broadwayacrossamerica.com

Chinatown ⑩

Map D5. Bounded by Kingston, Kneeland, Washington, & Essex Sts. Ⓣ *Chinatown.*

This is the third largest Chinatown in the US, after those in San Francisco and New York. Pagoda-topped telephone booths set the tone of the neighborhood, which is full of restaurants, and stores selling garments and Chinese medicine. Boston's Chinese colony was fully established by the turn of the 19th century, and in recent years the area's population has swelled with new arrivals from Korea, Vietnam, and Cambodia.

Typical store and restaurant façades in Boston's Chinatown

Sculptural fountain in Boston's Post Office Square

Post Office Square ⑪

Map E4. Cnr of Congress and Milk streets. Ⓣ *State, Downtown.*

Enclosed on the west side by the impressive Art-Deco former post office building, that gave the square its name, is the nerve center of Boston's financial district. The east side of the square faces the Renaissance-style former Federal Reserve Bank, now the Langham Boston Hotel, while the graceful Art-Moderne structure on the south side is a former Bell Telephone Company building, in which a small museum recreates the laboratory where Alexander Graham Bell invented the telephone, a device he first demonstrated in Boston in 1876. A public park provides an oasis of green among the high-rise buildings of the city. Local workers and tourists are able to relax on the lawns to the sound of water in the sculptural fountain.

Old South Meeting House ⑫

Map D4. 310 Washington St. ***Tel*** *(617) 482-6439.* Ⓣ *Park St, State, Government Center.* *Apr–Oct: 9:30am–5pm daily; Nov–Mar: 10am–4pm daily.* **www**.oldsouthmeetinghouse.org

Built for Puritan religious services in 1729, this edifice, with a tall octagonal steeple, had Colonial Boston's biggest capacity for town meetings. From 1765 on, it became the venue for large and vociferous crowds, led by a group of merchants called "the Sons of Liberty" to gather in protest against British taxation and the hated Stamp Act. During a protest rally on December 16, 1773, the fiery speechmaker Samuel Adams flashed the signal that led to the Boston Tea Party *(see p143)* at Griffin's Wharf several hours later. The British retaliated by turning Old South into an officers' tavern and a stable for army horses. Today, the Meeting House holds lectures and exhibitions, and has a multimedia show, which relives the events. The shop sells "Boston Tea Party" tea.

Alexander Graham Bell

King's Chapel & Burying Ground ⑬

Map D3. 58 Tremont St. ***Tel*** *(617) 523-1749.* Ⓣ *Park St, State, Government Center.* *late May–mid-Sep: 10am-4pm Mon, Thu, Fri, Sat, 10am–11:15am, 1:30pm–4pm Tue & Wed, 1:30–4pm Sun; mid-Sep–late May: 10am–4pm Sat, 1:30–4pm Sun (opening hours are subject to change during the ongoing restoration).* **Music Recitals** *12:15pm Tue.* **www**.kings-chapel.org

The first chapel on this site was built in 1689, but when the Governor of New England decided that a larger church was needed, the present granite edifice was begun in 1749. It was constructed around the original wooden chapel, which was then dismantled and heaved out of the windows of its replacement. High ceilings and open arches enhance the sense of spaciousness and light inside the chapel. Its other notable features include a pulpit shaped like a wine glass, which dates back to 1717, and a huge bell that was recast by the foundry of Revolutionary hero Paul Revere *(see p142)*.

The cemetery adjacent to the chapel is Boston's oldest.

The simply decorated interior of King's Chapel on Tremont Street

Old State House ⑭

Map D3. Washington & State Sts. ***Tel*** *(617) 720-1713.* Ⓣ *State.* *9am–5pm daily (reduced hours Jan, extended hours Jul & Aug).* **www**.bostonhistory.org

Now dwarfed by the towers of the Financial District, the Old State House was the seat of the British Colonial government between 1713 and 1776. The royal lion and unicorn still decorate each corner of its eastern façade. After independence, the Massachusetts legislature took possession of the building, and it has had many uses since, including a produce market, Masonic Lodge, and Boston City Hall. Its wine cellars now function as a subway station.

Old State House amid the skyscrapers of the Financial District

In 1776, the Declaration of Independence was read from the balcony on the East Façade. A circle of cobblestones below the balcony marks the site of the Boston Massacre. On March 5, 1770, colonists taunted British guardsmen with insults, rocks, and snowballs. The soldiers opened fire, killing five colonists. After the Boston Tea Party, this was one of the most inflammatory events leading up to the American Revolution *(see p44)*. Inside, exhibits include a multimedia presentation about the Boston Massacre.

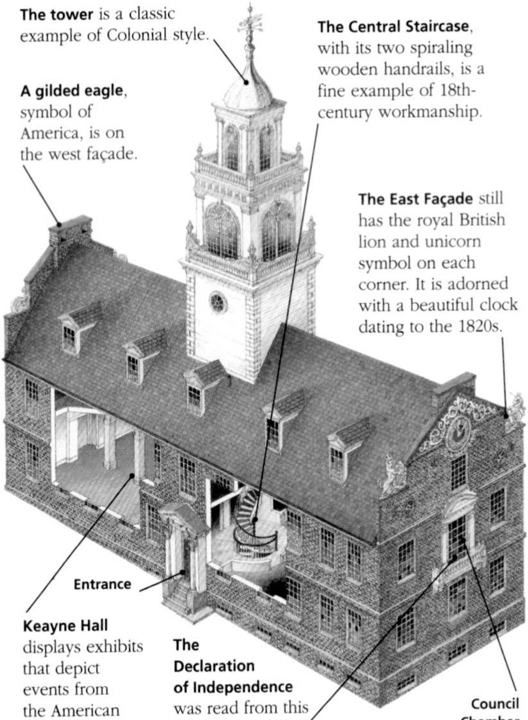

Greek Revival Custom House tower, one of Boston's most striking sights

Quincy Market ⑮

Map E3. Between Chatham & Clinton Sts. ***Tel*** *(617) 523-1300.* Ⓣ *Government Center, State.* *10am–9pm Mon–Sat, noon–6pm Sun.* **www**.faneuilhallmarketplace.com

This immensely popular shopping and dining complex attracts nearly 14 million people every year. It was developed from the old buildings of the city's meat, fish, and produce markets, which were beautifully restored in the 1970s. The 535-ft- (163-m-) long Greek Revival-style colonnaded hall is now filled with fast-food stands and tables beneath the spectacular central rotunda. Completing the ensemble are the twin North and South Market buildings, refurbished to house boutiques, restaurants, and business offices.

A short distance southeast of Quincy Market is the **Custom House** with its Greek Revival tower. The 495-ft (150m) tower with a four-sided clock was built in 1915 and for much of the 20th century was Boston's only skyscraper. There is a museum of maritime history in the rotunda. Call for the schedule of free tours of the tower, which offers spectacular city and harbor views.

Custom House
3 McKinley Square.
Tel *(617) 310-6300.*
Museum *8am–9pm daily.*
www.marriott.com/vacationclub

Slate tombstones of Boston's early settlers, Copp's Hill Burying Ground

Copp's Hill Burying Ground ⑯

Map E2. Entrances at Charter & Hull Sts. Ⓣ *Government Center, N Station.* *9am–5pm daily.*

Existing since 1659, this is Boston's second oldest cemetery, after the one by King's Chapel *(see p140).* Among those buried here are Robert Newton, the sexton who hung Paul Revere's signal lanterns in the belfry of the Old North Church, influential Colonial period Puritan ministers, as well as hundreds of black slaves and freedmen.

During the British occupation of Boston, King George III's troops were said to have used the slate headstones for target practice, and pockmarks from their musket balls are still visible. Copp's Hill Terrace, directly across Charter Street, is the site where, in 1919, a 2.3 million-gallon tank of molasses exploded, drowning 21 people in a huge, syrupy tidal wave.

Old North Church ⑰

Map E2. 193 Salem St. ***Tel*** *(617) 523-6676.* Ⓣ *Haymarket, Aquarium, N Station.* *9am–5pm daily (reduced hours Jan & Feb, extended hours Jun–Oct).* *9am, 11am Sun (also 5pm Jul–Aug).* *donation.* *Jun–Aug: "Behind the Scenes Tour" (fee charged).* **www**.oldnorth.com

Officially named Christ Episcopal Church, the Old North Church, which dates from 1723, is Boston's oldest surviving religious edifice. It is built of brick in the Georgian style, similar to that of St. Andrew's-by-the-Wardrobe in Blackfriars, London, designed by Sir Christopher Wren. The church was made famous on April 18, 1775, when sexton Robert Newman, aiding Paul Revere, hung a pair of lanterns in the belfry. These were to warn the patriots in Charlestown of the westward departure of British troops, on their way to engage the revolutionaries.

An imposing marble bust of George Washington, dating from 1815, adorns the church interior, which has unusual high-sided box pews. These were designed to enclose footwarmers, which were filled with hot coals or bricks during wintry weather. The tower contains the first set of church bells made in North America, cast in 1745. One of the first bellringers was a teenage Paul Revere.

Paul Revere Mall ⑱

Map E2. Hanover St. Ⓣ *Haymarket, Aquarium.*

This brick-paved plaza, between Hanover and Unity Streets, provides a precious stretch of open space in the crowded neighborhood of the North End, populated largely by people of Italian descent. Laid out in 1933, its focal point is an equestrian statue of Paul Revere (1735–1818). Benches, a fountain, and twin rows of linden trees give the space, much used by local people, a distinctly European feel. South of the Mall is busy Hanover Street, which is lined with Italian eateries.

Paul Revere House ⑲

Map E2. 19 N Square. ***Tel*** *(617) 523-2338.* Ⓣ *Haymarket, Aquarium.* *mid-Apr–Oct: 9:30am–5:15pm daily; Nov–mid-Apr: 9:30am–4:15pm daily.* *Jan–Mar: Mon.* **www**.paulreverehouse.org

Boston's oldest surviving clapboard frame house is historically significant, for it was here in 1775 that Paul Revere began his legendary horseback ride to warn his compatriots in Lexington *(see p149)* of the impending arrival of British troops. This historic event was later immortalized by Henry Wadsworth Longfellow *(see p148)* in his epic poem which begins, "Listen, my children, and you shall hear of the midnight ride of Paul Revere."

A versatile gold- and silversmith, and maker of church bells and cannons, Revere lived here from 1770 to 1800. Small leaded casement windows, an overhanging upper story, and nail-studded front door make the house a fine example of 18th-century Early American architecture. Three rooms in the house contain artifacts and furniture made in Revere's workshop. In the courtyard is a large bronze bell cast by Revere, who is known to have made nearly 200 church bells.

Paul Revere House, where Paul Revere began his midnight ride

Waterfront ⑳

Map E3. Atlantic Ave. **New England Aquarium** Central Wharf. ***Tel*** *(617) 973-5200.* Ⓣ *Aquarium.* *Sep–Jun: 9am–5pm Mon–Fri, 9am–6pm Sat & Sun; Jul–Aug: 9am–6pm Mon–Thu, 9am–7pm Fri–Sun.* **www**.neaq.org
Boston Tea Party Ship and Museum Congress St Bridge. ***Tel*** *(617) 338-1773.* Ⓣ *South Station.* *closed until at least summer 2010.* **www**.historictours.com/boston
Institute of Contemporary Art 100 Northern Ave. ***Tel*** *(617) 478-3100.* Ⓣ *Courthouse.* *10am–5pm Tue, Wed, Sat, Sun, 10am–9pm Thu, Fri.* **www**.icaboston.org
Children's Museum 300 Congress St. ***Tel*** *(617) 426-8855.* Ⓣ *S Station.* *10am–5pm daily, 10am–9pm Fri.* **www**.bostonkids.org

Boston's waterfront is one of the city's most fascinating areas. Fringed by wharves and warehouses – a reminder of the city's past as a key trading port – its attractions include a famous aquarium and two fine museums.

One of the largest wharves is **Long Wharf**, established in 1710. Once extending 2,000 ft (610 m) into Boston Harbor and lined with shops and warehouses, it provided secure mooring for the largest ships of the time.

Harbor Walk connects Long Wharf with other adjacent wharves, dating from the early 1800s. Most of them have now been converted to fashionable harborside apartments. **Rowes Wharf**, to the south of the waterfront is a particularly fine example of such revitalization. This modern red-brick development, with opulent condominiums and offices, features a large archway that links the city to the harbor.

The waterfront's prime attraction is the **New England Aquarium**, which dominates Central Wharf. Designed in 1969, the aquarium's core encloses a vast four-story ocean tank, which houses a Caribbean coral reef and contains a wide array of marine creatures such as sharks, moray eels, barracudas, and sea turtles, as well as exotic, brightly colored tropical fish. A curving walkway runs around the outside of the tank from the top to the bottom, and provides different viewpoints of the interior at many levels.

Exotic fish, New England Aquarium

A particularly popular section of the aquarium is the Penguin Pool, which runs around the base of the ocean tank, while the west wing has an outdoor tank with a lively colony of harbor seals. In 2001, the Simons IMAX® Theater was opened on the wharf, which presents changing programs of 3-D films on a giant screen. A highlight of the aquarium's programs are the boat trips from Boston Harbor, which take visitors to the whale feeding grounds far offshore. The aquarium also has a gift shop and a café with a beautiful view of the harbor.

Griffin's Wharf, where the Boston Tea Party took place on December 16, 1773, long ago buried beneath landfill, but anchored nearby on Fort Point Channel, the **Boston Tea Party Ships** replicate the British East India Company ships involved in the Tea Party protest *(see p44)*. At Fan Pier, the light-flooded galleries, performance space open to harbor views, and cutting-edge media center highlight the landmark building of the **Institute of Contemporary Art**, where exhibitions place strong emphasis on electronic media and performance art.

Overlooking Fort Point Channel is a rejuvenated 19th-century wool warehouse that houses the **Children's Museum**, one of the best in the country. Its many attractions and interactive exhibits include a climbing wall, and a hands-on recyling area with barrels of materials for children to use in self-instructive creative projects. They can also follow a giant maze or act in kidstage plays. An international flavor is added by a visit to the silk merchant's house, transplanted from Kyoto in Japan.

View down Long Wharf toward the waterfront and Custom House

Trinity Church ㉑

Bas-relief in Chancel

Routinely voted one of America's ten finest buildings, this masterpiece by Henry Hobson Richardson dates from 1877. The church is a beautiful granite and sandstone Romanesque structure, standing on wooden piles driven through mud into bedrock, surmounted by granite pyramids. John LaFarge designed the interior, while some of the windows were designed by Edward Burne-Jones and executed by William Morris.

VISITORS' CHECKLIST

Map B5. Copley Sq. ***Tel*** *(617) 536-0944.* Ⓣ *Copley.* *daily.* *7:45am, 9am, 11:15am, 6pm Sun.* ***Concerts*** *Sep–Jun: 12:15pm Fri.* *call for hours.* **www.**trinitychurchboston.org

★ North Transept Windows
Designed by Burne-Jones and executed by William Morris, the three stained-glass windows above the choir relate the story of Christmas.

The Chancel
Seven beautiful windows here show the life of Christ.

★ West Portico
The deeply sculpted west portico is modeled after St. Trophime in Arles, France.

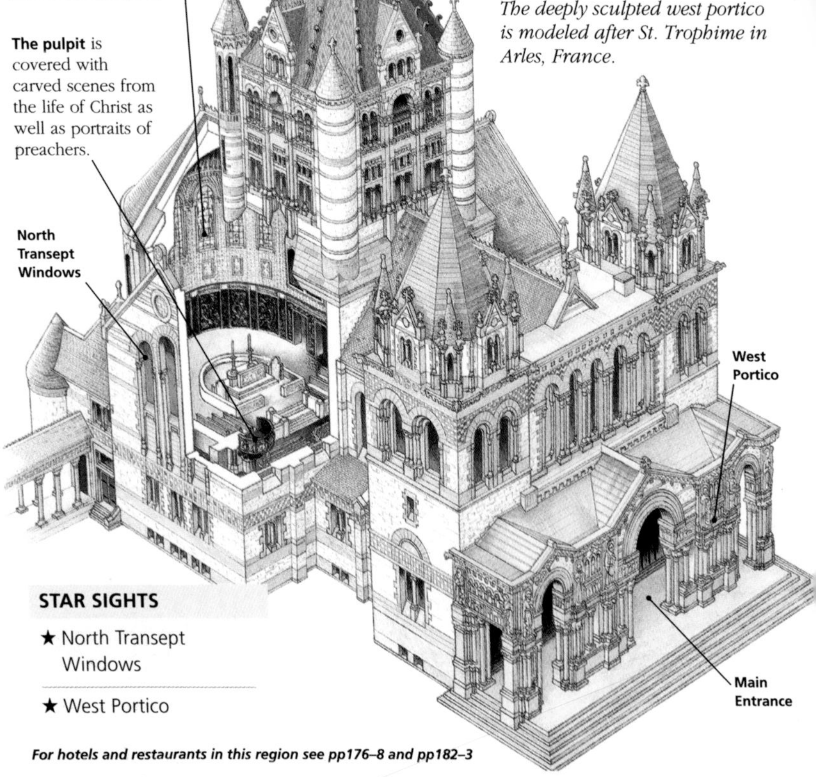

STAR SIGHTS

- ★ North Transept Windows
- ★ West Portico

View over Back Bay and Charles River from the John Hancock Tower

Copley Square ㉒

Map B5. Ⓣ *Copley.*

Named after the famous painter John Singleton Copley *(see p147)*, Copley Square was a marsh until 1870 and took on its present form only in the late 20th century. Today, this inviting plaza is an open space of trees and fountains, and a hive of civic activity with weekly farmers' markets and concerts in summer.

The **John Hancock Tower**, constructed in 1975, anchors the southeastern side of the Square. The tallest building in New England, the 740-ft (226-m) tower's mirrored façade reflects the beautiful Trinity Church and the original (1947) Hancock Building. Unfortunately, the observatory on the 60th floor has been closed following the events of September 11, 2001.

West of the Hancock Tower, across Copley Square, is the Italian palazzo-style **Boston Public Library**, built 1887–95. A marvel of fine wood and marble, the library has huge bronze doors, and murals by John Singer Sargent in a third-floor gallery. The vast Bates Hall on the second floor of this library is notable for its soaring barrel-vaulted ceiling. Close by, on the corner of Boylston and Dartmouth Streets, is the fabulous Italian Gothic-style **New Old South Church**, built in 1874–75.

John Hancock Tower
200 Clarendon St. ● *to the public.*

Boston Public Library
Copley Square. **Tel** *(617) 536-5400.*
◯ *Apr–Sep & Oct–May: 9am–9pm Mon–Thu, 9am–5pm Fri–Sat; Oct–May: 1–5pm Sun.* ● *public hols.* *2:30pm Mon, 6pm Tue & Thu, 11am Fri & Sat; (Oct–May: 2pm Sun).* **www**.bpl.org

Newbury Street ㉓

Map B5. Ⓣ *Arlington, Copley, Hynes Convention Center/ ICA.*

Newbury Street is a Boston synonym for "stylish." Lined with high-fashion outlets, art galleries, and chic restaurants, this is a great place for people-watching. Lower Newbury near the Public Garden is posh and elegant, while upper Newbury buzzes with youth-oriented shops and services. Churches provide vestiges of a more decorous era. Most notable is the **Church of the Covenant**, which contains the world's largest collection of Louis Comfort Tiffany stained-glass windows and an elaborate Tiffany lantern.

Church of the Covenant
67 Newbury St. **Tel** *(617) 266-7480.*
◯ *10am Sun.*
www.churchofthecovenant.org

Commonwealth Avenue ㉔

Map B4. Ⓣ *Arlington, Copley, Hynes Convention Center/ ICA.*

Envisioned as Boston's Champs Elysées, this avenue, 200-ft (61-m) wide, is lined with beautiful townhouses. In the second half of the 19th century, it became an arena for America's leading domestic architects, and a walk along it is like flicking through a catalog of architectural styles. Bronze statues of historic figures line the central mall. Abolitionist William Lloyd Garrison's statue, located between Exeter and Dartmouth Streets, is said to capture his air of moral superiority, while the best-loved memorial features sailor and historian Samuel Eliot Morison. In his statue, found between Exeter and Fairfield Streets, Morison strikes an informal pose, dangling his feet from a rock.

The Romanesque-style **First Baptist Church**, on the corner of Commonwealth Avenue and Clarendon Street, is one of the most distinctive buildings of the city skyline. Completed in 1872, its freestanding square bell tower, modeled on Italian campaniles, is topped with a decorative frieze by Bartholdi, the sculptor who created the Statue of Liberty. The faces in the frieze, which depict the sacraments, are likenesses of prominent Bostonians of the time, among them Henry Wadsworth Longfellow and Ralph Waldo Emerson.

First Baptist Church
110 Commonwealth Ave.
Tel *(617) 267-3148.* ◯ *for Sun worship.*

Greater Boston

Southwest of central Boston, what were once the marshlands of the Fenway now house two superb art museums – the Museum of Fine Arts and the Isabella Stewart Gardner Museum. West of the city, across the Charles River, is the college town of Cambridge, dominated by Harvard University. To its east is historic Charlestown, which forms a major part of Boston's Freedom Trail *(see pp136–7)*.

The dramatic structure of the John F. Kennedy Library and Museum

John F. Kennedy Library & Museum ㉕

Columbia Point, Dorchester.
Tel *(617) 514-1600. Ⓣ JFK/ U Mass.*
9am–5pm daily. Jan 1, Thanksgiving, Dec 25.
www.jfklibrary.org

Housed in a dramatic white concrete and black glass building designed by architect I.M. Pei, this museum chronicles the 1,000 days of the Kennedy presidency. The combination of video and film footage, papers, and memorabilia evoke the euphoria of "Camelot" as well as the numb horror of the assassination with an immediacy that is uncommon in historical museums. Some of the key chambers in the White House, including the Oval Office, are re-created here.

The house at 83 Beals Street in Brookline, where the late president was born in 1917, is now the **John F. Kennedy National Historic Site**. The Kennedy family moved to a larger house in 1921; in 1966 they repurchased this house, furnished it with their belongings circa 1917, and turned it into a memorial.

Isabella Stewart Gardner Museum ㉖

280 The Fenway. § (617) 566-1401
Ⓣ MFA. 11am–5pm Tue–Sun.
Jan 1, Thanksgiving, Dec 25.
call for concert schedule.
www.gardnermuseum.org

This Venetian-style palazzo houses a remarkable collection of over 2,500 works of art, including Old Masters and Italian Renaissance pieces. Advised by art scholar Bernard Berenson, the wealthy and strong-willed Isabella Stewart Gardner began collecting art in the late 19th century. Among the works she acquired were masterpieces by Titian, Rembrandt, and Matisse as well as by the American painters James McNeill Whistler and John Singer Sargent. The paintings, sculptures, and tapestries are displayed on three levels around the stunning skylit central courtyard.

Unfortunately, in 1990, 13 of these priceless works were stolen, including a rare Rembrandt seascape, *Storm on the Sea of Galilee*, then conservatively valued in the region of $200 million.

Museum of Fine Arts ㉗

Avenue of the Arts, 465 Huntington Ave. ***Tel*** *(617) 267-9300. Ⓣ MFA.*
10am–4:45pm Sat–Tue, 10am–9:45pm Wed–Fri (selected collections Thu & Fri). Jan 1, 3rd Mon in Apr, Jul 4, Thanksgiving, Dec 25.
Lectures, concerts, & films.
www.mfa.org

The largest art museum in New England, and one of the five largest in the US, the Museum of Fine Arts (MFA)

Central courtyard of the *palazzo*-style Isabella Stewart Gardner Museum

Japanese Temple Room, Museum of Fine Arts

has a permanent collection of approximately 450,000 objects, ranging from Egyptian artifacts to modern American paintings. Though founded in 1876, the MFA's present Classical-style building dates from 1909, with a west wing designed by I.M. Pei added in 1981. An extensive American Wing is scheduled to open in late 2010. Visitors are advised to check in advance for information on temporary gallery closings or works not on display during construction.

The Museum of Fine Art's excellent collection of ancient **Egyptian and Nubian Art** is unparalleled outside of Africa and derives primarily from the MFA-Harvard University excavations along the Nile, which began in 1905. It also includes a wonderful collection of mummies that is located on the first floor. The adjacent gallery of Ancient Near Eastern Art exhibits Babylonian, Assyrian, and Sumerian reliefs. On the second floor are several monumental sculptures of Nubian kings, dating from the 7th to 6th centuries BC.

Egyptian mummies

The MFA boasts one of America's top holdings of **Classical Art** as well. Among the highlights of this collection are Greek figured vases, carved Etruscan sarcophagi, and Roman portrait busts. Also on display are a series of wall panel paintings unearthed in Pompeii in 1901. The collections of **Asian Art** are said to be the most extensive under one roof anywhere in the world. They include Indian sculpture and narrative paintings, and exhibitions of Islamic miniature paintings that keep changing.

A beautiful stairway with carved lions leads to the Chinese and Japanese galleries on the second floor. Outstanding exhibits here include scroll and screen paintings. A highlight of the museum is the serene **Japanese Temple Room**, on the first floor, which is known for its exquisite examples of Buddhist art.

The **European Art** collections date from the 16th to the 20th centuries and begin with Dutch paintings, including several portraits by Rembrandt. The Koch Gallery, with its magnificent wooden coffered ceiling, displays masterpieces by El Greco, Titian, and Rubens.

Boston's 19th-century collectors enriched the MFA with wonderful French art: the museum features several paintings by Pierre François Millet as well as by 19th-century French artists such as Edouard Manet, Pierre-August Renoir, and Edgar Degas. It also has several paintings by Van Gogh, and holds the most important Monet collection outside of Paris. One of the most popular galleries displays *La Japonaise* by Monet and *Dance at Bougival* by Renoir. Some of the extensive European decorative arts collections remain in storage during the reconstruction works.

The **American Painting Galleries** on the first floor begin with portraits by the Boston artist John Singleton Copley, perhaps America's most talented 18th-century painter. Farther on are lush society portraits by John Singer Sargent, who also embellished the museum's domed rotunda with fine murals. The large and airy Lane Gallery exhibits the works of 20th-century American masters such as Stuart Davis, Jackson Pollock, and Georgia O'Keeffe.

The exhibits in the superb **American Decorative Arts** galleries include silver tea services made by Paul Revere *(see p142)*; 18th-century Boston-style desks, chests, and tall clocks; and a gallery of ship models and outstanding examples of contemporary crafts. The famed reconstructed rooms from a 19th-century mansion will be reinstalled as part of the American Wing.

In addition to these major collections, the Museum of Fine Arts also has important holdings in the multifarious arts of Africa, Oceania, and the ancient Americas, and collections of musical instruments and manuscripts.

John Singer Sargent's murals on the domed rotunda, MFA

The simple interior of Christ Church in Cambridge

Cambridge ㉘

Ⓣ *Harvard.* 🚌 *1, 69.* ℹ **Harvard Square Information Booth** *(617) 497-1630,* **Cambridge Office of Tourism** *(800) 862-5678, (617) 441-2884.* *Sun.* *River Festival (late Jun).* **www**.harvard.edu, **www**.cambridge-usa.org

Though part of the Greater Boston metropolitan area, Cambridge is a town in its own right, dominated by two world-famous universities, the **Massachusetts Institute of Technology** (MIT) and **Harvard**. It also has a number of sights associated with the American Revolution.

Among them is the historic house on Brattle Street, now known as the **Longfellow National Historic Site**. Built by Colonial-era merchants loyal to the British Crown during the Revolution, it was seized by American revolutionaries, and served as George Washington's headquarters during the Siege of Boston. From 1843 until his death in 1888 it was also the home of the famous poet Henry Wadsworth Longfellow, who wrote his most famous poems, including *The Song of Hiawatha*, here.

Harvard Square is the area's main shopping and entertainment district, full of cafés, inexpensive restaurants, trendy boutiques, and street performers. Harvard's large student population is much in evidence here, adding to the square's lively character.

Cambridge Common, north of Harvard Square, was set aside as a common pasture and military drill ground in the 1630s. It has served as a center for social, religious, and political activity ever since. The Common was used as an army encampment from 1775 to 1776, and a stone here marks the spot where George Washington took command of the Continental Army on July 3, 1775, beneath the Washington Elm. Today, its tree-shaded lawns and playgrounds are popular with families and students.

Christ Church, a short distance south of the Common, was designed in 1761 by Peter Harrison, the architect of Boston's King's Chapel *(see p140)*. In 1775, it served as a barracks for Continental Army troops, who melted down the organ pipes to cast musket balls. The church was restored for services on New Year's Eve, 1775, when George Washington and his wife were among the worshipers.

The 135-acre (55-ha) campus of the Massachusetts Institute of Technology (MIT), one of the world's leading universities in engineering and the sciences, stretches along the Charles River. Among the masterpieces of modern architecture that dot its campus are Eero Saarinen's Kresge Auditorium and Kresge Chapel, and the Wiesner Building designed by I.M. Pei, which houses a noted collection of avant-garde art in the List Visual Art Center. Art and Science are blended in the MIT Museum, with exhibits such as Harold Edgerton's stroboscopic flash photographs and the latest holographic art.

An altogether more old-world atmosphere prevails at the campus of Harvard University, with its red-brick, ivy-covered walls. Founded in 1636, Harvard is the oldest university in the US and one of the world's most prestigious centers of learning. At the heart of the campus, which encompasses more than 400 buildings, is the leafy **Old Harvard Yard**, dotted with student dormitories. Its focal point is the statue of its most famous benefactor, the cleric John Harvard. To the right of the statue is the imposing Widener Library which, with over 3 million volumes, is the third largest in the US. Another impressive building in the Yard is the Memorial Church, built in 1931, whose steeple is modeled on that of the Old North Church *(see p142)*. Standing out amid Harvard's Georgian-style buildings is the Carpenter Center for Visual Arts, designed by the avant-garde French architect Le Corbusier.

A major draw for visitors to Harvard are its outstanding museums. The **Harvard Art Museum** is in a state of flux that is expected to last until at least 2013 while the university renovates and enlarges the main museum building on Quincy Street, and prepares

Students strolling through Harvard Yard

to merge collections that were once distributed among the Fogg Art Museum, the Busch-Reisinger Museum, and the Sackler Museum. The **Fogg Art Museum** focused on European art from the late Middle Ages to the present, with particular strengths in pre-Renaissance and Renaissance painting, as well as the Wertheim Collection of Impressionist and Post-Impressionist art.

The separate **Busch-Reisinger Museum** focused on Germanic art, particularly of the 20th century, and contained works by such masters as Wassily Kandinsky, Paul Klee, Emil Nolde, and Oskar Kokoschka.

The **Sackler Museum** housed a rich collection of ancient Greek and Roman, Asian, Indian, and Near Eastern art, and some of the finest Chinese bronzes outside China. Work from all three museums will be presented in a coherent, integrated fashion in the renovated museum. While work continues on the building, the Sackler is displaying selections from all three museums.

The **Harvard Museum of Natural History** is the public face of three Harvard institutions: the Botanical Museum, the Museum of Comparative Zoology, and the Mineralogical and Geological Museum. Highlights include fascinating exhibits, from dinosaurs to whales to ants, and the "glass flowers" – 3,000 botanically correct, exquisite models of 850 plant species in hand-blown glass, created between 1887 and 1936 by father and son artisans Leopold and Rudolph Blaschka. Don't miss the spectacular geodes or the collections of mysterious meteorites.

The **Peabody Museum of Archaeology and Ethnology**, entered at the opposite side of the building from the Natural History Museum, has impressive collections of Egyptian, North American Indian, and Central American artifacts as well as objects from the South Pacific Islands. Outstanding exhibits include totem carvings by Pacific Northwest tribes, Navajo

Chinese statues from the Sackler Museum's collection

weavings, artifacts from the Lewis & Clark Expedition, and casts of objects unearthed at Chichen Itza in Mexico and Copán in Honduras.

Harvard Art Museum
485 Broadway.
Tel *(617) 495-9400.*
10am–5pm Mon–Sat, 1–5pm Sun. *public hols.*
www.artmuseums.harvard.edu

Peabody Museum of Archaeology & Ethnology
11 Divinity St.
Tel *(617) 496-1027.*
9am–5pm daily. *Jan 1, Jul 4, Thanksgiving, Dec 24 & 25.*
www.peabody.harvard.edu

Harvard Museum of Natural History
26 Oxford St. ***Tel*** *(617) 495-3045.*
9am–5pm daily. *Jul 4, Thanksgiving, Dec 24 & 25.*
www.hmnh.harvard.edu

Charlestown ㉙

Community College. *93.* *from Long Wharf.* *Wed.* *Jun 24.*

Historic Charlestown, its picturesque streets lined with Colonial houses, is the site of the infamous battle of Bunker Hill, which took place on June 17, 1775. This was the Revolution's first pitched battle between British and Colonial troops, and though the latter lost, they made a courageous stand, inflicting huge losses on the much larger British force. The **Bunker Hill Monument**, a 221-ft (67-m) granite obelisk, dedicated in 1843, commemorates this event. The building has no elevator but 294 stone steps lead to the top where climbers are rewarded with spectacular views of Boston Harbor and the new Zakim Bridge, the new northern gateway to Boston (staircase closes at 4:30pm). Exhibits in the base of the monument explain the history and significance of the battle, which bought time for Continental Army forces to assemble to keep the British occupying forces penned up on the Boston peninsula.

Charlestown Navy Yard, established in 1800, is the home of America's most famous warship, the USS *Constitution*. Built in 1797, and nicknamed "Old Ironsides" *(see p137)*, she is the oldest commissioned warship afloat and a veteran of 42 victorious battles at sea. Thoroughly overhauled for the 1997 bicentennial, she is taken out into the harbor on July 4 each year for a turnaround that reverses her position at the pier. Visitors must pass a security check before boarding.

Environs

The Colonial town of **Lexington**, 16 miles (26 km) northwest of Boston, is the site of the first bloody skirmish between armed colonists, called Minutemen, and British troops. This battle, on April 19, 1775, acted as a catalyst for the Revolutionary War *(see p44)*. The Lexington Battle Green, with its Minute Man statue, is the focal point of the town. Three historic buildings associated with the battle and maintained by the local Historical Society are open to visitors seasonally.

Granite obelisk of the Bunker Hill Monument in Charlestown

Massachusetts

Of all the New England states, Massachusetts may have the most diverse mix of natural and man-made attractions. Scenic seascapes and picturesque villages beckon along the eastern seaboard and Cape Cod. Venturing inland, visitors will find historic towns where America's early architecture has been well preserved. In the west, green mountains and valleys, and rich culture characterize the Berkshire Hills.

Salem ❷

38,000. From Boston's Long Wharf. 2 New Liberty St, (978) 740-1650. Haunted Halloween (Oct). **www**.salem.org

This coastal town, founded in 1626, is best known for the infamous witch trials of 1692, which resulted in the execution of 20 innocent people. A chilling, multi-media re-enactment of the witch-hunt and subsequent trials can be seen at the **Salem Witch Museum**.

In the 18th and 19th centuries, Salem was one of New England's busiest ports, its harbor filled with ships carrying treasures from around the globe. The **Peabody Essex Museum** contains some of the world's deepest holdings of Asian art and artifacts. Many of the museum's exhibits, such as jewelry, porcelain figures, costumes, and scrimshaw objects, were brought back from distant shores by Salem's sea captains. The town's historic waterfront has been preserved as the **Salem Maritime National Historic Site**. It maintains three restored 18th-century wharves and a reconstructed East Indiaman sailing ship built in 1797, the *Friendship*, which is moored at the dock.

Peabody Essex Museum
East India Sq. ***Tel*** *(978) 745-9500, (866) 745-1876. 10am–5pm Tue–Sun.* **www**.pem.org

Environs
Marblehead, just 4 miles (6 km) from Salem, is a picturesque and historic seaport village, with historic buildings, mansions, and cottages, most notable of which are Abbot Hall and the Jeremiah Lee Mansion.

Lowell ❸

103,000. 246 Market St, (978) 970-5000.

Lowell has the distinction of being the country's first industrial city. In the early 19th century, the first cloth mill equipped with a power loom opened here, and the town soon had a number of giant mill complexes. But after the Great Depression *(see p49)* the mills closed down, leaving Lowell a ghost town. Since 1978, many downtown buildings have been restored and the Lowell National Historical Park traces the history of the town's textile industry. Lowell is also home to the **New England Quilt Museum**, which has a varied collection of displays of beautiful antique as well as contemporary quilts.

Early accused: Rebecca Nurse

SALEM WITCH TRIALS

In 1692, Salem was swept by a wave of hysteria in which 200 citizens were accused of practicing witchcraft. In all, 150 people were jailed and 19 were hanged as witches, while another man was crushed to death with stones. No one was safe: two dogs were executed on the gallows for being witches. Not surprisingly, when the governor's wife became a suspect, the trials came to an abrupt and officially sanctioned end.

Concord's Old Manse, home to 19th-century literary giants

Concord ❹

17,750. 58 Main St, (978) 369-3120. Battle of Concord Re-enactment (Apr). **www**.concordmachamberofcommerce.org

This peaceful, prosperous town has an eventful past. It was here that the Battle of Concord took place on April 19, 1775 which, together with the battle at nearby Lexington *(see p149)*, signaled the beginning of the Revolutionary War. The 900-acre (400-ha) **Minute Man National Historical Park** preserves the site of the battle, where a group of ordinary citizens and colonist farmers, known as Minutemen *(see p44)*, fought against British troops, driving them back from the park's North Bridge and chasing them back to Boston.

In the 19th century, Concord blossomed into the literary heart and soul of the country, with many writers establishing homes here. Both Ralph Waldo Emerson and Nathaniel Hawthorne lived briefly in **The Old Manse**; Emerson lived for nearly 50 years, until his death in 1882, at **Emerson House**, where his furniture, books, and memorabilia are on display.

Also in Concord is **Walden Pond**, immortalized in the writings of the essayist Henry David Thoreau (1817–62). In his influential work, *Walden; or Life in the Woods*, Thoreau called for a return to simplicity in everyday life and a respect for nature. Walden is widely considered to be the birthplace of the conservationist movement. The pond and its surrounding 333 acres (135 ha) of undeveloped woodland are ideal for walks, swimming, and fishing.

Walden Pond State Reservation
915 Walden St. ***Tel*** *(978) 369-3254.*
call for hours.

Plymouth 5

52,000. to Provincetown (seasonal). 130 Water St, (508) 747-7533, (800) USA-1620.
www.visit-plymouth.com

***Mayflower II*, replica of the original Pilgrim ship, in Plymouth**

The ship *Mayflower*, with 102 Pilgrims aboard, sailed into Plymouth Harbor in 1620 and established the first permanent European settlement in New England. Today the town bustles with visitors exploring the sites of America's earliest days, including **Plimoth Plantation**. Plymouth itself is a popular seaside resort, with a 3.5-mile (6-km) beach, offering harbor cruises and fishing excursions. In the fall, the surrounding bogs turn ruby red as the annual cranberry harvest gets underway.

Most of the historic sights can be accessed on foot by the Pilgrim Path that stretches along the waterfront and downtown areas. A sightseeing trolley also connects points of interest. At the Harbor is **Plymouth Rock**, a boulder marking the spot where the Pilgrims are said to have first stepped ashore. Moored by it is the **Mayflower II**, a replica of the 17th-century sailing ship that carried the Pilgrims over from England. Many of those who survived the brutal crossing on this small, cramped ship succumbed to illness and malnutrition during their first winter in Plymouth. They are buried across the street on **Coles Hill**, where there is a statue of the Indian chief Massasoit, who became an ally of the survivors. There is a panoramic view of the harbor from here.

The **Pilgrim Hall Museum**, opened in 1824 has the largest existing collection of Pilgrim-era furniture, armor, and decorative arts. There are also several historic homes, including the 1677 **Harlow Old Fort House**, one of the few remaining 17th-century buildings in the town. It is operated by the Plymouth Antiquarian Society.

Plimoth Plantation
Rte 3A. *137 Warren Ave, (508) 746-1622. late Mar–Nov: 9:30am–5pm daily. limited access to certain parts of site; wheelchairs available on request.* **www**.plimoth.org

PLIMOTH PLANTATION

Encircled by a palisade, Plimoth Plantation is a re-creation of the Pilgrims' 1627 village, complete with costumed interpreters, portraying actual colonists, each with a story to tell. The Wampanoag Homesite depicts Native American life before settlers arrived.

Storehouse
Provisions were stored here, along with furs and other goods to be shipped to England.

Hopkins House
Stephen Hopkins' wife gave birth to their son Oceanus on the Mayflower.

Allerton House
The roof of this house is thatched with the long-lasting, virtually waterproof local reeds.

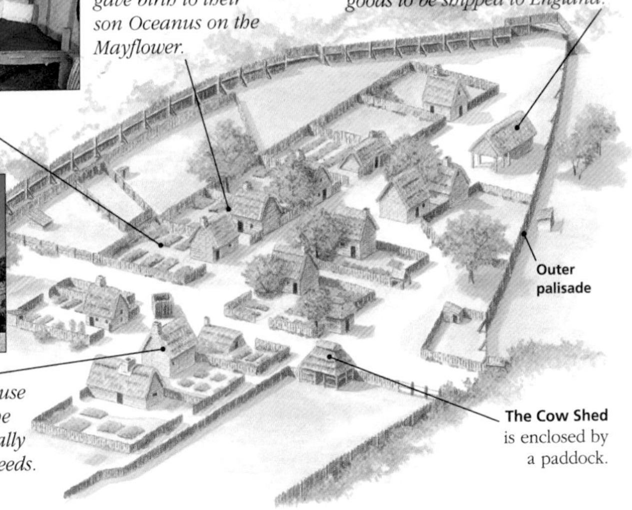

Cape Cod's Old Harbor Life-Saving Station, built in 1897

Cape Cod 6

Elm Ave, Hyannis. Ocean St, Hyannis; Railroad Ave, Woods Hole. Jct Rtes 132 & 6, Rte 25, Hyannis, (508) 362-3225, (888) 332-2732. Cape Cod Maritime Week (May), Annual Bourne Scallop Festival (Sep).

More than 13 million people arrive each summer to enjoy the boundless beaches, natural beauty, and quaint Colonial villages of Cape Cod, and the neighboring islands of Martha's Vineyard and Nantucket. A special attraction for visitors are whale-watching cruises, offered from April to mid-October. The Cape, shaped like an upraised arm bent at the elbow, extends some 70 miles (113 km) into the sea.

Cape Cod National Seashore, stretching more than 40 miles (64 km) along the northernmost section of the Cape, from Provincetown to Chatham, is famous for its horseshoe-shaped dunes, white sand beaches, salt marshes, glacial cliffs, and woodlands. Historical structures, such as the **Old Harbor Life-Saving Station** and the 18th-century Atwood Higgins House, are interspersed among the area's beautiful natural features.

One of the most popular destinations on the Cape is **Provincetown**. This picturesque town has a historic past – the Pilgrims first landed here in 1620 and stayed for five weeks before pushing on to the mainland. The 252-ft (77-m) **Pilgrim Monument**, the tallest granite structure in the US, commemorates this event. Today, Provincetown is especially vibrant during the summer months, when its population swells and it is a leading gay resort. Busy McMillan Wharf is the jumping off point for whale-watching cruises. Since the early 20th century, the town has also had a bustling artists' colony, counting among its famous residents the painters Mark Rothko and Jackson Pollock, and the writers Eugene O'Neill and Tennessee Williams. The work of local artists is also displayed in the Provincetown Art Association and Museum.

Pilgrim Monument

Chatham, an attractive, upscale community, offers fine inns, attractive shops, and a popular summer playhouse. Fishing boats stop and unload their catch at the pier, and the surrounding waters offer good opportunities for seasonal anglers. The Railroad Museum, housed in an 1887 Victorian train station, has photos, memorabilia, and vintage railroad cars.

Hyannis, the largest village in Cape Cod, is a busy shopping center and the main transportation hub for the region. It is also famous as the summer home of the country's most celebrated political dynasty, the Kennedys. The heavily screened Kennedy compound is best seen from the water aboard a sightseeing cruise. At its center is the "cottage" that multi-millionaire Joseph Kennedy (1888–1969) bought in 1926, expanding it into a sprawling vacation retreat for his nine children and their families. The Kennedy clan continues to gather here on family occasions. After John F. Kennedy's assassination in 1963, a simple memorial was erected in the town in his honor: a pool and fountain, and a circular wall bearing Kennedy's profile.

One of Hyannis' most popular forms of transportation is the **Cape Cod Central Railroad**, which offers a scenic two-hour round trip to the Cape Cod canal.

Hiking trails, salt marshes, tidal pools, and 12 miles (19 km) of beaches attract visitors to **Falmouth**, with its picturesque village green. It also has the 3.3-mile (5-km) Shining Sea Bike Path, with vistas of beach, harbor, and woodland. The path leads to the world's largest independent marine science research center, the Woods Hole Oceanographic Institute.

Sandwich, the oldest town in the Cape, is straight off a postcard: a church overlooking a picturesque pond, fed by a brook that powers the waterwheel of a Colonial-era gristmill. The church bell, dating to 1675, is said to be the oldest in the US. The town's most unusual attraction is **Heritage Museums & Gardens**, a 75-acre (30-ha) garden and museum housing the eclectic collection of the pharmaceutical tycoon, Josiah K. Lilly Jr. (1893–1966). Exhibits include 37 antique cars, Native American relics, and a 1912 carousel. The gardens are famous for their lovely rhododendrons. Just a 45-minute boatride away from the mainland lies

Popular sightseeing trip on the Cape Cod Central Railroad

For hotels and restaurants in this region see p178 and p183

Fishing boat moored outside a fishing shack, Martha's Vineyard

Martha's Vineyard. This 108-sq mile (280-sq km) island combines mesmerizing scenic beauty with the charms of a beach resort and abounds in opportunities for outdoor activities. Each town has its own distinctive atmosphere and architectural style.

Most visitors arrive by ferry at the island's commercial hub, Vineyard Haven. On the eastern shore is Edgartown, with the gracious 19th-century homes of the town's wealthy sea captains and merchants. The **Martha's Vineyard Historical Society** is housed in one of them – the Thomas Cooke House (c.1730), filled with antique furniture and ship models. From here, a short ferry ride goes to Chappaquiddick Island, where in 1969, a car driven by Senator Edward Kennedy went off the bridge, killing a woman passenger.

North of Edgartown is Oak Bluff, with its gingerbread cottages, while the Western Shoreline is tranquil and rural with pristine beaches.

Nantucket Island, a 14-mile (22-km) long enclave of tranquility with only one town, remains a largely untamed world of kettle ponds, quiet beaches, cranberry bogs, and fields of wild grapes and blueberries, punctuated by occasional houses. Nantucket was a prosperous center of the whaling industry in the early 1800s, and the mansions of sea captains and merchants reflect those glory days. The **Nantucket Historical Association** (NHA) operates 11 historical buildings in the town, one of which houses a fascinating Whaling Museum. A popular spot, 8 miles (13 km) from town, is Siasconset village, famous for its rose-colored bluffs and lanes with tiny cottages.

Cape Cod National Seashore
Rte 6, Cape Cod. *Salt Pond Visitor Center, Rte 6, Eastham, (508) 255-3421. year-round.*
www.nps.gov/caco

Heritage Museums & Gardens
67 Grove St, Sandwich. ***Tel*** *(508) 888-3300. Apr–Oct: 10am–5pm daily.* **www**.heritagemuseumsandgardens.org

Martha's Vineyard Historical Society
59 School St, Edgartown. ***Tel*** *(508) 627-4441. mid-Jun–Sep: 10am–5pm Tue–Sat; Oct–mid-Jun: 1–4pm Wed–Fri, 10am–4pm Sat; Jan–Feb:10am–4pm Sat.*

Nantucket Historical Association (NHA)
15 Broad St, Nantucket Island. ***Tel*** *(508) 228-1894.* **Historic buildings** *call for hours. Whaling Museum only.*
www.nha.org

Sturbridge 7

Old Sturbridge Village Rte 20, Sturbridge. ***Tel*** *(508) 347-3362. early Apr–late Oct: 9:30am–5pm daily; late Oct–early Apr: 9:30am–4pm Tue–Sun. Dec 25.* **www**.osv.org

This small town is home to **Old Sturbridge Village**, an open-air museum in the form of an early 19th-century village. At the heart of the museum are about 40 vintage buildings that have been restored and relocated from all over New England. They include the Federal-style Towne House, a meeting-house, a tavern, and a store, with authentic period settings.

The Berkshires 8

Pittsfield. 3 Hoosac St, Adams, (413) 743-4500. **www**.berkshires.org

Wooded hills, green valleys, rippling rivers, and waterfalls have long attracted visitors to this western corner of Massachusetts, which is rich in opportunities for outdoor as well as cultural activity. The area is speckled with scenic small towns and villages. **Pittsfield**, in the shadow of Mount Greylock, is famous as the home of Herman Melville (1819–91), where he wrote his masterpiece, *Moby Dick*. **Lenox** has the grand estates of prominent families such as the Carnegies. It also hosts the prestigious Tanglewood Musical Festival every summer. The main street of **Stockbridge** has been immortalized in the paintings of one of America's most beloved illustrators, Norman Rockwell (1894–1978), who lived here for 25 years. His works can be seen in the town's **Norman Rockwell Museum**.

Especially attractive to nature lovers is the **Mount Washington State Forest**, and the Mount Everett State Forest, nearby.

Norman Rockwell Museum
Rte 183. ***Tel*** *(413) 298-4100. May–Oct: 10am–5pm daily; Nov–Apr: 10am–4pm Mon–Fri, 10am–5pm Sat–Sun. Jan 1, Thanksgiving, Dec 25.*
www.nrm.org

Bash Bish Falls, Mount Washington State Forest in the Berkshires

Rhode Island

The smallest state in America, Rhode Island is not an island at all but has a shoreline dotted with lovely islets and beaches. Although known as the Ocean State, half of Rhode Island is woodland, ideal for nature walks and camping. The state's two major cities are Providence, the lively capital, and Newport, which has some of New England's most opulent mansions.

Stately buildings along Benefit Street's Mile of History in Providence

Providence 9

174,000. Providence Station, 100 Gaspee St. 1 Bonanza Way. Point St (to Newport). 1 Sabin St, (401) 274-1636 or (800) 233-1636. Festival of Historic Houses (Jun–Dec); International Film Festival (Aug).
www.goprovidence.com

Perched on seven hills on the banks of Narragansett Bay, Providence is an interesting blend of the historic and the modern. It started life as a farming community, established in 1636 by the clergyman Roger Williams, who was driven from the Massachusetts Bay colony for his outspoken beliefs on religious freedom. It soon became a flourishing seaport, and then evolved into a hub of industry in the 19th century, with immigrants from Europe pouring in to work in its textile mills.

Providence is bisected by the Providence River. On its west bank is the downtown district, revitalized by recent renewal projects, which have restored old buildings, constructed new malls and markets, and developed the waterfront. To the east is the campus of Brown University and several historic streets. The most outstanding of these is **Benefit Street's Mile of History**. This lovely tree-lined street has more than 100 houses ranging in style from Colonial and Federal to Greek Revival and Victorian. Its architectural gems include the **Providence Athenaeum**, a Greek Revival-style library, whose collection dates back to 1753, to the First Unitarian Church. Its 2,500-lb (1,350-kg) bell was one of the largest cast by Paul Revere's foundry. Also on Benefit Street is the Rhode Island School of Design's **RISD Museum of Art**, whose comprehensive collection ranges from Ancient Egyptian to contemporary American art. A short distance to the north, on Main Street, is the **First Baptist Church in America**. Built in 1774–75, it has an intricately carved wooden interior and a Waterford crystal chandelier.

Founded in 1764, **Brown University** is the seventh-oldest college in the US and one of the prestigious Ivy League schools. Its beautiful campus, a rich blend of Gothic and Beaux Arts styles, is worth exploring. Notable buildings here include the John Hay Library with its collection of memorabilia relating to President Abraham Lincoln, the John Carter Brown Library with a fascinating collection of Americana, and the List Art Center, a striking building designed by Philip Johnson, which features classical and contemporary art.

John Brown House, a Georgian mansion, built in 1786 for a wealthy merchant and shipowner, has been impeccably restored. Its interior is decorated with ornate plaster ornamented ceilings, a grand staircase with twisted balusters, and wallpapers from France. Its 12 rooms are a repository for some of the finest furniture and antiques of that period. Nearby, another house with fine 18th-century furnishings is the 1707 **Governor Stephen Hopkins House**.

One of the brightest additions to downtown Providence is **Waterplace Park and Riverwalk**, a 4-acre (1.6-ha) walkway located at the junction of three rivers – the Moshassuck, Providence, and Woonasquatucket. Visitors can also stroll along the park's cobblestone paths, float under footbridges in

Roger Williams Park and Zoo, a highlight of downtown Providence

For hotels and restaurants in this region see p179 and p184

canoes or gondolas, and enjoy free concerts at the amphitheater during the summer season.

Another successful downtown renewal project is **The Arcade**, an 1828 Greek Revival building that covers an entire block in the city's old financial district. The first indoor shopping mall in the US, this massive three-story stone complex with its high Ionic granite columns, has a skylight extending the entire length of the building, providing light even on rainy days. Restored in 1980, the arcade closed in 2008 so that an $8 million restoration could be carried out.

Downtown Providence is dominated by the imposing **Rhode Island State House** constructed in 1904. Its magnificent white marble dome is topped by a bronze statue called *Independent Man*, a symbol of Rhode Island's free spirit. Among the displays inside are the original state charter of 1663 and a full-length portrait of President George Washington by Gilbert Stuart.

The city's largest green space is the **Roger Williams Park and Zoo**. Once farmland, this 422-acre (171-ha) park now holds gardens, greenhouses, and ponds, a lake with paddleboats and rowboats, as well as jogging and cycling tracks and a tennis center. Children especially love the carousel rides and train, the planetarium, and the Museum of Natural History. The highlight of the park, however, is the zoo, which has more than 900 animals, including mammals such as zebras, giraffes, and cheetahs. An underwater window allows visitors to look at the penguins and polar bears as they cavort playfully in the water.

Rhode Island State House with its marble dome

RISD Museum of Art
224 Benefit St. ***Tel*** *(401) 454-6500.*
10am–5pm Tue–Sun, 10am–9pm third Thu of month. *public hols.*
www.risd.edu

John Brown House
52 Power St. ***Tel*** *(401) 273-7507.*
Jan–Mar: 10:30am–3pm Fri & Sat; Apr–Dec: 10:30am–3pm Tue–Sat.
Mon & public hols.

Rhode Island State House
82 Smith St. ***Tel*** *(401) 222-2357.*
8:30am–4:30pm Mon–Fri.
public hols. *self-guided, others by appt.*

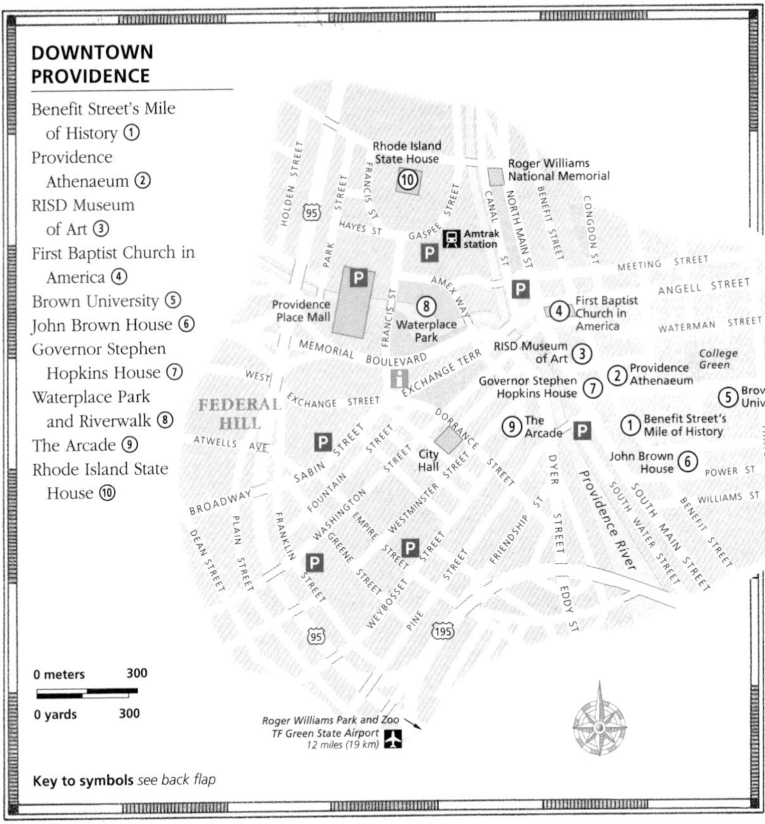

Scores of yachts in the harbor at Newport

Newport ⑩

28,000. Gateway Center, 23 America's Cup Ave. Perrotti Park (to Providence). 23 America's Cup Ave, (401) 849-8048, (800) 976-5122. Newport Tennis Week (Jul), JVC Jazz Festival (Aug). **www**.gonewport.com

A center of trade, culture, wealth, and military activity for more than 300 years, Newport is a true sightseeing mecca. The town's main attractions are its mansions, most of them located on Bellevue Avenue on the southeastern side of the city. Built between 1748 and 1902, when the rich and famous flocked here each summer to beat New York's heat, these summer "cottage" retreats of the country's wealthiest families, such as the Vanderbilts and the Astors, are some of America's grandest private homes. Modeled on European palaces and decorated with the finest artworks, the mansions were used for only 10 weeks of the year. **The Breakers** is one of the finest examples.

Newport is also home to the oldest synagogue in USA. Built in 1763 by Sephardic Jews who had fled Spain and Portugal in search of religious tolerance, the **Touro Synagogue** is an outstanding example of 18th-century architecture. It is located just east of Washington Square where a number of historic Colonial buildings have been preserved. Among them is the seasonal Brick Market Museum and Shop housed in the market, which was the center of commerce in Colonial times. Also on the Square is the White Horse Tavern *(see p184)*, which claims to be the oldest continuously operating tavern in America; it was granted its liquor license in 1673.

Apart from its mansions and historic sites, Newport also has numerous outdoor attractions. South of

THE BREAKERS

The architecture and ostentation of the Gilded Age of the late 1800s reached its pinnacle with The Breakers, the summer home of the railroad magnate Cornelius Vanderbilt II (1843–99). Completed in 1895, the four-story, 70-room limestone mansion was modeled after 16th-century palaces in Turin and Genoa. Its interior is adorned with marble, stained glass, gilt, and crystal.

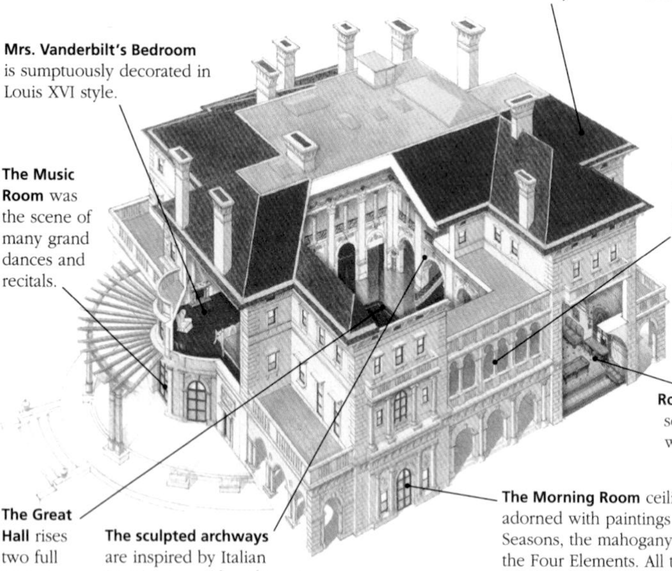

The Dining Room, a two-story room, has a stunning arched ceiling and two huge crystal chandeliers.

Mrs. Vanderbilt's Bedroom is sumptuously decorated in Louis XVI style.

The Upper Loggia has enchanting views of the Atlantic Ocean.

The Music Room was the scene of many grand dances and recitals.

The Billiard Room features several costly wall marbles.

The Morning Room ceiling is adorned with paintings of the Four Seasons, the mahogany doors with the Four Elements. All the cornices and panels were made in France.

The Great Hall rises two full stories.

The sculpted archways are inspired by Italian Renaissance-style palazzos.

The breathtaking Cliff Walk, popular with visitors in Newport

Washington Square is **Fort Adams State Park**, with Fort Adams, built in 1853, as its centerpiece. No longer in use as a garrison, the fort is surrounded with facilities for swimming and other sports. Each year, Newport's famous Jazz Festival is held here. The park also has the Museum of Yachting, with a collection of luxury yachts.

Another popular site is the 3.5-mile (5.5-km) long **Cliff Walk**, southwest of downtown. The trail, along the city's ragged cliffs, offers some fine views of the Gilded-Age mansions and has been designated a National Recreation Trail in 1975. The Forty Steps, each named for someone lost at sea, lead to the ocean.

The Breakers
Ochre Point Ave. ***Tel*** *(401) 847-1000.* *mid-Apr–Oct: 9am–5pm daily. Call for winter hours.* *Thanksgiving, Dec 24 & 25.* *every 15 minutes.* **www**.newportmansions.org

Touro Synagogue
85 Touro St. ***Tel*** *(401) 847-4794.* *call for times.* *every half hour.* *Shabbat & all Jewish hols.*

Fort Adams State Park
Harrison Ave. ***Tel*** *(401) 847-2400.* *sunrise to sunset daily.* **Museum of Yachting** ***Tel*** *(401) 847-1018.* *mid-May–Oct: 10am–5pm daily; Nov–mid-May: by appt.*

South County Beaches ⓫

Narragansett *36 Ocean Rd, (401) 783-7121.*
Charlestown *4945 Old Post Rd, (401) 364-3878.*

Southwest of Newport, between **Narragansett** and Watch Hill, are some 100 miles (161 km) of pristine white sand beaches and a series of tidal salt ponds. The ponds are big lures for birdwatchers hoping to study the egrets, sandpipers, and herons that swim and wade in the salty marshes. Many of the beaches are free to the public, except for parking fees. **Scarborough State Beach** is excellent for bodysurfing and surfboarding, while the sheltered, cove-protected **Roger Wheeler State Beach** is a favorite for families. **East Matunuck State Beach** is popular with surfers on windy days. The beautiful sandy stretch of **Charlestown Town Beach** has a boat ramp with access to the coastal ponds of the Ninigret National Wildlife Refuge.

Plaque to early English pioneers, Settlers Rock, Block Island

Farther west along the coast is **Misquamicut State Beach**. The largest beach in the state, it has gentle surf and an old-time amusement park with rides and many diversions for children.

Block Island ⓬

State Pier, Galilee. Ferries carry cars by advance bookings, (401) 783-7996. **www**.blockislandferry.com

Lying just 13 miles (21 km) off the coast, Block Island is a great destination for outdoor enthusiasts who enjoy such activities as swimming, fishing, sailing, bird-watching, canoeing, and horseback riding. Some 30 miles (48 km) of natural trails entice hikers and cyclists to experience the island's natural beauty.

The village of **Old Harbor** is the island's main hub of activity. Victorian houses, hotels, and shops line the streets, and anglers can charter boats to fish for striped bass, bluefish, flounder, and cod. South of the village are the dramatic 200-ft (61-m) high red clay cliffs of **Mohegan Bluffs**, and the Southeast Lighthouse, which was once the most powerful in New England.

A favorite with hikers is **Rodman's Hollow Natural Area**. This glacial depression, well marked with nature trails, is a refuge for hawks and white-tailed deer.

On Block Island's northwestern coast is **Great Salt Pond**, which is completely protected from the ocean. It is an excellent spot for kayaking and fishing. Nearby New Harbor is the island's prime marina and boating center. **Clayhead**, on the island's northeastern coast, offers wonderful views of the Atlantic Ocean, and is the starting point for a nature trail that goes all the way north to **Settler's Rock**. A plaque here honors the 16 Englishmen who landed here in 1661. The rock is at the edge of Sachem Pond, a favorite for swimming and kayaking. An 18-mile (29-km) driving tour of Block Island is a comfortable way to take in all these sites.

The dramatic red clay cliffs at Mohegan Bluffs, Block Island

Connecticut

Although compact enough to cross in a few hours, Connecticut has treasures that entice visitors to stay for days. Along its magnificent shoreline are beaches, marinas, and the remarkable maritime museum at Mystic Seaport. Inland, the Connecticut River Valley and the Litchfield Hills are dotted with scenic and historic villages. Hartford, the bustling capital, and New Haven, home of Yale University, are its main cities.

Hartford ⓭

139,000. 1 Union Place. 45 Pratt St, 4th floor, (860) 244-8181, (800) 793-4480. Mark Twain Days (summer).
www.enjoyhartford.com

Founded in 1636 by a group of English settlers from the Massachusetts Bay Colony, Hartford's golden age was in the 19th century when it became a flourishing center of the insurance industry. It also became a vibrant cultural center, thanks to resident authors such as Mark Twain. In recent years, an ambitious revitalization program has breathed new life into the city.

Dominating the cityscape is the gleaming gold-leaf dome of the **State Capitol**, a Victorian-Gothic building perched on a hilltop. Many of Hartford's attractions are accessible on foot from here. The Capitol overlooks the 40-acre (16-ha) **Bushnell Park**, the creation of Hartford native Frederick Law Olmsted (1822–1903), who also laid out New York's Central Park. There are 100 varieties of trees, and a 1914 carousel with 48 hand-carved horses.

The 1796 **Old State House**, designed by Charles Bulfinch *(see p134)*, is the country's oldest Capitol building. With its grand center hall and staircase, and ornate cupola, it is a superb example of Federal architecture. Nearby, the **Center Church** has five stained-glass windows designed by the US artist Louis Comfort Tiffany (1848–1933). To its south is the **Wadsworth Atheneum**, the oldest continuously operating public art museum in the country. Its collection includes Renaissance, Baroque, and Impressionist art, as well as works by American artists.

West of downtown is the 1874 **Mark Twain House and Museum**, a Gothic-style masterpiece with peaked gables, expansive upper balconies, and towering turrets. Constructed at the height of Twain's career, the 19-room home was based on a floor plan drawn up by his wife Olivia. Of special interest are

The Connecticut State Capitol, overlooking Bushnell Park

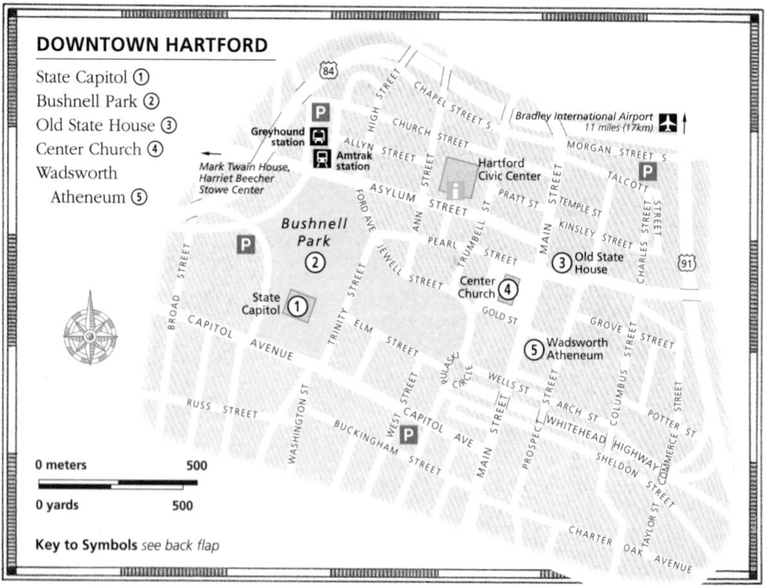

The Billiard Room, Mark Twain House, Hartford

the library with its ornate wooden fireplace mantel; the tranquil Billiard Room where Twain wrote some of his best known works, including *The Adventures of Tom Sawyer*; and the Master Bedroom with its beautifully carved bed. An informative visitor center illuminates Twain's life and work.

Next door is the **Harriet Beecher Stowe Center**, where the famous author of the anti-slavery novel, *Uncle Tom's Cabin* (1852), lived until her death in 1896. The house is adorned with gingerbread ornamentation typical of late 19th-century Victorian design, while the elegance of its interior displays Harriet's less well-known talent as a decorator.

Mark Twain House and Museum
351 Farmington Ave. ***Tel*** *(860) 247-0998. 9:30am–5:30pm Mon–Sat; noon–5:30pm Sun. Tue (Jan–Mar), Jan 1, Easter Sun, Thanksgiving. obligatory. 1st floor only.*
www.marktwainhouse.org

Litchfield ⓮

8,850. Litchfield Hills Visitors' Bureau, PO Box 968, (860) 567-4506.
www.northwestct.com

This picturesque and historic town is at the center of the Litchfield Hills region in northwestern Connecticut, which many people consider the most scenic part of the state. Anchored by the Housatonic River, the bucolic landscape of lovely woods, valleys, lakes, and wildlife offers great opportunities for sports such as canoeing, kayaking, whitewater rafting, tubing, fly-fishing, and hiking. In fall, the brilliant foliage along the region's roads entrances sightseers. Litchfield's many historic houses include the 1784 **Tapping Reeve House** and Law School, the country's first law school. On the outskirts of the town, on Route 202, **Mount Tom State Park** has trails leading to the 1,325-ft (404-m) summit. The lake is ideal for activities such as scuba diving, swimming, boating, and fishing.

Connecticut River Valley ⓯

Windsor *27,800. Hartford, (860) 244-8181.* **Old Lyme** *6,800. 32 Huntington St, New London, (860) 444-2206, (800) 863-6569.*
www.mysticcountry.com

The Connecticut River Valley is dotted with picture-postcard perfect little towns and villages. **Windsor**, settled in the early 1630s by Pilgrims from Plymouth *(see p151)* has a number of historic houses, open to visitors, such as the 1758 John & Sarah Strong House with its fine furnishings. Nearby is the Palisado Green, where nervous settlers built a walled stockade in their 1637 war with the Pequot Indians.

Wethersfield, settled in 1634, stands as a primer of American architecture from the 18th to the 20th centuries. Especially worth visiting is the Webb-Deane-Stevens Museum, which is a trio of dwellings that depict the lifestyles of three different 18th-century Americans – a diplomat, a wealthy merchant, and a leather tanner. The **Dinosaur State Park**, farther south, preserves some 500 prehistoric dinosaur tracks beneath a geodesic dome. It also has a display of a life-sized model of an 8-ft (2-m) tall Dilophosaurus.

Just outside the town of East Haddam is the bizarre and ostentatious **Gillette Castle**, built in 1919 by the actor William Gillette. This 24-room granite mansion is built like a medieval castle, complete with battlements and turrets, and is rife with oddities such as Gillette's homemade trick locks and furniture set on wheels and tracks.

Picturesque Old Lyme boasts several 18th- and 19th-century houses built for sea captains. It is also renowned for the **Florence Griswold Museum**, housed in an 1817 mansion. Paintings by some of America's leading artists, such as Childe Hassam and Clark Voorhees, adorn the walls of this museum, together with superb works by other artists who lived in art patron Florence Griswold's house and painted on its wall panels to repay her generosity.

Wethersfield
Greater Hartford Tourism District, 31 Pratt St, Hartford, (860) 244-8181, (800) 793-4480.
www.enjoyhartford.com

Gillette Castle
67 River Rd off Rte 82, Hadlyme. ***Tel*** *(860) 526-2336. late May–Columbus Day 10am–4:30pm daily.*

Florence Griswold Museum
96 Lyme St, Old Lyme. ***Tel*** *(860) 434-5542. 10am–5pm Tue–Sat, 1–5pm Sun.* **www**.flogris.org

The Harpist **by Alphonse Jongers at the Florence Griswold Museum**

New Haven 16

123, 626. 169 Orange St, (203) 777-8550. www.visitnewhaven.com **Yale University** Dwight Hall, (203) 432-2300. International Festival of Arts and Ideas (Jun). www.yale.edu

Founded in 1638, New Haven is located on the coast, where three rivers flow into Long Island Sound. Although this has helped make it a major manufacturing center, the city is better known as the home of **Yale University**, one of the world's most prestigious institutions of higher learning. Its alumni include no less than four American presidents, including the Bushes Sr. and Jr, and Bill Clinton. Yale, founded in 1701, has made New Haven a leading center for education, research, and technology, and has enriched its cultural life as well.

Tiffany stained-glass window, First Church of Christ

The main area of the town is the 16-acre (6-ha) **New Haven Green**, serving as the setting for many of New Haven's activities and festivals. Three beautiful early 19th-century churches are located on the Green, of which the **First Church of Christ**, with a Tiffany stained-glass window, is regarded as a masterpiece of American Georgian style.

Much of the core of downtown New Haven is covered by the Yale University campus, dotted with Georgian and Neo-Gothic buildings, as well as modern structures designed by Eero Saarinen and Philip Johnson. Major landmarks on the campus are the beautiful Gothic-style Memorial Quadrangle and the Harkness Tower, whose carillon rings out at intervals through the day.

Yale's outstanding museums are a prime attraction for visitors. The **Yale Center for British Art**, whose collection was donated by the philanthropist Paul Mellon (1907–99), has the largest collection of British art outside the UK and includes paintings by Gainsborough, Hogarth, and Turner. The treasures of the **Beinecke Rare Book and Manuscript Libraries** include one of the world's few remaining Gutenberg Bibles. The **Yale University Art Gallery**, reflecting the generosity and taste of the Yale alumni, houses works by artists such as Picasso, Van Gogh, Manet, and Monet, while the **Peabody Museum of Natural History** is famous for its collection of dinosaurs.

A must for the musically inclined is the **Yale Collection of Musical Instruments**. Its stunning exhibits consist of violins and harpsichords dating back centuries. These historical instruments are still played at concerts held here today.

Entrance to the Peabody Museum of Natural History, Yale University

The most popular park in New Haven is the 84-acre (34-ha) Lighthouse Point Park on Long Island Sound. It has nature trails, a bird sanctuary, as well as an 1840 lighthouse.

Yale Center for British Art
1080 Chapel St. *Tel (203) 432-2800.* *10am–5pm Tue–Sat, noon–5pm Sun.* *public hols.*

Beinecke Rare Book & Manuscript Libraries
121 Wall St. *Tel (203) 432-2977.* *8:30am–8pm Mon–Thu, 8:30am–5pm Fri, 10am–5pm Sat.* *Sat in Aug & public hols.*

Yale University Art Gallery
1111 Chapel St. *Tel (203) 432-0600.* *10am–5pm Tue–Sat (upto 8pm on Thu), 1–6pm Sun.* *public hols.* www.artgallery.yale.edu

Church spires around New Haven Green, the focal point of the town

For hotels and restaurants in this region see p179 and p184

The *Charles W. Morgan*, the last wooden whaling ship, in Mystic Seaport

Connecticut Coast ⑰

Mystic *2,600.* *14 Holmes St, (860) 572-9578.* **Madison** *16,000.* *22 Scotland Ave, (203) 245-7394.* **Stamford** Fairfield County. *117,083.* *297 West Ave, Norwalk, (203) 853-7770.*

Connecticut's magnificent 105-mile (170-km) long shoreline, is scalloped by coves, inlets, and harbors, dotted with beaches, marinas, and state parks. Historic towns and villages also lie along the coast.

One the most popular tourist destinations along the Connecticut Coast is **Mystic Seaport**. This authentic 18th- and 19th-century seafaring village, where nearly every home sports a nautical motif, also has the world's largest maritime museum. Mystic's main attraction is its preservation shipyard and its fleet of antique ships, including the whaling ship, *Charles W. Morgan*, currently in dry dock, built in 1841. Another highlight is the Mystic River Scale Model, with more than 250 detailed buildings. The impressive Mystic Aquarium has a huge gallery of penguins, stingrays, and sharks, while seals and sea lions can be seen cavorting in the outdoor Seal Island.

A short distance west of Mystic Seaport is **New London**. This historic town was torched by British forces during the American Revolution, but remarkably, many of the houses survived. Among them is the Joshua Hempsted House, built in 1678, which is insulated with seaweed. By the 19th century New London had recovered to become a prosperous center of the whaling industry – the row of colonnaded Greek Revival mansions on Whale Oil Row attest to the affluence of that era.

The resort town of **Madison**, full of antique stores and boutiques, also has several historic homes open for viewing. Among the fascinating artifacts on display at the **Deacon John Grave House** is the family bookkeeping ledger, with entries from 1678 to 1895. Also in Madison is **Hammonasset Beach State Park**, the largest shoreline park in the state, with a 2-mile (3-km) long beach that attracts swimmers, sailors, sunbathers, and divers. Neighboring **Guilford** has a Tudor Gothic-style granite fort. This three-story stronghold, built in 1640 by a group of Puritans settlers to protect themselves against attacks by the local Indians, is the oldest stone dwelling of its kind in New England.

From Guilford's Stony Creek Dock, travelers can cruise to the **Thimble Islands** aboard tour boats that operate in the area, watching seals or taking in the glorious fall colors. Many of the 365 islands are little more than large boulders, but some privately owned islands have small communities. Legend has it that the privateer Captain Kidd (1645–1701) hid plundered treasure on Money Island while being pursued by the British fleet.

The Thimbles, home to seals, whales, and colorful legends

Coastal Fairfield County, in the southernmost corner of the state, has attractions for every taste. The shoreline is dusted with beaches offering a variety of summer recreation opportunities, while naturalists are drawn to its nature preserves and zoo. The area also has numerous art galleries and museums.

Bridgeport is home to the Beardsley Zoo, the Barnum Museum (named after the circus impresario P.T. Barnum who was the town's mayor), and the Discovery Museum.

The charming town of **Westport** on the banks of the Saugatuck River has the Sherwood Island State Park. **Norwalk** has historic buildings, shops, and cafés along its waterfront, as well as a Maritime Aquarium. **New Canaan**, set in a landscape of woods, streams, and rolling fields, is spectacular in fall. **Stamford** has a unique First Presbyterian Church, shaped like a fish, and a lively downtown area.

Greenwich, blessed with a stunning coastline, is home to an art colony, the Bush-Holley Historic Site. A 44-mile (71-km) drive through Fairfield County gives a good overview of the Connecticut coast.

Mystic Seaport
75 Greenmanville Ave (Rte 7).
Tel (860) 572-5315.
Ships & exhibits
Apr–Oct: 9am–5pm; Nov–Mar: 10am–4pm. *Dec 24 & 25.*
www.mysticseaport.com

Deacon John Grave House
Madison, 581 Boston Post Rd.
Tel (203) 245-4798. *May–Sep: 1–4pm Wed–Sat.*

Hammonasset Beach State Park
I-95, exit 62. **Park** *Tel (203) 245-2785.* *8am–dusk daily.*
Campground reservations
Tel (877) 668-2267.

Vermont

Vermont's varied attractions are scattered throughout the state. Historic villages and the natural splendors of the Green Mountain National Forest grace the south, while in the northwest Lake Champlain provides a backdrop for the lively college town of Burlington. Famous ski resorts such as Stowe are perched amid the mountains that run the length of the state. In fall, Vermont's display of leaf colors is spectacular.

Woodward Reservoir in the Green Mountain National Forest

Green Mountain National Forest ⓲

Forest Supervisor, Green Mountain National Forest, 231 N Main St, Rutland. ***Tel*** *(802) 747-6700.*

This huge spine of greenery and mountains runs for 350,000 acres (142,850 ha) – almost the entire length of Vermont – along two-thirds of the Green Mountain Range. The mountains, many of them over 4,000 ft (1,200 m) high, have some of the best ski centers in the US, including Sugarbush and Mount Snow.

The National Forest is divided into northern and southern sectors, and encompasses six wilderness areas, many of them with no roads, electricity, or clearly marked trails. Less primitive areas of the forest, however, have picnic sites, camping grounds, and more than 500 miles (805 km) of hiking paths, including the famous Long and Appalachian Trails. The area's lakes, rivers, and reservoirs offer excellent boating and fishing, and there are designated paths for horseback riders as well as bikers.

In the southwest corner of the Green Mountain National Forest is **Bennington**, Vermont's third-largest city. An important manufacturing center, Bennington is also home to the small but prestigious Bennington College. Three 19th-century wooden covered bridges (just off Route 67) herald the approach to the town, which was established in 1749. A few decades later, Ethan Allen arrived on the scene to lead the Green Mountain Boys, a citizen's militia that scored several decisive victories against British forces during the Revolutionary War.

The town's most prominent landmark is the 306-ft (93-m) high **Bennington Battle Monument**, a granite obelisk commemorating a 1777 battle, when Colonial forces defeated the British. The monument looms over the Old Bennington Historic District, which has a village green ringed by Federal-style brick buildings. The 1806 First Congregational Church is particularly striking, with its vaulted plaster and wood ceilings. Next to the church is the Old Burying Ground where one of America's most loved poets, Robert Frost, is buried. A major attraction for visitors is the **Bennington Museum and Grandma Moses Gallery**. Apart from an impressive collection of Americana, the museum houses several paintings by famed folk artist Anna Mary "Grandma" Moses, who lived in the Bennington area. A farmer's wife with no formal art training, Grandma Moses (1860–1961) started painting landscapes as a hobby when she was in her mid-70s. "Discovered" by critics in 1940, her distinctive primitive paintings soon won international renown.

The 1891 Bennington Battle Monument

Bennington Museum & Grandma Moses Gallery
75 Main St. ***Tel*** *(802) 447-1571.* *10am–5pm Thu–Tue (daily Sep–Oct).* *Jan, Thanksg., Dec 25.*
www.benningtonmuseum.com

Manchester ⓳

3,860. Suite 1, 5046 Main St, (802) 362-2100.

This scenic town, ringed by mountains, is a favorite destination for both shoppers and skiers. Manchester Village and Manchester Center are major outlet centers in New England, offering brand-name goods in their designer outlets and factory stores. Visitors also enjoy following the Equinox Skyline Drive, with its panoramic views from the crest of Mount Equinox.

The town has two major ski areas – **Stratton**, with more than 90 trails and a hillside ski village with shops and restaurants, and **Bromley**, a busy, family-oriented ski area.

Manchester has been a vacation resort since the 19th century, and its gracious mansions evoke that era. One of the most elegant is **Hildene**, a 24-room Georgian manor built by Robert Todd Lincoln, son of President Abraham Lincoln. Among its notable features are a 1,000-pipe Aeolian organ.

Hildene
Rte 7A. ***Tel*** *(802) 362-1788.*
9:30am–4:30pm daily. *every 30 mins.*
www.hildene.org

For hotels and restaurants in this region see p180 and p185

Killington 20

1,000. Rte 4, West Killington, (802) 422-3333 or (800) 621-6867.

Sporty types who like outdoor adventure and a lively social life head for this year-round resort. Killington operates the largest ski center in the eastern United States, with 191 runs for alpine skiing and snowboarding spread across seven peaks, including nearby Pico Mountain. It also has superb cross-country ski centers at Mountain Top Inn and Mountain Meadows.

Killington itself is the second highest peak in Vermont, at 4,240 ft (1,295 m). The ski season here lasts eight months, longer than anywhere else in Vermont.

In summer as well as fall a gondola ferries visitors up to the peaks from where, on clear day, there are views of five states and distant Canada.

Woodstock 21

1,000. Mechanic St, (802) 457-3555, (888) 496-6378.
www.woodstockvt.com

Even in Vermont, where historic, picturesque villages are commonplace, Woodstock stands out. Founded in 1761, the town is an enclave of renovated brick and clapboard Georgian houses, many of them beautifully restored, thanks to the generosity of philanthropists such as the Rockefeller family, and the railroad magnate Frederick Billings (1823–90), who also financed the planting of 10,000 trees here. **Billings Farm and Museum** is still a working entity. The 1890 farmhouse has been restored, and visitors can attend seasonal events such as apple-cider pressing in the fall and plowing competitions in the spring. The museum's exhibits include vintage farm implements, butter churns, and ice cutters.

Nearby Quechee is home to the **Vermont Institute of Natural Science**, a reserve where injured birds of prey are cared for until they can be returned to the wild.

The SS *Ticonderoga*, in Shelburne Museum

Billings Farm & Museum
River Rd. **Tel** *(802) 457-2355.*
May–Oct: 10am–5pm daily. Call for winter hours.

Vermont Institute of Natural Science
Woodstock Rd, Quechee. **Tel** *(802) 359-5000. May–Oct: 10am–5pm daily; Nov–Apr: call for hours.*
www.vinsweb.org

Environs

Six miles (10 km) east of town is the stunningly beautiful **Quechee Gorge**. The best view of the chasm is on Route 4, which crosses the gorge via a steel bridge. A short hiking trail leads from the parking lot on the east side to the Ottauquechee River below.

One of the many beautiful homes in the village of Woodstock

Shelburne Museum & Farms 22

Rte 7, 7 miles (11 km) S of Burlington. **Tel** *(802) 985-3346. mid-May–mid-Oct: 10am–5pm daily. mid-Oct–Mar, Thanksgiving, Dec 25.*
www.shelburnemuseum.org

Established in 1947 by collector Electra Webb, Shelburne Museum's 37 historic structures and their contents constitute one of America's finest museums. Its eclectic collection, which celebrates three centuries of American ingenuity, includes folk art, antique tools, and circus memorabilia, along with scrimshaw, Native American artifacts, and paintings by artists such as Winslow Homer and Grandma Moses.

Among the relocated or replicated historic buildings on view are a horseshoe-shaped **Circus Building**, housing a 500-ft (152-m) long miniature circus parade, an 1890 **Railroad Station**, and an 1871 Lake Champlain lighthouse. Visitors can explore the SS *Ticonderoga*, a former Lake Champlain steamship, which was still operating when purchased by Webb in 1950. The visitor center is located in the 1901 Round Barn, which also features changing exhibits.

Shelburne is home to a historic 1,400-acre (566-ha) estate, Shelburne Farms, with its beautiful green rolling pastures and woodlands. There are tours of the dairy, and there are also special areas where children can pet and play with the animals.

First Unitarian Church, Burlington

Burlington ㉓

39,000. 345 Pine St. King St Dock. Suite 100, 60 Main St, (802) 863-3489, (877) 686-5253. *Discover Jazz Festival (Jun).* **www**.vermont.org

Vermont's largest city, Burlington is one of the most popular tourist destinations in the state. Half of the population of this lively town is made up of students from the University of Vermont and the city's four colleges. Rich in interesting shops and restaurants as well as grand old mansions and historic landmarks, Burlington is also Vermont's center of commerce and industry. It is scenically located on the shores of Lake Champlain.

The center of Burlington is compact and easy to explore on foot. It includes the historic district, at the core of which is the four-block section known as the **Church Street Marketplace**. The neighborhood has been converted into a pedestrian mall, complete with trendy boutiques, patio restaurants, and crafts shops. Many of them are housed in Queen Anne-style buildings from the late 1800s. The historical attractions in this neighborhood include the 1861 **First Unitarian Church**, the oldest house of worship in Burlington, and the **City Hall**, which marks the southern boundary of the marketplace. This graceful building, built of local brick, marble, and granite, dates to 1928. The City Hall Park is a popular outdoor concert venue, and in summer street performers and musicians add color and action to the area.

On the waterfront is **Battery Park**, the site of a battle between US soldiers and the British Royal Navy in 1812. Today, the park is a peaceful place, from where there are lovely views of Burlington Bay and the backdrop of the Adirondack Mountains on the other side of Lake Champlain. South of the park is the **Burlington Boat House**; here a three-decker cruise ship, *Spirit of Ethan Allen III*, takes visitors on a 90-minute trip, which gives a good historical overview, as the captain narrates tales of the Revolutionary War.

The **Robert Hull Fleming Museum**, on the campus of the University of Vermont, is on a hillside overlooking the city. The artifacts in this elegant 1931 Colonial Revival building range from ancient Mesopotamian objects to European paintings and sculptures and Native American crafts.

Robert Hull Fleming Museum
61 Colchester Ave. ***Tel*** *(802) 656-0750.* *early Sep–Apr: 9am–4pm Tue–Fri, 1–5pm Sat–Sun; May–early Sep: noon–4pm Tue–Fri, 1–5pm Sat–Sun.* *public hols.*

Lake Champlain ㉔

Vermont-New York border from Whitehall to Alburg. *60 Main St, Burlington, (802) 863-3489, (877) 686-5253.*

Sometimes called the sixth Great Lake because of its size, Lake Champlain is 120 miles (190 km) long, 12 miles (19 km) wide, and has 500 miles (800 km) of shoreline.

Statue in Burlington's Battery Park

Said to be the home of "Champ," a water serpent that could be a distant cousin of the Loch Ness monster, the lake is sprinkled with about 70 islands. At the northern end of the lake is **Isle La Motte**, which has a statue of Samuel de Champlain, the French explorer who discovered and explored much of the surrounding region. On nearby **Grand Isle** is America's oldest log cabin (1783). The lake has its western shore in New York State, and seasonal hour-long ferry rides run between Burlington and Port Kent, New York.

Some of Lake Champlain's treasures are underwater, preserved in a marine park

Sailing and boating, popular on beautiful Lake Champlain

For hotels and restaurants in this region see p180 and p185

where scuba divers can explore shipwrecks resting on sandbars and at the bottom of this clear-water lake.

The **Lake Champlain Maritime Museum** at Basin Harbor gives a complete overview of the region's marine history through fascinating displays of ship models, old divers' suits, and photographs of vintage Lake Champlain steamers.

Lake Champlain Maritime Museum
4472 Basin Harbor Rd, Vergennes. ***Tel*** *(802) 475-2022.* *late May–mid-Oct: 10am–5pm.* **www**.lcmm.org

Stowe ㉕

3,500. *51 Main St, (802) 253-7321, (800) 247-8693.*
www.gostowe.com

This mountain-ringed village is the skiing capital of New England and draws hordes of visitors in winter. Mountain Road begins in the village and is lined with chalets, motels, restaurants, and pubs; it leads to the area's highest peak, **Mount Mansfield** (4,393 ft/1,339 m).

In summer, too, there are plenty of outdoor activities on offer. Visitors can hike, rock-climb, fish, canoe, bike, or inline skate along the paved, meandering 5.5-mile (8.5-km) **Stowe Recreational Path**, which winds from the village church across the West Branch River, then through green woodlands.

Stowe's other claim to fame is as the home of the musical Von Trapp family, who were the inspiration behind the 1965 movie *The Sound of Music*. After their daring escape from Austria during World War II, they chose Stowe as their new home. Their **Trapp Family Lodge** is set in a 2,700-acre (1,092-ha) estate. This giant wooden chalet is now one of the most popular hotels in the area *(see p180)*.

The Austrian-style Trapp Family Lodge in Stowe

Ben & Jerry's Ice Cream Factory ㉖

Rte 100, Waterbury.
Tel *(866) BJTOURS.* *Jul–mid-Aug: 9am–9pm daily; mid-Aug–Oct: 9am–7pm daily; Nov–Jun: 10am–6pm daily.*

Although Ben Cohen and Jerry Greenfield hail from Long Island, New York, they have done more than any other "flatlanders" to put Vermont's dairy industry on the map. In 1977, these childhood friends paid $5 for a correspondence course on making ice cream, and soon parlayed their knowledge into what became an enormously successful ice-cream franchise.

No longer privately owned, the factory uses the richest dairy products to produce their ice cream and frozen yogurt. The Ben & Jerry trademark is the black and white Holstein cow, which embellishes everything on sale in the gift shop.

Tours of the factory start every 15 minutes and run for 30 minutes. Visitors learn all there is to know about making ice cream. They are given a bird's-eye view of the factory floor, and at the end of the tour they get a chance to sample the products and sometimes taste new flavors.

Ben & Jerry's bus, gaily decorated with dairy cows

A ski-lift in Vermont, one of the best skiing areas of the US

SKIING IN NEW ENGLAND

In New England, topnotch slopes and cross-country ski trails are never far away. The best skiing is concentrated in the three northern states. Vermont has the most high-quality peaks, and the world-famous resorts of Killington and Stowe. Two great trails in Vermont for skiers and snowshoers are the Catamount Trail and the Trapp Family Lodge Ski Center. New Hampshire's White Mountains have some of the best downhill, alpine, and cross-country ski trails in the Northeast. In Maine, Sugarloaf/USA and Sunday River are considered the best hills in the state. Downhill ski trails are rated by a standard code: Easier=green circle; More difficult=blue square; Most Difficult=black diamond; and Expert=double diamond. Equipment, and lessons for all levels are available at all the resorts.

New Hampshire

New Hampshire's natural beauty is evident all over the state. The northern part is rippled by the tall peaks of the White Mountain Range and the spectacular chasm of Franconia Notch. Ponds and lakes, such as the pristine Lake Winnipesaukee, dot central New Hampshire. The main cities – historic Concord and lively Portsmouth, with its scenic Atlantic coastline – nestle amid the tranquil farmlands of the south.

The striking exterior of the Mount Washington Hotel & Resort

Bretton Woods 27

550. *(800) 346-3687.* **www**.visitwhitemountains.com

This tiny enclave in the Mount Washington Valley has an unusual claim to fame. In 1944, with the need for currency stability after the economic upheavals of World War II, it hosted the United Nations conference that led to the establishment of the International Monetary Fund and, later, the World Bank. The setting for this historic meeting was the magnificent Spanish Renaissance-style **Mount Washington Hotel and Resort** *(see p180)*. Opened in 1902, the hotel's sparkling white exterior and crimson roof stand out in contrast to Mount Washington, looming behind it. The hotel has entertained several distinguished guests, including the British Prime Minister Winston Churchill, and three US presidents. Surrounded by 17,300 acres (7,000 ha) of parkland, its facilities include a 27-hole golf course. Nearby, Bretton Woods ski area offers alpine skiing and 62 miles (100 km) of cross-country trails.

Mount Washington Hotel & Resort
Rte 302, Bretton Woods. ***Tel*** *(603) 278-1000, (800) 258-0330.*

Environs

Dominating the Mount Washington Valley is the 6,288-ft (1,917-m) peak of **Mount Washington**, the highest in the northeastern United States. The peak has the dubious distinction of having the worst weather in the world, and in April 1934 clocked the highest wind ever recorded on earth: 230 mph (370 kph). On clear days, however, there are panoramic views from the top. There are hiking trails and an auto road to the summit, but the most exciting way up is by the **Mount Washington Cog Railroad**. This steam-powered train chugs the 3.5-mile (5.6-km) route to the top along a heart-stoppingly steep track. Some of the best alpine skiing is in Tuckerman Ravine on Mount Washington.

Franconia Notch 28

I-93, Franconia Notch Pkwy. *(603) 823-8800.* **Park** *daily.* **Flume Gorge Visitor Center** ***Tel*** *(603) 745-8391.* *May–Oct: 9am–5pm daily.* *for Flume Gorge, Visitor Center, & campsites.* **www**.flumegorge.com

This spectacular mountain pass, carved between the Kinsman and Franconia ranges, and designated as the Franconia Notch State Park, has some of the state's most stunning natural wonders. Foremost among them was the **Old Man of the Mountain**, a rocky outcrop on the side of a cliff that resembled a man's profile until the nose and forehead crashed down in May 2003. Other attractions compensate for the loss. The trout-filled **Profile Lake** reflects the brilliant colors of fall foliage on the slopes of **Cannon Mountain**. A boardwalk and stairways lead visitors through the **Flume Gorge**, a narrow, chasm whose granite walls tower more than 90 ft (27 m) above the boardwalk, while an aerial tramway speeds

FALL FOLIAGE IN NEW ENGLAND

Thousands of visitors head for New England in the fall, to gaze in wonder at the annual changing of leaf colors. The color change is not just a capricious act of Nature. As daylight hours diminish, the leaves of deciduous trees stop producing the green pigment chlorophyll, and other pigments hidden behind the chlorophyll's color now burst into view. More pigments are produced by sugars that remain trapped in the leaves. The result is a riotous display of shades of yellow, orange, crimson, and maroon. The peak period for "leaf-peeping" varies from early October in northern New England to late October in the southern section, but this can differ, depending on the weather *(see Fall Foliage Hotlines, p175)*.

Glorious colors lighting up the New England landscape in fall

Narrow Flume Gorge in Franconia Notch State Park

passengers to the 4,180-ft (1254-m) summit of Cannon Mountain in just 8 minutes.

Robert Frost (1874–1963), one of America's best-loved poets, settled in the Franconia Notch region in 1915. The majestic setting inspired him to pen many of his greatest works here, including the famous poem *Stopping By Woods on a Snowy Evening*.

White Mountain National Forest 29

719 N Main St, Laconia, (603) 528-8721.
Camping *Tel* *(877) 444-6777. Call for availability & reservations.*

New Hampshire's most beautiful wilderness area, the White Mountain National Forest, sprawls over 770,000 acres (311,600 ha). The area has an abundance of wildlife, including a large population of moose, which can often be seen from the road.

Outdoor activities offered in this region range from bird-watching and rock-climbing to skiing and kayaking. But even less sporty travelers will revel in the spectacular scenery visible from their car – valleys flanked by tall pine forests, waterfalls that tumble over rocky outcrops, and more than 20 summits that soar to over 4,000 ft (1,200 m). An especially scenic stretch of road is the 100-mile (161-km) long **White Mountains Trail** that loops across Mount Washington Valley through Crawford Notch and Franconia Notch. In autumn, brilliant fall foliage colors transform the rugged countryside into a palette of flaming red maples, golden birch, and maroon northern red oaks, interspersed with evergreens.

Another popular route is the **Kancamagus Highway**, touted by many as the most beautiful road in New England. This 34-mile (55-km) road, which runs through the White Mountain National Forest between Lincoln and Conway, offers exceptional vistas as it climbs 3,000 ft (914 m) through the Kancamagus Pass. The road descends into the Saco Valley and joins up with the trout-filled Swift River. There is easy access for fishermen from the highway to the river, and there are campgrounds and picnic areas along the entire length of the highway. Well-marked trails allow drivers to stretch their legs amid the beautiful scenery – a popular one is the short loop that leads to the lovely Sabbaday Falls.

Kancamagus Hwy
Rte 112 between Lincoln & Conway.
Saco District Ranger Station, 33 Kancamagus Hwy, (603) 447-5448.

Environs

Close to the White Mountains is the **Lincoln/ Woodstock** region, whose main attraction is **Clark's Trading Post**. This curious combination of circus acts, amusement park rides, and museums makes a welcome change for children after a leaf-peeping drive. Lincoln is a base camp for both backwoods adventurers and stick-to-the-road sightseers. Nearby **Loon Mountain** is one of the state's premier ski resorts. In summer, it offers activities such as nature walks, tours of caves, mountain biking, and horseback riding.

Loon Mountain
E of I-93, near Lincoln. ***Tel*** *(603) 745-8111, (800) 229-5666.*

Lake Winnipesaukee 30

Lakes Region Association, (800) 605-2537.
www.lakesregion.org

With a shoreline that meanders for 240 miles (386 km), and a surface area of 72 sq miles (187 sq km), this stunning lake has New Hampshire's largest stretch of waterfront. Ringed by mountains and scattered with 274 islands, Lake Winnispesaukee has sheltered bays, harbors, and resort towns around its shores. The largest and prettiest of these is **Wolfeboro**. Leaving from Weirs Beach, the M/S *Mount Washington* offers the best scenic cruise in all New England. To its north is upscale **Meredith**, with lovely lakeside homes.

North of Meredith is pristine **Squam Lake**, ideal for boating and fishing, where the movie *On Golden Pond* (1981) was filmed. The town of **Center Sandwich** is on Winnipesaukee's north shore. Surrounded by woodland, it is a favorite destination during fall foliage season. On the eastern shore, the Castle in the Clouds mansion crowns the crest of a hill that rises some 750 ft (229 m) above the lake. A 70-mile (113-km) drive around Lake Winnipesaukee takes in all these sights.

The beautiful scenery to be found in White Mountain National Forest

Canterbury Shaker Village ㉛

288 Shaker Rd, Canterbury. **Tel** *(603) 783-9511, (866) 783-9511.*
mid-May–Oct: 10am–5pm daily.
www.shakers.org

Founded in 1792, this village was occupied by Shakers for 200 years. The Shakers were a sect that broke away from the Quakers, who fled to America to escape religious persecution in Britain in the mid-18th century. Their belief in celibacy and strict separation from the rest of the world eventually led to their demise. The 690-acre (280-ha) site, which has several buildings open to visitors, is punctuated by millponds, nature trails, and traditional gardens. Skilled artisans can be seen re-creating Shaker crafts, known for their simple lines and beautiful workmanship.

Picturesque buildings at Canterbury Shaker Village

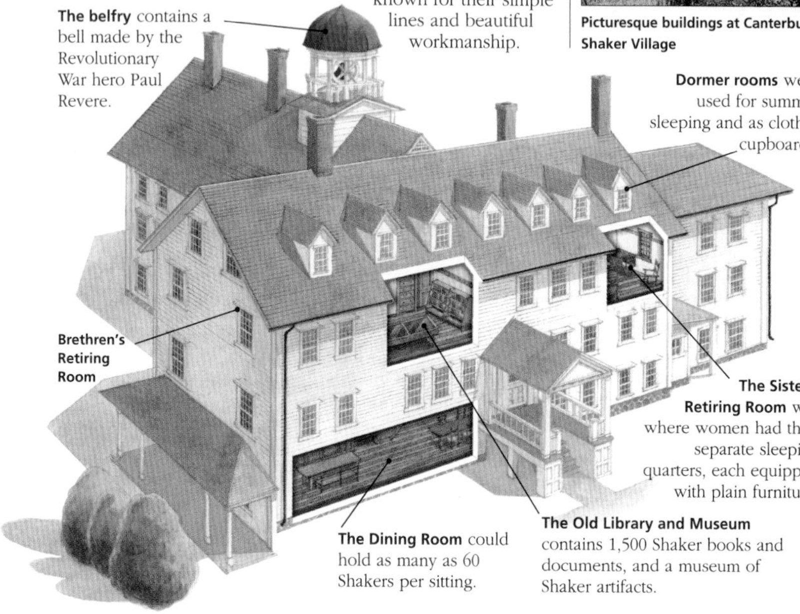

Concord ㉜

37,500. *40 Commercial St, (603) 224-2508.*

New Hampshire's capital is a quiet little town, dominated by its impressive **State House**. Built in 1819 from granite and marble, it is one of the oldest state houses in America. Another landmark is the giant glass pyramid of the **McAuliffe-Sheppard Discovery Center**. A Concord schoolteacher, McAuliffe (1948–86) was tragically killed when the *Challenger* Space Shuttle *(see p302)*, launched by NASA on January 28, 1986, exploded and crashed 73 seconds after lift-off. The astronomy and space exploration exhibits in the planetarium also include multi-media shows such as "Destination Mars."

McAuliffe-Sheppard Discovery Center
2 Institute Dr. **Tel** *(603) 271-7827.* *10am–2pm Mon–Wed, 10am–5pm Thu–Sat, 11:30am–5pm Sun.* *weekend after Labor Day*

Manchester ㉝

105,250. *889 Elm St, (603) 666-6600.* *(603) 622-7531.*

Once a major center of the textile industry, with its mills powered by waterpower from the Merrimack River, today Manchester is famous as the home of New Hampshire's premier art museum, the **Currier Gallery of Art**. The gallery opened a major new extension in 2008. Its collection includes works by such European masters as Claude Monet and Henri Matisse, as well as works of 20th-century American painters such as Andrew Wyeth (1917–2009) and Georgia O'Keeffe

The Currier Gallery of Art in Manchester

Portsmouth's Market Street, a favorite with tourists

(1887–1986). Also part of the museum is the Zimmerman House. The single-story home with its elegant exterior was built in 1950 by the pioneering American architect Frank Lloyd Wright. He also designed the furniture now displayed with the art collection.

The only indoor mall in the state is the Mall of New Hampshire in Manchester.

Currier Gallery of Art
150 Ash St. ***Tel*** *(603) 669-6144.*
11am–5pm Mon, Wed–Fri & Sun, 10am–5pm Sat.
www.currier.org

Portsmouth 34

26,000. *10 Ladd St.* *500 Market St or Market Sq, (603) 436-1118.* *mid-May–Oct: 8:30am–1pm daily.* *Market Square Day (Jun), Prescott Park Arts Festival (Jul–Aug daily).*
www.portsmouthchamber.org

Girded by the Piscataqua River and North and South Mill ponds, Portsmouth is a historic town, compact enough to be explored on foot. Established in 1623, it became a prosperous hub of maritime commerce by the 18th century. It was also a hotbed of revolutionary fervor, and the place where the Colonial naval hero John Paul Jones (1747–92) took command of the warship *Ranger*. During the American Revolution, Jones led several raids along the British coast, for which he was awarded a gold medal by Congress.

A number of Portsmouth's historic buildings, many of which have been turned into boutiques and restaurants, are in the downtown core, especially along **Market Street**. Historic houses and gardens can also be found along the **Portsmouth Harbor Trail**, a walking tour of the Historic District. Especially worth visiting is the elegant 1763 Moffatt-Ladd House on Market Street, one of the earliest examples of the Federal style of architecture. The Wentworth-Gardner House on Mechanic Street, is regarded as one of the finest examples of Georgian architecture in the country. Both houses have beautiful interiors and are open to visitors in summer and fall.

A popular destination in summer is Water Country, which has a huge wave pool, a pirate ship, and a man-made lagoon. Interactive exhibits are the highlight of the **Children's Museum of New Hampshire**, where children can enter a human-scale kaleidoscope or command a submarine. Visitors can explore the real thing at Albacore Park where a sleek submarine, the USS *Albacore*, is on display. When it was built in 1953, it was the fastest underwater vessel of its kind.

Portsmouth's most popular attraction is **Strawbery Banke**, a 10-acre (4-ha) site near the waterfront located at the very spot at which Portsmouth was founded. This outdoor museum, which can be explored on foot or in authentic horse-drawn carriages, contains more than 40 buildings that depict life from 1695 to 1955. Many buildings are set amid gardens cultivated according to their eras, from early pioneer herb gardens to formal Victorian flower beds. The houses open to the public are furnished in period style and contain interesting collections of decorative arts and ceramics.

The **Jones House**, a 1790 structure, displays artifacts excavated at the site. The elegant 1760s Chase House is furnished with sumptuous pieces from several periods, while the Sherburne House, built in 1695, now serves as an exhibit on 17th-century house design and construction. In the Dinsmore Shop, built in 1800, visitors can watch a cooper making barrels and casks in the traditional way.

Strawbery Banke also has a Colonial Revival Garden, the Aldrich Garden, planted with flowers mentioned in the poetry of Portsmouth native Thomas Bailey Aldrich.

Children's Museum of New Hampshire
6 Washington St, Dover. ***Tel*** *(603) 742-2002.* *10am–5pm Tue–Sat, noon–5pm Sun.*
www.childrens-museum.org

Strawbery Banke
Marcy St. ***Tel*** *(603) 433-1100.*
check for hours. *limited access to some buildings.*
www.strawberybanke.org

Inside lavishly furnished Chase House, Strawbery Banke, in Portsmouth

Maine

The largest state in New England, Maine is truly the Great Outdoors. Its most popular attractions are found along the spectacular coastline, beginning in the south-east with its largest and liveliest city, Portland, and the resort towns of the Kennebunks. Farther north, yachts and windjammers ply the waters of Penobscot Bay, while Acadia National Park stands as Maine's coastal jewel. World-class skiing, hiking, and boating opportunities are found inland, at Bethel and Sugarloaf.

Portland 35

65,000. 950 Congress St. Commercial & Franklin Sts. 99 Commercial St, (877) 833-1374, (207) 772-5800. Wed & Sat. Old Port Festival (Jun 4), Victorian Holiday (Nov 24–Dec 23).
www.visitportland.com

This historic city has a beautiful location on the crest of a peninsula, with expansive views of Casco Bay and the Calendar Islands. Once a flourishing port, Portland was devastated by no less than four major fires, the last one in 1866. Nevertheless, the city still has a number of sturdy stone Victorian buildings.

The West End has fine mansions and a splendid promenade overlooking the water. Portland's liveliest area, however, is around the Old Port, near the harbor. This restored neighborhood's narrow streets are filled with shops, restaurants, and art galleries. Dominating the area is the regal **United States Customs House**, with its gilded ceilings, marble staircases, and chandeliers. It was built after the Civil War (1861–65). From the docks, ships offer cruises to the Calendar Islands, harbor tours, and deep-sea fishing trips.

West of the Old Port, the **Portland Museum of Art**, displays works by the area's most famous artist, Winslow Homer (1836–1910), as well as by European masters such as Gauguin and Picasso. The **Children 's Museum of Maine** has three floors of interactive exhibits. The **Maine Narrow Gauge Railroad Co. & Museum** displays vintage locomotives and offers scenic trips along the waterfront.

Children's Museum banner

Several of Portland's fine historic houses are open to visitors. They include the **Wadsworth-Longfellow House** (1785) where poet Henry Wadsworth Longfellow grew up; and the **Victoria Mansion** with its painted trompe l'oeil walls. Portland's signature landmark is the Portland Head Light at Fort Williams Park. First illuminated in 1791, the lighthouse is surrounded by beach and picnic areas, and the keeper's house is now a museum.

Portland Museum of Art
7 Congress Sq. ***Tel** (207) 775-6148.*
mid-Oct–early May: 10am–5pm Tue, Wed, Thu, Sat, & Sun, 10am–9pm Fri; late May–mid-Oct: 10am–5pm Mon.
Oct–May: Mon.
www.portlandmuseum.org

Children's Museum of Maine
142 Free St. ***Tel** (207) 828-1234.*
year-round: 10am–5pm Tue–Sat, noon–5pm Sun; May–Sep: 10am–5pm Mon.
public hols.

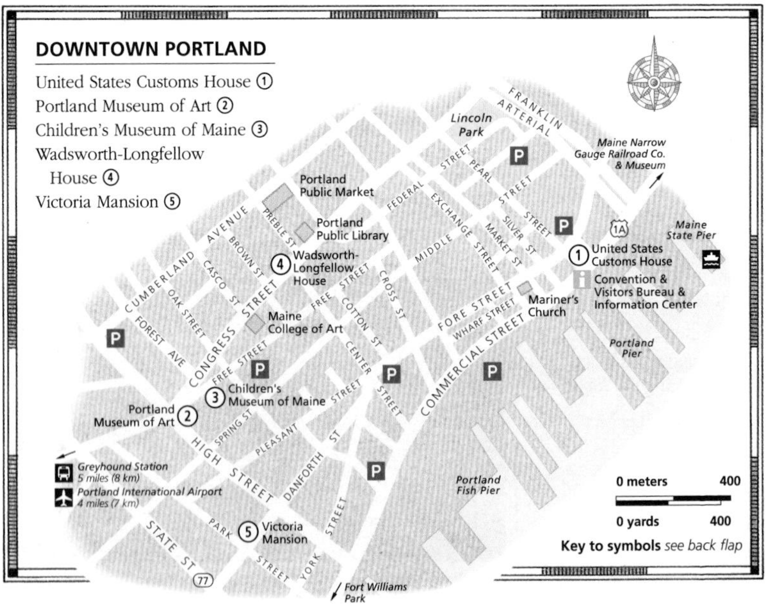

The Kennebunks 36

17 Western Ave, Kennebunk, (207) 967-0857. **www**.visitthekennebunks.com

First a thriving shipbuilding center and port, then a summer retreat for the rich, the Kennebunks are made up of two villages, Kennebunk and Kennebunkport.

Kennebunkport's historic village is graced by several Federal and Greek Revival structures, and the striking 1824 **South Congregational Church**, with its soaring white steeple. History of a different sort can be found at the **Seashore Trolley Museum**, where some 200 antique streetcars are housed, including one called "Desire." Tours of the countryside are offered on one of the restored trolleys. The scenic drive along Route 9 offers views of surf along rocky Cape Arundel. At **Cape Porpoise**, travelers can sample lobster pulled fresh from the Atlantic. Kennebunk is famous for its beaches, notably **Kennebunk Beach**, and for one of the most romantic houses in New England, the 1826 **Wedding Cake House**. According to local lore, George Bourne was unexpectedly called to sea before his marriage. Although a very hastily arranged wedding took place, there was no time to bake the traditional wedding cake. So the shipbuilder vowed to his bride that on his return he would remodel their home to look like a wedding cake. Today the ornate latticework offers proof that Bourne was a man of his word. Interesting architectural walking tours of Kennebunk's historic area are offered by the **Brick Store Museum**, housed in four restored 19th-century buildings.

Seashore Trolley Museum
195 Log Cabin Rd, Kennebunkport.
Tel *(207) 967-2800.* *call for times.*
www.trolleymuseum.org

Brick Store Museum
117 Main St, Kennebunk. ***Tel*** *(207) 985-4802.* *10am–4:30pm Tue–Fri, 10am–1pm Sat.* *Sun, public hols.*
www.brickstoremuseum.org

Boats on the waters of Penobscot Bay's Stonington village, Deer Isle

Penobscot Bay 37

Rockland *1 Park Dr, (207) 596-0376.* **Camden** *2 Public Landing, (207) 236-4404.* **Searsport** *Main & Steamboat, (207) 548-6510.* **Castine** *Emerson Hall, Court St, (207) 326-4502.* **Deer Isle** *Rte 15 at Eggemoggin Rd, (207) 348-6124.*

Penobscot Bay is picture-book Maine, with hills sloping down into the ocean, wave-pounded cliffs, sheltered harbors bobbing with boats, and lobster traps piled on the docks. Penobscot Bay is also famous for its islands, which can be visited on boat tours from the mainland.

Penobscot Bay's commercial center is the fishing town of **Rockland**, whose biggest event is the lobster festival on the first full weekend of August. A prime attraction is the Farnsworth Art Museum, displaying the works of leading American painters such as Edward Hopper and Andrew Wyeth.

A favorite destination for tourists is **Camden**, with its spired churches, elegant homes, and shops along the waterfront. A short distance from the village is Camden Hills State Park, which offers breathtaking views of the bay from the summit of Mount Battie. Standing on this point, the poet Edna St. Vincent Millay (1892–1950) was inspired to write her first volume of poetry. Nearby **Searsport** is regarded as the antiques capital of Maine and has large and busy fleamarkets on weekends in the summer.

Sailboats moored in Penobscot Bay's Camden Harbor

The more remote eastern shore leads to serene, perfectly preserved villages such as **Castine** and Blue Hill. In Castine is the historic Fort George, built by the British in 1799, and witness to the American Navy's worst defeat during the Revolutionary War. Blue Hill is a living postcard, surrounded by fields of blueberries, and with many of its clapboard buildings listed on the National Historic Register.

Deer Isle, reached from the mainland via a graceful suspension bridge, is actually a series of small islands linked by causeways. Island highlights include the scenic towns of Stonington and Deer Isle. From Stonington, it is an 8-mile (13-km) boat ride to the thickly wooded Isle au Haut, much of which belongs to Acadia National Park *(see p172)*. Another unspoiled haven is Monhegan Island with its dramatic cliffs and hiking trails. North Haven Island is a summer colony, covered with meadows of wildflowers. Vinalhaven, with its granite shoreline and inland moors, is a perfect place for a swim or a hike.

For hotels and restaurants in this region see p181 and p185

Bass Harbor Head, which exemplifies Maine's rock-bound shoreline

Acadia National Park 38

Hulls Cove Visitor Center, off Rte 3 in Hulls Cove, (207) 288-3338. mid-Apr–Oct: daily. Bangor-Bar Harbor. at Hulls Cove. **www**.nps.gov/acad

An unspoiled paradise, heavily visited in summer, the 35,000-acre (14,164-ha) Acadia National Park covers much of Mount Desert Island, off the southeast Maine coast.

The park's main attraction is the scenic Loop Road, a 27-mile (43-km) drive that climbs and dips with the pink granite mountains of the east coast of the island and takes in its main sights. Among these is the 1,527-ft (465-m) high **Cadillac Mountain**, the highest point on the Atlantic Coast. Hiking trails and an auto road lead to spectacular panoramas at the summit. The road continues south to the idyllic **Sand Beach**, but the icy water discourages many swimmers. Farther south there is a unique natural phenomenon known locally as **Thunder Hole** – when the tide rises during heavy winds, air trapped in this crevice is compressed and then expelled with a resounding boom. The Loop Road continues inland, swinging past Jordan Pond, Bubble Pond, and Eagle Lake.

On the southern shore of the park is the quaint village of **Bass Harbor**, where an 1858 lighthouse is perched on the rocky coastline, offering magnificent views of the ocean. The park is home to numerous animals, including woodchucks, white-tailed deer, and red foxes. Visitors who want a closer, more intimate look at the park's flora and fauna can do so on foot, bike, or horseback along the 45 miles (72 km) of old broken-stone carriage roads, which wind through the park.

Cutting through the center of Mount Desert Island is **Somes Sound**, a finger-shaped natural fjord that juts 5 miles (8 km) inland. It separates the quiet village of Southwest Harbor from Northeast Harbor, which is the center of Mount Desert Island's social scene, with its upscale shops and handsome mansions. Southwest Harbor is home to the **Mount Desert Oceanarium**, which features 20 tanks of sea animals.

The elegant resort town of **Bar Harbor** is a lively tourist center and a good base from which to explore the Acadia National Park. More than 5,000,000 visitors each year pass through Bar Harbor on their way to the wilds of the park. Located on Mount Desert Island's northeastern shore, it was the 19th century summer haven for some of America's richest people, including the Astors and the Vanderbilts. In 1947, a fire destroyed a third of the town's lavish homes, thus ending its reign as a high-society enclave. The town's attractions include the **Criterion Theater**, an Art Deco gem that shows both popular and art films, and the **Abbe Museum**, which celebrates Maine's Native American heritage with displays of tools, crafts, art, artifacts, and archaeology. The Wild Gardens of Acadia, with some 300 species of local plants, are located next to the museum.

Bar Harbor Oceanarium, situated 8.5 miles (14 km) northwest of the town, is the place to see harbor seals, explore a salt marsh on Thomas Bay Marsh Walk, or visit the Maine Lobster Museum and take in demonstrations of lobstering.

Acadia Zoo in Trenton, lying across the bridge from Mount Desert Island, is home to some 45 species of animals, including reindeer, wolves, monkeys, and moose.

Bar Harbor
1201 Bar Harbor Rd, Trenton (207) 288-5103.

Cadillac Mountain, the highest point on the Atlantic coast, with striking panoramas at the summit

For hotels and restaurants in this region see p181 and p185

Roosevelt Cottage, built in 1897, on Campobello Island

Campobello Island 39

Roosevelt Campobello International Park *(506) 752-2922.* **Island** *dawn–dusk;* **Park** *late May–mid-Oct.* *every 15 mins.* **www**.fdr.net

Located on Campobello Island is the **Roosevelt Campobello International Park**, established in 1964 as a memorial to President Franklin D. Roosevelt *(see p49)*. The island's main settlement of Welshpool was where the future president spent most of his summers until 1921, when he contracted polio. Despite his disability, Roosevelt was elected to four terms, leading the US through the Great Depression and World War II.

The highlight of the 2,800-acre (1,333-ha) park – which actually lies in Canada and is the only international park in the world – is **Roosevelt Cottage**. Built in 1897, this sprawling, 34-room wood-frame summer home displays mementos that had belonged to President F.D. Roosevelt.

At the island's southern tip is **Liberty Point**, where a pair of observation decks perched on the rugged cliffs offer far-ranging views of the Atlantic.

A short distance inland from here is **Lower Duck Pond Bog**, a prime habitat for the great blue heron, killdeer, and the American black duck.

On the island's western shore is **Mulholland Point**, with an 1885 lighthouse and a picnic site offering views of the FDR Memorial Bridge. Other good picnic sites are at Raccoon Beach located on the eastern shore.

Sugarloaf 40

(207) 237-2000, (800) 843-5623.

Maine's highest ski mountain, Sugarloaf is the center of this touristy village packed with hotels, restaurants, and condominiums. Downhill skiers, in particular, are attracted to **Sugarloaf /USA** ski center with its more than 130 trails and a vertical drop of 2,820 ft (860 m). The center also offers cross-country skiing, ice skating, and snowshoeing.

In summer, the emphasis shifts to the resort's 18-hole golf course, boating on the lakes and rivers, and hiking in the nearby Carrabassett Valley. The resort is also famous for its network of more than 50 miles (80 km) of mountain biking trails, through flat as well as steep and challenging terrain.

Sugarloaf/USA
Carrabassett Valley. ***Tel*** *(207) 237-2000, (800) 843-5623.* *8:30am–3:50pm daily.* *in lodge.* **www**.sugarloaf.com

Bethel 41

2,500. *8 Station Place; (207) 824-2282, (800) 442-5826.* **www**.bethelmaine.com

A picturesque historic district, a major ski resort, and proximity to the White Mountains give Bethel year-round appeal. First settled in 1796, the town was a farming and lumbering center until the coming of the railroad in 1851 made it a popular resort. The line-up of classic clapboard mansions on the town green includes the Federal-style **Moses Mason House** (c.1813), restored and furnished with period pieces.

There are scenic drives in all directions, taking in unspoiled Colonial hamlets such as Waterford to the south, and beautiful mountain terrain to the north. **Sunday River Ski Resort**, 6 miles (10 km) north of town in Newry, has more than 130 ski trails. **Grafton Notch State Park** has spectacular scenery along its drives and hiking trails. The park's special spots include waterfalls and sweeping views of the scenic surroundings from Table Rock and Old Speck Mountain.

Moses Mason House
10–14 Broad St. ***Tel*** *(207) 824-2908.* *Jul–early Sep: 1–4pm Tue–Sun; year round: by appt.*

Sunday River Ski Resort
Off Rte 2 in Newry. ***Tel*** *(207) 824-3000, (800) 5432-SKI.* *9am–4pm Mon–Fri, 8am–4pm Sat–Sun.*

Grafton Notch State Park
Rte 26 NW of Newry. ***Tel*** *(207) 824-2912.* *mid-May–mid-Oct.*

Screw Auger Falls in Grafton Notch State Park, Bethel

Practical Information

Although particularly popular during summer and fall, New England is a four-season vacation destination. The superb skiing facilities attract tourists during winter, which often lasts from mid-November to April. The region offers a wide variety of recreational activities within a relatively small area. On any weekend, vacationers can hike the White Mountains of New Hampshire, swim at Maine's Ogunquit Beach, and take in the Boston Symphony Orchestra. Outside of Boston, where public transportation is excellent, you definitely need a car for sightseeing.

TOURIST INFORMATION

State tourism offices are great sources of information and are happy to send road maps, brochures, and listings of attractions, accommodations, and events, free of charge. Some places also offer discount vouchers for lodgings, restaurants, and entry fees. Many towns have a visitors' bureau that offers information on local lodgings, events, and restaurants.

PERSONAL SECURITY

New England's comparatively low crime rate makes it a safe holiday destination. But it is good to take precautions. Since pickpockets tend to frequent popular tourist sights, use a money belt for cash and documents and keep cameras out of sight. Avoid wearing expensive jewelry and leave your valuables in the hotel safe.

NATURAL HAZARDS

The variety of outdoor activities in New England often entail risks, which can be minimized with proper precautions. Always be prepared for sudden changes in the weather, especially in higher elevations. Wear protective gear for adventure sports and never try to interfere with wildlife.

GETTING AROUND

Many bus companies serve particular sections of New England, making it relatively simple to get from state to state. In Boston and Cambridge, it is easier to get around by public transportation than by driving. Once outside the city you will need a car. In fact, much of New England's charm lies along scenic jaunts down the coast and driving tours during the fall-foliage season.

THE CLIMATE OF NEW ENGLAND

New England's weather can vary greatly from year to year. Generally, the short spring is cloudy and wet, with rainy skies and melting snow. Summer can be unpredictable, but is generally dry – July and August are usually the sunniest months. Bright fall days out among the colorful foliage are spectacular – the peak fall-foliage period usually lasts from mid-September to late October. Snow usually starts in December; the temperature can dip to 0° F (–18° C) or lower in winter. In general, it is warmer along the coast and in the southern section of New England.

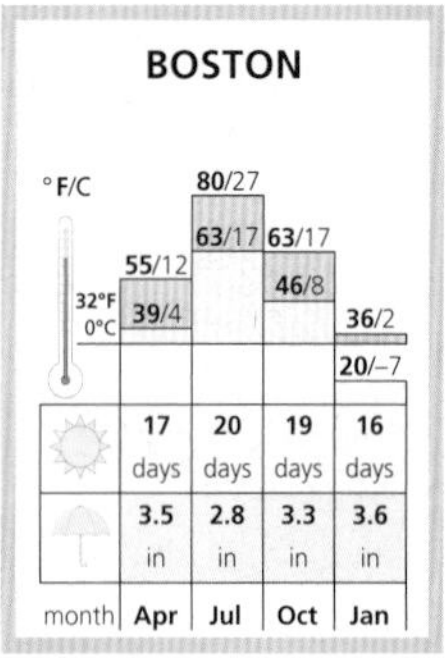

Several books list the best driving tours of the region. Yankee Magazine (www.yankeemagazine.com) details recommended routes, historic stops, and places to eat and stay.

SAFETY FOR DRIVERS

Large areas of New England are wild, so be prepared for any eventuality. This is doubly true in winter, when sudden blizzards and white-outs caused by blowing snow can leave motorists stranded. Stock salt, a snow brush, an ice scraper, and a small shovel. If you do get stuck in an out-of-the-way place, stay inside your car. Keep the motor running for warmth, but open your window slightly and keep the tailpipe clear to prevent carbon monoxide buildup. **American Automobile Association (AAA)** provides roadside assistance.

LAWS

The legal drinking age in New England is 21, and young people can be asked to produce a proof of age in order to buy alcohol or enter a bar. You can lose your driver's license if caught driving under the influence of alcohol. Cigarettes can be sold only to people 18 years of age or older. Smoking and drinking in public spaces is illegal. Some restaurants have separate areas for smokers.

SPORTS & OUTDOOR ACTIVITIES

With miles of coastline, mountain ranges, forests, and rivers, the region has much to offer to sports lovers. The choice of camping areas in national forests range from primitive sites to ones with various facilities. Hiking trails crisscross almost the entire region, with the most popular being the New England section of the Appalachian Trail and Vermont's Long Trail. The **Appalachian Trail Conservancy** runs various information and education programs on the Appalachian

Trail. Miles of quiet back roads in the region are a cyclist's paradise. Mountain bikers also have plenty to choose from. Some ski areas let bikers use their lifts and slopes in summer.

New England's Green and White Mountains offer superb rock climbing, hang gliding, and paragliding sites.

Anglers will love New England. Deep-sea fishing is best at Point Judith in Rhode Island. Brook trout and bass are plentiful in the inland streams and lakes, especially in Maine. The state's latticework of rivers is ideal for canoeing, kayaking, and whitewater rafting.

Penobscot Bay, Maine, and Newport, Rhode Island, are both considered sailing meccas. For those who want something calmer than the Atlantic Ocean, New England has countless lakes, and boats can be rented at many seaside and lakeside resorts. Whale-watching cruises have become a very popular activity. Take the cruise on a calm day, as choppy water can cause seasickness.

The region's northernmost reaches, with a thick annual blanket of snow, offer great skiing, skating, and snowmobiling opportunities. Stowe, located in Vermont, can claim the title of New England's ski capital. The world-famous **Stowe Mountain Resort** offers excellent trails for skiers of all levels.

ENTERTAINMENT

New England is a traveler's dream as it offers a wide range of entertainment. Free concerts and festivals abound in fall, spring, and summer, and there is no shortage of bars and nightclubs in which to slake, or build, your thirst. Boston's Harvard Square has been famous for four decades for its nightly and weekend scene of street performers. Mellow jazz lounges and smoky blues bars attract a devoted clientele.

Classical music, theater, and dance have long been the mainstays of the region's cultural identity. The larger towns and cities have good symphony orchestras, dance, and drama companies. But the hub of the region's performing arts is Boston. The **Boston Symphony Orchestra (BSO)** and its popular music doppleganger, the Boston Pops, are the city's cherished institutions. The BSO performs a full schedule of concerts at Symphony Hall from October to April. The Pops move in for performances in May and June.

Theater is alive and well across New England's six states, but the epicenter of this dynamic world is, again, Boston. The most avant-garde contemporary theater found in Boston is at the **American Repertory Theater (ART)**.

SHOPPING

New England's well-known factory outlets offer brand name clothing at huge discounts. Freeport, Maine has the famous outdoor equipment outlet **L.L. Bean**. The interconnected **Copley Place** and **Shops at Prudential Center** are Boston's leading upscale indoor shopping malls. The region is an antique hunter's dream, with stores and barns offering a wide array of objects from the past. The Charles Street section of Boston's Beacon Hill is one of the prime antiquing areas. Look for shops run by New Hampshire craftsmen, Vermont-made products, and Maine crafts. Tourists looking for gifts with a regional flavor should sample the maple syrup and maple sugar candy.

DIRECTORY

TOURIST OFFICES

Connecticut
www.ctvisit.com

Greater Boston
www.bostonusa.com

Maine
www.visitmaine.com

Massachusetts
www.massvacation.com

New Hampshire
www.visitnh.gov

Rhode Island
www.visitrhodeisland.com

Vermont
www.1-800-vermont.com

FALL FOLIAGE HOTLINES

Connecticut
Tel *(800) 288-4748.*

Maine
Tel *(800) 777-0317.*

Massachusetts
Tel *(800) 227-6277.*

New Hampshire
Tel *(800) 258-3608.*

Rhode Island
Tel *(800) 556-2484.*

Vermont
Tel *(800) 837-6668.*

ROAD EMERGENCY

American Automobile Assn. (AAA)
Tel *(800) 222-4357.*

HIKING

Appalachian Trail Conservancy
799 Washington St, PO Box 807, Harpers Ferry, WV 25425-0807.
Tel *(304) 535-6331.*
www.appalachiantrail.org

SKIING

Stowe Mountain Resort
5781 Mountain Rd, Stowe, VT 05672. ***Tel*** *(800) 253-4754.* **www**.stowe.com

ENTERTAINMENT

American Repertory Theater
64 Brattle St, Cambridge, MA. ***Tel*** *(617) 547-8300.*
www.amrep.org

Boston Symphony Orchestra
301 Massachusetts Ave, Boston, MA. ***Tel*** *(617) 266-1492.* **www**.bso.org

SHOPPING

Copley Place
100 Huntington Ave, Boston, MA.
Tel *(617) 369-5000.*
www.simon.com

L.L. Bean
95 Main Street, Freeport, ME. ***Tel*** *(877) 755-2326.*
www.llbean.com

Shops at Prudential Center
800 Boylston St, Boston, MA. ***Tel*** *(800) 746-7778.*
www.prudentialcenter.com

Choosing a Hotel

The incredibly varied accommodations of the New England states are tailored to suit all tastes and budgets. Rustic country inns and bed-and-breakfasts are plentiful, offering travelers quaint facilities and a more personal touch. Hotels are listed by area and then by price category, with symbols highlighting some of the amenities.

PRICE CATEGORIES IN US DOLLARS ($)
For a standard double room per night, including breakfast, service charges, and taxes.

($) Under $125
($)($) $125–$175
($)($)($) $175–$225
($)($)($)($) $225–$300
($)($)($)($)($) Over $300

BOSTON

BACK BAY AND SOUTH END 463 Beacon Street Guest House ($)($)

463 Beacon St, 02115 ***Tel*** *(617) 536-1302* ***Fax*** *(617) 247-8876* ***Rooms*** *20*

Budget lodging especially popular with young European travelers offers studio rooms and small furnished apartments (with some cooking facilities) by the day, week, or month. This Back Bay brownstone is a handsome building closer to the Charles River Esplanade than Back Bay attractions, but rates, especially off-season, can be a steal. **www.463beacon.com**

BACK BAY AND SOUTH END Newbury Guest House ($)($)($)

261 Newbury St, 02116 ***Tel*** *(617) 437-7666, (800) 437-7668* ***Fax*** *(617) 670-6100* ***Rooms*** *32*

When three Victorian homes were linked to form this inn, the owners were careful to preserve such period details as ceiling medallions, parquet floors, and decorative fireplaces. The rooms feature a comfortable mix of older furniture. Newbury Street can be noisy; ask for a room at the back. Breakfast is included. **www.newburyguesthouse.com**

BACK BAY AND SOUTH END Midtown Hotel ($)($)($)($)

220 Huntington Ave, 02115 ***Tel*** *(617) 262-1000, (800) 343-1177* ***Fax*** *(617) 262-8739* ***Rooms*** *159*

This classic 1960s-era motor inn is a rarity in Back Bay. Rooms offer simple style and good value in an otherwise expensive area near the Christian Science complex and Symphony Hall. Outdoor swimming pool and low-cost parking are significant bonuses. Pet-friendly. **www.midtownhotel.com**

BACK BAY AND SOUTH END Eliot Suites Hotel ($)($)($)($)($)

370 Commonwealth Ave, 02215 ***Tel*** *(617) 267-1607, (800) 443-5468* ***Fax*** *(617) 536-9114* ***Rooms*** *95*

Suites with separate sleeping and sitting rooms are equally convenient for guest musicians playing at nearby Symphony Hall, business people, and families (children under 18 stay free). Guests enjoy complimentary access to Boston Sports Club and the short stroll to Fenway Park. Restaurant Clio is one of the city's best. **www.eliothotel.com**

BACK BAY AND SOUTH END Jurys Boston Hotel ($)($)($)($)($)

350 Stuart St, 02116 ***Tel*** *(617) 266-7200* ***Fax*** *(617) 266-7203* ***Rooms*** *225*

An Irish boutique hotel chain took the elegance of this limestone-faced former Boston Police headquarters, doubled its size to add more rooms, and threw in all the right touches (feather pillows and duvets, heated towel racks, 24-hour room service) to make a modest-priced hotel feel like a luxury stay. **www.jurys-boston-hotels.com**

BACK BAY AND SOUTH END Lenox Hotel ($)($)($)($)($)

61 Exeter St, 02116 ***Tel*** *(617) 536-5300, (800) 225-7676* ***Fax*** *(617) 236-0351* ***Rooms*** *212*

This landmark hotel near the Boston Public Library features sumptuous Edwardian detail in the public areas. Several deluxe corner suites with woodburning fireplaces rival any upscale room in town. Mahogany furniture, marble baths, and muted fabrics create a soothing, elegant atmosphere. **www.lenoxhotel.com**

BEACON HILL AND THEATER DISTRICT John Jeffries House ($)($)

14 David Mugar Way, 02114 ***Tel*** *(617) 367-1866* ***Fax*** *(617) 742-0313* ***Rooms*** *46*

This red-brick building opened in 1909 as housing for nurses at the Massachusetts Eye and Ear Infirmary. Hardwood floors, original moldings, and traditional furnishings give the feel of a well-lived-in Beacon Hill townhouse. Popular with families of hospital patients and visitors alike. Most rooms have kitchenettes. **www.johnjeffrieshouse.com**

BEACON HILL AND THEATER DISTRICT Beacon Hill Hotel & Bistro ($)($)($)($)

25 Charles St, 02114 ***Tel*** *(617) 723-7575* ***Fax*** *(617) 723-7525* ***Rooms*** *13*

Paris meets Beacon Hill in this smart renovation of a townhouse steps from Boston Common and the Public Garden. Rooms are fairly small but chic with soothing colors, framed photos, plantation shutters, and flat-panel TVs. Guests can spread out in the second floor sitting room or on a private roof deck. Breakfast included. **www.beaconhillhotel.com**

BEACON HILL AND THEATER DISTRICT Boston Park Plaza Hotel & Towers ($)($)($)($)

64 Arlington St, 02116 ***Tel*** *(617) 426-2000, (888) 625-5144* ***Fax*** *(617) 426-5545* ***Rooms*** *941*

Opened in 1927 this 15-floor hotel is the city's largest historic lodging. Two ballrooms and an oversized but elegant lobby make the Park Plaza the scene of many local celebrations as well as business meetings and small conventions. Watch the action over afternoon tea in Swan's Café. **www.bostonparkplaza.com**

Key to Symbols *see back cover flap*

BEACON HILL AND THEATER DISTRICT Boston at Beacon Hill $$$$$

5 Blossom St, 02114 ***Tel*** *(617) 742-7630, (800) 972-3381* ***Fax*** *(617) 742-4192* ***Rooms*** *305*

It's worth walking the few extra steps away from Beacon Hill and Quincy Market for the savings that you make on the price of a room in this cluster of office buildings. Functioning largely as a tour group and conference facility, this hotel is part of the Holiday Inn chain. **www.ichotelsgroup.com**

BEACON HILL AND THEATER DISTRICT Charles Street Inn $$$$$

94 Charles St, 02114 ***Tel*** *(617) 314-8900, (877) 772-8900* ***Fax*** *(617) 371-0009* ***Rooms*** *9*

This time capsule was built in 1860 as a demonstration showpiece for new homes under construction in the Back Bay. Victorian features such as carved marble fireplaces harmonize with European furnishings and modern whirlpool tubs, mini-fridges, and CD players. Good base for exploring the antiques shops. Breakfast included. **www.charlesstreetinn.com**

BEACON HILL AND THEATER DISTRICT Courtyard Boston Tremont Hotel $$$$$

275 Tremont St, 02116 ***Tel*** *(617) 426-1400, (800) 321-2211* ***Fax*** *(617) 482-6730* ***Rooms*** *315*

This 1920s tower hotel in the Theater District has been completely restored. The dramatic lobby features marble columns, carved granite details, and glittering crystal chandeliers. Guest rooms are more simply furnished but with modern amenities including walk-in showers. **www.courtyardbostontremont.com**

BEACON HILL AND THEATER DISTRICT Four Seasons Hotel Boston $$$$$

200 Boylston St, 02116 ***Tel*** *(617) 338-4400, (800) 819-5053* ***Fax*** *(617) 423-0154* ***Rooms*** *274*

The low-key luxury at this modern hotel on a corner of the Public Garden at the edge of the Theater District draws rock stars, best-selling authors, corporate bigwigs, and visiting dignitaries. Lobby-level Bristol Lounge offers afternoon tea, full menu for children, and a fireplace ambience conducive to making business deals. **www.fourseasons.com**

GREATER BOSTON Constitution Inn $$

150 Third Ave, Charlestown, 02129 ***Tel*** *(617) 241-8400, (800) 495-9622* ***Fax*** *(617) 241-2856* ***Rooms*** *147*

Convenient to the Freedom Trail, this unique property offers the lowest rates to Armed Services personnel. However, it also welcomes casual visitors and its well-maintained rooms, fitness center, pool, and sauna are a good deal for all. The staff are especially welcoming. **www.constitutioninn.org**

GREATER BOSTON Isaac Harding House $$$

288 Harvard St, Cambridge, 02138 ***Tel*** *(617) 876-2888, (877) 489-2888* ***Fax*** *(617) 497-0953* ***Rooms*** *14*

This bed and breakfast occupies an 1860s Victorian house in a quiet Cambridge residential neighborhood halfway between Central and Harvard squares. Public areas combine comfort with elegance. Guest rooms are spacious and bright, some share baths. Free parking is available. **www.harding-house.com**

GREATER BOSTON Harvard Square Hotel $$$$

110 Mount Auburn St, Cambridge, 02138 ***Tel*** *(617) 864-5200, (800) 458-5886* ***Fax*** *(617) 864-2409* ***Rooms*** *73*

This four-story motor-inn boasts an excellent location in the midst of Harvard Square. There is a small lobby and basic but comfortable guest rooms featuring light wood furnishings and warm colors. Register for special deals offered only by e-mail. **www.harvardsquarehotel.com**

GREATER BOSTON Holiday Inn Express $$$$

250 Monsignor O'Brien Hwy, Cambridge, 02141 ***Tel*** *(617) 577-7600, (800) 972-3381* ***Fax*** *(617) 354-1313* ***Rooms*** *112*

This business hotel features rooms with luxurious bedding, deluxe continental breakfasts, a small business center, limited onsite parking, and free parking in the lot across the street. It is close to the Museum of Science and only a short walk to Lechmere T-stop. **www.ichotelsgroup.com**

GREATER BOSTON Irving House $$$$

24 Irving St, Cambridge, 02138 ***Tel*** *(617) 547-4600, (800) 547-4600* ***Fax*** *(617) 576-2814* ***Rooms*** *44*

This rambling Victorian building is a short walk from Harvard University's main campus. The rooms in the older rooming house turned bed and breakfast vary greatly in size and amenities. The Irving's quiet location and proximity to Harvard Yard and Harvard Square make it a favorite with visiting scholars on a budget. **www.irvinghouse.com**

GREATER BOSTON Le Méridien Cambridge $$$$$

20 Sidney St, Cambridge, 02139 ***Tel*** *(617) 577-0200, (800) 543-4300* ***Rooms*** *210*

Built as the Hotel@MIT, this high-tech Le Méridien is adjacent to the Massachusetts Institute of Technology. As one of Le Méridien's design hotels, the decor of the rooms here is sleek and contemporary, and the Central Square location is great for access to the area's shopping, ethnic restaurants, and music bars. **www.starwoodhotels.com**

NORTH END AND WATERFRONT Golden Slipper B&B Afloat $$$$

Lewis Wharf, 02110 ***Tel*** *(781) 545-2845* ***Rooms*** *2*

For a different perspective on Boston, this vintage Chris Craft yacht tied up at Lewis Wharf sleeps two in a comfortable bedroom, and two more can sleep on the lounge's pull-out couch. Galley kitchen, full bathroom, TV, and air conditioning. Convenient location in historic district, close to Faneuil Hall. **www.bostonsbedandbreakfastafloat.com**

NORTH END AND WATERFRONT Seaport Hotel $$$$$

1 Seaport Lane, 02210 ***Tel*** *(617) 385-4000, (800) 262-0608* ***Fax*** *(617) 385-4001* ***Rooms*** *426*

This modern business hotel is connected by walkway to the Seaport World Trade Center. Weekend specials often include good options for families. Shuttles run to North Station and the Financial District. Water taxi to Long Wharf, the North End, and Charlestown Navy Yard is a fun way to tour the Freedom Trail. **www.seaportboston.com**

OLD BOSTON AND FINANCIAL DISTRICT Harborside Inn $$$$

185 State St, 02109 ***Tel*** *(617) 723-7500, (888) 723-7565* ***Fax*** *(617) 670-6015* ***Rooms*** *54*

This modest boutique hotel in an 1858 granite spice warehouse building is located near Faneuil Hall Marketplace and the New England Aquarium. Small guest rooms have fresh, modern furnishings, and some have city views. **www.harborsideinnboston.com**

OLD BOSTON AND FINANCIAL DISTRICT Hilton Boston Financial District $$$$$

89 Broad St, 02110 ***Tel*** *(617) 556-0006, (800) 996-3426* ***Fax*** *(617) 556-0053* ***Rooms*** *362*

This 1928 Art Deco building was Boston's first skyscraper, built on the edge of the Financial District. A careful hotel conversion preserved the marble floors in the lobby and bathrooms and polished wood and brass details in the public areas. Business people favor the sedate library as a meeting place. **www.hilton.com**

OLD BOSTON AND FINANCIAL DISTRICT Langham Hotel Boston $$$$$

250 Franklin St, 02110 ***Tel*** *(617) 451-1900, (800) 223-6800* ***Fax*** *(617) 423-2844* ***Rooms*** *318*

Old money doesn't get much older than at the Langham, which occupies the Renaissance Revival palace on Post Office Square, originally constructed as the Federal Reserve Bank. The painted dome and gilded vaults of the foyer hint at comforts of 19th-century French decor in the rooms. Special family programs. **www.langhamboston.com**

OLD BOSTON AND FINANCIAL DISTRICT Liberty Hotel $$$$$

215 Charles St, 02114 ***Tel*** *(617) 224-4000* ***Fax*** *(617) 224-4001* ***Rooms*** *300*

Charles Street Jail, built in Boston granite in 1851, was transformed in 2007 into a sleek designer hotel with a soaring atrium lobby, three of Boston's best restaurants (including Lydia Shire's Scampo), and a swanky bar. Rooms are luxuriously comfortable and many have floor-to-ceiling views of the Charles River. **www.libertyhotel.com**

OLD BOSTON AND FINANCIAL DISTRICT Omni Parker House $$$$$

60 School St, 02108 ***Tel*** *(617) 227-8600, (800) 843-6664* ***Fax*** *(617) 742-5729* ***Rooms*** *551*

Memorabilia on display in the ornate lobby emphasize Parker House's status as America's longest continuously operating hotel. Rooms were recently updated, though some remain compact. Boston cream pie was first served here and Parkers Restaurant and Parkers Bar are favorites with politicians. Located on the Freedom Trail. **www.omnihotels.com**

MASSACHUSETTS

CONCORD Colonial Inn $$

48 Monument Sq, 01742 ***Tel*** *(978) 369-9200, (800) 370-9200* ***Fax*** *(508) 371-1533* ***Rooms*** *56*

This landmark structure was built in 1716 and has operated as an inn since 1889. The original inn has 15 rooms, while others are located in the newer wing and adjacent buildings. Colonial Revival furnishings contribute to the antiquarian air. The tavern is a key stop on the folk music circuit. **www.concordscolonialinn.com**

NANTUCKET Union Street Inn $$$$

7 Union St, 02554 ***Tel*** *(508) 228-9222, (800) 225-5116* ***Fax*** *(508) 325-0848* ***Rooms*** *12*

This c.1770 house, exemplifying Nantucket's historic, cedar-shingle architecture, sits in the midst of the island's main village, handy for walking to virtually all attractions. Wide-plank pine floors and fireplaces in several rooms are complemented by modern luxury linens and amenities. Full cooked breakfast served daily. Closed Jan–Mar. **www.unioninn.com**

PLYMOUTH Pilgrim Sands Motel $$

150 Warren Ave, 02360 ***Tel*** *(508) 747-0900, (800) 729-7263* ***Fax*** *(508) 746-8066* ***Rooms*** *64*

Directly across the street from Plimoth Plantation, this modern motel has spacious rooms, a whirlpool spa, indoor and outdoor heated pools, and its own private beach that adjoins Plymouth Long Beach. Two self-catering suites are also available. Continental breakfast in the coffee shop and wireless Internet access included. **www.pilgrimsands.com**

PLYMOUTH John Carver Inn $$$

25 Summer St, 02360 ***Tel*** *(508) 746-7100, (800) 274-1620* ***Fax*** *(508) 746-8299* ***Rooms*** *80*

This popular lodging combines Colonial Revival style, right down to pub-chair seating in the dining room, with a Pilgrim-themed indoor pool featuring an 80-foot water slide. Located on a hill across from an historic grist mill, the inn is a few minutes' walk from waterfront attractions. Popular with bus tours. **www.johncarverinn.com**

PROVINCETOWN Chateau Provincetown $$$$

105 Bradford St, 02657 ***Tel*** *(508) 487-1286* ***Fax*** *(508) 487-3557* ***Rooms*** *54*

This hilltop compound overlooking Provincetown harbor features luxuriant gardens, a large heated pool, and several decks. It offers surprisingly quiet private accommodations in a resort destination known for a certain edgy rowdiness. Continental breakfast is included. **www.chateauprovincetown.com**

SALEM Hawthorne Hotel $$$$

18 Washington Square W, 01970 ***Tel*** *(978) 744-4080, (800) 729-7829* ***Fax*** *(978) 745-9842* ***Rooms*** *93*

Built in 1925 in the Federal style of a century earlier, the Hawthorne is a civic and social center for Salem, hosting annual Halloween events including a costume ball. The city's only full-service hotel, it is located near Salem Common, the Peabody Essex Museum, and the pedestrian shopping district. Free wireless Internet access. **www.hawthornehotel.com**

Key to Price Guide *see p176* **Key to Symbols** *see back cover flap*

RHODE ISLAND

BLOCK ISLAND 1661 Inn and Hotel Manisses $$$

Spring St, 02807 ***Tel*** *(401) 466-2421, (800) 626-4773* ***Fax*** *(401) 466-3162* ***Rooms*** *26*

The 9-room inn is open all year and features the best appointed rooms, but the 17-room Victorian Hotel Manisses (closed mid-Oct–Mar) is a grand tradition on Block Island. There is no air conditioning, some rooms lack TVs, but all have private bathrooms. Hotel guest rooms are furnished with Victorian antiques. **www.blockislandresorts.com**

CHARLESTOWN General Stanton Inn $$

4115 Old Post Rd (Route 1A), 02813 ***Tel*** *(401) 364-8888, (800) 364-8011* ***Fax*** *(401) 364-3333* ***Rooms*** *17*

With a portion dating from 1667, the General Stanton claims to be one of the oldest continuously run hostelries in North America. Much of that atmosphere persists in the dining room's low ceilings, massive fireplaces, and exposed hand-hewn timbers. Site of popular weekend flea market in warm weather. **www.generalstantoninn.com**

NEWPORT Beech Tree Inn $$$

34 Rhode Island Ave, 02840 ***Tel*** *(401) 847-9794, (800) 748-6565* ***Rooms*** *8*

Located in a quiet residential area away from the waterfront hubbub, this Victorian bed and breakfast (built in 1887) is noted for offering the "biggest breakfast in Newport". Some rooms have gas fireplaces and whirlpool tubs, but all have air-conditioning and TV. Older children are welcome. The guest common area has a full kitchen. **www.beechtreeinn.com**

NEWPORT Castle Hill Inn and Resort $$$$$

590 Ocean Dr, 02840 ***Tel*** *(401) 849-3800, (888) 466-1355* ***Fax*** *(401) 849-3838* ***Rooms*** *25*

Perhaps the most exclusive of resorts in Newport, Castle Hill occupies a prime spot on the peninsula at the west end of Ocean Drive. The main mansion was built as a summer home for scientist/explorer Alexander Agassiz in 1874, and the property has a history of celebrity guests. Additional rooms in the chalet and beach houses. **www.castlehillinn.com**

PROVIDENCE The Westin $$$

One West Exchange St, 02903 ***Tel*** *(401) 598-8000, (800) 937-8461* ***Fax*** *(401) 598-8200* ***Rooms*** *364*

A massive convention hotel sandwiched between the R.I. Convention Center and Providence Place shopping mall in the heart of downtown manages to fit into the city's historic skyline with surprising aplomb. Top-of-the-line appointments (bedlinens and toiletries) make business travelers feel at home. Excellent restaurant. **www.westin.com/providence**

PROVIDENCE Hotel Providence $$$$

311 Westminster St, 02903 ***Tel*** *(401) 861-8000, (800) 861-8990* ***Fax*** *(401) 861-8002* ***Rooms*** *80*

Located in the central Providence business district, in an architecturally interesting area, is this minimalist, modern boutique hotel. Rooms and suites are well-equipped and have sophisticated, luxurious decor and furnishings. Each features original art by the Chairman of the Rhode Island School of Design. **www.thehotelprovidence.com**

CONNECTICUT

ESSEX Griswold Inn $$$

36 Main St, 06426 ***Tel*** *(860) 767-1776* ***Fax*** *(860) 767-0481* ***Rooms*** *30*

Located in the center of Essex village, the "Gris" has been an inn since at least 1801. Old-fashioned charm abounds and the original prints and oil paintings on the walls reflect the maritime history of this important port on the Connecticut River. Rooms are comfortable and furnished with antiques. Five dining rooms. **www.griswoldinn.com**

LITCHFIELD Litchfield Inn $$$

432 Bantam Rd, 06759 ***Tel*** *(860) 567-4503, (800) 499-3444* ***Fax*** *(860) 567-5358* ***Rooms*** *32*

Colonial decor belies the 1982 founding of this inn, the largest hostelry in Litchfield and the epicenter of the country squire lifestyle of the Connecticut hills. The lobby's chandelier and dramatic but delicately carved staircase set the tone. Eight luxury rooms go all-out with styling. Continental breakfast included. **www.litchfieldinnct.com**

MYSTIC Steamboat Inn $$$$

73 Steamboat Wharf, 06355 ***Tel*** *(860) 536-8300* ***Fax*** *(860) 536-9528* ***Rooms*** *11*

With each room named for a vessel from Mystic's sailing heyday, this inn beside the historic drawbridge is about as nautical as it gets. The architecture is quirky, rooms have odd angles, and views are sometimes blocked by a yacht docked outside. Breakfast buffet served in the morning; sherry and cookies in the afternoon. **www.steamboatinnmystic.com**

NEW HAVEN Swan Cove Bed & Breakfast $$

115 Sea St, 06519 ***Tel*** *(203) 776-3240* ***Rooms*** *4*

Located in historic Oyster Point, Swan Cove features mini-suites and rooms in a Queen Anne-style house on a Long Island Sound cove. All rooms and suites have private entrances and a dining area. There is a TV in the common room and in some suites. Breakfast included. **www.swancove.com**

VERMONT

BURLINGTON Hilton Hotel $$$$

60 Battery St, 05401 ***Tel*** *(802) 658-6500, (800) 9Hilton* ***Fax*** *(802) 658-4659* ***Rooms*** *258*

Location is everything for Burlington's most upscale hotel, which sits between the heart of downtown and the shore of Lake Champlain. The best rooms have breathtaking views of the lake with the Adirondack Mountains rising behind. It's set up for business travelers, with a good business center and work desks in rooms. **www.hilton.com**

KILLINGTON Mountain Meadows Lodge $$

285 Thundering Brook Rd, 05751 ***Tel*** *(802) 775-1010, (800) 370-4567* ***Rooms*** *20*

Set both on a glacial lake and on the Appalachian Trail, the lodge is a perfect base for outdoors enthusiasts in almost every season. Excellent fishing and boating in warm weather, top skiing in winter. Restaurant serves dinner at weekends in winter for guests only, and there's a massage therapist on staff. **www.mountainmeadowslodge.com**

MANCHESTER The Equinox Resort $$$$$

3567 Main St (Route 7A), 05254 ***Tel*** *(802) 362-4700, (800) 362-4747* ***Fax*** *(802) 362-4861* ***Rooms*** *183*

An historic 18th-century resort with stunning public spaces and spacious rooms. Situated between the Green and Taconic mountains, the vast property has sweeping views. Outdoor activities (most with extra charge) include boating, golf, falconry, flyfishing, and shooting, as well as nearby snowmobiling and skiing. **www.equinoxresort.com**

RICHMOND The Richmond Victorian Inn $$

191 E Main St, 05477 ***Tel*** *(802) 434-4410, (888) 242-3362* ***Fax*** *(802) 434-4411* ***Rooms*** *6*

Located in the foothills of the Green Mountains, just 12 miles (19.5 km) east of Lake Champlain, this modestly priced inn's guest rooms are furnished in a country Victorian style with antiques, quilts, and other homey touches. Rooms do not have air-conditioning or TVs. (TV in sitting room.) Children 12 and older welcome. **www.richmondvictorianinn.com**

SHELBURNE Inn at Shelburne Farms $$$$$

1611 Harbor Rd, 05482 ***Tel*** *(802) 985-8498* ***Rooms*** *24*

This late 19th-century mansion overlooking Lake Champlain is the centerpiece of a historic farm that makes cheese and offers garden and property tours. The grounds were designed by Frederick Law Olmsted, the father of US landscape architecture, while the English gardens were created by the owners. **www.shelburnefarms.org**

STOWE Alpenrose Motel $

2619 Mountain Rd, 05672 ***Tel*** *(802) 253-7277, (800) 253-4707* ***Rooms*** *8*

Located halfway between Stowe village and Stowe Mountain Ski Resort, and just steps off the Stowe Recreation Path, this motel offers bargain lodging in spacious rooms, many with a basic kitchen. Some two-room units can sleep up to five. Outdoor storage lockers for skis and snowboards. **www.gostowe.com/alpenrose**

STOWE Trapp Family Lodge $$$$

700 Trapp Hill Rd, 05672 ***Tel*** *(802) 253-8511, (800) 826-7000* ***Fax*** *(802) 253-5740* ***Rooms*** *96*

This is the world-famous resort of the family that inspired *The Sound of Music*. Set within massive grounds, there is a large Austrian-style main lodge, luxury villas, guest house chalets, nightly entertainment, a range of recreational activities, and exquisite cuisine. Some rooms are air-conditioned. **www.trappfamily.com**

NEW HAMPSHIRE

BRETTON WOODS The Mount Washington Hotel & Resort $$$$$

Route 302, 03575 ***Tel*** *(603) 278-1000, (800) 314-1752* ***Fax*** *(603) 278-8838* ***Rooms*** *200*

Since 1902 this elegant hotel has offered high-quality service in a beautiful natural setting. The mountain air keeps the rooms comfortable during the summer season. An indoor pool, a games room, and excellent dining round out the experience. **www.mtwashington.com**

CONCORD The Centennial Inn $$$

96 Pleasant St, 03301 ***Tel*** *(603) 227-9000, (800) 360-4839* ***Fax*** *(603) 225-5031* ***Rooms*** *32*

Housed in a restored 1892 Victorian brick mansion, this centrally located inn provides rooms and suites handsomely furnished in antiques and quality reproductions. Six of the suites occupy the inn's striking twin turrets. High-speed wireless Internet access throughout and there's a popular bar and bistro. **www.thecentennialinn.com**

FRANCONIA The Franconia Inn $$

1300 Easton Rd, 03580 ***Tel*** *(603) 823-5542, (800) 473-5299* ***Fax*** *(603) 823-8078* ***Rooms*** *32*

A cozy inn built in 1935 with striking views of the White Mountains rising directly behind the building. Outdoor enthusiasts will find a variety of sports activities in almost all seasons, from rock-climbing and trail hiking to skiing and snowshoeing. There's no air-conditioning, but it rarely gets hot. Closed Apr–mid-May. **www.franconiainn.com**

Key to Price Guide *see p176* **Key to Symbols** *see back cover flap*

FRANCONIA Lovett's Inn $$$

1474 Profile Rd, 03580 **Tel** *(603) 823-7761, (800) 356-3802* **Fax** *(603) 823-8802* **Rooms** *19*

For 70 years the distinctive hospitality of this former country estate has attracted such guests as movie star Bette Davis and members of the Kennedy clan. Some rooms have television and most have air-conditioning. The inn's dining room is a special draw, featuring well-crafted cuisine and a good wine list. Closed April. **www.lovettsinn.com**

MANCHESTER The Highlander Inn $$

2 Highlander Way, 03103 **Tel** *(603) 625-6426, (800) 548-9248* **Fax** *(603) 625-6466* **Rooms** *87*

This former boarding house and 1930s inn were completely transformed into a modern conference hotel aimed at business travelers. The Highlander is also a popular venue for weddings and graduation events. The location is convenient for Manchester airport. **www.highlanderinn.com**

MEREDITH Meredith Inn B&B $$

2 Wauwekan St, 03253 **Tel** *(603) 279-0000* **Fax** *(603) 279-4017* **Rooms** *8*

This Victorian home has been updated with modern amenities. It is handy for activities on Lake Winnipesaukee, and within walking distance to the beach on Lake Wauwekan. In another direction lie the artisans' shops and restaurants of downtown Meredith. Most rooms have air-conditioning. Reduced rates Nov–Apr. **www.meredithinn.com**

PORTSMOUTH The Inn at Christian Shore $$

335 Maplewood Ave, 03801 **Tel** *(603) 431-6770* **Fax** *(603) 373-8421* **Rooms** *5*

This well-preserved early Federal-era home is furnished with a mix of antiques, African art, and contemporary paintings that accord with the taste of the Argentine owner. The neighborhood is a close walk to the historic city center and waterfront. Gourmet breakfasts included. No children allowed. **www.innatchristianshore.com**

PORTSMOUTH Sheraton Harborside Portsmouth $$$$

250 Market St, 03801 **Tel** *(603) 431-2300, (888) 627-7138* **Fax** *(603) 433-5649* **Rooms** *219*

Located just two blocks from Market Square and adjacent to the docks for whale watching and harbor cruises, this Sheraton is a modern business hotel equally suited for the leisure traveler. A Redwood sauna, extensive fitness room, and large pool set it apart from other Portsmouth lodgings. **www.sheratonportsmouth.com**

MAINE

BAR HARBOR Mira Monte Inn and Suites $$$

69 Mount Desert St, 04609 **Tel** *(207) 288-4263, (800) 553-5109* **Fax** *(207) 288-3115* **Rooms** *17*

Constructed in 1864, this is one of the few B&Bs in town owned by Bar Harbor natives. It features two formal gardens and an inviting wrap-around porch for rocking and reading. The center of town is a five-minute walk away from this residential neighborhood. All rooms have a fireplace and/or balcony. Closed Nov–Apr. **www.miramonte.com**

BETHEL Bethel Inn and Country Club $$$

On the Common, 04217 **Tel** *(207) 824-2175, (800) 654-0125* **Fax** *(207) 824-2333* **Rooms** *150*

A premier Maine resort, with four Colonial-style buildings, this property has its own championship golf course, golf school, and tennis courts. Summer rates include golf, except for town-house guests. Winter rates include cross-country trail fees. Some packages include meals. Air-conditioning in some rooms. **www.bethelinn.com**

KENNEBUNKPORT Captain Jefferd's Inn $$$$

5 Pearl St, 04046 **Tel** *(207) 967-2311, (800) 839-6844* **Rooms** *15*

This sea captain's mansion, built in 1804, retains its antique charm and has beautifully landscaped gardens. There is also a wood-burning fireplace in the living room and some rooms have gas fireplaces. Ten rooms in the main inn, five more in the carriage house. It's conveniently located, one block from the old Town Green. **www.captainjefferdsinn.com**

OGUNQUIT The Cliff House Resort & Spa $$$$

Shore Rd, 03907 **Tel** *(207) 361-1000* **Fax** *(207) 361-2122* **Rooms** *196*

Iconic oceanside resort built in 1872 with a full floor devoted to recreation. All rooms have balconies. The resort also has a noted full-service spa. Cliff House trolley takes guests to spots of interest in the area in July and August, including Ogunquit's excellent swimming beaches. Closed mid-Dec–Mar. **www.cliffhousemaine.com**

PORTLAND Inn at St. John $

939 Congress, 04102 **Tel** *(207) 773-6481, (800) 636-9127* **Fax** *(207) 756-7629* **Rooms** *39*

Built in 1897 to accommodate rail passengers, this venerable inn stands just minutes from Portland's Old Port, Waterfront, and Arts districts. Rooms are tastefully decorated, but some share baths. The telephone is free if calling locally. Inexpensive extended stays are available off-season. Dogs are welcomed. **www.innatstjohn.com**

PORTLAND Portland Regency Hotel $$$$

20 Milk St, 04101 **Tel** *(207) 774-4200, (800) 727-3436* **Fax** *(207) 775-2150* **Rooms** *103*

Situated in the heart of the Old Port, this conversion of the city's former Armory is Portland's premiere full-service hotel. Colonial-style furnishings, flat-panel TVs, and wireless Internet access throughout. The fitness center is free for guests. A complimentary town car is available between hotel and transportation facilities. **www.theregency.com**

Choosing a Restaurant

New England's cuisine is a melting pot of different cultures – the English, Irish, and the Italians have each brought their own cuisines as well as adopted native ingredients. Restaurants have been selected across a wide price range for their value, good food, atmosphere, and location. They are listed by area and then by price.

PRICE CATEGORIES
For a three-course meal for one, half a bottle of house wine, and all unavoidable extra charges such as sales tax and service.
($) Under $25
($)($) $25–$40
($)($)($) $40–$50
($)($)($)($) $50–$65
($)($)($)($)($) Over $65

BOSTON

BACK BAY AND SOUTH END Mike's City Diner ($)

1714 Washington St, 02118 ***Tel*** *(617) 267-9393*

Show up early – very early. Mike's is open 6am–3pm every day, and there's usually a line out the door waiting for the luncheon specials rendered with just a little more care and finesse than you'll find on the Interstate. Political candidates always come by for a photo op during the quadrennial presidential nominating race. Breakfast and lunch daily.

BACK BAY AND SOUTH END Tapeo ($)($)($)

266 Newbury St, 02116 ***Tel*** *(617) 267-4799*

Authentically Spanish, this combination restaurant and tapas bar specializes in small plates that would be served with a glass of sherry in Spain. One of the few restaurants in Boston to serve true *jamón serrano* (the Spanish answer to Italian prosciutto), Tapeo also prepares exquisite bites like boneless pheasant breast and garlicky squid. Excellent sherry list.

BACK BAY AND SOUTH END Azure ($)($)($)($)

61 Exeter St, 02116 ***Tel*** *(617) 933-4800*

While the chef is known for his bold treatments of grilled meats such as lamb steak marinated in pomegranate juice, North Atlantic and Alaskan seafood dishes are the real stars. They are usually set off by an unusual fruit or vegetable, such as a mound of sweet and sour eggplant. The portions are large and Azure also serves a hearty breakfast.

BACK BAY AND SOUTH END Tremont 647 & Sister Sorel ($)($)($)($)

647 Tremont St, 02118 ***Tel*** *(617) 266-4600*

The extensively tattooed chef-owner is no shrinking violet, and his style of cooking favors big portions, bold flavors, and lots of smoke with the meat. South End trend-followers are always stopping in to determine what's *au courant*, whether it is high-alcohol caipirinhas or the weekend pajama brunches when diners show up in sleepware.

BEACON HILL AND THE THEATER DISTRICT Legal Sea Foods ($)($)($)

26 Park Plaza, 02116 ***Tel*** *(617) 426-4444*

This flagship restaurant is still a national leader in setting quality standards for fresh fish well prepared. Its amenities include an extensive wine cellar and a lounge popular for Back Bay business lunches and after-dinner drinks. Legal Seafoods offers an award-winning kids menu and a gluten-free menu for celiacs.

BEACON HILL AND THE THEATER DISTRICT Locke-Ober ($)($)($)($)($)

3 Winter Pl, 02108 ***Tel*** *(617) 542-1340*

The original 1890s decor has been lusciously restored in this bastion of fine dining in Old Boston. Locke-Ober did not permit women until the 1970s, but now its kitchen is run by a female chef-owner who fills the giant footsteps of Escoffier with modern interpretations of culinary classics. Lunch Mon–Fri, dinner Mon–Sat.

GREATER BOSTON Mr. Bartley's Burger and Salad Cottage ($)

1246 Massachusetts Ave, Cambridge, 02138 ***Tel*** *(617) 354-6559*

Harvard Square's quintessential burger shop specializes in a whopping piece of meat the size of a big man's fist. Other sandwiches have the sophomoric names linked to a celebrity, but the prices are right, the food is fresh, and it fills you up. On weekends it can take up to an hour to get in the door to order. Lunch and dinner daily.

GREATER BOSTON Craigie on Main ($)($)($)($)($)

853 Main St, Cambridge, 02139 ***Tel*** *(617) 497-5511*

The French-trained chef-owner creates new dishes each day as the menu comes together based on the fish, meat, dairy, and produce deliveries. House terrines, *pâtés*, and preserved vegetables provide some constancy, but each night's featured dishes tend to be surprises. Bargain fixed-price meals available. Dinner Tue–Sun.

NORTH END AND THE WATERFRONT La Famiglia Giorgio's ($)($)

112 Salem St, 02113 ***Tel*** *(617) 367-6711*

Upbeat Italian meals with generous portions at a price that will not break the bank. Great for couples and families on a casual night out. The menu is simple: pizzas, pastas with a choice of sauces, and filling chicken or veal dishes. Unlike many North End restaurants, they do serve dessert and coffee. Lunch Mon–Fri and dinner daily.

Key to Symbols *see back cover flap*

NORTH END AND THE WATERFRONT Pomodoro $$

319 Hanover St, 02113 ***Tel*** *(617) 367-4348*

The tiny Pomodoro often has long lines of diners waiting for tables. The eponymous tomato sauce is one of the North End's best, and the kitchen shines with its vegetable dishes. Even dedicated meat-eaters will find pleasure in a meal of cold grilled vegetable antipasti, great bread, and a warming bowl of soup. Payment in cash only.

NORTH END AND THE WATERFRONT Barking Crab $$$

88 Sleeper St, 02110 ***Tel*** *(617) 426-2722*

Although it is open all year, this Fort Point Channel restaurant is best in summer, when diners can sit outdoors at picnic tables and wield heavy stones to crush lobster and crab shells. Local cod, haddock, flounder, tuna, halibut, clams, and crab are available fried, steamed, or broiled. The Boston skyline views are an added bonus.

NORTH END AND THE WATERFRONT Terramia $$$

98 Salem St, 02113 ***Tel*** *(617) 523-3112*

This snug trattoria (the sister restaurant to Antico across the street) eschews the red-sauce neighborhood heritage in favor of Piedmontese roasted meats (including game), deeply savory dishes with dark mushrooms and caramelized onions, and bright Ligurian-style seafood lightly dressed with capers and lemon. There is sadly no coffee or dessert.

NORTH END AND THE WATERFRONT Meritage $$$$$

70 Rowes Wharf, 02110 ***Tel*** *(617) 439-3995*

Exquisite regional and seasonal contemporary American dishes are laid out on the menu to match choices from this hotel restaurant's wine list. Thus, the list leads with dishes for sparkling wines and light whites, proceeds through robust reds, and ends with rich desserts or a platter of fine cheese matched to ports and Sauternes. Dinner Tue–Sun, brunch Sun.

OLD BOSTON AND THE FINANCIAL DISTRICT Durgin Park $$

340 Faneuil Hall Marketplace, 02109 ***Tel*** *(617) 227-2038*

Legendary for its generous portions, Durgin Park began in 1826 as a lunch hall for produce and meat market workers. Family-style seating at long tables in the dining room makes for lively conversation. Traditional favorites include baked beans, Indian pudding, and grilled prime rib of beef big enough to hang over the edge of the plate.

MASSACHUSETTS

CAPE COD Scargo Café $$$

799 Main St, Route 6A, Dennis, 02638 ***Tel*** *(508) 385-8200*

The welcoming ambience is matched by creative cuisine and excellent service. Main dishes range from lightly seared tuna with pickled ginger to tenderloin steak on mushrooms topped with soft goat's cheese. The handy location across from the Cape Playhouse makes it a good bet for a pre-matinée lunch or early dinner before the curtain rises.

CONCORD Walden Grille $$

24 Walden St, 01742 ***Tel*** *(978) 371-2233*

This 20-year-old casual downtown spot is a favored gathering place for soccer moms at lunch and friends having after-work drinks and supper. The creative American fare gets more creative every year, branching out from old favorites such as cornbread-stuffed chicken to bistro dishes such as seared skate with pumpkin risotto. Lunch and dinner daily.

MARTHA'S VINEYARD Sweet Life Café $$$$$

63 Upper Circuit Ave, Oak Bluffs, 02557 ***Tel*** *(508) 696-0200*

Three intimate dining rooms and a garden terrace in an 1861 Victorian house serve as the stage for imaginative New American cooking. The cuisine shows the sure hand of an accomplished chef, with touches like balsamic-glazed red peppers as a balance to sweet corn chowder. Dinner Thu–Tue (closed Dec–May).

PLYMOUTH Lobster Hut $$

25 Town Wharf, 02360 ***Tel*** *(508) 746-2270*

On the waterfront, steps from the *Mayflower II*, this Plymouth institution has a classic fish shack menu and enough tables to serve the tourists hankering for baskets of fried clams or scallops, steamed or broiled lobster, or plates of fish and chips mounded high. Self-service, and food can be packed to take to the beach. Closed Jan.

SALEM Lyceum Bar & Grill $$$

43 Church St, 01970 ***Tel*** *(978) 745-7665*

In this historic building, where Alexander Graham Bell made the first long-distance telephone call in 1877, you'll find a good assortment of New American and grilled dishes. The elegant rooms have high ceilings and glass walls, and an intriguing wine list emphasizes lesser-known California vineyards. Lunch Mon–Fri, dinner daily, brunch Sun.

STURBRIDGE Publick House $$$$

295 Main St, 01566 ***Tel*** *(508) 347-3313*

This roadside inn has greeted and fed travelers since 1771, and in keeping with the preservationist spirit of nearby Old Sturbridge Village the inn maintains the open hearths and plain fare that the Founding Fathers would have sought. Favorites include lobster pie, roast prime rib of beef, and baked scrod. Breakfast, lunch & dinner daily; brunch Sun.

RHODE ISLAND

BLOCK ISLAND Finn's Seafood Restaurant $$

212 Water St, 02807 ***Tel** (401) 466-2473*

This restaurant sports a seafood market next door, a sure sign of fresh fish in these parts. Both fried and broiled fish are dependable, but species vary with the season and the luck of the fishing boats. Lobster, steamed mussels, clam rolls, and broiled swordfish are all tasty. The upstairs deck has great views. Closed mid-Oct–May.

NEWPORT White Horse Tavern $$$$

26 Marlborough St, 02840 ***Tel** (401) 849-3600*

The oldest operating tavern in America, with low-beamed ceilings, hearth fires, colonial bric-a-brac, and candlelit dining rooms. Good American food with modern touches. For a main dish treat, try the Beef Wellington topped with a pâte of *foie gras*. Lunch and dinner daily and brunch Sun.

NEWPORT The Black Pearl $$$$$

Bannister's Wharf, 02840 ***Tel** (401) 846-5264*

A rundown sail loft of Bannister's Wharf was transformed into one of Newport's most elegant dining spots. Famous for its clam chowder, this landmark blends classic French fare in the sedate Commodore Room with casual dining in the tavern and bar. Competition can be fierce for the best sunset tables. Closed Jan–mid-Feb.

PROVIDENCE Al Forno $$$$

577 S Main St, 02903 ***Tel** (401) 273-9760*

Wood-fire grilled meats, pizzas from stone-floor ovens, and baked pasta dishes are signatures of this popular, informal, place that has received top national reviews. The chef-owners keep inventing new and fabulous dishes that use fresh local ingredients and draw diners from as far away as Boston. Arrive early or prepare to wait. Dinner Tue–Sat.

PROVIDENCE Aspire $$$$

311 Westminster St, 02903 ***Tel** (401) 521-3333*

Regional Rhode Island cuisine gets an upscale, New American interpretation at this sophisticated restaurant where the emphasis is on local oysters and clams. Meats and vegetables are largely sourced locally, and the fresh pasta is particularly good. There's an excellent wine list, and the bar is a favorite with the business crowd. Dinner daily.

CONNECTICUT

HARTFORD Max Downtown $$$$

City Place, 185 Asylum St, 06103 ***Tel** (860) 522-2530*

Smart, modern, bustling, this favorite-with-locals downtown spot features excellent modern American dishes, including a selection of chophouse specials that range from a petite steak *au poivre* to a gigantic porterhouse that hangs off the plate. It is the flagship of the local group of Max restaurants here and in the suburbs. Lunch Mon–Fri, dinner nightly.

LITCHFIELD West Street Grill $$$$

43 West St, 06759 ***Tel** (860) 567-3885*

The area's most popular gathering place for big-name New Yorkers who weekend in the Litchfield Hills offers pace-setting food in a comfortably casual setting. Serves a relatively casual lunch (including burgers) and a more formal New American style. In summer and fall there can be extended waits for a table. Closed Mon–Tue in winter.

MYSTIC Mystic Pizza $

56 W Main St, 06355 ***Tel** (860) 536-3700*

This pizza-and-pasta parlor in downtown Mystic gained national attention in the Julia Roberts movie, but is more famous to diners for its "secret recipe" sauce. Order a house special pizza slathered with the sauce and smothered with pepperoni, meatballs, sausage, green peppers, onions, and mushrooms.

NEW HAVEN Zinc $$$$

964 Chapel St, 06510 ***Tel** (203) 624-0507*

Situated directly on New Haven Green, the stunning minimalist decor of Zinc suits the vibrant food – a stylish blend of New American with liberal touches of Southeast Asian influences, such as the tamari marinade for the grilled tuna. The menu draws extensively on local greenmarkets and organic suppliers. Lunch Tue–Sat, dinner nightly.

NEW HAVEN Union League Cafe $$$$$

1032 Chapel St, 06510 ***Tel** (203) 562-4299*

An historic building plays second fiddle to superb French food, impeccably prepared and served on formal tables with white linens. This is the real deal, with such treats as braised veal cheeks, wild bass steamed with fennel, and a casserole of vegetables enriched with truffle butter. Lunch Mon–Fri, dinner Mon–Sat.

Key to Price Guide *see p182* **Key to Symbols** *see back cover flap*

VERMONT

BURLINGTON India House Restaurant $$

207 Colchester Ave, 05401 ***Tel*** *(802) 862-7800*

A stalwart among the Burlington area's college students, this spot specializes in traditional North Indian food, with both vegetarian and non-vegetarian choices. Authentic *tandoori* cooking includes *reshimi kabob* and pork chunks seared in the clay oven's dry heat. There's a good choice of beers, including Kingfisher in large cans.

MANCHESTER CENTER Up for Breakfast $

4935 Main St, 05255 ***Tel*** *(802) 362-4204*

Delicious, nutritious breakfasts, with many varieties of eggs, pancakes, French toast, waffles, fruit plates, and tofu "eggs vegetarian" that will keep you going until dinner time. There's a good choice of coffees, including a maple latté, freshly squeezed grapefruit juice, or a champagne-and-orange juice mimosa. A full champagne menu is also available.

STOWE Norma's at Topnotch Resort and Spa $$$

4000 Mountain Rd, 05672 ***Tel*** *(802) 253-8585*

The primary dining option at the Topnotch Resort, Norma's serves creative, contemporary fare in a casual environment. This all-purpose bistro has an open kitchen, serving meals with an emphasis on locally grown organic ingredients. Terrace tables afford scenic views of Mount Mansfield, Vermont's highest peak.

NEW HAMPSHIRE

PORTSMOUTH The Blue Mermaid Island Grill $$

409 The Hill, 03801 ***Tel*** *(603) 427-2583*

A wonderful selection of internationally flavored dishes that includes spiced pork, marinated lamb, and a great choice of Caribbean-spiced seafoods prepared on a wood-burning grill. Grazers will find the long list of small plates appealing. The beverage list has nine margaritas, tropical coolers, martinis, and a good wine selection.

PORTSMOUTH The Dunway Restaurant at Strawberry Banke $$$$

66 Marcy St, 03801 ***Tel*** *(603) 373-6112*

In a Colonial home with a post and beam interior, on the grounds of Strawberry Banke Historical Museum, the menu here showcases modern American cuisine. It features local seafood and produce, herbs and vegetables from Strawberry Banke's gardens, and European cheeses. Dinner Mon–Sat; closed Sun.

PORTSMOUTH The Oar House $$$$

55 Ceres St, 03801 ***Tel*** *(603) 436-4025*

Located in a restored 1803 warehouse literally steps from the harbor, the decor reflect's Portsmouth's maritime heritage. But the menu is thoroughly up-to-date, featuring an excellent *bouillabaisse* and an apricot-glazed roast chicken. The wood-fire grill enriches the flavor of fish and beef steaks. Reservations recommended. Closed Jan.

MAINE

KENNEBUNKPORT The Clam Shack $

2 Western St, 04046 ***Tel*** *(207) 967-3321*

This take-out stand is the quintessential seaside experience of hot mollusks and crustaceans next to cool surf. The menu consists of some of the best fast seafood you'll find, including fried and steamed clams, scallops, and a truly memorable lobster roll. It's known for its fresh-cut onion rings. Closed mid-Oct–mid-May.

OGUNQUIT Barnacle Billy's $

Perkins Cove Rd, 03907 ***Tel*** *(207) 646-5575*

This is a classic, bare-bones Maine lobster house with a basic seafood menu, a casual atmosphere, and seaside surroundings. Set directly on the waterfront in Ogunquit, it is quite a bargain in an often pricey resort town. The more expensive but full-service Barnacle Billy's Etc. is right next door. Closed Nov–Apr.

PORTLAND Back Bay Grill $$$$

65 Portland St, 04101 ***Tel*** *(207) 772-8833*

The Back Bay Grill has a seasonal menu and offers elegant New American food in a modern setting that makes it Portland's most popular fine-dining restaurant. A *Wine Spectator Award of Excellence* winner, this restaurant has an enormous selection of wine and is also known for its superb desserts. Dinner Mon–Sat; closed Mon Jan–Feb.

WASHINGTON, DC & THE CAPITAL REGION

INTRODUCING WASHINGTON, DC & THE CAPITAL REGION 188–195

WASHINGTON, DC 196–211

VIRGINIA 212–219

WEST VIRGINIA 220–221

MARYLAND 222–225

DELAWARE 226–227

Washington, DC & the Capital Region at a Glance

Washington, DC and the four states that make up the Capital Region lie in the northeastern United States. This area played an important role in America's history – the earliest colonies were established here, and many battles of the Revolutionary War and Civil War were fought on its fields. The region is, therefore, dotted with magnificent historic sites. Washington, DC is one of America's most visited cities and offers a great range of cultural attractions. The surrounding region's rich variety of landscapes includes Virginia's lush, rolling countryside, West Virginia's rugged mountains, Maryland's picturesque bays and harbors, and Delaware's parks, beaches, and opulent country mansions.

New River Gorge National River (see p220), *in West Virginia, runs through dense forests. The dramatic gorge is a perfect white-water rafting destination.*

Blue Ridge Parkway (see p218), *stretching 215 miles (346 km) through Virginia, winds its way along the crest of the Appalachian Mountains all the way to North Carolina. This lovely route is at its best during spring and fall.*

◁ A dramatic nighttime view of the United States Capitol, one of the world's best-known symbols of democracy

Baltimore (see p222) *epitomizes the rich maritime heritage of Maryland. This pleasant port city's redeveloped waterfront features many shops and restaurants, as well as the stunning National Aquarium.*

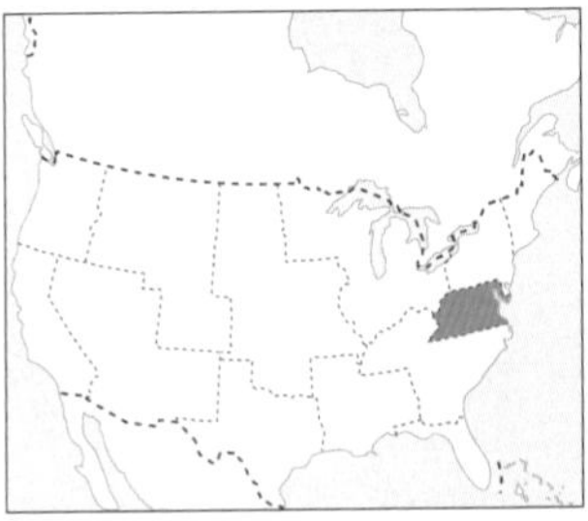

LOCATOR MAP

Rehoboth Beach (see p227), *along the Atlantic Ocean in Delaware, is one of the state's liveliest beach resorts, with restaurants and shopping malls, as well as a range of options for endless entertainment.*

Washington, DC (see pp196–211), *the nation's imposing capital, is dominated by the White House, the president's official residence since the 1820s. Millions of visitors take the tour of this elegantly decorated mansion, the city's signature landmark.*

WASHINGTON, DC & THE CAPITAL REGION

Center of government for the world's most powerful nation, Washington, DC is a stately, Neo-Classical city, with grand avenues and monumental public buildings that reflect the pride and ambitions that course through the corridors of power. Its surrounding region preserves important places where the young nation evolved from a Colonial outpost to an independent country.

Located midway along the Atlantic Coast, the nation's capital lies at the heart of the East Coast. This was also the heart of the Colonial landscape where the country began, and where many of its most significant events occurred. Besides its rich tapestry of historical events, this region also has one of the country's most beautiful and varied landscapes. Just 30 miles (48 km) east from the White House is Chesapeake Bay, the country's largest and most productive estuary, while to the west are the lush Appalachian hardwood forests. This wide variety of topography and scenery is paralleled by an equally wide range of social and economic situations; the area in and around the nation's capital is home to some of the wealthiest as well as the most deprived citizens in the United States.

HISTORY

The first Europeans to this area were a small band of Spanish explorers and Jesuit priests who tried unsuccessfully to set up a colony around Chesapeake Bay in 1570. They were followed by the English, who in honor of the "Virgin Queen" Elizabeth I, named the entire region between Spanish Florida and French Canada, "Virginia." But, it was not until 1607, under the reign of James I, that Virginia's first successful English settlement, Jamestown, was founded a few miles up the James River on Chesapeake Bay. Despite the initial hardships, the colonists' prospects improved after they learned to cultivate tobacco and corn. By the 1630s, Virginia had become the world's leading producer of tobacco.

Jamestown's eventual success led to the establishment of the Catholic

Natural chimney formations in the Shenandoah Valley at Front Royal, Virginia

◁ Attractive Colonial townhouses, a typical feature of Georgetown, Washington, DC

Nighttime view of Lincoln Memorial and Washington Monument with the US Capitol in the distance

colony of Maryland, named in honor of King James's wife, Queen Mary. Governed by Lord Baltimore, the colony attracted Catholics from England as well as Puritan and Quaker settlers from Virginia. Every year, thousands of English immigrants came to the new colonies in search of opportunities impossible back home. By the mid-1660s, both Virginia and Maryland had evolved into England's most profitable New World colonies. In 1664, the English took control of Delaware, founded and settled by the Dutch and the Swedish in the early 1600s. West Virginia, however, did not separate from Virginia until the Civil War.

By the 1670s, a simulataneous rise in taxes and a swift drop in tobacco prices caused widespread suffering and a short-lived rebellion. The situation stabilized in the early 1700s, when some of the tobacco farmers began to reap great fortunes. Much of their success was based on the shift from servant labor to that of African slaves, whose numbers grew from a few hundred in 1650 to over 150,000 in 1750, when blacks made up nearly half the total population.

KEY DATES IN HISTORY

1607 Establishment of the private English colony of Jamestown in Virginia

1624 Virginia becomes a royal colony

1632 King Charles I establishes Maryland

1664 Delaware comes under British rule

1699 Williamsburg becomes Virginia's capital

1774 Virginia's Peyton Randolph leads the first Continental Congress to discuss freedom

1775–81 The Revolutionary War

1791 George Washington obtains land for the capital city

1830 The Baltimore and Ohio Railroad (B&O) is the nation's first long-distance railroad

1846 The Smithsonian Institution is established

1865 Confederate General Robert E. Lee surrenders to the Union at Appomattox

1932 During the Great Depression, a "Bonus Army" of WWI veterans camp around the Capitol to plead for government aid

1935 US Supreme Court building is completed

1963 Martin Luther King Jr. delivers his "I have a Dream" speech before Lincoln Memorial

1989 L. Douglas Wilder is elected governor of Virginia, the first black to hold such high office

Sept 11, 2001 Terrorist attack on the Pentagon

2009 The nation's first African-American president, Barack Obama, is inaugurated

INDEPENDENCE & CIVIL WAR

Frustration over British rule eventually led to calls for independence. Although the Revolutionary War ended at Yorktown, Virginia, in 1781, it was only after the Treaty of Paris that American independence became a reality. Virginia, by far the largest and wealthiest of the American colonies, provided many of the "Founding Fathers," including George Washington, the military leader and first president; Thomas Jefferson, author of the Declaration of Independence and third president; and James Madison, author of the Constitution and two-term president.

In 1791, Washington, empowered by a Congressional act, selected the site for the nation's capital on land incorporated from Maryland and Virginia, a choice determined by its location midway between north and south. This independent federal territory, termed the District of Columbia (DC) was merged with the city of Washington in 1878. When the government moved to Washington in 1800, the US Capitol and the president's home (later renamed the "White House") were still under construction. Both were burned by the British during the War of 1812.

Nothing has been more divisive in the region's history than the issue of slavery. Many residents were slaveholders; others became ardent abolitionists. As racial tensions escalated, war between the North and the South became inevitable. Over the course of the four-year Civil War (1861–65), many significant battles, including General Robert E. Lee's surrender at Appomattox Court House, took place here. The area was also home to the rival capitals – Washington, DC and Richmond, Virginia.

Cycling, a pleasant way to explore Washington, DC

Between the 1880s and the 1930s, Washington, DC evolved into the grand city intended by its planners nearly a century before. Wide avenues were opened up, tawdry railroads were removed from the National Mall, and many grand buildings were constructed to house the expanding bureaucracy. Even so, it wasn't until the mid-1900s, with the advent of air conditioning, that the capital became a year-round, world-class city.

Lee's surrender at Appomattox Court House

PEOPLE & CULTURE

Washington and the surrounding area reflect less stereotypical aspects of contemporary US. Its residents range from "blue-bloods" with roots reaching back to before the *Mayflower* landed at Plymouth Rock, to more recent immigrants and descendants of African-American slaves. This diversity is often surprising. Some of the most patrician communities are in northern Virginia's anglophile "Hunt Country" and among Annapolis' nautical millionaires. Alongside are outposts of blue-collar industry, and many anachronistic communities, such as the Chesapeake's traditional fisherman ("watermen") villages and the proud holdouts of Appalachian mountain culture, still visible in West Virginia.

Washington itself offers very revealing images of class and character, with its many poor, minority neighborhoods seemingly a world away from the wealthy, mainly white enclave of Georgetown. Even more expressive are the anonymous postwar middle-class suburbs that lie on both sides of the busy "Beltway" surrounding the capital.

From these diverse social strata have emerged many remarkable people. Francis Scott Key composed the national anthem "The Star-Spangled Banner" in Baltimore, while Thurgood Marshall championed Civil Rights as an activist and later as a Supreme Court Justice. Writers include the poet and horror-story creator Edgar Allen Poe, the scholar, editor, and journalist H.L. Mencken, and contemporary novelist Anne Tyler. Singers include Patsy Cline and Ella Fitzgerald, from Virginia, and Baltimore's Billie Holliday and DC native Duke Ellington who made jazz and swing the nation's soundtrack.

Exploring Washington, DC & the Capital Region

Washington, DC, the nation's capital, with its magnificent monuments, superb museums, and cosmopolitan flavor, is a favorite destination for tourists. Within easy reach of the capital, the four states of Virginia, West Virginia, Maryland, and Delaware are equally rewarding to explore, offering a varied area of mountains, plains, beaches, and historic towns. Among the region's most popular attractions are the Colonial town of Williamsburg, the scenic splendours of the Shenandoah Valley and the Blue Ridge Parkway, and the unspoiled wilderness of West Virginia. The port city of Baltimore and the tranquil beaches of Delaware also draw many visitors.

Colorful furled sails on the Maryland coast

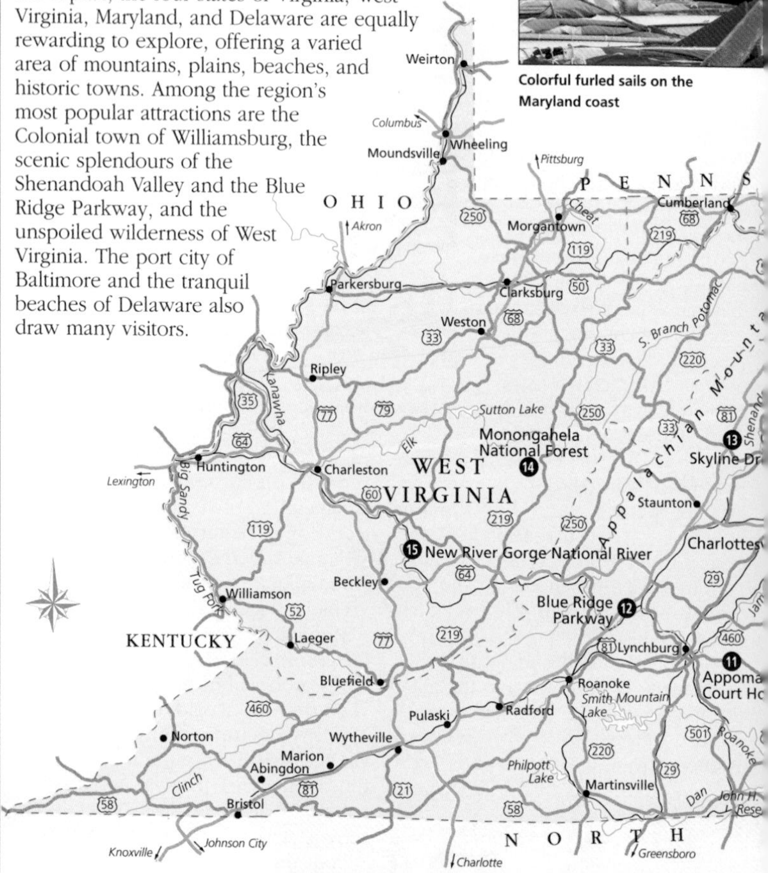

0 km 50

0 miles 50

KEY

- Airport
- Highway
- Major road
- Railroad
- State border

John Brown's Fort, Harpers Ferry National Park in West Virginia

For additional map symbols *see back flap*

The interior of the Oval Office in the White House, Washington, DC

SEE ALSO

- ***Practical Information*** pp228–9
- ***Where to Stay*** pp230–33
- ***Where to Eat*** pp234–7

MILEAGE CHART

WASHINGTON, DC

10 = Distance in miles
10 = Distance in kilometers

WASHINGTON, DC	ALEXANDRIA, VA	RICHMOND, VA	HARPERS FERRY, WV	BALTIMORE, MD	ANNAPOLIS, MD	WILMINGTON, DE	
7 / 11							ALEXANDRIA, VA
105 / 169	**102** / 164						RICHMOND, VA
69 / 111	**73** / 118	**167** / 269					HARPERS FERRY, WV
45 / 72	**51** / 82	**150** / 241	**67** / 108				BALTIMORE, MD
32 / 51	**41** / 66	**137** / 220	**89** / 143	**31** / 50			ANNAPOLIS, MD
107 / 172	**114** / 183	**224** / 360	**141** / 227	**70** / 113	**97** / 156		WILMINGTON, DE
106 / 170	**113** / 182	**222** / 357	**138** / 222	**69** / 111	**96** / 154	**6** / 10	NEW CASTLE, DE

SIGHTS AT A GLANCE

Washington, DC pp196–211 (1)

Virginia
Alexandria (2)
Mount Vernon pp212–13 (3)
Fredericksburg (4)
Colonial Williamsburg pp214–15 (5)
Jamestown & Yorktown (6)
Norfolk (7)
Richmond (8)
Chincoteague (9)
Charlottesville p217 (10)
Appomattox Court House and National Historical Park (11)
Blue Ridge Parkway (12)
Skyline Drive p219 (13)

West Virginia
Monongahela National Forest (14)
New River Gorge National River (15)
Harpers Ferry (16)

Maryland
Antietam National Battlefield (17)
Frederick (18)
Baltimore (19)
Annapolis (20)
North Bay (21)
St. Michaels (22)
Easton (23)
Crisfield (24)
Salisbury (25)
Ocean City (26)

Delaware
Wilmington (27)
Winterthur (28)
Hagley Museum/ Eleutherian Mills (29)
Nemours Mansion & Gardens (30)
New Castle (31)
Lewes (32)
Rehoboth Beach (33)

Washington, DC ❶

Washington, DC covers an area of 61 sq miles (158 sq km) and has a population of about 600,000. As the capital of the US and the seat of federal government, it is rich in grand monuments. It also has a vibrant cultural life, with superb museums, most of them free, and an array of entertainments. The city is made up of four quadrants, with the US Capitol at the central point. The northwest quadrant contains most of the tourist sights, with other sights and places of interest located round the Capitol and south of the Mall, in the southwest quadrant.

Tourists checking their routes at a tourist information kiosk

GETTING AROUND

Washington's excellent public transportation system is more convenient than driving a car. Traffic is heavy and parking spaces are limited. All the major tourist attractions in the city are accessible on foot, or by Metrorail, Metrobus, the Circulator bus, or taxi.

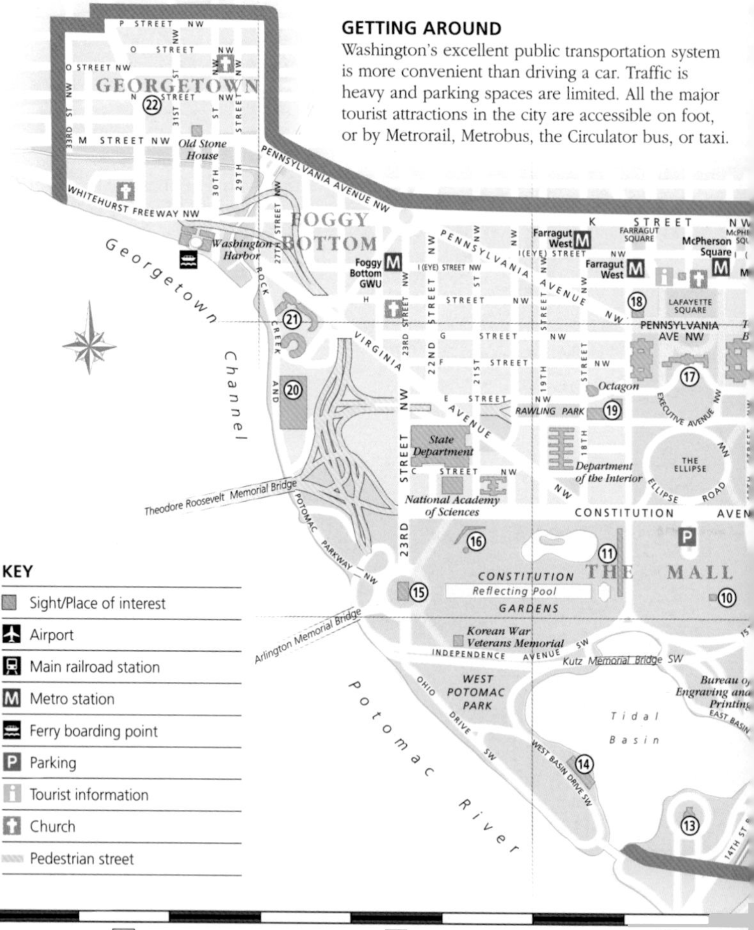

SIGHTS AT A GLANCE

United States Capitol pp198–9 ①
Library of Congress ②
US Supreme Court ③
National Air & Space Museum ④
National Gallery of Art ⑤
National Museum of Natural History ⑥
National Museum of African Art ⑦
National Museum of American History ⑧
Smithsonian American Art Museum & National Portrait Gallery ⑨
Washington Monument ⑩
National World War II Memorial ⑪
United States Holocaust Memorial Museum ⑫
Jefferson Memorial ⑬
Franklin D. Roosevelt Memorial ⑭
Lincoln Memorial ⑮
Vietnam Veterans Memorial ⑯
The White House pp206–207 ⑰
Renwick Gallery ⑱
Corcoran Gallery of Art ⑲
The Kennedy Center ⑳
Watergate Complex ㉑
Georgetown ㉒

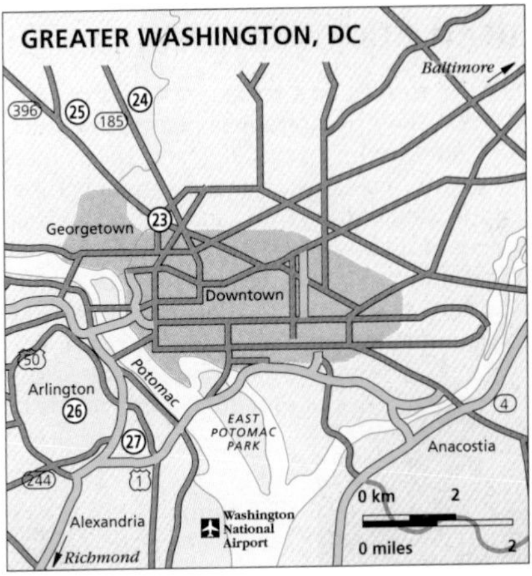

KEY

Area of main map

Greater Washington, DC
(see inset map)
Phillips Collection ㉓
National Zoological Park ㉔
Washington National Cathedral ㉕
Arlington National Cemetery ㉖
The Pentagon ㉗

SEE ALSO

- ***Where to Stay*** pp230–1
- ***Where to Eat*** pp234–6

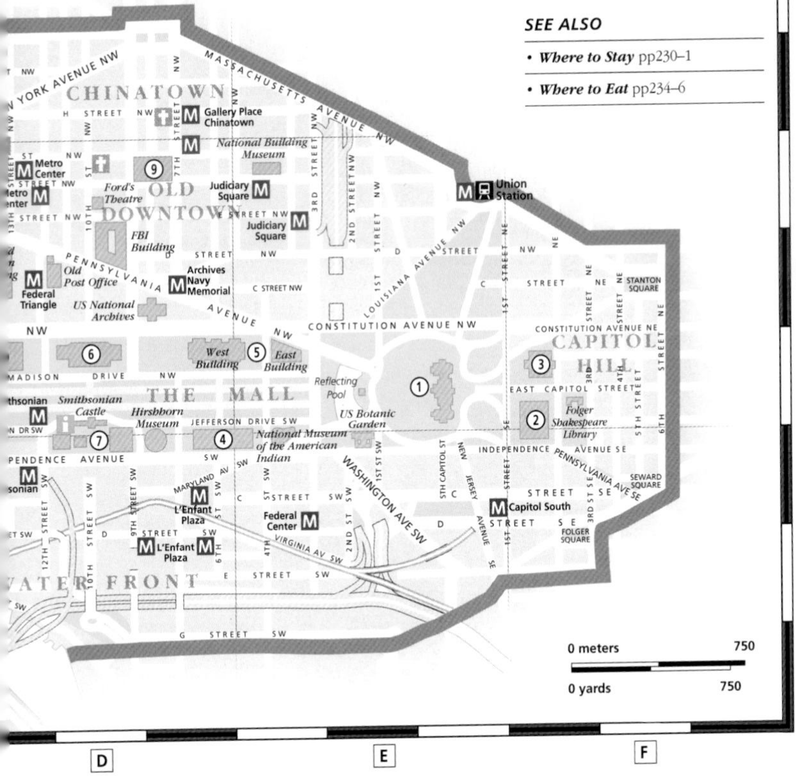

United States Capitol ①

One of the world's best known symbols of democracy, the US Capitol has been the legislative heart of America for over 200 years. The cornerstone of this grand Neo-Classical building was laid by George Washington in 1793, and by 1800 it was occupied, though unfinished. The British burned the Capitol in the War of 1812, and in 1815 work began on its restoration. Many architectural and artistic features, such as Constantino Brumidi's murals and the Statue of Freedom, were added later.

★ The Rotunda
Completed in 1824, the 180-ft (55-m) Rotunda is capped by Apotheosis of Washington, *a fresco by Brumidi.*

US Capitol
The Capitol also marks the center of Washington, DC. The city's four quadrants radiate out from the middle of the building.

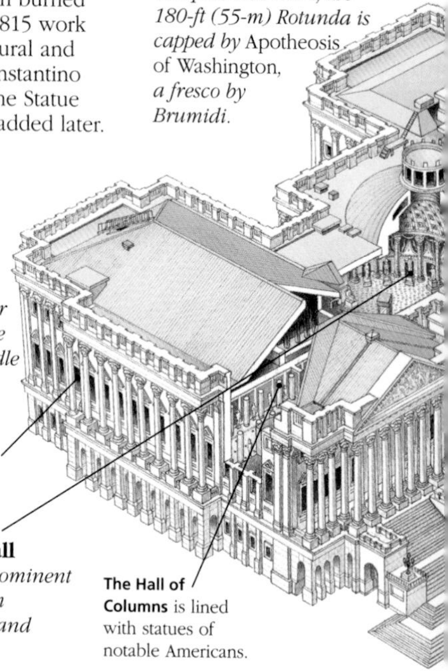

The House Chambers

★ National Statuary Hall
Statues of prominent citizens from each state stand in this hall.

The Hall of Columns is lined with statues of notable Americans.

Library of Congress ②

Map F4. 10 1st St, SE. ***Tel*** *(202) 707-5000.* *(202) 707-8000.* *Capitol S.* *32, 34, 36, 96.* *10am–5:30pm Mon–Sat.* *federal hols.* *For access to reading rooms, visitors must have a user card. The website or information desk can explain how this can be obtained.* **www**.loc.gov

The Library of Congress holds the largest collection of books, manuscripts, microfilms, maps, and music in the world. First established in the US Capitol in 1800, the library was destroyed when the Capitol was burned in 1814. Thomas Jefferson then offered his personal collection as a replacement, and from this seed the collection continued to grow. Since 1897, it has been housed in a grand Italian Renaissance-style main building, now known as the Thomas Jefferson Building. In front of it is a fountain with a striking bronze statue of the Roman sea god, Neptune.

One of the highlights of this marvel of art and architecture is the **Great Hall** with its splendid marble arches and columns, grand staircases, bronze statues, rich murals, and stained-glass skylights.

The Great Hall, with its splendid marble arches and columns

Equally impressive is the **Main Reading Room**, where eight huge marble columns, and 10-ft (3-m) high female figures, personifying aspects of human endeavor, dwarf the reading desks. The domed ceiling soars to a height of 160 ft (49 m). There are 10 other reading rooms in the Jefferson Building, notably the African and Asian Reading Rooms.

The staircase landing near the Visitors' Gallery, overlooking the Main Reading Room, is dominated by a beautiful marble mosaic figure of Minerva.

The Library's treasures include one of only three perfect vellum copies of the 15th-century Gutenberg Bible, the first book printed using movable metal type.

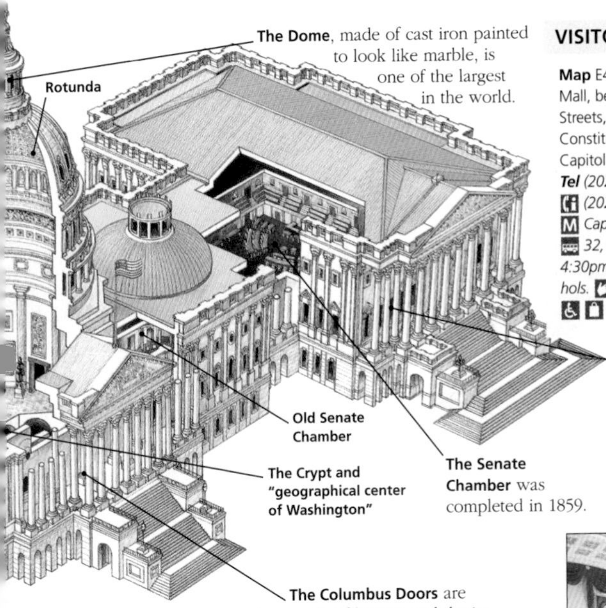

VISITORS' CHECKLIST

Map E4. Independence Mall, between 1st & 3rd Streets, & Independence & Constitution Aves (enter via the Capitol Visitor Center). ***Tel*** *(202) 224-3121.* *(202) 225-6827.* M *Capitol S, Union Station.* *32, 34, 36, 96.* *8:30am–4:30pm Mon–Sat.* *federal hols.* *except Sun.* **www**.visitthecapitol.gov

STAR FEATURES

★ National Statuary Hall

★ Old Senate Chamber

★ The Rotunda

★ Old Senate Chamber

This sumptuous chamber was occupied by the Senate until 1859, and then by the Supreme Court for 75 years. It is now used mainly as museum space.

US Supreme Court ③

Map F4. 1st St between E Capitol St & Maryland Ave NE. ***Tel*** *(202) 479-3211.* M *Capitol S.* *9am–4:30pm Mon–Fri.* *federal hols.* ***Lectures.*** **www**.supremecourtus.gov

The judicial branch of the US government and the highest court in the land, the Supreme Court is the last stop in the disposition of the nation's legal disputes and issues of constitutionality. Groundbreaking cases settled here include *Brown v. Board of Education*, which abolished racial segregation in schools, and *Miranda v. Arizona*, which declared that crime suspects were entitled to a lawyer before they were interrogated.

As recently as 1929, the Supreme Court was still meeting in various sections of the US Capitol. Then, at Chief Justice William Howard Taft's urging, Congress authorized a separate building to be constructed. The result was a magnificent Corinthian edifice designed by Cass Gilbert that opened in 1935. Allegorical sculptures depicting the Contemplation of Justice and the Authority of the Law stand beside the steps.

The impressive Neo-Classical façade of the US Supreme Court

The Great Hall that leads to the courtroom is an expanse of marble, lined with columns and the busts of former chief justices. The elegant court chamber itself has a coffered plaster ceiling decorated with gold leaf, and a frieze running around the walls that depicts both real and allegorical legal figures. The exhibit hall has displays on legal systems from around the world and an array of judges' robes.

Visitors may watch the court in session Monday to Wednesday from October through April. Admission is on a first-come, first-served basis. When the court is not in session, public lectures on the Supreme Court are held every hour on the half hour in the Courtroom.

The Mall

This boulevard, between the Capitol and the Washington Monument, stretches for 1 mile (1.6 km) and is the city's cultural heart; the many great museums of the Smithsonian Institution can be found along this green strip. At the northeast corner of the Mall is the National Gallery of Art. Directly opposite is one of the most popular museums in the world – the National Air & Space Museum – a soaring construction of glass and steel. Both the National Museum of American History and the National Museum of Natural History, on the north side of the Mall, draw huge numbers of visitors.

★ National Museum of Natural History
The central Rotunda was designed in the Neo-Classical style and opened to the public in 1910 ⑥

★ National Museum of American History
From George Washington's uniform to this 1940s Tucker Torpedo, US history is documented here ⑧

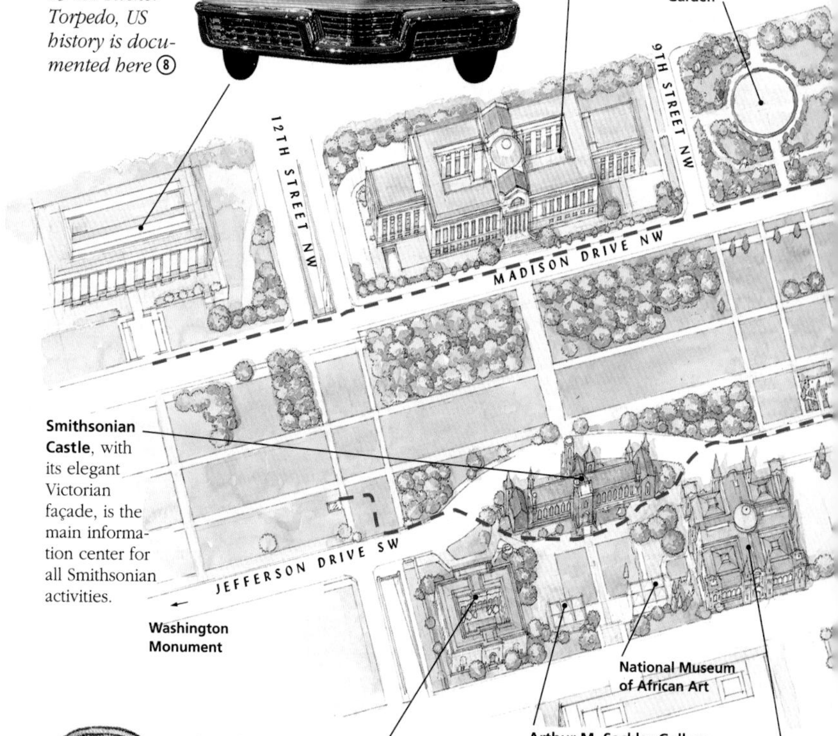

Smithsonian Castle, with its elegant Victorian façade, is the main information center for all Smithsonian activities.

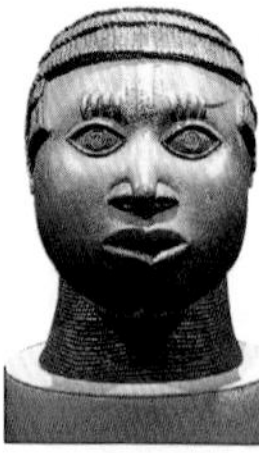

National Museum of African Art
Founded in 1965 and located underground, this museum houses a comprehensive collection of ancient and modern African art ⑦

Freer Gallery of Art displays masterpieces of American and Asian art.

Arthur M. Sackler Gallery holds an extensive collection of Asian art, which was donated to the nation by New Yorker Arthur Sackler.

Arts & Industries Building, a masterpiece of Victorian architecture, was built to contain exhibits from the Centennial Exposition in Philadelphia.

0 meters 100
0 yards 100

★ National Gallery of Art
This gallery's fine collection of art treasures, such as The Alba Madonna *(c.1510) by Raphael, chronicle the history of art from the Middle Ages to the 20th century* ⑤

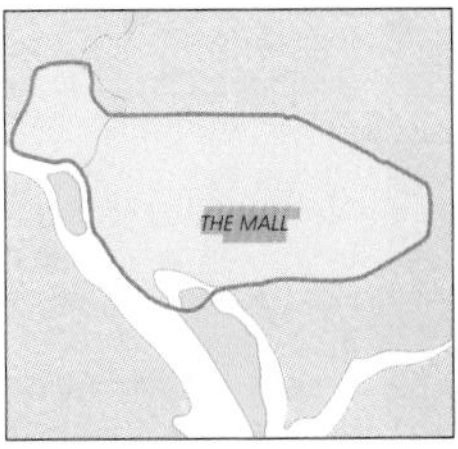

LOCATOR MAP
See Map pp196–7

KEY

– – – Suggested route

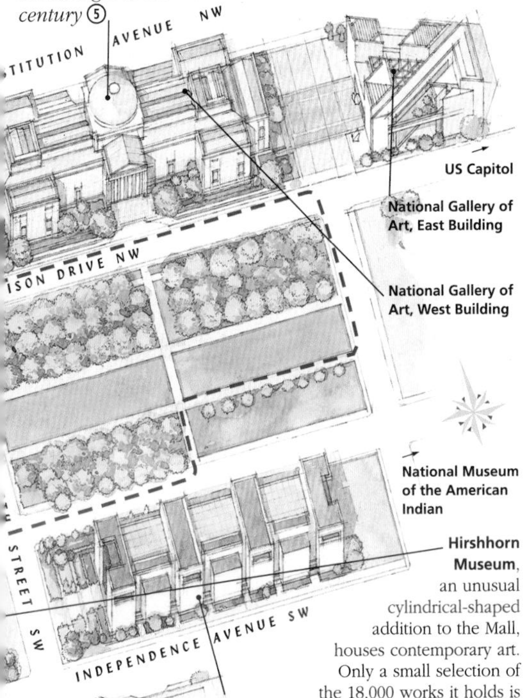

Hirshhorn Museum, an unusual cylindrical-shaped addition to the Mall, houses contemporary art. Only a small selection of the 18,000 works it holds is on display at any one time.

★ National Air & Space Museum
The clean, modern design of the National Air & Space Museum echoes the technological marvels on display inside ④

STAR SIGHTS

- ★ National Air & Space Museum
- ★ National Gallery of Art
- ★ National Museum of American History
- ★ National Museum of Natural History

National Air & Space Museum ④

Map D5. 601 Independence Ave, SW. ***Tel*** *(202) 633-1000.* Ⓜ *Smithsonian.* 🚌 *32, 34, 36, 52.* ◯ *10am–5:30pm daily.* ● *Dec 25.* *10:15am, 1pm.* www.nasm.si.edu

Opened on America's Bicentennial on July 1, 1976, the Air & Space Museum is today the most visited site in Washington. The museum's entrance leads into the lofty **Milestones of Flight** gallery, which displays many of the firsts in air and space travel. These include the 1903 Wright *Flyer*, the first powered, heavier-than-air machine to achieve controlled, sustained flight, built by the Wright Brothers; the *Spirit of St. Louis*, in which Charles Lindbergh made the first transatlantic solo flight in 1927; and the *Apollo 11* Command Module, which carried astronauts Buzz Aldrin, Neil Armstrong, and Michael Collins on their historic mission to the moon in 1969. Another gallery that attracts crowds is the **Space Race**, where exhibits include space suits, a working model of the *Columbia* Space Shuttle, and the Skylab, an orbiting workshop for three-person crews.

An eye-catching exhibit in the **Pioneers of Flight** gallery is the red Lockheed Vega in which Amelia Earhart became the first woman to make a solo transatlantic flight in 1932. The very popular **World War II Aviation** gallery displays fighter aircrafts from the American, British, German, and Japanese air forces.

Milestones of Flight gallery in the National Air & Space Museum

The façade of the National Gallery of Art

National Gallery of Art ⑤

Map E4. **West Building** Constitution Ave between 4th & 7th Sts, NW. **East Building** 4th St between Madison Drive & Constitution Ave, NW. ***Tel*** *(202) 737-4215.* Ⓜ *Archives/Navy Memorial, Judiciary Square, Penn Quarter, Smithsonian.* 🚌 *32, 34, 36, 70.* 🕒 *10am–5pm Mon–Sat, 11am–6pm Sun.* ● *Jan 1, Dec 25.* *call (202) 842-6690.* *call (202) 842-6176.* ♿ **www**.nga.gov

One of Washington, DC's top attractions, this superb museum was established when American financier Andrew Mellon bequeathed his collection of European art to form the basis of a National Gallery of Art. Spurred on by his example, other collectors left their art to the proposed museum.

Of the two main buildings, the stately Neo-Classical-style West Building, opened in 1941, features European art from the 13th to the 19th centuries. The modern East Building, completed in 1978, features 20th-century art. An underground concourse, with a cafeteria and shops, joins the two buildings.

Matching wings flank a central rotunda in the **West Building**. West of the rotunda are the galleries displaying Italian, Dutch, Flemish, and Spanish art. The Italian paintings include works by Giotto, Botticelli, Raphael and Leonardo da Vinci; and other masterpieces on display include works by Rembrandt, Van Dyck, Rubens, Goya, El Greco, and Velasquez. The sculpture galleries here display decorative arts from the Middle Ages to the 20th century. Galleries east of the rotunda house an outstanding collection of French Impressionist and Post-Impressionist art. Among its highlights are Monet's *Woman with a Parasol,* Degas' *Four Dancers*, and Toulouse-Lautrec's *Quadrille at the Moulin Rouge*. Portraits by John Singer Sargent and James McNeill Whistler are among the gallery's important collection of American paintings. Adjacent to the West Building is a Sculpture Garden, which is transformed into an ice skating rink in winter.

The huge **East Building** is designed to accommodate large pieces of modern art. Centered in its courtyard is a giant red, blue, and black mobile by Alexander Calder, completed in 1976. Near the entrance is a sculpture by Henry Moore; the atrium displays a 1977 tapestry by Joan Miró.

National Museum of Natural History ⑥

Map D4. Constitution Ave & 10th St, NW. ***Tel*** *(202) 633-1000 (recorded message after museum hours).* Ⓜ *Smithsonian.* 🚌 *32, 34, 36.* 🕒 *10am–5:30pm daily.* ● *Dec 25.* *10:30am & 1:30pm Mon–Fri.* ♿ **www**.nmnh.si.edu

Established in 1910, this vast museum's collection of 120 million artifacts includes samples from the world's diverse cultures, as well as fossils and living creatures from land and sea. The museum's entrance leads into the lofty Rotunda, where visitors are greeted by the impressive sight of a massive African Bush elephant. To the right of the Rotunda is one of the most popular areas of the museum, the **Dinosaur Hall**, featuring dinosaur skeletons and eggs, and Ice Age mammals, such as the woolly mammoth. Also on the ground floor is **Ocean Hall**, where exhibits explore the magnificence of the ocean, as well as man's relationship to it. To the left of the Rotunda is an IMAX® Theater and the Hall of Mammals with its huge 25,000 sq. ft of stunning displays.

On the second floor is the **Gems and Minerals** collection, whose highlight is the 45.52-carat Hope Diamond. The largest deep blue diamond in the world and famed for its stunning color and clarity, it once belonged to Louis XVI of France. Also on the second floor is the highly popular **Insect Zoo**, with its giant hissing cockroaches and large leaf-cutter ant colony.

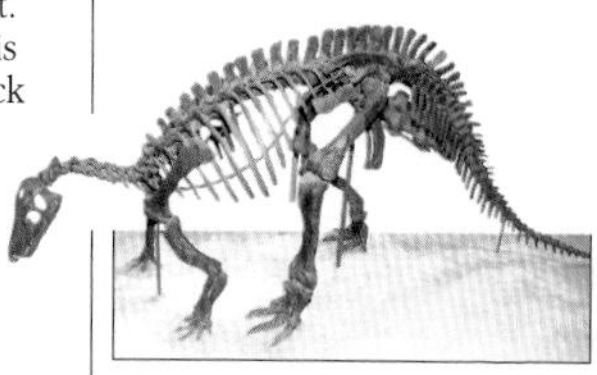

Dinosaur skeleton in the National Museum of Natural History

National Museum of African Art ⑦

Map D5. 950 Independence Ave, SW. ***Tel*** *(202) 633-1000.* Ⓜ *Smithsonian.* 🕒 *10am–5:30pm daily.* ● *Dec 25.* ♿ **www**.si.edu/nmafa

This quiet museum is missed by many visitors, perhaps because much of its exhibition space is underground. The small entrance pavilion at the ground level leads to three subterranean floors where the exhibits are displayed. The 7,000-piece permanent collection includes both modern and ancient art from Africa, although the majority of pieces date from the 19th and 20th centuries. Traditional African bronzes, ceramics, and pottery are on display, as are stunning ivory and gold objects, brightly colored *kente* textiles from Ghana, and photographs.

National Museum of American History ⑧

Map D4. 14th St & Constitution Ave. ***Tel*** *(202) 633-1000 (recorded message outside opening hours).* *Smithsonian–Federal Triangle.* *32, 34, 36.* *10am–5:30pm daily.* *Dec 25.* **www**.americanhistory.si.edu

This three-story museum showcases America's past. A dramatic, central five-story atrium is surrounded by displays of artifacts representing the breadth of the museum's collection. Fascinating and diverse exhibits cover the USA's cultural, social, technological, and political history.

The Hall of Invention in the west wing of the first floor features great innovators and their process of innovation, ranging from the microwave oven to an accessible snowboard for people who cannot use their legs.

Popular exhibits elsewhere in the museum include the 100-year-old Headsville Post Office from West Virginia, which was dismantled and reassembled here in 1971 and is still a working post office. Another popular exhibit is a *Model T* Ford. This vehicle was an engineering landmark that heralded the beginning of the motor age.

First ladies' gowns worn to the presidents' inaugural balls are also a memorable exhibit. Jackie Kennedy's and Nancy Reagan's haute couture gowns are all kept at the museum – as well as Rosalynn' Carter's "off the rack one."

Of great historical and cultural significance is the Star-Spangled Banner that flew over Fort McHenry in 1814, and which inspired the Francis Scott Key poem that later became the US national anthem. The fragile flag is dramatically displayed in an environmentally controlled exhibit on the second floor.

Ford's *Model T*, in the National Museum of American History

The extent of the museum's collection is huge, from science to objects that represent the lives and offices of the presidency, to American popular culture exhibits, such as the ruby slippers worn by Judy Garland in *The Wizard of Oz*.

Smithsonian American Art Museum & National Portrait Gallery ⑨

Map D4. **Smithsonian American Art Museum** 8th & G Sts NW. ***Tel*** *(202) 633-1000.* *11:30am–7pm daily.* *Dec 25.* **www**.americanart.si.edu
National Portrait Gallery 8th & F Sts NW. ***Tel*** *(202) 633-1000.* *11:30am–7pm daily.* *Dec 25.* *Gallery Place–Chinatown.* **www**.npg.si.edu

Nowhere in Washington is the city's penchant to copy Greek and Roman architecture more obvious than in the former US Patent Office building, now the home of the Smithsonian American Art Museum and the National Portrait Gallery. The Patent Office was converted into the twin museums in 1968. The art museum contains a wealth of works by American artists, reflecting the history and culture of the country. The highlight of the American folk art collection is an amazing piece of visionary art called *Throne of the Third Heaven of the Nations' Millenium* (c.1950–64), created out of light bulbs, silver and gold foil, and old furniture by a Washington janitor by the name of James Hampton. Among the 19th- and early 20th-century works, the Western landscapes by Albert Bierstadt stand out. Especially dramatic is his painting *Among the Sierra Nevada, California*, which captures the vastness of the American West. Another outstanding work from this period is *Achelous and Hercules* by Thomas Hart Benton (1889–1975). In this mythical analogy of early American life, Hercules symbolizes man taming the wild and then enjoying the fruits of his labor. Works by Modernists Jasper Johns, Andy Warhol, and Robert Rauschenberg are among the other treasures of this museum.

The National Portrait Gallery is America's family album, featuring paintings, sculptures, etchings, and photographs of thousands of famous Americans. Assembled here are such diverse works as Gilbert Stuart's famous portrait of George Washington (which features on the one-dollar bill), busts of Dr. Martin Luther King Jr. and the poet T.S. Eliot, and some photographs of actress Marilyn Monroe.

***George Washington* by Gilbert Stuart**

Washington Monument, which dominates the city skyline

Washington Monument ⑩

Map C4. Independence Ave at 17th St, SW. ***Tel*** *(202) 426-6841.* Ⓜ *Smithsonian.* 🚌 *13, 52.* ◯ *9am–4:45pm daily.* ● *Jul 4, Dec 25.* ♿ 🛈 ***Interpretive talks.*** **www**.nps.gov/wamo

Constructed from 36,000 pieces of marble and granite, the 555-ft (170-m) tall Washington Monument is one of the capital's most recognizable landmarks, clearly visible from almost all over the city. Conceived of as a tribute to the first president of the US, its construction began in 1848, but stopped in 1858 when funds ran out. The building work resumed in 1876 after public interest in the project revived – a slight change in the color of the stone indicates the point at which construction stopped and then began again. The original design included a circular colonnade around the monument, but lack of funds prevented its construction.

Cleaned to a gleaming white, the monument has a capstone weighing 3,300 pounds (2,000 kg). It is topped by an aluminum pyramid, and surrounded by 50 flagpoles. Inside the monument are 192 commemorative stones, donated by individuals, states, societies, and nations. There are stunning views across the city from the top (admission is free, but timed tickets are required).

National World War II Memorial ⑪

Map C4. 17th St, NW, between Constitution Ave & Independence Ave. ***Tel*** *(202) 426-6841.* Ⓜ *Smithsonian or Federal Triangle.* ◯ *24 hours daily.* 🛈 *on request.* ♿ **www**.nps.gov/nwwm

This 7.5-acre (3-ha) memorial was built to honor US veteran soldiers and civilians of World War II. It includes two 43-ft (13-m) pavilions, symbolic bas-relief panels, and fifty-six granite pillars, one for each of the country's states and territories. These are adorned with bronze wreaths of oak and wheat, which symbolize the nation's agricultural and industrial strength. The memorial was officially opened to the public in 2004.

United States Holocaust Memorial Museum ⑫

Map C5. 100 Raoul Wallenberg Place, SW. ***Tel*** *(202) 488-0400.* Ⓜ *Smithsonian.* 🚌 *13 (Pentagon shuttle).* ◯ *mid-Jun–Mar: 10am–5:30pm daily; Apr–mid-Jun: 10am–5:30pm daily (to 8pm Tue & Thu).* ● *Dec 25 & Yom Kippur. Time pass required for permanent exhibit. Advance passes: (800) 400-9373.* ♿ **www**.ushmm.org

Opened in 1993, the US Holocaust Memorial Museum bears witness to the systematic persecution and annihilation in Europe of six million Jews and others deemed undesirable by the Third Reich. The museum is meant to be experienced, not just seen. Within the exhibition space, which ranges from the intentionally claustrophobic to the soaringly majestic, are thousands of photographs and artifacts, 53 video monitors, and 30 interactive stations that contain graphic and emotionally disturbing images of violence, forcing visitors to confront the horror of the Holocaust.

Starting from the top, the fourth floor documents the early years of the Nazi regime, with exhibits exposing their ruthless persecution of Jews. The third floor exhibits are devoted to the "Final Solution," the killing of six million "undesirable" people. Artifacts include a box car that carried prisoners to concentration camps.

On the second floor is the **Hall of Remembrance**, which houses an eternal flame that pays homage to the victims of the Holocaust, and the **Hall of Witness** on the first floor features temporary exhibits.

At the Concourse Level is the **Children's Tile Wall**. Over 3,000 tiles, painted by children, constitute this moving memorial to the one-and-a-half million children murdered in the Holocaust.

Jefferson Memorial ⑬

Map C5. S bank of the Tidal Basin. ***Tel*** *(202) 426-6841.* Ⓜ *Smithsonian.* ◯ *9:30am–11:30pm.* ● *Dec 25.* ***Interpretive talks.*** ♿ 🛈 **www**.nps.gov/thje

When this Neo-Classical-style memorial to the third US president, Thomas Jefferson (1743–1826), was completed in 1943, critics gave it the derisive nickname "Jefferson's Muffin." It was dismissed as far too "feminine" for so bold and influential a man who had played a significant part in drafting the Declaration of Independence in 1776. The dome of this round, colonnaded building covers a majestic 19-ft (6-m) statue of Jefferson. The statue was originally cast in plaster since metal was rationed when the building was dedicated in 1943. It was recast in bronze after the end of World War II, and a museum is now in the basement of the building. Etched on the walls are Jefferson's words from the Declaration of Independence. Legend says that the architects

Majestic statue of Jefferson

For hotels and restaurants in this region see pp230–31 and pp234–6

The colonnaded domed Jefferson Memorial, housing the bronze statue

are said to have purposely misquoted and mispelled these words (they claimed because of lack of space).

Jefferson Memorial stands on the banks of the scenic **Tidal Basin**, built in 1897 to catch the overflow from the Potomac River. In the 1920s, hundreds of Japanese cherry trees were planted along its shores, and the sight of the trees in bloom is one of the most photographed in the city. Peak blooming time is for two weeks, between mid-March and mid-April. Rental paddle-boats are available at the Tidal Basin.

Franklin D. Roosevelt Memorial ⑭

Map C5. W Basin Dr, SW. ***Tel*** *(202) 426-6841.* *Smithsonian.* *13.* *8am–midnight daily.* *Dec 25.* ***Interpretive programs & talks.*** **www**.nps.gov/fdrm

The memorial to President Franklin D. Roosevelt, opened in 1997, is a mammoth park of four granite open-air rooms, one for each of Roosevelt's terms *(see p49)*. The first room has the visitor center, and a bas-relief of Roosevelt's first inaugural parade. In the second room is a sculpture titled *Hunger*, recalling the hard times of the Great Depression. A controversial statue of Roosevelt in the third room of this open air park shows the disabled president sitting in a wheelchair hidden by his Navy cape.

Dramatic waterfalls cascade into a series of pools in the fourth room, which also has a statue of Roosevelt's wife, Eleanor, and a relief of his funeral cortege carved into the granite wall. The water symbolizes the peace that Roosevelt was so eager to achieve before his death.

Lincoln Memorial ⑮

Map B4. Constitution Ave, between French & Bacon Drs. ***Tel*** *(202) 426-6841.* *Smithsonian, Foggy Bottom.* *9:30am–11:30pm daily.* *on request.* **www**.nps.gov/linc

The Lincoln Memorial is one of Washington's most awe-inspiring sights, with the seated figure of President Abraham Lincoln in his Neo-Classical "temple," looming over a reflecting pool.

The site chosen for the monument was a swamp, and before building could begin in 1914 it had to be drained. Concrete piers were poured for the foundation so that the building could be anchored in bedrock. As the memorial neared completion, architect Henry Bacon realized that the statue of Lincoln would be dwarfed inside the huge edifice. The original 10-ft (3-m) statue by Daniel Chester French was doubled in size and carved from 28 blocks of white marble. Engraved on the wall are the words of Lincoln's famous Gettysburg Address *(see p106)*.

In 1963, the memorial was the site of a mammoth gathering of 200,000 people in support of Civil Rights, where Dr. Martin Luther King Jr. made his historic "I have a Dream" speech. A direct result of this speech was the passing by Congress of Civil Rights legislation in 1964.

Vietnam Veterans Memorial ⑯

Map B4. 21st St & Constitution Ave, NW. ***Tel*** *(202) 426-6841.* *Foggy Bottom.* *9:30am–11:30pm daily.* *on request.* **www**.nps.gov/vive

Powerful in its symbolism and dramatic in its simplicity, this memorial was designed by Maya Lin, then a 21-year-old student at Yale University, whose design was selected from 1,421 entries. Dedicated in 1982, it consists of two triangular black walls, set into the earth at an angle of 125 degrees, one end pointing to the Lincoln Memorial and the other to the Washington Monument. The walls are inscribed with the names of the Americans who died in the Vietnam War, in chronological order from 1959 to 1975. The site is covered by tokens of remembrance placed by veterans and their families – poems, pictures, toys, and flowers – making this one of the most moving memorials on the Mall. A more conventional memorial was added in 1984 – a statue of three soldiers.

The Lincoln Memorial, one of Washington's most visited monuments

The White House ⑰

The official residence of the president, the White House was designed by Irish-born architect James Hoban. Known as the Executive Mansion, it was first occupied in 1800 by President John Adams. Burned by the British in 1814, the partially rebuilt edifice was reoccupied in 1817. In 1901, President Theodore Roosevelt renamed the building the White House and ordered the West Wing to be built. The East Wing was added in 1942, completing the building as it is today. Beautifully decorated with period furniture, valuable antiques, and paintings, the White House attracts more than a million and a half visitors every year.

The White House
The official residence of the US president for 200 years, the White House façade is familiar to millions of people around the world.

★ State Dining Room
Able to seat as many as 140 people, the State Dining Room was enlarged in 1902. A portrait of President Abraham Lincoln, by George P.A. Healy, hangs above the mantel.

The West Terrace leads to the West Wing and the Oval Office, the president's official office.

★ Red Room
One of four reception rooms, the Red Room is furnished in red in the Empire Style (1810–30). The fabrics were woven in the US from French designs.

The stonework has been painted over and over to maintain the building's white façade.

STAR ROOMS

- ★ Red Room
- ★ State Dining Room
- ★ Vermeil Room

For hotels and restaurants in this region see pp230–31 and pp234–6

Lincoln Bedroom
President Lincoln used this room as his Cabinet Room, then turned it into a bedroom, furnishing it with Lincoln-era decor. Today it is used as a guest room.

VISITORS' CHECKLIST

Map C4. 1600 Pennsylvania Ave, NW. *7:30am–12:30pm Tue–Sat only for groups with Congressional or embassy appointments. Contact Visitor Center for information.* *federal hols & official functions.* *obligatory.*
www.nps.gov
White House Visitor Center
1450 Pennsylvania Ave, NW.
Tel *(202) 208-1631.* *Federal Triangle.* *7:30am–4pm daily.* *Jan 1, Thanksgiving, Dec 25.*
www.nps.gov/whho

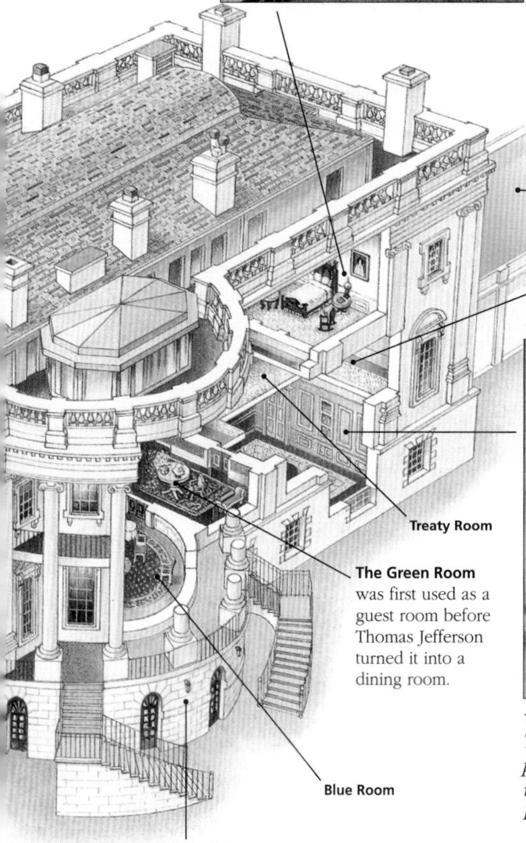

The East Terrace leads to the East Wing.

The East Room is used for large gatherings, such as dances and concerts.

Treaty Room

The Green Room was first used as a guest room before Thomas Jefferson turned it into a dining room.

Blue Room

★ Vermeil Room
This ivory room houses seven paintings of First Ladies, including this portrait of Eleanor Roosevelt by Douglas Chandor.

Diplomatic Reception
This room is used to welcome friends and ambassadors. It is elegantly furnished in the Federal Period style (1790–1820).

THE WHITE HOUSE VISITOR CENTER

The Visitor Center has interesting exhibits about the history of the White House as well as royal gifts on display. There are also seasonal lectures by famous speakers on aspects of history in and out of the White House. The center has a monthly Living History program with actors portraying historic figures. The gift shop carries an extensive range, including the annual White House Christmas ornament. Tours of the president's official residence in the White House are extremely limited at this time. Guided tours can be booked only by special arrangement through a member of Congress or an embassy.

Façade of the Visitor Center

The magnificent Renwick Gallery, a fine example of French Empire style

Renwick Gallery ⑱

Map C4. Pennsylvania Ave at 17th St, NW. ***Tel*** *(202) 633-1000.* Ⓜ *Farragut W.* *10am–5:30pm daily.* *Dec 25.* *noon Mon–Fri.* **www**.americanart.si.edu

This magnificent red-brick building was designed by James Renwick in 1859. It originally housed the art collection of William Wilson Corcoran until it was moved to the current Corcoran Gallery of Art in 1897.

After efforts by First Lady Jacqueline Kennedy saved the building from destruction, it was bought by the Smithsonian. Refurbished and renamed, the Renwick Gallery opened in 1972. It is dedicated primarily to 20th-century American crafts and houses some impressive exhibits in every material including clay, glass, and metal. *Gamefish* (1988) by Larry Fuente is a stunning example of mixed media art.

Corcoran Gallery of Art ⑲

Map C4. 500 17th St, NW. ***Tel*** *(202) 639-1700.* Ⓜ *Farragut W, Farragut N.* *10am–5pm Wed–Sun, 10am–9pm Thu (except Thanksgiving).* *Mon, Tue, Dec 25, Jan 1.* **www**.corcoran.edu

A treasure trove of fine art, this privately funded collection was founded by William Wilson Corcoran, a banker. His collection soon outgrew its original home in the Renwick Gallery and moved to this massive edifice in 1897. Many of the European works were added in 1925 by art collector and US Senator William A. Clark. The gallery's masterpieces now include 16th-century paintings, including 17th-century works by Rembrandt, and 19th-century Impressionist paintings by Monet and Renoir. It also has the largest collection of paintings by Jean-Baptist Camille Corot outside France, and fine examples of African-American art. Paintings from the 20th century include works by Picasso, John Singer Sargent, and de Kooning. Chamber music concerts take place some Sundays at 4pm. Call for the schedule.

Lion Statue, guarding the Corcoran Gallery

The Kennedy Center ⑳

Map B4. New Hampshire Ave & Rock Creek Pkwy, NW. ***Tel*** *(202) 467-4600, (800) 444-1324.* Ⓜ *Foggy Bottom.* *80.* *10am–9pm daily; 10am–9pm Mon–Sat, noon–9pm Sun & hols (box office).* *10am–5pm Mon–Fri, 10am–1pm Sat–Sun (call 416-8340).* **www**.kennedy-center.org

In 1958, President Eisenhower signed an act to begin fund-raising for a national cultural center that would attract the world's best opera, music, and dance companies to the US capital. His successor, John F. Kennedy, was also an ardent supporter and fund-raiser for this project but he was assassinated before the completion of the center, which was named in his honor.

Designed by Edward Durrell Stone, the center opened in 1971. The **Grand Foyer**, adorned with a remarkable bronze bust of Kennedy by sculptor Robert Berks, stretches 630 ft (192 m) and provides an impressive entrance to the three main theaters of this vast arts complex. In front of the foyer is the **JFK Terrace**, which runs the length of the center and offers glorious views of the Potomac River.

Of the three huge theaters, the **Eisenhower Theater**, with a bronze bust of Eisenhower, is at one end of the foyer. At the other end is the **Concert Hall**, which seats over 2,400 people and is the home of the National Symphony Orchestra. Between them is the sumptuous **Opera House**, hung with an enormous crystal chandelier, and with seating for more than 2,300 people. The Opera House is flanked by the **Hall of States**, with the flags of each of the 50 American states, and the **Hall of Nations**, with the flags of every country with which the US has diplomatic relations.

The impressive Grand Foyer of the Kennedy Center

Watergate Complex ㉑

Map B3. Virginia Ave between Rock Creek Pkwy & New Hampshire Ave, NW. M *Foggy Bottom-GWU.*

Located next to the Kennedy Center on the banks of the Potomac, the four rounded buildings that make up the Watergate Complex were completed in 1971 and designed to contain apartments, offices, and shops. The Watergate soon became one of Washington's most desirable addresses. In 1972, however, the complex found itself at the center of international news. Burglars, linked to President Nixon, broke into the offices of the Democratic Party headquarters in the complex to bug the telephones there, sparking off a major political scandal. Investigations by *Washington Post* reporters Bob Woodward and Carl Bernstein uncovered the extent of the president's involvement through incriminating tapes and proven bribery. This led to an impeachment hearing, but before Mr. Nixon could be impeached, he resigned. Vice-President Gerald Ford succeeded him.

Georgetown ㉒

Map A3. **Old Stone House** 3051 M St, NW. ***Tel*** *(202) 895-6015.* *phone ahead.* *30, 32, 34, 36, 38.* **www**.nps.gov/olst **Georgetown University** 37th & O Sts, NW. ***Tel*** *(202) 687-0100.* *varies.* *call 687-3600 for details.* **www**.georgetown.edu **Dumbarton Oaks** 1703 32nd St, NW. ***Tel*** *(202) 339-6401.* *2–5pm Tue–Sun.* *Federal hols, Dec 24.* *house only.* **www**.doaks.org

Georgetown developed well before Washington, DC. Native Americans had a settlement here, and by the mid-18th century Georgetown had a substantial population of immigrants from Scotland. With the construction of Washington Harbor and the Chesapeake and Ohio Canal in 1828, it soon grew into a wealthy port.

The picturesque Old Stone House in Georgetown, built in 1765

Today one of Washington, DC's most attractive neighborhoods, Georgetown is lined with elegant townhouses, many of them converted into upscale bars, restaurants, and boutiques. The two main business streets of the area are Wisconsin Avenue and M Street. On the latter is the historic **Old Stone House** (built in 1765), which may be the only building in Washington that predates the American Revolution. N Street, lined with historic buildings, has an array of 18th-century Federal-style mansions, as well as some fine Victorian townhouses. The 1794 Thomas **Beall House** (number 3017), is where Jackie Kennedy lived for a year after JFK's death.

More Federal houses can be seen lining the banks of the **Chesapeake and Ohio Canal**, which was built in 1828 and runs for 184 miles (296 km) from Georgetown to Cumberland, Maryland. The canal, with its ingenious transportation system of locks, aqueducts, and tunnels, fell out of use with the arrival of the railroad in the 19th century. It is now a protected national park, offering many recreational facilities. Park rangers in period costume guide tours of the canal in mule-drawn barges, and boating is also popular, especially between Georgetown and Violette's Lock – the first 22 miles (35 km) of the canal. The towpath along the canal is ideal for walks and bike rides.

The Riggs National Bank, on Wisconsin Avenue in Georgetown

A major center of activity in this district is **Georgetown University**, founded in 1789. Among the historic buildings on its campus is the Gothic-inspired Healy Building, topped by a fanciful spiral.

Sprawling over 22 acres (9 ha) of land in Georgetown is the historic **Dumbarton Oaks** estate. Its superbly landscaped gardens surround a grand Federal-style brick mansion, which houses a priceless art collection assembled by pharmaceutical heirs Robert and Mildred Bliss.

The historic Dumbarton Oaks Conference, attended by President Franklin Roosevelt and British Prime Minister Winston Churchill, was held in the music room of this house in 1944, laying the groundwork for the establishment of the United Nations.

The Blisses donated the house to Harvard University, and it now houses a library, research institution, and museum, the highlight of which is its superb collection of Byzantine art. A new wing of the house, designed by Philip Johnson, houses pre-Columbian masks, gold jewelry from Central America, frescoes, and Aztec carvings.

Auguste Renoir's masterpiece, *The Luncheon of the Boating Party* (1881)

Phillips Collection ㉓

1600 21st St at Q St, NW. ***Tel*** *(202) 387-2151.* Ⓜ *Dupont Circle.* *10am–5pm Tue–Wed & Fri–Sat, 10am–8:30pm Thu, 11am–6pm Sun.* *Mon, Jan 1, Jul 4, Thanksg., Dec 25.* *11am Fri & Sat.* **www**.phillipscollection.org

This is one of the finest collections of Impressionist art in the world, and the first museum in the US devoted to modern art of the 19th and 20th centuries. Housed in the beautiful 1897 Georgian Revival mansion of the collection's founders, Marjorie and Duncan Phillips, this museum has a more intimate and personal ambience than the larger Smithsonian art museums.

Among the wonderful selection of Impressionist and Post-Impressionist works on display are *Dancers at the Barre* by Degas, *Self-Portrait* by Cezanne, *Entrance to the Public Gardens at Arles* by Van Gogh, and Renoir's masterpiece, *The Luncheon of the Boating Party* (1881).

Other great paintings in the collection include El Greco's *The Repentant Saint Peter* (1600), *The Blue Room* (1901) by Picasso, Piet Mondrian's *Composition No III* (1921–25), and *Ochre on Red* (1954) by Mark Rothko.

The museum hosts a number of special events, such as gallery talks, film retrospectives, and live jazz concerts. Especially popular are its Sunday afternoon concerts, staged in the Music Room, with performances by classical artists of world renown. These popular concerts are free to anyone who has purchased a ticket for the gallery on that day.

National Zoological Park ㉔

3001 Connecticut Ave, NW. ***Tel*** *(202) 673-4800.* Ⓜ *Cleveland Park, Woodley Park-Zoo.* *Apr–Oct: 10am–6pm daily (buildings), 6am–8pm daily (grounds); Oct–Apr: 10am–4:30pm daily (buildings), 6am–6pm daily (grounds).* *Dec 25.* *call (202) 673-4671.* **www**.natzoo.si.edu/

Located in a sprawling 163-acre (66-ha) park designed by Frederick Law Olmsted (the landscape designer of New York's Central Park), the National Zoo was established in 1887. Since 1964 it has been part of the Smithsonian Institution, which has developed it as a dynamic "biopark" where animals are studied in environments that replicate their natural habitats.

The Komodo dragon, a rare lizard in the National Zoological Park

The zoo's most famous residents are the giant pandas, Mei Xiang, Tian Tian, and baby Tai Shan who can be seen roaming around the large trees, pools, and air-conditioned outdoor grottos in the **Giant Panda Exhibit**.

Equally popular with visitors is the **Great Ape House**, which houses lowland gorillas, each weighing around 400 lbs (180 kg), and arboreal orangutans.

The **Reptile Discovery Center** features the rare Komodo dragons, lizards that can grow up to a length of 10 ft (3 m) and weigh up to 200 lbs (90 kg).

In **Amazonia**, which re-creates the lush green Amazonian habitat, visitors can see poison arrow frogs and giant catfish, while the **Asia Trail** features red pandas and sloth bears.

Other rare creatures include the endangered Golden Lion Tamarins and red wolves.

Washington National Cathedral ㉕

Massachusetts & Wisconsin Aves, NW. ***Tel*** *(202) 537-6200.* *32, 34, 36.* *10am–3:30pm Mon–Sat, 12:45–4pm Sun.* *donation.* *group reservations call 537-6207.* *noon Mon–Sat, hourly 8am–11am & 4pm & 6:30pm Sun, 5:30pm Mon–Fri, 4pm Sat & Sun.* **www**.nationalcathedral.org

The building of the Church of St. Peter and St. Paul (its official name) was financed entirely by donations. It is the world's sixth largest cathedral, measuring 518 ft (158 m) in length and 301 ft (95 m) from grade to the top of the central tower. It uses building techniques of the Gothic style of architecture, evident in the pointed arches, rib vaulting, stained-glass windows, and exterior flying buttresses. Inside, sculpture, needlework, wrought iron, and wood carving depict the nation's history and biblical scenes.

Above the west entrance is a splendid relief of *The*

Gothic-style architecture of the Washington National Cathedral

Creation by Frederick Hart, which depicts mankind being formed from chaos. The pinnacles on the Cathedral towers are decorated with leaf-shaped ornaments. Above the south entrance is an exquisite stained-glass **Rose Window**, while in the nave another stained-glass window commemorates the *Apollo 11* space flight and contains a sliver of moon rock. The **High Altar** has carvings of 110 figures surrounding the central statue of Christ. The floor in front of the altar has stone from Mount Sinai. By the **Children's Chapel**, built to the scale of a six-year-old, is a statue of Jesus as a boy.

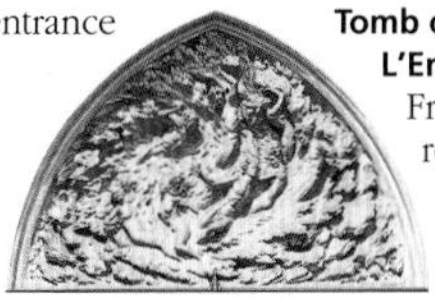

***The Creation,* National Cathedral**

Arlington National Cemetery ㉖

Arlington, VA. ***Tel*** *(703) 607-8000.* *Arlington National Cemetery.* *Oct–Mar: 8am–5pm daily; Apr–Sep: 8am–7pm daily.* *Dec 25.*

A sea of simple headstones covers Arlington National Cemetery, marking the graves of around 300,000 American servicemen killed in the nation's major conflicts – from the Revolution to the present. The focus of the cemetery, which sprawls over 624 acres (252 ha) of a hillside, is the **Tomb of the Unknowns**, honoring the thousands whose bodies were never found or identified. Its four vaults are for soldiers from World Wars I and II, Korea, and Vietnam. Each vault held one unidentified soldier until 1998, when the Vietnam soldier was identified by DNA analysis and reburied in his hometown. Near it is the **Memorial Amphitheater**, which has hosted many state funerals, and where annual services are held on Memorial Day.

North of the Tomb of the Unknowns, an eternal flame burns at the **Grave of John F. Kennedy**, lit by his wife Jacqueline on the day of his funeral in December 1963. She and their infant son Patrick and an unamed stillborn daughter are buried next to the late president. His brother Robert F. Kennedy is nearby. Close to Arlington House is the imposing **Tomb of Pierre L'Enfant**, the French architect responsible for planning the city of Washington. The cemetery also houses poignant memorials to the victims of the Lockerbie air crash and the *Challenger* Space Shuttle, which exploded seconds after take-off in January 1986.

The grand Georgian-Revival mansion at the top of the hill, above the Kennedy graves, is **Arlington House**, which was the home of the Confederate general Robert E. Lee (1807–70). When Lee left his home in 1861 to lead Virginia's armed forces during the Civil War, the Union confiscated the estate for a military cemetery. The house, now a memorial to the general, is open to visitors.

The Pentagon ㉗

1000 Defense Pentagon, Hwy 1-395, Arlington, VA. ***Tel*** *(703) 697-1776.* *Pentagon.* *tours by appointment only. For details call the above number.* **www**.pentagon.afis.osd.mil

The world's largest office building, the Pentagon is almost a city in itself. This enormous edifice houses 23,000 people who work for the US Department of Defense, which includes the Army, Navy, and Airforce, and 14 other defense agencies. Despite its enormous size – it has 17.5 miles (28 km) of corridors, and the entire US Capitol could fit into one of its five wedge-shaped sections – the building's efficient design ensures that it takes no more than seven minutes to walk between any two points in the Pentagon. Designed by army engineers, it is built from sand and gravel dredged from the Potomac and molded into concrete. The building was started in September 1941, and completed in January 1943 at a cost of $83 million.

The headquarters of the US military establishment and the ultimate symbol of America's military might, the Pentagon was one of the targets of terrorists who flew a hijacked American Airlines plane into one side of the building on September 11, 2001, killing 189 people. It has now been completely restored.

Uniform rows of headstones in Arlington National Cemetery

Virginia

There is enough history and natural beauty in Virginia to satisfy the most avid sightseer. Mount Vernon, the perfectly preserved home of President George Washington, is close to Washington, DC. In eastern Virginia is the old capital, Williamsburg, a living museum of the Colonial era. To its west, the Skyline Drive reveals the spectacular beauty of the Shenandoah National Park and the Blue Ridge Mountains. The state capital, Richmond, retains a charming Old South aura.

Alexandria ❷

128,000. Union Station, 110 Callahan St. M King Street. Ramsay House Visitor Center, 221 King St (703) 746-3301.
www.funside.com

Old Town Alexandria has kept a special historical flavor, dating back to its incorporation in 1749. Accessible by Metro from Washington, Alexandria is still a busy port, with its lively Market Square. Its tree-lined streets are filled with elegant, historic buildings, among them the 1753 **Carlyle House**, a Georgian Palladian mansion on Fairfax Street. A guided tour of the house, now beautifully restored, provides fascinating details about 18th-century everday life. On the same street is the **Stabler Leadbeater Apothecary Shop**, established in 1792. When it closed in 1933, the doors were locked with all its contents intact. Now reopened as a museum, the shop's 8,000 original objects include huge mortars and pestles, and jars of herbal remedies.

Façade of the elegant Carlyle House, built in 1752, Alexandria

The **Boyhood Home of Robert E. Lee**, a Federal townhouse where General Lee *(see 193)* lived from the age of 11 until he went to the West Point Military Academy, is currently a private residence and not open to the public. The **Lee-Fendall House Museum** nearby is rich with artifacts from the Revolution to the 1930s Labor Movement. To its south is the 1773 **Christ Church**, a Georgian edifice where George Washington's pew is still preserved with his nameplate, as is that of Robert E. Lee.

On Union Street is the **Torpedo Factory Art Center**, displaying the work of local

Mount Vernon ❸

This country estate on the Potomac River was George Washington's home for 45 years. The house is furnished as it would have been during Washington's presidency (1789–97), and the 500-acre (202-ha) grounds still retain aspects of the original farm, such as the flower and vegetable gardens, the sheep paddock, and quarters for the slaves who worked the plantation.

The Upper Garden
The plants in this colorful garden replicate those grown in Washington's time.

For hotels and restaurants in this region see pp232–3 and p237

artists and craftsmen. From the nearby waterfront, there are boat tours on the Potomac River.

The **Farmers Market** in the center of town dates back to 1753, and George Washington regularly sent produce from his farm at Mount Vernon to be sold here. Today, shoppers can find fresh vegetables and fruit, flowers, baked goods, preserves, and local crafts.

Carlyle House
121 N Fairfax St. ***Tel*** *(703) 549-2997.* *10am–5pm Tue–Sat, noon–5pm Sun; Nov–Mar: last tour 4pm.* *Mon, Jan 1, Thanksgiving, Dec 25.*

Lee-Fendall House Museum
614 Oronoco St. ***Tel*** *(703) 548-1789.* *10am–4pm Tue, Thu–Sat, 1–4pm Wed, Sun.* *Dec 25–Jan 31 (except 3rd Sun, Lee's birthday celebration).*

Torpedo Factory Art Center
105 N Union St. ***Tel*** *(703) 838-4565.* *10am–6pm daily (to 9pm Thu).* *Jan 1, Easter, Jul 4, Thanksgiving, Dec 25.*
www.torpedofactory.org

The elegant dining room at Kenmore House, Fredericksburg

Fredericksburg ❹

22,600. *706 Caroline St, (800) 678-4748.* *9am–5pm daily (Memorial Day & Labor Day until 7pm).* *Dec 25.* **www**.fredericksburgva.gov

Fredericksburg's attractions are its historic downtown district and four Civil War battlefields, including those at Chancellorsville and The Wilderness. The Rising Sun Tavern and Hugh Mercer Apothecary Shop in the old downtown offer living history accounts of life in a town that began as a 50-acre (20-ha) port on the Rappahannock River. **Kenmore Plantation and Gardens**, also in the heart of town, has beautiful rooms and gardens. The town's visitor center offers horse-and-carriage or trolley tours. The battlefields evoke the Union's long push toward Richmond during the Civil War *(see p46)*.

Kenmore Plantation & Gardens
1201 Washington Ave.
Tel *(540) 373-3381.*
Mar–Oct: 11am–5pm daily; Nov–Dec: 10am–5pm daily.
Jan–Feb, Thanksgiving, Dec 24–25, 31. **www**.kenmore.org

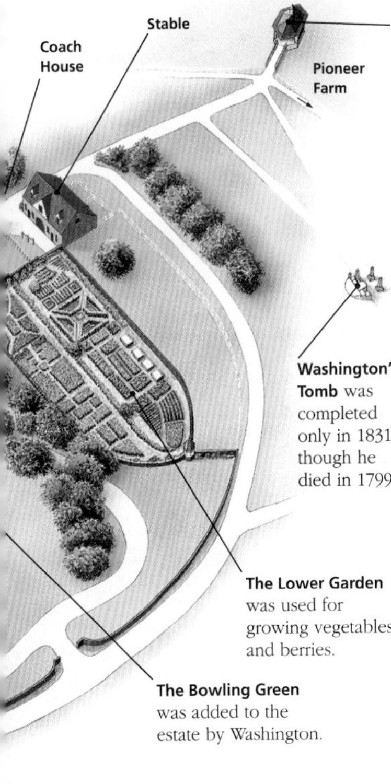

The Wharf is on the same site as it was in Washington's time. Today, visitors who come on day-trip boats from Washington, DC, disembark at this point. Potomac cruise boats also stop off here.

Washington's Tomb was completed only in 1831, though he died in 1799.

The Lower Garden was used for growing vegetables and berries.

The Bowling Green was added to the estate by Washington.

VISITORS' CHECKLIST

S end of George Washington Memorial Pkwy, Fairfax County, VA. ***Tel*** *(703) 780-2000.* *Yellow line to Huntington Station.* *Fairfax Connector bus 101 to Mount Vernon: call (703) 339-7200.* ***Tour bus services & boat cruises available.*** *Mar & Sep–Oct: 9am–5pm daily; Apr–Aug: 8am–5pm daily; Nov–Feb: 9am–4pm daily.* *first floor.*
www.mountvernon.org

The Pioneer Farm
This exhibit demonstrates farming techniques pioneered by Washington. There is also a replica of his unique 16-sided treading barn, created using authentic tools.

Colonial Williamsburg ❺

Colonial couple

As Virginia's capital from 1699 to 1780, Williamsburg was the hub of the loyal British colony. After 1780 the town went into decline. Then in 1926, John D. Rockefeller embarked on a massive restoration project. Today, in the midst of the modern-day city, the 18th-century city has been re-created. People in colonial dress portray the lifestyle of the original townspeople; blacksmiths, silversmiths, cabinet makers, and bakers show off their skills; and horse-drawn carriages pass through the streets, providing visitors with a fascinating insight into America's past.

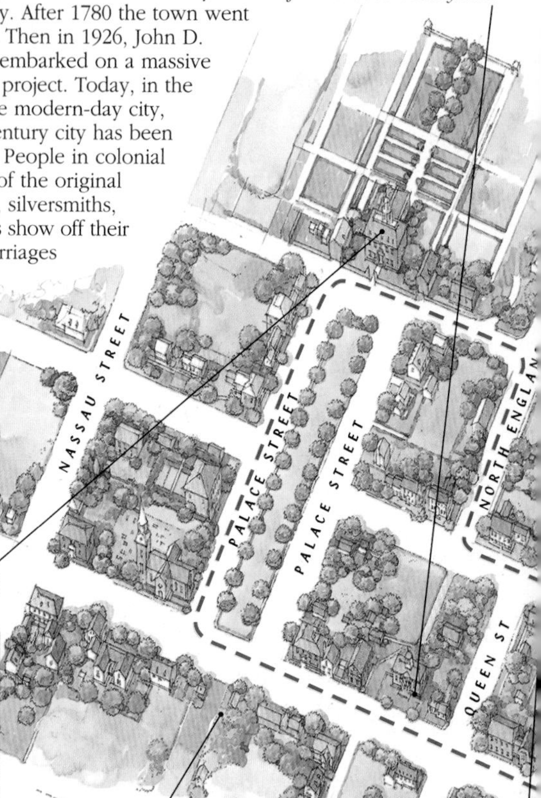

Courthouse
Built in 1770–71 this was the home of the county court for more than 150 years.

★ Governor's Palace
Originally built in 1720 by Governor Alexander Spotswood, the palace has been reconstructed in its full pre-Revolution glory.

Nursery
Costumed living-history interpreters work the land in Colonial Williamsburg using replica tools and the same techniques as the original settlers.

0 meters 200

0 yards 200

STAR SIGHTS

- ★ Capitol
- ★ Governor's Palace
- ★ Print Office

Robertson's Windmill
This reproduction stands on the site of the original 1723 windmill. The cart was a traditional means of transporting materials. Settlers' crafts are demonstrated nearby.

★ Print Office
This store stocks authentic 18th-century foods, including wine, Virginia ham, and peanuts.

VISITORS' CHECKLIST

421 N Boundary St.
(757) 229-6511.
www.colonialwilliamsburg.com
www.visitwilliamsburg.com

Milliner
Owned by Margaret Hunter, the milliner shop stocked a wide range of items. Imported clothes for women and children, jewelry, and toys could all be bought here.

Raleigh Tavern
The Raleigh was once an important center for social, political, and commercial gatherings. The building burned in 1859, but this reproduction evokes the original spirit.

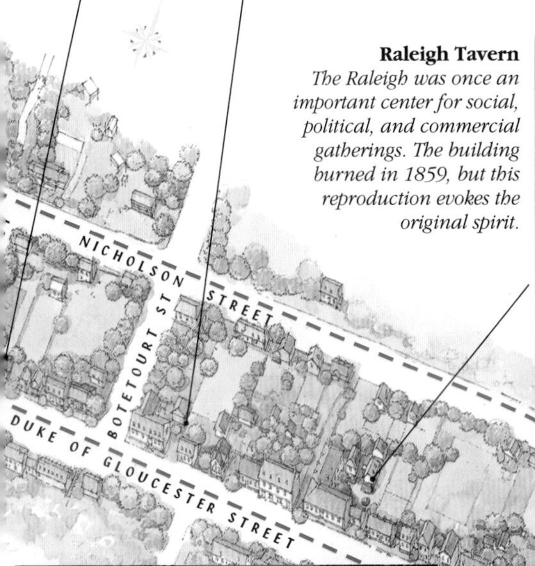

★ Capitol
This is a 1945 reconstruction of the original 1705 building. The government resided in the West Wing, while the General Court was in the East Wing.

KEY

– – – Suggested route

Jamestown Settlement, a re-creation of Colonial James Fort

Jamestown & Yorktown 6

York County Public Information Office, (757) 890-3300.

Jamestown, established in 1607 on the banks of the James River, was the first permanent English settlement in the US. One of the early settlers was John Rolfe, who married Pocahontas, daughter of the Indian chief, Powhatan. But the colony didn't last long – disease, famine, and attacks by Algonquin Indians caused heavy loss of life and in 1699, the colony was abandoned.

Present-day Jamestown Island contains 1,500 acres (607 ha) of marshland and forest. Close to the ruins of the colony, the **Jamestown Settlement** is a re-creation of the original colony, complete with costumed interpreters and replicas of James Fort, an Indian village, and the ships that brought the first successful colonists to Virginia.

On the opposite side of the peninsula, 15 miles (24 km) away, Yorktown was the site of the decisive battle of the American Revolution in 1781. Battlefield tours at **Colonial National Historical Park** explain the siege at Yorktown, which ended with the surrender of the British forces.

Jamestown Settlement
Tel *(757) 253-4838, (888) 593-4682. 9am–5pm daily (to 6pm Jun 15–Aug 15). Jan 1, Dec 25.* **www**.historyisfun.org

Colonial National Historical Park
Tel *(757) 898-3400. 9am–5pm daily. Jan 1, Thanksg., Dec 25.* **www**.nps.gov/colo

Norfolk 7

262,000. 232 E Main St, (800) 368-3097, (757) 664-6620. **www**.norfolkcvb.com

A historic Colonial port, located at the point where Chesapeake Bay meets the Atlantic Ocean, Norfolk is a busy maritime center with the world's largest naval base. The city's logo – a mermaid – is the theme of sculptures and emblems all over Norfolk. The downtown waterfront centers on the massive battleship USS *Wisconsin*, a part of the new **Nauticus, The National Maritime Center**. The center offers multimedia presentations about naval battles, ships, and deep-sea creatures.

Another top attraction is the **Chrysler Museum of Art**, which displays the eclectic personal collection of automobile tycoon Walter Chrysler Jr. The works of art include paintings by Velasquez, Rubens, Degas, Renoir, and modern masters such as Roy Lichtenstein.

Neighboring Virginia Beach is the site of the 18th-century lighthouse at Cape Henry, where the English first landed in 1607. The waterfront is also home to the Virginia Aquarium and Marine Science Museum.

Nauticus, The National Maritime Center
1 Waterside Dr. ***Tel*** *(757) 664-1000. 10am–5pm Tue–Sat, noon–5pm Sun; Jun 1–Sep 1:10am–5pm daily. Thanksgiving, Dec 24 & 25, Jan 1.* **www**.nauticus.org

Richmond 8

198,300. 405 N Third St, (804) 783-7450. **www**.visitrichmondva.com

The old capital of the Confederacy *(see p47)*, Richmond still retains an aura of Old South gentility. Bronze statues of Civil War generals and other heroes line Monument Avenue, while Victorian mansions and brownstones testify to this area's postwar prosperity.

Civil War artifacts, including General Robert E. Lee's coat and sword, are among the exhibits at the **Museum of the Confederacy**. Next door, the White House of the Confederacy is a treasure of the Victorian age.

The graceful Neo-Classical **State Capitol** dominating downtown houses a lifesize sculpture of George Washington by Jean Antoine Houdon. To its west is the serene **Hollywood Cemetery**, the resting place of presidents John Tyler and James Monroe, as well as of 18,000 Confederate soldiers who are buried under a communal pyramid. Palmer Chapel offers superb views of James River and Belle Isle. Farther uptown are two fine museums, the fascinating **Science Museum of Virginia** and the **Virginia Museum of Fine Arts**, which has collections ranging from ancient Egyptian, Indian, and Himalayan art to French Impressionist and modern American masterpieces. The museum's highlight, however, is the priceless Pratt Collection of Imperial Russian Art, which includes five fabulous jeweled Easter eggs made for the Csar by the jeweler Peter Carl Fabergé.

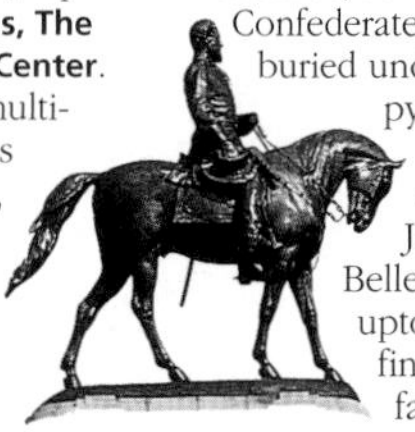

Statue of Robert E. Lee in Richmond

Virginia Museum of Fine Arts
200 North Blvd. ***Tel*** *(804) 340-1400. 11am–5pm Wed–Sun. Mon–Tue, Jan 1, Jul 4, Thanksg., Dec 25. only exhibitions.* **www**.vmfa.museum

For hotels and restaurants in this region see pp232–3 and p237

Chincoteague 9

4,300. *6733 Maddox Blvd, (757) 336-6161.*

The main tourist attraction on Virginia's sparsely developed Eastern Shore, Chincoteague draws fishermen, bird-watchers, and beachcombers. The town itself is primarily a service center, with hotels, motels, and restaurants catering to visitors bound for the **Chincoteague National Wildlife Refuge**, which protects a number of offshore islands, as well as coastal marshlands and a 10-mile (16-km) stretch of Atlantic Ocean beachfront.

A driving tour loops for over 3 miles (4.8 km) through the wildlife preserve, but the best way to see some of the numerous egrets, snow geese, herons, falcons, and other birds found here is by walking or paddling in a canoe.

Chincoteague National Wildlife Refuge
Tel *(757) 336-6122.* *6am–6pm daily.* *limited.*

Charlottesville 10

45,000. *610 E Main St, (434) 293-6789, (877) 386-1103.* **www**.pursuecharlottesville.com

Charlottesville was Thomas Jefferson's hometown. It is dominated by the University of Virginia, which he founded and designed, and also by his home, **Monticello**.

It took Jefferson 40 years to complete Monticello, which he began building in 1769. It is now one of the most celebrated houses in the country. The entrance hall doubled as a private museum, and the library held a collection of around 6,700 books.

The 5,000-acre (2,023-ha) grounds include a large terraced vegetable garden where Jefferson grew and experimented with varieties. The remains of the slaves' quarters still stand; nearly 200 slaves worked the estate's plantations, and recent evidence suggests that one of them, Sally Hemmings, bore Jefferson's child.

The obelisk over Jefferson's grave in the family cemetery lauds him as "Father of the University of Virginia." The university's Neo-Classical buildings and grounds are open to visitors. Vineyards and wineries surround Charlottesville. Michie Tavern *(see p237)*, joined to the Virginia Wine Museum, has been restored to its 18th-century appearance and serves typical Southern cuisine.

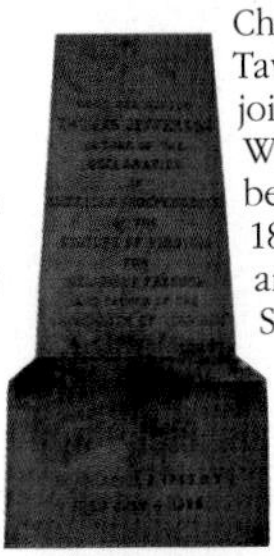

The obelisk over Jefferson's grave

Montpelier, on a 2,500-acre (1,012-ha) site, 25 miles (40 km) to the north, was the home of the fourth president, James Madison.

Monticello
Route 53, 3 miles (4.8 km) SE of Charlottesville. ***Tel*** *(434) 984-9822.* *Mar–Oct: 8am–5pm; Nov–Feb: 9am–4:30pm.* *Dec 25.* **www**.monticello.org

MONTICELLO, CHARLOTTESVILLE

Situated in the leafy foothills of the Blue Ridge Mountains, this Palladian masterpiece was built between 1769 and 1809 by Thomas Jefferson.

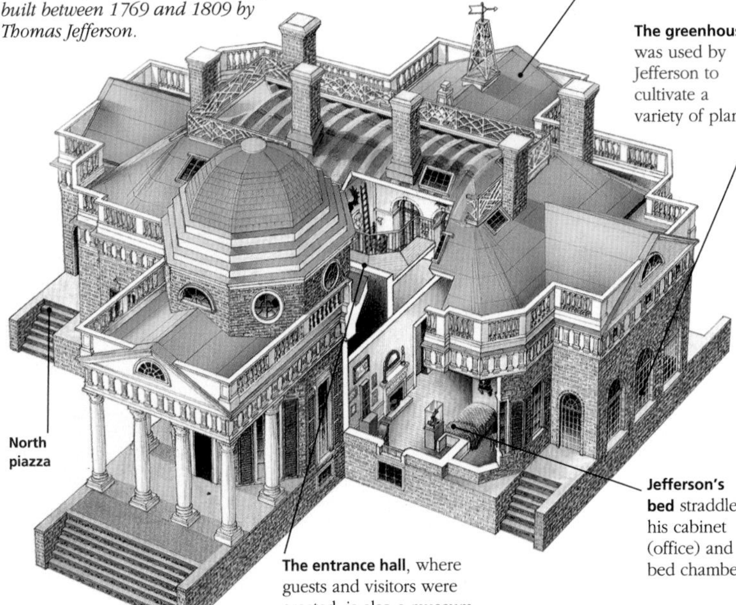

A reconstructed building, Appomattox Court House

Appomattox Court House and National Historical Park ⓫

(877) AT BLUE GREY, (434) 352-8999. 8:30am–5pm daily. Jan 1, Martin Luther King Day, Presidents Day, Thanksgiving, Dec 25.

This National Historic Park, located 3 miles (4.8 km) northeast of the town of Appomattox, re-creates the spot where Confederate General Robert E. Lee surrendered to US General Ulysses S. Grant to signal the end of the Civil War *(see p193)*. Today, markers trace the sites of the last skirmishes of the war, and 27 reconstructed and restored buildings replicate the scene where, on April 9, 1865, the two leaders and their armies put an end to that long, destructive war. In the last months of fighting, General Grant had captured the Confederate stronghold at Petersburg, while General Sherman's "March to the Sea" across Georgia surrounded Confederate forces from the South. With the fall of the Confederate capital at Richmond on April 2, General Lee realized that victory was impossible. The terms of surrender were generous, since Union leaders hoped to promote reconciliation. When the Confederates laid down their arms, the Northern soldiers saluted their opponents.

Much of the original setting was destroyed in battle or later dismantled by souvenir hunters. Most of what stands here today was reconstructed by the National Park Service in the 1940s.

Blue Ridge Parkway ⓬

***Tel** (828) 298-0398.*
www.nps.gov/blri

Stretching for 469 miles (755 km) along the crest of the Appalachian Mountains, the Blue Ridge Parkway *(see p41)* extends from the southern border of Shenandoah National Park all the way to North Carolina, ending finally at Great Smoky Mountains National Park *(see p262)*. Created as a public works project during the "New Deal" era in the depths of the 1930s Great Depression, the scenic route was begun in 1935 but was not completed until 1987. Mileposts along the way, measured from north to south, help travelers discover the points of interest along the route. Some of the highlights along the 216-mile (348-km) portion of the Blue Ridge Parkway in Virginia include a crossing of the James River at milepost 63 and the lakefront lodge in the Peaks of Otter section near milepost 86. The historic **Mabry Mill** at milepost 176 was in use as a backwoods sawmill and blacksmith shop until 1935.

This parkway passes through Asheville, North Carolina, and Roanoke, Virginia, and is primarily rural and scenic, with no advertising or commercial traffic allowed. Open all year, the peak travel season is fall.

The picturesque Mabry Mill at milepost 176 of the Blue Ridge Parkway

Skyline Drive ⓭

Skyline Drive runs along the backbone of the Shenandoah National Park's Blue Ridge Mountains. Originally farmland, the government designated the area a national park in 1926. Deer, wild turkey, bears, and bobcats inhabit the park, and wildflowers, azaleas, and mountain laurel are abundant. The park's many hiking trails and its 75 viewpoints offer stunning natural scenery.

North entrance station

Whiteoak Canyon ②
The Whiteoak Canyon Trail passes six waterfalls on its route.

Pinnacles Overlook ①
The view of Old Rag Mountain with its outcroppings of granite is spectacular.

Bearfence Mountain ⑤
Although this is a bit of a climb, partly on rock scramble, it is not too difficult, and the reward is a breathtaking 360-degree view of the surrounding landscape.

Big Meadows ③
Close to the visitor center, this meadow retains its centuries-old state. It was probably kept clear by fires or lightning strikes. Herds of deer can be seen.

KEY

- - Walk route
- Lookout point
- Road

0 km 10

0 miles 10

Rapidan Camp ④
At the end of Mill Prong Trail, this 164-acre (66-ha) resort was President Hoover's weekend retreat until 1932, when he donated it to the park.

Lewis Mountain ⑥
Quaint cabins, a campground, picnic area, camp store, laundry, and showers provide for campers and hikers here.

TIPS FOR DRIVERS

Starting point: *North at Front Royal, central at Thornton Gap or Swift Run Gap, south at Rockfish Gap.*
Length: *105 miles (168 km), duration of 4–8 hrs depending on the number of stops.*
When to go: *Mid-October for fall leaf colors; spring and summer for wildflowers.*
What it costs: *No fee to travel the Blue Ridge Parkway.*

Fall in Shenandoah National Park

West Virginia

Set entirely within the Appalachian Mountains, this "Mountain State" remains largely forested, despite centuries of aggressive lumbering and mining. The state was part of Virginia until the Civil War, and its early European pioneers were less wealthy and generally very different from the genteel planters of eastern Virginia. As talk of secession grew, western Virginia aligned with the Union. Four years after abolitionist John Brown raided a federal arsenal in Harpers Ferry in a failed attempt to inspire a slave rebellion in 1859, West Virginia was declared a separate state. Today it is known for its woodworking, quilting, and basketry crafts, and traditional Appalachian music and dancing.

Blackwater Falls State Park, in Monongahela National Forest

Monongahela National Forest ⓮

200 Sycamore St, Elkins. ***Tel** (304) 636-1800.* ◯ *8am–4:45pm Mon–Fri.*

The eastern half of the state lies deep within the Allegheny Mountains, a part of the longer Appalachian Range. Much of this rugged terrain is protected as the vast Monongahela National Forest, which encompasses five federally designated wilderness areas and serves as the headwaters for six major river systems. Its landscapes of rhododendron, black cherry, highland bogs, blueberry thickets, and exposed rocks are the habitat for black bear, white-tailed deer, bobcat, otter, mink, and many other species. The forest's trails attracts hikers, horseback riders, and mountain bikers, while in winter, the area is popular for downhill and cross-country skiing.

The small town of **Elkins**, the headquarters of the national forest, makes a convenient base to explore the area. The town's Augusta Heritage Center hosts residential summer programs on traditional folklife and folk arts, as well as bluegrass and old-time mountain music dances and concerts.

Northeast of Elkins, an 8-mile (13-km) stretch of the 124-mile (200-km) Allegheny Trail links two state parks – **Canaan Valley Resort State Park**, a downhill ski resort, and **Blackwater Falls State Park**, a good place for backcountry ski touring. Both parks have restaurants and provide facilities for lodging and camping. Farther south, Snowshoe Mountain Resort is the state's largest downhill resort in winter and a mountain biking center from spring to fall (rentals and guided trips are available). The nearby **Cass Scenic Railroad State Park** organizes vintage steam train rides across the mountaintops for panoramic views. Fall foliage rides are the most popular.

Southeast of Elkins, the **Spruce Knob–Seneca Rocks National Recreation Area** draws rockclimbers up the sandstone strata of Seneca Rocks, an hour's drive away. The 75-mile (121-km) Greenbrier River Trail, running parallel to the Virginia border, from White Sulphur Springs in the south all the way to the Cass Scenic Railroad State Park in the north, is a converted "rails-to-trails" rail bed route, which is quite popular for bicycle tours.

Spruce Knob-Seneca Rocks National Rec. Area
(304) 567-2827. ◯ *May–Sep: 9am–4:30pm Wed–Sun; Nov–Apr: 9am–4:30 pm Sat–Sun.* ♿

Cass Scenic Railroad
Route 66/Main St, Cass. ***Tel** (304) 456-4300.* ♿ ◯ *late May–Oct.*

New River Gorge National River ⓯

Canyon Rim Visitor Center US Hwy 19, Lansing. ***Tel** (304) 574-2115.* ◯ *9am–5pm daily.* ● *Jan 1, Thanksgiving, Dec 25.* ♿ **www**.nps.gov/neri

The New River courses through a deep gorge in the southeastern corner of the state, drawing rafters for some of the most exciting whitewater adventures in the eastern US. The National Park Service, located between Fayetteville and Hinton, oversees a stretch that falls 750 ft (225 m) within 50 miles (80 km), with a compact set of

Rock Climber above New River Gorge National River

For hotels and restaurants in this region see p233 and p237

Overlook at Hawk's Nest State Park, New River Gorge National River

Class V rapids. The modern Canyon Rim Visitor Center and gorge bridge provide easy access to panoramic overlooks and rim hiking trails. The visitor center also distributes comprehensive lists of local rafting outfitters, while the nearby **Hawk's Nest State Park** offers modest lodge rooms and operates an aerial tram down to the river for boat rides during summer. The former mining town of Fayetteville is also a popular base for rafters and outfitters, while the old industrial town of Hinton holds a grittier appeal and is easily accessible to visitors via Amtrak.

Hawk's Nest State Park
Hwy 60, Ansted. ***Tel*** *(304) 658-5212.*
Tram Rides, Boat Rides *Call for seasonal operating days and hours.*

Harpers Ferry ⓰

300. NPS Visitor Center, (304) 535-6298.

Nestled at the confluence of the Potomac and Shenandoah Rivers, where West Virginia meets Virginia and Maryland, is the tiny town of Harpers Ferry. Named after Robert Harper, the Philadelphia builder who constructed a ferry here in 1761, most of the historic downtown area is today the **Harpers Ferry National Historic Park**. It was here in 1859, that Maryland abolitionist John Brown led an ill fated raid on the federal arsenal. Although his attempt failed, this event ignited the Civil War two years later.

The town looks just as it did in the 19th century, with small clapboard storefronts clinging to steep hillsides that slope down to the rushing rivers. Several historic buildings, including John Brown's Fort and the arsenal, are open to visitors.

The famous Appalachian Trail *(see p174)*, which runs through town, has its headquarters at the **Appalachian Trail Conservancy**. The Trail is a 2,000-mile (3,220-km) footpath that stretches along the spine of the Appalachian Mountains from Georgia to Maine. With an Amtrak train station, Harpers Ferry is just an hour's ride from Washington, DC, making this remote region accessible for visitors without a car.

Appalachian Trail Conservancy
799 Washington St.
Tel *(304) 535-6331.*
9am–5pm daily.
www.appalachiantrail.org

Aerial view of Harpers Ferry, located at the confluence of the Potomac and Shenandoah Rivers

Maryland

Maryland has an abundance of both natural attractions and historical sites. The rolling farmlands around Antietam in western Maryland are rich in Civil War heritage. Water-related tourism is a mainstay of southern Maryland's Chesapeake Bay, the longest inland shoreline in the US, which attracts sailors, fishermen, and seafood lovers who can indulge in the delicious local specialty – soft-shell blue crabs. The Eastern Shore on the Delmarva Peninsula, dotted with picturesque villages, is also graced by the wild beauty of Assateague and Chincoteague Islands.

Antietam National Battlefield ⓱

Rte 65, 10 miles (16 km) S of Hagerstown. ***Tel** (301) 432-5124.* *Jun–Sep: 8am–7pm daily; Oct–May: 8:30am–5pm.* *Jan 1, Thanksgiving, Dec 25.* **www**.nps.gov/anti

One of the worst battles of the Civil War was waged here on September 17, 1862, culminating in 23,000 casualties among the Confederate as well as the Union armies.

An observation tower offers a panoramic view of this historic battlefield. Antietam Creek runs peacefully under the Burnside Bridge, where the fighting was severe and much blood was spilled. The whole site has a haunted atmosphere even today. Although the battle did not end in a decisive victory, the horrendous bloodshed at Antietam inspired President Lincoln to issue the Emancipation Proclamation. The visitor center movie recreating the battle should not be missed.

Frederick ⓲

50,000. *19 E Church St, (800) 999-3613, (301) 600-2888.* *9am–5pm daily.* **www**.fredericktourism.org

Frederick's historic center, dating back to the mid-18th century, was renovated in the 1970s and is now a popular tourist attraction.

This charming town is a major antique center and home to hundreds of antique dealers. Its shops, galleries, and eateries are all in 18th- and 19th-century settings, and several historic houses in the town, beautifully restored and furnished with period artifacts, are open to visitors. Francis Scott Key, author of "The Star Spangled Banner," is buried in Mt. Olivet Cemetery. Tourist information is available at the visitor center, which also conducts popular walking tours during the weekends.

Baltimore ⓳

675,500. *Inner Harbor West Wall, (410) 837-4636, (800) 282-6632.* **www**.baltimore.org

There is much to do and see in this pleasant port city of restaurants, antiques, arts, boats, and monuments. A good place to start is the Inner Harbor, the city's redeveloped waterfront, with its harborside shops and restaurants. The centerpiece, and one of Baltimore's most popular attractions, is the stunning **National Aquarium**, whose collection includes many exhibits, a seal pool, and a dolphin show.

The Harbor is also home to the **Maryland Science Center**, where "do touch" is the rule. It features a number of interactive exhibits, and the Planetarium and IMAX® Theater thrill visitors with images of earth and space.

The **American Visionary Art Museum**, also on the Inner Harbor, houses a collection of extraordinary works by self-taught artists whose materials range from matchsticks to faux pearls.

Uptown is the **Baltimore Museum of Art**, with its famous collection of modern art, including works by Matisse, Picasso, Degas, and Van Gogh. It also has a large collection of pieces by Andy Warhol and two sculpture gardens featuring works by Rodin and Calder.

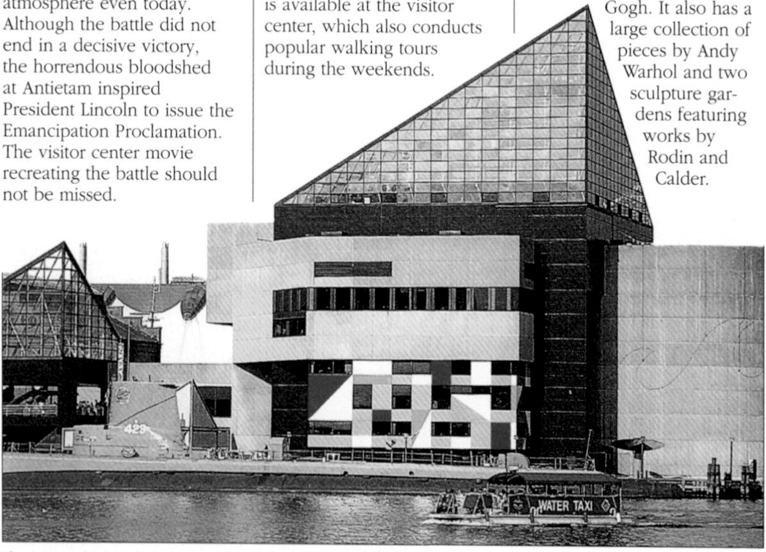

The eye-catching architecture of the National Aquarium, Baltimore

For hotels and restaurants in this region see p232 and p236

Also impressive is the **Walters Art Gallery** on the elegant Mount Vernon Square, lined with Colonial brick townhouses. The gallery's collection includes Greek and Roman classical art, Southeast Asian and Chinese artifacts, Byzantine silver, pre-Columbian carvings, and jeweled objects by Fabergé. There are also paintings by Rubens, Monet, Manet, and the Victorian artist Alma-Tadema, whose beautiful *Sappho and Alcaeus* (1881) should not be missed.

The lively neighborhood of Little Italy is also worth a visit for its knockout Italian restaurants and the games of bocce (Italian lawn bowling), played around Pratt or Stiles Street on warm evenings.

National Aquarium
501 E Pratt St, Pier 3. ***Tel*** *(410) 576-3800.* *Mar–Jun & Sep–Oct: 9am–5pm daily (to 8pm Fri); Jul–Aug: 9am–7:30pm Sun–Thu, 9am–9:30pm Fri–Sat; Nov–Feb: 10am–4pm Mon–Thu, 10am–8pm Fri, 10am–5pm Sat–Sun.* *Mon, Thnksg., Dec 24, 25.* **www**.aqua.org

Maryland Science Center
601 Light St. ***Tel*** *(410) 685-5225.* *10am–5pm Tue–Thu, 10am–8pm Fri, 10am–6pm Sat, 11am–5pm Sun.* *Mon, Thnksg., Dec 25.* **www**.mdsci.org

Baltimore Museum of Art
N Charles St & 31st St. ***Tel*** *(443) 573-1700.* *11am–5pm Wed–Fri, 11am– 6pm Sat–Sun.* *Mon, Tue, Jan 1, Jul 4, Thanksgiving, Dec 25.* **www**.artbma.org

Walters Art Museum
600 N Charles St. ***Tel*** *(410) 547-9000.* *10am–5pm Wed–Sun.* *Dec 24, 25, Jan 1, Jul 4, Thnksg.* *Sat, Sun.*

Annapolis ⓴

35,800. *Annapolis & Anne Arundel County Visitors Bureau, 26 West St, (410) 280-0445.* *9am–5pm daily.* **www**.visit-annapolis.org

The capital of Maryland, Annapolis, is regarded as the jewel of Chesapeake Bay. It is defined by the nautical character that comes with the 17 miles (27 km) of shoreline and the longtime presence of the **United States Naval Academy**. A walk down Main Street leads past the 200-year-old Maryland Inn, shops, and wonderful seafood restaurants that serve local fish, to the City Dock lined with boats. It is then a short walk to the 150-year-old US Naval Academy. Inside the visitor center is the *Freedom* 7 Space Capsule that carried the first American, Alan Shepard, into space. The US Naval Academy Museum in Preble Hall is also worth visiting, especially to see the gallery of detailed ship models.

The beautiful formal gardens of the William Paca House, in Annapolis

The **Maryland State House**, completed in 1779, is the oldest state capitol in continuous use. Its Old Senate Chamber is where the Continental Congress (delegates from each of the American colonies) met when Annapolis was briefly the capital of the United States in 1783–84. It was also here that the Treaty of Paris was ratified in 1784, formally ending the Revolutionary War.

Annapolis teems with Colonial-era buildings, most of them still in use. The 1765 **William Paca House**, home of Governor Paca who signed the Declaration of Independence, is a fine Georgian house with an enchanting garden, both of which have recently been lovingly restored. Another restored mansion worth visiting is the magnificent red-brick **Hammond Harwood House**, which boasts exceptionally fine woodcarving. Built in 1774, this masterpiece of Georgian design, a short walk west of the State House on Maryland Avenue, was named after the Hammond and Harwood families. Worth exploring are the Cornhill and Duke of Gloucester Streets, examples of the city's historic residential streets. Many tours are offered in Annapolis, including bus, boat, and walking tours. It is particularly enjoyable for tourists to view the city from the water by sightseeing boat, schooner, or kayak.

Tiffany window in the Naval Academy, Annapolis

US Naval Academy
Corner of King George, E of Randall St. ***Tel*** *(410) 293-8687.* *9am–5pm daily (photo i.d. required).* *Jan 1, Thanksgiving, Dec 25.*

Maryland State House
State Circle. ***Tel*** *(410) 974-3400.* *9am–5pm Mon–Fri, 10am–4pm Sat–Sun (call ahead; photo i.d. required).* *Dec 25.* *11am & 3pm.*

William Paca House
186 Prince George St. ***Tel*** *(410) 267-7619.* *Mar–Dec: 10am–5pm daily.* *Thanksgiving, Dec 24, 25.*

North Bay 21

121 N Union St, Ste. B, Havre de Grace, (410) 939-2100.

At the northern end of Chesapeake Bay, the lovely town of Havre de Grace is home to the Concord Point Lighthouse. Popular with artists and photographers, the lighthouse has been in continuous operation since the mid-1800s. The **Havre de Grace Decoy Museum** exhibits a fine collection of working decoys and chronicles how the craft evolved from a purely practical wildfowl lure into a highly sophisticated form of American folk art.

Across the bay to the east, the lush forests of **Elk Neck State Park** cover the tip of a peninsula crowned by Turkey Point Lighthouse, one of the bay's oldest. The park offers a sandy beach for swimming, boat rentals, miniature golf, and hiking trails.

Northeast of the park across the Elk River is Chesapeake City, where rooftops appear much as they did 100 years ago when the village grew to service the Chesapeake and Delaware Canal. Today, the village is a "boutique town," with fine shops and restaurants. The **C and D Canal Museum** is housed in the canal's original pumphouse. Working models of canal locks, the original steam power plant, and a giant water wheel are on display.

Havre de Grace Decoy Museum
215 Giles St. ***Tel*** *(410) 939-3739.* *10:30am–4:30pm Mon–Sat, noon–4pm Sun.* *public hols.*

Elk Neck State Park
End of Route 272. ***Tel*** *(410) 287-5333.*

C&D Canal Museum
End of 2nd St. ***Tel*** *(410) 885-5621.* *8am–4pm Mon–Fri.* *Hols.*

St. Michaels 22

1,900. *(800) 808-7622.*
www.stmichaelsmd.org

St. Michaels, founded in 1677, was once a haven for ship builders, privateers, and blockade-runners. Today, the town is a destination for pleasure boaters and yachts flying international colors. B&Bs, a variety of shops, and good restaurants abound.

Chesapeake Bay Maritime Museum is one of Maryland's top cultural attractions. The museum features interactive exhibits on boat building, historic boats, decoys, and various other aspects of Chesapeake Bay life. Several vessels unique to the area are anchored on the property, and the **Hooper Strait Lighthouse**, a fully restored 1879 screwpile wooden structure, is open for exploration.

Chesapeake Bay Maritime Museum
Navy Point at Mill St. ***Tel*** *(410) 745-2916.* *10am–5pm (until 6pm in summer, 4pm in winter).*
www.cbmm.org

The bay in Blackwater National Wildlife Refuge, Easton

Easton 23

11,700. *11 S Harrison St. (410) 770-8000.*
www.tourtalbot.org

A handsome little town, Easton is an interesting combination of unique shops and historic homes. A restored 1820s schoolhouse serves as the premises of the **Academy of the Arts**. Although the emphasis is on Eastern Shore artists, the gallery's permanent collection includes works by famous artists such as James Whistler and Grant Wood.

Once a farm used by muskrat trappers for the fur trade, **Blackwater National Wildlife Refuge** was established in 1933 to provide sanctuary for migrating waterfowl. Geese number 35,000 and ducks exceed 15,000 at the peak of the fall migration. The best time to observe migratory birds is from October through

Hooper Strait Lighthouse at Chesapeake Bay silhouetted by a pink and violet sunset

For hotels and restaurants in this region see p232 and p236

March; however, many songbirds and other animals can be seen all year round.

Academy Museum of the Arts
106 South St. ***Tel*** *(410) 822-2787.* *10am–8pm Tue–Thu, 10am–4pm Mon, Fri, Sat.* *Sun.* **www**.art-academy.org

Blackwater National Wildlife Refuge
2145 Key Wallace Dr, Cambridge. ***Tel*** *(410) 228-2677.* *8am–4pm Mon–Fri, 9am–5pm Sat–Sun.* *Thanksg., Dec 25.*

Crisfield ㉔

2,900. *906 W Main St, Crisfield, (800) 782-3913.*

This busy commercial seafood port supports a bustling sportfishing industry. From Mid-May through October, the fish are running. The **Governor J. Millard Tawes Historical Museum** is named after a resident who became Maryland's 54th governor. The museum has displays on local history and marine life. It also offers walking tours through a boatyard and a seafood processing plant as well as trolley tours through historic Crisfield to the Ward Brothers Waterfowl carving workshop and the crab-processing shanties of Jenkins Creek.

Crisfield Tawes Historical Museum
3 Ninth St, Somers Cove Marina. ***Tel*** *(410) 968-2501.* *9am–5pm Mon–Sat; winter: 10am–4pm Mon–Fri.* *Sun, week of Christmas, week after Christmas.*

Environs
Accessible only by boat, **Smith Island**, 10 miles (16 km) to the west, was chartered in 1608 by Captain John Smith, founder of the Jamestown settlement *(see p191)*. Ewell, at the north end of the island, is where most of the population lives. Some claim that the distinctive local speech is reminiscent of the Elizabethan/Cornwall dialect brought here in the 1770s.

Ferris wheel at Trimper's Rides, Ocean City

Salisbury ㉕

29,000. *8480 Ocean Hwy, (800) 332-8687.*

The largest city on the Eastern Shore, Salisbury is known for its fine antique shops. It developed as a mill community in 1732 and soon became the principal crossroads of the southern Delmarva Peninsula. Salisbury's **Ward Museum of Wildfowl Art** contains the world's premier collection of wildfowl art. Here, wood is carved and painted to resemble wild birds in natural settings. The museum looks at the history of the art, from antique working decoys to contemporary carvings. **Pemberton Historical Park** is the site of Pemberton Hall, built in 1741 for Isaac Handy, a British Army colonel. The grounds are threaded by self-guided nature trails, and the manor house contains a small museum maintained by the local historical society.

Captain John Smith (1580-1631)

Ward Museum of Wildfowl Art
909 S Schumaker Dr. ***Tel*** *(410) 742-4988.* *10am–5pm Mon–Sat, noon–5pm Sun.*

A specialist duck decoy maker at work in Crisfield

Ocean City ㉖

7,100. *4001 Coastal Hwy, (410) 289-2800.*

Soft beige sand extends endlessly along the Ocean City peninsula, fronted by miles of hotels. In summer, brightly colored umbrellas provide shade, while at night, the beach boardwalk that stretches from the inlet north past 27th Street is lively with strolling couples, singles, and families.

At the inlet, on the southern border of Ocean City, the **Ocean City Life-Saving Museum**, housed in a decommissioned 1891 Life-saving Station, relates the history of Ocean City and the US Life-saving Service.

North on the Boardwalk, **Trimper's Rides** began operating in 1902 with a steam-powered 45-animal carousel. Today, Trimper's includes a 1905 Herschel-Spellman merry-go-round glittering with jewels and fantasy animals, Ferris wheels, bumper rides, mechanized fortune-tellers, and a host of other entertainments.

Ocean City also has many miniature golf courses: visitors can play beneath plaster polar bears, bask in the tropics, or putt around rubber sharks.

Ocean City Life-Saving Station Museum
Boardwalk at the Inlet. ***Tel*** *(410) 289-4991.* *May & Oct: 10am–4pm daily; Jun–Sep: 10am–10pm daily; Nov–Apr: call for hours.* **www**.ocmuseum.org

Trimper's Rides
Baltimore & S 1st St on the boardwalk. ***Tel*** *(410) 289-8617.* *mid-May–mid-Sep: 1pm–midnight Mon–Fri, noon–midnight Sat–Sun; mid-Sep–mid-May: limited hours.*

Delaware

Although Delaware is the country's second-smallest state, larger only than tiny Rhode Island, its importance in industry, banking, and technology far exceeds its size. This is mainly due to the laissez faire tax and corporation laws that have attracted several large companies to base their headquarters here. Along with a significant history, stately country homes, and some of the nation's best museums, Delaware's 2,000 square miles (500,000 ha) also boasts more than 20 miles (32 km) of sandy beaches along the Atlantic Ocean.

Detail from *Washington Crossing the Delaware*, Delaware Art Museum

Wilmington 27

71,500.
100 W 10th St, (800) 489-6664.
www.visitwilmingtonde.com

This former Swedish colony is home to one of the country's finest art museums, the **Delaware Art Museum**. Its outstanding collections contain works by American illustrators such as Howard Pyle, and his students N.C. Wyeth and Maxfield Parrish. There are also paintings and sculpture by other 19th- and 20th-century American artists such as Winslow Homer. The galleries feature paintings and decorative arts from the English pre-Raphaelite movement, led by Dante Gabriel Rossetti. The romantic works, second only to those of London's Victoria and Albert Museum in the UK, were bequeathed to the museum in 1935 by the wealthy Wilmington industrialist Samuel Bancroft Jr.

Delaware Art Museum
2301 Kentmere Parkway.
***Tel** (302) 571-9590. 10am–4pm Wed–Sat, noon–4pm Sun.*
www.delart.org

Winterthur 28

SR 52. ***Tel** (302) 888-4600, (800) 448-3883. 10am–5pm Tue–Sun.*
Thanksgiving, Dec 25.
www.winterthur.org

Originally the home of Evelina du Pont and James Biderman, Winterthur was named after the Biderman ancestral home in Switzerland. Henry Francis du Pont inherited the house in 1927. Du Pont was one of the many post-World War I collectors, whose nationalistic sentiments caused them to take a fresh look at American decorative objects. His collection of American furniture is one of the most important assemblages of early American decorative arts in the world.

Winterthur showcases the du Pont family's fascination with American decorative arts and horticulture. The surrounding 982-acre (397-ha) grounds are landscaped beautifully, with miles of surfaced paths and scenic woodland trails. The part of the museum open to the public consists of two buildings, 175 period rooms, and two floors of exhibition galleries.

Hagley Museum/ Eleutherian Mills 29

Rte 141. ***Tel** (302) 658-2400.*
9:30am–4:30pm daily; Jan–mid-Mar: 1:30pm (for one tour only) Mon–Fri; 9:30am–4:30pm Sat–Sun.
Thanksgiving, Dec 25.
www.hagley.org

Picturesquely located on the banks of the Brandywine River, Hagley Yard is the origin of the du Pont fortune in America. Its serene setting is visible in spring when the river banks are ablaze with purple and pink rhododendrons and azaleas.

Eleuthere du Pont acquired the property and established a black powder (explosives) factory here in 1884. Factory buildings, storehouses, drying tables, and the workers' village are open to the public. Facing the river are the Eagle Roll Mill's "mixing rooms," with their 5-ft (1.5-m) thick walls, where powder explosions – there have been 299 blowouts in 20 years – did the least damage. Hagley Museum, at the entryway to the property, explores the history of the sites with exhibits and dioramas.

The modest du Pont family home, **Eleutherian Mills**, dates from 1803. It overlooks the powder works at the far end of the property and contains many original furnishings. The garden is verdant with a variety of native plants, shrubs, and trees.

Boxcar exhibit at Hagley, on the banks of the Brandywine River

For hotels and restaurants in this region see p233 and p237

The elegant French-style Nemours Mansion, built by Alfred I. du Pont

Nemours Mansion and Gardens 30

1600 Rockland Rd.
Tel *(302) 651-6912.* *May–Dec: Tue–Sat.* *9am, 11am, 1pm, 3pm; call to make reservations.*
www.nemoursmansion.org

Built by Alfred I. du Pont in 1909-1910, this Louis XVI-style château is named after the north-central French town that Pierre Samuel du Pont de Nemours, his great-great-grandfather, represented as a member of the French Estates General in 1789. The mansion's 102 rooms are opulently decorated with Oriental rugs, tapestries, and paintings dating from the 15th century. The 300-acre (12-ha) gardens are landscaped in the classic French style.

New Castle 31

4,800. *220 Delaware St, (302) 322-9801.*
www.newcastlecity.org

Delaware's former capital is today a well-preserved historic site, with restaurants, shops, and residential areas. The **New Castle Courthouse** displays artifacts that illuminate the town's multinational origins; Sweden, Holland, and Britain all have claimed New Castle as their own. Several historic homes lie a short stroll from each other. One, the **Amstel House**, was the home of Governor Van Dyke. The town's most elegant dwelling place in 1738, its most famous guest was George Washington.

New Castle Courthouse
211 Delaware St. **Tel** *(302) 323-4453.*
10am–3:30pm Tue–Sat, 1:30–4:30pm Sun. *Mon, public hols.*

Lewes 32

3,000. *120 Kings Hwy, (302) 645-8073.*
www.leweschamber.com

The site of Zwaanendael ("Valley of the Swans"), Delaware's original Dutch settlement in 1631, Lewes is a quiet town with a small beach, sophisticated restaurants, residences, and shops. The **Zwaanendael Museum**, built in 1931, is a striking replica of the Town Hall of Hoorn, home of most of the settlers. Its exhibits elaborate on the first encampment as well as the area's other historical aspects.

In 1682, the British Crown granted the colony of Delaware to Englishman William Penn *(see p98)* who established one of the nation's first public lands by setting aside Cape Henlopen for the citizens of Lewes. Besides a bay and ocean beaches, **Cape Henlopen State Park** contains Gordon's Pond Wildlife Area and the Great Dune, which rises 80 ft (24 m) above sea level. The park's varied habitats are home to many birds, reptiles, and mammals, including threatened shore-birds. Attractions include hiking trails, interpretive displays, a pier, camping, and swimming.

Zwaanendael Museum
Kings Hwy & Savannah Rd.
Tel *(302) 645-1148.* *10am–4:30pm Tue–Sat, 1:30–4:30pm Sun.* *Mon, hols.*

Cape Henlopen State Park
42 Cape Henlopen Dr.
Tel *(302) 645-8983.*

Rehoboth Beach 33

1,200. *501 Rehoboth Ave, (302) 227-2233.*
www.beach–fun.com

Rehoboth beach was originally a Methodist summer camp. A commercial strip of restaurants and shops stretches along Rehoboth Avenue, meeting sand beaches at Funland on the boardwalk. The Outlets, between Lewes and Rehoboth Beach, feature every major outlet store, taking advantage of the fact that there is no sales tax in Delaware.

Three miles (5 km) south of the beach, the 2,700-acre (1093-ha) **Delaware Seashore State Park** covers the strip of land between the Atlantic Ocean and Rehoboth Bay. **Millsboro**, west of Reheboth Bay, is home to the Nanticoke tribe. In mid-September, the tribe holds a public pow-wow to preserve their heritage and explain their beliefs.

South of the park, the 89-ft (27-m) Fenwick Island Lighthouse marks the Delaware-Maryland border. Built in 1852, it was decommissioned during World War II.

Delaware Seashore State Park
Inlet 850. **Tel** *(302) 227-2800.*
Mar 1–Nov 30.

A Nanticoke Indian at the annual pow-wow, Rehoboth Beach

Practical Information

Washington, DC and the capital region is very rich in museums, cultural events, and entertainment, as well as in scenic sites and outdoor activities around its seashores, rivers, and mountains. This region offers excellent amenities for the large numbers of tourists that it attracts. Spring and fall are the best times to visit, as the summers are hot and humid in much of the region, and the winters cold and damp. However, spring, summer, and fall see the largest number of visitors, so it is best to make reservations.

TOURIST INFORMATION

The capital region is well-equipped to cater to visitors' needs. Visitor information desks at airports and within cities will provide guides and maps, information on guided tours, events, and festivals. Major hotels also have guest services desks. The **Smithsonian Information** line is a useful resource for finding out about special events in the museums. State tourism bureaus are other reliable sources of comprehensive information.

PERSONAL SECURITY

In recent years, Washington has made great efforts to clean up its streets and bring down crime. If you stick to the tourist areas and avoid outlying neighborhoods, you should not run into any trouble. When visiting sights off the beaten track, stay alert and study your map properly before you set off. If you plan to hike alone, always carry a cell phone, and inform someone in advance about your itinerary.

GETTING AROUND

Travel within DC and the Capital Region is easy. Washington has a comprehensive public transportation system, and all major attractions in the capital are accessible on foot, or by **Metrorail, Metrobus** Circulator bus, or taxi. If you decide to drive in DC, be prepared for traffic jams and unexpected route changes. Avoid driving at night if you are unfamiliar with the area.

Several DC-based tour companies offer tours that include Mount Vernon, Williamsburg, and Monticello in Virginia. Baltimore and Annapolis, Maryland's major cities, are connected to DC by rail and bus. Car rental is widely available, but often expensive. Both **Amtrak** trains and **Greyhound** buses are cheaper alternatives, but your choice of destination may be more limited. To explore many of the scenic parts of the Capital Region, it is best to travel by car. Visitors should avoid shortcuts and stay on well-traveled roads.

ETIQUETTE

Smoking is prohibited in all public buildings, restaurants, bars, and stores in the region. Cigarettes can only be purchased by those over 18 years old; proof of age may be required. The legal age for drinking alcohol in Washington is 21, and you may need a photo identification (ID) as proof of your age in order to purchase alcohol and be allowed into bars. It is illegal to drink alcohol in public parks or to carry an open container of alcohol in your car while driving. Penalties for driving under the influence of alcohol are quite severe, and may even include a jail sentence.

OUTDOOR ACTIVITIES

Maryland's Chesapeake Bay and Eastern Shore offer wonderful opportunities for boating, sailing, and fishing. For outdoor enthusiasts, other highlights of the Capital Region include hiking the **Appalachian Trail** in Virginia and West Virginia, whitewater rafting in West Virginia, and cycling along the picturesque Chesapeake and Ohio Canal Towpath, which runs all the way from Washington to Maryland. There is also a 16-mile (26-km) biking trail from Washington to Mount Vernon. Delaware's Rehoboth Beach and Seashore State Park are a magnet for those in search of sea and sand.

Among spectator sports, the **Washington Redskins** (football), **Washington Nationals** (baseball) and the **Baltimore Orioles** (baseball) are hot tickets. If tickets have sold out, it is fun to watch the game along with other enthusiasts at a sports bar.

THE CLIMATE OF DC & CAPITAL REGION

The Capital Region's climate varies greatly. In winter, temperatures can plummet below freezing. During this time, Virginia's Appalachian Mountains are covered with snow, attracting skiers and snowboarders. Summers can be very hot and humid, with almost continuous sunshine. Summer is also the season for the heaviest rainfall, especially between May and August, when the rain comes as a welcome break from the humidity. The rains taper off in September and October, when the weather is pleasantly mild. The region is at its best in spring and fall.

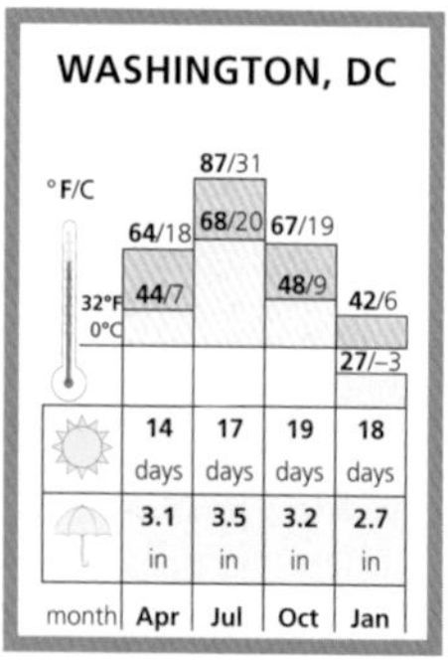

ENTERTAINMENT

Visitors to this region will never be at a loss for entertainment or cultural events. There are more free activities in DC than in any other American city. The weekend section of Friday's edition of the *Washington Post*, provides listings of free concerts, gallery talks, films, book signings, poetry readings, plays, and concerts.

The **Kennedy Center** in Washington is home to the **Washington Opera Company** and the **National Symphony Orchestra**, two of the capital's crown jewels. It offers a magnificent dance and ballet season as well, featuring the world's finest companies, including the Bolshoi, the American Ballet Theater, and the Dance Theater of Harlem. The center also hosts touring theater companies and many top jazz performers. Other good jazz and blues venues are **Blues Alley** in Georgetown, the **Merriweather Post Pavilion** in Columbia, Maryland, and the **Nissan Pavilion** in Manassas, Virginia.

Film classics and film premieres are shown at the American Film Institute in Silver Spring, MD, and documentaries at the Library of Congress. Many of the capital's museums have regular series of film shows, lectures, and concerts.

Washington holds many seasonal cultural events. In June, there are nightly performances by the **Shakespeare Theatre Free for All** at the Carter Barron Amphitheater. Independence Day celebrations are spectacular along the Mall, with fireworks from the base of the Washington Memorial. Labor Day Weekend in September is marked by a free concert by the National Symphony Orchestra on the lawns of Capitol Hill. Tours of the White House are limited at present. Check at the White House Visitor Center for the latest information.

SHOPPING

Washington, DC as well as Maryland and Virginia are famous for their antique stores. Frederick, Maryland, has the **Emporium at Creekside Antiques**, which houses over 100 antique shops. A great place to shop are the museum shops in DC, which stock an incredibly wide range of products, from African textiles and artwork reproductions to contemporary American crafts. Popular department stores are **Macy's** in DC and Nordstrom in Arlington, Virginia. There are large malls in the Virginia and Maryland suburbs, and at Fashion Center in Pentagon City. Discount hunters should head for the 230 outlets at Potomac Mills, situated 30 miles (48 km) south of DC on I-95, or to Rehoboth Beach in Delaware, with its huge concentration of outlet stores.

Many shops in the Washington, DC area are closed on federal holidays.

DIRECTORY

TOURIST INFORMATION

Delaware
99 King's Hwy, Dover, DE 19901.
Tel *(866) 284-7483.*
www.visitdelaware.com

Maryland
217 E Redwood St, Baltimore, MD 21202.
Tel *(866) 639-3526.*
www.visitmaryland.org

Smithsonian Information
1000 Jefferson Dr, SW Washington, DC.
Tel *(202) 633-1000.*

Virginia
901 E Byrd St, Richmond, VA 23219.
Tel *(800) 847-4882.*
www.virginia.org

Washington, DC
901 Seventh St NW, Suite 400, Washington, DC 20001.
Tel *(202) 789-7000.*
www.washington.org

West Virginia
Tel *(800)-225-5982.*
www.callwva.com

TRAVEL

Amtrak
Tel *(800) 872-7245.*
www.amtrak.com

Greyhound
Tel *(800) 231-2222.*
www.greyhound.com

Metrorail & Metrobus
600 Fifth St, NW, Washington, DC 20001.
Tel *(202) 637-7000, (202) 638-3780 (TTY for hearing-impaired callers).*
www.wmata.com

SPORTS & OUTDOOR ACTIVITIES

Baltimore Orioles
Oriole Park at Camden Yards, 333 W Camden St, Baltimore, MD 21201.
Tel *(888) 848-2473.*
www.theorioles.com

Washington Nationals
RFK Stadium, 2400 E Capitol St, SE.
Tel *(202) 675-6287.*
www.nationals.com

Washington Redskins
FedExField 1600, FedEx Way, Landover, MD 20785.
Tel *(301) 276-6050 (ticket office), (301) 276-6000.*
www.redskins.com

ENTERTAINMENT

Blues Alley
1073 Wisconsin Ave, NW.
Tel *(202) 337-4141.*

Kennedy Center
New Hampshire Ave & Rock Creek Pkwy, NW.
Tel *(202) 467-4600.*
www.kennedy-center. org

Merriweather Post Pavilion
Columbia, MD.
Tel *(410) 715-5550.*
www.merriweathermusic.com

National Symphony Orchestra
Tel *(202) 467-4600.*

Nissan Pavilion
7800 Cellar Door Dr, Haymarket, VA.
Tel *(703)754-6400.*

Shakespeare Theatre Free for All
Carter Barron Amphitheater, 16th St & Colorado Ave, NW.
Tel *(202) 334-4790.*
www.shakespeare theatre.org

SHOPPING

Emporium at Creekside Antiques
112 E Patrick St, Frederick, MD.
Tel *(301) 662-7099.*

Macy's Department Store
12th & G St, NW.
Tel *(202) 628-6661.*

Choosing a Hotel

Washington offers a wide choice of accommodations. For a relaxing holiday you may want to choose a hotel with all the amenities – pool, health club, deluxe restaurant, and room service – though cheaper options are also available. Hotels are listed by areas and within these by price.

PRICE CATEGORIES IN US DOLLARS ($)
For a standard double room per night, including breakfast, service charges, and taxes.
$ Under $125
$$ $125–$175
$$$ $175–$225
$$$$ $225–$300
$$$$$ Over $300

WASHINGTON, DC

CAPITOL HILL Hotel George $$$

15 E Street NW, 20001 ***Tel*** *(800) 576-8331* ***Rooms*** *139*

Stylish, contemporary, and eco-friendly, this chic boutique hotel is in the heart of Capitol Hill and within walking distance of Union Station, the National Mall, and the Smithsonian Museums. The modern, luxurious guestrooms are nestled in an historic building with modern conveniences for leisure and business travelers. **www.hotelgeorge.com**

CAPITOL HILL The Liaison Capitol Hill $$$

415 New Jersey Ave, NW, 20001 ***Tel*** *(202) 638-1616* ***Fax*** *(202) 347-1813* ***Rooms*** *343*

Within walking distance from the Smithsonian and close to the Capitol, this hotel offers a sophisticated urban retreat that appeals to business and leisure travelers. All of the rooms have MP3 players. There is an outdoor pool and the fitness center here is open 24 hours. The restaurant is one of Washington's favorites. **www.affinia.com**

CAPITOL HILL Hyatt Regency Washington Capitol Hill $$$$

400 New Jersey Ave, NW (at D St), 20001 ***Tel*** *(202) 737-1234* ***Fax*** *(202) 737-5773* ***Rooms*** *834*

Entrance to the Hyatt is through a five-story atrium. Rooms have wireless Internet, while many suites offer views of the Capitol. You'll find here the Article One American Grill, as well as the Article One Lounge. Children under 18 stay for free. Two and a half blocks from Union Station. **www.hyattregencywashington.com**

CAPITOL HILL Phoenix Park Hotel $$$$

520 N Capitol St, NW (at F St & N Capitol), 20001 ***Tel*** *(202) 638-6900* ***Fax*** *(202) 393-3236* ***Rooms*** *149*

Located one block from Union Station, this historic hotel features rooms furnished in an 18th-century Irish manor style. Three of the suites have spiral staircases and three have balconies. Irish entertainers perform nightly at The Dubliner, a pub with good Irish and American food. **www.phoenixparkhotel.com**

GEORGETOWN The Georgetown Inn $$$$

1310 Wisconsin Ave, NW, 20007 ***Tel*** *(202) 333-8900* ***Fax*** *(202) 333-8308* ***Rooms*** *95*

A small, boutique hotel built in the style of historic Georgetown. The large rooms have Colonial-style decor and luxurious bathrooms. The Daily Grill restaurant displays scenes of old Washington on the walls. Located in the heart of Georgetown. **www.georgetowninn.com**

GEORGETOWN Four Seasons Hotel $$$$$

2800 Pennsylvania Ave, NW, 20007 ***Tel*** *(202) 342-0444* ***Fax*** *(202) 944-2076* ***Rooms*** *211*

A modern exterior belies the old-world elegance of this hotel, which prides itself on its excellent service. Rooms are spacious, with mahogany paneling, antiques, and flowers. Afternoon tea is served on the Garden Terrace. Located near shops, restaurants, and the Washington Harbor. **www.fourseasons.com**

GREATER WASHINGTON The Churchill Hotel $$

1914 Connecticut Ave, NW, 20009 ***Tel*** *(202) 797-2000, (800) 424-2464* ***Fax*** *(202) 462-0944* ***Rooms*** *173*

A luxury boutique hotel with a predominantly European clientele, the Churchill Hotel was opened as an apartment building in 1906. Its rooms are huge and tastefully furnished. The Chartwell Grill restaurant features American cuisine. **www.thechurchillhotel.com**

GREATER WASHINGTON The Normandy Hotel $$

2118 Wyoming Ave, NW (Connecticut Ave & 23rd St), 20008 ***Tel*** *(202) 483-1350* ***Fax*** *(202) 387-8241* ***Rooms*** *75*

Converted from a dormitory in a private school, this is a small, cozy hotel. Books can be borrowed from the hotel library and read by the fireside. Continental breakfast is available. The building is surrounded by stately apartments and historic townhouses. **www.doylecollection.com**

GREATER WASHINGTON Tabard Inn $$

1739 N St, NW, 20036 ***Tel*** *(202) 785-1277* ***Fax*** *(202) 785-6173* ***Rooms*** *40*

This country-style inn, named after the inn in Chaucer's *The Canterbury Tales*, is converted from three townhouses. The rooms are charming and eclectic, some in Victorian style. Several of the rooms have a shared bath. The restaurant serves superb American/Continental cuisine. Passes to a gym are available. **www.tabardinn.com**

Key to Symbols *see back cover flap*

GREATER WASHINGTON Hotel Madera $$$
1310 New Hampshire Ave, NW (13th St), 20036 **Tel** *(202) 296-7600, (800) 430-1202* **Fax** *(202) 293-2476* **Rooms** *82*

This small boutique hotel, with dramatic lighting, is close to Dupont Circle. The hotel restaurant, The Firefly, is a modern American bistro. There is a complimentary wine hour from 5:30 to 6:30pm. Daily passes to a gym can be arranged. **www.hotelmadera.com**

GREATER WASHINGTON Swann House $$$
1808 New Hampshire Ave, NW, 20009 **Tel** *(202) 265-4414* **Fax** *(202) 265-6755* **Rooms** *9*

This bed and breakfast, in a Romanesque-style house built in 1883, is filled with beautiful antiques as well as "modern treasures." There is an outdoor pool in the courtyard and rooms are equipped with wireless Internet access. **www.swannhouse.com**

THE MALL L'Enfant Plaza Hotel $$$
480 L'Enfant Plaza, SW, 20024 **Tel** *(202) 484-1000* **Fax** *(202) 646-5060* **Rooms** *370*

Many of the rooms in this 3-star luxury hotel have spectacular views. Conveniently located near the Smithsonian with easy access to the metro station. The American Sea Grill features steaks and seafood. A good choice for families, the hotel has an indoor pool and is pet friendly. **www.lenfantplazahotel.com**

PENN QUARTER Washington International Youth Hostel $
1009 11th St, NW (at K St), 20001 **Tel** *(202) 737-2333* **Fax** *(202) 737-1508* **Rooms** *270*

Attracting an international clientele, it is located three blocks away from Metro Center. The rooms are clean, spacious, and air-conditioned. Amenities include a community kitchen, laundry, TV lounge, and luggage storage. Continental breakfast provided for a fee. Only MasterCard and Visa are accepted. **www.hiwashingtondc.org**

PENN QUARTER Hotel Washington $$$
515 15th St, NW, 20004 **Tel** *(202) 638-5900, (800) 424-9540* **Fax** *(202) 638-4275* **Rooms** *350*

A registered historic landmark and one of the oldest hotels in Washington. The Sky Terrace on the rooftop offers breathtaking views of the monuments. Conveniently located one block from the White House and three blocks from Metro Center. **www.washingtondchotels.com**

PENN QUARTER Willard Intercontinental Hotel $$$$$
1401 Pennsylvania Ave, NW (at 14th St), 20004 **Tel** *(202) 628-9100* **Fax** *(202) 637-7326* **Rooms** *332*

This grand historic hotel offers luxury rooms with marble bathrooms and high-speed Internet. Mark Twain, Abraham Lincoln, and Walt Whitman were once guests and it was here that Martin Luther King wrote his "I Have a Dream" speech. Located two blocks from the White House. **http://washington.intercontinental.com**

WHITE HOUSE & FOGGY BOTTOM Hotel Lombardy $$
2019 Pennsylvania Ave, NW (at I St), 20002 **Tel** *(202) 828-2600, (800) 424-5486* **Fax** *(202) 872-0503* **Rooms** *140*

This European-style boutique hotel has an accommodating multilingual staff. Café Lombardy serves American food and a limited menu is available in the Venetian Room lounge. Two blocks from the Farragut West Metro and three blocks from the White House. **www.hotellombardy.com**

WHITE HOUSE & FOGGY BOTTOM George Washington University Inn $$$
824 New Hampshire Ave, NW, 20037 **Tel** *(202) 337-6620, (800) 426-4455* **Fax** *(202) 298-7499* **Rooms** *95*

This boutique-style hotel has a marble lobby. All rooms, with a Williamsburg-inspired decor, come with a refrigerator, microwave, and coffee-maker, while some of them have complete kitchens. High-speed Internet available. Conveniently located near the University, Kennedy Center, and metro. **www.gwuinn.com**

WHITE HOUSE & FOGGY BOTTOM The Quincy $$$
1823 L St, NW, 20036 **Tel** *(202) 223-4320, (800) 424-2970* **Fax** *(202) 293-4977* **Rooms** *99*

A modern boutique hotel with studio apartments, some with full-size kitchens. The tariff includes Continental breakfast and a free daily *Washington Post*. Room service from Luigi's Italian restaurant. Free passes to Bally Fitness with gym and pool. **www.quincysuites.com**

WHITE HOUSE & FOGGY BOTTOM St. Regis Washington $$$$
923 16th St, NW (at K St), 20006 **Tel** *(202) 638-2626* **Fax** *(202) 347-4758* **Rooms** *178*

A historic, luxury hotel with a warm, European ambience. Elegantly furnished with antiques, chandeliers, and exquisite tapestries, reminiscent of a Renaissance palace. Guests will enjoy the romantic setting and cuisine in the elegant new restaurant. **www.stregis.com/washington**

WHITE HOUSE & FOGGY BOTTOM The Westin Grand $$$$
2350 M St, NW, 20037 **Tel** *(202) 429-0100* **Fax** *(202) 429-9759* **Rooms** *263*

CD players, coffee-makers, minibars, and luxurious marble bathrooms with extra-deep bathtubs are just a few of the amenities in the rooms of this well-appointed hotel. The Westin Café on M serves continental cuisine, while the M Street Grill serves American favorites. There is also an outdoor pool. **www.starwoodhotels.com**

WHITE HOUSE & FOGGY BOTTOM Hay-Adams Hotel $$$$$
800 16th St, NW (at H St), 20006 **Tel** *(202) 638-6600* **Fax** *(202) 638-2716* **Rooms** *145*

This historic Italian Renaissance-style hotel overlooking Lafayette Square and the White House combines the two homes of John Hay and Henry Adams, both renowned authors and diplomats. Beautifully renovated rooms feature antiques and ornamental ceilings. **www.hayadams.com**

MARYLAND

ANNAPOLIS, MD Maryland Inn $$$

16 Church Circle, 21401 ***Tel*** *(410) 263-2641* ***Fax*** *(410) 268-3613* ***Rooms*** *124*

This lovely, award-winning brick inn near the water was built in the 1760s. The Victorian-style rooms are comfortable and The Treaty of Paris is a warm, inviting restaurant. Reservations are made through the Historic Inns of Annapolis, which also runs the Governor Calvert House and the Robert Johnson House. **www.historicinnsofannapolis.com**

BALTIMORE, MD Homewood Suites by Hilton Baltimore $$$

625 S President St, 21202 ***Tel*** *(410) 234-0999* ***Fax*** *(410) 234-0399* ***Rooms*** *165*

Located at the inner harbor, with access to the National Aquarium, shopping, and restaurants, this all-suite hotel offers living and sleeping areas with kitchens, laundry facilities, Wi-Fi, and a complimentary grocery shopping service, daily breakfast buffet, and on weekdays an evening reception with snacks. **http://homewoodsuites1.hilton.com**

BALTIMORE, MD Renaissance Harborplace Hotel $$$$

202 E Pratt St, 21202 ***Tel*** *(410) 547-1200* ***Fax*** *(410) 539-5780* ***Rooms*** *622*

The rooms in this hotel have a view either of the harbor or the indoor courtyard. The staff are attentive and cordial. Windows restaurant has a beautiful view of the water and specializes in excellent seafood from Chesapeake Bay. **www.marriott.com**

BALTIMORE, MD Peabody Court, A Clarion Hotel $$$$$

612 Cathedral St, 21201 ***Tel*** *(410) 727-7101, (800) 292-5500* ***Fax*** *(410) 789-3312* ***Rooms*** *104*

A boutique-style hotel, with a Renaissance façade and a well-appointed lobby, it provides excellent service. Located close to the Walters Art Museum in a charming neighborhood. George's on Mt Vernon Sqaure restaurant offers casual fine dining. **www.peabodycourthotel.com**

TILGHMAN ISLAND, MD Chesapeake Wood Duck Inn $$$

Gibsontown Rd, at Dogwood Harbor, 21671 ***Tel*** *(410) 886-2070, (800) 956-2070* ***Fax*** *(410) 677-7526* ***Rooms*** *7*

Winner of the AAA and 3-star Mobil awards, this waterfront bed and breakfast, built in 1890, offers great hospitality and innovative cuisine. A three-course gourmet complimentary breakfast and a four-course dinner available Saturday evenings for inn guests, by reservation only. **www.woodduckinn.com**

VIRGINIA

ALEXANDRIA, VA Hotel Monaco $$$

480 King St (at S Pitt St), 22314 ***Tel*** *(703) 549-6080, (800) 368-5047* ***Fax*** *(703) 684-6508* ***Rooms*** *241*

This Kimpton Hotel is conveniently located in the heart of the historic Old Town. The four-star luxury hotel features stylish guestrooms and suites, and a destination restaurant. The hotel provides transportation to and from Reagan National Airport. **www.monaco-alexandria.com**

ALEXANDRIA, VA Morrison House $$$

116 S Alfred St, 22314 ***Tel*** *(703) 838-8000, (866) 834-6628* ***Fax*** *(703) 684-6283* ***Rooms*** *45*

Modeled after a Federal manor home, this hotel has attractive rooms with four-poster beds, armoires, and Italian marble bathrooms. The Grille restaurant offers fine dining and a varied menu in elegant surroundings. Pet friendly. **www.morrisonhouse.com**

CHARLOTTESVILLE, VA The Boar's Head Inn $$$$

Route 250 W, 22903 ***Tel*** *(434) 296-2181, (800) 476-1988* ***Fax*** *(434) 972-6024* ***Rooms*** *171*

A romantic and charming inn in a beautiful country setting near the foothills of the Blue Ridge Mountains, with two lakes in the grounds. Facilities include an 18-hole golf course, tennis, fishing, biking, four pools, and a spa. The Old Mill Room, built from the timbers of an old gristmill, offers fine dining. **www.boarsheadinn.com**

CHINCOTEAGUE, VA Refuge Inn $$$

7058 Maddox Blvd, 23336 ***Tel*** *(757) 336-5511, (888) 257-0038* ***Fax*** *(757) 336-6134* ***Rooms*** *72*

This inn is only half a mile away from the National Wildlife Refuge and close to the National Seashore. The convenient location, inexpensive rooms, and friendly atmosphere make it a good choice for families. Two of the suites are equipped with kitchens. **www.refugeinn.com**

FREDERICKSBURG, VA Dunning Mills Inn All-Suite Hotel $$

2305-C Jefferson Davis Hwy, 22401 ***Tel*** *(540) 373-1256* ***Fax*** *(540) 899-9041* ***Rooms*** *54*

This hotel is set in the woods near Civil War cemeteries and five major battlefields. George Washington's boyhood home is also close by. Each suite includes a queen-size bed, a sofa bed, a kitchen, and a dining area, while some also have Jacuzzis. Picnic areas, barbecues, and facilities for pets are also provided. **www.dunningmills.com**

Key to Price Guide *see p230* **Key to Symbols** *see back cover flap*

LURAY, VA Big Meadows Lodge $

PO Box 727 (Skyline Dr), 22835 ***Tel*** *(540) 999-2221, (888) 896-3833* ***Fax*** *(540) 999-2011* ***Rooms*** *97*

Located at Milepost 51 on the scenic Skyline Drive in the Shenandoah National Park. The rustic accommodations, which include cabins, suites, or guest rooms in the chestnut-paneled lodge, offer attractive views of the forest and the valley. Closed November to mid-May. **www.visitshenandoah.com**

RICHMOND, VA The Berkeley Hotel $$$

1200 E Cary St, 23219 ***Tel*** *(804) 780-1300, (888) 780-4422* ***Fax*** *(804) 648-4728* ***Rooms*** *55*

Situated in the heart of downtown Richmond, a warm welcome is given at this gracious hotel, with its lavish, traditional furnishings. The most popular rooms are those with balconies. Berkeley's four-diamond restaurant, The Dining Room, specializes in regional cuisine. **www.berkeleyhotel.com**

WEST VIRGINIA

CHARLESTON Marriott Charleston Town Center $$$

200 Lee St E, 25301 ***Tel*** *(304) 345-6500* ***Fax*** *(304) 353-3722* ***Rooms*** *352*

Situated in downtown Charleston, the Marriott Charleston Town Center hotel is located near the Tri State Racetrack & Gaming Center Casino, the Charleston Civic Center, white water rafting, and many other attractions. With its welcoming and comfy surroundings and wonderful service, this hotel in the chain lives up to the reputation. **www.marriott.com**

ELKINS Tunnel Mountain Bed & Breakfast $

Route 1, Box 59-1, 26241 ***Tel*** *(304) 636-1684, (888) 211-9123* ***Fax*** *(304) 728-5150* ***Rooms*** *3*

Take a break, relax, and refresh with a vacation at the Tunnel Mountain Bed & Breakfast. Nestled at the edge of the Monogahela National Forest, it offers breathtaking views of glorious Mother Nature. Romance abounds at this scenic retreat. No children under 12 permitted. **www.wvonline.com**

HARPERS FERRY The Jackson Rose Bed & Breakfast $$

1167 W Washington St, 25425 ***Tel*** *(304) 535-1528* ***Rooms*** *4*

Named for the fragrant roses that grew outside the window where Stonewall Jackson had his headquarters during the Civil War, this charming Federal-style mansion now houses a cozy B&B. The comfortable rooms have original pine floors and high ceilings. Breakfast features a hot entrée and home-made jams. **www.thejacksonrose.com**

WHEELING Oglebay Family Resort $$

Oglebay Park, 26003 ***Tel*** *(304) 243-4000, (800) 624-6988* ***Fax*** *(304) 243-4070* ***Rooms*** *271*

Bring the family together at the Oglebay Family Resort in Wheeling. This 1,650-acre historic resort has something for every member of the family, from golf and tennis to swimming and a children's activity center. The inviting, comfortable accommodations will be a welcome reprieve.

DELAWARE

DOVER Sheraton Dover Hotel $$

1570 N DuPont Hwy, 19901 ***Tel*** *(302) 678-8500, (800) 325-3535* ***Fax*** *(302) 678-9073* ***Rooms*** *152*

Near historic Dover, the Sheraton Dover Hotel welcomes guests with a plush, inviting atmosphere and good service. Attractions and shopping are just minutes away in downtown but the hotel also offers an indoor pool, whirlpool, and a fitness room. There is an in-house restaurant and bar. **www.sheratondover.com**

MONTCHANIN Inn at Montchanin Village $$$

Rte 100 and Kirk Rd, 19710 ***Tel*** *(302) 888-2133, (800) 269-2473* ***Fax*** *(302) 888-0389* ***Rooms*** *28*

Situated in historic Brandywine Valley, the Inn at Montchanin Village oozes 19th-century charm. White picket fences, winding walkways, and a manicured lawn greet travelers outside, while inside marble bathrooms, Victorian decor, and canopy beds are found. Great for a romantic getaway. **www.montchanin.com**

REHOBOTH BEACH Boardwalk Plaza Hotel $$

Olive Ave and the Boardwalk, 19971 ***Tel*** *(302) 227-7169, (800) 332-3224* ***Fax*** *(302) 227-0561* ***Rooms*** *217*

The Boardwalk Plaza Hotel is known as the place to stay while in Rehoboth Beach. This Victorian-style delight affords beautiful ocean views. Relax and rejuvenate on the beach or enjoy a dip in the Spa pool (indoor-outdoor). Dine on tasty cuisine at Victoria's, the in-house restaurant. **www.boardwalkplaza.com**

WILMINGTON Hotel DuPont $

11th St and Market, 19801 ***Tel*** *(302) 594-3100, (800) 441-9019* ***Rooms*** *217*

Delaware's only four-star hotel and a local institution, the Hotel DuPont has been providing elegant accommodations to guests since 1913. Imported linens and plush mahogany furnishings help create luxurious guestrooms. Located in Brandywine Valley, Wilmington affords many attractions with which to entertain travelers. **www.dupont.com/hotel**

Choosing a Restaurant

An eclectic choice of food is on offer across Washington, including many traditonal restaurants that serve classic American dishes as well as a vast number of Ethiopian, Vietnamese, and Italian restaurants. The restaurants have been selected across a range of price categories for their exceptional food, good value, and interesting location.

PRICE CATEGORIES
For a three-course meal for one, half a bottle of house wine, and all unavoidable extra charges such as sales tax and service.
$ Under $20
$$ $20–$30
$$$ $30–$45
$$$$ $45–$60
$$$$$ Over $60

WASHINGTON, DC

CAPITOL HILL America — $

Union Station, 50 Massachusetts Ave, NE, 20002 **Tel** *(202) 682-9555*

Located inside Union Station, with a great view of the Capitol, America features regional dishes. Death by Chocolate is a favorite dessert on the 200-item menu. An enormous restaurant with an enormous menu, the place is spread over three stories of Union Station.

CAPITOL HILL Market Lunch — $

Eastern Market, 225 7th St, SE (at C St), 20003 **Tel** *(202) 547-8444*

The menu features authentic regional food and extensive seafood delicacies, such as crab cakes, crab sandwiches, river fish, and flavorful salads. The cafeteria-style breakfast and lunch are as casual as they are delicious. Expect a long wait on Sunday mornings. Closed on Mondays.

CAPITOL HILL Tunnicliff's — $$

222 7th St, SE (opposite Eastern Market), 20003 **Tel** *(202) 544-5680*

The restaurant attracts a casual and diverse crowd. The popular Sunday brunch at Tunnicliff's features Eggs Chesapeake (a crab cake with two poached eggs), as well as peanut butter and jelly pizza. All major credit cards except Discover are accepted here.

CAPITOL HILL Bistro Bis — $$$$$

15 E St, NW, 20001 **Tel** *(202) 661-2700*

French food with an American twist is served in a beautiful, cozy dining area. This chic modern restaurant located near the Senate attracts a fashionable clientele. The duck confit and salmon Provençal come highly recommended. Valet parking is available after 5:30pm.

GEORGETOWN Zed's Ethiopian Cuisine — $

1201 28th St, NW, 20007 **Tel** *(202) 333-4710*

An Ethiopian restaurant, popular with vegetarians, Zed's offers traditional *wats* (red pepper sauces), *alechas* (stews), and *injera* (bread). The atmosphere is quiet and romantic and the decor features Ethiopian textiles, paintings, and woodcarvings.

GEORGETOWN Martin's Tavern — $$

1264 Wisconsin Ave, NW (at N St), 20007 **Tel** *(202) 333-7370*

Established in 1933, this is the oldest family-owned restaurant in DC. It is also a charming location for pub food. The front room can get noisy, but the booths in the back provide a quiet respite.The menu offers a range of prices. On Saturdays the bar stays open until 3am.

GEORGETOWN Old Glory All-American Bar-B-Que — $$

3139 M St, NW, 20007 **Tel** *(202) 337-3406*

This homey restaurant serves traditional American barbecue – spare ribs and hickory-smoked chicken. The menu also features wood-fried shrimp and desserts such as apple crisp and coconut cherry cobbler. There's a new rooftop deck with outdoor seating and views of Georgetown.

GEORGETOWN Sequoia — $$

Washington Harbor, 3000 K St, NW (at 30th St), 20007 **Tel** *(202) 944-4200*

A trendy restaurant combining American cuisine with fabulous views of the Potomac and Virginia skyline. The casual, large seating area outside is especially delightful. The brunch is excellent. Parking is in the building on the K St side. A jazz band performs every other Wednesday.

GEORGETOWN Café Divan — $$$

1834 Wisconsin Ave, NW (north of S St), 20007 **Tel** *(202) 338-1747*

The mezze platter makes a reasonable lunch. Café Divan has a small take-out area as well as a dining room with bay windows for a leisurely meal. Specialties include lamb, chicken, seafood, and *pides* (Turkish pizza with a thin crust and a choice of eight toppings).

Key to Symbols *see back cover flap*

GEORGETOWN Citronelle $$$$$

Latham Hotel, 3000 M St, NW (at 30th St), 20007 ***Tel*** *(202) 625-2150*

This award-winning restaurant serves sophisticated French dishes, such as pastry "cigars" stuffed with wild mushrooms, and potato-crusted halibut. *Prix fixe* for a three-course starts at $95. You can also splurge on a nine-course tasting menu for $150.

GREATER WASHINGTON Ben's Chili bowl $

1213 U St, NW, 20009 ***Tel*** *(202) 667-0909*

A timeless Washington institution, Ben's Chili Bowl is popular with anyone who loves a good, high-calorie meal. Bill Cosby is one such devoted fan. The chili dogs are known nationally and the milk shakes hit the spot. Best loved are its salmon cakes, grits, scrapple, and blueberry pancakes, offered during breakfast hours (6–11am).

GREATER WASHINGTON Hank's Oyster Bar $$$

1624 Q St, NW, 20009 ***Tel*** *(202) 462-4265*

Serving five oyster varieties nightly as well as comfort food such as molasses-braised short ribs and deep-fried Ipswich clams and popcorn shrimp. Other offerings at this intimate restaurant include salmon with Moroccan spices and seared scallops in walnut vinaigrette but the main draw is the Hog Island-style barbeque oyster.

GREATER WASHINGTON Iron Gate Inn $$$

1734 N St, NW, 20036 ***Tel*** *(202) 737-1370*

It's hard to find a more romantic spot with such reasonable prices. The interior is warm and cozy with working fireplaces, and the garden is lovely. Food is imaginatively prepared and nicely presented. Lunch from Monday to Friday and dinner from Monday to Saturday.

GREATER WASHINGTON Tabard Inn $$$

1739 N St, NW, 20036 ***Tel*** *(202) 331-8528*

The menu of this historic inn always offers a delicious surprise. The garden is lovely and the funky interior has several inviting nooks and crannies. Valet parking on Friday, Saturday evenings, and Sunday brunch. A jazz duo performs on Sundays 7:30–10:30pm.

GREATER WASHINGTON Restaurant Nora $$$$$

2132 Florida Ave, NW (corner of R St), 20008 ***Tel*** *(202) 462-5143*

One of the stalwarts of Washington dining, featuring organic seasonal ingredients and a varied menu of contemporary American cuisine. The decor is warm and cozy with Amish and Mennonite quilts adorning the walls. Open for dinner only and closed on Sundays.

THE MALL The Atrium Café $

National Museum of Natural History, Constitution Ave &10th St, NW, 20560 ***Tel*** *(202) 633-1000*

The atrium of Washington's National Museum of Natural History is six stories high.This large food court on the ground level of the museum offers a wide selection of food including pizza, sandwiches, soups, hot entrées, salads, and mouth-watering desserts.

THE MALL Cascade Café $

National Gallery of Art, Concourse level, Constitution Ave, NW, 20565 ***Tel*** *(202) 712-7460*

One of the better options for hungry museum-goers, this café offers fast and convenient buffet-style foods. The Cascade's "open-kitchens" allow you the added pleasure of watching food being freshly prepared. There is also a separate Espresso and Gelato Bar next to the café.

THE MALL Mitsitam Café $

National Museum of the American Indian, Independence Ave & 4th St, SW, 20560 ***Tel*** *(202) 633-1000*

Mitsitam means "let's eat" in the language of the Piscataway. It features an interesting menu inspired by Native Americans from the Northwest Coast, the Great Plains, Northern Woodlands, and Central and South America. The buffet-style café also has a range of prices.

THE MALL Pavilion Café $

Sculpture Garden, adjacent to the National Gallery West Building at 7th St, NW, 20565 ***Tel*** *(202) 289-3360*

This outdoor café offers a splendid view of the Sculpture Garden and of the ice-skating rink in winter. Choices include gourmet pizzas, wraps, and hot chocolate. There is a children's menu. Open Monday to Saturday 10am–4:30pm and Sunday 11am–5pm. Extended hours until 9pm during the ice-skating season.

PENN QUARTER Full Kee $

509 H St, NW, 20001 ***Tel*** *(202) 371-2233*

The Cantonese noodles, dumplings, and soups are excellent at this rather sparsely decorated Chinatown restaurant. Full Kee is certainly a great place to grab a cheap, as well as a quick meal before a Verizon Center event. Alcoholic beverages are not served here.

PENN QUARTER Hard Rock Café $$

999 E St, NW (at 10th St), 20004 ***Tel*** *(202) 737-7625*

All the American classics are available, including burgers, sandwiches, and salads. Videos, music, and memorabilia make the two floors of this restaurant an exciting tourist experience, though it can get a little hectic. Stained-glass windows honor rock-and-roll greats in this worldwide chain.

PENN QUARTER Old Ebbitt Grill $$

675 15th St, NW, 20005 ***Tel*** *(202) 347-4801*

Expect this upbeat American grill to be packed with both locals and tourists. It's a chance to sample the DC scene as well as savor quality seafood, pasta, steaks, an excellent raw bar, and wine list. The crab cakes and trout parmesan are house favorites.

PENN QUARTER Zaytinya's $$$

701 9th St, NW (at G St), 20001 ***Tel*** *(202) 638-0800*

This restaurant with a striking modern decor offers a superb variety of authentic Greek, Turkish, and Lebanese mezze with excellent vegetarian selections. The ambience is sophisticated, warm, and inviting, making this a favorite choice for Washingtonians.

WHITE HOUSE & FOGGY BOTTOM Aroma $$

1919 I St, NW, 20006 ***Tel*** *(202) 833-4700*

This North Indian restaurant is one of the best-kept secrets in Washington. It is casual yet elegant, and the food is excellent. Aroma offers an all-you-can-eat lunchtime buffet for a very reasonable price on Saturdays. The restaurant is closed on Sundays.

WHITE HOUSE & FOGGY BOTTOM Georgia Brown's $$

950 15th St, NW, 20005 ***Tel*** *(202) 393-4499*

Anyone who craves Carolina shrimp, grits (coarse grain), gumbo, or fried green tomatoes should come here. Low-country Southern cooking with style is served in an inviting but hectic atmosphere. A jazz trio performs during the Sunday brunch.

WHITE HOUSE & FOGGY BOTTOM Bombay Club $$$

815 Connecticut Ave, NW, 20006 ***Tel*** *(202) 659-3727*

The attentive service and exclusive clientele provide a glimpse of upper-crust Washington. Specialties include tandoori salmon and green chili chicken. A classical pianist performs nightly. Open for lunch from Monday to Friday, brunch on Sunday, and for dinner every night.

WHITE HOUSE & FOGGY BOTTOM Kinkead's $$$

2000 Pennsylvania Ave, NW, 20006 ***Tel*** *(202) 296-7700*

You won't be disappointed at this American brasserie with an excellent seafood menu, one of the finest in town. Bob Kinkead's creations, such as the pepita-crusted salmon, are wonderfully complemented by the extensive wine list. Live jazz is performed on every weeknight.

WHITE HOUSE & FOGGY BOTTOM Galileo $$$$

1110 21st St, NW, 20036 ***Tel*** *(202) 293-7191*

The most talked-about Italian restaurant in DC, this retaurant is known for its elaborate dishes. Chef Roberto Donna's fame rests on his innovative menu, which changes daily. Choose from Galileo's range of home-made pastas (linguini with lobster), risottos, and game dishes. There's also a fine selection of wines.

MARYLAND

ANNAPOLIS, MD Middleton Tavern Oyster Bar & Restaurant $$$

2 Market Space, 21401 ***Tel*** *(410) 263-3323*

Established in 1750, the historic Middleton Tavern Oyster Bar & Restaurant is located across the street from the harbor. This is an indoor/outdoor spot, perfect to soak up the view. The oyster shooters come with beer. Also on the menu are crab cakes, seafood, and pasta dishes.

BALTIMORE, MD Obrycki's Crab House $$

1727 E Pratt St, 21231 ***Tel*** *(410) 732-6399*

A seasonal restaurant offering superb seafood dining. Obrycki's Crab House is located in Fells Point, the historic district of downtown Baltimore. A favorite of the house is the hard-shell steamed crabs. Closed from mid-November to mid-March.

BETHESDA, MD Mon Ami Gabi $$$

7239 Woodmont Ave (at Bethesda Ave), 20814 ***Tel*** *(301) 654-1234*

Located in Bethesda's restaurant row, Mon Ami Gabi is a good choice for traditional French food in a casual atmosphere. While it has the authentic *steak frites*, *bouillabaisse*, crêpes, and quiches to choose from, the emphasis is on rustic simplicity. Live jazz performance on Tuesday and Thursday evenings. Valet parking is available at night.

BETHESDA, MD Persimmon $$$$

7003 Wisconsin Ave, 20815 ***Tel*** *(301) 654-9860*

Considered one of the best restaurants in Bethesda, Persimmon is an American bistro with a cozy, romantic atmosphere. Parking is available on the street and in the municipal lot behind the building. Open for lunch from Monday to Friday and for dinner daily.

Key to Price Guide *see p234* **Key to Symbols** *see back cover flap*

VIRGINIA

ALEXANDRIA, VA Gadsby's Tavern $$$

138 N Royal St, 22314 ***Tel*** *(703) 548-1288*

This establishment dates back to 1792 and is connected to the Gadsby's Tavern museum. The waiters are in Colonial costume, and the decor in the style of the 1700s. The menu includes duck, prime rib, seafood, and pies. Live music on Friday and Saturday evenings.

ALEXANDRIA, VA Le Refuge $$$$

127 N Washington St, 22314 ***Tel*** *(703) 548-4661*

Across the street from historic Christ Church, this small French restaurant has great charm and wonderful French country food. *Bouillabaisse* and soft shelled crabs (in season) are specialties of the house. Closed on Sundays. All major credit cards, except Discover, are accepted.

CHARLOTTESVILLE, VA Michie Tavern $

683 Thomas Jefferson Pkwy, 22902 ***Tel*** *(434) 977-1234*

Casual dining (buffet style) with a Colonial touch – the staff dress in period costume and the decor is rustic. Take a tour of the 200-year-old inn and outbuildings. The home-made Southern fare, based on 18th-century recipes, is hearty – try the outstanding Southern-fried chicken. Only lunch is served here.

WILLIAMSBURG, VA Christiana Campbell's Tavern $$$

Waller St (near the Capitol), 23187 ***Tel*** *(757) 229-2141*

Run by Colonial Williamsburg, this historic tavern offers seafood specialties. The menu includes sherried crab stew, crab cakes, and "sea pye" (made with crab, shrimp, lobster, and cream), all served with spoonbread or sweet potato muffins.

WILLIAMSBURG, VA The Trellis $$$

403 Duke of Gloucester St, 23187 ***Tel*** *(757) 229-8610*

Located near the historic district, this restaurant features contemporary American cuisine with an emphasis on fresh food – the menu changes every season. It also offers an extensive wine list with more than 20 wines from Virginia. Parking is available at Merchant Square lots.

WEST VIRGINIA

CHARLESTON Rio Grande Restaurant $$

160 Court St, 25301 ***Tel*** *(304) 344-8616*

The Rio Grande Restaurant receives guests from all over to savor its typical Tex-Mex menu. With its festive Mexican decor and prompt and courteous service, no wonder repeat business is customary. Start off with the mouthwatering fiery cheese dip before enjoying other menu items such as burritos, chicken, tacos, or any of the vegan items.

ELKINS Cheat River Inn $$

Route 1, 26241 ***Tel*** *(304) 636-6265*

While enjoying the wonder of nature in the Monogahela National Forest, stop by the Cheat River Inn to refuel. This restaurant has riverside dining, mounted fish on display, and a tasty American menu. Indulge in one of their specialty dishes – prime beef or rainbow trout.

DELAWARE

NEW CASTLE Jessop's Tavern $

114 Delaware St, 19720 ***Tel*** *(302) 322-6111*

Go back in time to Colonial days of old and enjoy dinner at Jessop's Tavern, where flavorful home-cooking and good service go hand-in-hand. The menu consists of authentic Early American entrees and appetizers served at wooden tables surrounded by Colonial decor. Reservations are recommended.

REHOBOTH BEACH The Back Porch Café $$

59 Rehoboth Ave, 19971 ***Tel*** *(302) 227-3674*

Open since 1974, The Back Porch Café in Rehoboth Beach is located in an old beach house. This café has an extensive wine list and an enticing seafood menu. Live music on the weekends draws the crowds. Reservations are recommended. Open daily June–September; open weekends in May and October.

THE SOUTHEAST

INTRODUCING THE SOUTHEAST 240–247

NORTH CAROLINA 248–251

SOUTH CAROLINA 252–255

GEORGIA 256–261

TENNESSEE 262–267

KENTUCKY 268–271

The Southeast at a Glance

Although the five Southeast states – North and South Carolina, Kentucky, Tennessee, and Georgia – share a common history and culture, they are quite distinct from one another. The region covers three different topographical areas. To the east, the low-lying coastal plains along the Atlantic include the historic cities of Savannah, Georgia, and Charleston, South Carolina, bordered by pristine beaches. The central Blue Ridge and Appalachian Mountains hold acres and acres of stunningly scenic wilderness, while in the inland foothills, linked to the Gulf of Mexico by the Mississippi and other broad rivers, are cities such as Louisville, Kentucky, and Tennessee's twin music capitals, Nashville and Memphis. Atlanta is the main commercial center.

Lexington (see p270) *is Kentucky's main horse-breeding center. Visitors are allowed access to most of the stud farms surrounding the city.*

Nashville (see pp264–5) *is Tennessee's state capital as well as the nation's country music capital. The town's revitalized downtown, with its lively restaurants, cafés, and nightclubs, is the center of action, day and night.*

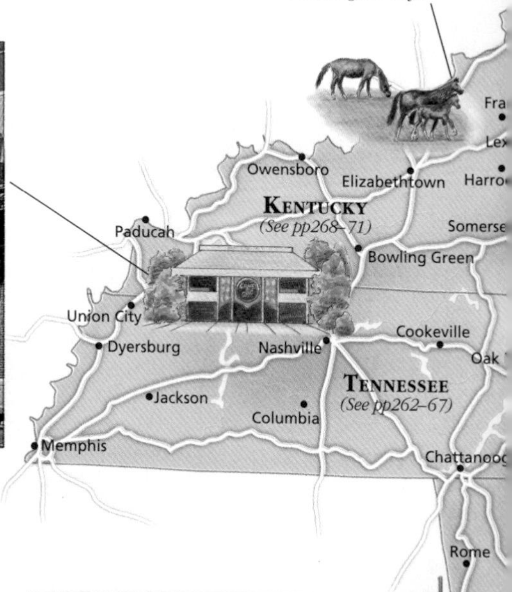

Atlanta (see pp260–61), *Georgia's capital, is the place where Coca-Cola was born in the 1880s. Since then, the drink has become an international favorite. The hard-hitting TV news channel, CNN, is also based in Atlanta.*

◁ **Acres of farmlands stretching across southwestern Georgia**

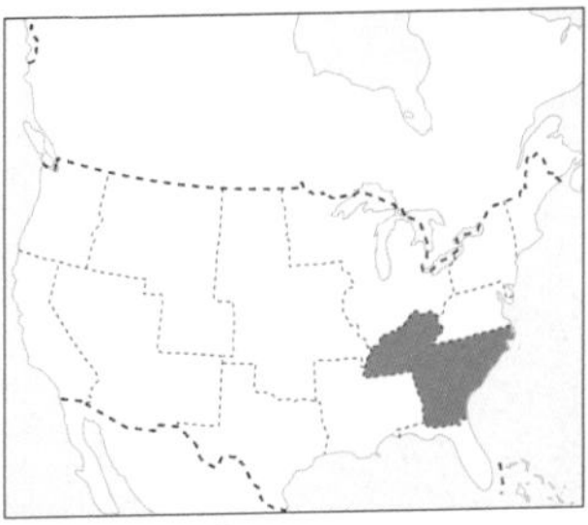

LOCATOR MAP

The Outer Banks (see p250) *are a long chain of narrow barrier islands that run along North Carolina's Atlantic Coast. Beside pristine beaches, the other attractions here include historic lighthouses and the site where the Wright Brothers launched their first successful flight.*

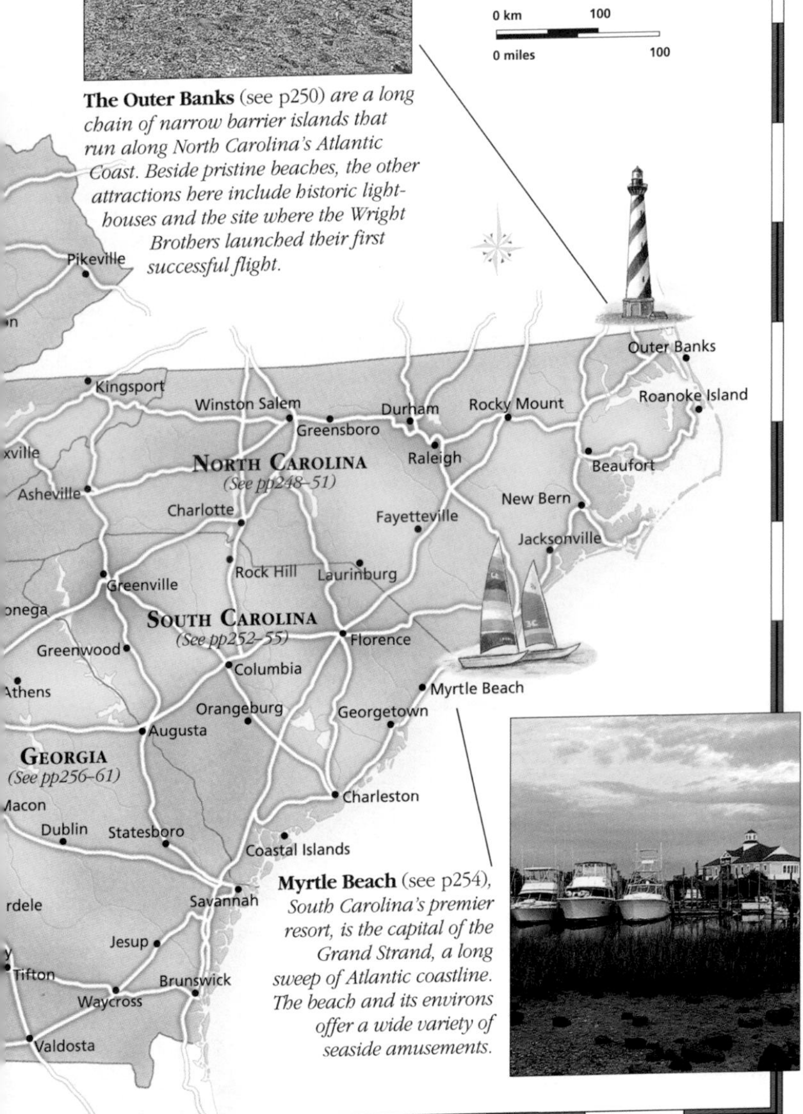

Myrtle Beach (see p254), *South Carolina's premier resort, is the capital of the Grand Strand, a long sweep of Atlantic coastline. The beach and its environs offer a wide variety of seaside amusements.*

THE SOUTHEAST

One of the country's most fascinating regions, the Southeast is home to two of America's most beautiful cities – Charleston and Savannah – as well as some of its most pristine beaches and expanses of primeval forests. Culturally, the region is famous for its vibrant musical traditons, as both country-western and the blues originated in Nashville and Memphis.

The Southeast's cities reflect the region's proud cultural heritage. Celebrated for their beauty and sophistication, Charleston and Savannah are urban gems, with lushly landscaped parks and gracious homes. Both actively preserve their stately architecture as well as support a fine range of hotels, restaurants, and cultural institutions. Other cities vary greatly. The quiet college town of Durham, North Carolina, rated the "most educated city in America," stands in direct contrast to burgeoning commercial centers such as Atlanta, Georgia, the economic capital of the "New South." Equally engaging are Nashville, the capital of country-western music, and Memphis, the birthplace of the blues.

The region's natural landscape is as memorable. Nearly a thousand miles of Atlantic coastline are formed by a long series of offshore barrier islands, ranging from Cape Hatteras to Cumberland Island on the Florida border. Just inland, and linked to the ocean by several broad rivers, is the heartland of the Colonial-era plantation country. Farther inland are the farmlands of North Carolina, the primary US producer of tobacco products, and the rolling bluegrass fields of Kentucky's verdant Horse Country. At the center lies unforgettable mountain scenery.

HISTORY

Long before the arrival of the first Europeans, the region was home to a highly developed Native American culture, known as the Moundbuilders. Evidence of their large cities can be seen at Georgia's Ocmulgee National Monument. Later Indians, especially the Cherokee who lived in western North Carolina and northern Georgia,

Kentucky Derby, the annual horse-racing event held in Louisville's Churchill Downs

◁ Colorful, patriotic roofline, South Carolina

Exhibits in the Civil War Museum, Bardstown, Kentucky

were among North America's most civilized tribes. Other tribes included the Creek, Tuscarora, Yamasee, and Catawba, but by the early 1800s, most of the Indians had been decimated by war and disease, or driven westward. Apart from a prominent Cherokee community in the far western corner of North Carolina, very few Indians survive in the region today.

In the early 1500s, explorers from Florida's Spanish colonies ventured here, lured by Indians' tales of great wealth. The Spanish were followed by the French and then the English. But it was only in 1670, under Charles II, that the first successful colony, called Carolina, was established near what is today Charleston. Carolina's first settlers came from the congested English colony on Barbados, and it was their agricultural expertise that made the land-owning "planters" the wealthiest in the American colonies. Their wealth, however, was based on slave labor, and thousands of Africans were imported to clear the swamps, dig canals, and harvest the crops. Along the coast where the main crops, rice and indigo, were grown, the white colonists were a small minority, outnumbered four to one by the workers whose labor they exploited.

The great fortunes made in Carolina inspired the creation in 1732 of another colony, Georgia, located to the south. In many ways Georgia was a novel colony, funded by the government rather than private interests and founded with social, rather than commercial, intentions. For the first time in the Americas, slavery was banned, as was drinking alcohol and the presence of lawyers. The new colony, however, faltered and came under the control of Carolina, which introduced the slave-holding practices.

In December 1860, the state of South Carolina declared itself independent from the rest of the country. Though Georgia followed soon after, the other Southeast states remained with the Union. It was only after South Carolina forces attacked the fortress at Fort Sumter near Charleston, on April 12, 1861, did Tennessee and North Carolina join the rebel cause. Ironically, only Kentucky, the birthplace of President Abraham Lincoln and Confederate President Jefferson Davis, remained divided – a true border state.

The impact of the four-year Civil War lasted for another 100 years, as the struggle against the iniquities of slavery gained momentum as the Civil Rights Movement. While primarily a grassroots

KEY DATES IN HISTORY

1587 Sir Walter Raleigh sponsors the establishment of an ill-fated colony at Roanoke in present-day North Carolina

1670 The first permanent English settlement in the Carolina colony is established at Charleston

1729 Carolina divided into North and South

1763 The Anglo-Spanish treaty fixes the Mississippi River as the western extent of the Southeast colonies

1792 Kentucky becomes the 15th US state

1795 The University of North Carolina, the country's first state-sponsored university, opens at Chapel Hill

1838 The government forcibly expels the Cherokees westward on the "Trail of Tears"

1861 Confederates attack on Fort Sumter

1864 General Sherman spares Savannah at the end of his notorious "March to the Sea"

1903 The Ohio-based Wright Brothers make the first successful powered airplane flight at Kitty Hawk, North Carolina

1976 Georgia Governor Jimmy Carter elected 39th president of the United States

1996 Atlanta hosts the centennial Olympics

2002 Jimmy Carter wins the Nobel Peace Prize

Grave of Dr. Martin Luther King Jr. in Atlanta, a pilgrimage site for people from all over the world

campaign, many of the battles were led by Atlanta-born Baptist minister Martin Luther King Jr, who practiced the use of nonviolent direct action to win equality for black people. Though Dr. King was assassinated while participating in a strike by black sanitation workers in Memphis in 1968, the movement for Civil Rights eventually saw his colleague Andrew Young elected to Congress from Georgia. Young was later elected mayor of Atlanta in 1981.

SOCIETY, CULTURE, & THE ARTS

The Southeast has been, and continues to be, a major contributor to American culture. Atlanta gave the world Coca-Cola and CNN, while Kentucky, particularly Colonel Sanders and his Kentucky Fried Chicken, spread the craze for fast food. Kentucky is also well known all over the world for its production of high-quality bourbon whiskey and high-speed horses.

Important though the region's cities are, they are also the conduit through which the outside world reaches into their hinterlands. Nashville's country music, for example, is deeply rooted in Appalachian folkways, while the blues and rock 'n' roll of Memphis emerge from the different ethnic and historical cultures of the broad Mississippi Delta. A roll call of the artists born and bred here spans all musical genres – the Everly Brothers, Bill Monroe, and Loretta Lynn are from Kentucky; John Coltrane, Doc Watson, Thelonius Monk, and Nina Simone hail from North Carolina; the Allman Brothers, James Brown, Otis Redding, and Gladys Knight came from Georgia; while Tennessee can take credit for Chet Atkins, Tina Turner, and Carl Perkins, and its favorite adopted son, Elvis Presley (1935–77).

This is also true of literature, which witnessed the creativity of such diverse writers as Alice Walker, Thomas Wolfe, Carson McCullers, and James Agee, and characters and settings such as "God's Little Acre" and "Catfish Row" from George Gershwin's opera *Porgy & Bess.* Music, literature, and the arts still dominate Southeastern culture, and numerous events and festivals are celebrated all over the region.

TOURISM

The Appalachain Mountains and their local constituents, the Blue Ridge and Great Smoky Mountains, offer miles of spectacular scenery in near-pristine condition. Much of the mountain landscape is now preserved in a series of local, state, and national parks, and forests. The Great Smoky Mountains National Park, in particular, is one of the country's most popular, drawing millions of visitors each year. Other attractions include the beach resorts that proliferate along the Outer Banks in North Carolina, and Louisville's Kentucky Derby, reputed to be the biggest racing event in the country.

Local band performing in one of the many clubs in downtown Nashville, Tennessee

Exploring the Southeast

Despite the Southeast's diverse landscape and topography, the region is compact enough to tour in about a week. The coastal cities of Charleston and Savannah, as well as the inland metropolises of Atlanta, Nashville, and Memphis, are well linked by road and short-haul airline flights. The broad crest of mountains that rise up at the center include such prime attractions as the scenic Blue Ridge Parkway and the Great Smoky Mountains National Park. Among the region's other highlights are Georgia's beautiful Golden Isles and Kentucky's spectacular mountain landscapes and bluegrass pasturelands, famous for their thoroughbred horse farms.

SIGHTS AT A GLANCE

North Carolina
Research Triangle Region 1
Winston-Salem 2
Blue Ridge Parkway 3
Asheville 4
Outer Banks 5
Roanoke Island 6
Beaufort 7

South Carolina
Charleston pp252–3 8
Columbia 9
Myrtle Beach 10
Georgetown 11
Coastal Islands 12

Georgia
Savannah 13
Golden Isles 14
Okefenokee Swamp National Wildlife Refuge 15
Americus 16
Macon 17
Athens 18
Dahlonega 19
Stone Mountain Park 20
Atlanta pp260–61 21

Tennessee
Great Smoky Mountains National Park 22
Chattanooga 23
Nashville pp264–5 24
Memphis pp266–7 25

Kentucky
Cumberland Gap National Historic Park 26
Mammoth Cave National Park 27
Berea 28
Daniel Boone National Forest 29
Lexington 30
Harrodsburg 31
Hodgenville 32
Bardstown 33
Louisville 34

For additional map symbols *see back flap*

KEY

- Airport
- Highway
- Major road
- Railroad
- State border

MILEAGE CHART

10 = Distance in miles
10 = Distance in kilometers

ATLANTA, GA							
248 399	SAVANNAH, GA						
207 333	**310** 499	ASHEVILLE, NC					
324 522	**115** 185	**268** 432	CHARLESTON, SC				
250 402	**497** 800	**294** 473	**551** 887	NASHVILLE, TN			
460 740	**711** 1143	**506** 814	**787** 1266	**213** 343	MEMPHIS, TN		
379 609	**583** 938	**283** 455	**540** 869	**213** 343	**423** 681	LEXINGTON, KY	
422 678	**658** 1058	**358** 576	**616** 991	**175** 281	**385** 619	**79** 127	LOUISVILLE, KY

View of smoky mist from Clingman's Dome, Great Smoky Mountains National Park

SEE ALSO

- ***Practical Information*** pp272–3
- ***Where to Stay*** pp274–7
- ***Where to Eat*** pp278–81

North Carolina

The site of the first English outpost in America in 1585, North Carolina became the 12th of the original 13 states in 1789 – it was also one of the country's 13 original colonies. While the population is increasingly based in cities, much of the state remains covered with fields of tobacco, a crop whose politics are the source of local and national debate. Still, the sight of green fields dotted with plank-wood, tin-roofed drying sheds continues to conjure up a classic image of North Carolina. Though tobacco-growing dominates the state's center, the east is lined by miles of pristine Atlantic Ocean beachfront, and the western mountains are among the most majestic found east of the Rockies.

Façade of North Carolina Museum of History, Raleigh

Research Triangle Region ❶

1,188,000. Durham Convention and Visitors' Bureau, 101 E Morgan St, Durham, (919) 687-0288, (800) 446-8604.

The state capital of Raleigh forms a regional triangle with the two major university towns of Durham and Chapel Hill. This region is the state's intellectual center, and has spawned the high-technology Research Triangle Park, a corporate campus located between the three cities.

Primarily a business region and gateway, the Triangle provides various urban conveniences and offers some interesting sights. Quiet downtown Raleigh includes a handful of modern state museums located across from the 1840 Greek Revival State Capitol, including the Sports Hall of Fame, the Museum of Natural Sciences, and the **North Carolina Museum of History**. The latter is well known for a Civil War exhibit describing the state's divided loyalties. Other exhibits feature pirates, Native Americans, and vehicles. A few miles north toward the airport, the **North Carolina Museum of Art** holds three floors of statuary and paintings. Among these is the 16th-century *Madonna and Child in a Landscape* by the artist Lucas Cranach the Elder, which had been stolen by the Nazis. When this was discovered, the museum returned the painting to its original owner, who in turn, has now loaned it back to the museum.

Of the two university towns, the smaller Chapel Hill, with its wooded **University of North Carolina (UNC)** campus, Morehead Planetarium, art museum, and genteel Carolina Inn with its aristocratic clientele, is by far the quainter of the two. Downtown Durham, wedged between the three-part **Duke University** campus, is home to the Durham Bulls minor-league baseball team. It also hosts the annual September Blues Festival. A major landmark on the West Campus is the superb Neo-Gothic Duke Chapel. Alumni and students of the two universities enjoy the lively rivalry between their respective sports teams – the Duke's Blue Devils and UNC's Tar Heels.

North Carolina Museum of History
5 E Edenton St, Raleigh. ***Tel*** *(919) 807-7900. 9am–5pm Mon–Sat, 1–5pm Sun.*
www.ncmuseumofhistory.org

North Carolina Museum of Art
2110 Blue Ridge Rd, Raleigh. ***Tel*** *(919) 839-6262. 9am–5pm Tue–Sat (to 9pm Fri), 10am–5pm Sun.* **www**.ncartmuseum.org

UNC Visitor Center
250 E Franklin St, Chapel Hill. ***Tel*** *(919) 962-1630. 9am–5pm Mon–Fri. Sat–Sun, public hols.*
www.unc.edu

Winston-Salem ❷

186,000. 200 Brookstown Ave 27101, (336) 728-4200.
www.visitwinstonsalem.com

North Carolina's close ties with the tobacco industry are evident in the fact that two major US cigarette brands have been named after this twin city. Moravian immigrants first settled here in 1766. Their descendants celebrate their roots at **Old Salem**, an interesting restoration of a Colonial village, where guides dressed in period costume demonstrate traditional crafts. They also relate the story of this Protestant sect's journey from Moravia to this region. Gift shops throughout the village offer such Moravian wares as handmade lace and pewter ornaments. The complex is set invitingly on a hill and is compact enough to be covered in an hour or two.

Adjacent to the village is the **Museum of Early Southern Decorative Arts**. Guides take

Actors dressed in period costume, Old Salem Colonial village

For hotels and restaurants in this region see p274 and p278

A panoramic view of lush vegetation and mountains from the Blue Ridge Parkway

visitors through 24 rooms exhibiting antebellum furnishings and artifacts from across the region. A children's museum is downstairs.

Old Salem
900 Old Salem Rd. ***Tel*** *(336) 721-7300.* *9am–5pm Tue–Sat, 1–5pm Sun.* *Easter, Thanksgiving, Dec 24, 25.* *museum.*
www.oldsalem.org

Blue Ridge Parkway ❸

(828) 298-0398.
www.nps.gov/blri

A scenic two-lane highway, the Blue Ridge Parkway *(see pp40–41)* runs 469 miles (755 km) south from Virginia along the Blue Ridge Mountain ridge-line. Its most scenic stretches lie in North Carolina, where the road meanders for 250 miles (402 km) past peaks, waterfalls, and the towering, 6,684-ft (2,037-m) Mount Mitchell.

The National Park Service's most popular destination with over 23 million visitors every year, the route has a maximum speed limit of 45 mph (72 km/h), which is strictly enforced. It is most scenic during spring and fall. Some sections close in winter. There are ample opportunities to detour to nearby trails and mountain towns such as Boone and Blowing Rock.

The parkway ends at the entrance to **Great Smoky Mountains National Park**, north of Cherokee *(see p262)*. Here, at the reservation of the Eastern Band of Cherokee Indians, a museum relates the history of the Cherokee people, focusing on the forcible removal of the tribe in 1838 to Oklahoma on the "Trail of Tears." The town of Cherokee itself has a large Indian-run gambling casino.

Asheville ❹

69,000.
151 Haywood St, (828) 258-6101.
www.exploreasheville.com

Surrounded by mountains, this town's commercial district retains many Art Deco buildings from its boom years as an early 20th century resort. Downtown Asheville evokes the period of local author, Thomas Wolfe (1900–38), who wrote about his hometown in *Look Homeward Angel*. Today the modest "Dixieland" boardinghouse described in the novel is preserved as the **Thomas Wolfe State Historic Site**. Asheville is said to be among the healthiest towns in the country, with many health-food stores, cafés, bookstores, bluegrass clubs, and a vibrant arts and music scene, patronized by a non-conformist and sophisticated populace. It is probably better known for its 250-room, art-studded, **Biltmore Estate** to the south of town. This French Renaissance-style mansion holds a collection of 18th- and 19th-century art and sculpture, and also has the distinction of being the largest residence in America. Beside the main Neo-Classical house, the splendid estate also has a winery, a deluxe inn *(see p274)*, and gardens designed by Frederick Law Olmsted, who also designed New York's Central Park. Visitors should expect long lines, as the estate attracts huge crowds, making it among the country's most visited house tours, along with the White House and Elvis Presley's "Graceland" *(see p267)*. Asheville also makes a great base for exploring the surrounding mountain region.

Biltmore Estate in Asheville, one of the most visited house tours in America

Thomas Wolfe State Historic Site
52 N Market St. ***Tel*** *(828) 253-8304.* *9am–5pm Tue–Sat, 1–5pm Sun.* **www**.wolfememorial.com

Biltmore Estate
Biltmore Ave (Hwy 25). ***Tel*** *(828) 225-1333.* *8:30am–5pm daily.* *public hols.*
www.biltmore.com

Cape Hatteras National Seashore, protecting the Outer Banks' northern coast

Outer Banks ❺

32,000. 1 Visitors Center Rd, Manteo, (252) 473-2138. www.outerbanks.org

North Carolina's Atlantic coastline is made up of a long chain of narrow barrier islands known as the Outer Banks. Most of the northern coast is protected as part of the **Cape Hatteras National Seashore**, where long stretches of pristine beach, dune, and marsh shelter wild ponies, sea turtles, and many varieties of waterbirds. Offshore, two jet streams that meet in a fury stir up the wild currents, storms, and hurricanes that have earned North Carolina's coast its reputation as "the Graveyard of the Atlantic." The coastline's many historic lighthouses, life-saving stations, and pirate lore are as important a part of the Outer Banks' maritime heritage as is its seafood industry.

In the early 20th century, bridges built from the mainland brought in the tourist trade, and now hotels and resort-home developments line the northernmost coast from Corolla all the way to Nags Head. In addition to the sun, surf, and sand, this tourist region offers many historic attractions and family amusements, in the town of **Kill Devil Hills**. The "First in Flight" slogan found on coins and the state's license plates commemorates the Wright Brothers' first historic flight, which took place here. The **Wright Brothers National Memorial** stands at the very site where Orville and Wilbur Wright launched *Flyer*, the first successful experiment in powered flight in 1903.

Wright Brothers commemorative marker

A few minutes drive south at **Jockey Ridge State Park**, hang-gliders participate in a modern version of the Wright Brothers' adventures, while "sandboarders" ride the largest sand dune on the East Coast. "Sandboarding," or running headfirst down the sheer 110-ft (34-m) high sand wall, is a revered local tradition. The dune is also a great spot to watch the sunset. Fewer people venture to the inland side of the island, where a slow kayak ride through the tidal marsh, or a walk through the scenic maritime forest at **Nags Head Woods Preserve**, hold a quieter appeal. Peculiar to barrier islands, these maritime forests, on the rough Atlantic Coast, are lined with banks of sturdy live oaks that protect the lush vegetation from the onslaughts of the water and wind. Follow the signs to the preserve west off Hwy 158 close to the Wright Brothers Memorial.

The drive along the National Seashore is one of the country's most scenic routes, with many opportunities to visit lighthouses and walk along dune and marsh boardwalks. Among the dozens of lighthouses, the 1847 Bodie Island Lighthouse is the only one still in operation. A free ferryride transports cars and passengers between **Hatteras Island** and **Ocracoke Island**. Hatteras's distinctive black-and-white spiral **Cape Hatteras Lighthouse**, built in 1870, is the tallest brick lighthouse in the world at 193 ft (59 m). The scenic village of Ocracoke has a good selection of inns, restaurants, and shops, which makes this remote port an inviting destination for an overnight stay. Visitors can connect with toll mainland ferries (reservations recommended) from here.

Wright Brothers National Memorial
US Hwy 158, milepost 8, Kill Devil Hills. ***Tel*** *(252) 441-7430. 9am–5pm daily (to 6pm Jun–Aug). Dec 25.*

Nags Head Woods Preserve
701 W Ocean Acres Dr, Kill Devil Hills. ***Tel*** *(252) 441-2525. dawn–dusk daily.*

Cape Hatteras Lighthouse
Hatteras Is, off Hwy 12, 1 mile (1.6 km) SE of Buxton. ***Tel*** *(252) 995-4474. mid-Apr–mid-Oct: 9am–4:30pm daily (to 5:30pm Jul–Aug).*

Ocracoke Island
Ocracoke Car Ferry to Cedar Island or Swan Quarter. ***Tel*** *(800) 293-3779 for fares & schedules (subject to change).*

Cape Hatteras Lighthouse, the world's tallest brick lighthouse

For hotels and restaurants in this region see p274 and p278

The landscaped Elizabethan Gardens on Roanoke Island

Roanoke Island ❻

1 Visitors Center Rd, Manteo, (800) 446-6262, (252) 473-2138. www.outerbanks.org

A marsh island lying between the Outer Banks and the mainland, Roanoke Island was the site of the first English settlement in North America. The first expedition to these shores, sponsored by by Sir Walter Raleigh, was in 1584. In 1587, another ship carrying more than 100 colonists disembarked at the island to create a permanent settlement. But when the next group arrived three years later, all the earlier colonists, including the first English women and children to land in the present-day US, had vanished without a trace. Today, the **Fort Raleigh National Historic Site**, the adjacent **Elizabethan Gardens**, an outdoor drama, and the nearby theme park with a replica of a 16th-century sailing ship as its centerpiece, all relate the mysterious story of this legendary "Lost Colony."

At the northern tip of the island, Fort Raleigh preserves the ruins of the colony's original disembarkation point, and ranger-led tours reveal what little is known about it. The Elizabethan Gardens are ideal for a walk through landscaped paths and lawns. A short drive south, at the port of Manteo, the **Roanoke Island Festival Park** tells the story of the first ship of explorers through tours aboard a recreation of the *Elizabeth II*, with costumed guides. There is also a museum that relates both the Native and European history of the region.

Fort Raleigh National Historic Site
US Hwy 64/264, Manteo. ***Tel*** *(252) 473-5772.* *9am–5pm daily.* *Dec 25.* *Elizabethan Gardens only.* www.nps.gov/fora

Roanoke Island Festival Park
Port of Manteo. ***Tel*** *(252) 475-1506.* *9am–4pm or 6pm daily (seasonal, call & check).* *Jan 1, Thanksgiving, Dec 24–25.*

Beaufort ❼

4,000. *(252) 726-8148 (Morehead City).*

Beaufort's considerable charms lie in its historic B&B inns, seafood markets, and restaurants. The highlight of this coastal resort's small attractive waterfront is the **North Carolina Maritime Museum**, which interprets the boating, fishing, and pirate history of this coastline. A swashbuckling robot of Edward "Blackbeard" Teach, a notorious pirate who was captured and killed off the Outer Banks in November of 1718, welcomes visitors in the shell room. A popular event is the family-oriented, educational Pirate Day, which is dedicated to pirate lore and has costumes, flag flying, and treasure hunts. Other activities include boat-building and net-making classes, and kayaking excursions. At the docks, private ferries take passengers out to the deserted sands of Lookout Island, preserved from development as the **Cape Lookout National Seashore**. The ecology of Lookout Island is similar to Cape Hatteras, with virgin beaches, marshland, and dunes, all rich in birdlife, but the limited access makes it more remote and less visited. The town at the island's northern tip was abandoned in the 1970s.

North Carolina Maritime Museum
315 Front St. ***Tel*** *(252) 728-7317.* *9am–5pm Mon–Fri, 10am–5pm Sat, 1–5pm Sun.* *Jan 1, Thanksgiving, Dec 25.* www.ncmaritime.org

Cape Lookout National Seashore
3601 Bridge St, Morehead City. ***Tel*** *(252) 728-2250.* *9am–5pm daily.* *Jan 1, Dec 25.* www.nps.gov/calo

The waterfront at Salt Marsh and Newport River, Beaufort

South Carolina

After separating from its sibling North Carolina in 1729, the South Carolina colony spread Upcountry, where Welsh, Irish, and Scottish immigrants established small owner-operated farms, in sharp contrast to the Lowcountry gentry. By the 1860s, however, the differences between the two had subsided and a unified South Carolina became the first Southern state to declare independence from the Union. Soon after, the first shot of the American Civil War was fired at Fort Sumter. Today, the state's "glory days" of resistance and revolution are re-created at plantations, museums, and monuments. Many visitors, however, head straight for the miles of beaches.

Charleston 8

100,000. *375 Meeting St, (843) 853-8000.* *Spoleto Festival (late May–early Jun).* **www**.charlestoncvb.com

One of the south's most beautiful cities and South Carolina's first capital, Charleston is situated on the tip of a peninsula between the Ashley and Cooper Rivers. Named after King Charles II of England, the city was founded in 1670 and soon became a wealthy colony of tobacco, rice, and indigo plantations. The first shot of the Civil War was fired just off the city's harbor, where people gathered to watch the Confederate seige of Fort Sumter. Today, Charleston retains much of its original period architecture and is a popular destination for antebellum house-and-garden tours, horse-and-carriage rides, fine Southern cuisine, and plantation retreats.

The historic district's beautifully preserved architecture evokes the city's Colonial and early American past. The civic and religious buildings here range from styles as varied as Colonial and Georgian, Greek and Gothic Revival, to Italianate and Victorian. Among the highlights are distinctive Charlestonian residences, set perpendicular to the street with grand piazzas running along their lengths. The only high structures are the towering church steeples. Horse-and-carriage rides through tree-lined streets provide a graceful overview.

A trip south from **Old City Market** to the Battery takes in many highlights along Church Street, including the old magazine, the Gothic French Huguenot Church, and the **Heyward-Washington House**. This 1772 house was built by rice planter Daniel Heyward and has a splendid collection of Charleston-made furniture. A half-block detour to the east on Chalmers leads to the Old Slave Mart, once one of the busiest in the American colonies. At the Battery, the **Edmondston-Alston House** features two floors of an opulent 1825 mansion overlooking the harbor. White Point Gardens Park lies to the south, while in the north, **Waterfront Park**, with its walk-through fountain, stands across from the popular restaurant row. Visitors can explore the cobblestone alleyways in search of hidden gardens, gargoyles, and harbor views. To the west of Waterfront Park, the **Gibbes Museum of Art** reveals local history through landscape paintings and portraits of famous South Carolinians.

The charming 1772 Heyward-Washington House

Heyward-Washington House
87 Church St. **Tel** *(843) 722-2996.* *10am–5pm Mon–Sat, 1–5pm Sun.* *major public hols.*

Edmondston-Alston House
21 E Battery. **Tel** *(843) 722-7171.* *10am–4:30pm Tue–Sat, 1:30–4:30pm Sun–Mon.* *major public hols.*

Gibbes Museum of Art 135 Meeting St. **Tel** *(843) 722-2706.* *10am–5pm Tue–Sat, 1–5pm Sun.* *major public hols.*

South Carolina Aquarium
100 Aquarium Wharf. **Tel** *(843) 720-1990.* *Apr 1–Aug 15: 9am–6pm Mon–Sat, noon–6pm Sun (to 5pm Aug 16–Mar 31).* *public hols.* **www**.scaquarium.org

Picturesquely set overlooking the harbor, Charleston's aquarium provides an excellent introduction to the indigenous creatures found within the state's aquatic habitats. These range from Appalachian rivers and blackwater swamps, to salt marshes and coral reefs. An IMAX® Theater lies adjacent.

Fort Sumter Visitor Center
340 Concord St. **Tel** *(843) 720-1990.* *8:30am–5:30pm daily.* *Jan 1, Dec 25.* *boat tours.* **www**.nps.gov/fosu

An embarkation point for boat tours to Fort Sumter, the visitor center relates the story of the

Civil War cannon lying preserved at Fort Sumter

For hotels and restaurants in this region see p275 and p279

American Civil War's first battle. The fort, which stands on an island at the entrance to Charleston harbor, was controlled by Union troops. In April 1861, the Confederate army besieged the fort. When Union troops tried to bring in supplies, the Confederates, who had occupied nearby Fort Johnson, unleashed a 34-hour bombardment. Union forces finally surrendered on April 14, 1861, and the fort remained under Confederate control until 1865. Ironically, General Beauregard, the Confederate leader, was a student of the defending Union commander, Major Robert Anderson, at the US Military Academy at West Point, New York *(see p91)*. Fort Sumter has been preserved unchanged since the end of the war. It is a National Monument.

Charleston Museum

360 Meeting St. ***Tel*** *(843) 722-2996.* *9am–5pm Mon–Sat, 1–5pm Sun.* *public hols.*
www.charlestonmuseum.org
This museum presents a comprehensive overview of the city's history from pre-Colonial days. Its most distinctive exhibits are in the Native American and Natural History galleries; the former has dug-out canoes and costumed mannequins, and the latter has a number of mounted skeletons of prehistoric animals such as the Cretaceous dinosaur *Thescelosaurus neglectus*.

Flowers in bloom at Audubon Swamp Gardens, Magnolia Plantation

Ashley River Plantations

Middleton Place 3550 Ashley River Rd. ***Tel*** *(843) 556-6020.* *9am–5pm daily.* *Dec 25.* **Drayton Hall** 3380 Ashley River Rd. ***Tel*** *(843) 769-2600.* *9:30am–3pm or 4pm (seasonal).* *Jan 1, 1st week Feb, Thanksgiving, Dec 24–25, Dec 31.* **Magnolia Plantation** Rte 4/Hwy 61. ***Tel*** *(843) 571-1266.* *8am–4:30pm or 5:30pm (seasonal) daily.*
Within a short drive upriver, three house tours provide a glimpse of Charleston-style country living. Of them, the grandest is **Middleton Place**, with its 1755 mansion located on a bluff overlooking the US's oldest landscaped gardens. Closeby, **Drayton Hall** is one of the country's finest examples of Colonial architecture. Built in 1738, the Georgian Palladian mansion has been preserved in its original condition without electricity or plumbing. A daily program on African-American heritage is held here.

Magnolia Plantation has a more modest house, with a petting zoo and a motorized train ride. Prized attractions are the acres of riverfront informal gardens with charming pathways that lead through a profusion of flowers, and **Audubon Swamp Gardens**, a lush tupelo-and-cypress sanctuary.

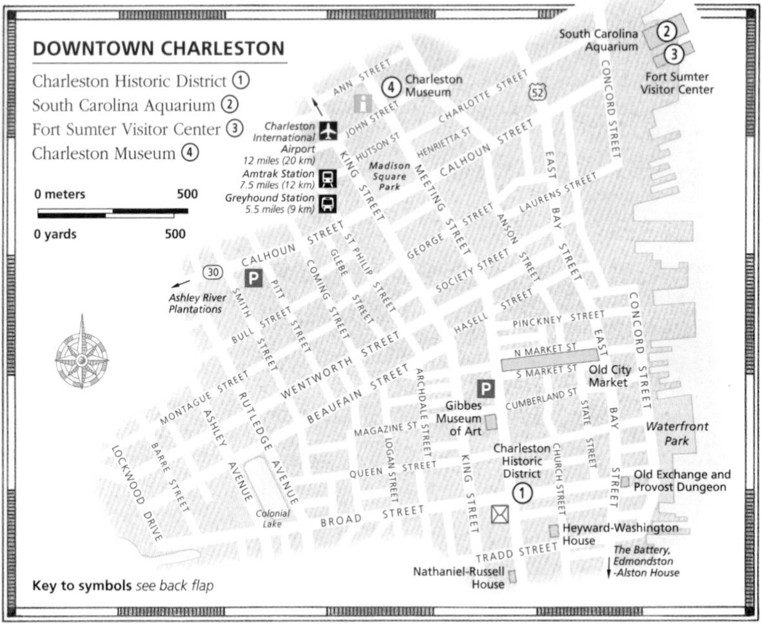

Columbia 9

116,000. 900 Assembly St, (803) 545-0000. www.columbiacvb.com

Situated at the fall line of the Congaree River – the area that marked the limit of inland navigation – this city was declared the state capital over Charleston in 1786. Although General William T. Sherman destroyed most of Columbia during the Civil War, the **State House** managed to survive intact. Today, six bronze stars mark the spots where Union cannonballs hit the 1855 copper-domed building, located in the center of the quiet downtown on Gervais Street.

On the banks of the river, the **South Carolina State Museum** is housed in an artfully recycled textile mill built in 1894. Informative exhibits on the state's natural, cultural, and industrial history are displayed. The adjacent **South Carolina Confederate Relic Room and Museum** maintains a huge collection of artifacts that trace the military history of South Carolina's participation in US wars from the Civil War onward, as well as an exhibit on the history and sometimes controversial meanings of the Confederate flag. While Southern traditionalists proclaim the flag a symbol of regional pride, many others see it as a symbol of white supremacy that should be abolished. A 20-minute drive south of town, the **Congaree Swamp National Park** offers visitors a close-up look of the biodiversity found within a cypress swamp ecosystem. The swamp is at its best from late fall to early spring.

A view of the Grand Strand on Myrtle Beach

South Carolina State Museum
301 Gervais St. ***Tel*** *(803) 898-4921.*
10am–5pm Tue–Sat, 1–5pm Sun.
Mon, Easter, Thanksg., Dec 25.
www.museum.state.sc.us

South Carolina Confederate Relic Room & Museum
301 Gervais St. ***Tel*** *(803) 737-8095.*
10am–5pm Tue–Sat; 1–5pm first Sun of month. *public hols.*
http://crr.sc.gov

Myrtle Beach 10

23,000. *1200 N Oak St, (843) 626-7444.*
www.myrtlebeachinfo.com

This popular beach is the center of the "Grand Strand," a long sweep of the Atlantic coastline south of the North Carolina border, which is dominated by hotels, golf courses, amusement parks, and arcades. Its heyday was in the 1950s, when as a Spring Break destination, college students descended on this beach town for a weeklong party. "The Shag," South Carolina's official state dance, was invented here and caused a craze all over the country. The elite crowd vacations at exclusive resort communities, but everyone ventures to the nearby fishing village of **Murrell's Inlet** for seafood.

South of Myrtle Beach two attractions make a worthwhile detour. On the inland side of the coastal Hwy 17, 16 miles (26 km) south of the beach, is **Brookgreen Gardens**, landscaped around 550 works of statuary by 250 artists. Oceanside, **Huntington Beach State Park** offers access to an undeveloped beach and saltmarsh boardwalk, as well as an art studio that once belonged to Anna Huntington, the sculptor who created Brookgreen Gardens in the 1930s.

Brookgreen Gardens
US Hwy 17. ***Tel*** *(843) 235-6000.*
9:30am–5pm daily. *Dec 25.*

Georgetown 11

10,000. *1001 Front St, (843) 546-8436.* **www**.georgetownchamber.com

Set along the banks of the Sampit River, Georgetown was the center of the state's lucrative rice trade, producing almost half the rice grown in the US in the 1840s. Downtown's **Rice Museum**, housed in the 1842 Old Market building, explains how the rice industry influenced almost every facet of life here. The museum's new maritime

Civil War arms on display at the South Carolina State Museum, Columbia

For hotels and restaurants in this region see p275 and p279

gallery features examples of historic local watercraft. The museum leads out to a waterfront park where a wooden boardwalk makes an attractive marsh-side promenade.

The commercial district is reminiscent of a Southern small town in the early-to-mid-1900s, a quiet contrast to the Grand Strand or the bustle of Charleston. About 15 miles (24 km) south of Georgetown, **Hampton Plantation State Park** is an unfurnished 1750 Georgian house. Visitors are able to explore the mansion, which overlooks the remains of the old rice fields. The well maintained grounds include enormous live oak trees and beautiful camellia gardens.

Hampton Plantation State Park, Georgetown

Rice Museum
Front & Screven Sts. ***Tel*** *(843) 546-7423.* *10am–4:30pm Mon–Sat.* *public hols.*
www.ricemuseum.org

Hampton Plantation State Park
US Hwy 17. ***Tel*** *(843) 546-9361.*
Mar–Oct: 9am–6pm daily (grounds), noon–4pm Tue–Sun (house); Nov–Feb: 9am–6pm daily (grounds), 1–4pm Thu–Sun (house). *house.*

Coastal Islands ⓬

Lowcountry Visitors Center & Museum, I95 exit 33 & US17, (843) 717-3090. **www**.southcarolinalowcountry.com

Extending from Georgetown south to beyond Savannah in Georgia, the remote islands of the Lowcountry are a semi-tropical region with a rich natural and cultural history. Shifting sand dunes, dense maritime forests of live oak draped with Spanish moss and muscadine vines, and numerous lagoons and marshes harbor a mix of wildlife such as sea turtles, sea birds, alligators, ospreys, and dolphins.

The area's unique African-American history evolved around the common heritage of slaves, brought here from the rice-growing regions of West Africa, to cultivate this crop along the tidal creeks. Isolated on these islands, the Lowcountry Africans were able to perpetuate their cultural traditions over the generations. Today, their "Gullah" heritage remains distinct in the local language, music, cuisine, and folkways. To the east of Beaufort, two islands preserve the natural and cultural history. Both are accessible by car via Hwy 21, which offers a panoramic view of the Port Royal Sound marsh landscape.

On St. Helena Island, the renowned **Penn Center** is a touchstone of Gullah culture. A former school established in 1862 by Pennsylvanian abolitionists during the Civil War, the center has a distinguished history from the Civil Rights era. National leaders such as Martin Luther King and groups such as the Southern Christian Leadership Conference met here to advance the Civil Rights Movement. A modest museum located in the old schoolhouse relates numerous events from the center's past through photographs and other displays. The center also sponsors storytelling programs and an annual festival that celebrates Gullah culture.

Canoeing at the Hilton Head Island Resort, Coastal Islands

Beyond St. Helena, **Hunting Island State Park** on Hunting Island preserves a natural barrier island environment. Its highlights include a pleasant, uncrowded beach, a coastside campground, and a 19th-century lighthouse.

Hilton Head Island, named after the English sea captain William Hilton who explored the island in 1664, is South Carolina's premier beach resort. It is dominated by several deluxe resort complexes, including the Westin Resort, Hyatt Regency, Crowne Plaza, Disney, and of course, the Hilton, providing golf, tennis, and spa facilities. Among the other recreational opportunities are horseback riding, fishing, boating, sailing, and a variety of other water sports.

Penn Center
Martin Luther King Dr, St. Helena. ***Tel*** *(843) 838-2432.* *11am–4pm Mon–Sat.* *public hols.*

Hunting Island State Park
Hwy 21. ***Tel*** *(843) 838-2011.*
Apr–Oct: 6am–9pm daily; Nov–Mar: 6am–6pm daily.

A view of the Port Royal Sound marshland at dusk, Coastal Islands

Georgia

The last of the 13 original colonies, Georgia was founded by a British general, James Oglethorpe, to stop Spanish expansion up from Florida. While the state initially banned slavery, economic pressures from competing slaveholding colonies led to its introduction. As a result, it grew wealthy from slave labor on rice, indigo, and cotton plantations. Georgia was devastated during the Civil War, when General Sherman's "March to the Sea" set ablaze a swath of land across the state. Led by pragmatic Atlanta *(see pp260–61)*, Georgia was able to overcome the many hardships of its troubled past, and was well positioned to benefit from the economic boom in the late 20th century.

A colorful Halloween display on River Street, Savannah

Savannah ⓭

251,000. 301 Martin Luther King Jr. Blvd, (912) 944-0455. **www**.savannahvisit.com

Labeled the "most beautiful city in America" by the Paris newspaper *Le Monde*, the lushly landscaped parks and gracious homes of Savannah have earned it a reputation for scenic beauty and sophistication. It was established in 1733 on the banks of the Savannah River, 16 miles (26 km) from the Atlantic Ocean. Its founder, James Oglethorpe, laid out a town grid dotted with small squares designed to deter invaders. Today, even after the turmoil of the Revolution and Civil War, his design remains intact, with the squares now serving as scenic parks filled with statues and fountains. The city has one of the largest, and perhaps most beautiful, urban historic districts in the US, which now thrives as the city's downtown commercial center. Horse-and-carriage tours provide an introduction to historic Savannah, though walking around is the best way to explore the area.

River Street is one of the city's central entertainment districts, lined with seafood restaurants, raucous taverns, and souvenir shops housed in old warehouses constructed of ballast-stones. Water taxis shuttle passengers to the modern Convention Center across the river on Hutchinson Island. Uphill, **Factors Walk** is a stately promenade on top of the bluff. A few blocks in from the river, **City Market** is another lively arts and entertainment district, housed in historic buildings.

Historic house museums throughout Savannah shed light on the city's history, architecture, and culture. Many homes and religious centers are open to tours year-round. Of these, the **Davenport House** on Columbia Square is considered one of the country's finest examples of Federal-style architecture, while nearby, the **Owens-Thomas House** on Oglethorpe Square is among the finest Regency buildings, built by English architect William Jay in 1816. Other houses can be seen on the popular **Tour of Homes and Gardens**, held in spring.

A handful of museums also highlight different aspects of the city's history. The **Telfair Academy of Arts**, at the center of the historic district, displays a fine collection of Impressionist paintings and decorative arts within an 1818 Regency-style mansion. At the western edge of the district, the **Ships of the Sea Maritime Museum** holds ship models of all shapes and sizes within the palatial 1819 Scarborough House. Located just beyond the historic district, the **Ralph Mark Gilbert Civil Rights Museum** has exhibits relating to the city's history. In-depth African-American heritage tours also start at the museum.

Many more attractions await in the surrounding Low-country – the marsh-laden coastal region of Georgia and South Carolina *(see p255)*. A drive out on Hwy 80, east of the **Tybee Island** beach resort (18 miles/29 km east of downtown), passes the **Bonaventure Cemetery**, where singer Johnny Mercer and writer Conrad Aitken are buried. Also located en route is the behemoth brick **Fort Pulaski National Monument**, which rises like a medieval fortress at the mouth of the Savannah River.

Davenport House
324 E State St. ***Tel*** *(912) 236-8097.* *10am–4pm Mon–Sat, 1–4pm Sun.* *Jan 1, Mar 17, Easter, Jul 4, Thanksgiving, Dec 25.*

Fort Pulaski National Monument, Savannah

Jekyll Island Club Hotel, one of many historic buildings on the Golden Isles

Golden Isles ⓮

68,000 (Glynn County).
4 Glynn Ave, (912) 265-0620.
www.bgicvb.com

The Spanish called the barrier islands off Georgia's southern coast "the Golden Isles" – possibly after lost treasure or the golden hue of the marshlands in fall – a term that tourism promoters were happy to revive. While they are primarily beach resorts, the islands retain a number of historic sights. **Fort Frederica National Monument**, located on St. Simons, along a scenic stretch of the Frederica River that lies adjacent to Christ Church, holds the ruins of a fortified village built by James Oglethorpe in 1736. Another significant site is the quiet expanse of marsh off Demere Road, south of Fort Frederica, where the Battle of Bloody Marsh was fought in 1742. This decisive battle between English and Spanish forces determined which Colonial power would control this part of the American continent. Near the island's southern tip, Neptune Park in downtown St. Simons has the historic 1872 **St. Simons Lighthouse**, where visitors can climb to the top. Lying across Bloody Marsh from St. Simons, Sea Island is home to the luxurious Cloister Hotel. At the turn of the 20th century, **Jekyll Island** was the exclusive preserve of the nation's premier industrialists, such as the Vanderbilts, Goodyears, and Rockefellers. With the advent of World War II, however, this vulnerable coastal island was deemed unsafe and the families moved elsewhere. Today, the island's historic district comprises the "cottages," as the millionaires' mansions were known, and the elegant Jekyll Island Club. The cottages have been restored and are now open as museums or inns. Among these are the 1892 Indian Mound Cottage, which passed into the hands of William Rockefeller in 1904, and Crane Cottage, which is now part of the **Jekyll Island Club Hotel** *(see p276)* and features a fine restaurant. Other highlights are a former stable, now a small museum, and Faith Chapel, with its Tiffany windows. The historic Jekyll River Wharf, next to the Jekyll Island Club Hotel, has a popular seafood restaurant serving raw seafood, mainly fresh oysters. On the ocean side, a selection of franchise motels and restaurants offer family lodging and dining. There is also a campground located at the island's northern tip near "Boneyard Beach," where sun-bleached driftwood gives the beach its name.

St. Simons Lighthouse

Fort Frederica National Monument
Frederica Rd, St. Simons Island. ***Tel*** *(912) 638-3639.* *9am–5pm.* *Dec 25.* **www**.nps.gov/fofr

Okefenokee Swamp National Wildlife Refuge ⓯

Hwy 121, Folkston. *(912) 496-7836.* *sunrise–5:30pm (7:30pm in summer).* *Dec 25.* *exhibits.*

In the remote southeastern corner of the state, the Okefenokee Swamp is an exotic, primeval landscape of blackwater and cypress that harbors alligators, softshell turtles, otters, and all kinds of birdlife. The Seminole Indian name "Okefenokee," loosely translated as "trembling earth," characterizes the peat moss hammocks that bubble up from the water as a natural part of swamp ecology. Boat tours provide a close-up view at three sections of the swamp, including the **Okefenokee Swamp Park** near Waycross, and the wildlife refuge headquarters at **Folkston**, which provides details about overnight paddling trips into the swamp. Fargo, near the swamp's western entrance, is the nearest town to the **Stephen C. Foster State Park**, 18 miles (29 km) to the northeast. This section is perched on a peninsula in the deep recesses of the swamp. Camping facilities and cabins are available here.

Okefenokee Swamp Park
Hwy 177, Waycross. ***Tel*** *(912) 283-0583.* *9am–5:30pm daily.* *Thanksg., Dec 25.* *exhibits only.*

Suwanee Canal Recreation Area, Okefenokee Swamp Refuge

Americus ⓰

18,000. 123 W Lamar St, (229) 928-6059.

Off the beaten track in south Georgia, the tidy county seat of Americus lies in a region of diverse attractions. The **Habitat for Humanity**, a worldwide organization offering "self-build" housing for the poor, has its headquarters downtown. In 2003 it opened its Global Village and Discovery Centre, which includes an international marketplace and up to 40 examples of habitat homes built around the world, including Papua New Guinea, Botswana, Ghana, and others.

Located 10 miles (16 km) north of town, Andersonville is the **National Prisoner of War (POW) Museum**. This marks a spot that was a notorious prisoner-of-war camp during the Civil War, which later became a veterans' cemetery. Almost 13,000 of the camp's inmates died from the terrible living conditions. Housed in a structure built to resemble a concentration camp, the museum's disturbing exhibits commemorate American POWs in conflicts from the Civil War through Vietnam to the Gulf and Iraqi Wars.

The local high school in Plains, 10 miles (16 km) west of Americus, is part of the **Jimmy Carter National Historic Site**. It was here that a teacher predicted that her student would become president. Carter proved her right, and the school is now dedicated to the life of the Plains-area peanut farmer's son who became the 39th president in 1976, in the wake of Nixon's resignation *(see p209)*. The former president, recipient of the Nobel Peace Prize in 2002, lives here and teaches Sunday school at the Maranatha Baptist Church when he is in town. An excursion train runs from Cordele in the east through Plains up to Carter's boyhood farm in Archery.

Headstones at the Andersonville cemetery near Americus

Habitat for Humanity
121 Habitat St at W Lamar St. **Tel** *(229) 924-6935. 9am–5pm Mon–Fri, 10am–2pm Sat. Sun.*

Macon ⓱

107,000. 200 Cherry St, (478) 743-3401. **www**.maconga.org

Founded on the south bank of the Ocmulgee River in 1823, Macon was laid out in a grid of avenues, which still exist in its historic district downtown. Uphill from here is one of the city's highlights, the Intown Historic District. This area has some of the city's most beautiful homes, a few of which are open to the public. The 1855 **Hay House Museum**, built in the Italian Renaissance style, features period characteristics such as trompe l'oeil marble, a ballroom, and hidden passages. The 1842 House Inn is also located here. Guided architectural tours begin at the visitor center. The city also has a vibrant musical history and was home to such greats as Little Richard and Otis Redding. The **Georgia Music Hall of Fame**, located in the historic district, provides an overview of the state's contribution to rhythm-and-blues, rock 'n' roll, gospel, country, and other genres. The nearby **Georgia Sports Hall of Fame** celebrates Georgia's athletes, such as Hank Aaron and Ty Cobb. Across the river from downtown, the **Ocmulgee National Monument** marks a historic mound complex built around 1100 as the capital of the Creek Confederacy.

Exterior of the Italianate Hay House Museum, Macon

Hay House Museum
934 Georgia Ave. **Tel** *(478) 742-8155. 10am–4:30pm Mon–Sat, 1–4:30pm Sun. Sun (Jan, Feb, Jul, Aug), public hols.*

Athens ⓲

80,000. 280 E Dougherty St, (706) 353-1820.

Home to the **University of Georgia** (UGA), Athens is well known as the state's intellectual and literary center. It has also gained repute as the originator of alternative music. Local bands such as REM, the B-52s, and Widespread Panic have made it big, and the 40-Watt Club on West Washington Street and the annual Athfest in June continue the tradition. The city is largely deserted in summer, while in fall it overflows with Georgia Bulldog fans for the home football games. The visitor center provides details about house and garden tours, such as the 1856 structure that now houses the Lyndon House Arts Center and the Founders Memorial Garden in North Campus. The university visitor center directs guests to the art museum, with its 19th- and 20th-century paintings and sculpture, and gives details on sports events and performances on campus.

UGA bulldog mascot

View from the Amicalola Falls, Amicalola State Park

Dahlonega ⓳

13 S Park St, (706) 864-3711.
www.dahlonega.org

The legendary Blue Ridge Mountain range extends across the state's northeastern corner. With abundant waterfalls and flowering forests, the region is well known for its cultural heritage of outstanding folk arts such as quilt-making, woodworking, and bluegrass music. The discovery of gold in the main town of Dahlonega in 1828 precipitated the nation's first gold rush, two decades before California's famous "Forty-Niners." The state's **Gold Museum**, housed in the 1836 courthouse in the center of Dahlonega's attractive town square, displays mining equipment, nuggets, and mining lore. The town also offers gold-panning and gold-mine tours as well as a complete set of coins minted in the US Mint that operated here from 1838 to 1861.

Gold Museum
1 Public Square.
Tel *(706) 864-2257.* *9am–5pm Mon–Sat, 10am–5pm Sun.* *Jan 1, Thanksgiving, Dec 25.*
www.gastateparks.org

Environs
About 18 miles (29 km) from Dahlonega, the **Amicalola Falls State Park** is the gateway to the southern terminus of the 2,144-mile (3,450-km) Appalachian Trail, a hiking route that leads from the top of Springer Mountain in Georgia north to Mount Katahdin, deep in Maine. Less ambitious hikers can head to the park's Len Foote Hike Inn, which offers ecologically sensitive, comfortably rustic overnight accommodations. The park also features a mountain-top lodge, restaurant, campground, and the Amicalola Falls. East of Dahlonega, along Hwy 441 at the Georgia–South Carolina border, the federally designated "Wild and Scenic" Chatooga River is considered one of the most daring rivers to navigate in eastern US. The book and the film *Deliverance* were based on this area (but locals don't appreciate being reminded of this). Visible from high above the river, Tallulah Gorge features a suspension bridge.

Amicalola Falls State Park & Lodge
Hwy 52. ***Tel*** *(706) 265-4703.* *8am–10pm daily.* *Jan 1, Thanksg., Dec 25.* www.gastateparks.org

Stone Mountain Park ⓴

US Hwy 78. *(770) 498-5690.* *6am–midnight (hours vary so call ahead).* *Dec 24–25.* *partial.*
www.stonemountainpark.com

The centerpiece of this popular park, located about a 30-minute drive east of downtown Atlanta, is a bas-relief carved into the side of a massive granite mountain. The sculpture depicts three Confederate heroes – Jefferson Davis, president of the Confederacy, and generals Robert E. Lee and Stonewall Jackson. Its creator, Gutzon Borglum, began work here in 1924 and later sculpted the faces of four American presidents at Mount Rushmore *(see p447)*.

A sky-lift takes visitors up to the summit, and the walk down affords a close-up view of the unusual "monadnock" habitat – it harbors many species of plants that are more commonly associated with the desert than the humid Southeast. The huge lawn, lying between the granite wall and Stone Mountain Park Inn, is the location of various events such as the summer laser light shows and the annual Fourth of July fireworks. Other attractions include an antebellum village, an ice rink, and paddlewheel riverboat rides around the lake. A number of lodging and dining options are also available here.

The centerpiece bas-relief sculpture at Stone Mountain Park

Atlanta 21

416,500. Underground Atlanta, (404) 521-6600.
www.atlanta.net

Founded as a terminus for two railroad routes in 1837, Atlanta's importance as a transportation hub made it a Union target during the Civil War. After a 75-day siege, General William T. Sherman broke the Confederate defenses and set most of the town ablaze, a history recounted romantically in Margaret Mitchell's Gone With the Wind. Today, the city claims to be the "Capital of the New South" and has since been considered more brash and faster paced than its Southern neighbors.

Exploring Atlanta

This cosmopolitan city is home to many industrial giants including Coca-Cola. Its entrepreneurial spirit led to an economic boom that lasted two decades, capped by a successful bid to host the Olympics in 1996. One of the city's landmarks, the **Centennial Olympic Park** downtown, commemorates this event. Yet another is **Turner Field**, where the former boxer Muhammad Ali famously lit the Olympic torch in the stadium. Downtown's attractions, **Georgia Aquarium**, **World of Coca-Cola**, and the **Martin Luther King Jr. Historic Site**, are all within a mile of these Olympic landmarks. A short Metro ride north leads to the city's exceptional **High Museum** in midtown. East of midtown lie the residential neighborhoods of Virginia Highlands and Little Five Points, with their superb specialty restaurants.

World of Coca-Cola

121 Baker St. ***Tel** (404) 676-5151. 9am–5:30pm daily (last adm: 4pm). Hours may vary so call or check website. Easter, Thanksgiving, Dec 25.*
World of Coca-Cola displays the world's largest collection of Coke memorabilia. Visitors can watch a 4D presentation, see a production line in operation, and sample from a range of 60 products.

The Centennial Olympic Park in downtown Atlanta

Georgia Aquarium

225 Baker St. ***Tel** (404) 581-4000. 10am–5pm Sun–Fri, 9am–6pm Sat.*
www.georgiaaquarium.org
One of the world's largest aquariums housing 500 marine species in five habitats. The Meso American Reef of Central America highlights the diversity of the region with 85,000 animals, including four whale sharks. Other habitats feature a brilliant rainbow of colored tropical fish.

CNN Studio

Marietta St at Techwood Dr. ***Tel** (404) 827-2300. 9am–5pm daily. Easter, Thanksgiving, Dec 25. with advance notice.*
A 55-minute guided tour of CNN Studio takes visitors through the inner workings of the world's first 24-hour news station, located in a 14-story atrium global headquarters. Book in advance for the tour. The lobby gift shop sells merchandise ranging from Atlanta Braves paraphernalia to videos of Desert Storm coverage.

Martin Luther King Jr. National Historic Site

450 Auburn Ave. ***Tel** (404) 331-5190. 9am–5pm or 6pm. Dec 25.*
Situated in a long reflecting pool beside an eternal flame, the crypt of the Nobel Peace Prize-winner Dr. Martin Luther King Jr. is a pilgrimage site for people from all over the world. The pool lies within the complex of the Center for Nonviolent Social Change, which has a gallery displaying portraits and memorabilia. Also located nearby is the original **Ebenezer Baptist Church**, where Martin Luther King Jr, his father, and grandfather presided. **The Martin Luther King Birthplace** is down the street to the east, while the **National Park Service Visitor Center**, housing portraits and exhibits that relate the area's role in the Civil Rights Movement, is right across the street.

This district preserves the heart of the **Sweet Auburn** neighborhood, which was the center of African-American life in the early 1900s.

Margaret Mitchell

Margaret Mitchell House and Museum

990 Peachtree St. ***Tel** (404) 249-7015. 9:30am–5pm Mon–Sat, noon–5pm Sun. Jan 1, Thanksgiving, Dec 24–25.*
Margaret Mitchell (1900–1949) wrote her magnum opus *Gone With the Wind* here in a basement apartment she affectionately called "the Dump." The three-story Tudor Revival house has had a dramatic history. It was abandoned, threatened by urban renewal, and then torched several times by

The reflecting pool, eternal flame, and crypt of Dr. Martin Luther King Jr.

For hotels and restaurants in this region see pp275–6 and pp279–80

High Museum of Art, Atlanta

arsonists, once on the eve of the Olympics opening. Various exhibits tell the story of the Georgia-born writer and reveal the extent of the house's restoration. Mementos from the famous film, such as Scarlett O'Hara's bonnet, are also on display.

High Museum of Art

1280 Peachtree St NE. **Tel** *(404) 733-4444.* *10am–5pm Tue–Sat, noon–5pm Sun.* *public hols.*
www.high.org

One of the country's best museums, the High Museum of Art lies in the city's premier arts district and is housed behind a colorful Alexander Calder sculpture in a strikingly modern Richard Meier structure. The museum doubled in size with the addition of Renzo Piano's sculpturally styled buildings and open plaza. Its extensive permanent collection careens from regional folk art and 19th-century American art to 18th-century Asian ceramics and sub-Saharan artifacts. Among the museum's packed calendar of events are blockbuster traveling exhibits, art films, make-art events, and lectures.

Atlanta History Center

130 W Paces Ferry Rd. **Tel** *(404) 814-4000.* *10am–5:30pm Mon–Sat, noon–5:30pm Sun.*

The center contains a museum and two historic houses. The museum is built in the style of a massive railroad depot. Exhibits such as **Fact or Myth?** shed light on antebellum life and the city's African-American community.

Contrasting examples of rural and urban life are presented in the two houses. The Tullie Smith Farm, with its livestock and traditional crafts demonstrations, is a typical mid-1800s farmhouse, while the elegant 1928 Swan House has a grand interior staircase and swan motifs throughout.

Fernbank Natural History Museum

767 Clifton Rd NE. **Tel** *(404) 929-6300.* *10am–5pm Mon–Sat, noon–5pm Sun.* *Thanksg., Dec 25.*

This museum is housed in a striking modern building centered around a skylit four-story atrium. It has natural history exhibits ranging from plate tectonics to bubble science. Of local interest is its coverage of Georgia's diverse ecosystems, including the Appalachian forest, the coastal plain, and a particular favorite, the exotic Okefenokee Swamp habitat *(see p257)*. The museum's IMAX® Theater features frequent "IMAX® and Martinis" nights, and there is also an on-site café. A number of in-town nature trails weave through the forest outside.

Jimmy Carter Library & Museum

441 Freedom Pkwy. **Tel** *(404) 865-7100.* *9am–4:45pm Mon–Sat, noon–4:45pm Sun.* *Jan 1, Thanksgiving, Dec 25.*
www.jimmycarterlibrary.org

Located on a hilltop site, the library highlights the humanitarian successes of President Carter's administration *(see p258)*. These include the Camp David accords, Panama Canal treaties, and human-rights and energy policies.

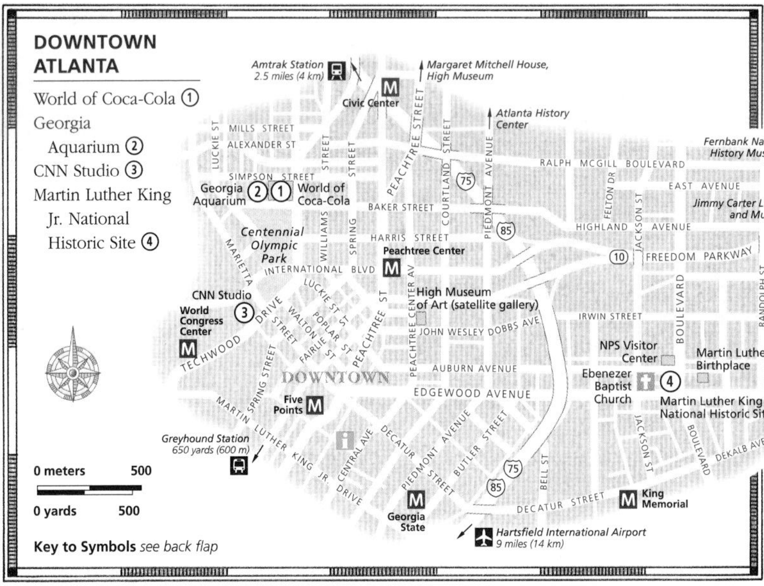

Tennessee

Tennessee is made up of three distinct regions. Memphis anchors the western lowlands along the Mississippi River; Nashville, the state capital, heads the central plateau; and the east is dominated by the Appalachian Mountains, with Knoxville as its urban base. With the Cumberland and Tennessee Rivers feeding into the Ohio, then into the Mississippi, the state was well positioned to prosper from the steamboat trade, and later, the railroads. During the Civil War, Chattanooga was the scene of battles, while Memphis and Nashville were occupied by Union forces. Today, Tennessee is known for its tremendous contribution to American roots music, from bluegrass, country, gospel, and blues, to rockabilly, rock 'n' roll, and soul.

Visitors at a preserved log cabin, Cades Cove

Great Smoky Mountains National Park ㉒

US Hwy 441, Gatlinburg, (865) 436-1200. *daily.*
www.nps.gov/grsm

The "Smokies," which earn their name from the smoke-like haze that clings to the ridge, hold some of the highest peaks in eastern US and support a diversity of plant life. With more than 10 million visitors each year, this is one of the country's most-visited parks. Established as a national park in 1934, half of it is in Tennessee and the other half in North Carolina. The Tennessee entrance is through Gatlinburg and Hwy 441, which bisects this sprawling park along the Newfound Gap Road and meets up with the Blue Ridge Parkway *(see p249)* on the North Carolina side.

Of the 800 miles (1,287 km) of trails, the most popular is the **Appalachian Trail**, which straddles the state border through the park. Trails to the park's many scenic waterfalls are also popular. The hike to **Mount LeConte** offers panoramic views, and there is even a hike-in lodge that provides rustic overnight accommodations, for which reservations are required. The 6,643-ft (2,025-m) tall **Clingman's Dome**, the state's highest peak, has an observation tower that offers fine views of the surrounding landscape. At the western end of the Great Smoky Mountains National Park, **Cades Cove** still preserves the historic farm buildings that were erected back in the 1820s. These include structures such as log cabins, barns, and a still operating gristmill. Bicycling, horseback riding, fishing, and white-water rafting are some of the popular activities available to adventurous tourists in this beautiful park and its surrounding region.

Spectacular view from Clingman's Dome

Sugar Maple

Magnolia

Mountain Laurel

Rhododendron

FLORA OF THE GREAT SMOKY MOUNTAINS

Famed for its incredible biodiversity, the Great Smoky Mountains shelter more than 1,500 species of flowering plants, including some 143 species of trees. The mountains' hardwood forests are made up of sugar maples, yellow birches, and poplars, while its spruce-fir forests are dominated by coniferous red spruce and Frasier fir. The understory consists of dense rhododendron and mountain laurel. Closely interwoven with Appalachian culture, the forest produces honeysuckle vines for basketry and various hardwoods for whittling and musical instruments, in addition to offering wild berries and fruits, medicinal plants (including ginseng), and harboring wild game.

Chattanooga 23

153,000.
2 Broad St, (423) 756-8687.
www.chattanoogafun.com

Located on the banks of the Tennessee River along the Georgia border, Chattanooga is surrounded by several high landmasses – the plateaus of Lookout Mountain, Signal Mountain, and Missionary Ridge. Founded as a ferry landing by the Cherokee Indian Chief John Ross in 1815, Chattanooga was later occupied by white settlers after the Cherokees were forced out from here along the tragic "Trail of Tears" to Oklahoma in 1838 *(see p46)*. The railroad leading to Atlanta provided a natural target for the Union Army during the Civil War, and several battles were fought on this dramatic terrain.

Downtown Chattanooga is today a revitalized center surrounding the original site of the ferry landing known as Ross's Landing. Within this compact area are many of the city's most popular attractions such as the Chattanooga Regional History Museum, which covers the area's local history – Native American, Civil War, and cultural; the **Tennessee Aquarium**; the attractive Riverwalk promenade; and the pedestrian-only Walnut Street Bridge that spans the river to Coolidge Park and Carousel. At the Tennessee Aquarium, visitors can trace the journey of a single drop of water from its origins in the Smoky Mountains through rivers, reservoirs, and deltas, then out into the Gulf of Mexico. Over 9,000 species of fish, amphibians, reptiles, mammals, and birds illustrate the state's varied habitats and ecosystems. An IMAX® Theater lies adjacent.

A short drive south of downtown on East Brow Road, the homespun **Battles for Chattanooga Electric Map** was originally known as "Confederama." It tells the story of local Civil War battles with 5,000 miniature soldiers and a series of tiny lights on large boards which are used to represent the advancing Confederate and Union troops. At the foot of Lookout Mountain, the station at St. Elmo Avenue is the start point for the mile-long **Lookout Mountain Incline Railway**. The train climbs a gradient of 72.7 percent up the side of Lookout Mountain for panoramic views. It was built in the 1890s to bring tourists up to the hotels that were once located on top. The **Chickamauga and Chattanooga National Military Park** of Point Park is a three-block walk away. The other section of the military park is the Chickamauga battlefield near Fort Oglethorpe across the border in northwest Georgia. The site at Point Park commemorates all the brave Confederate and Union soldiers who fought on the precipitous slopes of this steep plateau in the Battle Above the Clouds in 1863. This battle took place after Union forces were able to reverse an earlier Confederate victory and planted the US flag on the top of Lookout Mountain. At **Ruby Falls**, 3 miles (5 km) away, visitors descend by elevator to the floor of a cave, then walk past stalactites and stalagmites to the 145-ft (44-m) waterfall. A light show transforms the lovely natural surroundings of the falls into a somewhat gaudy display.

On the Georgia side of Lookout Mountain, **Rock City Gardens** has natural limestone rock formations beautified by the Enchanted Trail, a Lover's Leap, and little gnomes peering out from the crevices.

Former Chickamauga battlefield, with cannons, statuary, and memorials

Lookout Mountain Incline Railway

The Tennessee Aquarium, Chattanooga

Tennessee Aquarium
1 Broad St. ***Tel*** *(423) 265-0695.*
10am–6pm daily. *Thnksg., Dec 25.* **www**.tnaqua.org

Chickamauga & Chattanooga National Military Park
110 Point Park Rd. ***Tel*** *(423) 821-7786.*
8:30am–5pm daily. *Dec 25.*
www.nps.gov/chch

Ruby Falls
Tel *(423) 821-2544.*
8am–8pm daily. *Dec 25.*
www.rubyfalls.com

Nashville 24

570,000. *Broadway at Fifth St, (615) 259-4747.*
www.visitmusiccity.com

Best known today as the capital of country music, Nashville is a friendly and fun place to visit. Its musical history dates to 1927, when a radio broadcaster changing from music from the Grand Opera to the more popular Barn Dance show, introduced the upcoming selection as the "Grand Ole Opry." A musical legend was thus born and has flourished ever since. The city, however, has more to it than just music. It was founded as Fort Nashborough on the banks of the Cumberland River in 1779 and was named the state capital of Tennessee in 1843. It is also the financial center of the region and home to Vanderbilt University, one of the country's most prestigious institutions.

Exploring Nashville

Nashville's vibrant downtown area is anchored by the Country Music Hall of Fame. Most of the city's major attractions are within comfortable walking distance, such as the imposing **State Capitol** at the top of the hill, the historic and beautifully renovated Ryman Auditorium on Fifth Avenue, and the scenic riverfront with its reconstructed fort – a replica of the original outpost. Plenty of restaurants, cafés, and nightclubs lie in the surrounding area, locally known as "the District."

View of Nashville's colorful riverfront

Devoted country music fans might want to venture 10 miles (16 km) east to see the Grand Ole Opry House. A similar trip 1.5 miles (2.4 km) west of downtown to Music Row, the heart of Nashville's recording industry, might also interest ardent fans or aspiring songwriters.

Country Music Hall of Fame & Museum

222 Fifth Ave S. ***Tel*** *(615) 416-2001.* *9am–5pm daily.* *Thu (Jan–Feb), Jan 1, Thanksgiving, Dec 25.*
www.countrymusichalloffame.com

"Spreading the gospel of country music," the Country Music Hall of Fame honors scores of such outstanding musicians as Patsy Cline, Merle Haggard, and Hank Williams in a huge rotunda at a grand downtown location. In keeping with its exhibits, the building itself has been specially designed to resemble the black and white keys of a giant piano. Inside there is a beloved collection of vintage guitars, costumes, string ties, cowboy boots, well-known lyrics composed on bar napkins, and the celebrated golden Elvis Cadillac. A country music primer explains the academic distinctions between the subgenres of bluegrass, Cajun, honky-tonk, and rockabilly.

Legendary Hank Williams

Ryman Auditorium

116 Fifth Ave N. ***Tel*** *(615) 458-8700.* *9am–4pm.* *Thanksgiving, Dec 25.* **www**.ryman.com

This landmark auditorium is still an evocative setting for live performances. The Grand Ole Opry was broadcast from here for 31 years, from 1943 to 1974, when it moved to the new Opry House. Daytime tours of the Mother Church of Country Music are available, but the best way to see the 2,000-seat theater is by taking in a show; performers from B.B. King to the Dixie Chicks and Sheryl Crow are typical of the diverse all-star lineup. Within a few blocks of Ryman Auditorium, the modern **Nashville Convention Center**, **Gaylord Entertainment Center**, and nightclubs also feature all kinds of music – country, bluegrass, and blues.

Façade of the Ryman Auditorium, a Nashville landmark

Musicians Hall of Fame and Museum

301 Sixth Ave S. ***Tel*** *(615) 244-3263.* *10am–6pm Mon–Thu, 10am–5pm Fri–Sat.* *Jan 1, Easter, Jul 4, Thanksgiving, Dec 25.*
www.musicianshalloffame.com

Learn all about the musicians who created the greatest recordings of all time at the Musicians Hall of Fame. Visitors can see guitars, drums, and other instruments played by such famous musicians as Jimi Hendrix, as well as those played by such lesser-known session musicians as drummer Hal Blaine.

Tennessee State Museum

Fifth Ave btwn Union & Deaderick. ***Tel*** *(615) 741-2692.* *10am–5pm Tue–Sat, 1–5pm Sun.* *public hols.* **www**.tnmuseum.org

Although the main focus of this museum is the Civil War, it also covers other aspects of the state's past. Starting with a dugout canoe, exhibits showcase local Native American history, early pioneer life, slavery, the Civil Rights Movement, the river trade, and the Natchez Trace route. There is also a large collection of 19th-century decorative arts, such as European and American antique furnishings.

For hotels and restaurants in this region see pp276–7 and pp280–81

Exterior of the Grand Ole Opry House in Nashville

Grand Ole Opry House

2804 Opryland Dr. ***Tel** (615) 889-3060.* *some evenings, call in advance for tickets and show information.* **www**.opry.com

Located 10 miles (16 km) east of downtown in a gulch of Opry-themed development called Music Valley, the 4,400-seat modern Opry House continues the "world's longest running radio show" beyond its 75th year. The Who's Who of country music grace the stage of this legendary institution (live broadcast on 650 WSM-AM). The nearby Grand Ole Opry Museum tells the Opry story with wax figurines. The complex contains the fabulous Opryland Hotel.

Belle Meade Plantation

5025 Harding Rd. ***Tel** (615) 356-0501.* *9am–5pm Mon–Sat, 11am–5pm Sun.* *Jan 1, Thanksgiving, Dec 25.* *partial.*

A 20-minute drive southwest of downtown, Belle Meade is among the state's best-preserved antebellum estates. The 1853 Greek Revival mansion was once the centerpiece of a 5,300 acre (2144.8 ha) plantation and has been restored to its former splendor. Guides in period costume offer tours of the mansion and outbuildings, including an 1832 slave cabin. A Sunday summer concert series features live performances on the spacious grounds.

The Hermitage

4580 Rachel's Lane. ***Tel** (615) 889-2941.* *varies, check website.* *3rd week in Jan, Thanksg., Dec 25.* **www**.thehermitage.com

The home of Tennessee's foremost political and military hero, Andrew Jackson, this estate is a 20-minute drive east of downtown. After distinguishing himself as a military leader in the War of 1812, Jackson became the state's single Congressional representative before Tennessee gained statehood. He was elected the seventh president of the United States in 1828 and re-elected in 1832, serving two terms. Most of the contents of the house remain intact from Jackson's time. He is buried in the garden.

Natchez Trace Parkway

Originally a series of Indian trails, the Natchez Trace Parkway, which links Nashville with Natchez in Mississippi, is today a national historic parkway *(see p362).* Its northern terminus lies 15 miles (24 km) southwest of town. Here, the contour of the Trace is more rolling and deeply forested than farther down in Mississippi.

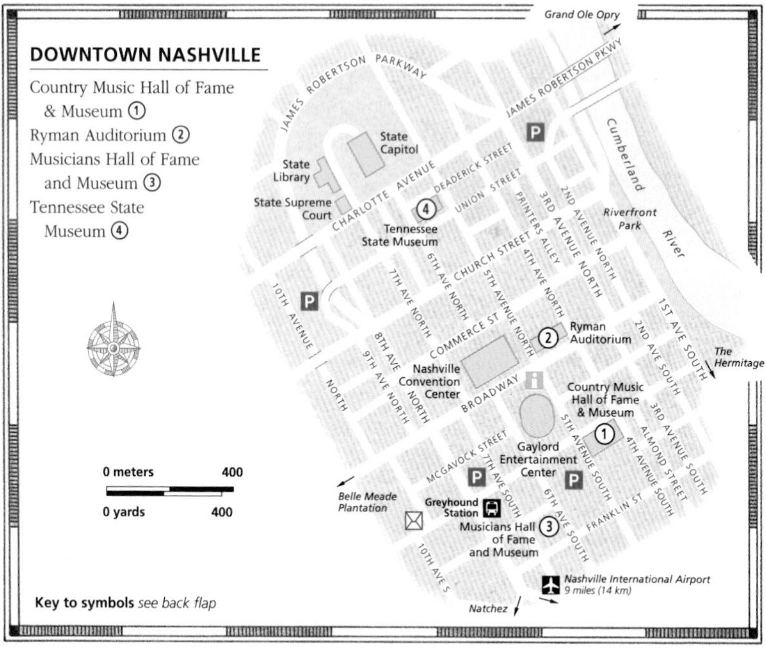

A neon B.B. King's Blues Club sign on Beale Street

Memphis 25

650,000. 119 N Riverside Dr, (901) 543-5333. **www**.memphistravel.com

Memphis sits on the banks of the Mississippi River at Tennessee's southwestern corner, where it meets the states of Arkansas and Mississippi. The city is most closely associated with two very different American icons – Civil Rights leader Dr. Martin Luther King Jr, and the singer Elvis Presley.

Since the early 20th century, Memphis has been synonymous with music. As the birthplace of rock 'n' roll, which originated from blues *(see p361)*, the city celebrates this legacy in its many nightclubs and saloons, and out on the streets. Even its festivals revolve around music. Highlights include Elvis's birthday on January 8; "Memphis in May," a month-long series of concerts and cookouts (Memphis is also famous for its barbecue); the W.C. Handy Awards, the blues answer to the Grammys, also in May; Elvis Week or "Tribute Week" around August 16; and the Music and Heritage Festival on Labor Day weekend.

Beale Street

A thriving commercial center for the city's African-American community, Beale Street's heyday was in the first half of the 20th century. After a period of decline, this historic street has now been resurrected as the heart of a vibrant entertainment district, rivaling New Orleans' Bourbon Street *(see p350)* in popularity. Restaurants, nightclubs, saloons, and shops line a four-block stretch. Many statues also punctuate the strip on either side. There is one of Elvis Presley across from Elvis Presley's Memphis Nightclub, which was established after his death, and one of W.C. Handy stands at the entrance to a plaza where many outdoor festivals take place. A block away, **W.C. Handy's Home**, a tiny white shotgun shack, is now a museum to the man who has often been called the "Father of the Blues." At the center of the strip stands the **A. Schwab's Dry Goods Store** at 163 Beale. This shop has been open here since 1876. Many nights Beale Street is closed to traffic, and people come to listen to live music emanating from every door. A short walk from Beale Street, **AutoZone Park** is the new red and green stadium of the Memphis Redbirds baseball franchise. It lies across from the landmark **Peabody Hotel** at 149 Union Avenue, where the famous ducks march twice a day to and from the lobby to the fountain where they can be seen frolicking all day *(see p277)*.

B.B. King, Rock-N-Soul Museum

National Civil Rights Museum

450 Mulberry St. ***Tel*** *(901) 521-9699.* *9am–5pm Mon–Sat, 1–5pm Sun.* *Tue.* **www**.civilrightsamuseum.org

The museum was once the Lorraine Motel, where Dr. Martin Luther King Jr. was tragically assassinated on April 4, 1968. Room 306 is preserved as it was on the day of his killing and a memorial wreath rests outside the window. Across the street, the assasination scene is recreated in the bathroom from which James Earl Ray apparently fired his fatal shot.

Memphis Rock-N-Soul Museum

Fedex Forum, 200 3rd St. ***Tel*** *(901) 205-2533.* *10am–7pm daily.* *Jan 1, Thanksg., Dec 25.* **www**.memphisrocknsoul.org

The intersection between history and race, and its expression in song, is explained with outstanding musical accompaniment at this museum. It is located opposite the Gibson Guitar factory, which offers a fascinating tour. The exhibit is sponsored by the Smithsonian Institute and examines the blues and country roots of rock 'n' roll with a fascinating movie, and displays of old instruments as well as vintage jukeboxes, stage costumes, and profiles of artists. A digital audio tour features more than six hours of fabulous music. Music fans may want to travel 10 minutes south to the Stax Museum of American Soul Music, in the old Stax Records recording studio.

Mud Island

Via Front & Main Sts. ***Tel*** *(901) 576-7241.* *10am–5pm or 6pm (seasonal) Tue–Sun.* **www**.mudisland.com

Reached via monorail, Mud Island holds the **Mississippi River Museum** that tells the story of the river with artifacts such as an 1870 steamboat replica. The museum also has many Native American exhibits. The most engaging exhibit, however, is located outside where water courses through a replica of the Mississippi for a five-block-long stretch, ending at a swimming pool shaped like the Gulf of Mexico.

Elvis Presley's grave in his lavish Graceland estate

Center for Southern Folklore

119 S Main St. ***Tel*** *(901) 525-3655.* *9:30am–5:30pm Mon–Fri.* *Thanksgiving, Dec 25.* *hourly.* *shows.*
www.southernfolklore.com

A touchstone for all that is authentically Southern, the center offers a great café, folk art gallery, gift shop, and a stage for shows ranging from jug bands to puppetry, with plenty of blues, soul, folk, rock, and gospel in between. It also sponsors the acclaimed Music and Heritage Festival.

Sun Studio

706 Union Ave. ***Tel*** *(901) 521-0664.* *10am–6pm daily.* *Thanksgiving, Dec 25.*
www.sunstudio.com

Famous musicians from all over the world come to record in the legendary studio that launched the careers of Elvis, B.B. King, Johnny Cash, Jerry Lee Lewis, Roy Orbison, and others. Founded in 1954 by Sam Philips, the studio's exhibits include Elvis's original drum set and microphone. Souvenir items with the familiar yellow rooster logo are on sale, and visitors can also make their own souvenir recordings.

Graceland

3734 Elvis Presley Blvd. ***Tel*** *(901) 332-3322.* *9am–5pm Mon–Sat, 10am–4pm Sun (but times can vary).* *Tue (Dec–Feb), Jan 1, Thanksgiving, Dec 25.* **www**.elvis.com

A 10-minute drive from downtown, Graceland attracts more than 700,000 visitors each year to the estate that Elvis Presley bought as a 22-year-old superstar and called his home until his death in 1977. Starting at the grand visitor complex, guests are taken by van through the metal gates up the drive to the house to view the front rooms, famous Jungle Room den, gallery, racquetball court, and Memorial Gardens, where he is buried. The tour is self-guided. Across the street, additional admission charges are needed to see Elvis's car collection, his two airplanes, and a **Sincerely Elvis** exhibit with home movies and personal effects. Unofficial souvenir shops along **Elvis Presley Boulevard** offer some bizarre but entertaining items, such as Elvis-emblazoned nail clippers and beach towels.

Full Gospel Tabernacle Church

787 Hale Rd. ***Tel*** *(901) 396-9192.* *11am Sun.* *donation.*

The Reverend Al Green left a successful recording career in the 1970s (his hits included songs such as "Tired of Being Alone") to pursue his calling. He often presides over Sunday services at his church in Southside Memphis, not far from Graceland. Visitors to the electric gospel service should show respect by wearing decent attire, donating a little, and staying for the entire service.

Kentucky

With its Appalachian Mountain landscapes and rolling rural pasturelands, where horses run on acres and acres of bluegrass, Kentucky is easily one of the most picturesque states in the country. The lands west of the mountains were once inhabited by Indian tribes who strenuously opposed the encroachment of white settlers. Today, Kentucky is widely known for its horses, and many thoroughbred stud farms are centered around Lexington. One of the most prestigious horse races, the Kentucky Derby, takes place in Louisville. This state is also famous for its downhome style of country music, and Hwy 23 along its eastern border has been designated the Country Music Highway.

A cannon at Fort McCook, Cumberland Gap National Historic Park

Cumberland Gap National Historic Park ㉖

US Hwy 25 E, Middlesboro. *(606) 248-2817.* *8am–5pm daily.* *Dec 25.* **www**.nps.gov/cuga

Situated in the southeastern corner where Kentucky meets the states of Virginia and Tennessee, the Cumberland Gap is a natural pass through the Cumberland Mountains, once used by migrating deer and bison. It was first explored by Dr. Thomas Walker in 1750 on behalf of a land company. Some five years later, the legendary fur trapper and explorer Daniel Boone ran his Wilderness Road through the Gap, thus opening the way for some 200,000 pioneers to establish homesteads in the interior wilderness.

This rugged area is thickly forested, and many sights, such as the Sand Cave sandstone overhang and White Rocks sandstone outcrop, are accessible only by hiking trails. The hardwood and softwood forests shelter wild turkeys, white-tailed deer, and many varieties of songbirds.

The Gap was also a strategic point in the Civil War. It was held alternately by Confederate and Union forces, and the fortifications can still be seen throughout the park. Today, a four-lane Interstate Highway and a railroad tunnel run through the Gap. A drive up to **Pinnacle Overlook** leads to a short trail for a view of three states, most dramatic during fall.

Mammoth Cave National Park ㉗

I-65 exit 53. *(270) 758-2180.* *Mar–Oct: 8am–6pm daily, Nov–Feb: 8:45am–5pm.* *Dec 25.* *fee.*

Halfway between Louisville *(see p271)* and Nashville *(see p264)*, this park offers guided tours of one of the largest cave systems known, formed by underground rivers that left a dramatic landscape of stalactites and stalagmites. Guests are free to choose from tours with names such as "Historic" or "Wild Cave Tour" (helmets provided). According to experts, evidence suggests that the cave had been inhabited as far back as 4,000 years ago. The Green River runs its course above Mammoth Cave, an area that is crisscrossed by several hiking trails.

Berea ㉘

9,000. *(800) 598-5263.* *Berea Crafts Festival (Jul).* **www**.berea.com

Home to Berea College, dedicated to educating disadvantaged Appalachian youth, Berea is known as a highlands crafts center. Typical crafts include woodworking, pottery, and textiles. The town hosts the Kentucky Guild of Artists Fair, the Craftmen's Fair, as well as the Berea Crafts Festival. Year-round, there are public tours of artisans' studios, such as **Weaver's Bottom**, founded in 1983.

Weaver's Bottom
140 N Broadway. ***Tel*** *(859) 986-8661.* *9am–5pm Mon–Sat.* *Dec 25.*

The path leading into the interior of Mammoth Cave

For hotels and restaurants in this region see p277 and p281

View of dense forest foliage from the Zilpo Road National Scenic Byway, Daniel Boone National Forest

Daniel Boone National Forest ㉙

1700 Bypass Rd, Winchester. *(859) 745-3100.* *8am–4:30pm daily.* *Jan 1, Thanksg., Dec 25.*

Named after the legendary pioneer and fur trapper David Boone, who lived in Kentucky, this National Forest protects some of the most dramatic scenery in Kentucky. The dense forest provides shelter to over 35 endangered species, including red-cockaded woodpeckers, big-eared bats, and bald eagles. The **Sheltowee Trace National Recreation Trail** runs the entire 260-mile (418-km) length of the forest, from Morehead near the Ohio border in the north to Pickett State Rustic Park in Tenessee. Also near Morehead, **Cave Run Lake** is popular for boating, and the **Zilpo Road National Scenic Byway** offers a good chance to see the forest's rich variety of wildlife on a short drive. The central area east of Stanton features the **Natural Bridge State Resort Park**, a naturally occuring archway surrounded by rugged terrain, and the picturesque **Red River Gorge**, both of which offer great hiking, canoeing, and whitewater rafting opportunities. At the southern end, **Cumberland Falls State Resort Park** offers lodging, camping, and swimming.

Cumberland Falls State Resort Park
7351 Hwy 90, Corbin.
Tel *(606) 528-4121.* *daily.*
www.parks.ky.gov

Environs

Visitors to the southern portion of the park might want to detour to **Corbin**, off I-75, 50 miles (80 km) north of the state's southern border with Tennessee. Corbin is notable as the original home of Kentucky Fried Chicken, where Colonel Harland Sanders first served the special recipe that went on to become a global franchise. The kitchen where the famous herbs and spices were first put together is on display, along with KFC artifacts.

Chairlifts carrying visitors up to the Natural Bridge

COUNTRY & BLUEGRASS MUSIC

Country singer Billy Ray Cyrus in concert

As the Mississippi Delta is to blues music, so the stretch of eastern Kentucky (along with West Virginia) is home to the greatest proportion of country music artists in America. British, Irish, and Scottish immigrants brought Elizabethan ballads, rhythms, and instruments to the area, which they then forged into a distinctly American style known as "country." It was characterized by fast fiddling, occasional yodeling, and laments on the hardscrabble life of the American Southeast. Hwy 23, which runs from Ashland to Pikeville along the state's eastern border, has been dubbed the "Country Music Highway" to commemorate the vast number of artists who come from here. Along its length, the route passes by the hometowns of Billy Ray Cyrus, the Judds, Loretta Lynn, Patty Loveless, and Dwight Yoakum.

Kentucky's vast bluegrass pasturelands defined a particular style of country music known as "bluegrass." This evolved from the musical style played in the late 1940s by Bill Monroe and his Bluegrass Boys. The name "bluegrass" stuck, and this acoustic folk style remains popular in the region today. Traditional bluegrass instruments include the fiddle, guitar, mandolin, five-string banjo, and bass and dobro guitars.

Thoroughbred race horses grazing in pastures near Lexington

Lexington 30

226,000. *301 E Vine St, (859) 233-1221.* **www**.visitlex.com

Kentucky's second largest city, Lexington is also the capital of the state's horse country. The surrounding bluegrass-covered countryside is lined with hundreds of throroughbred stud farms, where many Kentucky Derby winners are bred, reared, and trained. Most farms are open to visitors, who are welcome either on their own with advance reservations or as part of an organized tour. The visitor center supplies lists of farms and tour operators.

About 6 miles (9.6 km) north of town lies the **Kentucky Horse Park**, a state-operated working farm that serves as an equestrian theme park. Here, visitors can watch live shows, ride ponies, sign up for escorted trail rides, take carriage tours, and go swimming and camping. The park's **International Museum of the Horse** is a monument to the role of the horse in the development of human history. The adjacent **American Saddlebred Museum** is named for, and focuses on, America's first registered horse breed. Outside, the Man o' War Memorial marks the grave of the beloved thoroughbred who won several acclaimed races. In town, the 1803 **Mary Todd Lincoln House** preserves the girlhood home of Abraham Lincoln's wife.

Kentucky Horse Park
4089 Iron Works Pkwy. ***Tel** (859) 233-4303.* *mid-Mar–Oct: 9am–5pm daily.* *Nov–mid-Mar: Mon–Tue, major public hols.*
www.kyhorsepark.com

Harrodsburg 31

7,400. *124 S Main St, (859) 734-2364.*
www.harrodsburgky.com

A large number of Shaker families from New England relocated in and around Harrodsburg in 1805 and established a farming community renowned for its handicrafts. It grew to a sizeable population of around 500 in 1830 and then, in part due to the Shaker belief in celibacy, it grew less cohesive and became scattered by 1910. The area's premier attraction is the **Shaker Village of Pleasant Hill**, America's finest, largest, and most completely restored Shaker community and living history museum. The architecture and furnishings at the village reflect the spare, utilitarian style that typifies the Shaker values. Artisans demonstrate crafts such as woodworking and weaving.

Shaker Village of Pleasant Hill
3501 Lexington Rd. ***Tel** (859) 734-5411.* *10am–5pm daily (to 4:30pm Nov–Mar).*
Dec 24–25. *partial.*
www.shakervillageky.org

Hodgenville 32

2,700. *72 Lincoln Square, (270) 358-3411.*

Hodgenville is the base for the **Abraham Lincoln Birthplace National Historic Site**, located 3 miles (5 km) to its south. The site commemorates the 16th US president's Kentucky roots by preserving his childhood home. Here, 56 steps representing the years of Lincoln's life lead up to a granite-and-marble Memorial Building built around a 19th-century log cabin, where the

Barrel making in the Shaker Village of Pleasant Hill, Harrodsburg

For hotels and restaurants in this region see p277 and p281

president was born. The site also encompasses a large portion of the original Lincoln family farmland.

Abraham Lincoln Birthplace National Historic Site
7120 Bardstown Rd (Hwy 31 E). ***Tel*** *(270) 358-3137.* *8am–4:45pm or 6:45pm (seasonal).* *Jan 1, Thnksg., Dec 25.* **www**.nps.gov/abli

The Hodgenville log cabin in which Abraham Lincoln was born

Bardstown ㉝

6,800. *107 E Stephen Foster Ave, (502) 348-4877.*
www.visitbardstown.com

The self-proclaimed "Bourbon Capital of the World," Bardstown is surrounded by the state's largest whiskey distilleries, which have earned Kentucky its legendary reputation as the whiskey-making center of the US. (Bourbon is made from corn, malt, and rye, and is aged in charred white oak barrels.) The most popular distillery, James Beam, known in countless country songs as "Jim Beam," lies 14 miles (22.5 km) west of Bardstown, while a 20-mile (32-km) drive south leads to the famed Maker's Mark distillery, Kentucky's oldest distillery operating in the same site. However, Bardtown's most popular attraction is **My Old Kentucky Home State Park.** Here, guides lead visitors through the historic mansion that, according to legend, inspired composer Stephen Foster to write "My Old Kentucky Home," the state's beloved anthem. The park also hosts outdoor musicals.

My Old Kentucky Home State Park
US Hwy 150. ***Tel*** *(502) 348-3502.* *Sep–May: 9am–4:45pm; Jun–Aug: 8:30am–6:15pm.* *Jan 1, Thanksgiving, Dec 24–31.*

Stephen Foster statue, My Old Kentucky Home State Park, Bardstown

Louisville ㉞

269,000. *30 Market St, (502) 584-2121.*

Founded at the falls of the Ohio River in 1788, Louisville (pronounced "Looavul") is home to one of the world's most famous horse races, the Kentucky Derby. What Mardi Gras is to New Orleans, or the Masters Tournament is to Augusta, the Derby is to Louisville – it is the event around which all local calendars revolve. Since it first began in 1875, three-year-old horses have run the track at Churchill Downs on the first Saturday in May. Kentucky's high society turns out in spring finery for this social event of the year, with hats and seersucker suits constituting battle uniform. Mint juleps, the Southern concoction of bourbon, ice, sugar, and fresh mint are the unofficial beverage of choice. "My Old Kentucky Home" plays while the horses are led onto the track for an event that lasts less than two minutes. Winners take home the coveted trophy, decorated with lucky silver horseshoes in a "U" shape "so that the luck doesn't spill out." The adjacent **Kentucky Derby Museum** showcases horse-racing history and offers backside track tours" through the Churchill Downs track. A couple of blocks from the historic district on the waterfront, the **Louisville Slugger Museum** produces the worldclass baseball bat in a factory marked by a landmark 120-ft (36-m) high bat.

The **J.B. Speed Art Museum** on South 3rd Street displays a large collection of Renaissance paintings and sculpture. At the Riverfront Plaza on the banks of the Ohio River at Main and Fourth Streets, several paddlewheelers tour the area, and a fountain periodically shoots water 375 ft (114.3 m) into the air. The surrounding historic district's old warehouses have been recast as cafés, galleries, and shops.

Located 2 miles (3.2 km) northeast of downtown, Cave Hill Cemetery is one of the largest and most beautiful in the US. Many Louisvillians go visit the grounds just to feed the ducks, or take in the landscaped lawns. Thirty miles (48.2 km) southwest of Louisville, the exterior of the federal gold bullion repository at **Fort Knox** can be seen.

Gigantic baseball bat outside the Louisville Slugger Museum

Kentucky Derby Museum
704 Central Ave. ***Tel*** *(502) 637-1111.* *9am–5pm Mon–Sat (from 8am Mar 15–Nov 30), 11am–5pm Sun.* *Breeder's cupdays, first Fri–Sat in May, Thanksgiving, Dec 25.* **www**.derbymuseum.org

Louisville Slugger Museum
800 W Main St. ***Tel*** *(502) 588-7228.* *9am–5pm Mon–Sat, 1–5pm Sun (to 6pm daily Jul–mid-Aug).* **www**.sluggermuseum.org

Practical Information

Successful traveling around the Southeast requires a great deal of advance planning, as there is so much to see and do in the vast area. With miles of sandy beaches, picturesque historic cities such as Charleston, the stunning rugged wilderness of the Blue Ridge and Appalachian Mountains, and rolling hills and valleys of the foothills, the Southeast truly has it all. In addition to myriad natural wonders, the region also offers burgeoning commercial centers such as Atlanta, and engaging cultural towns including Memphis, the birthplace of the blues, and Nashville, the commercial and cultural capital of "country-western" music, arts, and entertainment.

TOURIST INFORMATION

Each of the five Southeast states, North Carolina, South Carolina, Kentucky, Tennessee, and Georgia, publishes travel information that can be ordered by phone or via web sites. State "Welcome Centers" located along most major highways greet visitors as soon as they enter each of the Southeast states. Open between 8am and 5pm daily, these centers offer free road maps and a full range of tourist information, covering climate, transportation, attractions, and accommodations. More information is available from a multitude of tourism bureaus across the five states.

NATURAL HAZARDS

The end of summer in the Southeast can be very pleasant, but this is also the main hurricane season, and potentially one of the most troubling times for visitors. Hurricane season stretches from August to the end of the year, but since storms form in the Atlantic Ocean near the Equator, emergency alert systems usually give at least a day or two warning before strong winds and heavy rains arrive.

Watch out for tornadoes and thunderstorms in late spring and summer, especially in the south, where they strike suddenly and create flash floods. If a tornado watch or warning is issued, take cover straight away.

GETTING AROUND

Like much of the US, the Southeast is a region where it can be hard to get around without a car. **Greyhound** buses do serve some larger towns and cities, and visitors can also take **Amtrak** trains to travel around the Southeast. Nevertheless, driving is the best way to get around the region, as public transportation can be limited. Seat belts are required for drivers and front seat passengers in all of the five states. Most states also require seat belts for back seat passengers, and child seats are required for all automobile occupants aged 4 and under. Speed limits vary, but are usually 70 to 75 mph (112 to 120 km/h) on Interstate Highways outside of densely populated urban areas, weather permitting.

ETIQUETTE

Compared to the rest of the country, Southerners are largely a teatotalling lot. Many of them are Baptists, a religion that frowns on the consumption of alcohol. "Dry" counties can still be found in some rural areas, particularly in the mountains where alcohol cannot be legally served or sold to the public. But exceptions to this tradition are legendary. Makers of "moonshine" a 100-proof home-made whisky typically distilled from corn, gained an outlaw reputation in the days of the Prohibition for evading federal agents by hiding stills deep in the woods and working them by cover of darkness – hence the name "moonshine".

Drinking mint juleps on the day of the Kentucky Derby in Louisville is such a revered local custom that girls start collecting the traditional sterling silver "julep cups" as young as 12 years of age.

FESTIVALS

The southeast states stage a diverse range of annual community, regional, and national festivals. In February, cultural sites all over the Southeast, especially the Martin Luther King Jr. Center for Non-Violent Social Change in Atlanta, celebrate the **Black History Month** with various special programs. In March, Savannah, Georgia, hosts a lively **St. Patrick's Day** celebration, when thousands come together to drink beer, dance, sing, and celebrate

THE CLIMATE OF THE SOUTHEAST

The region's states have a mild climate with temperatures rarely dipping below freezing in winter, though summer in the low-lying areas can be very hot. Spring sees azaleas and other blossom in the region's famous gardens. Summer, with its sunny days and warm water along sandy beaches, is the most popular time for travel. The end of summer is the primary hurricane season. In inland areas, leaves change color on mountain hardwood trees in October. In winter, snow can fall across many areas.

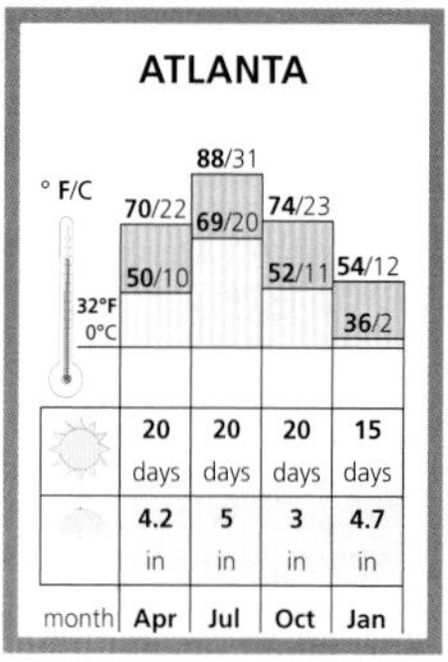

real or imagined Irishness. March and April are also ideal months for enjoying house-and-garden tours and the blossoms of the Southeast's many fruit trees, celebrated in events like the **Cherry Blossom Festival** of Macon, Georgia, where visitors can see more than 200,000 trees that line the city streets.

Throughout May, one of the country's largest music and arts festivals takes place in historic Charleston, South Carolina, as part of the **Spoleto Festival USA**.

Summer brings a deluge of outdoor events. Bands, fireworks, and street festivals are the norm for community celebrations of the July 4 Independence Day holiday. One of the largest fireworks displays in the US is staged at Stone Mountain, outside Atlanta. Numerous county and state fairs crop up around this time, as do music festivals such as **Old Time Fiddlers' Jamboree** in Smithville, Tennessee. The end of summer brings **Elvis Week** in Memphis, Tennessee, celebrating the life and times of Elvis Presley with a week-long festival around the anniversary of his death on August 16.

A highlight of autumn is the **Tennessee Fall Home-coming**, an Appalachian-themed crafts and culture festival that takes place annually at the Museum of Appalachia. At the end of the year, an old-fashioned Christmas is re-created at the living history village of Old Salem, outside Winston-Salem in North Carolina.

SPORTS & OUTDOOR ACTIVITIES

The cities of the Southeast host a wide array of professional and amateur sports teams, and there are many minor league teams in smaller cities. Especially in basketball and football, hundreds of high-quality and passionately supported sports teams are fielded by public and private colleges and universities. Atlanta has major league teams in all four main American spectator sports, baseball, football, hockey, and basketball, but professional NFL football is also played in Charlotte, North Carolina, and Nashville, Tennessee. At the minor league level, Memphis has an enormous new downtown stadium for their Class AAA baseball team, the Redbirds; Nashville, Charlotte, and Louisville also have high-quality Class AAA baseball teams. Baseball season runs from April to September, football from September through January, and basketball from winter through mid-spring.

In other sports, the **Kentucky Derby** in early May draws hundreds of thousands of horse-racing fans from all over the world.

Golf fans flock to Augusta, Georgia to watch the Masters tournament in April. **NASCAR** stock car races are the region's most popular attractions, drawing more than 200,000 people to weekly races at Atlanta, Bristol, Concord, Rockingham, and Darlington.

Numerous state parks provide opportunities for camping, boating, fishing, and hiking. The coastal states of the Southeast are known to excel in beach activities.

ENTERTAINMENT

The birthplace of the blues, rock 'n' roll, and country-western music, the Southeast is a great place to enjoy live music. Hundreds of events take place all over the region almost every night. Besides the various nightclubs hosting talented musicians, the major entertainment venues of the region include the legendary **Grand Old Opry** in Nashville and **B.B. King's Blues Club** in Memphis.

DIRECTORY

TOURIST OFFICES

Georgia
Tel (800) 847-4842.
www.exploregeorgia.org

Kentucky
Tel (800) 225-8747.
www.kentuckytourism.com

North Carolina
Tel (800) 847-4862.
www.visitnc.com

South Carolina
Tel (800) 872-3505.
www.discoversouthcarolina.com

Tennessee
Tel ((800) 462-8366.
www.tnvacation.com

TRAVEL

Amtrak
Tel (800) 872-7245.
www.amtrak.com

Greyhound
Tel (800) 231-2222.

PARKS & OUTDOOR INFORMATION

Georgia
205 SE Butler St, Atlanta.
Tel (800) 864-7275.
www.gastateparks.org

Kentucky
2200 Capital Plaza Tower, Frankfort.
Tel (800) 255-7275.
www.kystateparks.com

North Carolina
1615 Mail Service Center, Raleigh.
Tel (919) 733-4181.
www.ncsparks.net

South Carolina
1205 Pendleton St, Columbia.
Tel (803) 734-0159.
www.southcarolinaparks.com

Tennessee
401 Church St, Nashville.
Tel (615) 532-0001, (800) 421-6683.
www.tnstateparks.com

Kentucky Derby
Tel (800) 928-3378.
www.kdf.org

NASCAR
www.nascar.com

Atlanta Falcons
Tel (404) 223-8000.
www.atlantafalcons.com

Carolina Panthers
Tel (704) 358-7000.
www.panthers.com

Tennessee Titans
Tel (615) 565-4000.
www.titansonline.com

ENTERTAINMENT

B.B. King's Blues Club
143 Beale St, Memphis, Tennessee.
Tel (901) 524-5464.

Grand Old Opry
Nashville, Tennessee.
Tel (615) 889-3060.

Choosing a Hotel

One of the best ways to sample Southern hospitality is to stay in one of the Southeast's many distinctive hotels. Larger cities such as Atlanta offer the widest range of lodging choices, while hideaways can readily be found along the Atlantic shore. National chains offer affordable rooms, designed to be most convenient to motorists.

PRICE CATEGORIES
For a standard double room per night, including service charges and any additional taxes.

$ Under $100
$$ $100–$150
$$$ $150–$200
$$$$ $200–$300
$$$$$ Over $300

NORTH CAROLINA

ASHEVILLE Cedar Crest Victorian Inn $$$

674 Biltmore Ave, 28803 ***Tel*** *(828) 252-1389, (877) 251-1389* ***Fax*** *(828) 253-7667* ***Rooms*** *12*

Set on four acres of lovely grounds, this Queen Anne-style mansion offers luxurious and spacious guestrooms that are individually decorated with period furnishings. Seasonal hot breakfast and personalized service. Conveniently located half a mile south of downtown Asheville and four miles from the Blue Ridge Parkway. **www.cedarcrestvictorianinn.com**

ASHEVILLE Inn on Biltmore Estate $$$$$

1 Antler Hill Rd, 28803 ***Tel*** *(800) 411-3812, (828) 225-1600* ***Rooms*** *213*

This seven-story hotel located on the 8,000-acre (3237-ha) grounds of the Biltmore Estate offers elegant and luxurious accommodations. There are leisure activities for the entire family, including hiking, cycling, and cooking classes. The restaurant serves food and wine sourced straight from the estate. **www.biltmore.com**

BEAUFORT Beaufort Inn $$$

101 Ann St, 28516 ***Tel*** *(252) 728-2600, (800) 726-0321* ***Fax*** *(252) 728-1864* ***Rooms*** *44*

Overlooking the Gallants Channel, this small hotel is located within walking distance of the Maritime Museum and the waterfront area of Beaufort. The cozy wood-paneled lobby offers comfortable seating around the fireplace. The guestrooms are spacious, there is an outdoor hot tub, and complimentary breakfast. **www.beaufort-inn.com**

CHAPEL HILL Carolina Inn $$$$

211 Pittsboro St, 27516 ***Tel*** *(919) 933-2001, (800) 962-8519* ***Fax*** *(919) 962-3400* ***Rooms*** *184*

Elegant, historic hotel with antique furnishings and modern conveniences, located in the heart of downtown Chapel Hill adjacent to the University of North Carolina. Spacious guestrooms with large windows and fine furnishings offer luxury bedding, work desk, and high-speed Internet. The four-star restaurant serves regional fare. **www.carolinainn.com**

DURHAM Homewood Suites by Hilton $$

3600 Mt Moriah Road, 27707 ***Tel*** *(919) 401-0610* ***Fax*** *(919) 401-2441* ***Rooms*** *96*

This small modern hotel is tastefully decorated in neutral colors with a pleasant lobby and eating area where a complimentary breakfast is served. Spacious guest suites offer comfortable homelike furnishings with full kitchen, workspace, separate bedroom, and a living room with sofa, recliner and television. **www.hilton.com**

MANTEO The Tranquil House Inn $$$

405 Queen Elizabeth St, 27954 ***Tel*** *(252) 473-1404* ***Fax*** *(252) 473-1526* ***Rooms*** *25*

A classic Outer Banks-styled inn, located on the waterfront of downtown Manteo and close to the beaches and Roanoke Island Festival Park. This charming inn has custom cypress woodwork and stained glass details. The guestrooms are individually decorated with hand-tiled baths, some featuring four-poster or canopied beds. **www.1587.com**

NAGS HEAD First Colony Inn $$$$

6720 S Virginia Dare Trail, 27959 ***Tel*** *(252) 441-2343, (800) 368-9390* ***Fax*** *(252) 441-9234* ***Rooms*** *26*

The beach is just across the street from this attractive inn with spacious grounds, broad verandas, library, and swimming pool. The cozy guestrooms vary in size and are decorated with period furnishings, neutral colors, and comfortable chairs and couches. The breakfast buffet features a hot entrée. **www.firstcolonyinn.com**

OCRACOKE The Cove Bed & Breakfast $$$

21 Loop Rd, 27960 ***Tel*** *(252) 928-4192* ***Fax*** *(252) 928-4092* ***Rooms*** *6*

Charming and comfortable, this Outer Banks-styled B&B is located in a quiet residential neighborhood close to the lighthouse. The modest rooms are individually decorated and feature private balconies. Home-cooked breakfasts and evening wine and cheese reception for guests. Bicycles are provided to cycle into Ocracoke. **www.thecovebb.com**

RALEIGH Holiday Inn Raleigh – North $

2805 Highwoods Blvd, 27604 ***Tel*** *(919) 872-3500* ***Fax*** *(919) 863-3880* ***Rooms*** *130*

This modern six-story hotel is conveniently located near the I-440, the main highway around the city. Guestrooms are spacious, comfortable, and well-appointed, with dual phone lines and high-speed Internet access. There is an exercise room and large seasonal outdoor swimming pool. **www.ichotelsgroup.com**

Key to Symbols *see back cover flap*

SOUTH CAROLINA

COASTAL ISLANDS Palm Key $$$

330 Coosaw Way, 29936 **Tel** *(843) 726-6468* **Fax** *(843) 726-5030* **Rooms** *50*

Comfortable family cottages in a spectacular natural setting offer full kitchens and large porches with exceptional marsh or pond views. There is access to walking paths, bird watching, and kayaking, and the location is convenient for exploring the Coastal Islands, Beaufort, Hilton Head Island, and Hunting Island State Park. **www.palmkey.com**

CHARLESTON Indigo Inn $$$

1 Maiden Lane, 29401 **Tel** *(843) 577-5900, (800) 845-7639* **Fax** *(843) 577-0378* **Rooms** *40*

Located in the historical district, this charming luxury inn is close to the major attractions, fine restaurants, and shops. Each guestroom is individually decorated with period antique furnishings, modern baths, and many rooms have views into the tranquil central courtyard. Full Hunt breakfast and wine and cheese served each afternoon. **www.indigoinn.com**

CHARLESTON The Inn at Middleton Place $$$$

4290 Ashley River Rd, 29414 **Tel** *(843) 556-0500, (800) 543-4774* **Fax** *(843) 556-5673* **Rooms** *43*

Award-winning contemporary design, gracious accommodations, and a setting amid natural beauty are the hallmarks of this elegant inn adjoining the well-known 18th-century Middleton Place Plantation. Guestrooms feature floor-to-ceiling windows, hardwood floors with braided rugs, and wood-burning fires. **www.theinnatmiddletonplace.com**

CHARLESTON Charleston Place $$$$$

205 Meeting St, 29401 **Tel** *(843) 722-4900, (888) 635-2350* **Fax** *(843) 722-0728* **Rooms** *442*

Elegantly furnished luxury hotel located in Charleston's historic district close to restaurants, shops, and attractions. The comfortable guestrooms are tastefully decorated with fine period reproduction furnishings and marble baths. Amenities include boutique shops, several restaurants, and a spa and health club. **www.charlestonplacehotel.com**

COLUMBIA Columbia Marriott $$$

1200 Hampton St, 29201 **Tel** *(803) 771-7000, (800) 880-1885* **Fax** *(803) 254-2911* **Rooms** *300*

Centrally located in the heart of downtown, this 15-story high-rise hotel provides comfortable modern guestrooms with modern furniture, work desks, and elegant bedding. There is also a well-equipped fitness facility, swimming pool, valet parking, retail shops, sports bar, and fine dining. **www.marriottcolumbia.com**

MYRTLE BEACH The Breakers $$

2701 N Ocean Blvd, 29577 **Tel** *(843) 444-4444, (800) 952-4507* **Fax** *(843) 626-5001* **Rooms** *141*

Located on the beach, this 19-story family-friendly high-rise resort hotel is close to restaurants and attractions. Guests have access to three separate pools: a lazy river pool, an outdoor pool, or an indoor pool. There are Jacuzzi tubs and a bar that overlooks the ocean and the legendary beaches. **www.breakers.com**

GEORGIA

AMERICUS Americus Garden Inn Bed & Breakfast $$

504 Rees Park, 31709 **Tel** *(229) 931-0122, (888) 758-4749* **Rooms** *8*

This grand mansion was built in 1847. Located in a residential area a mile from the downtown historic district, the inn boasts broad verandas and an acre of lawn. Each of the large guestrooms is individually decorated, and some rooms have Jacuzzi tubs or private balconies. **www.americusgardeninn.com**

AMICALOLA FALLS Amicalola Falls State Park Lodge $$

418 Amicalola Falls State Park Rd, Hwy 52, 30534 **Tel** *(706) 265-8888* **Rooms** *57*

Surrounded by the Chattahoochee National Forest with stunning views of the Smoky Mountains, this lovely modern lodge is very popular with individuals and families. The 729-foot falls are within walking distance of the lodge, and the park offers many scenic walking trails. Hearty country meals are served in the restaurant. **www.gastateparks.org**

ATLANTA Omni Hotel at CNN Center $$$

100 CNN Center, 30303 **Tel** *(404) 659-0000* **Fax** *(404) 525-5050* **Rooms** *1067*

This 15-story hotel set on four acres within the CNN Center Complex offers travelers a great location close to Peachtree Street, the aquarium, museums, and other attractions. Large guestrooms feature cherry furnishings, marble and granite baths, and views of the city, atrium, or Centennial Olympic Park. **www.omnihotels.com**

ATLANTA Four Seasons Hotel $$$$$

75 14th St, 30309 **Tel** *(404) 881-9898, (800) 819-5053* **Fax** *(404) 873-4692* **Rooms** *244*

This stunning marble-and-granite, mid-town, high-rise hotel is known for impeccable service and for providing every conceivable modern amenity. The impressive lobby features a grand staircase in red Spanish marble. The Park 75 restaurant offers fine dining, and the guestrooms are large and comfortable. **www.fourseasons.com/atlanta/**

ATLANTA Westin Buckhead $$$$$

3391 Peachtree Rd, NE ***Tel*** *(404) 365-0065, (800) 937-8461* ***Fax*** *(404) 365-8787* ***Rooms*** *365*

A contemporary design with curved white-tile exterior sets the tone for this sleek, modern, and ultra-comfortable hotel. The interior spaces are decorated in a minimalist style with original contemporary paintings by renowned artists. Rooms provide spacious comfort with Westin's Heavenly Beds and marble bathrooms. **www.starwoodhotels.com/westin/**

DAHLONEGA Smith House $$

84 S Chestatee St, 30533 ***Tel*** *(706) 867-7000, (800) 852-9577* ***Fax*** *(706) 864-7564* ***Rooms*** *18*

Originally built in 1884, this charming inn stands atop a former gold mine. The cozy guestrooms are tastefully decorated with country-elegant furnishings. The renowned restaurant serves heaping platters of home-cooked Southern-style comfort food, and the inn is just a short walk from the town square. **www.smithhouse.com**

JEKYLL ISLAND The Beachview Club $$$

721 N Beachview Dr, 31527 ***Tel*** *(912) 635-2256, (800) 299-2228* ***Fax*** *(912) 635-3770* ***Rooms*** *37*

Miles of sandy beach, great old oak trees on well-kept grounds, and a location close to the historic district are highlights of this hotel. The guestrooms are an excercise in understated elegance, with small kitchenettes and many with ocean views. A great place to relax in the casual ambience of Jekyll Island. **www.beachviewclub.com**

MACON 1842 Inn $$$$

353 College St, 31201 ***Tel*** *(478) 741-1842, (877) 452-6599* ***Fax*** *(478) 741-1842* ***Rooms*** *19*

This gracious, Greek Revival inn with broad verandas and attractive grounds offers guests luxury and Southern hospitality in a relaxed country setting. The appealing guestrooms are furnished with English antiques and oriental carpets. Enjoy a full American breakfast served in the lovely courtyard, in the parlor, or in your room. **www.1842inn.com**

ST. SIMONS Epworth by the Sea $

100 Arthur J Moore Dr, 31522 ***Tel*** *(912) 638-8688* ***Fax*** *(912) 634-0642* ***Rooms*** *900*

This Methodist Conference and Retreat Center welcomes families and individuals on vacation. Located on the Frederica River, the lovely grounds have a swimming pool, tennis courts, and playgrounds. The accommodations are clean and modest; more upscale rooms are available for an extra charge. The service is excellent. **www.epworthbythesea.org**

SAVANNAH Mulberry Inn $$

601 E Bay St, 31401 ***Tel*** *(912) 238-1200, (877) 468-1200* ***Fax*** *(912) 236-2184* ***Rooms*** *145*

A charming boutique hotel located at Washington Square and housed in a c.1868 cotton warehouse. Southern elegance and period furnishings, art, and ornate details are an important part of the decor throughout. Afternoon tea features dessert and coffee accompanied by live piano music. **www.savannahhotel.com**

SAVANNAH River Street Inn $$$

124 E Bay St, 31401 ***Tel*** *(912) 234-6400, (800) 253-4229* ***Fax*** *(912) 234-1478* ***Rooms*** *86*

Located in the Landmark Historic District on the riverfront, this intimate hotel has rooms furnished in a variety of styles, from four-poster iron beds and hardwood floors to floor-length windows and private balconies. It's convenient to all of old Savannah, with cruise departures and a trolley stop right outside the front door. **www.riverstreetinn.com**

SAVANNAH Kehoe House $$$$$

123 Habersham St, 31401 ***Tel*** *(912) 232-1020, (800) 820-1020* ***Fax*** *(912) 231-0208* ***Rooms*** *13*

Elegant and historic, this refined boutique hotel housed in an exquisitely restored 1892 Renaissance Revival mansion is located in the historic district overlooking Columbia Square. Each of the guestrooms has antique furnishings, European linens, and wireless Internet. Afternoon tea and evening wine with hors d'oeuvres. **www.kehoehouse.com**

TENNESSEE

CHATTANOOGA Chattanooga Choo Choo Holiday Inn $$

1400 Market St, 37402 ***Tel*** *(423) 266-5000, (800) 872-2529* ***Fax*** *(423) 265-4635* ***Rooms*** *363*

Train enthusiasts and families find that the railroad history, decor, and activities make up for the modest, somewhat dated accommodations at this hotel. Arcades, model railroad museum, old-time portraits, shops, fish ponds, and gardens are just some of the activities on offer. Frequent shuttle service into downtown. **www.choochoo.com**

CHATTANOOGA Sheraton Read House Hotel $$$

827 Broad St, 37402 ***Tel*** *(423) 266-4121, (800) 937-8461* ***Fax*** *(423) 643-1294* ***Rooms*** *243*

This recently renovated, Georgian-style hotel creatively blends historic architecture with modern conveniences and contemporary decor. The grand lobby has marble floors, wood paneling, and relaxing seating areas and the guestrooms are comfortable. Free shuttle route to Chatanooga attractions. **www.starwoodhotels.com/sheraton**

GATLINBURG Carr's Northside Cottages & Motel $

421 Laurel Road W, 37738 ***Tel*** *(865) 436-4836, (800) 370-5593* ***Rooms*** *40*

Located on the river just a short walk from downtown Gatlinburg, the accommodations here are family-friendly. The grounds are park-like and include a picnic area and playground. The rooms range from simple, hotel-style accommodations to Jacuzzi suites and elegant cottages. **www.carrscottages.com**

Key to Price Guide *see p274* **Key to Symbols** *see back cover flap*

GATLINBURG Buckhorn Inn $$

2140 Tudor Mountain Rd, 37738 ***Tel*** *(865) 436-4668, (866) 941-0460* ***Fax*** *(865) 436-5009* ***Rooms*** *19*

Just a mile from the Great Smoky Mountains National Park entrance, this classic 1938 mountain lodge offers upscale accommodations with stunning views of the mountains and 25 acres of surrounding forest and meadow. There are rocking chairs on the porch, a huge stone fireplace in the common room, and hearty breakfasts. **www.buckhorninn.com**

GREAT SMOKY MOUNTAINS NATIONAL PARK Mt. Leconte Lodge $$$$

250 Apple Valley Rd, 37862 ***Tel*** *(865) 429-5704* ***Fax*** *(865) 774-0045* ***Rooms*** *50*

Rustic backcountry lodge only accessible by a 5-mile hike up one of the National Park's highest peaks. The cabins have no electricity, no showers, shared hot water faucet, flush toilets, kerosene lamps, propane heaters, and wooden bunks. Southern country-style meals are served. Reservations essential. Open late-Mar–mid-Nov. **www.leconte-lodge.com**

MEMPHIS Elvis Presley's Heartbreak Hotel $$

3677 Elvis Presley Blvd, 38116 ***Tel*** *(901) 332-1000, (877) 777-0606* ***Fax*** *(901) 332-2107* ***Rooms*** *128*

Elvis would have loved this kitschy small hotel with over-the-top 1950s-styled furniture and decor throughout. The spacious guestrooms, each with a kitchenette, are decorated with gold-flecked blue carpets, blond-wood furnishings, and blue harlequin bedspreads. Elvis videos play on the inhouse TV channel. **www.elvis.com/epheartbreakhotel/**

MEMPHIS Peabody Hotel $$$$

149 Union Ave, 38103 ***Tel*** *(901) 529-4000* ***Fax*** *(901) 529-3600* ***Rooms*** *464*

The twice-daily march of the ducks on a red carpet through the lobby is the entertainment highlight at this historic downtown hotel, known as the South's Grand Hotel. The remodeled guestrooms are spacious and luxurious, using a subtle blend of neutral colors, fine furnishings, and fabrics. **www.peabodymemphis.com**

NASHVILLE Union Station Hotel $$$

1001 Broadway, 37203 ***Tel*** *(615) 726-1001* ***Fax*** *(615) 248-3554* ***Rooms*** *125*

The dramatic barrel-vaulted lobby with stained glass and bas-relief sculptures was the main hall of Nashville's 1900s train station. This elegant hotel takes maximum advantage of the unique architectural charm of each guestroom, adding contemporary decor, high-speed Internet, and marble bathrooms. **www.unionstationhotelnashville.com**

KENTUCKY

BARDSTOWN Rosemark Haven $$

714 N Third St, 40004 ***Tel*** *(502) 348-8218, (888) 420-9703* ***Rooms*** *7*

A gracious Southern brick mansion with a three-story oval spiral staircase, high ceilings, antique furnishings, and wood floors. Individually decorated guestrooms, some with fireplaces or whirlpool tubs. The inn is lovely, the breakfast is delicious, and there is an Italian restaurant and wine bar on-site for dinner. **www.rosemarkhaven.com**

BEREA Boone Tavern Hotel $$

100 Main St, 40404 ***Tel*** *(859) 985-3700, (800) 366-9358* ***Fax*** *(859) 985-3715* ***Rooms*** *58*

This historic small hotel located on College Square adjacent to Berea College opened in 1909 to house college visitors. Still owned by the college, many of the staff members are student interns. The modern guestrooms are decorated with reproduction hand-crafted furnishings made by the college woodcraft department. **www.boonetavernhotel.com**

LEXINGTON SpringHill Suites Lexington $$

863 S Broadway, 40508 ***Tel*** *(859) 225-1500* ***Fax*** *(859) 225-1534* ***Rooms*** *108*

Attractive and stylish, this Marriott all-suites hotel is adjacent to the Red Mile Harness Race Track and just a short distance from downtown. The spacious suites are well laid out and provide a mini-refrigerator, microwave, and high-speed Internet access, as well as comfortable beds, chairs, and sofa, and pleasant decor. **www.marriott.com**

LEXINGTON Gratz Park Inn $$$

120 W Second St, 40507 ***Tel*** *(859) 231-1777, (800) 752-4166* ***Fax*** *(859) 233-7593* ***Rooms*** *44*

This intimate historic hotel housed in a 1906 brick building features antique reproduction mahogany furnishings, hardwood floors, and regional artwork. The guestrooms offer modern comforts with a harmonious blend of antique-reproduction furnishings, luxury bedding, and high-speed wireless Internet access. **www.gratzparkinn.com**

LOUISVILLE Rocking Horse Manor B&B $$

1022 S Third St, 40203 ***Tel*** *(502) 583-0408, (888) 467-7322* ***Fax*** *(502) 583-6408* ***Rooms*** *6*

Built in 1888, this Richardsonian Romanesque mansion is decorated in formal Victorian style with dark wood paneling and furnishings throughout the common areas. Each room is decorated with great attention to detail, with themes such as "country cottage" or "grand Victorian", with a four-poster bed and fireplace. **www.rockinghorse-bb.com**

LOUISVILLE Seelbach Hilton $$$

500 4th St, 40202 ***Tel*** *(502) 585-3200* ***Fax*** *(502) 585-9239* ***Rooms*** *321*

This opulent and historic hotel was built in 1905 and is decorated with imported marble, fine woodwork, and art from around the world. Many famous figures have stayed here, including nine Presidents, F. Scott Fitzgerald (who references the hotel in his book *The Great Gatsby*), and gangster Al Capone. **www.seelbachhilton.com**

Choosing a Restaurant

Traditional Southern food is affordable across the region. A typical country meal includes meat, bread, and two or three vegetables, washed down by sweet iced tea, and topped off by banana pudding. Innovators are now creating new dishes with local ingredients. There are plenty of family-friendly, relaxed restaurants.

PRICE CATEGORIES
For a three-course meal for one, including a glass of house wine (where served), and all other unavoidable charges such as sales tax.
$ Under $30
$$ $30–$40
$$$ $40–$50
$$$$ $50–$60
$$$$$ Over $60

NORTH CAROLINA

ASHEVILLE Tupelo Honey $

12 College St, 28801 ***Tel*** *(828) 255-4863*

This restaurant is charming and upscale yet casual, with homey decor featuring hanging plants, photographs on the walls, and small, linen-covered tables on hardwood floors. Creative twists embellish old Southern favorites, with healthier versions of classic comfort foods prepared with fresh local ingredients and organic foods. Closed Monday.

ASHEVILLE Zambras Tapas $$

85 W Walnut St, 28801 ***Tel*** *(828) 232-1060*

The flavors of Spain, Portugal, and North Africa are presented at this contemporary restaurant and tapas bar. The festive atmosphere is casual and relaxed, with floor pillows as well as formal tables. Menu choices include traditional entrees, seafood, vegetarian paellas, and pan-fried trout. Spanish and Portugese wines are available.

BEAUFORT Clawson's 1905 Restaurant & Pub $$

425 Front St, 28516 ***Tel*** *(252) 728-2133*

This popular restaurant and pub on the historic waterfront is housed in an early 1900s grocery store and the five-and-dime next door. The wood floors and brick walls are decorated with American memorabilia. The menu features large combination platters of seafood, ribs, steak, pork, and chicken, with North Carolina micro-brews and wine.

CHAPEL HILL Mama Dip's $$

408 W Rosemary St, 27516 ***Tel*** *(919) 942-5837*

Traditional Southern cooking is served up in this spacious but plain restaurant and the menus for breakfast, lunch, and dinner are extensive. Some of the favorites, which are also available for take-out, are Catfish gumbo and Brunswick stew made with chicken and butter beans. Banana pudding, cobbler, and pie are dessert choices.

DURHAM Magnolia Grill $$$

1002 9th St, 27705 ***Tel*** *(919) 286-3609*

A casual restaurant with wood floors, local art on the walls, and an open kitchen. The menu changes frequently and features fresh regional ingredients in sometimes spicy and complex entrées influenced by many cultures. Favorites include Charcoaled Hoisin-Marinated Angus Sirloin with Spicy Peanut Sauce. Closed Sunday and Monday.

MANTEO 1587 Restaurant $$$$

405 Queen Elizabeth St, 27954 ***Tel*** *(252) 473-1587*

Set within the Tranquil House Inn, 1587 is elegant yet relaxed, with large windows that offer views across the bay. The menu changes seasonally and takes full advantage of the fresh foods and herbs grown in the restaurant's garden. Atlantic seafood, meats, and fowl are complemented by an extensive wine list.

NAGS HEAD Sam & Omie's $$

7228 S Virginia Dare Trail, Milepost 16.5, 27959 ***Tel*** *(252) 441-7366*

Sam & Omies has been a downhome local place for more than 70 years. It started as a place for fishermen to have a hearty breakfast and now serves lunch and dinner as well. Casual and funky, with lots of seaside flavor and a friendly bar, standard fare includes local seafood and prime rib, burgers, and club sandwiches. Closed Dec–Feb.

OCRACOKE Howard's Pub & Raw Bar $$

1175 Irvin H Garris Hwy, 27960 ***Tel*** *(252) 928-4441*

The atmosphere here is laid-back and family-friendly, and the food is fresh and made to order. Burgers are hand-shaped, and the oysters and clams are never shucked till you place your order. Choose from over 200 micro-brewed, imported, or domestic beers, and sit back and watch the ocean. Live music some nights. Closed Jan–early Mar.

RALEIGH Sawasdee Thai Restaurant $

3601 Capital Blvd 107, 27604 ***Tel*** *(919) 878-0049*

The modest exterior of this excellent Thai restaurant conceals an eclectic interior with tangerine walls and homey decor. The authentic food is fresh and flavorful, and can be ordered mild or spicy hot. The standard offerings are on the menu, but the house specials such as Sizzling Spinach Beef and Kra Paw Catfish are especially savory.

Key to Symbols *see back cover flap*

SOUTH CAROLINA

BEAUFORT Plum's Café $

904 Bay St, 29902 ***Tel*** *(843) 525-1946*

Small and cozy, this popular casual restaurant, with tables out on the porch, has great views across the park to the waterfront. The menu features salads, soups, and creative sandwiches. The shrimp is fresh, the lamb is tasty, and favorites include chicken salad and pastas. After your meal walk across the park and sit in a waterfront bench swing.

CHARLESTON Basil $

460 King St, 29403 ***Tel*** *(843) 724-3490*

Upscale Thai cuisine draws the crowds to this popular restaurant. Seating is at tables or at the bar with views into the open kitchen where the talented chefs turn fresh ingredients into Nouveau-Asian entrées featuring mild or spicy beef, pork, shrimp, and tofu as well as curries, stir-fries, and noodle dishes. The portions are large here.

CHARLESTON Hominy Grill $

207 Rutledge Ave, 29403 ***Tel*** *(843) 937-0930*

This Charleston classic is famous for its Southern cooking prepared with the freshest local ingredients by skilled chefs. The casual dining room is housed in a charming old building. Entrées include comfort foods and Southern favorites such as fried chicken, shrimp creole, fresh vegetables, cheese grits, and outstanding desserts such as buttermilk pie.

CHARLESTON Magnolia's $$$$

185 E Bay St, 29401 ***Tel*** *(843) 577-7771*

This restaurant is in an old building with pine floors and walls decorated with wrought-iron magnolias and magnolia paintings. Service and attention to detail is excellent, and the menu features classic Southern dishes such as fried green tomatoes, cheese grits, rich bouillabaisse, pecan-encrusted flounder and rich desserts like Mocha Crème Brulée.

COLUMBIA Al's Upstairs Italian Restaurant $$

304 Meeting St, West Columbia, 29169 ***Tel*** *(803) 794-7404*

Elegant and romantic, Al's is located on the second floor of a hundred-year-old building with a window-lined dining room that offers stunning views of the Columbia skyline. Entrées feature fresh Atlantic seafood, hand-cut steaks, traditional veal and chicken Italian specialties, innovative pasta dishes, and desserts from the kitchen.

COLUMBIA Blue Marlin $$

1200 Lincoln St, 29201 ***Tel*** *(803) 799-3838*

Low Country cuisine is the specialty here, with an emphasis on seafood and hand-cut steaks. The inviting dining room features tables and booths in a converted train station, with wood detailing and the original ceiling. Shrimp and grits are popular, or sample the innovative house specialties such as a skillet of Oysters Bienville or Firecracker Flounder.

HILTON HEAD Charlie's L'Etoile Verte $$$

8 New Orleans Rd, 29928 ***Tel*** *(843) 785-9277*

One of the best restaurants on Hilton Head, Charlie's is charming and elegant with an eclectic country French atmosphere. The daily menu offers the freshest seafood, meats, and produce made into innovative and memorable entrées. The service is attentive, wine list extensive, and desserts superb. Reservations suggested. Closed Sunday.

MURRELLS INLET Capt. Dave's Dockside $$$

4037 Hwy 17 Business #A, 29576 ***Tel*** *(843) 651-5850*

This popular dockside restaurant on the waterfront overlooking Murrells Inlet has re-opened in a new two-story building that is casually elegant. The modern decor features wood flooring, a gleaming display kitchen with natural lump charcoal grill, and large windows offering superb views of the inlet. The menu features fresh seafood and beef.

GEORGIA

ATHENS Last Resort Grill $$

184 W Clayton St, 30601 ***Tel*** *(706) 549-0810*

New Southern cuisine is served in a casual and friendly atmosphere in this downtown restaurant that attracts a young crowd. The historic building features local art on the walls, and seating is in booths or outdoors in the courtyard. Southwestern-influenced entrées include salmon and grits as well as Adobo Salmon and Firecracker Filet.

ATLANTA La Grotta Ristorante Italiano $$

2637 Peachtree Rd NE, 30305 ***Tel*** *(404) 231-1368*

One of Atlanta's best Italian restaurants offers fine Northern Italian cuisine in a sophisticated and intimate environment. The menu is extensive, featuring exquisitely prepared seafood, beef, veal, and chicken entrées and fresh pasta choices. The desserts are decadent and the wine list is extensive. Closed Sunday.

ATLANTA Atlanta Grill at the Ritz Carlton $$$

181 Peachtree St, NE, 30303 ***Tel*** *(404) 659-0400*

This elegant restaurant with a warm, club feel is decorated with large murals and offers outdoor seating on a veranda with wrought-iron railings and flickering gas-lamp-style lighting. Grilled steaks, chops, and seafood, Southern-inspired dishes, and one of the city's best bars with an extensive wine list make this a choice place for dinner.

ATLANTA Bone's $$$$$

3130 Piedmont Rd NE, 30305 ***Tel*** *(404) 237-2663*

The best steakhouse in Atlanta and one of the best in the US, Bone's has provided outstanding service since it opened in 1979. Prime, aged, corn-fed Iowa beef, fresh seafood, and Maine lobster are the mainstays here, with regional side dishes, an impressive wine list, and decadent desserts. This restaurant is a favorite with the business crowd.

DAHLONEGA Wylie's Restaurant on the Square $$

19 North Chestatee St, 30533 ***Tel*** *(706) 867-6324*

This delightful three-floor restaurant and pub on the Square features hand-trimmed Black Angus steaks, as well as a variety of pasta and seafood. The main floor dining room is casual, with a relaxed atmosphere and small tables. The upstairs dining room is spacious and the basement pub features a full bar and live music Friday and Saturday nights.

JEKYLL ISLAND Grand Dining Room $$$$$

371 Riverview Dr, 31527 ***Tel*** *(912) 635-2400*

In keeping with the island's priveledged history, the Grand Dining Room is formal and elegantly decorated in Victorian style with columns, high-backed chairs, fireplaces, and sparkling crystal on fine linen tablecloths. Gentlemen must wear jackets. The Continental menu features cherry-smoked breast of duck and jerk-seared jumbo scallops with apple chutney.

MACON The Back Burner Restaurant $$

2242 Ingleside Ave, 31204 ***Tel*** *(478) 746-3336*

This cheerful, well-run French Country restaurant is set in a charming cottage with tables in small individually decorated rooms. The menu changes, with entrées such as Chilean halibut in a champagne and shallot sauce or rack of lamb in a Dijon thyme sauce. The desserts are decadent and there is a small wine list. Closed Sunday and Monday.

ST. SIMONS Crabdaddy's $$$

1219 Ocean Blvd, 31522 ***Tel*** *(912) 634-1120*

This popular seafood restaurant specializes in Southern hospitality and an extensive selection of fresh fish. The offerings include locally caught fish as well as Pacific Salmon. All fish is served grilled, blackened, or steamed and comes with salad, bread, and choice of side dish. Daily specials, fried shrimp, crab cakes, and meat entrées are also available.

SAVANNAH Mrs. Wilkes' Dining Room $

107 W Jones St, 31401 ***Tel*** *(912) 232-5997*

Arrive early and expect long lines for lunch at Mrs. Wilkes'. Bottomless platters and bowls of good home-cooked food are passed around large tables, boarding-house style. The menu varies seasonally and day to day, but fried or barbeque chicken is a standard, along with a succession of tasty sides. Lunch only, closed Saturday and Sunday.

SAVANNAH Il Pasticcio $$$

2 E Broughton St, 31401 ***Tel*** *(912) 231-8888*

One of the best Italian restaurants in the Southeast is located in Savannah's downtown shopping district. Great food, great service, and great atmosphere come together here. The pasta is home-made with savory sauces, the seafood is fresh, and the veal and meat entrées impressive. Reservations recommended.

TYBEE ISLAND Crab Shack $

40 Estill Hammock Rd, 31328 ***Tel*** *(912) 786-9857*

This family-friendly seafood restaurant has a long and varied menu, with regional favorites like Low Country boil and steamed oysters as well as crab, shrimp, pork barbeque, hotdogs, and much more. This is a casual place where you can sit inside or under the live oak trees outside with a view of the marsh. There is even a gator lagoon out front.

TENNESSEE

CHATTANOOGA Mt. Vernon Restaurant $$

3535 Broad St, 37409 ***Tel*** *(423) 266-6591*

This casual downtown restaurant has served satisfied customers for over 50 years. The menu features traditional favorites such as Southern fried chicken, slow-roasted turkey, and fresh fried corn. Many entrées are healthy selections, prepared with olive oil. The Amaretto Cream Pie is a house specialty. Closed Sundays.

CHATTANOOGA 212 Market Restaurant $$$

212 Market St, 37402 ***Tel*** *(423) 265-1212*

This restaurant features creative takes on contemporary American cuisine. The menu changes frequently to take advantage of fresh local ingredients, with offerings such as wild pacific salmon with blackberry-pomegranate coulis, or parmesan-crusted lamb chops. The decor is warm, artistic, and modern, and the dining room has balcony seating.

Key to Price Guide *see p278* **Key to Symbols** *see back cover flap*

GATLINBURG Buckhorn Inn $$

2140 Tudor Mountain Rd, 37738 ***Tel*** *(865) 436-4668*

This elegant inn is set on a hilltop with mountain views. Dinner is fixed-price by reservation only, and the beautifully prepared and presented four-course meal might feature a main entrée of rainbow trout, prime rib, or pork chops. Soup, salad, and dessert round out the offering, and although no alcohol is served you may bring your own.

MEMPHIS Corky's BBQ $

5259 Poplar Ave, 38119 ***Tel*** *(901) 685-9744*

Some of the favorites at this traditional hickory-smoked barbeque include hand-pulled pork shoulder, dry rub ribs, and tangy sauced ribs, and there are plenty of great sides.This is the original location, and the walls are covered with pictures of the famous Memphis folk who have eaten here. The atmosphere is boisterous, fun, and family-friendly.

MEMPHIS Automatic Slims' Tonga Club $$$

83 S Second St, 38103 ***Tel*** *(901) 525-7948*

The spicy and exotic flavors and foods of the Caribbean and Southwest are served in this hip downtown restaurant, with an arty decor. Lusty entrées include seafood-based Voodoo Stew or Jamaican Jerk Duck. The short wine list pairs well with spicy food, or try one of the martinis. And for dessert don't miss the Bourbon pecan tart.

MEMPHIS Paulette's $$$$

2110 Madison Ave, 38104 ***Tel*** *(901) 726-5128*

Romantic and elegant, this midtown restaurant features fine Continental dining with a Tennessee twist. Housed in an old mansion and decorated with antiques and paintings, the service is excellent. Entrées include seafood crêpes and pork tenderloin with cherry sauce. The desserts are decadent too.

NASHVILLE Da Vinci's Gourmet Pizza $

1812 Hayes St, 37203 ***Tel*** *(615) 329-8098*

This gourmet pizza house is situated in a cozy yet modern 1920s cottage with tall windows and a homey feel. Simple yet sophisticated, the pizza choices range from traditional pepperoni and mushroom to signature pies such as Bella Vita with spinach, roma tomato, onion, garlic, feta, and provolone cheeses.

NASHVILLE F. Scott's $$$

2210 Crestmoor Rd, 37215 ***Tel*** *(615) 269-5861*

This sophisticated restaurant, with a relaxed neighborhood atmosphere and attentive service, serves fine Contemporary American cuisine. Entrées include porcini and tomato-rubbed chicken or veal scalopini with wild mushroom sauce. The menu changes seasonally. The wine list is extensive and there is jazz music nightly in the lounge. Closed Sunday.

NASHVILLE Capitol Grille $$$$$

231 6th Ave N, 37219 ***Tel*** *(888) 888-9414*

This elegant and charming restaurant in the Hermitage Hotel attracts the Nashville business, political, and theatre-going crowd for fine regional cuisine and attentive service. Black Angus beef and game, fresh seafood, and the best local produce available are crafted into creative Southern cuisine. Reservations are essential for the Sunday brunch.

KENTUCKY

BEREA Boone Tavern Restaurant $$$

100 Main St, 40404 ***Tel*** *(859) 985-3700*

This homey dining room is part of historic Boone Hall at Berea College. The menu selections include both traditional and creative Southern and American cuisine. This is fine dining, with tablecloths and friendly attentive service and a selection of meats, poultry, and seafood. Signature dishes include Chicken Flakes in a Birds Nest and decadent desserts.

LEXINGTON Jonathan at Gratz Park $$$$

120 W Second St, 40507 ***Tel*** *(859) 252-4949*

Upscale and refined, the elegant dining room at the Gratz Park Inn serves some of Lexington's finest cuisine. The menu offers regional entrees with a contemporary twist, including selections such as pepper-crusted grilled tuna or mushroom-dusted beef tenderloin. The service is excellent and the decor is pleasant and relaxing.

LOUISVILLE Lynn's Paradise Café $

984 Barrett Ave, 40204 ***Tel*** *(502) 583-3447*

Fun, creative, and unusual, this eatery is popular with locals and visitors alike. With a nod to diner style, the modern decor features bright walls and funky accessories. Huge platters of comfort food are served, including melt-in-your-mouth buttermilk biscuits and decadent desserts. A memorable experience. Closed Monday.

LOUISVILLE Lilly's $$$$

1147 Bardstown Rd, 40204 ***Tel*** *(502) 451-0447*

Creative and innovative cuisine and a welcoming atmosphere make this charming bistro popular with locals and travelers. Lilly's specializes in garden-fresh produce and an original menu that changes seasonally, with selections such as Baked Halibut in Bouillabaisse Broth and the signature God Bless Our Farmers Plate. Closed Sunday.

FLORIDA

INTRODUCING FLORIDA 284–289
MIAMI 290–299
THE GOLD & TREASURE COASTS 300–301
ORLANDO & THE SPACE COAST 302–313
THE NORTHEAST 314–315
THE PANHANDLE 316–317
THE GULF COAST 318–319
THE EVERGLADES & THE KEYS 320–323

MARLIN
1200

FLORIDA

For the majority of Florida's 40 million-plus annual visitors, the typical travel poster images of Florida – sun, sea, sand, and Mickey Mouse – are reason enough to jump on the next plane. The Sunshine State deserves its reputation as the perfect family vacation spot, but Florida is much richer in its culture, landscape, and character than its stereotypical image suggests.

Both climatically and culturally, Florida is a state divided – a bridge between temperate North America and tropical Latin America and the Caribbean. In the north, roads are lined with stately live oak trees and people speak with a southern drawl, while, in the south, shade from the subtropical sun is cast by palm trees, and the inhabitants of Miami are as likely to speak Spanish as English.

For most visitors, Florida's prime attractions lie along the coasts, where the beaches are varied and abundant enough to satisfy every visitor. However, great rewards await those who want to explore farther. The lush forests and rolling hills of the north provide some of the loveliest countryside in the state. Equally exciting are the so-called "wild areas," such as the Everglades, which harbor an extraordinary diversity of plant and animal life, and where alligators and snakes are living reminders of the inhospitable place that Florida was not much more than 100 years ago.

HISTORY

At first glance, Florida appears to be a state without history. Yet behind its modern veneer lies a long and rich past, molded by different nationalities and cultures. Until the 16th century, Florida supported a large indigenous population, whose complex political and religious systems demonstrated a high degree of social organization. However, colonization soon decimated the Indians through warfare and disease. In 1513, the Spanish explorer Juan Ponce de León discovered Florida and named it after Pascua Florida, the Feast of the Flowers

Deerfield Beach, a quiet coastal resort within easy reach of Boca Raton

◁ **The Marlin Hotel in Miami's South Beach, a classic establishment illuminated in colorful neon**

(Easter). For almost 200 years several Spanish conquistadors attempted unsuccessfully to search for gold and colonize the region. Their primary concern was Florida's strategic position. The Gulf Stream carried Spanish galleons laden with gold and treasure from the New World colonies past Florida's coast on their journey back across the Atlantic, and it was thus vital that "La Florida" not fall into enemy hands.

Henry Flagler, 1830–1913

Initially the French troubled the Spanish, but the real threat to their control came in 1742 when English colonists from Georgia defeated them and finally acquired Florida about 20 years later. Though Florida was returned to Spain in 1783, numerous boundary disputes followed. It was only after Andrew Jackson, the ambitious US general, captured Pensacola that the official US occupation took place in 1821. During this period, the plantation system was firmly established in north Florida. The principal cash crop was cotton, for which intensive slave labor was required to work in the fields.

KEY DATES IN HISTORY

1513 Ponce de León discovers "La Florida"

1563 Pedro Menéndez de Avilés founds St. Augustine after defeating the French

1763 Britain acquires Florida

1783 Britain returns Florida to the Spanish

1785–1821 Spanish-American border disputes

1821 Florida becomes part of the US; Andrew Jackson becomes the first American governor

1835–42 Second Seminole War

1845 Florida becomes the 27th state

1852 Harriet Beecher Stowe publishes the anti-slavery epic, *Uncle Tom's Cabin*

1853 Third Seminole War begins

1886 Henry Flagler starts construction of the Florida East Coast Railway

1958 *Explorer I* is launched after NASA chooses Cape Canaveral as the site of its space program

1959 Over 300,000 Cubans flee to Florida

1980 125,00 Cubans arrive in the Mariel boatlift

1992 Hurricane Andrew devastates south Florida

2000 George W. Bush appointed president after the Florida election debacle

2003 Space Shuttle *Columbia* explodes on re-entry and *Spirit*, a rover, heads for Mars

American attempts to subdue the Seminole Indians and take over their land led to over 65 years of conflict. When the Third Seminole War ended in 1858, the Indians retreated to the Everglades, where they still live. Soon after came the Civil War, by the end of which, in 1865, Florida was in ruins. But the state recovered rapidly. Railroad barons, such as Henry Flagler and Henry Plant, built a network of railroads and opulent hotels, which attracted wealthy visitors from the north. Tourism flourished in the early 20th century, and by 1950 it had become Florida's top industry. The launch of the NASA space program at Cape Canaveral in the 1950s also helped boost the state's prosperity.

SOCIETY & CULTURE

The state "where everyone is from somewhere else," Florida has always been a cultural hodgepodge. The earliest inhabitants were the Seminole Indians and the early pioneers of the 1800s, the Cracker farmers, named perhaps from the cracking of their cattle whips or the cracking of corn to make grits. However, both groups are rarely encountered along the affluent, heavily populated coast.

Americans have poured into this land of opportunity since World War II; the twentieth most populous state in the US in 1950, Florida is now ranked fourth. The largest single group to move south has been the retirees, for whom Florida's climate, lifestyle of leisure, and low tax rates, hold great appeal after a life of hard work. While

Space shuttle *Discovery* lifts off from the Kennedy Space Center, Cape Canaveral

Mural inside the US Federal Courthouse, Miami

super-rich communities like Palm Beach fit the conservative and staid image that some people still have of Florida, the reality is very different. An increasing number of the new arrivals are young people for whom Florida is a land of opportunity, a place to enjoy the good life. Today, the younger generation has helped turn Miami's South Beach into one of the country's trendiest resorts.

From 1959 on, there has also been massive immigration from Latin America; Dade County in particular has a huge Hispanic community. This ethnic diversity is today celebrated in an endless cycle of exuberant festivals, music, and local food.

ECONOMICS & TOURISM

Economically, Florida is not in bad shape compared with the rest of the country. For most of its history, its main source of revenue has been agriculture – citrus fruits, vegetables, sugar, and cattle, which was originally introduced by the Spanish colonists. In fact, Florida produces over 70 percent of the citrus fruits consumed in the United States today, while Kissimmee is known as the "cow capital" of the state. High-tech industry is significant as well, and the proximity of Miami to Latin America and the Caribbean has made it the natural route for trade with the region. This proximity has also contributed to the state's flourishing cruise industry. Florida's warm climate has also generated high-profile moneyspinners, such as car racing, and the Daytona International Speedway attracts thousands of visitors every year. Spring baseball training also draws teams and lots of fans south, while the fashion trade brings models by the dozen and plenty of glamour to Miami.

It is tourism, however, that fills the state's coffers. The Walt Disney World Resort may appear to dominate the industry, but Florida makes the most of all its assets. Its superb beaches and the promise of winter sunshine have lured millions of vacationers through the years. Beside beaches and theme parks, there are natural habitats, state-of-the-art musems, and towns, such as St. Augustine and Pensacola, that still retain their Spanish Colonial ambience.

Beach buggie, Daytona Beach

Conservation is a major issue in Florida today. After decades of intense urban development, Floridians have finally learned the importance of preserving their rich and varied natural heritage. Great swathes of the natural landscape have already disappeared beneath factories, condos, and cabbage fields, but those involved in industry and agriculture are acting more responsibly, and water use is now strictly monitored. Florida's natural treasures, from its freshwater swamps and hardwood forests to its last remaining panthers, are now protected for posterity.

A vibrant mural in Key West's Bahama Village

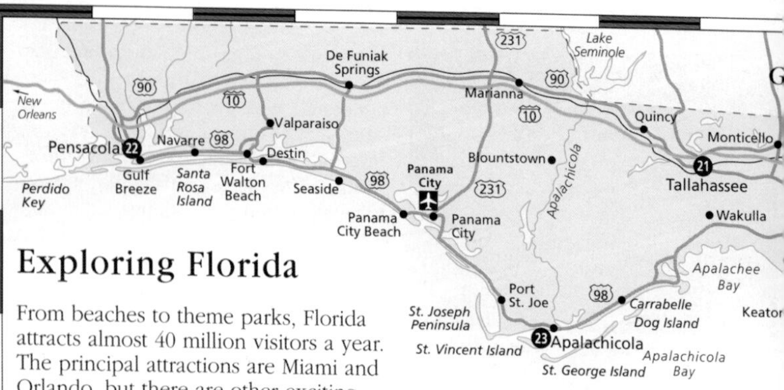

Exploring Florida

From beaches to theme parks, Florida attracts almost 40 million visitors a year. The principal attractions are Miami and Orlando, but there are other exciting destinations as well, such as St. Augustine and Pensacola, established by Spanish colonialists in the 16th century. For nature lovers, the Everglades is a thrilling experience, while the Keys offer a choice of activities, such as fishing, diving, and snorkeling. An extensive road network links the main towns, so traveling by car in Florida is both quick and enjoyable.

Art Deco motif, popular in Miami

SIGHTS AT A GLANCE

Miami pp290–99 ❶

The Gold & Treasure Coasts
Fort Lauderdale ❷
Boca Raton ❸
Loxahatchee National Wildlife Refuge ❹
Palm Beach ❺

Orlando & the Space Coast
Cocoa Beach ❻
Kennedy Space Center ❼
Canaveral National Seashore & Merritt Island ❽
Walt Disney World® Resort pp304–307 ❾
Universal Orlando pp308–309 ❿
SeaWorld Orlando & Discovery Cove pp310–11 ⓫
Orlando ⓬
Winter Park ⓭
International Drive ⓮
Kissimmee ⓯
Disney Wilderness Preserve ⓰

The Northeast
Daytona Beach ⓱
St. Augustine ⓲
Fernandina Beach ⓳
Ocala National Forest ⓴

The Panhandle
Tallahassee ㉑
Pensacola ㉒
Apalachicola ㉓

The Gulf Coast
Tampa ㉔
St. Petersburg ㉕
Sarasota p319 ㉖
Lee Island Coast ㉗

The Everglades & the Keys
Big Cypress Swamp ㉘
Everglades National Park ㉙
Biscayne National Park ㉚
The Keys ㉛
Key West ㉜

KEY

- Airport
- Cruise port
- Highway
- Major road
- Railroad
- State border

MILEAGE CHART

10 = Distance in miles
10 = Distance in kilometers

	MIAMI	PALM BEACH	ORLANDO	ST. AUGUSTINE	TALLAHASSEE	PENSACOLA	TAMPA	ST. PETERSBURG	SARASOTA
PALM BEACH	**70** 113								
ORLANDO	**237** 381	**171** 275							
ST. AUGUSTINE	**314** 505	**247** 398	**107** 172						
TALLAHASSEE	**504** 811	**438** 705	**257** 414	**205** 330					
PENSACOLA	**707** 1138	**642** 1033	**450** 724	**399** 642	**197** 317				
TAMPA	**279** 449	**200** 322	**84** 135	**190** 306	**274** 441	**468** 753			
ST. PETERSBURG	**262** 422	**228** 367	**106** 171	**212** 341	**299** 481	**490** 789	**24** 39		
SARASOTA	**230** 370	**195** 314	**131** 211	**236** 380	**333** 536	**520** 837	**60** 97	**35** 56	
KEY WEST	**161** 259	**233** 375	**394** 634	**478** 769	**641** 1032	**873** 1405	**426** 686	**410** 660	**376** 605

For additional map symbols *see back flap*

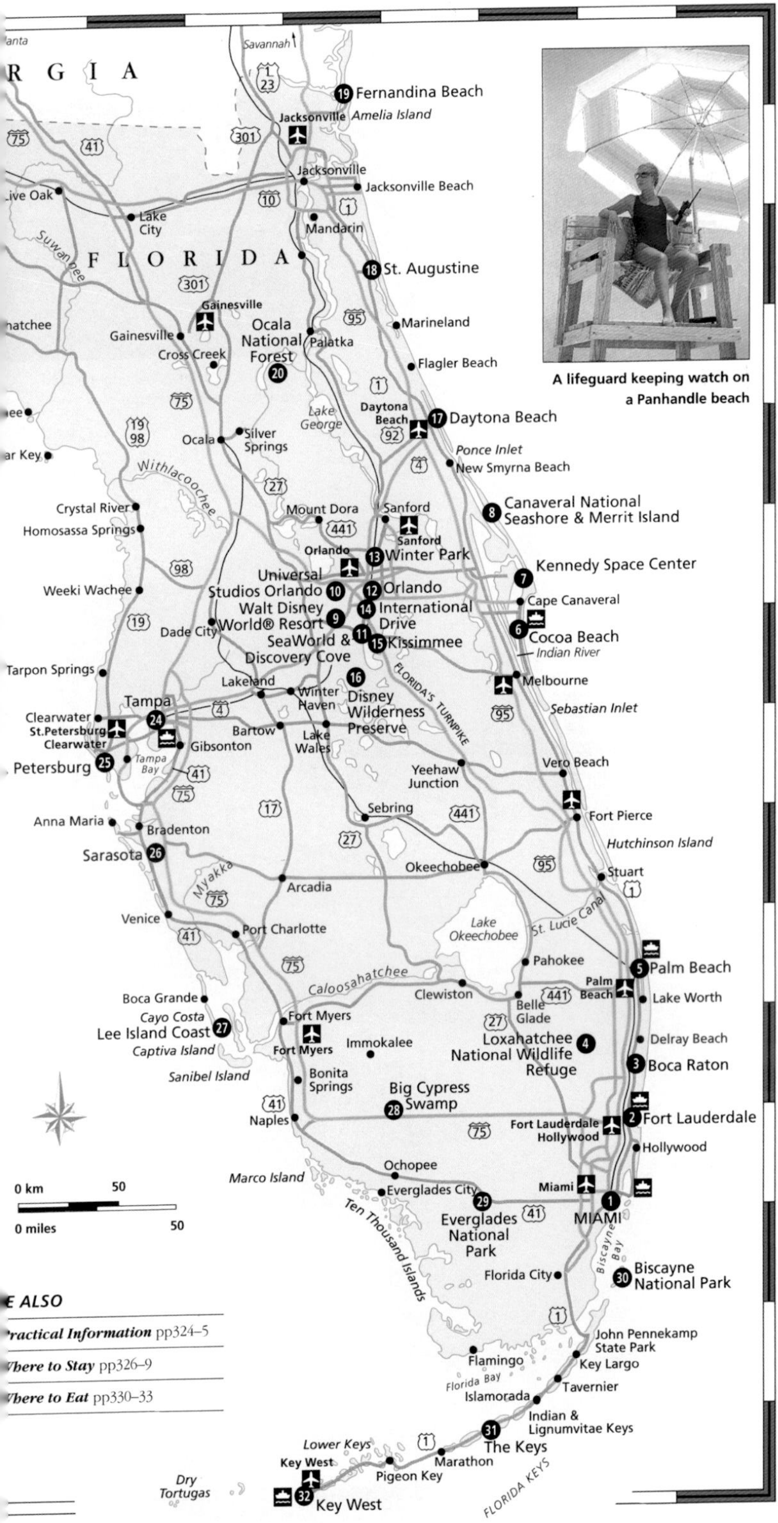

A lifeguard keeping watch on a Panhandle beach

E ALSO

ractical Information pp324–5

here to Stay pp326–9

here to Eat pp330–33

Miami ❶

A small trading post a century ago, Miami, or Greater Miami, now covers 2,000 sq miles (5,180 sq km) and has a population of two million. The metropolis incorporates many districts and cities and comprises Miami-Dade County. Miami's top sights are its beaches, especially fun-filled South Beach. Other sights include Little Havana, the heart of the city's Cuban population, and the leafy suburbs of Coral Gables and Coconut Grove.

Miami Beach, a city in its own right, linked by causeways to the mainland

KEY

- Sight/Place of interest
- Beach area
- Airport
- Metrorail station
- Boat boarding point
- Parking
- Tourist information
- Expressway

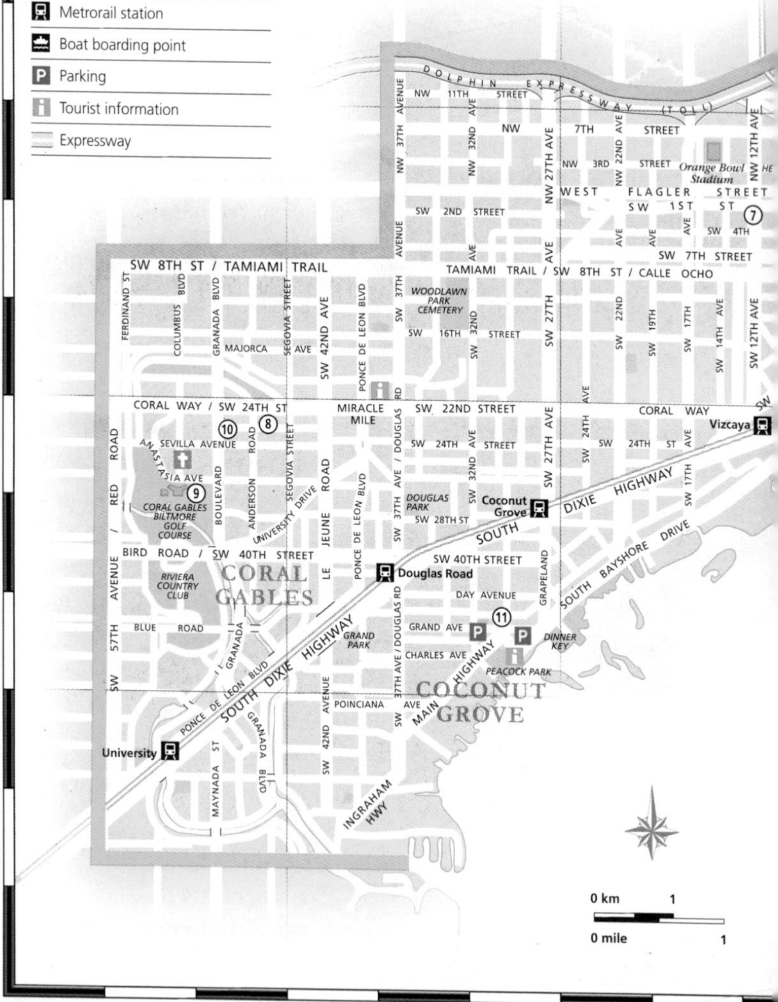

GETTING AROUND

Public transportation in Miami is run by the Miami-Dade Transit Agency, which operates the buses, the Metrorail commuter rail network, and downtown's elevated Metromover. However, the best way to get around is by car, while taxis are recommended at night.

SEE ALSO

- ***Where to Stay*** p326
- ***Where to Eat*** p330

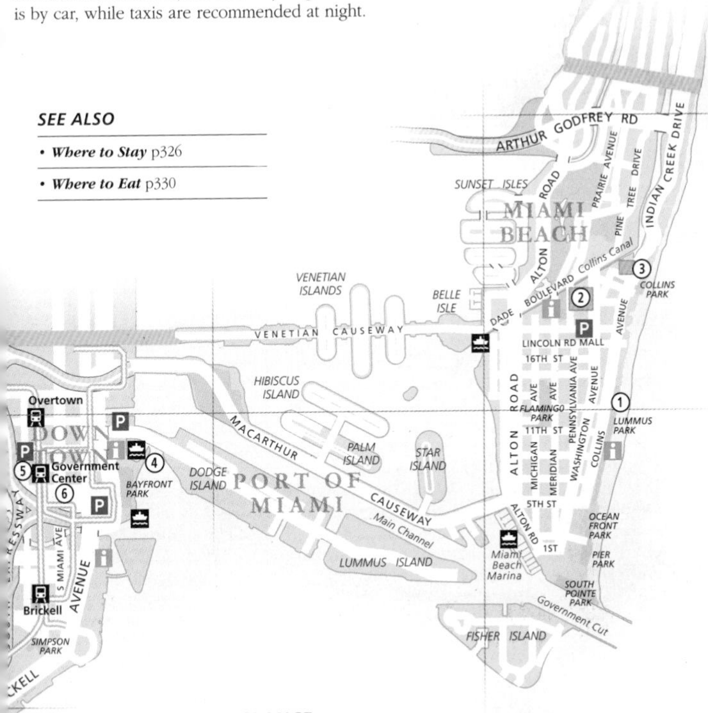

SIGHTS AT A GLANCE

South Beach ①
Holocaust Memorial ②
Bass Museum of Art ③
Biscayne Bay Boat Trips ④
Miami-Dade Cultural Center ⑤
Downtown ⑥
Little Havana ⑦
Coral Gables ⑧
Biltmore Hotel ⑨
Venetian Pool ⑩
Coconut Grove Village ⑪
Vizcaya p297 ⑫

Greater Miami
(see inset map)
North Beaches ⑬
Ancient Spanish Monastery p298 ⑭
Key Biscayne ⑮
Fairchild Tropical Garden ⑯
Miami Metrozoo ⑰
Wings Over Miami ⑱

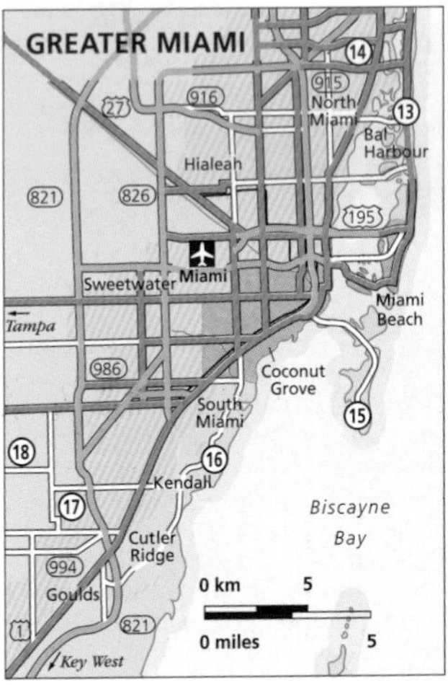

KEY

Area of main map

Lifeguard hut in South Beach to match buildings on Ocean Drive

South Beach ①

Map F2. M, S, C, H, G, L, F, M, *Night Owl, Airport Owl.* *1001, Ocean Drive, (305) 672-2014.* **www**.mdpl.org

This trendy district, also known as SoBe, extends from 6th to 23rd Streets between Lenox Avenue and Ocean Drive. A hedonistic playground, enlivened by an endless parade of fashion models, body builders, and drag queens, SoBe is also home to the world's largest concentration of well-preserved Art Deco buildings.

The 800-odd buildings along Ocean Drive were, in fact, modest hotels built in the 1930s by architects, the most famous of whom was Henry Hohauser, who used inexpensive materials to create an impression of stylishness. The present use of bright colors, known as Deco Dazzle, was introduced in the 1980s by designer Leonard Horowitz.

Collins and Washington Avenues, too, have their share of Art Deco buildings, such as the classic Marlin Hotel at 1200 Collins Avenue, one of the finest representations of Streamline Moderne. Farther north is the luxury Delano Hotel *(see p326)*, with its striking non-Deco interior of billowing white drapes and original Gaudi and Dali furniture. Other buildings of interest are the 1920s Mediterranean Revival Old City Hall and the austere Miami Beach Post Office on Washington Avenue. Inside the Post Office is a mural showing the arrival of Juan Ponce de León, the Spanish conquistador who discovered Florida in 1513. Also on Washington Avenue is the Wolfsonian Museum–FIU, built in the 1920s, which has an excellent collection of fine and decorative arts.

Between Washington and Drexel Avenues is **Española Way**, a small, pretty enclave of Mediterranean Revival buildings, where ornate arches, capitals, and balconies adorn salmon-colored, stuccoed frontages. Built from 1922–25, this street is said to be the inspiration for Addison Mizner's Worth Avenue in Palm Beach *(see p301)*. Off-beat art galleries and boutiques line this leafy street, and on weekends craft booths are set up here.

The pedestrian **Lincoln Road Mall** is Miami's up-and-coming cultural corner, dominated by the ArtCenter South Florida. Established in 1984, the ArtCenter has three exhibition areas and a dozen studios that double as work-in-progress and selling space, as well as independent galleries. The galleries are usually open in the evenings when the mall comes alive as theater-goers frequent the restored Art Deco Lincoln and Colony theaters. After a heavy dose of modern art, the stylish restaurants and cafés, such as Van Dyke at 846, along Lincoln Road, offer respite.

The Beach, extending for 10 miles (16 km) up the coast, evolved into a spectacular

OCEAN DRIVE: DECO STYLE

Deco detail, South Beach

The splendid array of buildings on Ocean Drive illustrates Miami's unique interpretation of the Art Deco style, popular all over the world in the 1920s and 30s. Florida's version, often called Tropical Deco, uses motifs such as flamingos, sunbursts, and jaunty nautical features, appropriate to South Beach's seaside location. Three main styles exist: traditional Art Deco, futuristic Streamline Moderne, and Mediterranean Revival, inspired by French, Italian, and Spanish architecture. A spirited preservation campaign, led by Barbara Capitman in the 1970s, made this area the first 20th-century district in the country's National Register of Historic Places.

A flamingo is etched into glass doors in the Beacon's lobby.

Beacon *(1936)*
A contemporary color scheme, an example of Horowitz's Deco Dazzle, brightens the abstract decoration above the ground floor windows.

winter playground after the bridge connecting the island with the mainland was built in 1913. Much of the sand flanking the beach was imported several decades ago, and it continues to be replenished to counter coastal erosion. The vast stretches of sand are still impressive and draw large crowds of people.

The beach constantly changes atmosphere. Surfers predominate up to 5th Street. The vast beach beyond is an extension of SoBe's lively persona, with colorful lifeguard huts and posing bathers. Alongside runs Lummus Park, where Yiddish is spoken by the mainly Jewish population. Around 21st Street, the clientele is predominately gay.

The stretch north of 23rd Street is sometimes known as **Central Miami Beach**. The most eye-catching sight here is the impressive Fontainebleau Hotel (pronounced "Fountain-blue" locally). Completed in 1954, this curvaceous structure was architect Morris Lapidus' (1903–2001) interpretation of a modern French château. With its grandeur, pool, and waterfall, the hotel was the ideal setting for the 1960s James Bond film classic, *Goldfinger*.

Holocaust Memorial ②

Map F2. 1933–45 Meridian Ave. ***Tel*** *(305) 538-1663.* A, FM, G, L, W. *9am–9pm daily.* **www**.holocaustmmb.org

Miami Beach has one of the largest populations of Holocaust survivors in the world, hence the great appropriateness of Kenneth Treister's gut-wrenching memorial, finished in 1990. The centerpiece is an enormous bronze arm and hand stretching skyward, representing the final grasp of a dying person. It is stamped with a number from Auschwitz and covered with more than 100 life-size bronze statues of men, women, and children in the throes of the most unbearable grief. Titled *The Sculpture of Love and Anguish*, this is one of the most powerful contemporary sculptures in Florida today. Around the central plaza is a tunnel lined with the names of Europe's concentration camps, a graphic pictorial history of the Holocaust, and a granite wall inscribed with the names of thousands of victims who perished.

The Holocaust Memorial

***Coronation of the Virgin* (c.1492) by Domenico Ghirlandaio**

Bass Museum of Art ③

Map F2. 2121 Park Ave. ***Tel*** *(305) 673-7530.* *M, S, C, H, G, L.* *10am–5pm Tue–Sat (until 9pm 2nd Thu of month), 1–5pm Sun.* *public hols.* *(free 2nd Thu of month)* **www**.bassmuseum.org

This Mayan-influenced, 1930s Deco building has a good collection of European paintings, sculpture, and textiles donated in 1964 by the philanthropists John and Johanna Bass. The collection, dating from the 15th to 17th centuries, includes Renaissance works, paintings from the northern European schools, featuring paintings by Rubens, and huge 16th-century Flemish tapestries. The permanent galleries have more than 2,800 pieces on display.

Adrian *(1934)*
Its Mediterranean inspiration and subdued colors make the Adrian stand out from other buildings.

Cardozo *(1939)*
A late Henry Hohauser work and Barbara Capitman's favorite, this Streamline gem replaces traditional Art Deco details with curved sides and aerodynamic racing stripes.

Biscayne Bay Boat Trips ④

Map D3. Bayside Marketplace. M *College/Bayside.* *16, 3, C, 95, BM, S, FM, Night Owl.* **Island Queen Cruises and Gondola Tours** *(305) 379-5119.* **Floridian Cruises** *(305) 445-8456.* **Duck Tours** *(786) 276-8300.*

A leisurely way to view the sprinkling of exclusive private island communities around Biscayne Bay is to take one of the many cruises from **Bayside Marketplace**. Tours, such as "Estates of the Rich and Famous" run by Island Queen Cruises, leave regularly and last about 90 minutes.

Biscayne Bay tour boat sign

Tours begin by sailing past Dodge and Lummus islands, where the world's busiest cruise port is situated. This port, which contributes an annual income of more than $5 billion to the local economy, handles more than three million cruise passengers a year.

Near the eastern end of MacArthur Causeway is the US Coastguard's fleet of high-speed craft. Opposite lies the unbridged Fisher Island, separated from South Beach by Government Cut, a water channel dredged in 1905. A restricted beach for African Americans in the 1920s, this is now, ironically, a highly exclusive residential enclave, with homes rarely costing less than $500,000. The tour continues north around the man-made Star, Palm, and Hibiscus islands, where real estate lots were sometimes sold "by the gallon." Among the lavish mansions are the former homes of Frank Sinatra and Al Capone, as well as the present abodes of stars such as Gloria Estefan and Julio Iglesias.

Other boat trips include nighttime cruises, deep-sea fishing excursions, and even gondola rides. Duck Tours take place on an amphibious vehicle that departs several times a day from South Beach, just off Lincoln Road. The tour takes in points of interest in South Beach and heads into Miami before "splashing" into Biscayne Bay for a closer look at the homes of the rich and famous on Star Island.

Bayside Marketplace is a fun complex with several shops, bars, and restaurants, including the Hard Rock Café, complete with a guitar erupting from its roof. **Bayfront Park** is nearby. At its center is the Torch of Friendship, commemorating John F. Kennedy, surrounded by the coats of arms of Central and South American countries; a plaque from the city's exiled Cuban community thanks the US for allowing them to settle here.

Miami-Dade Cultural Center ⑤

Map D3. 101 West Flagler St. M *Government Center.* *All buses to Miami Ave.* **Historical Museum of Southern Florida** ***Tel*** *(305) 375-1492.* *10am–5pm Mon–Wed & Fri–Sat, noon–5pm Sun.* **Miami Art Museum of Dade County** ***Tel*** *(305) 375-3000.* *Tue–Sun.* **Main Public Library** *daily.*

Designed by the celebrated American architect Philip Johnson in 1982, the Miami-Dade Cultural Center is a large complex, with a Mediterranean-style central courtyard and fountains. It includes an art gallery, museum, and library. Of these, the most interesting is the Historical Museum of Southern Florida, which concentrates on pre-1945 Miami. Besides displays on the Spanish colonization and Seminole culture, there is a fascinating collection of old photographs. These bring to life Miami's early history, from the hardships endured by the early pioneers to the fun-filled Roaring Twenties. The Miami Art Museum of Dade County, across the plaza, has a limited permanent collection and many short-term exhibitions, mainly on post-1945 American art.

Metro-Dade Cultural Center, in downtown Miami

Downtown ⑥

Map D3. M *various stations.* **US Federal Courthouse** 301 N Miami Ave. ***Tel*** *(305) 523-5100.* M *Arena/State Plaza.* *8am–5pm Mon–Fri.* *public hols.*

When the development of Miami took off with the arrival of the Florida East Coast Railway in 1896, the early city focused on one square mile (2.5 km) on the banks of the Miami River. Today, this is the site of present downtown and the hub of the city's financial district. Its futuristic skyscrapers are a monument to the banking boom of the 1980s, when the city emerged as a major financial and trade center. The raised track of the Metromover, a driverless shuttle launched in 1986, provides a swift but good overview of the area.

Among the most striking high-rises here are the Wachovia Financial Center

One of the lavish mansions seen during a Biscayne Bay boat tour

For hotels and restaurants in this region see p326 and p330

View of downtown Miami's skyline from the MacArthur Causeway

and the Bank of America Tower, constructed in 1983, and famous for its changing nighttime illuminations. Older structures include the Alfred I. DuPont Building (1938), home of the Florida National Bank, and the Ingraham Building (1927), a Neo-Classical/ Renaissance Revival work.

The **US Federal Courthouse**, completed in 1931, is an imposing Neo-Classical building, with a pleasant, very Mediterranean courtyard. It has hosted a number of high-profile trials, including that of Manuel Noriega, the former Panamanian president, in 1990. Its main attraction, how ever, is the mural on the second floor. Designed by Denman Fink *(see p296)*, it depicts Miami's transformation from a wilderness into a modern city. Entry is often restricted, especially during high-profile cases.

Miami's oldest Catholic parish, **Gesu Church**, built in 1925, is located on Northeast 2nd Street. It is noted for its fine stained-glass windows, which were made in Munich, Germany. The **Freedom Tower**, on Biscayne Boulevard, is loosely modeled on the Giralda in Seville. At first home to the now-defunct *Miami News*, it became the reception center for Cuban exiles in the 1960s. It now stands empty. Macy's (formerly Burdines, founded in 1898) is on Flagler Street.

Little Havana ⑦

Map C3. *8 from Downtown, 17, 12, 6.* **El Credito Cigar Factory** 1106 SW 8th St ***Tel*** *(305) 858-4162.* *8am–6pm Mon–Fri, 8am–4pm Sat.*

As its name suggests, the 3.5-sq mile (9-sq km) area comprising Little Havana has been the surrogate homeland of Cuban immigrants since the 1960s. The atmosphere here, especially on the streets, is vibrant and reflects the Cuban way of life. Spanish is spoken everywhere, while a salsa beat emanates from every other shop, and *bodegas* (canteens) sell Cuban specialties.

Freedom Tower (1925)

The main commercial thoroughfare and sentimental heart is **Calle Ocho** (Southwest 8th Street), with its liveliest stretch between 11th and 17th Avenues.

The small but authentic **El Crédito Cigar Factory**, near the corner of Calle Ocho and 11th Avenue, sells boxes of a wide range of cigars. The factory, set up in Havana in 1907, moved to Miami only in 1968. Cigar rollers can be seen at work here. The leaves are grown in the Dominican Republic, reputedly from Cuban tobacco seeds, the world's best.

The district's nationalistic focal point, **Cuban Memorial Boulevard**, as Southwest 13th Avenue is known, is dotted with memorials in honor of Cuban heroes. The most prominent is the Brigade 2506 Memorial's eternal flame commemorating the disastrous Bay of Pigs invasion in 1961. Every April 17, people gather here to remember the Cubans who died in the attempt to overthrow Fidel Castro's regime. Beyond are other memorials to heroes who fought against Cuba's Spanish colonialists in the 1880s. At intervals, too, along Calle Ocho between 12th and 17th Avenues, are stars on the pavement honoring more recent Latin celebrities such as Julio Iglesias and Gloria Estefan in Little Havana's version of Hollywood's Walk of Fame.

Salsa music album covers

North of Calle Ocho, at West Flagler Street and Southwest 17th Avenue, the Plaza de la Cubanidad has a map of Cuba sculpted in bronze. There's a flourish of banners advertising the headquarters of Alpha 66, Miami's most hard-line anti-Castro group.

Also in this district are the tiny Máximo Gómez Park, or Domino Park, and Woodlawn Cemetery. The Versailles restaurant, nearby, is the Cuban community's cultural and culinary bastion.

A Cuban mural in Little Havana, symbolizing nostalgia for the homeland

Coral Gables ⑧

Map A4. **Lowe Art Museum**
Tel *(305) 284-3535.* *Metrorail (University).* *52, 56, 72.* *10am–5pm Tue–Sat, noon–5pm Sun, noon–7pm Thu.* *major public hols.* **Miracle Mile** *Metrorail (Douglas Rd), then bus J or 40, 42, 24 from downtown.*

Aptly named the City Beautiful, Coral Gables is a separate city within Greater Miami. In the 1920s, George Merrick planned this aesthetic wonderland with Denman Fink as artistic advisor, Frank Button as landscaper, and Phineas Paist as architectural director. Regulations guarantee that new buildings follow the same part-Italian, part-Spanish style advocated by Merrick. Major landmarks here include the Spanish Baroque **Coral Gables Congregational Church**, the district's first church, the Spanish Renaissance Coral Gables City Hall, and the **Lowe Art Museum**, located in the University of Miami's campus.

Its main shopping street was named **Miracle Mile** (the walk along one side and down the other being the mile in question) by a developer in 1940. The Colonnade Hotel was built in 1926 by Merrick as the headquarters for his real estate business. Nearby, at Salzedo Street and Aragon Avenue, is the Old Police Station Building, built in 1939.

Coral Gables Congregational Church

South view of the Biltmore Hotel, Coral Gables' most famous landmark

Biltmore Hotel ⑨

Map A4. 1200 Anastasia Ave.
Tel *(305) 445-1926.* *Metrorail (S Miami) then bus 72.* *Sun free.*
www.biltmorehotel.com

During its heyday in the 1920s, this hotel *(see p326)* hosted figures such as Al Capone, Judy Garland, and the Duke and Duchess of Windsor. During World War II, it served as a military hospital and remained a veterans' hospital until 1968. After a $55-million restoration in 1986, it went bankrupt in 1990 but reopened two years later. The Biltmore's most striking feature is a 315-ft (96-m) near replica of Seville Cathedral's La Giralda, also the model for Miami's Freedom Tower *(see p295)*. Inside is a grand lobby, lined with Herculean pillars. The Biltmore has the largest hotel swimming pool in the US, where its famous instructor, Johnny Weismuller – known for his role as Tarzan – set a world record in the 1930s.

Venetian Pool ⑩

Map A4. 2701 De Soto Blvd.
Tel *(305) 460-5356.* *Metrorail (S Miami) then bus 72.* *mid-Jun–mid-Aug: 11am–7:30pm Mon–Fri; Apr–May & Sep–Oct: 11am–5:30pm; Nov–Mar: 10am–4:30pm; all year: 10am–4:30pm Sat & Sun.* *Mon Sep–May, Jan 1, Thanksgiving, Dec 24–25.*
www.venetianpool.com

Perhaps the most beautiful swimming pool in the world, the Venetian Pool was ingeniously fashioned from a coral rock quarry in 1923 by Denman Fink and Phineas Paist. Pink stucco towers and vine-covered loggias, candy-cane Venetian poles, a cobblestone bridge, fountains, waterfalls, and numerous caves surround crystal-clear, spring-fed waters, which are great for swimming. The pool was once one of the most fashionable social spots in Coral Gables – in the lobby are a series of photographs of beauty pageants staged here during the 1920s. This beautiful public swimming pool is definitely worth a visit, for a swim or just a look.

Venetian Pool, ingeniously created in the 1920s out of an old coral rock quarry

Coconut Grove Village ⑪

Map B4. *Metrorail (Coconut Grove).* *42 from Coral Gables, 48 from downtown, 6, 27, 22.*

Miami's oldest community, Coconut Grove was a fabled hippy hangout in the 1960s. Today, "the village," as it is simply known, is famous for its cafés and restaurants, especially at night or on weekends. This is also the city's most relaxed shopping area with many boutiques and two malls – the outdoor CocoWalk, and the stylish Streets of Mayfair. In contrast are the food stalls of the colorful farmers' market, held every Saturday at McDonald Street and Grand Avenue.

On Grand Avenue, too, are the simple homes of the local Bahamian community, descendants of the Wreckers *(see p323)*, who lived here from the mid-1800s. The exuberant Goombay Festival, a party with a parade, great food, and Caribbean music, is held here every June.

In a shady, affluent neighborhood south along Main Highway, is the **Barnacle**, home of Ralph Monroe, a Renaissance man who made his living from ship building and wrecking. At 3400 Devon Road is the picturesque **Plymouth Congregational Church**, built in 1916.

Coconut Grove Village, a lively area of shops, cafés, and bars

Vizcaya ⑫

Map C4. 3251 S Miami Ave. ***Tel*** *(305) 250-9133.* *Metrorail (Vizcaya).* *48.* *9:30am–5pm, gardens till 5:30pm (last adm: 4:30pm) daily.* *Dec 25.* *limited.* **www**.vizcayamuseum.org

Florida's grandest residence was completed in 1916 as the winter retreat for millionaire industrialist James Deering. His vision was to replicate a 16th-century Italian estate, but one that had been altered by succeeding generations. As a result, Vizcaya and its opulent rooms come in a blend of styles from Renaissance to Neo-Classical, furnished with the fruits of Deering's shopping sprees around Europe. The formal gardens, a rarity in Florida, beautifully combine Italian and French garden features with tropical foliage. They are dotted with sculptures and quaint buildings, including a Japanese tea house. Deering would always ask of his architect: "Must we be so grand?" fearing that Vizcaya would be too costly to support. After Deering's death in 1925, it proved to be so until it was bought by Dade County in 1952. The house and gardens were opened to the public thereafter.

Statue of Pulcinella

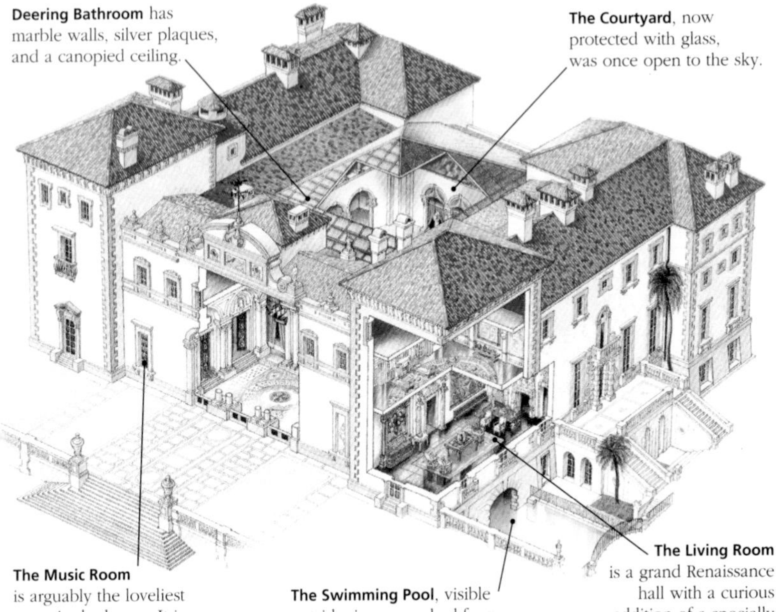

Deering Bathroom has marble walls, silver plaques, and a canopied ceiling.

The Courtyard, now protected with glass, was once open to the sky.

The Music Room is arguably the loveliest room in the house. It is lit by a striking chandelier.

The Swimming Pool, visible outside, is approached from a grotto behind the house.

The Living Room is a grand Renaissance hall with a curious addition of a specially made organ.

Greater Miami

The areas north of Miami Beach and downtown and south of Coral Gables are seldom very scenic, but they are still well worth exploring for the great beaches and family amusements. Many of the area's primary attractions, such as zoos, gardens, and citrus orchards, were badly damaged by Hurricane Andrew, which devastated southern Florida in August 1992. Most sights have reopened, although restoration work continues in some cases.

Beach at Haulover Park, under the protective eye of a lifeguard

North Beaches ⑬

Map F4. Collins Ave. *K, S, or T from South Beach or downtown.*

The Barrier Islands to the north along Collins Avenue are occupied mainly by posh residential areas and inexpensive resorts, popular with package tours. A quiet strip of sand between 79th and 87th Streets separates Miami Beach from **Surfside**, a simple community popular with French Canadians. At 96th Street Surfside merges with **Bal Harbour**, a stylish enclave known for its flashy hotels and one of Miami's swankiest malls, Bal Harbour Shops. To the north is the pleasant **Haulover Park**, with a marina on the creek side and dune-backed sands facing the ocean.

Ancient Spanish Monastery ⑭

Map F4. 16711 W Dixie Hwy, N Miami Beach. ***Tel*** *(305) 945-1462.* *H from South Beach, 3 from downtown.* *9am–5pm Mon-Fri, 10am–5pm Sat, 1:30–5pm Sun.* *public hols, may close Sat or Sun for special events.* **www**.spanishmonastery.org

These monastery cloisters have an unusual history. Built in Spain between 1133 and 1141, they were bought in 1925 by newspaper tycoon William Randolph Hearst *(see p688)*, who had their 35,000 stones packed into crates. An outbreak of foot-and-mouth disease led to the crates being opened (to check the packing straw), and the stones were repacked incorrectly. Once in New York, they remained there until 1952, when it was decided to piece together "the world's largest and most expensive jigsaw puzzle." The cloisters resemble the original, but there is still a pile of unidentified stones in a corner of the gardens.

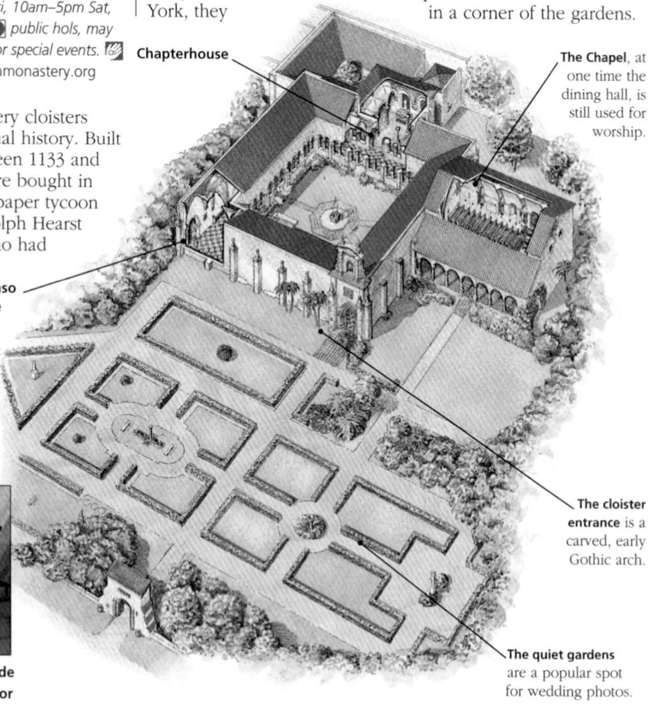

Chapterhouse

The Chapel, at one time the dining hall, is still used for worship.

Statue of Alphonso VII, patron of the monastery

The cloister entrance is a carved, early Gothic arch.

The quiet gardens are a popular spot for wedding photos.

The bell outside the chapel door

The tranquil, palm-fringed lakes of the Fairchild Tropical Garden

Key Biscayne ⑮

Map F5. 7 miles (11 km) SE of downtown. *B.* **Bill Baggs Cape Florida State Park** *Tel (305) 361-5811. daily.* **www**.floridastateparks.org

The view of downtown from Rickenbacker Causeway, connecting the mainland to Virginia Key and Key Biscayne, is one of Miami's best. Views aside, this has some of the city's top beaches. The most impressive is at Crandon Park in the upper half of the Key, which is 3 miles (5 km) long and enormously wide, with palm trees and picnic areas. At the southern end, the **Bill Baggs Cape Florida State Park** has a shorter beach joined to more picnic areas by boardwalks across the dunes.

Fairchild Tropical Garden ⑯

Map F5. 10901 Old Cutler Rd. *(305) 667-1651. 65 from Coconut Grove. 9:30am–4:30pm daily. Dec 25.* **www**.fairchildgarden.org **Mattheson Hammock Park** *Tel (305) 665-5475. 6am–sunset daily.*

Established in 1938, this beautiful tropical garden is also a major botanical research institution. One of world's largest collections of palm trees (550 of the 2,500 known species) stands around a series of man-made lakes. The garden also has an impressive array of cycads – relatives of palms and ferns that bear unusual giant red cones – as well as countless other trees and plants, including a comical-looking sausage tree.

Guides on the 40-minute tram tours describe how plants are used in the manufacture of medicines and perfumes (the flowers of the ylang-ylang tree, for example, are used in Chanel No. 5). The waterfront **Mattheson Hammock Park** is next door to the Fairchild Tropical Garden. Its highlight is the Atoll Pool, an artificial saltwater swimming pool circled by sand and palm trees alongside Biscayne Bay.

Palms in Fairchild Tropical Garden

Miami Metrozoo ⑰

Map E5. 12400 SW 152nd St, Miami. *(305) 251-0400. Metrorail (Dadeland North) then Zoo Bus. 9:30am–5:30pm daily.* **www**.miamimetrozoo.com

This enormous zoo is considered one of the country's best. Animals are kept in spacious landscaped habitats, separated from humans by moats. Highlights include lowland gorillas, Malayan sun bears, and white tigers. The Petting Zoo is a favorite with kids, and the Wildlife Show demonstrates the agility of the big cats. Take the 20-minute ride on the monorail for an overview, and then visit what you like; or take the monorail to Station 4 and then walk back.

Wings Over Miami ⑱

Map E5. 14710 SW 128th St, adjacent to Tamiami Airport. *(305) 233-5197. 10am–5pm Thu–Sat. public hols.* **www**.wingsovermiami.com

This museum is dedicated to the preservation of old aircraft. Its hangars contain a superb collection of finely preserved examples of aircraft that are still in operation. These include a 1943 AT6D Texan "Old Timer," a Douglas B-23 Dragon, and a British Provost Jet, as well as a wide range of other fascinating exhibits such as a machine-gun turret.

All these planes take to the sky during the Memorial Day weekend celebration. While in February, they are joined by B-17 and B-24 bombers in the Wings of Freedom event.

White tiger in front of a mock Khmer temple at Miami Metrozoo

Fort Lauderdale ❷

150,000. *100 East Broward Blvd, Ste 303, (954) 765-4466.*

Proclaimed the "Yachting Capital of the World," Fort Lauderdale's character is defined by its waterways, which branch from the New River. The area around the mouth of the river is known as the **Isles**. This is the city's prime area, with mansions behind lush foliage and luxurious yachts moored in the waterways.

Millions of visitors head for the barrier islands lying along the coast between the beaches and the Intracoastal Waterway. The waterway crosses **Port Everglades**, the world's second largest cruise port after Miami. Riverboat cruises and water taxis are also available.

Water taxi on the New River, Fort Lauderdale

Las Olas Boulevard, the city's busiest street, is lined with eateries and boutiques. The fine **Museum of Art**, also located here, is best known for its works by the CoBrA artists, a group of 20th-century Expressionist painters from Copenhagen, Brussels, and Amsterdam.

Downtown is the city's business and cultural center. **Riverwalk**, a 1.5-mile (2.4-km) stretch along the New River's north bank, links most of the city's historical and cultural landmarks; it starts at **Stranaham House** (1901), which originally served as a trading post, post office, and bank. **Old Fort Lauderdale** runs along Southwest 2nd Avenue and has a few early 1900s buildings, such as the Old Fort Lauderdale Museum of History. The city has the liveliest beaches on the Gold Coast, especially toward the end of Las Olas Boulevard, where skaters cruise past bars and shops. To the west is Sawgrass Mills, Florida's largest mall, with its own indoor theme park, Wannado City.

Peach-pink Mizner Park, one of Boca Raton's shopping malls

Boca Raton ❸

80,000. *1555 Palm Beach Lakes Blvd, (561) 233-3000.*

Affluent Boca Raton was originally a sleepy pineapple-growing settlement that architect Addison Mizner (1872–1933) envisaged as the "greatest resort in the world." The nucleus of his vision was the ultra-luxurious Cloister Inn, finished in 1926, with his trademark Spanish details. The hotel is now part of the exclusive **Boca Raton Resort and Club** *(see p326)*. Weekly tours for non-residents are arranged by the Boca Raton Historical Society, based at the Mizner-designed Town Hall.

Just opposite is the open-air **Mizner Park**, perhaps the most impressive of Boca Raton's dazzling malls. Located in a spectacular setting within Mizner Park is the **Boca Raton Museum of Art**. This museum contains 44,000 sq ft (4,088 sq m) of space for world-class exhibitions and an impressive display of contemporary art.

The verdant and historic **Old Floresta** district, a mile (1.6 km) west of the Town Hall, has 29 Mediterranean-style houses built by Mizner.

Boca Raton's long, undeveloped beach is reached via beachside parks, such as **Red Reef Park**, which also has the informative **Gumbo Limbo Nature Center**. The most northerly of the parks, **Spanish River Park** is also the most attractive, with pleasant picnic areas shaded by pines and palm trees. It also has a lovely lagoon on the Intracoastal Waterway, next to an observation tower.

Boca Raton Museum of Art
501 Plaza Real, Mizner Park.
Tel *(561) 392-2500.* *Tue–Sun.* *public hols.*
www.bocamuseum.org

Loxahatchee National Wildlife Refuge ❹

10216 Lee Rd. ***Tel*** *(561) 734-8303.* *Delray Beach.* **Refuge** *daily.* *Dec 25.* **Visitor Center** *Nov–Apr: daily; May–Oct: Wed–Sun.* *Dec 25.*

The northernmost part of the Everglades *(see p321)*, this 221-sq mile (572-sq km) refuge is known for its superb wildlife. The best time to visit is in winter, when migrating birds arrive here from the

Cyclists and skaters enjoying the beachfront in Fort Lauderdale

An alleyway along Worth Avenue, Palm Beach's most exclusive street

north. The visitor center, off Route 441, has a display that explains the Everglades' ecology, and there are also two trails. The Cypress Swamp Boardwalk is lined with wax myrtle trees; the longer Marsh Trail is a bird-watcher's paradise, with ibis, herons, and anhingas. Visitors can also spot turtles and alligators. Those with canoes can explore the 5.5-mile (9-km) canoe trail, and there are also numerous nature walks.

Palm Beach ❺

10,000. 45 Cocoanut Row, (561) 655-3282.

Essentially a winter resort for the rich and famous, Palm Beach was created at the end of the 19th century by the railroad baron Henry Flagler. In the 1920s Addison Mizner built luxurious Spanish-style mansions for its residents, a trend that established its unique look and influenced future architectural styles.

Palm Beach's major sights can be viewed in the area between Cocoanut Row and South County Road. Of these, the **Flagler Museum** (formerly Whitehall), Flagler's 55-room winter residence, has a grand marble entrance hall, an Italian Renaissance library, and a Louis XV ballroom. Flagler's private railroad car is on display on the South Lawn.

To the south, the **Society of the Four Arts**, founded in 1936, has two libraries, an exhibition space, and an auditorium for concerts and films. Other interesting buildings include the Town Hall, built in 1926, the Mizner Memorial Park, and **The Breakers**, a mammoth Italian Renaissance structure and Palm Beach's grandest hotel *(see p327)*.

The epitome of Palm Beach's opulent lifestyle, however, is **Worth Avenue**. Stretching across four blocks from Lake Worth to the Atlantic Ocean, this is the town's best known thoroughfare. It first became fashionable with the construction of the Everglades Club in 1918, a collaborative effort between Mizner and his patron, Paris Singer, heir to the sewing machine fortune. Today, Worth Avenue boasts a spectacular mix of glitzy fashion boutiques, art galleries, and shops.

Picturesque alleyways, reminiscent of the backstreets of Spanish villages, connect with Worth Avenue. These interlinking pedestrian alleys, created by Mizner, are a riot of arches, twisting flights of stairs, cascading bougainvillea, and courtyards. The Esplanade, an open-air mall, is at the eastern end.

The multimillion-dollar mansions of Palm Beach are located in the suburbs. Some were built by Mizner and his imitators in the 1920s, but since then hundreds of other houses have proliferated in styles from Neo-Classical to Art Deco. The most easily visible are on a ridge along South Ocean Boulevard, nicknamed "Mansion Row." The most elaborate residence, Mar-a-Lago (# 1100), is now a top-end private club owned by millionaire Donald Trump.

Flagler Museum

Cocoanut Row & Whitehall Way.
Tel *(561) 655-2833. 10am–5pm Tue–Sat, noon–5pm Sun. Jan 1, Thnksg., Dec 25. limited.*
www.flaglermuseum.us

Flagler Museum at Palm Beach, formerly Henry Flagler's winter home

Cocoa Beach ❻

14,000. Merritt Island. 400 Fortenberry Rd, (321) 459-2200.

This large, no-frills resort calls itself the East Coast's surfing capital. Surfing festivals set the tone, along with win-your-weight-in-beer competitions. Motels, restaurants, and gift and souvenir shops characterize the main street. The dazzling **Ron Jon Surf Shop** has surf boards galore (for sale and rent) and a huge T-shirt collection. In front of its flashing towers are sculptures of sports figures.

Kennedy Space Center ❼

Off Rte 405, 6 miles (9.6 km) E of Titusville. ***Tel** (321) 449-4444.*
Titusville. 9am–7pm daily. Dec 25. The center occasionally closes for operational requirements; always call ahead. wheelchairs available at Information Central.
***Tel** (321) 867-4636 for schedule of launches.*
www.kennedyspacecenter.com

When Cape Canaveral was chosen as the site for NASA's (National Aeronautics and Space Administration) space program in the 1960s, the area came to be known as the Space Coast. The Kennedy Space Center on Merritt Island is the only place in the Western Hemisphere where shuttles carrying humans are launched into space. It was also the site of the historic launch of *Apollo 11* in July 1969, when President John F. Kennedy's dream of landing a man on the moon was realized. The

Rockets on display at the Cape Canaveral Air Station

Visitor Complex, built in 1967 for astronauts and their families to view space center operations, is a 131-sq mile (340-sq km) facility that includes many attractions. Its highlight is the two **IMAX® Theaters**, which show films on space exploration on screens that are five floors high. Footage from the shuttle missions offer breathtaking views of Earth from space. West of the entrance, the **Rocket Garden** is where visitors can walk through a group of rockets, each representing different stages in space history. **Robot Scouts**, located to the east of Rocket Garden, reveals the latest planetary explorer robots, while **Exploration in the New Millennium** shows visitors what the future holds for space exploration; guests can even touch a piece of a Mars meteorite. The **Astronaut Encounter** in the same building is where visitors can meet real astronauts.

Guests can also climb aboard **Explorer** – a life-size replica of the Space Shuttle, at Shuttle Plaza in the northeastern corner of the Complex. The **Launch Status Center** is where briefings are held throughout the day that provide the latest mission details. Shuttles were the ingenious alternative to the very expensive, single-use crafts, used in the Apollo missions. Designed in the late 1970s, these re-usable spacecraft are now the backbone of the space program. Close by, the **Astronaut Memorial** honors the astronauts, from the *Apollo 1* to the Space Shuttle *Columbia* missions, who died in the service of space missions.

Close to the entrance of the Complex, an all-glass rotunda leads to **Early Space Exploration**, which showcases key figures from the early days of rocketry. In the **Mercury Mission Control Room**, visitors view the actual consoles from which the first eight manned missions were monitored.

A life-size replica of the space shuttle *Explorer*, Kennedy Space Center

TIMELINE OF SPACE EXPLORATION

1958 First American satellite, the *Explorer 1*, is launched (Jan 31)

1962 John Glenn orbits the earth in *Mercury* spacecraft

1975 American *Apollo* and Russian *Soyuz* vehicles dock in orbit (Jul 17)

1981 *Columbia* is the first shuttle in space (Apr 12)

1996 *Mars Pathfinder* sent to gather data from the surface of Mars

2001 Dennis Tito pays $20 million to spend one week on board an International Space Center

1950 | **1960** | **1970** | **1980** | **1990** | **2000**

1961 On May 5, Alan Shepherd becomes the first American in space. Kennedy commits nation to moon landing

1969 Neil Armstrong and Buzz Aldrin (*Apollo 11*) walk on the moon (Jul 24)

1986 The *Challenger* explodes, killing its crew (Jan 28)

1990 The Hubble telescope is launched (Apr 24)

2003 Space Shuttle *Columbia* breaks up upon re-entry into the atmosphere (Feb 1)

Launch pads seen on Kennedy Space Center Tours

Footage and interviews with some of the personnel are the highlights. Next are displays of some of the authentic Mercury and Gemini spacecraft, which help create some hands-on excitement of early space exploration.

The Center also offers a number of interesting tours. The **Kennedy Space Center (KSC) Bus Tour** leaves frequently from the Visitor Complex and offers an overall tour of two major facilities. Visitors enter secured areas, where guides explain the inner workings of each facility. Each tour can take between two and six hours, as visitors can take their time to explore each site.

At the tour's first stop – the **LC 39 Observation Gantry** – one can get a bird's-eye view of the launch pads from the 60-ft (18-m) observation tower. Back on the ground, a film and several exhibits tell the story of a shuttle launch. The second facility to visit is the **Apollo/Saturn V Center**, featuring an actual 363-ft (110-m) Saturn V moon rocket, used by the Apollo missions. Visitors can watch the launch of *Apollo 8*, the first manned mission to the moon, in the Firing Room Theater, followed by a film at the Lunar Theater, which shows footage of the moon landing. This is also the only place in the world where guests can dine next to a genuine moon rock, at the Moon Rock Café. There are two special-interest tours – **Cape Canaveral: Then & Now Tour**, a historic tour of the Mercury, Gemini, and Apollo launch pads; and the **NASA Up Close Tour**, an insider's view of the entire space shuttle program. This tour includes at the **International Space Station Center**, where visitors can peer inside the facility where each space station is readied for launch. Special tours to see actual shuttle launches can be arranged by booking at the Visitor Complex. However, missions were postponed after the *Columbia* disintegrated in 2003. Launches resumed in 2005, but have been dogged by safety concerns and weather conditions. Outside the center, prime viewing sites are in Titusville and Cocoa Beach.

Environs

The **US Astronaut Hall of Fame** at Titusville, 9 miles (14 km) west of KSC, offers exciting opportunities to experience weightlessness and ride flight simulators with G-forces.

Canaveral National Seashore & Merritt Island ❽

Titusville.

www.nps.gov/cana

These adjacent preserves on the Space Coast share an astounding variety of fauna and a range of habitats including estuaries and hardwood hammocks. Visitors can often see alligators and the endangered manatee, but the highlight is the rich birdlife.

The **Canaveral National Seashore** has a pristine 24-mile (39-km) stretch of beach. Apollo Beach at the northern end, and Playalinda Beach to the south are fine for sunbathing, but swimming can be hazardous, and there are no lifeguards. The top of Turtle Mound offers splendid views of Mosquito Lagoon (aptly named, so bring repellent in spring and summer).

Route 402 to Playalinda Beach has views of the Kennedy Space Center's launch pads. It also crosses **Merritt Island National Wildlife Refuge**, which covers an area of 220 sq miles (570 sq km). Much of the refuge lies within the Space Center and is out of bounds. Winter is the best season to visit. To view the local wildlife, follow the Black Point Wildlife Drive, which has the 5-mile (8-km) Cruickshank Trail. Be sure to pick up the informative leaflet at the drive's entrance. The Visitors' Information Center has displays on the habitats and wildlife in the refuge. One mile (1.6 km) farther east, the Oak Hammock and Palm Hammock trails have short boardwalks across the marshland for bird-watchers.

Canaveral National Seashore

Rte A1A, 20 miles (32 km) N of Titusville or Rte 402, 10 miles (16 km) E of Titusville. ***Tel*** *(321) 267-1110.*

daily. *for shuttle launches.*

Merritt Island National Wildlife Refuge

Rte 406, 4 miles (6.5 km) E of Titusville. ***Tel*** *(321) 861-0667.*

daily. *for shuttle launches.*

SPACE COAST BIRD LIFE

The Space Coast is a bird-watcher's paradise. Its magnificent and abundant birdlife is best viewed early in the morning or shortly before dusk. Between November and March, in particular, the marshes and lagoons teem with migratory ducks and waders, as up to 100,000 birds arrive from colder northern climates. Royal terns, white ibis, black skimmers, brown pelicans, and sandhill cranes are some of the birds that are frequently seen.

Brown pelican

Walt Disney World® Resort ❾

Walt Disney World, covering 43 sq miles (69 sq km), is the largest entertainment complex on earth. The main draw is its theme parks: Magic Kingdom, Epcot, Disney's Hollywood Studios, and Animal Kingdom. A self-sufficient vacation spot, the Resort supplies everything from hotels to golf courses, and each year brings a new wonder – Disney's Animal Kingdom is the biggest new attraction. Peerless in its imagination and attention to detail, the Resort is also a hermetic bubble cocooned from the real world. Everything runs like clockwork, and nothing shatters its illusions of fantasy. Unless you're a confirmed cynic, Walt Disney World Resort will amaze you.

WHEN TO VISIT

The busiest times of the year are Christmas and Easter, June to August, and the last week in February. At these times, the parks approach capacity – some 90,000 people in the Magic Kingdom alone. Even so, all the rides operate and the parks remain open for much longer. During the off-season, 10,000 visitors a day might visit the Magic Kingdom, and certain attractions may be closed for maintenance. The weather is also a factor – in July and August, hot and humid afternoons are regularly punctuated by thunderstorms. Between October and March, the temperatures and humidity are much more comfortable and permit a more energetic schedule.

LENGTH OF VISIT

Walt Disney World offers at least a week of entertainment. To enjoy it to the full, give Magic Kingdom and Epcot two days each, and a day each for Disney's Hollywood Studios and Animal Kingdom. Keep three nights to see the splendid fireworks displays of Fantasmic!, Fantasy in the Sky, and IllumiNations.

GETTING AROUND

An extensive transportation system handles an average of 200,000 guests each day. Even if you stay outside Walt Disney World Resort, many nearby hotels offer free shuttle services to and from the theme parks. Check when you make your reservation.

WALT DISNEY RESORT

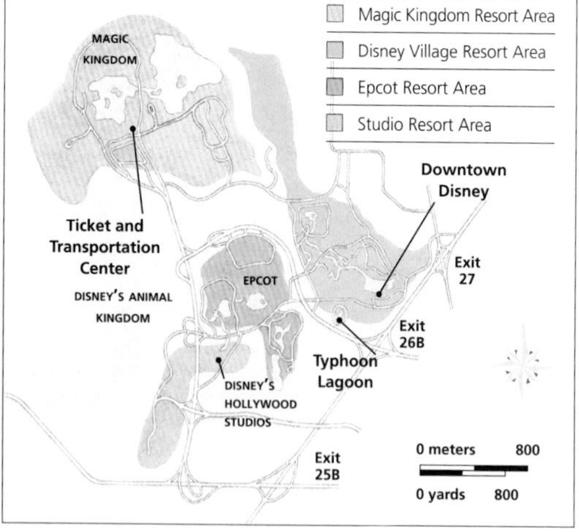

USEFUL NUMBERS

General information
Tel *(407) 824-4321.*

Accommodation information/reservations
Tel *(407) 934-7639.*

Dining reservations
Tel *(407) 939-3463.*
www.disney.go.com

The transport hub of Walt Disney World is the **Ticket and Transportation Center** (TTC). Connecting it to the Magic Kingdom are two monorail services. A third monorail links the TTC to Epcot. Ferries run from the TTC to the Magic Kingdom. They also connect the Magic Kingdom and Epcot with resorts in their areas. Buses link everything in Walt Disney World, including direct links to Magic Kingdom. Residents and pass holders can use the entire transportation system for free, while one-day tickets allow holders to use the ferries and monorails between the TTC and Magic Kingdom.

DISABLED TRAVELERS

Wheelchairs can be borrowed at the park entrance, and special bypass entrances allow disabled guests to board rides without waiting in line. Staff, however, are not allowed to assist with lifting for safety reasons.

VERY YOUNG CHILDREN

Parents with pre-school age kids can make use of the unique system known as "switching off," where they can enjoy various rides and attractions one at a time while the other parent stays with the child, without having to line up twice.

The Resort can be exhausting, so it is a good idea to rent a stroller from any park entrance. Take frequent breaks from the excitement and the heat by building in time for snacks or naps.

If you've come with young kids you should focus mainly on the Magic Kingdom.

SAFETY

The resort's first-rate security force means problems are dealt with promptly. Cast members are trained to watch out for unaccompanied children and escort them to lost children centers.

PARKING

Visitors to the Magic Kingdom must park at the TTC and use public transportation; Epcot and Disney's Hollywood Studios have their own parking lots. Parking is free for Disney Resort residents; others must pay, but only once a day regardless of how many times they move their vehicle.

ADVANTAGES OF STAYING IN THE RESORT

Lodging in the resorts and in Walt Disney World Swan and Dolphin (operated independently but Disneyesque in every other respect) are of a very high standard. However, even the lowest-priced places are more expensive than many hotels outside Walt Disney World.

However, a few practical reasons to stay there are:

- Proximity to parks and free use of Disney's transportation.
- Early entry privileges into the parks (up to 90 minutes). Check in advance with each park for details.
- Guaranteed admission to the theme parks even when the parks are otherwise full.
- The possibility of dining with your favorite Disney character in your hotel.
- The delivery of shopping purchases made anywhere within the Resort.
- Note that the hotels close to the Marketplace (which are not run by Disney) offer few of the above mentioned privileges. For information on hotel listings see pages 327–8.

RESORT DINING

Visitors should make reservations in advance for any full-service restaurant in Walt Disney World Resort, especially in the theme parks and above all in Epcot. Whether or not you are staying at one of the resorts, reservations for dining can be made 60 days in advance. Some tables are held for same-day reservations, so make your reservation as early in the morning as possible. For restaurant details, see page 332.

MEETING MICKEY

For many youngsters, meeting the Disney characters is the high point of their visit. Apart from seeing them in the parks, you can also meet them in numerous restaurants (usually at breakfast). Each park and many resorts also offer "character dining," but you must book ahead.

DIRECTORY

INFORMATION

Tickets & Types of Passes

You can buy one-day, one-park tickets, but if you're staying for over three days consider the following:
Park Hopper Pass: entitles one-day entry to each park on any four or five days.
All-in-One Hopper Pass: offers unlimited access to theme parks and water parks on any five, six, or seven days.
Length of Stay Pass: this useful pass is exclusively for Resort hotel guests; unlimited entry to theme parks, water parks, and Sports complex. Prices depend on length of stay.
Annual Pass and Premium Annual Pass: non-Disney guests visiting for over ten days should consider these, which cost little more than a 7-day park hopper. Child pricing applies to ages 3–9.
FastPass allows one to reserve time at 19 popular attractions rather than wait in line. Passes are available at the rides.

Busiest Days

Each of the theme parks is busiest on certain days:
Magic Kingdom: Monday, Thursday, and Saturday.
Epcot: Tuesday, Friday, and Saturday.
Disney's Hollywood Studios: Wednesday and Sunday.

Opening Hours

When the theme parks are busiest, opening hours are the longest: 9am to 10/11pm or midnight. In less busy periods, hours are 9am to 6/7/8pm. The parks open early for pass holders and guests at any of the Resort hotels. Call to check details.

The Ideal Schedule

To avoid the worst of the crowds and heat, arrive early and visit the popular attractions first. Take a break in the afternoon, when it is hot and parks are busy, and return in the evening to see parades and fireworks.

Top Tips

Lines are shortest at the start and end of the day, and during parade and meal times. The wait for a show is rarely longer than the show itself.

- Parks fill rapidly after the first hour of opening. Until then, you can often just walk onto rides for which there will be a line later.
- After a thunderstorm, the water parks are often almost empty, even at the busiest times of the year.
- Information regarding timings of shows, parades, and rides, and tips such as the waiting times at various attractions, are usually available at each park. Check at notice boards, Information Centers, and Guest Services.
- Ask for a Park Map.
- During parades, other attractions are quiet.
- Wear a comfortable pair of shoes, as the parks entail a lot of walking.
- There is very little shade, so be sure to wear a hat.

MAGIC KINGDOM

Magic Kingdom is the essential Disney theme park. Disney characters fill its cheerful acres, and seven lands evoke different themes.

It is best to head straight for **Space Mountain**, a superb coaster in Tomorrowland. It shoots around in stygian blackness against projections of asteroids and galaxies. **Stitch's Great Escape!** is a ride based on the film Lilo and Stitch, who is a crazy, uncontrollable space alien who manages to cause mayhem even out in space. Another popular attraction is **Monsters, Inc. Laugh Floor.** Guests find the power of laughter in an interactive adventure inspired by the movie. **Buzz Lightyear's Space Ranger Spin** is a fabulous journey in a two-seater car. It is fitted with laser cannons and a control, so you can shoot at targets with a laser beam.

Fantasyland, dominated by Cinderella's Castle, forms the core of the Magic Kingdom. **The Many Adventures of Winnie the Pooh** uses the latest technology, lighting, and sound effects to create an enchanting experience, while **Peter Pan's Flight** combines the feeling of flying with the delight of perfectly matched music and movement. **"It's a small world"** is a musical indoor voyage and one of the most popular rides at Disney. **The Haunted Mansion** in Liberty Square leads visitors through a spook-ridden mansion and graveyard.

Set in the Wild West, Frontierland offers a journey on a runaway train known as **Big Thunder Mountain Railroad**. The fun **Country Bear Jamboree** is an Audio-Animatronics® animal show, and **Splash Mountain** is an exciting flume ride.

Adventureland is a fusion of Africa and the Caribbean. **The Jungle Cruise** goes past an animatronically animated setting of Africa. Another voyage, **Pirates of the Caribbean**, leads you into underground prisons and past 16th-century galleons.

Main Street USA is famous for the **SpectroMagic Parade**, a fantasy of music, live action, and illuminated floats. In peak season, it takes place at 7pm and again at 9pm. The afternoon parade is best viewed from Frontierland. The evening parade also features **Wishes Nighttime Spectacular** – an extravaganza of fireworks and music. Mickey's ToonTown Fair (with numerous attractions for children), is the best place to watch the show.

EPCOT

Epcot, an acronym for the Experimental Prototype Community of Tomorrow, was Disney's dream of a technologically advanced community that represented a utopian vision of the future.

The enormous 250-acre (101 ha) park is divided into two halves: **Future World** with an emphasis on entertainment and education; and **World Showcase**, which represents the art, culture, and culinary skills of different countries around the globe. Boats cross the World Showcase Lagoon frequently and are a convenient method of getting here.

The unmistakable seven-and-a-half-thousand-ton globe of **Spaceship Earth** is the focal point of Future World. It takes visitors past superbly crafted tableaux and Animatronics® scenes portraying future possibilities in technology. Since most people visit here first, there are long lines in the mornings, so it is best seen in the afternoon.

Test Track, one of Epcot's top rides, places visitors in a simulator that moves on tracks at high speeds. You test a prototype sports car at over 66 mph (106 km/h) on a raised roadway. Try to visit this ride first in the morning. The popular **Mission: SPACE** uses state-of-the-art technology to simulate a ride to Mars in a rocket. This may cause motion sickness.

The Imagination Pavilion is best known for the hilarious "Honey, I Shrunk the Audience," which integrates Disney's unique 3-D film technology with special effects.

At **The Seas with Nemo & Friends Pavilion** visitors can watch sea life through transparent walls, climb aboard a "Clamobile" to search for Nemo, or enjoy the interactive show, "Turtle Talk with Crush."

The Land Pavilion has a tremendously popular attraction called Soarin. Visitors are lifted high off the ground in a simulated hang-glider trip. The wind whips through your hair and your feet dangle above treetops as you "fly" over California.

EATING & DRINKING

The typical fare at **Magic Kingdom** is fast food. However, try the Liberty Tree Tavern or Crystal Palace for quieter dining. Cinderella's Royal Table in the castle has a regal ambience, and the Plaza Restaurant is great for sandwiches.

The dining at **Epcot** is superb, particularly **World Showcase**, where reservations are required. Recommended are: **Mexico:** the San Angel Inn serves interesting but pricey Mexican cuisine. **Italy:** Tutto Italia Ristorante serves pasta and fine Italian specialties. **Japan:** you can eat communally, either in the Mitsukoshi Teppan Edo or at the bar of Mitsukoshi Tokyo Dining for sushi and tempura. **France:** the upscale Bistro de Paris (dinner only); Les Chefs de France, an exclusive restaurant with *haute cuisine*; and the terraced Le Cellier Steakhouse for steaks, and crêpes.

At **Disney's Hollywood Studios**, you can soak up the atmosphere at three of the full-service restaurants. The costly Hollywood Brown Derby replicates Hollywood's Original Brown Derby, where the stars met in the 1930s. Children prefer the Sci-Fi Dine-In Theater Restaurant, where you sit in mini-Cadillacs and watch old sci-fi films. For dining without a reservation, try Hollywood & Vine, which serves pasta, salads, seafood, ribs, and steaks.

World Showcase has architectural showpieces of 11 different countries, with replicas of famous buildings. Each pavilion is staffed by people from the country it represents, selling ethnic products and food. The best live shows are the acrobats at China and the Living Statues at Italy. Highlights include **Reflections of China** – a Circle-Vision film on China's ancient sites; **Maelstrom** in Norway – an exciting trip through fjords; and **Impressions de France** – a film offering a whirlwind tour of France. Do not miss **IllumiNations**, a *son-et-lumière* show with lasers, fire- and waterworks. It is staged near closing time around World Showcase Lagoon.

DISNEY'S HOLLYWOOD STUDIOS

Disney's Hollywood Studios, formerly known as Disney-MGM Studios, opened in 1989, both as a theme park and as a working film and TV studio. Although most of the working film section has been shut down, it combines top-notch shows and rides, based on Disney and Hollywood films (to which Disney bought the rights), with entertaining tours.

At Hollywood Boulevard, Art Deco styled buildings vie with a replica of Mann's Chinese Theater. The best shops are located here: Celebrity 5 & 10 has a range of affordable movie souvenirs, such as clapper boards and Oscars®, and the pricey Sid Cahuenga's One-Of-A-Kind stocks rare film memorabilia such as autographed photos and famous actors' clothes. **The Great Movie Ride** carries visitors past enormous movie sets, where scenes from films are re-created using live action.

Sunset Boulevard is an evocation of the famous Hollywood street in the 1940s. Re-created theaters and storefronts are dominated by the Hollywood Tower Hotel. This lightning-ravaged hotel is the spot for Orlando's scariest ride – **The Twilight Zone Tower of Terror** – in which you are strapped into an elevator for a voyage inspired by the 1950s TV show *The Twilight Zone*™. Its high point is the ghastly 13-story plunge, repeated no fewer than seven times. The **Rock 'n Roller Coaster Starring Aerosmith** accelerates to 60mph (96 km/h) in 2.8 seconds in the dark, and pulls 5G in the first corkscrew.

Animation Courtyard gives visitors a glimpse behind the scenes during the creation of Disney's Audio-Animatronics®. The **Magic of Disney-Animation** is a guided visit with a Disney artist, while **Playhouse Disney-Live on Stage!** is an interactive show featuring Disney Pals from Mickey Mouse Clubhouse and Little Einsteins™.

At Mickey Avenue, **Journey into Narnia** allows visitors to meet Prince Caspian. Pixar Place's **Toy Story Midway Mania!** is a 4-D midway-style game-playing adventure.

Streets of America Studio Backlot Tour has a tram ride that takes visitors for a peek at the camera, wardrobe, and lighting departments. It ends in Catastrophe Canyon, in the midst of a flood and explosions. The walking tour demonstrates special effects.

Streets of America is a clever re-creation of the Big Apple, San Francisco, Chicago, and other cities. Its highlight is the spectacular **Muppet™ Vision 3-D**, a slapstick 3-D movie starring the Muppets. Trombones, cars, and rocks launch themselves at you out of the screen – so realistic that children often grasp the air expecting to touch something.

Echo Lake offers the sensational **Star Tours** ride, based on the *Star Wars* films and includes an intergalactic battle. The **Indiana Jones™ Epic Spectacular** is a 30-minute live show featuring edge-of-your-seat stunts and adventures.

At 5pm, the park holds a parade based on one of Disney's animated films. The evening show, **Fantasmic!** is the finest of its kind in Florida. It combines music, lasers, animation, and over a hundred actors and dancers. Although it seats 10,000 people, you still need to arrive two hours early to get a good seat.

ANIMAL KINGDOM

This park has both real and mythical beasts, spread over seven different "lands."

At Discovery Island, the **It's Tough to be a Bug** show is a superb 3-D presentation. Camp Minnie-Mickey is where visitors meet Disney characters. The **Festival of the Lion King** show here is superb.

Africa offers the fabulous **Kilimanjaro Safaris**, where you see animals roaming freely.

Asia features gibbons, birds, and tigers in a re-creation of Indian ruins. Tapirs and Komodo dragons are found on the **Maharaja Jungle Trek**, the climax of which are the magnificent Bengal tigers that roam the ruins. **Expedition Everest – Legend of the Forbidden Mountain** is a huge new attraction where visitors ride a train through the misty unknown. Dinoland USA has the wild **DINOSAUR** ride, where a motion simulator bucks and weaves, trying to ensnare and avoid dinosaurs. **Primeval Whirl** and **Tricera Top Spin** attempt to spin visitors dizzy.

THE REST OF WALT DISNEY WORLD® RESORT

Walt Disney World has 22 resorts *(see p327)*, two water parks, a campground, nearly 300 restaurants, nightclubs, a shopping village, and half a dozen golf courses.

Of the waterparks, **Blizzard Beach**, a reconstructed Alpine ski resort, claims to have the tallest freefall slide in the world. At **Fort Wilderness Resort and Campground**, activities include horseback riding, fishing, and biking. Jet skiing, rental boats, and fishing gear are also available at the **Marketplace** and at all lakeside resorts. The Marketplace is an outdoor mall with lots of shops – The World of Disney sells mountains of merchandise; and **Disney's West Side** has blues clubs and the famous Cirque du Soleil, an avant-garde circus spectacle with more than 70 performers.

Universal Orlando ⑩

Once a single movie park, Universal Orlando now boasts two theme parks, an entertainment complex, and three resorts. Together, Universal Studios Florida, Islands of Adventure, and Universal CityWalk present a formidable reason to spend time away from Walt Disney World. The parking lot feeds into Universal CityWalk where there is a series of moving walkways to a fork leading to the two separate parks.

Universal's globe, the logo for the new combined complex of parks

TACKLING THE PARKS

The busiest seasons are during Christmas and Easter. During the off-season, check with Guest Services for special deals on tickets. Arrive early to combat the long lines for rides (the gates open an hour before opening time). Arrive 15 minutes early for shows to ensure a seat. Children may find most rides too intense but there are some child-friendly attractions: ET Adventure, the Woody Woodpecker's Nuthouse, A Day in the Park with Barney, Animal Actors on Location!, Jurassic Park, and the Seuss Landing.

EATING & SHOPPING

There are plenty of options for dining. The Hard Rock Café is the largest in the world. Lombard's Seafood Grill specializes in fish dishes, while Universal Studios Classic Monsters Café serves Californian and Italian cuisine, and has a great buffet. Most rides and attractions have their own stores. In Hitchcock's 3-D Theater, one can buy a Bates Motel Soap, while Universal Studio Store has everything from fake Oscars to oven mitts with the Universal logo.

UNIVERSAL STUDIOS FLORIDA

The entrance is known as Front Lot, as it is built to look like the front lot of a 1940s Hollywood film studio. Actors in costumes wander the streets playing characters from *Ghostbusters, Frankenstein*, and legends such as Marilyn Monroe and the Marx Brothers. The shooting schedule posted near the turnstiles has details of shows that are being filmed. Tickets for these are available at the booth located near Guest Services.

The next area is Production Central. The simulator ride here, **Jimmy Neutron's Nicktoon Blast**, is great fun. Also in this area is a new example of the increasing number of 3-D plus one attractions, **Shrek 4-D** allows visitors to experience 3-D film special effects.

The New York area has more than 60 façades, some of which replicate real buildings, others reproduce famous movie settings. There are cut-outs of the Guggenheim Museum and the New York Public Library, as well as Macy's department store, and Louie's Italian Restaurant, scene of a shootout in the original *Godfather* movie. The park's newest ride is the **Revenge of the Mummy**. This high-speed rollercoaster propels you though Egyptian passageways and includes frighteningly lifelike robotics. The other ride here is **Twister...Ride It Out**, which pits visitors against a simulated tornado, and lets them experience the terrifying power of the elements standing inside 20 ft (6 m) of the five-floor high funnel of winds.

In the section known as Hollywood, sets of Hollywood Boulevard and Rodeo Drive pay tribute to Hollywood's golden age, from the 1920s to the '50s – with the famous Mocambo nightclub, the luxurious Beverly Wilshire Hotel and top beauty salon, Max Factor. There is even a replica of the Hollywood Walk of Fame, with the names of stars embedded in the ground.

Hollywood's most popular attraction is **Terminator 2: 3-D**, a ride that uses superb robotics and the latest 3-D technology to catapult the audience into the action alongside the star of the *Terminator* films, Arnold Schwarzenegger.

The **Universal Horror Make-Up Show** offers a behind-the-scenes look at scary make-up effects.

The **Simpsons Ride** allows visitors to swoop, soar, and smash their way through Krustyland in this adventure starring the world's favorite animated family. In the incredibly addictive **Men In Black – Alien Attack**, visitors

Universal Studios' Terminator 2: 3-D, a state-of-the-art attraction

The thrilling river ride in Jurassic Park River Adventure, Jurassic Park

join Will Smith in a simulator, battling aliens with lasers and cannons. In Woody Woodpecker's Kid Zone, the enchanting **ET Adventure** is based on Steven Spielberg's 1982 film. Guests soar off to ET's home planet on a flying bicycle, gliding over a twinkling cityscape, before arriving at a world inhabited by ET look-alikes.

The San Francisco section's big draw is **Disaster!**™ Take a trip into the world of disaster movies, experience special effects, and board a moving subway train set, in the final scene of a disaster movie. At the end, watch the trailer starring you, in your very own "major movie motion picture."

At **Beetlejuice's Graveyard Revue**™ join the classic Universal Monsters as they unleash their hot sound in a spooktacular rock 'n' roll revue that is loud enough to wake the dead. A popular attraction is **Fear Factor Live**, the first ever theme park experience based on a reality TV show. Casting takes place 75 minutes before the show, which tests the courage and strength of participants.

THE ISLANDS OF ADVENTURE

One of the world's most technologically advanced theme parks, Islands of Adventure demands a day's visit of its own. The first island visitors encounter is the Marvel Super Hero Island where the theme draws from the Marvel Comics' Super Hero stable of characters. The **Incredible Hulk Coaster**, probably Florida's best, is a green leviathan that accelerates you to over 40 mph (64 km/h) in two seconds before turning upside down at 110 ft (33.5 m) above the ground. The **Amazing Adventures of Spider-man**, shows a stunning integration of 3-D technology with motion simulation. Toon Lagoon, where cartoons transmute into reality, hosts a wet ride – **Popeye & Bluto's Bilge-Rate Barges**, a twisting, churning, and splashing raft ride.

Jurassic Park boasts the **Jurassic Park River Adventure**, a cruise where visitors see friendly dinosaurs before being diverted due to a raptor breakout. The **Pteranodon Flyers** ride flies pairs of riders over the island on an 80-second trip, while the **Discovery Center** is an interactive natural history exhibit where guests can view the results of mixing DNA from various species, including themselves.

The Lost Continent is an island of myth and legend. For coaster addicts, **Duelling Dragons** is the ride of choice. Two coasters – Fire and Ice, battle to see who will arrive back first. Stage shows include the Eighth Voyage of Sinbad Stunt Show, and Poseidon's Fury, with a myriad special effects. Seuss Landing, based on the popular Dr. Seuss children's books, the creation of Theodor Seuss Geisel, caters to children. The **Cat in the Hat** ride serves as an introduction to the characters. There are also a host of innovative rides that captivate younger children.

The **Wizarding World of Harry Potter**, complete with Hogwarts Castle, is expected to open during 2010.

VISITORS' CHECKLIST

1000 Universal Studios Plaza, exits 29 or 30B on I-4. *(407) 363-8000. 21, 37, 40 from Orlando. 9am–6pm daily; extended evening hours in summer & on public hols.* **www**.universalorlando.com

UNIVERSAL CITYWALK

Inspired by many of popular culture's innovators such as Bob Marley, Universal CityWalk is a 30-acre (12-ha) entertainment complex of restaurants, nightclubs, and cinemas. Open between 11am and 2am, its dazzling array of restaurants range from Emeril's (a top TV chef) to the nostalgic Bubba Gump Shrimp Co., and the famous Hard Rock Café. A restaurant known as "Bob Marley – A Tribute to Freedom," is an exact replica of this famous musician's home. Among the many nightclubs are Hard Rock Live! and the groove dance club where visitors can watch live musical performances. The complex also has stores and movies, and its stages host concerts, art festivals, and celebrity appearances. A lagoon provides a picturesque setting to sip a cool drink or take a moonlight stroll.

The Hard Rock Café and music venue, Universal CityWalk

SeaWorld Orlando & Discovery Cove ⓫

In scale and sophistication, SeaWorld is one of the world's most impressive marine-life adventure parks. Established in 1973 to promote its educational, research, and conservation programs, the park abounds in fun as well as entertainment. SeaWorld's answer to the Disney mouse is Shamu the killer whale, and the Believe and Blue Horizons shows top the bill. Next to SeaWorld is Discovery Cove, an all-inclusive park, where guests can swim with rays, dolphins, and other fascinating sea creatures.

Dolphin Cove, where everyone can touch and feed the dolphins

EXPLORING SEAWORLD

SeaWorld is less crowded than Orlando's other theme parks. Most of the presentations are either walk-through exhibits or stadium shows. Arriving 15 minutes early guarantees a good seat. Show timings overlap, so guests cannot leave a show just in time for another. However, it is possible to get a seat in the Clyde and Seamore (Sea Lion and Otter) show by leaving the Shamu Stadium while the performers are taking their bows. The best time to see shows such as Wild Arctic and Shark Encounter is while visitors are busy watching the stadium events. Young children enjoy meeting the actors in furry suits who play the parts of Shamu and Crew – guests can normally find them near SeaWorld's exit around closing time. The 400-ft (122-m) Sky Tower ride offers a superb overview of the park. For more information, go to Guest Relations near the exit gate.

TOP TIPS

- *SeaWorld allows guests to feed many of the animals, but it restricts both the type and the amount of food, which must be purchased from them. If this is something you would like to do, check with guest services as soon as you enter the park for feeding times and food availablility.*
- *Build your schedule around the three main types of presentations: Believe, Sea Lion and Otter, and Blue Horizons shows.*
- *Bring a waterproof plastic bag for your camera as, especially during Believe and Blue Horizons shows, people sitting in the first 12 rows often get splashed by salt water.*
- *Journey to Atlantis is guaranteed to get you wet, so reserve this for the hottest part of the day.*
- *SeaWorld's gentle pace means that visiting after 3pm is a less crowded experience.*

EXHIBITS & RIDES

Three meticulously lanscaped habitats are incorporated in **Key West at SeaWorld**. Dolphin Cove, a wave pool in the style of a Caribbean beach, offers underwater viewing of bottlenose dolphins and the chance to pet and feed them. Visitors can also touch one of the 200-odd rays at Stingray Lagoon, while Turtle Point is home to rescued loggerhead, hawksbill, and green sea turtles, which are too injured to survive in the wild.

Shamu, the park's official mascot

Pacific Point Preserve recreates the rugged north Pacific Coast in the form of a large, rocky pool. One can watch harbor seals, South American fur seals, and noisy California sea lions basking on the rocks or gliding effortlessly through the water.

Most of the other wildlife at SeaWorld is viewed through glass. **Manatee Rescue** offers a splendid underwater view of these irresistibly appealing herbivores *(see p319)*.

In the fabulous **Penguin Encounter**, a moving walkway leads past a frozen landscape where a large colony of penguins demonstrate their comical waddling and elegant swimming. The gawky puffins are also a delight to watch.

Billed as the world's largest collection of dangerous sea creatures, **Shark Encounter** is very popular. Moray eels, barracuda, and pufferfish are the tantalizing appetizers before a main course of sharks, whose toothy grins are a short distance away, as visitors walk through a glass tunnel inside their aquarium. **Shamu: Close Up!**, next to the **Shamu Stadium**, is a research and breeding facility to study killer whale behavior – ten whales have been born here so far. **Wild Arctic** is a thrilling, hi-tech ride that simulates a helicopter flight through blizzards and avalanches. Visitors arrive at Base Station Wild Arctic, created around an old expedition ship, and encounter polar bears, harbor seals, walruses, and beluga whales.

SeaWorld's **Journey to Atlantis**, a water coaster with a mythological twist, and **Kraken**, a winner of the annual Orlando roller-coaster competition, are hot tickets. **Aquatica** is a water park that offers thrilling rides, including water slides and wave pools.

SHOWS & TOURS

The excitement of seeing a killer whale erupt out of the water carrying one of the SeaWorld trainers on its nose is hard to overstate. In the park's number one show, **Believe** is a revolutionary show that features SeaWorld's entire family of killer whales performing awe-inspiring choreography to an original score. The show has a magnificent three-story set, four rotating LED screens that can move together to make an 80-ft (24-m) wide panoramic screen, and a sound system with nearly 100 speakers.

Blue Horizons is another stunning theatrical spectacular that showcases graceful dolphins and false killer whales, a rainbow of exotic birds, and an entire cast of world-class divers and aerialists in elaborate costumes. The vivid imagination of a young girl sets the stage for an emotional adventure involving the power of the sea and the elegance of flight.

The **Clyde and Seamore Take Pirate Island** show, held in the Sea Lion and Otter Stadium, features two sea lions (Clyde and Seamore), otters, and a walrus in a swashbuckling adventure of lost loot, pirate ships, and hilarity on the high seas.

The Nautilis Theater hosts **A'Lure, the Call of the Ocean**, the spectacular tale of the Sea Sirens whose hypnotic calls have lured fishermen into their underwater lairs for centuries. It is a mariner's story that comes to life with athletic flying performers, gravity-defying aerial tumblers, and amazing silk yo-yo artists.

Another show, **Pets Ahoy**, features talented cats, birds, dogs, and pigs, all of whom have been rescued from animal shelters. Other exhibits include **Shamu's Happy Harbor**, a play area for smaller children, and **Dolphin Nursery** for new dolphin moms and their calves.

The **Hubbs–SeaWorld Research Institute** runs a number of nonprofit "Research, Rescue and Rehabilitation" projects. It has helped thousands of manatees, dolphins, and whales in difficulty – nursing and operating on them. Those that recover fully are released into the wild. Several tours such as The Sharks! tour, offer a glimpse of this work. If interested, inquire at Guest Relations.

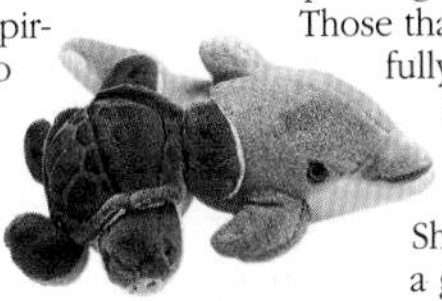

Cuddly versions of SeaWorld stars

The **Adventure Express Tour** offers exclusive guided park tours, reserved seats, feeding opportunities, and back door access to rides. **Mistify**, the laser-fireworks show held nightly at the Waterfront, constitutes a stunning finale to the day.

DISCOVERY COVE

Just across the road from SeaWorld, Discovery Cove is a quiet revolution in Florida's theme parks. With a capacity of only 1,000 guests a day (the car park is limited to only 500 cars), it offers some unforgettable experiences, the most vaunted of which is an opportunity to swim with Atlantic bottlenose dolphins.

Discovery Cove has been conceived as a private island. Its five main areas are set within beautifully landscaped grounds with waterfalls, pools, and niches connected by beaches. **Tropical Reef** abounds with grottos and a shipwreck, and offers the opportunity to swim alongside threateningly large sharks, separated from visitors by a transparent plexi-glass wall. At the **Free Flight Aviary**, guests can feed birds, while **Ray Lagoon** offers the chance to snorkel above rays, some of which grow up to a length of 5 ft (1.5 m). The warm waters of **Rainforest River** are inviting to swimmers and snorkelers who can float lazily past lagoons, a waterfall, and thick rainforest. There is also an underwater cave. The **Dolphin Lagoon** has a 15-minute orientation session, followed by 30 minutes of wading and swimming with these highly intelligent mammals.

It's a good idea to split your party into two for the dolphin experience, to be able to take each other's photographs. Do not bring any sunscreen, as the park has its own "fish friendly" one, the only brand permitted. If you decide not to visit the Dolphin Lagoon, the price of the visit is less. The package price (no child reductions) includes the dolphin experience (children under six cannot participate), all equipment, a free snorkel, a meal, and seven days admission to SeaWorld or Busch Gardens, Tampa Bay. Despite the price, the park is very popular, and it is better to book well in advance.

A performing killer whale, one of the star attractions at SeaWorld Orlando

VISITORS' CHECKLIST

7007 SeaWorld Drive, intersection of I-4 & Bee Line Expressway. *(407) 351-3600.*
8, 42 from Orlando.
minimum hours 9am–7pm daily (until 11pm in summer).
www.seaworld.com

Downtown Orlando, dominated by the SunTrust Center

Orlando 12

200,000. *8723 International Dr, (407) 425-1234.* **www**.orlandoinfo.com

Orlando was just a sleepy provincial town until the 1950s. However, its proximity to Cape Canaveral and the theme parks soon transformed it into a burgeoning business center. Downtown, with its glass-sided high-rises, comes to life only at night, when both visitors and locals flock to the many bars and restaurants around Orange Avenue, the town's main street.

During the day, the area around **Lake Eola**, east of Orange Avenue, offers views of the wooden homes of the town's earliest settlers. The residential districts north of downtown have many parks and museums, including the serenely beautiful Harry P. Leu Gardens and **Loch Haven Park**, which houses a trio of museums. The most highly regarded of these is the **Orlando Museum of Art**. Its collections include pre-Columbian artifacts with figurines from Peru, African art, and American paintings from the 19th and 20th centuries. The park is also home to the John and Rita Lowndes Shakespeare Center, which includes the 350-seat Margeson Theater and smaller Goldman Theater. The Center holds the Orlando-UCF Shakespeare Festival.

The **Maitland Art Center**, on Packwood Avenue in the leafy suburb of Maitland, occupies studios designed in the 1930s by artist André Smith as a winter retreat for fellow artists. Set around courtyards and gardens, the buildings show a profusion of Mayan and Aztec motifs. The studios are still used, and exhibitions of contemporary American crafts are held often here.

North of Lake Eola is the town's newest attraction, the **Orlando Science Center**. Covering 207,000 sq feet (19,200 sq m) of floor space, the center's aim is to offer a stimulating environment for experimental science learning. It thus provides a huge range of exciting state-of-the-art interactive exhibits. Among its attractions are the Dr. Philips CineDome, which also functions as a planetarium, its dinosaur fossils collection, and the ShowBiz Science exhibit, which reveals some of the tricks and special effects used in movies.

Loch Haven Park
N Mills Ave at Rollins St.
Orlando Museum of Art ***Tel*** *(407) 896-4231.* *Tue–Sun.* *public hols.* **www**.omart.org

Orlando Science Center
777 East Princeton St.
Tel *(407) 514-2000.* *9am–5pm Tue–Thu, 9am–9pm Fri–Sat, noon–5pm Sun.* **www**.osc.org

Winter Park 13

25,000. *507 N New York Ave, (407) 644-8281.* **Scenic Boat Tour** ***Tel*** *(407) 644-4056.* **www**.scenicboattours.com

Greater Orlando's most refined neighborhood took off in the 1880s, when wealthy northerners came south and began to build winter retreats here. The **Charles Hosmer Morse Museum of American Art** probably has the finest collection of works by Art Nouveau craftsman, Louis Comfort Tiffany. There are superb examples of his jewelry, lamps, and many of his windows, including the *The Four Seasons* (1899). To the south of Winter Park is **Rollins College**, dotted with 1930s Spanish-style buildings. The finest is the **Knowles Memorial Chapel**, whose main entrance has a relief of a meeting between the Seminole Indians and the Spanish conquistadors. The college's **Cornell Fine Arts Museum's** impressive collection of Italian Renaissance paintings is the oldest in Florida. The **Scenic Boat Tour** explores the nearby lakes and canals.

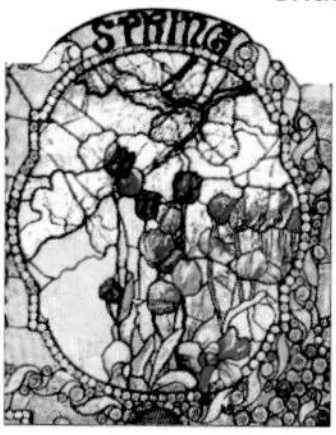

Tiffany's *Four Seasons* window, Winter Park

Charles Hosmer Morse Museum of American Art
445 Park Ave N. ***Tel*** *(407) 645-5311.* *Tue–Sun.* *public hols.* **www**.morsemuseum.org

Main entrance of Knowles Memorial Chapel, Winter Park

The sinking home of Ripley's Believe It or Not!, International Drive

International Drive ⓮

Orlando. *Orlando.*
Visitor Center, 8723 International Drive, (407) 363-5872.

A stone's throw from Walt Disney World, "I Drive" is a 3-mile (5-km) ribbon of hotels, shops, and theaters. Its most popular attraction is **Wet'n Wild**, known for its big-thrill rides. The Storm and Mach 5 feature terrifying descents down near-vertical slides, and there is also the watery Kid's Playground.

Filled with fantastic objects, illusions, and film footage of strange feats, **Ripley's Believe It or Not!** was created by the American cartoonist, Robert Ripley. It is housed in a building that appears to be falling into one of Florida's sinkholes, which occur due to the erosion of the limestone bedrock. **Titanic – Experience** displays artifacts, movie memorabilia, and re-creations of the ship's rooms and grand staircase. Two blocks from the mall is Orlando's **Official Visitor Information Center**, which has coupons for many attractions, such as discounts on admission and bargain meals.

Kissimmee ⓯

41,000. *1925 E Irlo Bronson Memorial Hwy, (407) 847-5000.* **www**.floridakiss.com

Meaning "Heaven's Place" in the language of the Calusa Indians, Kissimmee is said to be the cow capital of Florida. In the early 20th century, cows freely roamed the streets of this cattle boom town. Today, the only livestock visitors are likely to encounter are those that appear in the rodeos at **Silver Spur Arena**. Held every February and July, this is the biggest rodeo east of the Mississippi.

Most visitors headed for Walt Disney World often stop at Kissimmee, drawn by the many inexpensive motels, strung along the busy, traffic-ridden US 192. For those who want to linger, Kissimmee's Old Town is a re-created pedestrian street of early 20th-century buildings with several eccentric shops offering psychic readings and tattoos. **Warbird Adventures**, which is by the Kissimmee Municipal Airport, gives visitors the unforgettable opportunity to fly in an original World War II advanced T-6 navy trainer or a classic M.A.S.H. helicopter. Whether you want a thrilling acrobatic adventure or a smooth sightseeing flight, visitors can take the controls and learn about flying one of these historical aircraft from an experienced instructor.

Warbird Adventures
233 N Hoagland Blvd.
Tel *(407) 870-7366, (800) 386-1593.*
9am–5pm Mon–Sat, by appointment Sun.
www.warbirdadventures.com

Disney Wilderness Preserve ⓰

Road map E3. 2700 Scrub Jay Trail, 12 miles (18 km) SW of Kissimmee. ***Tel*** *(407) 935-0002.* *Kissimmee.* *Kissimmee.* *9am–5pm daily.* *Sat–Sun Jun–Sep.* *Sun 1:30pm Oct–May.* **www**.nature.org

Orlando's best wilderness preserve is a haven for native plants and animals, and also for people wanting to get away from the crowds. Unlike other Disney attractions, there are no thrill rides on these 12,000 acres (18.75 sq miles), but there is still plenty to do. There is an off-road buggy tour on Sundays, and three hiking trails that lead to Lake Russell. The interpretive trail is 0.8-mile (1.2-km) long and visitors can learn about nature along the way. The longer trails are mostly unshaded, so bring sunscreen, a hat, plenty of water, and insect repellent.

Lake Russell, one of many lakes at the Disney Wilderness Preserve

Daytona Beach ⓱

64,000. 126 E Orange Ave, (386) 255-0415.
www.daytonabeach.com

This resort is famous for its 23-mile (37-km) beach, lined with a wall of hotels. The old-fashioned boardwalk offers concerts in the bandstand, arcades, and go-karts. During the April Spring Break, nearly 200,000 college students descend on the beach for this ritual party.

This is also one of the few beaches in Florida where cars are allowed on the sands, a hangover from the days when motor enthusiasts, such as Louis Chevrolet and Henry Ford, raced on the beaches. The **Daytona International Speedway** nearby draws huge crowds, especially during the Speedweek in February and the Motorcycle Weeks in March and October *(see p28)*.

Across the Halifax River downtown, the **Halifax Historical Society Museum** occupies a 1910 bank building and displays local history. To the west, the **Museum of Arts and Sciences** has exhibits from 1640 to 1920. **Gamble Place**, run by the museum, is a hunting lodge built in 1907 for James N. Gamble, of Procter & Gamble fame. Museum tours include the Snow White House, built for Gamble's grandchildren.

Museum of Arts & Sciences
1040 Museum Blvd. ***Tel*** *(386) 255-0285.* *daily.* *public hols.*

Cars cruising the hard-packed sands of Daytona Beach

St. Augustine ⓲

16,000. 100 Malaga St, (904) 829-6401. 10 Castillo Dr, (904) 825-1000. Arts & Crafts Spring Festival (Apr). **www**.visitoldcity.com

America's oldest continuously occupied European settlement was founded by the Spanish colonist Pedro Menéndez de Avilés on the feast day of St. Augustine in 1565. Today, this town has many attractions for the modern tourist, not least its 43 miles (69 km) of beaches and the fact that it is within easy reach of several golf courses and marinas. St. Augustine burned down in 1702 but was soon rebuilt in the lee of the **Castillo de San Marcos**. This mighty fortress is the largest and most complete Spanish fort in the US. Constructed of coquina, a sedimentary limestone formed by seashells and corals that could withstand the impact of cannonballs, this is a superb example of 17th-century military architecture.

The historic heart of St. Augustine is compact and easy to explore on foot. Horsedrawn carriage tours are popular and depart from Avenida Menendez, north of the Bridge of Lions, which was built across Matanzas Bay in 1926. The 18th-century City Gate is the entrance to the **Old Town**. Its focus is the pedestrian St. George Street, lined with attractive stone buildings. Some of the main attractions here are the **Spanish Quarter Village**, a museum that recreates an 18th-century garrison town, and **Peña-Peck House**, a fine First Spanish Period home dating to the 1740s. The **Oldest Wooden Schoolhouse**, built from cypress and red cedar wood in the mid-1700s, is also located on this street. The heart of the Spanish settlement is **Plaza de la Constitution**, a leafy square flanked by Government House Museum and the grand Basilica Cathedral.

Cleopatra **(c.1890) by Romanelli, Lightner Museum**

The splendid **Flagler College** started out as the Ponce de Leon Hotel, built by Henry Flagler *(see p286)* in 1883, a year after he honeymooned in St. Augustine. Its gilded and stuccoed cupola has symbolic motifs representing Spain and Florida, notably the golden mask of the Timucuan Indian sun god and the lamb – a symbol of Spanish knighthood. The other resorts Flagler built here are the Cordoba and Alcazar Hotels. The latter, a three-floor Hispano-Moorish structure, is now the **Lightner Museum**, devoted to the country's Gilded Age. Its exhibits include glass works by Louis Tiffany, and its Grand Ballroom houses an eclectic exhibit of "American Castle" furniture. The lovely **Ximenez-Fatio House** is now a museum run by the National Society of Colonial Dames. It seeks to re-create the genteel boarding house that it was in the 1830s, when invalids and adventurers first visited Florida in order to escape from the harsh northern winters.

Castillo de San Marcos
1 S Castillo Dr. ***Tel*** *(904) 829-6506.* *8:45am–4:45pm daily.* *Dec 25.* *limited.* *call for details.*
www.nps.gov/casa

Lightner Museum
75 King St. ***Tel*** *(904) 824-2874.* *daily.* *Dec 25.*
www.lightnermuseum.org

For hotels and restaurants in this region see p328 and p332

Fernandina's Beech Street Grill with Chinese Chippendale motifs

Fernandina Beach ⓳

10,000. Jacksonville. Jacksonville. 961687 Gateway Blvd Ste 101 G, (904) 261-3248.

The town of Fernandina Beach on Amelia Island, just across the St. Mary's River from Georgia, was famous as a pirates' den until the early 1800s. Its harbor attracted a motley crew of foreign adventurers, whose various allegiances earned the island its soubriquet, the "Isle of Eight Flags." Today, Fernandina is better known as a charming Victorian resort and Florida's primary source of sweet Atlantic white shrimp: more than 2 million pounds (900,000 kilos) are harvested by shrimping fleets each year.

Occupying a large section of the town's **Historic District**, the Silk Stocking District was named after the affluence of its original residents. Sea captains and timber barons built homes here in a variety of styles. Queen Anne houses with turrets jostle with graceful Italianate residences and fine Chinese Chippendale structures, such as the **Beech Street Grill**. The weathered buildings on Centre Street once housed chandleries and naval stores. Antique shops and gift shops have now replaced them; the 1878 Palace Saloon, however, still serves a wicked Pirate's Punch at the mahogany bar adorned with hand-carved caryatids. Farther south, the **Amelia Island Museum of History** occupies the former jail and offers twice daily, 90-minute guided history tours recounting the island's turbulent past – from the time of its first Indian inhabitants to the early 1900s.

The **Fort Clinch State Park**, at the island's northern tip, has trails, beaches, and campsites, as well as a 19th-century fort built in 1847. Park rangers now dress in Civil War uniforms and perform 19th-century war re-enactments one weekend a month.

Amelia Island Museum of History
233 S 3rd St. ***Tel*** *(904) 261-7378. Mon–Sat. public hols. limited. compulsory, two tours daily.*

Ocala National Forest ⓴

daily. campgrounds & swimming areas. **Visitor Center** 3199 NE Co Rd. ***Tel*** *(352) 236-0288.* **Juniper Springs Canoe Rental** ***Tel*** *(352) 625-2808.*

Between Ocala and the St. John's River, the world's largest sand pine forest covers 366,000 acres (148,000 ha) and is crisscrossed by rivers and hiking trails. One of the last refuges of the endangered Florida black bear, it is also home to animals such as deer and otter, and a variety of birds such as bald eagles, barred owls, wild turkey, and several wading birds. Hiking trails vary from boardwalks and short loop trails to the 66-mile (106-km) stretch of the National Scenic Trail. Bass-fishing is popular, and there are swimming holes and campgrounds at the recreation areas of Salt Springs and Alexander Springs.

Canoe rental is widely available; the 7-mile (11-km) canoe run down Juniper Creek from the **Juniper Springs Recreation Area** is one of the finest in Florida. The Salt Springs trail is especially good for bird-watching. There are guides at the main visitor center on the forest's western fringe or at the centers at Salt Springs and Lake Dorr, on Route 19.

Environs

Silver Springs, on the western border of Ocala National Forest, 29 miles (46 km) west of the Juniper Springs Recreation Area, is the world's largest artesian spring and Florida's oldest tourist attraction. Its famous glass-bottomed boat tours have been running since 1878. Jeep safaris and "Jungle Cruises" also travel through the Florida outback, where the early Tarzan movies starring Johnny Weismuller were filmed. Wild Waters, next to the springs, is a lively water park. The quieter **Silver River State Park**, 2 miles (3 km) southeast, has a lovely walking trail through a hardwood hammock and cypress swamp, leading to a swimming hole in a bend of the crystal clear river.

Silver River State Park
1425 NE 58th Ave, Ocala. ***Tel*** *(352) 236-7148. daily.*

Juniper Springs, Ocala National Forest

Tallahassee ㉑

137,000. 918 Railroad Ave, (800) 872-7245. 106 E Jefferson, (850) 413-9200. Springtime Tallahassee (Mar–Apr).

Encircled by rolling hills, Florida's dignified state capital is gracious and uncompromisingly Southern. Tallahassee grew dramatically during the plantation era, and the elegant town houses built in the 1800s can still be seen around Park Avenue and Calhoun Street. The Chamber of Commerce, on Duval Street, is housed in the city's oldest building, a 1830 Classical-Revival mansion, known as "The Columns."

The **Old Capitol Building** in downtown Tallahasse has been beautifully restored to its 1902 state, with a pristine white dome and striped awnings. Once inside, guests can visit the Supreme Court chamber and the Senate. The high-rise **New Capitol Building** behind it offers a fabulous view of the city. The **Museum of Florida History** situated on Bronough Street, covers about 12,000 years of the region's history.

The Old and the New Capitol Buildings, Tallahassee

Environs
During the 1820s and '30s, the area around Tallahassee was Florida's most important cotton-growing region. A tour along the canopied roads of the old **Cotton Trail** takes visitors past former cotton plantations and cattle pastures. The **Goodwood Museum and Gardens** retains its lovely 1830s mansion; Bradley's Country Store, set up in 1927, still serves their famous homemade sausages. Located 15 miles (24 km) south of Tallahassee, **Wakulla Springs State Park** has one of the world's largest freshwater springs, which pumps 700,000 gal (2.6 million liters) of water a minute into a large pool. Here, visitors can swim or snorkel in its clear waters or ride in a glass-bottomed boat. Boat trips on the Wakulla River are the best way to see alligators and wading birds. The elegant Wakulla Springs Lodge was built in the 1930s.

Wakulla Springs State Park
550 Wakulla Park Dr, Wakulla Springs.
Tel *(850) 926-0700. daily.*
www.floridastateparks.org

Pensacola ㉒

294,000. 980 E Heinburg St, (850) 433-4966. (850) 476-4800. 1401 E Gregory St, (850) 434-1234. Fiesta of Five Flags (Jun). **www**.visitpensacola.com

Florida's earliest Spanish settlement, Pensacola was established by Don Tristan de Luna, who sailed into Pensacola Bay in 1559. The city features diverse architectural

The Beaches of the Panhandle

Lying between Perdido Key and Panama City Beach are some of Florida's most beautiful beaches. The brilliant sand, consisting mainly of quartz, is washed down from the Appalachian Mountains. One can choose between quiet, pristine beaches and more lively resorts, with ample opportunities for water sports. The main season is April–July.

Perdido Key ①
is the location of Florida's most westerly shores, which are inaccessible by car and quieter than most.

Quietwater Beach ②
On Santa Rosa Island, it's not the Panhandle's finest but is an easy hop from Pensacola.

Pensacola Beach ③
has miles of pristine sand and a string of shops, hotels, and bars. Large crowds gather here on weekends to sunbathe and swim.

Navarre Beach ④
is quieter than Pensacola but nevertheless has good facilities, water sports, and a pier for fishing.

0 km 15
0 miles 10

styles, from Colonial cottages to elegant Classical-Revival homes. Pensacola was wiped out by a hurricane two years after it was established, but it was soon rebuilt, and over the next 300 years the city was occupied by the Spanish, French, English, and the Americans. The 1800s were a period of prosperity ushered in by the timber boom, and much of today's downtown dates from this time.

Pensacola's oldest quarter, the **Historic Pensacola Village**, has a number of museums and houses, built by wealthy pioneers and traders. There are daily tours from Tivoli House on Zaragoza Street. Forming a backdrop to the Museum of Commerce is a cleverly constructed Victorian streetscape, complete with a printer's workshop, a saddlery, and an old-time music store. Florida's earliest church, the Old Christ Church (1832), stands in the leafy Seville Square shaded by oaks and magnolia trees.

The **TT Wentworth, Jr., Florida State Museum**, set in a Spanish Renaissance Revival building, has an eclectic collection that includes oddities such as a shrunken head from pre-Columbian times and old Coca-Cola bottles.

Farther north, the **North Hill Preservation District** has 19th- and 20th-century houses, built on the sites of British and Spanish forts. Even today, cannonballs are found in local gardens. A very striking home is the McCreary House on North Baylen Street. A Queen Anne home built in 1900, it has a gabled roof and tower. Lying between the two districts, **Palafox Street** is the city's commercial hub.

TT Wentworth, Jr., Florida State Museum
330 S Jefferson St. *(850) 595-5985.* *Mon–Fri.* *public hols.*
www.historicpensacola.org

Guides in 19th-century costume in the Historic Pensacola Village

Apalachicola ㉓

3,000. *Tallahassee.* *122 Commerce St, (850) 653-9419.*
www.apalachicolabay.org

A riverside customs station established in 1823, Apalachicola's first 100 years were its finest. It flourished first with the cotton trade, and later with the lumber boom. Today, pines and hardwoods still stand in the **Apalachicola National Forest**. The area offers hiking trails, canoeing opportunities, and campsites. Oystering in the Apalachicola River began in the 1920s. Oyster boats still pull up at the dockside, and Water Street has many places where fresh oysters are available.

A walking map of the old town, available at the Chamber of Commerce, takes in buildings from the cotton era, such as the 1838 Greek Revival Raney House. The **John Gorrie State Museum** houses a model of Gorrie's patent ice-making machine. Designed to cool yellow fever patients, the doctor's 1851 invention was the vanguard of modern refrigeration and air conditioning.

Fort Walton Beach ⑤
A relaxed resort, ideal for family holidays. It is also one of the best beaches for water sports.

Panama City Beach ⑨
Condos and amusement parks line buzzing Panama City Beach, the Panhandle's biggest resort. Water sports facilities are excellent here.

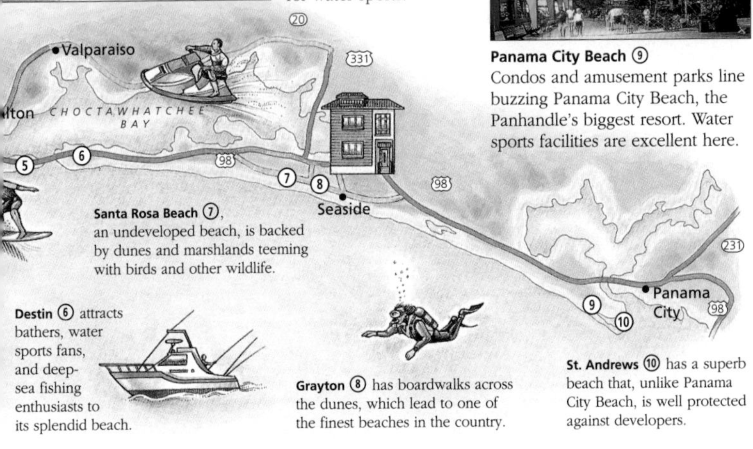

Santa Rosa Beach ⑦, an undeveloped beach, is backed by dunes and marshlands teeming with birds and other wildlife.

Destin ⑥ attracts bathers, water sports fans, and deep-sea fishing enthusiasts to its splendid beach.

Grayton ⑧ has boardwalks across the dunes, which lead to one of the finest beaches in the country.

St. Andrews ⑩ has a superb beach that, unlike Panama City Beach, is well protected against developers.

The high-rise skyline of downtown Tampa on the Gulf Coast

Tampa ㉔

300,000. 601 Nebraska Ave, (800) 872-7245. 610 Polk St, (800) 231-2222. Channelside Dr, (800) 741-2297. 615 Channelside Dr, (813) 223-1111. Gasparilla Festival (Feb). **www**.visittampabay.com

Situated at the mouth of the Hillsborough River, Tampa is one of Florida's fastest-growing cities. A perfect harbor, Tampa Bay was a magnet to the Spanish, who arrived here in 1539. However, the city's greatest period of prosperity was in the 1800s, when railroad baron Henry Plant extended his railroad here and made it an important center for trade.

Tampa's downtown area is centered around the partly pedestrian Franklin Street, which has the historic Tampa Theater. To its southeast, on North Ashley Drive, is the **Tampa Museum of Art**. This museum's exhibits range from Greek, Roman, and Etruscan antiquities to 20th-century American art.

The luxurious Tampa Bay Hotel, which houses the **Henry B. Plant Museum**, is the city's premier landmark, its Moorish minarets visible from all over the city. Plant commissioned the building in 1891, and its construction alone cost $3 million. Currently a part of the University of Tampa, the south wing has been preserved as a museum. Its splendidly furnished interior retains the original Wedgwood china, Venetian mirrors, and 18th-century French furniture.

The **Florida Aquarium** is on Channelside Drive. It displays a variety of sea creatures such as seabirds, otters, and baby alligators living in tanks that replicate their natural habitats.

Located 3 miles (5 km) east of downtown, **Ybor City** was created by Spaniard Don Vicente Martinez Ybor, when he moved his cigar business from Key West to Tampa in the late 1800s. About 20,000 migrant workers settled here, and the legacy of the cigar boom is still visible on 7th Avenue, with its Spanish tiles and wrought-iron balconies. Today, the area is known for its lively shops, clubs, and restaurants, including the Columbia Restaurant, Florida's oldest establishment.

Northeast of downtown, the **Museum of Science and Industry** features various exhibits including an IMAX® Cinema. The GTE Challenger Learning Center, a living memorial to the Space Shuttle *Challenger*, has simulators and a mission control room. Nearby is Tampa's biggest attraction – **Busch Gardens**. This theme park incorporates an unusual zoo that re-creates colonial-era Africa. The zoo supports over 2,600 animals, with giraffes and zebras roaming freely over the "Serengeti Plain." Lions and other African animals can be seen on a unique Edge of Africa safari ride.

Greek vase, Tampa Museum of Art

Busch Gardens
Busch Blvd, Tampa. *(813) 987-5082. 9:30am–6pm daily, extended hours for summer & hols.* **www**.buschgardens.com

St. Petersburg ㉕

265,000. 180 9th St North, (727) 898-1496. 100 2nd Ave N, (727) 821-4715. Festival of the States. **www**.stpete.com

Established in 1875, "St. Pete," as it is often called, was originally a retired person's mecca. Times have changed however, and extensive renovations have rejuvenated the downtown waterfront area.

The city's claim to fame is the prestigious **Salvador Dali Museum**, which has the largest private collection of the Spanish artist's work in the world, worth more than $350 million. It was opened in 1982, 40 years after the Ohio businessman Reynolds Morse first met Dali and began collecting his works. There are 95 oil paintings, 100 watercolors and drawings, 1,300 graphics, sculptures, and other objects. Spanning the years 1914–70, they range from Dali's early figurative paintings to his first experiments in Surrealism, as well as those mature, large-scale paintings described as his "masterworks."

The city's best-known landmark is **The Pier**, which has a string of shops and restaurants. Close by, the **St. Petersburg Museum of History** focuses on the city's history and has exhibits ranging from mastodon bones and native pottery to a replica of the sea plane that made the world's first flight with a paying passenger in 1914.

The modern Palladian-style **Museum of Fine Arts**, near the bay, is famous for its wide-ranging collection of European, American, and Asian works. Supreme among the French Impressionist paintings are *A Corner of the Woods* (1877) by Cézanne and Monet's classic *Parliament, Effect of Fog, London* (1904).

Salvador Dali Museum
1000 3rd St S. *(727) 823-3767. 4, 32, trolley from The Pier. 9:30am–5:30pm Mon–Sat (8pm Thu), noon–5:30pm Sun. Thanksgiving, Dec 25.* **www**.salvadordalimuseum.org

For hotels and restaurants in this region see p329 and p333

South Lido Park Beach on Lido Key, one Sarasota's off-shore islands

Environs
The Gulf Coast's much-advertised "361 days of sunshine a year," lures tourists from all over the world to the beaches between St. Petersburg and Clearwater. Known as the Holiday Isles or the Suncoast, the strip encompasses 28 miles (45 km) of barrier island beaches. St. Pete Beach is the busiest, with excellent water sports facilities; the **Fort de Soto Park** beaches have been ranked among the top 10 in the US. Florida's famous sea cows, or manatees, found all along in the coastal waters, are gentle herbivorous giants that grow to a length of 10 ft (3 m). Once plentiful, today only about 2,500 survive.

Sarasota 26

60,000. 575 N Washington Blvd, (941) 955-5735; Amtrak bus, (800) 872-7245. 655 N Tamiami Trail, (941) 957-1877. Circus Festival (Jan). **www**.sarasotafl.org

Known as Florida's cultural center, Sarasota's affluence is often credited to the millionaire circus owner, John Ringling, who invested much of his fortune, estimated at $200 million, in the area. His legacy is best seen at his house and in his splendid collection of European art, Sarasota's biggest attraction. The **Ringling Museum Complex** comprises the Museum of Art, a colorful Circus Museum, and the Ca' d'Zan – Ringling's winter residence overlooking Sarasota Bay. Ringling had a particular love for Italy, and his fine collection of Italian Baroque paintings are the cornerstone of his collection. The highlight of the Museum of Art is the Rubens Gallery. Also noteworthy are the Astor Rooms, displaying the lavish 19th-century interiors of a New York mansion.

Sarasota has an attractive waterfront setting, and numerous artists and writers have settled here. The restored storefronts in the downtown area around Palm Avenue and Main Street house antique shops, bars, and restaurants.

The nearby barrier islands – Longboat Key, Lido Key, and Siesta Key – have great beaches and excellent tourist accommodations. **South Lido Park Beach** on Lido Key has a lovely woodland trail. The broad **Siesta Key Beach** is always lively, while Turtle Beach is quieter and has the only campsite on these Keys. Longboat Key is well known for its golf courses. Most of the beaches offer excellent water sports facilities.

RINGLING MUSEUM COMPLEX: CA' D'ZAN

The Ca' d'Zan (House of John), modeled after a Venetian palace with Renaissance and Baroque features, is set off by a 200-ft (60-m) marble terrace. Its opulence epitomizes the life of the American super-rich of the early 20th-century.

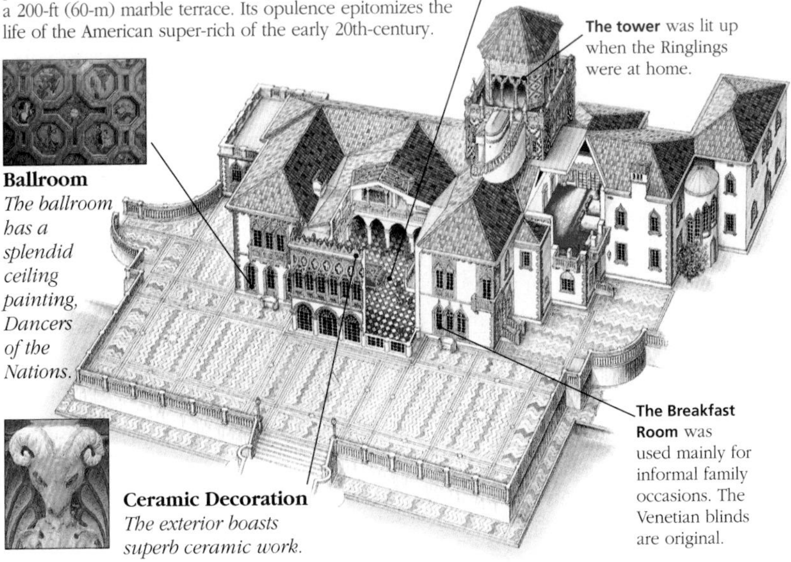

The court, with its marble floors and onyx columns, was the living room and the focal point of the house.

The tower was lit up when the Ringlings were at home.

Ballroom
The ballroom has a splendid ceiling painting, Dancers of the Nations.

The Breakfast Room was used mainly for informal family occasions. The Venetian blinds are original.

Ceramic Decoration
The exterior boasts superb ceramic work.

Beachfront cottages on Sanibel Island, Lee Island Coast

Lee Island Coast 27

2275 Cleveland Ave, Fort Myers, (800) 231-2222. *1159 Causeway Rd, Sanibel, (239) 472-1080.* **Boat Services** *Tropic Star (239) 283-0015; Captiva Cruises (239) 472-5300; North Captiva Island Club Resort (239) 395-1001.*

This coastline offers an irresistible combination of sandy beaches, beautiful sunsets, and exotic wildlife. Of the two most popular islands, **Sanibel** has manicured gardens and rows of shops and restaurants along Periwinkle Way, the town's hub. Most of the beaches with public access are along Gulf Drive, the best being Turner and Bowman's beaches.

The **Sanibel Captiva Conservation Foundation** on Sanibel-Captiva Road, protects a chunk of the island's wetland. It has 4 miles (6 km) of boardwalk trails and an observation tower, which is a vantage point for viewing birds. The **JN "Ding" Darling National Wildlife Refuge** occupies two-thirds of Sanibel. Its wildlife includes raccoons, alligators, and birds such as roseate spoonbills, bald eagles, and ospreys. The popular scenic "Wildlife Drive" can be covered by bike or car. Paths and canoe trails are lined with red mangrove and sea grape. Canoes and fishing boats are available for rent.

Captiva Island, the other popular island, is less developed. However, visitors can enjoy the ambience of the old-fashioned South Seas Plantation Resort with its busy marina, which is the starting point for boat trips to Cayo Costa Island – a beautiful, untouched barrier island.

Both islands are best known for their shells, and visitors soon get drawn into the shell-collecting culture. Other less developed islands lie close by and can be explored by boat.

JN "Ding" Darling National Wildlife Refuge
Mile Marker 2, Sanibel Captiva Rd.
Tel *(239) 472-1100.* *Sat–Thu.* *public hols.*

Environs

Fort Myers, about 25 miles (40 km) east of the Lee Island Coast, is an old-fashioned city that was put on the map in the 1880s by one of America's most famous inventors, Thomas Alva Edison (1847–1931). The Edison Winter Home is Fort Myers' most enduring attraction. Edison built his estate in 1886, and the house, laboratory, and botanical gardens are much as he left them. The laboratory contains his original equipment and is still lit by carbon filament light bulbs, which have been in constant use since Edison invented them. The museum displays personal items, phonographs, and a 1916 Model T car that was given to Edison by Henry Ford, his great friend. Next door, the Ford Winter Home has a few early Ford cars on display.

Original equipment in Thomas Edison's laboratory, Fort Myers

The Fort Myers Historical Museum, on Peck Street, is housed in the former railroad station. Interesting exhibits include a model of Fort Myers in the 1900s, and a P-39 bomber that crashed in the 1940s. To the south of the city are a handful of lively beaches.

Big Cypress Swamp 28

Big Cypress National Preserve ***Tel*** *(239) 695-1201.* *daily.* *Dec 25.* **Fakahatchee Strand Preserve State Park** ***Tel*** *(239) 695- 4593.* *daily.* **Audubon of Florida's Corkscrew Swamp Sanctuary** ***Tel*** *(239) 348-9151.* *daily.*

Home to several hundred plants and animals including the endangered Florida panther, this vast, wetland basin features islands of slash pine, prairies, and hardwood hammocks. A third of the swamp is covered by cypress trees growing in long, narrow forests or "strands." The Tamiami Trail (US 41) stretches from Tampa to Miami and cuts directly through the swamp.

Big Cypress National Preserve is the swamp's largest protected area. Visitors can stop at the Oasis Visitor Center for information and enjoy the views from US 41. The **Fakahatchee Strand Preserve State Park** lies to the west. The few remaining specimens of old growth cypresses, some of which are 600 years old, are found at Big Cypress Bend. The country's largest cluster of royal palms are also found here. Route 846 leads to **Audubon of Florida's Corkscrew Swamp Sanctuary**, with its old-growth cypresses. It is famous for its birds and is a winter nesting area for endangered wood storks.

For hotels and restaurants in this region see p329 and p333

Everglades National Park ㉙

daily. all centers open Dec–Apr: daily; check for rest of year. **Ernest F. Coe Visitor Center** ***Tel*** *(305) 242-7700.* *8am–4:30pm all year.* **Gulf Coast Visitor Center** *(Everglades City)* ***Tel*** *(239) 695-3311; boat tours & canoe rental (239) 695-2591.* **Shark Valley Information Center** ***Tel*** *(305) 221-8776; tram tours & cycle rental (305) 221-8455.* **Royal Palm Visitor Center** ***Tel*** *(305) 242-7700.* **Flamingo Visitor Center** ***Tel*** *(239) 695-2945. For canoe, bicycle rental & boat tours, call (239) 695-3101.* *most boardwalks are accessible.* *(800) 365-2267 to book.* **www**.nps.gov/ever

Covering 1.4 million acres (566,580 ha), the Everglades National Park makes up only a fifth of the world-famous Everglades – low lying wetlands formed from the overspill of Lake Okeechobee. The unique landscape consists of a vast expanse of sawgrass prairie, broken by tree islands, hammocks, and meandering channels. A paradise for wildlife, the park has a wide range of fauna, including 400 species of birds.

The main entrance lies 10 miles (16 km) west of Florida City. Inside are walking trails, most of them elevated boardwalks; some are suitable for bicycles. Boats and canoes can be rented. The best time to visit is during winter. South of the main entrance lies the informative Royal Palm Visitor Center and two boardwalk trails. The popular **Anhinga Trail** attracts wildlife in the dry winter months, and its open site is excellent for photographs. Alligators congregate at the "gator hole" (a pond that is hollowed out by alligators in the dry season to reach the water below) at the head of the trail, and a wide range of fauna, including deer, raccoons, and the splendid anhinga bird, can be spotted. Close by, the **Gumbo Limbo Trail** offers the best chance to explore a tropical hardwood hammock but is ridden with mosquitos. Watch for the pretty bromeliads, non-parasitic members of the pineapple family that grow on other plants, and the trail's namesake, the gumbo-limbo tree with its red bark.

A short distance to the west, **Long Pine Key's** campsite is beautifully situated and is one of the main reasons that people stop here. Several shady trails lead off from it: do not stray from the paths as the limestone bedrock has "solution holes" created by rain, which are deep and difficult to spot.

Shark Valley lies north of Long Pine Key, near the park boundary. The area is best visited by taking a tram tour or a bicycle along the 15-mile (25-km) loop road. A 60-ft (18-m) tower at its end offers great views. The valley is home to the Seminole Indians, who settled here in the 19th-century after being driven into the Everglades by land-hungry Europeans *(see p286)*.

The elevated **Pa-hay-okee Overlook** lies northwest of Long Key Pine. The expanse of sawgrass prairie seen from here is typical of the Everglades landscape. The view from the observation tower is worth the climb: tree islands break the horizon, and a multitude of birds, such as hawks, roseate spoonbills, great blue herons, and snail kites, can be easily spotted.

The **Mahogany Hammock Trail** leads through one of the park's largest hammocks, and it has a variety of fauna and flora. Trails such as West Lake Trail and Snake Bight Trail lie between Mahogany Hammock and **Flamingo** on Florida Bay and are especially rich in birdlife. Flamingo has the park's only hotel and also offers a wide choice of activities such as hiking, fishing, boating, and wildlife viewing. An overnight stay at the campsite is a must, especially for bird-watching. The bays around Flamingo have manatees *(see p319)*, as well as the rare, endangered American crocodile. The Flamingo Visitor Center has information about ranger-led activities: talks, slideshows, and walks through the swamp. Canoeing is the best way to explore the **watery trails around Flamingo**. These range from short trips to a week-long adventure of the remote Wilderness Waterway, leading past Whitewater Bay along the park's western coast. Northwest of Flamingo, the park's western entrance is marked by the island of Chokoloskee.

Park ranger

Today, the Everglades are under threat. Irrigation canals have disrupted the flow of water from Lake Okeechobee, which could prove disastrous for this delicate ecosystem.

Visitors should follow a few, simple safety tips. Bring insect repellent and protection against the sun. Follow park rules and respect all wildlife. Note that some shrubs and trees are poisonous, as are some caterpillars, spiders, and snakes. Do not wander off the pathways, and drive slowly because animals often venture onto the road.

Boardwalk through swamps in the Everglades National Park

Biscayne National Park 30

9700 SW 328th St, Convoy Point.
Miami. Tel (305) 230-7275.
daily. Dec 25. limited.
Boat Tours *Tel (305) 230-1100.*
www.nps.gov/bisc

Dense mangrove swamp protects the shoreline of Biscayne National Park, which incorporates the northernmost islands of the Florida Keys. Its waters hold the park's greatest draw – a living coral reef with myriad forms and over 200 types of tropical fish. The barrier islands are unoccupied, so the coral here is healthier and the water even clearer than in the more popular parks farther south. Activities include glass-bottomed boat tours, snorkeling, and diving – all arranged by the visitor center.

Bahia Honda's beautiful beach, the finest in the Florida Keys

The Keys 31

Miami.

Running southwest off the tip of the Florida peninsula are the Keys, a chain of fossilized coral islands protected by North America's only coral reef. Visitors flock to the resorts here to enjoy several activities ranging from fishing to snorkeling.

From the 1500s, the Keys lured a succession of settlers, pirates, and "wreckers." Its development, however, took off in the early 1900s, when rail baron Henry Flagler *(see p286)* constructed the Overseas Railroad across the Keys. It has since been replaced by the magnificent Overseas Highway, which ends at Key West.

The largest island in the Upper Keys is **Key Largo**, named "long island" by Spanish explorers. One of its highlights is the *African Queen*, the boat used in the eponymous 1951 film, which makes short pleasure trips. The island's greatest draws, however, are the diving and snorkeling opportunities just offshore in the **John Pennekamp Coral Reef State Park**. The park has a visitor center, swimming areas, and woodland trails, but it is best known for its fabulous underwater reaches, which provide a glimpse of the extraordinary forms of coral reef life.

Gold ornament from a treasure ship

Islamorada, south of Key Largo, declares itself as the "Sport Fishing Capital of the World." Encompassing seven islands, it is known for its outstanding big game fishing. The Whale Harbor Marina on Upper Matecumbe Key bristles with impressive deep-sea charter craft, used to catch blue-water fish. Fishing boats, based here, offer half-day trips, even if visitors are not expert anglers.

Long Key Bridge marks the beginning of the Middle Keys. The **Dolphin Research Center**, a nonprofit concern on Grassy Key, conducts the delightful "Dolphin Encounter," where one can swim with these endearing marine mammals. It is also a rest home for sick and injured dolphins.

The heavily developed **Marathon Key** is the main center of the Middle Keys. Its primary appeal lies in fertile fishing grounds, and enthusiasts can choose from a range of angling techniques, including spear-fishing and line-fishing. Crane Point Hammock has 64 acres (26 ha) of tropical forest and mangroves, and several trails, while the **Museum of Natural History of the Florida Keys** explains the islands' history, geology, and ecology.

The Lower Keys are more rugged and less developed than the Upper and Middle Keys. The vegetation is more wooded and supports a different flora and fauna. The most striking change, however, is in the slow and languid pace of life.

After crossing the Seven Mile Bridge, visitors can head for the **Bahia Honda State Park**, which has the finest beach in the Keys. Brilliant

FISHING IN THE FLORIDA KEYS

Deep-sea fishing from a sports boat

Islamorada, Marathon, and Key West are the area's major fishing centers, and small marinas throughout the region offer boats for rent. There are options to suit most budgets and abilities, and one can book places on fishing party boats or hire guides. Deep-sea fishing, an exhilarating option, appeals to the Hemingway spirit of the angler, while backcountry fishing calls for stealth and cunning. The numerous bait and tackle shops rent out gear and sell licenses.

white sand is backed by tropical forest, with unusual species of trees, such as silver palm and yellow satinwood. Canoes, kayaks, and water sports gear are available to rent. The adjacent **Looe Key National Marine Sanctuary** is a spectacular dive location, with abundant marine life.

The second largest island, **Big Pine Key** is the Lower Keys' main residential community and the best place to see the diminutive Key deer. The turning near MM 30 leads to the **Blue Hole**, a flooded quarry whose viewing platform is ideal for watching the deer and other wildlife.

Key Largo
MM 106, (305) 451-1414, (800) 822-1088. **www**.fla-key.com

John Pennekamp Coral Reef State Park
MM 102.5. ***Tel*** *(305) 451-1202.* *daily.* *limited.*

Key West 32

28,000. 402 Wall St, (305) 294-2587.

The southernmost settlement in the US, Key West is a magnet for people who want to leave the rest of America behind. In the 16th century, it became a haven for pirates and "wreckers." "Wrecking," or the salvage of shipwrecks on the Keys' coral reef, was the business that first made Key West rich.

It soon became Florida's wealthiest city, and its opportunistic lifestyle attracted a stream of settlers from the Americas, the Caribbean, and Europe; their legacy is visible in the island's unique architecture and cuisine. An influx of writers and a large gay community in recent years have added to Key West's cultural cocktail.

Most of the sights are within a few blocks of **Duval Street**, the main axis of Old Key West. Bylanes, such as Fleming Street, have many fine 19th-century wooden buildings, which contrast with the simple homes erected to house Cuban cigar-workers.

The **Wreckers' Museum** on Duval Street was originally the home of the wreck captain Francis B. Watlington. Built in 1829, its design displays some eccentric maritime influences, such as a hatch used for ventilation in the roof. It is stuffed with nautical bric-a-brac. Farther down, the **San Carlos Institute**, founded in 1871, is a Cuban heritage center. The garden of **Heritage House Museum**, on Caroline Street, has the Robert Frost cottage, named after the famous American poet who frequently stayed here. At the northern edge of the Old Town is **Mallory Square**, which comes to life at sunset, when a variety of performing artists amuse the crowds.

The **Bahama Village** on the western fringe of the Old Town is named after Key West's earliest settlers. It has a lively Caribbean flavor with a number of brightly painted clapboard buildings.

A prime attraction is the Spanish-colonial style **Hemingway Home**, where novelist Ernest Hemingway lived from 1931 to 1940. The room where he penned several of his most famous works, such as *To Have and Have Not* (the only book set in Key West), is above the carriage house. His library, travel mementos, and memorabilia, such as the cigar-maker's chair on which he sat and wrote, are on display.

The **Mel Fisher Maritime Museum** on Green Street, displays fabulous shipwreck treasures such as coins, jewels, and crucifixes. These were salvaged by the late Mel Fisher, who discovered the wrecks of the Spanish galleons *Nuestra Señora de Atocha* and *Santa Margarita*, about 40 miles (64 km) west of Key West, in 1985. Inside were 47 tons of gold and silver bars, and 70 lbs (32 kg) of raw emeralds that sank with the galleons in 1622.

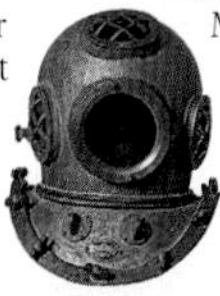

Diver's helmet, Mel Fisher Museum

The **Conch Train** and **the Old Town Trolley Tour** are convenient options for exploring the town.

Hemingway Home
907 Whitehead St. ***Tel*** *(305) 294-1136.* *daily.* *limited.*
www.hemingwayhome.com

FLORIDA'S CORAL REEF

North America's only live coral reef extends 200 miles (320 km) along the length of the Keys, from Miami to the Dry Tortugas. A complex and delicate ecosystem, it protects these islands from oceanic storms. Coral reefs are created over thousands of years by tiny marine organisms known as polyps and are home to a multitude of plants and sea creatures, including 500 species of fish.

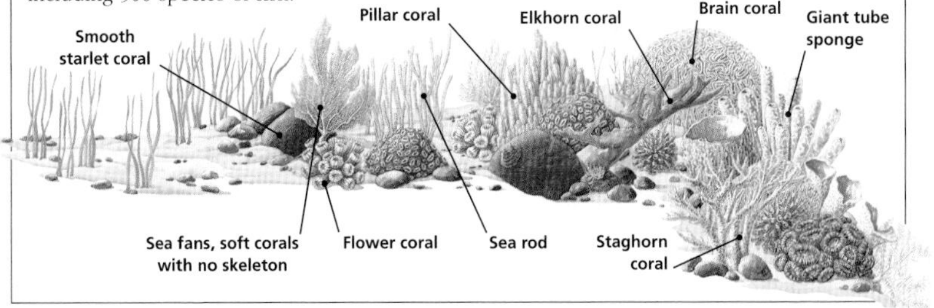

Practical Information

With over 40 million visitors a year, Florida is very well geared for catering to tourists' needs. It is the ultimate family vacation destination. A strong emphasis is placed on entertaining children, and the superb facilities available, make traveling with youngsters a real pleasure. Given its warm climate, Florida is a winter destination for many Americans. The peak season runs from December to April, when the beaches and other attractions are at their busiest. Anyone visiting Walt Disney World or other theme parks should be prepared for long lines during the peak season.

TOURIST INFORMATION

Most large cities in Florida have a Convention and Visitor's Bureau (CVB), offering a huge array of brochures. Most hotels also have a brochure rack or free "WHERE" magazines that list museums, entertainment, shopping, and dining. To get information before you leave home, call or write for a vacation pack, issued by the Florida Tourism group.

SECURITY & HEALTH

Though crimes against tourists have fallen since the 1990s, it is best to be take precautions in urban areas, especially in Miami. Avoid deserted neighborhoods at night. Carry as little money as possible, and leave valuables at home or check them at the hotel reception desk (it is best not to leave valuables in your hotel room). If attacked, hand over your wallet at once, and do not try to resist. In case of a serious illness or accident, hospitals provide good treatment. Minor ailments can be treated at the 24-hour walk-in clinics. Medical care is expensive, so be sure your insurance documents are up-to-date. In an emergency dial 911, or you can contact **Metro-Dade Police Information**.

NATURAL HAZARDS

Hurricanes are infrequent but devastating when they do occur. If a storm is imminent follow the announcements on local television and radio. The **National Hurricane Center** in Miami gives details on impending hurricanes. On beaches, keep an eye on children as riptides are a danger in some places.

The worst climatic hazard is the sun. Use sunscreen, wear hats, and drink plenty of fluids to avoid dehydration. Alligators are a thrilling sight in the Everglades but they can and do kill, so treat them with respect. Look out for spiders, scorpions, and venomous snakes native to Florida. It is best not to touch unfamiliar vegetation. Wear insect repellent when visiting parks and nature preserves.

DRIVING IN FLORIDA

Driving in Florida is a delight because of its excellent road network, inexpensive gasoline, and affordable car rentals. The fastest routes are the six-lane Interstate Highways, referred to as I-10, I-75, and so on. Be warned that local drivers change lanes frequently on expressways, so stick to the right and be alert near exits. Speed limits can vary within a few miles, from 55–70 mph (90–105 km/h) on highways, to 20–30 mph (32–48 km/h) in residential areas, and 15 mph (24 km/h) near schools Speed limits are rigorously enforced, and fines can be as much as $500.

In the event of a serious breakdown, call the emergency number on the rental agreement and the agency will provide a new vehicle. The **American Automobile Association (AAA)** also has its own breakdown service and will assist its members.

Miami has had a bad reputation for crimes against motorists, but be careful in other areas as well. Avoid driving in unfamiliar territory after dark. If you have to refer to a map, stop only when you are in a well-lit area. Ignore any attempt by anyone to stop you from driving.

ETIQUETTE

Dress in Florida is mostly casual, but it is illegal for women to go topless on beaches, except in a few places, such as Miami's South Beach. Drinking alcohol on beaches and in other public places is illegal, as is smoking in buses, trains, taxis, and in most public buildings. All restaurants and cafés are no-smoking in Florida.

THE CLIMATE OF FLORIDA

With its warm climate, Florida is a year-round destination. Its climatic divide between the temperate north and the subtropical south means that the state has two distinct tourist seaons. In south Florida (including Orlando), the busiest time is when tourists come to enjoy the mild winters. Here the summers can be uncomfortably hot. In the north, the Panhandle attracts most visitors in the summer. Despite this difference, the Sunshine State by and large lives up to its reputation of clear, blue skies and a pleasant climate.

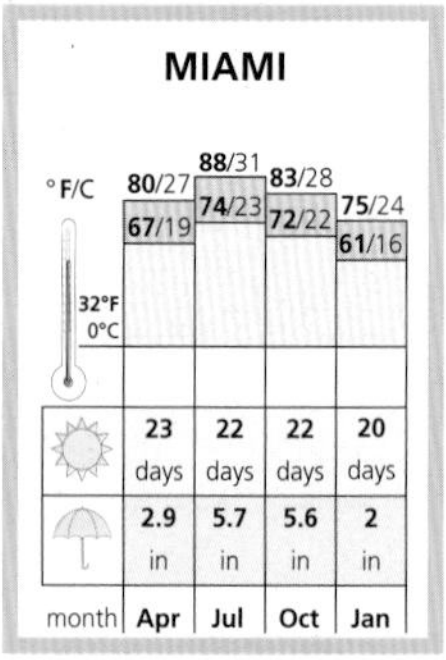

SPORTS & OUTDOOR ACTIVITIES

Florida's climate makes the state a top destination for all sports enthusiasts, from golfers and tennis players to canoeists and deep-sea divers. The best sources of information on outdoor activities are the **Florida Sports Foundation** and the **Department of Environmental Protection (DEP)**.

Water sports of all kinds are well represented, with wonderful beaches on both the Atlantic and Gulf coasts. Most resorts offer the full range from windsurfing to jetskiing. Water-skiing can also be enjoyed on lakes and inland waterways. The state provides ample opportunities for canoeing as well, with the Wilderness Waterway in the Everglades National Park being a favorite run.

Florida has superb diving and snorkeling sports. The country's only living coral reef skirts the state's southeast coast, stretching the length of the Keys. Excellent guided snorkeling trips are available to view the coast's coral and fish. For information on diving, contact the **Keys Association of Dive Operators**.

Fishing off the pier is popular at coastal spots, but the state is best known for its sport fishing. Deep-sea fishing boats can be chartered at seaside resorts; the biggest fleets are in the Panhandle and the Keys. Many rivers and parks offer freshwater fishing. The **Florida Game and Fresh Water Fish Commission** provides details on locations and licensing costs.

Outdoor adventure tours to wilder areas, such as the Everglades, are organized by some companies, including **Build a Field Trip.**

ENTERTAINMENT

Whether your preference is for a Broadway drama, a lavish Las Vegas-style floorshow, or a small cruise, Florida has something for everyone. **Walt Disney World® Resort, Universal Orlando** and other attractions offer the best in family entertainment, with theme parks galore to thrill children during the day and dinner shows at night. Here, meals are served, generally themed to the show you are watching. Water parks, throughout Florida, are also big draws.

Lavish road shows are the highest-quality productions in Florida. The state has its own theater groups, orchestras, and opera companies, such as the the **Symphony of the Americas** and the **Florida Grand Opera**. Some of the best places to dance are clubs offering live and varied music. Nightclubs require an ID to prove that you are over 18.

Florida is the world's leading departure point for cruises to the Caribbean. You can also go on mini-cruises, for a day or just an evening, for around $40. Evening cruises usually entail dinner and dancing; casino cruises, operating out of Miami and Port Everglades, are the new rage. Fort Lauderdale and St. Petersburg also have popular tour boats.

SHOPPING

Shopping is also a very popular pastime in Florida, with Miami attracting many overseas shoppers. Although the state has some very upscale stores, often clustered in shopping districts such as the exclusive Worth Avenue on Palm Beach, it is best known for its discount stores. If searching for gifts or souvenirs, the theme parks and seaside tourist centers offer a vast choice. Florida is also famed for its citrus fruit, which you can buy fresh or preserved as colorful candies and jellies. Other buys include seashells, Seminole crafts, Latin music, and hand-rolled cigars.

DIRECTORY

TOURIST INFORMATION

Tel (888) 735-2872.
www.visitflorida.com

EMERGENCY NUMBERS

All Emergencies
Tel 911 to alert police, fire, or medical services.

Miami-Dade Police Information
Tel (305) 595-6263.

National Hurricane Center
Tel (305) 229-4470, recorded message with hurricane details.

American Automobile Assn. (AAA)
Tel (407) 444-7000.

AAA General Breakdown Assistance
Tel (800) 222-4357.
NOTE: Rentals also provide 24-hour assistance.

SPORTS

Department of Environmental Protection (DEP)
3900 Commonwealth Blvd, Tallahassee, FL 32399.
Tel (850) 245-2118.

Florida Sports Foundation
Tallahassee, FL 32308.
Tel (850) 488-8347.
www.flasports.com

BACKCOUNTRY PURSUITS

Build a Field Trip
Fort Lauderdale, FL 33308.
Tel (954) 772-7800.

FISHING

Florida Game and Fresh Water Fish Commission
Tel (850) 488-4676.
Tel (888) 347-4356 (fishing licenses).
www.state.fl.us/fwc

DIVING & SNORKELING

Keys Association of Dive Operators (KADO)
www.divekeys.com

ENTERTAINMENT

Florida Grand Opera
1200 Coral Way, Miami.
Tel (305) 854-7890.

Symphony of the Americas
199 N Ocean Blvd, Pompano Beach.
Tel (954) 545-0088.

Universal Orlando
Tel (407) 363-8000.
www.universal orlando.com

Walt Disney World® Resort
Tel (407) 934-7639 (for reservations).
www.disneyworld.com

Choosing a Hotel

Florida has a large variety of places to stay suitable for all budgets and tastes – from rustic wooden cabins with minimal facilities to luxurious resort hotels that cater to their guests' every need. In between, visitors can choose from ordinary hotels, more charming bed and breakfasts, convenient motels, or fully-equipped apartments.

PRICE CATEGORIES
For a standard double room per night, including service charges and any additional taxes.

($) Under $100
($)($) $100–$150
($)($)($) $150–$200
($)($)($)($) $200–$250
($)($)($)($)($) Over $250

MIAMI

COCONUT GROVE Hampton Inn ($)($)($)

2800 SW 28th Terrace, 33133 ***Tel*** *(305) 448-2800* ***Fax*** *(305) 442-8655* ***Rooms*** *168*

Located directly at the entrance of the Grove and right near the Key Biscayne causeway, this chain motel has a convenient location and offers good value for money. Rooms are basic, yet clean. Although there is no restaurant or lounge here, it is good for the night if you're passing through. **www.hamptoninncoconutgrove.com**

COCONUT GROVE Mayfair Hotel and Spa ($)($)($)($)

3000 Florida Ave, 33133 ***Tel*** *(305) 441-0000* ***Fax*** *(305) 441-1647* ***Rooms*** *179*

Once a stuffy hotel of Miami Vice-era fame, this place is now a swank member of the exclusive Kimpton Group. Modern rooms throughout with plasma TVs, a restaurant, and a rooftop sundeck with pool, bar, and cabanas. Expect a South Beach-like scene. **www.kimptomhotels.com**

CORAL GABLES Courtyard by Marriott ($)($)

2051 S Le Jeune Rd, 33134 ***Tel*** *(305) 443-2301* ***Fax*** *(305) 446-6827* ***Rooms*** *168*

Located in the heart of Coral Gables Business District, this well-run hotel provides moderately-priced, clean guest rooms. Apart from basic modern amenities, business facilities are also offered, with free transportation to Miami Airport. Close to shopping, dining, and entertainment venues.

CORAL GABLES Hotel Place St. Michel ($)($)($)

162 Alcazar Ave, 33134 ***Tel*** *(305) 444-1666* ***Fax*** *(305) 529-0074* ***Rooms*** *27*

Reminiscent of old-world Europe, down to the rickety old elevator, this place is ideal for a romantic rendezvous. Rooms are decorated individually in a traditional European style. Service is stellar as is the Restaurant St. Michel, in which you could imagine you were dining on the Champs Elysées. **www.hotelstmichel.com**

GREATER MIAMI Ritz Carlton Key Biscayne ($)($)($)($)($)

455 Grand Bay Dr, Key Biscayne, 33149 ***Tel*** *(305) 365-4500* ***Fax*** *(305) 365-4501* ***Rooms*** *402*

The ritziest of all three Miami Ritz Carltons, this one is a beachfront haven for those seeking privacy, indulgence, and relaxation. Many Hollywood celebrities, royalty, and bigwigs choose to stay here for privacy over the glaring eye of South Beach paparazzi. The hotel spa is sublime and the ocean views priceless. **www.ritzcarlton.com**

MIAMI BEACH Clay Hotel and International Hostel ($)

1438 Washington Ave, 33139 ***Tel*** *(305) 534-2988* ***Fax*** *(305) 673-0346* ***Rooms*** *225*

Housed in a 1920s Spanish Mediterranean building on historic Espanola Way, ultra-hip Clay is popular with world travelers. While 90 rooms come with private baths, 12 have balconies overlooking the area. The occasional movie night and cocktail hour have been known to make strangers lifelong friends. Book early. **www.clayhotel.com**

MIAMI BEACH The Kent ($)($)($)

1131 Collins Ave, 33139 ***Tel*** *(305) 604-5068* ***Fax*** *(305) 531-0720* ***Rooms*** *54*

Funky and affordable, the Kent offers the best of both worlds, and is within walking distance of the beach. The ultra-modern rooms have been designed by Biba-creator, Barbara Hulanicki. Be sure to ask for a tour of the Lucite Suite with its James Bond feel. Free use of iMac computers is available in the lobby. **www.thekenthotel.com**

MIAMI BEACH Hotel Nash ($)($)($)($)

1120 Collins Ave, 33139 ***Tel*** *(305) 674-7800* ***Fax*** *(305) 538-8288* ***Rooms*** *50*

An $11-million renovation has turned this Art Deco place into one of the beach's best hotels. The Nash pumps scents of aromatherapy into every room and public space. Three tiny pools – freshwater, saltwater, and mineral water – and one of South Florida's best restaurants make this an attractive stay. **www.hotelnash.com**

MIAMI BEACH The Delano ($)($)($)($)($)

1685 Collins Ave, 33139 ***Tel*** *(305) 672-2000* ***Fax*** *(305) 532-0099* ***Rooms*** *195*

Designed by Starck-Ian, luxurious Delano has sparse rooms and a sizzling scene. At the photogenic wading pool, with priceless views, you may be sitting next to a Hollywood producer, starlet, music mogul, or royalty. One of the area's best restaurants, Blue Door, is here, as is the elegant Rose Bar. **www.morganshotelgroup.com**

Key to Symbols *see back cover flap*

THE GOLD & TREASURE COASTS

BOCA RATON Ocean Lodge $

531 N Ocean Blvd, 33432 **Tel** *(561) 395-7772* **Fax** *(561) 395-0554* **Rooms** *18*

A real bargain, this small two-story motel has large, well-appointed rooms. The best part about Ocean Lodge, besides its prices, is its proximity to the beach – just across the street. Don't expect frills or any pampering. An older and mainly Canadian clientele tends to frequent this place year after year.

BOCA RATON Boca Raton Resort and Club $$$$$

501 E Camino Real, 33431 **Tel** *(561) 395-3000* **Fax** *(561) 447-3183* **Rooms** *963*

This sophisticated 1926 Addison Mizner resort straddles the Intracoastal Waterway, encompassing acres of land. Some rooms are located in the original building and others in the more modern beach club accessible by water shuttle. Activities include 18-hole golf courses and a 25-slip marina. **www.bocaresort.com**

FORT LAUDERDALE Pillars Hotel $$$$

111 N Birch Rd, 33304 **Tel** *(954) 467-9639* **Fax** *(954) 763-2845* **Rooms** *23*

A sublime hideaway on the Intracoastal Waterway, this British Colonial Caribbean-style retreat has lavish rooms with rich furnishings. A welcome cocktail is served on arrival. There is a library with over 500 books as well as videos. A gorgeous pool and courtyard create a relaxed ambience. Water taxis available. **www.pillarshotel.com**

PALM BEACH The Breakers $$$$$

1 S County Rd, 33480 **Tel** *(561) 655-6611* **Fax** *(561) 659-8403* **Rooms** *560*

A Palm Beach landmark, this Italian Renaissance-style oceanfront hotel is where old money clashes with new. The Flagler Club, a hotel within the hotel, features butlers, concierges, doting service, and celebrities. The Oceanfront Spa and Beach Club is indulgent, as are the restaurants. Golf, spa, and family activities. **www.thebreakers.com**

ORLANDO & THE SPACE COAST

BAY LAKE Disney's Animal Kingdom Lodge $$$$$

2901 Osceola Parkway, 32830 **Tel** *(407) 938-3000* **Fax** *(407) 939-4799* **Rooms** *1293*

A stay at Disney's Animal Kingdom Lodge will make you feel as if you are staying on a thrilling African game reserve. The rooms are arranged in a semicircular layout, overlooking a vast savanna that allows for random sightings of birds, giraffe, and other wildlife. A fun spot for animal lovers. **www.disneyworld.com**

COCOA BEACH The Inn at Cocoa Beach $$

4300 Ocean Blvd, 32931 **Tel** *(321) 799-3460* **Fax** *(321) 784-8632* **Rooms** *50*

This seaside B&B is great for a romantic stay. All rooms are furnished with a mix of pine, tropical, and French country pieces. Other units open to a courtyard with swimming pool. There are honor bars from which you can pour your own drinks, as well as nightly wine-and-cheese socials and afternoon teas. **www.theinnatcocoabeach.com**

DOWNTOWN ORLANDO Grand Bohemian $$$$

325 S Orange Ave, 32801 **Tel** *(407) 313-9000* **Fax** *(407) 313-9001* **Rooms** *250*

Reputedly the best hotel in Downtown Orlando, the Grand Bohemian caters mainly to business people. The interior boasts more than 100 pieces of 19th- and 20th-century American fine art and attracts art aficionados who love the museum-like ambience here. **www.grandbohemianhotel.com**

KISSIMEE Gaylord Palms Resort & Convention Center $$$$$

6000 W Osceola Pkwy, 34747 **Tel** *(407) 586-0000* **Fax** *(407) 239-4822* **Rooms** *1406*

Gaylord Palms has its own restaurants, recreational facilities, shops, and the Canyon Ranch Spa Club. The glass dome-topped Grand Atrium surrounds a replica of the Castillo de San Marcos from St. Augustine. Waterfalls, foliage, and a rocky landscape add to the vibe. An elegant hotel, Emerald Bay, is also on site. **www.gaylordpalms.com**

LAKE BUENA VISTA Nickelodeon Family Suites by Holiday Inn $$$

14500 Continental Gateway, 32821 **Tel** *(407) 387-5437* **Fax** *(407) 387-1489* **Rooms** *770*

Voted as the best Holiday Inn in America in 2003, this family hotel has a second bedroom for children, with either bunk or twin beds, and full kitchens. It has themed activity nights and recreational services, and has teamed up with the Nickelodeon Channel. **www.nickhotel.com**

LAKE BUENA VISTA Disney's Boardwalk Inn and Villas $$$$$

2101 N Epcot Resorts Blvd, 32830 **Tel** *(407) 939-5100* **Fax** *(407) 939-5150* **Rooms** *371*

This 1940s-style property provides an array of clubs, restaurants, shops, and carnival-type entertainment on the boardwalk behind the resort and overlooking the water. Some of the Cape Cod-style rooms have balconies, and some overlook the pool with children's favorite, the Keiser Coaster water slide. **www.disneyworld.com**

LAKE BUENA VISTA Disney's Wilderness Lodge $$$$$

901 W Timberline Dr, 32830 **Tel** *(407) 824-3200* **Fax** *(407) 824-3232* **Rooms** *909*

Surrounded by tall timbers, spouting geysers, and mammoth stone hearths, the Wilderness Lodge is great for children looking to "rough it" in bunk beds. An old national park vibe and views of beautiful woods transport you to Yosemite. A perennial favorite, this one does not seem like Disney was trying too hard. **www.disneyworld.com**

ORLANDO Hyatt Place Orlando Universal $$

5895 Caravan Court, 32819 **Tel** *(407) 351-0627* **Fax** *(407) 351-3317* **Rooms** *151*

Great bargain for families looking for proximity to Universal's theme parks without having to pay the price to stay on park property. All suites are generously proportioned and come with kitchens that are a better option than the overpriced eateries found in the area. Free transport to local parks is a bonus. **www.hyatt.com**

ORLANDO The Villas of Grand Cypress $$$$$

1 N Jacaranda, 32836 **Tel** *(407) 239-4700* **Fax** *(407) 239-7219* **Rooms** *146*

With a remote location, this Mediterranean-inspired resort has junior suites featuring Roman baths, while bedroom villas come with kitchens, dining rooms, and patios. The landscaping is gorgeous and the resort shares facilities with its sister property, the Hyatt Regency Grand Cypress. It caters mostly to adults. **www.grandcypress.com**

THE NORTHEAST

AMELIA ISLAND Amelia Island Plantation $$$$$

6800 First Coast Hwy, 32035 **Tel** *(904) 261-6161* **Fax** *(904) 277-5945* **Rooms** *680*

This enormous all-inclusive property encompasses golf courses, lagoons, and bike trails. Hotel rooms are located within the cozy Amelia Inn and Beach Club; all units have balconies and are luxuriously decorated. There is a good choice of dining halls and restaurants. The sprawling on-site spa is sublime. **www.aipfl.com**

DAYTONA BEACH The Plaza Resort and Spa $$$

600 N Atlantic Ave, 32118 **Tel** *(386) 255-4471* **Fax** *(386) 253-7672* **Rooms** *323*

After a $26-million renovation, the Plaza boasts some of Daytona's best rooms. All units have balconies and microwaves, while some of the corner units come with sitting areas and two balconies overlooking the Atlantic. An on-site convenience store sells frozen dinners. Full-service Ocean Waters Spa. **www.plazaresortandspa.com**

FERNANDINA BEACH Hampton Inn and Suites $$

19 S 2nd St, 32034 **Tel** *(904) 491-4911* **Fax** *(904) 491-4910* **Rooms** *122*

Possibly the coolest Hampton Inn ever, this one was designed to fit in with the rest of its Victorian neighbors. There is a two-story lobby with wood floors taken from an old Jax church. Rooms feature king beds, fireplaces, and whirlpool tubs. Take pictures of the sign, because no one will believe that this is a chain hotel. **www.hamptoninn.com**

ST. AUGUSTINE Victorian House $$

11 Cadiz St, 32084 **Tel** *(904) 824-5214* **Fax** *(904) 824-7990* **Rooms** *8*

This 1897 vintage Victorian bed and breakfast features a wrap-around porch and adjoining old general store, known as the Carriage House, that is divided into four rooms. Children are not allowed in the main house but they can stay in the Carriage House. All units have private entrances. Antiques abound. **www.victorianhouse-inn.com**

THE PANHANDLE

APALACHICOLA Coombs House Inn $$$

80 6th St, 32320 **Tel** *(850) 653-9199* **Fax** *(850) 653-2785* **Rooms** *19*

The most luxurious bed and breakfast in the area, Coombs House occupies two 1905 homes, and all rooms are decorated in plush Victorian style. The Love Bungalow has its own private entrance, and the other building has a whirlpool tub. Guests receive complimentary wine on weekends. **www.coombshouseinn.com**

DESTIN Hilton Sandestin Beach Resort and Spa $$$$

4000 Sandestin Blvd, 32541 **Tel** *(850) 267-9500* **Fax** *(850) 267-3076* **Rooms** *598*

A splendid all-suites beachside resort, the rooms here are housed in two adjacent towers. The hotel is located on the grounds of Sandestin Beach and Golf Resort and shares its golf and tennis facilities. Thirteen tennis courts, a camp for kids, and a private beach are some of the great amenities. **www.hiltonsandestinbeach.com**

PANAMA CITY BEACH Edgewater Beach Resort $$

11212 Front Beach Rd, 32407 **Tel** *(850) 235-4044* **Fax** *(850) 235-6899* **Rooms** *500*

This sports-oriented facility is one of the area's largest condo-resorts. It has a gorgeous beachfront location and beautifully landscaped grounds. Rooms in the Gulf-side towers have great views. The pedestrian overpass leads to a 9-hole golf course. **www.edgewaterbeachresort.com**

Key to Price Guide *see p326* **Key to Symbols** *see back cover flap*

PENSACOLA BEACH Bay Beach Inn $

51 Gulf Breeze Pkwy, 32561 ***Tel*** *(850) 932-2214* ***Fax*** *(850) 932-0932* ***Rooms*** *168*

Offering great views of Pensacola Bay and a private beach, this hotel also houses one of the best restaurants in the area. While the rooms are not outstanding, there are a number of activities to choose from such as boating, kayaking, and jet skiing. **www.baybeachinn.com**

TALLAHASSEE Cabot Lodge North $

2735 N Monroe St, 32303 ***Tel*** *(850) 386-8880* ***Fax*** *(850) 386-4254* ***Rooms*** *160*

A charming motel with a tin roof and wrap-around porch. Rooms are unremarkable but clean. There is no restaurant, but the complimentary continental breakfast and evening cocktails ensure you do not starve or go thirsty. An excellent deal for reliable, no-frills budget accommodation. **www.cabotlodge.com**

THE GULF COAST

FORT MYERS BEACH Outrigger Beach Resort $$

6200 Estero Blvd, 33931 ***Tel*** *(239) 463-3131* ***Fax*** *(239) 463-6577* ***Rooms*** *144*

A charming, spick-and-span motel that's been owned and operated by the same family since 1965. The small cottages with backyard decks are quite lovely. Other motel-style rooms overlook the parking lot, so try to avoid those. The lively beachside bar is one of the area's best places for sunset views. **www.outriggerfmb.com**

ST. PETERSBURG Dickens House $$$$

335 8th Ave, 33701 ***Tel*** *(727) 822-8622* ***Rooms*** *5*

Located in St. Petersburg's historic district, two blocks back from Tampa Bay, is this restored 1912 Arts & Crafts house with comfortably furnished rooms. The gourmet breakfast menu includes a cooked Southern breakfast, fruit-filled pastries, French toast, and fresh fruit platters. Coffee available all day. **www.dickenshouse.com**

SANIBEL ISLAND Sanibel Inn $$$$$

937 E Gulf Dr, 33957 ***Tel*** *(239) 472-3181* ***Fax*** *(239) 472-5234* ***Rooms*** *94*

Nature lovers will adore this place – stunning beaches, butterfly gardens, and the most vibrant tropical flowers and foliage. This effect seems to spill into the decor and color schemes of the spacious rooms. Go bird-watching, hiking, or even kayaking. Special children's programs include shell safaris and dolphin watches. **www.sanibelinn.com**

SARASOTA The Cypress $$$$

621 Gulfstream Ave, 34236 ***Tel*** *(941) 955-4683* ***Rooms*** *5*

With a charming tin roof, this little inn is hidden amid mango trees and swaying palms. It also overlooks the bay. The decor includes lovely antiques and a grand piano. Rooms feature queen-sized beds, hardwood floors, and oriental rugs. Perhaps the best-kept secret in Sarasota. Delicious breakfasts too. **www.cypressbb.com**

TAMPA Westin Harbour Island $$$$$

725 S Harbour Island Blvd, 33602 ***Tel*** *(813) 229-5000* ***Fax*** *(813) 229-5322* ***Rooms*** *299*

Standing on its own island, this hotel is very close to downtown. Rooms overlook the harbor, and are very cosy with their pillow-top mattresses. The hotel's Italian waterfront restaurant serves great food. The Harbour Island Athletic Club has workout facilities, tennis courts, and a full-service spa. **www.wyndhamhotels.com**

THE EVERGLADES & THE KEYS

EVERGLADES Ivey House $$$

107 Camellia St, 34139 ***Tel*** *(239) 695-3299* ***Rooms*** *18*

Once the recreation center for the men who built the Tamiami Trail in the 1920s, Ivey House offers rooms with shared bathrooms in the main lodge as well as en suite rooms at the poolside inn. In the heart of historic Everglades City, day and overnight trips can be arranged to the Everglades back country and islands. **www.iveyhouse.com**

KEY LARGO Kona Kai Resort and Gallery $$$$$

97802 Overseas Hwy, 33037 ***Tel*** *(305) 852-7200* ***Fax*** *(305) 852-4629* ***Rooms*** *11*

A gorgeous garden of palms, ferns, and tropical fruit trees surrounds this landscaped escape from the ordinary. Rooms are private, airy, and cheerful, and bathrooms well-stocked with natural beauty products. An art gallery displaying local and international artworks attracts an eclectic crowd. Absolutely heavenly. **www.konakairesort.com**

KEY WEST The Grand $$$

1116 Grinnell St, 33040 ***Tel*** *(305) 294-0590* ***Fax*** *(305) 294-0477* ***Rooms*** *11*

Definitely one of the better bargains in town, this friendly guesthouse is five blocks from Duval Street. The rooms are cute and cosy, with private baths. The complimentary continental breakfast is tasty and satisfying. Not fancy but pleasant and functional, and a great place to stay for a few nights. **www.thegrandguesthouse.com**

Choosing a Restaurant

There is plenty of fresh produce in Florida, from tropical fruit and bountiful vegetables year-round to seafood, which all restaurants use to great effect. Restaurants cater to every palate and budget, from the trendy establishments in Miami to simpler restaurants in the interior, where food tends to be more homey.

PRICE CATEGORIES
For a three-course meal for one, including a glass of house wine (where served), and all other unavoidable charges such as sales tax.

($) Under $25
($)($) $25–$35
($)($)($) $35–$50
($)($)($)($) $50–$60
($)($)($)($)($) Over $60

MIAMI

CORAL GABLES Bugatti ($)($)($)

2504 Ponce de Leon Blvd, 33134 ***Tel*** *(305) 441-2545*

Many locals believe Bugatti to be the best Italian restaurant in the city. A personable and helpful staff is one reason. But most believe it is because of delicious dishes such as lobster ravioli and various risotto preparations. Daily specials usually tend to be quite remarkable.

CORAL GABLES Christy's ($)($)($)($)

3101 Ponce de Leon Blvd, 33134 ***Tel*** *(305) 446-1400*

A very popular steak house featuring succulent beef and seafood in a club-like setting. A tasty Caesar salad accompanies each entree. Christy's has been popular with Italian business-suit types for power lunches for decades. Immaculate and consistently top-notch service.

DOWNTOWN S & S Restaurant ($)

1757 NE 2nd Ave, 33132 ***Tel*** *(305) 373-4291*

A no-frills historic diner serving a good selection of staple American dishes for breakfast and lunch (until 6pm). Specials include pot roast, meat loaf, and fried chicken. It is a great place to experience the old South Florida color and atmosphere with old-time prices. Desserts are also good.

DOWNTOWN Big Fish ($)($)($)

55 SW Miami Ave, 33128 ***Tel*** *(305) 373-1770*

This is a comfortable and unassuming seafood restaurant on the shores of the Miami River. It offers a great view of the Downtown and Brickell Avenue skyline, along with some of the freshest fish in town. Try daily specials for the most innovative options, though it is difficult to go wrong here.

GREATER MIAMI Chef Allen's ($)($)($)($)($)

19088 NE 29th Ave, Aventura, 33180 ***Tel*** *(305) 935-2900*

Sleek and chic, this Miami landmark is known for its high-quality, daring New Florida cuisine. The activity in the kitchen, framed by a large picture window, is fascinating. Even that won't distract you from the culinary style of Allen Susser, one of the leading chefs in the region. You must try the pistachio-encrusted grouper and veal chops.

LITTLE HAVANA Hy Vong ($)($)

3458 SW 8th St, 33135 ***Tel*** *(305) 446-3674*

This mainstay in Little Havana is an oddity with its total emphasis on Vietnamese cuisine, which also happens to be extremely good. Long lines often form to sample specialties such as grilled lamb in curry sauce and other more exotic dishes. Samplers and newcomers to the cuisine are welcome.

MIAMI BEACH 11th Street Diner ($)

1065 Washington Ave, 33139 ***Tel*** *(305) 534-6373*

This old-time diner, which relocated to South Beach from Wilkes-Barre, Pennsylvania, has all the associated charm one would expect. The menu has all the diner classics such as meatloaf, fried chicken, pasta, and rice, and a good selection of sandwiches and burgers as well. All very reasonably priced.

MIAMI BEACH Joe's Stone Crab ($)($)($)

11 Washington Ave, 33139 ***Tel*** *(305) 673-0365*

This Miami institution is a must. There is lobster, shrimp, and fish, as well as the signature stone crab and surprisingly popular fried chicken. The key lime pie is also highly sought-after. Joe's now offers affordable take-out lunches. No reservations but worth the wait, which can be ample.

MIAMI BEACH The Forge ($)($)($)($)($)

432 41st St, 33140 ***Tel*** *(305) 538-8533*

Celebrities, both local and visiting, abound at this Miami institution. Its glitzy decor has opulent American cuisine to match; the desserts are sublime. The Forge also boasts the most sizeable wine list in the city. Time permitting, ask for the wine cellar tour. Wednesday nights are regular popular social occasions.

Key to Symbols *see back cover flap*

THE GOLD & TREASURE COASTS

BOCA RATON Bova $$$$$

1450 N Federal Hwy, 33432 ***Tel*** *(561) 362-7407*

Serving gourmet Italian cuisine, this elegant, modern restaurant is a trendy spot if you want to people watch – the long bar is always packed. The food is great, too, with tasty focaccia from the wood-fired ovens and delicious duck. The white-on-white decor gives a very chic "South Beach" look in Boca.

FORT LAUDERDALE Himmarshee Bar & Grille $$

210 SW 2nd St, 33301 ***Tel*** *(954) 524-1818*

Popular with the young and fashionable Fort Lauderdale crowd, Himmarshee Bar is usually packed, particularly on weekends. A wasabi-encrusted salmon and similar creative takes on American cuisine define the menu. Great bar and wine list. They also have a lovely outside seating area. Regulars rave about the charming service.

FORT LAUDERDALE Le Café de Paris $$$

715 E Las Olas Blvd, 33301 ***Tel*** *(954) 467-2900*

This well-established family restaurant offers good-value French cuisine. Set menus include an excellent escargot appetizer followed by a gourmet dinner. Make sure to leave room for tantalizing desserts. Good value for the price, with freshness abounding.

PALM BEACH L'Escalier $$$$$

1 S County Rd, 33480 ***Tel*** *(561) 655-6611*

The elegant dining room at the Breakers Hotel offers a memorable formal restaurant experience. French cuisine, always being refined, is featured with dishes such as seared foie gras, Colorado lamb, and Dover sole meunière. A dress code applies. Expensive but conservatism does not extend to the food, which is stellar.

ORLANDO & THE SPACE COAST

COCOA BEACH The Mango Tree Restaurant $$$$

118 N Atlantic Ave, 32931 ***Tel*** *(321) 799-0513*

This gourmet restaurant serves local dishes, with seafood as a specialty. Situated just yards from the Atlantic Ocean, there is a tropical garden with waterfowl, Japanese carp, and lush foliage to set the mood. The main course is complemented by salads and fresh vegetables.

DOWNTOWN ORLANDO Napasorn Thai Restaurant $

56 Pine St, 32801 ***Tel*** *(407) 245-8088*

A small restaurant in downtown Orlando with a menu that offers Thai dishes with great home-cooked flavor – the Pad Thai is excellent and basil duck is a stand-out dish. There's sushi too. Accompany your meal with a choice of more than 30 flavors of Saki and 20 different beers. There's live music on Thursdays and a DJ on Fridays and Saturdays.

DOWNTOWN ORLANDO Seasons 52 $$$

7700 W Sand Lake Rd, 32836 ***Tel*** *(407) 354-5212*

The emphasis is most definitely on healthy eating here, with every dish under 475 calories. However, the food is unfailingly delicious, and the seasonal menu includes grilled vegetables, crab-stuffed mushrooms, and rosemary and Parmesan cheese flatbreads. Everything is cooked using just a little olive oil.

INTERNATIONAL DRIVE Bahama Breeze $$$

8849 International Dr, 32819 ***Tel*** *(407) 248-2499*

Indulge your tropical fancy at this fun and frolicking eatery with a menu laden with tastes of the Tropics. Drinkers might want to sample the delicious Bahamarita. Jerk Chicken, coconut prawns, and pasta are especially good. The light-hearted environment helps make it amenable to the whole family. Good mingling for those unaccompanied.

INTERNATIONAL DRIVE The Crab House $$$

8291 International Dr, 32819 ***Tel*** *(407) 352-6140*

Choose from nine crab dishes at this informal and friendly restaurant. The seafood and salad bar is loaded with freshly shucked oysters, shrimp, marinated mussels, crawfish, and other seafood dishes. Lunch specials are good value. The well-known bar picks up in the evenings and on the weekends.

KISSIMEE Pacino's Italian Ristorante $$$

5795 W Hwy 192, 34746 ***Tel*** *(407) 396-8022*

Charbroiled food is the focus of this comfortable and family-friendly restaurant. A free delivery service is available to nearby hotels. Steaks tend to be the most favored of the menu items, but Pacino's does a good job at mixing up its entrées for broad appeal. The staff are hospitable and gracious.

WALT DISNEY WORLD California Grill $$$

Disney's Contemporary Resort,, 32830 ***Tel*** *(407) 939-3463*

An unpretentious restaurant – a great Disney antidote – that welcomes families. The food can range dramatically from seafood platters to shrimps sautéed in sauce. Spanish or Neo-Spanish dishes dominate the menu. The bustling, fast-paced, energetic environment sometimes detracts from conversation.

WALT DISNEY WORLD Whispering Canyon Café $$$

Disney Wilderness Lodge, 32830 ***Tel*** *(407) 939-3463*

Snap on your six-guns and settle in for an all-you-can-eat campfire cookout buffet in a Wild West setting. The café is also open for frontier-style breakfasts. Families with children will find this particularly appealing. The food is decent but entertainment value is quite high. Stop in for a unique local experience.

WALT DISNEY WORLD Victoria & Albert's $$$$$

Disney's Grand Floridian Resort, 32830 ***Tel*** *(407) 824-1089*

Reservations are a must at this lavish restaurant. The six-course fixed-price menu is superlative, and diners are waited on by a butler and a maid. Ask for the chef's table, the most exclusive one in the house. One of the most delightfully decadent dining experiences in the area, and not one for children.

THE NORTHEAST

DAYTONA BEACH Down the Hatch $$$

4894 Front St, Ponce Inlet, 32127 ***Tel*** *(386) 761-4831*

A homey, family-oriented restaurant serving delicious fresh fish and a few meat dishes. The eatery is set right on the water, and you can watch the boats unload their catch at the end of the day. A relaxing site that presents a fun-filled outing for the entire family. Good value for money.

FERNANDINA BEACH The Grill $$$$$

4750 Amelia Island Pkwy, 32034 ***Tel*** *(904) 277-1100*

Winner of the AAA Five Diamond award, this upscale restaurant is located in the Ritz-Carlton Amelia Island Hotel. Offers a minimum three-course meal and an elaborate, not-to-be-missed Sunday brunch. The menu changes daily and features seasonal and regional specialties. Ask for fresh Florida fish and game. Reservations recommended.

OCALA Arthur's $$$

3600 SW 36 Ave, 34474 ***Tel*** *(352) 854-1400*

Located in the elegant Hilton Ocala hotel, this stylish restaurant is well known for its lunch and dinner buffets. The highly renowned chef presents delicious traditional fare as well as old favorites. There is a different special every day, and a lavish Sunday brunch. Enjoy the view of lively horses at play in the paddock outside.

ST. AUGUSTINE Florida Cracker Cafe $$

81 St. George St, 32084 ***Tel*** *(904) 829-0397*

Situated in the city's historic district, this charming restaurant offers simple fare with some exotic local dishes, such as fried alligator. However, it is the large portions, consistently good food, and the cosy ambience that make it a favorite with all who visit. Very casual, comfortable, and family-friendly.

THE PANHANDLE

APALACHICOLA Seafood Grill & Steakhouse $$

100 Market St, 32320 ***Tel*** *(850) 653-9510*

Located downtown, this friendly grill features a wide range of meals. Tuck into the "world's largest" fried fish sandwich, try the area's famous oysters and fried shrimps, or pick one of the 30 or more beers offered at this energetic spot. The ambience is relaxed, and the service good. Packed on weekend nights.

DESTIN Marina Café $$$$

404 Hwy 98 E, 32541 ***Tel*** *(850) 837-7960*

A jewel on the Emerald Coast, this restaurant combines excellent service, a spectacular location, and creative, internationally inspired cuisine. The specialty here is seafood and you will definitely want to enquire about the daily specials and the fresh catch of the day. Also boasts an impressive wine list. Perfect for a romantic evening.

FORT WALTON BEACH Staff's Seafood Restaurant $$$

24 Miracle Strip Pkwy, 32548 ***Tel*** *(850) 243-3482*

Opened in 1913, this historic restaurant is well known for its fine local recipes. A favorite here are the seafood platters, which offer deliciously prepared crabs, scallops, shrimps, gumbo, and fish – all covered in tasty sauces. The menu also has steak, roast beef, and pork dishes. The service is friendly. Good value for money.

Key to Price Guide *see p330* **Key to Symbols** *see back cover flap*

PENSACOLA McGuire's Irish Pub $$

600 E Gregory St, 32501 ***Tel** (850) 433-6789*

A visit to Pensacola is not complete without a stop at this popular bar and eatery, which serves huge portions of steak, pasta, pizza, and pub fare. Wash it down with one of their home-brewed beers. A favorite stopping-off point with locals and tourists alike, McGuire's has lots of character and is great for experiencing the local color.

TALLAHASSEE Chez Pierre $$$

1215 Thomasville Rd, 32303 ***Tel** (850) 222-0936*

An incongruous, yet hugely successful combination of Southern hospitality and appetizing French food make this bistro a local favorite. The use of fresh regional ingredients accentuates the innovative dishes. The pastries and other desserts are definitely worth trying as well. The ambience is cosy and comfortable.

THE GULF COAST

FORT MYERS The Veranda $$$

2122 2nd St, 33901 ***Tel** (239) 332-2065*

One of the more acclaimed restaurants in the area, this charming eatery is housed in a 1902 building and offers original culinary creations such as artichoke fritters stuffed with blue crab. The decor is Deep South and the service attentive, but not overbearing. Ideal for those looking for a romantic and intimate getaway.

SARASOTA Michael's On East $$$$

1212 E Ave S, 34239 ***Tel** (941) 366-0007*

One of Sarasota's premier restaurants. Features contemporary American cuisine and a large selection of micro-brewed beers. A wide range of salads, sandwiches, pastas, and seafood is on offer here. The decor is stylish, with swirling designs and motifs, as well as plush seating. Reservations are strongly suggested.

ST. PETE BEACH Hurricane Seafood Restaurant $$$

809 Gulf Way Rd, 33706 ***Tel** (727) 360-9558*

Set right on the beach, this acclaimed restaurant prides itself on its crab cakes and fresh Florida grouper, which comes blackened, grilled, broiled, or in a sandwich. The cocktail deck is particularly popular and busy at sunset for the spectacular views, with a good selection of wines and cocktails.

TAMPA Columbia Restaurant $$$

2117 E 7th Ave, 33605 ***Tel** (813) 248-4961*

The Columbia is Florida's oldest restaurant, dating from 1905, and anchors a whole block in Ybor City. Excellent Spanish and Cuban cuisine served in a dining room that features stonework and handpainted Spanish tiles. The custard flan, made Cuban style, is a must-have dessert. Twice-nightly Flamenco shows (Mon–Sat).

TAMPA Mise en Place $$$$

442 W Kennedy Blvd, 33606 ***Tel** (813) 254-5373*

This adorable little restaurant is wildly popular with both locals and travelers. The innovative menu of the busy bistro changes daily, but the delicious fare, prepared with fresh regional ingredients, never fails to please. Offers a range of seafood, poultry, and meat dishes. Advance reservations are highly recommended.

THE EVERGLADES & THE KEYS

EVERGLADES Coopertown Airboat Rides and Restaurant $

22700 SW 8th St, 33144 ***Tel** (305) 226-6048*

A great place to stop in for a beer and some traditional country-style cooking. The diverse menu offers frog legs, alligator tail, steaks, shrimps, burgers, french fries, and more. This small restaurant also provides airboat rentals and tours. An interesting stopping-off point for those who want to absorb the local color.

KEY LARGO Fish House Restaurant and Seafood Market $$$

MM 102.4, 102401 Overseas Hwy, 33037 ***Tel** (305) 451-4665*

Although it resembles a shack, this small restaurant is one of the most preferred destinations by locals for the freshest fish and conch salad. No frills, just good seafood. The rustic charm will enchant many, including kids, as will the appetizing food. The affordably priced fare makes this an unusual eatery in the pricey Keys.

KEY WEST Antonia's Restaurant $$$$

615 Duval St, 33040 ***Tel** (305) 294-6565*

A local landmark, this beloved little restaurant offers appetizing Northern Italian cuisine. It presents classical and modern fare, featuring delicious homemade pastas and sauces, as well as fresh local and imported ingredients, and also boasts an exquisite wine list. It is extremely busy on weekends so reservations are highly recommended.

THE DEEP SOUTH

INTRODUCING THE DEEP SOUTH 336–343

NEW ORLEANS, LOUISIANA 344–353

LOUISIANA 354–357

ARKANSAS 358–359

MISSISSIPPI 360–363

ALABAMA 364–365

The Deep South at a Glance

Comprising the four states of Louisiana, Arkansas, Mississippi, and Alabama, the Deep South is one of the most distinctive parts of the United States. From the broad plains of the mighty Mississippi River and the bayous of Louisiana's Cajun Country to the hardscrabble forests of Arkansas's Ozark Mountains, the region is both geographically and culturally diverse. While opulent mansions, antebellum homes, and Civil Rights Movement sights are aspects of its past, the Deep South's special charms rest with the people and their natural appreciation of the good things in life. America's two most beloved musical creations – jazz and the blues – were born here, a legacy that is celebrated throughout the region, particularly in New Orleans. This city's universal reputation for nonstop fun is best experienced during Mardi Gras.

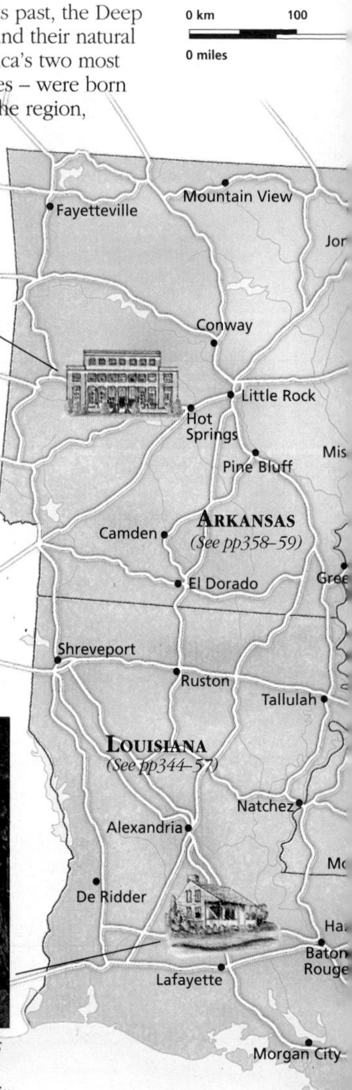

Hot Springs (see p358), *Arkansas, is home to the historic Bathhouse Row, where the Buckstaff Bathhouse still offers spa facilities. Former president Bill Clinton spent his youth in this city.*

Lafayette (see p356) *is the heart of Louisiana's Cajun Country, where the descendants of French Canadian immigrants still preserve their language and culture. Much of this local culture can be found in restaurants and nightclubs, at the city's museums and historic parks, as well as out in the surrounding swamps.*

◁ **Two rows of magnificent oak trees lining the drive to Oak Alley, a Lower Mississippi plantation**

Selma (see p364) *is one of the many towns in Alabama that played a significant role during the Civil Rights Movement in the 1950s and '60s. An important sight here is the National Voting Rights Museum, which tells the story of the successful Selma-to-Montogomery March led by Dr. Martin Luther King Jr. in 1965.*

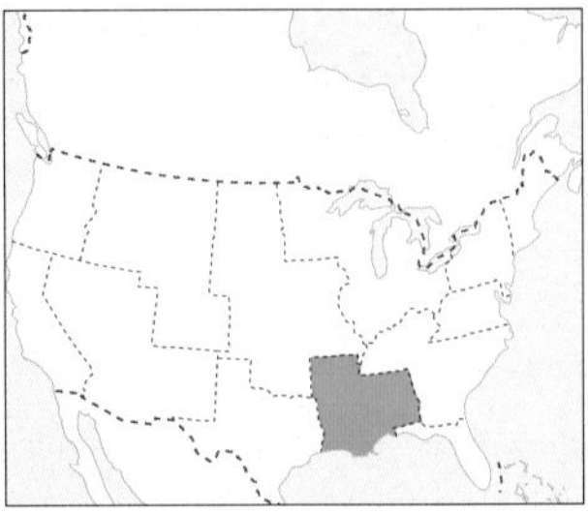

LOCATOR MAP

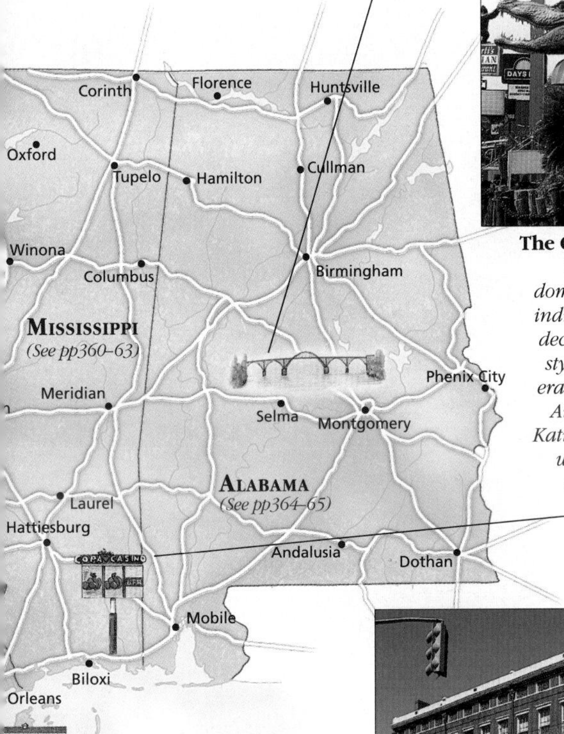

The Gulf Coast (see p363) *has traditionally been dominated by the seafood industry. But over the last decade, lavish Las Vegas-style casinos have proliferated along the coast. In August 2005 Hurricane Katrina hit the Gulf Coast with devastating effects and major rebuilding work is still going on.*

New Orleans (see pp344–53), *the region's cultural capital, is characterized by Colonial architecture, lively bars, and the annual Mardi Gras festivities.*

ROYAL
CAFE
BALCONY
DINING

THE DEEP SOUTH

With its warm, semitropical climate and easy-going temperament, the Deep South is perhaps the most culturally diverse region of the United States. Multiethnic and all-embracing in a friendly, hospitable way, the region offers visitors an unforgettable introduction to Southern charm, as embodied by the pleasure-seeking lifestyle of New Orleans.

Some 14 million people live in the Deep South, in a region covering about 200,000 sq miles (517,998 sq km), which is similar in size and population density to neighboring Texas. While the four states share a natural appreciation for the good things in life, they are otherwise quite different. Louisiana epitomizes French Catholic culture, whereas Mississippi and Alabama were the heart of the Confederacy during the Civil War. Arkansas differs in its rugged landscape matched by its people's pride in the state's mountain heritage. Most residents of the primarily rural Deep South have family roots reaching deep into history, and a rare continuity exists between past and present.

The rich bottomlands that line the meandering path of the Mississippi River across parts of Mississippi, Arkansas, and Louisiana once yielded the world's largest crops of cotton, and it was here that some of the greatest early American fortunes were made. However, the industry's labor-intensive demands were based on the iniquities of slavery, which has haunted the economy and culture of the Deep South for two centuries.

HISTORY

Some of the region's earliest known inhabitants were the city-based agricultural communities of the Mississippian culture, whose members cultivated extensive fields of corn, beans, and squash, and constructed elaborate mounds for their religious and political rituals. The 3,700-year-old effigy mounds at Poverty Point in northeastern Louisiana, one of North America's oldest, largest, and most significant archaeological remains, dates from this period.

The steamboat *Natchez* leaving Mississippi River port

◁ **Royal Café, a popular Cajun-Creole restaurant in the French Quarter, New Orleans**

Dennis Malone Carter's painting, *The Battle of New Orleans*

When Spanish conquistador Hernando de Soto and his troops first encountered the Mississippian cities, they soon decimated the people and their culture. Thereafter, other more dispersed Indian groups rose to power, most notably the Chickasaw, Choctaw, Quapaw, Creek, and Cherokee tribes. The Creek Indians of central and northern Alabama were perhaps the most successful, numbering some 15,000 at their peak. In the early 1700s, European colonists supported the Creeks, and supplied them with guns and ammunition in exchange for their help in vanquishing the other tribes. A century later, the Creeks themselves were under assault, and by 1816 they had been forced to give up their vast and fertile territory to the incoming Americans. The story of most other Deep South Indians is similar, ending tragically in the 1830s, when they were moved to distant Oklahoma. A few, including the Choctaw tribe in central Mississippi, still live on their ancestral lands.

While English-speaking Americans dominate the past and present, the French and Spanish carried out much of the early exploration and settlement. Louisiana and Arkansas were under nominal French control until 1803, while Alabama and Mississippi were part of the Spanish colony of West Florida until 1814. Boundaries and allegiances varied until the US took control, through the Louisiana Purchase of 1803, and by the multiple battles with England, Spain, and their Indian allies.

With the defeat of the British at the Battle of New Orleans in January 1815, the Deep South entered an era of unprecedented growth and prosperity. New Orleans became the fourth-largest US city and the nation's second-busiest port. Steamboats plied the Mississippi River, as chronicled by writer Mark Twain (1835–1910), himself a former steamboat captain.

By the mid-1800s, wealthy individuals from the Carolinas, in particular, introduced the slave-owning, cotton-growing plantation culture that would reap huge fortunes and lead inexorably toward the Civil War. Mississippi, the second state to secede from the US, provided the rebel Confederacy with its president, Jefferson Davis, while Montgomery, Alabama, served as its first capital. The fall of Vicksburg in 1863 effectively ended Confederate control of the Mississippi, and after the war much of the region lay in ruins.

KEY DATES IN HISTORY

1539 Hernando de Soto leads the first European expedition to the Deep South

1699 Fort de Maurepas, near present-day Biloxi, Mississippi, becomes capital of France's Louisiana colony

1723 Louisiana's capital moved to New Orleans

1803 Louisiana Territory purchased from Napoleonic France (the Louisiana Purchase)

1814 Creek and Chickasaw Indians are forced to relinquish their territorial claims

1812 Louisiana becomes a state

1817 Mississippi becomes a state

1819 Alabama becomes a state

1836 Arkansas becomes a state

1863 US forces take control of Vicksburg to end Confederate access to the Mississippi River

1935 Populist Louisiana Governor Huey "Kingfish" Long assassinated in Baton Rogue

1955 Montgomery Bus Boycott

1962 African-American student James Meredith becomes the first nonwhite person to attend classes at the University of Mississippi

1992 Former Arkansas Governor Bill Clinton is elected 42nd president of the United States

2005 Hurricane Katrina hits the southern US, destroying towns and cities and killing thousands of people in New Orleans and the Gulf Coast

The post-Civil War economic and social wasteland gave rise to a doctrine of white supremacy and racist violence that plagued the region the following century. It wasn't until the 1950s and 60s, when the dramatic confrontations of the Civil Rights Movement, such as those at Selma, Alabama, in 1965, began to change things for the better.

PEOPLE & THE ECONOMY

The Deep South is remembered for its often troubled history as well as its people's resolute and indomitable spirit to cope with the problems of the past. Despite a large exodus of African Americans to northern US cities after the Civil War, descendants of slaves still form a large percentage of the population, and the slow but steady process of overcoming racial segregation has transformed the region. Today, African Americans are legally entitled to equal treatment, although in reality there remains a distinct gap in opportunities between whites and nonwhites.

Another distinctive component is Louisiana's Cajuns, who live in the watery region north and west of New Orleans. A third very different culture is found in the densely forested mountains of Arkansas and northern Alabama. Long denigrated as "hillbillies" like their figurative cousins in Tennessee, Kentucky, and West Virginia, these mountain people have a fiercely protected independence and self-reliance. Hunting and fishing, both for recreation and sustenance, many still practice traditional crafts and perform the so-called "bluegrass" music derived from the folk music of their Scottish and Irish forebears.

As the cotton-based economy of plantation and Reconstruction days has disappeared, little has emerged to take its place. Thanks to inexpensive imports, the region's once-thriving textile industry has all but disappeared. Except for the steel mills of Birmingham, Alabama, the corridor of petrochemical factories along the Mississippi in Louisiana, or the gambling centers in the Mississippi Delta and along the Gulf of Mexico, the Deep South still suffers from a major lack of industry and employment opportunities. Success stories include Dillard's department stores and the world-dominating retail might of Wal-Mart, both of which started and still have their corporate headquarters in Arkansas. In contrast, one of the region's economic darlings of the 1990s, the Mississippi-based telecommunications company, WorldCom, crashed into bankruptcy in 2002.

CULTURE & ARTS

If culture and the arts were the most valuable market commodities, the Deep South would be the wealthiest region in the country. The region has been instrumental in creating some of the world's most popular forms of musical, literary, and culinary expression. Jazz, for example, grew from the bubbling melting pot of Creole culture that was New Orleans after the Civil War, while the blues and its offspring rock 'n' roll, emerged from the slave songs of the Mississippi Delta. Writers such as Tennessee Williams and William Faulkner, and novels like Harper Lee's classic *To Kill a Mockingbird*, helped earn the Deep South a place in world literature, while the melange of Cajun, Creole, "Soul Food," and barbecue make it a delicious place to travel.

Statue of William Faulkner in the courthouse square in downtown Oxford, Mississippi

Exploring the Deep South

Stretching from the Gulf Coast to the Appalachians in the north and the Great Plains in the west, the Deep South region sprawls across some 200,000 sq miles (517,998 sq km). Although large in area, the population is sparse and the transportation facilities limited. As elsewhere in the US, a car is the best way to get around. New Orleans, has the region's major airport, while smaller airports serve other cities. In 2005, Hurricane Katrina destroyed towns and cities in Mississippi, Alabama, and Louisiana *(see p366)*. Please check for the latest information before you travel.

KEY

- Airport
- Highway
- Major road
- Railroad
- State border

SIGHTS AT A GLANCE

Louisiana

New Orleans pp344–53 1
Plantation Alley 2
Baton Rouge p355 3
Lafayette 4
Bayou Teche 5
Natchitoches 6
Shreveport 7

Arkansas

Little Rock 8
Hot Springs 9
Mountain View 10
Eureka Springs 11

Mississippi

Mississippi Delta 12
Oxford 13
Tupelo 14
Vicksburg National Military Park 15
Jackson 16
Natchez Trace Parkway 17
Natchez 18
Gulf Coast 19

Alabama

Mobile 20
Selma 21
Montgomery 22
Tuskegee 23
Birmingham 24
Huntsville 25

SEE ALSO

- ***Practical Information*** pp366–7
- ***Where to Stay*** pp368–71
- ***Where to Eat*** pp372–5

A traditional sternwheeler riverboat cruising the Mississippi River

MILEAGE CHART

10 = Distance in miles
10 = Distance in kilometers

NEW ORLEANS, LA	BATON ROUGE, LA	LITTLE ROCK, AR	OXFORD, MS	JACKSON, MS	MOBILE, AL	
80 129						BATON ROUGE, LA
529 851	**480** 772					LITTLE ROCK, AR
345 555	**333** 536	**221** 356				OXFORD, MS
185 298	**173** 278	**344** 553	**174** 280			JACKSON, MS
144 232	**199** 320	**573** 922	**402** 647	**189** 304		MOBILE, AL
343 552	**399** 642	**377** 607	**187** 301	**238** 382	**258** 415	BIRMINGHAM, AL

Statue of General Tilghman, Vicksburg National Military Park

A jazz pub, one of many in New Orleans

New Orleans ❶

Located in southeast Louisiana, New Orleans lies between Lake Pontchartrain and a bend in the Mississippi. It covers an area of 199 sq miles (516 sq km) and prior to Hurricane Katrina (August 2005) it had a population of nearly 500,000. Since then the population has reached 223,000. The city's historic areas were largely unaffected by the storm. The topmost tourist destination is the French Quarter, where the legendary Royal and Bourbon Streets are located. Beyond this lie the Central Business District centered along the waterfront, the verdant Garden District, and the area around City Park.

Diners at the popular Acme Oyster House

SIGHTS AT A GLANCE

Old US Mint ①
Old Ursuline Convent ②
French Market ③
Café du Monde ④
Jackson Square ⑤
St. Louis Cathedral, Cabildo, & Presbytère ⑥
Washington Artillery Park and Moonwalk ⑦
St. Louis Cemetery #1 ⑧
Hermann-Grima Historic House ⑨
Bourbon Street ⑩
Royal Street ⑪
Steamboat Natchez ⑫
Custom House & Insectarium ⑬
Audubon Nature Institute ⑭
Ferry to Algiers & Mardi Gras World ⑮
Riverwalk Marketplace ⑯

Greater New Orleans ***(see inset map)***
Garden District ⑰
City Park ⑱

Royal Street and its well-known LaBranche buildings

GETTING AROUND

Although most of the city's popular tourist sights in and near the French Quarter are easily accessible on foot, New Orleans also has a useful public transportation system. Bus routes cover the city, and no visitor should miss the opportunity to take a trip on the city's streetcar. Riverboats also provide a relaxing and pleasant way to see the sights along the basin of the Mississippi River. Taxis are affordable and convenient, and are recommended for all trips planned for after dark.

SEE ALSO

- ***Where to Stay*** pp368–9
- ***Where to Eat*** pp372–4

KEY

- Sight/Place of interest
- Airport
- Train station
- Streetcar station
- Bus terminus
- Ferry terminal
- Tourist information
- Parking
- Highway

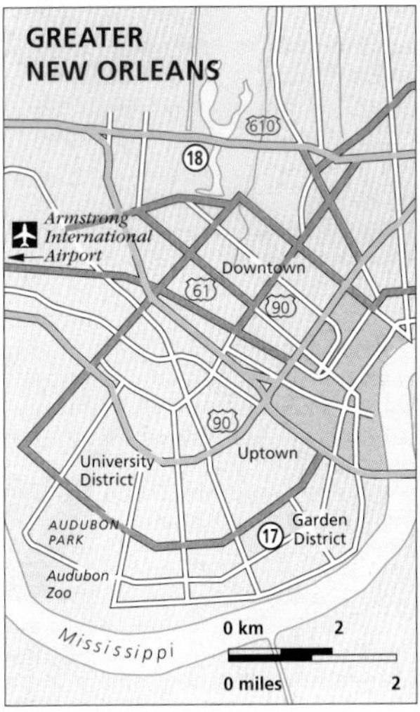

KEY

- Area of main map

Neo-Classical façade of the Old US Mint

Old US Mint ①

Map E2. 400 Esplanade Ave. ***Tel*** *(504) 568-6968.* *Riverfront.* *3, 55.* *9am–5pm Tue–Sun.* *public hols.*
www.sm.crt.state.la.us/mintex.htm

This Greek Revival building, built in 1835 by William Strickland, functioned as a mint until 1909, turning out a variety of coinage, including Confederate and Mexican currency. It then became a federal prison and was later used by the Coast Guard. In the late 1970s, it was taken over by the state and converted into a museum to house the **New Orleans Jazz Collection**. The exhibit tells the story of jazz *(see p349)* through a collection of original musical instruments, vintage photographs, and historic documents. Among the instruments displayed are the ebony clarinet George Lewis played on to record "Burgundy Street Blues," and the cornet Louis Armstrong learned to play on. At the entrance are a series of photographs of early bands and musicians, as well as a steamboat scale model.

The building also houses the **History of the Old US Mint Exhibition**, which displays gold and silver coins formerly minted here. The building lost its entire roof during Hurricane Katrina in 2005, but it has been carefully and completely restored.

Photograph, New Orleans Jazz Collection

Old Ursuline Convent ②

Map E2. 1100 Chartres St. ***Tel*** *(504) 529-3040.* *Riverfront.* *3, 55.* *10am–4pm Tue–Fri, 11am– 4pm Sat–Sun (guided tours only).*

The oldest building in the Mississippi Valley, the Old Ursuline Convent was built in 1752, some 25 years after the Ursuline Sisters first arrived in New Orleans. With its steep-pitched roof punctuated by a row of dormers and tall chimneys, it is a typical French Colonial structure and one of the few to remain from that period. In the 1820s, the nuns moved to new quarters, and the convent became the first official residence for the bishops and archbishops of New Orleans, and the home of the archdiocesan archives. Later, it became part of a parish.

The current chapel, now known as Our Lady of Victory, was consecrated in 1845. Inside, visitors can admire the splendid pine-and-cypress ceiling, two superb Bavarian stained-glass windows, and a window depicting the Battle of New Orleans, beneath an image of Our Lady of Prompt Succor. The nuns' old kitchen and laundry is now the rectory.

A formal French garden containing a handsome iron gazebo lies in front of the building. It is accessed via the porter's lodge.

Old Ursuline Convent, dating from 1752

French Market ③

Map E2. N Peters St, from St. Ann to Barracks St. *Riverfront.* *3, 5, 48.* *Shops: 9am–7pm daily; Farmers Market: 24 hours daily.*
www.frenchmarket.org

A New Orleans institution since 1791, this area served as a trading place for Native Americans much before European settlement. Officially the French Market is five blocks between St. Ann and Barracks Streets, beginning roughly at Café du Monde and ending at the Old Mint museum. In daily use, the term "French Market" usually denotes the open air markets from St. Philip to Barracks, which stock many New Orleans specialties. The Farmers Market (beginning at Ursulines Street) recently underwent an extensive restoration and offers fresh Louisiana produce, seafood, and spices. Strawberries in the spring and the pecans in the fall are especially prized.

The majority of the space is now given over to the **Flea Market** – all kinds of items, ranging from jewelry and pottery to African arts and crafts, can be bought at the stalls and tables around the French Market buildings. The Flea Market stands on the site of the notorious neighborhood around Gallatin Street, which was once inhabited by criminals, prostitutes, and visiting sailors.

Café du Monde ④

Map E2. 1039 Decatur. ***Tel*** *(504) 587-0833. Riverfront.* *3, 5, 55. 24 hours daily.* **www**.cafedumonde.com

Everyone who visits New Orleans stops here for a plate of sugar-dusted *beignets* (square French donuts) accompanied by plain *café au lait* or the famous chicory-flavored version. These are the only items offered at this 100-year old coffee house, where visitors can relax at a table under the arcade and listen to the street musicians, or simply watch people as they go by.

During the mid-19th century there were 500 similar coffee houses in the French Quarter. Coffee was one of the city's most important commodities, and the coffee trade helped the economy recover after the Civil War, when New Orleans vied with New York City to control coffee imports. Chicory-flavored coffee was conceived during the Civil War, when the root was used to stretch the coffee supply.

Taking a break at Café du Monde with coffee and *beignets*

Jackson Square ⑤

Map E2. *Riverfront.* *3, 5, 55.*

Once little more than a muddy field called the Place d' Armes where troops were drilled, criminals were placed in the stocks, and executions were carried out, this square lies in the heart of the French Quarter. It was renamed in honor of General Andrew Jackson *(see p265)* who defeated the British at the Battle of New Orleans in 1815.

Jazz band playing in Jackson Square

The gardens and pathways, as they exist today, were laid out in 1848, when the beautification of the square took place under the patronage of Baroness Micaela Pontalba, then one of the city's most colorful personalities. Under her auspices, the Pelanne brothers designed the handsome wrought-iron fence that encloses the square. At the center stands a statue of General Jackson astride a rearing horse, sculpted by Clark Mills for $30,000. The inscription "The Union must and shall be preserved," on the plinth was added by Union General Benjamin "Beast" Butler, when he occupied the city during the Civil War.

Today, the square is a lively meeting place, where artists exhibit their works and jazz musicians entertain visitors throughout the week.

A developer like her philanthropist father Don Andreés Almonester y Rojas *(see p348)*, the baroness also commissioned the **Pontalba Buildings**, flanking the uptown and downtown sides of Jackson Square. Built at a cost of over $300,000, they were considered the best and the largest apartments of their kind at that time. These elegant apartment buildings are based on plans the baroness brought back from Paris after she separated from her husband. The design of the initials A and P (for Almonester and Pontalba) in the cast-iron railings of the balconies and galleries is attributed to one of the baroness's sons, an artist.

The **National WWII Museum** is the world's most extensive museum commemorating World War II, with everything from tanks to personal diaries. It has been designated by Congress as the country's official World War II Museum. It is located in New Orleans because this is where Andrew Higgins designed and built the amphibious landing craft that Eisenhower considered essential for the Allies' victory.

National WWII Museum
945 Magazine St, Warehouse District. ***Tel*** *(504) 527-6012. 9am–5pm Tue–Sun. public hols.* **www**.nationalww2museum.org

NEW ORLEANS IRONWORK

The shadows cast by New Orleans ironwork add a romantic touch to the city. Wrought iron, which came first, was fashioned by hand into beautiful shapes by German, Irish, and African-American artisans. Cast iron, on the other hand, was poured into wooden molds and allowed to set. As a result, the latter has a somewhat solid, fixed appearance, unlike wrought iron, which is handmade and has a more fluid aspect. Both kinds of ironwork can be seen throughout the city, particularly in the French Quarter and the Garden District, where balconies, fences, window grilles, and gates are adorned with decorative motifs such as abstracts, cherubs, fruit, flowers, and animals.

Ironwork on the Pontalba Buildings

St. Louis Cathedral

St. Louis Cathedral, Cabildo, & Presbytère ⑥

Map D2. Jackson Square. ***Tel*** *(504) 525-9585 (St. Louis Cathedral), (504) 568-6968 (Cabildo & Presbytère).* *St. Charles Ave, Canal.* *3, 5, 55, 81.* *9am–5pm daily (St. Louis Cathedral); 9am–5pm Tue–Sun (Cabildo & Presbytère).* *Cabildo & Presbytère.* *St. Louis Cathedral, regular services throughout the day.*
www.saintlouiscathedral.org

This complex of buildings comprises the cathedral, Cabildo, and Presbytère. St. Louis Cathedral stands on the site of two earlier churches that were destroyed. The current building, begun in 1789, was dedicated as a cathedral in 1794. Inside are superb murals and a carved-wood Baroque main altar.

The Cabildo, designed by Guilberto Guillemard, was built and financed in 1795 by Don Andrés Almonester y Rojas. It served as a capitol for the legislative assembly of the Spanish Colonial government and subsequently as the City Hall. From 1853 to 1911 it housed the state Supreme Court. The Louisiana Purchase *(see p340)* was signed in the Sala Capitular in 1803.

The Casa Curial, or Presbytère, was built between 1794 and 1813, and used as a courthouse until 1911. It now houses the Mardi Gras Museum, featuring colorful objects and memorabilia.

Washington Artillery Park and Moonwalk ⑦

Map E2. Decatur St, between St Ann & St Peter sts. *3, 5, 55.* *Riverfront.*

Washington Artillery Park faces Jackson Square from Decatur Street. Inside the park is an austere concrete amphitheater with a central staircase leading to the Moonwalk. This community boardwalk was named after former New Orleans Mayor Maurice "Moon" Landrieu, who approved the construction of flood walls that made the riverfront area accessible to the public.

The park was built in 1976 and was once used as a military training ground, but today the amphitheater and Moonwalk are favored by street performers. Crowds often gather to enjoy performances by musicians, including guitarists, clarinettists, saxophonists, trombonists, and steel drummers, who play with an open case at their feet to collect donations.

The breeze along the waterfront can provide a welcome break from the humidity of the city, and it's also the perfect vantage point from which to see the river, Jackson Square, and the surrounding area. Stone steps lead down to where you can dangle your feet in the water, but don't attempt to stand in it, as the current is deceptively powerful.

St. Louis Cemetery #1 ⑧

Map D2. Basin St between St. Louis & Conti. ***Tel*** *(504) 596-3050.* *46, 48, 52, 57.* *9am–3pm Mon–Sat, 9am–noon Sun.*

The city's oldest surviving cemetery was established in 1789. This fascinating place, with its rows of mausoleums, is the resting place of many legendary local residents. The most famous of all is probably Marie Laveau. Crowds visit her tomb, marking it with an "X" (symbolically requesting that she grant a particular wish). By 1829, St. Louis Cemetery #1 was filled, mostly with victims of yellow fever, and the nearby **St. Louis Cemetery #2** was established as an extension. Many of the city's 19th-century Creole aristocracy are buried here in ornate mausoleums.

Statue of an angel, St. Louis Cemetery #1

However, the cemeteries should not be visited alone, as they are in secluded areas where muggers and pickpockets operate. It is advisable for visitors to join guided tours, given by the **Save Our Cemeteries** organization and by **Gray Line Tours**. Both companies provide plenty of excellent local information.

Gray Line Tours
Tel *(504) 569-1401.*
www.graylineneworleans.com

Save Our Cemeteries
Tel *(888) 721-7493*

VOODOO WORSHIP

Portrait of Marie Laveau

Voodoo arrived in New Orleans from Africa, via the Caribbean, where it originated as a form of ancestor worship among the West African tribes, who were brought to North America as slaves. During the slave uprising in Saint Dominigue in 1793, many of the planters from Haiti fled to New Orleans, bringing their slaves (and voodoo) with them. Marie Laveau (c.1794–1881), the voodoo queen, used Catholic elements such as prayer, incense, and saints in her rituals, which she opened to the public for an admission fee. The voodoo calendar's high point was the celebration she held along Bayou St. John on St. John's Eve.

New Orleans Jazz

Blue Lu Barker

Jazz is America's original contribution to world culture. It evolved slowly and almost imperceptibly from a number of sources – from the music played at balls, parades, dances, and funerals, and New Orleans' unique blend of cultures. Its musical inspirations included African work chants and spirituals, as well as European and American folk influences – the entire mélange of music that was played in 19th-century New Orleans.

Trumpeter Oscar "Papa" Celestin, *the founder of the Tuxedo Brass Band in 1911, also composed "Down by the Riverside."*

Kid Ory's trombone, *which he played while performing with King Oliver and others, is displayed at the Old US Mint.*

STORYVILLE JAZZ SALON

The 38-block area bounded by Iberville, Basin, Robertson, and St. Louis Streets, was the city's legal red-light district from 1897 to 1917. Known as Storyville, many early jazz artists, including Jelly Roll Morton, King Oliver, and Edward "Kid" Ory, entertained at the bordellos, playing behind screens.

Riverboat Jazz Bands *came into being after Storyville was closed down in 1917. New Orleans' best musicians either performed on boats or migrated to northern cities. Pianist Fate Marable's band included Louis Armstrong, who played the cornet.*

Congo Square *was where slaves gathered every Sunday to celebrate their one day off by playing music and dancing.*

Louis Armstrong, *the internationally famous jazz trumpeter, began singing on the streets of New Orleans. He played with Kid Ory before leaving the city in 1923 to join King Oliver's band in Chicago.*

Master bedroom at the Hermann-Grima Historic House

Hermann-Grima Historic House ⑨

Map D3. 820 St. Louis St. ***Tel*** *(504) 525-5661.* 3. *10am–3pm Mon–Fri.* *public hols.*
www.hgghh.org

This gabled brick house is one of the French Quarter's few examples of American Creole-style architecture. It was built in 1831 by William Brand for Samuel Hermann, a German-Jewish merchant who lost his fortune in 1837 and sold the house to Judge Felix Grima. It features a central doorway with a fan-light and marble steps; another window with a fanlight graces the second floor. Inside, the floors and doors are made of cypress. The three-story service quarters are in a building off the parterre behind the house. They contain a kitchen with a rare four-burner wood-fired stove with a beehive oven.

Bourbon Street ⑩

Map D3. *3, 55, 89.*

Today Bourbon Street, rather than Basin Street, is synonymous with sin. This legendary street, named after the French royal family of Bourbon, is lined with bars that offer vats of such lethal concoctions as Brain Freeze, Nuclear Kamikaze, and Sex on the Bayou, most often to the accompaniment of blasting rock or blues. Other places offer everything from peep shows, topless dancers, and strip joints, to drag shows and gay action. During Mardi Gras, the sidewalks and overhanging balconies are jammed with crowds and drinking revelers.

Some of the most famous establishments near this lively street include **Pat O'Brien's** (St. Peter Street), which is well-known for its rum-based "Hurricane" cocktail, **Preservation Hall** (St. Peter Street), a top-quality jazz venue, and **Arnaud's** (Bienville Street),

Fire fountain at Pat O'Brien's, near Bourbon Street

a restaurant that is a true New Orleans classic. **Galatoire's**, close to Arnaud's, is another premier New Orleans restaurant *(see p373)*. **Lafitte's Blacksmith Shop**, at 941 Bourbon Street, is considered one of the finest bars in New Orleans. Constructed sometime before 1772, it is a good example of the brick-between-posts French-style building, in which soft local bricks are supported by cypress timbers and protected by plaster. Inside, several small fireplaces warm the place on cool evenings, and there is also a small patio containing a sculpture of Adam and Eve, created by an artist as payment for his bar bill.

Despite its name, there is no concrete evidence that the pirate brothers, Jean and Pierre Lafitte, operated a smithy here as a front for their smuggling activities. They were also prominent slave traffickers, selling "black ivory" to Louisiana's prominent slave-holding families. The brothers earned local gratitude by warning the Americans of the planned British attack on New Orleans in 1815, and they fought bravely in the ensuing battle.

Just up from Lafitte's is the oldest gay bar in the country, **Lafitte's in Exile**. It is so called because, until the early 1950s, gays frequented the old Lafitte's; when the bar changed hands, its new owner refused to renew the lease, and its gay patrons established their new quarters here. It has remained a popular alternative ever since.

A VIEW OF ROYAL STREET

The pride of the French Quarter, Royal Street is lined with beautiful buildings that have been carefully restored. Today, they are occupied by elegant stores and restaurants.

Brennan's (#417)
Built around 1802 for a Spanish merchant, this building became a bank, and then a restaurant in 1954. Its balcony seal is made of cast iron.

Antoine Peychaud's Pharmacy (#437)
An antique shop offering a range of fine objects is now housed in the pharmacy where the cocktail was born.

Louisiana State Bank (#403)

Moss Antiques

Lafitte's Blacksmith Shop, Bourbon Street

Royal Street ⑪

Map D3. *St. Charles Ave.* *3, 5, 55, 81, 82.*

Antique shops filled with beautiful, often French, objects line Royal Street, undoubtedly the most fetching street in the French Quarter. In the early colony, this was the city's financial center and its main and most fashionable street. Today, many of the antique stores occupy handsome landmarks. Their merchandise includes crystal chandeliers, massive inlaid armoires, and ormolu furnishings – treasures associated with an opulent Southern lifestyle.

The **Historic New Orleans Collection**, born of one couple's interest in the Battle of New Orleans (1815), is housed in a complex of houses built for Jean François Merieult and his wife in 1792. The collectors were General and Mrs. L. Kemper Williams, who lived in the residence at the rear of the courtyard from the 1940s to the '60s.

The museum's 10 galleries display historical artifacts, ranging from maps and paintings to furnishings and decorative objects. The Empire Gallery displays tables, chests, and sofas, alongside portraits of such native New Orleanians as Madame Auguste de Gas, mother of artist Edgar Degas. The museum's other galleries include the Plantation Gallery, the Louisiana Purchase Gallery, the Victorian Gallery, and the Spanish Colonial Gallery.

Farther away are **Gallier House Museum**, an attractive 19th-century residence that combines Creole and American architectural elements, and the lovely **Lalaurie House**, associated with ghosts. Also on Royal Street is **Rumors**, a gift shop that sells Mardi Gras souvenirs all year long – masks, beads, krewe costumes, and posters are all available for sale here.

Historic New Orleans Collection
533 Royal St. ***Tel*** *(504) 523-4662.*
9:30am–4:30pm Tue–Sat.

Artifacts from the Historic New Orleans Collection on Royal Street

Steamboat *Natchez*, offering regular two-hour cruises

Steamboat Natchez ⑫

Map E3. Woldenberg Riverfront park wharf. ***Tel*** *(504) 586-8777, (800) 233-2628.* *Riverfront.* *45, 87.* *Harbor Jazz Cruises: board 11am Fri–Sun, 2pm Mon–Sun, 6pm Fri & Sat.*
www.steamboatnatchez.com

A reminder of the old days of river travel, the Steamboat *Natchez* is typical of the steamboats that traveled the length of the Mississippi, taking three to five days to get from Louisville, Kentucky *(see p271)*, to New Orleans. The boatmen, notorious brawlers in search of women and liquor at the end of a trip, established New Orleans' reputation as the "City of Sin." In their heyday, from 1830 to 1860, some 30 steamboats lined up at the levee. The era ended by the close of the 19th century as railroads and highways replaced them. Today, daily cruises offer visitors a glimpse into a forgotten lifestyle.

St. Anthony's Garden
This beautiful garden stands at the back of St. Louis Cathedral. Its serenity hides the fact that it was a staging ground for duels in the 18th century.

The LaBranche Buildings (#700)
Embellished with fine oak-leaf ironwork, these buildings were constructed in 1835 for sugar planter Jean Baptiste LaBranche.

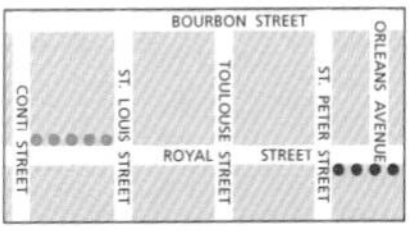

LOCATOR MAP

Custom House ⑬

Map D3. 423 Canal St. 3. Canal. *daily.* *some public hols.*
www.auduboninstitute.org

Perhaps the most important Federal-style structure in the South, this Quincy granite building took 33 years to complete (1848–81). The Marble Hall is a dramatic space under a ground-glass ceiling supported by 14 marble columns.

Audubon Nature Institute ⑭

Map E3. Canal St at Mississippi River. ***Tel*** *(504) 581-4629.* *Riverfront.* *3, 5, 55, 57.* *10am–5pm Tue–Sun.* *Dec 25 & Mardi Gras.*

Focusing on the waters around New Orleans, from the Mississippi and the swamps to the Gulf of Mexico and the Caribbean, this complex features some 560 species of marine life. Highlights include a tank containing a Caribbean reef, and a replica of an oil rig. Other tanks contain species that illustrate everything there is to know about life beneath the ocean, including how fish communicate. The complex also includes New Orleans Zoo, the Insectarium, and the Entergy IMAX® Theater. Daily riverboat cruises can also be taken from here.

The aquarium lost nearly all of its many forms of aquatic life because of power outages due to the devastation caused by Hurricane Katrina in August 2005. However, it was fully restored and enhanced and was reopened to great fanfare, with as many species on display as before.

Under the sea at the Audubon Nature Institute

Entrance to the Riverwalk Marketplace

Ferry to Algiers & Mardi Gras World ⑮

Map E4. Take the ferry at the end of Canal St. In Algiers take the shuttle. *Riverfront.* *55, 57.* *9am–4:30pm daily.* **Blaine Kern's Mardi Gras World** 233 Newton St, Algiers. ***Tel*** *(504) 361-7821.* *9:30am–5pm daily.*
www.mardigrasworld.com

A ferry takes visitors across the Mississippi to Algiers and the fascinating Blaine Kern's Mardi Gras World. Blaine Kern is often called "Mr. Mardi Gras" because many of the massive floats are constructed here in his warehouse.

The tour begins with coffee and the traditional King Cake. A short film shows the floats and the stages of their production, from the original drawings and molds to the end result. Visitors can try on some of the flamboyant costumes worn by Krewe members in past parades. Visitors can also wander through the warehouses and view huge decorative figures made of fiberglass or Styrofoam overlaid with papier-mâché. The cost of making the floats is usually borne by each Krewe and can range from anywhere between $300 and $3,000.

Riverwalk Marketplace ⑯

Map E4. 1 Poydras St. ***Tel*** *(504) 522-1555.* *Riverfront.* *3, 55, 57, 65.*
www.riverwalkmarketplace.com

This massive riverside shopping mall, designed by the same company that developed Boston's Faneuil Hall *(see p136)*, contains more than 140 stores, most of which are brand-name favorites such as Eddie Bauer, Banana Republic, and the Museum Company. The top floor is devoted to a food court, while a highlight of the ground floor is the Creole Delicacies Gourmet Shop, which offers a two-hour course in cooking. In addition to plentiful shopping opportunities, the mall has an outdoor walkway that runs along the Mississippi River, giving visitors one of the best views of the river and river traffic in the city. International and other cruise ships dock alongside the marketplace, the most notable being those operated by the Delta Queen Steamboat Company, which was established in 1890. Several information plaques attached to railings along the walkway describe everything from the types of boats plying the river to the seagulls that drift up from the Gulf of Mexico.

The **Spanish Plaza**, near the entrance, has a fountain in the center. Surrounding it is a circular mosaic bench, depicting the coats of arms of the city's Spanish immigrants.

St. Charles Avenue Streetcar, a New Orleans landmark

Garden District ⑰

Between Jackson & Louisiana Aves, & St. Charles Ave & Magazine St. *St. Charles.* *11, 14, 27.*

When the Americans arrived in New Orleans after the Louisiana Purchase in 1803, they settled upriver from the French Quarter. This area is referred to as the Garden District because of the lush gardens planted with magnolia, camellia, azalea, and jasmine. A residential neighborhood, it is filled with large mansions built by wealthy city planters and merchants. Some of the grand residences here are the Robinson House and Colonel Short's Villa, which has a handsome cast-iron cornstalk fence.

A romantic New Orleans experience is to take a ride on the slow-moving **St. Charles Avenue Streetcar** to uptown New Orleans. The last of the sort that featured in Tennessee Williams' *A Streetcar Named Desire*, it travels 6.5 miles (10.5 km) from Canal Street to Carrollton Avenue. Along the way it passes many famous landmarks. The most prominent are Lee Circle with its memorial to Confederate general Robert E. Lee, the Gothic Revival Christ Church, Touro Synagogue, the Latter Public Library, and Loyola and Tulane Universities.

Just off St. Charles Avenue is one of the loveliest urban parks in the country. The 340-acre (137-ha) Audubon Park was originally the sugar plantation of Jean Etienne Boré, who developed the commercially successful sugar granulation process. It was also the location of the 1884 World Exposition. The **Audubon Zoo** occupies 58 acres (23 ha) of the park's grounds. Beautifully landscaped, the zoo opened in 1938 but was completely redesigned in the 1980s. Today, the animals live in open paddocks that replicate their natural habitats. The Louisana Swamp, where white alligators bask along the banks or float in the muddy lagoon, is one of the most engaging exhibits.

Evocative statue in the City Park's New Orleans Botanical Gardens

City Park ⑱

45, 46, 48, 87, 90. **New Orleans Museum of Art** ***Tel*** *(504) 488-2631.* *10am–5pm Tue–Sun.* *public hols.* **www**.noma.org

The fifth largest urban park in the US, the 1,500-acre (607-ha) City Park is a New Orleans institution, where visitors can relax and enjoy the semitropical Louisiana weather. The **New Orleans Botanical Gardens** and the prestigious **New Orleans Museum of Art** share this space with moss-draped live oaks, lagoons for boating and fishing, and the championship Bayou Oaks Golf Course.

Housed in an impressive Beaux Arts building, the museum has an astonishingly varied collection. Originally the Delgado Museum of Art, it was founded in 1910 when Isaac Delgado, a millionaire bachelor, donated the original $150,000 to construct an art museum in City Park. In 1971 it was renamed the New Orleans Museum of Art in deference to some of its later benefactors. The New Orleans Botanical Garden was created in the 1930s. Then, it was primarily a rose garden, but today there are also spring and perennial gardens, featuring camellias, azaleas, and magnolias, as well as tropical plants and trees. City Park's grounds were flooded with brackish water following Hurricane Katrina, but the local people have made great efforts to restore them to their former pristine beauty.

Colorful costume for the Mardi Gras parade

MARDI GRAS

Culminating on the day before Ash Wednesday – Mardi Gras – the Carnival festivities in New Orleans are celebrated with lavish masked balls, presented by groups of citizens known as "Krewes." Although most balls are private, many Krewes also put on parades, with ornate costumes and colorful floats. Many Carnival traditions began with the Krewe of Rex. The symbolic purple, green, and gold colors used for masks, banners, and other decorations are derived from the original costume worn by Rex, the King of Mardi Gras, in the 1872 parade. The tradition of throwing souvenir doubloons (coins), beads, and dolls from the floats to the crowds began in 1881.

Louisiana

Old Plantation water pump

Renowned for its exotic landscape of bayous and swamps, antebellum plantation homes, jazz, and fine food, Louisiana is a state richly steeped in history and tradition. Its predominant French heritage is the legacy of the French settlers who named the colony for Louis XIV. Both France and Spain colonized Louisiana before the United States finally acquired the territory through the Louisiana Purchase of 1803. Louisiana became a state in 1812 and in the following decades played a strategic role in the Civil War and the painful struggle for Civil Rights. Today, the state preserves both its Colonial history as well as its distinct Creole and Cajun heritage. Highlights include the beautiful plantations along the Mississippi and the cultural delights of Cajun Country.

Plantation Alley ❷

Hwy 18 from New Orleans, which joins Hwy 1. *New Orleans Convention & Visitors' Bureau, (800) 672-6124; the bureau maintains a list of tour operators.*

Before the Civil War, the Mississippi River was lined with plantations producing first indigo, then cotton, rice, and sugar. At the time, this was one of the nation's wealthiest regions and home to two-thirds of America's millionaires. Of the 350 opulent estates that once flourished here, around 40 remain. Of these about a dozen are open to the public on a stretch of the Great River Road *(see pp40–41)* between New Orleans and Baton Rouge, known as "Plantation Alley."

Today, large neighboring petrochemical plants have replaced sugar cane and cotton as the mainstay of the riverside economy. High levees, reinforced by the Army Corps of Engineers after the flood of 1927, block the river from the road. The tradition since the 1880s has been to light bonfires atop them each Christmas Eve, to illuminate the way for Santa Claus.

Oak Alley Plantation in Vacherie, is 40 miles (64 km) west from New Orleans airport. An arcade of 28 arching live oaks, planted some 300 years ago, leads to this striking 1839 house. The picture of the Greek Revival mansion down the long arcade seems the archetypal Hollywood image. Both the recently refurbished house and garden have been used as a location for several movies, including *Interview with the Vampire* (1994). The mansion offers five B&B cottages for overnight stay. To its east, **Laura Plantation** has an 1805 Creole house constructed of cypress, designed by Senegalese builders. The plantation slaves are thought to be the source of various Senegalese folk tales, including the famous *Br'er Rabbit* stories translated into English by Joel Chandler Harris.

A 15-minute drive from New Orleans, **Destrehan Plantation**, built in 1787, is the oldest documented plantation home in the Lower Mississippi Valley. The French Colonial-style home features demonstrations of indigo dyeing and other crafts like bousillage construction, a method using a mixture of clay and Spanish moss. San Francisco Plantation, near Garyville, is a 40-minute drive away from New Orleans. Built in 1856, under centuries-old spreading live oak trees, this galleried home in the Creole open-suite style is listed as a National Historic Landmark. It has now fully reopened after being restored following a fire in 2005.

Closest to Baton Rouge and the area's largest plantation home, the palatial 1860 **Nottoway Plantation** occupies an area of 53,000 sq ft (4,924 sq m), and comprises 65 rooms, 165 doors, and 200 windows. Completed in 1859, its largest room happens to be the Grand White Ballroom, where the owner, John Hampden Randolph, celebrated his daughters' weddings.

In addition to guided house tours, several plantations now operate restaurants and comfortable B&B inns.

The Grand White Ballroom, Nottoway Mansion, in Plantation Alley

Oak Alley Plantation
3645 Hwy 18 Vacherie. ***Tel*** *(225) 265-2151.* *9am–5pm daily.* *Jan 1, Thanksgiving, Dec 25.*
www.oakalleyplantation.com

Laura Plantation
2247 Hwy 18. ***Tel*** *(225) 265-7690.* *9am–5pm daily.* *Jan 1, Mardi Gras, Easter, Thanksg., Dec 25.*
www.lauraplantation.com

Destrehan Plantation
13034 River Road, Destrehan. ***Tel*** *(985) 764-9315.* *9am–4pm daily.* *public hols.*
www.destrehanplantation.org

Nottoway Plantation
White Castle. ***Tel*** *(225) 545-2730.* *9am–5pm daily.* *Dec 25.*
www.nottoway.com

For hotels and restaurants in this region see pp368–9 and pp372–4

Louisiana Old State Capitol, Baton Rouge

Baton Rouge ❸

664,000. 1253 Florida Blvd, (225) 383-3811. 730 North Blvd, (800) 527-6843. Greater Baton Rouge State Fair (mid-Oct).
www.visitbatonrouge.com

Established by the French in 1699 to control access to the Mississippi, Baton Rouge ("Red Stick") was named for the spikes hung with bloody fish heads that marked the boundary between two Native American territories. The capital of Louisiana since 1849, this city is a favored tourist destination. Baton Rouge's population grew dramatically after Hurricane Katrina as people from New Orleans, made homeless, relocated here.

North of downtown, the **State Capitol** was built in 1932 under the tireless direction of ex-governor and US Senator Huey Long (1893–1935), who persuaded legislators to approve the $5 million construction budget. Ironically, Long was assassinated in the building in 1935. This 34-story structure, the country's tallest capitol, offers superb city views from its 27th-floor observation deck. To the south, the autocratic senator's penchant for lavish buildings is further reflected in the **Old Governor's Mansion**, built in 1930 and modeled on the White House. Today, this restored Greek Revival structure displays such memorabilia of past governors as Jimmie Davis's guitar and Huey Long's pajamas. The ornate 1849 Gothic Revival **Louisiana Old State Capitol**, to the southwest, holds interactive exhibits on the state's tumultuous political history.

Statue in the new State Capitol

Outside, an observation plaza overlooks the river, where the massive World War II-era destroyer, **USS *Kidd***, offers public tours. Farther south, visitors can get a feel of the antebellum era firsthand at the 1791 **Magnolia Mound Plantation**, a 16-acre (6-ha) French-Creole style home and working plantation.

A short, 10-minute drive southwest from downtown leads to the attractive, tree-shaded **Louisiana State University** campus and the **LSU Rural Life Museum**, maintained by the university. Unlike the grand plantation restorations, this museum, with its simple artifacts, reveals how the common owner-operated farming families lived in the 19th century.

Louisiana Old State Capitol
100 N Blvd. ***Tel*** *(225) 342-0500.*
10am–4pm Tue–Sat, noon–4pm Sun. Mon, public hols.

LSU Rural Life Museum
I-10 exit 160, at 4650 Essen Ln.
Tel *(225) 765-2437. 8:30am–5pm daily. Jan 1, Easter, Thanksgiving, Dec 24–25.*
www.rurallife.lsu.edu

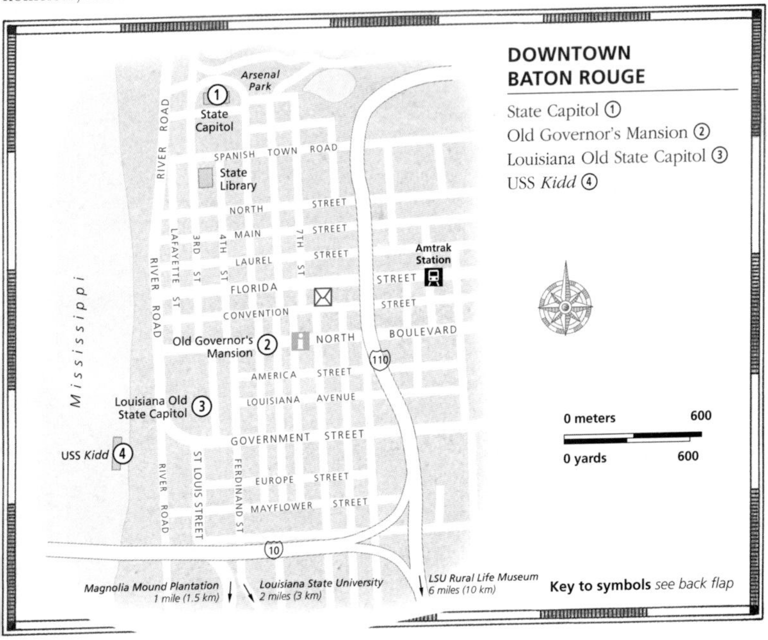

Cathedral of St. John the Baptist, Lafayette

Lafayette 4

115,000. 1400 NW Evangeline Thruway, (337) 232-3808. www.lafayettetravel.com

The unofficial "Capital of French Louisiana" is an entertaining introduction to the world of bayous, alligators, superb cuisine, and lilting Cajun accents. When the first Acadians arrived here in 1765, they settled along the bayous and prairies west of New Orleans, working as farmers to make a living from the swamps and marshes.

Lafayette evolved from a small settlement, set up in the 1821 around a church, now the towering **Cathedral of St. John the Baptist**, near the Vermilion River. Today, the town is the heart of Cajun Country, distinguished by its unique cultural heritage.

Lafayette's living history museum, **Vermilionville** (the original name of the town), evokes 19th-century Acadiana with its characteristic French-influenced architecture. The buildings here are constructed of bousillage *(see p354)*, and have high-pitched roofs. Both Vermilionville and nearby **Jean Lafitte National Historical Park Acadian Cultural Center** feature exhibits as well as demonstrations on the skills needed to survive in 18th- and 19th-century Louisiana. These include the netmaking that was vital for a life dependent on harvesting food from the bayou, and woodcraft that built plows and the shallow-draft wooden pirogue. The National Park Service, which operates the Jean Lafitte National Historic Park, also maintains other Acadian cultural centers in the wetlands region in Thibodaux (100 miles/160 km to the southeast), and in the prairie region in Eunice that lies about 30 miles (48 km) to the northwest.

Vermilionville
300 Fisher Rd. ***Tel*** *(337) 233-4077.* *10am–4pm Tue–Sun.* *Mon, Jan 1, Martin Luther King Jr. Day, Thanksgiving, Dec 24, 25, & 31.* **www**.vermillionville.org

Jean Lafitte National Historical Park Acadian Cultural Center
501 Fisher Rd. ***Tel*** *(337) 232-0789.* *8am–5pm daily.* *Dec 25.*

Bayou Teche 5

Hwy 31 runs from Breaux Bridge to New Iberia. *2513 Hwy 14, (337) 365-1540.* **www**.iberiatravel.com

Bayou Teche (pronounced "Tesh") meanders north-to-south alongside a scenic route between Lafayette and the Atchafalaya Swamp. Stretching between Breaux Bridge and New Iberia, the 25-mile (40-km) length of Hwy 31, with its lush vegetation and beautiful moss-draped oaks, offers a true flavor of the region.

In downtown **Breaux Bridge**, a tiny drawbridge over Bayou Teche proclaims the town "the Crawfish Capital of the World." The town also hosts the annual Crawfish Festival in May. At **Lake Martin**, the Nature Conservancy's Cypress Island Preserve offers an opportunity to see swamp wildlife from a hiking trail and boat tours. The preserve has the world's largest white ibis rookery.

Farther south, in **St. Martinville**, the famous Evangeline Oak marks the spot where Evangeline and her lover Gabriel were supposed to be reunited. Both their tragic tale and the Acadian saga are narrated in *Evangeline*, Henry Wadsworth Longfellow's 1847 poem. Nearby, St. Martin de Tours Church dates back to the town's founding in 1765. An adjacent museum displays carnival costumes.

Just outside town, the evocative **Longfellow-Evangeline State Historic Site** offers tours of an 18th-century sugar plantation house. Bayou Teche flows through the town of **New Iberia**, famous for its grand plantation home – the 1834 Shadows-on-the-Teche, which is now a museum.

A detour to Avery Island leads to the **McIlhenny Tabasco Company**, a popular stop for gourmands where a guide presents information

Shadows-on-the-Teche plantation house in New Iberia, Bayou Teche

The Fort St. Jean Baptiste reconstruction in Natchitoches

about the company's history and manufacturing. The adjacent **Jungle Gardens** is a natural swamp, which you can also take a tour of.

Longfellow-Evangeline State Commemorative Area
1200 N Main St, St. Martinville. ***Tel*** *(337) 394-3754.* *9am–5pm daily.* *Jan 1, Thanksgiving, Dec 25.*
www.ohwy.com/la/l/lonevasa

McIlhenny Tabasco Company
Avery Island. ***Tel*** *(337) 365-8173.* *9am–4pm daily.* *public hols.*

Natchitoches 6

39,000. *781 Front St, (318) 352-8072, (800) 259-1714.*
www.natchitoches.net

The oldest permanent settlement in Louisiana, Natchitoches ("Nack-a-tish") was founded on the banks of the Cane River by the French in 1714. The town's compact 33-block riverfront district retains much of its 18th-century Creole architecture, with elaborate ironwork and spiral staircases. South of downtown, **Fort St. Jean Baptiste** re-creates the 1732 frontier outpost designed to deter Spanish expansion eastward from Texas.

The surrounding Cane River Country has several plantation house tours. Of these, **Melrose Plantation** was visited by such writers as John Steinbeck and William Faulkner. The **Old Courthouse Museum** showcases aspects of Louisiana's culture and history in an imposing historic building. Changing exhibitions of art and artifacts feature such themes as creole history.

Melrose Plantation
LA 119. ***Tel*** *(318) 379-0055.* *noon–4pm daily.* *public hols.*

Old Courthouse Museum
600 2nd St. ***Tel*** *(318) 357-2270.* *9am–5pm Mon–Sat.* *public hols.*

Shreveport 7

402,000. *629 Spring St, (318) 222-9391.*
www.shreveport–bossier.org

Situated near the Texas border, Shreveport was founded on the Red River in 1839. Agriculture and river transport trade were mainstays of the local economy until the turn of the 20th century, when the discovery of oil made the city a boom town. Shreveport declined after the oil industry moved offshore. However, today the town is rapidly changing and has a friendly atmosphere with a number of cultural activities. The **Louisiana State Museum** illustrates the state's history through murals and exhibits, while the annual Louisiana State Fair, held here in late October or early November, attracts more than 300,000 visitors.

Environs

About 165 miles (265 km) from Shreveport in the far northeastern corner of Louisiana state is one of the most significant archaeological sites located in the eastern part of the country. **Poverty Point National Monument** *(see p339)* outside Epps retains the religious mounds built by the early civilization that flourished in the Lower Mississippi basin around 600 BC. Visitors can get here through Hwy 577.

Poverty Point National Monument
Hwy 577. ***Tel*** *(888) 926-5492.* *9am–5pm daily.* *Jan 1, Thanksgiving, Dec 25.*

Exterior of Louisiana State Museum in Shreveport

THE ACADIANS – CAJUN COUNTRY

The Acadians, or "Cajuns," were originally French immigrants who had founded a colony in Nova Scotia, Canada, in 1604, naming it l'Acadie after the legendary Greek paradise, Arcadia. Exiled by the British in 1755, they finally settled along the isolated bayous of Louisiana, where they developed a rich French-influenced culture, deeply rooted in its music and cuisine. Acadian culture is best seen in the region's many festivals. Of these the Courir de Mardi Gras, literally "the race," is a distinctly Cajun version of the Mardi Gras *(see p353)*. Colorfully dressed and masked horseback riders ride from house to house, ostensibly collecting ingredients for a community gumbo. They then triumphantly parade through the town, before gathering together for food, drink, music, and frivolity. "Acadiana" is a 22-parish region comprising the wetlands area near New Orleans, the prairies north of Lafayette, and the remote southwestern coast.

Acadian dress

Arkansas

Aptly known as the "Natural State," Arkansas abounds in mountains, valleys, dense woodlands, and fertile plains. Its two mountain ranges, the Ozark and the Ouachita, are separated by the Arkansas River, which flows through the state capital, Little Rock. The birthplace of former president Bill Clinton, the state actively promotes sights associated with him, including his birthplace, Hope, his boyhood home in Hot Springs, and Little Rock, where he served as governor and waged his campaign for presidency. This former frontier state remains largely wild even today, with vast areas of natural beauty, famous for adventure sports.

Display in the Central High Museum, Little Rock

Little Rock 8

185,000. 615 E Capitol Ave, (501) 370-3290. www.littlerock.com

Founded on the Arkansas River, near a boulder for which it is named, Little Rock was another modest-sized Southern state capital until native son Bill Clinton was elected 42nd US president in 1993. As a result, executive attention has helped revitalize the city. A center for much activity is Little Rock River Market District, lined with lively clubs, restaurants, cafés, and shops. Adjacent to the district is the **William J. Clinton Presidential Center**, which houses a library and museum where exhibits tell the inside story of the presidency. The **Old State House State History Museum**, west of Main Street, is where Clinton celebrated his 1992 and 1996 presidential victories.

In 1957, the contentious desegregation of Little Rock Central High School catapulted the city to the forefront of the national struggle for Civil Rights. Despite the Supreme Court ban, the governor refused to integrate the school, forcing President Eisenhower to send in the 101st Airborne Division to protect the "Little Rock Nine" (the first nine black students). Today, Central High School is a national historic site and the only operating school to be thus designated. **Central High Museum and Visitor Center** documents this story.

Central High Museum & Visitor Center
2125 W 14th St. *Tel (501) 374-1957.* *daily.* *some public hols.*

Old State House State History Museum
300 W Markham St. *Tel (501) 324-9685.* *daily.* *some public hols.*

William J. Clinton Presidential Center
1200 Pres. Clinton Ave. *Tel (501) 374-1957.* *daily.* *some public hols.*

Hot Springs 9

38,000. *629 Central Ave, (501) 321-2277.*

In its heyday in the early 20th century, this was a popular resort for people seeking restorative cures from the thermal springs flowing from the southwestern slope of Hot Springs Mountain. The area became the first US federal reserve park in 1832 and a national park in 1921. The original "Bathhouse Row" is now a National Historic Land-

Exterior of the Spanish-style Fordyce Bathhouse, the visitor center for Hot Springs National Park

For hotels and restaurants in this region see p370 and p374

mark District within **Hot Springs National Park**. The visitor center is housed in the opulent Spanish Renaissance-style 1915 Fordyce Bathhouse. Only the **Buckstaff Bathhouse** today remains in operation, offering spa facilities. Hotels, such as the Arlington Resort Hotel *(see p370)*, also offer full bathing facilities.

At the Row's south end, the city visitor center distributes maps to sights associated with President Clinton, who spent his childhood in the city. Hot Springs High School, where Clinton graduated in 1964, is now an apartment building with a "cultural campus" that has exhibits from Clinton's teenage years. Visitors can also tour sights such as Clinton's church and his favorite burger joint. A scenic drive to the summit of Hot Springs Mountain leads to an observation tower offering panoramic views of the Ouachita Mountains, the city, and the forests and lakes that surround it.

Hot Springs National Park
369 Central Ave. ***Tel*** *(501) 624-2701.* *9am–5pm daily.* *Jan 1, Thanksgiving, Dec 25.*

Buckstaff Bathhouse
509 Central Ave, Bathhouse Row.
Tel *(501) 623-2308.* *7am–noon Mon–Sat, 1:30–3pm Mon–Fri.* *Jan 1, Jul 4, Thanksgiving, Dec 25.*

Mountain View ⑩

3,200. *107 N Peabody, (888) 679-2859.*

Nestling deep in the hills and valleys of the remote Ozark Mountains, the secluded hamlet of Mountain View is a haven for outdoor enthusiasts. A short drive to the north is the **Ozark Folk Center State Park**. The park celebrates the Ozark Mountain region's cultural heritage with living history exhibits, crafts demonstrations, festivals, and traditional music performances held at the state park theater. It also offers hiking trails, a lodge open year round, a lively restaurant, and a swimming pool. The nearby "Wild and Scenic" **Buffalo National River** is highly popular for float fishing and canoeing; many local outfitters organize guided canoe trips of the river. The National Forest Service maintains several campgrounds in the area.

Steeply inclined streets of the Victorian commercial area, Eureka Springs

Ozark Folk Center State Park
1032 Park Ave. ***Tel*** *(870) 269-3851.* *check for times.*
www.ozarkfolkcenter.com

Environs
About 15 miles (24 km) northwest of Mountain View, via Hwy 14, lie **Blanchard Springs Caverns**, which feature an extensive collection of limestone cave formations and an underground stream open for public tours. The ever-changing crystalline formations in these "living" caves are the result of minerals deposited by dripping water. Exploring the magnificent caves can be difficult because of the damp air and cramped conditions. However, both the two main routes, the half-mile (1-km) Dripstone Trail as well as the 1.2-mile (2-km) Discovery Trail, offer an unforgettable experience of life underground. A visitor center features exhibits and videos that describe the caves and their long process of creation.

Christ of the Ozarks, Eureka Springs

Blanchard Springs Caverns
off Hwy 14. ***Tel*** *(870) 757-2211.* *mid-Apr–Oct: 9am–5pm daily; Oct–Apr: 9:30am–4pm Wed–Sun.* *Jan 1, Thanksgiving, Dec 25.*

Eureka Springs ⑪

2,400. *137 W Van Buren, (479) 253-8737, (888) 387-3520.*
www.eurekasprings.org

The world's second-largest statue of Jesus, the seven-story-high "**Christ of the Ozarks**," towers above the former resort town of Eureka Springs. After nearly a century of decline, the town has benefited by its development as an artists' community, as a romantic getaway, and by the establishment of country music performances in the style of Nashville's Grand Ole Opry *(see p264)* held at the Hoe-Down and Pine Mountain Jamboree. For almost 30 years running, the Great Passion Play has been performed at the **Sacred Arts Center**. This outdoor drama depicts the days leading up to the death of Jesus Christ.

The religious tone of the town is perpetuated in the **Bible Museum** with its collection of more than 6,000 Bible editions in 625 languages. Eureka Springs Historic Gardens and a scenic railroad are the town's other attractions. Many visitors also tour the well-preserved Victorian buildings and savor the magic of the town's forested mountain setting.

Sacred Arts Center
935 Passion Play Rd.
Tel *(800) 882-7529.* *Apr–Oct: call for times.*

Mississippi

The birthplace of Tennessee Williams, Elvis Presley, B.B. King, and Oprah Winfrey, Mississippi is a complex state best known for blues music, antebellum plantation homes, and a lamentable Civil Rights history. The endless horizon of cotton fields, most often associated with Mississippi, can be found in the northwest Delta region, while in the northeastern corner is the hardscrabble hill area around Tupelo. The state capital, Jackson, sits in the central plain and is the urban center of this largely rural state. Today, Mississippi offers such contrasting diversions as glittering Las Vegas-style casinos, excellent Vietnamese seafood restaurants, and ferry rides to deserted beaches.

Ventress Hall, University of Mississippi campus, Oxford

Mississippi Delta ⓬

23,000 (Clarksdale). Greenwood. 1540 DeSoto Ave, Hwy 49, Clarksdale, (662) 627-7337.

The Mississippi Delta, a vast, alluvial basin, cleared of its once-thick forests, and blanketed with cotton fields, is the birthplace of blues music. The **Delta Blues Museum** in downtown Clarksdale is the touchstone for music lovers from around the world. Located in a renovated 1920's freight depot, this museum is a virtual repository of blues music, with personal belongings, photographs, instruments, and videos of such resident legends as Robert Johnson, Howlin' Wolf, and Muddy Waters. Exhibits include the wooden "Muddywood" guitar created by Z.Z. Top with planks from the original House of Blues, the birthplace of Muddy Waters. The Sunflower River Blues and Gospel Festival is held outside the museum each August. The Delta's creative legacy extends beyond music. The annual Tennessee Williams festival celebrates the work of the famous playwright who spent his childhood in Clarksdale.

About 55 miles (88 km) south of Clarksdale, the **Cottonlandia Museum** in Greenwood documents the history of the Delta with a special emphasis on cotton, the industry that fueled the culture and economy of the region. A 24-mile (38-km) drive south brings visitors to Greenville, the largest town in the Delta. The visitor center of this major riverport occupies a riverboat docked at the foot of the bridge. The Mississippi Delta Blues Festival is held in town every September. Other sights include the tiny museum in Leland honoring Jim Henson, the creator of the Muppets; Belzoni, said to be the "Catfish capital of the World," located in the county that has the most farm-raised catfish; and Indianola, the hometown of B.B. King.

Catfish farm sign

Delta Blues Museum
1 Blues Alley, Clarksdale. ***Tel*** *(662) 627-6820. Mar–Oct: 9am–5pm Mon–Sat; Nov–Feb: 10am–5pm Mon– Sat. Jan 1, Jul 4, Thnksg., Dec 25.* **www**.deltabluesmuseum.org

Cottonlandia Museum
1608 Hwy 82 W. ***Tel*** *(662) 453-0925. 9am–5pm Mon–Fri, 2–5pm Sat–Sun. major public hols.* **www**.cottonlandia.org

Oxford ⓭

14,000. (662) 234-4680. **www**.touroxfordms.com

Home to the stately 1848 University of Mississippi, fondly known as "Ole Miss," the appealing college town of Oxford is the state's intellectual and cultural center. The local literary landmark is the secluded 1844 **Rowan Oak**, home of William Faulkner, one of the most influential writers of the time and pioneer of the Southern Gothic literature movement. The plot outline of *A Fable*, the book the Nobel Prize-winning author was working on at his death, can be seen inscribed on the walls. A Faulkner statue stands in downtown's classic courthouse square, surrounded by sophisticated galleries, restaurants, cafés, and live music venues.

The University of Mississippi campus houses the **University Museums**. In addition to classical Greek and Roman antiquities, the

One of the many riverboat casinos in the Mississippi Delta

For hotels and restaurants in this region see pp370–71 and p375

adjacent museums hold a small but dynamic collection of Southern folk art.

Rowan Oak
Old Taylor Rd. **Tel** (662) 234-3284. *10am–4pm Tue–Sat, 1–4pm Sun.* *some public & university hols.*

University Museums
University Ave at Fifth St. **Tel** (662) 915-7073. *10am–4:30pm Tue–Sat, 1–4 pm Sun.* *some public & university hols.*

Tupelo ⓮

37,000. *399 E Main St, (662) 841-6521.* **www**.tupelo.net

An hour's drive west from Oxford, Tupelo is the birthplace of Elvis Presley, one of the world's most enduring cultural icons. Here, in a modest, two-room shotgun shack on the eastern fringe of town, the King of Rock 'n' roll was born in 1935, along with his stillborn twin Jesse. Elvis lived in Tupelo until age 13, when the family was forced by financial constraints to move to Memphis *(see p266).* Today the **Elvis Presley Birthplace**, refurbished to look as it did in 1935, is a pilgrimage site for Elvis fans the world over. An adjacent museum holds a unique private collection of Elvis memorabilia. A chapel, which overlooks the birthplace, features Elvis' own bible.

The new Tupelo Automobile Museum, the first of its kind in the state, displays more than 100 restored cars and includes a replica of a vintage garage.

Tupelo offers all the basic necessities for lodging and dining, and serves as a pit stop for the famous Natchez Trace Parkway *(see p362).*

Statue of young Elvis at Tupelo, his birthplace

Elvis Presley Birthplace
306 Elvis Presley Dr. **Tel** (662) 841-1245. *9am–5pm Mon–Sat, 1–5pm Sun.* *Thanksgiving, Dec 25.* **www**. elvispresleybirthplace.com

Grave markers in Vicksburg National Military Park

Vicksburg National Military Park ⓯

3201 Clay St. *(601) 636-0583.* *8am–5pm daily.* *Dec 25.* **www**.nps.gov/vick

The Vicksburg National Military Park, established in 1899, commemorates one of the most tragic sieges in Civil War history *(see p47).* Its strategic location, high on the bluffs overlooking the Mississippi River, made Vicksburg the target of Union forces, which wanted to gain control of the vital river corridor and cut the Confederacy in half. On March 29, 1863, the Union Army surrounded the city. After a 47-day siege, the Confederates surrendered on July 4, 1863, giving the North undisputed control of the river and sounding the death knell of the Confederacy. The impact of defeat was so severe that Vicksburg's citizens refused to recognize the Fourth of July holiday until the mid-20th century. The campaign's story is retold in statuary headstones, earthworks, and artifacts at the park. Guided tours bring the landscape to life, where re-enactments of the Civil War are held from June through August.

BLUES MUSIC

The sound at the root of all contemporary popular music heard around the world springs from the large, flat, alluvial basin called the Mississippi Delta. Here African rhythms, work chants, and spirituals evolved into a distinctive style of music known as the blues. When Alabama musician W.C. Handy came through the Delta in 1903, he declared it "the weirdest music I ever heard," and carried the sound up to Memphis, where he recorded the Memphis Blues. Along with the Great Migration of African Americans from the rural South to the industrial North in the early 1900s, the blues reached Chicago, where such famous artists as Muddy Waters electrifed the sound. Rock 'n' roll is said to be born from this sound.

Muddy Waters figure in Delta Blues Museum

Old gas station at the Mississippi Agriculture and Forestry Museum

Jackson ⓰

220,000. 921 S President St, (601) 960-1891.

Founded on a bluff above the Pearl River, Mississippi's capital city was named after popular national hero General Andrew Jackson *(see p265)*. During the Civil War, the city was torched on three separate occasions by Union General William Tecumseh Sherman, earning it the nickname "Chimneyville." The few buildings that survive are treasured landmarks today. Of these, the old 1839 Capitol, now the **Old Capital Museum of Mississippi History**, presents an overview of the state's Civil Rights history, juxtaposing stark black-and-white video footage of violent clashes between the police and protesters, with plainspoken commentary. Upstairs, the museum features revolving exhibits on such topics as author Eudora Welty, a Jackson resident, or "Pride of the Fleet" about the battleship USS *Mississippi*. A small, 20th-century room elaborates on the impact of the cotton and lumber industries on the state's economy, ecology, and society. Yet, the city itself is the best historical exhibit. With its railroad trestles, smoky coffee shops, and franchise-free main street, downtown Jackson appears like a movie set from the 1950s. The **Mississippi State Capitol**, built in 1903, resembles the US Capitol in Washington, DC, and houses the legislative, judicial, and executive branches of the state government. Jackson is also home to the **Mississippi Agriculture and Forestry Museum**, a very appealing family attraction that celebrates the state's rural heritage. Among its exhibits are an 1850s homestead, complete with livestock and gardens, and a 1930s small-town Main Street with a general store selling penny candy. The Chimneyville Crafts Gallery, a handicraft store on the grounds, displays and sells folk arts, including Choctaw crafts. The expansive site also has a lively cafeteria and produce stand. The adjacent Sports Hall of Fame honors the state's beloved athletes and college teams with enjoyable interactive exhibits.

Other sights in Jackson include the local zoo, Mynelle Gardens, the Mississippi Museum of Natural Science, and the Mississippi Museum of Art, which displays the state's largest art collection. All these attractions, plus the city's growing reputation as a blues venue, make Jackson a pleasant stop for visitors coming through the Natchez Trace Parkway.

Old Capital Museum of Mississippi History
Old Capitol, 100 S State St. ***Tel*** *(601) 576-6920. daily. public hols.*

Mississippi Agriculture & Forestry Museum
1150 Lakeland Dr. ***Tel*** *(800) 844-8687. 9am–5pm Mon–Sat. Sun, Jan 1, Thnksg., Dec 25.*

Natchez Parkway sign

Natchez Trace Parkway ⓱

Visitor Center Mount Locust. ***Tel*** *(662) 680-4027. 8am–5pm daily.* **www**.nps.gov/natr

Established as a National Historic Parkway in 1938, this 450-mile (724-km) highway linking Natchez with Nashville, Tennessee *(see p264–5)*, was originally an animal trail. Later, it evolved into a footpath and played a vital role in the development of the country's midsection by linking the Ohio River Valley and the Gulf of Mexico. Pioneers used the route to transport their crops and produce downriver by barge to Natchez, where they sold both their goods and barges for scrap lumber, and then returned north on foot.

Today, the Natchez Trace Parkway *(see pp40–41)* is a scenic, year-round destination. No commercial traffic is permitted in this haven for hikers, motorists, and cyclists, and the speed limit is a leisurely 50 mph (80 km/h).

The parkway preserves several historical sites, such as **Emerald Mound**. Situated near Natchez, it dates from AD 1400 and is the second largest Native American ceremonial mound in the country. A detour west, along Hwy 552, leads to the "**Ruins of**

Natchez Trace Parkway, a historic wooded trail

Windsor," where a ghostly set of 23 towering Corinthian columns serves as a poignant reminder of a mansion that burned down in 1890. The **Mount Locust** visitor center is located 15 miles (24 km) northeast of Natchez in a restored 1783 inn.

Natchez ⓲

20,000. 640 S Canal St, (601) 442-5880.

Best known for its fine antebellum architecture, Natchez is an attractive little town on the bluffs above Mississippi River. Many of its historic buildings lie within easy walking distance of the compact downtown district. The coast here took the brunt of Hurricane Katrina's tidal surge, which destroyed many structures along the historic waterfront. The area is rapidly being rebuilt and many attractions have reopened. Some of these gems include the oldest house in town, the 1798 **House on Ellicott's Hill**; the stately and palatial **Stanton Hall** (1857); the unfinished **Longwood** (1860), whose construction was interrupted by the Civil War; and **Rosalie**, an 1829 brick mansion atop the bluff that served as Union headquarters during the Civil War.

Many house museums are open all year, but many more can be seen during the **Natchez Pilgrimage** held in March, April, October, and November *(see p28)*. A short drive east of downtown is **Melrose Plantation**, the US's most intact antebellum estate. Maintained by the National Park Service, it displays African-American history in slave quarters alongside the 1845 Greek Revival mansion. At the south end of town, a mile (1.6 km) off Hwy 61, is the Grand Village of the Natchez Indians, with Indian mounds, replicas of huts, nature trails, and a museum.

House on Ellicott's Hill
Jefferson & Canal Sts. ***Tel*** *(601) 442-2011. 9am–4:30pm daily. Dec 25.*

Natchez Pilgrimage Tour
Tel *(601) 446-6631, (800) 647-6742.*

Longwood, the octagonal, domed house, in Natchez

Gulf Coast ⓳

156,000 (Biloxi & Gulfport). 942 Beach Dr, Gulfport, (228) 896-6699. **www**.gulfcoast.org

Lingering French influences and a maritime heritage combine to make the scenic Gulf of Mexico coastline unlike the rest of Mississippi. In 1699, two Québcois brothers, Pierre le Moyne, Sieur d'Iberville, and Jean Baptiste le Moyne, Sieur de Bienville, reached what is now Ocean Springs, to set up France's first permanent settlement in the South. In 1704, the French government sponsored the transport of 20 young women as prospective brides for the male colonists. Armed with their trousseaux in state-issued suitcases or "cassettes," the "cassette girls" were housed on Ship Island. After the Americans gained control of the coast, they built **Fort Massachusetts** in the mid-1800s on Ship Island. During the Civil War, the Union used the fort to house POWs, including a troop of African-American Confederates from Louisiana.

Fishing schooners lining the waterfront on the Gulf Coast

In August 1965, Hurricane Camille, one of the worst storms to hit mainland US, split Ship Island into two – West Ship and East Ship (although it is still referred to locally in the singular). Today, both are part of the **Gulf Islands National Seashore**. A ferry transports passengers to the beach and for tours of the historic fort. Boating is a popular recreation – visitors can take boat and kayak trips to deserted islands, or fishing charters on traditional shrimp boats. The **Walter Anderson Museum of Art** exhibits works by the late painter, potter, naturalist, and writer Walter Anderson, reflecting his love for the Mississippi coast.

Gulf Islands National Seashore
3500 Park Rd, Ocean Springs. ***Tel*** *(228) 875-9057.* **www**.nps.gov/guis

Walter Anderson Museum of Art
510 Washington Avenue, Ocean Springs. *(228) 872-3164.*
www.walterandersonmuseum.org

Alabama

Alabama slopes from the Cumberland Plateau in the northeast, across forested ridges and fertile plains to the Gulf of Mexico at Mobile Bay. The first European presence was established by the French along the coast in the early 1700s. During the next 100 years, settlement increased as overland immigrants from Tennessee and Georgia moved here, ousting the Choctaw, Cherokee, and Creek Indians from their ancestral lands. With progress, cotton fed the port of Mobile, and the steel industry drove Birmingham's economy. Today, the state is known for its diverse landscape, its antebellum architecture, and, most importantly, its Civil Rights history.

Reconstructed Fort Conde, Mobile

Mobile ⓴

203,000. 1 S Water St, (251) 208-2000.

This beautiful port city was founded as a French colony in 1702. Later it served as a strategic Confederate port until the final days of the Civil War. Today, the city retains both its French and Southern flavor and is best known for its **Mardi Gras Cottage Museum**, which includes memorabilia dating from the early 1800s.

At the head of Mobile Bay is **Fort Conde**, a partially reconstructed fort built by the French. Moored nearby is the World War II battleship, USS *Alabama*. A scenic loop drive around the bay leads to two other historic forts, Fort Morgan to the east, and Fort Gaines on Dauphin Island. Both are havens for birdlife.

Fort Conde
150 Royal St. ***Tel** (251) 208-7304.*
8am–5pm daily. public hols, Mardi Gras.

Selma ㉑

21,000. 912 Selma Ave, (334) 875-7241. **www.**selmaalabama.com

Situated on a bluff high above the Alabama River, this city was the site of one the most notorious scenes in Civil Rights history. On March 7, 1965, a day that became known as "Bloody Sunday," 600 Civil Rights protesters heading toward Montgomery, the capital, violently clashed with the police at Edmund Pettus Bridge. A few weeks later, however, Dr. Martin Luther King Jr. led a successful march to the State Capitol steps. The **National Voting Rights Museum** encapsulates the story, and an annual re-enactment pays tribute to the event.

Before the Civil Rights era, Selma's place in history was assured as the "Arsenal of the Confederacy." It produced weapons, cannons, and iron-clad ships. Much of the city was destroyed during the war, but the townscape along the river remained intact. The city's 1891 cherry-red train depot has exhibits on local history.

Display inside the Voting Rights Museum in Selma

National Voting Rights Museum
1012 Water Ave. ***Tel** (334) 418-0800. 9am–5pm Mon–Fri, 10am–3pm Sat.*
www.voterights.org

Montgomery ㉒

224,000. 300 Water St, (334) 262-0013.

Alabama's capital city since 1846, Montgomery was also the Confederacy's first capital during the Civil War. In 1861, Jefferson Davis was sworn in as the Confederate president on the steps of the Greek Revival State Capitol. Across the street, the **First White House of the Confederacy** is now a museum related to those times.

The city also played a pivotal role during the Civil Rights Movement. The segregation of the city's transportation system led to an act of defiance by Rosa Parks, when she refused to surrender her bus seat to a white man. In 1956, the young Dr. Martin Luther King Jr. supported the year-long Montgomery Bus Boycott, which ultimately brought about the desegregation of the city's public transportation system. Its success was significant as it not only strengthened the movement, but also saw the rise of King as the campaign's leader. The city's landmark **Civil Rights Memorial**, designed by Vietnam Veterans Memorial artist Maya Lin

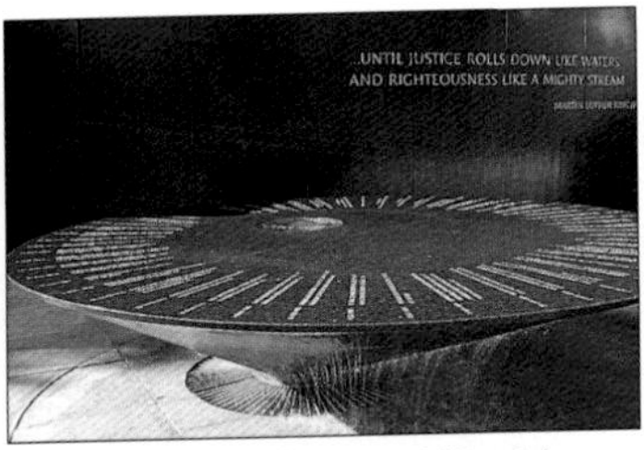

Montgomery's Civil Rights Memorial Fountain

(see p205), honors 40 martyrs who sacrificed their lives in the fight for racial equality.

Montgomery is also associated with two major figures of 20th-century arts. Local girl Zelda Fitzgerald and her husband, writer F. Scott Fitzgerald, lived here in 1931, while he was writing *Tender is the Night*. Their house is now a museum. In 1958, country singer Hank Williams played his final concert in the city three days before his death. Williams is buried in Oakwood Cemetery, and a statue of the singer stands downtown.

First White House of the Confederacy
644 Washington Ave. ***Tel*** *(334) 242-1861.* *8am–4:30pm Mon–Fri.* *Sat–Sun, state hols.*

Tuskegee ㉓

13,000. *121 Main St, (334) 727-6619.*

Former slave Booker T. Washington founded the Tuskegee Normal and Industrial Institute here in 1881 to improve educational opportunities for African Americans. The school evolved into **Tuskegee University**, best known for agriculturist George Washington Carver's innovations that revolutionized agricultural growth in the region. The "Tuskegee Airmen," the group of African American pilots who distinguished themselves in World War II, also graduated from the institute, now part of the Tuskegee Institute National Historic Site.

Birmingham ㉔

250,000. *2200 9th Ave N, (205) 458-8000.*

The largest city in Alabama, Birmingham was once the region's foremost producer of steel. Celebrating the city's industrial past is **Sloss Furnaces National Historic Landmark**, a museum housed in an old steel mill, and a 55-ft (17-m) high iron statue of Vulcan, the Roman god of fire, on the summit of Red Mountain, the source of the iron ore. Today, the city's attractions are typical of a modern Southern city – antebellum houses, botanical gardens, and the acclaimed **Birmingham Museum of Art**, with its fine collection of Wedgwood. Yet, the most moving landmarks are those that relate to the city's African-American history. These can be seen within walking distance of the central downtown district's visitor center, where maps as well as tours are available.

Dr. Martin Luther King Jr.

The **Birmingham Civil Rights Institute** uses vintage film footage to explain the city's Civil Rights Movement. Among the exhibits is the door of the cell in which Dr. Martin Luther King Jr. wrote his famous "Letter from a Birmingham Jail," arguing that individuals have the right to disobey unjust laws. Down the street, the restored Sixteenth Street Baptist Church stands as a memorial to four black girls killed by a Ku Klux Klan bomb in 1963. To its southeast, in the historic **Carver Theatre**, the Alabama Jazz Hall of Fame hosts live music performances and celebrates the achievements of such artists as Dinah Washington, Nat King Cole, W.C. Handy, and Duke Ellington. At the north end of town, the **Alabama Sports Hall of Fame** honors beloved native African-American athletes such as Joe Louis and Jesse Owens.

Birmingham Civil Rights Institute
520 16th St N. ***Tel*** *(205) 328-9696.* *10am–5pm Tue–Sat, 1–5pm Sun.* *public hols.* *(Sun free).* **www**.bcri.org

Huntsville ㉕

163,000. *500 Church St, (256) 533-5723.*

Set in a curving valley in northern Alabama, the cotton market town of Huntsville developed into a space and military research and development, and manufacturing center after World War II. Home to the NASA-Marshall Space Flight Center, the city's main attraction is the US Space and Rocket Center and the mission control tours. Exhibits include Apollo capsules and a life-size space shuttle. A camp here also teaches children about space exploration.

George Washington Carver Museum, Tuskegee University

Practical Information

Advance planning is necessary for a successful tour around the Deep South, simply because there is so much to see and do. New Orleans, the region's most exotic city, is packed with entertainment and music venues, clubs, hotels, and restaurants, while many small towns and the expansive and diverse areas between them often double as low-key resort areas, catering to city-dwellers in need of a change of pace. Depending upon the time, visitors can explore significant historical sights, appreciate stunning scenery, gaze at the well-manicured gardens of former plantation homes, take in a local celebration, or simply relax alongside a lazy river.

TOURIST INFORMATION

Each of the Deep South states publishes a wide variety of informative travel guides, which may be ordered by telephone or accessed via web sites. As soon as visitors enter Louisiana, Mississippi, Alabama, or Arkansas, they may check in one of a dozen official "Welcome Centers" along major highways. Staffed by helpful volunteers and open from 8am to 5pm daily, these centers offer free road maps and a full range of tourist information. Such information is also available from the multitude of local and regional tourism bureaus across all four states.

NATURAL HAZARDS

The Deep South is prone to hurricanes and occasional tornadoes from early June to November each year. In August 2005, Hurricane Katrina hit the Gulf Coast, destroying New Orleans and coastal towns and killing thousands of people. If planning a visit, visitors should follow the storm forecasts for the Gulf and Caribbean. The **National Hurricane Center** in Miami provides information on impending hurricanes. When a Hurricane Warning is posted in the area you are visiting, either cancel your trip or evacuate the area. Follow the broadcasts about emergency procedures on radio and television.

The biggest hazard is the sun. Use high-factor sunscreen and wear a hat. Also, drink plenty of fluids to avoid getting dehydrated. Biting and stinging insects, especially mosquitoes, are a nuisance between April and November, so remember to carry insect repellent.

GETTING AROUND

Like much of the US, the Deep South is a region where it can be difficult to get around without a car. Seat belts are mandatory for drivers and front-seat passengers in all Deep South states. Most states also require seat belts for back-seat passengers. All automobile occupants under the age of four require child safety seats.

Public transportation options are limited. **Greyhound** buses only serve some larger towns and cities, while **Amtrak** runs two train routes – north–south across the Mississippi Delta between Memphis and New Orleans, and east–west, connecting New Orleans with Mobile and Birmingham. However, an unusual way to get around the Deep South is to board a replica Mississippi riverboat. **Majestic American Line** offers tours along "Old Muddy," from New Orleans up to Baton Rouge, Natchez, and other cities.

ETIQUETTE

The old-world traditions of the Deep South hospitality and courtesy, especially toward women, are legendary. Addressing people politely, with a "sir" or "ma'am" will be much appreciated, and will help social interaction.

Check for non-smoking signs as smoking is prohibited in most public buildings, including stores and restaurants. Although the laws for drinking alcohol vary from state to state, the legal age is 21. Only in New Orleans is it permissible to drink on the streets, though only in plastic containers called "go cups."

FESTIVALS

The Deep South states stage a diverse range of annual community, regional, and national festivals. The nation's biggest party, and one of the world's most colorful and lively annual events, is the 10-day long series of celebrations leading up to **Mardi Gras**, French for "Fat Tuesday." The carnival parades, music, drinking, and dancing are at their liveliest at New Orleans, though smaller but no less energetic celebrations are also held in several

THE CLIMATE OF THE DEEP SOUTH

The climate across this region does not vary much from state to state, although seasonal differences are distinct. Winter is rather wet, while the summer heat and humidity can be sweltering. By September the weather is fine again, though late summer storms or hurricanes can put a damper on travel. Spring and autumn are the ideal times to plan an extended trip. Spring flowers, such as magnolia blossoms, set the tone for the early months of the year.

NEW ORLEANS

°F/C	Apr	Jul	Oct	Jan
High	77/25	90/32	79/26	62/17
Low	61/16	76/24	64/18	47/8
Sunshine	14 days	19 days	18 days	20 days
Rainfall	4.5 in	6.1 in	3 in	5 in
month	Apr	Jul	Oct	Jan

other Deep South towns, including Mobile, Alabama.

Spring is a fine time to be in Mississippi, especially if you can time your trip to enjoy the "*Gone With the Wind*"-like re-creations of the **Natchez Pilgrimage**, a month-long celebration of the antebellum "Old South." Many of the city's historic homes are open to the public, and several pageants and performances take place.

Summer brings a profusion of outdoor events, and fireworks, bands, and street festivals are the norm for community celebrations of the July 4 Independence Day holiday. Numerous county and state fairs take place in the countryside in July and August, as do a number of music festivals such as the **B.B. King Homecoming Festival** in Indianola Mississippi, the first of many blues-themed festivals that take place in and around the Mississippi Delta. Later in the summer comes the grand **Mississippi Delta Blues and Heritage Festival**, held in September in Greenville, Mississippi. In October, the historic homes of Natchez and Vicksburg are again opened to the public during the **Fall Pilgrimage**. During this time, lucky visitors may sample freshly-made, sugary pralines, sold by vendors.

SPORTS & OUTDOOR ACTIVITIES

The towns and cities of the Deep South are not large enough to support top-tier professional sports teams, but they field dozens of minor league teams and hundreds of high-quality sports teams of various public and private colleges and universities. New Orleans has the New Orleans Hornets basketball team and the New Orleans Saints football team, which plays in the **Superdome**, one of the world's largest indoor sports arenas. The main events of the college sporting seasons are football and basketball games between regional rivals, including Louisiana State University Tigers, the University of Alabama's Crimson Tide, and the Rebels of the University of Mississippi. Baseball season runs from April to September, football from September through January, and basketball from winter through mid-spring.

Although both fishing and boating are also prominent, fishing is by far the more popular of the two sports. Lake fishing for bass or crappie is available in many state parks, while Arkansas streams offer trout fishing. Deep-sea fishing for grouper, tarpon, or snapper, or by net for the shrimp, can be arranged from Gulf of Mexico ports such as Biloxi, Mississippi, Mobile, Alabama, or Grand Isle, Louisiana. Visitors should check with the various state fish and game departments to see which permits are required.

ENTERTAINMENT

The birthplace of jazz and a melting pot of American music, New Orleans is a showcase for all types of performances. Local newspapers such as the *Times-Picayune* or the weekly *New Orleans Magazine* carry detailed listings of the events and activities. A major venue for music in New Orleans is the historic **Preservation Hall**, where traditonal "Dixieland" jazz may be heard most nights. A huge range of nightclubs in the tourist-dominated French Quarter as well as in the uptown area offer live musical entertainment. For traditional Cajun music, head to Lafayette and the roadhouse restaurant, **Prejean's**, the most reliable of the music venues in the region.

Many other cities also host popular musical events. Blues festivals take place all over Mississippi and Arkansas during summer. A wonderful place to listen to the blues is **Ground Zero Blues Club**, in Clarksdale, Mississippi.

DIRECTORY

TOURIST OFFICES

Alabama
Tel (800) 252-2262.
www.tour.alabama.org

Arkansas
Tel (800) 628-8725.
www.arkansas.com

Louisiana
Tel (800) 994-8626.
www.louisianatravel.com

Mississippi
Tel (866) 733-6477.
www.visitmississippi.org

NATURAL HAZARDS

National Hurricane Center, Miami
Tel (305) 229-4470.
www.nhc.noaa.gov

TRAVEL

Amtrak
Tel (800) 872-7245.
www.amtrak.com

Greyhound
Tel (800) 231-2222.
www.greyhound.com

RIVER CRUISES

Majestic American Line
Robin St Wharf, 1380 Port of New Orleans Place.
Tel (800) 543-1949.

FESTIVALS

Mardi Gras, New Orleans
Tel (800) 672-6124.
www.neworleansonline.com

B.B. King Homecoming Festival
Tel (662) 887-4454.

SPORTS

Superdome
Tel (504) 587-3663.
www.superdome.com

DEPARTMENTS OF FISH & GAME

Arkansas
Tel (501) 223-6300.

Alabama
Tel (334) 242-3465.

Louisiana
Tel (225) 765-2800.

Mississippi
Tel (601) 432-2400.

ENTERTAINMENT

Preservation Hall
Tel (504) 522-2841.
www.preservationhall.com

Prejean's
Tel (337) 896-3247.
www.prejeans.com

Ground Zero Blues Club
Tel (662) 621-9009.
www.groundzerobluesclub.com

Choosing a Hotel

In the Deep South, New Orleans has plentiful accommodations with many historic and architecturally distinctive properties. The bayou country around Lafayette and the Mississippi town of Natchez also offer historic lodgings. Casino hotels along the Mississippi River and Gulf Coast generally offer low room rates.

PRICE CATEGORIES
For a standard double room per night, including service charges, and any additional taxes.

$ Under $100
$$ $100–$150
$$$ $150–$250
$$$$ $250–$350
$$$$$ Over $350

LOUISIANA

BATON ROUGE Courtyard Baton Rouge Acadian Center $$

2421 S Acadian Thruway, 70808 ***Tel*** *(225) 924-6400* ***Fax*** *(225) 923-3041* ***Rooms*** *149*

The large, comfortable rooms of this contemporary three-story hotel feature luxury bedding, work desk, and ergonomic chair. Hotel amenities include a swimming pool and whirlpool, exercise room, and the Market, which is open 24 hours for snacks and light meals. **www.marriott.com**

BATON ROUGE Hilton Baton Rouge Capitol Center $$$

201 Lafayette St, 70801 ***Tel*** *(225) 344-5866* ***Fax*** *(225) 906-0595* ***Rooms*** *290*

This beautiful boutique hotel has recreated the historical grandeur of the former Heidelberg Hotel and added modern amenities and excellent service. The third floor garden deck with pool overlooks the Mississippi River. Complimentary shuttle service within a five mile radius. **www.hilton.com**

BAYOU TECHE, IBERIA, Days Inn & Suites $

611 Queen City Dr, 70560 ***Tel*** *(337) 560-9500* ***Fax*** *(337) 560-5611* ***Rooms*** *59*

This modern hotel with helpful staff located near local attractions. The decor is chain-hotel pleasant, the rooms are comfortable and good-sized, featuring small refrigerators, a microwave, and coffee-makers. The business center offers free high-speed Internet access. **www.daysinn.com**

BAYOU TECHE, ST. MARTINVILLE, Bienvenue House $$

421 N Main St, 70582 ***Tel*** *(337) 394-9100* ***Rooms*** *4*

Southern hospitality abounds at this charming antebellum home with porch swings and artful decor. Each of the elegant, invinting guestrooms features a tastefully crafted theme such as "French Aristocracy", "Acadian Country", or "Southern Granduer." Gourmet breakfast is served daily. **www.bienvenuehouse.com**

LAFAYETTE Bois des Chenes B&B Inn $$

338 N Sterling St, 70501 ***Tel*** *(337) 233-7816* ***Fax*** *(337) 233-7816* ***Rooms*** *5*

Richly decorated with regional, French, and American antique furniture and collections of pottery and glass, this Acadian-style plantation home warmly welcomes guests to Cajun country. The rooms feature elegant furnishings, small refrigerators, and TVs. Boat tours into the neighboring Atchafalaya Swamp. **www.hometown.aol.com/boisdchene/bois.htm**

LAFAYETTE Drury Inn & Suites $$

120 Alcide Dominique, 70506 ***Tel*** *(337) 262-0202, (800) 378-7946* ***Fax*** *(337) 262-0202* ***Rooms*** *102*

This modern five-story chain hotel has an attractive lobby and the rooms are tastefully decorated and feature high-speed wireless Internet, a small refrigerator, and microwave. Hotel amenities include a swimming pool, exercise room, hot breakfast buffet, and one hour of free long-distance phone calls. **www.druryhotels.com**

LAFAYETTE Courtyard by Marriott $$$

214 E Kaliste Saloom Rd, 70508 ***Tel*** *(337) 232-5005* ***Fax*** *(337) 231-0049* ***Rooms*** *90*

This contemporary three-story hotel is conveniently located close to Lafayette's major attractions. Hotel amenities include a swimming pool and whirlpool, exercise room, breakfast restaurant, and the Market, which is open 24 hours for snacks and light meals. **www.marriott.com**

NATCHITOCHES Quality Inn $

5362 University Pkwy, 71457 ***Tel*** *(318) 352-7500, (888) 443-2784* ***Fax*** *(318) 352-7500* ***Rooms*** *59*

Located just off Interstate 49, this small, two-story hotel with exterior corridors is convenient for travelers heading to New Orleans and the nearby local attractions. The all-new decor is country-cozy without overdoing it, and there are small refrigerators and microwaves in the rooms, plus a free Continental breakfast. **www.qualityinn.com**

NEW ORLEANS – CENTRAL BUSINESS DISTRICT Lafayette Hotel $

600 St. Charles Ave, 70130 ***Tel*** *(504) 524-4441* ***Fax*** *(504) 523-7327* ***Rooms*** *44*

A small luxury hotel with wrought-iron balconies and French doors, just a short walk from the French Quarter. The lobby is decorated with a delightful blend of Italian marble, woodwork, English carpets, and warm mahogany. Each guestroom is individually decorated, with marble baths and plush robes. **www.neworleansfinehotels.com/thelafayettehotel/**

Key to Symbols *see back cover flap*

NEW ORLEANS – CENTRAL BUSINESS DISTRICT Le Pavillon $$

833 Poydras St, 70112 ***Tel*** *(504) 581-3111, (800) 535-9095* ***Fax*** *(504) 620-4130* ***Rooms*** *226*

This upscale historic hotel has a dazzling lobby with Czechoslovakian crystal chandeliers, antiques, and oil paintings. The generous guestrooms are lavishly appointed with plush bedding, handmade draperies, and marble bathrooms. The service is first class and the rooftop swimming pool is delightful. **www.lepavillon.com**

NEW ORLEANS – CENTRAL BUSINESS DISTRICT Hampton Inn New Orleans $$$

226 Carondelet, 70130 ***Tel*** *(504) 529-9990, (800) 292-0653* ***Fax*** *(504) 529-9996* ***Rooms*** *187*

This 14-story neo-classical hotel offers great value for a location just two blocks from the French Quarter. Historic charm and modern amenities with a complimentary Continental breakfast every morning. The rooms are clean and comfortable but vary in size. Parking available onsite for a fee. **www.neworleanshamptoninns.com/downtown.html**

NEW ORLEANS – CENTRAL BUSINESS DISTRICT Windsor Court Hotel $$$$

300 Gravier St, 70130 ***Tel*** *(504) 523-6000, (888) 596-0955* ***Fax*** *(504) 596-4513* ***Rooms*** *324*

Luxury, excellent service and tasteful English decor create an understated elegance that makes this hotel easy to enjoy. The guestrooms are exceptionally large and comfortable with fine English furnishings and fabrics. Museum-quality art from the 17th, 18th and 19th centuries is displayed in a small gallery. **www.windsorcourthotel.com**

NEW ORLEANS – FRENCH QUARTER La Dauphine $

2316 Rue Dauphine, 70117 ***Tel*** *(504) 948-2217* ***Fax*** *(504) 948-3420* ***Rooms*** *4*

Four blocks from the French Quarter, this bed and breakfast in the Bohemian area of New Orleans caters to art lovers and the budget-minded. The inviting rooms feature four-poster beds, ceiling fans, shared bathrooms, and lots of hanging art. There's also a lovely small courtyard garden. The laid-back hosts are multilingual. **www.ladauphine.com**

NEW ORLEANS – FRENCH QUARTER Chateau Hotel $$

1001 Rue Chartres, 70116 ***Tel*** *(504) 524-9636* ***Fax*** *(504) 525-2989* ***Rooms*** *48*

An ideal location within walking distance of Bourbon Street and impeccable service make this small hotel in a restored 18th-century mansion popular. The courtyard is charming, and the pool is outside with a bar and café. The rooms are richly appointed. Complimentary Continental breakfast and off-street parking. **www.chateauhotel.com**

NEW ORLEANS – FRENCH QUARTER Degas House B&B $$

2306 Esplanade Ave, 70119 ***Tel*** *(504) 821-5009* ***Rooms*** *9*

This charming restored inn outside the French Quarter was home to French Impressionist Edgar Degas for a time. Each of the rooms is named for one of Degas' family members and individually decorated to match, with reproductions of Degas' art and copies of books about Degas' stay in New Orleans. **www.degashouse.com**

NEW ORLEANS – FRENCH QUARTER Hotel St. Pierre $$

911 Burgundy St, 70116 ***Tel*** *(504) 524-4401* ***Fax*** *(504) 593-9425* ***Rooms*** *74*

This quaint hotel is loaded with New Orleans character and is located on a residential street two blocks from Bourbon Street and close to the French Quarter attractions. Several small historic buildings and Creole cottages are grouped around lovely courtyards and a pool. **www.frenchquarterinns.com/hotelstpierre/**

NEW ORLEANS – FRENCH QUARTER Monteleone Hotel $$$

214 Rue Royale, 70130 ***Tel*** *(504) 523-3341, (800) 535-9595* ***Fax*** *(504) 528-1019* ***Rooms*** *600*

Legendary hospitality and a prime French Quarter location are the hallmarks of this excellent family-owned and operated hotel. Historic and contemporary, the expansive grand lobby is elegant while the rooftop swimming pool is a favorite gathering spot. Guestrooms have new marble and granite bathrooms. **www.hotelmonteleone.com**

NEW ORLEANS – FRENCH QUARTER Royal Sonesta $$$

300 Bourbon St, 70130 ***Tel*** *(504) 586-0300, (800) 766-3782* ***Fax*** *(504) 586-0335* ***Rooms*** *483*

In the heart of the French Quarter, the Royal Sonesta offers New Orleans style with French flair. The decor includes wrought-iron lace balconies, French doors, and gabled windows. Amenities include a tropical courtyard, fine restaurant, live entertainment in the Mystick Lounge, heated pool, and indoor parking. **www.sonesta.com/RoyalNewOrleans**

NEW ORLEANS – FRENCH QUARTER Ritz Carlton New Orleans $$$$

921 Canal St, 70112 ***Tel*** *(504) 524-1331, (800) 542-8680* ***Fax*** *(504) 524-7675* ***Rooms*** *452*

Located on the Mississippi River in the French Quarter, the Ritz offers high-end luxury and excellent hospitality. Decorated in the grand style of a Garden District mansion, Southern ambience is created in the interior design, art, and furnishings throughout the hotel. The guestrooms have high ceilings and Italian marble baths. **www.ritzcarlton.com**

NEW ORLEANS – GARDEN DISTRICT Hampton Inn Garden $$$

3626 St Charles Ave, 70115 ***Tel*** *(504) 899-9990* ***Fax*** *(504) 899-9908* ***Rooms*** *100*

This six-story hotel is located in the lovely Garden District on the St. Charles Streetcar Line, three miles from the French Quarter. Thoroughly modern inside, the traditional exterior design blends with the old mansions in the neighborhood. Complimentary Continental breakfast and free onsite parking. **www.hilton.com**

NEW ORLEANS – GARDEN DISTRICT Henry Howard House $$$

2041 Prytania St, 70130 ***Tel*** *(504) 561-8550, (877) 563-1411* ***Fax*** *(504) 566-1518* ***Rooms*** *17*

This renovated 1850s Garden District mansion offers homey elegance, modern comforts, and a great location just a block from the St. Charles trolley line and two blocks from the restaurants, antique shops, and boutiques of Magazine Street. Rooms are bright and spacious; free wi-fi and long-distance calls. **www.henryhowardhouseinn.com**

ARKANSAS

EUREKA SPRINGS 1886 Crescent Hotel & Spa $$

75 Prospect Ave, 72632 **Tel** *(479) 253-9766, (877) 342-9766* **Fax** *(479) 253-5296* **Rooms** *72*

This historic four-story Victorian hotel is known for its ghosts and the 15 acres of beautiful gardens and grounds that are a popular place for weddings. Rich in atmosphere, the charming lobby, full-service spa, and porch with rocking chairs looking out over the gardens are highlights. **www.crescent-hotel.com**

HOT SPRINGS Arlington Resort Hotel & Spa $$

239 Central Ave, 71901 **Tel** *(501) 623-7771, (800) 643-1502* **Fax** *(501) 623-2243* **Rooms** *484*

This grand old Southern hotel has attracted guests since 1907 with its mineral waters. The mineral water spa and bath house, along with the early 1900s elegance and ambience are an experience reminiscent of the gracious past. The classic guestrooms are modest, yet clean and comfortable. **www.arlingtonhotel.com**

LITTLE ROCK Comfort Inn Downtown $$

707 Interstate 30, 72202 **Tel** *(501) 687-7700, (888) 472-6717* **Rooms** *150*

A modern chain hotel conveniently located in downtown Little Rock near the William J. Clinton Presidential Center and River Market. The rooms are attractive and comfortable with luxury bedding, desk, and comfortable chair. Roof-top swimming pool, free shuttle service within three miles, and free wireless Internet. **www.comfortinnlittlerock.com**

LITTLE ROCK The Capital Hotel $$$

111 W Markham, 72201 **Tel** *(501) 374-7474, (877) 637-0037* **Fax** *(501) 370-7091* **Rooms** *94*

This historic 1876 hotel has undergone an extensive renovation. An architectural gem known for its charm and grace, the hotel's two-story lobby is a masterpiece in marble with a sweeping staircase, and Italianate columns and arches defining inviting sitting areas. The newly enlarged guestrooms are tastefully appointed. **www.thecapitalhotel.com**

MOUNTAIN VIEW Ozark Folk Center Dry Creek Lodge $

1032 Park Ave, 72560 **Tel** *(870) 269-3871, (800) 264-3655* **Fax** *(870) 269-2909* **Rooms** *60*

The State Park Service operates this single-floor lodge as part of the Ozark Folk Center. The rooms offer homey decor and each has glass doors onto porches with views into the woods. The center offers many family, musical, and craft activities and the Skillet restaurant for breakfast, lunch, and dinner. **www.ozarkfolkcenter.com**

MISSISSIPPI

BILOXI Beau Rivage Resort & Casino $

875 Beach Blvd, 39530 **Tel** *(228) 386-7444* **Fax** *(228) 386-7414* **Rooms** *1740*

The Beau Rivage is designed to fulfill all your vacation needs without ever leaving the premises, with restaurants, casino, and entertainment adjoining the hotel, Las Vegas style. The large rooms are luxurious with traditional furnishings and soothing colors and the baths are large. **www.beaurivage.com**

CLARKSDALE Executive Inn $

710 S State St, 38614 **Tel** *(662) 627-9292* **Fax** *(662) 624-4763* **Rooms** *93*

Located just off Highway 61 South, Blues Alley, this two-story chain motel is close to the Delta Blues Museum. All of the rooms have microwaves and small refrigerators, and there is a heated swimming pool, basketball court, and free Continental breakfast in the morning.

JACKSON Best Western Executive Inn $$

725 Larson St, 39201 **Tel** *(601) 969-6555* **Fax** *(601) 353-7468* **Rooms** *63*

One of the downtown hotels located adjacent to the Capitol and near the Coliseum, the rooms here are large, clean, and tastefully decorated in neutral and blue tones with amenities such as in-room microwave, refrigerator, high-speed Internet, and Continental breakfast. **www.bestwesternmississippi.com**

JACKSON Roberts Walthall Hotel $$

225 E Capitol St, 39201 **Tel** *(601) 948-6161, (800) 932-6161* **Fax** *(601) 948-0088* **Rooms** *208*

This downtown hotel is a favorite gathering place for government and business people at lunch. Dark wood paneling and marble floors decorate the lovely lobby. The dining room and the club-like bar retain the flavor of the hotel's historic past. There is even a barbershop. Rooms are neat and clean with traditional furnishings.

NATCHEZ Natchez Eola Hotel $

110 Pearl St, 39120 **Tel** *(601) 445-6000, (866) 445-3652* **Fax** *(601) 446-5310* **Rooms** *131*

This historic 1927 downtown hotel has elegant common areas decorated with crystal chandeliers, antiques, and fine oil paintings. The lovely courtyard features gardens with an original fire-and-water fountain. The rooms are comfortably furnished and some feature fireplaces and balconies. **www.natchezeola.com**

Key to Price Guide *see p368* **Key to Symbols** *see back cover flap*

NATCHEZ Monmouth Plantation Inn $$$

36 Melrose Ave, 39120 **Tel** *(601) 442-5852, (800) 828-4531* **Fax** *(601) 446 7762* **Rooms** *30*

A member of Small Luxury Hotels of the World, and known as one of the most romantic inns in America, this luxury inn is housed in an 1818 plantation home surrounded by 26 acres of beautifully manicured grounds with live oak trees. Rooms are elegantly appointed in grand antebellum style with antique furnishings. **www.monmouthplantation.com**

OXFORD Downtown Oxford Inn and Suites $$

400 North Lamar Blvd, 38655 **Tel** *(662) 234-3031, (800) 606-1497* **Fax** *(662) 234-2834* **Rooms** *100*

One of Oxford's best lodging options, this modest but pleasant chain hotel is located one block from the restaurants and shops of Oxford Square, and near the University of Mississippi. The standard rooms are pleasant, clean, and tastefully decorated. Continental breakfast and high-speed Internet access. **www.downtownoxfordinnandsuites.com**

OXFORD The Five Twelve Inn $$

512 Van Buren Ave, 38655 **Tel** *(662) 234-8043, (866) 383-6547* **Rooms** *5*

This c.1905 Greek Revival manor house is a bed and breakfast loaded with Southern charm. Decorated in English country style with some antiques, the inn features an inviting wrap-around porch and serves breakfast on weekends. The rooms are delightful with comfortable beds and claw foot tub in the bathroom.

ALABAMA

BIRMINGHAM Best Western Carlton Suites $$

140 State Farm Pkwy, 35209 **Tel** *(205) 940-9990* **Fax** *(205) 940-9930* **Rooms** *104*

Exceptional customer service and special amenities distinguish this Best Western from others in the chain. An all-suites hotel, the rooms are spacious, clean, and decorated in a homey country style with comfortable beds. Complimentary hot breakfast buffet and free cocktails and appetizers every Monday–Thursday evenings. **www.carltonsuiteshotel.com**

BIRMINGHAM Hampton Inn & Suites Downtown Tutwiler $$$

2021 Park Pl N, 35203 **Tel** *(205) 322-2100* **Fax** *(205) 325-1198* **Rooms** *147*

This very nice Hampton Inn with quality service is in the financial district and close to museums and restaurants. The rooms are pleasant with understated decor, comfortable beds, free Internet, and in-room microwave and refrigerator. Complimentary hot breakfast or breakfast-bag. **www.hamptoninn.com**

BIRMINGHAM Hotel Highland at Five Points South $$$

1023 20th St S, 35205 **Tel** *(205) 933-9555* **Fax** *(205) 933-6918* **Rooms** *63*

The rooms of this ultra-chic boutique hotel are dressed out in modern handcrafted furnishings and the finest linens from Brazil. They also feature two large flat-screen TVs, a wet bar, and refrigerator. Located in the Five Points South neighborhood, the hotel offers a trendy Martini bar and excellent restaurants nearby, **www.thehotelhighland.com**

HUNTSVILLE Marriott Huntsville $$$

5 Tranquility Base, 35816 **Tel** *(256) 830-2222* **Fax** *(256) 895-9528* **Rooms** *142*

Adjacent to the NASA Space and Rocket Center, this bustling seven-story Marriott is close to the Space Camp and high-tech businesses. The service is good, with friendly and helpful staff. The generous rooms are quiet and offer a work desk, easy chair, and great beds. Swimming pool, whirlpool, and fitness area. **www.marriott.com**

MOBILE Kate Shepard House B&B $$$

1552 Monterey Pl, 36604 **Tel** *(251) 479-7048* **Rooms** *3*

This Queen Anne-style bed and breakfast built in 1897 is on the National Historic Register and located in a quiet historic district close to downtown. The house has original fireplace mantles, stained glass windows, and hardwood floors. Service is friendly and personal and the full breakfast features daily hot entrées. **www.bbonline.com/al/kateshepard**

MOBILE The Battle House $$$

26 N Royal St, 36602 **Tel** *(251) 338-2000* **Fax** *(251) 338-5300* **Rooms** *207*

This richly historic downtown hotel has enhanced its legendary classic Southern charm and grandeur with modern amenities and conveniences. The opulent, glass-domed lobby is stunning and the luxurious guestrooms are decorated with highlights of burgundy and gold. **www.marriott.com**

MONTGOMERY Hilton Garden Inn $$

1600 Interstate Park Dr, 36109 **Tel** *(334) 272-2225* **Fax** *(334) 277-4559* **Rooms** *97*

The guestrooms in this four-story small hotel are pleasantly decorated in neutral tones with comfortable beds, fluffy towels, desks, high-speed Internet, microwave, and refrigerator. The Pavillion store sells frozen and microwave meals for in-room cooking. Located in a quiet neighborhood location just off the interstate. **www.hiltongardeninn.com**

SELMA St. James Hotel $$

1200 Water Ave, 36701 **Tel** *(334) 872-3234, (866) 965-2637* **Fax** *(334) 872-0332* **Rooms** *42*

Steamboat passengers, plantation owners, and even the notorious outlaw Jesse James once slept in this wonderfully historic antebellum riverfront hotel. The broad wrap-around porches with their wrought-iron ballustrades offer views of the Alabama River and the Edmund Pettus bridge used by freedom marchers in 1965. **www.stjameshotelselma.com**

Choosing a Restaurant

The entire Deep South region is known for its outstanding and distinctive cuisine. Chefs in New Orleans enjoy the same celebrity status as film stars in Los Angeles. Creole and Cajun delicacies make the most of fresh local seafood such as crawfish, shrimp, soft-shell crabs, and Gulf Coast oysters.

PRICE CATEGORIES
For a three-course meal for one, including a glass of house wine (where served), and all other unavoidable charges such as sales tax.
($) Under $20
($)($) $20–$30
($)($)($) $30–$40
($)($)($)($) $40–$50
($)($)($)($)($) Over $50

LOUISIANA

BATON ROUGE Albasha ($)($)
5454 Bluebonnet Rd, Suite G, 70809 ***Tel*** *(225) 292-7988*

This cozy, casual café with murals on the walls offers a range of Lebanese and Greek dishes in a comfortable atmosphere. The service is friendly and the kitchen serves up fresh food cooked to perfection. Favorites include chicken schwarma, mousaka, and stuffed grape leaves. Or, order one of the plate specials for a variety of dishes.

BATON ROUGE Boutin's Cajun Restaurant ($)($)($)
8322 Bluebonnet Blvd, 70810 ***Tel*** *(225) 819-9862*

Renowned for authentic Cajun food and live Cajun music most evenings, in a dining room with a dance floor decorated with Cajun murals on the wall. Traditional favorites include Crawfish Etouffée and Shrimp and Oysters en Brochette. The menu includes items that add a nouveau twist, like Seafood Wonton and Pepper Jack Shrimp.

BATON ROUGE Maison Lacour ($)($)($)($)($)
11025 N Harrells Ferry Rd, 70816 ***Tel*** *(225) 275-3755*

This French restaurant is situated in a cozy cottage in a park-like setting. Five dining rooms with French Country decor create a casual, intimate environment. Traditional French cuisine is served along with a selection of seafood, meats, and game, all accompanied by home-made French bread and salad with a house vinaigrette. Closed Sunday.

LAFAYETTE Prejean's ($)($)($)
3480 US I-49 N, 70507 ***Tel*** *(337) 896-3247*

Prejean's fun and casual atmosphere coupled with great Cajun food draws crowds of locals and travelers. The service is efficient and friendly and there's live music every evening and weekend mornings. The menu offers gumbos and bisques, best-sellers like Blackened Catfish Etouffée and Grilled Seafood Platter, as well as seafood, meats, and game.

LAFAYETTE Don's Seafood Hut ($)($)($)($)
4309 Johnston St, 70503 ***Tel*** *(337) 981-1141*

This local downtown favorite with a friendly atmosphere has been in business since 1936. The menu offers large servings of carefully prepared authentic Cajun downhome seafood specialties, such as Broiled Tilapia with Crawfish Etouffee, gumbos loaded with seafood, numerous crab and crawfish dishes, and a fresh oyster dinner.

LAFAYETTE Café Vermilionville ($)($)($)($)($)
1304 W Pinhook Rd, 70503 ***Tel*** *(337) 237-0100*

Housed in a historic early 1800s inn with large windows and original cypress beams and floors, the cuisine is upscale Cajun with two dinner menus. The traditional menu offers the signature dishes that have made the Café popular, while the second menu offers chef creations using the freshest ingredients. Closed Sunday.

NATCHITOCHES The Landing ($)($)($)
530 Front St, 71457 ***Tel*** *(318) 352-1579*

Situated in the middle of the historic district of Natchitoches, this casual restaurant is a favorite lunch and dinner spot with good service. The po-boys are a lunch favorite, while the dinner menu offers a fine selection of original Creole- and Cajun-influenced seafood, meat, and pasta entrées.

NEW ORLEANS – CENTRAL BUSINESS DISTRICT Mother's ($)
401 Poydras St, 70130 ***Tel*** *(504) 523-9656*

This casual diner-style restaurant is favored for its breakfasts and heaping po-boys. It's a chaotic experience with often long lines waiting to place their order before finding a seat. The serving staff is bustling, the atmosphere is boisterous, and the food is very tasty. The po-boys are renowned, but they also serve a great chicken gumbo.

NEW ORLEANS – CENTRAL BUSINESS DISTRICT Jacques-Imo's ($)($)($)
8324 Oak St, 70118 ***Tel*** *(504) 861-0886*

This restaurant offers an unbeatable New Orleans combination: great food, excellent service, funky decor, and a fun time. The menu is an eclectic mix of Creole and Cajun with contemporary twists, including such popular dishes as fried chicken, shrimp Creole, and alligator cheesecake. Closed Sunday.

Key to Symbols *see back cover flap*

NEW ORLEANS – CENTRAL BUSINESS DISTRICT Palace Café $$$

605 Canal St, 70130 ***Tel*** *(504) 523-1661*

This charming and lively two-floor café located on Canal Street downtown serves up classic and contemporary Creole cuisine. Signature dishes include Andouille Crusted Gulf Fish. White Chocolate Bread Pudding was invented here and is often imitated in other New Orleans restaurants, but the Palace Cafe's is the best.

NEW ORLEANS – CENTRAL BUSINESS DISTRICT Herbsaint Bar & Restaurant $$$$

701 St. Charles Ave, 70130 ***Tel*** *(504) 524-4114*

Herbsaint is one of the more innovative New Orleans restaurants. The atmosphere is relaxed, the service is great, and the food features new twists on old favorites and daring new creations such as confit duck with dirty rice, rabbit fricassee, and beignets with a molten chocolate interior. Closed Sunday.

NEW ORLEANS – CENTRAL BUSINESS DISTRICT Emeril's $$$$$

800 Tchoupitoulas St, 70130 ***Tel*** *(504) 528-9393*

Emeril's is one of the finest contemporary Creole restaurants in the city. The menu is expansive, with Creole and American entrées that have been enhanced with Creole ingredients and flavors. The dining area is inviting, sleek, and modern with a view into the kitchen. The six-course tasting menu is exceptional, and the banana cream pie legendary.

NEW ORLEANS – FRENCH QUARTER Café du Monde $

800 Decatur St, 70116 ***Tel*** *(504) 525-4544*

Sit in the open-air section of this legendary café and soak in the sounds of jazz produced by top local musicians. There is one item on the menu – beignets, which are squares of dough fried and covered with powdered sugar. Coffee is served black or au lait with hot milk, and there are other drink choices. Open 24 hours daily, closed Christmas Day.

NEW ORLEANS – FRENCH QUARTER Johnny's Po-Boy $

511 St. Louis St, 70130 ***Tel*** *(504) 524-8129*

No-frills, family-friendly, and very popular, Johnny's is located in the busy part of the French Quarter. The service is fast and friendly, the po-boys are large, and the French rolls are light. The selection is huge, with seafood versions as well as meats and the French Fry po-boy. You can order to-go and eat it by the Mississippi River. Lunch only.

NEW ORLEANS – FRENCH QUARTER Port of Call $

838 Esplanade Ave, 70116 ***Tel*** *(504) 523-0120*

This small, dark, minimalist, and very popular restaurant serves up the best burgers in New Orleans, served with baked potatoes. The burgers come with cheddar cheese or mushrooms, and there is a choice of toppings for the potatoes. They also serve charbroiled steaks and the full bar serves up a variety of potent drinks.

NEW ORLEANS – FRENCH QUARTER Acme Oyster House $$$

724 Iberville St, 70130 ***Tel*** *(504) 522-5973*

This classic Oyster Bar has table seating as well as standing room at the bar, and offers a very casual atmosphere with ultra-fresh oysters served raw, fried, chargrilled, and in gumbos and po-boys. The hush puppies and beer are just as popular, and there is a sampler platter with red rice, beans, and jambalaya. Closed Monday.

NEW ORLEANS – FRENCH QUARTER Antoine's $$$$

713 St. Louis St, 70130 ***Tel*** *(504) 581-4422*

Antoine's is the legendary New Orleans restaurant that has been open for more than 150 years. Classic and elegant, there are a dozen upscale dining rooms and 150 items on the vintage French-Creole menu. Oysters Rockefeller is one of the signature dishes, served piping hot and covered with Antoine's secret sauce. Closed Sunday.

NEW ORLEANS – FRENCH QUARTER Arnaud's $$$$

813 Bienville St, 70112 ***Tel*** *(504) 523-5433*

This classic, historic, and upscale French-Creole restaurant features a glittering main dining room with gleaming chandeliers, etched-glass windows, and Italian mosaic-tiled floors. The lengthly menu offers many classic dishes as well as creative entrées, and the signature specialties such as Shrimp Arnaud and soufflé potatoes are legendary.

NEW ORLEANS – FRENCH QUARTER Bacco $$$$

310 Chartres St, 70130 ***Tel*** *(504) 522-2426*

Surrounded by Gothic arches, Baroque ceiling paintings, and hand-painted murals, the dining room is stunning. The creative cuisine begins with fresh regional seafood, wild game, and local produce and is then artistically embellished with Italian flavors and housemade pastas to produce Bacco's Lobster & Shrimp Ravioli and other acclaimed entrées.

NEW ORLEANS – FRENCH QUARTER Bayona $$$$

430 Dauphine St, 70112 ***Tel*** *(504) 525-4455*

One of New Orleans' best restaurants is housed in a Creole Cottage in the French Quarter. Several elegant dining rooms and the charming courtyard create a warm and friendly atmosphere. The famous cuisine is eclectic, with flavorful and complex entrees influenced by countries from around the world. Closed Sunday, reservations required.

NEW ORLEANS – FRENCH QUARTER Galatoire's $$$$

209 Bourbon St, 70130 ***Tel*** *(504) 525-2021*

This traditional restaurant is refined and upscale, yet with touches of the French countryside that form its roots. Family-owned and operated since 1905, Galatoire's prides itself on impeccable cuisine, service, and ambience. Many believe the remoulade is the best in town. Reservations for upstairs accepted. Closed Monday.

NEW ORLEANS – FRENCH QUARTER K-Paul's Louisiana Kitchen $$$$$

416 Chartres St, 70130 ***Tel*** *(504) 524-7394*

The Cajun craze began in this restaurant in the 1980s and K-Paul's has expanded greatly since then, still attracting crowds with its signature spicy-hot seasonings and rich sauces. Favorites include the roux-thickened gumbos, fresh blackened fish, and the jambalaya. The two-story restaurant is tastefully decorated. Closed Sunday.

NEW ORLEANS – MARIGNY Feelings Café $$

2600 Chartres St, 70117 ***Tel*** *(504) 945-2222*

This charming neighborhood restaurant draws a loyal crowd back again and again with its romantic courtyard and main dining room with old brick decor and shuttered French doors. The service is great and the Creole entrees reasonably priced, with dishes such as Seafood Baked Eggplant and Bleu Cheese Steak. Closed Monday–Wednesday.

NEW ORLEANS – UPTOWN/GARDEN DISTRICT Casamento's $$$

4330 Magazine St, 70115 ***Tel*** *(504) 895-9761*

For over 80 years Casamento's has served fresh New Orleans oysters and seafood in this small, gleaming, tiled restaurant. The oyster loaf, oyster gumbo, oyster po-boy, and the shucked-at-the-bar raw oysters have all received rave reviews. The short menu has other choices, including fried shrimp, oysters, calamari, and fish, with cheesecake for dessert.

NEW ORLEANS – UPTOWN/GARDEN DISTRICT Brigtsen's $$$$$

723 Dante St, 70118 ***Tel*** *(504) 861-7610*

Small and intimate, this local favorite is tucked into a charming cottage with pastel walls and candles on the table. The service is warm and welcoming, and the small wine list carefully chosen. The menu changes frequently, featuring Creole, Acadian, and New Orleans flavors with fresh seafood, rabbit, and duck entrees. Closed Sunday and Monday.

NEW ORLEANS – UPTOWN/GARDEN DISTRICT Commander's Palace $$$$$

1403 Washington Ave, 70130 ***Tel*** *(504) 899-8221*

Situated in the Garden District in a Victorian-era building, Commander's is a classic, sophisticated, and celebrated New Orleans restaurant. Dining in the lovely garden is popular, service is excellent, and the Creole cuisine is legendary. The menu varies, offering a selection of traditional and innovative dishes. The wine list is impressive too.

ARKANSAS

EUREKA SPRINGS The Balcony Restaurant $$$

12 Spring St, 72632 ***Tel*** *(479) 253-7837*

Located in the historic Basin Park Hotel in downtown Eureka Springs, this restaurant offers casual dining on the balcony overlooking historic Spring Street and the shopping district. The menu is extensive, with a variety of American family favorites, such as soups, salads, burgers, and sandwiches, as well as beef and chicken dinners. Only open Fri–Sun.

HOT SPRINGS McClard's BBQ $

505 Albert Pike, 71913 ***Tel*** *(501) 623-9665*

A favorite of then-Governor Bill Clinton, McClard's has been in business since 1928 and is considered Arkansas' premier barbeque house. The ribs are cooked and smoked in the old-fashioned pit-style and the special sauce is legendary. The hot tamales and coleslaw get rave reviews. Closed Sunday and Monday, mid-Dec–mid-Jan, and one week in August.

HOT SPRINGS Belle Arte Ristorante $$$

719 Central Ave, 71901 ***Tel*** *(501) 624-7474*

This friendly and relaxed restaurant has an old world ambience with high ceilings and arched entryways. Locals and visitors come for the fine Italian dining. The cuisine is artistically presented and the menu features steak, seafood, chicken, and pasta entrees. Fine wines and desserts finish off the menu. Reservations are recommended.

LITTLE ROCK Cajun's Wharf $$$

2400 Cantrell Rd, 72202 ***Tel*** *(501) 375-5351*

Cajun's is an upbeat restaurant featuring a good selection of fresh seafood and aged Angus Beef. The menu includes a large selection of American appetizers, soups, and salads, and other entrées as well. The wine list features moderately priced California wines. The outdoor deck, bar, and dance club draw a lively crowd. Closed Sunday.

LITTLE ROCK Doe's Eat Place $$$

1023 W Markham St, 72201 ***Tel*** *(501) 376-1195*

Great steaks are served family-style in this downhome eatery with well-worn linoleum floors, which attracts politicians and almost everyone else. T-Bone, porterhouse, and sirloin steaks are cooked to order and arrive at the table with marinated salad, new potatoes, French fries, and Texas Toast. Hot tamales are a popular appetizer. Closed Sunday.

MOUNTAIN VIEW Skillet Restaurant $$

Ozark Folk Center, 72560 ***Tel*** *(870) 269-3139*

This excellent country-style restaurant is part of the famous Ozark Folk Center and it is well worth dining here. Large windows offer views of a butterfly garden and wildlife feeding stations. The menu is extensive, and live music accompanies the weekend buffets. The staff here is friendly and the service professional. Closed Nov–mid-Apr.

Key to Price Guide *see p372* **Key to Symbols** *see back cover flap*

MISSISSIPPI

CLARKSDALE Madidi $$$$

164 Delta Ave, 38614 ***Tel*** *(662) 627-7770*

Co-owned by actor and local-resident Morgan Freeman, Madidi is a pleasant find. Housed in a historic downtown building, this intimate restaurant displays colorful regional art. The cuisine is French-influenced with a Southern flair, with entries such as rack of lamb and hybrid bass. The menu changes seasonally. Closed Sunday and Monday.

GULFPORT/BILOXI Mary Mahoney's Old French House $$$$

116 Rue Magnolia, 39530 ***Tel*** *(228) 374-0163*

This charming one-of-a-kind restaurant is set in a historical 1737 house with period decor and furnishings, and a courtyard shaded by a massive old oak tree. The distinctive menu features fresh Gulf seafood, such as seasoned flounder and stuffed snapper. There is also a selection of meats and a varied dessert menu. Closed Sunday.

JACKSON Julep Restaurant & Bar $$$

1305 E Northside Dr 105, Highland Village, 39211 ***Tel*** *(601) 362-1411*

Regional cuisine with a fun and very contemporary twist is found in this captivating restaurant. The chefs borrow from other food traditions to create Southern favorites with a delightful difference. The menu changes frequently but the award-winning Fried Chicken and Blackened Catfish Tacos with pepper jack cheese and remoulde is usually available.

NATCHEZ Carriage House Restaurant $

401 High St, 39120 ***Tel*** *(601) 445-5151*

Situated on the lovely grounds of Stanton Hall, this charming restaurant in the estate's Carriage House serves old-fashioned and contemporary Southern food. The menu offers a selection of salads and entrées, with fried chicken, tomato aspic, and Longwood Salad the specialties. Be sure to order the famous biscuits. Lunch only.

OXFORD Bottletree Bakery $

923 Van Buren Ave, 38655 ***Tel*** *(662) 236-5000*

This charming bakery just off the town square is very popular for breakfast and lunch. Bakery choices include giant croissants plain or stuffed with chocolate or other fillings, and pastries such as brioche and fruit Danish. For lunch there's soup and sandwiches served on fresh breads or croissants. The coffee is great and the apple pie famous. Closed Mon.

ALABAMA

BIRMINGHAM Café Dupont $$$$$

113 20th St N, 35203 ***Tel*** *(205) 322-1282*

Located in a storefront building with high ceilings and original floors in downtown Birmingham's historic North End, Café Dupont's menu supports the Slow Food Movement. It features dishes made with locally grown ingredients, and choices include steaks, seafood such fried oysters and okra with cayenne butter sauce, and classic beignets.

BIRMINGHAM METRO AREA Bob Sykes Bar-B-Q $

1724 9th Ave, 35020 ***Tel*** *(205) 426-1400*

A short drive out of Birmingham on I-20 W, Bob Sykes is a culinary landmark serving delicious barbeque. For more than 50 years this family-run business has been slow-roasting pork and chicken over hickory wood to produce tender, succulent, and flavorful barbeque. The restaurant also offers hamburgers and great pies. Closed Sunday.

HUNTSVILLE Little Paul's Gibson Barbeque $

815 Madison St SE, 35801 ***Tel*** *(256) 536-7227*

This popular family-owned restaurant has great service and is open for breakfast, lunch, and dinner. The excellent barbeque is hickory-smoked, offering pork, ribs, chicken, and beef. The famous fried catfish is just one of the other menu offerings. The portions are large here, but save room for a slice of the delightful homemade pie for dessert.

MOBILE The Pillars $$$$

1757 Government St, 36604 ***Tel*** *(251) 471-3411*

This upscale restaurant is housed in a lovely old plantation home furnished with antiques, with wide porches surrounded by oak trees. The menu features fresh Gulf seafood prepared in a variety of ways, including sauces such as white wine and cream or crabmeat and pecan Creole. Continental favorites are Angus beef and lamb. Closed Sunday.

MONTGOMERY Ox Yoke Steakhouse & Grill $$

4380 Wetumpka Hwy, 36101 ***Tel*** *(334) 274-0330*

Locals and visitors alike head to this upscale steakhouse primarily for its top-quality, handcut, chargrilled steaks, but the fish dishes are excellent too. The atmosphere is friendly and the service top-notch. Prices are reasonable for the quality ingredients and there are nightly specials. Closed Sun & Mon.

THE GREAT LAKES

INTRODUCING THE GREAT LAKES 378–385

CHICAGO, ILLINOIS 386–397

ILLINOIS 398–399

INDIANA 400–403

OHIO 404–407

MICHIGAN 408–411

WISCONSIN 412–415

MINNESOTA 416–421

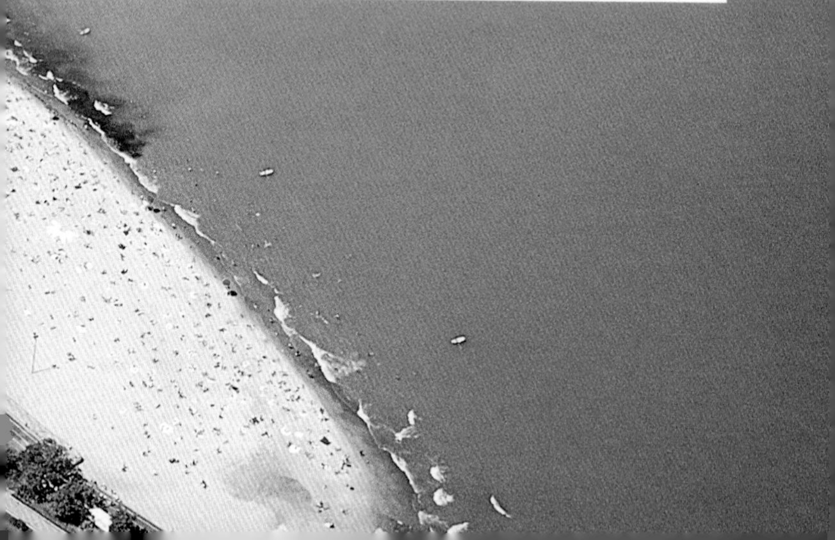

The Great Lakes at a Glance

Spreading between the Colonial-era landscapes of the East Coast and the wide open spaces of the Wild West, this region stakes a strong claim to being the most "American" part of the US. Home to more than one in five Americans, the Great Lakes is energetic and surprisingly varied. With its bustling big cities and sleepy small towns, idyllic rural scenes and sublime waterfront wilderness, industrial might and broad swaths of pristine natural beauty, the attractions here are as varied as the six states of Illinois, Ohio, Michigan, Indiana, Wisconsin, and Minnesota that form the center of America's heartland.

Voyageurs National Park (see p421) *in Minnesota covers endless stretches of watery wilderness near the Canadian border. The park, with its lakes, bogs, and islands, is a prime outdoor destination.*

Wisconsin's (see pp412–15) *natural wonders attract hikers, bikers, and campers who explore the state's glacial moraines, lakes, and valleys through well-marked trails.*

Springfield (see p399) *is the capital of Illinois, a state characterized by vast expanses of rich, flat farmland. Abraham Lincoln, who lived here for 31 years (1830–61), delivered his famous "House Divided" speech in 1858 at the Old State Capitol.*

◁ **Aerial view of Chicago's magnificent high-rises, towering above Lake Shore Drive**

Chicago (see pp386–97), *the region's largest city, is located on the southwestern edge of Lake Michigan. One of the world's most celebrated centers of architectural innovation, the city has attracted many of North America's most influential architects. The most significant of these was Frank Lloyd Wright.*

LOCATOR MAP

Detroit (see p408–409), *still known as the Motor City, is also Michigan's main city and commerical center. Downtown's Hart Plaza, at the riverfront, is the site of the city's lively summer festivals.*

Ohio (see pp404–407) *is a curious combination of a rural and heavily industrial state. It also contains some of the earliest examples of Native American cultures, such as the symbolic earthen Serpent Mound.*

Indianapolis (see p402) *Monument Circle is the dominant feature of downtown. The city's many excellent museums add to its status as Indiana's state capital.*

THE GREAT LAKES

Surrounding the world's largest bodies of fresh water, the Great Lakes region is a land of epic proportions. From the towering skyscrapers of Chicago, Illinois, and the factories of Detroit, Michigan, to the seemingly endless plains of Indiana, the bountiful pastures of Wisconsin, and Minnesota's watery wilderness, this is one of the most exciting destinations in the country.

Spreading west from the original American colonies to beyond the Mississippi River, the Great Lakes region formed the first frontier of the early United States. The lakes themselves – Ontario, Erie, Huron, Michigan, and Superior – were a conduit for trade and exploration, and a key to the region's development. Plentiful harvests from the fertile soils, lumber from the forests, and ore from the region's mines all came together to support the growth of such cities as Chicago, Cleveland, Detroit, and Minneapolis. From the mid-19th century on, immigrants from all over the country and around the world came here to work on farms and in factories, thus establishing the diverse cultures and traditions that still flavor Great Lakes life. While industry and agriculture have given way to the service economy, the region's history and heritage have now become important tourist attractions, enhancing the natural beauty of its many lakes, rivers, and forests.

HISTORY

Long before the United States was founded, the region surrounding the Great Lakes was home to some of the most developed and powerful Native American cultures. Evidence of one of the most significant archaeological remnants in North America can be found in southern Ohio and Illinois, where the enigmatic Moundbuilder culture constructed the largest cities north of Mexico. Of these, the most

A 1920s photograph showing parked automobiles at Detroit's Cadillac Square

◁ **Stacked icicle formations in the Sawtooth Mountain Range along Lake Superior's northern shore, Minnesota**

impressive is at Cahokia. Farther north, spanning the international border between the US and Canada – which runs right through the center of the Great Lakes – Native Americans were grouped together into many distinct though related tribes. The Huron and Ojibwe in the north, and the Fox, Shawnee, and Menominee in the south and west had developed intricate trade and cultural relationships. However, after some 100 years of European contact, large Native populations had been decimated through disease and internecine warfare.

Replica of Christopher Columbus's ship *Santa Maria* in Columbus, Ohio

Initially, early European exploration of this part of the New World was dominated by the French. Traveling from their colony at Quebec, the first French explorers were rapidly followed by fur trading "voyageurs" who bartered tools and weapons for beaver pelts. At the same time, French Jesuit missionaries began to establish commercial, military, and religious outposts at Sault Sainte Marie in 1668 and at Detroit in 1701. Until the mid-1700s, religion and the fur trade remained the main points of contact between Indians and Europeans.

The pace of settlement accelerated after the end of the Seven Years War in Europe in 1763, and the Americans and British acquired territorial control of the region. Within a few decades Ohio, Indiana, and Illinois had changed from isolated frontier territories to states. Following the completion of the Erie Canal in 1825, and improved transportation on the lakes, settlers were able to reach the previously distant lands of Michigan and Wisconsin. In 1858, Minnesota became the last of the Great Lakes states to join the nation.

KEY DATES IN HISTORY

1620 Etienne Brule is the first European to explore present-day Michigan and Wisconsin

1673 Jesuit missionary Jacques Marquette and explorer Louis Jolliet cross the northern Great Lakes and descend the Mississippi River

1750 The population of Detroit, the only large Great Lakes settlement, numbers 600

1763 France surrenders its Great Lakes territorial claims to Great Britain

1783 The US acquires the region from Britain, forms the Northwest Territory

1803 Ohio is the first to become a state in the Great Lakes area

1903 Henry Ford establishes the Ford Motor Company in Detroit

1936 A factory strike leads General Motors to accept the United Auto Workers union as the sole bargaining agent for its workers

1968 Chicago police attack anti-Vietnam War protestors at the Democratic National Convention

1995 Over 500 people die in Chicago heat wave

2000 Former WWF champion Jesse "The Body" Ventura is elected Governor of Minnesota

2009 Chicago resident Barack Obama becomes first African-American US president

IMMIGRANTS & INDUSTRY

The opening up of the Great Lakes region to settlement coincided with a major influx of immigrants. From the 1840s on, immigration increased tenfold as more than 200,000 people, mostly Irish and Germans fleeing the potato famine and political unrest respectively, came to America every

Historical Museum, Winona, MN, on the Mississippi

year. Many settled in ethnic enclaves in rapidly growing cities such as Chicago, Detroit, Cincinnati, and Cleveland, where some three-quarters of residents were either foreign-born or first-generation Americans.

Large numbers of other immigrants set up wheat and dairy farms on recently cleared forests, or found work in other resource-based industries. Copper mining in Michigan's Upper Peninsula, for example, produced more than 75 percent of the nation's supplies between 1850 and 1900. With a total value of nearly $10 billion, this mining boom was 10 times more lucrative than the legendary California Gold Rush of 1849. Another major industry was food processing. Meat-packing, which was concentrated on the huge stockyards of Chicago and Minneapolis, relied on the railroads to transport millions of cattle and pigs from across the Midwest. The Great Lakes also came to dominate grain processing, and some of the nation's largest companies, including the world-famous Kellogg's and General Mills, are still based here.

The early 20th century witnessed the largest and most enduring industrial boom, mainly because of the mutually dependent growth of the steel and automobile industries, both largely based in the Great Lakes region. Dearborn and Detroit, headquarters of Ford Motor Company as well as other smaller companies that evolved into the giant General Motors, emerged as the "Motor City." Despite competition from other countries, the Great Lakes automobile industry flourished and in turn supported a network of other industries, such as the iron mines in Minnesota, steel mills in Indiana, and rubber plants in Ohio.

POLITICS & CULTURE

The success of the industries may have reaped huge fortunes for their owners, but the workers' conditions were often dire. This exploitation led to a number of violent battles, particularly around Chicago, such as the riots in Haymarket Square in 1886 and the bitter strike against the Pullman Palace Car company in 1894. The growth of unions gave workers some semblance of political power, which in turn supported a number of left-leaning social movements. The Great Lakes in general, and Minnesota and Wisconsin in particular, were early strongholds of the Populist and Progressive movements, which in the early 1900s proposed such now-accepted innovations as the eight-hour workday and graduated rates of income tax.

This social awareness also influenced art and literature. One of the region's most famous works of art, Diego Rivera's massive mural on the walls of the Detroit Institute of Art, depicts workers struggling under the demands of industrialization. The region's great literary works include Hamlin Garland's depictions of life on the Wisconsin frontier, Sherwood Anderson's *Winesburg, Ohio*, the vivid exposés of Sinclair Lewis, and the stories of St. Paul native F. Scott Fitzgerald.

A view of Detroit's gleaming skyscrapers, including the Renaissance Center, from across the Detroit River

Exploring the Great Lakes

Encompassing large cities as well as vast stretches of farmland and places of natural beauty, the Great Lakes covers a broad area that is best explored by car. While the major towns and cities are linked by both Interstate highways and Amtrak trains, public transportation is otherwise limited, but there is a seasonal ferry service across Lake Michigan. Chicago is the region's largest and most cosmopolitan city; other cities include Indianapolis, Detroit, Cleveland, Cincinnati, Milwaukee, and Minnesota's twin cities of Minneapolis & St. Paul.

SEE ALSO

- ***Practical Information*** pp422–3
- ***Where to Stay*** pp424–7
- ***Where to Eat*** pp428–31

Visitors near Old Mission Lighthouse, Lake Michigan shore, Michigan

SIGHTS AT A GLANCE

Illinois
Chicago pp386–97 1
Rockford 2
Galena 3
Springfield 4
Southern Illinois 5

Indiana
New Harmony 6
Bloomington 7
Indiana Dunes National Lakeshore 8
South Bend 9
Shipshewana 10
Fort Wayne 11
Indianapolis 12
Columbus 13
Ohio River Valley 14

Ohio
Cincinnati 15
Dayton 16
Serpent Mound 17
Hopewell Culture National Historic Park 18
Columbus 19
Berlin 20
Cleveland 21
Lake Erie Islands 22
Sandusky 23
Toledo 24

Michigan
Detroit pp408–409 25
Ann Arbor 26
Lansing 27
Grand Rapids 28
Lake Michigan Shore 29
Mackinac Island 30
Upper Peninsula 31

Wisconsin
Milwaukee 32
Door County 33
Wisconsin Dells 34
Baraboo 35
Madison 36
Spring Green 37
La Crosse 38
Apostle Islands 39

Minnesota
Minneapolis & St. Paul pp416–17 40
Mississippi River Towns 41
Rochester 42
Pipestone National Monument 43
Brainerd Lakes Area 44
Duluth 45
Iron Range 46
Boundary Waters Canoe Area Wilderness 47
Voyageurs National Park 48

For additional map symbols *see back flap*

KEY

- Airport
- Highway
- Major road
- Railroad
- State border
- International border

MILEAGE CHART

10 = Distance in miles
10 = Distance in kilometers

	CHICAGO, IL	INDIANAPOLIS, IN	CINCINNATI, OH	CLEVELAND, OH	DETROIT, MI	MILWAUKEE, WI
INDIANAPOLIS, IN	**181** 291					
CINCINNATI, OH	**297** 478	**113** 182				
CLEVELAND, OH	**342** 550	**317** 510	**243** 391			
DETROIT, MI	**283** 455	**317** 510	**256** 412	**168** 270		
MILWAUKEE, WI	**93** 150	**278** 447	**395** 636	**435** 700	**375** 604	
MINNEAPOLIS, MN	**409** 658	**595** 958	**707** 1138	**751** 1207	**695** 1118	**336** 541

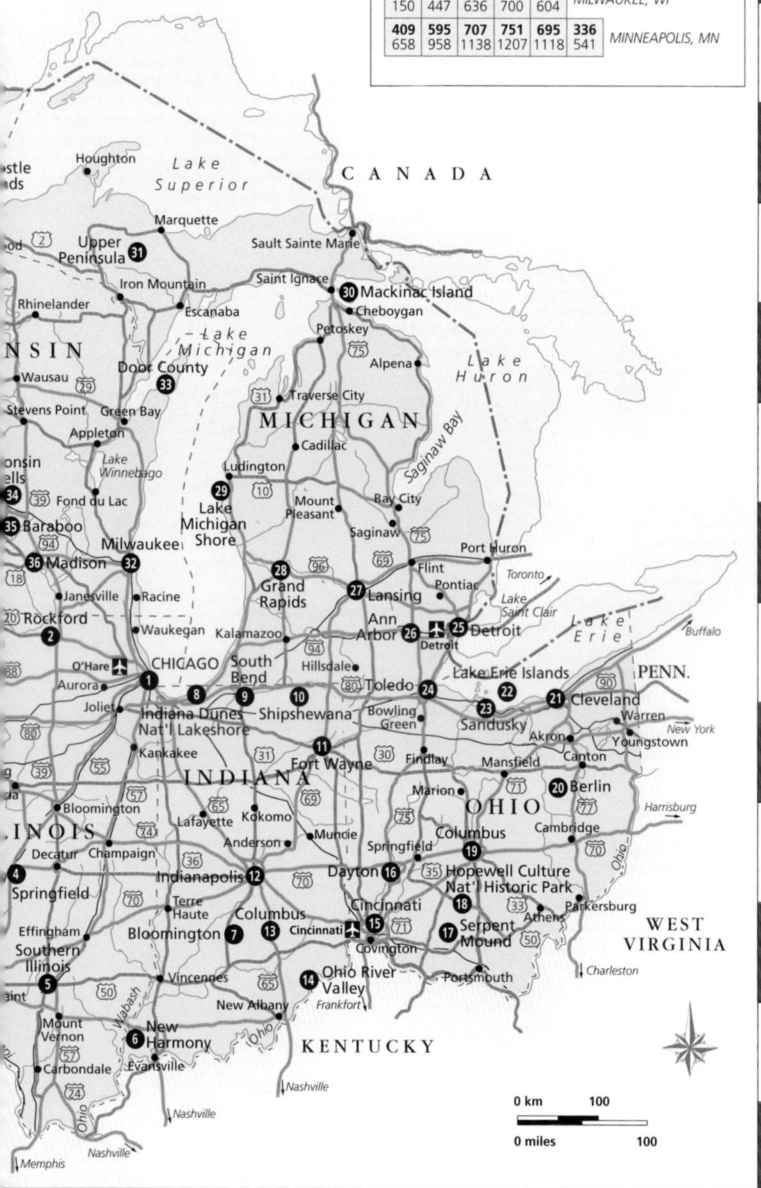

Chicago ❶

Chicago, a city of almost 3 million people, covers 228 sq miles (591 sq km) of the US's Midwest. Situated at the southwest edge of the vast Lake Michigan, the city claims 29 miles (47 km) of lakefront. Despite burning to the ground in 1871 and witnessing terrible social unrest, the city soon rebuilt itself to emerge as the financial capital of the Midwest. Today, this third largest city in the US is world famous for its innovative architecture, its vibrant cultural and educational institutions, and for its colorful and turbulent political history. It is also home to US president Barack Obama.

SIGHTS AT A GLANCE

Chicago History Museum ①
Newberry Library ②
Magnificent Mile ③
John Hancock Center ④
Navy Pier ⑤
Chicago Children's Museum ⑥
Millennium Park ⑦
Art Institute of Chicago ⑧
Sears Tower ⑨
The Loop pp390–91 ⑩
South Loop ⑪
Museum Campus ⑫

South Side
(see inset map)
Museum of Science & Industry ⑬
University of Chicago ⑭
DuSable Museum of African American History ⑮

Greater Chicago
(see inset map)
Lincoln Park Zoo ⑯
Oak Park pp396–7 ⑰

GETTING AROUND

Although Chicago is a sprawling Midwestern metropolis, many of the city's sights and main cultural centers are located downtown, making the city a walker's dream. The city's public transportation is inexpensive and efficient. The train system, known as the "L" for elevated, is the easiest way to get around. Buses crisscross the city and bus drivers are helpful. Free trolleys go to popular sites during summer. Taxis are affordable, convenient, and readily available.

KEY

- Sight/Place of interest
- Airport
- Metra train station
- CTA train station
- Tourist information
- Parking
- Railroad line
- Expressway

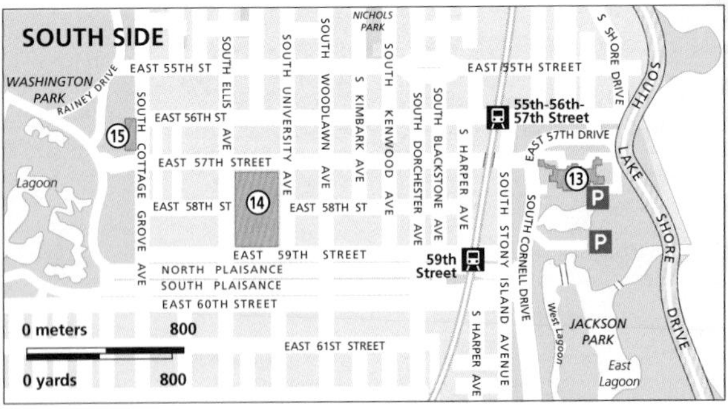

KEY

Area of main maps

0 meters 800

0 yards 800

SEE ALSO

• ***Where to Stay*** p424

• ***Where to Eat*** p428

The marquee and sign of the opulent Chicago Theater

Original Neo-Georgian entrance to the Chicago History Museum

Chicago History Museum ①

Map D1. 1601 N Clark St. ***Tel*** *(312) 642-4600.* [M] *Clark/Division then bus 22, 36.* [bus] *11, 151, 156.* [hours] *9:30am–4:30pm Mon–Sat (until 8pm Thu); noon–5pm Sun.* [closed] *Jan 1, Thanksg., Dec 25.* [admission] *(free Mon).* [wheelchair] [tours] *(call for times).* [P] ***Concerts, lectures, films.*** **www**.chicagohistory.org

The city's oldest cultural institution, the 1856 Chicago Historical Society is a major museum and research center, with a library open for public research. It traces the history of Chicago and Illinois, from its first explorers through the development of the city to the major events in modern-day Chicago. Miniature dioramas depict great events such as the Great Fire of 1871, the Chicago River during the Civil War, and the bustling LaSalle Street in the mid-1860s.

The American Wing holds one of only 23 copies of the Declaration of Independence, and a 1789 copy of the American Constitution, first printed in a Philadelphia newspaper. The building has two faces – the original 1932 Neo-Georgian structure, and a 1988 addition with a three-story, glass-and-steel atrium entrance.

Newberry Library ②

Map D2. 60 W Walton St. ***Tel*** *(312) 943-9090.* [M] *Chicago (red line) to Clark/Division then bus 22.* [hours] *hours for lobby, book rooms, & exhibits vary. Call ahead.* [closed] *public hols.* [wheelchair] [tours] *3pm Thu; 10:30am Sat.* [shop] ***Exhibits, lectures, concerts.*** **www**.newberry.org

Founded in 1887 by banker Walter Newberry, this independent research library for the humanities was designed by Henry Ives Cobb, master architect of the Richardsonian Romanesque style.

The superb collection includes cartography, Native American history, Renaissance studies, geneology, and such rarities as first editions of Milton's *Paradise Regained* and a 1481 edition of Dante's *Divine Comedy*.

Magnificent Mile ③

Michigan Ave, between E Walton Pl & E Kinzie St.

The Magnificent Mile, a stretch of Michigan Avenue north of the Chicago River, is the city's most fashionable street. Almost completely destroyed in the 1871 fire, the street grew into Chicago's premier shopping district after the opening of the Michigan Avenue Bridge in 1920. Exclusive shops line the wide boulevard, while modern retail outlets and skyscrapers rub shoulders with historic buildings.

To the north lies the Gothic Revival-style **Fourth Presbyterian Church**. Its exposed buttresses, stone spire, and recessed main window reflect the influences of medieval European churches.

To its right are two historic castellated structures, the **Water Tower** and the **Pumping Station**, among the few buildings that survived the 1871 fire. The tower, originally housing a standpipe, is now home to a photography gallery and a theater. The station still fulfills its original purpose of pumping water and houses a Visitor

Open-air skywalk topping the John Hancock Center

ARCHITECTURE IN CHICAGO

Chicago is world famous as a center of architectural innovation, a city where architects have pushed the boundaries of creativity. This reputation had its beginnings in the tragic fire of 1871. Working on a blank slate, architects rose to the challenge of reshaping a devastated city. It was in Chicago that the world's first skyscraper was built, and here that Frank Lloyd Wright developed his Prairie School of architecture.

Gothic Revival *style, represented by the Water Tower, drew from medieval European architecture.*

Italianate design *style was inspired by Renaissance palaces and villas of northern Italy. The elegant Drake Hotel exemplifies this style.*

Richardsonian Romanesque *style – typified by rough-cut stone, round arches, and recessed windows – can be seen in the Newberry Library.*

Information Center (163 E Pearson St) and café. Across the street, **Water Tower Place** contains eight floors of upscale boutiques and restaurants. Other "vertical shopping malls" on the street include Chicago Place and Westfield North Bridge. **Hershey's Chicago** is nearby and well-stocked, and has sugar-free versions of its most popular products.

Slightly south, the Gothic-style **Tribune Tower**, office of the *Chicago Tribune*, holds rock fragments from world-famous sites, such as St. Peter's Basilica in Rome, the Forbidden City in Beijing, and even a 3.3-billion-year-old piece of moon rock embedded in its exterior walls.

At the southernmost end of the street is the beloved two-part **Wrigley Building**. This white terra-cotta structure features a giant four-sided clock and a quiet courtyard, which is open to the public.

John Hancock Center ④

Map D2. 875 N Michigan Ave. **Observatory *Tel*** *(888) 875-8439.* *Chicago (red line).* *145, 146, 147, 151.* *9am–11pm daily.* *to observatory (children under 5 free).* **www**.hancock-observatory.com

Affectionately called "Big John" by Chicagoans, the 100-story, cross-braced steel John Hancock Center stands out in the Chicago skyline. The tapering obelisk tower's major attraction is the Hancock Observatory on the 94th floor. Here, 1,127 ft (344 m) above the Magnificent Mile, an open-air (screened) sky-walk offers spectacular views of the city. The elevator ride to the top at 20 miles (32 km) is one of the fastest in the US.

Designed by architect Bruce Graham of Skidmore Owings and Merrill and engineer Fazlur R. Khan, the center houses offices, condominiums, and shops in 2.8 million sq ft (0.26 million sq m) of space.

Navy Pier ⑤

Map D2. 600 E Grand Ave. ***Tel*** *(800) 595-7437.* *29, 56, 65, 66, 120, 121, 124.* *10am; closing times vary by day & season.* *Thanksgiving, Dec 25.* ***Lake cruises.*** **www**.navypier.com

Navy Pier is a bustling recreational and cultural center. Designed by Charles S. Frost, the 3,000-ft (915-m) long and 400-ft (120-m) wide pier was the largest in the world when built in 1916. Over 20,000 timber piles were used in its construction.

The giant Ferris wheel, Navy Pier Park

Originally a municipal wharf, the pier was used for naval training during World War II. After a four-year renovation, Navy Pier opened in its present incarnation in 1995. Navy Pier Park has a 150-ft (45-m) Ferris wheel, an old-fashioned carousel, an outdoor amphitheater, ice skating, miniature golf, and an IMAX® 3D Theater. The Smith Museum features stained glass.

Chicago Children's Museum ⑥

Map E3. 700 E Grand Ave. ***Tel*** *(312) 527-1000.* *29, 56, 65, 66, 120, 121, 124.* *10am–5pm daily (until 8pm Thu).* *Thanksg., Dec 25.* *(free first Mon of month).* ***Special activities daily.*** **www**.chichildrensmuseum.org

Chicago Children's Museum, focusing on activating the intellectual and creative potential of children ages 1 to 12, is an activity center for the whole family. "Kids Reinvent Chicago" will be a new theme when the museum moves to Grant Park and almost doubles in size. The Dinosaur Expedition is where children can dig for bones in an excavation pit, or simply slide, climb, and jump around.

Queen Anne *style, once a popular design for Chicago residences, is exemplified by row houses in Crilly Court.*

Chicago School, *developed here, led to an engineering and aesthetic revolution with commercial skyscrapers like the Reliance building.*

Neo-Classical *style has classical Greco-Roman elements, as seen in the Chicago Cultural Center.*

International Style *stresses severe geometry and large expanses of glass. Sears Tower is a fine example.*

Post-Modern *architecture, an eclectic style without strict rules, is seen in the Harold Washington Library Center.*

Millennium Park ⑦

Map D4. 55 N Michigan Ave. ***Tel*** *(312) 742-1168.* *Madison.* *6am–11pm daily.* *free tours at 11:30am & 1pm daily.* **www**.millenniumpark.org

The award-winning center for art, music, architecture, and landscape design opened in 2004 on 24.5 acres (10 ha) of former railroad property. The park is bordered by Michigan Avenue, Colombus Drive, and Randolph and Moore streets. The nearby Welcome Center, at 201 East Randolph Street, is a good place to find out about what the park has to offer.

Unusual design elements within the park include Frank Gehry's spectacular Jay Pritzker Pavilion with its roof of massive, curling, stainless steel ribbons that looms 120 feet (37 m) high. This outdoor concert venue hosts the Grant Park Music Festival series of concerts each summer, as well as other free concerts and events. Another Gehry-designed ribbon of the same material forms a 925-feet (282-m) long, winding bridge that connects the park to Daley Bicentennial Plaza.

The Neo-Classical façade of the Art Institute of Chicago

Video images of the faces of 1,000 local residents rotate over the two 50-feet (15-m) tall towers of glass blocks which make up the interactive Crown Fountain designed by Spanish artist Jaume Plensa. Water pours out of the towers from spring to fall, landing in a shallow reflecting pool that is popular with local families.

Other unique features within the park are the contemporary 5-acre (2-ha) Lurie Garden with its dramatically lit hedges and perennial garden, and British artist Anish Kapoor's Cloud Gate sculpture, which resembles a giant drop of mercury and allows visitors to view themselves as a part of the Chicago skyline.

The Art Institute of Chicago ⑧

Map D4. 111 S Michigan Ave. ***Tel*** *(312) 443-3600.* *Adams.* *1, 3, 6, 7, 126, 145, 147, 151.* *Van Buren St.* *10:30am–5pm Mon–Fri (to 8pm Thu); 10am– 5pm Sat, Sun.* *Jan 1, Thanksg., Dec 25.* *(under 12s free; separate adm to some exhibits).* ***Exhibits, lectures, films*.** **www**.artic.edu

The extensive collections at the Art Institute of Chicago repr-esent nearly 5,000 years of creativity through paintings, sculptures, textiles, photo-graphs, cultural objects, and decorative artifacts. Founded by civic leaders and art patrons in 1879 as The Chicago

The Loop ⑩

The Loop gets its name from the elevated track system that circles the center of downtown. Screeching trains and a steady stream of people add to its bustle. In the canyon vistas, through the historic buildings and modern edifices, you can catch glimpses of the bridges spanning the Chicago River. The renovation of warehouses and historic theaters is helping to enliven the Loop at night.

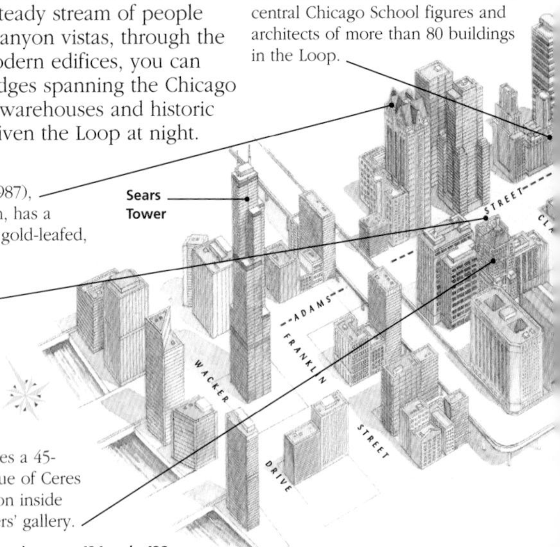

Marquette Building, an early skyscraper (1895), was designed by William Holabird and Martin Roche, central Chicago School figures and architects of more than 80 buildings in the Loop.

190 South LaSalle Street (1987), designed by Philip Johnson, has a white-marble lobby with a gold-leafed, vaulted ceiling.

The Rookery, designed by Burnham and Root in 1888, typifies the Richardsonian Romansque style.

Chicago Board of Trade occupies a 45-story Art Deco building, a statue of Ceres atop its roof. The frenetic action inside can be observed from a viewers' gallery.

For hotels and restaurants in this region see p424 and p428

Academy of Fine Arts, the museum became The Art Institute of Chicago in 1882. Outgrowing two homes as wealthy patrons donated their art collections, it finally settled in this Neo-Classical structure. The addition of the Modern Wing in 2009 made this the second largest museum in the United States.

The museum's holdings span from 3rd millennium BC Egyptian and Chinese artifacts to modern and contemporary American and European art. Though best known for its world famous Impressionist and Post-Impressionist collection with such masterpieces as Paul Cézanne's *The Basket of Apples* (c.1895), Henri de Toulouse-Lautrec's *At the Moulin Rouge* (1895), and Claude Monet's six versions of a wheat field, the museum represents almost every major artistic movement of the 19th and 20th centuries. Particularly strong are examples of Cubism, Surrealism, and German Expressionism.

The 35,000-strong exquisite Asian collection is also noteworthy for its Japanese woodblock prints, and Indian and Chinese historic artifacts.

Willis Tower ⑨

Map C4. 233 S Wacker Dr. **Observatory *Tel*** *(312) 875-9696.* *Quincy.* *7, 126.* *Apr–Sep: 10am–10pm daily; Oct–Mar: 10am–8pm daily; last adm 30 min before closing.* *(children under 3 free).*
www.theskydeck.com

At a height of 1,450 ft (442 m) Willis Tower (formerly known as the Sears Tower) is one of the world's tallest buildings. Boasting the highest occupied floor and the highest height to the rooftop, it was designed by Bruce Graham, of Skidmore Owings and Merrill, and engineer Fazlur Khan. Over 110 concrete caissons, anchored in bedrock, support the tower's 222,500 tons.

Today, the tower contains 3.5 million sq ft (0.3 million sq m) of office space, more than 100 elevators, and almost enough telephone cable to circle the Earth twice. The elevator to the glass-enclosed 103rd-floor Skydeck travels at 1,600 ft (490 m) per minute, and offers stunning views. Nearby, the 12-story **Rookery** building, the world's tallest when it opened in 1888, is one of the city's most photographed edifices. Its dark red-brick façade with terra-cotta trim gives way to a two-tiered court, remodeled in 1907 by Frank Lloyd Wright, who was nearing the peak of his fame. He covered the iron columns and staircases with white marble, inlaid with gold leaf.

View of the Sears Tower and Skydeck, looking northeast

The Rookery
209 S LaSalle St.
for tours, call Chicago Architectural Foundation, (312) 922-3432. *public hols.*

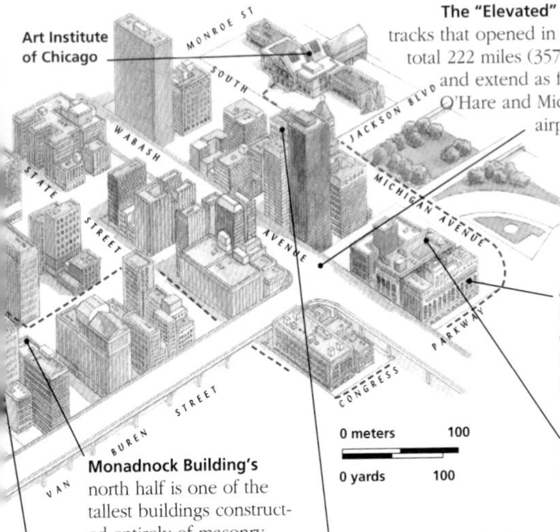

Art Institute of Chicago

The "Elevated" train tracks that opened in 1892 total 222 miles (357 km) and extend as far as O'Hare and Midway airports.

Auditorium Building, an 1889 multipurpose skyscraper, features one of Adler and Sullivan's best interiors in its seventh-floor, birch-paneled recital hall.

Monadnock Building's north half is one of the tallest buildings constructed entirely of masonry.

Fine Arts Building, designed by Solon S. Beman in 1885, was originally a wagon carriage showroom. It once also housed Frank Lloyd Wright's studio.

Santa Fe Center, a classic Chicago School building, with an elegant two-story atrium, houses the Chicago Architecture Foundation.

Federal Center is a three-building office complex designed around a central plaza by Ludwig Mies van der Rohe.

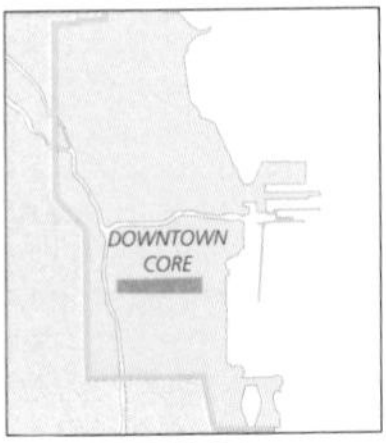

LOCATOR MAP

KEY
– – – – Suggested route

Rowe Building, Printing House Row District

South Loop ⑪

Map D4. *M Harrison, Roosevelt. via State St & Dearborn St buses (near South Side: Michigan Ave bus 3).*

Located a short walk south of the downtown core, the South Loop has changed dramatically in recent decades, from a run-down industrial district to a residential and retail neighborhood. The South Loop developed as an industrial area in the late 1800s, but after World War II, manufacturers left and the area declined. In the 1970s, with the conversion of the district's derelict warehouses to fashionable lofts, businesses sprang up as Chicagoans took advantage of the area's proximity to downtown.

This transformation is most evident in the two blocks of the **Printing House Row Historic District**, which in the 1890s had earned Chicago the title of the printing capital of the US. By the 1970s, with the closing of the nearby Dearborn Station, manufacturers withdrew and the area fell into decline. Many of the massive buildings erected for the printing trade remain today. Their conversion into stylish condominiums and office lofts has led to the revitalization of the neighborhood and an influx of commercial activity.

The Second Franklin Building has ornamental tilework illustrating the history of printing over its entranceway, while the Rowe Building houses Sandmeyer's bookstore specializing in local authors and travel literature. The nearby Richardsonian Romansque-style **Dearborn Station Galleria**, Chicago's oldest surviving passenger train station building, has also been converted into a shopping mall. Its square clock tower is a landmark. Dominating the South Loop, at State and Congress, is the world's largest public library building, the **Chicago Public Library, Harold Washington Library Center**, holding close to 9 million books and periodicals on its 70 miles (113 km) of shelving. This Post-Modern giant pays tribute to many of Chicago's historic buildings, through its varied architectural features. Artwork is displayed throughout the building, including work by Cheyenne artist Heap of Birds. The library also showcases exhibits relating to Chicago's history.

To the southeast, the **Museum of Contemporary Photography** focuses on American photography produced since 1936, with selections from its 7,000-strong collection and temporary exhibitions. On the same block, the **Spertus Museum** is Chicago's Jewish Museum. It is part of the Spertus Institute of Jewish Studies, which moved into a new facility in 2007. The museum invites visitors to learn about the Jewish experience through a series of thought-provoking exhibitions and programs on Jewish history, religion, art, and culture, over the centuries and today. Often these exhibitions draw from Spertus' own world-class collection of art and artifacts, including ritual objects, textiles and jewelry.

A computer lists the names of people lost in the Holocaust by Chicago families – it takes a full day to read the list – and an exhibition is geared to teaching young people about it.

The Asher Library, on the fifth floor, is the largest public Jewish library in the central US, with over 110,000 books and 1,000 Jewish films on video and DVD. A new and interactive Children's Center promotes literacy and storytelling.

A short walk east leads to Grant Park's Buckingham Fountain and **South Michigan Avenue**, one of Chicago's finest streets. Featuring a spectacular row of historic buildings, it is an excellent place to admire the varied architectural styles for which the city is famous. Farther along the street lies the opulent Hilton Chicago. Decorated in French Renaissance style, this 25-story hotel was the largest in the world when it opened in 1927. Across the street Buddy Guy's Legends presents big-names and local blues acts. Owner and blues legend Buddy Guy is often there himself.

Judaic art showcased in the Spertus Museum

Chicago Public Library, Harold Washington Library Center
400 S State St. ***Tel*** *(312) 747-4300.* *M Library. 9am–9pm Mon–Thu, 9am–5pm Fri–Sat, 1–5pm Sun. public hols. call (312) 747-4050.* ***Exhibits, lectures, films.*** **www**.chipublib.org

Spertus Museum
610 S Michigan Ave. ***Tel*** *(312) 322-1700. M Harrison. 10am–5pm Sun–Wed, 10am–6pm Thu, 10am–3pm Fri. Sat, public & Jewish hols. (children under 5 free; all get in free 10am–noon Wed, 2–6pm Thu).* ***Concerts, lectures, films.*** **www**.spertus.edu

For hotels and restaurants in this region see p424 and p428

Museum Campus ⑫

Map E5. S Lake Shore Dr. **M** *Roosevelt then free trolley.* 🚌 *12, 146.* 🚆 *Roosevelt then free trolley.*

The Museum Campus is a vast lakefront park connecting three world-famous natural science museums. This 57-acre (23-ha) extension of Burnham Park was created by the relocation of Lake Shore Drive in 1996.

Located in the southwest part of the lush green campus is the Daniel Burnham-designed Neo-Classical structure housing the **Field Museum**. This great natural history museum holds an encyclopedic collection of zoological, geological, and anthropological objects from around the world. Founded in 1894 (with funding from Marshall Field) to house objects from the 1893 World's Columbian Exposition, the museum now holds over 20 million objects.

Xochpilli, Aztec God of Flowers, Field Museum

Particular strengths of the museum include such dinosaur fossils as "Sue" – the most complete *Tyrannosaurus rex* skeleton ever found, Native Indian and Ancient Egyptian artifacts, and extensive displays on mammals and birds.

The permanent "Ancient Americas" exhibit covers Ice Age to Aztec cultures. The Hall of Jades displays more than 500 artifacts from Neolithic times to the Bronze Age and Chinese Dynasties. The highlight is a 300 lb (136 kg) jar from the palace of Emperor Quanlong. The Underground Adventure is a subterranean exhibit where visitors can walk through worm tunnels, meet giant bugs, and feel reduced to insect size.

The monumental Neo-Classical entrance to Field Museum

A short walk northeast along terraced gardens leads to the **John G. Shedd Aquarium**, housing nearly 8,000 saltwater and freshwater animals, representing 650 species of fish, birds, reptiles, amphibians, invertebrates, and mammals. Named for its benefactor, a prominent Chicago businessman, the aquarium opened in 1930 in a Neo-Classical building. The remodeled Oceanarium has a magnificent curved wall of glass facing Lake Michigan, whose water flows into its tank. This marine-mammal pavilion showcases beluga whales and dolphins. The aquarium's exhibits can be viewed from many viewpoints, some under water.

Farther east, the Museum Campus houses the **Adler Planetarium and Astronomy Museum** featuring one of the world's finest astronomical collections, with artifacts dating as far back as 12th-century Persia. It also has the world's first virtual-reality theater. Spectacular sky shows complement displays on navigation and space exploration. State-of-the-art technology enables visitors to explore exhibits hands-on. Funded by businessman Max Adler, this 12-sided, Art Deco structure was designed by Ernest Grunsfeld in 1930 and is now a historical landmark.

Beluga whale at the Oceanarium in the John G. Shedd Aquarium

Field Museum
1400 S Lake Shore Dr. (312) 922-9410. *10am–5pm daily (from 11am Sun). Dec 25. via east entrance. 11am, 2pm Mon–Fri.* ***Lectures, films, events.*** **www**.fieldmuseum.org

John G. Shedd Aquarium
1200 S Lake Shore Dr. ***Tel*** *(312) 939-2438. Memorial Day–Labor Day: 9am–6pm daily (Jun–Aug: 9am–10pm Thu, Oceanarium 9am–8pm Thu); Labor Day–Memorial Day: 9am–5pm Mon–Fri; 9am–6pm Sat, Sun, public hols. Dec 25. (free Sep–Feb: Mon & Tue; except special exhibits).* ***Lectures.*** **www**.shedd.org

Adler Planetarium & Astronomy Museum
1300 S Lake Shore Dr. ***Tel*** *(312) 922-7827. 9:30am–4pm daily (to 4:30pm Sat & Sun; 9:30am–10pm 1st Fri of each month). Thanksgiving, Dec 25. separate adm to theaters.* ***Lectures, films, light shows.*** **www**.adlerplanetarium.org

OLD MONEY

Potter Palmer

Chicago has a beautiful sound because Chicago means money – so the late actress Ruth Gordon reputedly said. By the beginning of the 20th century the city was home to 200 millionaires. One of the most prominent was dry-goods merchant and real-estate mogul Potter Palmer who, with his socialite wife Bertha Honoré, had an enormous impact on the city's cultural and economic life. In 1882, Palmer built an opulent home at North Lake Shore Drive. Perhaps no feature of the mansion epitomized the family's wealth as much as the doors: there were no outside handles, as the doors were always opened from inside, by servants. Department-store owner Marshall Field was less ostentatious. Although he rode in a carriage to work, he stopped short of his store to walk the last few blocks so people would not see his mode of transport. Likewise, he asked the architect of his $2-million, 25-room mansion not to include any frills.

View of the Museum of Science and Industry from across Columbia Basin

Museum of Science & Industry ⑬

Map B5. 57th St & S Lake Shore Dr. ***Tel*** *(773) 684-1414, (800) 468-6674.* *Garfield then eastbound bus 55.* *1, 6, 10.* *55th-56th-57th St, 59th St.* *9:30am–4pm Mon–Sat, 11am–4pm Sun.* *Dec 25.* *(free Jan & other occasional days).* ***Films.*** **www**.msichicago.org

The Museum of Science and Industry celebrates scientific and technological accomplishments, with an emphasis on achievements of the 20th and 21st centuries. With its collection of over 800 exhibits and 2,000 interactive displays, the museum makes the exploration of science and technology an accesssible experience.

Though best known for its exhibits on space exploration, biology, and transportation, this largest science museum in the Western Hemisphere has more than enough to keep visitors of all ages engaged for a full day.

The **Henry Crown Space Center** features the Apollo 8 Command Module, the first manned spacecraft to circle the moon, in 1968, a replica of NASA's Apollo Lunar Module Trainer, and a 6.5-oz (185-gm) piece of moon rock. A 20-minute movie simulates the experience of blasting off in a space shuttle, complete with shaking seats, allowing viewers to feel like astronauts, if only briefly.

The transportation section features outstanding examples of transport from train and plane to automobile. In **All Aboard the Silver Streak** visitors can climb aboard a record-breaking 1930s train that revolutionized industrial design. One of the most popular exhibits, **Take Flight** explores the inner workings of a 727 jetliner, cantilevered to the museum's balcony, and simulates a seven-minute San Francisco-to-Chicago flight.

Visitors can walk through a 16-ft (5-m) tall replica of the human heart, seeing it from the perspective of a blood cell, and calculate the number of times their heart has beaten since birth, or look inside the human body in a detailed exhibit on anatomy. **Genetics: Decoding Life** explores the ethical, biological, and social issues of this field of research.

A few exhibits fall outside the museum's defined focus but prove to be enduring crowd pleasers, such as a toy factory staffed by robots, and the five-story, wraparound Omnimax theater.

FROM PLASTER TO STONE

Originally built as the Palace of Fine Arts for the 1893 World's Fair, this structure later became the first home of the Field Museum of Natural History. Based on Classical Revival style, this plaster-clad building was designed by Charles B. Atwood. After the Field Museum moved out, the building sat in a state of disrepair until the mid-1920s, when Julius Rosenwald, chairman of Sears Roebuck and Co., campaigned to save it, launching a million-dollar reconstruction program. Exterior plaster was replaced with 28,000 tons of limestone and marble in an 11-year renovation. The Museum of Science and Industry opened in 1933, in time for the Century of Progress World's Exposition.

The original building during the 1893 World's Columbian Exposition

University of Chicago ⑭

Map A5. Bounded by 56th & 59th Sts, Ellis & Woodlawn Aves. *Garfield (green line) then bus 55.* *59th.*

The University of Chicago, was founded in 1890 with the endowment of John D. Rockefeller, on land donated by Marshall Field *(see p393).* Today, this outstanding private university has one of the greatest number of Nobel laureates among faculty, alumni, and researchers of any US university. It is particularly lauded in the fields of economics, chemistry, and physics. Henry Ives Cobb designed 18 of the university's limestone buildings

The Rockefeller Memorial Chapel, University of Chicago

For hotels and restaurants in this region see p424 and p428

Robie House, a masterpiece of the Prairie School of architecture

and developed its cloistered quadrangle plan (along the lines of Cambridge and Oxford), before the Boston firm Shepley Rutan and Coolidge took over as the main architects in 1901. Now the campus features designs from more than 70 architects.

The north entrance houses the ornamental Cobb Gate, a gargoyled ceremonial gateway donated by Henry Cobb in 1900. Across the street, the Regenstein Library holds rare book and manuscript collections, along with millions of other volumes.

Situated at the northern end of the campus is the light-filled, intimate **Smart Museum of Art**. Named after its benefactors, David and Alfred Smart, the museum holds more than 10,000 objects, including antiquities and Old Master prints, Asian paintings, calligraphies, and ceramics, spanning five centuries of Western and Eastern civilizations. The museum's café, with tall windows overlooking the tranquil sculpture garden, is a great spot for a quiet lunch. Outside the museum, sculptor Henry Moore's *Nuclear Energy*, marks the spot where, in 1942, a team of scientists led by Enrico Fermi ushered in the atomic age with the first controlled nuclear reaction.

In the southeast of the vast campus lies the **Oriental Institute Museum**, the exhibition arm of the university's Oriental Institute, whose scholars have excavated in virtually every region of the Near East since 1919. Highlights of the museum's collections include a reconstruction of an Assyrian palace (c.721–705 BC) and a 17-ft (5-m) sculpture of King Tutankhamen, the tallest ancient Egyptian statue in the Western Hemisphere (c.1334–25 BC). Opposite the museum, the massive Gothic-style **Rockefeller Memorial Chapel**, topped with a 207-ft (63-m) carillon tower, is the tallest building on campus. John D. Rockefeller had requested that this limestone-and-brick structure representing religion be the university's most dominant feature. Two blocks north lies Frank Lloyd Wright's world-famous **Robie House** (1908–1910), currently being restored. Designed for Frederick Robie, a bicycle and motorbike manufacturer, the home is one of Wright's last Prairie School houses: Wright left both his family and his Oak Park practice during its three-year construction. The exterior design of the house perfectly captures the prairie landscape of flat, open fields. The roof's sweeping planes embody the house's aesthetic of bold rectilinear simplicity. Steel beams support the overhanging roof. Also bold but simple, the interior is furnished with Wright-designed furniture. The house is an organic whole, underscored by the harmonious interplay between the exterior and interior.

Statue of King Tutankhamen, Oriental Institute Museum

Smart Museum of Art
5550 S Greenwood Ave. ***Tel*** *(773) 702-0200.* *10am–4pm Tue–Fri (until 8pm Thu), 11am–5pm Sat, Sun.* *public hols.*
www.smart-museum.uchicago.edu

Oriental Institute Museum
1155 E 58th St. ***Tel*** *(773) 702-9514.* *10am–6pm Tue & Thu–Sat (until 8:30pm Wed), noon–6pm Sun.* *public hols.* ***Special events***. **www**.oi.chicago.edu

Robie House
5757 S Woodlawn Ave.
Tel *(773) 834-1847.* *daily.* *Jan 1, Thanksgiving, Dec 25.* *(children under 4 free).* *mandatory: 11am, 1pm, 3pm Mon–Fri; noon Sat.*
www.wrightplus.org;
www.oi.uchicago.edu

DuSable Museum of African American History ⑮

Map A5. 740 E 56th Pl. ***Tel*** *(773) 947-0600.* *Garfield (green line) then bus 55.* *4, 10.* *10am–5pm Tue–Sat, noon–5pm Sun.* *public hols.* *(children under 6 free; free on Sun).* *book in advance.* ***Lectures, films.***
www.dusablemuseum.org

Founded in 1961 to preserve and interpret the diverse historical experiences and achievements of African Americans, the DuSable Museum highlights the accomplishments of the ordinary and extraordinary alike.

The museum's permanent exhibit, **Songs of My People**, brings together diverse images by Black photojournalists of African-American lives. Other exhibits include memorabilia from the life and political career of Chicago's first Black mayor, Harold Washington. The museum showcases local artwork, and traveling show topics have included black film history and African Americans on postage stamps.

Greater Chicago

Visitors eager to discover more of Chicago will not be disappointed by the rich mix of historical sights, recreational activities, and picturesque suburbs that the city's outlying areas have to offer. For lovers of architecture, Oak Park is a must-see for its Frank Lloyd Wright designs. Other Chicago neighborhoods, such as Wicker Park and Lakeview are ideal day-trip destinations. The vast expanse of Lincoln Park offers a respite from the bustle of the city in its lush gardens, flowering plants, and a zoo, famed for its naturalistic animal habitats.

A lowland gorilla at the zoo's Regenstein Center for African Apes

Lincoln Park Zoo ⑯

2200 N Cannon Dr. **Tel** *(312) 742-2000.* *Clark/Division.* *22, 36, 135, 136, 145, 146, 147, 151, 156.* *9am–6pm daily (Nov–Mar: 9am–5pm).* *on N Cannon Dr.* **Workshops, Special events www**.lpzoo.com

Located in the heart of Lincoln Park, this zoo is easily accessible from downtown. Established in 1868 with the gift of two swans from New York's Central Park, Lincoln Park Zoo is the country's oldest free public zoo. Today, more than 1,000 mammals, reptiles, and birds from around the world live here in realistic habitats. A world leader in wildlife conservation, the zoo shelters such animals as the threatened Grevy's zebra from Africa and the endangered Bactrian camel from Mongolia, as well as rare gazelles, deer, antelopes, and alpacas in its 11 outdoor habitats. A 1912 historic building houses rare cats, including Amur tigers. The zoo's large collection of lowland gorillas bears testimony to a successful breeding program. A working farm with cows, horses, pigs, and chickens, is popular with kids for the daily milking demonstrations.

Lincoln Park, Chicago's largest, offers walking and biking paths that wind along paddle-boating ponds, lagoons, and sandy beaches.

Frank Lloyd Wright's Home and Studio, Oak Park

Oak Park ⑰

Bounded by North Ave, Roosevelt Rd, Austin Blvd, & Harlem Ave. *(708) 848-1500.* *Oak Park (green line); Harlem/Lake (green line).* *Oak Park (Union Pacific/ West line).* **Visitor Center** 158 N Forest Ave. *10am–3:30pm Mon–Fri, 11am–3:30pm Sat–Sun.* *Jan 1, Thanksg., Dec 25.* **Frank Lloyd Wright Preservation Trust** 931 Chicago Ave. ***Tel*** *(708) 848-1976.* **www**.wrightplus.org, **www**.visitoakpark.com

Frank Lloyd Wright moved to Oak Park in 1889, at the age of 22. During the next 20 years here, he created many groundbreaking buildings as his legendary Prairie School style evolved. This tranquil community is now home to 25 Wright buildings – the largest grouping of his work anywhere. The best place to feast on Wright's achievement is the superbly restored **Frank Lloyd Wright Home and**

Pink flamingos in the Waterfowl Lagoon at Lincoln Park Zoo

For hotels and restaurants in this region see p424 and p428

Unity Temple, Frank Lloyd Wright's "little jewel," Oak Park

Studio, designed by Wright in 1889. This was also where he developed his influential architectural style.

Nearby are two private homes that reveal Wright's versatility. The 1902 **Arthur Heurtley House** is typically Prairie style, with its row of windows spanning the low roofline, and a simple but elegant entrance arch. The 1895 **Moore-Dugal House** across the street, is a hybrid of styles, rich with Tudor Revival and Gothic elements.

At the southern end of Oak Park is the masterful **Pleasant Home**, a 30-room Prairie-style mansion designed in 1897 by George W. Maher. The house holds extraordinary art glass – designed panels of leaded glass. It also includes intricate woodwork, and decorative motifs, and a display on the area's history.

Wright was especially proud of **Unity Temple**, his design for the Unitarian Universalist Congregation. He called this church one of his most important designs, his first expression of an "entirely new architecture." It was built between 1906 and 1908, using a then-unusual technique of poured reinforced concrete, in part because of a budget of only $45,000. Unity Temple is a masterpiece of powerful simplicity wedded with functional ornamentation.

Oak Park is also famous as the birthplace of the famed US writer Ernest Hemingway (1899–1960), who lived here until the age of 20. Although Hemingway *(see p323)* rejected the conservative mindset of this Chicago suburb saying it was full of "wide lawns and narrow minds," Oak Park continues to pride itself on its literary association. The **Ernest Hemingway Birthplace**, a grand Victorian home decorated with turn-of-the-20th-century furnishings, has displays on this Nobel Prize-winner's life. The **Ernest Hemingway Museum**, features several artifacts from Hemingway's early life.

The Victorian house in which Ernest Hemingway was born

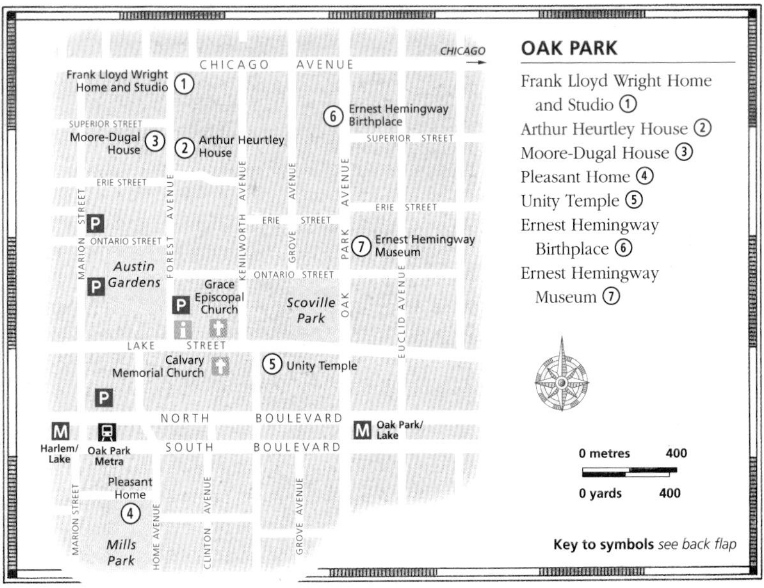

Illinois

Except for the densely populated area around Chicago *(see pp386–97)*, Illinois is a predominantly rural state. Large expanses of rich, flat farmland are dotted with the occasional small agricultural community or county seat. Known as the "Land of Lincoln," most of the sites related to the president are concentrated in Springfield, the heart of the state. Some rather unusual and picturesque scenery can be found in the hilly "Driftless Region" along the Mississippi in the northwest, and in the rugged "Illinois Ozarks" in the southeast.

Statue of Sac hero Black Hawk, southwest of Rockford

Rockford ❷

150,000. *102 N Main St, (800) 521-0849.* **www**.gorockford.com

Dubbed the Forest City in the late 1800s, Rockford today has beautiful public and private gardens and miles of parkland along the Rock River, which bisects the city. Of its two most-visited gardens, the **Klehm Arboretum and Botanic Garden** contains 150 acres (61 ha) of plants. The other, the **Sinnissippi Gardens**, runs south along the Rock River's east bank. Its features include an aviary, lagoon, and recreation path. The path offers views of downtown's historic buildings, including the restored Coronado Theater, a gilded 1927 Moorish movie palace.

On the town's east side, the **Midway Village and Museum Center** is both a living history center and local history museum. Exhibits tell the story of ethnic groups who flocked to the city's factories. The grounds have been turned into a 19th-century village, with restored buildings from the area.

The growth of Rockford followed the tragic 1830s Blackhawk War between the Sac Indians of northern Illinois and the US Army, determined to displace the tribes from their farmlands. After the Sacs lost, they were relocated to Iowa. A stone statue of the Sac warrior Chief Blackhawk is located 27 miles (43 km) southwest of Rockford.

Klehm Arboretum & Botanic Garden
2715 S Main St. ***Tel*** *(815) 965-8146.* *9am–4pm daily; Memorial Day–Labor Day: 9am–8pm daily.* **www**.klehm.org

Sinnissippi Gardens
1300 N 2nd St. ***Tel*** *(815) 987-8858.* **Greenhouse** *Apr–Nov: 9am–4pm Tue–Sun.* *Thanksgiving, Dec–Mar.* **www**.rockfordparkdistrict.org

Galena ❸

3,600. *101 Bouthillier, (877) 464-2536.* **www**.galena.org

Perched on a bluff overlooking the Galena River near its confluence with the Mississippi, this immaculately preserved town is a relaxing tourist destination with 19th-century homes, historical landmarks, and antique shops. Its status as the shipping center for the region's many lead mines made Galena the busiest Mississippi River Valley port between St. Louis and St. Paul in the 1840s.

The town's population peaked at 15,000 during the Civil War, when the elite erected many magnificent homes in a wide variety of ornate styles.

Many of Galena's historic homes are now open to visitors. **The Belvedere Mansion**, built in 1857 by a local steamboat owner, is a 22-room Italianate structure with a varied collection of period furnishings and some quaint recent additions, including the draperies from the *Gone with the Wind* movie set. Civil War general and US president Ulysses S. Grant lived quietly in Galena, between the signature events of his military career and time in the White House. His small, Federal-style 1860 home contains many of Grant's original possessions and furnishings.

The Galena/Jo Daviess County History Museum chronicles Galena's lead mining and Civil War shipping days. Informative one-hour walking tours of Main Street begin at 10am on Saturdays from May through to October.

The Belvedere Mansion
1008 Park Ave.
Tel *(815) 777-0747.* *mid-May–late Oct: 11am–4pm.*

Galena/Jo Daviess County History Museum
211 S Bench St. ***Tel*** *(815) 777-9129.* *9am–4:30pm daily.* *Jan 1, Easter, Thanksgiving, Dec 24, 25, 31.* **www**.galenahistorymuseum.org

A view of Galena with its historic landmarks

Cozy Dog Drive-in, a popular Route 66 café

Springfield 4

111,000.
109 N 7th St, (800) 545-7300.
www.visit-springfieldillinois.com

The state capital since 1837, Springfield gained fame as the adopted hometown of 16th US president, Abraham Lincoln, who lived here for 24 years before assuming the presidency in 1861. The **Abraham Lincoln Presidential Library and Museum** is full of artifacts, interactive displays, and special-effect theaters. The four-block **Lincoln Home National Historic Site** is a pedestrian-only historic district, with restored 19th-century homes, gaslights, and wooden sidewalks surrounding the neat frame house where Lincoln and his wife, Mary, lived for 16 years.

An on-site visitor center provides details about the city's other Lincoln-related attractions, including his law office, tomb, and the 1853 **Old State Capitol**. It was here that he delivered his famous 1858 "House Divided" speech, outlining the sectional differences that would soon plunge the nation into the Civil War. Lincoln's political career began in 1834, when he was elected to the Illinois General Assembly.

The town's other attraction is the elegant **Dana-Thomas House**, a 1904 Prairie-style home designed by Frank Lloyd Wright *(see p396)*. It contains much of Wright's original white oak furniture, light fixtures, art-glass doors, windows, and light panels. Many Wright experts consider this to be the best-preserved of the houses designed by the famous architect.

Springfield is also rich in Route 66 lore *(see pp40–41)*. The old road follows a clearly marked path through the city, leading to the southside **Cozy Dog Drive-in**, a legendary Route 66 eatery, which claims to have invented the corn-dog. The café's Route 66 Museum and its trademark "cozy dogs," still available at rock-bottom prices, make it a popular tourist destination (closed on Sunday).

Lincoln Home National Historic Site
413 S 8th St. **Tel** *(217) 391-3226.*
8:30 am–5pm daily. *Jan 1, Thanksgiving, Dec 25.*
www.nps.gov/liho

Old State Capitol
5th & Adams Sts, Springfield.
Tel *(217) 785-7960.* *9am–5pm Tue–Sat.* *public hols.*
www.illinois-history.gov

Southern Illinois 5

14967 Gun Creek Trail, Whittington, (888) 998-9397.
www.adventureillinois.com

In Southern Illinois, flat farmlands give way to rolling hills and forests along the Mississippi and Ohio Rivers. This terrain provided strategic vantage points from which Native Americans and, later, French traders and missionaries could monitor river traffic.

Near the confluence of the Mississippi, Missouri, and Illinois Rivers (90 miles/145 km southwest of Springfield) are the remains of the largest prehistoric Native American city north of Mexico. The **Cahokia Mounds State Historic and World Heritage Site** contains more than 100 earthen mounds dating from 1050–1250, when 15,000 people of the Mississippian culture are estimated to have occupied the city. The flat-topped Monks Mound covers 14 acres (6 ha) and rises, in four terraces, to a height of 100 ft (30 m), providing sweeping views of the nearby river valleys and the Gateway Arch *(see p454)*, about 12 miles (19 km) away in downtown St. Louis. The site's interpretive center recounts the fascinating story of these mounds, which were mysteriously abandoned by around 1500.

Further evidence of Native American habitation is abundant in the rugged, unglaciated "Illinois Ozarks," or "Little Egypt" region, where the Ohio River separates the state from Kentucky. The forested ridges and hollows of the sprawling **Shawnee National Forest** can be viewed most dramatically at the Garden of the Gods, a rocky outcropping marked by sandstone towers, boulders, and strangely shaped rocks.

Cahokia Mounds State Historic Site
30 Ramey Dr, Collinsville. **Tel** *(618) 346-5160.* *8am–sunset daily.*
Visitor Center *9am–5pm daily.* *public hols.*
www.cahokiamounds.com

Grass-covered mounds in the Cahokia Mounds State Historic Site

Indiana

Unlike the other states of the Great Lakes region, Indiana has only a short, 45-mile (72-km) stretch of shoreline along Lake Michigan. As a result, the state's history has centered on its extensive river systems – the Maumee/Wabash in the north, and the Ohio in the south – and the development of the railroads and highways that linked Indiana to key Midwestern and Eastern markets. Indiana today is an engaging place to explore by car, especially along its hilly Ohio River backroads and Amish-country scenic lanes.

New Harmony ❻

900. Atheneum, North & Arthur Sts, (800) 231-2168. **www**.newharmony.org

America's two most successful utopian communities flourished in this neat village on the eastern banks of the Wabash River. The first, the Harmonie Society, was founded by a Pennsylvania-based German Lutheran separatist group in 1814. The sect followed a doctrine of perfectionism and celibacy in anticipation of the second coming of Christ, focusing on the development of profitable agricultural and manufacturing enterprises.

In 1825, the Harmonists returned to Pennsylvania, after selling the town and the surrounding lands to Scottish textile magnate Robert Owen. The latter, too, sought to create an ideal society based on free education and the abolition of social classes and personal property ownership. The colony failed after two years, but Owen's sons, David and Robert, pursued their father's ideas and later established the Smithsonian Institution in Washington, DC.

The tree-lined town is now a State Historic Site with 25 well-preserved Harmonist buildings, an inn, and many beautiful manicured gardens. These include the reconstructed Labyrinth, a maze-like set of hedges arranged in concentric circles around a stone temple that stands at the center.

Historic New Harmony
410 Main St. ***Tel*** *(812) 682-4488. Mar–Dec daily, call for times.*

Monroe County Courthouse, Bloomington, a Beaux Arts building

Bloomington ❼

70,000. 2855 N Walnut St, (800) 800-0037. **www**.visitbloomington.com

Surrounded by rugged limestone outcrops, this city is home to the leafy Indiana University campus. Quarrying of the limestone deposits fueled Bloomington's 19th-century growth, the results of which can still be seen in the city's magnificent public buildings. A prime example is the 1906 Beaux Arts **Monroe County Courthouse**, at the center of the Courthouse Square Historic District located downtown.

On the campus are a variety of historic buildings and outdoor spaces. The 1941 Auditorium displays 20 panels of Thomas Hart Benton's controversial 1933 mural, *The Social and Industrial History of Indiana*, which ironically relates several key events of the state's history. The Tibetan Cultural Center is the only one in the U.S. and is a haven for meditation. The **Indiana University Art Center** was designed by architect I.M. Pei. It includes works by Henri Matisse, Claude Monet, Auguste Rodin, and Andy Warhol, as well as Picasso's 1934 *L'Atelier (The Studio)*.

Indiana University Art Center
1133 E 7th St. ***Tel*** *(812) 855-5445. 10am–5pm Tue–Sat, noon–5pm Sun. public hols.* **www**.artmuseum.iu.edu

Indiana Dunes National Lakeshore ❽

Dorothy Buell Memorial Visitor Center, Hwy 20 & Hwy 49. ***Tel*** *(219) 926-7561. 8:30am–4:30pm daily (to 6pm in summer). Jan 1, Thanksgiving, Dec 25.* **www**.nps.gov/indu

One of the nation's most diverse groups of ecosystems is contained within the 15,000-acre (6,070-ha) Indiana Dunes National Lakeshore. Only a 30-minute drive from downtown Chicago, this stunning refuge is located along the 25-mile (40-km) stretch of the Lake Michigan shore. Its ecosystems include bogs, swamps, marshes, glacial moraines, prairies, forests, oak savannas, and dunes linked by scenic roads and a network of hiking and biking trails. Home to a dizzying variety of native plant species, the park is also

Deer at the Indiana Dunes National Lakeshore

For hotels and restaurants in this region see p425 and p429

known as a bird-watcher's paradise as herons, cardinals, kingfishers, and towhees are frequently spotted here.

South Bend 9

107,789. 401 *E Colfax Ave, (800) 519-0577.* **www**.exploresouthbend.org

South Bend is widely known today as the home of the Roman Catholic **University of Notre Dame**. The 11,400-student institution was established in 1842 by Father Edward Sorin, a priest from the Congregation of the Holy Cross.

While religion is still important, the students and countless alumni are equally passionate about the Notre Dame "Fighting Irish" football team, one of the most successful in college football history. In fact, one of the most famous sculptures at the art-filled campus is a large mural of Christ known as *The Word of Life* that students call "Touchdown Jesus."

The **College Football Hall of Fame** relates the history of such legends as coaches Knute Rockne and Ara Parseghian, and players George Gipp, Paul Hornung, and Joe Montana. Extensive displays are enlivened by areas to test your own level of physical fitness and skill in passing, blocking, and kicking. A 360-degree theater literally surrounds visitors with its range of historical film and video highlights.

South of downtown, the **Studebaker National Museum** contains the horse-drawn carriages and early automobiles manufactured by the town's now-defunct Studebaker corporation. The collection includes the carriage in which President Lincoln rode to Ford's Theatre the night he was assassinated in Washington, DC, and a 1909 backward-forward automobile that shuttled US senators between their offices and the Capitol.

"Touchdown Jesus" mural at Notre Dame, South Bend

College Football Hall of Fame
111 S St Joseph. ***Tel*** *(800) 440-3263. 10am–5pm. Jan 1, Thanksg., Dec 25.* **www**.collegefootball.org

Shipshewana 10

525. *780 S Van Buren St, (800) 254-8090.* **www**.backroads.org

This small village, nestled in the rolling farmlands of northeastern Indiana, has one of the world's largest Amish communities *(see p109)*. The town's **Menno-Hof Mennonite Anabaptist Interpretive Center** provides a detailed background on the European Anabaptist movement, which gave rise to the Mennonite, Hutterite, and Amish sects. Religious persecution in the 19th century led to the large-scale immigration of Anabaptists to the US and Canada. Exhibits at the center re-create this dark period as well as examining the sects and their lifestyles as they are today.

Amish horse-drawn carriage

Local Amish farmers, with their distinctive black hats, white shirts, and black suits, riding horse-drawn buggies, are frequent sights in Shipshewana and the surrounding villages of Bristol, Elkhart, Goshen, Middlebury, Nappanee, and Wakarusa. Tourists come to the villages in search of furniture, dairy, baked goods, and quilts.

Menno-Hof Mennonite Anabaptist Interpretive Center
510 S Van Buren St. ***Tel*** *(260) 768-4117. Apr–Dec: 10am–5pm Mon–Sat (Jun–Aug: to 7pm Tue–Sat). Jan 1, Thanksgiving, Dec 25.* **www**.mennohof.org

Fort Wayne 11

206,000. *1021 S Calhoun St, (800) 767-7752.* **www**.visitfortwayne.com

Fort Wayne's location at the confluence of the St. Mary's, St. Joseph, and Maumee Rivers made it a strategic site for the Native Americans, French fur traders, British armies, and American settlers who sought to control the access to the Great Lakes. The city's prosperity during the railroad era is exemplified in the fascinating downtown Allen County Courthouse, constructed in 1902.

Visitors use the Sky Safari to glide over treetops and animal quarters at the **Fort Wayne Children's Zoo**, which is the city's biggest attraction. An extensive array of Australian animals has earned accolades nationally, while the new African Journey brings visitors up close to a menagerie of lions, hyenas, mongooses, and other species found on the continent.

Fort Wayne Children's Zoo
3411 Sherman Blvd. ***Tel*** *(260) 427-6800. 9am–5pm daily Apr–Oct.* **www**.kidszoo.org

A view of the Allen County Courthouse in Fort Wayne

A view of the architecture of modern Indianapolis

Indianapolis ⓬

860, 500. 30 S Meridian St, (800) 323-4639.
www.indy.org

Known as "The Crossroads of America," Indianapolis is much more than a transportation hub where multiple railroads and Interstate highways intersect. The city's many parks and monuments, and vibrant in-town neighborhoods make it one of the region's most surprising and satisfying destinations.

Selected as the state capital in 1820, Indianapolis was laid out on the banks of the shallow White River, with a network of wide boulevards radiating outward from the central **Monument Circle**, which is dominated by the towering 1901 Beaux Arts obelisk, the Soldiers' and Sailors' Monument.

The city's first-rate museums and lively arts and theater scenes are complemented by an active interest in sports. Every Memorial Day, the world's largest, single-day sporting event – the Indianapolis 500 auto race – fills the **Indianapolis Motor Speedway** with nearly 500,000 fans. Built in 1909 as a 2.5-mile (4-km) test track for the city's then-burgeoning automotive industry, the speedway played host to the first Indy 500 in 1911. The race was the brainchild of Indianapolis auto parts manufacturer Carl Fisher, who later gained fame as the tireless promoter of the Lincoln Hwy (now US 30), the nation's first transcontinental highway, from New York to San Francisco. The track's Hall of Fame displays more than 75 racing cars and other Indy 500 memorabilia, in addition to examples of the Stutz, Cole, Marmon, National, and Duesenberg automobiles built in the city before the industry centralized in Detroit. Visitors can also take a guided test drive around the famous track.

The five-story **Children's Museum of Indianapolis**, which opened in 1976, has been consistently rated as one of the country's best and is the largest in the world. The museum's 11 galleries and over 100,000 artifacts are displayed in a manner that encourages hands-on, interactive exploration of the sciences, history, world cultures, and the arts. Among the many highlights here are an authentic Indy 500 race car, a restored carousel, and a dinosaur discovery exhibit, where children work along side practicing paleontologists to excavate ancient fossils.

The **Indiana State Museum** relocated in early 2002 to a facility west of downtown in White River State Park, a 250-acre (101-ha) urban oasis. The spacious building is constructed of locally sourced materials, including Indiana limestone, sandstone, brick, steel, extruded aluminum, and glass. Focusing on Indiana's natural and cultural history, the museum displays extensive exhibits on sports and the early days of radio in this predominantly rural state.

Display in the Indianapolis Motor Speedway Hall of Fame

Lockerbie Square District, northeast of downtown, is the city's oldest surviving 19th-century immigrant neighborhood. Immortalized in the poetry of resident James Whitcomb Riley (1849–1916), the square has attracted recent attention for the dogged efforts to preserve its modest workers' cottages and restore its cobblestone streets and period street lights. Riley's 1872 brick Italianate home is now a museum and National Historic Landmark.

Situated on the grounds of the Oldfields estate of local pharmaceutical pioneer, J.K. Lilly Jr, 5 miles (8 km) north of downtown, the **Indianapolis Museum of Art** houses a wide-ranging collection of American, European, Asian, and African art. Among the museum's more acclaimed holdings are Winslow Homer's *The Boat Builders*, Edward Hopper's *Hotel Lobby*, Georgia O'Keeffe's *Jimson Weed*, and many of Paul Gauguin's works from his 1886 visit to the French artists' colony of Pont-Aven.

The restored Oldfields-Lilly house and superb gardens, designed by Percival Gallagher of the famed Olmsted Brothers landscape architecture firm, have been carefully restored to their original 1920s grandeur. The house and gardens are open for tours.

The **Eiteljorg Museum of American Indians and Western Art**, west of downtown, has one of the most impressive collections of Native American and Western American art in the US. A 100-acre (40-ha) art and nature park has been developed. Established in

For hotels and restaurants in this region see p425 and p429

George Carlson's *The Greeting* (1989) outside Eiteljorg Museum

1989 by Harrison Eiteljorg, a successful Indianapolis businessman and art collector, the museum is housed in a Southwest-inspired adobe building, in deference to Eiteljorg's large collection of works from the early 20th-century Taos Society of Artists *(see p544)*, who incorporated Native American, Western American, and Hispanic themes into their work.

On view are paintings by such celebrated artists as Georgia O'Keeffe, Frederic Remington, and Charles M. Russell, whose *Indians Crossing the Plains* is a famous depiction of vanishing Native American culture on the late 19th-century Great Plains. Many Native American artifacts are also displayed.

Indianapolis Motor Speedway
Hall of Fame, 4790 W 16th St.
Tel *(317) 492-6784. 9am–5pm daily (extended hours in May).*
Dec 25.
www.brickyard.com

Indianapolis Museum of Art
4000 Michigan Rd.
Tel *(317) 920-2660. 11am–5pm Tue–Sat (until 9pm Thu, Fri), noon–5pm Sun. Jan 1, Thanksgiving, Dec 25. for special exhibits.*
www.imamuseum.org

Eiteljorg Museum of American Indians & Western Art
500 W Washington St.
Tel *(317) 636-9378. 10am–5pm Mon–Sat, noon–5pm Sun.*
Jan 1, Thanksgiving, Dec 25. (children under 5 free). 1pm daily. **www**.eiteljorg.org

Columbus ⑬

39,000. 506 5th St, (800) 468-6564. **www**.columbus.in.us

One of the world's most concentrated collections of modern architecture can be found in this small southern Indiana city. From 1942 on, after the completion of architect Eliel Saarinen's **First Christian Church**, Columbus garnered international attention for the more than 60 churches, schools, banks, and commercial and public buildings constructed here. Today, the city's commitment to high-quality design has resulted in Columbus being ranked sixth on the American Institute of Architects list of cities marked by innovation in architecture and design.

A philanthropic foundation endowed by the city's largest employer, Cummins Engine, attracted some of the world's most distinguished architects. Among those who left their stamp on the city environment are Robert Trent Jones, Richard Meier, Robert Venturi, Alexander Girard, and I.M. Pei, whose 1969 Cleo Rodgers Memorial Library is at 536 5th Street. The **Columbus City Tours** allow visitors to catch a glimpse of these architectural delights.

Columbus City Tours
506 5th St. ***Tel*** *(800) 468-6564.*
10am Mon– Fri, 10am, 2pm Sat, 1pm Sun (Jan–Feb & Dec: Sat only).

Ohio River Valley ⑭

601 W First St, (800) 559-2956.
www.visitmadison.org

From Indiana's southeastern border with Kentucky, Route 56 and 156 follow the serpentine Ohio River for nearly 80 miles (129 km) as it winds lazily through the river towns of Rising Sun, Patriot, Florence, and Vevey. These two highways are the best way to explore both the river valley and the southern hill country.

The antebellum river port of **Madison**, 90 miles (145 km) southeast of Indianapolis, is one of the best-preserved towns on the river. Many of its residential and commercial buildings have benefited from a generous grant from the National Trust for Historic Preservation. The town's notable architectural charms include the Greek Revival **Lanier Mansion**, which was built in 1844 for railroad magnate James Lanier, and the Shrewsbury-Windle House, an 1849 riverboat entrepreneur's home featuring an elegant, free-standing circular staircase. Downtown is the restored 19th-century office of progressive frontier physician Dr. William D. Hutchings.

Lanier Mansion State Historic Site
601 W 1st St Madison.
Tel *(812) 265-3526. 9am–5pm Thu–Tue. Jan 1, Easter, Thanksgiving, Dec 25.*

Exterior of Eliel Saarinen's First Christian Church (1942), Columbus

Ohio

Ohio is a study in contrasts. As one of the nation's largest agricultural producers, the state is dotted with picturesque farmland, small towns steeped in history, and more recently settled Amish areas where horse-drawn buggies and barns are a thing of the present. Ohio also contains several of the country's most urbanized industrial centers along the Ohio River – the state's southern and eastern border – and in port cities that lie along the shores of Lake Erie.

Art Deco façade of the Union Terminal, Cincinnati

Cincinnati 15

331, 285. 525 Vine St, (800) 344-3445.
www.cincyusa.com

Built on a series of steep hills overlooking the Ohio River, Cincinnati was once called "Porkopolis" for its rank slaughterhouses and belching factories. Later, its winding side streets and stunning views from the hilltop Mount Adams neighborhood inspired British prime minister Winston Churchill to call it "the most beautiful of America's inland cities." The city is today a vibrant corporate center with a revitalized riverfront entertainment and parks district.

Cincinnati's location at the intersection of the Erie Canal and the Miami and Ohio Rivers, and its strategic perch on the border of the slave-holding South and the industrializing North made it a heterogeneous cultural and commercial crossroads. Many prominent locals, including writer Harriet Beecher Stowe, whose home is now a state historic site, strongly supported the anti-slavery movement. The dynamic **National Underground Railroad Freedom Center** focuses on the city's one-time heroic past.

Cincinnati's most celebrated landmark is the 1867 stone and steel suspension bridge, built by Brooklyn Bridge engineer John A. Roebling to link this city with Covington, Kentucky, across the Ohio River. Another landmark is the 1933 Art Deco **Union Terminal**, west of downtown. The refurbished terminal now houses a trio of attractions that specialize in city history, children's activities, and natural history/science. The enlarged **Center for Contemporary Art** adds creative energy downtown. The sixth-floor Un-Museum encourages interaction, especially among children.

On the eastern part of town, the **Cincinnati Art Museum** overlooks Eden Park. The museum's extensive collections include Roman, Greek, Egyptian, Asian, and African artifacts. Among its exhibits of contemporary art is a specially commissioned portrait by Andy Warhol of the controversial Cincinnati Reds baseball great, Pete Rose.

The Cincinnati Art Museum
953 Eden Park Dr. ***Tel*** *(877) 472-4226. 11am–5pm Tue–Sun (until 9pm Wed). public hols.*
www.cincinnatiartmuseum.org

Dayton 16

166,000. 1 Chamber Plaza, Suite A, (800) 221-8235.
www.daytoncvb.com

This pleasant city on the Great Miami River is known as the "Birthplace of Aviation." It was here that aviation pioneers, Wilbur and Orville Wright *(see p250)*, carried out much of their research and experimentation, which led to their successful flight in 1903 in Kitty Hawk, North Carolina. Five miles northeast lies the **Dayton Aviation Heritage National Historical Park** at the spot where the brothers tested their second and third aircraft in 1904 and 1905. The **Carillon Historical Park** holds the Wright *Flyer III* aircraft – the first capable of executing a turn. Over 300 aircraft and missiles from the post-Wright aviation era are at the **United States Air Force Museum**. Also within the National Aviation Heritage Area is the **National Aviation Hall of Fame**.

Overlooking the Great Miami River, the Italian Renaissance-style **Dayton Art Institute** features a large collection of European and American paintings, such as Claude Monet's *Waterlilies* and Edward Hopper's *High Noon*.

Carillon Historical Park
1000 Carillon Blvd. ***Tel*** *(937) 293-2841. Apr–Oct: 9:30am–5pm Tue–Sat, noon–5pm Sun & public hols.* **www**.carillonpark.org

Dayton Art Institute
456 Belmonte Park N. ***Tel*** *(937) 223-5277. 10am–4pm Tue–Sun (to 8pm Thu).* **www**.daytonartinstitute.org

Italian Renaissance-style Dayton Art Institute, Dayton

The 1,348-ft (411-m) Serpent Mound

Serpent Mound 17

3850 Rte 73, Peebles.
Tel (800) 752-2757. **Museum and Grounds** *May–Labor Day: 10am–5pm Fri–Sun; noon–5pm on public hols.*

The largest serpent-shaped effigy mound in the US, the 1,348-ft (411-m) long Serpent Mound overlooks Brush Creek in the Ohio River Valley. Although its exact age is unknown, research suggests that the mound was constructed between 800 BC and AD 400 by the ancient Adena people, Ohio's earliest farming Native American community.

The 5-ft (1.5-m) high, 20-ft (6-m) wide mound appears to represent an uncoiling serpent, with a tightly coiled tail at one end and a mouth-like opening, swallowing an oval-shaped egg, at the other. An on-site museum describes the mound's history and its protection under an 1888 law, the first in the US to safeguard important archeological sites.

Hopewell Culture National Historic Park 18

16062 Rte 104, Chillicothe. *Tel (740) 774-1126. 8:30am–5pm daily (until 6pm, Memorial Day to Labor Day). Jan 1, Thanksgiving, Dec 25.* **www**.nps.gov/hocu

Located in the Scioto River Valley, this 120-acre (48-ha) park preserves 23 Native American burial mounds built by the Hopewell people who lived here from 200 BC to AD 500. The Hopewell culture, which emerged from the Adena culture, covers a broad network of beliefs and practices among different Native groups spread over eastern US. As characteristic of the culture, the mounds are arranged in geometric shapes, ringed by an earthen wall. A visitor center provides an in-depth look at the social and economic life of the long-vanished Hopewell peoples, based on the archeological work conducted here.

Columbus 19

711,000. 277 W Nationwide Blvd, (614) 221-6623, (800) 354-2657. **www**.experiencecolumbus.org

Ohio's capital since 1816, Columbus has grown from a sleepy, swampy lowland site on the east bank of the Scioto River to become a bustling cultural, political, and economic center. Today, the city supports a thriving arts scene, with a superb symphony and ballet, in addition to revitalized historic neighborhoods and entertainment districts. Downtown's central feature is the Greek-Revival style **Ohio Statehouse**. Built between 1839 and 1861, the structure is surmounted by a unique drum-shaped cupola marked by a 29-ft (9-m) wide skylight.

Amish quilt patterns on display

The **Ohio Historical Center** is the best place to begin the exploration of Columbus. Its interactive displays trace Ohio's evolution from an 18th-century frontier outpost to its current urban and industrial status. Permanent exhibits detail the origin of the city's fine public architecture and parklands.

The **Franklin Park Conservatory and Botanical Garden**, built in 1895, has a bonsai and sculpture garden. It also has indoor simulations of exotic climates.

Sculpture in Franklin Park Conservatory and Botanical Garden

Ohio Historical Center
1982 Velma Ave.
Tel (614) 297-2300. 9am–5pm Tue–Sat (until 9pm Thu), noon–5pm Sun. most public hols. (children under 6 free)
www.ohiohistory.org/places/ohc

Franklin Park Conservatory & Botanical Garden
1777 E Broad St. *Tel (614) 645-8733, (800) 214-7275. 10am–5pm Tue–Sun (until 8pm Wed). Thanksgiving, Dec 25. (children under 2 free)*
www.fpconservatory.org

Berlin 20

3,100. 35 N Monroe St, Millersburg, (330) 674-3975, (877) 643-8824. **www**.visitamishcountry.com

Much of Ohio's large Amish population is concentrated in Holmes County in the north-central part of the state, about 90 miles (145 km) northeast of Columbus. Lying just outside Berlin village, **Schrock's Amish Farm** provides a good overview of the reclusive Amish, who have maintained their simplified 19th-century way of life. The farm has a multimedia visitor center and offers a tour of a working farm, complete with freshly baked goods and buggy rides.

Visitors are requested to drive carefully along the rural backroads and busier thoroughfares, out of respect for the slow-moving, horse-drawn carriages.

Schrock's Amish Farm
4363 SR 39. *Tel (330) 893-3232. Apr–Oct: 10am–5pm Mon–Fri, 10am–6pm Sat.*

View of the Cleveland skyline from The Flats

Cleveland 21

478,000.
Terminal Tower, Suite 3100, 100 Public Square, (800) 321-1001.
www.positivelycleveland.com

Although ranked as one of the poorest cities in the US, Cleveland is a hard-working, vibrant, and ever-changing place. Founded in 1796 by speculator Moses Cleaveland, the city evolved from a frontier town into a bustling commercial port in 1832, when the Ohio and Erie Canal linked Cleveland to the Ohio River.

Cleveland's steel industry was born after the Civil War, when railroads linked the city with Minnesota's Iron Range and the coalfields of western Pennsylvania. The industry thrived in the early 1900s, catering to the Detroit automobile industry's demand for easily transported steel. After World War II, however, the city's fortunes faded as industries moved away, leaving behind vast polluted landscapes and scores of unemployed workers.

Cleveland's "Rust Belt" image is today a thing of the past. The city now encompasses 19,000 acres (7,689 ha) of pristine parkland. **The East 4th Street District** and the historic **Warehouse District** are the entertainment hubs.

A signature feature since 1927, the 52-story Beaux Arts **Terminal Tower**, was designed as a "city within a city." It made maximum use of vertical space, squeezing an office building, railroad station, and hotel into its confines. The 42nd-floor observation deck offers grand views of the city and, on a clear day, one can see the Canadian shoreline.

The 1995 **Rock and Roll Hall of Fame and Museum** on the Lake Erie waterfront in downtown, put Cleveland at center stage of the nation's entertainment scene. The massive 150,000-sq-ft (13,935-sq-m) I.M. Pei-designed museum traces the development of the musical genre, beginning with its roots in the Mississippi Delta blues *(see pp360–61)* and Appalachian string bands. On display are memorabilia ranging from Chuck Berry's Gibson electric guitar to a Cub Scout shirt worn by Jim Morrison. To its west, the **Great Lakes Science Center** uses interactive exhibits to stimulate public interest in the fragile ecosystem of the Great Lakes region.

Cleveland's principal cultural attractions lie about 4 miles (6 km) east of downtown, around University Circle. Surrounding this expanse of parkland near the Case Western Reserve University campus are a series of early 20th-century buildings that now contain several fine museums. Among them is the **Cleveland Museum of Art**, with its superb collection of ancient Egyptian relics and pre-Columbian artifacts. Its European painting collection includes such masterpieces as Renoir's *Mother and Child* and Van Gogh's *Landscape with Wheelbarrow*. Facing this museum, the city's popular **Botanical Garden** features 10 acres (4 ha) of outdoor gardens, as well as a Japanese garden and a peace garden.

Rock and Roll Hall of Fame & Museum
1100 Rock and Roll Blvd. ***Tel*** *(216) 781-7625. 10am–5:30pm daily, 10am–9pm Wed; also 10am–9pm Sat (Memorial Day–Labor Day only). Thanksgiving, Dec 25. (under 12s free).* www.rockhall.com

Cleveland Museum of Art
11150 East Blvd. ***Tel*** *(216) 421-7340, (888) 262-0033. 10am–5pm Tue–Sun (until 9pm Wed, Fri, Sat). Mon, Jan 1, Jul 4, Thanksgiving, Dec 25.* www.clevelandart.org

Environs
Located 25 miles (40 km) west of Cleveland, **Oberlin** is home to Oberlin College, one of the first to admit African-American and female students. The Allen Memorial Art Museum on campus displays American, Asian, and European art.

The steel manufacturing center **Canton** 60 miles (96 km) south of Cleveland, is famed for the Pro Football Hall of Fame, which was opened in 1963 and has been visited by eight million fans.

The Rock and Roll Hall of Fame and Museum in downtown Cleveland

For hotels and restaurants in this region see pp426–7 and pp430–31

Perry's Victory Memorial at Put-in-Bay, Lake Erie Islands

Lake Erie Islands ㉒

770 SE Catawba Rd, Port Clinton, (800) 441-1271.
www.lake-erie.com

Located just offshore from the Marblehead Peninsula separating Sandusky Bay from Lake Erie, the Lake Erie Islands are a prime summer tourist destination. The islands include the bucolic, peaceful Kelleys Island and the rowdier South Bass Island, with the village of Put-in-Bay as its lively nightlife center.

Home of the Erie, Ottawa, and Huron Indian tribes until the 19th century, the Lake Erie Islands rose to national prominence during the War of 1812. On September 10, 1813, US Navy Commodore Oliver Hazard Perry defeated the more heavily fortified British fleet in the pivotal Battle of Lake Erie, fought off South Bass Island. A visitor center and a 352-ft (107-m) granite column at Put-in-Bay, **Perry's Victory and International Peace Memorial**, commemorates his victory and his famous message to US General William Henry Harrison: "We have met the enemy and they are ours."

Kelleys Island State Park has the fascinating Glacial Grooves, a series of deep limestone grooves caused by the movement of a heavy glacial wall. These grooves have been protected from quarrying since 1923.

Short ferry rides from nearby Sandusky and Marblehead are available. The Marblehead Lighthouse, built in 1821, is a popular regional icon.

Perry's Victory & International Peace Memorial
93 Delaware Ave, Put-in-Bay, S Bass Island.
Tel *(419) 285-2184.*
late-Apr–Oct: 10am–6pm daily; by appointment rest of year. (children under 16 free).
www.nps.gov/pevi

Kelleys Island State Park
Kelleys Island.
Tel *(419) 746-2546.*
Apr–Nov: sunrise–sunset.
www.ohiostateparks.org

Sandusky ㉓

29,800. 4424 Milan Rd, Sandusky, (800) 255-3743.
www.shoreislands.com

Sandusky was once one of the Great Lakes' largest coal-shipping ports. Today, its ferry terminal provides easy access to many of the Lake Erie Islands. The city is, however, best known for the 364-acre (147-ha) **Cedar Point Amusement Park**, one of the busiest summer tourist spots in the Midwest. The park claims to have the world's largest collection of roller coasters, ranging from rickety old wooden ones to the high-speed Magnum, Millennium Force, and Top Thrill Dragster. Cedar Point also includes a water park, the children-centered Camp Snoopy and a sandy Lake Erie beach.

Cedar Point Amusement Park
One Cedar Point Dr. ***Tel*** *(419) 627-2350. mid-May–Labor Day: 10am–7pm or later daily; Labor Day–end of Oct: days vary, call first.*
www.cedarpoint.com

Toledo ㉔

314,000. 401 Jefferson Ave, (800) 243-4667.
www.dotoledo.com

One of the world's leading glass manufacturing centers and the third busiest Great Lakes port, Toledo occupies a Maumee River site steeped in history. The 1794 Battle of Fallen Timbers that took place nearby opened northwestern Ohio and Indiana to white settlement. The area was also a strategic one during the War of 1812. The reconstructed Fort Meigs, about 10 miles (16 km) south of Toledo in Perrysburg, commemorates the stockade that withstood two British and Native American sieges in 1813.

Today, the city is famed for the **Toledo Museum of Art**, a Neo-Classical marble structure in the historic Old West End founded by local glass tycoon Edward Drummond Libbey. The museum features one of the world's largest collections of ornamental glass, housed in the Post-Modern Glass Pavilion which opened in 2008. The nearby **Fort Meigs State Memorial**, which is a reconstructed fort dating from the War of 1812, was rebuilt in 2003. It features a museum and interactive displays, and various outdoor re-enactments are organized throughout the summer by staff and volunteers in period costume.

Toledo Museum of Art
2445 Monroe St. ***Tel*** *(419) 255-8000. 10am–4pm Tue–Sat (to 10pm Fri, 6pm Sat), noon–6pm Sun. Jan 1, Jul 4, Thnksg., Dec 25.*
www.toledomuseum.org

A roller-coaster ride at Cedar Point Amusement Park, Sandusky

Michigan

This inland state has a rich maritime history. Michigan's principal land mass, the so-called Lower Peninsula, is a mitten-shaped area surrounded by three Great Lakes – Michigan, Huron, and Erie. This landmass contains the largest cities, including Detroit, and accounts for most of Michigan's industry and population. In the 19th century, the Lower Peninsula, with its wind-blown dunes and rolling cherry orchards, was a prime destination. The rugged Upper Peninsula to the northwest, whose northern border is Lake Superior, only became part of the state in 1834. It has also become a popular tourist getaway.

Crowds enjoying the annual jazz festival in Detroit's Hart Plaza

Detroit ㉕

951,270.
211 W Fort St, (800) 338-7648.
www.visitdetroit.com

Known today as the "Motor City," Detroit (meaning "the Strait" in French) was founded in 1701 by the French fur trader Antoine de la Mothe Cadillac. The city has since evolved from a shipbuilding center into a leading manufacturer of railroad equipment, cars, and bicycles. Its massive industrial growth, however, took place after Henry Ford began manufacturing automobiles in Detroit in 1896. By the 1920s, most American automobile manufacturers – Ford, General Motors, Pontiac, and Chrysler – had moved their headquarters and production facilities to the city.

The automobile industry still dominates Detroit. A web of highways fans out from the city's revitalized downtown. The city's present focal point is the huge riverfront **Renaissance Center**, General Motors' current headquarters. Nearby, **Hart Plaza** hosts year-round riverfront festivals, including the Detroit International Jazz Festival during Labor Day weekend. Directly across, the 25-ft (8-m) Big Fist outdoor sculpture on Woodward Avenue, is a tribute to the local African-American boxer Joe Louis, known as "The Brown Bomber." East of downtown is the lively Greek neighborhood and restaurant district centered on Monroe Avenue. Just north of downtown are **Comerica Park** and **Ford Field**, two famous sports venues.

Charles H. Wright Museum of African American History

315 E Warren Ave. ***Tel*** *(313) 494-5800.* *9am–5pm Tue–Sat, 1–5pm Sun.* *Mon, public hols.*
www.maah-detroit.org

Built in 1997, this center commemorates the contributions made by Detroit's large African-American population to the city's commercial and cultural progress. It depicts the Middle Passage of enslaved Africans across the Atlantic, the Underground Railroad, the Civil Rights Movement, and other milestones in African-American history. There is an exciting program of changing exhibits, as well as some that are long-term. One of these, aimed at very young children, is called "A is for Africa" and has 26 interactive stations and a three-dimensional "dictionary."

Detroit Institute of Arts

5200 Woodward Ave, Detroit Cultural Center. ***Tel*** *(313) 833-7900.* *10am–4pm Wed–Thu, 10am–10pm Fri, 10am–5pm Sat–Sun.* *Mon, Tue, public hols.* *(children under 6 free).* **www**.dia.org

The museum's centerpiece is a monumental 27-panel mural by Mexico City artist Diego Rivera. His controversial *Detroit Industry* depicts the automobile manufacturing process in a stark way, reflecting the artist's Leftist views of the relationship between management and labor.

The museum's outstanding collections range from pre-Columbian, Native American, and African art to 17th-century Dutch and Flemish paintings. It has a large selection of 19th-century American paintings.

Detroit Historical Museum

Detroit Historical Museums & Society 5401 Woodward Ave. ***Tel*** *(313) 833-1805.* *9:30am–3pm Wed–Fri, 10am–5pm Sat, noon–5pm Sun.* *public hols.* *(children under 4 free).*
www.detroithistorical.org

The renovated "Streets of Old Detroit" display, as well as a permanent exhibit on Detroit's automotive heritage, are the main features of this museum located in the Detroit

Nymph and Eros**, on display at The Detroit Institute of Arts**

For hotels and restaurants in this region see pp425–6 and pp429–30

Cultural Corridor near Wayne State University.

The society's **Historic Fort Wayne and Tuskegee Airmen Museum**, along the Detroit River on the city's southwest side, incorporates many of the surviving buildings from Fort Wayne, the last military bastion to defend the city. A bigger Tuskegee Airmen facility is planned, but for now the fort only is open on special occasions. The society also operates the **Dossin Great Lakes Museum** in Belle Isle Park in the Detroit River.

Exterior of Henry Ford Museum in Dearborn, a suburb of Detroit

Motown Historical Museum

2648 W Grand Blvd. ***Tel** (313) 875-2264.* *10am–6pm Tue–Sat (also Mon during summer).* *Sun, public hols.*
www.motownmuseum.org

During the early 1960s, the Motown record label revolutionized American popular music with its trademark "Motown Sound," which is a melodic blend of pop, soul, and rhythm and blues. The creative genius of label founder Berry Gordy Jr. and his stable of talented artists such as Marvin Gaye, Smokey Robinson, Stevie Wonder, the Temptations, and Diana Ross and the Supremes are honored in this museum, housed in the original brick building where hit records such as "Heard It Through the Grapevine" and "Baby Love" were produced. The renovated building, called Hitsville USA by Gordy, has a good display of a wide range of old photographs, instruments, and recording equipment, including the original "Studio A" where the classic sounds were first created. Displays narrate the story of Motown as the singlemost successful independent African-American-controlled record label in the history of the country. Today this label is owned by the PolyGram Corporation.

Environs

The suburb of Dearborn, 8 miles (13 km) west of Detroit, is home to **The Henry Ford**, an indoor and outdoor museum that has one of the nation's most impressive collections of Americana. Within the complex is the Henry Ford Museum, which displays a range of vintage cars, and is the starting point for the high-tech Ford Rouge Factory Tour. The open-air Greenfield Village exhibits Ford's eclectic collection of historical artifacts. These include diverse objects: a cot used by George Washington; the chair in which Abraham Lincoln was shot; inventor Thomas Edison's laboratory; and the Dayton home and bicycle shop of Orville and Wilbur Wright.

University of Michigan campus, Ann Arbor

Ann Arbor 26

114, 000. 120 W Huron St, (800) 888-9487. **www**.annarbor.org

A picturesque, midsized city, with a vibrant pedestrian-friendly downtown, Ann Arbor is a bastion of laid-back liberalism and environmental activism on the western fringe of conservative Detroit. The city's independent streak springs from the professors and students affiliated with the **University of Michigan**, the city's largest employer.

Music, film, and art festivals are a year-round tradition. One of the nation's largest outdoor art fairs is held in the city. This annual July event attracts more than 1,000 artists and 500,000 art fans and dealers. Ann Arbor is also home to many new and used bookstores, including **Border's Books**, a global chain that began in 1973. Its downtown Liberty Street store is still a focal point of the city.

The 2,800-acre (1,133-ha) Gothic central campus of the University of Michigan straddles Washtenaw Avenue, southeast of downtown. The **Kelsey Museum of Archaeology**, on the main campus, houses a variety of Greek, Roman, Egyptian, and Near Eastern artifacts. It reopened following renovation work in October 2009.

Lansing 27

119,128. 1223 Turner St, (888) 252-6746. **www**.lansing.org

A government and industrial center, this city benefits from its proximity to the Michigan State University in adjacent East Lansing. Selected as the state capital in 1847, the subsequent arrival of railroads in 1871 and the completion of the downtown statehouse in 1879 fueled the city's growth. The **Michigan Historical Museum** recounts the construction of the Second Renaissance Revival-style State Capitol and traces the state's history from the prehistoric era to the present through various interactive exhibits.

Exhibit from the Olds Museum

Lansing's status as a major automotive manufacturing center is linked to the business founded by Ransom E. Olds, who began building prototype vehicles here in 1885. He later produced the Curved Dash Olds, considered by many to have been the world's first mass-produced automobile. The **R.E. Olds Transportation Museum** has the distinction of showcasing an original 1901 Curved Dash Olds Runabout and a variety of classic Oldsmobiles from the 1930s and 1940s. Also in the collection is the last model, manufactured in 2004. Displays change quarterly.

R.E. Olds Transportation Museum
240 Museum Dr. ***Tel*** *(517) 372-0529.* *10am–5pm Tue–Sat, noon–5pm Sun.* *Nov–Mar: Sun.*

Grand Rapids 28

197,800. 171 Monroe Ave, Suite 700, (800) 678-9859. **www**.visitgrandrapids.org

Grand Rapids owes its reputation as a major furniture manufacturing center to the Grand River that flows through the heart of the city. The water-powered lumber mills that were set up along its banks in the 19th century formed the foundation for the growth of fine furniture makers such as Herman Miller and Steelcase.

East of downtown is the fashionable **Heritage Hill Neighborhood**, a historic district where several of the city's industrial moguls once lived. The stately 1895 **Voigt House Victorian Museum**, with its grand period furnishings, is now a museum, and the 1909 **Meyer May House** is one of Frank Lloyd Wright's last Prairie-style family homes. A scenic gathering spot is the spacious **Frederik Meijer Gardens and Sculpture Park**.

Also in town is the **Gerald R. Ford Museum**. It traces the career of the 38th president, who grew up in Grand Rapids, where his father ran a paint and varnish company. The museum includes a holographic tour of the White House and a replica of the Oval Office.

Voigt House Victorian Museum
115 College Ave SE. ***Tel*** *(616) 456-4600.* *11am–3pm Tue, 1–3pm 2nd & 4th Sun of month.* **www**.grmuseum.org/voigt

Frank Lloyd Wright's 1909 Meyer May House in Grand Rapids

Hikers at Sleeping Bear Dunes Lakeshore, Lake Michigan Shore

Lake Michigan Shore ㉙

741 Kenmoor Ave, Grand Rapids, (800) 442-2084. www.wmta.org

A major tourist destination since wealthy Chicagoans first came here in the late 1800s, Lake Michigan Shore is lined with sandy beaches, 19th-century resorts, working ports, and more than 25 scenic lighthouses. The resort town of Saugatuck makes an ideal base to explore the shore. A noteworthy attraction 20 miles (32 km) south is the excellent **Michigan Maritime Museum** narrates the history of fishing, shipping, and ship-building on the Great Lakes.

Located 200 miles (322 km) to the north on US 31, **Sleeping Bear Dunes National Lakeshore** incorporates many ecosystems and its signature sand dunes, which tower some 460 ft (140 m) above the lakefront beaches and an inland lake. The park's ghost forest of sand-buried trees can be explored through hiking trails or a 7-mile (11-km) drive.

The busy community of **Traverse City**, 25 miles (40 km) north of Sleeping Bear Dunes, is a convenient base to visit the picturesque Old Mission Peninsula. A short trip toward the north along Route 37 provides beautiful views of green rolling hills, cherry orchards, and the lake. At its tip stands the Old Mission Point Lighthouse, built in 1870. The white wooden structure sits exactly on the 45th parallel.

Sleeping Bear Dunes National Lakeshore
9922 Front St, Empire. ***Tel*** *(231) 326-5134. Park: year-round. Visitor Center: Memorial Day–Labor Day: 8am–6pm daily; Labor Day–Memorial Day: 8:15am–4pm daily. Jan 1, Thanksgiving, Dec 25.* **www**.nps.gov/slbe

Michigan Maritime Museum
260 Dyckman Rd, South Haven. ***Tel*** *(800) 747-3810. Memorial Day–Labor Day: 10am–5pm Mon–Sat, noon–5pm Sun; Labor Day–Memorial Day: noon–5pm Fri–Sun. public holidays.* **www**.michiganmaritimemuseum.org

Mackinac Island ㉚

500. Main St, (906) 847-3783. **www**.mackinacisland.org

The limestone outcrop of Mackinac Island, covering 6 sq miles (16 sq km), sits in the middle of the Straits of Mackinac, separating the Lower and Upper Peninsulas. Ferries that depart regularly from Mackinaw City and St. Ignace on the mainland are the only way to reach the island, where no cars are permitted. The principal landmark here is the 1887 **Grand Hotel** *(see p425)*, a classic Gilded Age summer resort that has the world's longest front porch at 660 ft (201 m). Fort Mackinac, overlooking the harbor, is in the **Mackinac Island State Park**. This restored fort commemorates the island's 18th-century past as a French, British, and American military outpost through a variety of demonstrations as well as multimedia shows.

Upper Peninsula ㉛

Iron Mountain, (906) 774-5180, (800) 562-7134. **www**.uptravel.com **Soo Locks Boat Tours** Dock #1, 1157 E Portage Ave, Sault Ste. Marie. ***Tel*** *(800) 432-6301. May 1–Oct 15; call for tour schedule. (children under 5 free).* **www**.soolocks.com

The sparsely populated wilderness of the 384-mile (618-km) wide Upper Peninsula is dotted with old lumber, mining, and fishing towns, and some of Michigan's most striking natural attractions. Also called the "UP," this region was first explored by 17th-century French adventurers, one of whom, Etienne Brule, established Michigan's oldest community, **Sault Sainte Marie**, on its north-eastern tip.

One of its most popular attractions, **Pictured Rocks National Lakeshore**, stretches along Lake Superior. Although accessible by car from Hwy 28, this 40-mile (64-km) stretch of beaches and bluffs can be viewed more dramatically on guided cruises, departing from Munising.

For more rugged scenery, head west to **Porcupine Mountains Wilderness State Park** along Lake Superior. It is known for its forests, lakes, rivers, and a 90-mile (145-km) network of hiking trails.

Canon at the British Landing, Mackinac Island State Park

Wisconsin

Most Americans associate Wisconsin either with cheese – because of its advertised nickname of "America's Dairyland" – or with beer, from Milwaukee's many historic breweries. While both images are accurate, this predominantly agricultural state is also famed as the Midwest's premier vacation destination. Wisconsin's recreational jewels range from the gorgeous Apostle Islands on its northern Lake Superior coast to 99 carefully maintained state parks, forests, and trails that allow hikers and bikers to explore glacial moraines, rugged lakeside cliffs, broad rivers, dense forests, and lush green valleys.

Façade of the 1892 Pabst Mansion in Milwaukee

Milwaukee 32

597,000. 400 W Wisconsin Ave, (800) 554-1448. Summerfest. **www**.milwaukee.org

Like Chicago, its more famous neighbor 90 miles (145 km) to the south, this manufacturing and brewing center grew up on a swampy Lake Michigan marshland. Treaties signed with local Indian tribes opened the area to white settlement in the 1830s. The city's strong German ambience dates to the arrival of "Forty-Eighters," the revolutionaries who fled Germany after an aborted attempt to overthrow the monarchy in 1848. By the 1870s, Milwaukee had as many as six daily German-language newspapers.

Pabst, Blatz, Schlitz, and Miller were the beers that "made Milwaukee famous." This tradition took such strong root in the city that even the local baseball team came to be called the Brewers. Milwaukee's wealthy beer barons were active philanthropists, investing in the arts, architecture, and social causes. The city's spectacular Lake Michigan shoreline hosts a long schedule of festivals, the most popular being Summerfest, an 11-day culinary and musical extravaganza that takes place in late June and early July.

The **Harley-Davidson Museum**, which sits in a 20-acre (8-ha) campus, opened in 2008. It celebrates a century of motorcycle manufacturing in Milwaukee and is a global mecca for bikers. The building's industrial design includes 80-ft (24-m) high towers of exposed galvanized steel. Inside are about 140 Harley vehicles and 16,000 smaller artifacts. Interactive features engage the interest of both children and adults.

The **Milwaukee County Historical Society** is located in the heart of downtown. Housed in a stately Beaux Arts bank building, which is being restored, the institution provides an excellent introduction to the city's economic, political, and social history.

To its southwest, the 150,000-square-ft (13,935-m) **Milwaukee Public Museum** is part science museum, part local and cultural history center. Its interactive, child-targeted science holdings include the world's largest dinosaur skull and a glass-enclosed tropical butterfly garden. The museum's pre-Columbian and Native American exhibits paint a vivid and honest portrait of the culture and fate of the continent's Native Americans, while the "Streets of Old Milwaukee" provides a fascinating glimpse of this metropolitan melting pot.

Captain Frederick Pabst, a successful Milwaukee brewer, amassed a fortune with his popular Pabst Blue Ribbon beer brand and real estate investments. The cornerstone of his empire, the 1892 Flemish Renaissance Revival-style **Pabst Mansion**, lies at the west end of the city's grand Wisconsin Avenue. At that time the 37-room palace was considered one of the world's most technologically sophisticated houses, as it was equipped with full electrical service, a heating system, and nine bathrooms.

Located in the city's Historic Third Ward warehouse district south of downtown and a mecca for upscale shopping and entertainment, the **Eisner: American Museum of Advertising and Design** critically assesses the impact of advertising on culture and society. It is one of the few

Spectacular new entrance of the Milwaukee Art Museum

For hotels and restaurants in this region see p427 and p431

museums in the country dedicated to this subject. Exhibits focus on topics as diverse as the marketing of US presidents, the use of sports heroes to market beers, and the legendary Burma-Shave advertising campaigns. The precursor to billboards on America's earliest highways, the signs for one of the world's first brushless shaving creams were often humorous jingles placed at intervals along the road.

Eastward, the lakefront **Milwaukee Art Museum** was established in 1888 and holds a 20,000-piece collection, renovated galleries, and a vast reception hall, designed by Spanish architect Santiago Calatrava. This pavilion has a grand, winglike sunshade to complement the museum's windswept setting. Its signature collections are its Frank Lloyd Wright decorative arts holdings and the modern and contemporary galleries, which include Mark Rothko's *Green, Red, Blue* and Picasso's *The Cock of the Liberation*.

The Miller Brewing Company, the only longtime brewer still in operation in the city, is at the town's western edge. This firm, which produces the top-selling Miller beers, opened in 1855, when immigrant brewer Frederick Miller purchased the floundering Plank Road Brewery. Today, it is the second-largest brewer in the US, after the St. Louis-based Anheuser-Busch *(see p455)*. The **Miller Brewing Company Tour** takes visitors on a tour of its brewery and the nearby Caves Museum, where beer was naturally cooled deep inside Milwaukee's bluffs. Complimentary Miller beverages, including water and sodas for children, are offered at the end of the tour. Milwaukee's other major sight is the Annunciation Greek Orthodox Church, one of Frank Lloyd Wright's last commissions. Designed in 1956, it was opened in 1961, two years after Wright's death.

Sign of the Miller Brewing Company

The Eisner: American Museum of Advertising & Design
208 N Water St. ***Tel*** *(414) 847-3290.* *11am–5pm Wed–Fri, (until 8pm Thu), noon–5pm Sat, 1–5pm Sun.* *public hols.* *(children under 12 free).* **www**.eisnermuseum.org

Harley-Davidson Museum
400 Canal St. ***Tel*** *(877) 436-8738.* *May–Oct: 9am–6pm daily (until 8pm Wed); Nov–Apr: 10am–6pm Mon–Fri, 9am–6pm Sat–Sun.* *(children under 5 free).* **www**.harley-davidson.com

Milwaukee Art Museum
700 N Art Museum Dr. ***Tel*** *(414) 224-3200.* *10am–5pm Tue–Sun, (until 8pm Thu).* *(children under 13 free).* **www**.mam.org

Miller Brewing Company Tour
4251 W State St. ***Tel*** *(800) 944-5483.* *10:30am–3:30pm Mon–Sat; call (414) 931-2337 for free guided tours Mon–Sat.* *Sun, public hols.* **www**.millerbrewing.com

Door County 33

1015 Green Bay Rd, Sturgeon Bay, (920) 743-4456, (800) 527-3529. **www**.doorcounty.com

Stretching like the spout of a teapot, between Green Bay and Lake Michigan, the Door Peninsula is a rugged New England-like expanse of rolling hills, lakeside cliffs, and pretty port villages. The county comprises the northern two-thirds of the peninsula and derives its name from the French-Canadian voyageurs' sobriquet for the treacherous shipping channel off the peninsula's northern point – Porte des Morts, or "Death's Door." The area's fishing and shipping heritage is on display at the **Door County Maritime Museum**, in downtown Sturgeon Bay, the county's largest port and southernmost city. A few miles north, on Hwy 57, is **The Farm**, a traditional Wisconsin dairy farm and petting zoo, replete with an array of animals – cows, goats, pigs, chickens, horses, and barn cats.

A view of Eagle Bluff Lighthouse, Door County

The peninsula's 250-mile (402-km) shoreline is lined with more than a dozen county parks and five magnificent state parks. The largest of these is the 3,776-acre (1,528-ha) **Peninsula State Park**, between the picturesque communities of Fish Creek and Ephraim on the northwestern coast. After traversing the park's miles of hiking and biking trails and visiting the restored Eagle Bluff Lighthouse, visitors can take in a performance by the Peninsula Players, the nation's oldest resident summer stock theater company.

Washington Island, 6 miles (10 km) across the Porte des Morts Straits to the northeast of Newport State Park, can be reached, year-round, via a short ferry ride. The island was home to the Potawatomi Indians until a hardy group of Icelandic immigrants arrived in the 19th century. The latter's descendants continue to farm the island's fertile soil and to welcome day-trippers who come in search of peace, quiet, and splendid lake views.

Door County Maritime Museum
120 N Madison Ave, Sturgeon Bay. ***Tel*** *(920) 743-5958.* *Memorial Day–Labor Day: 9am–6pm daily; 10am–5pm daily other times of year.* *some public hols.* **www**.dcmm.org

Peninsula State Park
9462 Shore Rd, Fish Creek. ***Tel*** *(920) 868-3258.* *6am–11pm daily.* **www**.dnr.state.wi.us

Guided boat tour along the Wisconsin River

Wisconsin Dells 34

2,400. 701 Superior St, (800) 223-3557. www.wisdells.com

Wisconsin Dells has one of the most spectacular locations along the Wisconsin River as it winds through an awe-inspiring, 15-mile (24-km) stretch of deep sandstone canyons. The area's natural beauty and a variety of manmade attractions make it a prime summer vacation destination. Among the highlights are the guided **Dells Boat Tours**, which offer excursions past the storied cliffs through the Upper and Lower Dells. The highest concentration of water parks in the world – 18 are indoors – make the area popular with families in winter too.

The region owes much of its popularity to photographer H.H. Bennett, whose late-19th-century photographs of the Wisconsin River's rugged landscapes became famous throughout America. The Wisconsin Historical Society operates the **H.H. Bennett Studio and History Center**.

Dells Boat Tours
Upper & Lower Dells Docks. ***Tel*** *(608) 254-8555.* *mid-Mar–Oct: 9:30am–7pm daily (until 4:30pm spring, fall).* **www**.dellsboats.com

H.H. Bennett Studio & History Center
215 Broadway, Wisconsin Dells. ***Tel*** *(608) 253-3523.* *May–Oct: 10am–5pm daily; Nov–Apr: 10am–4pm Sat–Sun.* *(children under 5 free).* **www**.wisconsinhistory.org/hhbennett

Baraboo 35

10,700. *600 W Chestnut St, (800) 227-2266.* **www**.baraboo.com

This tiny town was the winter base of the Ringling Brothers Circus *(see p319)* from 1884 until 1918. Thereafter, the troupe merged with its popular rival Barnum and Bailey to create the Ringling Brothers, Barnum and Bailey Circus, the largest in the United States. The **Circus World Museum**, located on the original Ringling wintering grounds, has live performances, music, parades, calliope concerts, and demonstrations. The museum also contains one of the world's largest collections of carved and painted circus wagons.

Circus World Museum, Baraboo

Circus World Museum
550 Water St. ***Tel*** *(866) 693-1500.* *mid-Apr–mid-May: 10am–4pm daily; mid-May–end-Aug: 9am–6pm daily; Sep–mid-Apr: 10am–4pm Sat–Sun.* *Jan 1, Easter, Thanksgiving, Dec 24–25, 31.* *(children under 5 free).* **www**.circusworldmuseum.com

Madison 36

210,000. *21 New Park St, (800) 373-6376.* **www**.visitmadison.com

Nestled on a narrow isthmus of land between Lake Mendota and Lake Monona, Madison is one of the country's most attractively situated capital cities. Established as the territorial capital in 1836, it became the state capital and home of the lakeside University of Wisconsin campus when Wisconsin achieved statehood, in 1848.

The majestic, 200-ft (60-m) dome of the **Wisconsin State Capitol** rises above the city's beautiful downtown. Among its key interior features are a rotunda encircled by marble Corinthian columns and an exquisite four-panel, glass mosaic symbolizing the themes of liberty and justice.

Madison is considered one of the nation's best places to live and work. The University of Wisconsin and the city's liberal political leanings have drawn scores of artists, environmentalists, and health-food devotees to the area. As a result, downtown features a variety of bookshops, galleries, and restaurants that are vegetarian-friendly. A network of biking and walking trails provides access to the shimmering lakes around the city of Madison.

The **Monona Terrace Community and Convention Center**, completed in 1997 from plans proposed by Frank Lloyd Wright *(see p396)*, has a tranquil rooftop garden that provides great views of downtown and Lake Monona. It includes a memorial to soul singer Otis Redding, who died in a plane crash on the lake in 1967.

Monona Terrace Community & Convention Center
2 blocks E of Capitol Square. ***Tel*** *(608) 261-4000.* *8am–5pm daily.* *1pm daily.* **www**.mononaterrace.com

Wisconsin State Capitol
2 E Main St. ***Tel*** *(608) 266-0382.* *8am–6pm Mon–Fri, 8am–4pm Sat–Sun.* *9am, 10am, 11am, 1pm, 2pm, 3pm Mon–Sat; 1pm, 2pm, 3pm Sun.*

Majestic dome of the Wisconsin State Capitol, Madison

Taliesin, architect Frank Lloyd Wright's sprawling estate in Spring Green

Spring Green ㊲

1,300. 150 E Jefferson St, (800) 588-2042.
www.springgreen.com

This handsome farming community lies just north of the Wisconsin River. In 1911, architect Frank Lloyd Wright, who spent his childhood in nearby Richland Center, built **Taliesin** ("Shining Brow" in Welsh) on a bluff overlooking the river. The 600-acre (240-ha) estate was Wright's home until his death in 1959 and included a school where his disciples were instructed in his Prairie-style design philosophy. Today, the Taliesin Fellowship runs the school and an architectural firm on the grounds. Guided tours lead visitors through Wright's eclectic home and gardens. About 9 miles (14 km) north of Spring Green is the **House on the Rock**. This sprawling resort complex has a home built on top of a 60-ft (18-m) chimney rock. The house, built in the 1940s by eccentric architect Alex Jordan, is the focal point for a rambling museum exhibiting Jordan's vast collection of Americana.

Taliesin
5607 County Rd C, Spring Green.
Tel *(608) 588-7900, (877) 588-7900. May–Oct: 9am–4:30pm daily.*
www.taliesinpreservation.org

House on the Rock
5754 Hwy 23.
Tel *(608) 935-3639. May–mid-Sep: 9am–6pm daily; mid-Sep–Nov: 9am–5pm daily. Jan–Apr, Thanksgiving, Dec 25.*
www.houseontherock.com

La Crosse ㊳

51,000. 410 Veterans Memorial Dr, (800) 658-9424. www.explorelacrosse.com

Founded as a trading post in 1842, La Crosse emerged as a key railroad junction after the Civil War. The city's well-preserved downtown district, and tree-lined neighborhoods around the University of Wisconsin-La Crosse campus, add to its charm. It also makes a fine base for exploring the Mississippi River towns along the Great River Road Scenic Byway *(see p41)* as it passes through the state.

East of downtown, **Grandad Bluff**, 600 ft (180 m) above the city, offers superb views of La Crosse and the Mississippi River Valley. Two restored paddlewheel steamboats offer great views of the river. A good alternative may be **Perrot State Park**, 30 miles (48 km) north of La Crosse. In Trempeleau, south of the park entrance, stands the Trempeleau Hotel *(see p427)*, the town's only building to have survived a fire that took place in 1888.

Grandad Bluff, an observation point east of downtown La Crosse

Apostle Islands ㊴

Bayfield. (800) 447-4094.
www.bayfield.org

Off the state's northeastern Lake Superior coast lie a group of 22 islands, the remains of retreating glaciers from the last Ice Age. They were named the Apostle Islands by 17th-century French missionaries, who incorrectly assumed that the archipelago included only 12 islands. Today, 21 islands form part of the **Apostle Islands National Lakeshore**. The old-growth forests here provide the habitat for resident bald eagles and black bears, while vast stretches of sand beaches with sea caves, carved by the wind and lake into craggy, brownstone cliffs, make the Apostle Islands a popular destination for those interested in eco-tourism.

Sailor mannequins for sale at Bayfield

A local cruise service from **Bayfield**, on the mainland, ferries visitors to the islands, one of which holds the 1881 Sand Island Light Station, with its octagonal tower built from locally quarried sandstone. The 22-chain archipelago offers the area's best sea kayaking. Various outfitters in Bayfield rent kayaks and provide guided charter tours.

Apostle Islands National Lakeshore
415 Washington Ave, Bayfield.
Tel *(715) 779-3397.* **Visitor Center** *8am–4:30pm daily (to 6pm Jun–Aug). Sat & Sun (mid-Oct–mid-May), most federal holidays.*
www.nps.gov/apis

Minnesota

Minnesota has been seductively nicknamed "The Land of 10,000 Lakes." While beautiful lakes have added to the state's appeal as an affordable outdoors destination, it was the meandering rivers that actually shaped Minnesota's history as an important trading and agricultural hub. Many of these rivers, streams, and lakes have now been preserved and offer a rare solitude and natural splendor in vast stretches of its watery wilderness.

Spoonbridge and Cherry **at the Walker Art Center**

Minneapolis & St. Paul 40

Minneapolis *368,400. 250 Marquette Ave S, (888) 676-6757.* **www**.minneapolis.org
St. Paul *287,150. 175 W Kellogg Blvd, (800) 627-6101.* **www**.visitstpaul.com

The twin cities, separated by the Mississippi, are a study in contrasts. Flamboyant Minneapolis, with its modern skyscrapers, is an urbane, commercial center where most of the state's corporate headquarters, museums, and high-end retail stores are located. St. Paul, the state capital, is more sedate, but has a colorful history, well-preserved downtown, and architectural and cultural attractions.

Exploring Minneapolis

Downtown revolves around the pedestrian **Nicollet Mall**, which hosts various cultural events, including occasional free concerts during Minnesota Orchestra's annual Sommerfest. The **Uptown** neighborhood, on the southwest, revolves around the Chain of Lakes, with its network of biking and jogging trails. The country's largest enclosed shopping mall, the **Mall of America**, is in the southern suburb of Bloomington. A 12-mile (19-km) light rail system links Mall of America, the international airport, and downtown Minneapolis.

Walker Art Center

1750 Hennepin Ave. ***Tel*** *(612) 375-7600. 11am–5pm Tue–Sun (until 9pm Thu). public hols. (free 5–9pm Thu; children under 13 free). 2pm Thu–Sun.* **www**.walkerart.org

The performing, visual, and media arts are the focus of the exhibits at the Twin Cities' most complete contemporary art resource. Among the highlights of the permanent and revolving exhibits are the minimalist work of sculptor Donald Judd, including the restored 1971 *Untitled*, a group of six, large-scale aluminium cubes, and Edward Hopper's *Office at Night* (1940).

Minneapolis Institute of Arts

2400 3rd Ave S. ***Tel*** *(612) 870-3131, (888) 642-2787. 10am–5pm Tue–Sat, 11am–5pm Sun. Jul 4, Thanksg., Dec 25.* **www**.artsmia.org

Established in 1915, this is one of the region's largest and most highly regarded museums. Its traditional collection includes a wide range of Greek and Roman statuary, Italian and Dutch Renaissance paintings, as well as American works by John Singleton Copley, Benjamin West, Georgia O'Keeffe, and regionalist Grant Wood.

The **Ulrich Architecture and Design Gallery** houses an astonishing collection of Prairie School furniture, architectural fragments, art-glass windows, and silver.

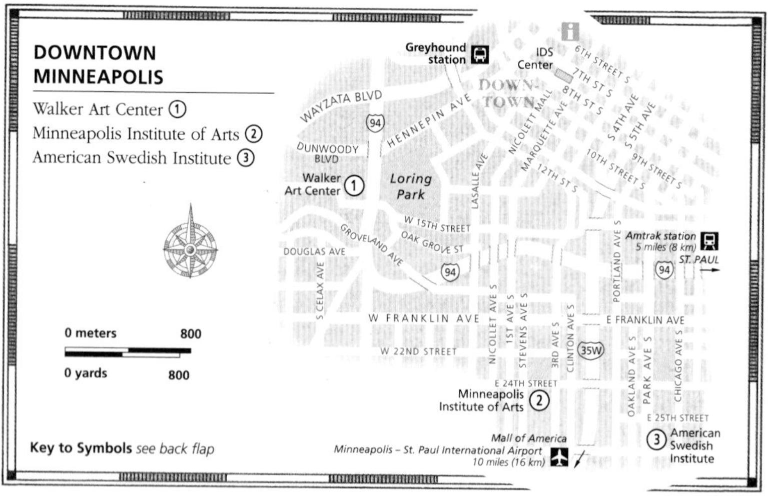

For hotels and restaurants in this region see p426 and p430

American Swedish Institute

2600 Park Ave. **Tel** *(612) 871-4907.* *noon–4pm Tue–Sat (until 8pm Wed, 1–5pm Sun.* *public hols.*
www.americanswedishinst.org

Housed in a grand 1907 Romanesque mansion, this institute chronicles the contributions of Swedish-Americans to the state's history and culture. Guided tours of the house, built by Swedish newspaper publisher Swan Turnblad, allow visitors to view his collection of Swedish-American *kakelugnar* (porcelain tile stoves), woodcarvings, textiles, and immigration artifacts. A revolving exhibit traces the journey of Swedes to the Twin Cities and explores the popular culture of early 20th-century Swedish-American districts.

Exploring St. Paul

Founded in 1841 on the site of Pig's Eye, the notorious French-Canadian trading post, St. Paul flourished as the busiest river port on the Upper Mississippi. By the late 19th century, the new state capital had emerged as a railroad hub, powered by the completion of the railroad between St. Paul and Seattle in 1893. The stately Romanesque, Queen Anne, and Jacobean mansions along **Summit Avenue** date from those prosperous days.

Downtown centers on the Art Deco City Hall and Courthouse on Kellogg Boulevard and St. Peter Street. The popular Minnesota Public Radio program, *A Prairie Home Companion*, is recorded live on many Saturdays at the **Fitzgerald Theater**, a beautifully restored 1910 vaudeville and movie palace at Exchange and Wabasha Streets. The city also hosts the Minnesota State Fair in late August and early September.

Minnesota State Capitol

75 Rev. Dr. Martin Luther King Jr. Blvd. *(651) 296-2881.* *9am–3pm Mon–Fri, 10am–2pm Sat, 1–3pm Sun.* *most public holidays.*

Designed by Cass Gilbert, architect of the US Supreme Court *(see p199)*, the Minnesota State Capitol is a monumental domed Beaux Arts structure. It features the sculpture, *Progress of the State*, a group of gold-leafed copper and steel statues in the front.

The sculpture *Progress of the State*, Minnesota State Capitol

City Hall & Courthouse

15 W Kellogg Blvd. **Tel** *(651) 266-8500.* *8am–4:30pm Mon–Fri.*

This Art Deco masterpiece, painstakingly restored from 1990 to 1993, is built of Indiana limestone and black Wisconsin granite. Its three-story base steps back to the central tower, making the structure appear to soar above the surrounding downtown. No detail was spared in the building's construction, with every light fixture, elevator door, railing, mailbox, door handle, and lock specially crafted in the ornate style of Art Deco.

Minnesota History Center

345 Kellogg Blvd W. **Tel** *(800) 657-3773.* *10am–5pm Mon (public hols only), 10am–8pm Tue, 10am–5pm Wed–Sat, noon–5pm Sun.* *most public hols (except when on Mon).*
www.mnhs.org/historycenter

A treasure trove of interactive exhibits that chronicles the state's 19th century history is housed in this granite and limestone building. Exhibits such as a huge boxcar, giant grain elevator, lifelike meat-packing plant, and a replica of a 1930s dairy farm help visitors relive history from the point of view of a farmer or factory worker. The center's pop culture highlight, **Sounds Good to Me: Music in Minnesota**, showcases the music that originated here.

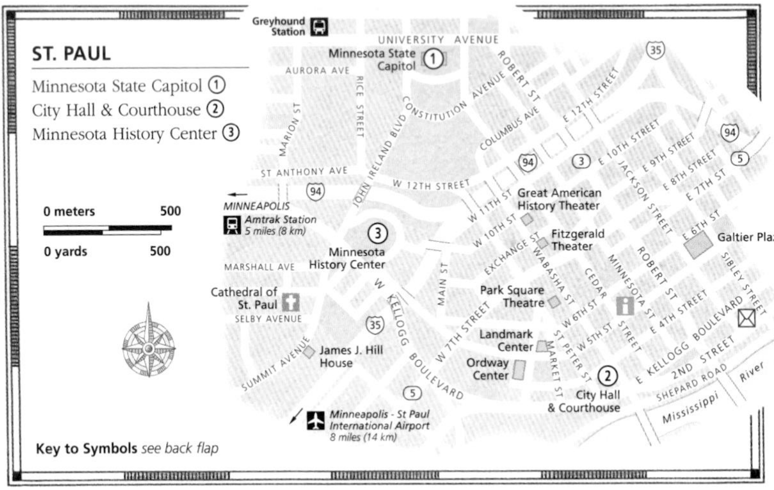

View of the Mississippi River from the Great River Bluffs State Park, southeast of the river town Winona

Mississippi River Towns ❹❶

(763) 212-8556.
www.mnmississippiriver.com

The Mississippi River courses 572 miles (921 km) through Minnesota. It originates in the north-central part of the state and continues until its confluence with the St. Croix River near Hastings. South of the confluence, it widens and picks up speed, rushing through deep, fog-laden valleys along the Minnesota-Wisconsin border. The Great River Road Scenic Byway *(see p41)*, or US 61, hugs the river's west bank, revealing breathtaking views of attractive towns and parks.

The 19th-century town of **Red Wing** was built on the site of a Dakota Sioux farming village. Today, the town is known primarily as the headquarters of the Red Wing Shoe Company, the popular work boot manufacturer, established in 1905. A downtown museum showcases its manufacturing process. The restored 1904 Sheldon Theater presents a musical history of the city.

About 10 miles (16 km) southeast of Red Wing is **Frontenac State Park**, one of the premier bird-watching sites along the river, where over 260 species pause on their journeys north and south every year. Bald eagles and warblers flock to the diverse habitats of Lake Pepin, the widest stretch of the river.

Picturesque **Winona**, 65 miles (105 km) southeast of Red Wing, is located on an island in the river. It prospered in the 19th century as a steamboat refueling stop, mill town, and wheat-shipping depot.

The beautiful **Great River Bluffs State Park**, about 20 miles (32 km) southeast of Winona, occupies one of the river's most scenic stretches.

Rochester ❹❷

90,000. 30 Civic Center Drive SE, (800) 634-8277. **www**.visitrochestermn.com

The primary attraction in this southeastern Minnesota city is the **Mayo Clinic**, founded by the physician brothers Will and Charles Mayo in the early 1900s. They initiated the first collaborative medical practice, integrating the findings of a group of medical specialists to more effectively diagnose and treat serious illnesses. About 2,500 physicians and scientists, plus 42,000 health staff, work at three Mayo sites, treating 500,000 people per year.

Mayo Clinic
200 1st St SW. ***Tel*** *(507) 538-0440.* *general tours at 10am Mon–Fri; art tours at 1:30pm Mon–Fri.* **www**.mayoclinic.org

Pipestone National Monument ❹❸

4,600. 36 Reservation Ave, (507) 825-5464. **Visitor Center** *8am–5pm daily. Jan 1, Thnksg., Dec 25.* **www**.nps.gov/pipe

Pipestone sits in the state's southwestern corner. The name derives from Dakota Sioux Indians who lived here for generations, quarrying the region's soft red quartzite to craft elegant ceremonial pipes. The stone catlinite has been named in honor of artist George Catlin, who depicted this place in his 1838 masterpiece, *Pipestone Quarry*.

Indian craftsmen continue the tradition in the remains of the quarries. The pipes are then sold at the adjoining Cultural Center.

Visitors negotiating a trail through Pipestone's quarries

Brainerd Lakes Area 44

65,000. 124 N 6th St, Brainerd, (800) 450-2838.
www.explorebrainerdlakes.com

Founded by the Northern Pacific Railroad in 1871, the Upper Mississippi River city of Brainerd was carved out of a dense forest, felled to meet the demands of the state's lumber boom. The area's heritage as a hard-working railroad and lumber town is personified in the flannel-shirted, bearded character of Paul Bunyan, the mythical Herculean Minnesota woodsman, and his massive pet, Babe, the Blue Ox. His name seems to appear at every turn; the Paul Bunyan Trail bike route, and Paul Bunyan Scenic Byway backroads auto tour are two examples.

Crow Wing State Park, located 9 miles (14 km) south of Brainerd, offers canoeing on the placid Crow Wing, which feeds into the less predictable Mississippi.

Brainerd is also the gateway to north-central Minnesota's lake region, where the state's trademark lodge-resorts were first developed on the shores of more than 500 freshwater lakes. **Mille Lacs Lake**, 40 miles (64 km) southeast of Brainerd, is bordered by beautiful state parks and the Mille Lacs Band of Ojibwe tribal reservation. The Minnesota Historical Society collaborated with the tribe to develop the Mille Lacs Indian Museum, on the lake's southwest shore.

The restored railroad Depot, the centerpiece of downtown Duluth

Duluth 45

87,000. 21 W Superior St, (800) 438-5884.
www.visitduluth.com

Minnesota's third largest city, Duluth is one of the Midwest's most enjoyable destinations. Clinging to the sides of the 800-ft (240-m) high granite slopes that ring its lively downtown, this city successfully juxtaposes numerous nature preserves with operating industries, which fuel its bustling port.

Babe, the Blue Ox

Its most striking feature is the **Aerial Lift Bridge**, a huge steel structure linking the mainland to the mouth of the Duluth harbor with a 385-ft (115-m) span. The bridge can raise at the rate of 138 ft (41 m) a minute to allow hulking freighters to pass into the harbor. One of these massive ships, the docked 610-ft (186-m) SS *William A. Irwin*, is now a museum.

The **Great Lakes Aquarium and Freshwater Discovery Center**, an "all-freshwater" aquarium, provides a close-up view of the bridge in action.

In Canal Park, next to the bridge, the **Lake Superior Maritime Visitor Center** details the shipping history of the Upper Great Lakes. It also relates the US Army Corps of Engineers' feat of constructing the Aerial Lift Bridge in 1930.

The centerpiece of the redbrick-paved streets of Duluth's attractive downtown is the 1892 **Depot**, or **St. Louis County Heritage and Arts Center**. The restored brownstone railroad depot houses the Duluth Art Institute, Duluth Children's Museum, Lake Superior Railroad Museum, and other types of exhibits. Depot Square, a re-creation of early 20th-century Duluth, features the waiting room where US immigration officials processed many of the state's Scandinavian and German immigrants.

The **North Shore Scenic Railroad** offers sightseeing trips from the depot in period trains. The excursions head north along the shore of Lake Superior, yielding spectacular views of waterfalls and cliffs plunging down to the shoreline. Motorists can also experience this magical trip on the North Shore Scenic Drive, a section of old Hwy 61 that runs along the lakeshore from Duluth all the way to the Canadian border.

The Depot/St. Louis County Heritage & Arts Center
506 W Michigan St. ***Tel*** *(218) 727-8025.* *Jun–Sep: 9:30am–6pm daily; Sep–May: 10am–5pm Mon–Sat, 1–5pm Sun.*
www.duluthdepot.org

Mille Lacs Lake, Minnesota's second largest lake, southeast of Brainerd

A view of Mesabi, one of the three ranges that comprise the Iron Range

Iron Range ㊻

10–2nd Ave W, Chisholm, (800) 422-0806.

When iron ore was discovered in northeastern Minnesota in the 1880s, waves of immigrant workers came to boomtowns that grew up along three ranges – the Vermilion, Mesabi, and Cuyana. These ranges collectively came to be known as the Iron Range district. By the 1960s, the mines' productivity diminished and many were shut down, decimating local communities and leaving behind empty mining pits. But in the past two decades, a growing tourist interest in the mining era has revitalized the Iron Range district.

About 225 miles (362 km) north of Minneapolis, the **Soudan Underground Mine** is Minnesota's oldest and deepest iron mine. It opened in 1884, closed in 1962, and is now part of a 1,300-acre (520-ha) state park. Visitors can go a half-mile (1 km) underground into the heart of the mine that also holds an operating atomic physics lab.

Statue outside Ironworld

The Iron Range city of Chisholm, 45 miles (72 km) southwest of Soudan, is home to the **Ironworld Discovery Center**. The center presents a glitzier, theme-park version of the Iron Range story with living history interpreters and trolley rides. Its highlight is the Minnesota CCC History Museum, commemorating the achievements of the state's Civilian Conservation Corps, a Depression-era program that put 84,000 young men to work on soil and forest conservation projects.

Soudan Underground Mine State Park
1379 Stuntz Bay Rd, Soudan. ***Tel*** *(218) 753-2245. May–Sep: 9:30am–5:30pm; Oct–Apr: 8am–4:30pm.*

Ironworld Discovery Center
801 SW Hwy 169 W, Chisholm. ***Tel*** *(800) 372-6437. 10am–5pm Tue–Sat (to 9pm Thu). (children under 7 free).* **www**.ironworld.com

Boundary Waters Canoe Area Wilderness ㊼

1600 E Sheridan St, Ely, (800) 777-7281, (218) 626-4300. **www**.ely.org; **www**.bwcaw.org

The largest wilderness preserve east of the Rocky Mountains, the Boundary Waters Canoe Area Wilderness stretches for almost 200 miles (322 km) along the Canadian border in the state's northeastern corner. One of the country's most unspoiled natural regions, this vast area attracts adventurers seeking an escape from civilization. The region is also one of the world's largest canoeing and fishing destinations, with more than 1,200 miles (1,932 km) of canoe routes which snake through 1,000 streams and lakes in the dense Superior National Forest.

To preserve the area's unique appeal, there is a limit on the number of campers as well as restrictions on the use of motorized watercraft. The area has no roads, and campers have to carry their equipment from lake to lake via portage methods perfected by the Ojibwe Indians. Still, visitors throng to the area either to canoe in waters teeming with northern pike or to spot rare Canadian lynx or wolverine.

Most camping parties begin their exploration at Ely, 240 miles (386 km) north of Minneapolis. One of the park's far-western entry points. The **Dorothy Molter Museum** is a memorial to the wilderness area's last human resident, who ran a resort here and died in 1986. The **International Wolf Center** in town promotes the survival of the region's once-threatened wolf population through interactive exhibits and close views of the resident gray and Arctic wolf.

Visitors can also take the 63-mile (101-km) Gunflint Trail, a scenic auto road into the northeastern corner of the Boundary Waters area. Motorists are encouraged to fill up the tank, pack food and water, and drive carefully to avoid moose.

Dorothy Molter Museum
2002 E Sheridan St. ***Tel*** *(218) 365-4451. Memorial Day–Labor Day: 10am–5:30pm Mon–Sat, noon–5:30pm Sun; May: weekends. (children under 6 free).* **www**.rootbeerlady.com

International Wolf Center
1396 Hwy 169 Ely. ***Tel*** *(218) 365-4695. 10am–5pm (to 7pm Jun–Aug). Mon–Thu (Oct–May); Sun (Nov–May). (children under 3 free).* **www**.wolf.org

Kayakers on Moose Lake, near Ely, Boundary Waters Wilderness

Voyageurs National Park ⓸⓼

Pelicans on one of the numerous lakes of Voyageurs National Park

3131 Highway 53 S, International 'alls, (218) 283-6600.
www.nps.gov/voya

'he watery Rainy Lake ›orderlands west of Superior Vational Forest contain the ›ld Voyageur Highway, an ›ld network of lakes, streams, ınd portage routes used by Vative Americans and French-Canadian trappers to move urs from the Minnesota and Northern Ontario forests ıcross the Great Lakes to Montreal. The route vas taken over by he British after the 'rench and Indian War, and extended s far west as the Canadian province of Alberta.

Today, 218,000 ıcres (87,200 ha) of his largely empty Canadian Shield vilderness are ›reserved in the Voyageurs Vational Park, a water-based ›ark with 30 lakes and ountless bogs, swamps, ›eaver ponds, and islands – ıabitat of large packs of Eastern timber wolves.

Rainy Lake, the finest fishing ake in the park, abounds in valleye, pike, and bass. The Rainy Lake Visitor Center, near nternational Falls, 295 miles (475 km) north of Minneapolis and 160 miles (258 km) west of Duluth, is one of three staffed access points to the park and the only one open year-round. The center features interactive exhibits concerning the fur trade and provides information about naturalist-guided tours. Although most vistors traverse the park's vast area using boat (motorized watercrafts are permitted here) and canoe, hikers can take advantage of a network of hiking trails, including a self-guided trek to Locater Lake and the Cruiser Lake Trail. This trail is the only means of exploring the roadless Kabetogama Peninsula. Shorter guided tours are available at the park visitor centers.

Lithograph of a fur trapper's cabin

For those people keen on boating, the border city of International Falls is the home base for stocking up on supplies or arranging a boat or canoe rental. The town's Boise Paper Solutions houses what the company claims to be the "largest, fastest paper machine in the world." In winter, the Voyageurs National Park offers opportunities for snowmobiling, ice fishing, and cross-country skiing.

WOLVES

Voyageurs National Park is one of the largest wolf sanctuaries in the US. The animals that roam here are gray wolves, one of three species of wolves in the world. Wolves live in packs, dominated by two adult parents, their offspring of the past 2–3 years, and several unrelated members. Contrary to folklore, wolves tend to shy away from humans.

Gray Wolf

Aerial view of the many islets in wild, spectacular Voyageurs National Park

Practical Information

Traveling around the Great Lakes states requires a lot of planning, since there is so much to see and do in such a wide area. From the towering skyscrapers of bustling big cities such as Chicago to the idyllic pastures of Wisconsin, the attractions here are as varied as the six states that form the Great Lakes region. With its rolling hills, endless farmlands, and sublime waterfront wilderness, America's heartland abounds in pristine wonders that offer a wide choice of outdoor pursuits.

TOURIST INFORMATION

Each of the Great Lakes states houses at least one state Welcome Center that offers a full range of tourist information, as well as clean restrooms. Most airports have information desks stocked with free brochures and maps. All the larger cities and many smaller towns have Convention & Visitors' Bureaus or Chambers of Commerce, with free directories of attractions, accommodations, and events.

NATURAL HAZARDS

Winters in the northern parts of Michigan, Minnesota, and Wisconsin can be very cold, with blizzards and snowstorms a common occurrence. Visitors should dress warmly and pack a small snow shovel, gloves, and a hat when traversing this region between November and April. Ice and snow can make driving extremely treacherous.

GETTING AROUND

Most major cities have limited public bus systems. Light rail, subway, and commuter train services only run in Chicago and Cleveland. A new public rail transit system is in operation in the Twin Cities, serving Minneapolis, St. Paul, and the surrounding metro area.

However, driving is the best way to get around this region. Seat belts are a must for drivers, front seat passengers, and back seat passengers. Child seats are mandatory for occupants aged four and under (8 and under in Illinois, 7 and under in Indiana). Helmets are compulsory for motorcyclists under the age of 18 in all of the Great Lakes states, except Michigan where all motorcyclists must wear helmets, and Illinois, which has no restrictions regarding helmet usage. Speed limits vary, but are usually 65–70 mph (105–113 km/hour) on Interstate Highways outside urban areas.

THE CLIMATE OF THE GREAT LAKES

Weather in most of the Great Lakes states is fairly consistent. Temperatures tend to be cooler in the northern states of Michigan, Wisconsin, and Minnesota where cold, snowy winters lure residents to ski. The southern regions of Ohio, Indiana, and Illinois witness a more temperate climate. Summer months are ideal for touring the lakeside areas in Ohio, Wisconsin, Michigan, and Minnesota. Cooler temperatures and fall colors make Sep–Oct ideal for an extended trip to Chicago and scenic drives through the rugged forests of Michigan's Upper Peninsula.

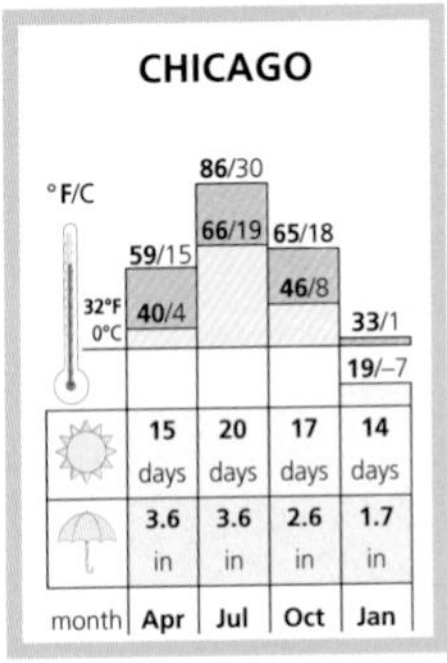

ETIQUETTE

Residents of the Great Lakes are friendly and polite – especially in Minnesota, where the phrase, "you bet," epitomizes their helpful attitude. Visitors to the Amish communities in Indiana and Ohio will be impressed by the shy, reserved manner of the Amish, whose simple, black outfits and horse-driven buggies are common sights on the roads. Many prefer not to be photographed, so ask their permission first.

FESTIVALS

The Great Lakes states stage a diverse range of annual, community, regional, state, and cultural festivals. As an expression of Chicago's strong Irish heritage, the city actually dyes the Chicago River green as part of its boisterous **St. Patrick's Day Parade**. The Mexican-American population residing in the region celebrates **Cinco de Mayo** (early May) festivals in many of the Great Lakes cities; it is celebrated in a big way especially in Chicago. Summer brings a deluge of outdoor events, starting on Memorial Day weekend with the Indianapolis 500 auto race. Fireworks and street festivals are the norm for various county and state fairs that crop up in July and August. The Minnesota State Fair (August), held in St. Paul is one of the largest summer events, along with Milwaukee's immensely popular **Summerfest**. Milwaukee also hosts a series of ethnic summer festivals on its lakefront, such as the Irish Fest, a huge celebration of Irish culture.

SPORTS

The Great Lakes region harbors a wide array of professional and amateur sports teams, with major pro baseball, football, and basketball franchises operating in nearly all of the major cities. The onset of spring signals the beginning of the baseball season, with fans flocking to historic **Wrigley Field**, home of the Chicago Cubs. Ohio boasts some of the region's best minor league parks in Toledo, Akron, and Dayton. This region also loves its football. The gregarious fans of the Chicago Bears and Cleveland Browns pro teams go head-to-head with the Wisconsin "Cheeseheads," who strip to the waist in the freezing cold to cheer on the Green Bay Packers. Several universities compete in the **Big Ten** conference that draws over 100,000 fans.

Winter brings basketball and hockey to the frozen region, with four NHL hockey teams, and many college teams active across the region.

OUTDOOR ACTIVITIES

Relatively short summers and long winters do not deter Great Lakes residents from enjoying the outdoors. On the contrary, the region's climate seems to encourage a more passionate pursuit of recreational activities, with mountain biking and cycling enthusiasts thronging paths and trails from April through early November. Northern Minnesota and Wisconsin are favorite canoe and kayak destinations, while sail and motorboats are omnipresent on all of the Great Lakes throughout summer. Many fishing enthusiasts look forward to ice fishing in winter. Skiing and snowmobiling are also extremely popular.

Some of the region's best outdoors outfitters are located at Ely, entrance to the Boundary Waters Area Canoe Wilderness, and in Bayfield, gateway to the Apostle Islands National Lakeshore. For a list of outfitters in these locations, contact the **Ely Chamber of Commerce** or the **Bayfield Chamber**.

ENTERTAINMENT

Most of the region's most famous live music and theatrical venues are in Chicago. **Buddy Guy's Legends** and the **Kingston Mines** are the best places to hear authentic electric Chicago blues. The **House of Blues** hosts a wide range of blues and alternative rock acts. Comedy fans flock to Chicago's **Second City**, training ground for many *Saturday Night Live* cast members, and to St. Paul's **Fitzgerald Theater**, home base for Minnesota humorist Garrison Keillor's long-running *A Prairie Home Companion* radio program.

The summertime **Big Top Chautauqua**, situated near Wisconsin's Apostle Islands, holds similar, old-time comic and musical shows. Visitors can also check out rides at the region's largest amusement parks: **Cedar Point** in Sandusky and **Kings Island** in Cincinnati.

SHOPPING

The region's premier retail destination is Chicago's **Magnificent Mile**. This dense stretch of Michigan Avenue north of the Chicago River holds some the nation's premier specialty shops, augmenting the classic **Macy's** (formerly Marshall Field's) department store on State Street in the heart of the Loop. Another popular shopping destination is the pedestrian **Nicollet Mall** in Minneapolis. This pleasantly designed downtown district is far removed from the Twin Cities' 520-store **Mall of America**, the country's largest indoor shopping mall, which is being expanded. Tourists can also travel to the Amish communities in northern Indiana. **Shipshewana** has a busy flea market, where quilts, rugs, and baked goods can be bought at reasonable prices.

DIRECTORY

TOURIST OFFICES

Illinois
Tel *(800) 226-6632.*
www.enjoyillinois.com

Indiana
Tel *(800) 677-9800.*
www.enjoyindiana.com

Michigan
Tel *(800) 644-2489.*
www.michigan.org

Minnesota
Tel *(888) 868-7476.*
www.exploreminnesota.com

Ohio
Tel *(800) 282-5393.*
www.ohiotourism.com

Wisconsin
Tel *(800) 432-8747.*
www.travelwisconsin.com

SPORTS & OUTDOOR ACTIVITIES

Bayfield Chamber of Commerce
Tel *(800) 472-4094.*

Ely Chamber of Commerce
Tel *(800) 777-7281.*

Fitzgerald Theatre
10 East Exchange Street
Tel *(651) 290-1200.*

ENTERTAINMENT

Big Top Chautauqua
Ski Hill Rd.
Tel *(888) 244-8368.*

Buddy Guy's Legends
754 S Wabash.
Tel *(312) 427-0333.*

Cedar Point
1 Cedar Point Dr.
Tel *(419) 627-2350.*

House of Blues
329 N Dearborn St.
Tel *(312) 923-2000.*

Kings Island
6300 Kings Island Dr.
Tel *(800) 288-0808.*

Kingston Mines
2548 N Halsted St.
Tel *(773) 477-4646.*

Second City
1616 N Wells.
Tel *(877) 778-4707.*

SHOPPING

Macy's
Tel *(312) 781-1000.*
www.macys.com

Magnificent Mile
Tel *(312) 642-3570.*
www.themagnificentmile.com

Mall of America
Tel *(952) 883-8800.*
www.mallofamerica.com

Nicollet Mall
Tel *(888) 676-6757.*
www.minneapolis.org

Shipshewana Flea Market
Tel *(260) 768 4129.*
www.tradingplaceamerica.com

Choosing a Hotel

Most Great Lakes cities have a range of chain hotels and motels. While larger centers such as Chicago, St. Paul, Cincinnati, and Indianapolis have historic boutique hotels and bed-and-breakfast inns, the remote areas of Minnesota, Wisconsin, and Michigan's Upper Peninsula harbor a choice of relaxing lakeside lodge and cabin resorts.

PRICE CATEGORIES
For a standard double room per night, including service charges and any additional taxes.

$ Under $100
$$ $100–$150
$$$ $150–$200
$$$$ $200–$300
$$$$$ Over $300

ILLINOIS

CHICAGO J. Ira & Nicki Harris Family Hostel — $

24 E Congress Prkwy, 60605 ***Tel*** *(312) 360-0300* ***Fax*** *(312) 360-0313* ***Rooms*** *55*

Located in a renovated 1886 building, a short walk from Lake Michigan and Grant Park, is this award-winning hoste which charges budget prices in a good location. Accommodation is in safe, clean dormitory rooms, most of which have a bathroom. Breakfast is included in the price and guests have use of a large kitchen. **www.hichicago.org**

CHICAGO Ohio House Motel — $

600 N LaSalle St, 60610 ***Tel*** *(312) 943-6000, (866) 601-6446* ***Fax*** *(312) 943-6063* ***Rooms*** *50*

This throwback, 1950s-style hotel boasts great rates, modest accommodations, and a prime location in the heart of the River North gallery district. You'll find no frills here – amenities include little more than cable TV, shower, and bat – but for exploring downtown on a budget, it doesn't get much more affordable. **www.ohiohousemotel.com**

CHICAGO Hotel Burnham — $$$

1 W Washington St, 60602 ***Tel*** *(312) 782-1111, (877) 294-9712* ***Fax*** *(312) 782-0899* ***Rooms*** *122*

Set in the magnificent Daniel Burnham-designed Reliance Building, this stunning hotel is both classic and cheerfully contemporary, with lovely touches such as mosaic floors and metal elevator grills. Many of the stylish rooms have grea Loop views. The lobby-level Atwood Café serves up three-star contemporary American fare. **www.burnhamhotel.cor**

CHICAGO Hotel Sax — $$$

333 Dearborn St, 60610 ***Tel*** *(312) 245-0333, (877) 569-3742* ***Fax*** *(312) 923-2444* ***Rooms*** *361*

Surrounded by some of River North's top dining and nightlife destinations, this trendy luxury property has undergon massive renovation to its rooms and now boasts a look described as "17th-century French salon with a 21st-century twist." Strong emphasis on service. **www.hotelsaxchicago.com**

CHICAGO Silversmith Hotel & Suites — $$$

10 S Wabash Ave, 60603 ***Tel*** *(312) 372-7696, (800) 979-0084* ***Fax*** *(312) 372-7320* ***Rooms*** *143*

Set in the landmark Silversmith building, this terra-cotta-clad Arts and Crafts-style structure was designed by legendary Chicago architects D.H. Burnham and Company. Rooms here are stylish and subdued, with microwave, CD player, two-line phones, in-room safe, and high-speed Internet access. **www.silversmithchicagohotel.com**

CHICAGO Drake Hotel — $$$$

140 E Walton Pl, 60611 ***Tel*** *(312) 787-2200, (800) 553-7253* ***Fax*** *(312) 787-1431* ***Rooms*** *537*

The grande dame of Chicago hotels, this luxurious Michigan Avenue destination still attracts luminaries from all ove the world. Rooms boast stunning views of Lake Michigan or the Mag Mile. Onsite restaurants include the Cape Cod Room seafood restaurant and the Palm Court for high tea. **www.thedrakehotel.com**

CHICAGO Ritz-Carlton Chicago — $$$$

160 E Pearson St, 60611 ***Tel*** *(312) 266-1000, (800) 819-5053* ***Fax*** *(312) 266-1194* ***Rooms*** *435*

Perched above Water Tower Place on Michigan Avenue, this grand luxury hotel is all about old-fashioned elegance, from the rooms' antique cherrywood furnishings and marble bathrooms to the famously service-oriented staff. All rooms have large picture windows with views of the city or lake. **www.fourseasons.com/chicagorc/**

GALENA Stoney Creek Inn — $$

940 Galena Square Dr, 61036 ***Tel*** *(815) 777-2223, (800) 659-2220* ***Fax*** *(815) 777-6762* ***Rooms*** *76*

This family-friendly chain hotel is all about rustic atmosphere, from furniture made from logs to theme suites with wilderness wall murals. Room amenities include TV and wireless Internet access. Continental breakfast, gift shop, indoor heated pool, whirlpool, and sauna also available. **www.stoneycreekinn.com**

OAK PARK Carleton of Oak Park Hotel — $$

1110 Pleasant St, 60302 ***Tel*** *(708) 848-5000, (888) 227-5386* ***Fax*** *(708) 848-0537* ***Rooms*** *154*

Set in an historic 1928 brick building, this boutique hotel is a short stroll from Frank Lloyd Wright's Unity Temple. Most of the comfortably furnished rooms have a kitchen with microwave and refrigerator, as well as wireless Internet access. Classic American restaurant Philander's features live jazz nightly. **www.carletonhotel.com**

Key to Symbols *see back cover flap*

INDIANA

BLOOMINGTON Fourwinds Resort $$

9301 Fairfax Rd, 47401 **Tel** *(812) 824-2628, (800) 824-2628* **Fax** *(812) 824-9816* **Rooms** *123*

Located in the hills of the Hoosier National Forest, with views of Lake Monroe and just 10 miles from Bloomington, this modern facility provides guests with such opportunities as boating, basketball, miniature golf, and volleyball. The brick-and-wood exterior resort has a restaurant, bar, children's activity area, and beach. **www.fourwindsresort.com**

FORT WAYNE Don Hall's Guesthouse $

1313 W Washington Center Rd, 46825 **Tel** *(260) 489-2524, (800) 348-1999* **Fax** *(260) 489-7067* **Rooms** *130*

Plush furnishings and a stone fireplace greet travelers to Don Hall's Guesthouse. The inn has standard rooms along with studio rooms and hospitality suites. The water fun area has two pools and a whirlpool, perfect for the family. Don Hall's also offers free transportation to the local library and Glenbrook Mall. **www.donhalls.com**

FRENCH LICK French Lick Springs Resort & Casino $$$$

8670 W Hwy 56, 47432 **Tel** *(812) 936-9300, (888) 936-9360* **Fax** *(812) 936-2100* **Rooms** *686*

Renovated to their original opulence, the resort's two hotels, French Lick Springs and West Baden Springs, offer excellent service and luxurious accommodations. Nestled among mineral springs, blooming flowers, and plush gardens, this facility provides guests with golf courses, tennis courts, spa services, and a riverboat casino. **www.frenchlick.com**

INDIANAPOLIS The Canterbury Hotel $$$$

123 S Illinois St, 46225 **Tel** *(317) 634-3000, (800) 538-8186* **Fax** *(317) 685-2519* **Rooms** *99*

Listed on the National Register of Historic Places, the charming mid-19th century Canterbury Hotel welcomes guests to downtown Indianapolis in style with its mahogany furniture and traditional artwork. The hotel offers a private entrance to the mall next door, filled with restaurants, cinemas, and specialty shops. **www.canterburyhotel.com**

MADISON Hillside Inn $

831 E Main St, 47250 **Tel** *(812) 265-3721, (877) 265-3232* **Rooms** *30*

The Hillside Inn in Madison was the site of the 1958 film *Some Came Running* with stars Frank Sinatra and Dean Martin. This historic inn welcomes travelers with comfortable rooms and offers views of the Ohio River with its traveling riverboats and barges. **www.hillsidemadison.com**

NEW HARMONY The New Harmony Inn $$

504 North St, 47631 **Tel** *(812) 682-4431, (800) 782-8605* **Fax** *(812) 682-3423* **Rooms** *90*

Nestled on the bend of the Wabash River, the New Harmony Inn was built in the simple style of the bygone era of the Harmonists, combined with modern conveniences such as complimentary wireless Internet. The inn features a tranquil setting with winding paths, labyrinth gardens, fountains, and waterfalls. **www.newharmonyinn.com**

MICHIGAN

DETROIT The Atheneum Suite Hotel $$$$

1000 Brush Ave, 48226 **Tel** *(313) 962-2323, (800) 772-2323* **Fax** *(313) 962-2424* **Rooms** *174*

The Atheneum Suite Hotel is situated in the middle of Greektown and provides access to the Renaissance Center in downtown Detroit and to Greektown dining and nightlife. This 174-suites luxury hotel has a lobby decorated with murals of Trojan warriors. **www.atheneumsuites.com**

GRAND RAPIDS Homewood Suites by Hilton $

3920 Stahl Dr SE, 49546 **Tel** *(616) 285-7100* **Fax** *(616) 285-1505* **Rooms** *78*

Homewood Suites in Grand Rapids is a comfortably modern hotel. It offers two-bedroom suites with efficiency kitchens among the standard rooms. The hotel has interior corridors with elevator access. Pets are allowed but a fee will be assessed. Rooms are being renovated a few at a time. **www.homewoodsuites.hilton.com**

KALAMAZOO Stuart Avenue ınn Bed & Breakfast $$

229 Stuart Ave, 49007 **Tel** *(269) 342-0230, (800) 461-0621* **Fax** *(269) 385-3442* **Rooms** *7*

Guests are greeted with hand-painted wallpapers, period antiques, and Belgian lace curtains at this elegant Victorian house. This is a three-story home without elevators and is a smoke-free environment. A complimentary full breakfast is provided. **www.stuartavenueinn.com**

MACKINAC ISLAND The Grand Hotel $$$$

1 Grand Ave, 49757 **Tel** *(906) 847-3331, (800) 334-7263* **Fax** *(906) 847-3259* **Rooms** *381*

An elegant 1887 building, this was the perfect setting for the romantic film *Somewhere in Time*, starring Christopher Reeve. Perched high over the Straits of Mackinac, the hotel offers picturesque lake views and rooms filled with antiques. Rates include breakfast and dinner. Motorized vehicles are not allowed on the historic island. **www.grandhotel.com**

MACKINAW CITY Best Western – Dockside Waterfront Inn $$$

505 S Huron Ave, 49701 ***Tel*** *(231) 436-5001* ***Fax*** *(231) 436-5933* ***Rooms*** *112*

Located on Lake Huron, guests can enjoy a lakefront room with a private balcony overlooking the view. Take advantage of the sun deck, paddleboat rentals, and the 1,400 feet of private sandy beach. A complimentary full breakfast is provided. **www.bestwestern.com**

TRAVERSE CITY Bayshore Resort $$$$

833 E Front St, 49686 ***Tel*** *(231) 935-4400, (800) 634-4401* ***Fax*** *(231) 935-0262* ***Rooms*** *120*

This beachside, Victorian-style resort provides breathtaking views of the West Grand Traverse Bay. The only transportation to the inn is by boat or float plane. Nearby towns provide free shuttle boats that depart daily. This is a smoke-free establishment. Free Continental breakfast. **www.bayshore-resort.com**

MINNESOTA

DETROIT LAKES The Lodge on Lake Detroit $$$

1200 E Shore Dr, 56501 ***Tel*** *(218) 847-8439, (800) 761-8439* ***Rooms*** *55*

Surrounded by a beautifully wooded area and a 150-ft private sandy beach, The Lodge on Lake Detroit is a welcome addition to the area. The resort opened in 2006 and provides a variety of activities for the entire family. Canoes and paddle boats are available as well as a spa with massage, manicures, and pedicures. **www.thelodgeonlakedetroit.com**

DULUTH South Pier Inn on the Canal $$$

701 Lake Ave S, 55802 ***Tel*** *(218) 786-9007, (800) 430-7437* ***Rooms*** *29*

South Pier Inn offers the most spectacular views of Lake Superior from your own private balcony. It's said you can see "eye-to-eye" with ships' captains. This inn with 400 feet of private shoreline provides plenty of "Kodak" moments with its romantic settings. **www.southpierinn.com**

LAKE KABETOGAMA Kettle Falls Hotel $

10502 Gamma Rd, 56669 ***Tel*** *(218) 240-1724* ***Rooms*** *12*

Accessible only by boat or plane, the Kettle Falls Hotel & Resort offers 12 different rooms for guests seeking to get away from city life. This resort was built in 1913, with original guests being loggers, prospectors, and prostitutes. The hotel provides a restaurant and bar for guests. **www.kettlefallshotel.com**

MINNEAPOLIS Minneapolis Grand Hotel $$$$

615 Second Ave S, 55402 ***Tel*** *(612) 288-8888, (866) 843-4726* ***Fax*** *(612) 373-0407* ***Rooms*** *140*

The Minneapolis Grand Hotel is just that – grand. This downtown hotel has 140 uniquely different rooms from which to choose. It is known for its innovative two-story fitness center and spa. Business services such as Internet access are provided. **www.grandhotelminneapolis.com**

MINNEAPOLIS Chambers, The Luxury Art Hotel $$$$$

901 Hennepin Ave, 55403 ***Tel*** *(612) 767-6900, (877) 767-6990* ***Fax*** *(612) 767-6801* ***Rooms*** *60*

This hotel combines art, design, and culinary skill in its presentation to guests and lives up to its name with luxury at every corner. Special amenities include in-room massage therapy and beauty services. A guest pass for the local fitness center is also provided. **www.chambersminneapolis.com**

ST. PAUL St. Paul Hotel $$$$$

350 Market St, 55102 ***Tel*** *(651) 292-9292, (800) 292-9292* ***Fax*** *(651) 228-9506* ***Rooms*** *254*

Celebrating its centennial year of business in 2010, the St. Paul is a landmark Minnesota hotel that has had a reputation for fine luxury lodging since its inception. All rooms have classic decor with modern amenities. Central location and free local transportation. **www.stpaulhotel.com**

OHIO

CINCINNATI The Vernon Manor Hotel $$

400 Oak St, 45219 ***Tel*** *(513) 281-3300, (800) 543-3999* ***Fax*** *(513) 281-8933* ***Rooms*** *177*

The Vernon Manor Hotel greets guests with a cobblestone drive. This historic hotel, fashioned after an English home, overlooks the city. The spacious guestrooms are filled with antiques. The hotel offers an English pub, fine dining, a florist, and a massage therapist. Pets are allowed with a fee assessed. **www.vernonmanorhotel.com**

CINCINNATI The Cincinnatian Hotel $$$$

601 Vine St, 45202 ***Tel*** *(513) 381-3000, (800) 942-9000* ***Fax*** *(513) 651-0256* ***Rooms*** *146*

In operation since 1882, the Cincinnatian Hotel is a downtown institution. Listed on the National Register of Historic Places, the Cincinnatian was one of the first hotels to have elevators. It has an eight-story atrium for guests to relax and take in the ambience of the hotel with its fireplaces, balconies, and contemporary design. **www.cincinnatianhotel.com**

Key to Price Guide *see p424* **Key to Symbols** *see back cover flap*

CLEVELAND Baricelli Inn $$$

2203 Cornell Rd, 44106 ***Tel*** *(216) 791-6500* ***Fax*** *(216) 791-9131* ***Rooms*** *7*

The Baricelli Inn is known for its savory restaurant. Each of the seven rooms in this quaint brownstone (1896) is individually and charmingly decorated. This three-story inn provides a complimentary Continental breakfast for its guests. **www.baricelli.com**

COLUMBUS The Lofts Hotel $$$$

55 E Nationwide Blvd, 43215 ***Tel*** *(614) 461-2663, (800) 735-6381* ***Fax*** *(614) 461-2630* ***Rooms*** *44*

Located at the heart of Columbus, The Lofts has floor-to-ceiling windows from which to view the bustling activities of downtown. Built from a 100-plus-year-old warehouse, this inn has used contemporary design to treat guests during a night's stay. Travelers have a choice of a loft-style room with plush furnishings. **www.55lofts.com**

PAINESVILLE Renaissance Quail Hollow Resort $$$

11080 Concord Hambden Rd, 44077 ***Tel*** *(440) 497-1100* ***Fax*** *(440) 497-1111* ***Rooms*** *176*

Renaissance Quail Hollow Resort is a nice, tranquil getaway from the hustle and bustle of everyday life. This modern resort has 36 holes of golf, swimming, tennis, spa, and other facilities to enjoy. Fine dining is available, serving different specialty dishes. Early check-in and late check-out is a plus. **www.quailhollowresort.com**

TOLEDO Mansion View Inn $$

2035 Collingwood Ave, 43620 ***Tel*** *(419) 244-5676* ***Fax*** *(419) 244-9268* ***Rooms*** *4*

The Mansion View Inn provides guests with comfortable rooms made cozy with Victorian decor. This inn encompasses 11,000 feet (1022 m) of land and is within walking distance of the Toledo Museum of Art. **www.mansionviewtoledo.com**

WISCONSIN

GREEN BAY Hilton Garden Inn $$$

1015 Lombardi Ave, 54304 ***Tel*** *(920) 405-0400* ***Fax*** *(920) 405-0512* ***Rooms*** *125*

The Hilton Garden Inn near Lambeau Field (home of the Green Bay Packers) encompasses five stories, with elevators provided. The comfortable, clean inn offers customers a good service. Some rooms are available with whirlpools. **www.hiltongardeninn.com**

MADISON Edgewater Hotel $$$

666 Wisconsin Ave, 53703 ***Tel*** *(608) 256-9071, (800) 922-5512* ***Fax*** *(608) 256-0910* ***Rooms*** *107*

Within walking distance of the downtown attractions yet far enough from the bustle to be a peaceful destination, some of the rooms and the restaurant at the Edgewater overlook Lake Mendota. Guests can enjoy cocktails on the pier during warm weather. An expansion program is underway in the hotel. **www.theedgewater.com**

MILWAUKEE Hyatt Regency Milwaukee $$$

333 W Kilbourn Ave, 53203 ***Tel*** *(414) 276-1234* ***Fax*** *(414) 276-6338* ***Rooms*** *484*

The Hyatt Regency is located in downtown Milwaukee. Skywalks bring the Midwest Airlines Center, Federal Plaza, Grand Avenue shopping, and the Entertainment District closer and make them easily accessible. After a day of exploring, enjoy the deluxe accommodations that the Hyatt provides. **www.hyatt.com**

MILWAUKEE Pfister Hotel $$$$

424 E Wisconsin Ave, 53202 ***Tel*** *(414) 273-8222, (800) 558-8222* ***Fax*** *(414) 273-5025* ***Rooms*** *307*

The Pfister Hotel offers luxurious accommodations and excellent service. Guido Pfister, a successful Milwaukee merchant, built this grand downtown hotel in 1893 and it has since been restored to its former glory. This hotel, home to a huge Victorian art collection, is now a historic landmark. **www.thepfisterhotel.com**

STURGEON BAY White Lace Inn $$

16 N 5th Ave, 54235 ***Tel*** *(920) 743-1105, (877) 948-5223* ***Fax*** *(920) 743-8180* ***Rooms*** *18*

Close to downtown, White Lace Inn is a glorious bed and breakfast that includes four historic homes. A smoke-free environment, the facilities are two-story but there is no elevator. A complimentary full breakfast is served in the main house. **www.whitelaceinn.com**

TREMPELEAU Trempealeau Hotel $

150 Main St, 54661 ***Tel*** *(608) 534-6898* ***Fax*** *(608) 534-6054* ***Rooms*** *11*

With amazing views of the Mississippi River, the Trempeleau Hotel offers a relaxing, refreshing atmosphere with comfortable rooms. Built in 1871 this quaint hotel also offers a casual, vegetarian-friendly restaurant. Outside activities and live music are also available. **www.trempealeauhotel.com**

WISCONSIN DELLS Kalahari Resort $$$$

1305 Kalahari Dr, 53965 ***Tel*** *(608) 254-5466, (877) 525-2427* ***Fax*** *(608) 254-2381* ***Rooms*** *750*

Both families and business travelers converge at the Kalahari Resort, a year-round destination. The African safari-themed resort incorporates an indoor theme park with a six-story high Ferris wheel, an indoor waterpark, go-karting, bowling, and miniature golf. Rooms and suites are comfortable and well equipped. **www.kalahariresorts.com**

Choosing a Restaurant

Although family-style dining establishments are numerous in all the Great Lakes states, nearly every sizable community contains a variety of fine-dining alternatives. The cosmopolitan, ethnically diverse dining scenes of the major cities challenge notions about traditional Midwestern meat and potatoes fare.

PRICE CATEGORIES
For a three-course meal for one, including a glass of house wine (where served), and all other unavoidable charges such as sales tax.
$ Under $20
$$ $20–$40
$$$ $40–$60
$$$$ $60–$80
$$$$$ Over $80

ILLINOIS

CHICAGO Ed Debevic's — $$
640 N Wells St, 60620 ***Tel** (312) 664-1707*

One-part diner, one-part theme restaurant, this '50s-style hangout is all about sassy, entertaining service – your waiter may excuse himself to hop up on the counter and do a dance routine – offered up with a menu of classic American favorites such as hamburgers, nachos, chili, hot dogs, and milkshakes. Hugely popular with teens and school groups.

CHICAGO Heaven on Seven — $$
Garland Building, 111 N Wabash Ave (7th Floor), 60602 ***Tel** (312) 263-6443*

Gregarious chef/owner Jimmy Bannos has been whipping up spicy Cajun and Creole fare on the seventh floor of the historic Garland Building for more than 25 years. Breakfast draws a crowd of Loop regulars, while the lunch menu offers jambalaya, Louisiana crab cakes, and po-boys. Lunch and breakfast only (dinner served third Friday of the month).

CHICAGO Carson's "The Place for Ribs" — $$$
612 N Wells St, 60610 ***Tel** (312) 280-9200*

Chicago's most famous barbecue restaurant, this legendary River North spot has been serving up plates of sauce-slicked baby back ribs and barbecued pork chops, chicken, and shrimp since 1976. Decked out with hunter green walls, floral carpeting, and dark wood accents, the room has a slightly dated supper club feel.

CHICAGO Trattoria No. 10 — $$$
10 N Dearborn St, 60602 ***Tel** (312) 984-1718*

Close to the downtown Theater District, this restaurant is quite popular as a pre-show destination – and for its weeknight $12 appetizer buffet. On the meal menu, expect a modern take on Italian classics, from Kobe skirt steak with cremini mushrooms and Parmigiano-Reggiano to farfalle pasta with duck confit and asparagus.

CHICAGO North Pond — $$$$
2610 N Cannon Dr, 60614 ***Tel** (773) 477-5845*

Nestled on a quiet pond in the middle of Lincoln Park, this contemporary American restaurant boasts one of the loveliest settings in the city. The airy, light-filled space is handsomely decorated in Arts and Crafts style. Award-winning chef Bruce Sherman works closely with local farmers and uses fresh, seasonal ingredients.

CHICAGO Russian Tea Time — $$$$
77 E Adams St, 60603 ***Tel** (312) 360-0000*

Dining at this Loop restaurant can feel like being in a Moscow tea room. Russian speakers dig into cold borscht and warm potato pancakes with sour cream and applesauce, as well as meat-stuffed pelmeni (dumplings) and chicken kebabs. Afternoon tea is served daily; the restaurant offers traditional vodka flights with pumpernickel and a pickle.

CHICAGO Everest — $$$$$
Chicago Stock Exchange, 440 S LaSalle St, 40th Floor, 60605 ***Tel** (312) 663-8920*

Perched 40 floors above the city, this exquisitely appointed French restaurant is considered one of the world's finest dining destinations. This is special occasion dining as it used to be: tuxedoed staff, hushed atmosphere, crystal chandeliers, and a strict jacket-required policy for gentlemen. There are several tasting menu options.

GALENA Fried Green Tomatoes — $$$
213 N Main St, 61036 ***Tel** (815) 777-3938*

Set in an historic 1838 building that has been a grocery, leather store, and monument shop, this charming storefront is now an Italian-inspired restaurant, popular for special-occasion dining. Must-try dishes include the namesake appetizer, plus traditional pasta and meat such as fettucine alfredo and veal marsala. Award-winning wine list.

OAK PARK Winberie's Restaurant and Bar — $
151 N Oak Park Ave, 60301 ***Tel** (708) 386-2600*

A bright, busy restaurant on Oak Park's main strip, this corner restaurant and wine bar is one of the area's top dining options. Antiques and framed posters give the space a charming feel; the eclectic menu is casual but creative, with fried calamari and wild mushroom potato cakes and parmesan shrimp po-boys. Extensive wine list.

Key to Symbols *see back cover flap*

INDIANA

BLOOMINGTON Michael's Uptown Café $$$

102 E Kirkwood Ave, 47408 ***Tel*** *(812) 339-0900*

Fiercely independent since 1976, Michaels' Uptown Café offers a chic jazz ambience right off the courthouse square. Citing "Real Food, Real Drinks, Real People," the café serves adventurous continental fare plus Cuban, Creole, and Cajun creations. Breakfast is delicious. People have written songs about the cottage cheese pancakes.

FORT WAYNE Biaggi's Ristorante Italiano $$

4010 W Jefferson Blvd, 46804 ***Tel*** *(260) 459-6700*

Biaggi's Ristorante Italiano is a well-regarded chain that entices diners with a menu consisting of steak, seafood, and pasta dishes. Try the savory home-made ravioli. The main dining room is an elegant but welcoming room with hardwood floors. Reservations are recommended.

INDIANAPOLIS Yats $

5363 N College Ave, 46220 ***Tel*** *(317) 253-8817*

An institution in Indianapolis, the Yats Cajun/Creole menu keeps diners coming back for more. A chalkboard behind the cashier greets diners with the daily menu. Some of the menu items listed might be savory stews, flavorful jambalayas, or enticing vegetarian entrées. No credit cards accepted.

INDIANAPOLIS St. Elmo's Steak House $$$$$

127 S Illinois, 46225 ***Tel*** *(317) 635-0636*

An Indianapolis landmark since 1902, St. Elmo's Steak House features a popular menu that rarely changes and a tuxedo-clad wait staff that has been there for decades. Highlights include a photo gallery of celebrity diners, a 20,000-bottle wine cellar, and a signature shrimp cocktail with horseradish sauce.

MADISON Key West Shrimp House $$$

117 Ferry St, 47250 ***Tel*** *(812) 265-2831*

Indulge yourself at the Key West Shrimp House. Diners can enjoy their meal in a century-old, blue-and-white building that once housed a mussel-button factory. Surrounded by exposed wood beams, wooden floors, and courteous service, guests can savor menu items such as fried shrimp or the daily fresh fish special.

RICHMOND Jade House Chinese Restaurant $

4710 National Rd E, 47374 ***Tel*** *(765) 935-4575*

The Jade House Chinese Restaurant is a casual, buffet-style facility known for its good food, good service, and good prices. Lunch and dinner are both served. Vegetarian dishes are on the menu, but the kids' favorite is the dessert bar complete with a creamy ice cream machine.

SOUTH BEND Sorin's at the Morris Inn $$$

N Notre Dame Ave, 46556 ***Tel*** *(574) 631-2000, (800) 280-7256*

Nestled on the University of Notre Dame's campus, Sorin's at the Morris Inn is named after the college's founder and decorated with murals of the famed campus. Sorin's American/French fare menu has something for everyone but make sure to save room for the heavenly desserts. Reservations are recommended.

MICHIGAN

AUBURN HILLS Lelli's Restaurant $$$$

885 N Opdyke Rd, 48326 ***Tel*** *(248) 373-4440*

Lelli's, a revered Italian restaurant, is a well-known Detroit institution. Patrons keep returning for the mouth-watering filet mignon among other dishes. Their signature dish, Shrimp Lelli, is a delightful seafood dish and was originally made famous at the restaurant's first location.

DETROIT Cuisine $$$

670 Lothrop Rd, 48202 ***Tel*** *(313) 872-5110*

"Cuisine – generally recognized as the city's best and most creative restaurant", reports the *New York Times*. Located behind the Fisher Theatre, guests go to dine on the innovative French/American cuisine. This upscale establishment has an excellent wine list and the desserts are heavenly so it's hard to choose just one.

FARMINGTON HILLS Tribute Restaurant $$$

31425 W 12 Mile Rd, 48334 ***Tel*** *(248) 848-9393*

Known as a prime power-dining spot in Detroit, the Tribute pleasures diners with a fusion of French/Contemporary cuisine. It addresses every aspect of dining, from the artistic presentation, exquisite flavors, and great service to the elegant ambience. They are among the top 50 restaurants in the USA. Reservations required.

GRAND RAPIDS San Chez a Tapas Bistro $$

38 Fulton St W Ste 100, 49503 ***Tel*** *(616) 774-8272*

San Chez a Tapas Bistro exploded on to the Grand Rapids scene in 1992. This high-quality, award-winning bistro specializes in *tapas* ("little plates"). A spectacular wine list is available. Sundays are made special by the "loosen your belt" Sunday brunches.

MACKINAW CITY Dixie's Saloon $$

401 E Central St, 49701 ***Tel*** *(231) 436-5449*

Located across from the Mackinac Island Ferry, the Dixie Saloon is the perfect place to stop for a bite before or after (or both) your trip to the island. With booths situated alongside the windows, guests can enjoy their meal with a view of the comings and goings on the waterfront. Menu choices include Dixie's famous BBQ ribs.

MINNESOTA

DULUTH New Scenic Cafe $$

5461 N Shore Scenic Dr, 55804 ***Tel*** *(218) 525-6274*

The New Scenic Café has diners traveling from all over just to enjoy their delicious seasonal menu with local dishes such as Northern Shores smoked salmon. Colorful gardens entice patrons outside to view the many types of flowers in bloom. The café has a small but good wine list. Local artists are promoted at the restaurant.

MINNEAPOLIS Nye's Polonaise Room $$

112 E Hennepin Ave, 55414 ***Tel*** *(612) 379-2021*

In operation since 1949, this Polish/American cuisine supper club boasts that it has not changed a bit. While enjoying a *pierogi* dinner or sauerkraut and sausage, guests can sing along to favorite songs played by the piano singer. The live polka music will make you want to kick up your feet.

MINNEAPOLIS Capital Grille $$$$

801 Hennepin Ave, LaSalle Plaza, 55402 ***Tel*** *(612) 692-9000*

The Capital Grille is considered one of the superb fine-dining establishments in Minneapolis. The restaurant is within walking distance of the Riverwalk and the US Cellular Arena. Enjoy a glass of wine from their 5000-bottle collection or try their signature drink, The Stoli Doli martini. Don't leave without trying one of their sinfully delicious desserts.

PLYMOUTH Tea House Restaurant $$

88 Nathan Ln, 55441 ***Tel*** *(763) 544-3422*

The Tea House Restaurant in Plymouth serves authentic Chinese cuisine in a casual but elegant atmosphere. It is open for lunch and dinner with take-out available during those hours. Vegetarian and Szechwan dishes are also available along with a lunch buffet.

ST. PAUL Mickey's Diner $

36 7th St, 55116 ***Tel*** *(651) 222-5633*

Locals consider Mickey's Diner, a city landmark built in 1937, serves the best breakfast food, burgers, and signature dish – mulligan stew. The unique surroundings has Mickey's standing out in the crowd, with its streamlined dining car sporting Art Deco neon signage, and its mirrored glass, stainless steel, and mahogany interior.

ST. PAUL Forepaugh's Restaurant $$$$

276 S Exchange St, 55102 ***Tel*** *(651) 224-5606*

An elegant Victorian mansion is the setting for this restaurant serving inventive New American cuisine. There are seven small dining rooms and an upper level patio area where drinks are served in warm weather. The Three-way Lamb is a specialty – it brings together home-made sausage, braised shank, and loin of lamb. Extensive wine list.

OHIO

CINCINNATI The Celestial $$

1071 Celestial St, 45202 ***Tel*** *(513) 241-4455*

One of the finest and most romantic restaurants in Cincinnati, the panoramic views of the Ohio River just might make you forget you're dining until your food arrives. But the heavenly scents and uniquely plated entrées will make you take notice. Though considered a steakhouse, the seafood and scrumptious Veal Chop Schnitzel refute that.

CLEVELAND Blue Point Grill $$$

700 W St. Clair, 44113 ***Tel*** *(216) 875-7827*

Blue Point Grill seafood restaurant is located in Cleveland's warehouse district. Its elegant but comfortable dining atmosphere allows guests to enjoy the sophisticated but innovative menu. Items include grouper, salmon, and the more exotic sea bass with red curry coconut sauce. Reservations are suggested. A good wine list is available.

Key to Price Guide *see p428* **Key to Symbols** *see back cover flap*

COLUMBUS Schmidt's Restaurant und Sausage Haus $

240 E Kossuth St, 43206 ***Tel*** *(614) 444-6808*

Schmidt's Restaurant und Sausage Haus is a quaint German restaurant, as the name implies. Located in Columbus' German Village, the staff, dressed in traditional costumes, provide great service delivering schnitzel, red cabbage, and other traditional German fare. Make sure to enjoy a micro-brewed beer with your meal.

LEBANON The Golden Lamb Dining Room $$$

27 S Broadway, 45036 ***Tel*** *(513) 932-5065*

The Golden Lamb Dining Room is a historic landmark in Lebanon, Ohio. Formerly a stagecoach tavern, this family-style inn serves enticing American-Colonial dishes such as roast leg of lamb, the house specialty. Check out the gift shop before leaving. Reservations are recommended.

TOLEDO Tony Packo's Café $

1902 Front St, 43605 ***Tel*** *(419) 691-6054*

Made famous by Maxwell Klinger on the TV series *M*A*S*H*, Tony Packo's Café is a local icon. Enjoy the spicy Hungarian hot dogs but don't forget to view the celebrity-autographed bun collection. Live Dixieland jazz is performed on the weekends. Five locations in the Toledo area.

WEST CHESTER Jag's Steak & Seafood $$$

5980 W Chester Rd, 45069 ***Tel*** *(513) 860-5353*

Jag's Steak and Seafood is one of the best dining experiences in the area. Each of their six dining rooms has an inviting atmosphere with its fireplace, artwork, and floral decor. Jag's specialty is the porterhouse but some consider the Japanese Kobe beef the "crown jewel" of the menu. Seafood entrees include Chilean sea bass and Maryland crab cakes.

WISCONSIN

MADISON Marigold Kitchen $$

118 S Pinckney St, 53703 ***Tel*** *(608) 661-5559*

Situated one block away from the State Capitol and the nation's largest outdoor farmers' market (on Saturday), Marigold's menu contains an abundance of local organic ingredients. These are used to create inventive variations of familiar dishes, such as omelette with artisan cheese or hash with lean duck. Open breakfast and lunch Mon–Sat.

MILWAUKEE Balisteri's Bluemound Inn $

6501 W Bluemound Rd, 53213 ***Tel*** *(414) 258-9881*

Its location near Miller Park (the city's baseball stadium) is why Balistreri's Bluemound Inn offers a fine dining spot for a post- or pre-game meal. Balistreri's menu includes savory Italian dishes and special signature entrées of fresh fish, poultry, and steaks.

MILWAUKEE Dream Dance $$$$$

1721 W Canal St, 53233 ***Tel*** *(414) 847-7883*

Dream Dance is a dream of a restaurant. The restaurant adds elegance and sophistication to the Potawatomi Bingo Casino where it is located. Most regulars will tell you that the farm-raised, free-range venison is their favorite dish. There's a seven-course tasting menu and the Cognac cart is presented with style.

SISTER BAY Mission Grille $$$

Hwys 42 & 52, 54234 ***Tel*** *(920) 854-9070*

The Mission Grille is appropriately named, being housed in a former church, which also explains the "choir loft" and "sanctuary" dining areas. "One of the top twelve restaurants in Wisconsin", says *Gourmet Magazine*. The seasonally changing menu includes fresh fish, lamb, and poultry, using local fruit and vegetables when possible.

SPRING GREEN Spring Green General Store $

137 S Albany St, 53588 ***Tel*** *(608) 588-7070*

The Spring Green General Store is located in a converted cheese warehouse. The menu consists of ethnic/healthy-eating cuisine. The adjoining store also sells groceries, following the restaurant's lead of natural and gourmet items. Good facilities for children. Beer is served.

WEST ALLIS Crawdaddy's $

6414 W Greenfield Ave, 53214 ***Tel*** *(414) 778-2228*

Walk by Crawdaddy's, close your eyes, and you'll hear the sounds and smell the fragrance of New Orleans. Milwaukee's first Creole/Cajun-style restaurant puts one in mind of New Orleans with its Cajun Zydeco and blues music and, of course, the original po-boy sandwich, the muffuletta sandwich, and entrée made with crawfish.

WISCONSIN DELLS Moosejaw Pizza & Brewing $$

110 Wisconsin Dells Pkwy S, 53965 ***Tel*** *(608) 254-1122*

Moosejaw Pizza and Brewing is a local's hangout. With its pool tables and video games, the menu is not the only draw. The natural, woodsy decor goes well with the tavern-like menu of pizza, hotdogs, and elk burgers, as well as New York strip steaks. A brewpub is on the premises.

THE GREAT PLAINS

INTRODUCING THE GREAT PLAINS 434–441

NORTH DAKOTA 442–443

SOUTH DAKOTA 444–447

NEBRASKA 448–451

IOWA 452–453

MISSOURI 454–457

KANSAS 458–459

OKLAHOMA 460–461

The Great Plains at a Glance

Centering on the midway longitude, the 100th meridian – which divides the United States roughly into East and West – this region is the essence of Middle America. Stretching from Canada to Texas, and sloping gradually from the foot of the Rocky Mountains to the floodplain of the Mississippi River, the Great Plains covers seven states, from North and South Dakota across Iowa, Nebraska, Missouri, Kansas, and Oklahoma. This largely rural and agricultural region is a place of small towns, wide open spaces, and distant horizons. Museums, historic sights, and entertainment options can be found in cities such as Tulsa, St. Louis, Kansas City, and Oklahoma City.

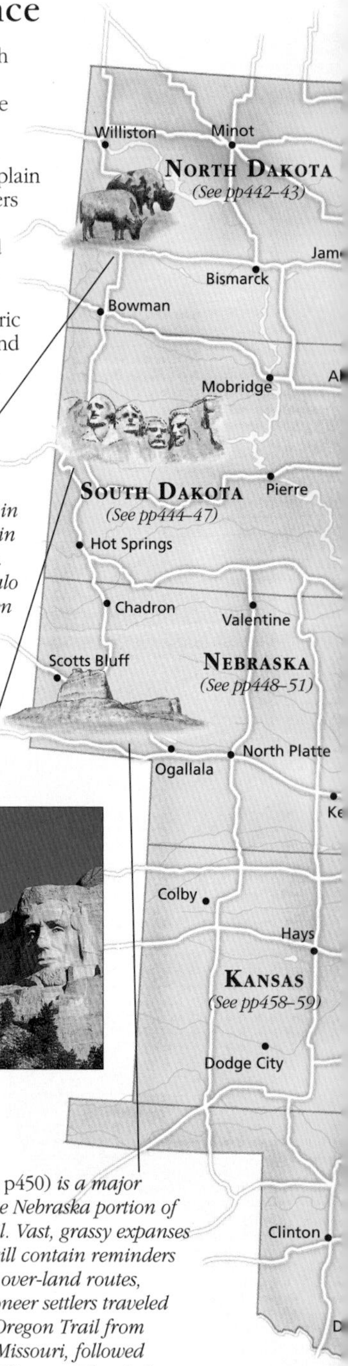

Theodore Roosevelt National Park (see p443), *in North Dakota, was created in 1947 as a memorial in the president's honor. Today, herds of buffalo can frequently be seen roaming the park's stark but beautiful badlands.*

Black Hills (see pp446–7), *South Dakota's main attraction, has six Native American reservations, as well as Mount Rushmore, with its giant, sculpted heads of four US presidents.*

Scotts Bluff (see p450) *is a major landmark on the Nebraska portion of the Oregon Trail. Vast, grassy expanses of open range still contain reminders of 19th-century over-land routes, along which pioneer settlers traveled westward. The Oregon Trail from Independence, Missouri, followed the North Platte River as it headed northwest across the Rocky Mountains.*

◁ **Endless expanse of cornfields, a common sight in rural Iowa**

Des Moines (see p452) *is the state capital of Iowa, one of the country's largest agricultural producers, with a rich stock of hard-working farming communities. Iowa's green river valleys and lush cornfields encapsulate an idyllic image of a nearly vanished rural America.*

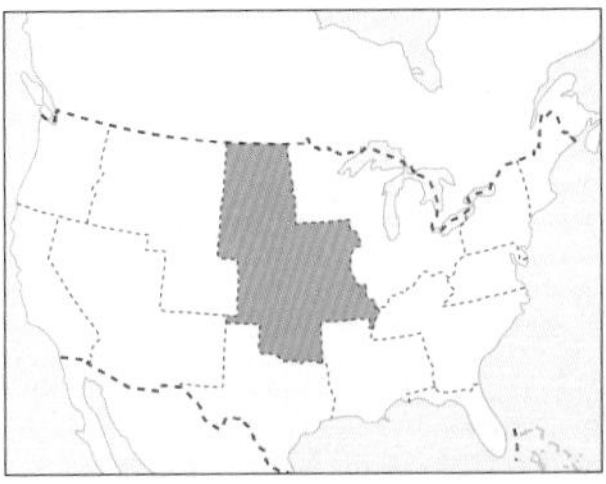

LOCATOR MAP

St. Louis (see pp454–5) *is one of Missouri's largest and most cosmopolitan cities. Its location on the route leading west made St. Louis an active commercial and cultural crossroads, a role symbolized by the Gateway Arch.*

Wichita (see p459), *Kansas, was once a cattle drive destination, where cowboys stopped to let off steam. The town's colorful past is displayed at the Old Cowtown Museum. Dodge City is the state's other Old West town.*

Oklahoma (see pp460–61) *boasts more miles of the original Old Route 66 highway than any other state. This historic road, famous as the "mother road" in John Steinbeck's* The Grapes of Wrath, *has also been celebrated in blues and jazz. Old gas pumps, signboards, and other exhibits can be seen at some Route 66 museums, especially in Clinton.*

THE GREAT PLAINS

From an airplane, the Great Plains look like a repeated pattern of rectangular fields and arrow-straight highways, prompting urban Americans to dub it "fly-over country." This predominately rural and agricultural region, which stretches clear across the center of the country, embodies the all-American ideals of independence and hard-working self-sufficiency.

The Great Plains are deeply rooted, both literally and figuratively, at the center of the American psyche. Though city-dwellers on both the East and West coasts may deride the region's general lack of sophistication, its residents' obvious pride in traditional values and old-fashioned lifestyles explains why this area is still the ideal location for all that is essentially American.

In fiction and film, the region has spawned such all-American creations as Mark Twain's *Huckleberry Finn*, Dorothy in *The Wizard of Oz*, the pioneer family of *Little House on the Prairie*, and the homespun sentimentality of *Field of Dreams* and *The Bridges of Madison County*.

Its rural reaches, with their vast expanses of fertile farmlands, form the basis of the Great Plains identity. Larger cities, such as Tulsa, St. Louis, Kansas City, and Oklahoma City, hold the bulk of the population as well as the museums, historic sights, and a wide range of hotels and resturants. Visitors can get a better sense of the region's culture by spending some time in bucolic, smaller towns.

HISTORY

Throughout the 17th and 18th centuries, French traders and fur trappers explored the region, coming into contact with the diverse Native American tribes who lived here. These tribes varied from the sedentary, agriculture-based cultures of the Caddo and Mandan people to the Pawnee, Osage, and Comanche Indians, whose livelihoods depended on hunting migratory herds of bison (or buffalo). As Europeans settled along the East Coast, other tribes relocated westward to the Great Plains. The most tragic mass migration to this region took place in 1838, when the

Herd of bison roaming the grasslands of Custer State Park, South Dakota

◁ **Eroded sandstone forms at Theodore Roosevelt National Park, North Dakota**

Lewis and Clark expedition mural at the Lewis & Clark Interpretive Center, Washburn, North Dakota

Cherokee Nation was forced to relinquish all lands east of the Mississippi River. In exchange, they were granted land for "as long as the grass grows and the waters run," in what was then known as Indian Territory (present-day Oklahoma). More than 4,000 people died from hunger, disease, and exposure on the long journey, dubbed the "Trail of Tears," from North Carolina to Oklahoma. Native American influence on the region is hard to quantify, but its heritage survives in numerous place names, including those of each state – Iowa, Missouri, Oklahoma, Kansas, Nebraska, and the Dakotas.

KEY DATES IN HISTORY

1738-43 French fur trader Pierre Gaultier du Varennes, Sieur de la Verendrye, explores the northern Great Plains

1764 St. Louis established

1803 The US buys much of the region from France as part of the Louisiana Purchase

1833 German artist Karl Bodmer documents Native American lifestyles

1882 "Buffalo Bill" stages the world's first rodeo in North Platte, Nebraska

1890 Massacre of 300 Sioux Indians by the US Army at Wounded Knee on Pine Ridge Reservation, South Dakota

1907 Hollywood actor John Wayne is born in Winterset, Iowa

1930-37 Extended drought and sustained winds create the Dust Bowl

1941 Mount Rushmore completed

1993 Disastrous springtime floods in Iowa and across the Great Plains

1995 The Federal Building in downtown Oklahoma City is destroyed by a truck bomb

2000 White supremacist Timothy McVeigh is executed for his role in the Oklahoma City bombing

Among the first Americans to explore the Great Plains were the legendary Lewis and Clark, whose expedition to the Pacific Ocean and back took almost three years, from 1803 to 1806. Remarkable as their journey was, the later expedition of the German Prince Maximilian made perhaps the most enduring contribution to the region's lore. Maximilian's journals, as well as artist Karl Bodmer's drawings and paintings of Indians, were published in Germany in 1838, and finally put the Great Plains on the international map.

Both expeditions embarked from St. Louis, the region's oldest city founded as a distant French fur-trading frontier outpost. By the mid-19th century, Kansas City had joined St. Louis as an outpost for pioneers crossing the Great Plains on the legendary Santa Fe, California, and Oregon Trails.

After the Civil War, a series of transcontinental railroads followed many of the same routes, cutting down on travel time and transportation costs. The railroads, however, sliced across the migration routes for the bison herds, whose numbers dwindled from millions to near extinction. As the railroads opened up the land, the Indians were forced onto reservations, while homesteading settlers took their place. These family-run farms, growing wheat, corn, cattle, and pigs, are still emblematic of the region, though many farms are now operated on an industrial scale by absentee landlords. The high point of agriculture was the World War I era, when farm prices were high and mechanization had yet to replace horse-drawn plows and other labor-intensive methods. The economic low point came soon afterward, when a sudden postwar drop in prices and a decade of drought turned the region into the "Dust Bowl," forcing some 200,000 farmers and their families to move west to California, a saga movingly documented in John Steinbeck's *The Grapes of Wrath*.

Prairie dog, Badlands

GEOLOGY & CLIMATE

The land is what defines life in the Great Plains. Some 500 million years ago, a deep inland sea laid the foundation of layers of sedimentary rock, with their rich array of ancient fossils as well as the fossil fuels that industries rely on today. Above this solid rock, a series of Ice Age glaciers, scraping their way south from Canada, deposited the pulverized soil that makes the eastern half of the Great Plains – and Iowa in particular – some of the world's most fertile farmland. Exceptions to the typically horizontal landscape are found at its fringes. The rugged Ozark Mountains lie in southern Missouri and Oklahoma, while in western South Dakota, the densely forested, gold-bearing granite peaks of the Black Hills rise high above the eroded sandstone of Badlands National Park.

While the underlying geology may make for uneventful scenery, the climate is anything but mild. The Great Plains experiences some of the nation's most extreme weather, particularly its fierce tornados. These powerful windstorms form with little warning in late spring and are most frequent along the "Tornado Alley," which runs through eastern Kansas and Oklahoma. The region also frequently suffers from flood-inducing rains and thunderstorms, scorching summer heat and humidity, and frigid winter blizzards.

PEOPLE & CULTURE

The Great Plains is, by and large, conservative, with patriotism and religion the dominating cultural values. Yet it also is a region of varied cultural and political traditions. In the 19th century, Kansas was one of the prime anti-slavery battlegrounds, but at the turn of the 21st century the state insisted that biblical ideas of creationism be taught in school science classes.

Ethnically, however, the population is surprisingly diverse. Many of the original immigrants were lured here from similar terrain in Europe, notably the steppes of eastern Europe, by promises of land ownership. A significant number were adherents of nonconformist religions, such as the Mennonites who came from German-speaking regions of Russia to settle in central Kansas and the Dakotas. Their past explains the presence of the many German-style pastry shops in what may seem like quintessentially American small towns.

Native Americans also play an increasingly visible role in the region's identity, thanks both to burgeoning casinos operated by the various tribes and to a growing respect for their culture and heritage. Oklahoma, for example, has one of the country's largest Native American populations, numbering nearly 10 percent of the state's 3 million inhabitants.

Pine Ridge Indian Reservation in South Dakota

Exploring the Great Plains

The Great Plains draws visitors in search of a taste of wholesome America. Its singular attraction is the countryside with its wide-open, seemingly endless spaces, where visitors can travel for miles without seeing more than a few railroad tracks, a set of power lines, or perhaps an occasional windmill or grain elevator. For those who want to explore farther, the Great Plains' highlights include the magnificent, sculpted monument of Mount Rushmore, the eerie landscape of Badlands National Park, and historic frontier outposts such as St. Louis and Kansas City, two of the region's largest cities. A car is essential to make the most of a visit to the Great Plains.

SIGHTS AT A GLANCE

North Dakota
- Grand Forks 1
- Devils Lake 2
- Washburn 3
- Theodore Roosevelt National Park 4
- Bismarck & Mandan 5
- Fargo 6

South Dakota
- Mitchell 7
- Pierre 8
- Badlands National Park 9
- Wall 10
- Pine Ridge Indian Reservation 11
- *Black Hills pp446–47* 12

Nebraska
- Chadron 13
- Ogallala 14
- North Platte 15
- Lincoln 16
- Nebraska City 17
- Omaha 18

Iowa
- Sioux City 19
- Des Moines 20
- Amana Colonies 21
- Cedar Rapids 22
- Dubuque 23
- Quad Cities (Davenport) 24
- Iowa City 25

Missouri
- *St. Louis pp454–55* 26
- Jefferson City 27
- Branson 28
- Kansas City 29
- St. Joseph 30

Kansas
- Lawrence 31
- Topeka 32
- Flint Hills 33
- Wichita 34
- Dodge City 35

Oklahoma
- Bartlesville 36
- Tulsa 37
- Tahlequah 38
- Oklahoma City 39

MILEAGE CHART

10 = Distance in miles
10 = Distance in kilometers

	BISMARCK, ND	RAPID CITY, SD	OMAHA, NE	DES MOINES, IA	ST. LOUIS, MO	KANSAS CITY, MO	WICHITA, KS
RAPID CITY, SD	**350** 563						
OMAHA, NE	**607** 977	**524** 843					
DES MOINES, IA	**667** 1073	**624** 1004	**135** 217				
ST. LOUIS, MO	**1039** 1672	**953** 1534	**434** 698	**434** 698			
KANSAS CITY, MO	**786** 1265	**702** 1130	**183** 295	**194** 312	**247** 397		
WICHITA, KS	**1034** 1664	**952** 1532	**385** 620	**393** 632	**444** 715	**203** 327	
OKLAHOMA CITY, OK	**1123** 1807	**1040** 1674	**519** 835	**546** 879	**500** 805	**349** 562	**161** 259

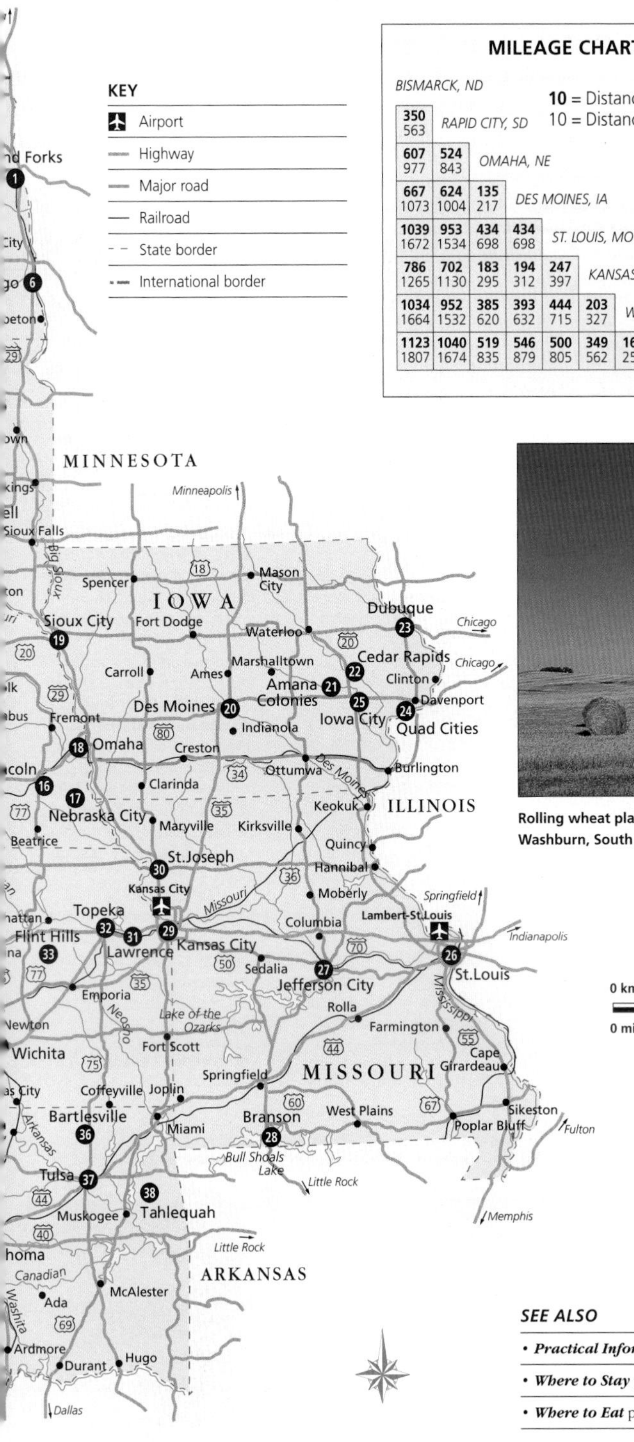

Rolling wheat plains near Washburn, South Dakota

SEE ALSO

• ***Practical Information*** pp462–3
• ***Where to Stay*** pp464–7
• ***Where to Eat*** pp468–71

North Dakota

Fort Lincoln State Park

A state of unexpected variety, North Dakota's vast blue skies, tiny farming communities, and endless wheat fields along its eastern half can lull visitors into a state of quiet contemplation. Toward the west, North Dakota's drier, more rugged Missouri Plateau contains the stark badlands of Theodore Roosevelt National Park and more than a dozen historic sites visited by Lewis and Clark *(see p570)* on their 1803–06 expedition up the Missouri River. The explorers spent 146 days in North Dakota on their outbound and return journeys. Vast tracts of undeveloped areas along the river north of the pleasant capital city of Bismarck still look much like they did in the early 19th century.

Grand Forks ❶

97,000. 4251 Gateway Dr, (800) 866-4566.
www.visitgrandforks.com

Located at the junction of the Red and Red Lake Rivers, the city attracted international attention in 1997, when the Red River flooded downtown, destroying many historic structures and inflicting huge damage. Massive clean-up, water control, and reconstruction efforts have helped Grand Forks overcome much of the flood's disastrous effects.

The **Empire Arts Center**, housed in the restored 1919 Empire Theatre, is now downtown's vibrant performing arts center. The University of North Dakota campus, 2 miles (3 km) west of downtown, is home to the **North Dakota Museum of Art**, with its good collection of contemporary art.

Empire Arts Center
415 Demers Ave. ***Tel*** *(701) 746-0500.* *call for times.*
www.empireartscenter.org

Devils Lake ❷

7,900. 208 Hwy 2 W, (800) 233-8048.
www.devilslakend.com

The primary recreational attraction in northeastern North Dakota is the 120,000-acre (48,600-ha) glacial Devils Lake, 90 miles (150 km) west of Grand Forks. With miles of shoreline and no natural outlet, the lake is an excellent spot for fishing and boating.

Fort Totten State Historic Site, 14 miles (22 km) to the south, is one of the best-preserved United States Army bases from the post-Civil War era. Built in 1867, it remained in use as a military reservation until 1890, when it became a boarding school for Native American children. The restored buildings around the parade ground contain period furniture.

Fort Totten State Historic Site
Rte 57. ***Tel*** *(701) 766-4441.* *May–Sep: 8am–5pm.* **http://**history.nd.gov/historicsites/totten

Washburn ❸

1,700.
(701) 462-8530.
www.washburnnd.com

The key attraction in the area surrounding the sleepy Missouri River town of Washburn is the **Lewis and Clark Interpretive Center**. A stunning view of the Missouri River Valley greets visitors, who can also don buffalo robes, listen to Native American music, and view exhibits tracing the river's shifting course over the past 200 years.

The center is an ideal starting point for a tour of the sites associated with Lewis and Clark's historic expedition. About 2 miles (3 km) north of the visitor center is the reconstructed **Fort Mandan**. It was here that Lewis and Clark's 44-man Corps of Discovery wintered between 1804 and 1805, en route to the Pacific Ocean.

The **Knife River Indian Village National Historic Site**, 20 miles (32 km) west of Washburn, contains the remains of the largest villages of the interrelated Mandan, Hidatsa, and Arikara tribes. Among these are a restored 50ft x 12-ft (15m x 12-m) earth lodge. The French trapper Charbonneau, and his Native American wife, Sacagawea, joined the Lewis and Clark expedition near this spot in 1804.

Lewis & Clark Interpretive Center
US 83 & Rte 200A.
Tel *(877) 462-8535.*
9am–5pm Mon–Sat, noon–5pm Sun.
www.fortmandan.com

The reconstructed, high-stockaded façade of Fort Mandan, near Washburn

For hotels and restaurants in this region see p464 and p468

The Painted Canyon, Theodore Roosevelt National Park

Theodore Roosevelt National Park ❹

Medora. *Tel (701) 623-4466.* *8am–4:30pm daily.* *Jan 1, Thanksgiving, Dec 25.*
www.nps.gov/thro

The tiny western North Dakota town of Medora is the gateway to the Theodore Roosevelt National Park and the remote, beautiful North Dakota badlands. The bill that created this park as a memorial to Roosevelt was signed on April 25, 1947, by President Truman. On November 10, 1978, the area was given national park status by virtue of another bill signed by President Carter.

The Theodore Roosevelt National Park is a sprawling one, covering over 70,000 acres (28,328 ha) of land. It is divided into three areas – the North and South Units and Elkhorn Ranch. The butte-studded South Unit has the phantasmagoric **Painted Canyon** and can be explored on horseback or seen from an overlook from a 36-mile (58-km) self-guided auto tour. The North Unit features a dramatic, oxbow bend in the Little Missouri River. Its moon-like landscape is dotted with mushroom-shaped stone formations and windswept grasslands. Unlike the much-visited South Unit, this pocket lies in very isolated country. However, a 14-mile (22-km) auto route through this rugged landscape provides access to nature trails and numerous scenic overlooks.

Bismarck & Mandan ❺

67,000. *1600 Burnt Boat Dr, Bismarck, (800) 767-3555.*
www.discoverbismarckmandan.com

Riverboat traffic, railroads, and the government were instrumental in the development of the state capital of Bismarck, founded in 1872 on the east bank of the Missouri River. The 19-story, Art Deco **North Dakota State Capitol** dominates the city's leafy, low-slung skyline. Known as the "Skyscraper of the Prairies," the 1933 structure is visible for miles in every direction, mainly because of its location on top of a small rise north of downtown. The **North Dakota Heritage Center**, abutting the Capitol, provides a fascinating introduction to the state's Native American heritage and territorial settlement. It also traces the story of the Capitol's design and construction.

The shipping and warehousing center of Mandan lies just across the Missouri. To the south of downtown is **Fort Abraham Lincoln State Park**, which contains On-a-Slant Indian Village, the excavated remains of a 17th-century Mandan Native American community, and several other reconstructed buildings. The fort was the last base for reckless George Armstrong Custer, who led the 7th Calvary from here to their disastrous defeat at the Battle of Little Bighorn *(see p581)* in 1876.

North Dakota Heritage Center
Capitol Mall, Bismarck. ***Tel** (701) 328-2666.* *8am–5pm Mon–Fri, 10am– 5pm Sat, Sun.*

Fort Abraham Lincoln State Park
4480 Fort Lincoln Rd. ***Tel** (701) 667-6340.* *Apr 1–Memorial Day: 9am–5pm daily; Memorial Day–Labor Day: 9am–7pm; Labor Day–Sep 30: 9am–5pm.*

Fargo ❻

187,000.
2001 44th St S, (800) 235-7654.
www.fargomoorhead.org

A grain processing center, Fargo lies directly across the Red River from its sister city, Moorhead, Minnesota. Fargo's historic downtown includes the renovated 1926 **Fargo Theatre**, an Art Moderne structure that still presents art and period films as well as live performances. Southwest of the theater is the superb **Plains Art Museum**, housed in a restored 1904 International Harvester Company warehouse. This museum has the state's largest public art collection, with works by the region's Native American and folk artists. The **Roger Maris Baseball Museum**, in the West Acres Shopping Center, celebrates the achievements of Fargo's most famous native son, who hit 61 home runs in 1961, setting a record for most home runs in a season.

Fargo Theatre
314 Broadway. ***Tel** (701) 239-8385.* *call for schedule.*

Exterior of the historic Fargo Theatre, Fargo

South Dakota

Pine Ridge Reservation

Rivers, hills, buttes, rolling prairies, and badlands are South Dakota's defining geographical features. The Missouri River bisects the state from north to south, with the corn and soybean fields of the flatter eastern plains giving way to shortgrass prairie and rocky badlands as one heads west on the state's main east–west corridor, I-90. Culturally, the state is dominated by the heritage of the Dakota, Lakota, and Nakota Sioux tribes, who roamed and hunted the buffalo-rich area until they were moved onto reservations in the late 1800s. Over 60,000 Native Americans still reside here.

Mitchell 7

16,000. 601 N Main St, (866) 273-2676. **www**.cornpalace.com

Located in the fertile James River Valley, Mitchell is the state's corn, grain, and cattle center. The city's claim to fame is the well-known **Corn Palace**, a Moorish auditorium that was built in 1921 to house the city's Corn Belt Exposition. Colorful domes, minarets, and kiosks are the only permanent design features on the ever-changing façade of the palace. Every year, local artists use more than 3,000 bushels of corn and grasses to create new murals, which depict agricultural scenes from South Dakota. This tradition dates back to 1892, when the Corn Real Estate Association constructed the first palace to showcase the area's crops, in an endeavor to lure settlers.

Corn Palace
8am–9pm daily except Apr–May & Sep–Nov: 8am–5pm daily; Dec–Mar: 8am–5pm Mon–Sat.

Pierre 8

14,000. 800 W Dakota Ave, (800) 962-2034. **www**.pierre.org

The second smallest capital in the US, Pierre lies in the Missouri River Valley, and forms a leafy oasis in the shortgrass, largely treeless plains of central South Dakota. The 1910 **South Dakota State Capitol** has a grand marble staircase and overlooks a lake visited each spring and fall by thousands of migratory birds. A huge display of Christmas trees inside the Capitol begins at Thanksgiving.

The excellent **South Dakota Cultural Heritage Center** is built into the side of a Missouri River bluff, covered with shortgrass prairie. Its exhibits trace the history of South Dakota's Sioux tribes and also provide information on the diverse ethnic backgrounds of the state's homesteading white settlers. On display is a lead plate that was buried in a nearby river bluff in 1743 by the French-sponsored Verendrye expedition to mark the site as French territory. The **Verendrye Museum**, across the river in Fort Pierre, focuses on French trading and exploration activities.

Mural at the Corn Palace, Mitchell

Exterior of the South Dakota State Capitol in Pierre

South Dakota State Capitol
500 E Capitol Ave. ***Tel** (605) 773-3765. 8am–7pm Mon–Fri, 8am–5pm Sat–Sun.*

South Dakota Cultural Heritage Center
900 Governors Dr. ***Tel** (605) 773-3458. 9am–4:30pm Mon–Fri, 1–4:30pm Sat–Sun. Jan 1, Easter, Thanksgiving, Dec 25.*

Badlands National Park 9

*Ben Reifel Visitor Center, Rte 240, S of I-90 exit 131. **Tel** (605) 433-5361. Jun–Aug: 7am–8pm; Sep–Oct: 8am–6pm; Nov–May: 8am–4pm.* **www**.nps.gov/badl

The eerie desolation of Badlands National Park is an awe-inspiring sight for travelers unprepared for such a stark, rugged landscape after miles of gentle, rolling South Dakota prairie. Formed over 14 million years ago from silt and sediment washing down from the Black Hills *(see pp446–7)*, the badlands were sculpted into their present craggy form by harsh sun and powerful winds.

Some of the region's most dramatically eroded buttes, pinnacles, and spires are contained in this 244,000-acre (98,744-ha) park. The **Ben Reifel Visitor Center** is the gateway to several self-guided hiking tours and the 30-mile (48-km) Badlands Loop Road (Route 240). The scenic drive follows the northern rim of the 450-ft (137-m) high Badlands Wall escarpment and leads to several overlooks and trails that provide breath-taking vistas of the eroded

View of the eroded gullies from Changing Scenes Overlook in Badlands National Park

gullies below. The road loops back north to I-90 near **Sage Creek Wilderness Area**, where golden eagles, hawks, and various songbirds gather in a vast expanse of steep grasslands, festooned each summer with wildflowers. The park-managed buffalo herd can be seen grazing on large stretches of prairie.

Wall Drug, a shopping and entertainment complex

Wall ⑩

800. 501 Main St, (888) 852-9255.
www.wall–badlands.com

Wall has done a thriving tourist trade since 1936, when local pharmacist Ted Hustead put up signs along the highway offering free ice water. This primitive roadside advertising tactic soon grew into a statewide slew of billboards, which still line I-90 all the way across South Dakota. Hustead's small-town pharmacy, **Wall Drug**, is now a sprawling Wild West shopping and entertainment complex. Along with Western and Native American souvenirs are interactive exhibits of cowboys, homesteaders, gunfighters, and medicine-show hucksters.

The sprawling **Buffalo Gap National Grassland** lies south, west, and east of Wall. Its visitor center describes the ecological and cultural history of the grasslands. Exhibits outline the various habitats and illustrate the astonishing biodiversity of the shortgrass, mixed-grass, and tallgrass prairies, which once covered most of the region.

Wall Drug
510 Main St. ***Tel*** *(605) 279-2175.*
7am–5:30pm daily (extended summer hours).
www.walldrug.com

Buffalo Gap National Grassland
708 Main St, (605) 279-2125.
Memorial–Labor Day: 8am–4:30pm daily; Labor Day–Memorial Day: 8am–4:30pm Mon–Fri.

Pine Ridge Indian Reservation ⑪

Oglala Sioux Tribe, Pine Ridge, (605) 867-6075.

Home to the Oglala Sioux tribe, the Pine Ridge Reservation is the nation's second-largest Native American reservation. The reservation lands abut the South Dakota–Nebraska border and extend west into the badlands region. The Oglala and their chief, Red Cloud, were relocated here in 1876. On December 29, 1890, the US Army's 7th Cavalry massacred about 300 Lakota men, women, and children at **Wounded Knee**. This was the last in a series of misunderstandings concerning the ceremonial Ghost Dance, which the tribe believed would reunite them with their ancestors, bring the buffalo back, and help them regain their lost lands. A lone stone monument, about 10 miles (16 km) east of the village of Pine Ridge, marks the site.

The **Red Cloud Heritage Center**, on the Red Cloud Indian School campus near Pine Ridge, contains the gravesite of Chief Red Cloud. It also displays a range of Native American artifacts.

Red Cloud Heritage Center
4.5 miles (7 km) N of Pine Ridge Village on Hwy 18. ***Tel*** *(605) 867-5491. 8am–6pm Mon–Fri. public hols.*
www.redcloudschool.org

The Red Cloud Heritage Center at the Pine Ridge Indian Reservation

Black Hills ⓬

Known to the Lakota Sioux as Paha Sapa, these majestic hills were a mysterious, sacred place where Native Americans would retreat to seek guidance from the Great Spirit. In 1874, George Armstrong Custer's *(see p581)* expedition discovered evidence of gold deposits in the thickly forested, oddly shaped granite hills. A series of misleading treaties followed, forcing the Sioux to relinquish their land, as miners, speculators, and settlers rushed into these once-sacred hills to stake their claims. Today, the Black Hills harbor some of the state's most visited attractions, particularly Mount Rushmore National Memorial. The 125-mile x 65-mile (201-km x 105-km) area is linked by US 385 and US 16, which meanders from Rapid City, the main center in the area, to Wyoming.

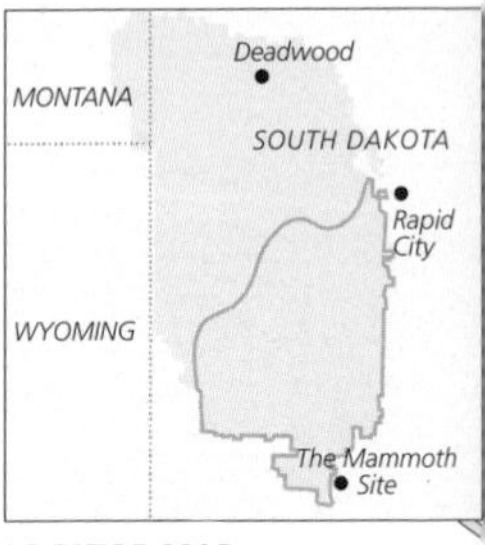

LOCATOR MAP

☐ *Black Hills* ☐ *Area illustrated*

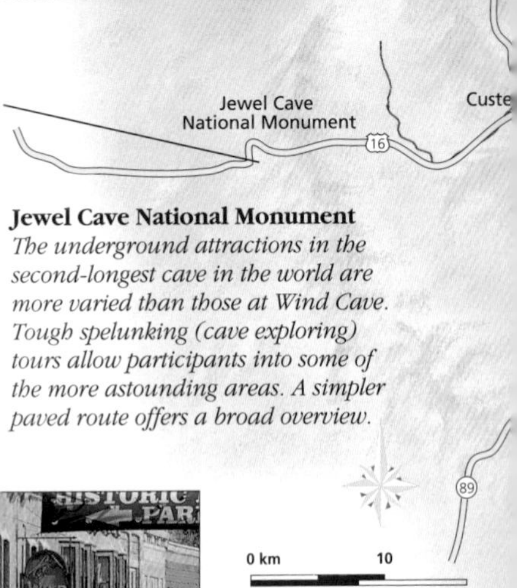

Crazy Horse Memorial
When complete, the statue of the great Sioux warrior, Crazy Horse, will be the world's largest sculpture. So far only the nine-story high face and the 219-ft (68-m) high horse's head are finished.

Jewel Cave National Monument
The underground attractions in the second-longest cave in the world are more varied than those at Wind Cave. Tough spelunking (cave exploring) tours allow participants into some of the more astounding areas. A simpler paved route offers a broad overview.

Deadwood
The restored downtown re-creates Deadwood's past as a wild, lawless gold mining town. Gunfighter Wild Bill Hickock was shot here in 1876, and Calamity Jane also left her mark here. Today, visitors try their luck in the historic gaming halls.

KEY

- Custer State Park boundary
- Wind Cave NP boundary
- Major road

Mount Rushmore National Memorial
An American icon since its completion in 1941, the giant, sculpted heads of presidents George Washington, Thomas Jefferson, Abraham Lincoln, and Theodore Roosevelt took 14 years to create. Sculptor Gutzon Borglum's studio, tools, and models are preserved on site.

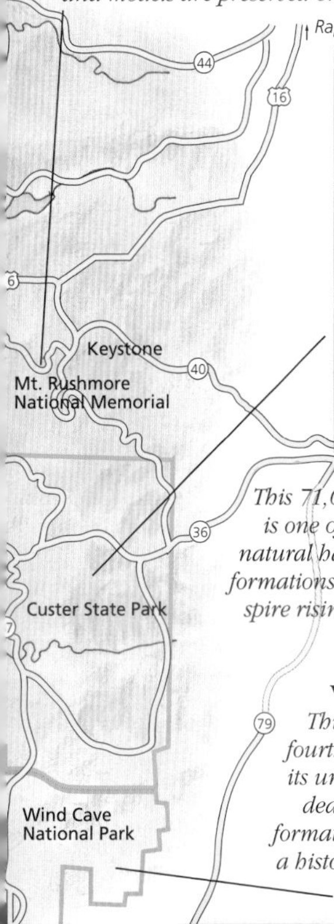

Custer State Park
This 71,000-acre (28,733 ha) park is one of the region's most pristine natural habitats, with towering rock formations such as the Needles Eye, a spire rising 30–40 ft (9–12 m) high.

Wind Cave National Park
This park contains the world's fourth-longest limestone cavern, its underground labyrinth studded with strange, popcorn-like formations. Guided tours include a historical candlelight tour, and the Natural Entrance tour.

The Mammoth Site
Discovered in 1974, this site displays the world's largest concentration of Columbian mammoth fossils. Originally a spring-fed sinkhole where animals were trapped and preserved, only 30 percent of the 26,000-year-old site has been explored so far.

VISITORS' CHECKLIST

Rapid City. *Rapid City.* *Black Hills Visitor Information Center, Exit 61 off I-90, Rapid City, (605) 355-3700.* **www**.blackhillsbadlands.com

Mount Rushmore National Memorial ***Tel*** *(605) 574-3165.* *call for timings.* **www**.nps.gov/moru

Crazy Horse Memorial ***Tel*** *(605) 673-4681.* *call for timings.* **www**.crazyhorsememorial.org

Custer State Park ***Tel*** *(605) 255-4515.* *call for timings.* **www**.custerstatepark.info

Wind Cave National Park ***Tel*** *(605) 745-4600.* *call for timings.* **www**.nps.gov/wica

Jewel Cave National Monument ***Tel*** *(605) 673-8300.* *call for timings.* *Jan 1, Thanksgiving, Dec 25.* *Visitor center only.* **www**.nps.gov/jeca

The Mammoth Site ***Tel*** *(605) 745-6017.* *call for timings.* **www**.mammothsite.com

Deadwood ***Tel*** *(800) 999-1876.* *call for timings.* **www**.deadwood.org

Nebraska

Indian tepee, Chadron

Nebraska's vast, grassy expanses of open range, and ruts from old overland wagon routes, epitomize the geography and history of the Great Plains. The modern I-80 freeway stretches westward in the shadow of the wide Platte River Valley, the historic Oregon, Mormon, and Pony Express Trails, and the original Lincoln Hwy (now US 30). Farther north, the sparsely settled central Nebraska Sandhills contain some of the nation's largest expanses of unbroken, mixed-grass prairie, while the Panhandle in the northwest is studded with rocky outcrops and jagged canyons. The state's two largest cities, Omaha and Lincoln, are in the southeast.

Chadron ⓭

5,600. *706 W 3rd St, (800) 603-2937.* **www**.chadron.com

Chadron is the ideal base to tour the Pine Ridge and Sandhills regions as well as explore aspects of the state's fascinating past. About 3 miles (5 km) east of town is the **Museum of the Fur Trade**. Built on the grounds of an 1833–49 American Fur Company post, the museum traces the history of the complex North American fur trade and its effect on Native American communities. One of its main features is a reconstructed trading post built into the sides of a low hill.

The area's key historical attraction is **Fort Robinson State Park**, just west of Crawford, which itself is 23 miles (37 km) west of Chadron. The park occupies the parade grounds, barracks, and officers' quarters of the US Army's Fort Robinson. The fort was built in 1874 to protect the nearby Red Cloud Indian Agency, where Sioux chief Red Cloud and his followers moved to before being relocated at Pine Ridge *(see p445)*. In 1877, the great Oglala Sioux chief, Crazy Horse *(see p446)*, and 900 of his tribe surrendered and set up camp outside of the fort. In a series of tragic events, Crazy Horse was killed while federal troops attempted to imprison him. A restored blockhouse commemorates the site where he fell.

The excellent Fort Robinson Museum details the fort's other lives as an experimental cattle ranch and a training ground for the army's World War II canine corps. The fort's restored quarters provide accommodation for visitors, while horseback trails lead through the surrounding lonesome buttes and grassy plains. The park also harbors a large herd of longhorn cattle and more than 400 bison.

Chadron State Park, 8 miles (13 km) south of Chadron, is a quieter, more scenic alternative, with ample campgrounds and cabin facilities. Hiking and biking trails from the park crisscross the spine of the 230-mile (370-km) long Pine Ridge escarpment. Hikers and mountain bikers seeking more challenging routes can follow the 25-mile (40-km) Pine Ridge Trail, a steep, meandering route through patches of meadows and thick stands of ponderosa pine. The trail is part of the Pine Ridge National Recreation Area, a craggy portion of the vast Nebraska National Forest, which runs along the brow of the escarpment, south of US 20, between Chadron and Crawford.

Restored officers' quarters in Fort Robinson State Park, Chadron

Fort Robinson State Park
US 20, 3 miles (5 km) W of Crawford. ***Tel*** *(308) 665-2900.* *daily.*
www.outdoornebraska.org

Martin Bay in Lake McConaughy State Recreation Area, near Ogallala

Ogallala ⓮

5,100. *204 E A St, (800) 658-4390.* **www**.visitogallala.com

Located on the South Platte River near the junction of I-80, US 26, and Route 92, Ogallala is the gateway to the Panhandle part of the Oregon Trail tour *(see p450)*. The city gained a rowdy reputation as the "Gomorrah of the Plains" soon after its founding in 1867, when the arrival of the railroad drew herds of cattle and hordes of Texas cowboys. Most modern visitors now come seeking camping, boating, hunting, and fishing supplies for their exploration of **Lake McConaughy State Recreation Area**, about 9 miles (14 km), to the north.

A refreshing oasis in the middle of the dry Panhandle

plains, Lake McConaughy is the state's largest reservoir. Known locally as "Big Mac," its cool waters are a prime breeding ground for rainbow trout, catfish, walleye, and white bass. The north shore is lined with fine sand beaches, while the marshes, woodlands, and grasslands on the lake's western end attract a wide variety of waterfowl. Loons, ducks, mergansers, and western grebes frequent Big Mac, making it one of the richest birding spots in the Great Plains region.

Lake McConaughy State Recreation Area
1475 Hwy 61 N. ***Tel*** *(308) 284-8800.* *Memorial Day–Labor Day: 8am–8pm daily.* *Visitor center only.* **www**.ngpc.state.ne.us

North Platte ⓯

27,000. *219 S Dewey, (800) 955-4528.* **www**.visitnorthplatte.com

Now one of the country's major railroad centers, North Platte was the late-19th-century home of the famed William "Buffalo Bill" Cody *(see p582)*. The comfortable ranch house he built on the outskirts of town was the base of operations for his spectacular traveling Wild West show until 1902, when he founded Cody in Wyoming. Cody's home is now part of the **Buffalo Bill Ranch State Historical Park** that includes a horse barn and log cabin from one of his previous ranches. The nearby **Lincoln County Historical Museum** exhibits a replica of the famous North Platte Canteen, which served countless pots of coffee and quantities of snacks to the military troops who passed through the town during World War II.

Buffalo Bill Ranch State Historical Park
2921 Scouts Rest Ranch Rd. ***Tel*** *(308) 535-8035.* *Mar 24–Memorial Day: 10am–4pm Mon–Fri; Memorial–Labor Day: 9am–5pm daily; Labor Day–Oct: 10am–4pm Mon–Fri.* *Oct–Apr.* **www**.ngpc.state.ne.us

Lincoln County Historical Museum
2403 Buffalo Bill Ave. ***Tel*** *(308) 534-5640.* *May–Sep: 9am–5pm Mon–Sat, 1–5pm Sun; winter: by appointment.*

Cody's house in North Platte's Buffalo Bill Ranch State Historical Park

Lincoln ⓰

252,000. *201 N 7th St, (402) 434-5348.* **www**.lincoln.org

State capital and Nebraska's second-largest city, Lincoln is also home to the University of Nebraska, whose Cornhuskers football team is so popular that it has sold out every home game at the 77,000-seat Memorial Stadium since 1962. The city's principal landmark, however, is the 400-ft (120-m) Indiana limestone tower of the **Nebraska State Capitol**. Completed in 1932, the "Tower of the Plains" is surmounted by a bronze statue of a man sowing grain and visible for miles around. Intricate murals and ornate ceilings adorn the interior. The building houses the nation's only unicameral legislature, a vestige of cost-saving measures introduced by the state during the Great Depression of the 1930s.

Bronze statue surmounting the Nebraska State Capitol in Lincoln

The state's political history is related alongside its rich Native American heritage in the excellent **Museum of Nebraska History**, located on 15th and P Streets. The **University of Nebraska State Museum**, in the downtown campus, has a wide-ranging collection of elephant fossils and Native American artifacts. In the nearby historic Haymarket District, several 19th-century warehouses have been converted into bars, restaurants, and shops.

Museum of Nebraska History
15th & P Sts. ***Tel*** *(800) 833-6747.* *9am–4:30pm Tue–Fri, 1–4:30pm Sat & Sun.* *public hols.* **www**.nebraskahistory.org

University of Nebraska State Museum
Morrill Hall, 14th & Vine Sts. ***Tel*** *(402) 472-2642.* *9:30am–4:30pm Mon–Sat, 1:30–4:30pm Sun.* *public hols.* **www**.museum.unl.edu

A colorful billboard in a parking lot welcoming visitors to North Platte

The Oregon Trail

Founded by trader William Sublette in 1830, this formidable 2,000-mile (3,200-km) trail was the main wagon route between Independence, Missouri *(see p457)* in the east and Oregon to the west. The original route curved northwest after crossing the Missouri River near present-day Kansas City, passing through northeastern Kansas and southeastern Nebraska on the way to the Platte River. Between 1841 and 1866, a staggering 500,000 settlers bound for the fertile farmlands of Oregon and the goldfields of northern California passed through Nebraska, following the northern banks of the Platte, past a string of army forts to Ogallala. As the trail veered northwest, away from the flat landscape of the Platte River Valley and up into the craggy Panhandle plateau along the North Platte River, pioneers were awestruck by the massive rock formations that signaled the Rockies to the west.

Trail marker, North Platte

THE OREGON TRAIL IN NEBRASKA
More than 428 miles (689 km) of the original Oregon Trail passed through the flat grasslands of Nebraska before it turned northwestward. Today, most of the old routes are easily accessible, with historic markers guiding travelers on I-80, along the Platte River, or Route 92 and US 26, which follows the trail's northwestern ascent of the North Platte. This undated illustration by William H. Jackson depicts the first covered wagon caravan, led by Smith-Jackson-Sublette, consisting of ten wagons drawn by five mules each, heading for Wind River Valley near present-day Lander in Wyoming.

LOCATOR MAP
The Oregon Trail

Chimney Rock, *east of the town of Scottsbluff, rises 500 ft (152 m) above the mixed-grass plains. This was one of the more frequently noted sights in travelers' diaries and sketchbooks.*

Scotts Bluff National Monument *has a well-staffed visitor center, which runs various interpretive and living history programs. These include an excellent overview of the Oregon Trail history as well as exhibits on the Mormon Trail. Visitors can hike to the summit of the 800-ft (244-m) sandstone outcropping and walk along still-visible Oregon Trail ruts.*

Morton's mansion at Arbor Lodge State Historical Park, Nebraska City

Nebraska City ⓱

7,200. 806 1st Ave, (800) 514-9113. www.nebraskacity.com

Sedate, tree-lined Nebraska City's origins were as a rowdy Missouri River way station, where families and adventurers bound for the Oregon Trail mingled with trappers, traders, and riverboat employees. Today, the city is best known as the birthplace of Arbor Day, established by Nebraska politician and newspaper editor Julius Sterling Morton (1832–1902). When he was Secretary of Agriculture under President Grover Cleveland, Morton introduced a resolution to make April 10 a state holiday to encourage farmers in Nebraska to plant trees as protection from high plains winds and soil erosion. Later, the date was changed to April 22, Morton's birthday. Arbor Day is still commemorated throughout the United States, although the date varies from state to state.

The city is also well known as the home of **Arbor Day Farm**, a 260-acre (105-ha) experimental farm, conference center, and forestry research center. Scenic hiking trails and guided tours offer casual explorations of the farm's apple orchards, windbreak arboretum, and a renewable energy plant.

The **Arbor Lodge State Historical Park** contains Morton's Georgian Revival mansion, greenhouse, and grounds. The park includes tours of the formal Italian garden and 52-room mansion, completed in 1902, and a carriage house with a stagecoach once driven by Wild West impresario Buffalo Bill *(see p582)*.

Arbor Day Farm
2611 Arbor Ave. ***Tel*** *(402) 873-8717.* *9am–5pm Mon–Sat, 11am–5pm Sun.* *Jan 1, Dec 25.*
www.arborday.org

Omaha ⓲

771,000. *1001 Farnam St, Ste 200, (402) 444-4660.*
www.visitomaha.com

Omaha evolved from a rough-and-tumble Missouri River town and outfitting post into a major railroad terminus with the construction of the transcontinental railroad in 1868 *(see p571)*. The restored Old Market warehouse district just south of downtown preserves the city's historical roots. Its old commercial buildings and cobblestone streets are now home to some of the region's best restaurants, bookstores, and antique shops. A few blocks south, the city's landmark 1931 Art Deco Union Station has been refurbished and converted into the **Durham Western Heritage Museum**. This splendid local history museum features displays on Omaha's railroad and transportation heritage.

Just west of downtown is the pink marble **Joslyn Art Museum**, a Smithsonian affiliate and the crown jewel of Omaha's cultural attractions. The museum features 19th and 20th century European and American art. It also is a treasure trove of Western American art, with paintings, sculpture, and photographs by George Catlin, Frederic Remington, George Caleb Bingham, and Edward S. Curtis. The centerpiece of its Western collection are the watercolors and prints by Swiss artist Karl Bodmer *(see p438)*, who documented life on the upper Plains when he traveled across North America with German naturalist, Prince Maximilian of Wied, in 1833.

North of downtown, the **Great Plains Black History Museum** relates the rarely told story of African-American migration and settlement on the Great Plains, beginning with the Exoduster group of freed slaves that left Reconstruction-ravaged Tennessee in the 1870s to homestead in Kansas. The **Mormon Trail Center**, about 5 miles (8 km) to the north, commemorates the 1846-48 migration of Mormons from the Midwest to Utah *(see p519)*. Located on the pioneers' late-19th-century Winter Quarters campsite, a visitor center explains the religious persecution that led to the migration. It also displays a reconstructed Mormon Trail handcart and wagon.

Durham Western Heritage Museum
801 S 10th St. ***Tel*** *(402) 444-5071.*
10am–8pm Tue, 10am–5pm Wed–Sat, 1–5pm Sun.
www.durhammuseum.org

Joslyn Art Museum
2200 Dodge St. ***Tel*** *(402) 342-3300.*
10am–4pm Tue–Sat, noon–4pm Sun. www.josyln.org

Art Deco façade of Omaha's Durham Western Heritage Museum

Iowa

Stretching from the Mississippi on its eastern border to the Missouri River on the west, Iowa offers seemingly endless vistas of rolling hills, lush cornfields, old-fashioned barns, and clapboard, country churches. It is one of the nation's largest agricultural producers, with a rich stock of tidy, hard-working farming communities. These are the images that make the state a perfect setting for Hollywood movies seeking to capture a nearly vanished rural America. Iowa also has a handful of lively cities, including the state capital Des Moines, with its excellent art and history museums.

Sioux City 19

123,000. 801 4th St, (800) 593-2228. **www**.downtownsiouxcity.com

A busy railroad center and Missouri River port, Sioux City sits on the northern cusp of Iowa's green, shaggy Loess Hills. This unique ecosystem is comprehensively explained at the **Dorothy Pecaut Nature Center** in Stone State Park, about 3 miles (5 km) north of the city. The northern tip of the 200-mile (320-km) Loess Hills Scenic Byway, which traverses the hills, can be accessed from the park. The park also has one of the state's few surviving stands of tallgrass prairie and a network of bike and hiking trails.

Just south of downtown, the **Floyd Monument** standing on a loess bluff marks the 1804 burial of Sargent Charles Floyd, who was a member of Lewis and Clark's *(see p570)* Corps of Discovery. Floyd was the first and only member to die on the transcontinental journey of the three-year long expedition. Exhibits from the voyage can be seen in the **Sergeant Floyd River Museum & Welcome Center** on the riverfront.

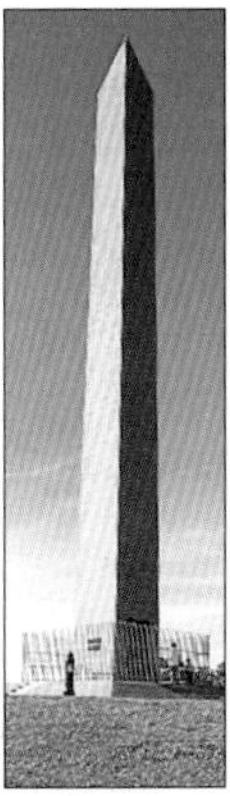

Floyd Monument

Dorothy Pecaut Nature Center
4500 Sioux River Rd. ***Tel*** *(712) 258-0838. 9am–5pm Tue–Sat, 1–5pm Sun. public hols.*

Des Moines 20

600,000. 400 Locust St, (800) 451-2625. **www**.seedesmoines.com

The state capital draws its name from French voyageurs who explored the Raccoon and Des Moines River Valleys, calling the latter *La Rivière des Moines*, "River of the Monks." The city is now an important agricultural and entertainment center and home of the massive Iowa State Fair, which lures more than a million visitors every August.

Dominating the area east of downtown is the gold-leafed central dome of the **Iowa State Capitol**. Nearby is the **Iowa Historical Building**, with its displays on the state's Native American, geological, and cultural history. West of the Capitol, the Eliel Saarinen-designed **Des Moines Art Center** exhibits an impressive collection of paintings by Henri Matisse, Jasper Johns, Andy Warhol, and Georgia O'Keeffe. The center's modern sculpture gallery was designed by I.M. Pei.

Des Moines Art Center
4700 Grand Ave. ***Tel*** *(515) 277-4405. 11am–4pm Tue, Wed, Fri, 11am–9pm Thu, 10am– 4pm Sat, noon–4pm Sun.*
www.desmoinesartcenter.org

Environs

Winterset, located about 35 miles (56 km) to the south, is the attractive seat of **Madison County** and birthplac of Hollywood Western star John Wayne. The four-room house where the actor grew up is a much-visited museum today. The local Chamber of Commerce provides a map of the five covered bridges that inspired author Robert Waller' famous 1992 novel, *The Bridges of Madison County.*

A typical family home in the Aman Colonies

Amana Colonies 21

622 46th Ave, Amana, (800) 579 2294. **www**.amanacolonies.com

The seven Amana Colonies, along the Iowa River were settled in the 1850s by the Inspirationists, a mainly German religious sect. The colonists prospered, building a profitable woolen mill and a series of communal kitchens, shops, and factories. In 1932, residents voted to end their communal lifestyle, setting up a profit-sharing society instead.

One of the community businesses has since evolved into the Amana appliance manufacturer, while the 1857 Amana Woolen Mill is the state's only woolen mill still in operation. The **Museums of the Amana Heritage Society** commemorate the success of the colonies' enterprises and its unique history in six separate museums.

Museums of the Amana Heritage Society
705 44th Ave. ***Tel*** *(319) 622-3567. Apr–Oct: 10am–5pm Mon–Sat, noon–5pm Sun.*
www.amanaheritage.org

Cedar Rapids ㉒

112,000. 119 1st Ave SE, (800) 735-5557.
www.cedar-rapids.com

This town's downtown straddles the Cedar River. The Iowa artist Grant Wood lived in Cedar Rapids for much of his adult life and developed a Regionalist style that celebrated the people and landscapes of his home state. The **Cedar Rapids Museum of Art** has one of the country's largest collection of Wood's paintings, including the well-known *Young Corn*.

The recently renovated History Center details the area's early history, while the **National Czech and Slovak Museum** celebrates the city's large Czechoslovak immigrant population. Czech Village, a corridor along 16th Avenue SW, is still lined with shops selling kolaches, babovkas, and other Czech delicacies.

Dubuque ㉓

57,000. 300 Main St, (800) 798-8844.
www.traveldubuque.com

Iowa's oldest city was established in 1788 by a French voyageur, Julian Dubuque. During the 19th century, the city's nouveau riche constructed luxurious homes atop the bluffs ringing the city. These citizens rode to and from downtown, 189 ft (57 m) below, via the **Fenelon Place Elevator**, an incline railway that is a major tourist attraction today.

View of Dubuque from the Fenelon Place Elevator

The city's main attraction is the **Mississippi River Museum**, a riverfront complex with exhibits on the mighty river's history and ecology. A series of aquariums replicate the habitat and ecosystem of the country's different rivers.

Quad Cities (Davenport) ㉔

104,000. 102 South Harrison St, Davenport, (563) 322-3911. **www**.visitquadcities.com

Davenport is one of the four Mississippi River communities that comprise the sprawling 400,000-person "Quad Cities" area on both sides of the Iowa and Illinois border. It is the only city not blocked off from the river by flood control walls. The excellent **Figge Art Museum** west of downtown has one of the better collections of early-20th-century American Regionalist paintings. It displays works by Missouri's Thomas Hart Benton and Kansas-born John Steuart Curry, as well as the only painted self-portrait of Grant Wood. The **Putnam Museum** charts the early history of the Mississippi River Valley and includes an aquarium. Its newest addition is the IMAX® Theater at the Putnam.

Figge Art Museum
225 W 2nd St. ***Tel*** *(563) 326-7804.* *10am–5pm Tue, Wed, Fri, Sat, 10am–9pm Thu, noon–5pm Sun.* *Mon, public hols.*
www.figgeartmuseum.org

Iowa City ㉕

65,300. 900 1st Ave, Coralville, (800) 283-6592.
www.iowacitycoralville.org

Easygoing Iowa City is home to the 1,900-acre (769-ha) University of Iowa campus and the school's noteworthy American Writers' Workshop. The town served as the territorial and state capital until 1857 and the Old Capitol, now the **Old Capitol Museum**, is on campus.

About 10 miles (16 km) east of Iowa City is the **Herbert Hoover National Historic Site**. The president's boyhood cottage has been restored, along with a number of buildings constructed by the local Quaker community.

Boats sailing below a bridge that spans the mighty Mississippi River, Davenport

Missouri

The Missouri River and the I-70 Interstate Highway bisect the state of Missouri, linking its two largest cities – St. Louis and Kansas City – and providing quick access to the centrally located state capital of Jefferson City. In the southwestern corner of Missouri, the rugged Ozark Mountain region is veined with beautiful streams and rivers, making the area a popular camping and canoeing destination.

Gateway Arch, symbol of the city of St. Louis

St. Louis ㉖

398,000. 308 Washington Ave, (314) 241-1764. **www**.explorestlouis.com

Located just south of the point where the Missouri empties into the Mississippi River, St. Louis has been one of the country's most active crossroads. Founded by a French fur trader in 1764, this frontier city became a part of the US as a result of the Louisiana Purchase in 1803. It soon established itself as the "Gateway to the West," as steamboats chugged up the Missouri River into territories opened up by the Lewis and Clark expedition.

Scott trial plaque in the Old Courthouse

Gateway Arch-Jefferson National Expansion Memorial

Memorial Dr & Market St. ***Tel*** *(314) 655-1600. 9am–6pm Labor Day–Memorial Day; 8am–10pm Memorial Day–Labor Day (summer). Jan 1, Thanksgiving, Dec 25.* **Old Courthouse** 11 N 4th St. ***Tel*** *(314) 655-1700. 8am–4:30pm daily. Jan 1, Thanksgiving, Dec 25.* **www**.nps.gov/jeff **Museum of Westward Expansion** ***Tel*** *(314) 655-1600. Jun–Sep: 8am–10pm; Oct–May: 9am–6pm.* **www**.stlouisarch.com

Completed in 1965 on the site of fur trader Pierre Laclede's original 1764 settlement, Eero Saarinen's 630-ft (192-m) tall **Gateway Arch** symbolizes the city's role as a commercial and cultural gateway between the settled eastern US and the wide-open lands to the west. The excellent **Museum of Westward Expansion** at the base of the arch features several detailed exhibits on the 1803–1806 expedition by the explorers Lewis and Clark *(see p570)* and other 19th-century expeditions. The museum also includes two movie theaters. Elevator-like tram rides transport visitors to the top of the arch, where picturesque views of the surrounding city and Illinois farmlands make the cramped quarters well worth the one-hour round trip.

The stately, domed **Old Courthouse** (1839–62) is one of the oldest buildings in the city of St. Louis. This Greek Revival structure was the site of two of the initial trials in the landmark Dred Scott case, which resulted in an 1857 decision by the US Supreme Court stating that African Americans were not citizens of the country and had no rights under the laws of the US. The decision overturned an earlier suit by Scott, an African-American slave who had returned to St. Louis with his owners after nine years in free states, to win his freedom. It also deepened the sectional and racial differences that finally erupted in the American Civil War that lasted from 1861 to 1865.

A museum that stands within the Old Courthouse recounts the events of the famous Dred Scott trial for the benefit of visitors and depicts what life must have been like for ordinary people living in 18th-century St. Louis under the yoke of French and Spanish rule.

Laclede's Landing

Morgan St & Lucas St between I-70 & the Mississippi River. ***Tel*** *(314) 241-5875. area open year-round; individual restaurant and club hours vary.* **www**.lacledeslanding.org

This vibrant restaurant and entertainment district consists of several blocks of restored 19th-century cotton, tobacco, and food warehouses that lie along the riverfront. The popular restaurants and blues clubs are known to attract large crowds, especially during the annual Big Muddy Blues Festival during the Labor Day weekend. The tall, six-story, cast-iron Raeder Place Building located on 719-727 N 1st Street, was built in 1873 and is one of the best-preserved warehouses in St. Louis. The 1874 Eads Bridge defines the Landing's southern boundary.

Raeder Building in Laclede's Landing area

Brick exterior of Anheuser-Busch Brewery

Forest Park

St. Louis Art Museum 1 Fine Arts Dr. ***Tel*** *(314) 721-0072.* *10am–5pm Tue–Sun (until 9pm Fri).* *Jan 1, Thanksgiving, Dec 25.* **www**.slam.org

Missouri History Museum Jefferson Memorial Bldg. ***Tel*** *(314) 746-4599.* *10am–6pm Wed–Mon, 10pm– 8pm Tue.* **www**.mohistory.org

Designed in 1876 by German-trained landscape architect Maximilian Kern, this 1,300-acre (526-ha) park is one of the nation's largest urban green spaces. The 1904 World's Fair, known officially as the Louisiana Purchase Exposition, was held on the grounds, drawing nearly 20 million visitors. After the fair, nearly all the grand Beaux Arts structures designed by Cass Gilbert were demolished. The only exception, the Palace of Fine Arts, is now home to the **St. Louis Art Museum**. Its sweeping collection of American art includes paintings by Missourians George Caleb Bingham and Thomas Hart Benton, and artists Georgia O'Keeffe, Winslow Homer, and Andy Warhol. The **Missouri History Museum**, originally the Jefferson Memorial Building, sits on the site of the main entrance to the 1904 fair. The Beaux Arts building houses impressive exhibits depicting the multicultural history of St. Louis. Its holdings include an original Louisiana Purchase transfer document, a replica of aviator Charles Lindberg's 1927 *Spirit of St. Louis* airplane, and extensive displays on the World's Fair. An interactive arts gallery explores the city's rich musical history.

Anheuser-Busch Brewery

1127 Pestalozzi St. ***Tel*** *(314) 577-2626.* *Jun–Aug: 9am–6:30pm Mon–Sat, 11:30am–5pm Sun; Sep–May: 10am–5:30pm Mon–Sat, 11:30am–5:30pm Sun.* **www**.budweisertours.com

The world's largest brewery, Anheuser-Busch, was founded in 1860 by entrepreneurial German immigrants. Its famous trademark Budweiser lager brand is still very popular. The complex contains many of the company's 19th-century brick structures. Tours include a visit to the famous Clydesdale horse stables.

Missouri Botanical Garden

4344 Shaw Blvd. ***Tel*** *(800) 642-8842, (314) 577-5100.* *9am–5pm daily.* *Dec 25.* **www**.mobot.org

This garden was created in 1859 by a wealthy St. Louis businessman on the grounds of his estate. The grounds contain an English garden, a Japanese garden, a Turkish-style Ottoman garden, as well as a scented garden for the visually impaired. The geodesic domed Climatron® has exotic birds and over 1,200 species of tropical plants, including banana trees, orchids, and epiphytes.

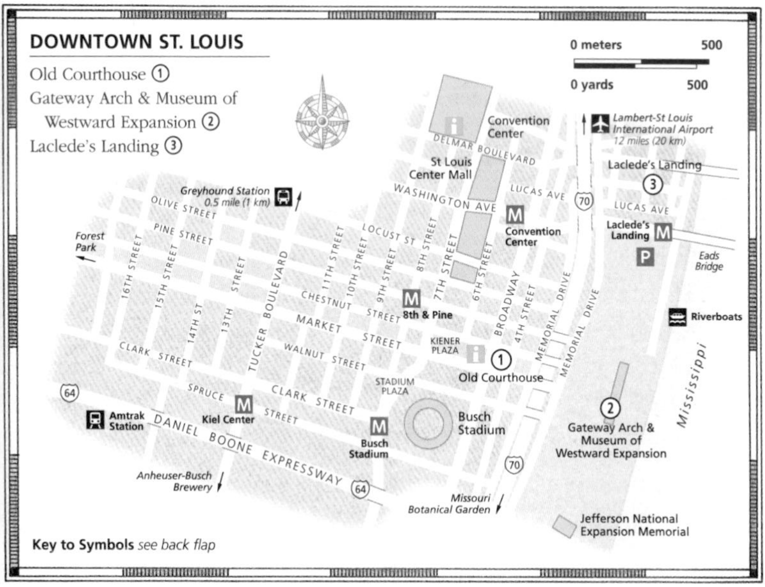

The Classic Revival Missouri State Capitol, Jefferson City

Jefferson City 27

44,200. 100 E High St, (800) 769-4183.
www.visitjeffersoncity.com

Soon after its founding as the state capital in 1821, Jefferson City grew into a busy Missouri River port. The **Jefferson Landing State Historic Site** preserves many structures from its original waterfront, including the 1839 Lohman Building. The Classic Revival **Missouri State Capitol**, completed in 1917, now houses the Missouri State Museum and a mural by Thomas Hart Benton. His bold 1935 *A Social History of the State of the Missouri* was criticized by Missouri's conservative power brokers for its stark depiction of the state's widespread poverty and seamier underclass.

Jefferson Landing State Historic Site
Jefferson St, (573) 751-2854. 10am–4pm Tue–Sat. Jan 1, Thnksg., Dec 25.

Branson 28

6,800. 269 State Hwy 248, (800) 214-3661.
www.explorebranson.com

This sleepy Ozark Mountain resort was radically transformed over the past 40 years, thanks to the phenomenal success of several family-oriented tourist attractions. A musical pageant revolving around the Ozarks-based novel, *The Shepherd of the Hills*, was one of the area's first big hits. It is still staged every night in a picturesque, outdoor arena attached to a working, mountain farm.

The Silver Dollar City amusement park features high-tech roller coasters and water rides in a 19th-century Ozark pioneer setting, about 9 miles (14 km) west of town. The area's biggest draws are Branson's nightly music programs, presented at more than 30 alcohol-free performance venues crowded together on the "The Strip" (Route 76 W).

Shepherd of the Hills Homestead
5586 W Hwy 76, 2 miles W of Branson. **Tel** *(800) 653-6288. May–Oct: 9am–4pm.*
www.oldmatt.com

Kansas City 29

1,900,000. 1100 Main St, (800) 767-7700.
www.visitkc.com

A delightful study in contrasts, Kansas City is rife with imagery associated with the Wild West. This vibrant city now contains beautifully landscaped parks and boulevards, sophisticated museums, fine public architecture, and high-end urban retail districts.

On the bluffs overlooking the Missouri River, just north of downtown, the **City Market** sits on the site of the town's original Westport Landing business district. The riverfront's 19th-century brick and cast-iron warehouses were converted into loft apartments and restaurants in the 1970s. Today, the 1930s City Market building houses an eclectic collection of shops, farmers' markets, retail outlets, and the Arabia Steamboat Museum, which displays artifacts salvaged from a 1856 wreck.

Northeast of the City Market, the **Kansas City Museum** is housed in a 50-room mansion in one of the city's most exclusive 19th-century neighborhoods. Its collections trace the city's evolution from a fur trading post into a powerful railroad and agricultural center. Walking tours are on offer at the visitor center, showing the limited exhibits that remain open during the museum's renovation, due for completion in 2011.

The newly minted "**Crossroads Arts District**" refers to the area stretching south of downtown to Penn Valley Park and Crown Center, roughly bounded on the east and west by Main Street and Broadway. The city's two most prominent architectural landmarks, **Union Station** and **Liberty Memorial** are located here. The magnificent Beaux Arts Union Station, built in 1914, was one of the country's busiest and most glamorous railroad terminals. It rose to national prominence in 1933 when outlaw Pretty Boy Floyd gunned down an accomplice and several police officers in what became known as the Union Station Massacre. Renovated after years of neglect, the station is now a local history museum,

Kansas City skyline with Union Station in the foreground

For hotels and restaurants in this region see p466 and p470

Sprawling lawn of the Nelson-Atkins Art Museum, Kansas City

children's science museum, and restaurant complex.

The recently restored 217-ft (66-m) Liberty Memorial overlooks the old train depot on the grassy bluffs of Penn Valley Park. It houses the nation's only World War I museum. The "Torch of Liberty" observation tower offers a sweeping view of the city. To its south, the **Hallmark Visitors Center** presents the history of Hallmark, the well-known greeting card company.

Southeast of downtown, the **18th & Vine Historic Jazz District** commemorates the city's rich African-American heritage. In the 1930s, all-night jazz clubs showcased the innovative riffs of local musicians such as Count Basie, Lester Young, and Charlie Parker. This was Kansas City's heyday, when under the free-wheeling "rule" of Tom Pendergast, a local concrete contractor, it was known as a "wide-open" town that stayed awake all night. Refurbished to form the backdrop for Robert Altman's 1996 film *Kansas City*, the district's premier attractions include the **American Jazz Museum**, which re-creates the city's swinging jazz era, and the **Negro Leagues Baseball Museum**, which honors talented African-American baseball players who toiled in low-paid obscurity for all-black teams in the US, Canada, and Latin America. In 1945, Kansas City Monarchs shortstop Jackie Robinson broke the color barrier by signing with the all-white Brooklyn Dodgers in the National League.

Mural at the American Jazz Museum

Once an outfitting post for travelers on the Santa Fe and Oregon Trails, the village of **Westport** became part of Kansas City in 1899. In the retail district along Westport Road, shops and restaurants now occupy some of the city's oldest buildings, such as Kelly's Westport Inn, an 1837 tavern. Several blocks south of Westport, the **Country Club Plaza**, the nation's first planned subur ban shopping district, was designed in 1922. To its east, the **Nelson-Atkins Museum of Art** has a stellar collection of paintings by Missouri's George Caleb Bingham and Thomas Hart Benton. The outdoor sculpture garden features 13 exclusive works by British artist Henry Moore.

American Jazz Museum
1616 E 18th St. ***Tel*** *(816) 474-8463.* *9am–6pm Tue–Sat, noon– 6pm Sun.* *public hols.*
www.americanjazzmuseum.com

Nelson-Atkins Museum of Art
45th St & Oak St. ***Tel*** *(816) 751-1278.* *10am–4pm Wed–Fri, 10am–5pm Sat, noon–5pm Sun.* *public hols.*
www.nelson-atkins.org

Kansas City Museum
3218 Gladstone Blvd. ***Tel*** *(816) 483-8300.* *9:30am–4:30pm Tue–Sat, noon–4:30pm Sun.* *Jan 1, Thanksgiving, Dec 25.*

Environs

The suburb of **Independence**, 15 miles (24 km) east of downtown Kansas City, has one of the country's best westward expansion museums, the National Frontier Trails Center. It was also the home of Harry S. Truman, 33rd US president. His simple downtown home is now a national historic site.

St. Joseph 30

73,200. *502 N Woodbine Rd, (800) 785-0360.* **www**.stjomo.com

Like many Missouri River communities, St. Joseph grew from a fur trading post into a wagon train outfitting center. Its position as the nation's westernmost railroad terminal instigated local entrepreneurs to launch the Pony Express in the mid-1800s. This service sought to deliver mail from St. Joseph to Sacramento – a 1,966 -mile (3,214-km) trip – in less than 10 days. Informative displays in the **Pony Express Museum** relate the story of this short-lived enterprise, while the Patee House Museum preserves an 1858 hotel that served as the headquarters of the Express. On its grounds is the house where the notorious Missouri outlaw, Jesse James, was killed by one of his former gang members in 1882.

Pony Express Museum
914 Penn St. ***Tel*** *(800) 530-5930.* *9am–5pm Mon–Sat, 1–5pm Sun.* *Jan 1, Thanksg., Dec 24–25 & 31.*
www.ponyexpress.org

Bronze statue of a Pony Express rider, St. Joseph

Kansas

For most Americans, Kansas conjures up images of rolling wheat fields, flatlands, sunflowers, and scenes from the 1939 film *The Wizard of Oz*. The real Kansas, however, is infinitely more interesting, both historically and geographically. Reminders of the state's turbulent 19th-century history as an Indian resettlement territory, anti-slavery battleground, and cattle drive destination can be seen frequently as one traverses the principal Interstate Highways, I-70 and I-35, and the meandering backroads. Kansas is also home to two of the country's few remaining stands of unbroken, tallgrass prairie, preserved in the undulating Flint Hills, just south of the lovely Kansas State University town of Manhattan.

Entrance to the Kansas Natural History Museum, Lawrence

Lawrence ㉛

67,000. 402 N 2nd St, (785) 865-4499.
www.visitlawrence.com

Founded by New England abolitionists in 1854, Lawrence's strong "free state" leanings made it a target for Missouri's pro-slavery "border ruffians," only 40 miles (64 km) to the east. The attractive, downtown retail district is lined with 19th-century stone and brick commercial buildings, reminders of the city's massive reconstruction drive after a destructive 1863 raid led by Confederate guerrilla William Quantrill.

A restored 1889 railroad depot houses the **Lawrence Visitor Information Center**, which relates key episodes in the city's history and provides information about the University of Kansas campus, just southwest of downtown. Situated astride a hill, known locally as Mount Oread, the campus includes the **Kansas Natural History Museum** and the **Spencer Museum of Art**. Its broad sampling of American and contemporary art makes this one of the finest university art museums in the United States.

Spencer Museum of Art
1301 Mississippi St. ***Tel*** *(785) 864-4710. 10am–4pm Tue–Sat (until 8pm Thu), noon–4pm Sun. public hols.*
www.spencerart.ku.edu

Topeka ㉜

125,000. 1275 SW Topeka Blvd, (800) 235-1030.
www.visittopeka.travel

A quiet government center, Topeka's most significant historical attraction is Kansas Regionalist painter John Steuart Curry's mural in the **Kansas State Capitol**. His mural, *The Settlement of Kansas*, depicts abolitionist John Brown in a dramatic confrontation with pro-slavery forces that threatened to make Kansas a slave state in the 1850s. More background on this tense period and the state's settlement can be found at the superb **Kansas History Center**, to the city's west.

Kansas History Center
6425 SW 6th Ave.
Tel *(785) 272-8681. 9am–5pm Tue–Sat, 1–5pm Sun. public hols.*
www.kshs.org

Flint Hills ㉝

501 Poyntz Ave, (800) 759-0134.
www.manhattancvb.org

The shaggy, rolling Flint Hills are among Kansas's most spectacular natural features. The best way to explore the area is to drive along the scenic 85-mile (137-km) stretch of Route 177, running south from the university town of **Manhattan**, across I-70, and down to Cassody at I-35. About 6 miles (10 km) southeast of Manhattan is **Konza Prairie**, the country's largest remaining parcel of virgin tallgrass prairie. The 8,600-acre (3,482-ha) preserve contains a variety of spectacular hiking trails that wind up and down the chert-studded hills, providing awe-inspiring views of the surrounding landscape.

Route 177 intersects US 56 at **Council Grove** (40 miles/64 km south of Manhattan). The town takes its name from a huge oak tree, the Council Oak, which commemorates the spot where the Kansa and Osage tribes agreed to allow the old Santa Fe Trail to pass through their ancestral lands. The **Kaw Mission School**, now a state historic site, was set up by the Methodists from 1851 to 1854 in an attempt to "westernize" male children from the Kaw (also known as Kansa or Kanza) tribe. This experiment did not succeed. The site now displays artifacts from the Mission school.

The red-roofed Chase County Courthouse, Cottonwood Falls, Flint Hills

For hotels and restaurants in this region see pp466–7 and p471

Hikers at the Tallgrass Prairie National Preserve, Flint Hills

The **Tallgrass Prairie National Preserve**, 20 miles (32 km) south of Council Grove, protects what remains of an 11,000-acre (4451-ha) 19th-century cattle ranch. A hiking trail leads visitors from the ranch's Second Empire main house through large stands of native prairie. The ranching community of **Cottonwood Falls**, located about 3 miles (5 km) south on Route 177, contains another impressive Second Empire structure. Built in 1873, the red-roofed, limestone **Chase County Court-house** is the oldest still in use in Kansas.

Konza Prairie
McDowell Creek Rd. ***Tel*** *(785) 587-0441.* *sunrise-sunset daily.*
www.naturalkansas.org

Tallgrass Prairie National Preserve
Hwy 177, 2 miles (3 km) N of Strong City. ***Tel*** *(620) 273-8494.*
9am–4:30pm daily.
www.parktrust.org

Wichita 34

550,000. *515 S Main St, (800) 288-9424.*
www.visitwichita.com

Wichita developed in 1865 as a lawless railhead town, where cowboys driving cattle north from Texas on the Chisholm Trail *(see p481)* would stop to let off steam in the city's rowdy saloons and brothels. Those early cattle hands would not recognize today's Wichita, which has grown into a busy aircraft manufacturing and oil refining center. The town's colorful past is recreated at the **Old Cowtown Museum**. The original jail and period houses, as well as stores and saloons from surrounding rural communities are on display here. To its southeast is the **Mid-America All-Indian Center**, which depicts the 19th-century Great Plains lifestyles of the Kiowa, Cheyenne, and Lakota tribes. The main feature at the center is a reconstructed village. The "Gallery of Nations" features the flags of over 500 Indian nations.

Artifact, Indian Center Museum, Wichita

Old Cowtown Museum
1865 Museum Blvd.
Tel *(316) 219-1871.* *Apr–Oct: 10am–5pm Mon–Sat, noon–5pm Sun.*
www.old-cowtown.org

Mid-America All-Indian Center
650 N Seneca St. ***Tel*** *(316) 262-5221.* *10am–4pm Tue–Sat.* *public hols.*
www.theindiancenter.org

Dodge City 35

23,000. *400 W Wyatt Earp Blvd, (800) 653-9378.*
www.dodgecity.org

The Wild West's two most colorful characters, lawmen Wyatt Earp and Bat Masterson, earned their tough reputations in Dodge City during its brief but boisterous heyday. Between 1872 and 1884, the town flourished as a High Plains buffalo-hunting, cattle-driving, and railroad center. The **Boot Hill Museum** re-creates the infamous Front Street strip of saloons and burlesque houses that earned Dodge City the sobriquet of "Hell on the Plains." The museum organizes various shows and stagecoach rides. On the museum grounds is Boot Hill cemetery.

Before hordes of cowboys and gun-toting buffalo hunters came to town, Dodge City was just another stop on the Santa Fe Trail. Ruts from the old wagon trail can still be seen 9 miles (14 km) west of Dodge City along US 50 and at the **Fort Larned National Historic Site**, 55 miles (88 km) east of Dodge City. The site contains several restored original sandstone structures from the US Army fort that protected travelers along the Santa Fe Trail from 1859 to 1878.

Boot Hill Museum
Front St & 5th Sts. ***Tel*** *(620) 227-8188.* *Jun–Aug: 8am–8pm daily, Sep–May: 9am–5pm Mon–Sat, 1–5pm Sun.* *Jan 1, Thanksgiving, Dec 25.* **www**.boothill.org

Fort Larned National Historic Site, east of Dodge City

Oklahoma

Tribe mask

Bordered by six states, Oklahoma is a cultural, geographical, and historical crossroads, where jagged mountain ranges and High Plains mesas merge with forests, flatland wheat fields, and vast grassy ranges. The state has the nation's largest Native American population – more than 250,000 people representing 67 tribes – as a result of forced 19th-century migrations to the region, then known as the Indian Territory. Several "land runs" between 1889 and 1895 brought a huge influx of white and African-American settlers to this area, which joined the US in 1907 after oil was discovered.

***Praying Hands* at Oral Roberts University, Tulsa**

Bartlesville 36

36,700. 201 SW Keeler, (800) 364-8708. **www**.bartlesville.com

The state's first commercial oil well was drilled here in 1897, kicking off a large-scale oil boom. A replica of the original well, the Nellie Johnstone #1, now stands as a memorial in a downtown park. Today, the city's largest employer is still the ConocoPhillips company, founded in 1917 as Phillips Petroleum, by two speculators from Iowa.

Environs

Frank Phillips's extensive 3,600-acre (1456-ha) rural estate, **Woolaroc Lodge & Ranch**, is located 12 miles (19 km) southwest of Bartlesville. The picturesque ranch includes a superb Western art collection, the Native American Heritage Center, and a wildlife preserve. About 45 miles (72 km) northwest of Bartlesville (by way of Pawhuska) is the Nature Conservancy's **Tallgrass Prairie Preserve**. In this vast expanse of rolling prairie, a herd of bison graze among stands of big bluestem grasses, coneflowers, and blazing star wildflowers.

Woolaroc Lodge & Ranch
Rte 123, 12 miles (19 km) SW of Bartlesville. ***Tel** (918) 336-0307.*
Jun–Sep: 10am–5pm Tue–Sat; Oct–May: 10am–5pm Tue–Sun.
Mon, Thanksgiving, Dec 25.
www.woolaroc.org

Tulsa 37

805,000. Williams Center Tower 2, 2 W 2nd St, (800) 558-3311. **www**.visittulsa.com

Originally a railroad town, Tulsa prospered after the discovery of oil in 1901. Fortunes were made literally overnight, leading to the construction of Art Deco commercial buildings, roads, and bridges across the Arkansas River. Although Tulsa is still a major oil center, it also contains numerous man-made lakes, parks, and Arkansas River bike trails. Its top attraction is the **Thomas Gilcrease Institute**, a comprehensive art museum founded by a wealthy local oilman. Its collection includes a wide range of Native and Western American paintings by such well known artists as George Catlin and Frederic Remington. The city's most popular roadside sight is the Prayer Tower Visitor Center and the 80-ft (24-m) bronze statue of a pair of hands folded in prayer at the entrance to Tulsa's **Oral Roberts University**.

Thomas Gilcrease Institute
1400 N Gilcrease Museum Rd, off US 64. ***Tel** (918) 596-2700.*
10am–5pm Tue–Sun. *Mon & Dec 25.*
www.gilcrease.org

Tahlequah 38

14,300. 123 E Delaware St, (800) 456-4860. **www**.tourtahlequah.com

The capital of the Cherokee Nation, Tahlequah lies in the eastern Oklahoma Ozark Mountain foothills, the tribe's home since 1839. The city preserves several late 19th-century buildings, including the prison and the Cherokee National Capitol Building.

Of primary interest here is the **Cherokee Heritage Center**. Its attractions include a village dating from the 1875–90 Indian Territory era and a re-creation of a 17th-century settlement from the

Carriage on display at Woolaroc Ranch Museum, near Bartlesville

For hotels and restaurants in this region see p467 and p471

Earth lodges in the Cherokee Heritage Center, Tahlequah

tribe's ancestral lands in the Appalachian Mountains. Exhibits at the Cherokee National Museum chronicle the tribe's forced march along the "Trail of Tears" from North Carolina to Oklahoma in the 1830s *(see p438)*. This tragic event is also dramatized every year in June.

Cherokee Heritage Center
US 62, 3 miles (5 km) S of Tahlequah. ***Tel*** *(888) 999-6007.* *10am–5pm Mon–Sat* *public hols.*
www.cherokeeheritage.org

Oklahoma City 39

1,158,000. *189 W Sheridan, (800) 225-5652.*
www.visitokc.com

Oklahoma City was built and founded in a single day, April 22, 1889, as part of the first Oklahoma Territory land rush. Over 10,000 land claims were filed on that day, creating a city out of thin air. The city became the state capital in 1910 and saw its first oil strike in 1928. Today, there are more than 2,000 still-active oil wells, including one on the grounds of the Oklahoma State Capitol, within the city limits.

The **Oklahoma History Center** chronicles the state's intimate relationship with oil, as well as its pre-settlement history. The **National Cowboy Museum** contains one of the country's most comprehensive collections of Western-related art. Among its exhibits are works by such artists as Charles Russell, and Albert Bierstadt. It also features a giant statue of the famed Wild West figure Buffalo Bill and a collection of Western actor John Wayne memorabilia. On a more somber note, the city has paid homage to the 168 people killed in the tragic 1995 Federal Building bombing incident *(see p438)* with the dignified **Oklahoma City National Memorial**. The 3.3-acre (1.3-ha) downtown memorial includes a museum, reflecting pool, and 60-year-old American elm tree.

National Cowboy Museum
1700 NE 63rd St. ***Tel*** *(405) 478-2250.* *9am–5pm daily.* *Jan 1, Thanksgiving, Dec 25.*
www.nationalcowboymuseum.com

Oklahama History Center
2401 N Laird Ave. ***Tel*** *(405) 521-2491.* *9am–5pm Mon–Sat.* *public hols.*
www.okhistory.org

The reflecting pool at the Oklahoma City National Memorial

OLD ROUTE 66: THE HISTORIC "MOTHER ROAD"

Route 66 has been immortalized as the "mother road" traveled by the migrant Oklahoma family in author John Steinbeck's 1939 novel, *The Grapes of Wrath*, as they fled the drought-stricken Dust Bowl on the way to California. This historic highway, charted in 1926, was the first to link Chicago to Los Angeles. Old Route 66 heads southwest from the state's northeastern corner to its western border with Texas, meandering along the original two-lane alignment much of the way, frequently within sight of the modern interstates, I-44 and I-40 that parallel its original route. West of Oklahoma City, the route runs alongside I-40, with several sections of old road veering off the Interstate. The **Oklahoma Route 66 Museum** in Clinton sits across from a Best Western Motel where Elvis Presley slept on four separate occasions. The recently renovated museum has one of the country's best Route 66 collections. The **National Route 66 Museum** in Elk City (30 miles/48 km west of Clinton) sports a smaller but equally engaging array of exhibits, including a pickup truck modeled after the one used in director John Ford's 1940 film adaptation of *The Grapes of Wrath*. Other sights along the route include the **Totem Pole Park** (about 4 miles/6 km east of Foyil), and the **Will Rogers Memorial Museum** at Claremore (27 miles/43 km east of Tulsa). Oklahoma's favorite son, humorist Will Rogers, was born in a log cabin in nearby Oologah. The museum relates the life story of this colorful actor and newspaper columnist, and screens several of his films.

Totem Pole Park

Practical Information

Up-to-date information is essential when planning an itinerary across the Great Plains, where cities and attractions are often separated by miles and miles of rolling prairie. A region of small towns, wide-open spaces, and distant horizons, the beautiful landscape of the Great Plains draws visitors searching for a taste of wholesome Americana. The best time to plan a trip is from mid-April through late October, but bear in mind that many of the historical sights are open only from Memorial Day (end May) to Labor Day (end August).

TOURIST INFORMATION

Travelers entering the Great Plains via a principal Interstate Highway are greeted with signs advertising a state "Welcome Center." These centers provide a full range of tourist information, as well as clean restrooms and free coffee. Most of the region's major airports and train stations have information desks stocked with free brochures and maps. All of the larger cities and smaller towns operate Convention & Visitors' Bureaus, which provide free directories of events, attractions, accommodations, and restaurants, both in print and online.

NATURAL HAZARDS

Tornadoes usually occur during summer, particularly in the eastern portions of Kansas and Oklahoma, called "Tornado Alley." In the event of a tornado warning, travelers should first seek shelter in the basement of a solidly constructed building and then tune into a local radio station for additional information.

GETTING AROUND

Most of the major cities in the Great Plains have public bus systems that provide affordable but limited service. However, the convenient St. Louis Metrorail system is the only public rail transit system in the region.

DRIVING IN THE GREAT PLAINS

Driving is the best way to explore the region, since most sights are usually situated far away from each other. Thus certain precautions are necessary to ensure a safe journey. Seat belts are a must for drivers and front-seat passengers in all the states. Most states also require seat belts for back-seat passengers. Child seats are also mandatory, but age restrictions may vary from one state to another. Motorcyclists are required to wear helmets in all of the states except Iowa, which has no restrictions.

Speed limits vary but are usually between 70–75 mph (112–120 km/h) on Interstate Highways, which are located outside crowded urban areas. Radar detectors are permitted in all the states.

ETIQUETTE

Great Plains residents tend to be friendly and polite. Drivers on the empty back roads usually acknowledge an oncoming car or truck by raising one or two fingers off of the steering wheel in a modified version of a wave. The polite response is to offer the same in return.

FESTIVALS

The Great Plains states stage a wide range of annual community, regional, and state festivals. The largest of the region's many fairs is the **Iowa State Fair**, held in August in Des Moines, while one of the country's friendliest Independence Day celebrations takes place in historic Independence, Missouri. All through summer, Native Americans in South Dakota hold several traditional "pow-wow" get-togethers. Other summertime events are the historical productions staged by the Great Plains Chautauqua Society.

Musical festivals also abound in the region, with summer blues festivals in Kansas City, St. Louis, and Lincoln vying for top billing. The Walnut Valley bluegrass festival in Winfield, Kansas, and **Woody Guthrie Free Folk Festival** in his hometown Okemah, Oklahoma, are also very popular. Polka music, beer, and German food end the festival season at Missouri's **Oktoberfest**, in the Missouri River community of Hermann.

SPORTS

Missouri has a monopoly on professional sports teams in the region, with Kansas City and St. Louis operating the region's only pro baseball (Kansas City Royals and St.

THE CLIMATE OF THE GREAT PLAINS

This is a region of extremes, with hot summers and cold winters, especially in North and South Dakota. The southern states – Kansas, Missouri, and Oklahoma – have a more temperate climate, with milder winters. With its cooler nights and sunny days, June is perfect for touring the region's historic sites. Wildflowers are most colorful in May and September, while October's changing colors make it ideal for scenic drives through the wooded Ozark Mountains.

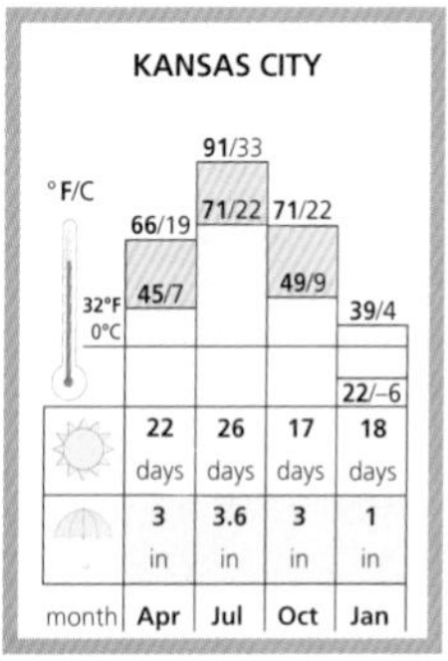

Louis Cardinals) and football (Kansas City Chiefs and St. Louis Rams) franchises. Many of the states have minor league baseball teams as well, providing travelers with opportunities to watch up-and-coming players in cozier settings. Iowa is a mecca for minor league fans, with A-level teams in Burlington, Cedar Rapids, Clinton, and Davenport, and the AAA affiliate of the Chicago Cubs in Des Moines.

College football and basketball are also very popular, particularly in the southern Plains states. The annual **Kansas–Kansas State** football game is the seasonal climax to one of college football's most colorful intrastate rivalries.

OUTDOOR ACTIVITIES

In defiance of the stereotypical image of the Great Plains as flat and devoid of topography, hikers, cyclists, and mountain bikers flock to the region's hilly areas. Nebraska's Pine Ridge country, South Dakota's Badlands and Black Hills, and the Kansas Flint Hills are havens for campers and hikers. The 200-mile (320-km) **Katy Trail** bike path winds along the Missouri River for much of its route. Iowa's seven-day 500-mile **RAGBRAI** cycling event is one of the world's largest, while the August motorcycle rally and race in Sturgis, South Dakota, draws thousands of participants and spectators. Fishing and boating enthusiasts can choose from a range of mainly man-made lakes, such as Nebraska's Lake McConaughy. Streams and rivers in the Missouri Ozarks near Branson provide opportunities to fish and canoe. Visitors should contact the state tourist offices for lists of outfitters for a particular region.

ENTERTAINMENT

The busiest live music and theatrical venues in the Great Plains are in Kansas City and St. Louis, with an array of clubs and theaters sprinkled in cities such as Tulsa, Lawrence, Lincoln, Omaha, Grand Forks, and Des Moines. The region's most spectacular outdoor performance venues include **The Muny** in Forest Park in St. Louis, Kansas City's **Starlight Theater**, in the city's bucolic Swope Park; and North Dakota's **Medora Musical**, featuring live Wild West musical programs on summer nights against the backdrop of the Theodore Roosevelt National Park badlands. A dizzying array of rides and activities awaits those who are more adventurous at the region's largest amusement parks, Kansas City's Worlds of Fun and Six Flags St. Louis.

SHOPPING

The region's premier retail destination is Kansas City's elegantly designed Country Club Plaza. This 1920s urban shopping district has several higher-end specialty shops and department stores. A popular suburban shopping destination is the upscale Galleria mall in Clayton.

Iowa's Amana Colonies offer some of the best locally made products at the Amana Woolen Mill and Millstream Brewing Company. The best place to visit for Native American crafts and other merchandise is South Dakota. The Native American Educational and Cultural Center at the Crazy Horse Memorial in the Black Hills, and the Red Cloud Heritage Center on the Pine Ridge Reservation offer a wide selection of handmade rugs, apparel, and other items. For Wild West souvenirs, travelers should visit Wall Drug, in Wall, located in South Dakota, for the widest selection.

DIRECTORY

TOURIST OFFICES

Iowa
Tel (888) 472-6035.
www.traveliowa.com

Kansas
Tel (800) 252-6727.
www.travelks.org

Missouri
Tel (800) 411-5110.
www.visitmo.com

Nebraska
Tel (800) 228-4307.
www.visitnebraska.org

North Dakota
Tel (800) 435-5663.

Oklahoma
Tel (800) 652-6552.
www.travelok.com

South Dakota
Tel (605) 773-3301; (800) 732-5682.
www.travelsd.com

ROAD CONDITIONS

Iowa
Tel (800) 288-1047.

Kansas
Tel (800) 585-7623.

Nebraska
Tel (402) 479-4512.

Oklahoma
Tel (405) 425-2385.

South Dakota
Tel (866) 697-3511.

FESTIVALS

Iowa State Fair
P.O. Box 57130. Des Moines, IA 50317-0003
Tel (515) 262-3111.
www.iowastatefair.com

Oktoberfest
Hermann, MO.
Tel (800) 932-8687.
www.hermannmo.info

Woody Guthrie Free Folk Festival
Okemah Industrial Park, Okemah, OK.
Tel (918) 623-2440.
www.woodyguthrie.com

ENTERTAINMENT

The Muny
Forest Park, St. Louis, MO.
Tel (314) 361-1900.

Starlight Theater
4600 Starlight Rd, KC, MO.
Tel (800) 776-1730.
www.kcstarlight.com

Medora Musical
Burning Hills Amphitheater, Medora, ND
Tel (800) 633-6721.
www.medora.com

Choosing a Hotel

This region's unique natural features and vibrant cities offer visitors a wide range of accommodations. There are a variety of historic hotels, chain hotels, and luxurious bed-and-breakfast inns in larger centers, while guest ranches, mountain lodges, and state park cabins provide comfortable lodgings in spectacular natural settings.

PRICE CATEGORIES
For a standard double room per night, including service charges and any additional taxes.

(\$) Under \$100
(\$)(\$) \$100–\$150
(\$)(\$)(\$) \$150–\$200
(\$)(\$)(\$)(\$) \$200–\$250
(\$)(\$)(\$)(\$)(\$) Over \$250

NORTH DAKOTA

DEVILS LAKE Totten Trail Historic Inn (\$)(\$)

Fort Totten Historic Site, 58335 ***Tel*** *(701) 766-4874* ***Fax*** *(701) 662-5334* ***Rooms*** *10*

The Totten Trail Historic Inn is a bed and breakfast open in summer at the Fort Totten State Historic Site. Furnished in frontier decor, it has rooms in the former officers' quarters with private baths or baths shared with another room. A complimentary Victorian-style tea and breakfast are made available to guests. **www.tottentrailinn.com**

FARGO Best Western Fargo Doublewood Inn (\$)

3333 S 13th Ave, 58103 ***Tel*** *(701) 235-3333, (800) 937-8376* ***Fax*** *(701) 280-9482* ***Rooms*** *172*

Minutes from downtown, the Best Western Fargo Doublewood Inn affords guests great service, great rates, and great sleeping accommodations. You can relax in a poolside lounge chair, shop at the West Acres Mall, or even visit the local Plains Art Museum. A restaurant and lounge are also on-site. **www.bestwestern.com**

FARGO Radisson Hotel Fargo (\$)

201 5th St N, 58102 ***Tel*** *(701) 232-7363* ***Fax*** *(701) 298-9134* ***Rooms*** *151*

Connection to the city's skywalk system allows guests of The Radisson Hotel Fargo easy access to downtown shopping and entertainment. The spacious rooms provide magnificent views of the area. Amenities provided include free newspaper, fitness center, sauna, and airport shuttle transportation. Pets allowed. **www.radisson.com/fargond**

MANDAN Best Western Seven Seas Hotel & Waterpark (\$)(\$)

2611 Old Red Trail, 58554 ***Tel*** *(701) 663-7401, (800) 597-7327* ***Fax*** *(701) 663-0025* ***Rooms*** *122*

Best Western Seven Seas Hotel & Waterpark is so-named because of its large indoor waterpark. The hotel's location is near many attractions including the Lewis & Clark Trail, championship golf courses, snow skiing, casino, and fresh-water fishing. Or enjoy the amenities at the hotel such as fitness center and on-site restaurant. **www.bestwestern.com**

SOUTH DAKOTA

CUSTER Sylvan Lake Lodge & Resort (\$)(\$)

13389 US Hwy 16A, 57730 ***Tel*** *(605) 574-2561, (888) 875-0001* ***Fax*** *(605) 574-4943* ***Rooms*** *66*

Sylvan Lake Lodge & Resort is located on Sylvan Lake in the Black Hills mountain region. Enjoy a peaceful stay in one of the private cabins complete with kitchenettes and fireplaces. Cozy guest rooms are also available in the main lodge. Enjoy activities such as hiking, bird-watching, and swimming. **www.custerresorts.com**

DEADWOOD Bullock Hotel (\$)(\$)

633 Main St, 57732 ***Tel*** *(605) 578-1745, (800) 336-1876* ***Fax*** *(605) 578-1382* ***Rooms*** *36*

Named for Deadwood's first sheriff, Seth Bullock, the historic Bullock Hotel has been restored to its former glory. Victorian decor and modern amenities greet guests. Each of the accommodations is different, from the Roosevelt Suite, named for Seth's best friend, Teddy, to the "haunted" 313 Suite. **www.deadwood.org**

INTERIOR Cedar Pass Lodge (\$)

Badlands National Park, 20681 SD Hwy 240, 57750 ***Tel*** *(605) 433-5460* ***Fax*** *(605) 433-5560* ***Rooms*** *22*

Located in the heart of the Badlands National Park, the Cedar Pass Lodge is for those who wish to get away from the hustle and bustle of city life. Enjoy your stay in one of the rustic cabins while listening to the sounds of nature all around. Hike one of the many trails around the park area. **www.cedarpasslodge.com**

PIERRE Governor's Inn (\$)

700 W Sioux Ave, 57501 ***Tel*** *(605) 224-4200* ***Rooms*** *82*

Governor's Inn gives the feel of a home away from home with its comfortable and spacious rooms that provide microwaves and refrigerators. Convenient to downtown Pierre, this remodeled hotel is a great place to stay when in South Dakota. A complimentary Continental breakfast is served. **www.govinn.com**

Key to Symbols *see back cover flap*

RAPID CITY Abend Haus Cottages & Audrie's Bed & Breakfast $$$

23029 Thunderhead Falls Rd, 57702 ***Tel*** *(605) 342-7788* ***Rooms*** *10*

Surrounded by the Black Hills National Forest, the Abend Haus Cottages & Audrie's Bed and Breakfast has amazing views and sounds of nature. Each room or cottage has its own private entrance, patio, and hot tub. A charming place to stay. **www.audriesbb.com**

RAPID CITY Alex Johnson Hotel $$$

523 6th St, 57701 ***Tel*** *(605) 342-1210, (800) 888-2539* ***Fax*** *(605) 342-1210* ***Rooms*** *143*

Alex Johnson Hotel, once known as "The Showplace of the West", is a part of American history. This Rapid City landmark, housed in an historic 1928 building with Native American decor, provides comfort and a unique overnight experience to patrons. **www.alexjohnson.com**

NEBRASKA

CRAWFORD Fort Robinson State Park $

US 20, 3 miles W of Crawford, 69339 ***Tel*** *(402) 471-1414* ***Fax*** *(308) 665-2906* ***Rooms*** *57*

Fort Robinson State Park (over 7,000 acres) makes facilities available to overnight guests from early Apr to mid-Nov. Nebraska's largest state park has reconstructed historic buildings, such as a ranch house, lodge, and cabins for public use. Activities include horse riding, hiking, cycling, and fishing. A park permit is required. **www.outdoornebraska.org**

LINCOLN Cornhusker Hotel $$

333 S 13th St, 68508 ***Tel*** *(402) 474-7474, (866) 706-7706* ***Fax*** *(402) 474-1847* ***Rooms*** *297*

Part of the Marriott chain, The Cornhusker Hotel advertises itself as "old-world charm meets modern convenience". The walls of the hotel contain beautifully painted murals and the airy elegant rooms are luxurious. Nearby attractions include the Sheldon Art Gallery, Memorial Stadium, and the Sunken Gardens. **www.thecornhusker.com**

MITCHELL Barn Anew Bed & Breakfast $$

170549 County Rd L, 69357 ***Tel*** *(308) 632-8647* ***Rooms*** *4*

Converted from an old roofless barn, the Barn Anew Bed & Breakfast is a great place to stay when visiting the Panhandle area. It has four comfortable rooms available with private baths. The view from the sitting room is of the Scott's Bluff National Monument. **www.barnanew.com**

NEBRASKA CITY Whispering Pines B&B $$

2018 6th Ave, 68410 ***Tel*** *(402) 873-5850* ***Rooms*** *5*

Within large gardens on the edge of town, this 1878 Victorian farmhouse has five themed guest rooms with private bathrooms. Outside, guests can enjoy the use of a hot tub and take in the waterlily garden, ponds, and waterfalls. The rate includes breakfast and other meals can be made on request. **www.bbwhisperingpines.com**

NORTH PLATTE Royal Colonial Inn $

1402 S Jeffers St, 69103 ***Tel*** *(308) 534-3630, (800) 624-4643* ***Fax*** *(308) 534-0110* ***Rooms*** *65*

The Royal Colonial Inn offers charming bed and breakfast accommodations, including some suites. The inn is filled with country decor and is a warm and cozy place to stay while enjoying the North Platte area. The rate includes a Continental breakfast.

OMAHA Marriott Omaha $$$

10220 Regency Circle, 68114 ***Tel*** *(402) 399-9000* ***Fax*** *(402) 399-0223* ***Rooms*** *300*

The Marriott Omaha greets guests with an airy and elegant lobby and the rooms are just as welcoming. The staff is accommodating and works to make your stay more enjoyable. There is an indoor pool and fitness facilities for your use. **www.marriott.com**

IOWA

AMANA COLONIES Die Heimat Country Inn Bed & Breakfast $

4434 V St, Homestead #10, 52236 ***Tel*** *(319) 622-3937, (888) 613-5463* ***Rooms*** *18*

The Die Heimat Country Inn Bed & Breakfast is said to have once been a stagecoach stop. This inn offers simple country rooms furnished with antiques and handmade quilts. A grandfather clock welcomes guests in the lobby. Sit on the "Amana" glider swing to take in the beautiful landscape. **www.dheimat.com**

CEDAR FALLS The Blackhawk Hotel $

115 Main St, 50613 ***Tel*** *(319) 277-1161, (800) 488-4295* ***Rooms*** *44*

Nestled among a block of refined brick buildings is the Blackhawk Hotel, which has undergone renovations to keep the old charm. Free bicycles are available to enjoy the 30-mile bike trail system in the area. Other activities include live theater, art festivals, and museums. Smoke-free hotel. **www.blackhawk-hotel.com**

DAVENPORT Radisson Quad City Plaza Hotel $$

111 E 2nd St, 52801 ***Tel*** *(563) 322-2200* ***Fax*** *(563) 322-9939* ***Rooms*** *221*

The cities of Davenport, Rock Island, Moline, and East Moline define the "Quad" in the Radisson Quad City Plaza. This hotel, along with its luxury accommodations, affords guests with amazing views of the Mississippi River. Enjoy the Waterfall Lounge with its lush foliage and plush burgundy seating. **www.radissondavenport.com**

DES MOINES Hotel Fort Des Moines $$

1000 Walnut St, 50309 ***Tel*** *(515) 243-1161, (800) 532-1466* ***Fax*** *(515) 243-4317* ***Rooms*** *242*

Renovated back to its former glory, the Hotel Fort Des Moines has grand decor and is a popular place to stay when visiting the State Capitol. This 11-story historic hotel spoils guests, both business and leisure. Airport transportation available. **www.hotelfortdesmoines.com**

MISSOURI

BRANSON Chateau on the Lake $$$

415 N Hwy 265, 65616 ***Tel*** *(417) 334-1161, (888) 333-5253* ***Fax*** *(417) 339-5566* ***Rooms*** *300*

The Chateau on the Lake features an amazing 10-story atrium that is engulfed with waterfalls, trees, and greenery. Visitors have a unique viewpoint from the glass elevators stationed on each side of the atrium. Each room has a private balcony and the resort offers a child activity area, full service marina, and library. **www.jqhhotels.com**

KANSAS CITY Hotel Savoy $$

219 W 9th St, 64105 ***Tel*** *(816) 842-3575, (800) 728-6922* ***Fax*** *(816) 842-3575* ***Rooms*** *22*

Famous guests such as Teddy Roosevelt, John D. Rockefeller, and Sara Bernhardt have stayed at the Hotel Savoy. Built in 1888, this historic building has a stained-glass skylight designed by Frank Anderson. The rooms are elegant and comfortably designed. **www.savoyhotel.net**

KANSAS CITY Hotel Phillips $$$

106 W 12th St, 64105 ***Tel*** *(816) 221-7000* ***Fax*** *(816) 221-3477* ***Rooms*** *215*

At the Hotel Phillips, the goddess of Dawn is considered the "patron saint of travelers passing through Kansas City", which explains the 11-foot statue in the lobby. Once the tallest hotel in town, the decor is amazing and elegant. The eye-catching black glass on the ceiling is described as an "illusion of endless space". **www.hotelphillips.com**

ST. LOUIS Napoleon's Retreat Bed & Breakfast $$

1815 Lafayette Ave, 63104 ***Tel*** *(314) 772-6979, (800) 700-9980* ***Fax*** *(314) 772-7675* ***Rooms*** *5*

"An elegant mansion in the heart of Victorian St. Louis" reports the *Chicago Herald* about Napoleon's Retreat Bed & Breakfast. The guest rooms are spacious and equipped with cozy, queen-size beds and private baths. Enjoy your breakfast in the courtyard, which is reminiscent of New Orleans. **www.napoleonsretreat.com**

ST. LOUIS Chase Park Plaza $$$$

212 N Kingshighway Blvd, 63108 ***Tel*** *(314) 633-3000, (877) 587-2427* ***Fax*** *(314) 633-1144* ***Rooms*** *250*

Said to encompass over one million square feet, the Chase Park Plaza is pure luxury and contemporary elegance. All guest needs are addressed and amenities include a movie theater, spa, barber shop, golf, and shopping. Something for everyone. **www.chaseparkplaza.com**

SPRINGFIELD Walnut Street Inn $$

900 E Walnut St, 65806 ***Tel*** *(417) 864-6346, (800) 593-6346* ***Fax*** *(417) 864-6184* ***Rooms*** *12*

Voted "best bed and breakfast in the Ozarks", this Queen Anne-style Victorian inn is a charming and inviting place to stay. One block from "Historic Route 66", antique and flea market shopping, sightseeing in Silver Dollar City, and live shows in Branson. **www.walnutstreetinn.com**

KANSAS

COTTONWOOD FALLS Grand Central Hotel $$$

215 Broadway, 66845 ***Tel*** *(620) 273-6763, (800) 951-6763* ***Fax*** *(620) 273-8381* ***Rooms*** *10*

The Grand Central Hotel located in tiny Cottonwood Falls is a two-story hotel built in 1884. The accommodations are luscious with thick comforters on iron beds and spa-like robes provided for extra comfort. The suites are each named for ranches in the immediate area. **www.grandcentralhotel.com**

LAWRENCE Circle S Ranch & Country Inn $$$

3325 Circle S Ln, 66044 ***Tel*** *(785) 843-4124, (800) 625-2839* ***Fax*** *(785) 843-4474* ***Rooms*** *12*

This true working ranch with small herds of cattle and bison covers over 1,200 acres of rich land ripe with tall prairie grasses, hand-dug ponds, and breathtaking scenery. There are 12 unique rooms with names such as Garden, Fishing, Floral, and Cowboy, and there's a style to suit everyone's tastes. Breakfast is included. **www.circlesranch.com**

Key to Price Guide *see p464* **Key to Symbols** *see back cover flap*

LAWRENCE Eldridge Hotel $$$

7th & Massachusetts St, 66044 **Tel** *(785) 749-5011, (800) 527-0909* **Fax** *(785) 749-4512* **Rooms** *48*

Located near the University of Kansas, the Eldridge Hotel is an integral part of American history. Built in 1855, this facility was once a Free State Hostelry for abolitionists. As told, many fights of the Civil War took place here. The rooms are comfortable and inviting. **www.eldridgehotel.com**

OVERLAND PARK Marriott Overland Park $$$

10800 Metcalf Ave, 66210 **Tel** *(913) 451-8000, (800) 228-9290* **Fax** *(913) 451-5914* **Rooms** *390*

The Marriott Overland Park is situated in the suburbs of Kansas City. Spacious, efficient, and comfortable rooms are provided for business and leisure guests. This full-service facility has an on-site restaurant, bar, indoor and outdoor pool, and fitness room. Shopping is just minutes away at the local mall. **www.marriott.com**

TOPEKA Senate Luxury Suites $

900 SW Tyler, 66612 **Tel** *(785) 233-5050, (800) 488-3188* **Fax** *(785) 233-1614* **Rooms** *52*

Nestled in the business district, this Victorian brick building with arched doorways and landscaped courtyards invites guests to rest, relax, and rejuvenate. The private balconies have lovely views of the Capitol dome and the towers of Grace Cathedral. **www.senatesuites.com**

WICHITA Courtyard Wichita at Old Town $$$

820 E 2nd St N, 67202 **Tel** *(316) 264-5300, (800) 321-2211* **Fax** *(316) 264-5302* **Rooms** *128*

Courtyard Wichita at Old Town is one of the Marriott chain's newest facilities. Guests can enjoy beautifully plush rooms, an atrium lush with flowers and foliage, and wide stairways overlooking the open and airy courtyard café. Area attractions include the Sedgwick County Zoo, Warren Theater, and Old Town. **www.marriott.com**

OKLAHOMA

BARTLESVILLE Hotel Phillips $

821 S Johnstone St, 74003 **Tel** *(918) 336-5600, (800) 331-0706* **Fax** *(918) 336-0350* **Rooms** *157*

A beautiful, flower-filled landscape and green canvas awning entrance greet travelers at the elegant Hotel Phillips. The hotel offers luxurious surroundings and excellent service. A complimentary full breakfast is served and complimentary daily newspapers are also provided. This is a smoke-free environment. **www.hotelphillips66.com**

CLINTON Trade Winds Courtyard Inn $

2128 W Gary Blvd, 73601 **Tel** *(580) 323-2610* **Fax** *(580) 323-4655* **Rooms** *76*

Located on Historic Route 66, the Trade Winds Courtyard Inn provides travelers with reasonable rates, good service, and comfortable rooms. The Route 66 Museum is across the road. Other nearby attractions include the Cheyenne Cultural Center, Washita National Wildlife Preserve, and Foss Lake. **www.tradewindsinnclinton.com**

OKLAHOMA CITY Marriott Waterford $$

6300 Waterford Blvd, 73118 **Tel** *(405) 848-4782, (800) 992-2009* **Fax** *(405) 843-9161* **Rooms** *197*

The Marriott Waterford Hotel provides excellent service and accommodations – the rooms are inviting and warm. The hotel has volleyball and squash facilities or take a dip in the outdoor pool. The Waterford Lounge is also available for cocktails. **www.marriott.com**

OKLAHOMA CITY Colcord Hotel $$$

15 N Robinson Ave, 73102 **Tel** *(405) 601-4300, (866) 781-3800* **Fax** *(405) 208-4399* **Rooms** *108*

The 1910 Colcord Hotel is a "luxury inn" with its classic, elegant black and marble decor. Spacious and airy rooms are equipped with the highest quality linen to complete the plush bedding. Amenities include HD TVs and a French restaurant. **www.colcordhotel.com**

STILLWATER Hampton Inn & Suites Stillwater $$

717 E Hall of Fame Ave, 74074 **Tel** *(405) 743-1306, (800) 426-7866* **Fax** *(405) 743-1382* **Rooms** *81*

Guest accommodations are laced with traditional old-world charm at this warm and inviting inn. The courtyard contains a pool, a hot tub, and an outdoor fireplace with a lovely sitting area. A complimentary hot breakfast is provided. Guests also have access to a fitness center nearby. **www.hamptoninn.hilton.com**

TULSA Hilton Garden Inn Tulsa South $$

8202 S 100th East Ave, 74133 **Tel** *(918) 392-2000* **Fax** *(918) 392-2099* **Rooms** *104*

Warm, comfortable rooms are provided at this hotel, as expected with this chain. A coin laundry and babysitting service are a couple of the features. Nearby attractions include the Oklahoma Aquarium, Tulsa Zoo, and Oral Roberts University. **hiltongardeninn.hilton.com**

TULSA Hotel Ambassador $$$$

1324 S Main St, 74119 **Tel** *(918) 587-8200, (888) 408-8282* **Fax** *(918) 587-8208* **Rooms** *55*

With seven rooms to a floor, the Hotel Ambassador guestrooms are certainly spacious. Pampering travelers with Italian marble baths and monogrammed bath robes, sophistication is the watchword. A great place for a romantic getaway. The Hurley Library is a must-see. **www.hotelambassador-tulsa.com**

Choosing a Restaurant

The Great Plains is the United States' largest cattle-producing area. As a result, red meat is a staple at most of the region's small-town cafés and big-city steakhouses. However, less hearty dining alternatives are also available in abundance. The following restaurants have been chosen for their good value and exceptional food.

PRICE CATEGORIES
For a three-course meal for one, including a glass of house wine (where served), and all other unavoidable charges such as sales tax.

- $ Under $25
- $$ $25–$50
- $$$ $50–$75
- $$$$ $75–$100
- $$$$$ Over $100

NORTH DAKOTA

BISMARCK Fiesta Villa Restaurant & Lounge $$

411 E Main St, 58501 ***Tel*** *(701) 222-8075*

The Fiesta Villa Restaurant and Lounge summons diners into its colorful, festive atmosphere with enticing smells of Mexican food. This local favorite is housed in the Northern Railroad Depot building providing a wonderful place to serve up this typical Mexican cuisine including burritos, tacos, and fiery salsa.

BISMARCK Peacock Alley $$

422 E Main St, 58501 ***Tel*** *(701) 255-7917*

The innovative flavors emanating from the kitchen of the Peacock Alley restaurant aren't the only attraction. This International/Fusion cuisine restaurant serves up delicious dishes in a historic 1915 hotel. The early 20th-century decor gives a feel of elegance and sophistication. Reservations are suggested.

DICKINSON The BrickHouse Grille $$$$

2 West Villard, 58601 ***Tel*** *(701) 483-9900*

This fine dining establishment, in a 1912 building across the road from the North Pacific Railroad Depot, offers fresh, simple, in-season ingredients turned into creative dishes. The Angus beef is hand-cut and exotic seafood is flown in daily. There's also wild game such as kangaroo, elk, and boar. Try one of the 17 types of Martini.

FARGO Café Aladdin $

530 6th Ave N, 58102 ***Tel*** *(701) 298-0880*

Café Aladdin presents customers with a unique menu of savory and enticing Greek and Mediterranean flavors. Enjoy a casual dining atmosphere with good food and good service. Locals choose the Café Aladdin as a good place for takeout.

GRAND FORKS Sanders 1907 Dakota Cuisine $$

22 S 3rd St, 58201 ***Tel*** *(701) 746-8970*

The Sanders 1907 Dakota Cuisine restaurant is a favorite among locals, serving up "Dakota cuisine" dishes such as grilled salmon, walleye, and lamb chops. Great service and savory food in a cozy atmosphere is provided in this downtown Grand Forks restaurant.

SOUTH DAKOTA

CUSTER The Pheasant Dining Room $$

State Game Lodge, 13389 US 16 A, 57730 ***Tel*** *(605) 255-4541*

The Pheasant Dining Room presents diners with unusual selections of enticing game dishes such as venison, elk, buffalo, and pheasant. This historic restaurant in the State Game Lodge affords breathtaking views of a pine forest and mountain valley. Open May–Oct.

DEADWOOD Jakes Atop the Midnight Star $$

677 Main St, 57732 ***Tel*** *(605) 578-1555*

Located in downtown Deadwood, Jakes Atop the Midnight Star is owned by *Field of Dreams* star, Kevin Costner. The restaurant is so-named for being "atop" the Midnight Star Casino in South Dakota. Jakes' chefs are renowned for their creative gourmet fare.

HILL CITY Alpine Inn $

133 Main St, 57745 ***Tel*** *(605) 574-2749*

The Alpine Inn is a favorite among locals. Former location of the Harney Peak Hotel, this restaurant is known for its tender filet mignon and lunches consisting of bratwurst and schnitzel. You'll have a hard time deciding on dessert as there are more than 30 mouthwatering selections. Reservations are not accepted, nor are credit cards.

Key to Symbols *see back cover flap*

PIERRE La Minestra $$

106 E Dakota Ave, 57501 ***Tel*** *(605) 224-8090*

La Minestra is one of Pierre's finest Italian restaurants. The pan-fried, pistachio-crusted walleye is one of their savory signature dishes; other delectable entrees include seafood, meat, and poultry dishes. This restaurant, with its sophisticated decor and excellent service, is a local favorite so reservations for dinner are suggested.

RAPID CITY Firehouse Brewing Company $

610 Main St, 57701 ***Tel*** *(605) 348-1915*

Firehouse Brewing Company, located in downtown, is so-named for its setting in a 1915 historic firehouse and is Rapid City's first brewpub. Come in for a glass of the handcrafted ales and stay to enjoy one of the heavenly desserts. For something more substantial try the home-made three-cheese pasta.

NEBRASKA

LINCOLN La Paz Mexican Restaurant $

321 N Cotner Blvd, 68505 ***Tel*** *(402) 466-9111*

Have a South-of-the-Border good time at La Paz Mexican Restaurant. La Paz is a restaurant for the whole family with its festive atmosphere and good portions. Try the spicy cream cheese and chicken enchiladas and wash it down with a tangy margarita.

LINCOLN Billy's $$

1301 H St, 68508 ***Tel*** *(402) 474-0084*

Billy's Restaurant is an historic landmark a half block from the Governor's Mansion in Lincoln. Each of the three dining rooms is named for famous Nebraskans – William Jennings Bryan, Charles Dawes, and George W. Norris. his fine-dining establishment serves delicious steak, lamb, duck, and vegetarian items among others.

OGALLALA Hilltop Inn $

197 Kingsley Dr, 69153 ***Tel*** *(308) 284-4534*

The Hilltop Inn is nestled on top of a scenic hill overlooking a lake, hence the name. Not all tables look out over the beautiful views so it's worth asking for one that does. This family restaurant serves up enticing comfort food. Their home-made apple butter is delicious!

OMAHA Flatiron Café $$$

1722 St. Marys Ave, 68102 ***Tel*** *(402) 344-3040*

Opened in December 1995 in the triangle-shaped Flatiron Building, the Flatiron Café near the Old Market in downtown Omaha offers an imaginative gourmet menu. The elegant dining room features faux-Italian marble walls, imported light fixtures, and a wall of windows. Open Mon–Sat for dinner only.

OMAHA French Café $$$

1017 Howard St, 68102 ***Tel*** *(402) 341-3547*

A substantial wine cellar, unbeatable French cuisine, non-intrusive service, and elegant decor make this a top-notch restaurant. The signature French onion soup in a traditional crock is a great start before rich entrées such as filet au poivre with brandy sauce.

YORK Chances R $

124 W 5th St, 68467 ***Tel*** *(402) 362-7755*

With its turn-of-the-century decor, wood paneling, antique furnishing, and brass galore, Chances R offers old-fashioned, home-cooked meals such as pan-fried chicken and lemon pie with mile-high meringue. It also serves mouthwatering country breakfasts and has a popular bar area called the Hob Knob Lounge.

IOWA

AMANA COLONIES Ox Yoke Inn $

4420 220th Trail, 52236 ***Tel*** *(319) 622-3441, (800) 233-3441*

Set in a home built in 1856, the Ox Yoke Inn at the Amana Colonies features family-style cooking and plenty of it. Menu selections include country-fried chicken, wiener schnitzel, smoked ham, and hand-trimmed steaks cut from Iowa's finest beef loins. Refillable bowls are passed around, with fluffy potatoes, creamy gravy, and tangy German sauerkraut.

CLIVE Cosi Cucina Italian Grill $$

1975 NW 86th St, 50325 ***Tel*** *(515) 278-8148*

Known for its Italian and French cuisine, this upscale restaurant boasts creative menus with items such as ostrich and mako shark. Subtle lighting and fresh flowers on the table add to the ambience. Famed for its triangular dinner rolls served with a splash of infused olive oil, Cosi Cucina also offers a great wood-fired oven pizza.

CORALVILLE Iowa River Power Restaurant $

501 First Ave, 52241 ***Tel*** *(319) 351-1904*

The Iowa River Power Restaurant is located in a historic building that once housed a flour mill, then a power generating station, and now a multi-tiered, fine restaurant. The locals favor the Steak Oscar and the surf 'n' turf options from their seafood/steak offerings. A Sunday brunch is served.

DAVENPORT Thunder Bay Grille $$

6511 Brady St, 52806 ***Tel*** *(563) 386-2722*

The Thunder Bay Grille offers a casual dining atmosphere in an interesting bi-level restaurant. The food selections are outstanding. Steak, seafood, and Cajun cuisine make this place a local favorite. Hand-cut steaks, rotisseries chicken, New Orleans catfish, and jambalaya are just a few of the choices. But save room for a heavenly dessert.

DES MOINES Christopher's $$

2816 Beaver Ave, 50310 ***Tel*** *(515) 274-3694*

Made with fresh ingredients, the Italian/American food at Christopher's draws repeated diners. The restaurant serves great spaghetti and meatballs and also offers more creative dishes such as flavorful tequila shrimp and olive chicken with capers, green olives, and fresh spinach. A friendly casual atmosphere makes Christopher's a local favorite.

DUBUQUE The Star $$

600 Star Brewery Dr, 52001 ***Tel*** *(563) 556-4800*

Located on the second floor of a 19th-century brick building that once housed the Dubuque Star Brewery, this restaurant serves steaks, pasta, and seafood in a casual atmosphere. Outdoor patios give great views of the Mississippi River. Close to Dubuque's museums and casinos.

IOWA CITY Lou Henri $

630 Iowa Ave, 52240 ***Tel*** *(319) 351-3637*

This restaurant provides guests with a laid-back, casual atmosphere. The good food and friendly staff make this a great place for Sunday morning breakfast. Their mouthwatering banana bread French toast is a favorite. The eclectic/American fare is diverse, also including spicy huevos rancheros quesadillas.

MISSOURI

BRANSON Candlestick Inn $$$

127 Taney St, 65616 ***Tel*** *(417) 334-3633*

This exquisite French restaurant is situated away from the hustle and bustle of downtown Branson. One of the enticing menu items is the grilled rack of lamb with an apple-mint chutney. Dine outside on the patio with gorgeous views of Lake Taneycomo. The inn is open until midnight so dine late and enjoy the lights of Branson.

CLAYTON Remy's Kitchen & Wine Bar $$

222 S Bemiston Ave, 63105 ***Tel*** *(314) 726-5757*

Located in the heart of Clayton, Remy's has a telltale motto: "Water separates the people of the world, wine unites them." Not surprisingly, Remy's has an award-winning wine list and a bar where high-top bar tables are spread with white tablecloths. The menu features Mediterranean cuisine. Save room for the bread pudding.

COTTONWOOD FALLS Grand Central Hotel & Grill $

215 Broadway, 66845 ***Tel*** *(620) 273-6763*

In the heart of the Flint Hills, the Grand Central Hotel & Grill is located in an historic hotel built in 1884. The restaurant features Old West charm with New World hospitality. A serene courtyard, original brick walls, and stockyard brick flooring add to the ambience. Tender steaks are a specialty.

KANSAS CITY Blue Bird Bistro $$$

1700 Summit St, 64108 ***Tel*** *(816) 221-7559*

This colorful West Side bistro has a wide-ranging vegetarian menu plus a succulent choice of meat dishes, including organic beef, bison, and free-range chicken. Located in an 1890s building with a bright yellow door, Blue Bird Bistro features an original pressed-tin ceiling, old drugstore tile flooring, and the welcoming aroma of savory spices and herbs.

KANSAS CITY EBT $$$$

1310 Carondelet Dr, 64114 ***Tel*** *(816) 942-8870*

Since 1979 EBT evokes the charm and grace of the Victorian era. Two brass elevators and mid-1900s sandstone columns help set the stage for a fine dining experience. Entrées include crab-stuffed halibut, Kobe strip steak, and cherry wood-smoked breast of duck.

ST. LOUIS Cunetto House of Pasta $

5453 Magnolia Ave, 63139 ***Tel*** *(314) 781-1135*

Located in the Italian neighborhood known as The Hill, Cunetto House of Pasta offers a dizzying array of pastas and entrees, as well as a hearty toasted ravioli appetizer. Family-owned since 1974 and a St. Louis tradition, Cunetto's is popular for its entrées served with a glass of house wine.

Key to Price Guide *see p468* **Key to Symbols** *see back cover flap*

KANSAS

COUNCIL GROVE Hays House Restaurant Tavern $

112 W Main St, 66846 ***Tel*** *(620) 767-5911*

Built in 1857 on the old Santa Fe Trail, the Hays House Restaurant Tavern has served many a fine meal. It's the oldest continuously operated restaurant west of the Mississippi. Try Beulah's ham or pan-fried chicken, with home-made ice cream for dessert. The original owner, Seth Hays, was the great grandson of legendary pioneer and hunter Daniel Boone.

LAWRENCE Pachamama's $$$

800 New Hampshire St, 66044 ***Tel*** *(785) 841-0990*

An eclectic upscale delight, Pachamama's opened in 1986 and moved to its current location in 2006. The menu offers an appetizing array of regional, Asian, and Italian favorites with at least one wonderful vegetarian special every evening. The Star Bar features its own imbedded solar system for star-gazing enjoyment.

OVERLAND PARK J. Gilbert's Wood Fired Steaks $$

8901 Metcalf Ave, 66212 ***Tel*** *(913) 642-8070*

Exposed wood and stone and soft lighting set the mood here. The name says it all as the restaurant specializes in prime, aged, center-cut beef cooked over an open wood-fired grill. It takes 15 minutes prep time for decadent chocolate Pompeii souffle – chocolate cake souffle with a liquid center, almonds, dried cherries, and whipped cream.

TOPEKA Carlos O'Kelly's $

3425 S Kansas Ave, 66611 ***Tel*** *(785) 266-3457*

Carlos O'Kelly's features Mexican/American food and chilled margaritas. Prairie Fire Fajitas include charbroiled steak or chicken served sizzling with caramelized onion, sweet red and green peppers, flour tortillas, cheese, sour cream, pico de gallo, and guacamole. For dessert try the traditional buñuelos.

WICHITA Olive Tree Bistro $

2949 N Rock Rd, 67225 ***Tel*** *(316) 636-1100*

Wichita's first Middle Eastern restaurant has attracted a steady stream of devoted diners since opening in 1979. The bistro features Continental cuisine and an extensive wine list. Try the kabobs and baba ghanoug (roasted eggplant and tahini spread). AAA has awarded the bistro its Four Diamond rating for more than 15 years.

OKLAHOMA

BARTLESVILLE Sterling's Grille $$

2905 E Frank Phillips Blvd, 74006 ***Tel*** *(918) 335-0707*

You expect good steaks in Oklahoma and Sterling's Grille certainly delivers. A favorite is the filet mignon pepper steak with a shallot wine reduction sauce. Seafood lovers will also find some good choices on the menu. Outdoor seating and three separate rooms with different motifs allow plenty of room for diners.

CATOOSA Molly's Landing $$

3700 N Hwy 66, 74015 ***Tel*** *(918) 266-7853*

A roadside attraction since 1979, this log house restaurant is set by the river near the woods on old Route 66. With a rustic lodge interior, Molly's Landing is furnished with leather, rawhide chairs, and stuffed animals. Steak is a popular choice here, as is smoked salmon and spicy grilled quail.

OKLAHOMA CITY The Coach House $$$

6437 Avondale Dr, 73116 ***Tel*** *(405) 842-1000*

Since 1985 The Coach House has been offering fine dining and an extensive wine list in a gracious setting. A warm oak-paneled dining room features delicious cuisine from world-renowned chef Kurt Fleischfresser. It is the city's only four-star rated restaurant from AAA. Try the pecan-cornbread-crusted salmon with tomato butter and you'll see why.

TULSA Garlic Rose $$$

3509 S Peoria Ave, 74105 ***Tel*** *(918) 746-4900*

Located in the heart of Brookside, the Garlic Rose specializes in Continental/Italian cuisine in a bistro-style setting with a courtyard and fireplace. Home-made bread, pasta, and desserts are delicious. So is the Sicilian chicken – sautéed chicken breast with lump crabmeat, asparagus, and a basil bearnaise on angel hair with a mozzarella-stuffed tomato.

TULSA Warren Duck Club $$$

6110 S Yale Ave, 74136 ***Tel*** *(918) 495-1000*

Those signature warm cookies at the Doubletree Hotel in Tulsa are tempting but save room for the Warren Duck Club. This fine-dining restaurant is known for its duck served with a selection of five different sauces. It features a wine list, a view of the lawn, and a dessert buffet for a fitting end to a fine meal. AAA Four Diamond rating.

TEXAS

INTRODUCING TEXAS 474–477

DALLAS 478–479

FORT WORTH 480–481

AUSTIN 482–483

SAN ANTONIO 484–485

HOUSTON 486–487

TEXAS

By almost any standard Texas is big. Stretching nearly 1,000 miles (1,600 km) across, and even longer north to south, it is by far the largest of the "Lower 48" states and also among the most populous, with 20 million residents. While its size has inspired a love of all things large, its past as an independent nation has given Texans a sense of pride and spirit of freedom, as is evident by the state flag that still carries the Lone Star, emblem of the Republic.

Dome of Texas State Capitol, Austin

The huge scale of Texas seems to have encouraged a culture of exaggeration, and according to residents, everything about the state is bigger, better, and brasher than anywhere else. The horns on the emblematic longhorn cattle, the great fortunes made from the state's supplies of oil, and even the one-time role of the Dallas Cowboys football team as "America's Team" – almost every aspect of life is imbued with a sense of superiority. Whether this is deserved or not is a matter of opinion, but contradiction is not what many Texans want to hear. As signs and songs all over the state say: "Don't Mess With Texas."

HISTORY

In Texas, history begins at the Alamo, a former Spanish mission and Mexican fort. "Remember the Alamo" was the battle cry of the Texas war of independence from Mexico. In December 1835, a band of rebellious American settlers commandeered the fort. Two months later, the vanquished Mexican army retaliated by attacking the fort for 13 days until all the 189 Americans inside were killed. Despite this setback, the freelance Americans under General Samual Houston defeated the Mexicans in 1836 and declared the independent Republic of Texas. The Republic, which included parts of what are now New Mexico, Oklahoma, Colorado, and Wyoming, was annexed by the US in 1845. This move ignited the Mexican War, and after two years of sporadic fighting Mexico was forced to accept the loss of Texas, and the rest of the West, in 1848.

Plaque depicting a scene from the Texas War of Independence, the Alamo complex, San Antonio

◁ Cowboy boots on display at M.L. Leddy's Boots and Saddlery in San Angelo, southwest of Abilene

Sculpture of longhorn cattle outside the Dallas Convention Center

The second half of the 19th century was the heyday of the great cattle drives of the Wild West. Huge herds of Texas longhorn cattle, descendants of animals introduced by the Spanish colonists centuries before, roamed the open range. Rounded up and driven by cowboys to towns such as Fort Worth and Dallas, these cattle were loaded onto trains and shipped to different markets located in the eastern US. After working on the range for weeks at a time, the cowboys' arrival into town was often heralded by a frenzy of gunplay and general debauchery.

KEY DATES IN HISTORY

1519 Spanish explorer Alonso Alvarez de Pineda sets foot in what is now Texas

1528 Cabeza de Vaca and a black African slave spend six years traveling across Texas

1685 Rene-Robert Cavelier, Sieur de la Salle, establishes a short-lived French colony on the Gulf of Mexico at Matagorda Bay

1716 Spain establishes Catholic missions in southern Texas

1822 American immigrant Stephen F. Austin establishes a settlement along the Brazos River

1836 Battle of the Alamo; Texas becomes a Republic

1845 Texas becomes a state

1870 Texas readmitted to the Union

1900 Hurricane hits Galveston, killing 6,000

1901 Oil is discovered at Spindletop

1962 NASA's "Mission Control" in Houston

1963 President John F. Kennedy assassinated in Dallas; Texas native Vice President Lyndon B. Johnson assumes leadership

1986 Crude oil prices fall, damaging economy

2001 Texas Governor George W. Bush is named as 43rd president, despite losing the popular vote

2004 George W. Bush is re-elected US president

ECONOMY & CULTURE

Though Texas has one of the nation's most diversified economies, historically it has been dependent upon two main industries, oil and agriculture. Since the discovery of oil in the early 1900s, the state has remained the center of the US petroleum industry, producing one-third of the nation's output and controlling most of the vast quantities imported from overseas. In fact, it is hard to think of Texas without reference to the oil industry, thanks to images of gushers, "Texas Tea," and the machinations of the Ewing family on the 1980s TV show *Dallas*.

Agriculture, too, is very important. The livestock industry is still big business, so identified with its "cowboy culture" roots that boots, jeans, and a Stetson hat seem to be the official state costume. However, Texas also produces other crops such as cotton and citrus. The state's high-tech industry is led by Texas Instruments and Austin-based Dell Computer, while the huge military presence supports a major aeronautical engineering industry, particularly at NASA's "Mission Control" in Houston.

These frequently booming and often busting industries have created many fortunes. Texan wealth supports not only glitzy shops and fancy restaurants but has also endowed several excellent museums in Houston, Fort Worth, and other cities. However, the most authentic images of Texas are not of urban sophistication but of the down-home informality and vast open spaces of its rural reaches. Perhaps the best way to find its heart is to follow a dusty country road, stopping for coffee in a small-town café, with its parking lot full of pickup trucks, or watching the sun set over the ever-distant horizon.

Cowboys relaxing on a Texas ranch at sunset

Exploring Texas

Texas is so large that it is a challenge to see all of it. Public transportation is negligible in this fossil-fueled state, where driving is an essential part of life. Many visitors fly between the main cities of Dallas, Austin, and Houston, and then rent a car to get around. About 90 percent of the state's 20 million residents live in the cities, which are equipped with restaurants, hotels, and visitor attractions. Out in the countryside, where the "real" Texas lives, facilities are few and far between. Even in the more popular areas such as the Hill Country outside Austin, hotels and restaurants tend to be basic, and distances are so great that travel time can take up a large portion of the day.

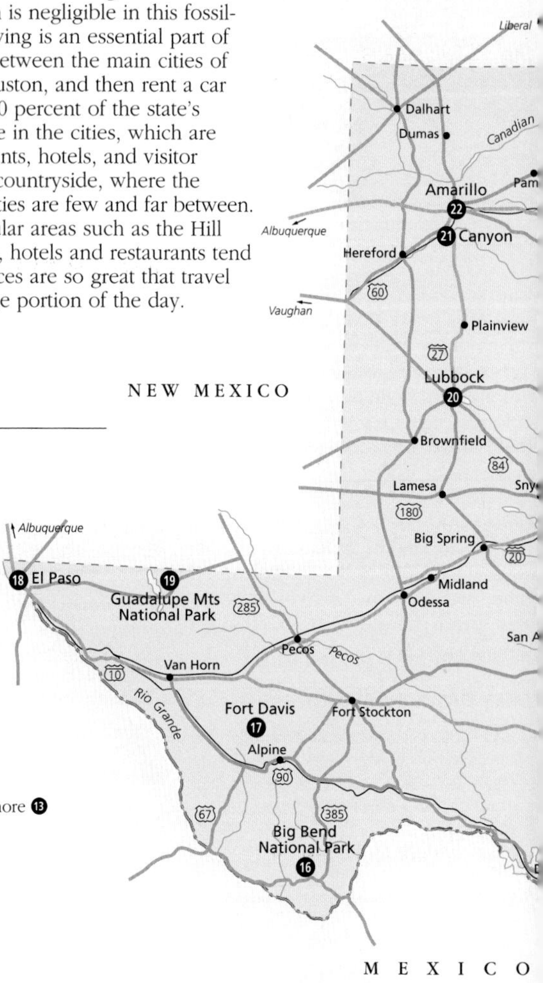

SIGHTS AT A GLANCE

Dallas pp478–9 ❶
Fort Worth pp480–81 ❷
Austin ❸
Fredericksburg ❹
Kerrville ❺
New Braunfels ❻
San Antonio pp484–5 ❼
Houston pp486–7 ❽
Big Thicket National Preserve ❾
Galveston ❿
Aransas National Wildlife Refuge ⓫
Corpus Christi ⓬
Padre Island National Seashore ⓭
Laredo ⓮
Rio Grande Valley ⓯
Big Bend National Park ⓰
Fort Davis ⓱
El Paso ⓲
Guadalupe Mountains National Park ⓳
Lubbock ⓴
Canyon ㉑
Amarillo ㉒
Abilene ㉓

KEY

- Airport
- Highway
- Major road
- Railroad
- State border
- International border

Sparkling glass office towers, dominating the Dallas skyline

For additional map symbols *see back flap*

SEE ALSO

- ***Practical Information*** pp494–5
- ***Where to Stay*** pp496–7
- ***Where to Eat*** pp498–9

MILEAGE CHART

10 = Distance in miles
10 = Distance in kilometers

	Dallas	Fort Worth	Austin	Fredericksburg	San Antonio	Houston	Galveston	El Paso
Fort Worth	**33** 53							
Austin	**196** 315	**187** 301						
Fredericksburg	**260** 418	**232** 373	**78** 126					
San Antonio	**273** 439	**264** 425	**79** 127	**71** 114				
Houston	**239** 385	**269** 433	**164** 264	**240** 386	**197** 317			
Galveston	**289** 465	**321** 517	**217** 349	**293** 472	**251** 404	**51** 82		
El Paso	**634** 1020	**608** 978	**577** 929	**497** 800	**551** 887	**747** 1202	**802** 1291	
Amarillo	**360** 579	**340** 547	**506** 814	**444** 715	**512** 824	**599** 964	**649** 1044	**432** 695

Amarillo's Cadillac Ranch, a pop-art display in northern Texas

View of Dallas from the Reunion Tower Observation area

Dallas 1

1,888,000. *Union Station, 400 S Houston St.* *Greyhound, 205 S Lamar St.* *100 S Houston St, (214) 571-1300.* *Cotton Bowl Parade (Jan 1); Dallas Blooms (mid-Mar–mid-Apr); Texas State Fair (Sep–Oct).* **www**.visitdallas.com

When most people think of Texas, they think of Dallas, even though it is neither the state capital nor the biggest city. Located in the north-eastern corner of the state, this is where the cotton fields and oil wells of East Texas meet the wide-open West Texas rangelands. With a forest of sparkling glass office towers dominating the downtown area, Dallas is the commercial and financial center of the "Lone Star" state, a role it has played since its days as the junction between the two main southwestern railroads. This fast-growing metropolis devoted to business has a huge concentration of technology firms, corporate headquarters, and wholesale markets. Infamous as the place where President Kennedy was assassinated, Dallas is nonetheless an energetic, enjoyable city, home to many prestigious museums, restaurants, and cultural venues.

Dallas is a sprawling city, merging into neighboring Fort Worth *(see pp480–81)*. The nation's eighth-largest city features a lively downtown, where most of the visitor attractions are located. A square-mile grid of streets centering on Main Street holds the main commercial district that is also the home of some of Texas' best museums. The lively West End and hip Deep Ellum districts lie at the edges of downtown. Walking in Dallas is an option, but a car, a cab, or the new DART trams can help make the most of a visitor's time.

Reunion Tower

300 Reunion Blvd E. ***Tel*** *(214) 651-1234.* *10am–10pm Sun–Thu, 10am–midnight Fri–Sat.* *may close for special events.*

Looking over Dallas from the western edge of downtown, this 50-story landmark is topped by a geodesic sphere containing a restaurant, a cocktail bar, and an observation area. Although not the city's tallest building, a title held by the 72-story Bank of America Tower located on Main Street, Reunion Tower does offer an unforgettable panoramic view of Dallas and its surrounding suburbs, and remains one of the city's most distinctive landmarks.

Sixth Floor Museum

411 Elm St. ***Tel*** *(214) 747-6660.* *noon–6pm Mon, 10am–6pm Tue–Sun.* *Thanksg., Dec 25.*

At the west end of downtown Dallas, this private museum meticulously re-creates the context while describing the controversial events of November 22, 1963, when President Kennedy was assassinated. Located in the former warehouse from which Lee Harvey Oswald shot and killed Kennedy, the exhibition concentrates on the life and times of Kennedy.

The corner window from which the shots were fired has been rebuilt to look like it did on the day of the assassination. A portion of the floor space documents the many conspiracy theories that question the official version of the president's murder.

West End Historic District

Bounded by highways and railroad tracks, this compact district of the century-old warehouses has been revitalized as the city's prime recreation center. At the north end, a former candy factory has been resurrected as the West End Marketplace, a four-story complex of shops, restaurants, nightclubs, and movie theaters.

Dallas Museum of Art

1717 N Harwood St. ***Tel*** *(214) 922-1200.* *11am–5pm Tue–Sun (until 9pm Thu).* *Jan 1, Thanksgiving, Dec 25.*

Housed in an expansive modern building north of downtown, the wide-ranging

Modernist façade of the Dallas Museum of Art

collection of this museum gives a fine overview of art history. The main galleries are arranged by continent, with works shown in chronological order. Noteworthy among these is the Art of the Americas gallery, displaying treasures from ancient Maya and Inca civilizations through paintings by such American artists as Frederic Church and Thomas Hart Benton, with a special focus on Texas-made art of the Wild West.

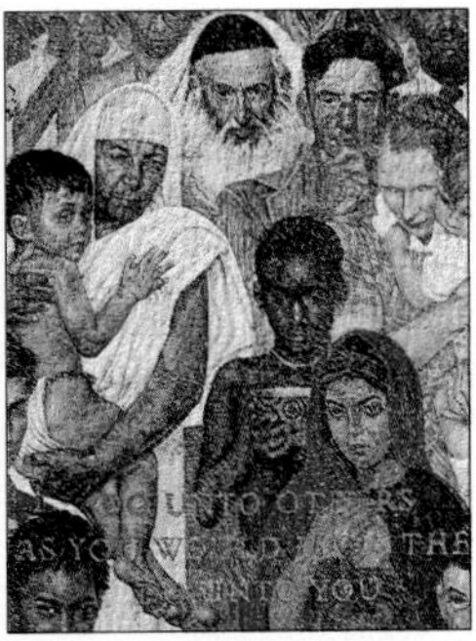

Mosaic mural in downtown's Thanks-giving Square

The European Sculpture and Painting gallery traces the evolution of art from Greek and Roman antiquities through the Renaissance, ending with a fine display of Modernist paintings. The world's most extensive collection of works by influential Dutch artist Piet Mondrian (1872–1944) is also on display.

Thanks-giving Square

Pacific Ave. ***Tel*** *(214) 969-1977.* **www**.thanksgiving.org

A peaceful and quiet oasis in bustling downtown, this pocket-sized park is packed with waterfalls, gardens, a belltower, and an all-faiths chapel. A small museum traces the history of the American custom of Thanksgiving and expresses gratitude for life in all its myriad forms.

Fair Park

First Ave. ***Tel*** *(214) 421-9600.*

This 277-acre (111-ha) exhibition center is the site of the annual Texas State Fair. It hosts the famous annual Cotton Bowl football game as well as many concerts and theater festivals. Alongside an aquarium, a natural history museum, and an African-American history museum, a highlight here is the Hall of State, a huge Art Deco repository of exhibits tracing all things Texan.

Nasher Sculpture Center

2001 Flora St. ***Tel*** *(214) 242-5100.* *11am–5pm Tue–Sun (to 9pm Thu).* **www**.nashersculpturecenter.org

The Nasher Sculpture Center offers a peaceful oasis in the urban center of Dallas. The internationally important collection of more than 300 modern and contemporary sculptures was acquired by the late Raymond and Patsy Nasher. Works by such noted artists as Joan Miró, Jeff Koons, and Anish Kapoor are displayed in a handsome Italian travertine stone building with a glass roof. The outside space is used to display further sculptures in a garden-like setting, with fountains and many trees.

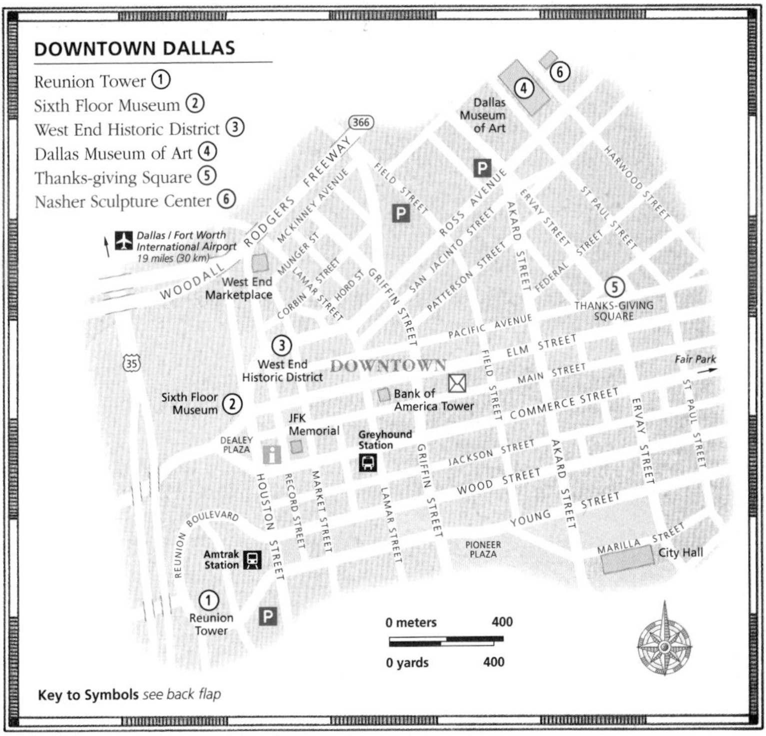

Fort Worth 2

1,702,625. Greyhound Lines, 901 Commerce St. 415 Throckmorton St, (817) 336-8791. Fort Worth Stock Show & Rodeo (late Jan–early Feb); Van Cliburn International Piano Competition (Jun).
www.fortworth.com

Unlike its flashy neighbor, Dallas, 25 miles (40 km) to the east, Fort Worth is smaller, much calmer, and more down-to-earth. In many ways it is also truer to its Texas roots. Founded in 1849 as a US Army outpost, Fort Worth boomed after the Civil War, when Chisholm Trail cattle drives made the city one of the country's largest livestock markets. Although cowboy culture lives on in the Stockyards District and the Amon Carter Museum, Fort Worth is also a capital of "high" culture, with some of the nation's finest performing arts spaces and organizations.

Fort Worth has three main areas of interest. Downtown Fort Worth revolves around Sundance Square, comprising more than a dozen blocks of historic buildings at the center of the city. To the north is the Stockyards District, where the Wild West culture is alive and well. About 2 miles (3 km) to the west, the Fort Worth Cultural District has some of the country's best museums. These are centered around the landmark Kimbell Art Museum, which along with the Amon Carter Museum traces the highpoints of European and American art. Other museums include the excellent Modern Art Museum, and the Museum of Science and History, which also houses a planetarium.

The Water Gardens, designed by the architect Philip Johnson

While walking is enjoyable in and around downtown, a car is essential to get around the rest of city.

Sundance Square

***Tel** (817) 255-5700.*

The heart of downtown Fort Worth, Sundance Square's name is a reminder of the city's Wild West past, when Chisholm Trail cattle drives used to come right through town, and cowboys and outlaws such as Butch Cassidy and the Sundance Kid frequented the city's many saloons. Filled with well-restored commercial buildings dating from the turn of the 20th century, the brick-paved streets of Sundance Square are now lined with theaters, shops, and restaurants. The city's symphony, ballet, and opera companies are all housed here. An important museum in this area is the **Sid Richardson Collection of Western Art** on Main Street. Housed in a replica of an 1895 building, the museum exhibits 60 paintings of the famed artists Frederic Remington and Charles M. Russell. Also on Main Street is the trompe l'oeil mural of the Chisholm Trail by Richard Haas.

Water Gardens

Houston & Commerce Sts.
***Tel** (817) 871-5755.*

Located on the site of Fort Worth's historic red-light district of Wild West saloons, this 5-acre (2-ha) park features a variety of waterfalls, cascades, streams, and fountains. Constructed in concrete and designed by architect Philip Johnson, the Water Gardens provide a welcome relief on hot summer days.

Advertisement for Western wear in the Stockyards District

Fort Worth Stockyards National Historic District

***Tel** (817) 626-7921.*

With its cobblestoned streets, raised wooden sidewalks, and streetlights designed to resemble old-fashioned gas lights, this small but engaging 10-block neighborhood is located 2 miles (3 km) north of downtown. Known as the Stockyards District, it developed alongside the sprawling Fort Worth Stockyards, where each day more than a million head of cattle were sold and shipped to markets in the eastern United States. Though the stockyards ceased to be commercially viable many years ago, the complex preserves the old wooden pens and holds daily livestock auctions.

Today, the neighborhood offers a glimpse of what life in Texas was like a century

View of Stockyards District with its many saloons

For hotels and restaurants in this region see p497 and p499

Longhorn cattle being led through Stockyards National Historic District

ago. A number of lively cowboy-themed saloons and honky-tonk nightclubs, many featuring live music, are also located here. The oldest and most atmospheric of these is the White Elephant Saloon. Also nearby are the Longhorn Saloon and **Billy Bob's Texas** *(see p495)*. Said to be the largest nightclub in the world, Billy Bob's Texas is housed in a huge building and boasts 42 bar areas. Live bull-riding demonstrations also take place here on weekend nights. The district includes a small museum and a steam train. Other attractions include weekend rodeos and a daily parade of longhorn cattle down Exchange Avenue. Today, this is an up-and-coming area, where trendy bars and cafés spring up almost every day.

Sign for Billy Bob's Texas nightclub

Kimbell Art Museum

3333 Camp Bowie Blvd. ***Tel** (817) 332-8451.* *10am–5pm Tue–Thu, noon–8pm Fri, 10am–5pm Sat, noon–5pm Sun.* *Jan 1, Jul 4, Thnksg., Dec 25.* *exhibitions only.* **www**.kimbellart.org

One of the most unforgettable museums and art collections in the United States, the Kimbell Museum is an architectural masterpiece, designed by Louis Kahn in 1971 as a series of vaulted roofs that seem to hover in mid-air. The gallery spaces are bathed in natural light, showing off the varied beauty of the diverse collections, which include pre-Columbian Mayan pottery, and jewelry, as well as rare ancient Asian bronzes. Paintings on display range from Renaissance and Baroque masterpieces by Rubens, Rembrandt, Tiepolo, and Tintoretto to a world-class collection of Post-Impressionist and early Modernist paintings by such celebrated masters as Cezanne, Picasso, and others.

Amon Carter Museum

3501 Camp Bowie Blvd. ***Tel** (817) 738-1933.* *10am–5pm Tue, Wed, Fri & Sat, 10am–8pm Thu, noon–5pm Sun.* *Jan 1, Jul 4, Thanksg., Dec 25.* **www**.cartermuseum.org

Along with the Kimbell Art Museum across the street, the Amon Carter Museum anchors Fort Worth's much-vaunted Cultural District, which is located 2.5 miles (4 km) west of downtown. The Amon Carter Museum concentrates entirely on American art of the Wild West, housing seminal paintings, drawings, and sculptures by Thomas Moran, Frederic Remington, Charlie Russell, and Georgia O'Keeffe among others. Said to be one of the foremost collections of cowboy art, the Amon Carter Museum also has the distinction of possessing the world's most extensive library. It has more than 100,000 photographs documenting the discovery, exploration, and settlement of the country's western frontier.

The Amon Carter Museum, which features cowboy art

Magazine cover depicting cowboy in action, 1913

COWBOYS

The romanticized image of the cowboy, as portrayed by Hollywood Westerns, was far removed from reality. During the 1880s, the demand for beef in the East and Midwest led to the Texas cattle trails, which linked the open ranges with railroads. Of these, the most famous was the Chisholm Trail to Abilene, Kansas. Cowboys traveled across the country on trail drives that were often fraught with danger. These poorly paid young men mostly rode the flanks of a herd to prevent cattle from wandering off. Those at the rear faced even more difficult conditions: Indian attacks, choking dust, long hours, and outlaw hustlers. From this tough life emerged the myth of the cowboy, celebrated in films, literature, music, and fashion. The first cowboy star was Buffalo Bill *(see p582)*. Since then, the rugged roles played by John Wayne and Clint Eastwood fashioned popular perceptions of cowboys and life in the Wild West.

Exterior of the Texas State Capitol in Austin

Austin ❸

735,000. 209 E 6th St; (512) 478-0098, (800) 926-2282. www.austintexas.org

The capital city of Texas, Austin is also home to a thriving high-tech industry as well as the state's main university. However, it is best known for hosting one of the liveliest popular music scenes in the country since the 1960s. Musicians as diverse as Janis Joplin and Willie Nelson achieved prominence in Austin. The exodus of musicians from New Orleans following Hurricane Katrina has further enhanced the city's vibrant music scene.

Nightclub sign, Austin

Showcasing the Texan love of all things large, the **Texas State Capitol**, in the heart of downtown, is the largest such structure in the US. Built in 1888, it has 500 rooms covering some 8.5 acres (3.5 ha) of floor space. With its over 300-ft (92-m) high pink granite dome dominating the downtown skyline, the building is taller than the US Capitol in Washington *(see pp198–9)*. In the rotunda beneath the dome, the floor contains the official seals of the six nations – Spain, France, Mexico, the Republic of Texas, the Confederacy, and the US – whose flags have all flown over Texas.

North of the Capitol complex, the expansive campus of the **University of Texas** spreads east from Guadalupe Street. Centering on a landmark tower, the campus holds a number of museums and libraries. The new **Blanton Museum of Art** has over 13,000 works of art, from the Renaissance to Abstract Expressionism, many of which were donated by novelist James Michener.

The **Lyndon Baines Johnson Presidential Library**, at the northeast edge of the campus, is a repository for all official documents of the Texas-born Johnson (1908–73), who served as US senator, vice-president, and US president following the assassination of John F. Kennedy *(see p478)*. Videotapes trace the Civil Rights Movement, the Vietnam War, and other key events of his tumultuous career. A 7/8th scale reproduction of his Oval Office is displayed on the top floor of this monumental building.

Texas State Capitol
11th St & Congress Ave. ***Tel*** *(512) 463-0063.* *7am–10pm Mon–Fri, 9am–8pm Sat–Sun.* *Jan 1, Easter, Thanksgiving, Dec 24–25.*

Blanton Museum of Art
Congress Ave. ***Tel*** *(512) 471-7324.* *10am–5pm Tue–Fri (to 9pm every third Thu), 1–5pm Sat–Sun.* *public hols.*

Fredericksburg ❹

8,400. *302 E Austin St, (830) 997-6523.* **www.**fredericksburg.texas.com

One of the loveliest small towns in Texas, and centerpiece of the rolling Hill Country that spreads over 25,000 sq miles (64,749 sq km) west of Austin, Fredericksburg was first settled by German immigrants in 1846. The town's strong Germanic heritage is kept alive by a number of biergartens and Bavarian-style buildings such as the reconstructed Vereinskirche (community or union church) in the Marktplatz, off Main Street.

The town is also home to the **National Museum of the Pacific War**, which traces the history of US military activities in the South Pacific during World War II. The museum includes the steamboat-shaped Nimitz Hotel. The hotel was built in the 1850s by the family of US Admiral Chester Nimitz, the commander-in-chief of US forces, who was born in Fredericksburg. It operated as a hotel until the early 1960s and opened as a museum in 1967. The museum has been greatly expanded since, but the appearance of the old hotel has been preserved. The tranquil Japanese Peace Garden, gifted by the Japanese government, is at the back.

Located midway between Fredericksburg and Austin, the boyhood home of the Vietnam War-era, 36th US president has been preserved

Tank display in the National Museum of the Pacific War, Fredericksburg

For hotels and restaurants in this region see pp496–7 and pp498–9

as the **Lyndon B. Johnson National Historical Park**. Other features of the park, which includes some sites spread out over the surrounding area, are Johnson's one-room rural school, the ranch that served as his "Texas White House," and his grave.

National Museum of the Pacific War
340 E Main St. ***Tel*** *(830) 997-4379.* *9am–5pm daily.* *Dec 25.*
www.nimitz-museum.org

Lyndon B. Johnson National Historical Park
US 290 in Johnson City. ***Tel*** *(830) 868-7128.* *8:45am–5pm daily.* *Jan 1, Thanksg., Dec 25.*
www.nps.gov/lyjo

Kerrville 5

21,000. *2108 Sidney Baker St, (830) 896-1155.*
www.kerrvilletx.com

A picturesque resort and retirement community located in the rugged hills above the Guadalupe River, Kerrville is one of the largest towns in the Texas Hill Country. This friendly town is famous for the 18-day folk music festival it hosts annually at the Quiet Valley Ranch just south of town, starting Thursday before Memorial Day. While the festival now attracts singers and fans from all over the world, it still retains the homey, intimate atmosphere of the early years.

Another highlight in town is the **Museum of Western Art**, which showcases contemporary painting and sculpture depicting the working life of cowboys. Hundreds of musicians are attracted to the **Kerrville Folk Festival** held from late May to early June, and which is outdoors and encourages camping and bonfires.

Museum of Western Art
1550 Bandera Hwy.
Tel *(830) 896-2553.* *9am–5pm Tue–Sat, 1–5pm Sun.* *some public hols.* www.museumofwesternart.org

German-style architecture in New Braunfels

New Braunfels 6

28,000. *390 S Seguin St, (830) 625-2385.*
www.nbcham.org

A popular day-trip from San Antonio *(see pp484–5)*, New Braunfels was one of many towns settled by German immigrants in the tumultuous 1840s, when Texas was an independent republic offering land grants to Anglo-Saxon settlers. The German heritage still thrives in local architecture, cuisine, language, and festivals. Many historic and restored German-style buildings can be seen across the town. However, German influence is most evident in the numerous annual festivals celebrated here, such as the sausage and beer festivals and the Polka Festival, all of which help preserve the town's strong German roots.

Built on the site that the town's aristocratic founder Prince Carl of Solms-Braunfels, Germany, chose for his castle (it was never built), the **Sophienburg-New Braunfells Archives and Museum of History** documents the town's history. Exhibits include several local artifacts and re-creations of pioneers' homes and shops, an early bakery, a doctor's office, and a pharmacy.

Sophienburg-New Braunfells Archives & Museum of History
401 W Coll St. ***Tel*** *(830) 629-1572.* *10am–4pm Tue–Sat.* *public hols.*

Gallery inside Kerrville's Museum of Western Art, displaying paintings and sculptures exemplifying the life of cowboys.

San Antonio ❼

The Arneson River Theater

Detail, Alamo Memorial

The most historic city in Texas, San Antonio is also the most popular, both for its pivotal historic role and its natural beauty. Once home to the Comanche Indians, the riverside site drew the attention of Spanish missionaries, who founded Mission San Antonio de Valero in 1718. Later converted into a military outpost and renamed the Alamo, it was the site of the most heroic episode of the Texan revolution. Predominantly Hispanic and Mexican in character, San Antonio balances a thriving economy with a careful preservation of its past. Most of the historic sites lie within a block of the pedestrian-friendly Riverwalk in the downtown core.

★ Riverwalk (Paseo del Rio)

This tree-shaded path along the San Antonio River was built as a flood-control project during the Depression-era New Deal. Now a horseshoe-shaped, open-air promenade lined with shops, Riverwalk is a peaceful oasis in the middle of the city.

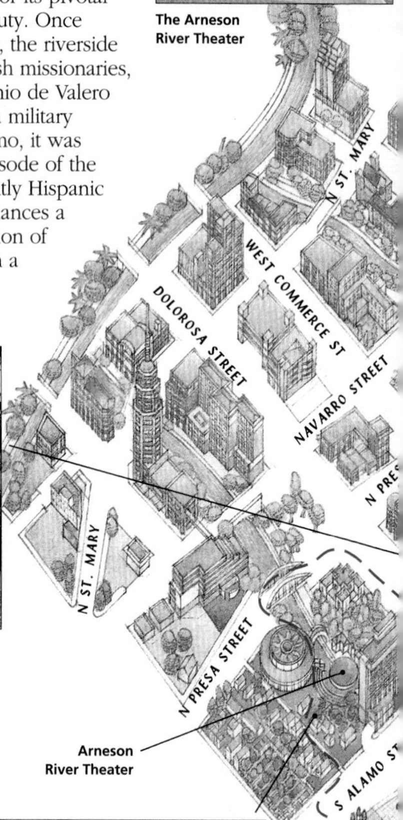

★ La Villita

It was in this early 19th-century "little village," that the Mexicans officially surrendered to the Republic of Texas. The quaint village of stone and adobe buildings now houses craft workshops and boutique shops.

Mission San Jose

MISSIONS NATIONAL HISTORICAL PARK

This 819-acre (331-ha) historic park preserves four Spanish frontier missions, which, along with the Alamo, formed the northern edge of Spain's North American colonies in the 18th century. Still in use as Catholic parish churches, the former missions such as Missions San Jose, San Juan, Espada, and Concepcion spread south from downtown San Antonio along the 9-mile (14-km) "Mission Trail." The finest of the group, Mission San Jose, is known for the intricately carved stonework of the Rose Window adjacent to the sacristy.

For hotels and restaurants in this region see p497 and p499

KEY

- - - Suggested route

0 meters 200

0 yards 200

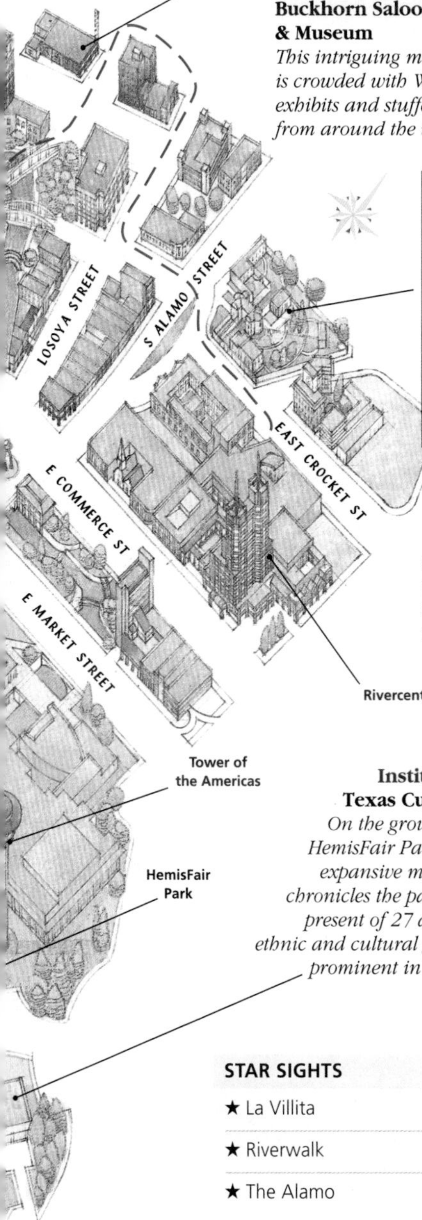

Buckhorn Saloon & Museum

This intriguing museum is crowded with Wild West exhibits and stuffed animals from around the world.

★ The Alamo

"Remember the Alamo" was the battle cry that inspired Texans during their war for independence against Mexico (1835–36). The secularized mission was the site of a long, bloody siege that took the lives of 189 Americans, shortly after which the Texas Republic was born.

Institute of Texas Cultures

On the grounds of HemisFair Park, this expansive museum chronicles the past and present of 27 distinct ethnic and cultural groups prominent in Texas.

STAR SIGHTS

- ★ La Villita
- ★ Riverwalk
- ★ The Alamo

VISITORS' CHECKLIST

1,592,000. *224 Hoefgren Ave, (210) 223-3226.* *Greyhound Lines, 500 N St. Mary's St.* *203 S St. Mary's St, (210) 207-6700.* *Riverwalk Mud Festival (Jan), Fiesta San Antonio (late Apr).* **www**.sanantoniocvb.com

The Alamo *300 Alamo Plaza, (210) 225-1391.* *9am–5:30pm Mon–Sat, 10am–5:30pm Sun.* *Dec 24, 25.* *donation.* **www**.thealamo.org

Houston 8

1,953,000. 902 Washington Ave. Greyhound Lines, 2121 S Main St. 901 Bagby St, (713) 437-5200. Houston Livestock Show (late Feb–early Mar); Art Car Parade (May); Thanksgiving Day Parade (Nov). **www**.visithoustontexas.com

A city of constant change and great diversity, the story of Houston is a typical Texas success story. Founded in 1836 in what was then a swamp, the city was named in honor of Texas hero General Sam Houston *(see p474)* and served as capital of the Texas Republic until 1839. A center for shipping cotton, Houston's fortunes faded after the Civil War, but it developed into a major port following the construction of a shipping channel to the Gulf of Mexico. The discovery of oil turned the city into a major petrochemical producer, and it has grown into the biggest city in Texas and the fourth-largest in the US. It has some of the world's finest art museums.

A huge, sprawling city that has grown to cover over 600 sq miles (1554 sq km), Houston is a thoroughly confusing place, lacking in an overall plan. The absence of any real visual order, the frequent changes in street names and directions, and the lack of public transportation and often heavy road traffic, can make matters worse.

In short, to see Houston visitors should be prepared to drive, and to get lost more than once. The main attractions for visitors lie southwest of downtown, on and around the **Rice University** campus.

Expansive gardens surrounding Ima Hogg's mansion, Bayou Bend

Menil Collection

1515 Sul Ross. ***Tel*** *(713) 525-9400.* *11am–7pm Wed–Sun.* *Jan 1, Easter, Jul 4, Thanksgiving, Dec 25.* **www**.menil.org

One of the world's better assemblies of painting and sculpture, this collection was endowed by the family of Houston philanthropist Dominque de Menil, who died in 1997. It is housed in a striking modern building designed by Italian architect Renzo Piano, one of the designers of the Pompidou Center in Paris. The most extensive display here is of Surrealist paintings, notably by Rene Magritte and Max Ernst. The museum also has a world-class collection of Cubist painting by Picasso and Braque in particular, as well as a full survey of 20th-century American paintings by Jackson Pollock, Jasper Johns, Robert Rauschenberg, and Cy Twombly. Separate galleries display ancient and medieval art of the Mediterranean. Also on view is a show of works by Native peoples of Africa, the South Pacific, and the Pacific Northwest region of North America.

A short walk east from the main museum stands the ecumenical **Rothko Chapel**, a spare concrete space designed around a series of large, dark-colored abstract paintings by the artist Mark Rothko. Commissioned by the de Menil family and completed by architect Philip Johnson in 1971, the chapel is open from 10am to 6pm daily. Two blocks to its south lies the Menil-sponsored **Byzantine Fresco Chapel Museum**, a detailed replica of a 13th-century Eastern Orthodox chapel, which displays the only Byzantine frescos on view in the Western Hemisphere.

Museum of Fine Arts

1001 Bissonnet St. ***Tel*** *(713) 639-7300.* *10am–5pm Tue & Wed, 10am–9pm Thu, 10am–7pm Fri & Sat, 12:15pm–7pm Sun.* *Jan 1, Thnksg., Dec 25.* **www**.mfah.org

The oldest art museum in Texas, and one of the largest in the US, the collections here range from Greek and Roman antiquities to Wild West sculptures by Frederic Remington. The striking new Beck Building has European art of the late 19th and early 20th century, with a survey of works by Manet, Pisarro, Renoir, and other masters.

Bayou Bend

1 Wescott St. ***Tel*** *(713) 639-7750.* *10–11:30am, 1–2:45pm Tue–Fri, 10–11:15am Sat.* *Jan 1, Thanksgiving, Dec 25.*

The largest public gardens in Houston surround the pink stucco mansion of oil heiress Ima Hogg (1882–1975), who survived her somewhat unfortunate name to become one of Houston's greatest benefactors. The wealthy philanthrope was

A view of downtown Houston and Memorial Park

Neon signs light up the lively Montrose District

not only famous as a patron of the arts but was also passionately concerned with the well-being of the city. Now run by the Museum of Fine Arts, her home displays a collection of decorative arts, highlighted by a sugar bowl crafted by Colonial hero Paul Revere *(see p142)*, and 5,000 pieces of furniture, ceramics, and textiles. Also on display are portraits by early American artists John Singleton Copley and Charles Willson Peale.

Montrose District

"Montrose" is a catch name for the lively collection of countercultural-flavored galleries, shops, nightclubs, cafés, and restaurants that can be found along Montrose Street and its intersection with Westheimer Road. Apart from the shopping malls and downtown business district, Montrose District is one of the few walkable neighborhoods in Houston and is especially popular on weekend nights.

Space Center Houston

1601 Nasa Rd 1. ***Tel*** *(281) 244-2100.* *times vary. Call to check.* *Dec 25.*
www.spacecenter.org

Adjacent to the Johnson Space Center, the mission control for all manned US explorations of space since 1965, this visitor-friendly attraction traces the full story of the Space Race. Hands-on exhibits are particularly appealing to young people and let visitors try on space helmets, touch moon rocks, or peer into actual spaceships such as those from the Mercury, Gemini, and Apollo programs. Computer simulations let visitors fly the space shuttle or land on the moon. There are also various changing exhibits. The major attraction of the Space Center is the tour of the still-in-use mission control facilities, where the historic missions to the moon and back were guided.

San Jacinto Battleground

Hwy 134, 21 miles (34 km) SE of downtown. ***Tel*** *(281) 479-2431.*
9am–6pm daily.

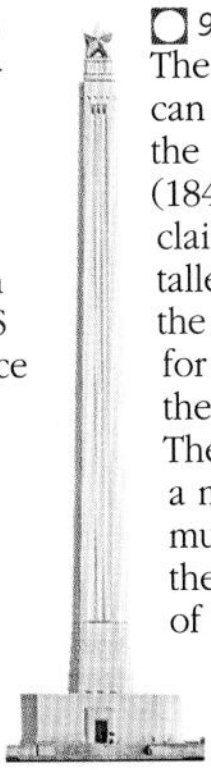
San Jacinto tower

The vast plains of Texas can be seen for miles from the foot of this 605-ft (184-m) tall monument, claimed to be one of the tallest in the world. It marks the site of the final battle for the independence of the Texas Republic in 1836. The slim shaft is topped by a massive "Lone Star." A museum at the base traces the history and culture of the state, while an adjacent theater hosts a popular 42-projector, multi-image slide show.

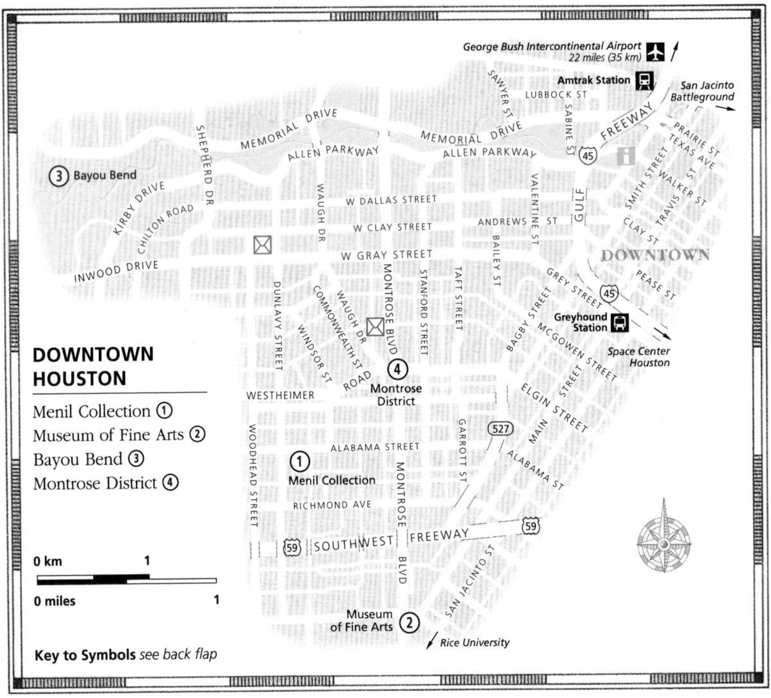

Dense cypress swamp in the Big Thicket National Preserve

Big Thicket National Preserve ❾

Junction of US 69 & Hwy 420, 7 miles (11 km) N of Kountze. **Tel** *(409) 951-6725.* *9am–5pm daily.* *Jan 1, Thanksgiving, Dec 25.* **www**.nps.gov/bith

Maintaining a unique mixture of mountains, plains, swamps, and forests, the Big Thicket National Preserve protects 15 distinct biologically diverse areas (nine land units and six water corridors) spread over 97,000 acres (39,255 ha) along the Texas/Louisiana border.

Although much of the preserve is relatively inaccessible, the area once served as a hideout for runaway slaves and outlaws. Today, it is best known for housing a wide range of plants and animals. A series of short hiking trails offer close-up views of dense groves of resident oaks, cactus, carnivorous "pitcher plants," and millions of mosquitoes.

Galveston ❿

60,000. *2328 Broadway, (409) 763-4311.*

Though comparatively smaller than other Texas cities, Galveston rivals the rest of the state for historical significance and character. Originally a notorious hideout for slave-trading Gulf Coast pirate Jean Lafitte *(see p350)*, Galveston was burned to the ground by US forces in 1821. But by the 1890s the port had grown to be the largest and wealthiest city in Texas. The economy soon declined following a devastating hurricane in 1900, which killed as many as 6,000 people. The subsequent rise of Houston also contributed to Galveston's fading fortunes.

In recent years, many of the city's grand Victorian mansions and 19th-century storefronts have been restored to their original glory. Many exuberantly designed buildings from that period survive in the Strand National Historic Landmark District, near the waterfront. **Ashton Villa** is one such building, but it is currently closed for repairs to damage caused by Hurricane Ike in 2008.

Often hailed as one of the state's best resorts on the Gulf of Mexico, the charming island city features more than 30 miles (48 km) of pristine, sandy beaches. Visitors can also indulge in the family-friendly fun of **Moody Gardens**, with its waterpark pools, a 10-story Rainforest Pyramid offering an incredible tropical environment, and a series of massive aquariums showcasing life from the world's oceans.

Ashton Villa
2328 Broadway.
Tel *(409) 762- 3933.* *Closed for renovations to damage caused by Hurricane Ike.*

Moody Gardens
1 Hope Blvd. **Tel** *(409) 744-4673.*
Apr–Oct: 10am–8pm daily; Nov– Mar: 10am–6pm daily.
Dec 25.

Aransas National Wildlife Refuge ⓫

Hwy 239. 65 miles (105 km) NE of Corpus Christi. **Tel** *(361) 286-3559.* *dawn–dusk.* *Thanksgiving, Dec 25.*

While sun worshipers flock to the Gulf Coast beaches throughout winter, birds and bird-watchers congregate slightly inland at the 70,000-acre (28,328-ha) Aransas National Wildlife Refuge. Established in 1937 to protect the vanishing wildlife of coastal Texas, Aransas is today home to alligators, armadillo, boars, javelinas, coyotes, white-tailed deer, and many other species of wildlife. The most famous visitors here are the endangered whooping cranes, the

Bird-watching in Aransas

Pyramid-shaped greenhouse in Moody Gardens, Galveston

Padre Island National Seashore – a popular vacation destination

tallest birds native to North America. Standing 5 ft (1.5 m) tall, with white bodies, black-tipped wings, and red heads, the cranes migrate here from Canada between November and March, feeding in the saltwater marshes.

Ringed by tidal marshes and broken by long, narrow ponds, Aransas is an ever-changing land that is still being shaped by the turquoise-blue waters of San Antonio Bay and the storms of the Gulf of Mexico. Grasslands, live oaks, and red bay thickets that cover deep, sandy soils provide spectacular background scenery.

Corpus Christi ⓬

380,000. 1201 N Shoreline, (361) 881-1888.

The deepest commercial port in Texas and an extensive US military presence have made Corpus Christi one of the fastest-growing cities in the state. Its military importance is marked by the famous 910-ft (277-m) long aircraft carrier, the USS *Lexington*, moored along the 2-mile (3-km) downtown waterfront. To its south, the **Texas State Aquarium** explores the sea life of the Gulf of Mexico with whales, rays, and sharks, and re-creations of reefs similar to those that have grown around the Gulf's many offshore oil rigs. Texas river otters and the Kemp's Ridley sea turtle are also found here.

"Corpus," as residents call the city, looks out across the harbor to **Mustang Island State Park**, where over 5 miles (8 km) of sandy beach stretch along the Gulf of Mexico. At the park's north end, modern condominium resorts detract from the natural scene, overshadowing the historic community of Port Aransas at the island's northern tip.

Texas State Aquarium
2710 N Shoreline Blvd.
Tel *(361) 881-1200. 9am–5pm daily (to 6pm Memorial Day–Labor Day). Thanksg., Dec 25.*
www.texasstateaquarium.org

Padre Island National Seashore ⓭

Malaquite Visitor Center, (361) 949-8068. **www**.nps.gov/pais

Bordered by a pair of tourist resorts at its north and south ends, Padre Island is a slender sandbar that stretches for more than 110 miles (177 km) between Corpus Christi and the Mexican border. The central 65 miles (105 km) have been preserved as the Padre Island National Seashore, which, with few roads and no commercial development, is among the longest wild stretches of coastline in the country. The park is open throughout the year for camping, beach-combing, surfing, swimming, hiking, fishing, and various other activities. Coyotes and other native wild animals still roam the heart of the island.

This is one of the nation's most popular vacation spots. It receives an average of 800,000 visitors per year, especially during the Spring Break, when university students from colder climes in the northern Midwest flock here to unwind and party. South Padre Island marks the southern end of the Gulf Coast of Texas.

A view of the Corpus Christi waterfront

Republic of the Rio Grande Museum, San Augustin Plaza, Laredo

Laredo ⓮

200,000. 501 San Augustin St, (956) 795-2200.

Located on the north bank of the legendary Rio Grande (or Rio Bravo, as it is known in Mexico), Laredo is often referred to as the "Gateway to Mexico." It operates two international bridges to Mexico and is hence one of the principal US ports of entry into Mexico.

Located north of the Rio Grande, the original center of Laredo has been well preserved around the historic San Augustin Plaza. Here, the intriguing **Republic of the Rio Grande Museum** is housed in a building that once served as the Capitol of the short-lived independent republic that in 1840 included southern Texas and the three northernmost states of Mexico. The museum traces Laredo's role under six different national flags.

Republic of the Rio Grande Museum
1005 Zaragoza St. *Tel (956) 727-3480.* *9am–4pm Tue–Sat, 1–4pm Sun.* *public hols.*

Rio Grande Valley ⓯

FM 1015 Expressway 83, Welasco, (956) 968-3141.

Stretching along the Rio Grande for 200 miles (322 km) between Laredo and the Gulf of Mexico, the Rio Grande Valley is a bustling corridor of agricultural, commercial, and retirement communities all jumbled together in a complicated sprawl. Linked by east-west US 83, which becomes increasingly busy as it gets closer to the Gulf, the valley feels very different from the rest of Texas, thanks in part to the lush, temperate climate softened by moisture-laden breezes. Numerous roadside stands sell bags of grapefruits and bunches of red chili peppers, while convoys of trucks lumber past between warehouses and factories on both sides of the river.

The region's story from border banditry to bilateral trade is traced with permanent and changing exhibits at the **Rio Grande Valley Museum**, while numerous parks try to protect the region's varied natural heritage. The 525-acre (212-ha) **Sabal Palm Audubon Sanctuary** preserves the last stand of the stumpy native Sabal palm trees, which once lined the river for miles upstream.

Rio Grande Valley Museum
24–25 Boxwood & Raintree Sts, Harlingen. *Tel (956) 216-4906.* *10am–4pm Wed–Sat, 1–4pm Sun.* *by appointment.*

Sabal Palm Audubon Sanctuary
International Blvd, 6 miles (10 km) SE of Brownsville. *Tel (956) 541-8034.* *7am–5pm daily.* *Jan 1, Thanksgiving, Dec 25.*

Big Bend National Park ⓰

Panther Junction, (432) 477-2251. **www**.nps.gov/bibe

One of the wildest and most isolated corners of the US, this diverse park covers 801,000 acres (324,154 ha) of southwest Texas. The name "Big Bend" comes from the 90-degree turn made by the Rio Grande as it carves its way toward the Gulf of Mexico through the volcanic rock of the San Vicente and Sierra del Carmen Mountains. Ranging from 1,500-ft (457-m) deep river canyons along the Rio Grande to the pine-forested Chisos Mountains, Big Bend offers a complete experience of the rivers, mountains, canyons, and deserts that define the American Southwest. These contrasts in topography have created a unique

Fascinating rock formations at Big Bend National Park

For hotels and restaurants in this region see pp496–7 and pp498–9

diversity of plant and animal habitats. Coyotes, roadrunners, and javelinas roam among spring wildflowers and cacti.

Fort Davis ⓱

600. *Town Square, (432) 426-3015.* **www**.ftdavis.com

Situated in the scenic Davis Mountains at a height of 4,900 ft (1,494 m), Fort Davis is a popular destination for visitors seeking relief from a typical Texas summer. A key site during the Indian Wars of the 19th century, it was originally established in 1854 as a US Army fort along the main road between El Paso and San Antonio *(see pp484–5)*. Today, it has been preserved as the **Fort Davis National Historic Site**. In summer, costumed interpreters help visitors on self-guided tours through some of the site's restored structures.

Guide dressed as an 1880s cavalry soldier in Fort Davis

The area's high altitude and isolation from large cities has also made it a fine location for astronomical research. Located atop the 6,791-ft (2,070-m) Mount Locke, 17 miles (27 km) northwest of town, the **McDonald Observatory** gives visitors the opportunity to see stars and planets. The Hobby-Eberle spectroscope here has a 430-inch (1,092-cm) mirror, the world's largest.

Fort Davis National Historic Site
Hwy 17. ***Tel*** *(432) 426-3224.* *8am–5pm daily.* *major public hols.*

McDonald Observatory
Hwy 118. ***Tel*** *(432) 426-3640.* *10am–5:30pm daily (call for evening schedule).* *Jan 1, Thanksgiving, Dec 25.*
www.mcdonaldobservatory.org

El Paso ⓲

722,000. *1 Civic Center Plaza, (915) 534-0600.* **www**.visitelpaso.com

Catholic Ysleta Mission in El Paso

Located on the northern bank of the Rio Grande, at one of the river's safest natural crossing places, El Paso has long been part of the largest and liveliest international community along the US/Mexico border. In 1598, Spanish explorer Juan de Onate crossed the river from Mexico and named the place "El Paso del Rio del Norte." It took another 80 years before the city was established with a trio of Catholic missions at Ysleta, Socorro, and San Elizario. Still in operation, the missions are among the oldest communities in Texas. The story of the varying course of the Rio Grande (and so the international border) until a concrete channel was built in 1963, is detailed in a museum at the **Chamizal National Memorial**, a 55-acre (22-ha) park on the US side. Outside, a 1.8 mile (2.9 km) walking trail circles the park.

Chamizal National Memorial
800 S San Marcial St. ***Tel*** *(915) 532-7273.* **Exhibits** *10am–5pm Tue–Sat.* **Grounds** *5am–10pm daily.* *Jan 1, Thanksgiving, Dec 25.* **www**.nps.gov/cham

VISITING MEXICO

A short, easy walk over the "International Bridge" from San Augustin Plaza, Laredo, leads visitors across the border in the typical Mexican border town of Nuevo Laredo. This trip gives visitors a deeper appreciation of the interdependence of these two very different yet increasingly similar countries. There is so much shared culture that, in the border areas at least, the differences between the US and Mexico are less striking than the similarities. Thanks mainly to the "Mexicanization" of the American side, where the population is more than 80 percent Latino, the food, music, and language is much the same. Nuevo Laredo, Juarez, and other Mexican cities are far larger and busier than their American counterparts, with a huge array of shops, restaurants, and bars offering a taste of Mexico. Elsewhere, along the more than 1,000-mile (1,609-km) border, dozens of small towns and villages are less frenetic, letting visitors sample a taco while soaking up some south-of-the-border ambience. For US citizens, a trip across the border requires a passport. For non-citizens, however, it is vital to confirm their legal status and ensure that they can return to the US. For all travelers, it is far easier and usually quicker to cross the border on foot.

"International Bridge" across the river to Nuevo Laredo, Mexico

Towering El Capitan in Guadalupe Mountains

Guadalupe Mountains National Park ⑲

US 62/180, (915) 828-3251.
www.nps.gov/gumo

An almost road-free region on the Texas/New Mexico border, this national park covers 85,000 acres (34,398 ha) of rugged mountains that make up portions of the world's most extensive Permian limestone fossil reef, El Capitan, and the 8,749-ft (2,667-m) Guadalupe Peak, the highest point in Texas. Formed as part of the same prehistoric limestone that makes up the nearby (and more popular) Carlsbad Caverns National Park *(see p552)*, the Guadalupe Mountains reward visitors with lofty peaks, spectacular views, unusual flora and fauna, and a colorful record of the past.

A short trail from the visitor center leads to the remains of a stone wall and foundations of a former frontier stage-coach station. This was built as part of the **Butterfield Trail**, which first established a link between St. Louis and California in 1858.

A few miles northeast of the visitor center, a forest of hardwood trees lines the trail of **McKittrick Canyon**. Here lies the site's most famous attraction, the spectacular red-and-orange foliage in October and November. The hiking trails between the canyon walls that shelter a perennial stream are also very popular.

Lubbock ⑳

258,000.
1301 Broadway, (806) 747-5232.

Home to 30,000 sports-crazy students at Texas Tech University, Lubbock is a cattle-ranching and cotton-growing city that is perhaps best known for its musical progeny. Local musicians including Roy Orbison, Joe Ely, Waylon Jennings, and Tanya Tucker are all honored in Lubbock's guitar-shaped **Buddy Holly Center**, a musical Hall of Fame named for the city's favorite son, Charles Hardin Holley. A statue of Buddy Holly, one of rock 'n' roll's most enduring icons, stands along 8th Street and Avenue Q.

Other aspects of Lubbock history are covered in the Texas Tech University's **Ranching Heritage Center**, an outdoor assembly of historic structures collected from all over Texas. On display are more than 30 original ranch buildings, from cowboy huts to stately overseers' mansions.

Buddy Holly Center
1801 Ave G. ***Tel*** *(806) 775-3560.*
10am–5pm Tue–Sat, 1–5pm Sun. *Jan 1, Easter, Jul 4, Thanksgiving, Dec 25.*
www.buddyhollycenter.org

Ranching Heritage Center
3121 4th St. ***Tel*** *(806) 742-0498.*
10am–5pm Mon–Sat, 1–5pm Sun. *Jan 1, Thanksg., Dec 24–25.*

Canyon ㉑

13,000. *1518 5th Ave, (806) 655-7815.*

Taking its name from the beautifully sculpted geology of nearby Palo Duro Canyon, this medium-sized Texas town is also home to the largest and best-known historical museum in the state. **The Panhandle-Plains Historical Museum**, housed in a stately 1930s complex on the campus of West Texas A&M University, holds over three million exhibits tracing the history of north-central Texas. Flint arrowheads from the Alibates quarry, north of Amarillo, highlight the culture of the region's prehistoric people, while geology and paleontology come together in exhibits exploring pre-historic dinosaurs and their relation to the region's prime industry, petroleum. The story of another great Texas tradition, cattle ranching, is explored through the life of Wild West rancher Charles Goodnight, who owned a

BUDDY HOLLY (1936–59)

Buddy Holly's statue, Lubbock

Singer, instrumentalist, and songwriter, Buddy Holly was one of the first major rock 'n' roll music performers. Deeply influenced by local blues and country music, he began to sing in country groups while still in high school. By the mid-1950s, Holly was playing in small clubs throughout the Southwest. Drawn increasingly to rock music as exemplified by Elvis Presley, he recorded both alone and as lead performer with the Crickets. The group's energetic style, combining elements of country music and a strong background rhythm, together with Holly's unique hiccoughing vocals, quickly made them a success. Songs such as "Maybe Baby" and Holly's solo hit "Peggy Sue" became runaway hits. Holly's phenomenal career came to an abrupt end in 1959 when he died in a plane crash in Iowa.

View of Palo Duro Canyon, the "Grand Canyon of Texas"

500,000-acre (202,344-ha) ranch, and later led the fight to save native bison from extinction. Goodnight's home is now preserved in the enjoyable "Pioneer Town," located behind the museum.

About 12 miles (19 km) east of town, **Palo Duro Canyon State Park** protects the 60-mile (97-km) long, 1,100-ft (335-m) deep red and yellow sandstone gorge also known as the "Grand Canyon of Texas." A number of scenic drives and hiking routes run between the rim and the canyon floor, offering views of such geological oddities as the 300-ft (91-m) tall stone "Lighthouse." Palo Duro is also home to a wide variety of flora and fauna, including spring wildflowers, mule deer, and wild turkeys. In summer, one of the canyon's 600-ft (183-m) cliffs forms the backdrop for the pageantry of *Texas*, a popular play on the history of the state.

A sculpturally implanted Cadillac car at Cadillac Ranch, Amarillo

Panhandle-Plains Historical Museum
2503 4th Ave. ***Tel*** *(806) 651-2244.* *Jun–Aug: 9am–6pm Mon–Sat, 1–6pm Sun; Sep–May: 9am–5pm Mon–Sat, 1–6pm Sun.* *Jan 1, Thanksgiving, Dec 24–25.*

Palo Duro Canyon State Park
Hwy 217. ***Tel*** *(806) 488-2227.* *8am–6pm daily (later closing times Mar–Nov).*

Amarillo 22

185,000. *4th & Buchanan Sts, (806) 374-1497.*
www.visitamarillotx.com

The commercial heart of the sprawling Texas Panhandle region, and a key center for agriculture as well as oil, natural gas, and nuclear power industries, Amarillo was first settled in 1887 along the Santa Fe Railroad. The city later thrived thanks to its location along the legendary Route 66 *(see p40)*. The route is now immortalized by **Cadillac Ranch**, a Pop Art work created from 10 classic Cadillac cars planted nose-down in a pasture west of downtown. Another more typically Texas experience is the **Amarillo Livestock Auction**, where modern-day cowboys buy and sell their cattle.

Cadillac Ranch
S side of I-40 between Hope Rd & Arnot Rd exits. ***Tel*** *24 hours.*

Abilene 23

116,000. *1101 N 1st St, (325) 676-2556.*

Although named for the notorious Wild West town in Kansas, Abilene evolved from a frontier settlement to a solid, stable community. Also known as the "Buckle of the Bible Belt," thanks to its predominantly Christian colleges where 8,000 students study, Abilene's past is kept alive at **Buffalo Gap Historical Village**, 14 miles (23 km) southwest of downtown. Founded in 1878, Buffalo Gap maintains over a dozen old buildings such as a courthouse, a train station, and a schoolhouse. Exhibits on display include Paleo-Indian artifacts and a frontier weapons collection.

Buffalo Gap Historical Village
Hwy 89. ***Tel*** *(325) 572-3365.* *10am–5pm Mon–Sat, noon–5pm Sun.* *Thnksg., Dec 25.*
www.buffalogap.com

Cowboy in Buffalo Gap Historical Village, Abilene

Practical Information

In a state as vast as Texas, it helps greatly that information for travelers is readily accessible. Images of oil and cattle ranches immediately spring to mind, and while this is true for much of the state, Texas has much variety to offer. Stretching for nearly 800 miles (1,287 km) from east to west, the state offers everything from bayous and forests to prairies, bare windswept plains, and beautiful beaches. The dynamic, bustling big cities of Dallas and Houston are a contrast to the laid-back charm of the capital city of Austin with its lush riverside parks, and historic San Antonio with its predominantly Hispanic cultural ambience.

TOURIST INFORMATION

Along most major highways in Texas, there are "Welcome Centers," operated by the **Travel Division** of the Texas Department of Transportation. Open between 8am and 5pm daily, these centers offer a full range of tourist information, including details of weather and road conditions, attractions and accommodations. Texas also publishes a magazine called *Texas Monthly* with travel stories and photographic essays on the wonders of the "Lone Star" state.

Most airports have information desks, and all major towns and cities have tourist-oriented Visitors' Bureaus or Chambers of Commerce.

NATURAL HAZARDS

Texas has its fair share of natural hazards. Winter blizzards block roads and strand drivers under heavy snows, while in spring, torrential rains that occur along with tornadoes and severe thunderstorms flood towns and cities located along streams and rivers. The most dangerous hazards are hurricanes, which can strike the Gulf Coast from June till December. Hurricane winds reach speeds of 75 to 150 mph (121 to 241 km/hr) or more, but even more dangerous than the high winds is the storm surge, a dome of ocean water that can cause severe flooding along coastal rivers and bays. Fortunately, sophisticated warning systems are in place to give visitors plenty of time to get out of harm's way. Radio and TV stations broadcast storm watches and evacuation warnings.

GETTING AROUND

Public transportation is almost negligible in this state, although a few **Greyhound** routes cover some major cities. A single **Amtrak** route also shuttles along the southern part of the state. There is an excellent network of airports across the state, and many visitors fly between the major cities, and then rent a car to get around the surrounding region.

Driving is essential in Texas and the comparatively low price of gas makes it a convenient option. Seat belts are required for drivers and front seat passengers, as well as back seat passengers under 15 years of age. Child seats are mandatory for all occupants aged 2 and under. Motorcyclists under 21 years of age must wear helmets, while riders over 21 years. must have proof of health insurance before they ride without a helmet. Radar detectors are permitted.

Speed limits for vehicles vary in Texas, with a statewide maximum of 70 mph (113 km/hour) allowed on Interstate Highways during daylight hours.

ANNUAL EVENTS & FESTIVALS

One of the best ways for visitors to get a feel for Texas is to take part in one of the state's huge range of annual events and festivals. Soon after the New Year sets in, the annual cleaning of the Riverwalk Canal in San Antonio launches the Mud Week, a 10-day festival of arts and entertainment. In March, Austin hosts the youthful South by Southwest festival of popular music.

But the festival season really gets going in summer, starting at the end of May with the nationally acclaimed **Kerrville Folk Festival**. Many other local festivals, fairs and events take place in towns all over the state, winding up with the massive **Texas State Fair**. This is one of the largest state fairs in the country, and is held in October in Dallas' extensive Fair Park. In addition to the national holidays, Texas also celebrates Confederate Heroes Day (Jan 19), Emancipation Day (June 19), and Lyndon Johnson's Birthday (Aug 27).

THE CLIMATE OF TEXAS

Despite its generally mild climate, weather across the vast state tends to vary greatly. Spring is ideal for travel, when the days are cool and wildflowers are in full bloom. Summer can be very hot and humid, with severe rains often causing floods along rivers and in low-lying areas. October is also good for travel, as temperatures are mild and the skies clear. In winter, snow storms blow down from the Great Plains, and hurricanes hit the Gulf Coast.

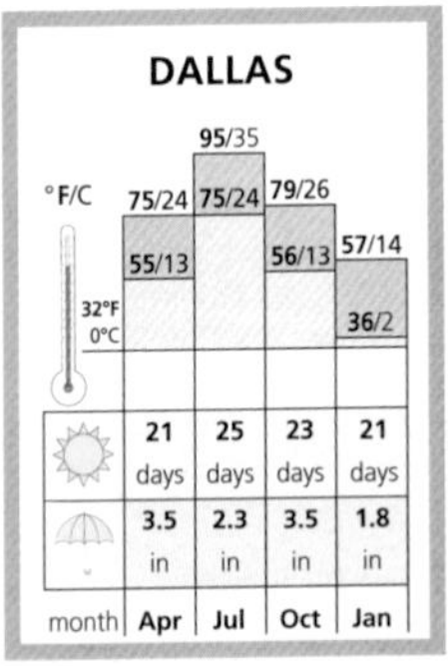

SPORTS

Springtime in Texas is synonymous with baseball, which is played at a variety of levels all over the state. Major league baseball is represented here by the Houston Astros and the Texas Rangers, both of whom play in state-of-the-art stadiums, though the Astros no longer play in the Astrodome – once the world's largest indoor space. Tickets for major league baseball games, however, can be expensive and hard to come by. In any case, a better sense of the game and its importance to Texas can be experienced by attending a Texas League baseball game, which may not be as slick, but is often more fun. Played in smaller arenas in front of a close-knit crowd of enthusiastic fans, the main Texas League teams include the El Paso Diablos and the San Antonio Missions.

As summer fades into fall, the American football season begins. A number of intense intrastate rivalries, such as that between the University of Texas and Texas A&M University, enliven the college football season. At the professional National Football League (NFL) level, the pride of Texas is the Dallas Cowboys, self-proclaimed "America's Team." The New Year kicks off in Dallas with the Cotton Bowl, a championship football game played between two of the top universities in the country.

Winter is also basketball season, and games are played at all levels throughout the state. At the professional National Basketball Association level, Texas has the Houston Rockets, the Dallas Mavericks, and the San Antonio Spurs.

OUTDOOR ACTIVITIES

Visitors can participate in a vast range of outdoor activities all over Texas. From golf to fishing, river rafting to cycling, Texas has something for everyone at all levels and abilities. There are golf courses all over the state, most of them open to the public. Fishing, in a variety of freshwater lakes and in the Gulf of Mexico, is regulated by the **Texas Parks Department**. River rafting along the Rio Grande through **Big Bend National Park** draws people from all over the world, so advance reservations are essential. Biking is also a popular activity, and bicycles can easily be rented from shops in most Texas towns.

ENTERTAINMENT

Located in Fort Worth's lively Stockyard District, **Billy Bob's**, the world's largest honky-tonk, is just one of hundreds of nightclubs and performance venues all over this music-loving state. More upscale and refined music can also be enjoyed, thanks to the many orchestras in Texas. Fort Worth has one of the finest music venues, the **Bass Performance Hall**, home to the city's symphony, opera, and ballet.

SHOPPING

Visitors wanting to bring home a souvenir of Texas should try cowboy boots. Western wear shops all over the state may have the perfect pair, but some visitors may wish to take advantage of the discounts offered close by at El Paso-based **Tony Lama Boots**, one of the country's largest and most famous boot makers. For more upscale needs, nothing beats **Neiman-Marcus**, one of the nation's most exclusive department stores, which started in Dallas and is still in business downtown. The sales tax in Texas is 6.25 percent, and cities and counties may impose an additional tax of 2 percent.

DIRECTORY

TOURIST INFORMATION

Travel Division
Dept. of Transportation,
PO Box 149248,
Austin, TX 78714.
Tel *(512) 486-5800.*
Road Conditions Info:
Tel *(800) 452-9292.*

NATURAL HAZARDS

National Hurricane Center
Tel *(305) 229-4470.*

GETTING AROUND

Amtrak
Tel *(800) 872-7245.*

Greyhound
Tel *(800) 231-2222.*

ANNUAL EVENTS & FESTIVALS

Kerrville Folk Festival
www.kerrville-music.com

Texas State Fair
www.bigtex.com

SPORTS

Dallas Cowboys
Tel *(972) 556-9900.*

Dallas Mavericks
Tel *(214) 747-6287.*

El Paso Diablos
Tel *(915) 755-2000.*

Houston Astros
Tel *(877) 927-8767.*

Houston Rockets
Tel *(713) 627-3865.*

San Antonio Missions
Tel *(210) 675-7275.*

San Antonio Spurs
Tel *(210) 554-7787.*

Texas Rangers
Tel *(817) 273-5100.*

OUTDOOR ACTIVITIES

Big Bend National Park
Tel *(432) 477-2251.*

Texas Parks Dept.
Tel *(512) 389-4800.*

ENTERTAINMENT

Bass Performance Hall
525 Commerce St,
Fort Worth.
Tel *(817) 212-4200.*

Billy Bob's
Texas Rodeo Plaza,
Fort Worth.
Tel *(817) 624-7117.*

SHOPPING

Neiman-Marcus
1618 Main St, Dallas.
Tel *(214) 741-6911.*
www.neimanmarcus.com

Tony Lama Boots
7156 E Gateway, El Paso.
Tel *(915) 772-4327.*

Choosing a Hotel

Travelers to Texas can choose from a wide variety of places to stay, from anonymous highway motels to atmospheric lodgings in historic buildings. Larger cities such as San Antonio and Dallas offer the best range of options. The Gulf Coast has many beach resorts, and there are also unique rural accommodations.

PRICE CATEGORIES
For a standard double room per night, including service charges and any additional taxes.

$ Under $100
$$ $100–$150
$$$ $150–$200
$$$$ $200–$300
$$$$$ Over $300

TEXAS

AMARILLO Big Texan Motel — $

7701 E I-40, 79118 ***Tel*** *(806) 372-5000, (800) 657-7177* ***Fax*** *(806) 371-0099* ***Rooms*** *54*

Part of the famous Big Texan Steak Ranch, this roadside motel is designed to resemble the main street of an Old West town. Each room in this two-story motel is full of character and individually decorated with Texan and Old West kitsch. The swimming pool is the shape of the state of Texas. Free limo service to the airport. **www.bigtexan.com**

AUSTIN Holiday Inn Austin Town Lake — $$$

20 N I-35 (exit 233), Riverside Dr, 78701 ***Tel*** *(512) 472-8211, (800) 593-5676* ***Fax*** *(512) 472-4636* ***Rooms*** *320*

Overlooking Town Lake, this high-rise hotel is conveniently located in the heart of Austin, adjacent to the Town Lake hike and bike trail, and close to the State Capitol, 6th Street, and the Warehouse District. Many guestrooms have sofa sleepers, children stay free, and children under 12 also eat free at the hotel restaurant.

AUSTIN Driskill Hotel — $$$$

604 Brazos St, 78701 ***Tel*** *(512) 474-5911, (800) 252-9367* ***Fax*** *(512) 474-2214* ***Rooms*** *188*

The magnificent lobby of this historic hotel, with its marble floors, three-story columns, and stained glass dome ceiling exudes luxury and opulence. Built in 1886 and extensively renovated and upgraded, the Driskill offers finely appointed, comfortable guestrooms with luxury bedding, terry robes, and high-speed Internet. **www.driskillhotel.com**

BIG BEND NATIONAL PARK Chisos Mountains Lodge — $$

Big Bend National Park, Basin Rural Station, 79834 ***Tel*** *(432) 477-2292* ***Rooms*** *72*

This large complex of accommodations comprised of a modern motel, rustic lodge, and period stone cottages is one of the few lodging options in the breathtakingly beautiful and remote Big Bend National Park. Well located for exploring the park, the views are excellent. The adjacent restaurant serves a varied menu. **www.chisosmountainslodge.com**

DALLAS The Magnolia — $$$

1401 Commerce St, 75201 ***Tel*** *(214) 915-6500, (888) 915-1110* ***Fax*** *(214) 253-0053* ***Rooms*** *330*

Thoroughly modern, this trendy hotel is housed in the historic 1920s Petroleum building downtown. The lobby and common areas are period-chic, with historic architectural details and decorative accents in bright colors. The spacious guestrooms are cozy and comfortable with contemporary furnishings and neutral decor. **www.magnoliahoteldallas.com**

DALLAS The Mansion on Turtle Creek — $$$$$

2821 Turtle Creek Blvd, 75219 ***Tel*** *(214) 559-2100, (888) 767-3966* ***Fax*** *(214) 528-4187* ***Rooms*** *143*

This luxurious small hotel, housed in the former palatial mansion of cotton magnate Sheppard King, offers a refined residential-style ambience. All guestrooms have recently been redecorated in a classical style, but retaining the elegant marble bathrooms and private balconies. **www.mansiononturtlecreek.com**

EL PASO Camino Real Hotel — $$

101 S El Paso St, 79901 ***Tel*** *(915) 534-3000, (800) 769-4300* ***Fax*** *(915) 534-3024* ***Rooms*** *359*

This 1912 landmark hotel has retained its historical grandeur, including the impressive lobby and grand staircase, Italian crafted marble details, and stunning Tiffany glass dome. The modern guestrooms are spacious, comfortable, and well-equipped. **www.caminoreal.com/elpaso**

FORT DAVIS Indian Lodge — $

PO Box 1707, 79734 ***Tel*** *(432) 426-3254* ***Rooms*** *39*

This 1930s pueblo-style lodge is set in the rugged foothills of Davis Mountain State Park. All of the rooms have modern decor, new vanities, and restored furnishings while maintaining a cozy and inviting rustic ambience. Reservations are essential. **www.tpwd.state.tx.us**

FORT DAVIS Prude Guest Ranch — $$

Hwy 118, 79734 ***Tel*** *(432) 426-3202, (800) 458-6232* ***Fax*** *(432) 426-4401* ***Rooms*** *41*

This great Texas Dude Ranch is part of an operating 1,000ha cattle ranch. The accommodations are rustic, the atmosphere is informal, and the list of activities is impressive. Guests can participate in ranch activities, horseback riding, bird-watching, or swim while enjoying wide-open spaces, scenic mountain ranges, and pure air. **www.prude-ranch.com**

Key to Symbols *see back cover flap*

FORT WORTH Etta's Place $$$

200 W 3rd St, 76106 ***Tel*** *(817) 255-5760, (866) 355-5760* ***Fax*** *(817) 878-2560* ***Rooms*** *10*

A cozy B&B-style inn located in Sundance Square with a personality all its own. There's a library with comfortable leather chairs and a music room with a Steinway piano. Each guestroom is individually decorated with antiques, period pieces, and fine fabrics. Well suited to both business and leisure travelers. **www.ettas-place.com**

FORT WORTH Stockyards Hotel $$$

109 E Exchange Ave, 76106 ***Tel*** *(817) 625-6427, (800) 423-8471* ***Fax*** *(817) 624-2571* ***Rooms*** *52*

This restored early 20th-century hotel is located in the Stockyards National Historic District. Through the years cowboys, cattle barons, country music stars, and outlaws have all stayed here. The lobby is filled with Western furniture, antiques, and art, and many of the guestrooms have antique furnishings. **www.stockyardshotel.com**

GALVESTON Tremont House $$$

2300 Ship's Mechanic Row, 77550 ***Tel*** *(409) 763-0300, (800) 996-3426* ***Fax*** *(409) 763-1539* ***Rooms*** *119*

Housed in a lavishly ornate 1879 Victorian building, Tremont House is located in Galveston's Strand Historic District. The four-story atrium lobby features birdcage elevators, Victorian furnishings are used throughout, and the Rooftop Terrace is a relaxing place to watch the sunset and the ships of Galveston's port. **www.galveston.com/thetremonthouse**

HARLINGEN La Quinta Inn $

1002 S Expressway 83, 78552 ***Tel*** *(956) 428-6888, (800) 642-4241* ***Fax*** *(956) 425-5840* ***Rooms*** *129*

Located in the heart of the Rio Grande Valley, this comfortable small chain hotel offers consistent quality and great service. Guests appreciate the rooms, with work spaces and high-speed Internet access, and there is a swimming pool as well as a complimentary Continental breakfast every morning. **www.lq.com**

HOUSTON Lovett Inn $$

501 Lovett Blvd, 77006 ***Tel*** *(713) 522-5224, (800) 779-5224* ***Fax*** *(713) 528-6708* ***Rooms*** *12*

Located in a lovely 1923 colonial-style home on a tree-lined boulevard in the Montrose Museum District, this friendly B&B-style inn is known for its gracious service. The grounds are lovely, with gazebo, pool, outdoor Jacuzzi, and a sunroom overlooking the pool. Continental breakfast is available every morning. **www.lovettinn.com**

HOUSTON Hotel ZaZa $$$$

5701 Main St, 77005 ***Tel*** *(713) 526-1991* ***Rooms*** *300*

Conveniently situated within walking distance of the Museum of Fine Arts, this modern, trendy hotel is housed in an historic building. Hip and surprising, this is a fun spot that knows how to pamper business travelers and provide a decadent setting for a romantic weekend. Hi-tech amenities blend with comfort. **www.hotelzaza.com/houston/**

LAREDO La Posada Hotel $$

1000 Zaragoza St, 78040 ***Tel*** *(956) 722-1701, (800) 444-2099* ***Fax*** *(956) 726-8524* ***Rooms*** *208*

This Spanish Colonial-style hotel is situated on the bluff above the Rio Grande River within walking distance of the shops along San Bernardo Avenue. Modern conveniences, helpful and courteous staff, and attractive rooms make this a pleasant place to stay. Free shuttle service to and from the airport. **www.laposadahotel.com**

LUBBOCK Arbor Inn & Suites $

5310 Englewood Ave, 79424 ***Tel*** *(806) 722-2726, (866) 644-2319* ***Rooms*** *73*

Personal service and an excellent location in the newer area of Lubbock just off the Loop Road make this family-owned hotel a popular choice. The comfortable rooms feature a sitting area and kitchenette. Larger suites are also available. Complimentary breakfast bar and cookies and lemonade every evening. **www.arborinnandsuites.com**

MARATHON Gage Hotel $$$

102 W Highway 90, 79842 ***Tel*** *(432) 386-4205, (800) 884-4243* ***Fax*** *(432) 386-4510* ***Rooms*** *43*

Surrounded by the mountains of Big Bend National Park, this rustic historic hotel offers a variety of accommodations. Rooms in the original 1927 two-story hotel are small and basic, not all with private baths.A modern extension features larger rooms with private baths, inviting decor, and museum-quality antiques. **www.gagehotel.com**

SAN ANTONIO Best Western Sunset Suites $$

1103 E Commerce St, 78205 ***Tel*** *(210) 223-4400, (866) 878-9595* ***Fax*** *(210) 223-4402* ***Rooms*** *64*

A sparkling all-suites hotel in a beautifully converted turn-of-the-century building located a short walk or streetcar ride from the Alamo and RiverWalk. This gem is located just north of Sunset Station and offers large comfortable rooms and extras such as free parking, buffet breakfast, fitness center, and high-speed Internet. **www.bestwesternsunsetsuites.com**

SAN ANTONIO Beckman Inn & Carriage House $$$

222 E Guenther St, 78204 ***Tel*** *(210) 229-1449, (800) 945-1449* ***Fax*** *(210) 229-1061* ***Rooms*** *5*

This lovely 1886 home in the King William Historic District was built by Albert Beckmann as a wedding gift for his bride. Beautifully landscaped grounds, gracious wrap-around porch, and a pleasant sun room are highlights of the home. The guestrooms are spacious, with Victorian decor that is solid and comfortable. **www.beckmanninn.com**

SAN ANTONIO Menger Hotel $$$$

204 Alamo Plaza, 78205 ***Tel*** *(210) 223-4361, (800) 345-9285* ***Fax*** *(210) 228-0022* ***Rooms*** *315*

Built in 1859 next door to the Alamo, this hotel has hosted notables throughout its long history. The lovely three-story Victorian lobby is decorated with antiques, the Menger Bar is a legendary San Antonio tavern, and the hotel is reputedly home to numerous ghosts. Guestrooms vary from modern to Victorian in decor. **www.mengerhotel.com**

Choosing a Restaurant

The best places to eat in Texas are those that offer variations within the state's traditional cuisines. "Tex-Mex" is the predominant food style, mixing Mexican dishes with large quantities of Texas beef. Beef also features prominently in the steakhouses and barbecue restaurants.

PRICE CATEGORIES
For a three-course meal for one, including a glass of house wine (where served), and all other unavoidable charges such as sales tax.

- $ Under $25
- $$ $25–$35
- $$$ $35–$50
- $$$$ $50–$70
- $$$$$ Over $70

TEXAS

ABILENE Perini Ranch $$$

Hwy 89 in Buffalo Gap, 79508 ***Tel*** *(325) 572-3339*

This is the place to get real Texas food with Texas ambience, plain and simple. The rustic ranch setting and chuck-wagon recipes have created their own legend. All of the hand-cut steaks are dry-rubbed and then grilled over mesquite. Reservations recommended. Closed Monday and Tuesday.

AMARILLO Golden Light Café $

2908 W 6th St, 79107 ***Tel*** *(806) 374-9237*

For some of the best burgers, crispiest fries, coldest beers, and coolest live music along historic Route 66, stop at this funky roadside diner that's been serving hungry travellers since 1946. It doesn't look like much from the outside, but the folks are friendly, there's lots of atmosphere, and the chili is hearty and delicious. Closed Sunday.

AUSTIN Threadgill's $

6416½ N Lamar Blvd, 78752 ***Tel*** *(512) 451-5440*

This historic 1930s restaurant housed in a former gas station serves American diner food with a Texan twist, with fried Mississippi catfish, chicken-fried steak, and pecan pie some of the most popular dishes. Janis Joplin sang here in the '60s and Jimmie Dale Gilmore in the '80s. It's worth a visit to see the huge collection of neon signs and memorabilia.

AUSTIN Roaring Fork $$$

701 Congress Ave, 78701 ***Tel*** *(512) 583-0000*

Rugged Old West-style meats and seafood are served in a fine dining atmosphere inside the InterContinental Hotel. Many entrées are prepared by wood-fired rotisserie, open-flame grill, or roasted in a wood-fired oven. Try the hearty green chili pork stew, crusted Gulf snapper, or roasted and smoked long bone ribs. Reservations recommended.

CORPUS CHRISTI Snoopy's Pier $$

13313 S Padre Island Dr, 78418 ***Tel*** *(361) 949-8815*

Hugely popular with the locals, Snoopy's is a great place for casual dining out on the patio. The sunsets are beautiful, the atmosphere fun, and the seafood fresh. The decor is rustic waterside with old fishing rods. The fried shrimp is delicious, and there are burgers and fish-and-chips as well as a chalk-board menu of fresh fish selections.

CORPUS CHRISTI Republic of Texas Bar & Grill $$$$

900 N Shoreline Blvd, 78401 ***Tel*** *(361) 886-3515*

Fine dining on the 20th floor of the Bayfront Tower offers beautiful panoramic views out across the Corpus Christi Bay. The classic American menu at this top-notch restaurant features USDA prime cuts of beef, wild game entrées of venison, buffalo, and quail, and fresh Gulf seafood. The award-winning wine list is extensive.

DALLAS Sonny Bryan's Smokehouse $

2202 Inwood Rd, 75235 ***Tel*** *(214) 357-7120*

Since 1910 the original Sonny Bryan's has served up legendary Texas barbecue. They take their time do it right, and their savory sauce compliments the rich, smoky flavor of the meats. Brisket is traditional, but the pulled pork, chicken, ribs, sausage, ham, and turkey are all good. When the brisket is gone they close for the day. Closed Sunday.

DALLAS Zodiac $$

1618 Main St, 75201 ***Tel*** *(214) 573-5800*

This elegant restaurant inside Neiman Marcus Downtown has attracted business people and shoppers for over 50 years with upscale cuisine. The menu changes seasonally, with contemporary and classic offerings such as Maine lobster sandwich or mandarin orange soufflé with chicken salad. Lunch only, reservations recommended. Closed Sunday.

DALLAS Abacus $$$$

4511 McKinney Ave, 75205 ***Tel*** *(214) 559-3111*

Quiet and romantic, Abacus is one of the hottest restaurants in town. The contemporary global cuisine features Mediterranean, Cajun/Creole, southwest, and Pacific Rim flavors. The menu changes monthly, and offers tantalizing treats like chili-rubbed elk loin served with charred corn. Finish with an East Texas peach turnover.

Key to Symbols *see back cover flap*

DALLAS Mansion on Turtle Creek Restaurant $$$$$

2821 Turtle Creek Blvd, 75219 ***Tel*** *(214) 559-2100*

This top-rated elegant restaurant housed in the historic Sheppard King Mansion received a sweeping redesign in 2007. The decor, including soft leather chairs and commissioned artwork, complements the menu featuring contemporary American cuisine. The new Chef's Room has a refined ambience and specializes in formal dining.

EL PASO H&H Car Wash & Coffee Shop $

701 E Yandell Dr, 79902 ***Tel*** *(915) 533-1144*

Some of the best Tex-Mex food in El Paso is served at H&H, and this small weathered ultra-casual shop is filled with locals and savy travellers enjoying specialties such as huevos rancheros and chiles rellenos. And yes, you can get your car washed while you eat, but arrive before 3pm when they close up shop for the day. Closed Sunday.

EL PASO Café Central $$$$

109 N Oregon St #1, 79901 ***Tel*** *(915) 545-2233*

Fine contemporary dining in a relaxed atmosphere that is simple and elegant. Located in the Arts District, the gourmet cuisine has a contemporary Southwest twist with a menu that changes seasonally. Typical selections include cream of green chile soup, ahi tuna served over a crab cake, and Mango Colada Pie for dessert. Closed Sunday.

FORT WORTH Joe T. Garcia's $

2201 N Commerce St, 76164 ***Tel*** *(817) 626-4356*

In business for over 60 years, this family-owned restaurant is a favorite with locals. Housed in a hacienda-style complex, the Tex-Mex menu is simple with a choice of enchiladas or fajitas with beans, rice, guacamole, and pico de gallo. Get a seat in the beautiful garden courtyard, order a margarita, and enjoy tortilla chips and home-made salsa.

FORT WORTH Cattlemen's Steakhouse $$$

2458 N Main St, 76164 ***Tel*** *(817) 624-3945*

Cattlemen's is a fun, noisy, and very popular steakhouse in the Stockyards that serves juicy charcoal-grilled steaks. Select a thick sirloin, rib-eye, or T-bone steak from the glass butcher case, or choose from menu items such as chicken, shrimp, or lobster. The price is right and the restaurant attracts a mixed crowd of families and steak-lovers.

FREDERICKSBURG Altdorf Biergarten $$

301 W Main St, 78624 ***Tel*** *(830) 997-7865*

Housed in a historic building on Main St, the Altdorf offers casual dining and a large selection of beers. The most popular seating is on the shady biergarten patio. The menu offers something for every taste, from steak to Tex-Mex and burgers. Specialties include German sausage or schnitzel with red cabbage and sauerkraut. Closed Tue.

GALVESTON Gaido's $$$

3802 Seawall Blvd, 77550 ***Tel*** *(409) 762-9625*

Located on the Gulf, this family-run landmark has been serving fresh-caught seafood and shrimp for generations. Nautical decor, huge windows with views of the Gulf, great service, and large servings of fresh seafood make this one of Galveston's most popular restaurants. The menu varies seasonally and includes beef and chicken and wicked desserts.

HOUSTON Americas $$$

1800 Post Oak Blvd #164, 77056 ***Tel*** *(713) 961-1492*

Americas is one of Houston's most popular and most unique restaurants. The dramatic decor captures the essence of the rain forest, with traces of mountains, caves, and greenery with flower-like hand-blown glass chandeliers. The New World cuisine is crafted with the flavors of South and Central America, producing satisfying seafood and meat entrées.

LUBBOCK Cattle Baron $$

8201 Quaker Ave #170, 79424 ***Tel*** *(806) 798-7033*

This upscale steak and seafood restaurant with attractive Western decor specializes in hand-cut steaks and fresh fish, with some chicken and pasta as well. Prime rib is the house favorite and the menu offers a great selection of seafood that includes Gulf shrimp, Mountain trout, and lobster. The cheese sticks are hand-breaded and the desserts are tasty.

MARATHON Café Cenizo $$$

101 W US-90, 79842 ***Tel*** *(432) 386-4205*

This charming restaurant in the historic Gage Hotel offers fine dining in an intimate setting with wood floors and Southwest decor. Both the dining room and the lovely courtyard have fireplaces, and the service is excellent. Mesquite-grilled Black Angus steaks, wild game, and regional favorites are featured on the menu; also a five-course Chef's Tasting.

SAN ANTONIO Boudros $$

421 E Commerce St, 78205 ***Tel*** *(210) 224-8484*

This trendy River Walk restaurant with patio seating is a local favorite noted for great food and consistently good service. Fresh local Texas beef, Gulf seafood, and Hill Country produce are combined to create delicious New American cuisine such as Blackened Prime Rib seared in Cajun spices and Gulf Yellowfin Tuna marinated in achiote.

SAN ANTONIO Mi Tierra Café & Bakery $$

218 Produce Row, 78207 ***Tel*** *(210) 225-1262*

This legendary and very busy Mexican restaurant has fed guests for over 60 years, offering a uniquely Mexican festive atmosphere. Festooned with lights and hanging piñatas, the café bustles with strolling mariachis and waiters carrying enormous trays of food. The juicy fajitas are famously good, and the bakery offers a huge selection of sweets.

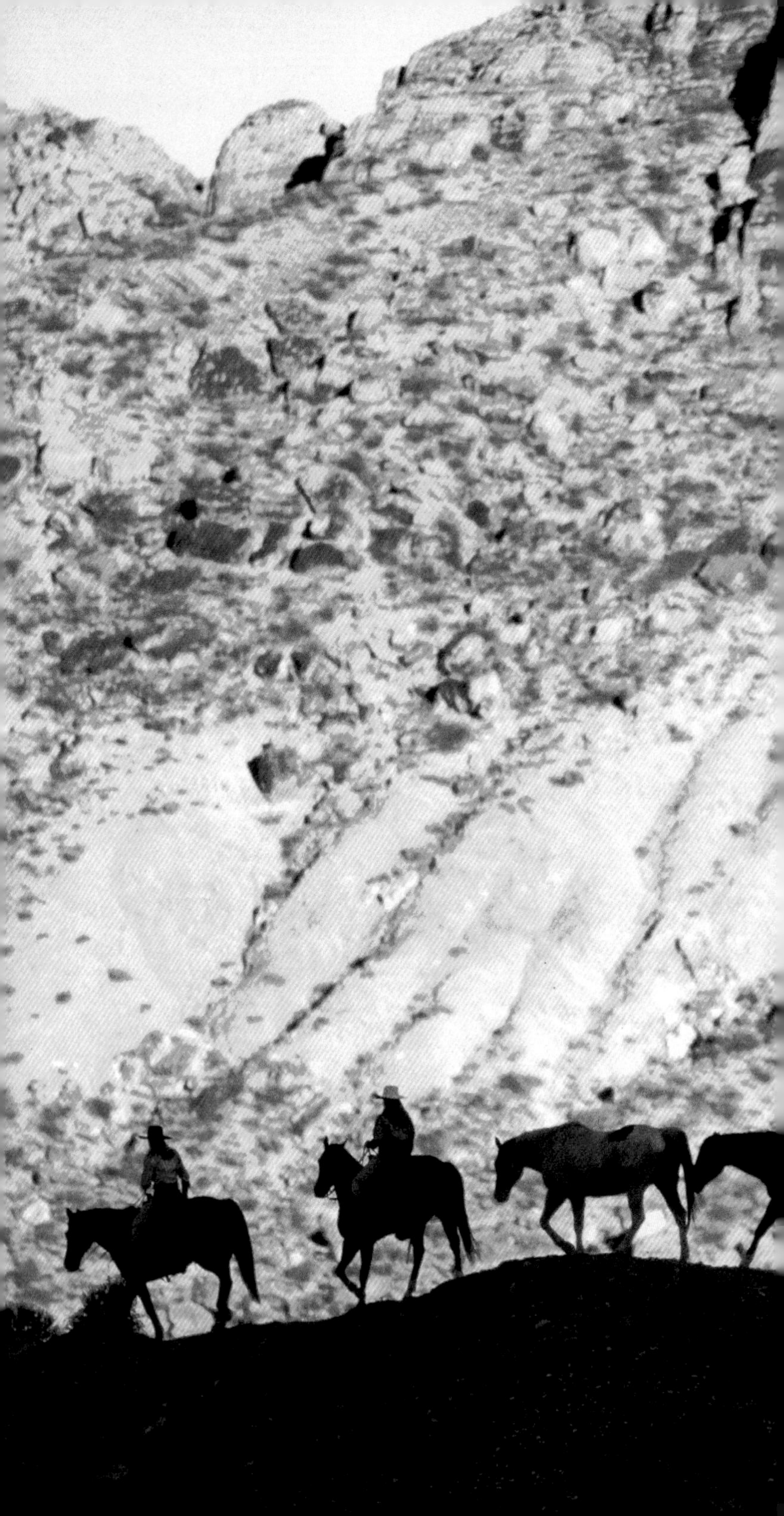

THE SOUTHWEST

INTRODUCING THE SOUTHWEST 502–509

LAS VEGAS, NEVADA 510–515

NEVADA 516–517

UTAH 518–527

ARIZONA 528–543

NEW MEXICO 544–553

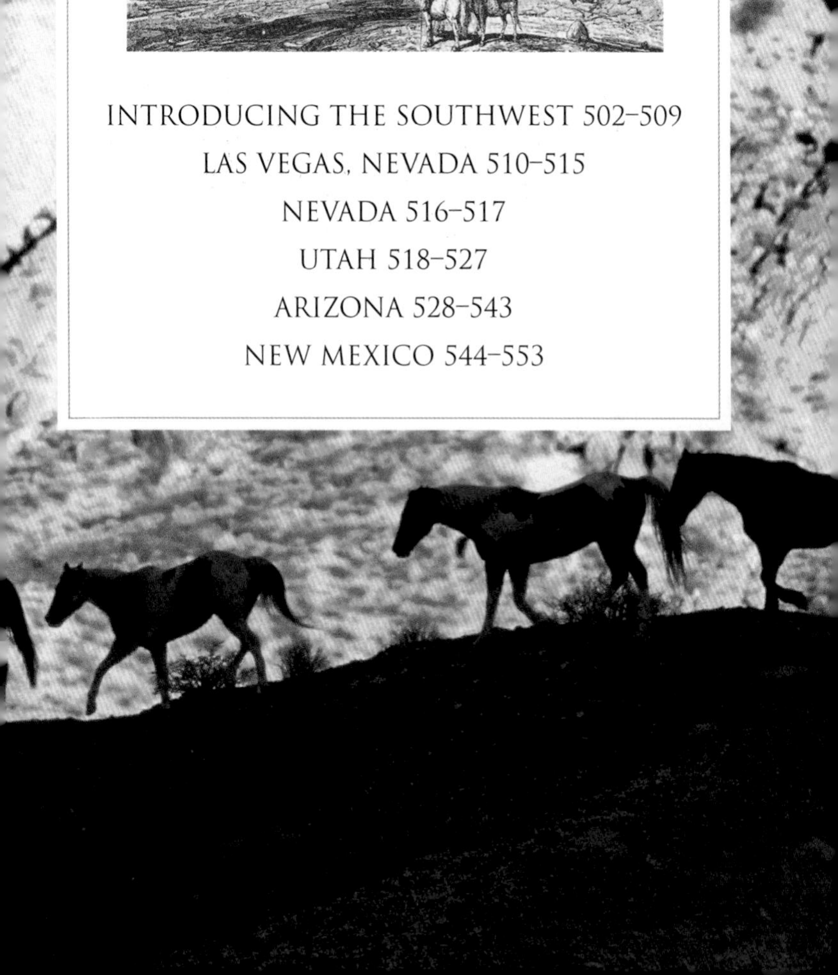

The Southwest at a Glance

America's Southwest is made up of the states of Nevada, Utah, Arizona, and New Mexico. It also includes the Four Corners area, the only place in the US where four states – parts of Utah, Arizona, New Mexico, and Colorado – meet at a central point. The region boasts spectacular landscapes, dominated by desert, deep canyons, and high mesas. Equally fascinating is its multicultural heritage, influenced by Native American, Hispanic, and Anglo-American settlers. Today, this region offers visitors a range of sights, most of which are concentrated in the cities of Phoenix, Tucson, Albuquerque, Santa Fe, and Las Vegas.

Hopi-made coiled basket made of willow or yucca leaves

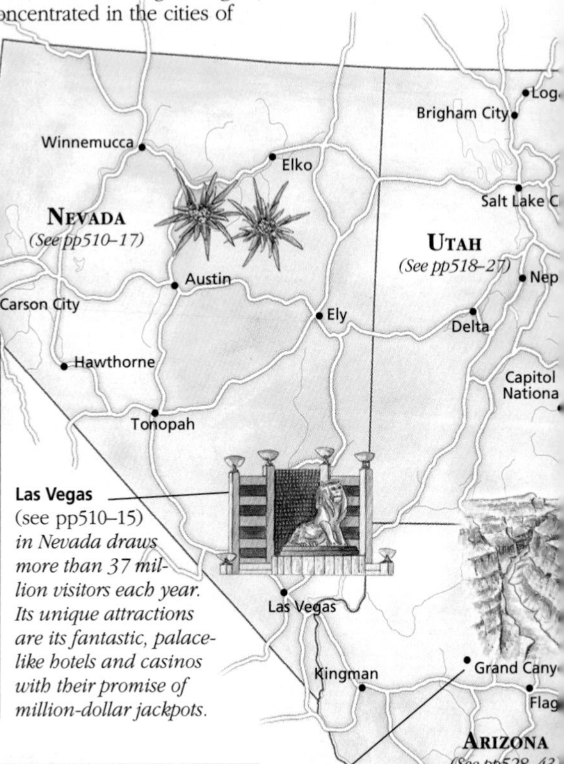

Las Vegas (see pp510–15) *in Nevada draws more than 37 million visitors each year. Its unique attractions are its fantastic, palace-like hotels and casinos with their promise of million-dollar jackpots.*

The **Grand Canyon** (see pp536–9) *in Arizona is the second most-visited national park in the country. This is, however, one of the many natural wonders in a state well-known for its stunning landscapes of pristine deserts, forested hills, and fertile meadows.*

◁ **Horseback riders negotiating a steep trail along a canyon, southern Utah**

Cacti and dried chilies adorning a flower shop, Tucson

LOCATOR MAP

Arches National Park (see pp520-21) *is just one of the many geological wonders in Utah, a state with the highest concentration of national parks in the United States. The dramatic and unpromising landscape of Utah also became the spiritual and worldly base of the Mormons. Salt Lake City, the state capital, is located northwest of the park.*

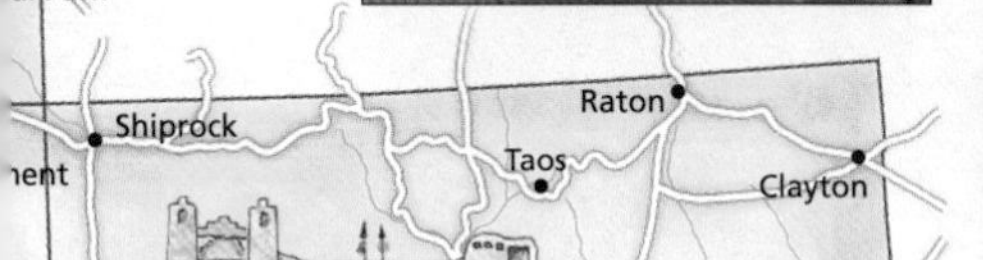

New Mexico (see pp544–53) *is one of the Southwest's most popular destinations. Its scenic beauty and rich cultural heritage have lured generations of artists, who have made Santa Fe and Taos vibrant creative centers. Albuquerque, the largest city, has many fine museums.*

IERA
OF THE YEAR
Splash
VOTED SHOW
OF THE YEAR
Pizza Hut

THE SOUTHWEST

Distinguished by its dramatic landscape, the Southwest is a land of twisting canyons, cactus-studded deserts, and rugged mountains. For more than 15,000 years, the region was inhabited by Native Americans, but by the 20th century Anglo-American traditions had mingled with those of the Hispanic and Native peoples to create the region's multicultural heritage.

The states of Nevada, Utah, Arizona, and New Mexico make up America's Southwest. Perceptions of this region are influenced by the landscape – the red sandstone mesas of Monument Valley, the tall saguaro cacti of Arizona's Sonoran Desert, the staggering scale of the Grand Canyon, and New Mexico's adobe architecture. At its heart is its defining geological feature – the Colorado Plateau – a rock tableland rising more than 12,000 ft (3,660 m) above sea level and covering a vast area of around 130,000 sq miles (336,700 sq km). The plateau was created by the same geological upheavals that formed the Rocky Mountains. Subsequent erosion by wind, water, and sand molded both hard and soft rock to form the mesas, canyons, and mountains. Many of these natural wonders have been preserved as national parks.

The region's main city, Las Vegas, has been synonymous with glamor and entertainment ever since Nevada legalized gambling in 1931. Mobster Bugsy Siegel opened the first luxury hotel, the Flamingo, in 1946, and soon there was a proliferation of casinos. Some of the biggest names in show business, such as Frank Sinatra and Elvis Presley, as well as eccentric millionaire Howard Hughes, have all contributed to Vegas's image as the fun city of limos, showgirls, and glitzy lifestyles. This city of megaresorts and casinos is as popular for its wedding chapels, where more than 100,000 couples get married each year.

HISTORY

The first Native American people were a society of hunters who inhabited the region between 10,000 and 8,000 BC. The introduction of new farming techniques and crops, especially corn from Mexico, saw the start of settled farming communities in around 800 BC. By AD 500 an agrarian society

The desert floor dotted with sagebrush, Monument Valley, Arizona

◁ Sparkling neon stars of the Riviera Hotel in Las Vegas, Nevada was well established, and large villages or pueblos began to develop. By 700 the three main cultures in the region were the Hohokam, the Mogollon, and the Ancestral Puebloan. Ancestral Puebloan people constructed elaborate dwellings that grew into large cities such as Chaco Canyon. However, in the 12th and 13th centuries, these settlements were mysteriously abandoned. It is thought that the people migrated to the Pueblo Indian settlements along the Rio Grande Valley and northwest New Mexico, where their descendants still live. The 15th century saw the arrival of the Navajo, who were hunters, and the fierce Apache warriors from Canada.

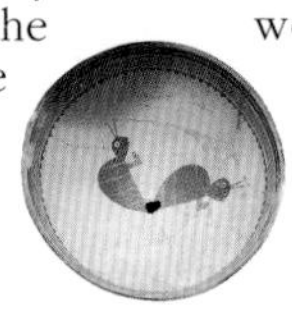
Ancient pottery bowl

In the 1500s, the Spanish quest for wealth, particularly gold, led to the establishment of a permanent colony called New Mexico, which included all of the present-day states of New Mexico and Arizona, as well as parts of Colorado, Utah, Nevada, and California. Mexican independence from Spain was declared in 1821, paving the way for Anglo-American traders.

KEY DATES IN HISTORY

1800 BC Corn brought from Mexico

AD 800 Chaco Canyon under construction

1400 Migrations of the Navajo and Apache

1540–42 Francisco Vasquez de Coronado leads the search for gold in New Mexico

1610 Santa Fe established as capital of New Mexico

1680 The Pueblo revolt against the Spanish

1821 Santa Fe Trail opened

1848 Treaty of Guadalupe-Hidalgo cedes Mexican territory to the US

1868 Navajo reservation founded in Four Corners region

1869 The coming of the railroad

1912 New Mexico and Arizona become 47th and 48th states of the United States

1931–36 Hoover Dam constructed in Arizona

1945 First atomic bomb tested in New Mexico

1974 Central Arizona Project begins to extract water from the Colorado River

1996 President Clinton signs Navajo-Hopi Land Dispute Settlement Act

2000 Forest fires devastate large parts of northern New Mexico and Arizona

The first Anglos (non-Spanish people of European descent) in the Southwest were "mountain men" or fur trappers, who helped open up the trade routes to the west. With the establishment of the Old Spanish and the Santa Fe Trails, this remote region became more accessible.

The US government's vigorous expansion led to conflict with Mexico, and the region became a part of the United States in 1848. Soon, the settlers began to forcibly acquire Native land, and more than 8,000 Navajo were made to march "The Long Walk" to a reservation in New Mexico in 1864. Resentment against the Anglos instigated the Indian Wars, which finally ended with the surrender of Apache leader Geronimo in 1886.

At the same time, rich lodes of gold, silver, and copper were discovered in Arizona, and mining camps such as Bisbee and Tombstone became boomtowns. This was the Wild West of mining prospectors, ranch cowboys, and notorious outlaws, such as Billy the Kid, whose exploits form part of American folklore

SOCIETY & CULTURE

The Southwest is a crossroads of the three great cultures that shaped America – Native American, Hispanic, and Anglo-American. The Spanish language is prominent, not only in bilingual New Mexico but also in Arizona. A host of Native American languages are also spoken, reflecting the far longer history of the region's Native inhabitants. The Hopi and other Pueblo peoples trace their ancestry back to the Ancestral Puebloan peoples, while the Navajo occupy the country's largest reservation, stretching across the northern ends of both Arizona and New Mexico. The Apache and many other tribes have land here as well. Today, Native populations have a hand in governing their own lands, and many have diversified their business interests to regenerate their economy and are involved in tourism, running casinos, and the production of such crafts as pottery and rugs.

A colorful Navajo rug

A variety of religions coexist in the Southwest. The most visible is Roman Catholicism, which was introduced in the 16th century by the Spanish colonists. It is today the main religion, although several Protestant denominations exist as well. Utah's residents, however, are predominantly Mormon. Native American spiritual beliefs are complex, as each tribe has its own practices.

One of the region's most famous attributes is the quality of light found in the hills of northern New Mexico. Georgia O'Keeffe's landscape paintings in the 1940s helped to make the area around Santa Fe a mecca for artists. Today, the city has the country's second largest art trade after New York City. The smaller resort town of Taos is also famous for its resident painters and sculptors.

Route 66 Flagstaff sign

Santa Fe, as well as Phoenix, Tucson, and Albuquerque also offer opera, ballet, classical music, and major theatrical productions. The Phoenix Symphony and New Mexico Symphony Orchestra, based in Albuquerque, are best known for their concerts, while jazz and country music can be heard in almost every city and major town.

ECONOMICS & TOURISM

Today, New Mexico and Arizona are the country's fifth and sixth largest states. Despite the fact that the region's population is increasing, it remains one of the least populated in the United States. The cities of Phoenix, Tucson, Santa Fe, and Albuquerque account for around 60 percent of the region's population. Such intense urbanization has put tremendous pressure on the region's resources, particularly water, which has become one of the Southwest's most pressing issues.

The legacy of the two World Wars changed the Southwest's economic course. In the 1940s, New Mexico's sparsely populated and remote desert area of Los Alamos was chosen as the location for the top secret Manhattan Project, which developed the world's first atomic bomb. Since then, the region has been a major center for national defense research and development of nuclear weapon technology, as well as for research into space travel, with both state and federal governments as major employers. Today, other research projects, including bio-technology, especially the Genome Project (which maps all human genes) and computer technology, attract scientists to the Southwest.

Tourism is another of the region's principal employers. Vast wilderness areas and a warm climate make outdoor leisure popular in the Southwest. Its national parks, established in the early 1900s, draw ever-increasing numbers of tourists each year. There are also miles of hiking trails, rivers for whitewater rafting, lakes for water sports, ski resorts, and some of the nation's finest golf-courses. One of the best ways to experience the landscape is on a trail ride, and armchair cowboys can attend that great Southwestern event – the rodeo.

The Southwest is as much a state of mind as it is a geographical region. The attractions of the landscape and a romantic sense of the past combine to conjure up the idealized legends of the "Wild West." For many, it is the chance to indulge the cowboy in their soul.

Horseback riding, a popular pastime in the Sonoran Desert near Tucson, Arizona

Exploring the Southwest

The four states of the Southwest encompass many natural wonders, such as the Grand Canyon and Monument Valley in Arizona, and Zion National Park in Utah. Beyond the scenic are the pueblo villages along the Rio Grande in New Mexico and the glitter of Las Vegas, Nevada's fastest growing city. Above all, the region conjures up images of the Wild West, as portrayed by Hollywood and preserved by the myths around old mining towns, such as Bisbee and Tombstone.

Chili wreath, Santa Fe

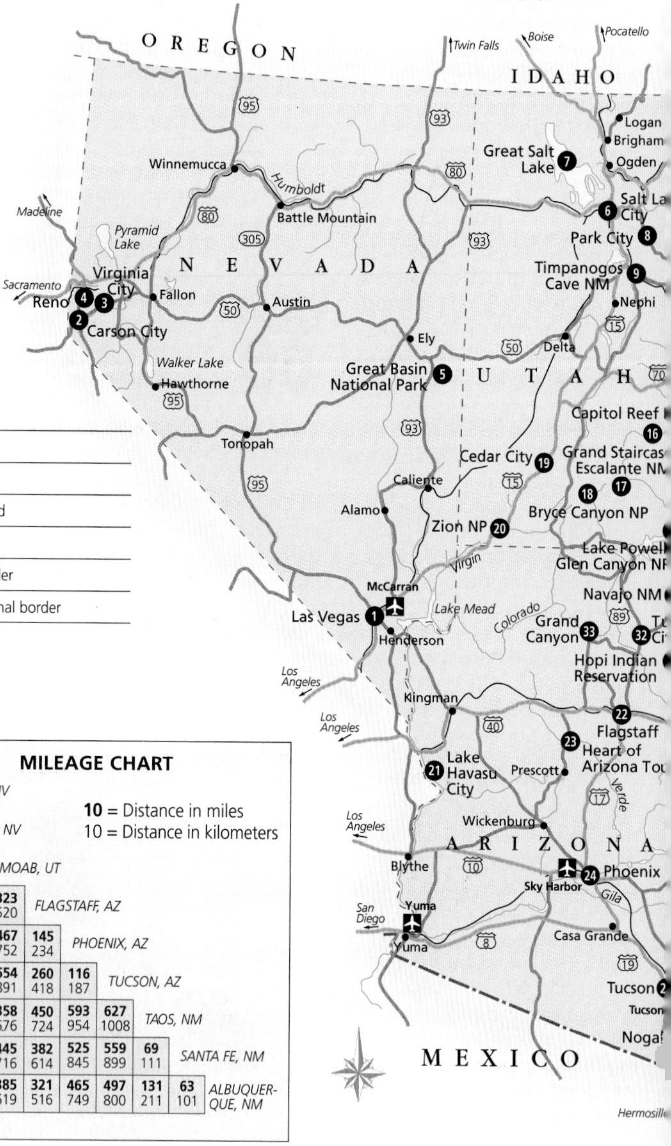

KEY

- Airport
- Highway
- Major road
- Railroad
- State border
- International border

MILEAGE CHART

10 = Distance in miles
10 = Distance in kilometers

	LAS VEGAS, NV	RENO, NV	MOAB, UT	FLAGSTAFF, AZ	PHOENIX, AZ	TUCSON, AZ	TAOS, NM	SANTA FE, NM
RENO, NV	**447** 719							
MOAB, UT	**458** 737	**750** 1207						
FLAGSTAFF, AZ	**251** 404	**697** 1121	**323** 520					
PHOENIX, AZ	**286** 460	**888** 1429	**467** 752	**145** 234				
TUCSON, AZ	**506** 814	**1003** 1614	**554** 891	**260** 418	**116** 187			
TAOS, NM	**701** 1128	**1375** 2213	**358** 576	**450** 724	**593** 954	**627** 1008		
SANTA FE, NM	**633** 1018	**1307** 2103	**445** 716	**382** 614	**525** 845	**559** 899	**69** 111	
ALBUQUERQUE, NM	**572** 920	**1246** 2005	**385** 619	**321** 516	**465** 749	**497** 800	**131** 211	**63** 101

For additional map symbols *see back flap*

SIGHTS AT A GLANCE

Nevada

Las Vegas pp510–15 ❶
Carson City ❷
Virginia City ❸
Reno ❹
Great Basin National Park ❺

Utah

Salt Lake City ❻
Great Salt Lake ❼
Park City ❽
Timpanogos Cave National Monument ❾
Arches National Park pp520–21 ❿
Moab ⓫
Canyonlands National Park p522 ⓬
Green River ⓭
Hovenweep National Monument ⓮
Lake Powell & Glen Canyon National Recreation Area ⓯
Capitol Reef National Park ⓰
Grand Staircase–Escalante National Monument ⓱
Bryce Canyon National Park pp526–7 ⓲
Cedar City ⓳
Zion National Park p525 ⓴

Arizona

Lake Havasu City 21
Flagstaff 22
Heart of Arizona Tour p529 23
Phoenix pp530–31 24
Tucson 25
Nogales 26
Bisbee 27
Amerind Foundation 28
Petrified Forest National Park 29
Window Rock 30
Hopi Indian Reservation 31
Tuba City 32
Grand Canyon pp536–9 33
Navajo National Monument 34
Monument Valley pp540–41 35
Canyon de Chelly National Monument pp542–3 36

New Mexico

Chaco Culture National Historical Park 37
Taos 38
Northern Pueblos Tour p545 39
Santa Fe pp546–7 40
Albuquerque pp548–50 41
Roswell 42
Carlsbad Caverns National Park 43
White Sands National Monument 44
Gila Cliff Dwellings National Monument 45

SEE ALSO

- ***Practical Information*** pp554–5
- ***Where to Stay*** pp556–9
- ***Where to Eat*** pp560–63

Mummy Cave Overlook in Canyon de Chelly, Arizona

Las Vegas ❶

The heart of Las Vegas, Nevada's most famous city, lies along Las Vegas Boulevard, a sparkling vista of neon known simply as "the Strip." The southern stretch of this 3.5-mile (6-km) long street that runs northeast through the city is home to a cluster of lavishly themed hotels, with their own shops, restaurants, and gaming casinos. They lure almost 37 million visitors every year, making Vegas the entertainment capital of the world. When the lights come on in the evening, these new megaresorts become a fantasyland with riotous design and architecture, such as that of the Luxor's striking pyramid with its sphinx. The exotically themed Aladdin Hotel is evidence of the city's ability to reinvent itself quickly – it took only two years to build.

A dazzling nighttime view of the Strip

New York New York
A replica of the Statue of Liberty forms part of the façade of this hotel, which is composed of a host of such Manhattan landmarks as the Empire State Building.

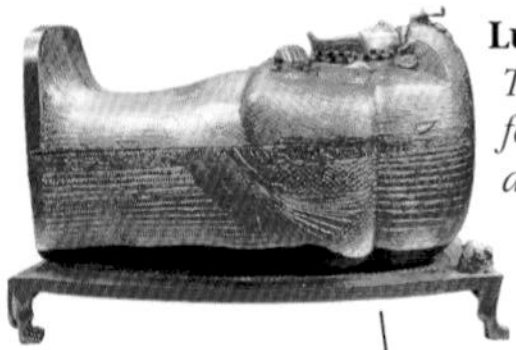

Luxor
The hotel's Egyptian features include a reproduction of Tutankhamun's tomb in the King Tut Museum.

The Monte Carlo is filled with Corinthian colonnades and arches.

Mandalay Bay's interior, with its palm trees and bamboo, re-creates a 19th-century tropical paradise.

Excalibur's towers are a kitsch fantasy of medieval England.

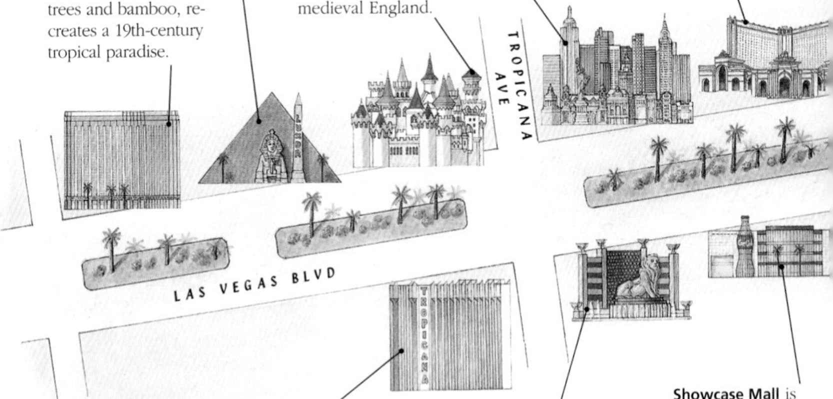

Showcase Mall is a striking building, with its giant neon Coca-Cola bottle. A huge games arcade makes the mall very popular with families.

Tropicana
This casino was rebuilt in the late 1970s with a stunning Art Nouveau-style stained-glass ceiling and glass lamps.

MGM Grand Hotel
One of the largest hotels in the US with more than 5,000 rooms, the Grand displays a 45-ft (15-m) high statue of Leo, symbol of the Hollywood film studio, MGM.

For hotels and restaurants in this region see p556 and p560

Caesars Palace
Reproduction Roman statuary adorns the grounds of Caesars Palace. One of the Strip's oldest and most glamorous hotels, Caesars was built in 1966. Inside, the lavish Forum Shops mall features moving statues.

Imperial Palace
A pagoda fronts this Asian-themed hotel, famous for its classic car collection, which is open to all visitors.

Bellagio
Built in 1998, this luxury resort's elegant lobby is hung with sculpted glass flowers, designed by glass artist Dale Chihuly (see p628).

Paris, with its half-scale replica of the Eiffel Tower, is a $760-million resort modeled on the French capital.

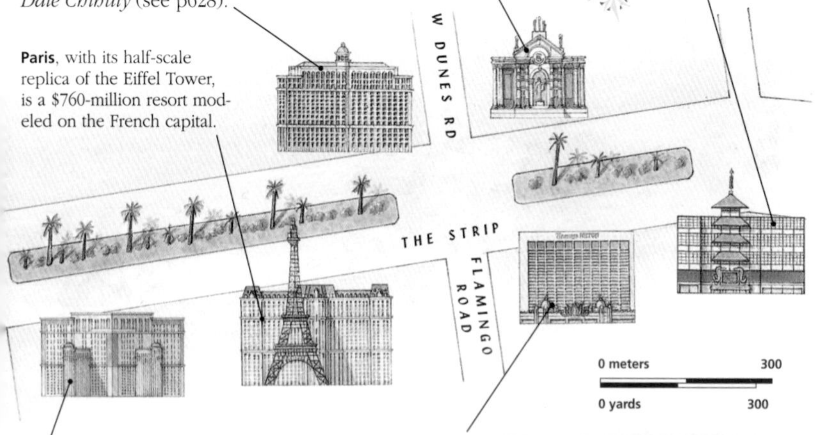

Planet Hollywood Resort & Casino
The hotel became Planet Hollywood Resort & Casino in 2007. Originally opened in 1963, as Aladdin Hotel, this is one of the glitziest Strip hotels made famous as the venue where Elvis Presley married Priscilla in 1967.

Flamingo
The flaming pink and orange neon plume of the Flamingo hotel's façade is a famous Strip icon. New York City Gangster Bugsy Siegel created the hotel and casino in 1946. He was killed, just a year later, by fellow investors.

Las Vegas (The Strip Continued)

The legalization of gambling in Nevada paved the way for Las Vegas' casino-based growth. The first casino resort, the El Rancho Vegas Hotel-Casino, opened in 1941 and was located on the northern section of the Strip. A building boom followed in the 1950s, resulting in a plethora of resorts. The Sands, Desert Inn, Sahara, and Stardust hotels began the process that transformed the Strip into a high-rise adult theme park. Although many of these north Strip resorts remain, they are now unrecognizable, thanks to million-dollar rebuilding programs. The façades of the new casinos are designed now to encourage people to walk up and spectacular shows are staged outside.

Roulette is very popular in Vegas – gambling was legalized in Nevada in 1931

TI
The pirate-themed world of Treasure Island lures passers-by to the spectacular Sirens of TI *show, held each evening on the hotel's Strip-side lagoon* ❹

The Mirage is both stylish and tacky – its beautiful, Strip-facing gardens feature an "erupting" volcano.

The Fashion Show Mall is currently the largest shopping destination in Vegas, with more than 200 stores, an entertainment complex, and a food court serving both fast and fresh food.

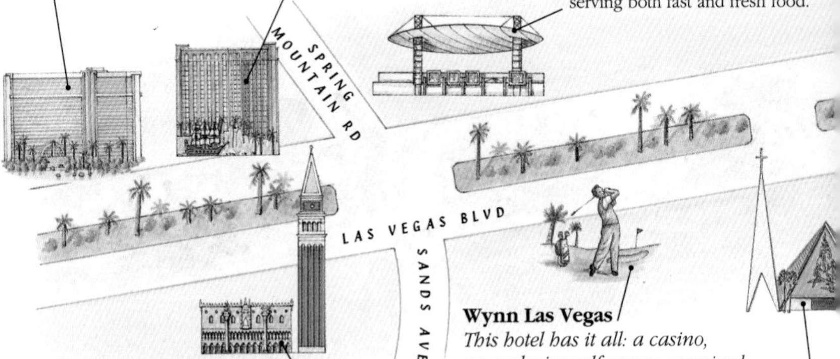

Wynn Las Vegas
This hotel has it all: a casino, an exclusive golf course, oversized luxurious rooms, restaurants with award-winning chefs, nightclubs, and dozens of designer shops.

Guardian Angel Cathedral
Located on Desert Inn Road, this chapel has elegant marble floors and imposing buttress support columns ❼

Venetian
One of the world's most luxurious hotels, this has mock canals flowing through its shopping area. Madame Tussaud's Wax Museum is located inside the hotel.

For hotels and restaurants in this region see p556 and p560

The Strip at dusk
Although the Strip is very busy with traffic it is increasingly pedestrian-friendly and an enjoyable walk.

Stratosphere Tower
An observation deck at the top of this 1,149-ft (350-m) tower offers fine views of the city and the ring of mountains that rise from the desert.

Circus Circus
Lucky the Clown beckons visitors to this resort, which offers circus acts and traditional carnival games on the mezzanine floor above the casino.

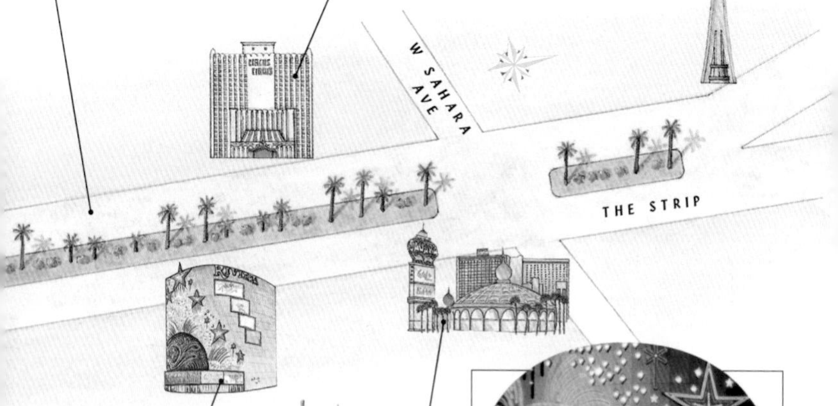

Riviera
The colorful, neon-lit, and seemingly jewel-encrusted façade of Riviera highlights the hotel's hit shows, and is one of the most dazzling landmarks along North Strip ❾

Sahara
This Moroccan-themed hotel opened in 1952 and is one of the city's oldest hotels. It features two of the most popular attractions on the Strip – the fast-paced Cyber Speedway and the thrilling roller coaster ride, Speed ⓬

0 meters 300

0 yards 300

Neon lights at the Riviera Hotel

LAS VEGAS NEON

The neon sign remains the dominant icon of Las Vegas, even though several of the new megaresorts have opted for a more understated look. Neon is a gas discovered by British chemist Sir William Ramsey in 1898. But it was a French inventor, Georges Claude, who, in 1910, discovered that an electric current passed through a glass tube of neon emitted a powerful, shimmering light. In the 1940s and 1950s the craft of neon sign-making became an art form in Las Vegas.

Exploring Las Vegas

Rising like a mirage out of Nevada's beautiful southern desert, Las Vegas is a fascinating wonderland that promises fun to all its visitors. Beyond the allure of the Strip are the glittering malls and museums in the downtown area. For those who can tear themselves away from the city, the surrounding canyons, mountains, deserts, and parks offer a wealth of natural beauty and outdoor pleasures. Apart from tourism and gaming, Las Vegas is also famous for wedding chapels that offer a wide range of customized ceremonies.

Liberace Museum

1775 E Tropicana Ave. ***Tel*** *(702) 798-5595.* *10am–5pm Tue–Sat; noon–4pm Sun.* *Mon, major hols.* **www**.liberace.org

This museum, founded in 1979, celebrates the life and work of one of Las Vegas's best-loved performers, Liberace (1919–87). It displays 18 of his 39 pianos, his lavish costumes, trademark capes, and stage jewelry. The costumes worn at his final 1986 performance took six seamstresses, wearing protective sunglasses against the glare of the stones, several months to make. The customized cars include a rare Rolls Royce covered with mirror tiles, in which the flamboyant artist would arrive at his show. Collections of objects from around the world include a piano-shaped ring, set with 260 diamonds.

Fremont Street Experience

Light Shows *6pm–midnight daily.* **www**.vegasexperience.com **Binion's Horseshoe** 128 E Fremont St. ***Tel*** *(702) 382-1600.* *24 hours.* **www**.binions.com **Four Queens** 202 E Fremont St. ***Tel*** *(702) 385-4011.* *24 hours.* **www**.fourqueens.com

Known as "Glitter Gulch," Fremont Street was where the first casinos with neon signs and illuminated icons were located. However, during the 1980s and 1990s as the Strip became more glamorous, this street went into decline. To reverse the process, an ambitious $70-million project was initiated by the city in 1994 to revitalize the area. The street is now a colorful, bustling pedestrian mall, covered by a vast steel canopy, extending for five blocks, and from which the spectacular sound-and-light shows are projected every night. Gaze upward to experience high-resolution images presented by more than 12 million LED modules with concert-quality sound.

Façade of Binion's Horseshoe

Established by Dallas bootlegger and gambler Benny Binion, the landmark **Binion's Horseshoe** retains an old-style Vegas atmosphere. Now managed by Harrah's Casinos, the legend continues with table games, slots, keno, and poker. Another historic casino along the Street is **Four Queens**. Named for the owner's four daughters, the casino has chandeliers and gilt mirrors, reminscent of 19th-century New Orleans. It also claims to have the largest slot machine in the world.

Lied Discovery Children's Museum

833 Las Vegas Blvd N. ***Tel*** *(702) 382-5437.* *Sep–May: 9am–4pm Tue–Fri, 10am–5pm Sat, noon–5pm Sun; Jun–Labor Day: 10am–5pm Mon–Sat, noon–5pm Sun.* *Mon (except school hols), Jan 1, Thanksgiving, Dec 25.* **www**.ldcm.org

A conical, concrete teepee forms part of this striking museum devoted to interactive exhibits. Children can stand inside a gigantic bubble, visit a totally green village, or even work in the in-house television studio.

The Las Vegas Natural History Museum

900 Las Vegas Blvd. ***Tel*** *(702) 384-3466.* *9am–4pm daily.* *Jan 1, Thanksgiving, Dec 25.* **www**.lvnhm.org

A popular choice with families who need a break from the Strip resorts, this museum has an appealing range of exhibits. Dioramas re-create the African savanna, complete with leopards, cheetahs, and antelopes. The marine exhibit offers a chance to view live sharks and eels at close quarters. Animatronic dinosaurs and the hands-on discovery room, where visitors can dig fossils and operate a robotic baby dinosaur, are popular with children.

Boulder City & Hoover Dam

12,500. ***Tel*** *(702) 494-2517.* *summer: 9am–5pm; winter: 9am–4pm.*

Named after Herbert Hoover, the 31st president, the historic Hoover Dam lies about 30 miles (48 km) east of Las Vegas. Before its construction, the Colorado River frequently flooded acres of farmland in Mexico and southern California. After much consideration, the dam was built between 1931 and 1935 across the Colorado River's Black Canyon. Hailed as an engineering marvel, it gave this desert region a reliable water supply and provided inexpensive electricity to Nevada, Arizona, and

An animatronic *Tyrannosaurus rex* in roaring form at the Las Vegas Natural History Museum

For hotels and restaurants in this region see p556 and p560

View of the Hoover Dam

California. This colossus of concrete is today a huge tourist attraction. Guided tours take visitors into the depths of the dam. The top of the visitor center offers superb views of the dam.

Just 8 miles (13 km) west of the dam, Boulder City was built to house the dam's construction workers. It is one of Nevada's most attractive well-ordered towns. Several of its 1930s buildings remain, including the historic Boulder Dam Hotel, which houses the Hoover Dam Museum.

Hoover Dam sign

Lake Mead National Recreation Area

Las Vegas. ***Tel*** *(702) 293-8906, (702) 293-8990.*
8:30am–4:30pm daily.
Jan 1, Thanksgiving, Dec 25. *limited.*
www.nps.gov/lame

After the completion of Hoover Dam, the waters of the Colorado River filled the deep canyons, which once towered above the river, to create Lake Mead. This huge reservoir is the largest man-made body of water in the US. Its 700-mile (1,130-km) shoreline is home to forests, canyons, and flower-rich meadows. Dotted with beaches, marinas, and campgrounds, the reservoir area offers water sports such as sailing, waterskiing, swimming, and fishing. Striped bass and rainbow trout are popular catches.

Valley of Fire State Park

Las Vegas. ***Tel*** *(702) 397-2088.*
partial.
www.desertusa.com/nvval

Lost City Museum of Archaeology
721 S Moapa Valley Blvd, Overton.
Tel *(702) 397-2193.*
8:30am–4:30pm daily.
Jan 1, Thnksg., Dec 25.

This spectacularly scenic state park is in a remote desert location some 60 miles (97 km) northeast of Las Vegas. It derives its name from the red sandstone formations that began as huge, shifting sand dunes about 150 million years ago. The extreme summer temperatures mean that spring or fall are the best times to explore the wilderness. Of the four well-maintained trails, the Petroglyph Canyon Trail is an easy half-mile (0.8 km) loop, which takes in several fine prehistoric Ancestral Puebloan rock carvings. One of the most famous depicts an *atlatl*, a notched stick used to add speed and distance to a thrown spear. Ancestral Puebloan people settled in the nearby town of Overton along Muddy River, around 300 BC. They left some 1,500 years later, perhaps because of a long drought. Archaeologists have discovered hundreds of prehistoric artifacts in the area, many of which are housed in Overton's **Lost City Museum of Archaeology**, just outside the town. Its large collection includes pottery, beads, woven baskets, and delicate turquoise jewelry, which was a local specialty.

Red Rock Canyon

Las Vegas. ***Tel*** *(702) 515-5350.*
8am–4:30pm daily. *public hols.* *limited.*
www.nv.blm.gov/redrockcanyon/

From downtown Las Vegas it is a short, 10-mile (16-km) drive west to the low hills and steep gullies of the Red Rock Canyon National Conservation Area. Here, baked by the summer sun, a gnarled escarpment rises out of the desert, its gray limestone and red sandstone the geological residue of an ancient ocean and the huge sand dunes that succeeded it. The canyon is easily explored on a 13-mile (21-km) long scenic road that loops off Hwy 159 providing a good overview and great picnic spots, but the best way to explore these steep winding canyons is on foot. Watch for the bighorn sheep and desert tortoises when hiking.

Extraordinary rock formations in the Valley of Fire State Park

Nevada

Nevada was known as the "Silver State" mainly because of the immense wealth that came out of the late 19th-century silver mines of the Comstock Lode, east of Reno. Today, it is synonymous with adult fun, thanks to the presence of the world's largest gambling and entertainment mecca at glittering Las Vegas *(see pp510–15)*. Away from its few cities, Nevada is mostly uninhabited desert, with ridge after ridge of rugged mountains dividing the endless sagebrush plains.

Façade of the impressive State Capitol in Carson City

Carson City ❷

55,000. *1900 S Carson St Suite 100, (775) 687-7410.* **www**.visitcarsoncity.com

The state capital and third largest city in Nevada, Carson City was named in honor of the Wild West explorer Kit Carson. Nestled at the base of the eastern escarpment of the Sierra Nevada, the city was founded in 1858, a year before the discovery of the Comstock Lode mines. It still retains a few old-fashioned casinos in its downtown core.

The excellent **Nevada State Museum**, down the street from the impressive State Capitol, is housed inside the 1870 US Mint building, where coins were made from Comstock silver. The museum holds a full-scale replica of a working mine, as well as displays on the natural history of Nevada and the Great Basin.

On the south side of Carson City, the **Nevada State Railroad Museum** preserves 60 steam engines and freight cars from the old Virginia & Truckee Railroad, which carried ore from the Comstock Lode between 1869 and the 1930s. Later used in Hollywood films, the trains also offer excursions on summer weekends.

Nevada State Museum
600 N Carson St. ***Tel*** *(775) 687-4810.* *8:30am–4:30pm daily.* *Jan 1, Thanksgiving, Dec 25.*

Nevada State Railroad Museum
2180 S Carson St. ***Tel*** *(775) 687-6953.* *8:30am–4:30pm daily.* *Jan 1, Thanksgiving, Dec 25.*

Virginia City ❸

1,000. *86 S C St, (775) 847-0311.* **www**.virginiacity–nv.org

Prospectors following the gold deposits up the slopes of Mount Davidson discovered one of the world's richest strikes, the Comstock Lode, in 1859. Almost overnight, the bustling camp of Virginia City grew into the largest settlement between Chicago and San Francisco. It had over 100 saloons and 25,000 residents, among whom was a journalist from Missouri who later became famous under the pseudonym Mark Twain.

Old timers in a Wild West-themed saloon in Virginia City

Over the next 20 years, tons of gold and silver were mined here, but by the turn of the 20th century the town had begun to fade. However, the popular 1960s TV show *Bonanza* has given the city a new lease on life as one of Nevada's most enjoyable destinations. A National Historic Landmark, the city is located at an elevation of 6,220 ft (1,896 m); its steep streets offer fine views of the surrounding mountains. The old main street, **C Street**, is packed with historic sites dotted alongside Wild West-themed saloons and souvenir shops. Up the hill along B Street, the elegant **Castle** is the state's best-preserved mansion. It was built in 1863–68 and in its heyday it was considered to be one of the finest mansions in the west. Although the interior is now closed to the public, you can still gain a glimpse of the amount of wealth that flowed through here in the 1860s.

The city's main historical museum fills the old **Fourth Ward School**, the Victorian Gothic landmark at the south end of C Street. It showcases the city's lively history with exhibits ranging from mining tools to Mark Twain, who began his career at the city's *Territorial Enterprise*. An intact classroom is preserved as it was in 1936, when the last class graduated.

Fourth Ward School
537 South C St. ***Tel*** *(775) 847-0975.* *May–Oct: 10am–5pm daily.* *Nov–Apr.*

Reno ❹

190,000. *4590 S Virginia St, (800) 367-7366.* **www**.visitrenotahoe.com

Self-proclaimed "The Biggest Little City in the World," Reno was Nevada's main gambling destination until it was surpassed by glitzy Las Vegas in the 1950S. The city also achieved national prominence

For hotels and restaurants in this region see p556 and p560

Archway over Virginia Street in downtown Reno

in the 1930s as a center for quick divorces. Although smaller than Las Vegas, Reno has a similar array of 24-hour-a-day casino-fueled fun. It also offers a huge variety of winter and outdoor activities, including 18 alpine ski resorts within one hour of Tahoe, dog sled tours, sleigh rides, sledding, snowshoeing, and cross-country skiing. The **Truckee River Whitewater Park** in downtown Reno is one of the premier white-water parks in the country, with 11 pools over a half-mile course. Kayaking, tubing, and rafting can be enjoyed by novice and experienced enthusiasts. All equipment is available for hire at the park.

The **National Automobile Museum**, on the south bank of the Truckee River, has one of the country's most extensive car collections. From early classics to 1960s hot rods, the museum – styled like a late-1940s Chrysler – show-cases the cars in stage-set "streets" that provide evocative period backgrounds.

Truckee River Whitewater Park
Wingfield (off W 1st St). ***Tel*** *(775) 334-2262.*

National Automobile Museum
10 S Lake St. ***Tel*** *(775) 333-9300.* *9:30am–5:30pm Mon–Sat, 10am–4pm Sun.* *Thanksgiving, Dec 25.* **www**.automuseum.org

Environs

West of Reno, the startling beauty of **Lake Tahoe** *(see p718)* greets visitors at the Nevada/California border. Surrounded by summer resorts and winter ski areas, this is one of the most popular destinations in western US.

Great Basin National Park ❺

100 Great Basin Hwy, Baker, (775) 234-7331. *8am–4:30pm daily (extended summer hours).* *Jan 1, Thanksgiving, Dec 25.* *limited.* **www**.nps.gov/grba

Travelers driving along the "Loneliest Road in America" are beckoned by the towering silhouette of the 13,063-ft (3,982-m) Wheeler Peak which stands at the center of Great Basin National Park. Below the peak lies the park's centerpiece, the **Lehman Caves**, discovered when homesteader Absalom Lehman stumbled upon their small entrance in 1885. Their fantastic limestone formations, including thousands of stalactites and shields, can be seen on various guided tours that take place at intervals all through the day.

Tours start from the park visitor center, which offers hiking and camping details, along with exhibits on Great Basin's wildlife. The well-maintained **Wheeler Peak Scenic Drive** starts near the visitor center and passes through all the major Great Basin climate zones while climbing from 6,500 ft (1,982 m) to over 10,000 ft (3,048 m) in 12 steep miles (19 km). Great Basin National Park's remote location has made it one of the least-visited national parks in the country, so hikers and campers can find immense solitude among the limestone caves, alpine forests, ancient bristlecone pines, and glacial lakes.

Picturesque Wheeler Peak at Great Basin National Park

THE LONELIEST ROAD IN AMERICA

One of the country's most compelling drives, the Nevada portion of transcontinental US 50, stretching between Lake Tahoe in the west and Great Basin National Park on the Utah border, traverses over 400 miles (644 km) of corrugated country. Early explorers mapped this region, Pony Express riders raced across it, and the long-distance Lincoln Highway finally tamed it. But US 50 has long played second fiddle to busy I-80, the more popular route across the state. The Nevada Commission on Tourism now sponsors a tongue-in-cheek promotion where travelers on US 50 can get a certificate saying "I Survived the Loneliest Road in America."

Sign on US 50 highway

Utah

Best known as world headquarters for the Mormon Church, Utah is also home to some of the most remarkable landscapes in the US. The inhospitably rugged sandstone canyons of the Colorado Plateau, which covers the southern half of the state, have been preserved within a series of unforgettably beautiful national parks, forests, and monuments. The towering snow-capped peaks of the Wasatch Mountains in the northern half of the state, a haven for skiers worldwide, played host to the 2000 Winter Olympics. West of the mountains sits the Mormon-dominated state capital Salt Lake City, Utah's only major city, bordered by its namesake lake.

Salt Lake City 6

181,700. *90 South West Temple St, (801) 534-4902.* **www**.visitsaltlake.com

Pleasant and friendly Salt Lake City makes a great stopover for weary travelers between Denver and San Francisco. Although its name derives from the undrinkable alkaline Great Salt Lake that spreads to the west, the city actually has abundant fresh water, thanks to the rain and snowmelt of the Wasatch Range, which rises to the east. Founded and controlled by the Mormons since 1847, the city spreads for miles and miles along the base of the snowcapped peaks.

Apart from its spectacular natural setting, Salt Lake City is known as the spiritual base of the Mormon church, which has its worldwide headquarters in Temple Square downtown. Here, the six spires of the main Mormon temple and the famous oblong auditorium of the **Mormon Tabernacle**, built in 1867, stand side by side. The Mormon Tabernacle choir rehearsals are open to the public.

To the west of Temple Square, the amazing **Family History Library** holds records of Mormon family trees dating back to the mid-16th century. Eastward, the 1850 Beehive House has been preserved as it was when Mormon leader Brigham Young lived here. At its entrance stands the stately 76-ft (23-m) Eagle Gate, capped by a 4,000-pound eagle with an impressive wingspan of 20 ft (6 m). To the north, the domed **Utah State Capitol**, modeled after the US Capitol, features a series of exhibits on Utah's history.

Mormon Tabernacle
Temple Square. ***Tel*** *(801) 240-4872.*
9am–9pm daily.
www.visittemplesquare.com

Family History Library
35 NW Temple St.
Tel *(801) 240-1794. 8am–5pm Mon, 8am–9pm Tue–Sat.*
Sun, Jan 1, Jul 4, Thanksgiving, Dec 24, 25, 26.
www.familysearch.org

View of "Eagle Gate" looking toward the Utah State Capitol

For hotels and restaurants in this region see p557 and p561

Visitors enjoying the view from the Great Salt Lake shore

Great Salt Lake 7

Great Salt Lake State Park, I-80 exit 104. *(801) 250-1898. Apr–Oct: 7am–8pm daily; Nov–Mar 8am–5pm daily. limited.*

The largest salt lake in North America, the Great Salt Lake is a shallow remnant of the prehistoric Lake Bonneville. Depending on the weather, the lake covers an area ranging from 1,000 sq miles (2,590 sq km) to 2,500 sq miles (6,477 sq km). The salt flats stretching west from the lake to the Nevada border are so hard and expansive that they have long been used as a proving ground for automobile racers. Apart from some algae and microscopic brine shrimp, the lake itself supports almost no life. However, the **Antelope Island State Park**, located in the middle of the lake, is home to resident herds of bighorn sheep, mule deer, bison, and its namesake, the pronghorn antelope. Access to the island, lying about 40 miles (64 km) northwest of Salt Lake City, is by way of a 7-mile (11-km) long causeway. Visitors can camp or swim along the shore or take guided lake cruises.

West from Salt Lake City, toward the lake's south shore, the **Great Salt Lake State Park** offers a broad, sandy beach with a marina and observation deck.

Antelope Island State Park
I-15 exit 335. ***Tel*** *(801) 773-2941.*
7am onward, hours vary.
limited.

Park City 8

7,300. Cnr Olympic Blvd & Hwy 224, (435) 649-6100. www.parkcityinfo.com

An hour's drive east from downtown Salt Lake City, through the Wasatch Mountains, leads to this popular resort. The city started life in the 1860s as a silver mining camp and still retains several turn-of-20th-century buildings along its photogenic Main Street. In recent years, it has become world-famous as the home of the prestigious **Sundance Film Festival**. Founded by actor and director Robert Redford in 1981, the annual festival focuses on independent and documentary films and has become America's foremost venue for innovative cinema. The festival's popularity is linked to Park City's excellent skiing facilities, showcased in the 2000 Winter Olympics. A sense of the town's history can be obtained at **Park City Museum** in the old City Hall.

Park City Museum
528 Main St. ***Tel*** *(435) 658-9625.* *May & Nov: 11am–5pm Mon–Sat, noon–6pm Sun; rest of the year: 10am–7pm Mon-Sat, noon–6pm Sun.* *Jan 1, Thanksgiving, Dec 25.* *limited.*

Historic houses lining Main Street in Park City

Timpanogos Cave National Monument 9

Hwy 92, American Fork. ***Tel*** *(801) 756-5238.* *mid-May–mid-Oct: 7am–5:30pm daily* *Nov–mid-May* **www**.nps.gov/tica

One of the the most popular destinations around Salt Lake City, the Timpanogos Cave National Monument lies deep beneath the 11,750-ft (3,581-m) summit of Mount Timpanogos. The site preserves a trio of massive limestone caverns stretching nearly 1,800 ft (549 m) deep into the mountain. Reached by way of a steep, 1.5 mile (2 km) uphill hike from the visitor center, and linked by man-made tunnels, the three caves are very cool (43° F/ 6° C), very damp, and full of spectacular limestone formations. Electric lights showcase the sundry stalactites, stalagmites, crystalline helictites, and other water-sculpted formations, all of which are still being formed. Only a limited number of people are allowed inside, so visitors should come early in the day or during the week, or call ahead for reservations.

Timpanogos Cave is one of the many highlights of the drive along the 40-mile (64-km) **Alpine Loop**, which follows Highway 92 around the landmark mountain. Many campgrounds, picnic spots, scenic views, and hiking trails can be enjoyed by trekkers along the way.

Scenic view along Alpine Loop following Highway 92

THE MORMONS

The Church of Jesus Christ of Latter Day Saints, a large Christian denomination, was founded by Joseph Smith (1805–44), a farm worker from New York State. In 1820 Smith claimed to have seen visions of the Angel Moroni, who led him to a set of golden tablets, which he translated and later published as the *Book of Mormon*, thus establishing the Mormon Church. Although this new faith grew rapidly, it attracted hostility because of its political and economic beliefs, and the practice of polygamy. Seeking refuge, the Mormons moved to Illinois in 1839, where Smith was killed by an angry mob. Leadership passed to Brigham Young, who led the members on an arduous journey west, in the hope of escaping persecution and setting up a safe haven in the unpromising landscape of Salt Lake Valley. The pioneers traveled across bleak prairies and mountains in primitive wagons, braving the fierce weather. Young's followers finally established successful farming communities across Utah's wilderness. Today, Mormons form 70 percent of Utah's population.

Portrait of Brigham Young (1801–77)

Arches National Park ⑩

Wildflowers in the park

Arches National Park has the the highest concentration of natural sandstone arches in the world. More than 80 of these natural wonders have formed over millions of years. The park "floats" on a salt bed, which once liquefied under the pressure exerted by the rock above it. About 300 million years ago, this salt layer bulged upward, cracking the sandstone above. Over time the cracks eroded, leaving long "fins" of rock. As these fins eroded, the hard overhead rock formed arches, which range today from the solid looking Turret Arch to the graceful Delicate and Landscape Arches.

Devil's Garden
This area contains several of the park's most beautiful arches, including Landscape Arch, a slender curve of sandstone more than 300 ft (91 m) long, which is thought to be the longest natural arch in the world.

Sunset Watch at Delicate Arch
A natural amphitheater surrounds the arch, creating seating from which vistas of the La Sal Mountains are framed.

THE WINDOWS SECTION

In the park's Windows Section, a one-mile loop trail leads to Turret Arch, then the North and South Windows Arches, located side by side. With excellent viewing spots available, many visitors photograph the North and South arches framed by the sandstone Turner Arch, as seen here.

EXPLORING THE PARK

The scenic drive to these spectacular arches starts at the visitor center at the park's south end, just off Highway 191. Several easy trails start from parking lots at the road's viewpoints. The loop at Balanced Rock is a suitable trail for children, and the Delicate Arch Viewpoint Trail has disabled access. Although permitted, camping is not popular because of the heat and water scarcity in the area.

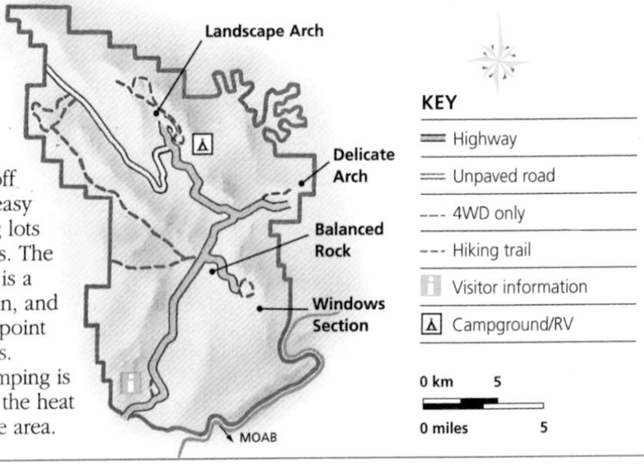

Delicate Arch
The most celebrated of all the arches here, and a state symbol, Delicate Arch appears on many Utah license plates. It is reached by a moderate 45-minute walk over sandstone.

VISITORS' CHECKLIST

(435) 259-8161.
Center Apr–Oct: 7:30am–6:30pm; Nov–Mar: 8am–4:30pm. (campground, Park Avenue Viewpoint, Delicate Arch Viewpoint Trail & Balanced Rock Trail.)
www.nps.gov/arch

Arches are formed through a process that takes millions of years; today's arches continue to erode and will eventually collapse.

Balanced Rock
This precariously balanced boulder atop a sandstone spire is one of the park's landmarks. Good views are available from the trail as well as the scenic road route.

Park Avenue and the Courthouse Towers
The large, rock monoliths known as Courthouse Towers bear an uncanny resemblance to city skyscrapers. They can be seen from Park Avenue, an easy, short trail.

Western-style, timber-clad gift store on Main Street, Moab

Moab ⓫

6500. Main & Center Sts, (435) 259-8825.
www.discovermoab.com

A town of dramatic ups and downs, Moab is currently riding its second great boom of the last 50 years. Once a quiet Mormon settlement, the discovery in 1952 of several major uranium deposits outside town made Moab one of America's wealthiest communities. When the uranium market declined in the 1970s, the town was saved by tourism and its proximity to Arches and Canyonlands National Parks. Many movies, including some John Wayne Westerns and the Indiana Jones classics were shot here.

Today, Moab is a top destination for lovers of the outdoors. Mountain bikers come here for the challenging ride from Moab Rim, reached by Moab Skyway, a scenic tram ride offering panoramic views of the area. Numerous hiking trails and 4WD routes take in some of this region's fabulous landscapes. Moab is also a major center for whitewater rafting on the Colorado River. **Matheson Wetlands Preserve** off Kane Creek Boulevard has 2 miles (3 km) of hiking trails along a riverside wetland, home to birds and indigenous wildlife.

Matheson Wetlands Preserve
Off Kane Creek Blvd. ***Tel*** *(435) 259-4629.* *dawn–dusk daily.*

Canyonlands National Park ⓬

Millions of years ago, the Colorado and Green Rivers cut winding paths deep into rock, creating a labyrinth of rocky canyons that form the heart of this stunning wilderness. At its center, the rivers' confluence divides the park's 527 sq miles (1,365 sq km) into three districts – the Needles, the Maze, and the grassy plateau of the Island in the Sky. Established as a national park in 1964, Canyonlands is growing in popularity. Most wilderness travel here requires a permit.

VISITORS' CHECKLIST

2282 South West Resource Blvd, Moab, (435) 719-2313. visitor center: 9am–4:30pm daily (longer during spring & fall). Jan 1, Thanksgiving, Dec 25.

www.nps.gov/cany

KEY

- Highway
- 4WD only
- Hiking route
- Campground/RV
- Picnic area
- Visitor information
- National Park boundary
- Viewpoint

Mesa Arch
An easy and rewarding 500-yard (455-m) trail leads to Mesa Arch, a long, low curve of stone that perfectly frames the snowcapped La Sal Mountains in the distance.

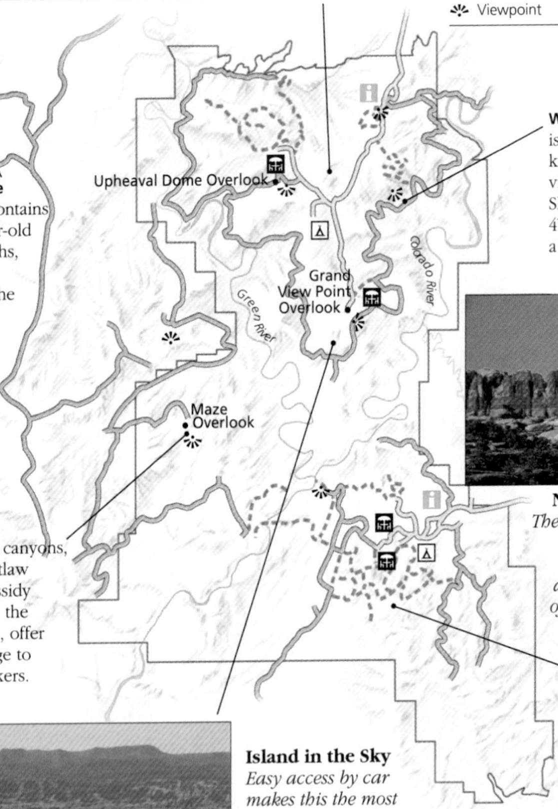

Horseshoe Canyon contains 6,000-year-old petroglyphs, said to be some of the oldest in existence.

White Rim Road is a 100-mile (160-km) trail accessed via the exhilarating Shafer Road, a 4WD track down a steep cliff.

Needles District
The most interesting features in this remote district are the hundreds of red rock spires, or needles, for which it was named.

The Maze canyons, where outlaw Butch Cassidy hid out in the late 1800s, offer a challenge to skilled hikers.

0 km 5
0 miles 5

Island in the Sky
Easy access by car makes this the most visited district of the park. A popular stop here is the Grandview Overlook, which offers panoramic views of the rocky canyons of the Green and Colorado Rivers.

For hotels and restaurants in this region see p557 and p561

The deep crevices of the canyons in the wide valley around Green River

Green River ⓭

1,000. 885 E Main St, (435) 564-3526. Apr–Oct: 8am–8pm; Nov–Mar: 8am–5pm daily.

Located in a broad, bowl-shaped valley, the town grew around a ford of the wild Green River in the 19th and early 20th centuries. Today, it is a launching spot for whitewater rafting on the Green and Colorado Rivers.

American geologist and ethnologist John Wesley Powell (1834–1902) began his exploration of the Colorado River and Grand Canyon from here in 1871. The **John Wesley Powell River History Museum** at Green River has 20,000 sq ft (1,860 sq m) of displays tracing the history of the area's exploration.

John Wesley Powell River History Museum
1765 E Main St. ***Tel*** *(435) 564-3427. Apr–Oct: 8am–8pm daily; Nov–Mar: 9am–5pm daily. public hols.*

Hovenweep National Monument ⓮

E of Hwy 191. ***Tel*** *(970) 562-4282. 8am–5pm daily (to 6pm May–Oct). Jan 1, Thanksgiving, Dec 25.* **www**.nps.gov/hove

The six separate sets of ruins at this Ancestral Puebloan site were discovered by W.D. Huntington, leader of a Mormon expedition, in 1854. The culture at Hovenweep, a Ute word meaning "Deserted Valley," reached its peak between 1200 and 1275. Little is known of the Utes beyond the clues found in the round, square, and D-shaped towers, and pottery and tools that they left behind.

Researchers have speculated that the towers might have been built as defensive fortifications, astronomical observatories, storage silos, or as religious structures for the entire community.

Lake Powell & Glen Canyon National Recreation Area ⓯

2 miles (3 km) N of Page on Hwy 98, off Hwy 160. *Carl Hayden Visitor Center, (928) 608-6404. Apr–Oct: 8am–5pm daily; Nov–Mar: 8am–4:30pm daily. visitor center only. Page & Wahweap only.* **www**.nps.gov/glca, **www**.lakepowell.com

The Glen Canyon National Recreation Area (NRA), established in 1972, covers more than one million acres of dramatic desert and canyon country around the 185-mile (298-km) long Lake Powell, named after John Wesley Powell. The lake was created by damming the Colorado River and its tributaries to supply electricity to the region's growing population.

The construction of the Glen Canyon Dam, completed in 1963, was controversial from the start. The spirited campaign, led by the environmentalist Sierra Club, continues to argue for the restoration of Glen Canyon, believing that ancient ecosystems are being ruined. Pro-dam advocates, however, firmly believe in its ability to store water, generate power, and provide recreation.

The "Y"-shaped recreation area follows the San Juan River east almost to the town of Mexican Hat, and heads northeast along the Colorado toward Canyonlands National Park. Within the area is the **Antelope Canyon**, a famously deep "slot" canyon. Other highlights include Lees Ferry, a 19th-century Mormon settlement that now offers tourist facilities, and the **Rainbow Bridge National Monument**. Rising 309 ft (94 m), this is the largest natural bridge in the world.

Today, the lake is busy with water sports enthusiasts and houseboat parties, exploring the myriad sandstone side canyons. Glen Canyon is also one of the most popular hiking, biking, and 4WD destinations in the country.

Rose-colored sandstone of Antelope Canyon, in Glen Canyon NRA

Capitol Reef National Park ⓰

10 miles (16 km) E of Torrey, Hwy 24. *(435) 425-3791. Jun–Sep: 8am–6pm daily; Oct–May: 8am–4:30pm daily. Dec 25.* **www**.nps.gov/care

Covering 378 miles sq (980 km sq), this spectacular park encloses a 100-mile (160-km) long, colorful wall of rock that was thrust up by the earth 65 million years ago. The strata that buckled upward folded back on itself, trapping water in the process. Around 100 years ago, prospectors crossing the desert were forced to stop at this wind-carved Waterpocket Fold. They likened the rock barrier to an ocean reef and thought its round white domes looked just like the US Capitol building, hence the park's name.

An adventurous drive along the partly unpaved Notom-Bullfrog Road provides a good overview of the area. Cars can negotiate the road in dry weather, but extra gas and water are essential. Capitol Gorge, to the north, can be reached via a scenic route, extending about 10 miles (16 km) into the heart of the park. Guided walking tours are available during summer, but be aware that only experienced hikers should attempt to explore the back country here.

To the north lies the 1908 **Gifford Farmhouse**. Now a cultural center, it is dedicated to the 1880s Mormon settlement that once flourished here. Fremont Canyon, on its right, features the famous Fremont Petroglyphs, created by the Ancestral Puebloans between 700 and 1250. Farther north, is the Cathedral Valley, named for the rock monoliths that tower over the desert.

Grand Staircase-Escalante National Monument ⓱

755 W Main St, Escalante, (435) 826-5499. Mar–Oct: 7:30am–5:30pm daily; Nov: 8am–4:30pm daily; Dec–Apr: 8am–4:30pm. **www**.ut.blm.gov/monument

Established by President Clinton in 1996, this monument encompasses 1.9 million acres (769,000 ha) of pristine rock canyons, mountains, and high desert plateaus. It was named for its four 12-million-year-old cliff faces that rise in tiered steps across the Colorado Plateau. To preserve its wild state, no new roads, facilities, or campgrounds are being built here. This vast untamed area is best explored on scenic drives combined with daylong hikes. About 9 miles (14 km) south of Highway 12 stands **Kodachrome Basin State Park**, a distinctive landscape noted for its 67 free-standing sand pipes or rock chimneys, formed millions of years ago as geyser vents.

Kodachrome Basin State Park
(435) 679-8562. dawn–dusk daily.

Bryce Canyon National Park ⓲

See pp 526–7.

Cedar City ⓳

20,500. *581 N Main St, (435) 586-5124.* **www**.scenicsouthernutah.com

Founded by Mormons in 1851, Cedar City developed as a center for mining and smelting iron. The Iron Mission State Park and Museum offers a glimpse of this pioneering spirit and features a large collection of early vehicles. The town offers a choice of hotels within an hour's drive of Zion National Park. Cedar City is popular for its annual Shakespeare Festival, staged in a replica of London's Globe Theatre. East of town, the spectacular **Cedar Breaks National Monument** features limestone cliffs and a lake topped by a deep green forest. In winter, the area is a popular skiing resort.

Vintage wagon outside Cedar City's museum

Cedar Breaks National Monument
Tel (435) 586-9451. daily. **Visitor Center** *8am–6pm daily.* **www**.nps.gov/cebr

Fishing in the lake at Cedar Breaks National Monument, near Cedar City

For hotels and restaurants in this region see p557 and p561

Zion National Park ⓴

Wild-
flowers

At the heart of this beautiful national park lies Zion Canyon, perhaps the most popular of all of Utah's natural wonders. It was carved by the powerful waters of the Virgin River and then widened, sculpted, and reshaped by wind, rain, and ice. Its majestic walls rise up to 2,000 ft (600 m) and are shaped into jagged peaks and formations in shades of red and white. Wild meadows and luxuriant foliage along the river account for the area's abundant wildlife. The park shuttle s the only way into the canyon. A number of short valks, beginning at the shuttle stops, follow marked rails to the tough 16-mile (26-km) hike through the :anyon and involves wading through the river.

VISITORS' CHECKLIST

Hwy 9, near Springdale. *Zion Canyon Visitor Center, (435) 772-3256.* *late Mar–early Nov: 8am–6pm daily (to 8pm in summer); early Nov–late Mar: 8am–5pm daily.* *partial.* www.nps.gov/zion

The spectacular Zion–Mt. Carmel Highway

ZION CANYON
The Virgin River meanders quietly through banks of wildflowers, cottonwood, oak, and willow trees, which grow beneath the sloping walls of the canyon. Be aware that sudden summer rainstorms may cause floods, so visitors are advised to check conditions first.

Iiking
Jumerous guided walking nd hiking tours of Zion's eology and history leave laily from the visitor center. merald Pools Trail and Canyon Overlook Trail are articularly popular trails.

EXPLORING ZION CANYON

A guided trail takes visitors along the 6-mile (10-km) scenic road that follows the Virgin River into an ever-narrowing canyon. In summer a shuttle bus operates along the Zion Canyon Scenic Drive and from the Information Center to the turn of Springdale.

KEY

- Highway
- Hiking trail
- Ranger station
- Campground/RV

0 meters 500
0 yards 500

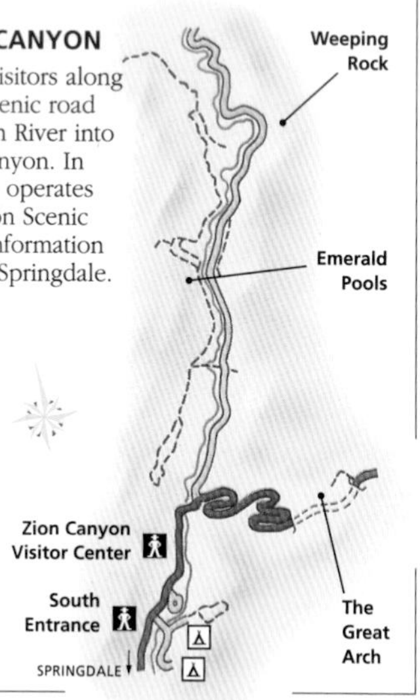

Bryce Canyon National Park ⓲

A series of deep amphitheaters filled with flame-colored rock formations called hoodoos are the hallmark of Bryce Canyon National Park. Bryce is high in altitude, reaching elevations of 6,000–8,000 ft (1,829–2,438 m), with a 18-mile (30-km) scenic road running along the rim of Paunsaugunt Plateau. Highlights include views of vast fields of pink, orange, and red spires; the Paiute Indians, once hunters here, described them as "red rocks standing like men in a bowl-shaped recess." The canyon's maze of pillars and channels is best appreciated on foot.

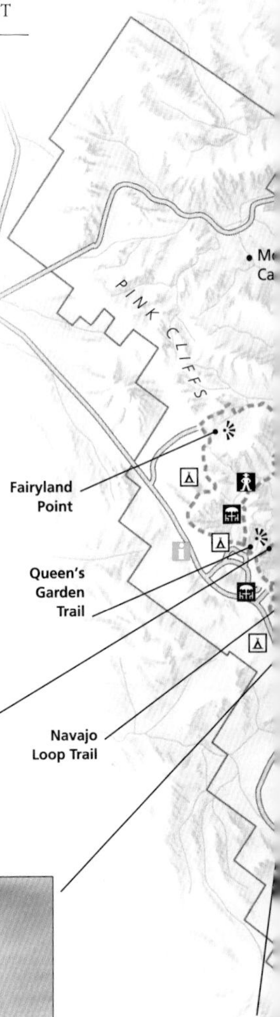

Sunrise Point
From this lookout it is easy to see why early settler and Mormon farmer Ebenezer Bryce, after whom the park is named, called it "a helluva place to lose a cow."

Thor's Hammer
Carved into the pink cliffs of the highest "step" of the Grand Staircase (see p524)*, this unusual landscape consists of eroded sandstone. Hoodoos such as Thor's Hammer are formed as rain and wind erode "fins" of harder rock that become columns, then further erode into strangely shaped hoodoos. The high altitude, ice, and wind continue the "carving" process today.*

Sunset Point is one of the major lookouts in Bryce Canyon. Inspite of its name it faces east, so while sunrises can be spectacular here, sunsets can be a little anticlimactic.

KEY
- Highway
- Hiking route
- Ranger station
- Campground/RV
- Picnic area
- Visitor information
- Viewpoint

Navajo Loop
This 1.4-mile (2-km) round-trip trail zigzags sharply down the cliff face for 500 ft (150 m) to finish in a slow meander among slot canyons and rock stands. The climb back up the trail is particularly strenuous.

For hotels and restaurants in this region see p557 and p561

Bryce Amphitheater
This panoramic vista of snow-covered rock spires is among the most popular views of the park. In both winter and summer the amphitheater is best seen from Inspiration Point.

VISITORS' CHECKLIST

Hwy 63 off Hwy 12. PO Box 170001, UT 84717 (435) 834-5322. regular shuttle service between the entrance & Bryce Point from Memorial Day to Labor Day. daily. Jan 1, Thanksg., Dec 25. **Visitor Center** *mid-Apr–Jun: 8am–6pm; Jun–Oct: 8am–8pm; Oct–Apr: 8am–4:30pm. limited.*
www.nps.gov/brca

Natural Bridge
This graceful natural bridge is located a few yards from the park's scenic highway. It frames a picturesque view of the distant valley below. Officially, it is a natural arch and not a bridge, as it was formed not by a river but by the same natural forces (of wind, rain, and ice) that created the park's hoodoos.

Agua Canyon
This overlook features some of the most delicate and beautiful of the park's formations, as well as a good view of the layered pink sandstone cliffs typical of the Paunsaugunt Plateau.

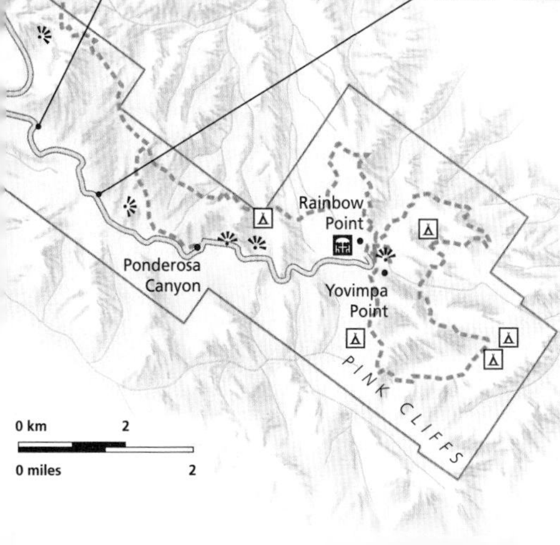

Utah Prairie Dog
Now threatened, the Utah prairie dog lives only in southern Utah; those living in the park today constitute the largest remaining group.

Arizona

Often referred to as the Grand Canyon State after its most famous sight, Arizona offers a range of stunning natural beauty. Its southwest corner features the hostile but eerily beautiful Sonoran Desert, bordered by the state's economic hub, Phoenix, and the city of Tucson. To the north, the landscape changes, rising through high desert plateaus, toward canyons and mountains, the romanticized "Wild West" of cowboy films. Here, the city of Flagstaff and the picturesque towns of Sedona and Jerome attract thousands of visitors. Over 25 percent of Arizona is Native American reservation land. The state also houses several Ancient Puebloan ruins.

London Bridge spanning a man-made waterway in Lake Havasu City

Lake Havasu City 21

45,000. 314 London Bridge Rd, (928) 453-3444. **www**.golakehavasu.com

California businessman Robert McCulloch founded Lake Havasu City in 1964. The resort city he built on the Colorado River was popular with the landlocked citizens of Arizona. His real brainwave, however, came four years later when he bought London Bridge and painstakingly transported it stone-by-stone from England to Lake Havasu. Some mocked McCulloch, suggesting that he had thought he was buying London's Gothic Tower Bridge, not this more ordinary one. There was more hilarity when it appeared that there was nothing in Havasu City for the bridge to span. Undaunted, McCulloch simply created the waterway he needed by digging a channel to divert water from Lake Havasu. The bridge and its adjoining mock-Tudor village complex have since become one of Arizona's most popular tourist attractions.

Flagstaff 22

58,000. Amtrak Flagstaff Station, 1 E Rte 66. Flagstaff bus station, 399 S Malpais Lane. Amtrak depot, 1 E Rte 66, (928) 774-9541. 8am–5pm daily. public hols. Flagstaff Festival of the Arts (early Jul–mid-Aug). **www**.flagstaff.org

Nestling among the pine forests of northern Arizona's San Francisco Peaks, Flagstaff is one of the region's most attractive towns. Its historic downtown, an attractive ensemble of red-brick buildings housing bars and restaurants, dates from the 1890s, when the town developed as a lumber center.

Flagstaff's lively café society owes much to the students of the **Northern Arizona University**, home to two campus art galleries. The Beasley Gallery holds temporary exhibitions and student work, while the Old Main Art Museum and Gallery has the permanent Weiss collection, which includes works by the Mexican artist Diego Rivera.

Situated on Mars Hill is the 1894 **Lowell Observatory**, named for its benefactor, Percival Lowell, a member of one of Boston's wealthiest families. Lowell wanted to look for life on Mars and although he did not succeed, the observatory earned repute with its documented evidence of an expanding universe, along with the discovery of Pluto by astronomer Clyde Tombaugh.

A few miles northwest of downtown, set picturesquely in a pine forest, is the **Museum of Northern Arizona**. It holds one of the Southwest's most comprehensive collections of Southwestern archaeological artifacts, as well as fine art and natural science exhibits. The museum presents an excellent overview of Anasazi history and contemporary Navajo, Hopi, and Pai cultures.

The collections are arranged in a series of galleries around a central courtyard. The Archaeology Gallery provides a fine introduction to the region's historic cultures. The award-winning anthropology exhibition in the Ethnology Gallery documents 12,000 years of Hopi, Zuni, Navajo, and Pai tribal cultures on the Colorado Plateau. The museum shop sells Native American arts and crafts. A section has exhibits that focus on the variety of plants and animals found on the Colorado Plateau through the ages.

Museum of Northern Arizona
3101 N Fort Valley Rd. ***Tel*** *(928) 774-5213. 9am–5pm daily. public hols.*
www.musnaz.org

Native American exhibits, Museum of Northern Arizona in Flagstaff

For hotels and restaurants in this region see pp557–9 and pp561–3

Heart of Arizona Tour ㉓

The Verde River passes through the wooded hills and fertile meadows of central Arizona, before opening into a wide, green valley between Flagstaff and Phoenix. The heart of Arizona is full of charming towns such as Sedona, hidden away among stunning scenery, and the former mining town of Jerome. Over the hills lies Prescott, once the state capital and now a busy, likable little town with a center full of dignified Victorian buildings. The area's ancient history can be seen in its two beautiful pueblo ruins, Montezuma Castle and Tuzigoot.

TIPS FOR DRIVERS

Recommended route: *From Sedona, take Hwy 89A to Tuzigoot, Jerome, & Prescott. Hwy 69 runs east from Prescott to Interstate Hwy 17, which connects to Camp Verde, Fort Verde, & Montezuma Castle.*
Tour length: *85 miles (137 km).*
When to go: *Spring & fall are delightful; summer is very hot.*

Sedona ①
Set among dramatic red rock hills, Sedona is a popular resort, known for its New Age stores and galleries as well as for its friendly ambience.

KEY

Tour route

Other road

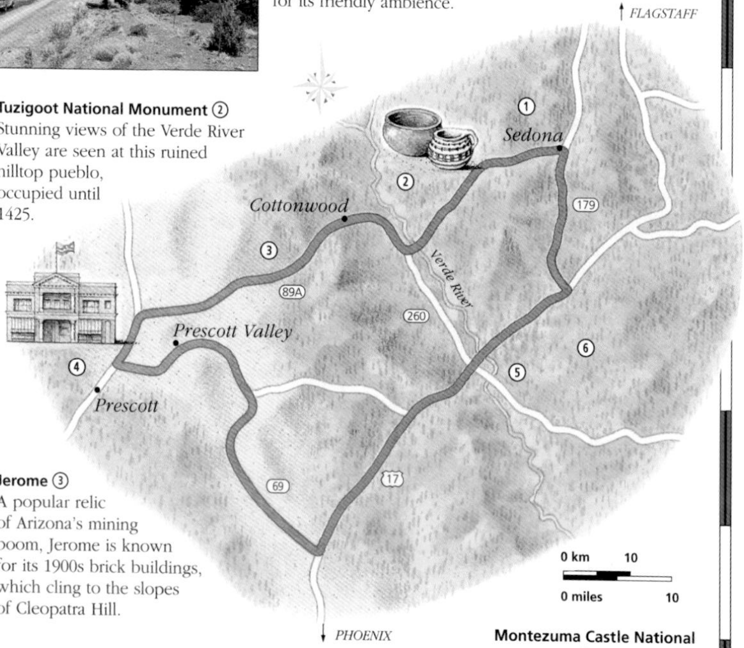

Tuzigoot National Monument ②
Stunning views of the Verde River Valley are seen at this ruined hilltop pueblo, occupied until 1425.

Jerome ③
A popular relic of Arizona's mining boom, Jerome is known for its 1900s brick buildings, which cling to the slopes of Cleopatra Hill.

Montezuma Castle National Monument ⑥
The Ancestral Puebloan ruins here date from the 1100s and occupy one of the loveliest sites in the Southwest.

Prescott ④
This cool hilltop town is set among the rugged peaks and lush woods of Prescott National Forest, making it a popular center for many outdoor activities.

Camp Verde ⑤
A highlight of this little town is Fort Verde. Built by the US Army in 1865, this stone fort is manned by costumed guides.

Phoenix ㉔

1,300,000 (city only). Greyhound Bus, 2115 E Buckeye Rd. 50 North 2nd St, (602) 254-6500. The PGA's Phoenix Golf Open (Jan).

Stretching across the entire Salt River Valley, Arizona's capital, Phoenix, started out as a farming town in the 1860s and soon developed into the economic hub of the state. As it grew, it gradually absorbed the surrounding towns of Scottsdale, Mesa, and Tempe, and now has over a million people within the city and almost three million in Metropolitan Phoenix. Downtown Phoenix has many historic attractions while the metropolitan area, famed for the design studio Taliesin West, is also popular with tourists for its spas and resorts during the warm winter months.

Exploring Downtown Phoenix

Downtown, where the city began in the 19th century, covers a few blocks east and west of Central Avenue and north and south of Washington Street. Washington Street houses the copper-domed **Arizona State Capitol Museum**, originally the state legislature. Among the exhibits are a series of sepia photographs documenting the city's political history. To its west is the **Arizona Mining and Mineral Museum** that traces Arizona's colorful mining history, which made millionaires of some and destitutes of many. Exhibits include photographs, historic tools, and quarried rocks.

More glimpses of the city's history can be seen in the attractive restored Victorian houses on the tree-lined **Heritage Square**, some of which have been converted into tearooms and small museums. Visitors can get a better impression of the city's early history at the inventive **Phoenix Museum of History** across the street. It features unusual artifacts, such as a steam-powered bicycle, and re-creates the city's first jail.

Cash register at the Museum of History

In between these historic attractions stands the ultra-modern **Arizona Science Center**, with over 300 interactive science exhibits offering virtual reality trips through the human body.

A short drive north of downtown leads to the highly acclaimed **Phoenix Art Museum**, renowned for its stimulating temporary exhibitions. The museum's second floor houses works by 18th- and 19th-century American artists, particularly those painters connected with the Southwest. Among the exhibits are works by Georgia O'Keeffe and Gilbert Stewart, whose celebrated *Portrait of George Washington* (1796) is seen on every dollar bill.

The **Heard Museum**, farther north, was founded in 1929 by Dwight Heard, a wealthy rancher and newspaper tycoon, whose wife, Maie, amassed an extraordinary collection of Native Southwestern American art. The museum exhibits over 30,000 works, but its star attraction is the display of more than 500 *kachina* dolls. Apart from dolls, there's an award-winning display of Native American pottery, jewelry, and textiles called Home: Native Peoples In The Southwest. Other interesting galleries are the Sandra Day O'Connor Gallery, which documents the museum's history and showcases the Heard family's early collection, and the Freeman Gallery, with its interactive hands-on display, which shows how artists interpret their environment through art.

Heard Museum
2301 North Central Ave. ***Tel*** *(602) 252-8840.* *(602) 252-8848.*
9:30am–5pm Mon–Sat, 11am–5pm Sun. *public hols.*
www.heard.org

The 1900 façade of the Arizona State Capitol Building, Phoenix

Environs

About 12 miles (19 km) northeast of downtown lies the former town of **Scottsdale**, founded in the late 19th century. Replete with air-conditioned malls, designer stores, hotels, cafés, and restaurants, it is also famous for its world-class golf courses. Scottsdale's quiet, tree-lined streets and desert setting attracted the visionary architect Frank Lloyd Wright *(see p396)* to establish his winter studio **Taliesin West** here in 1937. The 600-acre (240-ha) complex is now an architecture school and a working design studio. The muted tones of its low-lying buildings and use of local stone for irregular walls reflects Wright's enthusiasm for the desert setting.

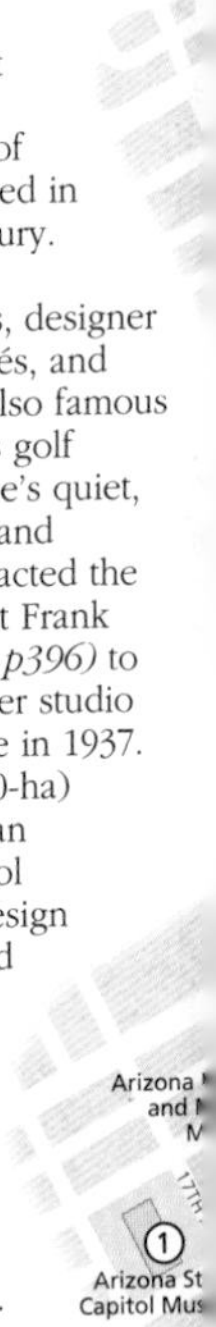

The **Cosanti Foundation**, 4 miles (6 km) west of Taliesin West, was established by the Italian architect and student of Wright, Paolo Soleri (b.1919), to further his

Taliesin West façade, designed to blend with the desert landscape

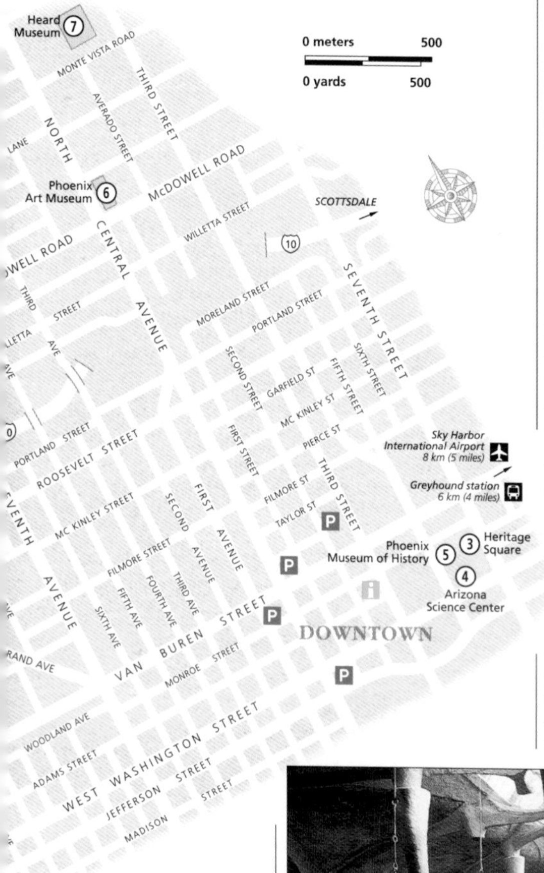

study of what he termed "arcology": a combination of architecture and ecology to create new urban habitats. Today, the site consists of simple, low structures housing studios, a gallery, and craft workshops, where Soleri and his workers make and sell their trademark windbells and cast bronzes.

South of the Cosanti Foundation is the **Camelback Mountain**, named for its humped shape. One of Phoenix's most distinctive landmarks, the mountain is a granite and sandstone out-crop formed by prehistoric volcanic forces. A steep climb, covering 1,200 ft (366 m) in the space of just over a mile, leads to the summit.

More glimpses of the area's Native American past can be found at the **Pueblo Grande Museum.** Located next to the ruins of a 1,500-year-old Hohokam settlement it is dedicated to the study and understanding of the people who lived there from the 8th to the 14th centuries. Full-scale reproductions of original adobe Hohokam homes can be viewed along the museum trail, as well as some of the ancient artifacts such as cooking utensils and pottery. Many of these pieces come from the Archaeological Park, site of the settlement, originally excavated in 1887. The museum operates a varied program of educational workshops and activities, for both adults and children, to promote its mission of enhancing an understanding of the Hohokam culture.

SIGHTS AT A GLANCE

- Arizona State Capitol Museum ①
- Arizona Mining and Mineral Museum ②
- Heritage Square ③
- Arizona Science Center ④
- Phoenix Museum of History ⑤
- Phoenix Art Museum ⑥
- Heard Museum ⑦

Innovative design of the Cosanti Foundation gift shop, Scottsdale

Tucson 25

750,000. Amtrak Station, 400 E Toole Ave. Greyhound Lines, 2 S 4th Ave. 110 S Church Ave, (520) 624-1817, (800) 638-8350. *La Fiesta de los Vaqueros (late Feb); Tucson Folk Music Festival (May).* **www**.visittucson.org

The second largest city in Arizona, Tucson (pronounced too-sahn) is located on the northern boundary of the Sonoran Desert, in a basin surrounded by five mountain ranges. The town's Colonial past dates to the 1770s, when strong resistance from the local Tohono O'odham and Pima Native tribes forced the Spanish to move their regional fortress, or presidio, from nearby Tubac to Tucson.

The city's main sights are clustered around the University of Arizona campus and the historic downtown area. The **Barrio** and **El Presidio** historic districts are located here. El Presidio occupies the area where the original Spanish fortress was built. Today, many of the historic buildings have been converted into restaurants, shops, and offices. Five of El Presidio's oldest dwellings, including the J. Knox Corbett House, are located in the Historic Block. They form a part of the **Tucson Museum of Art**, with its excellent collection of pre-Columbian artifacts, and exhibitions of contemporary American and European work. Southeast of the museum, the Pima County Courthouse, built in 1927, is a fine example of Spanish Colonial Revival Style.

The **St. Augustine Cathedral**, with its imposing sandstone façade, is southwest of El Presidio. Begun in 1896, the cathedral is modeled after the Spanish Colonial style of the Cathedral of Querétaro in central Mexico. The Barrio Historic District, farther south, was once a business district. Today, its quiet streets are lined with brightly painted adobe houses. On nearby Main Street is the "wishing shrine" of El Tiradito, where a young man was killed as a consequence of a lovers' triangle. The locals believe that if a candle lit here burns through a night, their wishes will come true.

Stained-glass window in the Cathedral

The University of Arizona campus houses several museums. The most notable is the **Arizona State Museum**, renowned for its collections of artifacts covering 2,000 years of Native history. Beyond downtown, Metropolitan Tucson extends into the surrounding mountain ranges. **Mount Lemmon** (9,157 ft/2,790 m), the highest peak, is to the north, while to the west is one part of the Saguaro National Park (the other is to the east), where vistas of the tall saguaro cacti can be seen.

About 14 miles (22 km) west of the university, lies the fascinating **Arizona-Sonora Desert Museum**. Covering more than 21 acres (8.5 ha), it includes a botanical garden, zoo, and natural history museum with displays describing the history, geology, and flora and fauna of the Sonoran Desert.

Nearby is the **Old Tucson Studios**, a Wild West theme park originally built as a set for a Western movie in 1939. Some of Hollywood's most famous Westerns, such as *Gunfight at the OK Corral* (1957) and *Rio Bravo* (1958) were filmed here.

The Southwest's oldest and best preserved Mission church lies south of Tucson. The **San Xavier del Bac Mission**, completed in 1797 by Franciscan missionaries, is built of adobe brick and is considered the finest example of Spanish Colonial architecture in the US. Its highlights include an ornate Baroque façade decorated with carved figures of saints, a glorious painted ceiling, and a spectacular main altar.

San Xavier del Bac Mission
1950 W San Xavier Rd, 10 miles (16 km) S of Tucson on I-19. ***Tel*** *(520) 294-2624.* *8am–5pm daily.*

SOUTHWEST ARCHITECTURE

The Southwest has been witness to a range of architecture styles from Ancestral Puebloan adobe to Spanish Colonial, and 19th- and early 20th-century Mission and Pueblo Revival. Colonizers brought their own forms that mingled with the Native, creating a unique plethora of multicultural styles.

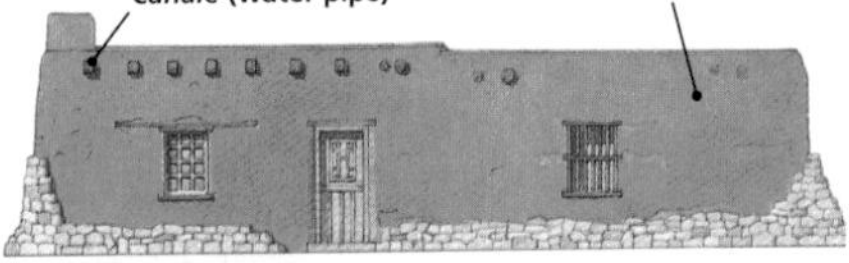

This adobe home *in El Rancho de las Golondrinas Museum in Santa Fe is made of adobe (sun-baked bricks that are a mixture of mud, sand, and straw), cemented with similar material, and replastered with mud.*

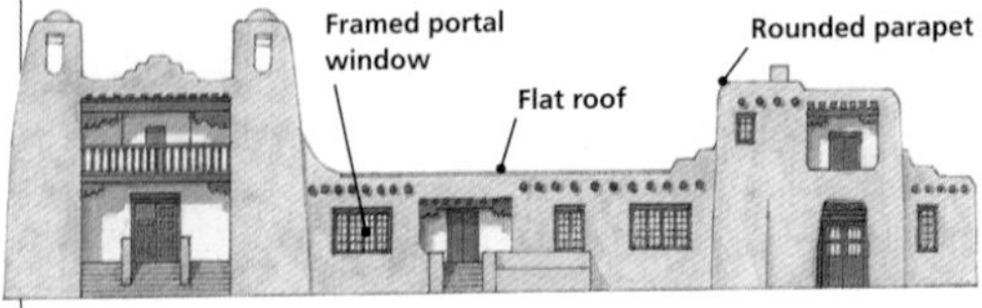

The Santa Fe Museum of Fine Arts *was the city's first building in Pueblo Revival style, with adobe walls, rounded parapets, framed portal windows, and pueblo-style multitiered stories.*

For hotels and restaurants in this region see pp557–9 and pp561–3

Statue of Virgin Mary at the San Xavier del Bac Mission, Tucson

Nogales 26

20,800. 123 W Kino Park, (520) 287-3685.

The birthplace of jazz star Charles Mingus, Nogales is really two towns that straddle the US border with Mexico. It is a busy port of entry, handling huge amounts of freight, including 75 percent of all winter fruit and vegetables sold in North America. The town attracts large numbers of visitors in search of bargains at shopping districts on both sides of the border. There is a profound contrast between the quiet, ordered streets of the US side, and the ramshackle houses and bustling, large-scale street market across the border. Visas are required only for visitors traveling beyond town limits. US citizens should carry a passport or birth certificate for identification, while foreign nationals should carry their passport and make sure that their visa status enables them to re-enter the US.

Mexican pottery from Nogales

Bisbee 27

6,500. Bisbee Chamber of Commerce, 1 Main St, (520) 432-5421.

The discovery of copper here in the 1880s sparked a mining rush, and by the turn of the century Bisbee was the largest city between St. Louis and San Francisco. Today, this is one of the Southwest's most atmospheric mining towns. Victorian buildings such as the landmark Copper Queen Hotel still dominate the historic town center, while attractive clusters of houses cling to the sides of the surrounding mountains. Visitors can tour the mines that once flourished here. The Bisbee Mining and Historical Museum illustrates the realities of mining and frontier life.

Environs

Some 25 miles (40 km) north of Bisbee is **Tombstone**, one of the wildest towns in the West. Founded by a prospector in 1877, its name derives from the warning he received that "all you'll find out there is your tombstone." Instead, the silver he found led to a silver rush. Today, Tombstone is a living legend, famous as the site of the 1881 gunfight at OK Corral between the Earp brothers and the Clanton gang. The OK Corral is now a museum, where the infamous gunfight is re-enacted. The old seat of justice, Tombstone Courthouse, is a historic site.

Amerind Foundation 28

***Tel** (520) 586-3666.*
10am–4pm Tue–Sun.
Mon; public hols.
www.amerind.org

The Amerind Foundation is one of the country's most important private archaeological and ethnological museums. The name Amerind is a contraction of "American Indian," and this collection depicts all aspects of Native American life through thousands of artifacts of different cultures. The displays include Inuit masks, Cree tools, and sculpted effigy figures from Mexico's Casas Grandes.

The adjacent Amerind Art Gallery has a fine collection of Western art by such artists as William Leigh and Frederic Remington. The delightful pink buildings, designed in the Spanish Colonial Revival style, are also interesting.

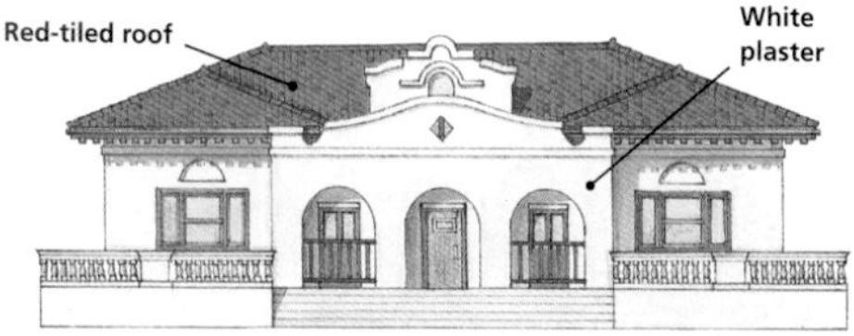

J. Knox Corbett House *in Tucson was designed in the 20th-century Mission Revival style by the Chicago architect David Holmes in 1906. It is characterized by white stucco walls, flat roofs, courtyards, and minimal ornamentation.*

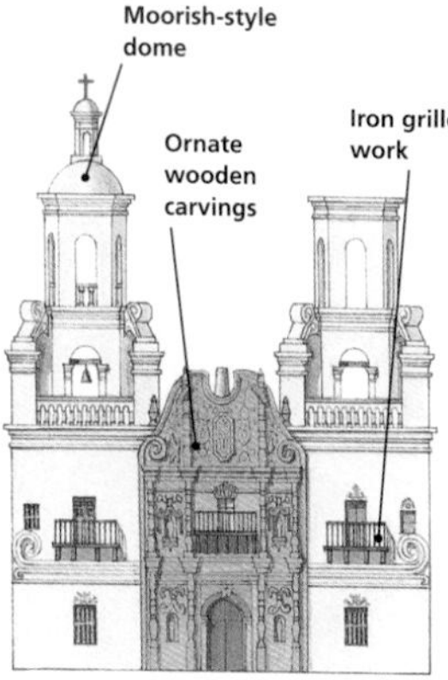

San Xavier del Bac Mission *is a fine example of the Baroque tradition of Spanish Colonial churches. The style saw a resurgence in the 20th century as Spanish Colonial Revival, with red-tiled roofs, ornamental terra-cotta, iron grille work, and white walls.*

Petrified Forest National Park ㉙

Off I-40. **Tel** *(928) 524-6228.* *8am–5pm daily.* *Dec 25.* *partial.*
www.nps.gov/pefo

This fossilized Prehistoric forest is one of Arizona's most unusual attractions. Millions of years ago, rivers swept trees downstream into a vast swamp that once covered this whole area. Groundwater transported silica dioxide into downed timber, eventually turning it into the quartz stone logs seen today, with colored crystals preserving the shape and structure of the trees.

Running the entire length of the forest is the famous Painted Desert. This is an area of colored bands of sand and rock that change from blues to reds throughout the day as the shifting light catches the different mineral deposits.

A 28-mile (45-km) scenic road starting at the visitor center travels the length of the park. There are nine overlooks along the way, including Kachina Point, where the Painted Wilderness trailhead is located. A permit is required to camp in the wilderness area. Near the south end of the road is the fine **Rainbow Forest Museum**.

Rainbow Forest Museum
Off Hwy 180 (S entrance). **Tel** *(928) 524-6822.* *8am–5pm daily.*

Eroded sandstone opening of Window Rock, near Highway 12

Window Rock ㉚

4,500. *Hwy 264, (928) 871-6436.*

Window Rock is the capital of the Navajo Nation, the largest Native American reservation in the Southwest. The town is named for the natural arch found in the sandstone cliffs located about a mile north of the main strip on Highway 12.

The **Navajo Nation Museum** located in Window Rock is one of the largest Native American museums in the country. Opened in 1997, the huge *hogan*-shaped building houses displays that cover the history of the Ancestral Puebloans and the Navajo.

Navajo Nation Museum
Hwy 264 & Post Office Loop Rd, *(928) 871-7941.* *8am–5pm Mon, 8am–8pm Tue–Fri, 9am–5pm Sat.* *Sun.*

Hopi Indian Reservation ㉛

10,000. *Hwy 264, Second Mesa, (928) 734-2401.* *Mar–Oct: 6am–9pm daily; Oct–Feb: 7am–8pm daily.* *Jan 1, Thanksgiving, Dec 25.*

Believed to be direct descendants of the Ancestral Puebloans, the Hopi Indians have lived in and cultivated this harsh and barren reservation area for almost a thousand years. They worship through the *kachina*, the living spirits of plants and animals, believed to visit the tribe during the growing season. Most Hopi villages are located on or near one of three mesas (flat-topped elevations), named First, Second, and Third Mesa. Artisans of each mesa specialize in particular crafts.

Visitors can take a guided walking tour of the impressive pueblo, **Walpi**, on the

Historic pueblo town of Walpi on First Mesa at the Hopi Indian Reservation

Ancestral Puebloan ruins of Keet Seel at the Navajo National Monument

First Mesa. Inhabited in the 12th century, it was built to be easily defended against possible Spanish or Navajo attacks. It straddles a dramatic knife-edge of rock, extending from the tip of the First Mesa. In places, Walpi is less than 100 ft (33m) wide with a drop of several hundred feet on both sides. The Walpi tour includes several stops where visitors can purchase *kachina* figurines, distinctive hand-crafted pottery, rugs, and baskets, or sample the Hopi *piki* bread. A wider range of Hopi arts and crafts are available in the galleries and stores of the Second Mesa. The Hopi Cultural Center here has a restaurant and the only hotel for miles around, as well as a museum that has an excellent collection of photographs depicting various aspects of Hopi life.

Kachina doll

On the Third Mesa, Old Oraibi pueblo, thought to have been founded in the 12th century, is fascinating because of claims that it is the oldest continually occupied human settlement in North America.

Walpi
(928) 737-2262.
Walking Tours *9:30am–3pm daily.*

Tuba City 32

17,300. Tuba City Trading Post, (928) 283-5441.

Named for Tuuvi, a Hopi Indian who converted to the Mormon faith, Tuba City is best known for the 65-million-year-old dinosaur tracks found just off the main highway, 5 miles (8 km) southwest of the town. This is also the largest community in the western section of the Navajo Reservation and is a good spot from which to explore both the Navajo National Monument and the Hopi Reservation.

Grand Canyon 33

See pp536–9.

Navajo National Monument 34

Tel *(928) 672-2700. 8am–5pm daily (extended summer hours). Jan 1, Thanksgiving, Dec 25. free.*
www.nps.gov/nava

Although named because of its location on the Navajo Reservation, this monument is actually known for its Ancestral Puebloan ruins. The most accessible ruin here is the beautifully preserved, 135-room pueblo of Betatakin, which fills a vast, curved niche in the cliffs of Tsegi Canyon. An easy, 1-mile (1.6-km) trail from the visitor center leads to an overlook, which provides a captivating view of Betatakin. For a closer look at these ancient houses, visitors can take the strenuous five-hour hiking tours held daily from late May to early September.

A more demanding 17-mile (27-km) hike leads to **Keet Seel**, a more impressive ruin. Only a limited number of permits to visit the ruin are issued each day. This hike requires overnight camping at a campsite with the most basic facilities. Keet Seel was a larger and more successful community than Betatakin. Construction began here in about 1250, but the site is thought to have been abandoned by 1300.

The Keet Seel ruins at the Navajo National Monument

Grand Canyon ㉝

One of the world's great natural wonders, the Grand Canyon is an instantly recognizable symbol of the Southwest. Running through Grand Canyon National Park *(see pp538–9)*, it is 217 miles (349 km) long, about 4 to 18 miles (6 to 29 km) wide, and over 5,000 ft (1,500 m) deep. It was formed over a period of six million years by the Colorado River, whose fast-flowing waters sliced their way through the Colorado Plateau, which includes the gorge, most of northern Arizona, and the Four Corners region. The plateau's geological vagaries have defined the river's course, and exposed vast cliffs are ringed by rocks of different color, variegated hues of limestone, sandstone, and shale. By any standard, the canyon, with its vast scale, is spectacular. But its special beauty is in the ever-shifting patterns of light and shadow and the colors of the rock, bleached white at midday, but bathed in red and ocher at sunset.

Mule Trip Convoy
A mule ride is a popular method of exploring the canyon's narrow trails.

Havasu Canyon
Since 1300 Havasu Canyon has been home to the Havasupai Indians. A population of around 500 Indians lives on the Havasupai Reservation, making a living from the tourist trade.

Grandview Point
At 7,400 ft (2,250 m), this is one of the highest places on the South Rim, the canyon's southern edge. It is one of the stops along the breathtaking Desert View Drive (see p538). *The point is thought to be the spot from where the Spaniards had their first glimpse of the canyon in 1540.*

North Rim

The North Rim receives roughly one-tenth the number of visitors of the South Rim. While less accessible, it is a more peaceful destination offering a sense of unexplored wilderness. Hikes include the North Kaibab Trail, a steep descent down to Phantom Ranch, the only lodge on the canyon floor.

VISITORS' CHECKLIST

Canyon View Information Plaza, S of Mather Point, Arizona, (928) 638-7888.
Grand Canyon Airport, Tusayan. Grand Canyon Railway from Williams daily.
From Flagstaff & Williams.
South Rim: year-round: daily. North Rim: summer only.
North Rim: late Nov–mid-May: closed because of snow.
partial.
www.nps.gov/grca

Bright Angel Trail

Used by both Native Americans and early settlers, the Bright Angel Trail follows a natural route along one of the canyon's enormous fault lines. It is an appealing option for day-hikers; unlike some other trails in the area, it offers plenty of shade and several seasonal water sources.

YAVAPAI POINT AT THE SOUTH RIM

Situated 5 miles (8 km) north of the canyon's South Entrance, along a stretch of the Rim Trail, is Yavapai Point. Its observation station offers superb views, and a viewing panel identifies several of the central canyon's landmarks.

HOW THE CANYON WAS FORMED

While the Colorado River, which changed course four million years ago, accounts for the canyon's depth, its width and formations are the work of even greater forces. Wind rushing through the canyon erodes the limestone and sandstone a few grains at a time, and rain pouring over the rim cuts deep side canyons through the softer rock. Perhaps the greatest force is ice. Water from rain and snowmelt works into cracks in the rock. When frozen, it expands, forcing the rock away from the canyon walls. Soft layers erode quickly into sloped faces, while harder rock resists erosion, leaving sheer vertical faces.

Cracks formed by water erosion

Exploring Grand Canyon National Park

Bell near Hermits Rest

A World Heritage Site, Grand Canyon National Park covers 1,904 sq miles (4,930 sq km), and consists of the canyon itself, which starts where the Paria River empties into the Colorado, and stretches from Lees Ferry to Lake Mead *(see p515)*. The park has two main entrances, on the North and South Rims of the canyon. Its main roads, Hermit Road and Desert View Drive, both accessible from the south entrance, overlook the canyon. Visitors can also enter the park from the north, although this route (Hwy 67) is closed during winter. Walking trails along the North and South Rims offer staggering views but to experience the canyon at its most fascinating, the trails that head down toward the canyon floor should be explored. The Bright Angel Trail on the South Rim and the North Kaibab Trail on the North Rim descend to the canyon floor and are tough hikes involving an overnight stop.

Adobe, Pueblo-style architecture of Hopi House, Grand Canyon Village

Grand Canyon Village

Grand Canyon National Park.
Tel *(928) 638-7888.* *partial.*

Grand Canyon Village has its roots in the late 19th century. The extensive building of visitor accommodations started after the Santa Fe Railroad opened a branch line here from Williams in 1901, although some hotels had been built in the late 1890s. The Fred Harvey Company constructed a clutch of well-designed, attractive buildings. The most prominent is the El Tovar Hotel *(see p562)*. Opened in 1905, it is named after Spanish explorers who reached the gorge in 1540. The Hopi House also opened in 1905 – a rendition of a traditional Hopi dwelling, where locals could sell their craftwork as souvenirs. It was built by Hopi craftsmen and designed by Mary E.J. Colter, an ex-schoolteacher and architect, who drew on Southwestern influences, mixing both Native American and Hispanic styles. She is responsible for many of the historic structures that now grace the South Rim, including the 1914 Lookout Studio and Hermits Rest, and the rustic 1922 Phantom Ranch *(see p562)* on the canyon floor.

Today, Grand Canyon Village has a wide range of hotels, restaurants, and stores. It can be surprisingly easy to get lost here since the buildings are spread out and discreetly placed among wooded areas. The village is the starting point for most of the mule trips through the canyon. It is also the terminus for the Grand Canyon Railway, restored steam trains that make the 64-mile (103-km) journey from Williams.

The South Rim

Most of the Grand Canyon's 4.4 million annual visitors come to the South Rim, since, unlike the North Rim, it is open year-round and is easily accessible along Highway 180/64 from Flagstaff *(see p528)* or Williams. **Hermit Road** and **Desert View Drive** (Hwy 64) start at Grand Canyon Village and include some of the best views of the gorge. Hermit Drive is closed to private vehicles from March to November, but there are free shuttle buses, and Desert View Drive is open all year.

From the village, Hermit Road meanders along the South Rim, extending for 8 miles (13 km). Its first viewpoint is **Trailview Overlook**, which provides an overview of the canyon and the winding course of the Bright Angel Trail. Moving on, **Maricopa Point** offers especially panoramic views of the canyon but not of the Colorado River, which is more apparent from nearby **Hopi Point**. At the end of Hermit Road lies **Hermits Rest**, where a gift shop, decorated in rustic style, is located in yet another Mary Colter-designed building. The longer Desert View Drive runs in the opposite direction, and covers 26 miles (42 km). It winds for 12 miles (20 km) before reaching **Grandview Point**, where the Spaniards may have had their first glimpse of the canyon in 1540.

The interior of the Hermits Rest gift store with crafts for sale lining the walls

For hotels and restaurants in this region see pp557–9 and pp561–3

Desert View's stone Watchtower on Desert View Drive

CALIFORNIA CONDORS

America's largest bird, the California condor, has a wingspan of over 9 ft (2.7 m). Nearly extinct in the 1980s, the last 22 condors were captured for breeding in captivity. In 1996, the first captive-bred birds were released in Northern Arizona. Today, about 50 condors fly the skies over Northern Arizona. They are frequent visitors to the South Rim, though visitors should not approach or attempt to feed them.

A pair of California condors

Ten miles (16 km) farther on lie the pueblo remains of Tusayan Ruin, where there is a small museum with exhibits on Ancestral Puebloan life. The road finally ends at the stunning overlook of **Desert View**. The Watchtower here was Colter's most fanciful creation, its upper floor decorated with early 20th-century Hopi murals.

Just east of Grand Canyon Village is **Yavapai Point** from where it is possible to see Phantom Ranch. This is the only roofed accommodation available on the canyon floor, across the Colorado River.

The North Rim

Standing at about 8,000 ft (2,400 m), the North Rim is higher, cooler, and greener than the South Rim, with dense forests of ponderosa pine, aspen, and Douglas fir. Visitors are most likely to spot wildlife on the North Rim. Mule deer, Kaibab squirrel, and wild turkey are among the most common sights. The North Rim is reached via Highway 67, off Highway 89A, ending at **Grand Canyon Lodge** *(see p558)* where there are visitor services, a campground, a gas station, restaurant, and a general store. Nearby there is a National Park Service information center, which offers maps of the area. The North Rim and all its facilities are closed between mid-October and mid-May, when it is often snowed in. The North Rim is twice as far from the river as the South Rim, and the canyon really stretches out from the overlooks giving a sense of its 10-mile (16-km) width. There are about 30 miles (45 km) of scenic roads along the North Rim as well as hiking trails to high viewpoints or down to the canyon floor (particularly the North Kaibab Trail that links to the South Rim's Bright Angel Trail).

The picturesque **Cape Royal Drive** starts north of Grand Canyon Lodge and travels 23 miles (37 km) to Cape Royal on the Walhalla Plateau. From here, several famous buttes and peaks can be seen, including Wotans Throne and Vishnu Temple. There are also several short, easy walking trails around Cape Royal, along the top. A 3-mile (5-km) detour leads to **Point Imperial**, the highest point on the canyon rim, while along the way the **Vista Encantada** has delightful views and picnic tables overlooking the gorge.

Mule deer on the canyon's North Rim

The Bright Angel Trail

This is the most popular of all Grand Canyon hiking trails. The Bright Angel trailhead is at Grand Canyon Village on the South Rim. The trail begins near the Kolb Studio at the western end of the village. It then switches dramatically down the side of the canyon for 9 miles (13 km). The trail crosses the river over a suspension bridge, ending a little farther on at Phantom Ranch. There are two rest-houses and a fully equipped campground along the way. It is not advisable to attempt the whole trip in one day. Many walk from the South Rim to one of the rest stops and then return up to the rim. Temperatures at the bottom of the canyon can reach 110°F (43°C) or higher during the summer. Day-hikers should therefore carry a quart (just under a liter) of water per person per hour for summer hiking. Carrying a first-aid kit is also recommended.

Hikers taking a break on the South Rim's Bright Angel Trail

Monument Valley ㉟

From scenic Highway 163, which crosses the border of Utah and Arizona, it is possible to see the famous buttes and mesas of Monument Valley. These ancient rocks, soaring upward from a seemingly boundless desert, have come to symbolize the American West, since they have been used as a backdrop for countless movies and TV shows.

The area's visitor center sits within the boundary of Monument Valley Tribal Park, but many of the valley's spectacular rock formations and other sites are found just outside the park boundary.

Guided Tours
A row of kiosks at the visitor center offer Navajo-guided 4WD tours of the valley. The marketing tactics can be aggressive, but the tours offer an excellent way to see places in the park that are otherwise inaccessible.

Three Sisters
One of several distinctive pinnacle rock formations at the valley, the closest view of the Three Sisters can be seen from John Ford's Point, and is one of the most photographed sights here.

Art & Ruins
Petroglyphs such as this deer can be seen on Navajo-guided tours of rock art sites, which are dotted around the valley's ancient ruins.

MONUMENT VALLEY
Monument Valley is not really a valley. The tops of the mesas mark what was once a flat plain. Millions of years ago, this plain was cracked by upheavals within the earth. The cracks widened and eroded, leaving the formations rising from the desert floor.

EXPLORING THE VALLEY
The awe-inspiring beauty of Monument Valley's buttes and mesas can be viewed by travelers from Highway 163. Visitors can also pay a fee to travel on a 17-mile (27-km) self-guided drive along a well-marked dirt road. (Fees are collected at the visitor center.) Alternatively, Navajo guides may be hired for hiking, horseback, or 4WD tours to fascinating and less-visited parts of the valley.

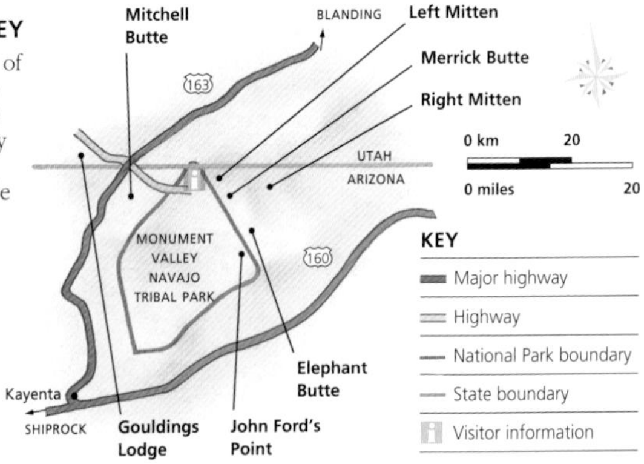

For hotels and restaurants in this region see pp557–9 and pp561–3

John Ford's Point

The most popular stop along the valley drive is John Ford's Point, which is said to be the film director's favorite view of the valley. Various stands offer a range of Navajo crafts. A nearby native hogan *(Navajo dwelling) serves as a gift shop where Navajo weavers demonstrate their craft.*

VISITORS' CHECKLIST

PO Box 360289, Monument Valley, (435) 727-5870.
sunrise–sunset daily.
Dec 25.
visitor center only.
www.navajonationparks.org

Navajo Weaver

Navajo women are usually considered to be the finest weavers in the Southwest. One rug can take months to complete and sell for thousands of dollars. Using the natural colors of the land, the weavers often add a "spirit line" to their work to prevent their spirit being "trapped" within the rug.

THE WILD WEST

Romanticized in cowboy movies, the "Wild West" conjures up images of tough men herding cattle across the country before living it up in a saloon. But frontier life was far from romantic. Settlers arriving in this wilderness were caught up in a first-come first-served battle for land and wealth, fighting Native Americans and each other for land. The rugged life of the mining prospectors and ranch cowboys helped to create the idea of the American West. Today, visitors can still see former mining towns such as Bisbee or enjoy re-enacted gunfights on the streets of Tombstone *(see p533)*, the site of one of the Wild West's most famous tales. In the late 19th-century, however, such survival skills as good shooting often co-existed with a kill-or-be-killed ethos. Guided trail rides, offered at many dude ranches, are a great way to explore the contemporary Wild West.

Guided trail rides, conducted to explore the Wild West

Canyon de Chelly National Monument 36

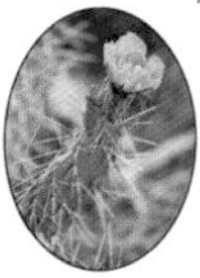

Flowering cactus

The awesome thousand-foot cliffs of the Canyon de Chelly boast of a long and eventful history of human habitation.. Archaeologists have found evidence of four periods of Native culture, starting with the Basketmaker people around AD 300, followed by the Great Pueblo Builders, who created the cliff dwellings in the 12th century. They were succeeded by the Hopi, who lived here seasonally for around 300 years, taking advantage of the canyon's fertile soil. Today, the canyon is the cultural and geographic heart of the Navajo Nation, where Navajo farmers still live tending the sheep, introduced by the Spanish, and women weave rugs at outdoor looms. Pronounced "d'Shay," de Chelly is a Spanish corruption of the Native name *tsegi*, meaning rock canyon.

Yucca House Ruin
Perched on the mesa top, this ruin of an Ancestral Puebloan house sits in a rock hollow, precariously overhanging a sheer drop to the valley floor.

Canyon Vegetation
Within the canyon, cottonwood and oak trees line the river washes; the land itself is a fertile oasis of meadows, alfalfa and corn fields, and fruit orchards.

Stone and adobe cliff dwellings were home to the Ancestral Puebloans from the 12th to the 14th centuries and were built to face south toward the sun, with cooler areas within.

Navajo Fortress
This imposing rock tower was the site of a three-month siege in 1863, when a group of Navajos reached the summit via pole ladders. They were trying to escape a US government patrol led by Kit Carson (see p544) *to settle the Navajo raids. Carson's persistence finally led them to surrender and they were marched to a camp in New Mexico.*

Hiking in the Canyon
Canyon de Chelly is a popular destination for hikers, but apart from the White House Ruins Trail, visitors can enter the canyons only with a Navajo guide.

VISITORS' CHECKLIST

2 miles (3.5 km) E of Chinle & Hwy 191. *PO Box 588, Chinle, (928) 674-5500.* *8am–5pm daily.* *Dec 25.* *guided tours are obligatory within the canyon except at the White House.*
www.nps.gov/cach

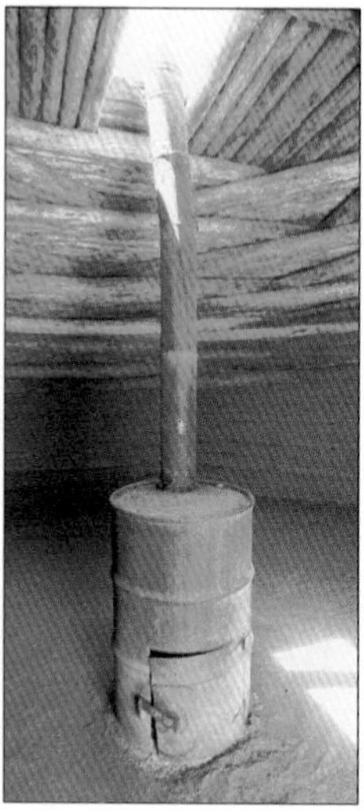

Hogan Interior
The hogan *is the center of Navajo family life. Made of horizontal logs, a smoke hole in the center provides contact with the sky, while the dirt floor gives contact with the earth. A door faces east to greet the rising sun.*

The pale walls of the White House cliff drop 550 ft (160 m) to the canyon floor.

WHITE HOUSE RUINS

This group of rooms, tucked into a tiny hollow in the cliff, seem barely touched by time. The dwellings were originally situated above a larger pueblo, much of which has now disappeared. It is the only site within the canyon that can be visited without a Navajo guide, reached via a steep 2.5-mile (5-km) round-trip trail that winds to the canyon floor and offers magnificent views.

MASSACRE CAVE

The canyon's darkest hour was in 1805, when a Spanish force under Lieutenant Antonio Narbona entered the area. The Spanish wanted to subdue the Navajo, claiming they were raiding their settlements. While some Navajo fled by climbing to the canyon rim, others took refuge in a cave high in the cliffs. The Spanish fired into the cave, and Narbona boasted that he had killed 115 Navajo including 90 warriors. Navajo accounts are different, claiming that most of the warriors were absent (probably hunting) and those killed were mostly women, children, and the elderly. The only Spanish fatality came when a Spaniard attempting to climb into the cave was attacked by a Navajo woman and both plunged over the cliff, gaining the Navajo name "Two Fell Over." The Anglo name is "Massacre Cave."

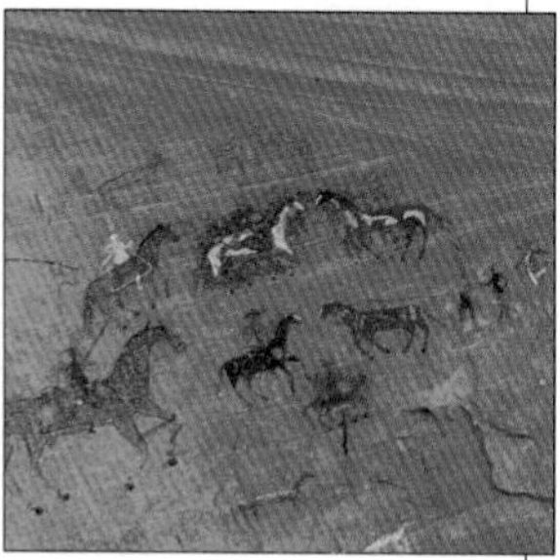

Pictograph on a canyon wall showing invading Spanish soldiers

New Mexico

New Mexico's rich cultural heritage and unique mix of Native American, Hispanic, and Anglo American people make it a fascinating place to visit. The forested peaks of the Rocky Mountains offer ski resorts in winter and cool retreats in summer. Northern New Mexico, with its soft colors and vivid desert landscapes, has attracted generations of artists to the creative centers of Santa Fe and Taos. In the vast, wild south visitors can explore ancient Native ruins at Bandelier National Monument and the fascinating cave systems of Carlsbad Caverns.

Fajada Butte in Chaco Culture National Historical Park

Chaco Culture National Historical Park ㊲

25 miles (5 km) SE of Nageezi off US 550. *(505) 786-7014.*
8am–5pm daily.
public hols.
www.nps.gov/chcu

One of the Southwest's most impressive cultural sites, Chaco Canyon reflects the sophistication of the Ancestral Puebloan civilization that existed here. With its six "great houses" (pueblos that contained hundreds of rooms) and many lesser sites, the canyon was once the political, religious, and cultural center for settlements that spread across much of the Four Corners.

Visitors can access the site via a 16-mile (26-km) dirt road that is affected by flash floods in wet weather. A paved loop road in the site passes several of Chaco's highlights. The major stop is **Pueblo Bonito**, the largest of the "great houses," a D-shaped, four-story structure with more than 600 rooms, and 40 *kivas*, round, pit-like rooms used for religious ceremonies. Begun around AD 850, it was built in stages over the course of 300 years. **Casa Riconada**, the largest religious chamber at Chaco, measuring 62 ft (19m) in diameter, lies to the southeast.

A short trail from Pueblo Bonito leads to another great house, **Chetro Ketl**, covering 3 acres (2 ha). The masonry used to build the later portions of this structure is among the most sophisticated found in any Ancestral Puebloan site. A two-hour hike northward leads to **Pueblo Alto**, built on top of the mesa at the junction of many ancient Chacoan roads.

Finely wrought stonework at Chaco Canyon

Taos ㊳

6,000. Greyhound, Taos Bus Center, Hwy 68.
1139 Paseo del Pueblo Sur (575) 751-8800, (800) 732-8267.
www.taoschamber.com

The city of Taos, home to Indians for around 1,000 years, is now a vibrant artistic center. In 1898, artists Ernest Blumenschein and Bert Phillips stopped here to repair a wagon wheel and never left. In 1915 they established the Taos Society of Artists, which continues to promote the work of local artists. Some of these are exhibited at the **Harwood Museum of Art**, located in a tranquil, 19th-century adobe compound. More works by the society's artists are housed in the **Blumenschein Home and Museum**, nearby.

The tree-lined, old Spanish **Plaza** at the heart of Taos makes for a pleasant stroll. To its east is the **Kit Carson Home and Museum**. A fur trapper and soldier, Carson's (1809–68) remarkable life is the focus of this museum.

A few miles north of the town center, Taos' main street, Paseo del Pueblo Norte, leads to the **Millicent Rogers Museum**, with its brilliant collection of Native arts and crafts, and black-on-black pottery of Puebloan artist Maria Martinez. This road leads to the dramatic Rio Grande Gorge Bridge, the country's second-highest suspension bridge, built in 1965. It offers awesome views of the gorge and the surrounding stark, sweeping plateau.

Taos Pueblo is north of the city. It features two multistory communal adobe houses still inhabited by villagers, making it one of the oldest communities in the country.

The Hacienda Martinez *(see p551)* at **Rancho de Taos**, south of the city, is a well-preserved Spanish Colonial house with thick adobe walls and heavy gates. The 18th-century adobe church of San Francisco de Asis was often painted by Georgia O'Keeffe, one of New Mexico's best known artists.

Northern Pueblos Tour ㊴

Redware pottery

The fertile valley of the Rio Grande between Santa Fe and Taos is home to eight pueblos of the 19 Native American pueblos in New Mexico. Although geographically close, each pueblo has its own government and traditions, and many offer attractions to visitors. Nambe gives stunning views of the surrounding mountains, mesas, and high desert. San Idelfonso is famous for its fine pottery, and other villages produce handcrafted jewelry or rugs.

TIPS FOR DRIVERS

Starting point: *Tesuque Pueblo, N of Santa Fe on Hwy 84.*
Length: *45 miles (70 km). Local roads leading to pueblos are often dirt tracks, so allow extra time.*
Note: *Visitors are welcome, but respect their laws & etiquette (see p554). Indian Pueblo Cultural Center, (505) 843-7270 (9am–5pm).* **www**.indianpueblo.org

Santa Clara Pueblo ⑤
This small pueblo is known for its artisans and their work. As in many pueblos, it contains a number of craft shops and small studios, often run by the Native artisans themselves.

Puye Cliff Dwellings ⑥
Now deserted, this site contains over 700 rooms, complete with stone carvings, which were home to Native peoples until 1500.

Ohkay Owingeh ⑦
Declared the first capital of New Mexico in 1598, this village, once known as San Juan Pueblo, is now a center for the visual arts.

San Ildefonso Pueblo ④
Occupied since AD 1300, this pueblo is best known for its etched black pottery, the proceeds of which saved its people from the Depression of the 1930s.

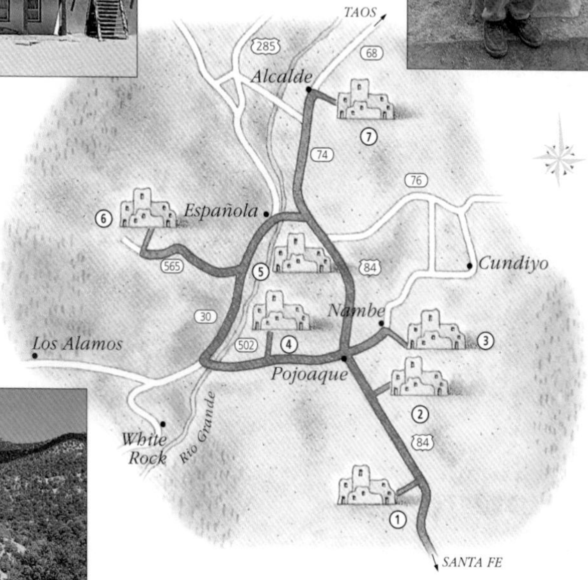

Nambe Pueblo ③
Set in a beautiful fertile valley, this village is bordered by a lakeside hiking trail with waterfall views and a buffalo ranch.

Pojoaque Pueblo ②
The new Peoh Cultural Center and Museum here is an excellent introduction to the pueblo way of life in these small communities.

Tesuque Pueblo ①
The Tewa people here have concentrated on farming and pottery-making for centuries.

0 km 10
0 miles 10

KEY

Tour route

Other road

Santa Fe ⓴

The oldest state capital in North America, Santa Fe was founded by the Spanish conquistador Don Pedro de Peralta, who established a colony here in 1610. This colony was abandoned in 1680 after the Pueblo Revolt, but was later recaptured. When Mexico gained independence in 1821, traders and settlers from Missouri poured into the area via the Santa Fe Trail. Perched on a high plateau, this beautiful city is surrounded by mountains. Its heart, since its founding, is the central Plaza, and there is no better place to begin exploring the city. Today, it houses a Native American market under the portal of the Palace of the Governors, and the square is lined with shops, cafés, and several galleries.

★ Museum of Fine Arts
Built of adobe in 1917, this museum focuses on the paintings and sculpture of Southwestern artists.

★ Palace of the Governors
This single-story adobe building, built in 1600, was the seat of regional government for 300 years. Now part of the Museum of New Mexico, it houses displays on the city's history.

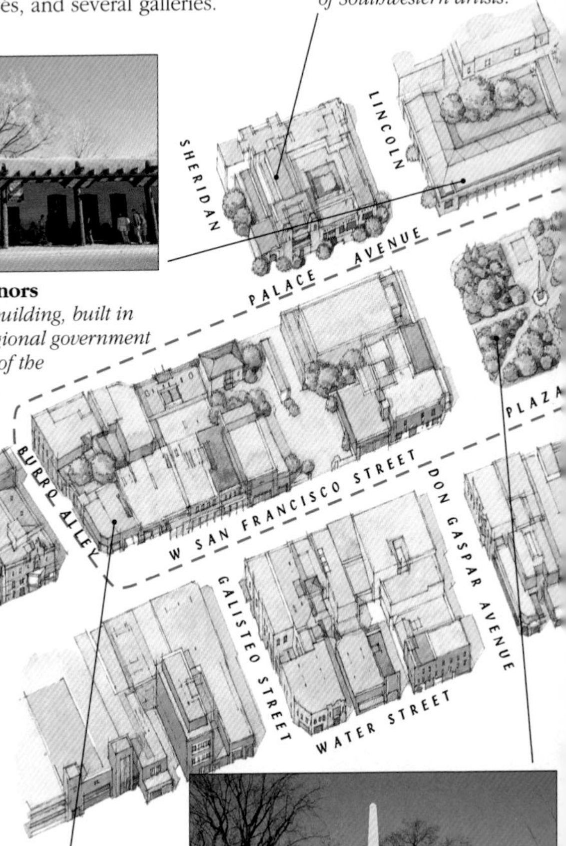

0 meters 100

0 yards 100

KEY

– – – Suggested route

STAR SIGHTS

★ Museum of Fine Arts

★ Palace of the Governors

Original Trading Post sells Hispanic art, antiques, and Native American crafts.

The Plaza
The obelisk at the center of this main square commemorates Santa Fe's war veterans. The Plaza is lined with old Colonial buildings, including the Palace of Governors.

For hotels and restaurants in this region see p559 and p563

Saint Francis Cathedral
This colorful, carved wooden statue of the Virgin stands in a side chapel belonging to the original 17th-century church on which the present cathedral was built in 1869.

VISITORS' CHECKLIST

65,000. *Santa Fe Municipal Airport, 10 miles (16 km) SW of Santa Fe.* *Lamy, 18 miles (29 km) S of city.* *858 St. Michael's Drive.* *60 E. San Francisco St, (505) 955-6200, (800) 777-2489.* *Spanish Market (Jul); Santa Fe Opera Season (Jul & Aug); Indian Market (Aug); Fiestas de Santa Fe (Sep).* **www**.santafe.org

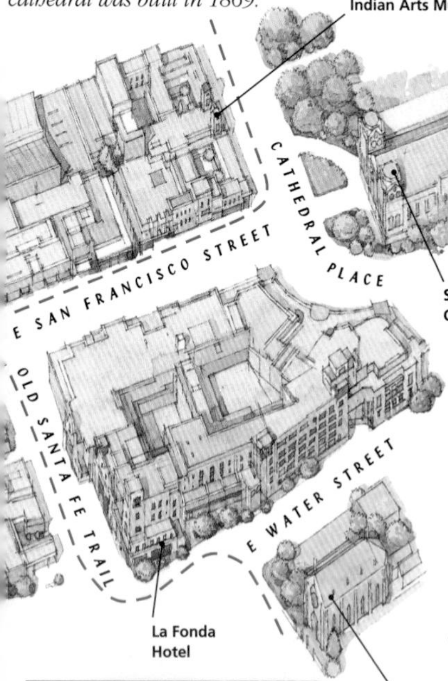

Loretto Chapel
Built in Gothic style by French architects in the 1870s, the Loretto Chapel was modeled on the Sainte-Chappelle in Paris. Its elegant spiral staircase has no nails or center support, and its perfect craftsmanship is all that keeps it aloft.

Exploring Santa Fe

This city's rich history and beautiful architecture have made it one of the country's most popular destinations. It is famous for its adobe buildings, art galleries, and the Museum of New Mexico's four museums. In addition to the Palace of the Governors and Museum of Fine Arts, there is the **Georgia O'Keeffe Museum**, northwest of the Plaza. This has the world's largest collection of O'Keeffe's works, including several of her best-loved paintings such as *Jimson Weed* (1932), *Purple Hills II*, and *Ghost Ranch, New Mexico* (1934).

Across the Santa Fe River is the fourth museum, the **Museum of International Folk Art**, with its stunning collection of folk art from all over the world. Alongside, on Museum Hill, the **Museum of Indian Art and Culture** is dedicated to traditional Native American arts and culture. Its main exhibit, "Here, Now and Always," tells the story of the region's oldest communities, in the words of Pueblo, Navajo, and Apache people.

Girard Collection toy, Museum of International Folk Art

Running parallel to the river, the gallery-lined **Canyon Road** was originally an Indian track between the Rio Grande and Pecos pueblo. To its west, on the Old Santa Fe Trail, is the **San Miguel Mission**, built in 1610. To the northwest, the 1795 **Santuario de Guadelupe**, dedicated to the Virgin of Guadelupe, patron saint of Mexican and Pueblo peoples, marked the end of Camino Real, the main trade route from Mexico. About 15 miles (24 km) south of Santa Fe, **El Rancho de las Golondrinas**, now a living history museum, was a historic stopping-off point on the Camino Real.

Museum of International Folk Art
706 Camino Lejo. ***Tel*** *(505) 476-1200.* *10am–5pm Tue–Sun.* *public hols.*

Albuquerque ❹❶

580,000. *401 2nd St NW, (505) 842-9918, (800) 284-2282.* **www**.itsatrip.com

Occupied by Native peoples from 1100 to 1300, the first inhabitants of Albuquerque were a small group of Colonial pioneers who settled by the Rio Grande in the wake of late 16th-century Spanish explorers. In 1706, a band of 18 families won formal approval for their town from the Spanish crown by naming the city after the Spanish Duke of Alburquerque, (the first "r" in the name was later dropped). Albuquerque's Old Town, today, still has many original adobe buildings dating from the 1790s, while downtown, to its east, is much more contemporary. Many of the city's shops, museums, and high-tech industries are located here.

Modern sculpture

Exploring Albuquerque

Dominating the historic Old Town is the Plaza, which was the center of Albuquerque for over 200 years. Today, this charming square is a pleasant open space where both locals and visitors relax on benches, surrounded by lovely adobe buildings. Opposite is the imposing **San Felipe de Neri Church**. Completed in 1793, this was the city's first civic structure. Despite many renovations, the church retains its original adobe walls. The nearby streets are lined with museums, colorful craft shops, and restaurants, such as the Church Street Café *(see p563)*. Said to occupy the oldest house in the city, this café serves excellent New Mexican cuisine. Beyond is a craft store, the Agape Pueblo Pottery, which stocks hand-crafted pueblo pottery.

Albuquerque BioPark

2601 Central Ave NW. ***Tel*** *(505) 764-6200.* *9am–5pm daily.* *Jan 1, Thanksgiving, Dec 25.* **www**.cabq.gov/biopark

The park encompasses the Albuquerque Aquarium and the Rio Grande Botanic Garden. The Rio Grande Zoological Park is located nearby. The botanic garden occupies 10 acres (4 ha) of woodland along the Rio Grande and has a wide variety of rare plants and gardens.

The aquarium focuses on the marine life of the Rio Grande, one of America's great rivers, and features a fascinating walk-through eel cave containing moray eels. There is also an impressive 285,000-gallon (1,078,842-liter), floor-to-ceiling shark tank.

San Felipe de Neri Church, at the north end of Old Town Plaza

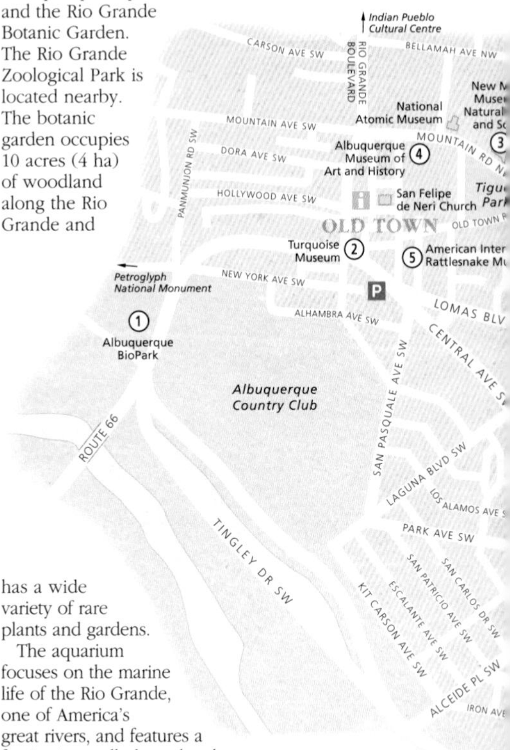

Turquoise Museum

2107 Central Ave NW. ***Tel*** *(505) 247-8650.* *9:30am–5pm Mon–Fri, 9:30am–4pm Sat.* *Thanksgiving, Dec 25.*

The fascinating displays in this museum focus on consumer education, helping visitors to judge the quality of turquoise gemstones. The entrance is a replica mine tunnel that leads to the "vault," which contains an unsurpassed collection of rare and varied turquoise specimens from around the world.

Glasshouse at Rio Grande Botanic Garden, Albuquerque BioPark

For hotels and restaurants in this region see p559 and p563

New Mexico Museum of Natural History and Science

1801 Mountain Rd NW. ***Tel*** *(505) 841-2800.* *9am–5pm daily.* *Jan & Sep: Mon, public hols.* **www**.nmnaturalhistory.org

This entertaining museum has a series of interactive exhibits. Visitors can stand inside a simulated live volcano or explore an ice cave. The "Evolator" is a ride through 38 million years of the region's evolution using the latest video technology. Replica dinosaurs, a state-of-the-art planetarium, and a large-screen film theater are all highly popular with children.

Albuquerque Museum of Art and History

2000 Mountain Rd NW. ***Tel*** *(505) 242-4600.* *9am–5pm Tue–Sun.* *public hols.* **www**.cabq.gov/museum

This excellent museum depicts four centuries of history in the middle of Rio Grande Valley. The well-chosen artifacts are expertly arranged for maximum impact. Exhibits focus on the Spanish Colonial period (1598–1821) and include a reconstructed 18th-century house and chapel. From March to December, the museum organizes walking tours of the Old Town.

Colorful tiles decorating the Art Deco-style façade of the KiMo Theater

American International Rattlesnake Museum

202 San Felipe Ave N. ***Tel*** *(505) 242-6569.* *10am–6pm Mon–Sat, 1–5pm Sun; winter: 11:30am–5.30pm Mon–Fri, 10am–6pm Sat, 1–5pm Sun.* *public hols.* **www**.rattlesnakes.com

This animal conservation museum explains the life cycles and ecological importance of some of Earth's most misunderstood creatures. It contains the world's largest collection of live rattlesnakes, including natives of North, Central, and South America. The snakes are displayed in glass tanks that simulate their natural habitat as closely as possible and are accompanied by explanatory notices suitable for both adults and children. The museum features other much-maligned venomous animals such as tarantulas and the Gila monster lizard.

KiMo Theater

423 Central Ave NW. ***Tel*** *(505) 768-3522.* *call for program.* **www**.cabq.gov/kimo

Built in 1927, the KiMo Theater was one of many entertainment venues constructed in the city during the 1920s and 30s. The building's distinctive design was inspired by that of the nearby Native American pueblos and created a fusion of Pueblo Revival and Art Deco styles. Today, the KiMo Theater presents an eclectic range of musical and theatrical performances.

Rio Grande Zoological Park

903 10th St SW ***Tel*** *(505) 764-6200.* *9am–5pm daily (to 6pm Sat–Sun in summer).* *Thnksg, Dec 25.*

The Rio Grande Zoo forms part of the Albuquerque BioPark. The zoo is noted for its imaginative layout with enclosures designed to simulate the animals' natural habitats, including the African savanna. Among the most popular species here are lowland gorillas and white Bengal tigers.

Key to Symbols *see back flap*

SIGHTS AT A GLANCE

Albuquerque BioPark ①
Turquoise Museum ②
New Mexico Museum of Natural History and Science ③
Albuquerque Museum of Art and History ④
American International Rattlesnake Museum ⑤
KiMo Theater ⑥
Rio Grande Zoological Park ⑦

Indian Pueblo Cultural Center courtyard

Albuquerque: Farther Afield

New Mexico's largest city, Albuquerque, has grown to fill the valley that stretches westward from the foothills of the Manzano and Sandia Mountains and across the banks of the Rio Grande. The coming of the railroad during the 1880s brought increasing numbers of settlers and greater prosperity. Today, the best way to explore the city is by car. The major sights, including the historic Old Town *(see p548)*, are all located near highway exits.

Indian Pueblo Cultural Center

2401 12th St NW. ***Tel*** *(866) 855-7902.* *9am–5pm daily.* *Jan 1, Thanksgiving, Dec 25.* **www**.indianpueblo.org

This impressive museum and cultural center is run by the 19 Indian pueblos that lie along the Rio Grande around Albuquerque and Santa Fe. It traces the Puebloan peoples' complex history and varied culture through their oral history and presents it from their viewpoint.

The building is designed to resemble the layout of a pueblo dwelling, and is set around the Puebloan Central Courtyard. This large courtyard, with its red adobe walls decorated with murals and hung chilies, emulates the layout of a Pueblo dwelling. Each weekend exuberant dance performances are held. The center also has a restaurant serving Pueblo Indian cooking, and an excellent group of gift shops offering high-quality pottery, jewelry, and other crafts.

University of New Mexico & Art Museum

Welcome Center, Central & Cornell, (505) 277-1989. **www**.unm.edu **University Art Museum *Tel*** *(505) 277-4001.* *9am–4pm Tue–Fri, 5–8pm Tue, 1–4pm Sun.* *Mon, Sat, University holidays.* **Maxwell Museum of Anthropology *Tel*** *(505) 277-4405.* *9am–4pm Tue–Fri, 10am–4pm Sat.* *Mon, Sun.*

The campus of New Mexico's largest university (UNM) is known for its Pueblo Revival-style architecture and its museums. The **University Art Museum** has one of the state's largest fine arts collection, including paintings and sculpture by Old Masters, and other works from the 17th to the 20th centuries.

The **Maxwell Museum of Anthropology**, one of the finest of its kind in the US, emphasizes the culture of the Southwest, with an important collection of art and artifacts. The museum also has traveling exhibits on regional and international themes, as well as a permanent exhibition entitled "Ancestors," which traces human development.

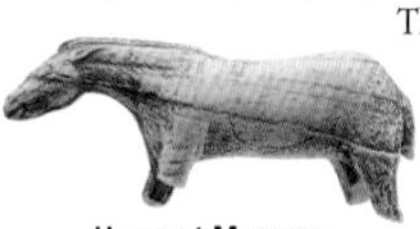

Horse at Museum of Anthropology, UNM

Anderson-Abruzzo International Balloon Museum

9201 Balloon Museum Dr NE. ***Tel*** *(505) 880-0500.* *9am–5pm Tue–Sun.* **www**.balloonmuseum.com

Named after pioneering Albuquerque balloonists Maxie Anderson and Ben Abruzzo, the museum highlights the history of ballooning. Colorful balloons and gondolas hang from the ceiling, while exhibits showcase historic gondolas and wicker baskets related to scientific and record-setting flights. Displays of memorabilia feature key events in ballooning history.

National Museum of Nuclear Science & History

601 Eubank Blvd SE. ***Tel*** *(505) 245-2137.* *9am–5pm daily.* *Jan 1, Easter, Thanksgiving, Dec 25.* **www**.nuclearmuseum.org

Inside this museum, exhibits and displays tell the story of the Atomic Age and nuclear science, including the history of nuclear development, weapons, and atomic energy, as well as today's peaceful uses of nuclear technology. Outside, the Heritage Park displays aircraft, missiles, railcars, and nuclear submarines.

Petroglyph National Monument

4735 Unser Blvd NW, (505) 899-0205. *8am–5pm daily.* *public hols.* *limited.* **www**.nps.gov/petr

This site, on the western outskirts of Albuquerque, was established in 1990 to preserve nearly 20,000 images carved into rock along the 17-mile (27-km) West Mesa escarpment. The earliest date back to 1,000 BC, but the most prolific period is thought to be between 1300 and 1680. The pictures range from human figures such as musicians and dancers to animals, including snakes, birds, and insects. Spirals and other geometric symbols are common, as are hands, feet, and animal tracks. The meanings of some petroglyphs have been lost over time, but others have great cultural significance to today's Puebloan population.

Hundreds of petroglyphs are accessible along Boca Negra Canyon, 2 miles (3 km) north of the park visitor center, where three trails wind past them. Visitors should not touch the petroglyphs; they are easily damaged.

Hispanic Culture in New Mexico

The heart of Hispanic culture in the Southwest is found in New Mexico. Here, the Hispanic population, descendants of the original Spanish colonizers of the 16th century, outnumbers that of the Anglo-Americans. The Spanish introduced sheep and horses to the region, as well as bringing Catholicism with its saints' festivals and colorful church decorations. Centuries of mixing with both the Southwest's Native and Anglo cultures have also influenced every aspect of modern Hispanic society, from language and cooking to festivals and the arts. Contemporary New Mexican residents bear the Hispanic surnames of their ancestors, and speak English with a Spanish accent. Even English speakers pepper their speech with Spanish terms.

Chili *ristras*, garlands of dried red chilies

SPANISH INFLUENCE
The restored El Rancho de las Golondrinas *(see p547)* is today a living museum, centered on the hacienda, pioneered in the Southwest by Spanish colonists. In a hacienda, a large number of rooms (approximately 20) would be set around one or two courtyards, reflecting the extended family style of living favored by the Spanish.

Wells were located in the middle of the main courtyard to be easily accessible.

Adobe beehive ovens *(hornos)* were introduced by the Spanish for baking bread. They were originally of Moorish design.

Hacienda Martínez (see p544) *was built south of Taos in 1804 by Don Antonio Martínez, an early mayor of the town. It is one of the few Spanish haciendas to be preserved in more or less its original form. Today, it is open to visitors who can watch local artisans demonstrating a variety of traditional folk arts.*

Navajo rug

Carved wooden *bulto* of St. Joseph

CRAFTS
Navajo rugs are considered a Native handicraft, but their designs also show signs of Moorish patterns brought by colonizers from Spain. Other folk art forms include artistic pottery, intricate silverwork, and carved wooden figures known as *bultos*, which combine religious beliefs and artistic expression.

Corn, *the region's staple food since pre-Columbian times, is used to make tortilla chips, which are served with guacamole (avocado dip).*

Roswell 42

50,000. 426 N Main St, (575) 623-5695. 8:30am–5:30pm Mon–Fri, 10am–3pm Sat & Sun. **www**.roswellnm.com

This small ranching town is a byword for aliens and UFOs since the night of July 4, 1947, when an unidentified airborne object crashlanded here. Jim Ragsdale, camping nearby, later claimed in 1995 to have seen a flash and a craft, hurtling through the trees and the bodies of four "little people," with skin like snakeskin. The US Air Force issued a statement that a flying saucer had been recovered, and despite a denial later on, the story caught people's imagination.

Witnesses were allegedly sworn to secrecy, fueling rumors of a cover-up and alien conspiracy theories to this day. The **International UFO Museum and Research Center** features a collection of newspaper clippings and photographs of the crash site, and a film with over 400 interviews of various people connected to the incident.

Roswell's Alien Zone symbol

Roswell's **Museum and Art Center** houses a large collection of artifacts on the history of the American West. The fascinating Robert H. Goddard Collection details 11 years of experiments by the famous rocket scientist.

Limestone columns in the Big Room at Carlsbad Caverns

Carlsbad Caverns National Park 43

3225 National Parks Hwy, Carlsbad. *to Carlsbad. to White's City.* ***Tel** (575) 785-2232, (800) 967-2283 (tour reservations). May–Aug: 8:30am–3:30pm daily; Sep–mid-May: 8:30am–2pm (Natural Entrance). Call for last entry times. Dec 25. partial.* **www**.nps.gov/cave

Located in the state's remote southeastern corner, this park protects one of the world's largest cave systems. Geological forces carved out this complex of chambers, and their decorations began to be formed around 500,000 years ago when dripping water deposited drops of the crystalized mineral calcite. Native pictographs near the Natural Entrance indicate that they had been visited by Native peoples, but it was cowboy Jim White who brought them to national attention in 1901. Concrete trails and electric lights have been laid out through this underground gallery of limestone caves. From the visitor center, elevators drop 750 ft (229 m) down to the **Big Room**. This space can also be reached via the **Natural Entrance Route**, which involves a half-hour walk over a steep, paved trail.

A self-guided tour leads to the Big Room, 25 stories high and 8.2 acres (3.3 ha) in area, festooned with stalagmites, stalactites, and flowstone formations. The adjoining ranger-led **King's Palace Tour** takes in the deepest cave open to the public, 830 ft (250 m) below ground. To its right, a paved section serves as the popular **Underground Lunchroom**, a diner and souvenir shop.

The caverns' recesses are the summer abode of almost a million free-tailed bats. They emerge at dusk to cross the desert in search of food.

White Sands National Monument 44

***Tel** (575) 679-2599. 8am–7pm daily (5pm winter). Dec 25.* **www**.nps.gov/whsa

The glistening dunes of the White Sands National Monument rise up from the Tularosa Basin at the northern end of the Chihuahuan Desert. It is the world's largest gypsum

DESERT FLORA AND FAUNA

Desert scorpion

Most of the Southwest is covered by four deserts, yet it is not an arid wasteland. The Sonoran Desert, with its rich array of flora and fauna, is famed for its saguaro cactus. The climatic extremes of the Chihuahuan Desert support hardy agaves and coyotes. The cooler Great Basin is home to many grasses and desert animals. The winter rain in the Mojave Desert results in a spectacular display of wildflowers in spring.

Prickly pear cacti *flower in spring and are among the largest of the many types of cacti that flourish in the Sonoran Desert.*

Bighorn sheep *are shy, elusive creatures and are not easily spotted. Now a protected species, they are being gradually reintroduced throughout the desert areas.*

For hotels and restaurants in this region see p559 and p563

Soaptree yucca plant in the White Sands National Monument

dune field, covering around 300 sq miles (800 sq km). Gypsum is a water soluble mineral, rarely found as sand. But here, with no drainage outlet to the sea, the sediment washed by the rain into the basin becomes trapped. As the rain evaporates, dry lakes form and strong winds blow the gypsum up into the vast fields of rippling dunes.

Visitors can explore White Sands by car on the Dunes Drive, a 16-mile (26-km) loop. Four clearly marked trails lead from points along the way, including the wheelchair-accessible Interdune Boardwalk. Year-round ranger-led walks introduce visitors to the dunes' flora and fauna. Only plants that grow quickly enough not to be buried survive, such as the hardy soaptree yucca. Most of the animals are nocturnal and include foxes, coyotes, and porcupines.

The park is surrounded by the White Sands Missile Range, a military testing site. For safety, the park and the road leading to it (Hwy 70) may close for up to three hours when testing is underway. The **White Sands Missile Range Museum** displays many of the missiles tested here, as well as the V-2 rockets used in World War II.

Gila Cliff Dwellings National Monument ㊺

Tel *(575) 536-9461. late May–early Sep: 8am–6pm daily; mid-Sep–mid-May: 9am–4pm daily. Jan 1, Dec 25.* **www**.nps.gov/gicl

The Gila (pronounced hee-la) Cliff Dwellings are one of the most remote archaeological sites in the Southwest, situated among the piñon, juniper, and ponderosa evergreens of the Gila National Forest. The dwellings occupy five natural caves in the side of a sandstone bluff high above the Gila River.

Hunter-gatherers and farmers called the Tularosa Mogollon established their 40-room village here in the late 13th century. The Mimbres Mogollon people, famous for their abstract black-and-white pottery designs on hand-coiled earthenware, also lived in this area. The cliff dwellers hunted the local wildlife, including whitetail and mule deer. They probably farmed the fields alongside the Gila River, growing corn and squash. A granary still holds a dessicated reserve of tiny corn. The ruins are accessed by a 1-mile (1.6-km) round-trip hike from the footbridge crossing the Gila River's West Fork. Allow two hours to navigate the 40-mile (64-km) road to the site from Silver City as it winds and climbs through the mountains and canyons of the forest.

The Joshua tree *was named by Mormons who saw the upraised arms of Joshua in its branches.*

Yucca plants *have been gathered for centuries and have many uses: their fruit can be eaten, and the roots make shampoo.*

The javelina *is a strange pig-like mammal that wanders the Chihuahuan and Sonoran Deserts in small packs.*

Golden eagles *can be seen high in the sky in daytime as they hunt for prey across the Great Basin Desert.*

Practical Information

Dotted with dramatic rock formations, canyons, ancient sites, and wild deserts, the Southwest offers visitors a range of outdoor pleasures. The cities feature superb museums, good dining, and accommodations, along with a laid-back culture. A major draw for visitors are the casinos of Las Vegas. The Southwest is a year-round destination. The high-lying areas of Arizona, New Mexico, and Utah have cold, snowy winters, making them popular for skiing, while the states' southern areas offer warm and sunny winters. But the less-crowded and milder spring and fall are the ideal seasons to visit.

TOURIST INFORMATION

Each state and major towns and cities have departments of tourism. Many of the Southwest's attractions on Indian reservation lands are managed by Native American tribal councils. For advice on these contact the local office of the **Navajo Tourism Department**.

PERSONAL SECURITY

Most tourist areas in the Southwest are friendly and unthreatening, but it is wise to be cautious. Find out which parts of town are unsafe at night. Never carry too much cash, and lock your valuables in the hotel safe.

NATURAL HAZARDS

Rapid weather changes in the Southwest often present dangerous situations. In parts of southern Utah and Arizona, sudden summer storms can cause flash floods. Visitors often underestimate the dry heat of the region's summers. Hikers must carry at least a gallon (4 liters) of drinking water per person for each day of walking.

The Southwest's wilderness harbors venomous creatures such as scorpions, snakes, and the Gila monster lizard; but it is unlikely you will be bitten if you avoid their habitats. Insect bites may hurt but are rarely fatal to adults. But, if bitten, seek medical help.

GETTING AROUND

Though slower than car and plane travel, trains and buses are enjoyable means of exploring the region. Visitors can take special railroad trips to enjoy some of the Southwest's most delightful scenery. The Grand Canyon Railway's diesel and steam rail trips from Williams to Grand Canyon feature packages that include Western entertainments.

Long-distance buses are the least expensive mode of travel. A bus tour is often the most convenient way of seeing both major city sights and some of the more remote scenery of the Southwest. In major cities, local bus routes cover most attractions. Taxis are also an efficient way of traveling around cities.

DRIVING IN THE SOUTHWEST

A car is often the only means of reaching remote areas. There are car rental agencies all over the region, but it is best to arrange a fly-drive deal for cities such as Las Vegas. Pay attention to road signs especially in remote areas where they may issue warnings about local hazards. Check your route to see if a Four-Wheel Drive (4WD) vehicle is required. Most backcountry areas now have roads that can carry conventional cars, but a 4WD is essential in some wild areas. When traveling between remote destinations, inform someone of your plans. Be wary of seasonal dangers such as flash floods in Utah's canyonlands. Carry plenty of food and water, and a cell phone as a precaution. If your vehicle breaks down, stay with it since it offers protection from the elements, and telephone for help.

ETIQUETTE

Dress in the Southwest is informal, practical, and dependent on the climate. Some of the region's most famous sights are located on reservation land. Visitors are welcome but must be sensitive as to what may cause offense. It is illegal to bring alcohol onto reservations – even a bottle visible in a locked car will land you in trouble. Ask before photographing anything, especially ceremonial dances or Native homes, and bear in mind that a fee may be requested. Do not wander off marked trails, as this is forbidden.

THE CLIMATE OF THE SOUTHWEST

The weather in this region ranges from the heat of the desert to the ice and snow of the mountains. Temperatures usually vary with altitude. As a result the higher elevations in the north, especially Utah, northern Arizona, and New Mexico, experience cold, snowy winters. The southern areas, on the other hand, have mild, sunny winters and hot, dry summers. Summer temperatures in the desert often reach more than 100°F (38°C), but can drop to almost 30°F (10°C) after sunset. Except for violent summer storms, rainfall is scarce in the Southwest.

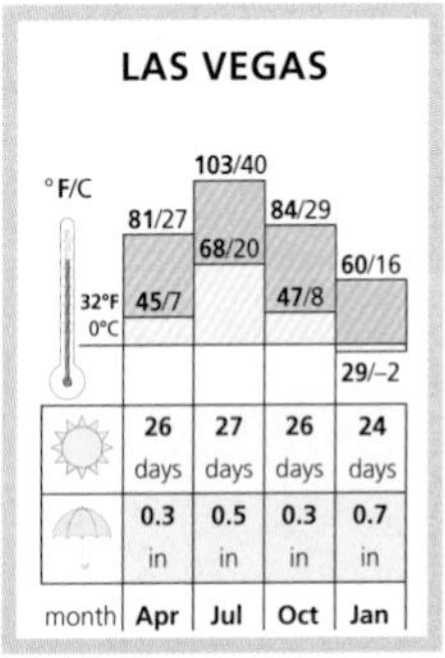

OUTDOOR ACTIVITIES

With thousands of miles of rock canyons, spectacular deserts, and snow-capped peaks, the Southwest is a magnet for climbers, hikers, mountain bikers, 4WD drivers, and skiers. All national parks have well-marked trails and ranger-led hikes, focusing on the local flora, fauna, and geology.

Utah considers itself the world's mountain bike capital, and Moab is a pilgrimage site for such bikers. **Poison Spider Bicycles** sells and repairs bikes as well as runs Nichols Tours, which leads groups through wilderness areas.

The Green, San Juan, and Colorado Rivers are ideal for whitewater rafting. A thrilling 6–16 day rafting trip along the Colorado River through the Grand Canyon is offered by many outfitters, including **Canyon Explorations**. Water sports, such as powerboating, jetskiing, and fishing, are popular in the artificial lakes.

Air tours are a good option for time-restricted travelers who wish to see the remote attractions. **Slickrock Air Guides of Moab** offer three-hour tours that cover Canyonlands, Lake Powell, Capitol Reef National Park, and the Grand Canyon's North Rim. However, helicopter tours of the Grand Canyon have a reputation for bad safety.

Arizona's 275 golf courses make the Southwest a golfer's paradise. Scottsdale, considered America's premier golf spot, is famous for its **Boulders Resort**. The ski season runs from November to April. Utah has some of the best skiing in the region, while New Mexico's **Taos Ski Valley** includes world-class slopes.

ENTERTAINMENT

The Southwest's blend of cultures has made the region a lively center for arts and entertainment. The cities of Phoenix, Santa Fe, Tucson, and Albuquerque offer opera, ballet, classical music, and theatrical productions. The small resort towns of Sedona and Taos, famed for their resident artists, regularly host touring productions and theater and musical shows. Most cities and major towns have a lively nightlife that includes country music, jazz, and rock as well as dinner theater and standup comedy.

The Southwest is a mecca for Western-style entertainment such as rodeo contests. Historic frontier towns such as Tombstone also stage mock gunfights. Check with the **Tombstone Visitor Center** for details. For sports fans, there are major league and college football, baseball, and basketball games.

GAMBLING IN LAS VEGAS

Despite its growing fame as the entertainment capital of the world, Las Vegas is popular mainly for its casinos. They can seem daunting at first, but with a basic understanding of the rules, most games are relatively easy. Some hotels have gaming guides on their in-house TV channels, and many casinos give free lessons at the tables. If you are winning, it is customary to tip the dealers.

SHOPPING

The Southwest's exciting range of Indian, Hispanic, and Anglo-American products make shopping a cultural adventure. Native crafts, including rugs and jewelry, can be bought in reservation posts or Pueblo stores.

Santa Fe is famous for its galleries selling Georgia O'Keeffe-inspired landscapes, contemporary art, and bronze cowboy sculptures.

Across the region, specialty grocery stores stock local products such as hot chili sauces and blue corn chips.

The big cities offer a choice of air-conditioned malls. The biggest concentration is in Phoenix, and its **Metrocenter Mall** is the region's largest. Las Vegas' fantasy-themed malls make shopping one of its many attractions.

DIRECTORY

TOURIST OFFICES

Arizona
Tel (602) 364-3700, (866) 298-3795.
www.arizonaguide.com

Colorado
Tel (800) 265-6723.
www.colorado.com

New Mexico
Tel (505) 827-7400; (800) 545-2070.
www.newmexico.org

Utah
Tel (801) 538-1030.
www.utah.com

Navajo Tourism Department
PO Box 663, Window Rock, AZ 86515.
Tel (928) 871-6436.
www.discovernavajo.com

MOUNTAIN BIKING

Poison Spider Bicycles
497 N Main St, Moab, UT 84532.
Tel (800) 635-1792, (435) 259-7882.

WHITEWATER RAFTING

Canyon Explorations
PO Box 310, Flagstaff, AZ 86002. *Tel (928) 774-4559, (800) 654-0723.*

AIR TOURS

Slickrock Air Guides of Moab
Tel (435) 259-6216.

SKIING

Taos Ski Valley
PO Box 90 Taos Ski Valley, NM 87525
Tel (866) 968-7386.

GOLF

Boulders Resort
34631 N. Tom Darlington Dr, Carefree, AZ 85377.
Tel (866) 397-6520.

RODEOS & WILD WEST SHOWS

Tombstone Visitor Center
Tel (520) 457-3929, (800) 457-3423.

SHOPPING

Metrocenter Mall
9617 Metro Pkwy, Phoenix, AZ 85051.
Tel (602) 997-2641.

Choosing a Hotel

The Southwest has a long history of hospitality that is reflected in the wide variety of accommodations on offer. There is a wealth of options for visitors, ranging from luxurious five-star resorts to simple rustic lodges. Las Vegas hotels are noted for their themes and size. Across the region prices tend to vary according to the season.

PRICE CATEGORIES
For a standard double room per night, including breakfast, service charges, and any additional taxes.

$ Under $100
$$ $100–$150
$$$ $150–$300
$$$$ $300–$500
$$$$$ Over $500

NEVADA

DOWNTOWN LAS VEGAS Binion's Gambling Hall & Hotel $

128 E Fremont St, 89101 ***Tel*** *(702) 382-1600, (800) 937-6537* ***Fax*** *(702) 384-9246* ***Rooms*** *366*

For 35 years this hotel was synonymous with the World Series Poker Championship. Binion's neon horseshoe is now gone, and the Poker Series has moved on, but the hotel's Gambling Hall still has its regulars. Affordable rooms are decorated in pink, and the Ride the Bull venue is popular. Guests can relax in the rooftop pool. **www.binions.com**

DOWNTOWN LAS VEGAS Four Queens Hotel & Casino $

202 E Fremont St, 89101 ***Tel*** *(702) 385-4011, (800) 634-6045* ***Fax*** *(702) 385-4011* ***Rooms*** *690*

One of the most prominent hotels on Fremont Street, the Four Queens occupies an entire downtown block. Renovated rooms have 32-in flat-screen TVs and wireless Internet access. Popular with locals, the hotel is ideal for budget-conscious visitors. Home of Hugo's Cellar restaurant. **www.fourqueens.com**

LAS VEGAS – THE STRIP MGM Grand Hotel & Casino $$$

3799 Las Vegas Blvd S, 89109 ***Tel*** *(702) 891-7777, (877) 880-0880* ***Fax*** *(702) 891-3036* ***Rooms*** *5,044*

The MGM Grand is presided over by a huge bronze lion and the Habitat area inside houses six real lions. The Grand Tower rooms are contemporary, while those in the West Wing have a sleek, upscale look. Bring walking shoes to get around the vast casino. An arena features performers such as Beyoncé and Kelly Clarkson. **www.mgmgrand.com**

LAS VEGAS – THE STRIP TI $$$

3300 Las Vegas Blvd S, 89109 ***Tel*** *(702) 894-7111, (800) 944-7444* ***Fax*** *(702) 894-7623* ***Rooms*** *2,885*

Two warships sit in front of the TI, where nightly battles take place between singing sirens and renegade pirates. The tastefully decorated rooms are priced well for such a central hotel. Adjacent to the Fashion Show Mall, the hotel offers a free tram to the Mirage *(see below)*. See the Cirque du Soleil's *Mystère*. **www.treasureisland.com**

LAS VEGAS – THE STRIP Bellagio $$$$

3600 Las Vegas Blvd S, 89109 ***Tel*** *(702) 693-7111, (888) 987-6667* ***Fax*** *(702) 693-8585* ***Rooms*** *3,933*

The east-facing rooms at the Bellagio overlook dancing-to-music fountains, as do several excellent restaurants. This Tuscan-themed hotel is dressed in marble and silk, with mosaic floors and the garden-of-glass lobby ceiling. The Gallery of Fine Art features outstanding exhibitions, including one showing Picasso ceramics. **www.bellagio.com**

LAS VEGAS – THE STRIP Caesars Palace $$$$

3570 Las Vegas Blvd S, 89109 ***Tel*** *(702) 731-7110, (877) 427-7243* ***Fax*** *(702) 697-5706* ***Rooms*** *3,340*

The ever-expanding Caesars is a Vegas institution. Its Roman-statuary theme carries over to the Forum shops, while the Coliseum arena hosts huge showbiz names such as Elton John and Bette Midler. The swanky rooms, all with marble baths, are housed in five separate towers. Great restaurants and a gorgeous pool area. **www.caesarspalace.com**

LAS VEGAS – THE STRIP The Mirage $$$$

3400 Las Vegas Blvd S, 89109 ***Tel*** *(702) 791-7111, (800) 374-9000* ***Fax*** *(702) 791-7414* ***Rooms*** *3,044*

A gamble that paid off, the Mirage is fronted by a booming, fiery volcano exploding over waterfalls. Check in at the lobby's long, tropical aquarium, and walk through a lush garden to the casino. Out back you can see the famous Secret Garden, filled with exotic lions and tigers, and the Dolphin Habitat. Rooms are pleasant. **www.mirage.com**

LAS VEGAS – THE STRIP Tropicana Resort & Casino $$$$

3801 Las Vegas Blvd S, 89109 ***Tel*** *(702) 739-2222, (888) 826-8767* ***Fax*** *(702) 739-3648* ***Rooms*** *1,874*

The Tropicana has been on a prime South Strip corner for 50 years, and the views are spectacular. Waterfalls in lush gardens spill into lagoon pools famed for summertime swim-up blackjack, and the casino ceiling is beautiful. Bedspreads in the rooms have tropical colors. See the *Folies Bergere* showgirl review. **www.tropicanalv.com**

LAS VEGAS – THE STRIP The Venetian Resort Hotel Casino $$$$

3355 Las Vegas Blvd S, 89109 ***Tel*** *(702) 414-1000, (877) 883-6423* ***Fax*** *(702) 414-1100* ***Rooms*** *4,027*

Stop by the canal for a gondola ride and marvel at the exquisite architectural facade replicating Venice's main landmarks (sadly marred by banners promoting inside attractions, like *Phantom of the Opera*). The beautiful rooms have sunken seating areas. Sidewalk cafés surround a replica of St. Mark's Square. **www.venetian.com**

UTAH

BRYCE CANYON Best Western Ruby's Inn $$$

1000 S Hwy 63, 84764 ***Tel*** *(435) 834-5341* ***Fax*** *(435) 834-5265* ***Rooms*** *368*

This bustling family-run hotel has been open for 90 years. The has-it-all complex starts with a grand lobby and offers both rooms in the main building and motel-style accommodation, not to mention restaurants, a general store, gas station, post office, and an art gallery. Several tour desks offer adventure activities. **www.rubysinn.com**

BRYCE CANYON Bryce Canyon Lodge $$$

Bryce Canyon National Park, 84717 ***Tel*** *(303) 297-2757, (888) 297-2757* ***Fax*** *(435) 834-8700* ***Rooms*** *115*

Built in the 1920s of sandstone and pine, the Bryce Canyon Lodge has a cozy, rustic feel. Decorated with replica hickory furniture, rooms are comfortable – as are the cabins with their gas-log fireplaces. There are no TVs, so guests spend their time walking along nearby trails. Open Apr–Oct. **www.brycecanyonlodge.com**

CEDAR CITY Crystal Inn Cedar City $$

1575 W 200 North St, 84720 ***Tel*** *(435) 586-8888, (888) 787-6661* ***Fax*** *(435) 586-1010* ***Rooms*** *100*

Conveniently located close to a major highway, the Crystal Inn sits at the gateway to several national parks. It offers a shuttle service to the airport and has an outdoor pool, as well as an indoor hot tub and sauna. Those attending the famous Utah Shakespearean Festival should make early reservations. **www.crystalinncedar.com**

ESCALANTE Prospector Inn $

380 W Main St, 84726 ***Tel*** *(435) 826-4653* ***Fax*** *(435) 826-4285* ***Rooms*** *50*

The Grand Staircase–Escalante, a nearly roadless, rugged terrain in remote Utah, is one of America's newest national monuments. Close to it, the Prospector Inn, on scenic Byway 12, is a family-run establishment with spacious rooms and a restaurant on site. Check out the glass-encased giant bear in the lobby. **www.prospectorinn.com**

MOAB Redstone Inn $

535 S Main St, 84532 ***Tel*** *(435) 259-3500, (800) 772-1972* ***Fax*** *(435) 259-2717* ***Rooms*** *52*

The downtown Redstone caters to adventure travelers, with packages for white-water rafting, four-wheel jeep trips, and other extreme (and not-so-extreme) sports. Cyclists may keep bikes in their rooms, each of which has a kitchen corner. Those returning from places such as the Slickrock Bike Trail can relax in the hot tub. **www.moabredstone.com**

MOAB The Gonzo Inn $$$

100 W 200 South St, 84532 ***Tel*** *(435) 259-2515, (800) 791-4044* ***Fax*** *(435) 259-6992* ***Rooms*** *43*

The Gonzo is a trendy inn with a mix of colorful Southwestern and retro 1970s decor. There's a large outdoor pool and a hot tub, and a Continental breakfast is included in the price. The Espresso Bar offers beverages 24/7. Guests without bikes can arrange rental. Bike storage, wipe-down, and repairs are also available. **www.gonzoinn.com**

TORREY Wonderland Inn $

875 E Hwy 24, 84775 ***Tel*** *(435) 425-3775, (800) 458-0216* ***Fax*** *(435) 425-3212* ***Rooms*** *50*

At the top of the world, close to Capitol Reef National Park, this inn is named for all the surrounding natural wonders – from canyons and mountains, to deserts and thick forests. It has clean, cheerful rooms. The surprise here is a swimming pool completely enclosed by glass, with stunning views. **www.capitolreefwonderland.com**

ZION NATIONAL PARK Zion Lodge $$$

Springdale, 84767 ***Tel*** *(303) 297-2757, (888) 297-2757* ***Fax*** *(303) 297-3175* ***Rooms*** *121*

This lodge is nestled in a wooded area deep inside Zion Canyon, with massive sandstone walls soaring all around, up to 3,800 ft (1,160 m). The rebuilt main lodge has maintained its original appearance and offers some historic cabins, as well as motel-style rooms. Rates are particularly attractive in the winter months. **www.zionlodge.com**

ARIZONA

BISBEE Copper Queen Hotel $$$

11 Howell Ave, 85603 ***Tel*** *(520) 432-2216* ***Fax*** *(520) 432-3819* ***Rooms*** *53*

With its rolltop desk at reception and antique-filled rooms decorated with period wallpaper, the Copper Queen is an early 1900s hotel that welcomed dignitaries in the city's long-gone boomtown days. Today, visitors can cool off in a claw-foot tub (some rooms only) or take a dip in the second-floor pool. **www.copperqueen.com**

FLAGSTAFF Hotel Monte Vista $$

100 San Francisco St, 86001 ***Tel*** *(928) 779-6971, (800) 545-3068* ***Fax*** *(928) 779-2904* ***Rooms*** *50*

This 1926 four-story brick hotel boasts an illustrious past. Rooms are named for celebrities who have stayed here, from Bob Hope, John Wayne, Freddie Mercury and Anthony Hopkins amongst others. There's a long list of resident ghosts too. The Monte Vista is close to the railroad, so you might need to ask for earplugs. **www.hotelmontevista.com**

FLAGSTAFF Hilton Garden Inn $$$

350 W Forest Meadows St, 86001 ***Tel*** *(928) 226-8888* ***Fax*** *(928) 556-9059* ***Rooms*** *90*

Hikers and bikers appreciate the indoor pool, sauna, and whirlpool spa of this hotel, located near downtown and Northern Arizona University. Rooms are equipped with microwaves and refrigerators, two phones, and free Internet. Take advantage of a Stay-Fit Kit – mat, ball, and dumbbells – for an in-room workout. **www.hiltongardeninn.**

GRAND CANYON Phantom Ranch $

Grand Canyon, 86023 ***Tel*** *(303) 297-2757, (888) 297-2757* ***Fax*** *(303) 297-3175* ***Rooms*** *40*

Few visitors to the Grand Canyon are given the opportunity to stay in the beautiful Phantom Ranch, just below the Canyon rim. The rustic lodge and timber cabins are reached by rafting the Colorado River, by hiking, or by mule. Segregated accommodation is dormitory-style, in bunk beds. Book very early. **www.grandcanyonlodges.com**

GRAND CANYON (NORTH RIM) Grand Canyon Lodge $$

Grand Canyon, 86052 ***Tel*** *(303) 297-2757, (888) 297-2757* ***Fax*** *(303) 297-3175* ***Rooms*** *205*

It's a long drive to the Canyon's North Rim, with more convenient access from Utah. Even then, it's a long way to the rim's edge, from where this rustic limestone lodge with motel-style rooms overlooks the Kaibab Plateau. Its log cabins are popular. The lodge is open seasonally, and reservations are a must. **www.grandcanyonlodges.com**

GRAND CANYON (SOUTH RIM) Bright Angel Lodge $

Grand Canyon Village, 86023 ***Tel*** *(303) 297-2757, (888) 297-2757* ***Fax*** *(303) 297-3175* ***Rooms*** *89*

Make bookings well in advance to get one of the edge-of-the-canyon cabins, priced well below similar lodgings at El Tovar. Designed by Mary Elizabeth Colter in 1935, this historic log-and-stone lodge is very popular. Low-priced motel-like rooms and cabins have been spruced up. **www.grandcanyonlodges.com**

GRAND CANYON (SOUTH RIM) Maswik Lodge $

Grand Canyon Village, 86023 ***Tel*** *(303) 297-2757, (888) 297-2757* ***Fax*** *(303) 297-3175* ***Rooms*** *278*

This family-friendly lodge, consisting of two buildings sitting among ponderosa pines, is a quarter-mile south of the Canyon rim. The south-facing rooms have all the basics but no air-conditioning, while the more spacious north rooms have all mod-cons. The rustic cabins can be booked only during the summer. **www.grandcanyonlodges.com**

GREEN VALLEY Best Western Green Valley $$

111 S La Cañada, 85614 ***Tel*** *(520) 625-2250* ***Fax*** *(520) 625-0215* ***Rooms*** *108*

Located mere minutes from the "white dove of the desert," the San Xavier del Bac church, this reliable chain hotel has comfortable rooms and attractive landscaping. Save some time for a swim in the pool after birdwatching at the nearby Madera Canyon, part of a migratory corridor for over 300 bird species. **www.bestwesterngreenvalley.com**

JEROME Ghost City Inn Bed & Breakfast $$

541 N Main St, 86331 ***Tel*** *(928) 634-4678, (888) 634-4678* ***Rooms*** *6*

Nestled among Jerome's ghosts and galleries, this 1890s copper miners' boarding house has been made into a tasteful inn. Perched high atop Cleopatra Hill, with views over the Verde River Valley, it has individually decorated rooms. Breakfast is served in the drawing room or on the back patio, next to a waterfall. **www.ghostcityinn.com**

LAKE HAVASU CITY Hampton Inn $$

245 London Bridge Rd, 86403 ***Tel*** *(928) 855-4071* ***Fax*** *(928) 855-2379* ***Rooms*** *162*

The Hampton Inn is one of the most popular hotels in town. Just a quarter-mile from the lake, it has many rooms with balconies and lake views. All rooms have refrigerators and microwaves. Guests can try their skill at the horseshoe pit, or take the walking trail to the beach. **www.hamptoninn.com**

PHOENIX Best Western Central Phoenix Inn & Suites $$

1100 N Central Ave, 85004 ***Tel*** *(602) 252-2100* ***Fax*** *(602) 252-2731* ***Rooms*** *107*

As its name implies, this hotel is indeed centrally located, within walking distance of the city's famous museums and Copper Square. It has an outdoor pool and spa, and a dry sauna in which to chill out after using the fitness center. There are beautiful views of downtown from the rooms on its upper floors. **www.bestwesternarizona.com**

PHOENIX Hotel San Carlos $$$

202 N Central Ave, 85004 ***Tel*** *(602) 253-4121, (866) 253-4121* ***Fax*** *(602) 253-6668* ***Rooms*** *121*

This historic hotel is full of character and charm. Despite some small rooms, it's priced right and filled with nostalgia. Its legendary guest roster includes the likes of Mae West, Clark Gable, and Marilyn Monroe, plus, of course, the obligatory resident ghost. A rooftop pool and a sidewalk café complete the picture. **www.hotelsancarlos.com**

PHOENIX Arizona Grand Resort $$$$

8000 S Arizona Grand Pkwy, 85044 ***Tel*** *(602) 438-9000, (866) 267-1321* ***Fax*** *(602) 431-6535* ***Rooms*** *640*

This family-friendly resort offers golf, tennis, horseback riding, and a spa. Its pièce de résistance, exclusive to guests, is The Oasis – a waterpark with a slide, a wave pool, and the Zuni River. Each balcony suite has a living room and a wet bar. There are miles of hiking trails in the adjacent South Mountain Preserve. **www.pointesouthmtn.com**

SCOTTSDALE Fairmont Scottsdale Princess $$$$$

7575 E Princess Dr, 85255 ***Tel*** *(800) 257-7544* ***Fax*** *(480) 585-0091* ***Rooms*** *651*

This relaxed resort features Spanish Colonial architecture, with a tiled roof, arches, pink stucco, and fountains. Rooms are spacious, luxurious, and decorated in earthy accents, with many amenities. The Princess is noted for its two Tournament Players Club golf courses, the Willow Stream spa, and a kids' club. **www.fairmont.com**

Key to Price Guide *see p556* **Key to Symbols** *see back cover flap*

SEDONA Star Motel $

295 Jordan Rd, 86336 ***Tel*** *(928) 282-3641* ***Rooms*** *11*

Located smack in the center of uptown Sedona, this small, unassuming motel is a real find for budget-minded families. Rooms might be short on romance or atmosphere, but they are spotlessly clean. The Star Motel's main claim to fame is that it's close to everything, and it even has views of Sedona's beautiful red rocks.

TUCSON El Presidio Bed & Breakfast Inn $$

297 N Main Ave, 85701 ***Tel*** *(520) 623-6151, (800) 349-6151* ***Fax*** *(520) 623-3860* ***Rooms*** *4*

Close to Old Town Artisans and the Tucson Museum of Art, this Victorian adobe inn, an American Territorial-style home from 1886, is located in a neighborhood of elegant mansions known as Snob Hollow. Filled with antiques, it has a lush and shady courtyard garden and offers fine gourmet breakfasts. **www.bbonline.com/az/elpresidio**

TUCSON Hacienda del Sol Guest Ranch Resort $$$

5601 N Hacienda del Sol Rd, 85718 ***Tel*** *(520) 299-1501, (800) 728-6514* ***Fax*** *(520) 299-5554* ***Rooms*** *30*

At the foot of the Santa Catalina Mountains, the Hacienda del Sol once housed a school attended by the rich and famous. It is now a relaxing luxury resort with exquisite rooms decorated in warm Southwestern tones and Spanish Colonial design. Go horseback riding, or get a jade-stone massage at the spa. **www.haciendadelsol.com**

NEW MEXICO

ALBUQUERQUE Albuquerque Doubletree Hotel $$$

201 Marquette Ave NW, 87102 ***Tel*** *(505) 247-3344, (888) 223-4113* ***Fax*** *(505) 247-7025* ***Rooms*** *295*

Close to the Old Town, the Doubletree is accessible from the Convention Center via an underground concourse. Many of its bright, airy rooms have balconies and views of the mountains. Guests can enjoy a cocktail at the Lobby Bar to the tune of a cascading waterfall. Good business facilities. **www.doubletreealbuquerque.com**

ALBUQUERQUE Casas de Sueños $$$

310 Rio Grande Blvd SW, 87104 ***Tel*** *(505) 247-4560, (800) 665-7002* ***Fax*** *(505) 242-2162* ***Rooms*** *21*

The Casas de Sueños (House of Dreams) used to house a 1930s artists' colony. Charming adobe-style *casitas* are hidden among the courtyards and gardens. Each room is uniquely decorated, some with *kiva* fireplaces or *saltillo* tiled floors, others with patios or Jacuzzi tubs. A full American breakfast is served. **www.casasdesuenos.com**

ALBUQUERQUE Hilton Albuquerque $$$

1901 University Blvd NE, 87102 ***Tel*** *(505) 884-2500, (800) 274-6835* ***Fax*** *(505) 880-1196* ***Rooms*** *263*

The Hilton is in the midtown district, close to the university, on a sprawling resort-like property. The cabanas are convenient to the pool, whirlpool, fitness center, and sauna. The tower rooms have balconies and splendid views of volcanoes and mountains. Decor is New Mexican throughout, with Indian rugs and pueblo art. **www.hilton.com**

CHAMA Branding Iron Motel $$

1511 Hwy 17, 87520 ***Tel*** *(505) 756-2162, (800)-446-2650* ***Rooms*** *39*

Close to the Colorado border, high up in the Rocky Mountains of New Mexico, the Branding Iron has pleasant rooms. It's located within walking distance of the depot for America's highest and longest narrow-gauge railroad, the Cumbres and Toltec Scenic Railroad. Closed Nov–Apr. **www.brandingironmotel.com**

SANTA FE El Rey Inn $$

1862 Cerrillos Rd, 87505 ***Tel*** *(505) 982-1931, (800) 521-1349* ***Fax*** *(505) 989-9249* ***Rooms*** *86*

With a gracious lobby in a white adobe-style building, the El Rey is a mini oasis in Santa Fe. Gardens are filled with chile ristras, fountains, and sculptures; rooms are comfortably decorated with Southwestern accents. One of the best lower-priced hotels in the area, the El Rey is near the Greer Garson Theater. **www.elreyinnsantafe.com**

SANTA FE Inn of the Turquoise Bear $$$

342 E Buena Vista St, 87505 ***Tel*** *(505) 983-0798, (800) 396-4104* ***Fax*** *(505) 988-4225* ***Rooms*** *11*

An historic, rambling adobe villa surrounded by gardens, this elegant inn is a tribute to its owner, Witter Brynner, and his literary and artistic friends. Gracious rooms with *kiva* fireplaces and *viga* ceilings are named for Brynner's visitors, such as Igor Stravinsky, Ansel Adams, and Edna Millay. Delicious breakfasts. **www.turquoisebear.com**

SANTA FE La Fonda Hotel $$$$

100 E San Francisco St, 87501 ***Tel*** *(505) 982-5511, (800) 523-5002* ***Fax*** *(505) 988-2952* ***Rooms*** *167*

This grande dame on the Plaza sits on the site of a 1610 adobe inn. Artworks are everywhere: the guest-room headboards, the blanket boxes, and even the light switches have been painted by the hotel's resident artist. Modern amenities include a swimming pool and a state-of-the art fitness center and spa. **www.lafondasantafe.com**

TAOS Taos Inn $$

125 Paseo del Pueblo Norte, 87571 ***Tel*** *(575) 758-2233* ***Fax*** *(575) 758-5776* ***Rooms*** *44*

Four buildings beyond the lobby house guest rooms decorated with vibrant colors and artworks; many also have antiques, fireplaces, and wood-beamed ceilings. The on-site Adobe Bar is known as Taos' "living room" and has drawn the likes of Greta Garbo, D.H. Lawrence, and, more recently, Robert Redford. **www.taosinn.com**

Choosing a Restaurant

The Southwest offers a top-class regional cuisine, as well as a diverse range of other eating experiences, especially in the larger cities. Mexican food is often best at local restaurants in New Mexico and Arizona, while Utah favors American fare. In small towns, hotel restaurants often serve the best food.

PRICE CATEGORIES
For a three-course meal for one, half a bottle of house wine, and all unavoidable extra charges such as sales tax and service.
$ Under $30
$$ $30–$40
$$$ $40–$60
$$$$ $60–$80
$$$$$ Over $80

NEVADA

DOWNTOWN LAS VEGAS Binion's Ranch Steakhouse — $$$

Binion's, 128 E Fremont St, 89101 **Tel** *(702) 382-1600*

If you manage to take your eyes off the Strip view from the 24th floor of Binion's you'll be able to admire the plush Victorian setting, enhanced by live piano on weekends. Choose a booth and dine on the specialties that made this place popular: lobster bisque, porterhouse steak, and seafood, including the signature Chicken Fried Lobster.

LAS VEGAS – THE STRIP Witchcraft — $

MGM Grand, 3799 Las Vegas Blvd S, 89109 **Tel** *(702) 891-3166*

Only a witch could concoct refreshing, inventive sandwiches like those served in this casual spot off Studio Walk, at the MGM Grand. Order a sublime sandwich such as the chicken breast with roasted red pepper, mozzarella, and pesto on country bread. Complete the experience with a glass of wine and a scrumptious dessert.

LAS VEGAS – THE STRIP California Pizza Kitchen — $$

The Mirage, 3400 Las Vegas Blvd S, 89109 **Tel** *(702) 791-7111*

Popular with families, California Pizza Kitchen offers unique wood-fired pizzas that come out of the hearth with a crisp crust and some unusual toppings. Among its bestsellers are the BBQ Chicken, with smoked cheeses and red onions, and the Portobello, loaded with gourmet mushrooms.

LAS VEGAS – THE STRIP Border Grill — $$$

Mandalay Bay, 3950 Las Vegas Blvd S, 89109 **Tel** *(702) 632-7403*

Authentic Mexican home cooking with a fresh twist is produced by Food Network's "Two Hot Tamales", Susan Feniger and Mary Sue Milliken. The restaurant is decorated with bright, bold colors and has courtyards and balconies overlooking the beach area. Fresh seafood, traditional spicy Mexican dishes, with excellent desserts and margaritas.

LAS VEGAS – THE STRIP Andre's — $$$$

Monte Carlo, 3770 Las Vegas Blvd, 89109 **Tel** *(702) 798-7151*

Old world charm and modern decor combine to create an elegant backdrop to the fine French cuisine served in three dining rooms. Rack of Colorado Lamb with Eggplant (aubergine) Parmesan and Live Maine Lobster are the signature entrées. There's a vast wine list and an enticing choice of Cognacs and Armagnacs. Reservations recommended.

LAS VEGAS – THE STRIP Emeril's New Orleans Fish House — $$$$

MGM Grand, 3799 Las Vegas Blvd S, 89109 **Tel** *(702) 891-7374*

The famed TV-star chef Emeril has brought his delicious Creole and Cajun recipes to Las Vegas. The New Orleans Fish House's modern decor has a casual elegance, and diners here are tempted by the gumbo soup or the signature BBQ shrimp for starters, and tasty roasted Gulf snapper. The extensive wine list is embodied by a 2,200-bottle tower.

LAS VEGAS – THE STRIP Hyakumi — $$$$

Caesars Palace, 3570 Las Vegas Blvd S, 89109 **Tel** *(702) 731-7110*

The tea garden atmosphere offers a relaxed oasis in the middle of the busy casino. Sushi chefs prepare 40 different varieties featuring fresh fish and seafood. The dining room offers *teppanyaki* feasts with grilled tenderloin, lobster tail, chicken, or jumbo shrimp. The *teriyaki*, *tempura*, and noodle soups are popular. There's also a fixed-price menu.

LAS VEGAS – THE STRIP Rosewood Grille — $$$$$

3763 Las Vegas Blvd S, 89109 **Tel** *(702) 792-5965*

Nothing much has changed in this long-standing and popular restaurant. You can sip martinis just as the crooners from the Rat Pack did, in an Old Vegas atmosphere. Settle into a comfy leather booth and feast on Maine lobster (sold by the pound). Several cuts of aged beef will please meat lovers, and the wine list is also outstanding.

LAS VEGAS – THE STRIP Top of the World — $$$$$

Stratosphere Tower, 2000 Las Vegas Blvd S, 89104 **Tel** *(702) 380-7711*

View Las Vegas as far as the eye can reach – downtown, the Strip, and the surrounding mountains – as this 833-ft- (254-m-) high restaurant slowly revolves around Sin City. The romantic atmosphere might even prompt a proposal in this marrying town. Colorado rack of lamb, crab-stuffed veal, and Chilean sea bass are the house specials.

Key to Symbols *see back cover flap*

UTAH

BRYCE CANYON Foster's Family Steakhouse $$

1150 Hwy 12, Bryce, 84759 ***Tel*** *(435) 834-5227*

Located just on the outskirts of the national park, Foster's is a family place, as the name implies. Hearty meals are served at breakfast, lunch, and dinner. Fresh pastries and bread are baked daily, and slow-roasted prime rib is a popular choice in the evening. Good sandwiches and soups can be enjoyed at lunchtime.

BRYCE CANYON NATIONAL PARK Bryce Canyon Dining Room $$$

Bryce Canyon Lodge, Bryce Canyon National Park, 84717 ***Tel*** *(435) 834-8760*

Nestled among ponderosa pines at the canyon, the Dining Room is both rustic and elegant. Its atmosphere is relaxing and very cozy, especially near the large stone fireplaces. Interesting items on the menu include Fairyland Crème Brie and Apple Stuffed Chicken. Be sure to save room for the fudge lava cake. Reservations are a must. Closed Nov–Mar.

CEDAR CITY Market Grill $

2290 W 400 North St, 84720 ***Tel*** *(435) 586-9325*

The Market Grill started up three decades ago to feed hungry cattle ranchers at the adjacent livestock auction. It offers "good ole' home cookin'," and you can eat until the cows come home in a Western atmosphere. A firm favorite among locals is the chicken-fried steak, served with mashed potatoes, gravy, and vegetables.

CEDAR CITY Rusty's Ranch House $$$

2275 E Hwy 14, 84721 ***Tel*** *(435) 586-3839*

Travel up Cedar Canyon to Rusty's and enjoy the canyon views through the windows overlooking Cold Creek. The typically Western decor sees mounted heads of moose, deer, and elk all around the dining room. They serve an outstanding filet mignon, tasty coconut shrimp, and honey-glazed ribs. At dinner, you can mingle with the locals.

MOAB Eddie McStiff's $$$

57 S Main St, 84532 ***Tel*** *(435) 259-2337*

A centrally located, down-to-earth place, Eddie McStiff's pours 14 house microbrews at its 20-seat bar. Its sought-after pizzas are reasonably priced, as are its pasta dishes and steaks. Bite into the gourmet ravioli filled with roasted tomato, goat's cheese, and mozzarella. In addition to the main dining area, there is a covered garden terrace.

MOAB Center Café $$$$

60 N 100 West, 84532 ***Tel*** *(435) 259-4295*

After a day of sporting or touring, stop for a bite to eat at this unassuming restaurant. Dressed in wood, with a stone fireplace and white tablecloths, the Center Café has a friendly, contemporary feel. Specials have global influences and may include an exotic ostrich or bison dish. The Small Bites bistro menu is served 3:30–6pm.

TORREY Capitol Reef Café $$

360 W Main St, 84775 ***Tel*** *(435) 425-3271*

The locally farmed trout is a specialty at this café, which hangs its hat on healthy food. The fish comes grilled, broiled, or smoked, and is served with a ten-vegetable salad. The Capitol Reef is open only during the warmer months, from mid-March to mid-October, and it is located close to its namesake national park.

ZION NATIONAL PARK Red Rock Grill $$

Zion Lodge, Springdale, 84767 ***Tel*** *(435) 772-7760*

Nestled among the cottonwoods, deep inside the canyon, the rustic Red Rock Grill boasts splendid views. Interesting menu items include the spicy-sweet *chipotle tilapia* fish and a vegetarian Navajo eggplant with a *tomatillo* cream sauce. Those who have been here before know to save room for the Moose Tracks ice-cream sundae.

ARIZONA

FLAGSTAFF Charly's Pub & Grill $$$

23 N Leroux St, 86001 ***Tel*** *(928) 779-1919*

Popular for people-watching at its sidewalk tables, Charly's serves Navajo tacos, fresh soups, and delicious pies, as well as posole steaks and vegetarian dishes. Late at night diners can expect varied music acts, from blues to jazz. Located in the Hotel Weatherford, which offers a selection of bars and restaurants on each floor.

FLAGSTAFF Cottage Place Restaurant $$$$

126 W Cottage Ave, 86001 ***Tel*** *(928) 774-8431*

Dine in an airy, bungalow-style residence-turned-restaurant with tables dressed in pink linen. The menu offers inspired Continental dishes such as pan-seared tenderloin filet topped with Gorgonzola and served with Port demi-glaze. A good selection of seafood and vegetarian dishes is also available. Closed Mon–Tue.

GRAND CANYON Phantom Ranch Canteen $$

Grand Canyon, 86023 ***Tel*** *(928) 638-2631*

Adventurers traveling to the canyon bottom – by raft, mule, or on foot – must be early risers. Dinner tends to be an early affair, too. Breakfast and dinner are at specific times here, and reservations are a must; email in advance, along with any lodging requests *(see p558)*. Choose steak, Hiker's Stew, or a vegetarian dish. Sack lunch is also available.

GRAND CANYON (SOUTH RIM) Bright Angel Restaurant $$

Grand Canyon Village, 86023 ***Tel*** *(928) 638-2631*

Open all year, the Bright Angel offers family-style casual dining and Southwestern fare named for the people who helped build the lodge. Try the Colter Quesadilla (for the architect who designed the building in 1935) or a Harvey House Steak. Seating is on a first-come, first-served basis, but in high season you can put your name on a waiting list.

GRAND CANYON (SOUTH RIM) El Tovar $$$

Grand Canyon Village, 86023 ***Tel*** *(928) 638-2631 ext. 6432*

Unquestionably, the best dining in the park can be found at El Tovar, where the menu offers a mix of classic and Southwestern flavors. The impressive dining room has a few window tables overlooking the Grand Canyon – meals are pricier in this section, and you must reserve in advance. For views and a light meal, head for the veranda.

JEROME Flatiron Café $

416 N Main St, 86331 ***Tel*** *(928) 634-2733*

If you travel the tortuous road up to Jerome, a one-time copper boomtown, you can't miss the tiny Flatiron Café, facing downhill where the road splits. Order chicken quesadilla with blue cheese, spinach, and homemade cilantro pesto, followed by an exceptionally strong espresso. Be sure not to slip on the café's slanted floors.

JEROME The Asylum $$$

200 Hill St, 86331 ***Tel*** *(928) 639-3197*

Inside the Grand Hotel, The Asylum offers fine dining and an award-winning wine list in a fun and classy setting with delightful mountain views. Dinner entrées include Prickly Pear Barbeque Pork Tenderloin, Sonoran Spiced Chicken Pasta, and Mesquite Bacon-wrapped Filet Mignon. The lunch menu features burgers, sandwiches, and salads.

LAKE HAVASU CITY Mudshark Brewing Co. $$$

210 Swanson Ave, 86403 ***Tel*** *(928) 453-2981*

Named for a local beach, Mudshark is a popular spot for handcrafted beer on tap. Its varied menu includes burgers, sandwiches, and slow-cooked pork chops. Try the Margarita Shrimp Pizza, with tomato, garlic, and feta cheese, and chase it with a glass of Scorpion Amber Ale. Huge, eye-catching wall murals add to the pleasant ambience.

PHOENIX Matt's Big Breakfast $

801 N 1st St, 85004 ***Tel*** *(602) 254-1074*

Matt's uses only grain-fed meats, organic produce, and cage-free eggs. During the week it's busy with downtown office workers wanting sandwiches and salads; at weekends people come for a salami scramble, Belgian waffles, and freshly squeezed orange juice. Decorated with '50s dinette tables, a bright-orange counter, and vintage artwork.

PHOENIX Aunt Chilada's at Squaw Peak $$

7330 N Dreamy Draw Dr, 85020 ***Tel*** *(602) 944-1286*

Casual, rustic, and spilling over with flowers, this out-of-the-way Mexican restaurant offers pleasant alfresco dining on a patio. In the late 19th century it was a general store serving the local mercury miners. Select the chicken breast mole with sesame seeds, and chase it with a margarita. Colorful murals complement the atmospheric decor.

PHOENIX Sam's Café $$$

2566 E Camelback Rd, 85016 ***Tel*** *(602) 954-7100*

Inside Biltmore Fashion Park, Sam's Café provides affordable homemade specialties with a Southwestern twist. A delicious entrée is lightly smoked Atlantic salmon with spicy pecans, served over sautéed spinach and mashed sweet potatoes, and topped with a red papaya-and-cilantro sauce. They're also proud of their margaritas.

PHOENIX Vincent on Camelback $$$$

3930 E Camelback Rd, 85018 ***Tel*** *(602) 224-0225*

Since 1986 Vincent has set a standard for fine dining, with an inventive menu that blends Southwestern ingredients with a Provençal flair. Start with the corn ravioli with white-truffle oil, followed by poached organic chicken with wild mushrooms, leeks, and thyme broth. Attentive service and an extensive wine list. Closed Sun.

SCOTTSDALE La Hacienda $$$$

Fairmont Scottsdale Princess, 7575 E Princess Dr, 85255 ***Tel*** *(480) 585-4848*

The aroma of mesquite and the sounds of mariachi guitars fill the air at this ranch house offering gourmet Mexican cuisine. The house specialty is *cochinillo asado* – slowly roasted, whole, barbecue-style suckling pig. On milder evenings you can dine on the patio and enjoy the view.

SEDONA Shugrue's Hillside Grill $$$$

Hillside Courtyard, 671 Hwy 179, 86336 ***Tel*** *(928) 282-5300*

It's all about the views in Sedona, and Shugrue's lofty floor-to-ceiling windows provide just that. They also have a large outdoor viewing terrace. Considered by many to have great steaks, the restaurant is also known for grilled, sautéed, or blackened seafood, such as blackened shrimp and sambuca sauce with fried saganaki cheese.

Key to Price Guide *see p560* **Key to Symbols** *see back cover flap*

TOMBSTONE Big Nose Kate's $

417 E Allen St, 85638 ***Tel*** *(520) 457-3107*

Named for Tombstone's first prostitute (allegedly) and Doc Holliday's girlfriend, Big Nose Kate's was built as a hotel in 1881. These days the bustling saloon is filled with Western memorabilia, steer heads, and stained glass. The Goldie's Over-Stuffed Reuben Sandwich has corned beef, sauerkraut, and Swiss cheese. Live country music daily.

TUCSON El Charro Café $$$

311 N Court Ave, 85701 ***Tel*** *(520) 622-1922*

The famous El Charro, located in the El Presidio historic district downtown, serves superb Mexican food prepared from ancient family recipes. No one should leave without trying the much sought-after *carne seca* – shredded sundried Angus beef marinated in garlic and lime juice, and grilled with fresh green chili, tomatoes, and onions.

TUCSON Janos $$$$$

Westin La Paloma Resort, 3770 E Sunrise Dr, 85718 ***Tel*** *(520) 615-6100*

At this much-celebrated fine-dining restaurant, Janos Wilder creates Southwestern dishes with a French twist and presents them with imaginative decorative touches. In addition to beautiful views of Tucson and an extensive wine list, there's also a prix-fixe menu with wine pairings. Take the time to read the delectable, detailed menu. Closed Sun.

NEW MEXICO

ALBUQUERQUE Church Street Café $$

2111 Church St NW, 87104 ***Tel*** *(505) 247-8522*

This café is located within the Casa de Ruiz, which was built with 1800s adobe and has antique Native Indian art and rugs on its walls. Dine inside by the *kiva* fireplace, or outdoors among the grapevines. Order the *carne adovada al horno*, a northern New Mexico dish of oven-cooked pork marinated in red chili. Sara, a friendly ghost, may pay a visit.

ALBUQUERQUE High Noon Restaurant and Saloon $$$

425 San Felipe NW, 87104 ***Tel*** *(505) 765-1455*

Parts of this rambling restaurant, one of the Old Town's historic treasures, date back to 1785. Many *santos* (icons of saints) stand in small, arched coves, and each room has a theme: Hispanic culture, early pioneers, *kachina* dolls, and Native Indian rugs. The cuisine is typically Southwestern, including bison rib eye and rack of lamb.

ALBUQUERQUE The Artichoke Café $$$$

424 Central Ave SE, 87102 ***Tel*** *(505) 243-0200*

This stylish downtown restaurant is like an art gallery, with rotating exhibits and a refined, contemporary look. The menu offers excellent French, Italian, and New American items. Tiger prawns served on fettuccini with a vodka and cream sauce come with sugarsnap peas, tomatoes, and artichoke hearts. Good wines.

CARLSBAD The Flume Room $$$

Stevens Inn, 1829 S Canal St, 88220 ***Tel*** *(575) 887-2851*

Named for the famous Pecos River aqueduct, built over a century ago, this restaurant features three large arches and an enormous etched-glass sculpture replicating the river structure. The Cattleman, a 12-oz (340-g) cut of prime rib, is the specialty here, but steaks, chicken, and seafood dishes are all on the menu. Casual and family-friendly.

SANTA FE Maria's New Mexican Kitchen $$

555 W Cordova Rd, 87501 ***Tel*** *(505) 983-7929*

Start (or end) your meal with a margarita; alternatively, if you are concerned about high-altitude drinking you can buy the proprietor's book (foreword by Robert Redford) and learn about margaritas. Chicken, beef, and vegetarian dishes are served on a sizzling platter with guacamole and *pico de gallo* (tomatoes, onions, and chili sauce).

SANTA FE The Shed $$

113 1/2 E Palace Ave, 87501 ***Tel*** *(505) 982-9030*

One of downtown Santa Fe's most popular lunch spots is housed in a rambling 1692 adobe hacienda with a courtyard. Try the red-chili enchiladas, tacos, or the charbroiled Shedburger, and be sure to have the locally made red-chili sauce which receives rave reviews. Exceptional homemade desserts and friendly service. Closed Sun.

SANTA FE Old House Restaurant $$$$

309 W San Francisco St, 87501 ***Tel*** *(505) 988-4455*

Frequented by pre-opera diners, the Old House offers fine food and impeccable service. Menus change according to the seasons. The tasting menu might have Dungeness crab bisque or seared Maine diver scallops for appetizers, a roasted duckling entrée, and huckleberry strudel for dessert. A superior wine collection completes the picture.

TAOS Doc Martin's Restaurant $$$$

125 Paseo del Pueblo Norte, 87571 ***Tel*** *(575) 758-1977*

Thomas-Paul Martin was the first physician in the county, and he would travel miles to mend bones and birth babies. Named for the famous doctor, this restaurant now heals appetites with superior regional cuisine. Dine à la carte or try the prix-fixe three-course menu, featuring pepper-crusted buffalo steak. Excellent wines.

THE ROCKIES

INTRODUCING THE ROCKIES 566–573

IDAHO 574–577

MONTANA 578–581

WYOMING 582–587

COLORADO 588–597

The Rockies at a Glance

The four states of Montana, Idaho, Wyoming, and Colorado form the heart of the Rockies, the mountain range that dominates the landscape of North America. This beautiful but sparsely populated region encompasses a wealth of natural wonders such as the geysers of Wyoming's Yellowstone National Park, the varied landscapes of Montana's Glacier National Park, and the cliff dwellings of Colorado's Mesa Verde National Park. Colorado is also celebrated as the skiing capital of the United States. The area's human history lends itself to superlatives as much as the land does. Throughout the Rockies there are tangible signs of such legendary 19th-century Native Americans and cowboys as Sitting Bull and "Buffalo Bill" Cody.

Coeur d'Alene (see p574) *in Idaho is located along Lake Coeur d'Alene. This popular vacation destination is famous for its unique floating golf green on the 14th hole.*

Sun Valley (see p576), *in southern Idaho, is one of the oldest and most exclusive winter resorts in the country. Its picturesque environs also offer many recreational options.*

Yellowstone National Park (see pp584–5) *is perhaps one of the country's most visited parks. The highlights of this wild wonderland are the hot springs, particularly Old Faithful Geyser and its steaming plume.*

◁ **Mountain summit reflected in the placid waters of Lake Josephine, Glacier National Park, Montana**

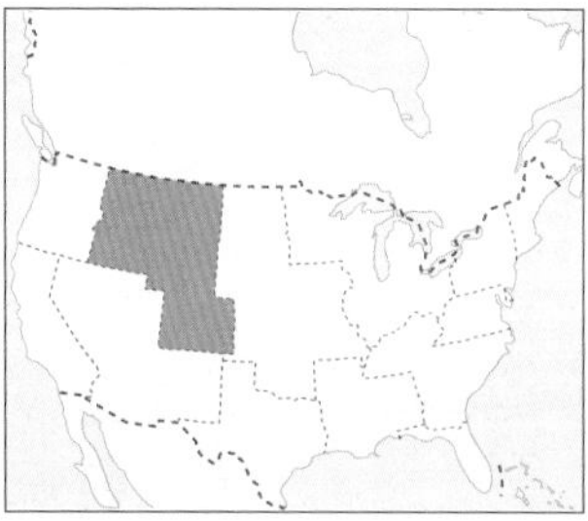

LOCATOR MAP

Billings (see p581) *evolved from a small frontier town into Montana's largest city. Its cowboy heritage can be seen at Yellowstone Art Museum.*

Denver (see pp588–9), *the region's main city, is also Colorado's state capital. This vibrant city is also known for its museums and parks.*

Mesa Verde National Park (see p596–597), *one of the country's most significant archaeological finds, preserves the elaborate cliff dwellings of the Ancestral Puebloan people.*

THE ROCKIES

One of the world's great outdoor regions, the Rockies offer a variety of experiences not found anywhere else. The sheer scale of the landscape is breathtaking, and words can hardly express the thrill of seeing firsthand the broad expanses of the Wyoming plains, Idaho's deep river canyons, the towering peaks of Colorado, or the rugged vastness of Montana.

The underlying geology of the Rocky Mountains is ancient, with some of the country's oldest rocks forming the highly stratified Precambrian peaks and valleys of Glacier National Park. The rest of the range is varied, with mineral-rich granite batholiths sharing space with the vast red-rock mesas of the Colorado Plateau. Evidence of volcanic activity, forming and reforming the landscape from deep beneath the surface, is also omnipresent, most prominently in Idaho's Craters of the Moon National Monument, and most famously in the geysers, mudpots, and hot springs of Yellowstone National Park in Wyoming.

This region has also been shaped by some of North America's mightiest rivers. Beside the terrifying white-water rapids of the Snake and other tumultuous rivers, the Rockies form the headwaters of many major western rivers, including the Colorado, the Missouri, the Columbia, and the Rio Grande. These rivers and their many tributaries offer some of the finest fishing in the world. Wildflowers are abundant, especially in the alpine meadows, while the dense forests are the habitat of a wide range of wildlife. Moose, elk, and bald eagles are spotted frequently along trails and roads, and the backwoods areas hold some of the nation's last wild populations of carnivores, including mountain lions, wolves, and massive grizzly bears.

HISTORY

The history of the Rockies is as wild and larger-than-life as the land itself. From the late 18th century, intrepid "mountain men" – French-Canadian and American fur trappers – traveled throughout the Rockies, trapping beavers and other animals for their valuable skins. After the Louisiana Purchase in 1803, the fledgling country acquired control of the Rockies, and the first official American

Pool along the Firehole Lake Drive, Yellowstone National Park, Wyoming

◁ Cross-country skiing at Steamboat Springs, one of Colorado's popular ski resorts presence was established between 1803 and 1806 by explorers Meriwether Lewis and William Clark. These daring men were accompanied by a "Corps of Discovery" made up of 29 soldiers and fur trappers, and joined by the legendary Indian guide Sacagawea and her baby son. They followed the Missouri upstream from the frontier outpost of St. Louis, traveling by boat and later by foot across Montana and Idaho on an epic 5,000-mile (8,047-km) journey to the Pacific Ocean and back. Also in 1806, Zebulon Pike led an expedition to Colorado, following the Arkansas River and spotting the majestic mountain that bears his name.

These explorers' published accounts, describing the sublime landscape and its wealth of wildlife, attracted increasing numbers of trappers and hunters, and by the 1830s several commercial outposts had been established, usually at the confluence of major rivers. Their routes across what had once been seen as an impenetrable barrier slowly but surely paved the way for transcontinental travelers. By the mid-1800s, thousands of pioneers following the Oregon Trail and other routes crossed the Rocky Mountains, bound for the Pacific Northwest, the California gold fields, and the Mormon lands in Utah. As a result, conflicts between immigrants and Native Americans increased dramatically. In the mountains, the Nez Percé and other small tribes lived comparatively peaceful and sedentary lives, while east of the mountains were migratory bands of Plains Indians, including such diverse and often rival tribes as the Sioux, Cheyenne, Crow, Arapahoe, and Shoshone. Most of these eastern tribes were themselves recent arrivals. Living in mobile encampments of tepees, they had mastered the art of riding horses and hunting buffalo. As cowboys and ranchers moved into the rich grazing lands, some 50 million native bison were all but eradicated, and the tribes whose entire culture was based on these mighty herds came under desperate threat.

Lewis & Clark National Historic Trail Interpretive Center, Great Falls, Montana

By the beginning of the 20th century, all the tribes had been contained in small reservations, far from their previous homelands. Ironically, one of the country's greatest Native American cultural repositories is in Wyoming's Buffalo Bill Historical Center, a memorial to the man who, as buffalo hunter and Indian fighter, contributed greatly to their destruction.

KEY DATES IN HISTORY

1200 Ancestral Pueblo Indians abandon their cliff dwellings at Mesa Verde, Colorado

1700–1800 French-Canadian fur trappers explore the Rockies

1803 The US acquires much of this region through the Louisiana Purchase

1803 The Lewis and Clark expedition begins

1806 Zebulon Pike explores the Arkansas River in southern Colorado

1843 The Oregon Trail is opened

1858 Gold is discovered outside Denver

1869 Wyoming gives women the vote

1872 US Congress establishes the world's first national park at Yellowstone

1876 Battle of Little Bighorn

1915 The Lincoln Highway, the first transcontinental route from New York City to San Francisco, runs across southern Wyoming

1951 Warren Air Force Base in Cheyenne is declared the base of operations for all US Intercontinental Ballistic Missiles (ICBMs)

1988 Forest fires across the Rockies cause serious damage to Yellowstone National Park

2003 Memorial commemorating the Native American victory at the Battle of Little Bighorn is dedicated at the site of the battle in Montana

Tepees, Buffalo Bill Historical Center, Wyoming

The former silver-mining town of Wallace, near Coeur d'Alene, Idaho

PROGRESS & DEVELOPMENT

The first transcontinental railroad crossed southern Wyoming in the late 1860s, followed in the 1870s and 1880s by other railroads, such as the Northern Pacific and Great Northern. Carrying cattle to eastern markets, and bringing weapons and supplies to the Wild West, it was these railroads that actually consolidated American settlement.

The search for and discovery of valuable minerals, mainly gold, silver, and copper, was another primary impetus to settlement. Because of the region's expansive forests, the lumber industry, too, had been an economic mainstay since pioneer times, and over the previous century oil and coal deposits have been the source underlying numerous booms and busts, especially in Colorado and Wyoming.

TOURISM & THE ECONOMY

Natural resource-based industries are still active all over the Rockies, though the main economic force today is tourism. These four states contain the highest mountains, the densest forests, the wildest rivers, and the most rugged canyons in the "Lower 48" states. Consequently, the Rockies is a magical place offering sublime scenery as well as a wide variety of attractions, such as historic train rides, summer "dude ranches," and historic sites. Many places also feature music festivals, Plains Indian pow-wows, or theatrical re-creations of Wild West shootouts.

This is also the best place to appreciate the great outdoors. Intrepid guides offer unforgettable trips such as whitewater rafting or fly-fishing for trout. The proliferation of ski resorts has also added to the state's tourism potential. When gold was discovered outside Denver in 1850, several mining camps sprang up at such evocatively named places as Silverton and Cripple Creek in Colorado and "Last Chance Gulch," now Helena, Montana. Many of these erstwhile mining centers are now deluxe winter resorts, such as Crested Butte, Telluride, and Aspen in Colorado, and Idaho's Sun Valley.

Neon sign for the Cowboy Bar, Jackson, Wyoming

Exploring the Rockies

The sheer vastness of the Rocky Mountains landscape and the relative shortness of the tourism season means that visitors need to plan well ahead. Many attractions on this 1,000-mile (1,609-km) long swath of mountains are on such high elevations that they are inaccessible during the long winter, with snow blocking roads from late October until June. The heavy snowfalls, however, enhance the region's phenomenal winter sports, and Denver, the main city, is a prime starting point for most visitors. Driving is the best way to explore the area, because public transportation is limited, and the national parks and most of the other attractions are far away.

KEY

- Airport
- Highway
- Major road
- Railroad
- State border
- International border

SIGHTS AT A GLANCE

Idaho

Coeur d'Alene 1
Hells Canyon National Recreation Area 2
Salmon 3
Sawtooth National Recreation Area 4
Boise 5
Sun Valley 6
Three Island Crossing State Park 7
Bruneau Dunes State Park 8
Twin Falls 9
Craters of the Moon National Monument 10
Idaho Falls 11

Montana

Big Hole National Battlefield 12
Missoula 13
Flathead Valley 14
Glacier National Park p579 15
Great Falls 16
Helena 17
Butte 18
Bozeman 19
Virginia City 20
Billings 21
Little Bighorn Battlefield National Monument 22

Wyoming

Cody 23
Yellowstone National Park pp584–5 24
Jackson 25
Grand Teton National Park p583 26
Bighorn Mountains 27
Devil's Tower National Monument 28
Casper 29
Guernsey 30
Laramie 31
Cheyenne 32

Colorado

Denver pp588–9 33
Boulder 34
Golden 35
Idaho Springs & Georgetown 36
Rocky Mountain National Park 37
Manitou Springs 38
Colorado Springs 39
Cripple Creek 40
Cañon City 41
Colorado Ski Resorts pp594–5 42
Great Sand Dunes National Monument & Preserve 43
Durango 44
Mesa Verde National Park 45
Ouray 46
Black Canyon of the Gunnison National Park 47
Colorado National Monument 48

For additional map symbols *see back flap*

SEE ALSO

- ***Practical Information*** pp598–9
- ***Where to Stay*** pp600–603
- ***Where to Eat*** pp604–607

MILEAGE CHART

10 = Distance in miles
10 = Distance in kilometers

DENVER, CO					
29 47	*BOULDER, CO*				
832 1339	**822** 1323	*BOISE, ID*			
792 1274	**784** 1261	**550** 885	*HELENA, MT*		
528 850	**518** 834	**367** 591	**379** 610	*JACKSON, WY*	
279 449	**269** 433	**912** 1468	**516** 830	**279** 449	*CASPER, WY*

Telluride, nestling beneath Mount Crested Butte

Trekkers at Maroon Bells, Aspen, Colorado

Idaho

One of the country's least populous states, Idaho has vast tracts of unexplored wilderness – remote mountain ranges, dense forests, frozen lakes, and deep river gorges. It is an ideal vacation spot for adventure sports enthusiasts, offering abundant opportunities for hiking, mountain biking, and whitewater rafting. To the north lie resorts such as Coeur d'Alene; the center has the majestic Sawtooth Mountains; while the south consists mainly of cultivated fields, prompting automobile license plates in the state to declare Idaho's pride in its primary product, "Famous Potatoes."

Coeur d'Alene ❶

38,000. *105 N First St, (208) 664-3194.* **www**.coeurdalene.org

A major vacation destination, Coeur d'Alene was founded in the 1870s as a US Army outpost. Its present "four star" status refers to the luxury available at the town's world-famous **Coeur d'Alene Resort** *(see p600)*. Located along the shore of the beautiful Lake Coeur d'Alene, this exclusive resort is well known for its unique floating golf green on the 14th hole. On the resort's east side, the 120-acre (49-ha) **Tubbs Hill Park** is a nature preserve with hiking trails, dense pine forests, and great views. Lake Coeur d'Alene is also home to one of the country's largest populations of ospreys and bald eagles, which can be seen frequently in winter diving for salmon in the waters of Wolf Lodge Bay.

A century ago, Coeur d'Alene was a busy service center for the prosperous silver mines in mountains east of the lake. A number of Victorian-era towns still stand in the former mining districts, and museums and mine tours offer a glimpse into this lost world. The town of Wallace, 52 miles (84 km) east, offers the **Sierra Silver Mine Tour**, which guides visitors through an 1890s silver mine.

Tubbs Hill Park
Tel *(208) 769-2252.* *dawn–dusk daily.*

Sierra Silver Mine Tour
420 5th St, Wallace. ***Tel*** *(208) 752-5151.* *May–Sep: daily. First tour at 9am, then every half hour.* **www**.silverminetour.org

A view of the scenic Lake Coeur d'Alene, near the resort

Hells Canyon National Recreation Area ❷

PO Box 832, Riggins. ***Tel*** *(208) 628-3916.* **www**.fs.fed.us/hellscanyon

The deepest river gorge in North America, Hells Canyon was carved from the craggy granite of the Seven Devils Mountains by the Snake River. Over a mile (1.6 km) deep and straddling the three-state border where Idaho, Washington, and Oregon meet, the canyon and its surroundings are now a recreational area that includes some 215,000 acres (87,008 ha) of wilderness where no motor vehicles are permitted. Nearly 100 miles (161 km) of undeveloped and turbulent whitewater draws kayakers, rafters, and other thrillseekers. Hells Canyon lies downstream from Hells Canyon Dam. The main visitor center is on the Oregon *(see pp640–41)* side of the dam, while in Idaho, the best introduction to the area is from Riggins, where there are many outfitters who provide rental gear.

Kayaking, Hells Canyon

Salmon ❸

3,120. *200 Main St, (208) 756-2100.* **Sacajawea Center** *May–Oct: Sat–Sun; daily in summer.* **www**.salmonidaho.com

Situated along the banks of the wild and scenic Salmon River, this was an important point along the Lewis and Clark Trail *(see p570)*. Essentially a supply town and resort center, Salmon makes a fine base for exploring the surrounding region. Among the activities offered are raft trips, kayaking, skiing, horseback riding, mountain biking, and snowmobiling. It is also possible to hike along parts of the legendary route that the explorers Lewis and Clark followed in the early 1800s while traveling from Illinois to find a navigable water route to the Pacific Ocean. Salmon was the birthplace of Lewis and Clark's guide, Sacajawea, and there is an interpretive center on Main Street that explores the significance of her role in their expedition.

The main highway, scenic US 93, winds along the main stream of the Salmon River, while smaller roads follow tributaries into the wild. At the hamlet of North Fork, Salmon River Road turns west from the highway, heading downstream along impassable rapids that Lewis and Clark aptly dubbed the "River of No Return."

For hotels and restaurants in this region see p600 and p604

A view of the Sawtooth Mountains, from the shores of Redfish Lake

Sawtooth National Recreation Area ❹

Hwy 75, 8 miles (13 km) N of Ketchum. *(800) 260-5970.* **Campground**. *year-round.*

This superb destination for hiking and camping encompasses 765,000 acres (309,586 ha) of rivers, mountain meadows, forests, and jagged peaks of the Sawtooth Range. For visitors driving up Hwy 75 from Sun Valley *(see p576)*, the best introduction to the area is at the 8,701-ft (2,652-m) high **Galena Summit**, where a spectacular panorama looks north over the Salmon River.

At an elevation of 6,200 ft (1,890 m), surrounded by the Sawtooth Mountains, the tiny hamlet of **Stanley** (population 75), has one of the most beautiful settings of any town in the US. The unpaved streets and wood-fronted frontier-style buildings make visitors feel like they have, at last, arrived in the Wild West, despite the fact that the glitzy resort of Sun Valley is barely an hour away to the south. Another attraction is **Redfish Lake**, 10 miles (16 km) south of Stanley, where rustic Redfish Lake Lodge is found near the foot of Mount Heyburn.

Boise ❺

210,000. 1220 S Vista Av and Grove Plaza (800) 635-5240.

French trappers in the 19th-century named this outpost "Boise," meaning wooded. Even today, this homespun, slow-paced city presents a picture-postcard image of America. Locals and visitors walk, ride bicycles, or enjoy an afternoon picnic on the grass in the vast Greenbelt parkland that adjoins the Boise River in the heart of downtown.

Boise is also the state capital and the largest city in rural Idaho. Its focal point is the domed **State Capitol**, which was completed in 1920 after 15 years of construction. The building's main distinction is that it is the only US capitol to be heated by naturally occurring geothermal water. It was built of sandstone blocks quarried by inmates at the **Old Idaho Penitentiary**, 2 miles (3 km) east of the capitol.

Now open to visitors, the state penitentiary was in use from 1870 to 1970. Apart from the prison, the grounds also house a series of museums dedicated to such subjects as transportation, the uses of electricity, and mining.

The city's historic center is three blocks south of the capitol. Here a dozen late-Victorian commercial buildings have been restored and house a lively set of coffee houses, bars, restaurants, and boutiques. Boise's oldest building, completed in 1864, now houses the **Basque Museum and Cultural Center**, which traces the presence of Basque sheep-herders in Boise and across western US, and is also known for celebrating Basque culture. A cluster of museums and cultural centers lie in **Julia Davis Park**, a 40-acre (16-ha) green area that straddles the Boise River at the heart of the Greenbelt.

A 15-minute drive by car away from the city is the **Peregrine Fund World Center for Birds of Prey**. One of the most successful organizations for breeding as well as studying raptors, the world center has been instrumental in recovering endangered populations of peregrine falcons in the US, a species that was nearly wiped out by lethal pesticides in the 1970s. Visitors also have the rare opportunity to see a variety of birds including eagles, condors, and falcons while enjoying a hilltop view of the surrounding sagebrush plains.

Peregrine Fund World Center for Birds of Prey
5668 West Flying Hawk Lane.
Tel *(208) 362-3716. Mar–Oct: 9am–5pm daily; Nov–Feb: 10am–4pm Tue–Sun. Jan 1, Easter, Thanksgiving, Dec 25.*

The beautiful exterior of the Idaho State Capitol in Boise

Skaters outside Sun Valley Lodge, Sun Valley

Sun Valley 6

251 Washington Ave, Ketchum, (208) 726-3423.
www.visitsunvalley.com

Developed in the late 1930s by the Union Pacific Railroad baron Averell Harriman, Sun Valley is one of the oldest and highest-profile winter resorts in the US. The construction of the Tyrolean-style **Sun Valley Lodge** *(see p600)* and the adjacent ski area was completed in 1936, after which Harriman was inspired to invite Hollywood movie stars and other members of the glitterati to enjoy his facilities. Sun Valley's fame was thus ensured by the presence of celebrities such as Errol Flynn, Gary Cooper, Clark Gable, and Ernest Hemingway. Since then, the Olympic-quality skiing on the well-groomed slopes of the 9,151-ft (2,789-m) Bald Mountain has continued to draw an exclusive clientele during the season between November and April. The resort also commissioned the world's first ski-lift.

Before the 1930s, however, the area was a mining and sheep-ranching center, based in the adjacent town of Ketchum. This town still retains many of its rugged frontier characteristics, despite the influx of multi-million-dollar vacation homes. The region's history is on view in the **Ketchum Sun Valley Heritage & Ski Museum**. Although most visitors never stray beyond Sun Valley and Ketchum, the surrounding landscape is filled with other recreational options. Bicyclists can follow the 20-mile (32-km) **Wood River Trail**, along the old Union Pacific Railroad right-of-way. The Wood River is also a prime trout-fishing stream, while to the north, the majestic Sawtooth National Recreation Area *(see p575)* offers pristine hiking and camping country.

Ketchum Sun Valley Heritage & Ski Museum
180 1st Ave E. ***Tel*** *(208) 726-8118.*
noon–5pm Mon–Sat.
www.ksvhs.org

Three Island Crossing State Park 7

Off I-84, Glenns Ferry Exit. *Glenns Ferry, (208) 366-2394.* ***Campground.***
www.parksandrecreation.idaho.gov

One of the most evocative sights along the historic Oregon Trail *(see p450)* is the famous Three Islands Crossing, which provided one of the few safe places for emigrants to cross the dangerous Snake River. The ford was in use until 1869, when Gus Glenn constructed a ferry 2 miles (3 km) upstream. Not all attempts at crossing, however, were successful. Depending on the time of year and the level of the water, it sometimes proved fatal to the pioneers in the westward-bound wagons. Some pioneers avoided the crossing. Instead, they would continue along the river's barren south bank before rejoining the main trail west of Boise.

The Hemingway Memorial, Sun Valley

Today, the park offers a campground and numerous picnic areas. Visitors can still experience the dangers of the 1800s if they visit the park on the second Saturday in August, when the ford crossing is re-created by history enthusiasts wearing period costumes and driving replica wagons.

Bruneau Dunes State Park 8

Hwy 78 (off State Hwy 51). ***Tel*** *Mountain Home, (208) 366-7919.* *9am–5pm daily.* ***Campground***

Immediately south of the Snake River, at the foot of the high-desert Owyhee Mountains, a surprising sight arises from the surrounding sagebush plains. Some of the largest sand dunes in North America, the Bruneau Dunes rise to heights of nearly 500 ft (152 m). They are protected from the destructive impacts of cars, motorcycles, and dune buggies within one of Idaho's largest state parks.

A visitor center explains how these quartz and feldspar sand dunes were formed, and why they are not blown away. The reason for this phenomenon is simple: prevailing winds blow from opposite directions for roughly equal amounts of time, which keep the dunes fairly stable. There are also specimens of local wildlife on display, including a short-eared owl. A small astronomical observatory is often open to the public.

The park encompasses a variety of habitats such as marsh, prairie, and desert. Wildlife includes snakes and lizards, and birds such as owls and eagles. A few small lakes lie at the foot of the dunes where visitors can go fishing in canoes or rubber rafts. Other activities offered are camping and horseback riding.

Snake River Gorge, Twin Falls

Twin Falls ⑨

36,000. Hwy 93, (208) 733-3974.
www.twinfallschamber.com

The falls for which the city was named have been diminished by dams and irrigation, but Twin Falls is still home to a splendid waterfall. Called the "Niagara of the West," the 212-ft (65-m) high and 1,000-ft (305-m) wide **Shoshone Falls** is an impressive sight, especially in spring when the water flows are at their peak.

Located 5 miles (8 km) northeast of the city, the falls are framed by the deep **Snake River Gorge**, famous for the ill-fated attempt by motorcycle daredevil Evel Knievel to leap across it in 1974. He survived, but with many injuries. The city stretches along the level plains to the south of the gorge, and is the center for potato-growing farms and cattle ranches.

Craters of the Moon National Monument ⑩

US 20. ***Tel*** *(208) 527-3257.*
(Campground only).
www.nps.gov/crmo

Sprawled across 83 sq miles (215 sq km) in central Idaho, the Craters of the Moon National Monument showcases one of the most extraordinary landscapes in the country. The most accessible section can be explored via the numerous short trails that lead through rippling, jagged, lava fields, strewn with cones and craters. They range from 15,000 to 2,000 years of age. The fields were formed by molten lava, which seeped out from gaps in the earth's crust over a period of 13,000 years. Despite their forbidding, blackened appearance, the lava fields harbor more than 50 species of mammals, 170 species of birds, and millions of resplendent wildflowers, which bloom in summer each year. Numerous caves and lava tubes also run beneath the surface.

The name "Craters of the Moon" was coined in the 1920s, when the monument was established. The visitor center near the entrance recounts the park's geological and natural history. Visitors can also improve their Hawaiian lava vocabulary, learning the scientific terms for sharp lava *(a'a)*, layered lava *(kipukas)*, and smooth lava *(pa'hoe'hoe)*.

In the 1960s, astronauts from the *Apollo 14* space mission visited the monument to learn more about volcanic geology that was similar to that of the moon.

Camping is also available in the park during the summer, and the main loop road draws crowds of cross-country skiers during winter.

Idaho Falls ⑪

50,730. 630 W Broadway, (866) 365-6943.
www.visitidahofalls.com

Set along the banks of the Snake River, with Wyoming's Grand Teton Mountains rising to the east, Idaho Falls is a charming and mainly agricultural city with a large Mormon population *(see p519)*. Dominated by the towering Mormon temple, the city has a vast "Greenbelt" area where people can jog and inline skate. Although the Idaho Falls, which lent their name to the city, have now been dammed, they still provide a scenic setting to the parkland. The **Museum of Idaho** showcases the state's history and hosts traveling exhibits. The **Idaho National Laboratory** (INL), located 50 miles (80 km) west of the city, was established in 1949 to design, build, and test nuclear reactors for military and civilian purposes. The world's first reactor, the EBR-1, was built here in 1951 and is open for viewing. On July 17, 1955, INL was the site of the world's first peaceful use of atomic power, when INL engineers sent 2,000 kilowatts (2 megawatts) of electricity to light up the nearby town of Arco.

Museum of Idaho
200 N Eastern Ave. ***Tel*** *(208) 522-1400.* *9am–8pm Mon–Tue, 9am–5pm Wed–Sat.*

Idaho National Laboratory
Hwy 20/26. ***Tel*** *(208) 526-0050.*
Jun–Aug: 8am–4pm daily
Jul 4. **www**.inl.gov

Blackened volcanic cones, Craters of the Moon National Monument

Montana

The northernmost of the Rocky Mountain states, Montana abounds in tall, rugged mountains, snow-capped peaks, lush valleys, and seemingly endless plains stretching beneath its trademark "big sky." The sheer scale and majesty of its wide open spaces and the larger-than-life character of its inhabitants, past and present, prompted Nobel Prize-winning novelist John Steinbeck to write "Montana seems to me to be what a small boy would think Texas is like from hearing Texans. Of all the states it is my favorite and my love."

Big Hole National Battlefield, surrounded by mountains

Big Hole National Battlefield ⓬

Hwy 43 near Wisdom. ***Tel*** *(406) 689-3155.* *May–Sep: 9am–6pm; Oct–Apr: 10am–5pm daily.* *Jan 1, Thanksgiving, Dec 25.*

Located near the Idaho border at an altitude of some 7,000 ft (2,134 m) in the Bitterroot Mountains, this battlefield site sits at the head of the lush Big Hole Valley, famed for its cattle ranches and trout-fishing opportunities. This serene pastoral scene is far removed from the terrible suffering experienced here on August 9, 1877. On that day, the flight north by 750 Nez Perce Indians, mostly women and children, was cut short by a surprise attack by US Army soldiers and civilian volunteers, leading to the death of nearly 100 Indians. The tribe continued their journey toward Canada, traveling another 1,500 miles (2,414 km) before finally surrendering in October, just 30 miles (48 km) short of the Canadian border.

Missoula ⓭

58,000. *1121 E Broadway, Suite 103, (800) 526-3465.*

Nestling in the Rocky Mountains of western Montana, Missoula is still dependent upon traditional Montana industries, such as timber and transportation. This lively city is also home to the University of Montana.

Surrounded by acres of magnificent wilderness, this picturesque city formed the backdrop of the book and subsequent movie *A River Runs Through It*. The city also houses the **Smokejumpers Base**, a national center for fighting forest fires in the Rockies. Exhibits explore fire-fighting techniques and equipment, and depending on the time of year (summer is forest-fire season), guests are able to tour the airplanes and meet fire-fighters.

To the south, the Bitterroot Valley has ranches and small towns, hemmed in by a pair of towering mountain ranges.

Smokejumpers Base Visitor Center
Aerial Fire Depot, Missoula Int'l Airport, Hwy 93. ***Tel*** *(406) 329-4934.* *Memorial Day–Labor Day: daily; Labor Day–Memorial Day: by appt.*

Flathead Valley ⓮

Bigfork Chamber of Commerce, 8155 Hwy 35, (406) 837-5888. **Salish & Kootenai Tribal Council** ***Tel*** *(406) 675-2700.*

Most of the valley's land, which stretches between the 40-mile (64-km) long and 15-mile (24-km) wide Flathead Lake and Missoula, is part of the Flathead Indian Reservation. Since 1855 this has been home to descendants of the region's Salish, Kootenai, and Pend d'Oreille Indian tribes. In summer, communities such as Elmo and Arlee celebrate Native traditions in numerous pow-wows, which are traditional gatherings featuring rodeo competitions, craft demonstrations, and sales.

The **People's Center** in Pablo traces the history of the Flathead region from a Native American perspective. To the west, some 18,500 acres (7,487 ha) of rolling ranchland were set aside in 1908 as the National Bison Range, housing bison, deer, bighorn sheep, and pronghorn.

The largest natural freshwater lake west of the Mississippi River, Flathead Lake is a deep-blue jewel at the western foot of the Rocky Mountains. Cherry orchards and towns like Bigfork line Hwy 35 on the lake's eastern shore, while to the west the busier US 93 hugs the water for over 35 miles (56 km). Rent bikes or kayaks, or take guided boat tours into the scenic lake.

People's Center
53253 Hwy 93, Pablo. ***Tel*** *(406) 883-5344.* *9am–5pm Mon–Fri; also 10am–5pm Sat from Memorial Day to Labor Day only.*

Flathead Lake, nestling at the foot of the Rocky Mountains

For hotels and restaurants in this region see p601 and p605

Glacier National Park ⓯

North of W Glacier. (406) 888-7800. *most visitor facilities open late May–mid-Sep.* **www**.nps.gov/glac

Hiking, a popular activity in Glacier National Park

Spreading nearly a million acres (404,690 ha) over the northern Rocky Mountains, Glacier National Park holds some of the world's most sublime scenery. With elevations ranging from 3,200 ft (975 m) along the Flathead River to summits topping 10,000 ft (3,048 m), the park contains a wide variety of landscapes. Alongside four dozen glaciers (which gave the park its name) and ancient limestone cliffs, there are lakes, waterfalls, and abundant wildlife, including moose, wolves, and bears. The flora ranges from high grassy plains to alpine tundra. In July, the park's higher altitudes are ablaze with meadows of blue gentians, yellow lilies, pink heathers, and feathery white Bear Grass.

Avalanche Creek drops through dense forests down a red rock gorge. A boardwalk nature trail runs along its length.

Going-to-the-Sun Mountain Road runs past St. Mary's Lake. This 50-mile (80-km) road is the main access for touring the park, joining the park headquarters to the east entrance.

Swiftcurrent Lake sits at the foot of deeply glaciated valleys. Its shores offer rustic lodgings.

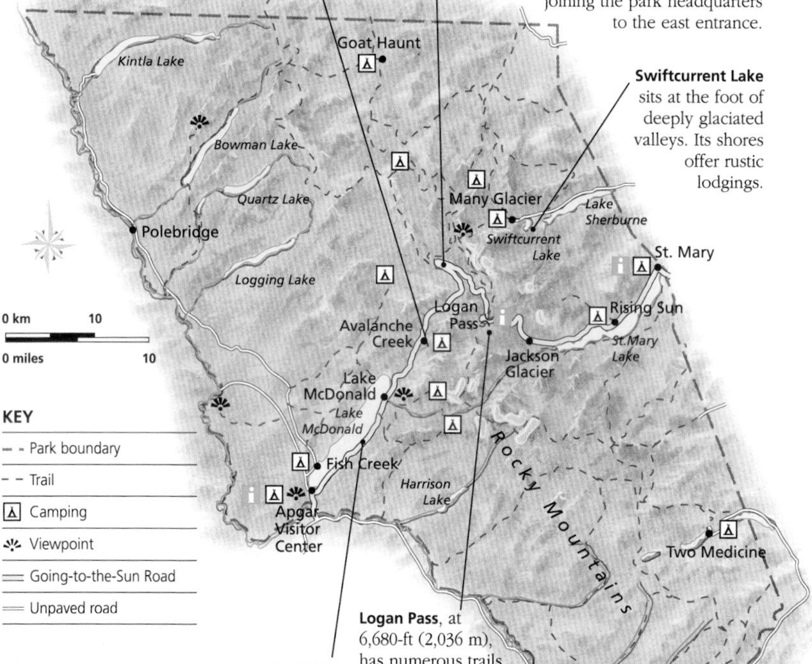

Logan Pass, at 6,680-ft (2,036 m), has numerous trails that lead from the road to alpine lakes and wildflower-rich meadows.

Lake McDonald

Surrounded by dense conifer forests and a circle of high peaks, this 10-mile (16-km) long glacier-carved lake is the largest in the park.

Great Falls 16

56,700. 15 Upper River Rd, (406) 761-4434.
www.greatfallschamber.org

Nestling picturesquely between the majestic Rocky Mountains to the west and Little Belt Mountains to the east, this rural city owes its name to its location along the Missouri River. As the river cuts through the city, it drops over 500 ft (152 m) in a series of rapids and five breathtaking waterfalls, first noted by explorers Lewis and Clark *(see p570)* in 1805.

The city is best known for its two excellent museums. One, the **Charles M. Russell Museum**, traces the history of the American West, focusing on the life and work of resident cowboy and prolific Wild West artist "Charlie" Russell, who gave the city much of its cultural flavor. His home and log cabin studio are next to the expansive museum.

On a bluff overlooking the Missouri River, 2 miles (3 km) northeast of downtown, is the **Lewis and Clark National Historic Trail Interpretive Center**, which details the epic explorations of the Corps of Discovery, the cross-country expedition led by Meriwether Lewis and William Clark from 1803 to 1806.

For 45 miles (72 km) downstream from the center, the Missouri River runs as a "Wild and Scenic" river on one of its virgin stretches, a route paralleled by a bike trail and driving tour along US 87. The route ends at Fort Benton, historic head of navigation on the Missouri River.

Charles M. Russell Museum
400 13th St N. ***Tel*** *(406) 727-8787.* *Jun–Aug: 9am–6pm daily; Sep–May: 10am–5pm Tue–Sat.* *Jan 1, Easter, Thanksgiving, Dec 25.*

Lewis & Clark National Historic Trail Interpretive Center
4201 Giant Springs Rd. ***Tel*** *(406) 727-8733.* *Memorial Day–Sep: 9am–6pm daily; Oct–Memorial Day: 9am–5pm Tue–Sat, noon–5pm Sun.* *Jan 1, Thanksgiving, Dec 25.*

Helena 17

27,500. 225 Cruse Ave, (406) 442-4120.

The state capital, Helena makes a fine base for exploring Montana. Originally known as "Last Chance Gulch," Helena was founded as a gold-mining camp in the 1860s. Fortunately much of the wealth generated here remained, as is evident from the number of mansions built by mining millionaires. Many of these exuberantly designed Victorian-era homes have been converted into B&B inns. The centerpiece of Helena is the copper-domed **Montana State Capitol**, decorated with several fine historical murals, including one of explorers Lewis and Clark painted by Charlie Russell. A statue on the grounds portrays Helena resident Jeanette Rankin, who in 1917 was the first woman to be elected to the United States Congress.

Statue of Jeanette Rankin, Montana State Capitol

Butte 18

34,000. 1000 George St, (406) 723-3177, (800) 735-6814.

Located in the heart of the Rocky Mountains, Butte is named for the prominent conical hill, Big Butte, which guards its northwest corner. That Butte has some of the world's richest mineral reserves is evident by the extensive signs of the gold, silver, and copper mining industry that thrived here from the 1870s through the first half of the 20th century. Glimpses of Butte's multi-ethnic, immigrant culture are also visible in such events as the St. Patrick's Day celebration by the town's Irish Catholic population. Of Butte's many fine museums, the **World Museum of Mining** occupies the site of an early gold mine. Its superb collection of mineral specimens, mining machinery, and mementos of the town's proud industrial heritage, also includes displays on Butte's leading role in the development of mine-workers' unions. Outside, some 30 historic buildings dating from 1880 to 1910 re-create an early mining camp, complete with a church, a schoolhouse, bordellos, and boarding houses.

Sites such as the **Granite Mountain Mine Memorial** commemorate the 168 men killed in a 1917 mine disaster. High above the city, the 90-ft (27-m) statue of "Our Lady of the Rockies" stands as a proud symbol of Butte's strength and endurance.

World Museum of Mining
155 Museum Way, off Park St. ***Tel*** *(406) 723-7211.* *Apr–Oct: 9am–5:30pm daily (to 9pm Jun–Aug).*

Lewis and Clark National Historic Trail Interpretive Center, Great Falls

Exterior of the Museum of the Rockies, Bozeman

Bozeman ⑲

27,500. 2000 Commerce Way, (406) 586-5421.

Situated in the heart of the Gallatin Valley, Bozeman lies in the middle of a sacred Sioux Indian hunting ground, which is now the state's most productive agricultural region. Founded in the 1860s, the city is one of the few Montana towns where the economy and history are not based on mining or railroads. Its present prominence is due mainly to the Montana State University. Established in 1893, it is the state's largest university and houses the **Museum of the Rockies**. The museum takes visitors through Earth's history, delving into everything from displays of dinosaurs and dinosaur eggs unearthed in Montana Plains, to pioneer history, Indian artifacts, and Western art. A planetarium presents astronomy and laser light shows.

Downtown's tree-lined streets are pleasant to stroll through. Visitors can also learn about local history at the **Gallatin Pioneer Museum**, housed in the former jail.

Museum of the Rockies
600 W Kagy Blvd on the Montana State University Campus. ***Tel*** *(406) 994-2251. May–Sep: 8am–8pm daily; Oct–Apr: 9am–5pm Mon–Sat, 12:30–5pm Sun. Thnksg., Dec 25.*

Gallatin Pioneer Museum
317 W Main St. ***Tel*** *(406) 522-8122. Jun–Aug: 10am–5pm Mon–Sat; Sep–May: 11am–4pm Tue–Sat. public hols.*

Virginia City ⑳

100. 300 Wallace St, (406) 843-5247. **www**.virginiacity.com

Gold was discovered here in 1863 and the ensuing stampede created a boom town. More than 100 historic buildings have been preserved, and visitors can enjoy stagecoach tours and panning for gold. On the **Alder Gulch Short Line Railroad**, a 1910 steam train makes the 30-minute trip to Nevada City, where the entire town is a state museum.

Billings ㉑

90,000. 815 S 27th St, (406) 245-4111. **www**.visitbillings.com

Founded by the Northern Pacific Railroad in 1882, and now Montana's largest city, Billings was named after the railroad company's president. In just a few months, Billings grew into a bustling community of 2,000 people. Visitors can get a feel of the town's frontier days, and of Montana's cowboy traditions, from the Wild West paintings and sculptures displayed in the **Yellowstone Art Museum**, located in the old county jail.

However, the most striking feature of Billings is the Rimrocks, a 400-ft (122-m) high sandstone wall that runs the length of the city along the Yellowstone River.

Outside the city the scenery is even more spectacular, especially along the Beartooth Highway that runs southwest toward Yellowstone National Park *(see pp584–5)*. The 65-mile (105-km) section between Red Lodge and the Wyoming border is stunning.

Yellowstone Art Museum
401 N 27th St. ***Tel*** *(406) 256-6804. 10am–5pm Mon (summer only), 10am–5pm Tue–Sat (until 8pm on Thu), noon–5pm Sun. public hols.*

Little Bighorn Battlefield National Monument ㉒

Exit 510 off I-90, Hwy 212, Crow Agency. *(406) 638-3204.* **www**.nps.gov/libi

Located on the Crow Indian Reservation, this battlefield preserves the site of a key moment in American history, known as "Custer's Last Stand." In June 1876, the impetuous US Army Lieutenant Colonel George Armstrong Custer *(see p446)* led his troop of 210 soldiers of the 7th Cavalry in an attack on a large Indian encampment along the Little Bighorn River. They were quickly surrounded by more than 2,000 combined Sioux and Cheyenne Indian warriors under the leadership of legendary Chief Sitting Bull. Custer's soldiers were wiped out. A sandstone marker stands above the soldiers' mass grave, and a small museum describes the disastrous battle.

Memorial to Custer's Last Stand, Little Bighorn Battlefield

Wyoming

The Wyoming state insignia, an image of a cowboy waving his Stetson hat while riding on the back of a bucking horse, says it all. This is classic cowboy country, a land of wide-open grasslands stretching for miles in every direction, where fewer than a half-million people inhabit an area of nearly 100,000 sq miles (260,000 sq km). For visitors, the main draws of Wyoming lie in its northwestern corner, where the twin spectacles of Yellowstone and Grand Teton National Parks attract some three million visitors annually.

Buffalo Bill Historical Center, Cody

Cody ㉓

9,000. 836 Sheridan Ave, (307) 587-2777.

Cody was founded by Wild West impresario "Buffalo Bill" Cody in 1896. Long the symbol of the American West, the city maintains its frontier look and is home to two museums that document this unique era. The smaller of these is **Trail Town**, a homespun collection of artifacts and buildings assembled on the original site of Cody. One highlight here is a log cabin reputedly used as a hideout by outlaws Butch Cassidy and the Sundance Kid.

Cody's main attraction, however, is the **Buffalo Bill Historical Center**, a 240,000-sq-ft (22,300-sq-m) complex of galleries that trace the natural, cultural, and military history of the Wild West. It holds more than 500 weapons, a superb collection of Western art, and Plains Indians artifacts, as well as a museum on Buffalo Bill himself.

In keeping with Buffalo Bill's pursuit of public spectacle, Cody's other great attraction is the **Cody Night Rodeo**, the nation's longest-running rodeo, held daily between late June and August.

Buffalo Bill Historical Center
720 Sheridan Ave. ***Tel*** *(307) 587-4771. Nov–Mar: 10am–5pm Thu–Sun; Apr: 10am–5pm daily; May–Aug: 8am–6pm daily; Sep–Oct: 10am–5pm daily. Jan 1, Thanksgiving, Dec 25.*

Yellowstone National Park ㉔

See pp584–5.

Jackson ㉕

9,000. 532 N Cache St, (307) 733-3316.

A popular stop since the days of the fur-trapping mountain men, Jackson is perhaps Wyoming's most visited city. Located at the southern entrance to Grand Teton and Yellowstone National Parks, much of its natural beauty is giving way to vacation homes and ski resorts. But Jackson retains its Wild West ambience despite the boutiques and art galleries that surround its tree-lined central square, and the congested summer traffic.

Alongside the national parks, dude ranches, and Wild West re-enactments, the main attraction is wildlife. The 25,000-acre (10,120-ha) **National Elk Refuge**, stretching between Jackson and the Grand Teton National Park, is home to some 7,500 native elk that congregate here in winter. Its entrance lies one mile (1.6 km) northeast of Jackson. Guided tours on horse-drawn sleighs are offered between November and April. In summer, the main gondola at Jackson Hole Ski Area (rated as one of the country's most challenging) lifts sightseers over 4,000 ft (1,219 m) to the top of Rendezvous Peak for a grand panorama.

National Elk Refuge
E Broadway at Elk Refuge Rd. ***Tel*** *(307) 733-9212. 8am–5pm daily (until 7pm Memorial Day–Labor Day). Thnksg., Dec 25. sleigh rides.*

BUFFALO BILL

One of the most colorful Wild West figures, William Frederick Cody (1846–1917) started out as a teenage rider for the Pony Express. He then served as US Army scout during the Civil War. When the war ended in 1865, he began supplying buffalo meat to workers of the transcontinental railroad, earning himself the nickname "Buffalo Bill." Cody was the model for a series of newspaper stories and "dime novels" written by Ned Buntline. The real-life Buffalo Bill soon parlayed his credentials into worldwide fame and fortune. Star of a spectacular circus in which historical scenes were acted out by cowboys and Indians, including such figures as Chief Sitting Bull, Cody toured the world between 1883 and World War I. Despite his fortune, by 1913 he was bankrupt, and died four years later in Denver *(see pp588–9)*.

Statue of Buffalo Bill

Grand Teton National Park 26

Moose. *Grand Teton National Park Headquarters, (307) 739-3300.*

www.nps.gov/grte

The youngest peaks in the Rockies, the Grand Tetons are among the sharpest and most dramatic mountains in the world. Their silver granite peaks rise over a mile above the lush Snake River Valley of Jackson Hole, all of which has been protected within the boundaries of the 485-sq-mile (1,256-sq-km) Grand Teton National Park. There are miles of hiking trails that lead to numerous glaciers and lakes. Wildlife, such as elk, bison, and bears, abounds. In summer, kayakers and rafters float the Snake River, while powerboats and canoes take more leisurely cruises on Jackson and Jenny Lakes. In winter, all hiking trails are open to skiers who make their way through the wilderness.

A view of the Grand Teton summits and fall colors

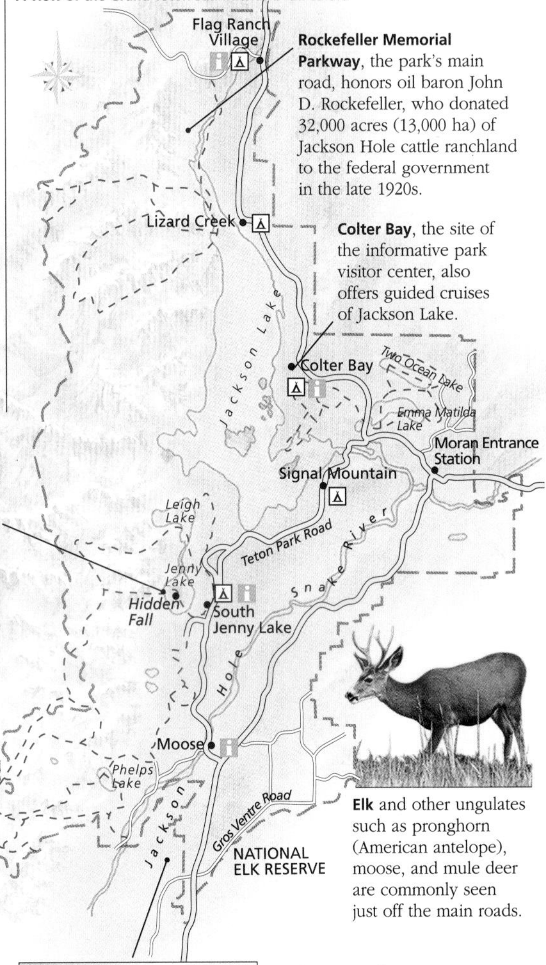

Rockefeller Memorial Parkway, the park's main road, honors oil baron John D. Rockefeller, who donated 32,000 acres (13,000 ha) of Jackson Hole cattle ranchland to the federal government in the late 1920s.

Colter Bay, the site of the informative park visitor center, also offers guided cruises of Jackson Lake.

Jenny Lake
The popular Jenny Lake lies at the base of the 13,770-ft (4,197-m) Grand Teton. Trails lead along forested shores to quiet beaches, with the mountains reflecting in the distance.

Elk and other ungulates such as pronghorn (American antelope), moose, and mule deer are commonly seen just off the main roads.

0 km 10

0 miles 10

KEY

- Park boundary
- Trail
- Camping
- Major road
- Unpaved road

Jackson Hole
Frontier fur trappers referred to a large valley ringed by mountains as a "hole." This valley of the Snake River runs between the Grand Teton and Gros Ventre Mountains, upstream from Jackson.

Yellowstone National Park ㉔

Official park sign

One of the marvels of the world, and the country's oldest national park, this wild wonderland spreads across the three states of Wyoming, Montana, and Idaho. Its heart is a volcanic plateau at an average elevation of 8,000 ft (2,438 m), housing over 10,000 hot springs and geysers – more than half of the world's total. Alongside the spectacular shows of geothermal activity, it has dense forests, towering peaks, deep river canyons, and enough outdoor recreation to last a lifetime. The 175-mile (282-km) Grand Loop Road does a full circuit of the main sights. Lodging is often booked solid, so visitors should reserve in advance.

An elk crossing the road in the park

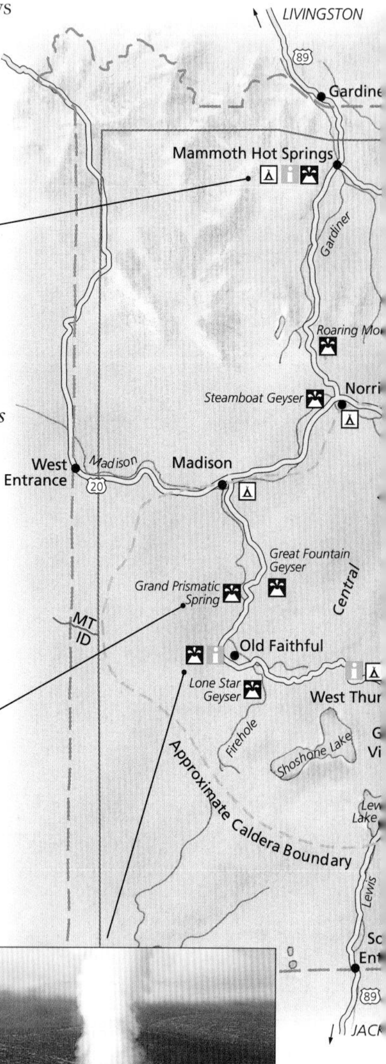

★ Mammoth Hot Springs
Hundreds of geothermal springs bubble up in Yellowstone, forming colored pools of boiling hot, mineral-rich water. The mineral content drapes delicate curtains of marble-like travertine over the cascading terraces of stone.

Grand Prismatic Spring
The 370-ft (113-m) wide Grand Prismatic Spring lies close to Old Faithful. The rainbow-colored hot spring, lining the bank of the Firehole River, is one of the world's largest.

★ Old Faithful Geyser
Named for its precise 90-minute eruption cycle, Old Faithful is the park's icon. Its steaming plume shoots as high as 120–180 ft (36–55 m) and lasts 2 to 5 minutes. Visitors line up on the wooden boardwalk to watch it spurt nearly 8,400 gallons (31,797 liters) of water per eruption.

For hotels and restaurants in this region see p602 and p606

Bison
With over 3,000 bison, Yellowstone has the world's largest herd. They roam freely across the park, often even disrupting traffic. Despite their docile appearance, bison can be dangerous, so visitors should avoid contact with them or any other wild animal.

VISITORS' CHECKLIST

US 26 in Moose. *YNP Headquarters, Mammoth Hot Springs, (307) 344-7381.* *year-round, but most facilities & roads are closed from October to May due to winter snows. The only open road is US 212, along the northern edge, between Gardiner & Cooke City, Montana.* **www**.nps.gov/yell

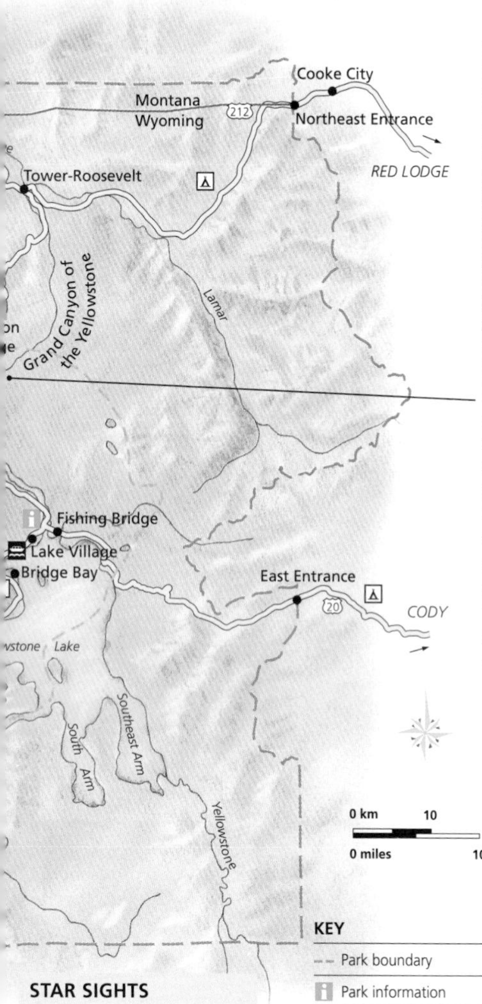

★ Grand Canyon
Plunging 500 ft (152 m) in a pair of falls – Upper and Lower Falls – the Yellowstone River has carved this 20-mile (32-km) long canyon into the mineral-rich yellow and orange rhyolite rock. Many trails along its rim offer splendid vistas. "Uncle Tom's Trail" drops down a steep staircase on to a platform, offering a close-up view of the falls.

Bears
Bears are plentiful in the park. Black bears are the most common, and more than 200 grizzlies inhabit its wilder reaches. Most animals avoid contact with humans, and rangers advise that humans should avoid any contact with bears.

STAR SIGHTS

- ★ Grand Canyon
- ★ Mammoth Hot Springs
- ★ Old Faithful Geyser

KEY

- Park boundary
- Park information
- Camping
- Ferry
- Geyser
- Major road
- State border

The Medicine Wheel on Medicine Mountain, the Bighorn Scenic Byway (US 14)

Bighorn Mountains 27

Bighorn National Forest
Tel *(307) 674-2600.*

Standing at the western edge of the historic plains of the Powder River Basin, the Bighorn Mountains were named for the bighorn sheep that were once abundant here. Crowned by the 13,175-ft (4,016-m) Cloud Peak, the mountains are crossed by a pair of very scenic highways, US 16 in the south (the old Yellowstone Trail) and US 14 in the north, which divides into two forks. The northernmost section of US 14 climbs past one of the country's most enigmatic archaeological sites, the **Medicine Wheel**, an 80-ft (24-m) diameter stone circle, which is located 27 miles (43 km) east of Lovell. This ancient circle is held sacred by Native Sioux and Cheyenne Indians, and offers a vast panorama from its 10,000-ft (3,048-m) elevation.

Devil's Tower National Monument 28

(307) 467-5283.
www.nps.gov/deto

Rising over 1,200 ft (366 m) above the surrounding plains, Devil's Tower is a flat-topped volcanic plug that looks like a giant tree stump. Featured in the 1977 Steven Spielberg movie *Close Encounters of the Third Kind*, this geological landmark is located in Wyoming's northeastern corner, looming over the banks of the Belle Fourche River. Set aside as a national monument by President Theodore Roosevelt in 1906, Devil's Tower (also known as Bear's Lodge) is a sacred site of worship for many Native Americans. The rolling hills of this 1,347-acre (545-ha) park are covered with pine forests, deciduous woodlands, and prairie grasslands, and abound in deer, prairie dogs, and other wildlife. The site's vertical rock walls and scenic trails are a magnet for rock-climbers and hikers.

Casper 29

50,000. 992 N Poplar and 500 N Center, (307) 234-5362.
www.casperwyoming.info

Located in the heart of Wyoming, Casper has been the center of the state's large petroleum industry since 1890. Surrounded by miles of broad, flat plains, this large, busy city grew up around the 1860s Fort Caspar, now a historical site and museum, known as the **Fort Caspar Museum**. Many of the fort buildings have been reconstructed at the point where the historic Oregon Trail *(see p450)* crossed the North Platte River, west of downtown. The museum features a variety of cultural and natural history exhibits pertaining to central Wyoming.

North and west of Casper lie miles of arid badlands, including such sites as the legendary "Hole in the Wall," where outlaws such as Butch Cassidy had hideouts. More accessible to visitors is the weirdly eroded forest of figures known as "Hell's Half Acre," located 35 miles (56 km) west of town on the south side of US 20.

Fort Caspar Museum
4001 Fort Caspar Rd. ***Tel*** *(307) 235-8462.* *daily, hours vary.*

A view of the exterior of Fort Caspar Museum, Casper

For hotels and restaurants in this region see p602 and p606

Guernsey 30

1,150. 90 S Wyoming St (summer only).

Set along the banks of the North Platte River, this is a small town whose size belies a wealth of historical interest. Just south of town are two of the most palpable reminders of the pioneer migrations westward along the Oregon Trail. The **Oregon Trail Ruts State Historic Site** preserves a set of 4–6-ft (1–1.8-m) deep gouges carved by wagon wheels into the soft riverside sandstone. A mile south, the Register Cliff has been inscribed with the names of hundreds of explorers, fur trappers, and Oregon Trail pioneers who crossed the area in the mid-1800s.

Evocative as these sights are, Guernsey's most important historic spot is the **Fort Laramie National Historic Site**, a reconstruction of a fur-trapping and US cavalry outpost. Between its founding in the 1830s and its abandonment in 1890s, the fort was a prime point of contact between Europeans, Americans, and Native Americans. Many of the buildings have been restored, and costumed interpreters act out roles from the fort's history.

Fort Laramie National Historic Site
US 26. *Tel (307) 837-2221.* *May–Sep: 8am–7pm daily; Oct–Apr: 8am–4:30pm daily.* *Jan 1, Thanksgiving, Dec 25.*

Laramie 31

27,200. 800 S 3rd St, (307) 745-7339. www.laramie.org

Home to the main state university campus, the small city of Laramie exudes an infectious youthful vitality, which is rare in other Wyoming cities. Located east of downtown at an elevation of 7,200 ft (2,195 m), the University of Wyoming is the highest college in the country. The campus is dominated by the strikingly modern **American Heritage Center**, an art museum and library documenting Wyoming history and culture. The town also housed Wyoming's first prison, now restored to its 1880s condition, when Butch Cassidy and other outlaws served time here. Located west of downtown, the old prison is now the centerpiece of the **Wyoming Territorial Prison State Historic Park**, which includes a re-creation of a frontier town.

The area around Laramie is rich historically and scenically. The 50-mile (80-km) stretch of the Lincoln Highway between Laramie and Cheyenne preserves part of the first transcontinental road in the US. To the west of Laramie, Hwy 130 follows the Snowy Range Scenic Byway through the beautiful Medicine Bow Mountains.

American Heritage Center
22nd St & Willett Dr. *Tel (307) 766-6622.* *10am–5pm Mon–Sat, 1–5pm Sun (summer only).* *public hols.* www.uwyo.edu/artmuseum

Wyoming Territorial Prison State Historic Park
975 Snowy Range Rd. *Tel (307) 745-6161.* *May–Oct: 9am–6pm daily.*

Cheyenne 32

55,000. 121 W 15th St, Suite 202, (307) 778-3133.

Founded in 1867 as a US Army fort along the newly constructed Union Pacific Railroad, Cheyenne later matured from a typical Wild West town into Wyoming's state capital and the largest city in the area.

The 10-day Cheyenne Frontier Days festival, held every July, brings to life the old days with parades, Indian pow-wows, horse races, and the world's largest outdoor rodeo. Visitors can also get a sense of Cheyenne heritage at the **Cheyenne Frontier Days Old West Museum**, which displays hundreds of antique saddles and wagons, such as the historic Deadwood Stage. During the 1870s and 1880s, this coach made a three-day trip between Cheyenne and the gold mines at Deadwood in South Dakota *(see p446)*.

Statue of cowboy, Old West Museum, Cheyenne

Downtown Cheyenne features two landmark buildings – the 1917 State Capitol and the former Union Pacific Depot, an elaborate Romanesque-style structure that has been restored to its original 1886 splendor. The western edge of Cheyenne features Warren Air Force Base, the primary command center of the US arsenal of nuclear-tipped intercontinental ballistic missiles, which are known as ICBMs.

Cheyenne Frontier Days Old West Museum
Frontier Park on N Carey Ave. *Tel (307) 778-7290.* *8:30am–5:30pm Mon–Fri, 9am–5pm Sat–Sun.* *public hols.*

The prison in Wyoming Territorial Park, Laramie

Colorado

The name "Colorado" dates back to the 16th century, when Spanish explorers first used the moniker in reference to the red rock formations that skirt the Front Range of the Rocky Mountains. Over 400 years later, the term conjures images of majestic peaks and snow-clad ski slopes, with good reason. Colorado is the most mountainous state in the US, with 54 summits that measure more than 14,000 ft (4,267 m) above sea level. Officially a state since 1876, during the past century Colorado has evolved from a sparsely inhabited mining and trapping country to become the most populous business center for the Rocky Mountain region.

Denver skyline with the Rockies forming a backdrop

Denver ㉝

*554,600. 1600 California St. **Tel** (303) 892-1505.*
www.visitdenver.com

Founded at the junction of the Platte River and Cherry Creek as a supply base for miners in 1858, Denver's mild climate attracted settlers. Soon after, it emerged as the region's primary trade and population center, and eventually became the state capital in 1876.

In the new millennium, abundant parklands, a vibrant downtown, and a number of well-known museums define this growing city. Denver is set picturesquely at the foothills of the Rocky Mountains.

Civic Center Park

Between Colfax Ave & 14th Ave Pkwy, Broadway & Bannock St. **Colorado History Museum** 1300 Broadway. ***Tel** (303) 866-3682. 10am–5pm Mon–Sat, noon–5pm Sun.* **www**.coloradohistory.org **Denver Art Museum** 100 W 14th Ave Pkwy. ***Tel** (720) 865-5000. 10am–5pm Tue–Thu, Sat, 10am–10pm Fri, noon–5pm Sun. public hols.* **www**.denverartmuseum.org
The geographical, cultural, and political heart of Denver, the Civic Center Park is dominated by the gold-domed **Colorado State Capitol**. This ornate structure houses the state legislature and governor's office. To the south stands the **Colorado History Museum**, where a comprehensive, wall-mounted timeline traces the state's history. Rotating exhibits also focus on varied aspects of Colorado's past. Continuing clockwise around the park is the tiled, seven-story high **Denver Art Museum**. This is one of the city's best museums and has impressive collections of both Western as well as Native American objects. Its latest addition is the ultra-modern landmark Frederic C. Hamilton Building. Finally, a block west of the park is the **Denver Mint**, one of four mints in the country, which presses more than ten billion coins in a year.

Molly Brown House

1340 Pennsylvania St. ***Tel** (303) 832-4092. 10am–4pm Tue–Sat, noon–4pm Sun.*
This restored mansion, now a museum, was the home of "The Unsinkable Molly Brown," so-called for her survival of the *Titanic* in 1912. Margaret Tobin Brown was a flamboyant and persistent woman whose life story exemplifies the boom-and-bust backdrop that is Colorado history. Born in 1867 in Hannibal, Missouri, she came west to the boomtown of Leadville, Colorado, in 1886, where she married a well-known mining man, J.J. Brown. When the silver market collapsed, J.J. persevered until he laid claim to one of Colorado's richest veins of gold in 1893. The couple then moved to Denver, where they lived in luxury, despite not being accepted by the city's elite. Her courageous rescue efforts during the sinking of the *Titanic* made her a national celebrity. With this came the society approval that had previously eluded her. However, she died in New York in 1932, penniless and alone. Later, in the 1960s, she was immortalized on stage and screen.

Larimer Square & Lower Downtown (LoDo)

Larimer Square Larimer St between 14th & 15th Sts. *(303) 685-8143.* **www**.larimersquare.com **LoDo District** Bordered by Market & Wynkoop St. *(303) 628-5428.*
The birthplace of Denver, Larimer Square remains a commercial and cultural hub for the city. Lying adjacent to Confluence Park, where the Platte River and Cherry Creek meet, this was the site where white settlers first set up camp. The square bustles with activity both day and night, mainly because of its many boutiques, galleries, bars, and restaurants.

After a disastrous fire in 1863, wooden structures were prohibited. As a result, red-brick Victorian architecture dominates both the square and the neighboring Lower

Larimer Square, the birthplace of Denver

For hotels and restaurants in this region see p603 and pp606–7

Downtown area (nicknamed "LoDo"). Centered on Union Station, LoDo experienced a renaissance of sorts in the 1990s, thanks to the arrival of the city's professional baseball team and their Coors Field stadium. Today, this is a favorite club-hopping district, well known for its smoky jazz joints, dance clubs, and famous microbreweries.

City Park

Between 17th & 26th Avenues from York St to Colorado Blvd. *24 hours daily.* **Denver Zoo** 2300 Steele St. ***Tel** (303) 376-4800.* *Apr–Sep: 9am–6pm daily; Oct–Mar: 10am–5pm daily.* **www**.denverzoo.org **Denver Museum of Nature & Science** 2001 Colorado Blvd. ***Tel** (303) 322-7009.* *9am–5pm daily.* *Dec 25.* **www**.dmns.org

About 2 miles (3 km) east of downtown is Denver's largest park, which offers a wide range of activities. It has a well-stocked fishing lake, running trails, a golf course, shady picnic areas, and sports fields. The park also contains the city's two most popular attractions – the **Denver Zoo** and the **Denver Museum of Nature and Science**. The zoo, the seventh largest in the country, is noted especially for its innovative animal habitats, which include the world's largest indoor Komodo dragon exhibit. The Denver Museum of Nature and Science, on the eastern edge of the City Park, features a wide range of exhibits.

Black American West Museum & Heritage Center

3091 California St. ***Tel** (303) 482-2242.* *Jun–Aug: 10am–5pm daily; Sep–May: 10am–2pm Tue–Sat.* *Jan 1, Easter, Thanksgiving, Dec 25.*

A hidden gem in the Five Points neighborhood, this fascinating museum is housed in a Victorian home, previously the abode of Justina Ford. In 1902 she became Denver's first female African-American doctor. The museum's founder, Paul Stewart, opened the museum in 1971 to commemorate Ford's life and to educate people about the African-American contribution to the American West. The museum's collection includes letters, photographs, and assorted memorabilia that effectively re-create the incredible stories of African Americans in pioneer times.

Black American West Museum and Heritage Center

Museo de las Americas

861 Santa Fe Dr. ***Tel** (303) 571-4401.* *10am–5pm Tue–Fri, noon–5pm Sat, Sun.* *Jan 1, July 4, Thanksgiving, Dec 25.*

Founded in the early 1990s, the Museo de las Americas is a touchstone for Denver's sizable Hispanic population. The first such museum in the region, it relates Mexican and Latin American history, as well as offers fascinating glimpses of their artistic and cultural traditions. The permanent collections are dedicated to the pre-Colombian Aztec as well as the Colonial period. Among the exhibits on display are a replica of an Aztec Sun Stone and a wall-size mural of the Aztec metropolis Tenochtitlán.

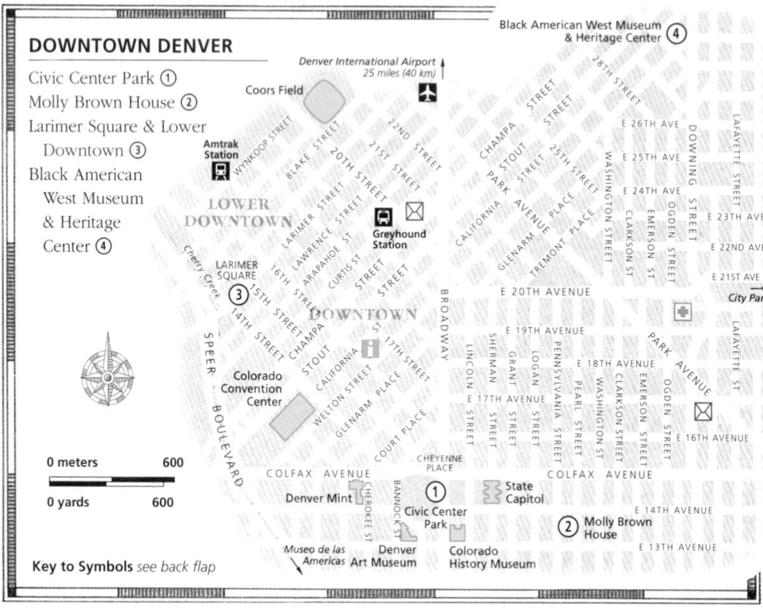

The attractive University of Colorado, Boulder

Boulder 34

95,000. 2440 Pearl St, (303) 442-2911.

An idyllic college town set at the foot of the Rockies, Boulder is best known for its bohemian culture, liberal politics, and thriving high-tech industry. The city was founded in 1858 as a commercial hub for the miners and farmers who settled nearby. After Colorado gained statehood, the **University of Colorado** (CU) was established here, at an altitude of 5,400 ft (1,646 m). Since then, the attractive Victorian-era campus and its coinciding vibrant culture have defined Boulder, attracting intellectuals, radicals, and individualists.

Northwest of the campus, the pedestrian-only Pearl Street Mall, lined with lively restaurants, bars, and shops, is the stage for many street performers. Nearby, the Hill District forms the center of Boulder's energetic nightlife and music scene. The I.M. Pei-designed **National Center for Atmospheric Research** is to the southeast. The center also features an art gallery and is a start-off point for some lovely nature trails.

West of Boulder, the jagged and forested crags of the Rockies provide a scenic backdrop to the city below. The nearby Flatiron Range, Eldorado Canyon, and Indian Peaks Wilderness Area are popular with climbers, hikers, and backpackers.

Cycling across Boulder Canyon, minutes from downtown Boulder

National Center for Atmospheric Research
1850 Table Mesa Dr. ***Tel*** *(303) 497-1174.* *8am–5pm Mon–Fri, 9am–4pm Sat–Sun.*

Indian Peaks Wilderness Area
20 miles (32 km) W of Boulder, US Forest Service. ***Tel*** *(303) 444-6600.* *24 hours daily.*

Golden 35

18,000. 1010 Washington Ave, (303) 279-3113, (800) 590-3113.

Golden's history as an early nexus of trade and politics remains visible today. Its origins date to the early 1840s, when hunter Rufus Sage, one of the first Anglos to camp in this area, spotted flakes of gold in the waters of Clear Creek. His findings led to an influx of Easterners in the 1850s, and by the 1860s the city emerged as a regional railroad hub and was declared the capital of the newly formed Colorado Territory. The original Territorial Capitol in the Loveland Building, which forms the center of downtown, dates from that period.

Golden's past is visible at the **Golden History Center** and at the impeccably restored **Astor House Museum**. Several rooms here re-create the 1867–1908 era when it served as a boarding house. The **Old Armory** nearby is the largest cobblestone building in the US. The 3-acre (1.2-ha) **Clear Creek History Park** houses many historic structures such as a 1876 schoolhouse. The town is also home to **Coors Brewery**, which offers tours.

The gravesite and museum of William "Buffalo Bill" Cody *(see p582)* overlooks the city on Lookout Mountain and there is an observation deck offering beautiful panoramic views.

Golden History Center
923 10th St. ***Tel*** *(303) 278-3557.* *10am–4:30pm Tue–Sat.* *Jan 1, Jul 4, Thnksg., Dec 24–25.*

Astor House Museum
822 12th St. ***Tel*** *(303) 278-3557.* *10am–4:30pm Tue–Sat.* *Jan 1, Jul 4, Thnksg., Dec 24–25.*
www.astorhousemuseum.org

Clear Creek History Park
11th St between Arapahoe & Cheyenne St.
Tel *(303) 277-2337.* *daily.*
www clearcreekhistorypark.org

Cobblestone exterior of the Old Armory, near Astor House, Golden

Idaho Springs & Georgetown 36

2,000. 2060 Miner St, (303) 567-4382.

Situated within an hour's drive from downtown Denver, the well-preserved 1860s mining towns of Idaho Springs and Georgetown are best known for their unblemished Victorian architecture, stunning mountains, and some excellent museums.

Idaho Springs was founded in 1859 and quickly emerged as a mining center when the surrounding streams and mountains were found to be exceptional sources of gold. The town's mining history is traced through exhibits that include equipment, payroll records, receipts, and photographs at the **Argo Gold Mine, Mill, and Museum**.

Georgetown, another mining town set up during the mid-19th century gold rush, is 15 miles (24 km) west of Idaho Springs. It is a vision of Victorian elegance tucked into an alpine valley 8,500 ft (2,591 m) above sea level.

One of the attractions here is the **Hamill House Museum**, which was built in 1867. It was enlarged in 1879 and now presents the public with the elegant, spacious lifestyle of a silver-mining magnate. There's also a carriage house, office building, and privy.

South from Idaho Springs, summer drivers can wind their way up the highest road in the United States. The Mount Evans Scenic Byway follows Hwy 103 and Hwy 5 through the Pike National Forest toward the 14,264-ft (4,347-m) high summit of Mount Evans.

Victorian architecture in downtown Georgetown

Argo Gold Mine, Mill, & Museum
S of I-70, exit from 241A.
***Tel** (303) 567-2421. mid-Apr–mid-Oct: 9am–6pm daily.*
www.historicargotours.com

Hamill House Museum
305 Argentine St.
***Tel** (303) 569-2840. summer: 10am–4pm daily; Sep–Dec 25: 10am–4pm Sat–Sun.*
www.historicgeorgetown.org

Rocky Mountain National Park 37

*1000 US Hwy 36. **Tel** (970) 586-1206. 24 hours daily. (Trail Ridge Road closed between Nov–May).*
www.nps.gov/romo

This National Park offers some of the most spectacular mountain views in the United States. Established in 1915, the park spreads across 416 sq miles (1,077 sq km) and includes 114 named peaks that measure more than 10,000 ft (3,048 m). The tallest of these, Longs Peak, is 14,255 ft (4,345 m) high. Snaking through the alpine scenery is the Continental Divide, which separates the western part of the US from the east, and where snowmelt flows down and eventually empties into the Atlantic or Pacific Oceans. Almost 150 lakes originate here, some occupying pastoral, forested settings, while others are perched on almost inaccessible shelves, high in the wilderness.

The majority of the three million annual visitors to the park drive 50 miles (80 km) on **Trail Ridge Road**, a spectacular stretch of highway that showcases the park's brilliant panoramas. After leaving the resort environment of Estes Park, the road climbs to its highest point of 12,183 ft (3,713 km) near the center of the park, before descending into a scenic valley north of the small town of Grand Lake. The tundra in the park's high country is an island of arctic vegetation surrounded by plants of lower latitudes. Wildlife watchers are likely to see elk, moose, black bear, and bighorn sheep.

Popular summer activities within the park include hiking, biking, backpacking, and fishing, while winter attracts snowshoers and skiers. Although there are no hotels inside the park, there are five fee-based campgrounds and numerous accommodations in both Estes Park and Grand Lake.

A view of the myriad peaks from the pinnacle of Trail Ridge Road, Rocky Mountain National Park

Pikes Peak Cog Railway atop the mountain, Manitou Springs

Manitou Springs 38

5,500. 354 Manitou Ave, (800) 642-2567.
www.manitousprings.org

This charming Victorian community attracts weekend visitors who come to explore its art galleries, shops, and restaurants. A product of the Gold Rush of the 1850s, it later became a popular spa town because of the natural mineral springs found here. Manitou (meaning "Full of Spirit" in Native Algonquian) is one of the largest national historic districts in the country. It is famous for two attractions that predate it by centuries, the **Cave of the Winds**, an impressive limestone cavern (now with light shows and tours) and the **Manitou Springs Cliff Dwellings**, dating from 1100 to 1300.

Manitou Springs is also the gateway to Pikes Peak *(see p570)*. The **Pikes Peak Cog Railway**, a historic train that climbs to the summit of the 14,110-ft (4,300-m) mountain, has its depot here.

Cave of the Winds
US 24, exit 141. ***Tel** (719) 685-5444. Jun–Aug: 9am–9pm daily; Sep–May: 10am–5pm daily.* **www**.caveofthewinds.com

Pikes Peak Cog Railway
515 Ruxton Ave. ***Tel** (719) 685-5401. Apr–Oct: several departures daily; Nov–Mar: limited schedule.*
www.cograilway.com

Manitou Springs Cliff Dwellings
10 Cliff Dwellings Rd. ***Tel** (800) 354-9971. 9am–5pm daily.*
www.cliffdwellingsmuseum.

Clocktower, Manitou Springs

Colorado Springs 39

380,000. 515 S Cascade Ave, (719) 635-7506.

Established by railroad baron William Jackson Palmer in 1871, Colorado Springs nestles below the looming beauty of Pikes Peak. The first resort town in the western US, it was initially nicknamed "Little London" because of the scores of English tourists that it attracted. The **Garden of the Gods** on the west side of town lures hikers and climbers with its awe-inspiring red sandstone formations, rife with arches, overhangs, stately walls, and precarious balancing rocks. One of the most recognizable – and most photographed – formations is Kissing Camels, so named for its resemblance to a pair of lip-locked dromedaries. Also located here is the Rock Ledge Ranch Historic Site, a preserved ranch that dates to the 1880s. The Italian Renaissance-style **Broadmoor Resort** *(see p603)* on Lake Circle, initially opened in 1918, epitomizes this era.

In the 1950s, Colorado Springs was chosen to be the home of the prestigious **US Air Force Academy** and the National Missile Defense Headquarters (NORAD). The latter is situated on the city's southwestern fringe, deep within the bomb-proof Cheyenne Mountain.

Culturally more conservative than Denver *(see pp588–9)*, modern-day Colorado Springs is one of the fastest-growing cities in the US, with rows of houses extending into the foothills to the west, and the vast plains to the east. The spirit of the Wild West remains alive even today at the **Pro Rodeo Hall of Fame**, which documents the origins of rodeo as well as the stories of prominent American rodeo stars through the ages. The **Colorado Springs Pioneers Museum** presents the area's history in the restored 1903 El Paso County Courthouse.

Garden of the Gods
1805 North 30th St. ***Tel** (719) 634-6666. Jun–Aug: 8am–8pm daily; Sep–May: 9am–5pm daily. Tue (Jan & Feb), Jan 1, Thnksg., Dec 25. only for Rock Ledge Ranch Historic Site (summer only).*

Broadmoor Resort
1 Lake Dr. ***Tel** (719) 634-7711. daily, but can vary. Call ahead to check.* **www**.broadmoor.com

Pro Rodeo Hall of Fame
101 Pro Rodeo Dr. ***Tel** (719) 528-4764. May–Sep: 9am–5pm daily; Oct–Apr: 9am–5pm Wed–Sun. Jan 1, Easter, Thanksgiving, Dec 24, 25, 31.* **www**.prorodeohalloffame.com

Colorado Springs Pioneers Museum
215 S Tejon St. ***Tel** (719) 385-5990. 10am–5pm Tue–Sat.*
www.cspm.org

Kissing Camels formations, Garden of the Gods in Colorado Springs

The magnifient view over the Royal Gorge Bridge and Park located in Cañon City

Cripple Creek 40

1,200. 513 E Bennett Ave, (719) 689-3315.

Known as "Poverty Gulch" before a gold strike in 1890 transformed it, this is one of the best-preserved 19th-century mining towns in the entire state. The fascinating **Mollie Kathleen Gold Mine** is the best place to explore the town's mining history. Discovered by Mollie Kathleen Gortner in 1891, this gold mine on the southwest face of Pikes Peak is the country's only vertical-shaft mine that offers tours. Even though mining operations ended in 1961, gold veins are still visible on its walls.

The surrounding area is still mined for gold though mining has ceased in most other Colorado boomtowns. Gambling was legalized here in 1990, with casinos housed behind original 1896 brick façades. The historic **Butte Opera House** puts on theater performances in summer.

Interior of Mollie Kathleen Gold Mine, Cripple Creek

Mollie Kathleen Gold Mine
Hwy 67. ***Tel*** *(719) 689-2466.* *May–Oct: 8am–6pm daily; winter tours by appt.* **www**.goldminetours.com

Butte Opera House
139 E Bennett Ave. ***Tel*** *(719) 689-6402.* **www**.butteoperahouse.com

Cañon City 41

16,000. 403 Royal Gorge Blvd, (719) 275-2331, (800) 876-7922.

A colorful place, blessed with clear skies, sunshine, and spectacular scenery, Cañon City, surprisingly, is also the "Prison Capital of Colorado." It acquired this title in 1876, after it chose to house the state prison instead of the state university. Today, prisons remain a key component of the regional economy. The **Museum of Colorado Prisons** is housed in a former women's prison built in 1935. Just 12 miles (19 km) west of the city stands the well-known **Royal Gorge Bridge & Park**. Etched into the granite bedrock for three million years by the Arkansas River, this beautiful, breathtaking gorge is over 1,000 ft (305 m) from rim to river at its deepest, but only 40 ft (12 m) wide at its base. Traversed by the world's highest suspension bridge and 12 miles (19 km) of railroad – the **Royal Gorge Route Railroad** – the park also attracts whitewater rafters to the challenging stretch of the river below.

Museum of Colorado Prisons
201 N 1st St. ***Tel*** *(719) 269-3015.* *Jun–Aug: 8:30am–6pm daily; Sep–May: 10am–5pm Wed–Sun.* **www**.prisonmuseum.org

Royal Gorge Bridge & Park
US Hwy 50. ***Tel*** *(888) 333-5597.* *Apr–early Oct: 10am–7pm daily; mid-Oct–Mar: 10am–4pm daily.* **www**.royalgorgebridge.com

Royal Gorge Route Railroad
Tel *(888) 724-5748.* *Jun–Sep: daily; Oct–Dec & Feb–May: Sat–Sun.* *Jan.* **www**.royalgorgeroute.com

WHITEWATER RAFTING IN COLORADO

The best way to enjoy the pristine Colorado wilderness is to take a whitewater rafting trip on the Arkansas River. The picturesque towns of Salida and nearby Buena Vista, 26 miles (42 km) to the north, are hubs for outfitters who offer guided river trips. With about 100 rafting companies in operation, this is the most intensively rafted river in the US. The Colorado River Outfitters Association (303-280-2554), is one of the best sources of information on rafting trips.

Rafting on the Arkansas River, Colorado

Colorado Ski Resorts ㊷

One of Colorado's most enduring symbols is of pristine white mountains dotted with skiers. The state's recreational ski industry dates to 1935 when Berthoud Pass, northwest of Denver, became the destination ski resort for pioneering skiers. As the sport's economic potential developed after World War II, many old mining towns emerged as popular ski resort towns. Today the state is undoubtedly the country's skiing capital, with more than 24 resorts. In recent years, other winter sports, such as snowboarding, have become very popular, and most ski mountains now allow snowboarders.

Steamboat Springs, *the cowboy cousin to the conservative luxury of Aspen, wears its rambunctious Western spirit as a badge of honor. It has some of the state's best snow (a dry, feathery powder), a 3,668-ft (1,118-m) vertical drop, and a total of 142 runs.*
Max altitude: *10,564 ft (3,220 m)*
Geared to: *all levels*
Ski level: 13% 56% 31%

Aspen, *a favorite of the rich and famous, has more than 200 different runs on four striking mountains. It developed when the Aspen Skiing Company opened its first lift in 1947. Sleek restaurants and boutiques housed behind Victorian-era storefronts complement the splendid ski terrain. Aspen also has a vibrant art and culture scene.*
Max altitude: *11,675 ft (3,559 m)*
Geared to: *all levels*
Ski level: 16% 61% 23%

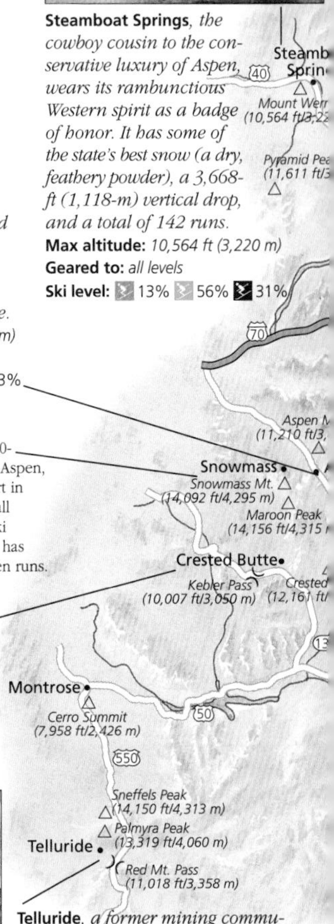

Snowmass, just a 30-minute drive from Aspen, is a complete resort in itself. Larger than all three of Aspen's ski areas combined, it has plenty of wide-open runs.

Crested Butte draws serious skiers to its unparalleled expert terrain. The town sits at the base of Mount Crested Butte, with a vertical drop of 2,775 ft (846 m) and 824 acres (333 ha) for "extreme" skiing.

Telluride, *a former mining community, opened as a ski resort in 1971. The nearby valley was once a hideout for outlaw Butch Cassidy. The town is also known for its bohemian politics, a lively nightlife, and trails that lead to such scenic areas as Bridal Veil Falls.*
Max altitude: *12,255 ft (3,736 m)*
Geared to: *all levels*
Ski level: 22% 38% 40%

Winter Park, *Colorado's oldest full-service ski resort, is linked to Denver by the Ski Train – 67 miles (108 km) of track that connect the slopes with LoDo's Union Station. The resort's five ski mountain areas offer downhill terrain for every skill level, and there are also numerous cross-country trails nearby.*
Max altitude: *12,060 ft (3,676 m)*
Geared to: *experts*
Ski level: 9% 21% 70%

Keystone, with its 12-hour ski day, is now famous for being Colorado's best night-skiing resort. Open eight months a year, it has three ski mountains and offers a variety of activities such as snowboarding, ice skating, sleigh rides, and indoor tennis.

Copper Mountain offers some of the most advanced skiing and snowboarding terrain in Colorado, as well as areas for novice and intermediate skiers. Once maligned, the newly re-designed village now brims with shops, bars, and restaurants.

Leadville, at an elevation of 10,152 ft (3,094 m), is the highest town in the US. This boom-and-bust mining town was once the site of the richest mines in the country – its story is told at the National Mining Hall of Fame and Museum. Today, it has a small, crowd-free ski resort.

SKI RESORTS & COMPANIES

Aspen Skiing Company (Aspen-Snowmass)
Tel (970) 925-1220, (800) 308-6935. Dec–mid-Apr: 9am–4pm daily.
www.aspensnowmass.com

Breckenridge Ski Resort
Tel (800) 427-8308. late Oct–May: 8:30am–4pm daily.
www.breckenridge.com

Keystone
Tel (800) 427-8308. mid-Oct–Apr: 8:30am– 8:30pm daily.
www.keystoneresort.com

Steamboat Ski Corp.
Tel (970) 879-6111. mid-Nov–mid-Apr: 8:30am–4pm daily.
www.steamboat.com

Telluride Ski Company
Tel (800) 801-4832. late Nov–mid-Apr: 8:30am–4pm daily.
www.tellurideskiresort.com

Vail Mountain
Tel (800) 404-3535, (970) 476-5601. mid-Nov–Apr: 8:30am–4pm daily.
www.vail.snow.com

Winter Park
Tel (970) 726-5514. mid-Nov–late Apr: 8:30am–4pm daily.
www.skiwinterpark.com

Ski Train
Tel (303) 296-4754.
See also pp598–9.
www.skitrain.com

Breckenridge *boasts an interesting history, recreation facilities including ice skating* (above), *and nightlife. The resort is spread across four peaks on the west side of town.*
Max altitude: *12,998 ft (3,962 m)*
Geared to: *all levels*
Ski level: 13% 32% 55%

Vail, *the largest single-mountain ski resort in the US, attracts skiers and snowboarders alike. The domain of Native tribes until the 1870s mining boom, the town actually developed when Vail Mountain opened to skiers in 1962. It has more than 2,000 trails and a 3,450-ft (1,052-m) vertical drop.*
Max altitude: *11,570 ft (3,527 m)*
Geared to: *all levels*
Ski level: 18% 29% 53%

KEY

- Major road
- Minor road
- Good for beginners
- Good for intermediate skiers
- Good for advanced skiers
- △ Peak
-)(Pass

Great Sand Dunes National Monument & Preserve

Great Sand Dunes National Monument & Preserve ㊸

11500 Colorado Hwy 150, NE of Alamosa. **Tel** *(719) 378-6399.* *24 hrs daily.* www.nps.gov/grsa

North America's tallest sand dunes sit at the foot of the gnarled Sangre de Cristo Mountains. Their sand was carried to this scenic spot by wind, melting glaciers, and the Rio Grande River, creating a 30 sq-mile (78 sq-km) dune-field. This unusual ecosystem is home to several equally unusual animals and insects, such as a species of kangaroo rat that never drinks water, and the Great Sand Dunes tiger beetle, found nowhere else in the world.

The park has a popular campground, which fills up quickly on weekends during summer, and a mix of long and short trails. Many visitors scale the dunes, which sometimes measure up to 750 ft (229 m).

Durango ㊹

Tel *16,000.* *111 South Camino del Rio, (888) 414-0835, (970) 247-0312.*

Once described by American humorist Will Rogers as "out of the way and glad of it," Durango was established in the Animas River Valley in 1881 as a rail station for the mines in the nearby San Juan Mountains. After the mining boom ended, Durango emerged as a major tourism center and cultural symbol of the West. This modern city is today a model of historic preservation, with late-19th-century saloons and hotels lining Main Avenue, and elegant mansions from the same era on Third Street. One thing, however, has changed – diehard mountain bikers, entrepreneurs, and artists have replaced the rugged miners.

Many visitors take a day trip on the **Durango & Silverton Narrow Gauge Railroad**. A fully functional 1882 steam engine, it follows a scenic 50-mile (80-km) journey, traveling from the valley floor to rock ledges en route to the former mining town of Silverton. Durango's other prime attraction is the great outdoors of the **San Juan National Forest**, where mountain biking is the top sport. Other popular activities are hiking, horseback riding, backpacking, rock-climbing, and river rafting.

Durango & Silverton Narrow Gauge Railroad & Museum
479 Main Ave. **Tel** *(970) 247-2733, (888) 872-4607.* *daily. Hours may vary, call for details.* www.durangotrain.com

San Juan National Forest
15 Burnett Court. **Tel** *(970) 247-4874.* *24 hrs daily.*

Mesa Verde National Park ㊺

East of Cortez via US Hwy 160. **Tel** *(970) 529-4465.* *8am–5pm daily; open 5pm to sunset in summer.* www.nps.gov/meve

When it was established in 1906, Mesa Verde became the first archaeological site in the US to receive national park status. Tucked into the recesses of canyon walls, the park's defining features are 600 fascinating cliff dwellings last inhabited by the indigenous Puebloan people before they abandoned them in 1300. The dwellings range from small houses to the 150-room **Cliff Palace** and are significant archaeological finds.

Park rangers lead tours between April and November to some of the most impressive dwellings, including Cliff Palace. Visitors can also explore several structures on their own, including the well-preserved Spruce Tree House. Square Tower House, the park's tallest ruin, can be viewed from an overlook. The **Chapin Mesa Archaeological Museum** displays a fascinating collection of items used by Puebloan people.

There are also 18 miles (29 km) of hiking trails within the park. One of them, the

Durango & Silverton Narrow Gauge Railroad

For hotels and restaurants in this region see p603 and pp606–607

Petroglyph Point Trail, offers visitors a chance to view ancient rock art. Camping and wildlife viewing (including foxes, mountain lions, and elk) are among the other activities. In winter, cross-country skiing and snowshoeing are popular.

Chapin Mesa Archaeological Museum
Tel (970) 529-4631. 8am–5pm daily.

Square Tower House, Mesa Verde National Park

Ouray 46

800. 1230 N Main, (970) 325-4746, (800) 228-1876.

Nicknamed the "Switzerland of America" for its resemblance to a village in the Alps, Ouray is located 80 miles (128 km) north of Durango. It was named after the Ute chief whose people hunted in the area before gold and silver prospectors established the town in 1876. Today the entire town is listed on the National Register of Historic Places, a testament to the number of well-maintained 19th-century structures still here. Two natural wonders – the massive geothermal-powered **Ouray Hot Springs Pool**, and the stunning **Box Canyon Falls**, which cascades 285 ft (87 m) down a natural cliff-side chute – are easily accessible from the town.

Ouray is also on the **San Juan Skyway**, a 236-mile (380-km) loop that includes the "Million Dollar Highway" to Silverton. Its surrounding wild-lands lure rock- and ice-climbers, four-wheel-drive enthusiasts, and other outdoors adventurers.

Ouray Hot Springs Pool
US Hwy 550, at the northern end of Ouray. *Tel (970) 325-7073. May–Sep: 10am–10pm daily; Oct–Apr: noon–9pm daily.*

Box Canyon Falls & Park
S of Ouray via US Hwy 550. *Tel (970) 325-7080.* **Visitor Center** *May 15–Oct 15: 8am–8pm daily. Oct 16–May 14.*

Black Canyon of the Gunnison National Park 47

E of Montrose via US Hwy 50.
Tel (970) 641-2337. 24 hrs daily.
www.nps.gov/blca

Though not as vast as Arizona's Grand Canyon *(see pp536–9)*, the Black Canyon is strikingly deep with steep sides. The canyon was created by the Gunnison River as it slowly sliced through solid stone for two million years. Its north and south rims have completely different ecosystems and are separated by a crevice 2,400 ft (732 m) at its deepest point and just 40 ft (12 m) at its narrowest point.

The **South Rim Road** meanders for about 7 miles (11 km) past several overlooks, including a fantastic vista of a multihued rock face known as Painted Wall, which is twice the height of New York's Empire State Building *(see p73)*. Although the park's northern edge is more isolated, it has a campground and offers magnificent sunset views.

Climbing is a popular sport in the park, as is hiking, camping, and fishing. Among the many trails is one particularly difficult one that descends to the canyon's floor.

The park's varied wildlife includes a variety of birds such as the peregrine falcons who nest on the canyon's sheer walls. Wildcats and bears also roam the vast park.

Colorado National Monument 48

W of Grand Junction via I-70 or 7 miles (11 km) S of Fruita on US Hwy 340. *Tel (970) 858-3617. 24 hrs daily.* **Visitors center** *summer: 8am–6pm; winter: 9am–5pm daily.*
www.nps.gov/colm

Carved by wind and water over the last 225 million years, this immense 20,500-acre (8,296-ha) national monument has been molded into an eeire high desert landscape of spectacular canyons, and red sandstone arches. A driving tour on the 22-mile (35-km) **Rim Rock Drive** offers several splendid panoramas, while numerous trails lead visitors right into the heart of the landscape. The park's two geological highlights are the incredible sandstone arches of Rattlesnake Canyon, and Miracle Rock, which is considered to be the largest balanced rock in the world.

The eerie high desert landscape of Colorado National Monument

Practical Information

Exploring the four Rocky Mountain states requires some advance planning, simply because of the sheer size and diversity of the region's landscape. The boundaries of this mountainous region stretch from the Canadian border in the north to New Mexico in the south. To the west, the area is bordered by the plateaus and basins of the Intermontane region. The breathtaking scenery, rugged terrain, scanty resources, and sparse population of the Rockies are spread across elevations that range from under 1,000 ft (305 m) to over 14,000 ft (4,267 m) above sea level.

TOURIST INFORMATION

Travelers entering the Rocky Mountain states via an Interstate Highway are greeted with signs advertising a state "Welcome Center." These centers provide a full range of tourist information as well as clean restrooms and free coffee. Denver's International Airport (DIA), and most of the region's other major airports and train stations have information desks with free brochures and maps. Most larger cities and smaller towns operate **Convention & Visitors Bureaus** or **Chambers of Commerce**, which provide free travel information.

NATURAL HAZARDS

The short summers of the Rockies region are warm and glorious, but can bring sudden thunderstorms, especially in the mountains. Rock slides, bugs, and wildlife are other hazards. Elevation across the four states can vary from under 1,000 ft (305 m) to over 14,000 ft (4,267 m) above sea level. At higher elevations, in areas such as Yellowstone National Park, roads may be closed by snow between late October and early June. The Interstate Highways and access routes to the region's many ski areas are kept open all year round.

The high altitude of the area means that the sun's rays are more intense so it is essential to wear sunscreen and to drink plenty of water. It is also important to be aware of altitude sickness, which can be life-threatening. Symptoms include shortness of breath, dizziness, lethargy, headache, and dehydration. Keep drinking plenty of water, limit alcohol, and do not hesitate to seek medical attention.

Winters are long and often bitterly cold with heavy winter and spring snows. Drivers should make sure that they possess, and know how to install, snow chains or other traction devices, which are required by law. Be especially careful while driving on icy surfaces.

In remote areas, hikers should be prepared for all weather conditions in winter as well as summer. Carry basic emergency supplies, including food and water, and extra clothing in case the weather changes for the worse.

GETTING AROUND

For visitors coming from the East or West Coast, Denver is a prime starting point. Smaller regional cities throughout the Rockies have airports, such as the Missoula, (MT) County International Airport. Other than organized bus tours, public transportation is limited. Denver has city buses, a light-rail system, and free shuttle buses. Having a car is essential in this region since most national parks and other sights are located at great distances from the major cities.

Seat belts are required for drivers and front seat passengers in all four states. Child seats are compulsory for all passengers aged eight and under. Helmets are required for all motorcyclists under the age of 18.

Speed limits vary but are usually 70–75 mph (112–120 km/hr) on Interstate Highways outside the populated urban areas. Radar detectors are permitted in the entire Rocky Mountain region.

ETIQUETTE

Some of the region's most famous sights are located on Native American reservation land. Visitors are welcome but must be sensitive as to what may cause offense. It is illegal to bring alcohol onto reservations, and taking photographs may not be allowed.

FESTIVALS

Summer in the Rockies brings a deluge of outdoor events, including community and state fairs, in addition to regional and national music, and art festivals. Fireworks, bands, and festivals abound for the July 4th celebrations, while

THE CLIMATE OF THE ROCKIES

Weather across the Rocky Mountain region is marked by long, snowy winters, short springs and fall, and hot summers. The main factor determining weather is elevation – temperatures are cooler and snowfalls heavier the higher you go. Visitors should be prepared for winter conditions at any time of year. Yet, months like October offer crisp days, ideal for scenic drives through the mountains when you can enjoy the fall colors of the aspens.

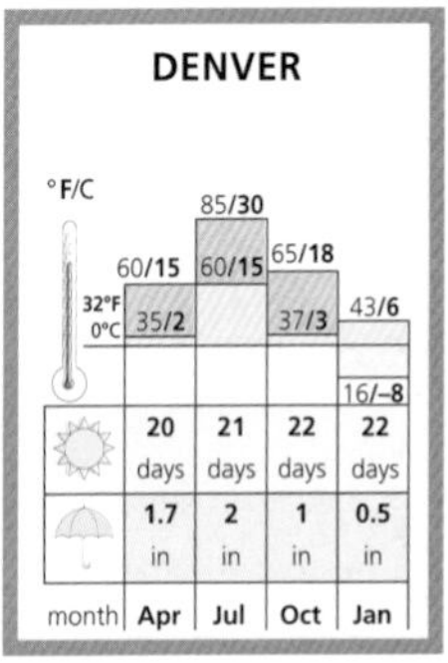

the region's strong Native American heritage is also celebrated with a number of pow-wows in July and August on selected reservations. Music and various cultural events, such as the ever popular **Telluride Bluegrass Festival**, the world-famous Aspen Music Festival & School (970-925-3254), and the Big Sky Arts Fesitval take place throughout the summer months.

SPORTS

The Rocky Mountain states all offer a wide variety of sports throughout the year. Denver is home to many of the region's professional teams. The **Colorado Rockies** play baseball all summer at the old-fashioned Coors Field downtown. The **Colorado Rapids** play professional soccer and the **Denver Broncos** play American football. Winter sees the **Denver Nuggets** on the basketball court. Many of the region's universities and colleges play seasonal games, often with heated regional rivalries.

One spectator sport characteristic of the Rockies is the rodeo, and many national competitions are held here. Events such as bull- and bronco-riding, calf roping, and steer wrestling showcase a cowboy's skill. Cheyenne, Wyoming, hosts the "World's Largest Outdoor Rodeo" when more than 250,000 fans flock here during **Frontier Days** at the end of July (800-227-6336). Dude ranches often offer special rodeos for guests.

OUTDOOR ACTIVITIES

The most popular outdoor activity is downhill skiing, which draws many participants and billions of dollars to the region's world-class resorts. Colorado has many of the biggest and most highly regarded resorts in the US, but there is also excellent skiing at Idaho's Sun Valley, Wyoming's Jackson Hole, and at smaller resorts throughout the region. Snowboarding is also popular, and cross-country skiing can be enjoyed in the stunning landscape of the region's many parks and forests. The ski season is from December to March, but many resorts are open until May or June depending on the weather.

Montana is home to such famous trout-fishing spots as the Madison and Yellowstone Rivers, while Idaho, Wyoming, and Colorado all offer excellent fly-fishing. Licenses are required, and catch-and-release is encouraged. Visitors can contact the **Montana Fish, Wildlife & Parks Department** or the **Idaho Fish & Game Department** for details.

Other popular warm-weather activities include hiking, mountain biking, and rafting. Rafting the Snake River through Grand Teton National Park is very popular, as is the wilder Salmon River in Idaho. The Colorado River Outfitters Association is one of the best sources of information on guided river-rafting trips. Lewis & Clark Trail Adventures lead whitewater raft trips through miles of Idaho rivers. Snow King Ski Resort near Jackson, Wyoming also offers historical hiking and rafting trips. Bicycle and motorcycle riding is gaining as much popularity as hiking, fishing, and skiing. Open Road Bicycles in Missoula, Montana, rents bikes for a day or by the week (406-549-2453). They will also help outfit and plan trips.

ENTERTAINMENT

The ski resorts and dude ranches in the area offer evening entertainment from cabaret and local theater productions to first-run movies. However, many evenings at these resorts are spent in hot tubs, relaxing around the bar, or at in-house casinos. College towns, such as Bozeman and Missoula, Montana, have many of the amenities that the back-country lacks: good bookstores, brew pubs, museums, and events that appeal to both urban and cowboy culture.

DIRECTORY

TOURIST INFORMATION

Colorado
1675 Broadway, Suite 1700 Denver, CO 80202.
***Tel** (800) 265-6723.*
www.colorado.com

Idaho
700 W State St, Boise.
***Tel** (208) 334-2470, (800) 847- 4843.*
www.visitidaho.org

Montana
301 S Park Ave, Helena.
***Tel** (800) 847-4868.*
www.visitmt.com

Wyoming
I-25 at College Dr, Cheyenne. ***Tel** (800) 225-5996.* **www**.wyomingtourism.org

ROAD CONDITIONS

Idaho
***Tel** (888) 432-7623.*

Montana
***Tel** (800) 226-7623.*
www.mdt511.com

FESTIVALS

Colorado State Fair
***Tel** (719) 561-8484.*
www.coloradostatefair.com

Eastern Idaho State Fair
***Tel** (208) 785-2480.*
www.idaho-state-fair.com

Montana State Fair
***Tel** (406) 727-8900.*
www.mtexpopark.com

Telluride Bluegrass Festival
***Tel** (800) 624-2422.*
www.bluegrass.com

Wyoming State Fair and Rodeo
***Tel** (307) 358-2398.*
www.wystatefair.com

SPORTS

Colorado Rapids
***Tel** (303) 727-3500.*
www.coloradorapids.com

Colorado Rockies
***Tel** (303) 292-0200.*
www.colorado.com

Denver Broncos
***Tel** (303) 649-9000.*
www.denverbroncos.com

Denver Nuggets
***Tel** (303) 405-1111.*
www.nba.com/nuggets

FISHING

Idaho Fish & Game Dept.
600 S Walnut St
Boise, ID 83712.
***Tel** (208) 334-3700.*

Montana Fish, Wildlife & Parks Department
1420 E 6th Ave
Helena, MT 59620.
***Tel** (406) 444-2535.*

Choosing a Hotel

Places to stay in the Rocky Mountains region are as varied as the landscape. In towns, visitors can choose from historic hotels and quaint bed-and-breakfast inns, but in rural areas the choice is usually limited to highway motels. Most national parks have large rustic lodges and there are several "dude ranches" where guests can play cowboy.

PRICE CATEGORIES
For a standard double room per night, including service charges and any additional taxes.

($) Under $100
($)($) $100–$200
($)($)($) $200–$350
($)($)($)($) $350–$450
($)($)($)($)($) Over $450

IDAHO

BOISE Idaho Heritage Inn ($)
109 West Idaho St, 83702 ***Tel*** *(208) 342-8066, (800) 342-8445* ***Rooms*** *8*

Within walking distance of downtown and Old Boise, this home was built in 1904 for a prominent businessman and later owned by Governor Clark. Period character and comfortable furnishings are found throughout, with modern amenities and hot water that comes from thermal springs. Cookies and wine in the evening. **www.idheritageinn.com**

BOISE Oxford Suites Boise ($)($)
1426 S Entertainment Ave, 83709 ***Tel*** *(208) 322-8000, (888) 322-8001* ***Fax*** *(208) 322-8002* ***Rooms*** *132*

This new small hotel is stylish and comfortable, great for business and leisure travelers. Located a mile from the airport, it offers free airport shuttle service as well as a complimentary breakfast buffet, evening reception with hors d'oeuvres, beer, wine, and soft drinks, and indoor pool area with whirlpool, sauna, and steam room. **www.oxfordsuitesboise.com**

COEUR D'ALENE Resort City Inn ($)($)
621 E Sherman Ave, 83814 ***Tel*** *(208) 676-1225, (877) 446-4667* ***Fax*** *(208) 676-8757* ***Rooms*** *18*

With its excellent downtown location, this two-story motel-style inn is within walking distance of the lake, beaches, restaurants, and attractions. The accommodations are a comfortable value-oriented choice with free wireless Internet, a small refrigerator, and microwave. There is a rooftop patio. **www.resortcityinn.com**

COEUR D'ALENE Coeur d'Alene Resort ($)($)($)
115 S 2nd St, 83814 ***Tel*** *(208) 765-4000, (800) 688-5253* ***Fax*** *(208) 664-7276* ***Rooms*** *338*

This year-round deluxe lakefront golf and spa resort is nestled on the shores of Lake Coeur d'Alene with pristine views of the mountains across the lake. Famous for its floating golf green, the resort offers a range of activities such as parasailing, lake cruises, fishing, and skiing. Rooms feature luxury furnishings and hi-tech amenities. **www.cdaresort.com**

KETCHUM Best Western Tyrolean Lodge ($)($)
260 Cottonwood St, 83340 ***Tel*** *(208) 726-5336, (800) 333-7912* ***Fax*** *(208) 726-2081* ***Rooms*** *56*

This attractive Austrian-style lodge is located at the base of Bald Mountain about 400 yards from Sun Valley's River Run ski facility and within walking distance of the river and the downtown restaurants. Continental breakfast is included. The outdoor hot tub and heated swimming pool are open year-round. **www.bestwesternidaho.com**

RIGGINS Best Western Salmon Rapids Lodge ($)($)
1010 S Main St, 83549 ***Tel*** *(208) 628-2743, (877) 957-2743* ***Fax*** *(208) 628-3834* ***Rooms*** *55*

A modern timber-and-stone Western- style lodge overlooking the confluence of the Salmon and Little Salmon Rivers. Popular with whitewater rafters and visitors to Hells Canyon, the lobby features two-story windows, a large stone fireplace, cozy couch, and rocking chairs. Guestrooms have a small fridge and wireless Internet. **www.salmonrapids.com**

SALMON Twin Peaks Ranch ($)($)($)
Twin Peaks, 83467 ***Tel*** *(208) 894-2290, (800) 659-4899* ***Fax*** *(208) 894-2429* ***Rooms*** *24*

This dude-ranch is located on 2,900 acres in the rugged mountains above the Salmon River. Activities include horseback riding to high mountain camps, trail drives, fishing in alpine lakes, and whitewater rafting on the Salmon. There is a three-night minimum stay. Open Jun–Aug. **www.twinpeaksranch.com**

STANLEY Idaho Rocky Mountain Ranch ($)($)($)($)
Hwy 75, 83278 ***Tel*** *(208) 774-3544* ***Fax*** *(208) 774-3477* ***Rooms*** *13*

This mountain ranch in the beautiful Sawtooth Valley offers stunning vistas of rugged mountain peaks. Accommodations include well-appointed rooms in the lodge or private log cabins. Guests can relax and soak in the natural hot springs pool, sit by the fire, or on the porch and take in the view. Meals included. **www.idahorocky.com**

SUN VALLEY Sun Valley Lodge ($)($)($)($)($)
Sun Valley, 83353 ***Tel*** *(208) 622-2151* ***Fax*** *(208) 622-2030* ***Rooms*** *148*

This luxurious hotel, built in 1936, is the lodging centerpiece of the famous and exclusive Sun Valley ski resort. Fully modern, the accommodations provide luxury, comfort, and contemporary amenities. The four-season lodge offers elegant dining options, spa and exercise facilities, children's activities, and a magnificent pool. **www.sunvalley.com**

Key to Symbols *see back cover flap*

MONTANA

BOZEMAN Fox Hollow B&B $$

545 Mary Rd, 59718 ***Tel*** *(406) 582-8440* ***Rooms*** *5*

Warm and inviting, this bed and breakfast offers panoramic views of the mountains and meadows from the porch, and a relaxed homey atmosphere inside. The large guestrooms are clean, comfortable, and tastefully decorated. The multi-course hot breakfasts are delicious, and there are fresh-baked cookies in the evening. **www.foxhollowbandb.com**

BUTTE Copper King Mansion $

219 W Granite St, 59701 ***Tel*** *(406) 782-7580* ***Rooms*** *5*

This Victorian mansion built in 1884 was the residence of William Clarke, one of Montana's famous Copper Kings. Architectural details include fresco-painted ceilings, hand-carved woodwork, and stained-glass windows. Tours of the mansion are conducted daily May–Oct. A full hot breakfast is served. **www.thecopperkingmansion.com**

GLACIER NATIONAL PARK Glacier Park Lodge $$

US-2, East Glacier Park, 59912 ***Tel*** *(406) 892-2525* ***Fax*** *(406) 892-1375* ***Rooms*** *161*

This rustic landmark hotel built in 1912 by the Great Northern Railroad has a dramatic lobby with a massive stone fireplace and 40-ft high Douglas fir pillars. Evening entertainment, a heated swimming pool, and nine-hole golf course available. The comfortable, traditional rooms vary in size. Closed Oct–Memorial Day **www.glacierparkinc.com**

GLACIER NATIONAL PARK Izaak Walton Inn $$

290 Izaak Walton Inn Rd, 59916 ***Tel*** *(406) 888-5700* ***Fax*** *(406) 888-5200* ***Rooms*** *33*

Surrounded by wilderness, this alpine lodge was constructed in 1939 to house the winter snow-removal railroad crews. The spacious wood-paneled lobby features a stone fireplace, rustic western furnishings, and railroad memorabilia. Lodging is also available in six cabins and four railroad cabooses. **www.izaakwaltoninn.com**

GLACIER NATIONAL PARK Lake McDonald Lodge $$

Lake McDonald, 59916 ***Tel*** *(406) 888-5431* ***Fax*** *(406) 892-1375* ***Rooms*** *100*

Surrounded by stunning scenery and nestled on the shores of the park's largest lake, this lodge was built as a hunting retreat in 1913. It radiates rustic charm with its large stone fireplace and massive wood timbers. There are multi-unit cottages and '70s-style motor-lodge rooms further into the woods. Closed Oct–Memorial Day **www.glacierparkinc.com**

GLACIER NATIONAL PARK Many Glacier Hotel $$

Many Glacier, 59916 ***Tel*** *(406) 892-2525* ***Fax*** *(406) 892-1375* ***Rooms*** *211*

Built in a Swiss Chalet style in 1915, the largest hotel in the park is decorated with a Swiss theme throughout. The massive lobby has a stone fireplace and cozy sitting area. The scenery here is stunning, with panoramic views of the mountains; mountain goats and big horn sheep are often spotted from here. **www.glacierparkinc.com**

GREAT FALLS Collins Mansion B&B $$

1003 2nd Ave NW, 59404 ***Tel*** *(406) 452-4444, (866) 939-4262* ***Fax*** *(406) 452-6787* ***Rooms*** *5*

Built in 1891, Collins Mansion was turned into a stylish B&B in 1998, retaining its Queen Anne-style gables, bay windows, wood moldings, and wrap-around veranda. Guestrooms are comfortably furnished, with cozy sitting areas and private bathrooms. A full breakfast is included. **www.thecollinsmansion.com**

GREAT FALLS, CHOTEAU Pine Butte Guest Ranch $$$

351 South Fork Rd, 59422 ***Tel*** *(406) 466-2158* ***Fax*** *(406) 466-5462* ***Rooms*** *10*

Nestled among the mountain peaks of the rugged East Front, this Guest Ranch operated by the Nature Conservancy is surrounded by lands protected for wildlife. The ranch is a great place to study natural history, hike mountain trails, ride horseback, or relax by the pool. **www.nature.org/wherewework/northamerica/states/montana/pinebutte**

HELENA The Sanders Bed & Breakfast $$

328 North Ewing, 59601 ***Tel*** *(406) 442-3309* ***Fax*** *(406) 443-2361* ***Rooms*** *7*

This charming B&B is housed in an 1875 residence built for the first US Senator from Montana. Thoroughly modern, this cheery home is elegantly decorated with antiques, artwork, and historical family memorabilia. Guestrooms range from relaxed to formal in style, with cozy beds and private baths. Full breakfast with hot entrée. **www.sandersbb.com**

MISSOULA Goldsmith's Inn $$

809 E Front St, 59802 ***Tel*** *(406) 728-1585, (866) 666-9945* ***Rooms*** *7*

Housed in a classic 1911 brick riverfront home, this lovely B&B is located within walking distance of downtown and the University of Montana. The guestrooms are individually decorated and some have balconies with scenic views. Each room features hand-tiled baths, hardwood floors with oriental carpets, and elegant beds. **www.goldsmithsinn.com**

POLSON, FLATHEAD VALLEY Best Western KwaTaqNuk Resort $$

49708 US Highway 93 E, 59860 ***Tel*** *(406) 883-3636, (800) 882-6363* ***Fax*** *(406) 883-5392* ***Rooms*** *112*

Located on the South Bay of Flathead Lake (the third largest freshwater lake in the world and the largest west of the Mississippi), the KwaTaqNuk Resort is owned and operated by the Confederated Salish and Kootenai Tribes. Restaurant, lounge, marina, 24-hour casino, indoor and outdoor pools, and gift shop. **www.kwataqnuk.com**

WYOMING

CHEYENNE Nagle Warren Mansion Bed & Breakfast $$

222 E 17th St, 82001 **Tel** *(307) 637-3333, (800) 811-2610* **Rooms** *12*

Luxurious comfort is the hallmark of this charming inn housed in a Romanesque-style 1888 mansion that was converted to an inn in 1997. Decorated in western Victorian style with antiques and period furnishings, the inn offers a well-stocked library, sitting room, cozy tower get-a-way, and a lovely garden with hot tub. **www.naglewarrenmansion.com**

CODY Hotel Irma $$

1192 Sheridan Ave, 82414 **Tel** *(307) 587-4221, (800) 745-4762* **Fax** *(307) 587-1775* **Rooms** *40*

Buffalo Bill Cody built this hotel in 1902, named it for his youngest daughter, and maintained two private suites and an office for his own use here. It maintains its Wild West atmosphere today, with free staged gunfights in front of the hotel six days a week. Guestrooms vary but all have a rustic quaintness. **www.irmahotel.com**

GRAND TETON NATIONAL PARK Flagg Ranch Resort $$

PO Box 187 Moran, 83013 **Tel** *(307) 543-2861, (800) 443-2311* **Fax** *(307) 543-2356* **Rooms** *92*

Conveniently located between Grand Teton and Yellowstone National Parks on the banks of the Snake River this log-cabin-style village offers comfortable, if basic, accommodations. The modern, Western-style log cabins contain two or four units, simply furnished with basic decor. Closed mid-October to mid-May. **www.flaggranch.com**

GRAND TETON NATIONAL PARK Jenny Lake Lodge $$$$$

Jenny Lake, 83012 **Tel** *(307) 733 4647, (800) 628-9988* **Fax** *(307) 543-3358* **Rooms** *37*

Surrounded by lake and mountain views, this rustic lodge offers elegance and luxury. Old West in appearance, the lodge is located within Grand Teton National Park with hiking and horseback riding trails nearby. Breakfast, five-course dinner, horseback riding, and bicycles included. Closed Oct–May. **www.gtlc.com**

JACKSON Wort Hotel $$$

50 N Glenwood St, 83001 **Tel** *(307) 733-2190, (800) 322-2727* **Fax** *(307) 733-2067* **Rooms** *59*

This elegant small hotel is located near Jackson's town square and close to boutiques, dining, and galleries. Built in 1941, the hotel is decorated in luxurious Western style with a two-story wood paneled lobby and stone fireplace. The welcoming guestrooms are decorated with pine furniture and goose-down comforters. **www.worthotel.com**

JACKSON HOLE Inn on the Creek $$$

295 N Milward, 83001 **Tel** *(307) 739-1565, (800) 669-9534* **Rooms** *9*

This romantic inn is just beyond the bustle of Jackson, yet within walking distance of the town square. The charming living room has comfortable furnishings and books on the area, and the rooms offer luxuries such as down comforters and chocolates on the pillows. Fresh cookies in the afternoon and breakfast in your room. **www.innonthecreek.com**

LARAMIE Vee Bar Guest Ranch $$$$

38 Vee Bar Ranch Rd, 82070 **Tel** *(307) 745-7036, (800) 483-3227* **Fax** *(307) 745-7433* **Rooms** *9*

This guest ranch in the Medicine Bow Mountains offers family-oriented outdoor activities, such as horseback rides in the meadows and mountains of the ranch as well as hiking, fly-fishing, river tubing, and cattle drives. The cozy, rustic cabins are set along the Little Laramie River. Open all year. **www.veebar.com**

MORAN Jackson Lake Lodge $$$

Hwy 89, 5 miles N of Moran, 83013 **Tel** *(307) 543-2811, (800) 628-9988* **Fax** *(307) 543-3143* **Rooms** *385*

Located within Grand Teton National Park, with spectacular views of Jackson Lake, this hotel offers upscale amenities in a wilderness setting. Snake River and the many lake activities are great for families, and the lodge itself has several dining options. Closed Oct–May. **www.gtlc.com/lodgeJac.aspx**

YELLOWSTONE NATIONAL PARK Bill Cody Ranch $$

2604 Yellowstone Hwy, 82414 **Tel** *(307) 587 2097, (800) 615-2934* **Fax** *(307) 587 6272* **Rooms** *17*

Located at 6,100 feet in the Rocky Mountains just 25 miles from the eastern entrance to Yellowstone National Park, this guest ranch decorated in the style of the Old West is great for family get-togethers and retreats. Days begin with early morning trail rides and breakfast in the lodge. Closed October to mid-May. **www.billcodyranch.com**

YELLOWSTONE NATIONAL PARK Lake Yellowstone Hotel $$

Lake Yellowstone, 59758 **Tel** *(307) 344-7311, (866) 439-7375* **Fax** *(307) 344-7456* **Rooms** *300*

Located within Yellowstone National Park along the shores of Yellowstone Lake, this delightful hotel offers a casual elegance reminiscent of the 1920s. The guestrooms in the hotel are decorated in 1920s style, while the small cabins nearby offer simpler and more economical accommodations. Closed mid-Sep–Jun. **www.travelyellowstone.com**

YELLOWSTONE NATIONAL PARK Old Faithful Inn $$

Old Faithful, 59758 **Tel** *(307) 344-7311, (866) 439-7375* **Fax** *(307) 344-7456* **Rooms** *329*

Situated within viewing distance of Old Faithful geyser, the lobby of this very popular lodge features a dramatic log and timber lobby with massive central fireplace and soaring ceilings. Built in 1904, the lodge was expanded twice with each section offering different accommodations. Closed mid-Sept–June. **www.travelyellowstone.com**

Key to Price Guide *see p600* **Key to Symbols** *see back cover flap*

COLORADO

ASPEN Hotel Jerome $$$$$

330 E Main St, 81611 **Tel** *(970) 920-1000, (877) 412-7625* **Rooms** *94*

Aspen's finest hotel provides exceptional service and luxury accommodations in a charming Victorian setting. Built in 1889 this elegant hotel continues to delight guests with attention to detail and modern conveniences. Lavish and richly appointed guestrooms have Victorian decor, fine bedding, and expansive bathrooms. **www.hoteljerome.rockresorts.com**

BOULDER Hotel Boulderado $$$

2115 13th St, 80302 **Tel** *(303) 442-4344, (800) 433-4344* **Fax** *(303) 442-4378* **Rooms** *160*

Boulder's oldest hotel offers an excellent downtown location just one block off Pearl Street. The two-story lobby with stained-glass domed ceiling and cantilevered cherry staircase is luxuriously Victorian in ambience. Spacious and comfortable, the guestrooms are decorated in Victorian style. **www.boulderado.com**

COLORADO SPRINGS Broadmoor $$$$$

1 Lake Ave, 80906 **Tel** *(719) 634-7711, (866) 837-9520* **Fax** *(719) 577-5700* **Rooms** *700*

Old World elegance, impeccable service, and a stunning location on Cheyenne Lake make this one of Colorado's premier resorts. Surrounded by 3,000 acres of manicured grounds, the resort offers three golf courses, tennis club, and luxury spa. The Italian Renaissance-style main building showcases a priceless art collection. **www.broadmoor.com**

DENVER Hotel Monaco $$$

1717 Champa St at 17th, 80202 **Tel** *(303) 296-1717, (800) 990-1303* **Fax** *(303) 296-1818* **Rooms** *189*

Bold, bright, and whimsical decor set the tone at this boutique hotel in downtown Denver located just a block from the 16th Street Mall and near the LODO entertainment district. The service is excellent with trendy innovations such as pet goldfish for your room, massages, and nightly complimentary wine hour. **www.monaco-denver.com**

DURANGO Strater Hotel $$

699 Main Ave, 81301 **Tel** *(970) 247-4431, (800) 247-4431* **Fax** *(970) 259-2208* **Rooms** *93*

This historic hotel situated in the center of downtown Durango features Victorian antiques, walnut furniture, historical memorabilia, and period wallpaper throughout the common areas. The fun saloon has a honky-tonk piano and costumed wait staff. Period guestrooms are comfortable and nicely decorated. **www.strater.com**

ESTES PARK (ROCKY MOUNTAIN NATIONAL PARK) Stanley Hotel $$$

333 Wonderview Ave, 80517 **Tel** *(970) 577-4000, (800) 976-1377* **Fax** *(970) 586-4964* **Rooms** *160*

Old World charm and stately elegance characterize this historic hotel created by steam power pioneer F.O. Stanley in 1909. Located near Rocky Mountain National Park and surrounded by spectacular mountain views, there are rocking chairs on the porch and polished wood floors. The hotel was used in the film *The Shining*. **www.stanleyhotel.com**

MANITOU SPRINGS The Cliff House $$$

306 Cañon Ave, 80829 **Tel** *(719) 685-3000, (888) 212-7000* **Rooms** *54*

This Victorian country inn with modern conveniences, located at the base of Pike's Peak, is a favorite luxury and romantic hideaway. Individually decorated guestrooms feature spacious comfort, tasteful decor, and modern baths. Many of the rooms have mountain views or amenities such as fireplaces or steam showers. **www.thecliffhouse.com**

MESA VERDE NATIONAL PARK Far View Lodge $$

MM 15 Park Rd 81330 **Tel** *(970) 529-4422, (888) 896-3831* **Fax** *(970) 564-4311* **Rooms** *150*

The only roofed accommodations within Mesa Verde National Park, this lodge sits high up on the ridge in the heart of the park. Although the rooms are basic, every one has a balcony with views out across three states, and the star-gazing is awesome. The major sights are just a short drive away. Closed Nov–Apr. **www.visitmesaverde.com**

STEAMBOAT SPRINGS Sheraton Steamboat Resort $$$

2200 Village Inn Court, 80477 **Tel** *(970) 879-2220* **Fax** *(970) 879-7686* **Rooms** *209*

The Sheraton is located in the heart of Ski Time Square at the base of the ski slopes. The ski-in, ski-out lobby, with ski rental shop, opens directly to the gondola. The resort features an outdoor heated pool, hot tubs, a cross-country ski trail in winter and a golf course in summer. Closed one month each Spring and Fall. **www.starwoodhotels.com**

TELLURIDE New Sheridan Hotel $$$

231 W Colorado Ave, 81435 **Tel** *(970) 728-4351, (800) 200-1891* **Fax** *(970) 728-5024* **Rooms** *26*

Built in 1895, this charming downtown hotel is committed to historic preservation. It was thoroughly renovated in 2008 and returned to its original historic elegance and furnished with fine antiques. Additional rooms were added along with a restaurant and rooftop hot-tubs. Most rooms have a private bath. **www.newsheridan.com**

VAIL Vail Cascade Resort & Spa $$$$$

1300 Westhaven Dr, 81657 **Tel** *(970) 476-7111, (800) 282-4183* **Rooms** *292*

This contemporary Western-styled luxury resort offers pampering and excellent amenities in a stunning mountain setting. The ski-in lobby is next to the chair-lift, and the resort offers a trendy spa and athletic club, heated outdoor swimming pools and hot tubs, along with 24-hour room service and baby-sitting service. **www.vailcascade.com**

Choosing a Restaurant

Restaurants in the Rockies area reflect the rugged character of the region and are often decorated to evoke the region's Wild West heritage. Most eateries are unpretentious and tend to close by 9pm but in cities they often aspire to cosmopolitan sophistication with a varied choice of dishes.

PRICE CATEGORIES
For a three-course meal for one, including a glass of house wine (where served), and all other unavoidable charges such as sales tax.

$ Under $25
$$ $25–$35
$$$ $35–$50
$$$$ $50–$70
$$$$$ Over $70

IDAHO

BOISE Brick Oven Bistro — $

801 W Main St, 83702 ***Tel*** *(208) 342-3456*

Centrally located in downtown Boise, this restaurant has been a local gathering spot for all who enjoy great made-from-scratch American regional fare since 1984. The menu features Southwest, Cajun, Midwest, and New England favorites, as well as desserts, beer, wine by the glass, and old-fashioned shakes, malts, and soda fountain treats.

BOISE Cottonwood Grille — $$$

913 W River St 913, 83702 ***Tel*** *(208) 333-9800*

This casually elegant restaurant has a stunning two-story stone fireplace surrounded by windows that offer a view into surrounding woodlands. The service is excellent, and the food is carefully selected from local sources or flown in fresh. Fresh Idaho trout and prime beef are featured, with fine wines and decadent desserts.

COEUR D'ALENE Takara Japanese Restaurant — $

309 E Lakeside Ave, 83814 ***Tel*** *(208) 765-8014*

Beyond the modest exterior façade of this café there is an elegantly simple main dining area and several private Tatami rooms with seating on floor cushions. The Japanese cuisine is the main show here, with a nice selection of sushi, light crispy tempura, tasty teriyaki, and specialties such as the 8oz Wafu steak. Closed Sunday.

COEUR D'ALENE Cedars Floating Restaurant — $$$

1 Marina Dr, 83814 ***Tel*** *(208) 664-2922*

The view of Lake Coeur d'Alene from this circular floating restaurant is enchanting, and the decor is simple and relaxed. The menu features an impressive list of fresh seafood such as wild salmon, pistachio-crusted halibut, and many others. The prime rib and steaks are flown in from the Midwest. Save room for the outstanding desserts.

IDAHO FALLS Rutabaga's — $$$

415 River Pkwy, 83402 ***Tel*** *(208) 529-3990*

Small and intimate, this delightful restaurant has tables outside overlooking the river in summer. The menu changes frequently and features entrees with global influences and interesting flavors. Thai roasted rack of lamb, miso-marinated sea bass, and free-range chicken with truffle are representative offerings. Closed Mon.

KETCHUM Sawtooth Club — $$

231 N Main St, 83340 ***Tel*** *(208) 726-5233*

This popular family-friendly restaurant overlooking the ski slopes of Mount Baldy is decorated in warm colors and offers a relaxed atmosphere. The dining room serves first-rate mesquite-grilled steaks, lamb, and seafood with a good wine list. The western bar serves cocktails and also lighter meals, such as excellent burgers and fries.

SUN VALLEY Gretchen's — $$$

Sun Valley Lodge, 83353 ***Tel*** *(208) 622-2225*

Located on the first floor of the Sun Valley Lodge, this is a favorite for breakfast, lunch, or dinner. The warm family-friendly atmosphere is comfortable and the dinner menu offers a selection of flavorful meats and seafood, such as grilled ruby trout with dry barbecue rub. Breakfasts vary from light and healthy to hearty and filling.

TWIN FALLS Buffalo Café — $

218 4th Ave W, 83301 ***Tel*** *(208) 734-0271*

Start the day with an enormous breakfast at this small, ever-popular café where the portions are large and everything is made from scratch. The friendly staff create a welcoming downhome feel. Try the buffalo chip – a hefty omelet with eggs, bacon, cheese, and fried potatoes. The lunch menu offers soups, salads, sandwiches, and buffalo burgers.

TWIN FALLS Rock Creek — $$

200 Addison Ave W, 83301 ***Tel*** *(208) 734-4154*

This old-style steakhouse is a local favorite with great ambience. The dark paneled walls are decorated with mounted animal heads. The menu features a nice selection of hand-cut steaks and a variety of freshly flown-in seafood. The wine menu is exceptional. Rock Creek has received the Wine Spectator Award of Excellence.

Key to Symbols *see back cover flap*

MONTANA

BIGFORK Bigfork Inn $$

604 Electric Ave, 59911 ***Tel*** *(406) 837-6680*

Housed in a Swiss chalet-style building, this charming inn is the favorite dining and gathering spot in the area. The service is warm and professional, the atmosphere is relaxed, and the cuisine is upscale. The menu is eclectic, with regional favorites such as bison rib chop, fresh Atlantic salmon baked in parchment, or crispy farmhouse duck.

BIGFORK Showthyme $$$

548 Electric Ave, 59911 ***Tel*** *(406) 837-0707*

Top-notch service in a fun yet elegant restaurant located next to the summer playhouse downtown. Great food is the star performer here, with an eclectic menu. The featured entrées include dishes like Espresso Rubbed Montana Beef Filet, Chili Releno, and Rack of Lamb. Reservations suggested. Closed January.

BILLINGS Walkers Grill $$$

2700 1st Ave N, 59101 ***Tel*** *(406) 245-9291*

The finest restaurant in Billings offers excellent service in a comfortable contemporary setting. The decor is stunning, combining elegant modern furnishings with painted ceilings and wall murals. The creative menu features beef, poultry, wild game, and seafood accompanied by fresh sides, with entrées such as braised buffalo osso buco.

BOZEMAN McKenzie River Pizza Company $

232 E Main St, 59715 ***Tel*** *(406) 587-0055*

Gourmet pizza is served in an upbeat and friendly atmosphere with plenty of Montana timber and outdoor memoribilia as decor. The pizza is excellent, with a choice of sourdough, natural grain, deep dish, and thin crusts covered with traditional and gourmet ingredients. The menu also offers huge sandwiches, pasta, soups, and salads.

BUTTE Matt's Place $

2339 Placer St, 59701 ***Tel*** *(406) 782-8049*

This historic landmark drive-in restaurant, open since 1930, is Butte's favorite lunch spot. The cozy dining room features a soda fountain and murals of the Rocky Mountains. The menu offers hearty fare, with fabulous burgers, onion rings, and malts, shakes, and sundaes. The local special is the legendary nutburger with peanuts. Open Apr–Nov.

GLACIER NATIONAL PARK Izaak Walton Inn $$

290 Izaak Walton Inn Rd, 59916 ***Tel*** *(406) 888.5700*

The dining room at the historic Izaak Walton Inn serves up excellent hearty meals in a rustic setting with great views of the Montana scenery. The menu includes long-standing favorites as well as creative offerings that change with the seasons and the availability of local foods such as buffalo, rainbow trout, and wild huckleberries.

GLACIER NATIONAL PARK Russell's Fireside Dining Room $$$

Lake McDonald Lodge, 59916 ***Tel*** *(406) 888-5431*

This charming restaurant is decorated in hunting lodge-style with wood walls, a massive stone fireplace, and rough hewn beams of western red cedar. The mountain cuisine features wild game and local favorites, accompanied by a frosty Montana micro-brew or glass of wine.

GREAT FALLS Dante's Creative Cuisine $$

1325 8th Ave N, 59401 ***Tel*** *(406) 453-9599*

Located in a 1908 red-brick building that was once an ironworks, Dante's is a gem of a restaurant. The service is excellent, the staff is friendly, and the atmosphere is upscale, relaxed, and casual. The eclectic menu features a nice mix of steaks, seafood, traditional Italian, and a few Mexican entrées, as well as salads with outstanding dressings.

HELENA Windbag Saloon & Grill $$

19 S Last Chance Gulch St, 59601 ***Tel*** *(406) 443-9669*

Located on legendary Last Chance Gulch Street in central Helena, this charming restaurant situated in an historic building bustles at lunch and dinner. The decor is old-time rustic and the service is friendly. Entrées feature large portions of classic comfort foods, including handcut steaks and gourmet hamburgers. Closed Sunday.

MISSOULA The Shack Café $

222 W Main St, 59802 ***Tel*** *(406) 549-9903*

The ambience is friendly and comfortable with an impressive decor that feaures real Montana antiques, including a bar that arrived by steamboat in 1881. The food is innovative, great tasting, and crafted with fresh ingredients. Try the huckleberry pancakes for breakfast or select from Angus sirloin and shrimp etouffée for dinner.

MISSOULA Lolo Creek Steakhouse $$

6600 Highway 12 W, 59847 ***Tel*** *(406) 273-2622*

Located in the foothills south of Missoula along Lolo Creek, this casual restaurant is housed in a massive log cabin. The menu includes steak, seafood, and chicken, with salads and great desserts. The Western-style sirloin, rib-eye, and New York steaks are grilled on an open-pit barbecue. Beer and wine available. Closed Monday.

WYOMING

BUFFALO Bozeman's Trail Steakhouse $$

675 Hart St, 82834 ***Tel*** *(307) 684-5555*

Located in the historic cowboy town of Buffalo, this casual family-friendly restaurant has a Western and Plains Indian decor. The house specialties are steaks, baby back ribs, and prime rib entrees. The restaurant also serves buffalo steaks, while the bar area offers lighter fare and burgers. There is also a good selection of micro-brews.

CASPER Poor Boy's Steakhouse $$

739 N Center St, 82601 ***Tel*** *(307) 237-8325*

This American-style family restaurant is very popular with the local crowd. The decor is Western with lots of wood paneling and a lovely long bar. Large portions of filling steaks, salads, and tasty desserts are the favorites here. There are also daily specials and a varied menu with chicken, seafood, and burgers. Micro-beers are on tap.

CODY Cassie's Supper Club & Dance Hall $$

214 Yellowstone Ave, 82414 ***Tel*** *(307) 527-5500*

This popular steakhouse and dance club is proud of its historic past. Cassie opened her sportin' house in 1922 and during prohibition she brewed bootleg whiskey in the basement. Today Cassie's is famous for its fine dining, western atmosphere, and weekend dances. Steaks are cut to order and grilled. The menu also has seafood, chicken, and pasta.

GRAND TETON NATIONAL PARK Dorman's Chuckwagon $

10 Moose Rd, 83013 ***Tel*** *(307) 733-2415*

For 60 years the Chuckwagon has offered a unique family dining experience at Moose Junction inside Grand Teton National Park. With seating at tables outdoors along the Snake River, or inside one of the large teepees, diners can have sourdough pancakes for breakfast, burgers and sandwiches for lunch, or a full Chuckwagon dinner. Closed Oct–May.

GRAND TETON NATIONAL PARK Jenny Lake Lodge Dining Room $$$$

Inner Park Rd, 83013 ***Tel*** *(307) 733-4647*

Fine dining in this stunning yet rustic dining room is a memorable experience. Dinner is a five-course gourmet affair, with appetizers such as elk carpaccio and main entrées such as venison strip loin, followed by a decadent dessert. Dinner is included in the room charge for lodge guests. Reservations required. Jackets suggested. Closed Oct–May.

JACKSON Jedediah's Original House of Sourdough $

135 E Broadway, 83001 ***Tel*** *(307) 733-5671*

Housed in an original log cabin just a block east of town square, this neat and tidy family-friendly restaurant serves breakfast and lunch. Popular with locals and visitors, the breakfast specialty is sourdough pancakes. Lunch selections include burgers and sandwiches. The menu is in the form of a "newspaper", with stories about historic Jackson Hole.

JACKSON Granary Restaurant at Spring Creek Ranch $$$

1800 Spirit Dance Rd, 83001 ***Tel*** *(307) 733-8833*

Set atop Gros Ventre Butte, this elegant Western dining room offers spectacular floor-to-ceiling views of the Grand Tetons. The unique cuisine features regional ingredients with international embellishments to produce creations such as blackened elk with a New Orleans sauce or Trout Meuniere in the French style.

YELLOWSTONE NATIONAL PARK Old Faithful Inn Dining Room $$

Old Faithful Bypass, 59758 ***Tel*** *(307) 545-4999*

The experience of eating in this historic dining room, with its lodgepole walls and massive stone fireplace, is exceptional. Open for breakfast, lunch, and dinner, the cuisine features Western entrées such as buffalo prime rib or elk tenderloin. The signature dessert is a rich chocolate Caldera. Closed mid-Sep–mid-May.

COLORADO

BOULDER John's Restaurant $$$

2328 Pearl St, 80302 ***Tel*** *(303) 444-5232*

This charming restaurant housed in a small cottage offers fine dining and a quiet, relaxed atmosphere. The cuisine is a blend of classic and contemporary Southern European and American, influenced by flavors from Asia, the Caribbean, Louisiana, and the American Southwest. The menu changes to incorporate fresh foods. Closed Sunday and Monday.

BOULDER Flagstaff House $$$$$

1138 Flagstaff Rd, 80302 ***Tel*** *(303) 442-4640*

Flagstaff House is perched high up Flagstaff Mountain offering incredible views of Boulder and the surrounding mountains from the dining room or the outdoor terraces. The cuisine is French/American with Asian influences, and incorporates the freshest seasonal organic ingredients and fresh fish flown in daily.

Key to Price Guide *see p604* **Key to Symbols** *see back cover flap*

BRECKENRIDGE (SUMMIT COUNTY) Café Alpine $$$

106 E Adams Ave, 80424 ***Tel*** *(970) 453-8218*

This cozy upscale restaurant offers summer dining on the deck and winter dining beside a warm crackling fireplace. Creative regional American cuisine is the forte, with a seasonal menu that changes daily to take advantage of the freshest ingredients available. A Breckenridge tradition in the middle of town.

COLORADO SPRINGS Blue Star $$$

1645 S Tejon St, 80906 ***Tel*** *(719) 632-1086*

This sleek, sophisticated restaurant in an upbeat contemporary setting offers attentive and personalized service. There are two dining rooms, one casual and the other offering sophisticated fine dining. The food is innovative American enhanced by the flavors of the Pacific Rim and the Mediterranean, and the menu changes monthly.

DENVER Jack-N-Grill $

2524 Federal Blvd, 80211 ***Tel*** *(303) 964-9544*

This cozy, kitsch family-owned cantina serves New Mexican dishes such as shrimp tacos and chile rellenos. Eat all of the seven-pound (3 kg) breakfast burrito and they'll hang your photo on the wall. Custom order the heat of the chile, from "regular" to "nuclear waste".

DENVER Wynkoop Brewing Company $$

1634 18th St, 80202 ***Tel*** *(303) 297-2700*

The Wynkoop was Denver's first brewpub and led the way in the resurgence of lower downtown. Housed in a red-brick building with pressed-tin ceiling, hardwood floors, and plenty of polished woodwork, the atmosphere is fun and casual. The ales and beers are excellent, and the menu includes favorites such as lamb and venison.

DENVER Buckhorn Exchange $$$$

1000 Osage St, 80204 ***Tel*** *(303) 534-9505*

This historic and famous steakhouse is set in a rustic building adorned with an amazing collection of mounted animal trophy heads, guns, and Wild West memorabilia. Denver's oldest restaurant is best known for its steaks and exotic game. The favorite choices are the buffalo steaks and elk medallions, and the appetizers of rattlesnake and buffalo sausage.

DURANGO Randy's $$

152 E College Dr, 81301 ***Tel*** *(970) 247-9083*

One of Durango's most romantic restaurants is hidden behind a modest exterior. For intimate dining, sit in one of the curtained private booths, or choose a window table with a view. The American menu features steaks, seafood, pasta, and poultry with nightly specials. The prime rib is one of the best in town, and the desserts are excellent.

GOLDEN Table Mountain Inn $$

1310 Washington Ave, 80401 ***Tel*** *(303) 277-9898*

Southwestern decor sets the stage for enjoying the finest Southwestern cuisine in the area. The service is attentive and the ambience is relaxed and casual. House specialties include entrées such as Rocky Mountain Rainbow Trout, Mango-Barbecued Pork Chops, and Chili Rellenos. Micro-brews are on tap and the margaritas are tangy.

MANITOU SPRINGS Briarhurst Manor $$$

404 Manitou Ave, 80829 ***Tel*** *(719) 685-1864*

Step back in time and enjoy fine dining in the elegant 1878 stone mansion owned by one of the founders of Manitou Springs. Romantic and elegant decor features hardwood floors, soft lighting, and antiques. This landmark restaurant is known for its regional Rocky Mountain cuisine, including bison steak, elk, Rocky Mountain trout, and fine beef steaks.

MORRISON The Fort $$$

19192 Hwy 8, 80465 ***Tel*** *(303) 697-4771*

Housed in a modern rendition of an historic Colorado fort, a classic Western theme is carried throughout this restaurant. The excellent cuisine features traditional and contemporary Western entrees including buffalo steaks and buffalo smoked ribs, as well as dishes featuring elk, quail, steak, and seafood. For dessert try the Chocolate Chile Bourbon Cake.

STEAMBOAT SPRINGS Rio Grande $$

628 N Lincoln Ave, 80487 ***Tel*** *(970) 871-6277*

Watch ski jumping from the front window on the rooftop patio while enjoying a legendary margarita, then tuck into Mexican cuisine from the Yucatan area. Rio Grande is popular with both locals and visitors who come for the friendly atmosphere and the homemade dishes which include tortillas and guacamole, fajitas, enchiladas, and quesadillas.

TELLURIDE Honga's Lotus Petal $$$

135 E Colorado, 81435 ***Tel*** *(970) 728-5134*

This local favorite serves excellent fusion Asian cuisine in a warm and friendly atmosphere. The creative menu draws on the food traditions of many countries, including Japan, China. and Thailand as well as India, Malaysia, and Indonesia. Regional ranchers and farmers provide organic and free-range ingredients, which are used whenever possible.

VAIL Sweet Basil $$$$

193 Gore Creek Dr #201, 81657 ***Tel*** *(970) 476-0125*

This casual contemporary restaurant with an understated modern mountain decor is located in the heart of Vail, and is very popular with locals and travelers. The cuisine is contemporary American with specialties including Colorado lamb. For dessert try the hot sticky toffee pudding cake.

THE PACIFIC NORTHWEST

INTRODUCING THE PACIFIC NORTHWEST 610–615

WASHINGTON 616–629

OREGON 630–641

THE PACIFIC NORTHWEST

Some of North America's most rugged and spectacular terrain unfolds across the Pacific Northwest. Native cultures have lived here for thousands of years, while European settlement is as recent as the early 19th century. The region is now home to two of North America's most sophisticated cities, Portland and Seattle, surrounded by soaring mountains, dense forests, and sparkling water.

The call of the wild is what draws visitors to Oregon and Washington, the states that comprise the Pacific Northwest. This region's vast landscapes bear the imprint of the geological forces that carved deep gorges and thrust up soaring mountain peaks. Despite urban development, the wilderness areas retain a certain pristine quality, especially when one encounters the 800-year-old Sitka spruce trees in a coastal rainforest or the lava fields flanking Mount St. Helens, formed during the volcano's eruption in 1980.

The weather in this region is as varied as its topography. West of the mountains, the north Pacific Ocean currents ensure pleasant summers and wet, mild winters. On the eastern plateaus, however, temperatures dip to well below freezing in the winter, often accompanied by heavy snow, and in the summer they soar. In the central mountain region, inland deserts usually experience harsh winters with frequent road closures and dry hot summers.

HISTORY

The region's Native peoples have lived in harmony with the land since their ancestors migrated here almost 15,000 years ago. The abundance of food and resources, west of the Cascade Mountains and along the coast, enabled many tribes to live in well-established settlements, hunting and fishing. Those tribes, living in the harsher landscapes east of the mountains, pursued more nomadic lifestyles, migrating across the high-desert hunting grounds in search of bison and deer. In spring and summer, they moved up the mountain

Mount Rainier towering above Tacoma's Commencement Bay and its industrial tideflats, Washington

◁ The Pinnacles, spires of volcanic ash inside the caldera, at Crater Lake National Park, Oregon

slopes to pick berries and dig roots. This tranquil existence was abruptly disturbed with the arrival of European traders and settlers.

The quest to discover the Northwest Passage – a quick ocean route linking Europe with the Far East – lured early European explorers to this region in the 16th century. The first was Spanish explorer Juan Rodriguez, who sailed from Mexico to southern Oregon in 1543. He was followed by Britain's Sir Francis Drake, who ventured as far north as the Strait of Juan de Fuca in 1592.

Portland, City of Roses

Britain's next major expedition was in the 1770s, when Captain James Cook, accompanied by George Vancouver and Peter Puget, sailed up the coasts of Oregon and Washington. In 1791, Vancouver and Puget also charted what is now Puget Sound in Washington. Their explorations coincided with those of an American fur trader from the East Coast, Captain Robert Gray, who discovered the Columbia River in 1792, naming it after his ship. Soon, other American vessels arrived in search of animal pelts and other bounty.

The battle to control the Pacific Northwest was waged by the British and Americans with trade, not gunfire. The 1803–06 Lewis and Clark expedition opened up the region to American fur traders, who were determined to wrest this very lucrative trade from the British. At that time, the dominant player was Britain's Hudson Bay Company (HBC), which continued to more or less rule the region until the middle of the 19th century.

Between 1843 and 1860, thousands of American settlers migrated westward on the 2,000-mile (3,218-km) Oregon Trail. As a result, America and Britain divided the region in 1846, using the 49th parallel as the new boundary between British Columbia to the north and Oregon to the south. Oregon, which included the present-day states of Oregon, Washington, and Idaho, became a US territory two years later. In 1852, this territory was further divided into Washington and Oregon.

Those who profited least from the division of spoils were the Native peoples. Diseases had already decimated many tribes, but now, those who survived were removed from their lands and moved to reservations.

KEY DATES IN HISTORY

1543 Spanish explorer Juan Rodriguez Cabrillo sails to the coast of southern Oregon

1765 Robert Rogers maps the vast territory he refers to as Oregon

1792 Robert Gray crosses the Columbia River

1829 Oregon City is the first town west of the Rocky Mountains

1846 US acquires Oregon and Washington

1848 Oregon Territory established

1851 Portland is incorporated

1852 Washington Territory is formed

1859 Oregon becomes 33rd state

1865 Seattle is incorporated

1897 Klondike Gold Rush brings prosperity to Seattle

1889 Washington becomes 42nd state

1905 Portland hosts World's Fair with Lewis & Clark Exposition

1916 Boeing Air Company founded in Seattle

1949 Seattle earthquake

1980 Mt. St. Helens erupts in Washington

1995 Amazon.com launched from Seattle

2002 Seahawks stadium opens in Seattle

PEOPLE & POLITICS

Nearly ten million people call the Pacific Northwest region their home. The nationwide spurt in growth of the Hispanic population in the 1990s is visible in this region as well. Hispanics,

Romantic interpretation of the Oregon Trail's westward trek, painted c.1904

Snowboarding at Mount Hood, Oregon

today, constitute the largest ethnic group in Oregon, representing almost 10 percent of the state's population. Hispanics also form 10 percent of Washington's local population. Native Americans have a significant presence here as well, having recovered from the decline that took place after European settlement. Many of the tribes continue to live in traditional communities, preserving their identities.

Portland and Seattle are among the continent's fastest-growing cities. Though both tend to be liberal in their politics, other areas in the Pacific Northwest region remain conservative. Even so, a unique political climate has emerged. Oregonians are the first in the US to have approved assisted suicide for the terminally ill, while Washingtonians had the distinction of electing the country's first Asian-American governor. Culturally, the region has cultivated a rich tradition of excellence in the arts, sciences, public services, and creative entrepreneurship. Some of the region's best creative talents include Dale Chihuly (b. 1941), one of the world's leading glass sculpturists, rock legend Jimi Hendrix (1942–70), Matt Groening (b. 1954), creator of the popular TV show *The Simpsons*, and Linus Pauling (1901–94), winner of two Noble Prizes, for chemistry in 1954 and peace in 1962.

Neon sign at Seattle's Pike Place Market

ECONOMY & INDUSTRY

In recent years, the region's economy had undergone great changes. While traditional industries such as fishing, mining, and logging struggle for survival, those based on services and technology flourish. Since the 1980s, when Bill Gates, the founder of Mircosoft, the world's foremost computer software company, established his headquarters in Redmond, there has been a proliferation of high-tech companies. Some 3,000 software and e-commerce businesses operate in the Seattle area alone. Jeff Bezos, another Seattle-based entrepreneur, set up Amazon.com, the world's largest online retailer. Among the other major companies with interests here are computer industry giants Intel, Adobe, and Hewlett-Packard, the aerospace leader Boeing, which operates several plants in western Washington, and the sportswear chain Nike. Starbucks, the coffee house that first opened in Seattle's Pike Place Market in the 1970s, now has coffee bars all over the world.

Amid this economic transformation, one industry has done consistently well. Increasingly, tourists are spending healthy sums to enjoy what the locals have long considered their greatest resource – the Pacific Northwest's natural beauty. The region not only offers great opportunities for some of the world's finest adventure sports such as whitewater rafting, kayaking, hiking, skiing, and rockclimbing, but for those who prefer more placid pastimes, the opportunities for sitting next to a mountain stream, or strolling along a remote beach are seemingly endless.

Portlanders relaxing at one of the city's local cafés and wine bars

Exploring the Pacific Northwest

The Pacific Northwest, comprising Oregon and Washington, is a region of great natural beauty. Its lofty mountains, deep canyons, crystal clear lakes, mighty rivers, and rugged shoreline offer visitors a chance to enjoy a wide range of outdoor activities. Equally alluring are its two principal cities – Portland and Seattle, with their excellent museums and vibrant cultural scene. Both cities are well-connected by air, road, and rail. However, the best way to explore the region, especially remote areas, such as Oregon's Hell Canyon and Washington's Olympic Peninsula, is by car.

The Space Needle, dominating the Seattle skyline

SIGHTS AT A GLANCE

Washington
Seattle pp616–19 1
Olympic National Park 2
Port Townsend 3
Bellingham 4
San Juan Islands pp622–3 5
North Cascades Highway 6
Lake Chelan 7
Leavenworth 8
Spokane 9
Walla Walla 10
Yakima Valley 11
Maryhill 12
Mount Rainier National Park pp626–7 13
Tacoma 14
Olympia 15
Mount St. Helens National Volcanic Monument 16
Fort Vancouver 17

Oregon
Portland pp630–31 18
Columbia River Gorge 19
Mount Hood 20
Astoria 21
Oregon Coast 22
Salem 23
Eugene 24
Madras & Warm Springs 25
Sisters 26
Bend 27
Newberry National Volcanic Monument 28
Crater Lake National Park pp636–7 29
Oregon Caves National Monument 30
Ashland 31
Steens Mountain 32
Malheur National Wildlife Refuge 33
John Day Fossil Beds National Monument 34
Pendleton 35
Wallowa Mountains 36
Hell's Canyon National Recreation Area pp640–41 37

For additional map symbols *see back flap*

MILEAGE CHART

10 = Distance in miles
10 = Distance in kilometers

SEATTLE, WA							
109 175	PORT TOWNSEND, WA						
280 451	**367** 591	SPOKANE, WA					
273 439	**374** 602	**157** 253	WALLA WALLA, WA				
172 277	**205** 330	**352** 566	**243** 391	PORTLAND, OR			
179 288	**190** 306	**445** 716	**330** 531	**87** 140	ASTORIA, OR		
219 352	**251** 404	**398** 640	**289** 465	**46** 74	**125** 201	SALEM, OR	
461 742	**494** 795	**642** 1033	**536** 863	**289** 465	**368** 592	**244** 393	ASHLAND, OR

KEY

- Airport
- Highway
- Major road
- Railroad
- State border
- International border

SEE ALSO

• ***Practical Information*** pp642–3
• ***Where to Stay*** pp644–5
• ***Where to Eat*** pp646–7

Painted Hill in the John Day Fossil Beds, Oregon

Washington

The only US state named for a president, Washington has an extraordinary geographical diversity within its 68,139 sq miles (176,466 sq km) of land. Of its three distinct geographic regions, the coastal Olympic Peninsula is dominated by great tracts of forest. Most of the state's largest cities are in the damp, green western region, scattered around Puget Sound. A drive through the spectacular peaks of the North Cascades takes visitors to the sunny, dry eastern part of the state.

Seattle 1

594,000. 800 Convention Place, Street Level, (206) 461-5840. **www**.visitseattle.org

Nestled between Puget Sound and Lake Washington, with Mount Rainier in the background, Seattle has a spectacular setting. The home of Microsoft and Amazon.com, the city's growth since the Klondike Gold Rush of 1897 *(see p737)* has been vigorous. Its prime geographic location and enviable lifestyle make Seattle one of America's most attractive cities.

Pioneer Square

Bounded by Alaskan & Yesler Ways, 4th Ave & S King St. *15, 16, 18, 22, 56.* *Occidental Park.* **Klondike National Historical Park** 319 2nd Ave S. ***Tel** (206) 220-4240. 9am–5pm daily. Jan 1, Thanksg., Dec 25.* **www**.nps.gov/klse

Seattle's first downtown and later a decrepit skid row, Pioneer Square is now a revitalized business neighborhood and National Historic District with a thriving art and music scene. Many of its buildings were constructed in the years between the two pivotal events in Seattle's history – the Great Fire of 1889 and the Klondike Gold Rush of 1897– 98. The handsome **Pioneer Building** on 1st Avenue, for instance, was completed three years after the fire.

The story of Seattle's role in the Gold Rush is told in the **Klondike National Historical Park** on South Jackson Street. A Seattle institution, the **Elliott Bay Book Company** nearby, occupies the site of the city's first hospital and stocks around 150,000 titles.

A display in Klondike Gold Rush National Historical Park

Opened in 1914, Seattle's first skyscraper, the terra-cotta **Smith Tower**, offers superb views from its wraparound observation deck.

Pike Place Market

Bounded by Pike & Virginia Sts, from 1st to Western Aves. ***Tel** (206) 682-7453. 10, 12, 21, 22, 56. 10am–6pm Mon–Sat, 11am–5pm Sun; may vary. public hols.* **www**.pikeplacemarket.org

Said to be the soul of Seattle, Pike Place Market is known as much for its colorful personality as for its abundant local produce. Established in 1907, the country's oldest continuously operating farmers' market is now a historic district bustling with farmers, artists, and street performers. Rachel, an enormous piggy bank, stands at the main entrance to the market, whose heart is the **Main Arcade** and the adjacent **North Arcade**. Here, low counters display fresh fruit, vegetables, herbs, and flowers grown by local farmers. Shoppers get to "meet the producer," as promised by the market's signature green sign. Attractions include the Pike Place Starbucks, birthplace of the omnipresent chain, and **Pike Place Fish**, the market's best-known seafood vendor. Here, fish-flinging fishmongers are a long-standing tradition.

Seattle Aquarium

Pier 59, 1483 Alaskan Way. ***Tel** (206) 386-4320. 10, 12, 15, 18, 21, 22, 56. Pike. 9.30am–5pm daily.* **www**.seattleaquarium.org

One of the country's top aquariums, the Seattle Aquarium showcases more than 400 species of animals, plants, and mammals indigenous to the Pacific Northwest. A highlight is the huge underwater glass dome, filled with sharks, octopus, and other Puget Sound creatures. The world's first aquarium-based salmon ladder – the fish jumping up the rungs to the maturing pond – explains the entire life cycle of the Pacific salmon. In the **Discovery Lab**, children can touch starfish and hermit crabs and examine live plankton through a high-resolution video microscope.

Pike Place Fish in Pike Place Market, which offers both fish and fun

For hotels and restaurants in this region see pp644–5 and pp646–7

Seattle Art Museum

100 University St. ***Tel** (206) 654-3100.* *10, 12, 174.* *10am–5pm Tue–Sun, 10am–9pm Thu & Fri.* *(free 1st Thu of month).* **www**.seattleartmuseum.org **Benaroya Hall** 200 University St. ***Tel** (206) 215-4700.* *174.* *noon & 1pm Tue & Fri.* **www**.seattlesymphony.org

At the entrance of the Seattle Art Museum stands the giant *Hammering Man*, a 48-ft (15-m) animated steel sculpture created as a tribute to workers. The bold limestone-and-sandstone museum building is as impressive. Its permanent collection includes 23,000 objects ranging from ancient Egyptian reliefs and wooden African sculptures to Old Master paintings and contemporary American art. Traveling exhibits are on the second floor. Also part of the museum are the Seattle Asian Art Museum in Volunteer Park in Capitol Hill *(see p618)*, and the Olympic Sculpture Park, which is located on Seattle's waterfront. Across the street, **Benaroya Hall**, home of the Seattle Symphony, occupies an entire city block. Of its two performing halls, Taper Auditorium, acclaimed for its fine acoustics, has 2,500 seats. The multilevel Grand Lobby, dramatic at night when lit, offers stunning views of the city skyline. Benaroya Hall has some excellent tours and an impressive private art collections.

Belltown

Bounded by Denny Way, Virginia St, Elliot Ave, & Broad St. *15, 18, 21, 22, 56.* **Austin A. Bell Building** 2326 1st Ave. **Virginia Inn** 1937 1st Ave. ***Tel** (206) 728-1937.* *11am–2am daily.*

South of the Seattle Center lies trendy Belltown. With its broad avenues lined with hip clubs, chic restaurants, and eclectic shops, it has been compared to Manhattan's Upper West Side. Earlier an area filled with car lots and sailors' taverns, its identity began to change in the 1970s when artists, attracted by cheap rents and studio space, moved in. Belltown now bears little resemblance to its early days. The handsome four-story brick **Austin A. Bell Building** is one of the few remaining original structures. Commissioned in 1888 by Austin Americus Bell, the son of Seattle pioneer William M. Bell, for whom Belltown is named, it is listed on the National Register of Historic Places. The building now houses pricey condominiums. The brick-and-tile **Virginia Inn** *(see p646)*, on the southern boundary of Belltown, is another historic building. A popular watering hole for more than a century, it is now Seattle's hottest art bar.

The *Hammering Man* sculpture at the entrance of Seattle Art Museum

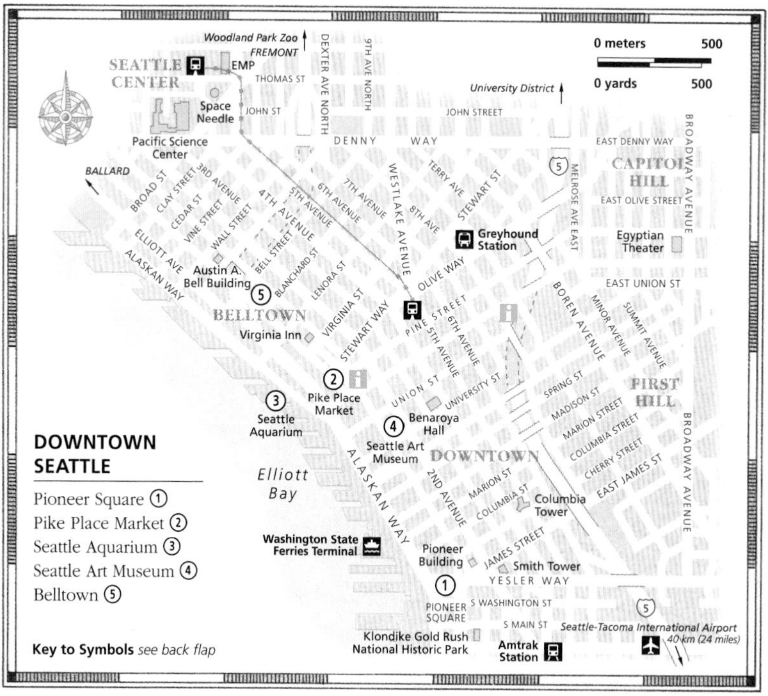

Seattle: Beyond Downtown

This extensive city offers plenty of opportunities for exploration and recreation. Immediately north of downtown are the prime cultural venues of Seattle Center, while to its northeast is the prominent Capitol Hill. Farther afield are the lively University District, Woodland Park Zoo, and the characterful neighborhoods of Fremont and Ballard.

Seattle Center

Bounded by Denny Way & 1st Ave N, Mercer & Broad Sts. *(206) 684-7200.* *Seattle Center.* *1, 2, 3, 4, 13, 16, 18.* **www**.seattlecenter.com

Space Needle 400 Broad St. ***Tel*** *(206) 905-2100.* *check for times.* **www**.spaceneedle.com

Experience Music Project/Science Fiction Museum 325 5th Ave N. ***Tel*** *(206) 770-2700.* *10am–7pm daily.* *Thanksgiving, Dec 25.* **www**.empsfm.org

The proud legacy of the city's second World's Fair in 1962, this 74-acre (30-ha) urban park contains several innovative structures, cultural venues, and excellent museums. Among the most striking is the **Space Needle**. Supported by three curved steel legs, the needle's glass-enclosed tophouse features an observation deck and a revolving restaurant. At the base of the Space Needle, the exuberant Frank Gehry-designed **Experience Music Project/Science Fiction Museum** celebrates music with rare memorabilia, interactive exhibits, and live performance space. Visitors can listen to musicians telling their own stories. Also here is the world's first museum devoted to science fiction. The museum incorporates exhibitions and a Hall of Fame, which presents respected writers, artists, publishers, and filmmakers from the world of science fiction.

The **Pacific Science Center** features six buildings of white pre-cast concrete surrounding five arches that soar over reflecting pools and fountains. Its hands-on science and math exhibits are especially appealing to children.

The center is best reached by the **Seattle Monorail**. It covers the 1.2-mile (2-km) distance between the downtown station (5th Avenue at Pine Street) and the Seattle Center in 90 seconds.

Space Needle, Seattle's best-known landmark and prime tourist attraction

The Experience Music Project building, in Seattle Center

Capitol Hill

Bounded by Montlake Blvds E & NE, E Pike & E Madison Sts, 23rd Ave E & I-5. *9, 10, 11, 12.*

Lively Capitol Hill is a colorful neighborhood where no one blinks at spiked purple hair and multiple body piercings. Broadway, the district's major avenue, is lined with shops and ethnic restaurants. Bronze footsteps, to teach passersby the tango and fox trot, are embedded in the sidewalk of Broadway.

While people-watching is a major source of entertainment, Capitol Hill also features two vintage movie houses: the **Egyptian Theater** on East Pine Street, and the **Harvard Exit** on East Roy Street. The hill is also home to **St. Mark's Episcopal Cathedral** on 10th Avenue Street, known for its magnificent Flentrop organ, consisting of 3,944 pipes.

Fremont

Bounded by N 50th St, Lake Washington Ship Canal, Stone Way Ave N, & 8th Ave NW. *26, 28.*

This funky district declared itself an "artists' republic" in the 1960s, one consisting of students, artists, and bohemians attracted here by low rents. By the late 1990s, its character began to change, after a high-tech firm set up office here. However, Fremont has managed to hold on to cherished traditions, such as the Summer Solstice Parade and an outdoor film series.

Public art is a fixture of Fremont. A 13.5-ft (4-m) tall statue of Lenin towers above pedestrians at Fremont Place, and a 15-ft (4.5-m) tall Volkswagen-eating troll lurks under the north end of the Aurora Bridge. On 34th Street, sculptor Richard Beyer's *People Waiting for the Interurban* is regularly clothed by locals. The dog's face in the sculpture is modeled after an honorary mayor, with whom the artist had a dispute.

Museum of Flight

9404 E Marginal Way S (exit 158 from I-5). ***Tel*** *(206) 764-5720.* *154, 173, 174.* *10am–5pm daily (to 9pm 1st Thu of month).* *Thanksgiving, Dec 25.* **www**.museumofflight.org

For hotels and restaurants in this region see pp644–5 and pp646–7

Richard Beyer's aluminium sculpture in Fremont

As the largest air and space museum on the West Coast, this is one of Seattle's premier attractions. The focal point is the Great Gallery, a dramatic six-story steel and glass structure that holds 39 full-size aircraft. Highlights include an M/D-21 Blackbird – one of the fastest aircraft ever built – and a replica of the International Space Station.

Many more planes sit on the tarmac outside, and visitors can walk through Air Force One, the plane used by presidents Eisenhower, Kennedy, Johnson, and Nixon, as well as the supersonic Concorde.

Also popular are the museum's flight simulators. Visitors can experience what flight is like in a World War II fighter plane or on a hang-glider.

Nearby is the Red Barn, with exhibits on the history of human flight. A multitude of kid-friendly exhibits are available, plus a full-size control tower where visitors can listen in on air traffic from the adjacent Boeing Field.

University District

Bounded by NE 55th St, Portage Bay, Montlake Blvd NE, & I-5. *4014 University Way NE, (206) 543-9198.* *18 lines serve this district.* *8am–5pm Mon–Fri.* **Washington Park Arboretum** 2300 Arboretum Dr E. ***Tel** (206) 543-8800.* **Visitor Center** *10am–4pm.* **Grounds** *dawn–dusk.* *to Japanese Garden.* **www**.depts.washington.edu/wpa

The hub of the energetic U-District is the University of Washington, the premier institute of higher learning in the Northwest. Located on the site of the 1909 World's Fair, the lovely 693-acre (280-ha) parklike campus is home to more than 35,000 students and 218 buildings in a mix of architectural styles. Just inside the main campus entrance is the **Burke Museum of Natural History and Culture**, featuring dinosaur fossils and Northwest Native art. On the western edge of the campus sits the **Henry Art Gallery**, the first public art museum in the state. The university's main avenue **University Way Northeast**, just west of the campus, is lined with bookstores, pubs, and inexpensive restaurants. University Village, east of the campus, offers an upscale shopping and dining experience.

A must-see is the **Washington Park Arboretum**, a 230-acre (93-ha) garden and living plant museum, with 4,600 species. Its Japanese Garden has carp-filled ponds and a teahouse.

Woodland Park Zoo

5500 Phinney Ave N. ***Tel** (206) 684-4800.* *5.* *summer: 9:30am–6pm daily; winter: 9:30am–4pm daily.* **www**.zoo.org

Designed in 1899, this is one of the oldest zoos on the West Coast and a major Seattle attraction. The nearly 300 animal species residing at the 92-acre (37-ha) zoo are grouped together in eco-systems rather than by species, in habitats designed to resemble their natural habitats. A visitor center at the main entrance provides maps and other information, such as animal feeding times. Among the excellent naturalistic habitats are the **Elephant Forest** – with its enormous elephant pool and Thai logging camp replica – and the **Trail of Vines**, which includes the first open-forested canopy for orangutans to be created within a zoo. The **Family Farm** includes a popular petting zoo, and a Bug World exhibit featuring many species of arthropods. Indigenous North American animals can be seen in their natural habitats along the **Northern Trail**.

Ballard

Bounded by Salmon Bay, Shilshole Bay, & Phinney Ridge. *10 lines serve this area.* **Hiram M. Chittenden Locks** 3015 NW 54th St. ***Tel** (206) 783-7059.* **Grounds** *7am–9pm daily.* **Visitor Center** *May–Sep: 10am–6pm daily; Oct–Apr: 10am–4pm Thu–Mon.*

Historic belltower in Ballard

Located in northwest Seattle, Ballard's distinct Scandinavian accent dates to its settlement by Scandinavian fishermen and loggers in 1853. At the turn of the 19th century, Ballard was a mill town, producing an impressive three million wooden shingles a day. North of the shingle mills, **Ballard Avenue** was the commercial center of this area and is now a historic district, which features a wide array of ethnic cafés and lively music clubs.

The area's Scandinavian heritage is celebrated at the annual Norwegian Constitution Day Parade on May 17, at the excellent **Nordic Heritage Museum** on Northwest 67th Street.

Located at the west end of Ballard, the **Hiram M. Chittenden Locks** allow boats to travel between saltwater Puget Sound and freshwater Lake Union and Lake Washington. Its grounds include 7 acres (3 ha) of botanical gardens.

The Olympic Peninsula ❷

Olympic National Park Headquarters *3002 Mt Angeles Rd, 1 mile S of Port Angeles, (360) 565-3130.*
www.nps.gov/olym

Bordered by the Pacific Ocean, the Strait of Juan de Fuca, and Puget Sound, Washington's Olympic Peninsula is an extraordinary piece of land. Its coastline, etched with bays and inlets, is peppered with majestic sea stacks – portions of wave-eroded headlands that remain as offshore mounds. Some of the country's most pristine mountains, beaches, and forestlands can be found in this remote region.

Sitting on the northwest tip of the peninsula, historic **Port Townsend** is known for its Victorian architecture and vibrant arts community. The 1982 movie, *An Officer and a Gentleman*, was filmed here. To its south, **Port Gamble**, a former logging town on the Kitsap Peninsula, has retained its original New England Victorian-style homes, country store, and church.

The centerpiece of the peninsula is the sprawling **Olympic National Park** *(p34)*, a UNESCO biosphere reserve and World Heritage Site. Encompassing 923,000 acres (373,540 ha), this biologically diverse park is a treasure-trove of snowcapped mountain peaks, lakes, waterfalls, rivers, and rainforests. Running through the center of the park are the jagged, glacier-covered Olympic Mountains. With its West Peak rising to a height of 7,965 ft (2,428 m), the three-peaked Mount Olympus is the highest mountain in the range.

The peninsula's Lake Crescent Lodge

The park headquarters are located in **Port Angeles**, a working port town. Sitting in the rain shadow of the Olympic Mountains, Sequim (pronounced "Squim") features an elk viewing site and the Olympic Game Farm, home to endangered animals. Southwest of Sequim, **Hurricane Ridge** offers panoramic views of the Olympic Mountains, the Strait of Juan de Fuca, and Vancouver Island from its 5,230-ft (1,594-m) high summit. In spring, the ridge is covered with wildflowers.

To the west, is the picturesque Lake Crescent area. Trout fishing is the main draw in this 625-ft (190-m) deep freshwater lake whose crystal clear waters also make it a favorite with divers. The historic resort, **Lake Crescent Lodge** *(see p644)*, located on the lake's southern shore, is a lovely place to stay. Farther west, the 4-mile (6.5-km) long **Rialto Beach** offers superb views of the Pacific Coast, with its tide pools, sea stacks, rocky islands, and the Hole in the Wall, a tunnel carved by waves into a cliff. The coastline receives the highest rainfall in the state. As a result, rainforests carpet much of the region. The **Hoh Rainforest**, with its annual rainfall of 14 ft (4 m), is a magical place, lush with Sitka spruce, Douglas fir, yew, and red cedar, draped with moss. Ancient trees here tower to nearly 300 ft (91 m) in height, and even the ferns grow taller than the hikers. Rainforests also surround the shores of Lake Quinalt. Snowcapped mountains encircle this glacial lake, which attracts fishermen and swimmers alike.

Wildlife is plentiful in the Olympic Peninsula – deer and bear abound, and the Olympic National Park has the country's largest herd of Roosevelt elk. The peninsula offers a wide range of outdoor recreation activities; among the most popular pursuits are fly- and deep-sea fishing, kayaking, whitewater rafting, mountain biking, hiking, and bird-watching. Skiing and snowshoeing are popular winter activities.

The majestic Olympic Mountains in Olympic National Park

Point Wilson Lighthouse, in Port Townsend's Fort Worden State Park

Port Townsend ❸

8,800. from Keystone on Whidbey Island & from Edmonds. 2437 E Sims Way, (888) 365-6978. www.ptchamber.org

This seaport, a National Historic Landmark, is one of only three seaports on the National Registry. A building boom in the late 1800s left the town with several grand Victorian mansions, which now form the cornerstone of its thriving tourism industry.

Downtown's Romanesque **Jefferson County Courthouse** with its 124-ft (38-m) tall clock tower, is claimed to be the jewel of Port Townsend's Victorian architecture. Farther away, the old City Hall is now the **Jefferson County Historical Society**, home to the city council, as well as an excellent museum. Other famous buildings include the Ann Starrett Mansion and the Rothschild House.

The **Fire Bell Tower**, on the bluff overlooking downtown, was built to summon the town's voluntary fire fighters. **Point Wilson Lighthouse**, in Fort Worden State Park, first lit in 1879, is still in operation. The fort is dotted with dozens of historic buildings and the grounds make a delightful stroll.

Port Townsend is also an excellent base from which to make whale-watching, kayaking, and cycling day-trips.

Bellingham ❹

75,000. 904 Potter St, (800) 487-2032. www.bellingham.org

Overlooking Bellingham Bay and many of the San Juan Islands *(see pp622–3)*, this town consists of four original towns – Whatcom, Sehome, Bellingham, and Fairhaven – consolidated into a single entity in 1904. The town's historic architecture includes Old Whatcom County Courthouse on East Street, the first brick building north of San Francisco, built in 1858, and the majestic City Hall. Built in 1892 in the Victorian Second Empire style, the City Hall is now the heart of the **Whatcom Museum of History and Art**. Highlights at this four-building campus include exhibits on children's toys from 1890–1930, an interactive art space for children, the Northwest Coast Native Americans, and the birds of the Pacific Northwest. The downtown area has several restaurants, art galleries, and specialty shops. South of downtown, the historic Fairhaven district is an artsy enclave of Victorian buildings housing galleries, restaurants, and bookstores.

Tower of Bellingham's former City Hall

Just up the hill from downtown sits the campus of **Western Washington University**, with its famous collection of outdoor sculptures, including artworks by noted American artists Richard Serra, Mark di Suvero, and Richard Beyer.

From Bellingham's ports, passenger ferries leave for whale-watch cruises and tours to Vancouver Island and the San Juan Islands. Near the city are several waterfront parks, hiking and biking trails, and recreational areas. South of the city, Chuckanut Drive (Hwy 11) is a scenic 21-mile (34-km) loop. Some 55 miles (88.5 km) east of Bellingham is the 10,778-ft (3,285-m) high Mount Baker, which is a popular location for skiing and snowboarding.

Whatcom Museum of History & Art
121 Prospect St.
Tel *(360) 778-8930.* *noon–5pm Tue–Sun.*
www.whatcommuseum.org

Western Washington University
S College Dr & College Way.
Tel *(360) 650-3424.*
Campus Information *mid-Sep–mid-Jun: 7:15am–8pm Mon–Fri; mid-Jun–mid-Sep: 7:15am–5pm Mon–Fri.* *public hols.*
www.wwu.edu

Crab traps on a boat ready to set out from Bellingham Harbor

San Juan Islands ❺

A Washington State ferry sailing from the mainland to the islands

Scattered between the Washington mainland and Vancouver Island, the San Juan archipelago consists of over 700 islands, 172 of them named. Ferries sail from Anacortes to the four largest islands – Lopez, Shaw, Orcas, and San Juan. Affectionately called "Slopez" because of its laidback nature, Lopez's gently rolling roads, numerous stopping points, and friendly drivers make it a popular destination for cycling. Horseshoe-shaped Orcas, the hilliest island in the chain, offers breathtaking views from atop 2,409-ft (734-m) Mount Constitution. The best destination for walk-on passengers, San Juan Island is home to Friday Harbor, the largest town in the archipelago. The nationally renowned Whale Museum is located here. Primarily residential, Shaw Island has very limited visitor facilities.

Sailboats in the Channel
Sailors love the many harbors and good winds in the San Juan Channel.

★ Roche Harbor
A charming seaside village, Roche Harbor features a marina, Victorian gardens, a chapel, and the historic Hotel de Haro, built in 1886.

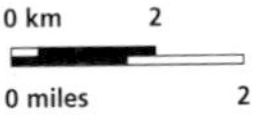

Lime Kiln Point State Park
This state park, with its picturesque lighthouse, is the only park in the country dedicated to whale-watching.

STAR SIGHTS

- ★ Deer Harbor
- ★ Friday Harbor
- ★ Lopez
- ★ Roche Harbor

For hotels and restaurants in this region see pp644–5 and pp646–7

★ **Deer Harbor**
Sea kayakers flock to Deer Harbor and the other waters surrounding the islands of Orcas, Lopez, and San Juan.

VISITORS' CHECKLIST

Washington State Ferries from Anacortes to Lopez, Shaw, Orcas, & San Juan Islands. **Tel** (206) 464-6400. **www.**wsdot.wa.gov/ferries Visitor Information, (888) 468-3701. **www**.visitsanjuans.com

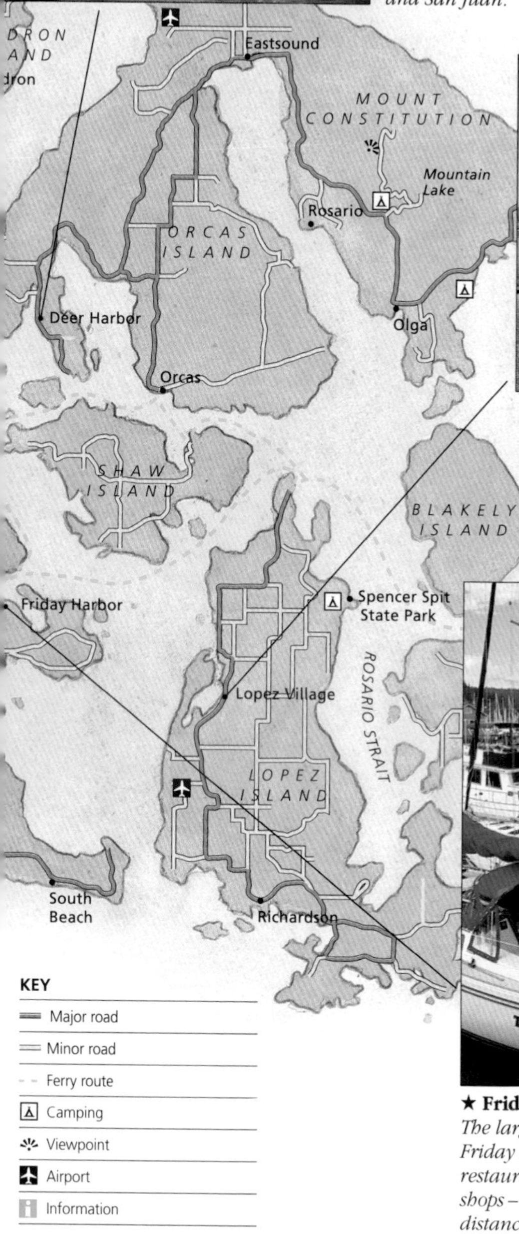

★ **Lopez**
Lopez, with its gentle slopes, is the flattest of the San Juan Islands, making it a popular destination for recreational cyclists.

★ **Friday Harbor**
The largest town in the San Juans, Friday Harbor offers a number of restaurants, inns, galleries, and shops – all within easy walking distance of the ferry dock.

Turquoise-colored Diablo Lake in North Cascades National Park

North Cascades Highway 6

State Rte 20.

The scenic North Cascades Highway is the northernmost mountain pass route in Washington. It is the 132-mile (213-km) section of Highway 20 between Winthrop in the east and I-5 to the west. Bisecting the **North Cascades National Park**, it offers access to the many wonders of this breathtakingly beautiful eco-system of jagged snowcapped peaks, forested valleys, and cascading waterfalls. The entire route is open from mid-April to mid-October.

The road follows the Skagit River, passing Gorge Creek Falls, Lake Diablo, and Ruby Creek. Along the way, the Ross Lake Overview is an ideal spot to view the scenic lake. At 5,477 ft (1,669 m), **Washington Pass Overlook** provides heart-pounding vistas of the steep pass up Liberty Bell Mountain. A dominant feature of the park, **Mount Shuksan** at the height of 9,131 ft (2,783 m), is one of the state's highest mountains.

The heavily glaciated park is home to a variety of animals – bald eagles, gray wolves, and bears. Many hiking trails link the highway to the quiet town of Stehekin at the northern-most tip of Lake Chelan.

North Cascades National Park
SR 20, near milepost 120 & Newhalem, (360) 854-7200. **www**.nps.gov/noca

Lake Chelan 7

102 E Johnson Ave, (800) 424-3526. **www**.lakechelan.com

Magnificent Lake Chelan, in the remote northwest end of the Cascades, Claims the distinction of being the country's third-deepest lake, reaching 1,500 ft (457 m) at its deepest point. Fed by 27 glaciers and 59 streams, the lake, which is less than 2 miles (3 km) wide, stretches for 55 miles (89 km). In summer, it buzzes with activity – boating, fishing, snorkeling, water-skiing, and wind surfing. The resort town of **Chelan** at the southeastern end of the lake has been a popular summer vacation destination for generations of Western Washingtonians seeking the sunny, dry weather on the eastern side of the state. Basking in the rain shadow of the Cascade Mountains, the town enjoys 300 days of sunshine each year. The town's vintage **Ruby Theatre** on East Woodin Avenue is one of the oldest continuously running movie theaters in the Northwest. Chelan's other highlights are the murals on buildings, which depict the history of the Lake Chelan Valley.

About 9 miles (14 km) from downtown Chelan is the town of **Manson**, whose main attraction is the Scenic Loop Trail. It offers easy exploration of the nearby orchards and hilly countryside. Farther north, the lakeside town of **Stehekin** can be reached by ferry.

Sign welcoming visitors to Lake Chelan

Leavenworth 8

2,000. 220 9th St, (509) 548-5807. **www**.leavenworth.org

Once a logging town, Leavenworth, at the foot of the Cascade Mountains in central Washington, is now a quaint little Bavarian-style town seemingly straight out of a fairy tale. This theme was consciously developed in the 1960s to help revitalize the town and, today, every commercial building in town, Starbucks and McDonald's included, looks as though it belongs in the Alps.

The town now bustles with festivals, art shows, and summer theater productions, attracting more than a million visitors each year. Among its popular festivals are Fasching, a classic Bavarian carnival held in February; Maifest, with its 16th-century costumes, maypole dances, and jousting; and Oktoberfest *(see p30)*, the traditional celebration of German food, beer, and music. Teeming with Bavarian specialty shops and restaurants, the town also has the fascinating **Leavenworth Nutcracker Museum**, which showcases 5,000 nutcrackers from 38 countries, some dating back 500 years.

Leavenworth Nutcracker Museum
735 Front St. ***Tel*** *(509) 548-4573.*
May–Oct: 2–5pm daily; Nov–Apr: 2–5pm Sat–Sun. for groups by appt.

A traditional horse-drawn 13-barrel beer wagon in Leavenworth

Spokane 9

202,000. 201 W Main St, (888) 776-5263.
www.visitspokane.com

Washington's largest inland city, this is the Inland Northwest's commercial and cultural center. The city was rebuilt in brick and terra-cotta after a disastrous fire in 1889 – its many handsome buildings are reminders of that building boom.

Spokane is the smallest city to host a world's fair (Expo '74). The fair site is now the sprawling **Riverfront Park**, a 100-acre (40-ha) expanse in the heart of the city. Of the town's two museum's, the **Northwest Museum of Arts & Culture** showcases regional history, while **Campbell House** (1898) nearby is an interactive museum. Other attractions are an IMAX® Theater and a 1909 carousel. A 37-mile (60-km) trail connects the city with Riverside State Park, located 6 miles (10 km) to the northwest.

Northwest Museum of Arts & Culture
2316 W 1st Ave. ***Tel*** *(509) 456-3931.* *11am–5pm Tue–Sun.* *public hols.*
www.northwestmuseum.org

Walla Walla 10

30,000. 29 E Sumac St, (509) 525-0850. **www**.wwvchamber.com

Located in the southeast corner of the state, Walla Walla is a green oasis in the midst of an arid landscape. The town features several National Register buildings, lovely parks, and a wealth of public art. The attractive campus of **Whitman College**, one of the nation's top-rated liberal arts colleges, is three blocks from downtown.

A popular destination for wine connoisseurs, the Walla Walla Valley has more than 35 wineries – several right in the heart of downtown. Among the town's other claims to fame are its delicious sweet Walla Walla onions and its annual Hot Air Balloon Stampede, a rally of some 45 pilots, held in May. The stampede also features live music, arts-and-crafts booths, and various events.

Grapes from Yakima Valley

Fort Walla Walla Museum, on Myra Road, consisting of original and replica pioneer buildings, gives a historical perspective of the area. The **Whitman Mission National Historic Site**, about 7 miles (11 km) west of town, is a memorial to pioneer missionaries Marcus and Narcissa Whitman who were massacred by Cayuse Indians. On weekends, the Living History Company honors the area's history through music and dance.

Fort Walla Walla Museum
755 Myra Rd. ***Tel*** *(509) 525-7703.* *Apr–Oct: 10am–5pm daily.* *(call ahead).* *by arrangement.*
www.fortwallawallamuseum.org

Whitman Mission National Historic Site
Hwy 12. ***Tel*** *(509) 522-6360.* *Jun–Sep: 8am–6pm daily; Oct–May: 8am–4:30pm daily.* *Jan 1, Thanksgiving, Dec 25.* *(except Monument Hill).*
www.nps.gov/whmi

Balloons over Walla Walla during the annual Hot Air Balloon Stampede

Yakima Valley 11

10 N 8th St, Yakima, (800) 221-0751. **www**.visityakima.com

With its rich volcanic soil, abundance of irrigation water, and 300 days of annual sunshine, the Yakima Valley is the fifth largest producer of fruits and vegetables in the US, and home to more than 40 regional wineries. Yakima, the valley's largest community and commercial hub, is a good base for visiting the valley's award-winning wineries.

A 40-minute drive away is White Pass and Chinook Pass, where you can hike, fish or go mountain bike riding and white water rafting. Otherwise, soak up some native culture at the Yakama Nation Cultural Center.

Maryhill 12

100. Klickitat County Visitor Information Center, (509) 773-4395.

A remote sagebrush bluff overlooking the Columbia River is where entrepreneur Sam Hill chose to build his palatial residence. In 1907, he purchased 7,000 acres (2,833 ha) here, with the vision of creating a utopian colony for Quaker farmers. He called the community Maryhill, in honor of his daughter, Mary. The ideal community did not materialize, and Hill turned his unfinished mansion into a museum. The treasures of the **Maryhill Museum of Art** include the throne and gold coronation gown of his friend Queen Marie of Romania, 87 sculptures and drawings by Auguste Rodin, and an impressive collection of Native American art. The beautifully landscaped grounds include a picnic area.

Maryhill Museum of Art
35 Maryhill Museum Dr, Goldendale. ***Tel*** *(509) 773-3733.* *Mar 15–Nov 15: 9am–5pm daily.*
www.maryhillmuseum.org

Mount Rainier National Park ⓭

Jeep with outdoor equipment

Established in 1899, Mount Rainier National Park encompasses 337 sq miles (872 sq km), of which 97 percent is designated wilderness. Its centerpiece is Mount Rainier, an active volcano towering 14,410 ft (4,392 m) above sea level. Surrounded by old-growth forest and wildflower meadows, Mount Rainier was named in 1792 by Captain George Vancouver *(see p612)* for fellow British naval officer Peter Rainier. Designated a National Historic Landmark District in 1997, the park, which features 1920s and 30s National Park Service rustic architecture, attracts two million visitors a year. The summer draws hikers, mountain climbers, and campers; the winter lures snowshoers and cross-country skiers.

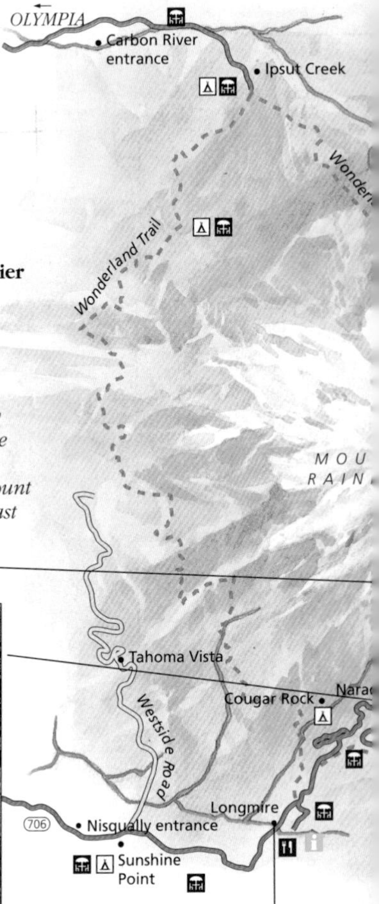

Mount Rainier Nisqually Glacier
Close to the Paradise entrance, the Nisqually Glacier is one of the most visible on Mount Rainier. Its last retreat was 1985–91.

Mount Rainier Narada Falls
One of the more spectacular and easily accessible cascades along the Paradise River, Narada Falls is just a short, steep hike from Route 706. The falls plummet 168 ft (51 m).

National Park Inn
This small, cozy inn, located in Longmire and open year round, is a perfect spot from which to enjoy stunning views of Mount Rainier.

STAR SIGHTS

★ Emmons Glacier

★ Paradise

★ Sunrise

VISITORS' CHECKLIST

Hwy 706 near Ashford. ***Tel*** *(360) 569-2211.* *Jackson Visitor Center, Paradise* *May–Oct: 10am–5pm daily; Nov–Apr: 10am–5pm Sat, Sun, hols.* **Nisqually Entrance** *year-round.* **White River Entrance** *summer only, hours vary.* **www**.nps.gov/mora

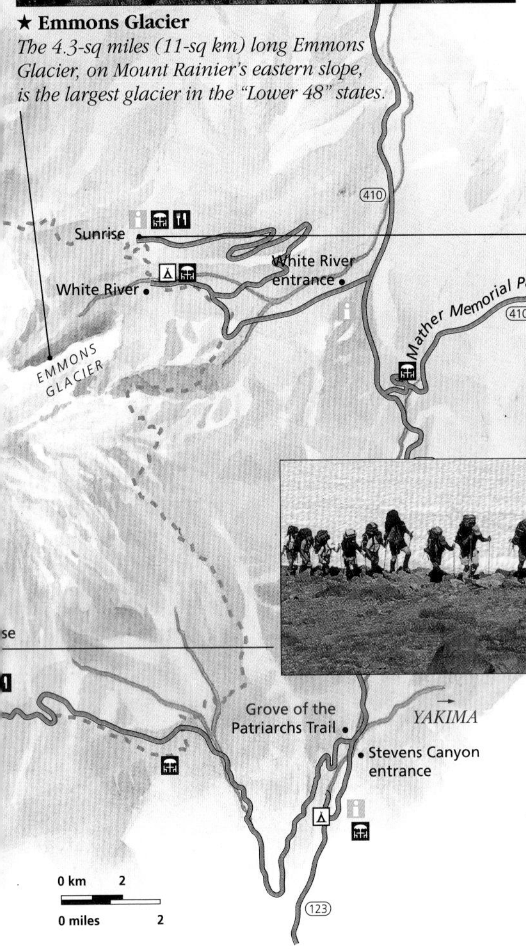

★ Emmons Glacier

The 4.3-sq miles (11-sq km) long Emmons Glacier, on Mount Rainier's eastern slope, is the largest glacier in the "Lower 48" states.

★ Sunrise

At 6,400 ft (1,950 m), Sunrise is the highest point to which visitors can drive in the park. It is open only during summer, when wildflowers can be admired.

★ Paradise

Paradise, the park's most popular destination, is open year-round and has an excellent visitor information center and well-marked trails.

GETTING AROUND

From the southwest (Hwy 706), enter the park via the Nisqually gate. Open year round, this is the primary entrance in winter. Drive 6 miles (10 km) to Longmire, where facilities include an inn and museum, and the Wilderness Information Center, open from late May to October. The 12-mile (19-km) road between Paradise and Longmire is steep; drive carefully. Carry chains when traveling by car during winter. Check the status of the roads before setting out as conditions can change quickly and closures may be made at short notice.

KEY

- Minor road
- Dirt or four-wheel-drive road
- Hiking trail
- Camping
- Picnic area
- Tourist information
- Restaurant

The modern stainless steel exterior of the Tacoma Museum of Glass

Tacoma ⑭

195,000. *1119 Pacific Ave, (253) 627-2836, (800) 272-2662.* **www**.traveltacoma.com

Washington's third-largest city, located south of Seattle, Tacoma was founded as a sawmill town in the 1860s. It prospered with the arrival of the railroad in the late 1880s, becoming a major shipping port for important commodities such as lumber, coal, and grain. Many of the Pacific Northwest's railroad, timber, and shipping barons settled in Tacoma's Stadium District. This historic area, with its stately turn-of-the-20th-century mansions, is named for the French château-style **Stadium High School**, also known as the "Castle."

The undisputed star of the city's revitalized waterfront is the striking **Museum of Glass**. The 75,000-sq-ft (6,968-sq-m) landmark building showcases contemporary art, with a focus on glass. A dramatic 90-ft (37-m) metal-encased cone houses a spacious glass-blowing studio.

The stunning Chihuly Bridge of Glass serves as a pedestrian walkway linking the museum to downtown Tacoma and the innovative **Washington State History Museum**. The museum features interactive exhibits, high-tech displays, and theatrical storytelling by actors in period costume, who relate stories of the state's past history.

The 50,000-sq-ft (4,645-sq-m), stainless-steel-wrapped **Tacoma Art Museum** was designed to be a dynamic cultural center and a showpiece for the city. Its growing collection of works, from the 18th century to the present day, include a large assembly of Pacific Northwest art, European Impressionist pieces, Japanese woodblock prints, and Tacoma artist Dale Chihuly'sd *(see p613)* glassworks. In keeping with its vision of creating a place that "builds community through art," the museum's facilities include the Bill and Melinda Gates Resource Center, providing visitors with access to a range of state-of-the-art research equipment. Children of all ages can also make use of the in-house, interactive art-making studio, ArtWORKS.

Sign denoting the old town of Tacoma

Tacoma's most popular attraction is **Point Defiance Park**, ranked among the 20 largest urban parks in the US. Encompassing 700 acres (285 ha), its grounds include Fort Nisqually, the first European settlement on Puget Sound and a major fur-trading establishment. Also in the park are seven specialty gardens, a scenic drive, hiking and biking trails, beaches, a boat marina, and a picnic area.

Highlighting a Pacific Rim theme, the **Point Defiance Zoo and Aquarium** on Pearl Street features more than 5,000 animals. A vantage point at the park's west end offers superb views of Mount Rainier *(see p626–7)*, Puget Sound, and the Tacoma Narrows Bridge, famous as one of the longest suspension bridges in the world.

The fishing village of **Gig Harbor**, 11 miles (17 km) south of Tacoma, has shops and restaurants that reflect the Scandinavian and Croatian heritage of its 6,500 inhabitants.

Museum of Glass
1801 E Dock St. ***Tel*** *(253) 284-4750, (866) 468-7386.* *10am–5pm Wed–Sat, noon–5pm Sun (Jun–Aug: Mon, Tue also).* *Jan 1, Thanksgiving, Dec 25.* **www**.museumofglass.org

Washington State History Museum
1911 Pacific Ave. ***Tel*** *(253) 272-9747.* *10am–5pm Tue–Sat, noon–5pm Sun.* *public hols.* *for groups.* **www**.wshs.org

Olympia ⑮

43,000. *809 Legion Way SE, (360) 704-7544.* **www**.visitolympia.com

Named for its magnificent view of the Olympic Mountains, Washington's state capital is located at the southern tip of Puget Sound. The city's **State Capitol Campus** is dominated by the 28-story Legislative Building (the Capitol), whose

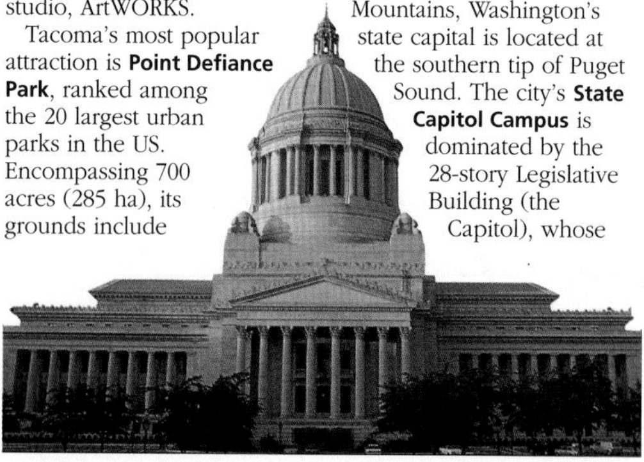
The Romanesque Legislative Building on the State Capitol Campus, Olympia

287-ft (87-m) brick-and-sandstone dome is one of the tallest masonry domes in the world. One of the most impressive in the nation, the campus encompasses superb buildings, several fountains, and monuments. Its landscaped grounds were designed in 1928 by the Olmsted Brothers, sons of Frederick Olmsted, one of the creators of New York City's Central Park *(see p78)*.

The **State Capital Museum** provides a historical perspective of Washington's early pioneer settlements, through its collections of early photographs and documents. The **State Archives**, with its historical records and artifacts, is another institution related to the state's past. Visitors can access such unique treasures as documents from the Canwell Committee, which blacklisted suspected Communists during the 1950s *(see p50)*.

Tree-lined streets, old homes, a picturesque waterfront, and a thriving cultural community all contribute to Olympia's charm. Tucked among downtown's historic buildings are several shops, restaurants, and galleries. Within walking distance are attractions such as the lively **Olympia Farmers Market,** offering local produce, seafood, and crafts, along with dining and entertainment.

Percival Landing, a 1.5-mile (2.5-km) boardwalk along Budd Inlet, offers views of the Olympic Mountains, the Capitol dome, Puget Sound, and ships in port.

State Capitol Campus
409 13th Ave SW, (360) 586-3460. Jan 1, Thanksgiving, Dec 25. **Legislative Building** *Memorial Day–Labor Day: 8am–5pm Mon–Fri, 9am–4pm Sat–Sun; Labor Day–Memorial Day: 8am–5pm Mon–Fri. Campus: hourly 10am–3pm daily; Temple of Justice: 8am–5pm Mon–Fri.*
www.ga.wa.gov/visitor

State Capital Museum
211 21st Ave SW. ***Tel*** *(360) 753-2580. 11am–3pm Wed–Sat. public hols.*
www.wshs.org

State Archives
1129 Washington St SE.
Tel *(360) 586-1492.*

Mount St. Helens and the surrounding area after the 1980 explosion

Mount St. Helens National Volcanic Monument 16

Tel *(360) 449-7800.*
www.fs.fed.us/gpnf/mshnvm

On the morning of May 18, 1980, Mount St. Helens literally exploded. Triggered by a powerful earthquake, the peak erupted, spewing one cubic mile (4.17 cubic km) of rock into the air and causing the largest recorded avalanche in history. In the blink of an eye, the mountain lost 1,314 ft (400 m), and 234 sq miles (606 sq km) of forestlands were destroyed. The eruption also claimed 57 human lives and those of millions of animals and fish.

The 110,000-acre (44,000-ha) monument was created in 1982 to allow the environment to recover naturally while encouraging research, recreation, and education. Roads and trails allow visitors to explore this fascinating region by car and foot. On the mountain's west side, Hwy 504 leads to five visitor centers, which document the disaster and recovery efforts. Mount St. Helens National Volcanic Monument Visitor Center, at milepost 5, features interpretative exhibits of the mountain's history. The visitor center at Hoffstadt Bluffs, at milepost 27, gives visitors their first full view of Mount St. Helens and offers helicopter tours into the blast zone from May to September. **Johnson Ridge Observatory**, at the end of the road, offers panoramic views.

Fort Vancouver 17

Tel *(360) 816-6230. Apr–Oct: 9am–5pm daily; Nov–Mar: 9am–4pm daily. Jan 1, Thanksgiving, Dec 24, 25, & 31. partial.*
www.nps.gov/fova

Between 1825 and 1849, Fort Vancouver was an important trading outpost for the British-based Hudson's Bay Company, the giant fur-trading organization. Located close to major tributaries and natural resources, it was the center of political and commercial activities in the Pacific Northwest during these years. During the 1830s and 1840s, the fort also provided essential supplies to settlers.

A National Historic Site, Fort Vancouver features accurate reconstructions of nine of the original buildings, including the jail, fur store, and wash house, all on their original sites. Guided tours and re-enactments offer a window into the fort's past. Over a million artifacts have been excavated from this site.

The three-story bastion, dating from 1845, at Fort Vancouver

Oregon

Oregon is best known for its many scenic wonders – snowcapped mountains, flowing rivers, verdant forests, and desert vistas are just some of the attractions in this incredibly diverse state. This rugged landscape was first settled by pioneers who migrated along the Oregon Trail *(see p450)*. Today, the state is known not only for its scenic beauty but also for its cosmopolitan pleasures. Portlanders are eager to claim their city as one of the most sophisticated and cultured anywhere.

Evening view of the Portland skyline and the Willamette River

Portland ⑱

575,000. *701 SW 6th Ave, (503) 275-8355, (877) 678-5263.* **www**.travelportland.com

Known as the City of Roses, Portland was founded in 1843, on the west bank of the Willamette River. It grew into a major port, but later, with the arrival of the railroad and decline in river trade, the city center moved inland. This area, with its steel-framed buildings, is now the city's downtown, while Old Town encompasses the former port and riverfront quarter. Portland's beautiful parks and gardens and well-preserved historic landmarks are a tribute to foresight and successful urban planning.

Pioneer Courthouse Square

SW Broadway & Yamhill St. ***Tel*** *(503) 223-1613.* **Pioneer Courthouse** 701 SW 6th Ave. ***Tel*** *(503) 326-2115.* *9am–5pm Mon–Fri.* *public hols.* **www**.pioneercourthousesquare.org

This one-block, brick-paved pedestrian square, in eastern downtown, is the heart of Portland, where Portlanders gather for free lunchtime concerts, flower shows, and other events, or simply for a chance to sit and enjoy their beautiful city. Underground spaces next to the square accommodate offices and businesses, which include the Portland Visitors Association Information Center, a coffee shop, and a branch of Powell's City of Books, a well-known store specializing in travel books.

Opposite is the **Pioneer Courthouse**, the first federal building to be built in the Pacific Northwest region. The US Court of Appeals and a US post office branch are housed here. Its octagonal tower has been a fixture of the Portland skyline from 1873.

South Park Blocks

Bounded by SW Salmon St & I-405, SW Park & SW 9th Aves. **Oregon Historical Society** 1200 SW Park Ave. ***Tel*** *(503) 222-1741.* *10am–5pm Tue–Sat.* *public hols.* **www**.ohs.org **Portland Art Museum** 1219 SW Park Ave. ***Tel*** *(503) 226-2811.* *10am–5pm Tue–Wed & Sat, 10am–8pm Thu–Fri, noon–5pm Sun.* *public hols.* **www**.portlandartmuseum.org

A green ribbon of elm-shaded lawns laid out by frontier businessman and legislator Daniel Lownsdale in 1852, the so-called South Park Blocks is a 12-block stretch running through the central city. Among its distinctive features are statuary and some 40 ornamental fountains. South Park Blocks is also the venue for a colorful local market, held every Saturday, where farmers sell their wares to locals and visitors alike.

The **Oregon Historical Society** to the south of the park has huge murals on its façades that depict scenes from the Lewis and Clarke expedition *(see p570)* and other significant moments in the state's history. On display in the galleries, which extend through three buildings, are paintings, photographs, maps, and historical documents that make this museum the largest repository of Oregon's historical artifacts.

The **Portland Art Museum**, opposite South Park Blocks in Southwest Park Avenue, is the oldest museum in the Pacific Northwest. Its sizable collection of European works, includes paintings by Picasso, Van Gogh, and Monet, and sculpture by Rodin and Brancusi. Its Grand Ronde Center for Native American Art displays masks, jewelry, and totem poles created by the indigenous peoples of North America. It has undergone a program of expansion, including the renovation and restoration of the North Building, and the creation of an underground gallery linking the two main buildings.

Governor Tom McCall Waterfront Park

Bounded by SW Harrison & NW Glisan Sts, SW Naito Pkwy & Willamette River.

Buried beneath an expressway from the 1940s to the 1970s, this 1.5-mile- (2.5-km-) long

The Saturday Farmers Market in South Park Blocks

Main gateway to Portland's Saturday Market

stretch of Willamette River waterfront was reclaimed and transformed into a park. Named after Tom McCall, Oregon's environmentally minded governor from 1967 to 1975, the park is now a frequently used riverside promenade and the venue for many local festivals, including the annual Rose Festival, held between May and June.

One of its most popular attractions is **Salmon Street Springs**, a fountain whose 100 jets splash water directly onto the pavement, providing relief on a hot day. Another highlight is the **Battleship Oregon Memorial**, at its southern end. Built in 1956, the memorial honors an 1893 US Navy ship. A time capsule sealed in its base in 1976 is to be opened in 2076.

RiverPlace Marina at the southwest end of Tom McCall Park offers many amenities including restaurants, one of the city's higher-end hotels – the RiverPlace Hotel *(see p645)*, upscale shops, sloping lawns, riverside walks, and a large marina.

Old Town & Chinatown

Bounded by SW Naito Pkwy & NW Glisan St, NW 3rd Ave & SW Pine St.

Elegant brick façades and quiet streets belie Old Town's raucous, 19th-century frontier-town past. A National Historic Landmark today, this river-front district once drew dockworkers, shipbuilders, and traders from all over the world during its heyday as a major port and the city's commercial center. Old Town is now a trendy, colorful neighborhood, especially during weekends, when vendors gather for the **Portland Saturday Market**, America's largest handicrafts bazaar. Chinatown Gate, a five-tiered, dragon-festooned gateway leads to Chinatown, home to the city's many Asian immigrants, who first arrived in Portland more than 135 years ago. The neighborhood's tranquil **Classical Chinese Garden** is a 15th century Ming-style walled enclave, with waterways and pavilions.

Pearl District

W Burnside to NW Lovejoy Sts, from NW 8th to NW 15th Aves.

Portland Streetcar

East- & southbound on NW Lovejoy St & 11th Ave, north- & westbound on 10th Ave & NW Northrup St. *every 15 mins, 5:30am–11pm Mon–Thu, 5:30am–1am Fri, 7:30am–1am Sat, 7:30am–11pm Sun.*

www.shopthepearl.com

Often called Portland's "newest" neighborhood, Pearl District actually occupies an old industrial area on the north side of Burnside Street. Many former warehouses and factories have been refurbished to house chic galleries, designer shops, design studios, clubs, cafés, restaurants, and breweries. A good time to visit Pearl District is during a First Thursday event, which takes place the first Thursday of every month. At this time, the many art galleries in the area remain open until late, usually 9pm. The district has a calendar of events, from small-dog playgroups, to a regular Farmers' Market held every Thursday in summer. The website has details.

A quaint way to travel between Pearl District and Nob Hill, a gracious, late-19th-century neighborhood, is to take the **Portland Streetcar**. These low-slung Czech-built trams are not only a convenient way to get around but are also free within the city center.

Washington Park

SW Park Pl. ***Tel*** *(503) 823-2223.* *24 hrs daily (not all sights).* *to some exhibits.*

www.portlandonline.com/parks

Washington Park, a popular outdoor playground, is surrounded by the city on all its sides. Its attractions include the Hoyt Arboretum, which has more than 8,000 trees and shrubs, the Japanese Garden, the International Rose Test Garden, and the popular **Oregon Zoo**, which has the largest number of elephants bred in captivity.

Oregon Museum of Science and Industry

1945 SE Water Ave. ***Tel*** *(503) 797-4000.* *Labor Day–mid-Jun: 9:30am–5:30pm Tue–Sun; mid-Jun–Labor Day: 9:30am–7pm daily.* *public hols.* *of submarine.*

www.omsi.edu

Sign at Oregon Zoo

Eastbank Esplanade

Bounded by Willamette River & I-5, Steel & Hawthorne Bridges.

East of the river, the Oregon Museum of Science and Industry (OMSI) is a top US science museum. A favorite among the hundreds of interactive exhibits is the earthquake simulator, in which visitors are shaken and rattled while learning about the tectonic plates that still shift beneath Portland.

Nearby, the **Eastbank Esplanade** is a pedestrian and bicycle path following the east bank of the Willamette River. A 1,200-ft (365-m) section floats on water, while a cantilevered portion is suspended above one of the city's original commercial piers, providing unobstructed river views.

Columbia River Gorge and the Cascade Mountains

Columbia River Gorge 19

775 Summer St NE, Salem, (800) 984-6743. **www**.crgva.org

This magnificent fir- and maple-covered river canyon cuts through the Cascade Mountains, forming a boundary between the states of Washington and Oregon. The best way to explore the area is to take the **Historic Columbia River Highway**. Blasted out of narrow cliffs, this road was designed to maximize viewing pleasure while minimizing environmental damage as much as possible. Along the route are the spectacular **Multnomah Falls**, tumbling 620 ft (186 m) in two picturesque cascades, and the cosy, rustic Timberline Lodge dating from the 1930s *(see p645)*.

Mount Hood 20

24403 E Welches Rd, Welches, (503) 622-3017. **www**.mthood.org

The spectacular snow-covered peak of Mount Hood, the tallest of Oregon's Cascade peaks, rises south of the Columbia River Gorge. Home to year-round skiing and snowboarding, the valleys below are famous for their produce of apples, apricots, pears, and peaches.

The **Mount Hood Loop** is a good way to explore the area; the highest point on the loop, known as **Barlow Pass**, is so steep that at one time, wagons had to be lowered down the hillsides with ropes. The Hood River Valley offers blossoming fruit trees in season and lovely views of the majestic Mount Hood throughout the year. **Hood River**, a riverside town called the "Windsurfing Capital of the World," also offers great opportunities for sports such as mountain biking.

Astoria 21

10,000. 111 W Marine Dr. ***Tel*** *(800) 875-6807.*
www.oldoregon.com

The oldest American settlement west of the Rocky Mountains, Astoria was established when John Jacob Astor sent fur traders around Cape Horn to establish a trading post at the mouth of the Columbia River in 1811. Earlier, explorers Lewis and Clark *(see p570)* spent the winter of 1805–1806 at a crude stockade near Astoria, making moccasins, preserving fish, and recording in their journals accounts of bear attacks and the almost continual rain. The stockade has since been rebuilt at Fort Clatsop National Memorial.

These days, the town is a bustling port; its old Victorian homes climb a hillside above the river. One such home, the stately **Captain George Flavel House Museum**, retains the cupola from which the captain and his wife once watched river traffic. An even better view can be enjoyed from atop the 164-step spiral staircase of the **Astoria Column**, encircled with friezes paying homage to the history of the Pacific Northwest.

Astoria Column

The town honors its seafaring past at the **Columbia River Maritime Museum**, where riverside galleries house fishing dories as well as Native American dugout canoes and other river-oriented artifacts. The lightship *Columbia*, berthed in front, once guided ships across the treacherous area at the mouth of the river.

Captain George Flavel House Museum
441 8th St. ***Tel*** *(503) 325-2203.*
May–Sep: 10am–5pm daily; Oct–Apr: 11am–4pm daily. *Jan 1, Thanksg., Dec 24–25.*

Columbia River Maritime Museum
1792 Marine Dr. ***Tel*** *(503) 325-2323.* *9:30am–5pm daily.*
Thanksgiving, Dec 25.
www.crmm.org

The majestic peak of Mount Hood as seen from Hood River Valley

Sea stacks rise off Bandon coast, with houses in the background

Oregon Coast ㉒

137 NE 1st St, Newport, Oregon, (541) 574-2679, (888) 628-2101. **www**.visittheoregoncoast.com

Hundreds of miles of pristine beaches make the Oregon Coast one of the the state's best-loved tourist destinations. The developed northern part has some of Oregon's most popular resorts, while the southern part is more wild and rugged. The coast is ideal for a range of recreational activities such as driving, cycling, hiking, camping, shell-fishing, and whale- or bird-watching.

Oregon's favorite beach town, **Cannon Beach**, south of Astoria, retains a quiet charm. Haystack Rock, one of the tallest coastal monoliths in the world, towers 235 ft (72 m) above a long beach and tidal pools. Ecola State Park, at the beach's north end, carpets Tillamook Head, a basalt headland, with verdant forests. Viewpoints look across raging surf to Tillamook Rock Lighthouse, which was built in 1880.

Picturesque house on Hemlock Street, Cannon Beach

Nature is the main attraction along the 35-mile (56-km) **Three Capes Scenic Route**, farther south. The rocks below Cape Meares State Scenic Viewpoint and Cape Meares Lighthouse are home to one of the largest colonies of nesting seabirds in North America. The Cape Lookout State Park is a good place to spot migrating gray whales. The Oregon State Parks Association provides detailed information about the sights along this stunning route.

The **Cape Perpetua Scenic Area** has the highest viewpoint on the coast. A road ascends to the top at 800 ft (240 m), and an easy hike along the Giant Spruce Trail leads to a majestic, 500-year-old Sitka spruce. From Cape Perpetua, Hwy 101 leads to Heceta Head State Park, with its ocean views – birds nest on rocks and sea lions and gray whales swim offshore. Rising high above the surf, the Heceta Head Lighthouse was first lit in 1894. Steller's sea lions inhabit the Sea Lion Caves, the only wild sea lion rookery on the North American mainland.

The massive sand dunes of the **Oregon Dunes National Recreation Area** stretch south from Florence for 40 miles (64 km). Towering sand formations, lakes, pine forests, grasslands, and open beaches attract a variety of recreation enthusiasts. Boardwalks make it easy to enjoy stunning vistas from Oregon Dunes Overlook, about 20 miles (32 km) south of Florence, while the mile-long Umpqua Scenic Dunes Trail, 30 miles (48 km) south of Florence, skirts the tallest dunes.

Bandon, near the mouth of the Coquille River, is so small and weathered that it is difficult to imagine that it was once a major port. Craggy rock formations rise from the ocean just off the beach. These wind-sculpted shapes include Face Rock, allegedly an Indian maiden who was frozen into stone by an evil spirit.

Dune buggy, Oregon Dunes National Recreation Area

A wild landscape of dunes and sea grass can be seen at the Bullards Beach State Park, which lies across the marshy, bird-filled Coquille Estuary.

Three Capes Scenic Route
Oregon State Parks. ***Tel*** *(800) 551-6949.* **www**.oregon.gov/oprd

Cape Perpetua Scenic Area
Interpretive Center. ***Tel*** *(541) 547-3289. Jun–Aug: 10am–5:30pm daily; Sep–May: 10am–4pm daily. public hols.*

Oregon Dunes National Recreation Area
855 Highway Ave, Reedsport. ***Tel*** *(541) 271-6000. dawn–dusk daily.* **www**.fs.fed.us/r6/siuslaw/recreation

Local arts and crafts on display at the Saturday Market in Eugene

Salem 23

143,000. 1313 Mill St SE, (800) 874-7012. www.travelsalem.com

Once a thriving trading and lumber port on the Willamette River, Salem became the capital of the Oregon Territory in 1851.

At the edge of Bush's Pasture Park stand **Asahel Bush House**, an 1878 home with a conservatory said to be the first greenhouse west of the Mississippi River, and the historic **Deepwood Estate**. The **Mission Mill Museum** preserves some of the state's earliest structures. These include the 1841 home of Jason Lee, who helped found Salem, and the Kay Woolen Mill, where waterwheels from the 1890s are still intact.

Asahel Bush House, Salem

The state's history is also in evidence around the **Oregon State Capitol**. A gilded pioneer stands atop the rotunda, marble sculptures of Lewis and Clark *(see 570)* flank the entrance, and the murals inside depict Captain Robert Gray's discovery of the Columbia River *(see p612)*.

Waller Hall, built in 1867, houses the **Hallie Ford Museum of Art** with its outstanding collection of 20th-century Native American basketry and paintings.

Mission Mill Museum
1313 Mill St SE. ***Tel*** *(503) 585-7012.* *10am–5pm Mon–Sat.* *major hols.* www.missionmill.org

Eugene 24

149,000. 754 Olive St, (541) 484-5307, (800) 547-5445. www.visitlanecounty.org

The University of Oregon brings culture and distinction to Eugene, which straddles the banks of the Willamette River at the south end of the river valley. The glass-and-timber **Hult Center for the Performing Arts**, is regarded as one of the best-designed performing arts complexes in the world. The **University of Oregon Museum of Natural History** counts among its holdings some ancient shoes – a pair of sagebrush sandals dating from as early as 9500 BC.

Local artisans sell their wares at the **Saturday Market**, in downtown Park Blocks. The **Fifth Street Public Market**, an assemblage of shops and restaurants in a converted feed mill, bustles with locals and university students.

Madras & Warm Springs 25

Madras *274 SW 4th St, (541) 475-2350.* www.madraschamber.com **Warm Springs** *1233 Veterans St, (541) 553-1161.* www.warmsprings.com

Madras is a desert ranching town surrounded by rimrock and vast tracts of wilderness recreation lands. **Crooked River National Grassland** provides endless vistas as well as fishing and rafting opportunities on two US National Wild and Scenic Rivers – the Deschutes and the Crooked – that weave through thousands of acres of juniper and sage brush. **Cove Palisades State Park** surrounds the deep waters of Lake Billy Chinook, a popular destination for boaters.

The Treaty of 1855 between the US government and the Wasco, Walla Walla, and Paiute tribes established lands for the tribes located on the 640,000-acre (256,000-ha) Warm Springs Reservation in central Oregon. Today, these Confederated Tribes preserve their cultural heritage at the **Museum at Warm Springs** with a stunningly beautiful collection of basketry and beadwork, haunting historic photographs, and videotapes of tribal ceremonies. The tribes also manage a casino and a resort, where a large pool is heated by hot springs.

Museum at Warm Springs
Hwy 26, Warm Springs. ***Tel*** *(503) 553-3331.* *9am–5pm daily.* *Mon & Tue (Dec–Feb), Jan 1, Thanksgiving, Dec 25.* www.museumatwarmsprings.org

Swimming pool fed by hot springs at the Warm Springs Reservation resort

Galloping horses near Sisters, the peaks of the Three Sisters Mountains visible in the distance

Sisters 26

9000. 164 N Elm St, (541) 549-0251.
www.sisterschamber.com

This Wild-West style ranching town is surrounded by lush pine forests, alpine meadows, and rushing streams. The peaks of the Three Sisters, each above 10,000 ft (3,000 m), rise majestically in the background.

Environs
The McKenzie Pass climbs from Sisters to a 1-mile (1.6-km) summit amid a massive lava flow. The **Dee Wright Observatory** provides panoramic views of more than a dozen Cascade Mountain peaks, buttes, and sweeping lava fields.

Dee Wright Observatory
Hwy 242, 15 miles (24 km) west of Sisters. *mid-Jun–Oct: dawn–dusk daily. Oct–mid-Jun.*

Bend's High Desert Museum, which showcases life in the region

Bend 27

75,000. 917 NW Harriman, (541) 382-8048, (877) 245-8484.
www.visitbend.com

Busy Bend, once a sleepy lumber town, is alluringly close to the ski slopes, lakes, streams, and many other natural attractions. While unsightly development is quickly replacing the juniper- and sage-covered grazing lands on the outskirts, the old brick business district retains its small-town charm. Drake Park is a grassy downtown retreat on both banks of the Deschutes River, and **Pilot Butte State Scenic Viewpoint**, atop a volcanic cinder cone that rises from the center of town, overlooks the High Desert and snow-capped Cascade peaks.

The **High Desert Museum** celebrates life in the rugged terrain that covers much of central and eastern Oregon. Walk-through dioramas use lighting and sound effects in authentic re-creations of Native American dwellings. A trail leads to replicas of a settler's cabin and a sawmill, and to natural habitats, including a trout stream and an aviary full of hawks and other raptors.

High Desert Museum
59800 S Hwy 97. ***Tel** (541) 382-4754. May–Oct: 8am–5pm daily; Nov–Apr: 10am–4pm daily. Jan 1, Thanksgiving, Dec 25.*
www.highdesertmuseum.org

Environs
The best way to explore the magnificent South Cascades Mountains is to take the **Cascade Lakes Highway**, a 95-mile (153-km) long loop, starting from Bend. Southward, the route passes Lava Butte, which offers fine mountain views. Also located along the highway is Elk Lake, popular for sailing, fishing, and windsurfing. Another interesting sight is Mount Bachelor, 12 miles (20 km) west of Bend. It offers some of the best skiing and snowboarding in the region. An enormous, 45-sq-mile (117-sq-km) lava flow (Devil's Garden) lies northwest of Mount Bachelor. Astronauts used it to train on foot and in moon buggies for their historic 1969 moonwalk.

Newberry National Volcanic Monument 28

Apr–Oct: dawn–dusk daily.
www.fs.fed.us/r6/centraloregon/newberrynvm *Lava Lands Visitor Center, 11 miles S of Bend on US 97, (541) 593-2421.*

Encompassing eerie and bleak landscapes of black lava, as well as sparkling mountain lakes, waterfalls, hemlock forests, and snow-capped peaks, the Newberry National Volcanic Monument occupies an area of 55,000 acres (22,000 ha). Exhibits at the **Lava Lands Visitor Center** explain how the volcano has been built by thousands of eruptions which, seismic activity suggests, may begin again. Other exhibits here highlight central Oregon's cultural history.

At Lava River Cave, a passage extends for almost one mile (0.8 km) into a lava tube, through which molten lava once flowed. The Lava Cast Forest has a trail through a forest of hollow molds, formed by molten lava that created casts around the tree trunks.

A jagged outcrop at the Newberry National Volcanic Monument

Crater Lake National Park ㉙

Oregon's only national park surrounds Crater Lake. At 1,943 ft (592 m), this lake is the deepest in the country and the seventh deepest in the world. Its creation began about 7,700 years ago when Mount Mazama erupted and then collapsed, forming the caldera in which the lake now sits. The rim of the crater rises to an average of 1,000 ft (300 m) above the lake. On the drive encircling the lake, 90 miles (144 km) of trails, various overlooks, and a beautiful lodge offer magnificent views.

KEY

- Tour route
- Other road
- Viewpoint
- Information

Merriam Point ④
This is an excellent spot from which to admire the west side of the lake, with the cone-shaped Wizard Island and the black volcanic blocks that surround it.

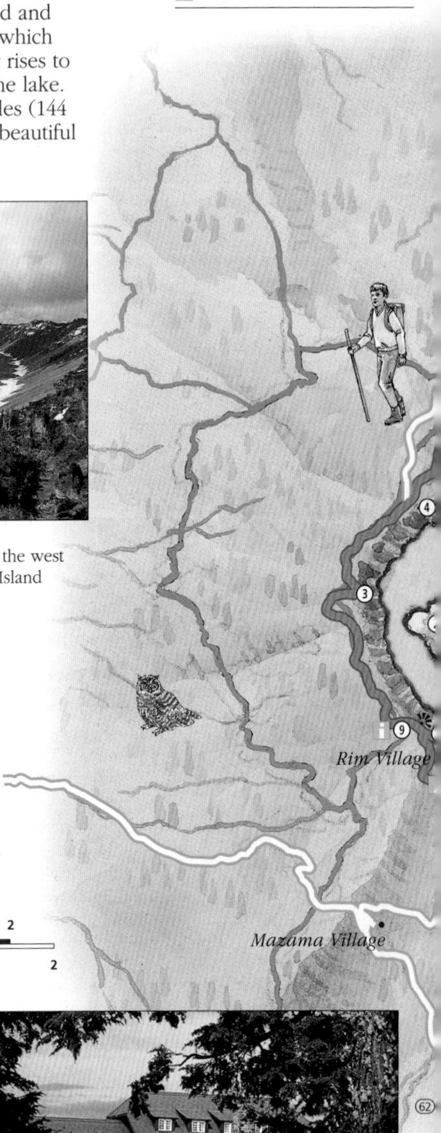

The Watchman ③
Named for its historic fire tower, the Watchman can be reached after a moderate climb. It is the nearest lookout to Wizard Island.

Wizard Island ②
A 300-ft (90-m) wide crater sits at the summit of this small cone-shaped volcanic island that juts 764 ft (233 m) above the surface of the lake.

Crater Lake Lodge ①
Perched on top of the caldera rim, this rustic hotel *(see p645)* has been welcoming guests since 1915. Extensive renovations have restored the structural integrity of the building, which was once at risk of collapsing under its own weight and of the snow that could accumulate in winter. Magnificent views can be enjoyed from this lodge.

Rim Drive ⑤
Spectacular views of the lake, the islands, and the surrounding mountains unfold at every turn of this 33-mile (53-km) circuit.

TIPS FOR DRIVERS

Tour length: *33 miles (53 km).*
Starting point: *Steel Information Center, on Rim Drive 4 miles (6.5 km) north of Rte 62.*
When to go: *Rim Drive is open from the end of June to mid-October, weather permitting.*
Stopping-off points: *Breakfast, lunch, and dinner are offered at Crater Lake Lodge; snacks are sold in Rim Village. Two-hour narrated boat trips (late Jun–mid-Sep: 10am–4pm daily) depart from Cleetwood Cove, at the bottom of a steep 1-mile (1.6-km) trail.*

Cleetwood Trail ⑥
This 1-mile (1.6-km) strenuous trail, which drops a steep 700 ft (210 m), is the only access to the lake. In summer, a boat tour departs from the dock at the base of the trail.

Mount Scott ⑦
When the weather allows, views from the peak extend as far as Mount Shasta in California.

The Pinnacles ⑧
Pumice spires, also known as fossil fumaroles, rise from the caldera's eastern base and form this eerie landscape. Many of the spires are hollow.

Sinnott Memorial Overlook ⑨
Beautiful views reward the intrepid traveler who attempts the short descent to Sinnott Memorial Overlook just below the caldera rim. Here, knowledgeable park rangers give geology talks.

A park ranger with tourists in the Oregon Caves National Monument

Oregon Caves National Monument ㉚

19000 Caves Hwy, Caves Junction, (541) 592-3400. Tours are organized daily from late Mar–late Nov. Hours vary. Dec–mid-Mar.
www.nps.gov/orca

Visitors on the 70-minute guided tours of these vast underground caverns follow lighted trails past strange formations, cross underground rivers, squeeze through giant ribs of marble, and clamber up and down staircases into huge chambers hung with stalactites. Discovered in 1874 by a hunter chasing his dog into a dark hole in the side of Elijah Mountain, the caves have been formed by the steady trickling of water over hundreds of thousands of years.

Ashland ㉛

20,000. 110 E Main St, (541) 482-3486.
www.ashlandchamber.com

Every year, some 350,000 theatergoers descend on this amiable town. The major draw is the **Oregon Shakespeare Festival**, which annually presents a schedule of 11 plays by Shakespeare as well as by classical and contemporary playwrights. Theater buffs can also see props and costumes from past performances and take detailed backstage tours of the festival's three venues – Elizabethan Theatre, Angus Bowmer Theatre, and the modern New Theatre.

Oregon Shakespeare Festival
15 S Pioneer St. ***Tel*** *(541) 482-2111.* **www**.orshakes.org

Steens Mountain ㉜

Steens Mountain Loop Rd (for 58 miles/93.5 km), starting North Loop Rd in Frenchglen. *484 N Broadway, Burns 97720, (541) 573-2636.* **www**.harneycounty.com/SteensMtn.htm

Scenery does not get much grander than it does here on this 9,700-ft (2,910-m) mountain in southeastern Oregon. The west slope rises gradually from sagebrush country, while the eastern slope drops more steeply. Antelope, bighorn sheep, and wild horses roam gorges and alpine tundra carpeted with wildflowers; eagles and falcons soar overhead.

The **Steens Mountain Loop Road** traverses this remarkable landscape. Lovely, marsh-fringed Lily Lake, on the west side of the Warner Mountains, is slowly silting up. However, it is popular with anglers because of its trout-fishing opportunities. The nearby Donner and Blitzen River was named "Thunder and Lightning" by an army officer attempting to cross it during a thunderstorm in 1864. Kiger Gorge to the east affords views of four immense gorges scooped out from the mountainside by massive glaciers. **East Rim Viewpoint** is a full mile (1.6 km) above the alkali flats of the Alvord Desert. Sitting in the mountain's rain shadow, this desert receives a mere 6 inches (15 cm) of rain a year.

Resting mule deer in the Malheur National Wildlife Refuge

Malheur National Wildlife Refuge ㉝

Tel (541) 493-2612. **Refuge & Museum** *dawn–dusk daily.* *public hols.* **Visitor Center** *8am–4pm daily (reduced winter hours).* *public hols.* **www**.fws.gov/malheur

One of the nation's largest wildlife refuges, Malheur spreads across 186,500 acres (74,600 ha) of the Blitzen Valley floor. More than 320 species of birds and 58 species of mammals are found here. Sandhill cranes, tundra swans, snowy white egrets, white-faced ibis, pronghorn antelope, mule deer, and redband trout are among the most numerous of the refuge's denizens.

Spring and fall are the best times to view birds, which alight in the refuge on their annual migrations up and down the Pacific Flyway, which is a major north–south route for migrating North American waterfowl. A small museum houses specimens of birds commonly seen in the refuge.

Environs

From the refuge, the 69-mile (110.5-km) **Diamond Loop National Back Country Byway** heads into sage-covered hills and red rimrock canyons. Along the route are Diamond Craters, a volcanic landscape; the Round Barn, a distinctive 19th-century structure; and Diamond, a small, poplar-shaded ranch town.

Diamond Loop National Back Country Byway
28910 Hwy 20 W, Hines, (541) 573-4400. **www**.blm.gov/or

John Day Fossil Beds National Monument ㉞

Hwy 19, 40 miles (64 km) W of John Day. ***Tel** (541) 987-2333.* *dawn–dusk daily.* **Visitor Center (Sheep Rock Unit)** *9am–4pm daily.* *public hols between Thanksgiving & Presidents Day.* **www**.nps.gov/joda

Prehistoric fossil beds litter the John Day Fossil Beds National Monument, where sedimentary rocks preserve the plants and animals that flourished in jungles and

View of the Steens Mountain from the East Rim Viewpoint, above the alkali flats of the desolate Alvord Desert

For hotels and restaurants in this region see p645 and p647

Formations at John Day Fossil Beds National Monument's Sheep Rock unit

savannas for 40 million years, between the extinction of the dinosaurs and the start of the most recent Ice Age. The monument's 14,000 acres (5,600 ha) comprise three units – Sheep Rock, Painted Hills, and Clarno. At all three, trails provide opportunities for the close-up observation of the fossil beds. Painted Hills presents the most dramatic landscapes – volcanic rock formations in vivid hues of red, pink, bronze, tan, and black. Clarno contains some of the oldest formations, dating back 54 million years and including some of the finest fossil plant remains on earth. At Sheep Rock, the visitor center displays many important finds from the beds.

Pendleton ㉟

16,000. 501 S Main St, (541) 276-7411, (800) 547-8911. **www**.pendletonchamber.com

Pendleton's outsized reputation for raucous cowboys and lawless cattle rustlers is matched by the fact that it is eastern Oregon's largest town. But visitors may be disappointed to learn that these colorful days belong to the past. However, cowboy lore comes alive during the Pendleton Round-Up each September, when rodeo stunt performers and some 50,000 spectators crowd into town. Previous rodeos are honored at the entertaining **Round-Up Hall of Fame**.

The town's biggest business, the **Pendleton Woolen Mills**, is known for its warm clothing and blankets, particularly its "legendary" blankets whose designs are a tribute to Native American tribes. The mill wove its first Indian trade blanket in 1895.

The **Pendleton Underground Tours** begin in a subterranean labyrinth of opium dens, gaming rooms, and Prohibition-era drinking establishments and include stops at a bordello and the cramped 19th-century living quarters of Chinese laborers.

The **Tamástslikt Cultural Institute** commemorates local history by displaying re-creations of historic structures, exhibits of war bonnets, and other artifacts.

Pendleton Woolen Mills
1307 SE Court Pl. ***Tel*** *(541) 278-0815.* **Salesroom** *8am–5pm Mon–Sat, 11am–3pm Sun.* *Jan 1, Thanksgiving, Dec 25.* *9am, 11am, 1:30pm, 3pm Mon–Fri.*
www.pendleton-usa.com

Round-Up Hall of Fame
1205 SW Court Ave. ***Tel*** *(541) 278-0815.* *May–Sep: 10am–4pm Mon–Sat; Oct–Apr: by appointment.* *public hols.*
www.pendletonroundup.com

A rodeo rider at the popular Pendleton Round-Up

Wallowa Mountains ㊱

Elkhorn Drive National Scenic Byway (for 83 miles/134 km), starting at Baker City.

The Wallowa Mountains form a 10,000-ft (3,050-m) high, 40-mile (64-km) long wall of granite in northeastern Oregon. Driving through the region takes in some of the finest scenery in the state.

The best way to explore the Wallowa Mountains is to take the **Elkhorn Drive National Scenic Byway**, a two-lane paved road, which begins from Baker City. Nestled between the Wallowa Mountains and the Elkhorn Range, the town has some lovely downtown blocks and fine Victorian houses. Farther north, the National Historic Oregon Trail Interpretive Center displays replicas of pioneer scenes.

Wallowa Lake

Surrounded by dense wilderness, the sleepy town of **Joseph** lies to the east of the Wallowa Mountains. Named after Chief Joseph, leader of the Nez Percé peoples, Joseph is a popular destination for recreation enthusiasts and artisans. One of Joseph's main attractions is the **Wallowa County Museum**, which is devoted to Chief Joseph's famous retreat, and to the history of both Indians and settlers of the area.

The crystal-clear waters of the **Wallowa Lake** sparkle at the foot of the Wallowa Mountains. The Wallowa Lake Lodge, a log building dating from the 1920s, still provides accommodations and meals. The popular Wallowa Lake Tramway whisks riders up to the summit of Mount Howard, to enjoy spectacular views of the sparkling lake below and majestic peaks rising up.

Wallowa County Museum
110 S Main St, Joseph. ***Tel*** *(541) 432-6095.* *Memorial Day–late-Sep: 10am–5pm daily.*
www.co.wallowa.or.us/museum

Hells Canyon National Recreation Area ㊲

Local prickly pear cactus

Some of the wildest terrain in North America clings to the sides of craggy, 9,400-ft (2,865-m) peaks at Hells Canyon before plunging to the famed basin far below. Here, the Snake River rushes through the world's deepest river-carved gorge. Visitors revel in the massive canyon walls rising 6,000 ft (1,830 m), the upland pine forests, and the delicate wildflower-covered alpine meadows – 652,000 wilderness acres (264,000 ha) in all. Much of the terrain is too rugged to cross, even on foot, making long sections of the Snake River accessible only by boat. Many visitors settle for the stunning views from several lookouts, and no one is disappointed.

Hells Canyon National Recreation Area Viewpoint

Buckhorn Lookout ①
One of several scenic overlooks situated in the Hells Canyon area, superb views of the Wallowa-Whitman National Forest and the Imnaha River canyon are afforded from this remote spot.

Nee-Me-Poo Trail ②
Visitors hiking along this National historic trail follow in the footsteps of the famous Chief Joseph and 700 Nez Percé Indians who, in 1877, embarked on an 1,800-mile (2,897-km) trek toward freedom in Canada.

Hells Canyon Reservoir ⑥
This 25-mile- (40-km-) long reservoir, part of a huge power-generating complex on the Snake River, is formed by Oxbow Dam to the south and Hells Canyon Dam to the north. A private road along the east shore provides access to the river.

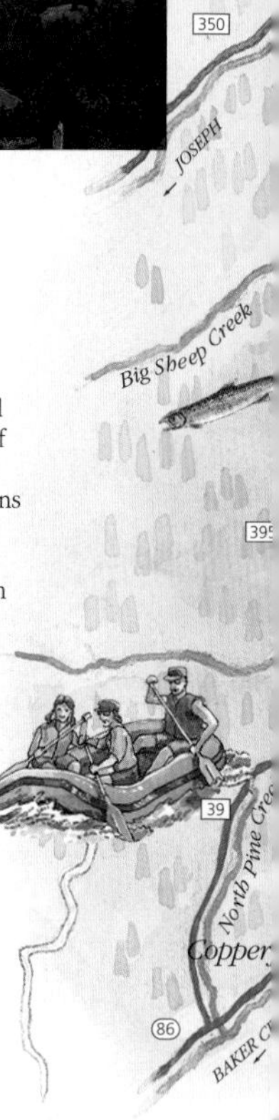

TIPS FOR WALKERS

Tour length: *214 miles (344 km), including all turnoffs.*
Starting point: *Oregon SR 350, 8 miles (13 km) east of Joseph.*
When to go: *Summer months only. Some roads are not suitable for every type of vehicle. For information, call the area's visitor center at (541) 426-5546.*
Stopping off points: *Picnic areas are widely available. Imnaha offers restaurants and lodging.*

Imnaha River ③
A road from the town of Imnaha follows this frothy river through a pine-scented valley, isolated ranches, and a fish weir where Chinook salmon, having migrated from the Pacific Ocean, can be seen swimming upstream.

KEY

- Tour route
- Other road
- Information
- Viewpoint

Hat Point Road ④
A steep, dizzying, 23-mile (37-km) gravel road takes visitors up to Hat Point, located at an elevation of 7,000 ft (2,100 m).

0 km 10
0 miles 10

Wild and Scenic River ⑤
A 31.5-mile (50.5-km) stretch of the Snake River, from Hells Canyon Dam to Upper Pittsburg Landing, is designated a Wild River. Experienced guides pilot rafters over the many stretches of rapids, but searing temperatures, bears, rattlesnakes, poison ivy, and generally inhospitable terrain discourage overland treks.

A boat negotiating rapids on the Snake River

Practical Information

The stunning scenery of the Pacific Northwest attracts visitors from around the world. Booming tourism – and in more recent years, ecotourism – has spawned a vast network of facilities and services: internationally acclaimed restaurants and accommodations abound, and efficient transportation by air, land, and water takes travelers virtually anywhere they want to go. The peak tourist season extends from mid-May through September. Winter is also a great time to visit the region as it is ideal for skiing and other snow sports.

TOURIST INFORMATION

Maps and information about sights, events, accommodations, and tours are available free of charge from **Washington State Tourism** and the **Oregon Tourism Commission**. These agencies also provide either free reservations services for a wide range of accommodations or referrals to these services. Most Pacific Northwest communities operate visitor centers or tourism booths, offering information about local activities, lodgings, and restaurants.

PERSONAL SECURITY

The Pacific Northwest prides itself on its safe cities and its welcoming attitude toward visitors. Street crime is rare, and the police are a visible presence in all major cities. However, it is wise to be careful and find out which parts of town are less safe than others. Your hotel or a tourist information center will provide information about which areas are best to stay away from. In the country, wildlife and natural dangers can be avoided by heeding local warnings and advice.

In an emergency, call 911 for the fire department, police, or an ambulance; if you are not in a major city, dial 0. The call can be placed from any phone free of charge. Hospitals are listed in phone books, and each has an emergency room that can be accessed 24 hours a day.

NATURAL HAZARDS

Before heading out on a hike or going camping, check in with the forest service for information on the conditions in the surrounding area and recommended safety precautions. Skiers and snowboarders should always heed warning signs and stay on groomed runs.

Insects can be annoying while hiking or camping – blackflies in the spring or mosquitoes in the summer. Ticks, which can be carriers of Lyme disease, are found in dry, wooded areas. Protect yourself by using tick repellant and wear long trousers, long sleeves, and socks. In case of a rash or flu-like symptoms, contact a doctor immediately.

On the beach, heed the red tide warnings that alert shellfish collectors to contamination. When camping, beware of cougars, wolves, coyotes, and bears. Be advised that leaving any food or garbage out will attract dangerous wildlife.

Potential safety hazards for drivers include gravel roads, which may become very slippery with rain, heavy snowfalls, black ice, and fog. To be safe, always carry a spare tire, and salt or sand in winter, also a flashlight, jumper cables, blankets, water, emergency food, and a shovel. Always carry a cell phone.

THE CLIMATE OF THE PACIFIC NORTHWEST

Rain is a distinctive presence in only half the Pacific Northwest – the part west of the mountains that divide the region. The weather in this western, coastal region remains mild throughout the year, and snow is rare in all but the higher elevations. The mountains see heavy winter snowfall, much to the delight of skiers. East of the mountains, the summers are hot, dry, and sunny, and winters more severe than west of the mountains.

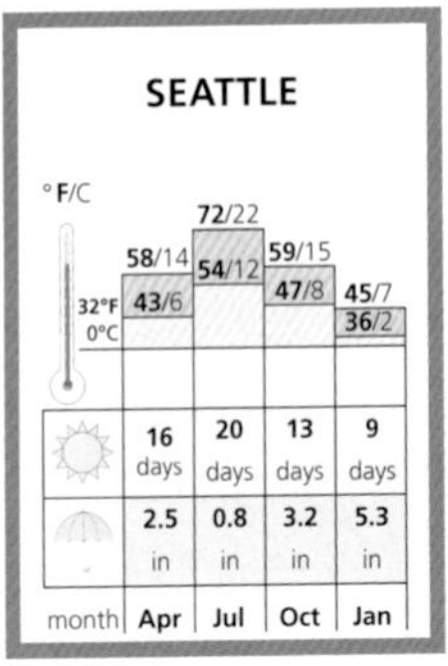

GETTING AROUND

Visitors to the Pacific Northwest have a wide range of transportation options. **United Airlines** offers flights to the major cities of the Pacific Northwest, while **Alaska Airlines** and its subsidiary **Horizon Airlines** fly to these and regional destinations.

Although the bus may be the slowest way of getting to the Pacific Northwest, it is probably the most economical. **Greyhound** has bus routes throughout the region; **Gray Line** offers sightseeing tours. Discounts are available for children, students, and senior citizens. The train is a good way to get to the Pacific Northwest and to travel within it. **Amtrak** offers daily service to Oregon and Washington from the Midwest and California and has daily runs between Seattle, Portland, and Eugene. **Washington State Ferries** connect 20 ports throughout Puget Sound, including Seattle.

Driving is by far the best mode of transport in the region, especially to enjoy the spectacular beauty of more remote areas. Remember to tune into local television and radio news channels for regular reports on traffic and road conditions, particularly during the winter.

ETIQUETTE

Dress in the Pacific Northwest tends to be casual, practical, and dependent on the weather. Stricter clothing requirements apply in theaters, high-end restaurants, and other more formal places. Designated beaches allow topless and nude sunbathing. The legal drinking age is 21. Smoking in public places is prohibited.

LAWS

The Seattle and Portland Police Departments are a visible presence, either on foot, bicycle, or squad car. There are also neighborhood security teams made up of citizen volunteers, which patrol on foot. Outside the metropolitan areas, there are county police and sheriff's offices to assist you.

It is illegal and insensitive to comment on or joke about bombs, guns, and terrorism in places such as airports. Drunk driving is also taken seriously; remember that open alcohol containers in a car are illegal. Narcotics users can face criminal charges and severe penalties.

SPORTS & OUTDOOR ACTIVITIES

The dramatically varied terrain and beautiful landscape of the Pacific Northwest make this the ideal region for a wide variety of outdoor activities. Both Washington and Oregon provide great conditions for adventure sports such as hang gliding and paragliding. Whitewater rafting is also popular, especially in the waters of the Cascades Range. Skiing and snowboarding are other popular activities.

For those interested in more placid pastimes, the **Oregon Department of Fish and Wildlife** or the **Washington Department of Fish and Wildlife**, provide information on freshwater fishing.

One of the most exciting ways to explore the scenic Pacific Northwest is by foot. Visitor centers and the **American Hiking Society** provide information about hiking; and the **Pacific Northwest Trail Association** offers details about the beautiful 1,200-mile (1,931-km) trail, which runs from the Continental Divide to the Pacific Ocean.

In summer, the region's many beaches are ideal for relaxing and offer refreshing waters to swim in. The coasts are also a delight for birdwatchers who can catch sight of gulls, sandpipers, plovers, and ducks. Birdwatchers can also enjoy the **Malheur National Wildlife Refuge** in Oregon. Canoeing and kayaking provide environmentally friendly ways of seeing the region's beautiful waters and abundant marine life. Washington's Puget Sound and San Juan Islands are the most popular destinations for sea kayaking, while Olympic National Park is the hot spot for canoeists. In Oregon, the Columbia River provides stretches of calmer water for paddling.

Cycling and inline skating are inexpensive ways of traveling. Bicycle Adventures offers cycling tours.

SHOPPING

Downtown districts in the Pacific Northwest provide everything from luxury goods in exclusive stores to flea market bargains. Outdoor gear manufactured by world-famous local companies such as REI are popular with tourists interested in adventure sports. Other items to shop for are antiques, books, and music from both the chain stores and independents, first-class wines (Pinot Noirs, Chardonnays, Rieslings, and dessert wines), and smoked Pacific salmon. Native American jewelry, carvings, paintings, and other handicrafts are also available throughout the region.

DIRECTORY

TOURIST INFORMATION

Oregon Tourism Commission
775 Summer St NE, Salem, OR 97301-1282
Tel *(503) 986-0000, (800) 547-7842.*
www.traveloregon.com

Washington State Tourism
P.O. Box 42500. Olympia, WA 98504-2500
Tel *(800) 544-1800.*
www.experiencewa.com

TRAVEL

Alaska Airlines
Tel *(800) 426-0333.*
www.alaskaair.com

Horizon Airlines
Tel *(800) 547-9308.*

United Airlines
Tel *(800) 241-6522.*

Gray Line
Tel *In Portland: (888) 684-3322. In Seattle: (800) 426-7532.* **www**.grayline.com

Greyhound
Tel *(800) 229-9424.*
www.greyhound.com

Amtrak
Tel *(800) 872-7245.*
www.amtrak.com

Washington State Ferries
Tel *(206) 464-6400.*
www.wsdot.wa.gov/ferries

FRESHWATER FISHING

Oregon Dept of Fish and Wildlife
Tel *(508) 947-6000, (800) 720-6339.*
www.dfw.state.or.us

Washington Dept of Fish & Wildlife
Tel *(360) 902-2200.*
www.wdfw.wa.gov

HIKING

American Hiking Society
Tel *(800) 972-8608.*
www.americanhiking.org

Pacific Northwest Trail Association
Tel *(877) 854-9415.*
www.pnt.org

BIRD-WATCHING

Malheur National Wildlife Refuge
Tel *(541) 493-2612.*
www.fws.gov/malheur

Choosing a Hotel

Whether you are looking for a relaxing oceanside inn, a small bed and breakfast, or a perfectly appointed hotel in the heart of the city, the Pacific Northwest offers accommodations to suit every taste and budget. In addition, rustic lodges and guest ranches, usually near scenic areas, provide unforgettable outdoor experiences.

PRICE CATEGORIES
For a standard double room per night, including service charges and any additional taxes.

$ Under $100
$$ $100–$150
$$$ $150–$200
$$$$ Over $200

WASHINGTON

CHELAN Campbell's Resort — $$$$

104 W Woodin Ave, 98816 ***Tel*** *(509) 682-2561, (800) 553-8225* ***Fax*** *(509) 682-2177* ***Rooms*** *170*

With a prime beachfront location, this long-time local favorite offers a host of on-site facilities including spa, conference facilities, outdoor heated pool, and beach bar. All of the spacious rooms include balcony or patio, and some have fireplaces and kitchens. There's even a boat moorage for water arrivals. **www.campbellsresort.com**

LEAVENWORTH Hotel Pension Anna — $$$

926 Commercial St, 98826 ***Tel*** *(509) 548-6273, (800) 509-2662* ***Fax*** *(509) 548-4656* ***Rooms*** *16*

This delightful German-style inn features rooms and suites with imported furniture from Austria and Germany; all have private baths. The most luxurious suite occupies part of an adjacent renovated church, complete with soaring ceilings and two twin beds in the old choir loft. Rates include full German-style breakfast. **www.pensionanna.com**

MT. RAINIER NATIONAL PARK National Park Inn — $$

Mount Rainier National Park, 98304 ***Tel*** *(360) 569-2275* ***Fax*** *(360) 569-2770* ***Rooms*** *25*

The smaller of Mt. Rainier National Park's two lodges, this 1920 inn in Longmire, at the southwest corner of the park, is a rustic retreat with charming but basic rooms. Open year-round, it attracts hikers and climbers in the summer and snowshoers and cross-country skiers in the winter. **www.mtrainierguestservices.com**

PORT ANGELES Lake Crescent Lodge — $$

416 Lake Crescent Rd, 98363 ***Tel*** *(360) 928-3211* ***Fax*** *(360) 928-3253* ***Rooms*** *52*

Set in a secluded spot on the shore of the fjord-like Lake Crescent, this lodge makes a fine base for exploring the northern reaches of Olympic National Park. Guests can choose among rooms in the 1916 main building or the many adjacent cottages. The lodge is closed in winter. **www.lakecrescentlodge.com**

QUINAULT Lake Quinault Lodge — $$$

345 South Shore Rd, 98575 ***Tel*** *(360) 288-2900, (888) 896-3827* ***Fax*** *(360) 288-2901* ***Rooms*** *92*

This grand 1926 lodge sits by the rainforest above the shore of Lake Quinault, in the remote southwestern corner of Olympic National Park. It offers old-style comfort, with few televisions and phones, but the rooms are comfortable, the views excellent, and the food worth a visit on its own. **www.visitlakequinault.com**

SEATTLE Ace Hotel — $$

2423 1st Ave, 98121 ***Tel*** *(206) 448-4721* ***Fax*** *(206) 374-0745* ***Rooms*** *28*

Chic white-on-white decor and friendly service are the hallmarks of this modern, minimalist Belltown hotel, which is popular with artists and musicians. Rooms in the updated old rooming house have high ceilings and low platform beds with army-surplus blankets; half share baths. Complimentary Continental breakfast included. **www.acehotel.com**

SEATTLE Mayflower Park Hotel — $$$

405 Olive Way, 98101 ***Tel*** *(206) 623-8700, (800) 426-5100* ***Fax*** *(206) 382-6996* ***Rooms*** *171*

One of the last of Seattle's independently owned classic hotels, this refurbished 1927 property is ideally located for shoppers. It opens directly into the upscale Westlake Center mall, and is just a block away from the flagship Nordstrom's and Macy's. The on-site Andaluca restaurant serves fine Mediterranean cuisine. **www.mayflowerpark.com**

SEATTLE Inn at Harbor Steps — $$$$

1221 1st Ave, 98101 ***Tel*** *(206) 748-0973, (888) 728-8910* ***Fax*** *(206) 748-0533* ***Rooms*** *28*

This boutique hotel at the base of a modern residential high-rise boasts an unsurpassed location for business and leisure travelers alike, with all of downtown, Pioneer Square, the waterfront, and Pike Place Market within easy walking distance. Rooms are bright, cozy, and spacious, most with garden views and fireplaces. **www.innatharborsteps.com**

SEATTLE MarQueen Hotel — $$$$

600 Queen Anne Ave N, 98109 ***Tel*** *(206) 282-7407, (888) 445-3076* ***Fax*** *(206) 283-1499* ***Rooms*** *56*

Built in 1918 as an apartment building, this quaint small hotel is close to the McCaw Opera House and other performance venues at Seattle Center. All of the tastefully appointed rooms have kitchens, hardwood floors with area rugs, and upscale toiletries and robes. Salon and spa services are also available. **www.marqueen.com**

Key to Symbols *see back cover flap*

WALLA WALLA Marcus Whitman Hotel $$$

6 W Rose St, 99362 ***Tel*** *(509) 525-5501, (866) 826-9422* ***Fax*** *(509) 525-2200* ***Rooms*** *127*

This 1928 high-rise is a focal point of downtown Walla Walla, providing both fine accommodations and dining in the heart of Washington's wine country. Guestrooms are divided between the original tower and a newer addition; the tower suites are the nicest rooms in town. **www.marcuswhitmanhotel.com**

YAKIMA Birchfield Country Manor $$

2018 Birchfield Rd, 98901 ***Tel*** *(509) 452-1960, (800) 375-3420* ***Fax*** *(509) 452-2334* ***Rooms*** *11*

Just two miles outside of Yakima, this 1910 farmhouse offers elegant rooms furnished with antiques in both the manor house and guest cottage (manor rooms have no phone or television). Thursday through Friday, the dining room is one of the Yakima Valley's finest restaurants, with an award-winning wine list. **www.birchfieldmanor.com**

OREGON

ASHLAND Columbia Hotel $$

262½ E Main St, 97520 ***Tel*** *(541) 482-3726, (800) 718-2530* ***Rooms*** *24*

An inexpensive, well-worn antique, this homey spot in the center of Ashland is just a few minutes' walk from Shakespeare festival venues. Guest rooms are tidy and tastefully furnished, and skylights offer abundant natural light in the spacious lobby, where you can relax with coffee and the morning paper. **www.columbiahotel.com**

ASTORIA Hotel Elliott $$$

357 12th St, 97103 ***Tel*** *(503) 325-2222, (877) 378-1924* ***Fax*** *(503) 325-6868* ***Rooms*** *32*

Located in the heart of downtown and given a three-year, multi-million-dollar renovation in 2003, this is Astoria's top boutique hotel. The building retains many of its original 1924 details, while the amenities are fresh and luxurious: beds have thick duvets, goose-down pillows, and 440-count cotton sheets. **www.hotelelliott.com**

BEND McMenamin's Old St. Francis School $$$

700 NW Bond St, 97701 ***Tel*** *(541) 382-5174, (877) 661-4228* ***Fax*** *(541) 330-8561* ***Rooms*** *19*

Central Oregon's first parochial school now welcomes guests for food, drink, movies, and overnight stays. Guestrooms in the 1936 structure feature private baths and modern conveniences, and memorabilia from the school and community adorns the walls. Also on-site are three pubs, four cottages, and a Turkish-style soaking pool. **www.mcmenamins.com**

BEND Inn of the Seventh Mountain $$$$

18575 SW Century Dr, 97702 ***Tel*** *(541) 382-8711, (800) 452-6810* ***Fax*** *(541) 382-3517* ***Rooms*** *220*

Situated on the banks of the Deschutes River, this popular resort makes a fine base for skiers, rafters, anglers, and other outdoors-loving travelers. The homey, condo-style accommodations range from simple bedroom units to fully-equipped suites, and amenities include heated pools, hot tubs, tennis courts, and hiking trails. **www.seventhmountain.com**

CRATER LAKE NATIONAL PARK Crater Lake Lodge $$$

565 Rim Village Dr, 97604 ***Tel*** *(541) 830-8700, (888) 774-2728* ***Fax*** *(541) 830-8514* ***Rooms*** *71*

Built in 1915 and extensively renovated, this grand lodge sits in a spectacular location on the rim of Crater Lake. Built of native stone and wood, it offers claw-foot tubs in guest bathrooms, a massive fireplace in the Great Hall, and fine Northwest cuisine in the restaurant. **www.craterlakelodges.com**

PORTLAND Hotel de Luxe $$$

729 SW 15th Ave, 97205 ***Tel*** *(503) 219-2094, (866) 986-8085* ***Fax*** *(503) 219-2095* ***Rooms*** *130*

Just a short walk from the Pearl District, this historic downtown hotel gets rave reviews from guests who appreciate the charming atmosphere and attentive service. The Art Deco decor pays homage to vintage Hollywood, but with modern amenities and a fine restaurant. Easy access via the city's light rail system. **www.hoteldeluxeportland.com**

PORTLAND Heathman Hotel $$$$

1001 SW Broadway, 97205 ***Tel*** *(503) 241-4100, (800) 551-0011* ***Fax*** *(503) 790-7110* ***Rooms*** *150*

With its Old World charm and proximity to Portland's cultural district, this handsome 1927 institution is a magnet for visiting musicians and writers. Rooms feature city views and works by local artists. Amenities include a cozy library, an extensive movie collection, afternoon tea, and a first-rate restaurant and bar. **www.heathmanhotel.com**

PORTLAND Governor Hotel $$$$

614 SW 11th Ave, 97205 ***Tel*** *(503) 224-3400, (800) 554-3456* ***Fax*** *(503) 241-2122* ***Rooms*** *100*

On the National Register of Historic Places, this 1909 gem is full of Arts and Crafts details inside and out. The former lobby (now part of Jake's Grill) features historic murals depicting scenes from the Lewis and Clark expedition, and some of the elegantly furnished rooms offer fireplaces and balconies. **www.governorhotel.com**

PORTLAND Westin Portland $$$$

750 SW Alder St, 97205 ***Tel*** *(503) 294-9000* ***Fax*** *(503) 241-9565* ***Rooms*** *205*

One of Portland's most luxurious hotels, this member of the Westin chain offers roomy, plush guestrooms and superb service. Especially well-equipped for business travelers, it offers work desks with ergonomic chairs, wireless Internet, three meeting rooms with floor-to-ceiling windows, and a central location. **www.westinportland.com**

Choosing a Restaurant

Known for its vast range of local seafood, the Pacific Northwest also boasts a large number of coffee bars. Seattle and Portland are in the midst of a culinary revolution – small restaurants popping up on every block with a variety of fare ranging from wildberry pancakes to pumpkin soup.

PRICE CATEGORIES
For a three-course meal for one, including a glass of house wine (where served), and all other unavoidable charges such as sales tax.
$ Under $30
$$ $30–$45
$$$ $45–$60
$$$$ $60–$80
$$$$$ Over $80

WASHINGTON

BELLINGHAM The Oyster Bar $$$$

Chuckanut Drive 25787, 98232 ***Tel*** *(360) 766-6185*

A venerable institution dating back to the 1920s, this lodge-like restaurant boasts stellar seafood and jaw-dropping views of the San Juan Islands. As the name suggests, a variety of local oysters leads the menu, which also offers such options as crab cakes, steamed mussels, bouillabaisse, wild mushroom ravioli, and a daily game special.

LEAVENWORTH Café Mozart $$$$

829 Front St, 98826 ***Tel*** *(509) 548-0600*

Upstairs from Andreas Keller, this elegant spot serves refined Middle-European fare accompanied on weekends by live harp music. The menu features pork, veal, and chicken *schnitzels*, *sauerbraten* and *spaetzle*, along with roast duck and other hearty dishes. The wine list features examples from both the USA and Europe.

ORCAS ISLAND Inn at Ship Bay $$$

326 Olga Rd, Eastsound, 98245 ***Tel*** *(360) 376-5886*

This fine restaurant on Orcas Island in the San Juan Islands specializes in fresh seafood. The menu changes often, and typically includes organic vegetables from the front gardens. The quiet country setting is perfect for romantic dining. There's a choice of menus. A few guestrooms are also available. Closed Sun, Mon, mid-Dec–mid-Feb.

PORT TOWNSEND Khu Larb Thai $

225 Adams St, 98368 ***Tel*** *(360) 385-5023*

In the heart of historic downtown, this was the first Thai restaurant on the Olympic peninsula and still the standard-bearer. The long menu is particularly strong on seafood and vegetarian dishes, such as mussels with curry paste and stir-fried vegetables with bamboo shoots and Thai basil. You can get things as searingly spicy as you like.

SEATTLE Athenian Inn $$

1517 Pike Pl #1517, 98101 ***Tel*** *(206) 624-7166*

More renowned for its view and its appearance in the movie *Sleepless in Seattle* than for the food itself, this beloved, well-worn old-timer in Pike Place Market offers friendly service along with an extensive menu of American fare and microbrews. The menu leans toward seafood, with oyster omelets, mussel soup, grilled fish, and salmon and chips.

SEATTLE Elliott's Oyster House $$$

1201 Alaskan Way, 98101 ***Tel*** *(206) 623-4340*

Tourists and locals rub elbows at this busy, convivial seafood house located at the heart of Seattle's downtown waterfront. The focal point of the teak- and copper-accented interior is the 21-ft- (7-m-) long oyster bar, where guests can order from as many as 20 different varieties of the bivalves. King Salmon and Dungeness crab are also specialties.

SEATTLE Ivar's Acres of Clams $$$

1001 Alaskan Way, 98104 ***Tel*** *(206) 624-6852*

A venerable Seattle institution, this popular waterfront spot offers terrific crab, clam, oyster, and salmon dishes, as well as the classic fish and chips they've been serving since 1938. You can watch the ferries gliding by out the window, and many diners like to sit outside on the dock and feed the seagulls their spare French fries.

SPOKANE Steam Plant Grill $$

159 S Lincoln St, 99201 ***Tel*** *(509) 777-3900*

As the name suggests, this stylish grill is located in the striking, unusual location of an old steam and electric plant, complete with towering smokestacks. The scene is vibrant, with power lunches and a bustling bar after work. The menu includes sandwiches, pastas, and creative preparations of meat and fish.

TACOMA Café Divino $$

2112 N 30th St, 98403 ***Tel*** *(253) 779-4226*

Located in historic Old Town Tacoma, a quiet business district abutting Commencement Bay, this is a friendly, unpretentious little spot two blocks from the waterfront. Casual and convivial, it serves a loosely Italian menu ranging from cannelloni and lasagna to smoked salmon quesadillas, baked brie with pears, and a crab-laden sandwich on focaccia.

Key to Symbols *see back cover flap*

WALLA WALLA Merchants LTD $

21 E Main St, 99362 ***Tel*** *(509) 525-0900*

Occupying three red-brick storefronts on Main Street, this deli is a great spot for healthy, hearty breakfasts and lunches such as Eggs Benedict, cheese blintzes, and hot and cold sandwiches. It's also a gourmet grocery with a huge inventory of everything from vinegars and jams to cheeses and bottled sauces, and a full-service bakery.

WALLA WALLA Whitehouse-Crawford $$$

55 W Cherry St, 99362 ***Tel*** *(509) 525-2222*

In a converted sawmill shared with the barrel room of Seven Hills Winery, this elegant restaurant has helped to transform Walla Walla's culinary culture. Part of an exodus from Seattle's best restaurants, chef Jamie Guerin follows the seasons with his menu and draws heavily on local producers for his ingredients. Even the burgers are first-class.

YAKIMA Café Mélange $$$

7 N Front St, 98901 ***Tel*** *(509) 453-0571*

Small and understated, and a long-time Yakima favorite. Situated in the North Front Street Historical District, it offers a variety of pasta dishes as well hearty entrées such as beef tenderloin with shiitake mushrooms, veal marsala, and roast duck with marionberry port sauce. The superb wine list features many local producers.

OREGON

ASTORIA Columbian Café $

1114 Marine Dr, 97103 ***Tel*** *(503) 325-2233*

Cramped and funky, this hole-in-the-wall diner is an Astoria institution. From the excellent hearty breakfasts to dinner, there's always good vegetarian fare as well as meats and, appropriately, seafood. Crêpes are a specialty, and among the condiments are Uriah's St. Diablo jellies (in red pepper, jalapeño and garlic flavors); you'll want to buy a few jars to go.

BEND Deschutes Brewery and Public House $

1044 Bond St, 97701 ***Tel*** *(541) 382-9242*

Award-winning Deschutes Brewery is one of the West's top beer producers, with popular brews such as Mirror Pond Pale Ale and Black Butte Porter. Fare at the spacious brewpub is better than most, with hearty specialty sandwiches and house-made sausage, bread, and mustard.

BEND Cork $$$

150 NW Oregon St, 97701 ***Tel*** *(541) 382-6881*

Sophisticated and romantic, Cork is in the vanguard of a new breed of Bend restaurants. Chef Greg Unruh's cuisine is seasonal American with plenty of Pacific Rim influence, as in the ahi poke with wasabi, glazed scallops with black sesame-seed pesto, and pressed duck salad with hoisin sauce. As befits the restaurant's name, the wine list is extensive.

EUGENE Oregon Electric Station $$$

27 E 5th Ave, 97401 ***Tel*** *(541) 485-4444*

Housed in the beautiful 1912 depot of a long-defunct electric railway, this charming restaurant serves top-notch steak, fish, and pasta dishes complemented by over 250 wines. Guests can dine in the high-ceilinged depot, in one of several lounges, aboard antique train cars, or outside on the broad patio.

PORTLAND The Heathman Restaurant $$$

1001 SW Broadway, 97205 ***Tel*** *(503) 241-4100*

Normandy meets the Northwest in the cooking of award-winning chef Philippe Boulot, whose menus follow the seasons in search of the freshest, finest ingredients. Standout dishes may include pistachio-stuffed rabbit leg, Peking duck à l'orange, and, for breakfast, smoked salmon hash. France and Oregon dominate the extensive wine list.

PORTLAND Jake's Famous Crawfish $$$

401 SW 12th Ave, 97205 ***Tel*** *(503) 226-1419*

A Portland institution and tourist destination, this 1892 fish house boasts nearly three dozen kinds of fresh fish and seafood daily. The menu offers them steamed, stuffed, seared, sautéed, and sauced, but you can get most things simply grilled – often the best choice. Polished paneling, old artwork, and crisply attired waiters create a club feel.

PORTLAND Paley's Place $$$$

1204 NW 21st Ave, 97209 ***Tel*** *(503) 243-2403*

Chef Vitaly Paley is one of Portland's star chefs, and his intimate eatery, located in a Victorian house in an historic neighborhood, is a shrine of Northwest cuisine. Highlights include bacon, prune, and chestnut-stuffed quail, mushroom-crusted sweetbreads, Dungeness crab salad, and arguably the best burger in the city.

SALEM Morton's Bistro Northwest $$

1128 Edgewater St W, 97304 ***Tel*** *(503) 585-1113*

One of Salem's finest restaurants is this basement bistro located across the Willamette River from downtown. The menu features seasonal, sustainable cuisine with distinctive combinations such as penne with Dungeness crab and Andouille sausage. Cioppino and Spanish-style prawns are standouts, and diners may choose between big and small plates.

CALIFORNIA

INTRODUCING CALIFORNIA 650–657

LOS ANGELES 658–677

SAN DIEGO COUNTY 678–681

THE DESERTS 682–685

CENTRAL COAST 686–693

SAN FRANCISCO 694–711

THE WINE COUNTRY 712–713

NORTHERN CALIFORNIA 714–715

THE GOLD COUNTRY 716–717

THE HIGH SIERRAS 718–719

California at a Glance

Situated on the Pacific Coast, California is 800 miles (1,300 km) long and 250 miles (400 km) wide, covering an area of 158,710 sq miles (411,060 sq km). An area of startling contrasts, the scorching deserts and snowcapped mountains of the south lead to the vast wilderness areas of the north. Los Angeles and San Francisco are the state's two major cities, and the state capital is Sacramento.

Sacramento (see p717) *in Gold Country is California's capital city. Its primary landmark is the California State Capitol, completed in 1874. In the old city, along the river, are many historic buildings built for the gold miners of 1849.*

Napa Valley (see p712), *a long, sliver of land, lies in the heart of Northern California's Wine Country. Hundreds of wineries dot the entire length of the valley; most offer tours and wine tastings.*

San Francisco's (see pp694–711) *Golden Gate Bridge connects the city with Marin County. This famous landmark was opened in 1937.*

Santa Barbara (see p686), *on the Central Coast, is a repository of the region's Spanish heritage. Its legendary mission, referred to as the "Queen of Missions," was built four years after the city was established as an important garrison in 1782.*

◁ **Rocks and crashing surf at Big Sur, Central Coast**

Yosemite National Park (see p718) *in the High Sierras is an unforgettable wilderness of forests, alpine meadows, breathtaking waterfalls, and imposing granite rocks. The giant sequoia trees here were California's first tourist attraction.*

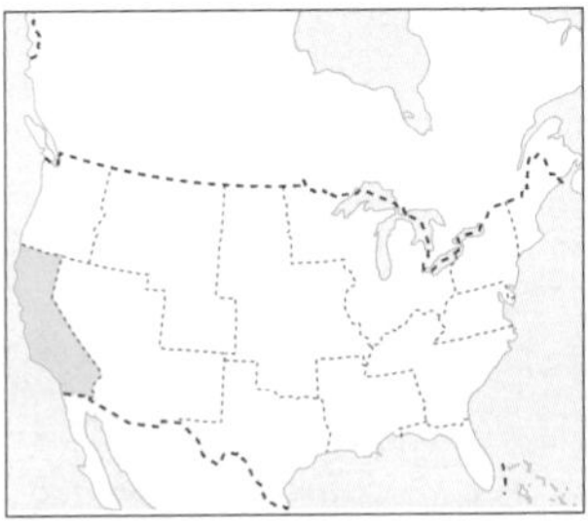

LOCATOR MAP

0 km 100

0 miles 100

Death Valley National Park (see pp684–5) *shows the California desert at its harshest and most awe-inspiring. The Native Americans called the valley Tomesha, "the land where the ground is on fire," an apt name for this extremely hot place.*

San Diego (see p678) *was the site of the first Spanish mission. Today, it is a major commerical and military port, where aircraft carriers, cruise ships, fishing boats, and pleasure craft are a common sight.*

Los Angeles (see pp658–77) *is a city dominated by wealth, fame, and glamor, as perceived by Hollywood. Its popular beaches along the Pacific Ocean attract more than 30 million people a year.*

CALIFORNIA

Impressive for both its size and its sway over modern culture, California symbolizes the United States' diversity and sense of prosperity. Here can be found towering forests, high mountain peaks, deserts within half a day's drive of ocean beaches, and two of the world's foremost cities, San Francisco and Los Angeles.

Perceptions of California vary so greatly that some people now joke that there are two states. The first is geographic – California is the Union's third-largest state (after Alaska and Texas). It claims some high mountain peaks such as Mount Whitney as well as the country's lowest expanse of dry land – Death Valley. Roughly one in every eight Americans is a Californian, making this the most populous of the 50 states, represented by the largest Congressional delegation.

State Seal

The other California is a realm of romance, formed by flickering celluloid images. Think "California" and pictures are immediately conjured up of bikini-clad beachcombers, middle-class suburban families in sprawling ranch houses, and glamorous film stars emerging from limousines before hordes of autograph seekers. These stereotypes are perpetuated by the tourism and entertainment media, especially Hollywood. The earlier Spanish legends had glorified Califorina as exotic, while the later Gold Rush elevated it to a land of fortune and opportunity. Whatever the truth may be, such were the eulogies that created California's colorful and seductive image.

HISTORY

Although the Spanish first "discovered" California in 1542, they colonized the area only in the 18th century. Their rule was enforced through three institutions – the mission (church), the presidio (fort), and the pueblo (town). Of these the mission was the most influential, and Franciscan friars set up 21 missions at

Window-shopping along Ocean Avenue, Carmel's most exclusive street

◁ The Los Angeles skyline with snowy Mount Baldy in the background, a view from Baldwin Hills

approximately 30-mile (48-km) intervals along El Camino Real ("the Royal Road") from San Diego to Sonoma. Still, the territory remained remote until 1848 when Mexico ceded California to the US, and gold was found in the Sierra Nevada foothills. The Gold Rush of 1849 drew hordes of prospectors, known as "Forty-Niners" after the year of their arrival. The discovery of silver deposits in the western Sierras, as well as the completion of the transcontinental railroad in 1869, brought greater prosperity. But along with the changes came racial tensions, ignited by the influx of Chinese immigrants, who were brought to help build the railroad. Immigrants have since contributed to the state's cultural richness as well as its overpopulation and social tensions.

The popular Third Street Promenade, Santa Monica

On April 18, 1906, San Francisco was struck by the country's worst ever earthquake, and many believed that California's heyday was over. However, the state's subsequent revival was linked to Hollywood's lucrative film industry. Movies and the new medium of television made California the symbol of America's postwar resurgence – suddenly everybody wanted the prosperous middle-class existence they believed was common here. At the same time racial discrimination and violence persisted, state schools lacked funds, and Hollywood found itself attacked by politicians as a hotbed of Marxist Communism.

Since the 1960s, however, California has been the birthplace of some of the country's most significant social movements. The University of California at Berkeley was home to the Free Speech Movement, and Haight Ashbury in San Francisco was the mecca for "hippies." Today, Silicon Valley is a leading center of the computer industry, and many world-class high-tech firms are based here. Yet, despite progress and prosperity, California is still earthquake prone.

KEY DATES IN HISTORY

1542 Spanish explorer Juan Rodríguez Cabrilho discovers California

1769 The first mission is set up at San Diego

1776 New presidio set up in San Francisco

1781 Pueblo of Los Angeles founded

1848 US annexes California. Gold discovered

1853 Levi Strauss lands in the Bay Area and begins selling his canvas trousers

1854 Sacramento becomes the state capital

1869 Transcontinental railroad completed

1891 Stanford University opens

1893 San Andreas Fault discovered

1906 Earthquake strikes San Francisco

1911 *The Law of the Range* is the first film made in Hollywood

1929 Actor Douglas Fairbanks Sr. hosts the first Academy Awards presentation

1945 UN Charter signed in San Francisco

1968 Senator Robert F. Kennedy assassinated

1978 Apple Computer's first personal computer

1984 Los Angeles hosts its second Olympics

1992 Statewide racial riots

2001 Energy crisis; rolling blackouts conserve electricity

2003 Election of Arnold Schwarzenegger as 38th Governer of California

SOCIETY & POLITICS

If the US as a whole is a melting pot of people, California is an ethnic microcosm. It receives the highest number of immigrants (more than 200,000 every year), and its racial makeup is the nation's most diverse. The percentage of whites and African Americans is lower than the national average, but the Asian population is more than triple the national level. Hispanics too, account for more than a quarter of all Californians. This ethnic cocktail is most visible in such cities as San Diego, Los Angeles, and San Francisco. Population growth has inevitably disturbed the balance between rural and urban sectors. Since the 1950s, farmlands have declined as the need for housing has arisen. Today, the fast-expanding job markets are in the service industries and in the Silicon Valley.

Most visitors usually come to see California's two main cities – San Francisco and Los Angeles. In the north and south of the state respectively, they define the opposing sides of its character. San Francisco is more compact, and prides itself on its nonconformity and openmindedness. It has evolved into a pro-labor hotbed, with a history of activism (the Bay Area led the anti-Vietnam War movement). It also has one of the world's largest concentrations of gays and lesbians. Los Angeles, in contrast, is a sprawling city without a focal point, where illusions of wealth, fame, and glamor have created a dimensionless image of bright lights and conservative politics. The conflicting power that the two cities exert on the politics of the state and the nation explains why California may appear a little schizophrenic.

Beat writer Jack Kerouac

CULTURE & THE ARTS

For most people, California's contributions to culture are Hollywood blockbusters or televised sitcoms. But another creativity reveals itself through its history of landscape painting, portraiture, and 20th-century avant-garde art. Modern artists such as John McLaughlin and Elmer Bischoff, and such pioneers of photographic art as Imogen Cunningham and Ansel Adams, have all achieved international recognition. British artist David Hockney lived here for many years, capturing the state's sun-soaked image on canvas. California is also home to some of the world's finest art museums, including the Los Angeles County Museum of Art, the San Francisco Museum of Modern Art, and the J. Paul Getty Museum. The Bay Area's Victorian architecture has always been a major tourist attraction, and visiting designers Frank Lloyd Wright and Daniel Burnham have left their mark here as well. Recent influential architects include residents Frank Gehry and Joe Esherick.

Over the years, California has been home to scores of successful writers, including Nobel Prize-winner John Steinbeck and Beat authors Jack Kerouac and Allen Ginsburg. The tradition continues with Amy Tan *(The Joy Luck Club)*, and detective novelist Sue Grafton, among others. Pop music also plays a major role, for this is where the Beach Boys, Janis Joplin, the Grateful Dead, and the Red Hot Chili Peppers launched their careers.

Californians love to eat out, and chefs Wolfgang Puck and Alice Waters have achieved fame promoting "California cuisine" – a blend of local ingredients and Asian techniques. This, combined with a selection of world-class local wines, is proof that Californians take good care of their palates. They are generally body-conscious and frequent gyms, or participate enthusiastically in sports and a wide range of activities. Luckily, surrounded by some of the nation's most beautiful countryside and the gentlest climate, they don't have to go far to enjoy a satisfying outdoor experience.

San Francisco's cable car, a good way to get around

Exploring California

Beyond Los Angeles and San Francisco are other interesting towns and sights to visit. Highlights include San Diego and the Death Valley National Park in the south, and Monterey, Sacramento, and the Yosemite National Park in the north. Most visitors arrive at airports in Los Angeles and San Francisco. Both cities are linked to the rest of the state by an extensive road and rail network.

Shelter Island yacht harbor in San Diego Bay

SIGHTS AT A GLANCE

Los Angeles pp658–77 1

San Diego County
San Diego 2
SeaWorld 3
La Jolla 4
Tijuana, Mexico 5

The Deserts
Palm Springs 6
Anza-Borrego Desert State Park 7
Salton Sea State Recreation Area 8
Joshua Tree National Park 9
Mojave Desert 10
Death Valley National Park pp684–5 11

Central Coast
Santa Barbara 12
Channel Islands National Park 13
Lompoc Valley 14
San Luis Obispo 15
Hearst Castle™ pp688–9 16
Big Sur pp690–91 17
Carmel 18
Monterey 19
Santa Cruz 20
San Francisco pp694–711 21

The Wine Country
Sonoma Valley 22
Napa Valley 23
Russian River Valley 24
Fort Ross State Historic Park 25
Mendocino 26

Northern California
Humboldt Redwoods State Park 27
Eureka 28
Redwood National Park 29
Weaverville 30
Mount Shasta 31
Lava Beds National Monument 32
Lassen Volcanic National Park 33

The Gold Country
Nevada City 34
Grass Valley 35
Marshall Gold Discovery State Park 36
Sacramento p717 37
Highway 49 38
Columbia State Historic Park 39

The High Sierras
Lake Tahoe 40
Yosemite National Park 41
Eastern Sierras 42
Sequoia & Kings Canyon National Parks 43

SEE ALSO

- ***Practical Information*** pp720–21
- ***Where to Stay*** pp722–5
- ***Where to Eat*** pp726–9

Giant sequoia trees in Yosemite National Park

MILEAGE CHART

10 = Distance in miles
10 = Distance in kilometers

	Los Angeles	San Diego	Palm Springs	Santa Barbara	Monterey	Santa Cruz	San Francisco	Sonoma
San Diego	**121** 195							
Palm Springs	**107** 172	**138** 222						
Santa Barbara	**95** 153	**220** 354	**202** 325					
Monterey	**320** 515	**468** 753	**425** 684	**250** 402				
Santa Cruz	**363** 584	**492** 792	**467** 752	**272** 438	**43** 69			
San Francisco	**380** 612	**556** 895	**485** 781	**337** 542	**112** 180	**73** 117		
Sonoma	**409** 658	**599** 964	**513** 826	**380** 612	**158** 254	**118** 190	**45** 72	
Sacramento	**384** 618	**504** 811	**488** 785	**404** 650	**195** 314	**156** 251	**87** 140	**69** 111

Los Angeles ❶

Sitting in a broad, flat basin, surrounded by beaches, mountains, and deserts, the 468-sq-mile (1,200-sq-km) city of Los Angeles has a population of 3.8 million. The city's celluloid self-image, with its palm trees, shopping malls, and opulent lifestyles, has been idealized as the ultimate "American Dream." While known for its museums and galleries, it is still the fantasy worlds of Hollywood and Disneyland that draw most people to Los Angeles.

Waterskiing, a popular activity along the south Los Angeles coastline

SIGHTS AT A GLANCE

The Getty Center (1)
Santa Monica (2)
Venice (3)
Museum of Tolerance (4)
Westwood & UCLA (5)
The Golden Triangle (6)
Sunset Boulevard pp664–5 (7)
Mulholland Drive (8)
Hollywood Boulevard (9)
Hollywood Bowl (10)
Farmers Market (11)
Miracle Mile (12)
Exposition Park & University of Southern California (13)
Los Angeles Central Library (14)
Los Angeles City Hall (15)
Music Center (16)
Grand Central Market (17)
Little Tokyo (18)
Museum of Contemporary Art (19)
El Pueblo (20)
Lummis Home and Garden (21)
Southwest Museum of the American Indian (22)
Griffith Park (23)
Hollywood Sign (24)
Universal Studios (25)

Greater Los Angeles (see inset map)

Malibu (26)
Pasadena (27)
Watts Towers (28)
Long Beach (29)
Knott's Berry Farm (30)
Mission San Juan Capistrano (31)
Newport Beach (32)
Disneyland® Resort pp674–5 (33)

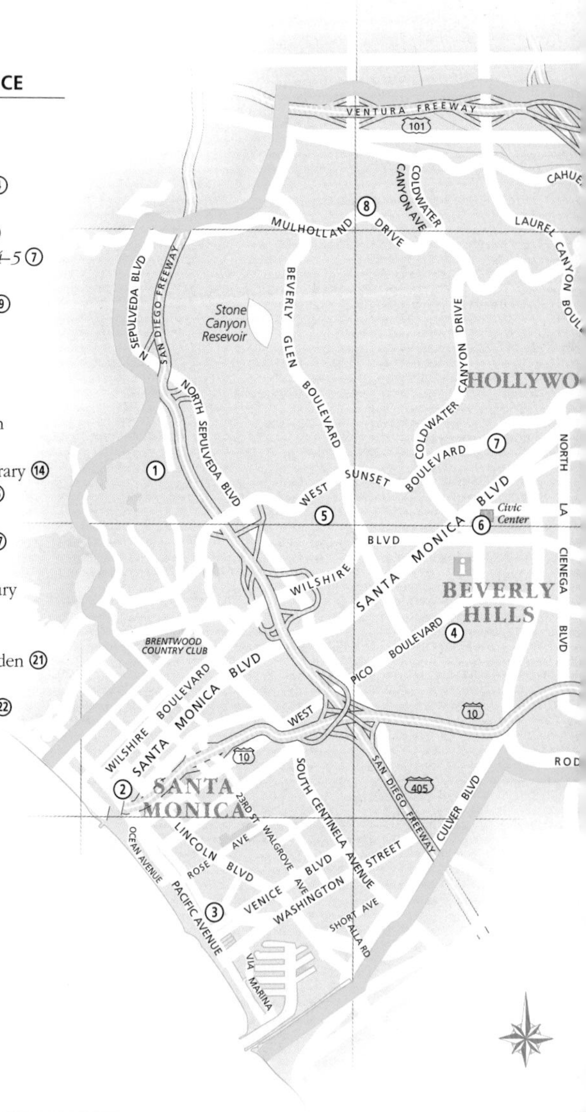

KEY

- Sight/Place of interest
- Amtrak station
- Metro station
- Tourist information
- Freeway

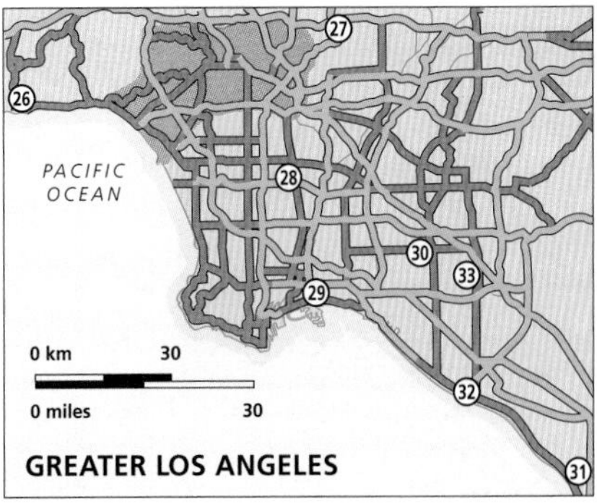

KEY

- Area of main map

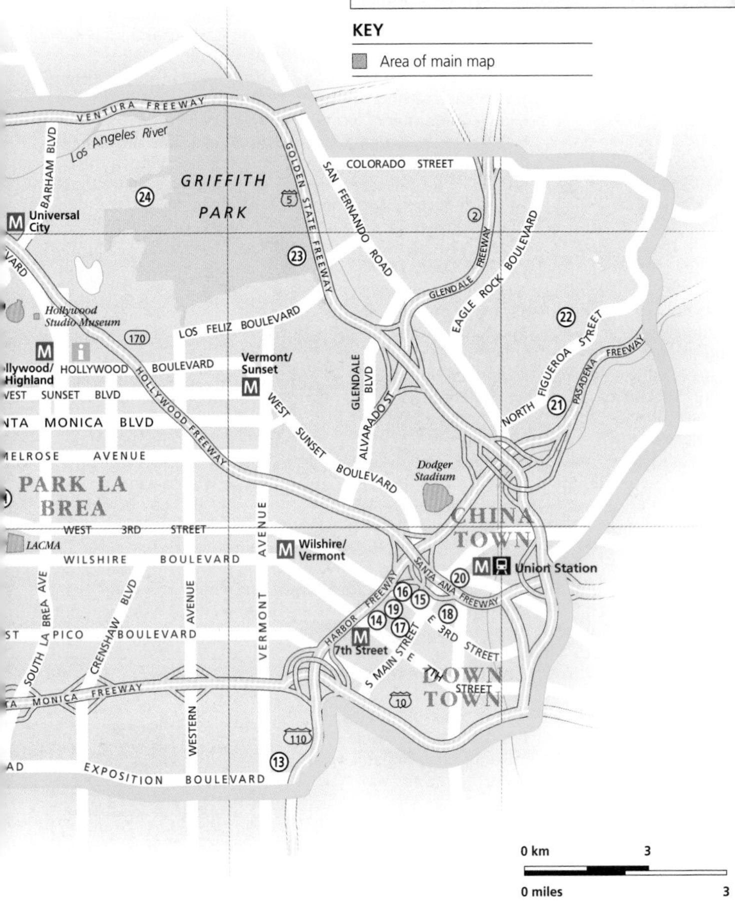

GETTING AROUND

With its well-knit network of freeways, Los Angeles is best explored by car, although public transportation works well in the downtown area and Hollywood. Buses are often crowded and slow, but they run on most of the main streets. The Metro is useful for touring the business district, while some neighborhoods are best seen on foot.

SEE ALSO

- ***L.A. Practical*** pp676–7
- ***Where to Stay*** p722
- ***Where to Eat*** p726

Adoration of the Magi **(c.1495–1505) by Andrea Mantegna, Getty Museum**

The Getty Center ①

Map B3. 1200 Getty Center Dr. ***Tel*** *(310) 440-7300.* *10am–5:30pm Tue–Thu & Sun, 10am–9pm Fri–Sat. No parking reservations needed Sat–Sun.* *public hols.* **www**.getty.edu

Situated amid the untamed beauty of the Santa Monica Mountains in the Sepulveda Pass, The Getty Center holds a commanding physical and cultural position in the area. Opened in 1997, the 110-acre (45-ha) complex houses not only the Getty Museum but also the center's research, conservation, and grant programs, dedicated to art and cultural heritage.

J. Paul Getty (1892–1976) made his fortune in the oil business and became an ardent collector of art. He amassed a remarkable collection of European art works, focusing on pre-20th-century artistic movements, from the Renaissance to Post-Impressionism. A bold collector, Getty enjoyed the pursuit of an object almost more than the possession of it. He wanted his collection to be open to the public free of charge. His original home, the Getty Villa in Malibu, was the site of the first Getty Museum. It displays objects from ancient Greece, Rome, and Etruria.

Since Getty's death, the Trust has purchased works of the highest quality to complement the existing collection. New departments such as manuscripts and drawing have also been added.

From below, the center may look like a fortress, but once inside, the scale is intimate, with fountains, walkways, courtyards, and niches. An electric tram brings visitors from the parking lot to the complex. The museum has a tall, airy foyer that opens onto a central courtyard. Facing this courtyard are the five two-story pavilions that feature the varied art collections. European paintings in the museum date from the 13th to the late 19th centuries and include masterpieces such as Andrea Mantegna's *Adoration of the Magi* (c.1495–1505), Rembrandt's *The Abduction of Europa* (1632), Paul Cézanne's *Still Life with Apples* (1900), and Vincent Van Gogh's *Irises* (1889). The last was painted by the artist when he was in the asylum at St-Remy. The Getty's collection of sculpture contains fine examples of Baroque and Neo-Classical works, including François Girardon's *Pluto Abducting Proserpine* (c.1693–1710) and statues – *Venus*, *Juno*, and *Minerva* (1773) – by Joseph Nollekens.

The museum's photography department features works of many of the pioneers of photography, such as Louis-Jacques-Mande Daguerre (inventor of the daguerreotypes) and William Henry Fox Talbott (the first to make prints from negatives).

Decorative arts were Getty's first love as a collector, after he rented a New York penthouse furnished with 18th-century French and English antiques. The museum holds a superb collection of ornate French furniture and decorative arts, with coffers, chandeliers, wall-lights, and tapestries, dating from the reign of Louis XIV to the Napoleonic era (1643–1815).

The museum traces the development of handwritten and illuminated manuscripts from the sixth to the 16th century, and holds an impressive collection of masterpieces from different historical periods such as the Byzantine, Ottoman, Romanesque, Gothic, and the Renaissance.

Santa Monica ②

Map B4. *90,000.* *1920 Main St, (310) 393-7593.* *Santa Monica Festival (May).* **www**.santamonica.com

With its fresh sea breezes, mild climate, and friendly streets, Santa Monica has been the star of the Los Angeles coastline since the 1890s, when trolleys linked it to the city, and beach parties became the rage. In the early days, it lived a dual life as a sleepy coastal town and the headquarters for offshore gambling ships. In the 1920s and 30s, movie stars such as Cary Grant and Mary Pickford bought land here, creating "the Gold Coast." Following the success of the television series *Baywatch*, the popular beach and pier gained worldwide fame. But the city, perched on a high yellow cliff overlooking Santa Monica Bay, is also noted for its restaurants, shopping areas, and vibrant arts scene. Lush parks dot the city's landscape, with none quite as beautiful as **Palisades Park**, on the bluff overlooking the ocean. Stretching 1.5 miles

Street entertainer playing guitar

Tall palm trees lining the road in Palisades Park, Santa Monica

For hotels and restaurants in this region see p722 and p726

The Chiat Day Mojo Advertising Agency, designed by Frank Gehry

(2.5 km) along the cliff's edge, this narrow, well-manicured park is one of the best spots to watch the sun set. For the quintessential California experience, take a walk or jog along the paths, with the ocean as a backdrop and the towering palms overhead. At the northern end, the aptly named Inspiration Point has great views of the bay, stretching from Malibu to Palos Verdes.

Inland, between Wilshire Boulevard and Broadway, is **Third Street Promenade**. Once a decaying shopping street, this boulevard has undergone a major face-lift and is now one of the liveliest places in Los Angeles. Its three pedestrian blocks are lined with shops, cafés, bookstores, and theaters. At night the mood is especially festive, with street performers entertaining visitors with music, dance, and magic tricks.

Santa Monica's other important shopping area is Main Street, which runs south toward Venice. It abounds in a wide range of shops, restaurants, and galleries. Many examples of public art are displayed along the street, such as Paul Conrad's *Chain Reaction*, a stainless-steel and copper-link chain statement against nuclear war. The Frank Gehry-designed **Chiat Day Mojo Advertising Agency** building, shaped like a pair of binoculars, dominates the street. Main Street also features the California Heritage Museum, which has the distinction of showcasing various periods in the state's history.

Northeast of the beach, the 1908 **Santa Monica Pier** is the West Coast's oldest amusement pier, with bumper cars, roller coasters, and a giant Ferris wheel. There is also the 1922 carousel that featured in Paul Newman's 1973 film, *The Sting*. **Bergamot Station** is a large, sprawling 5.5-acre (2-ha) arts complex that stands on the site of an abandoned trolley station. The crude buildings are constructed out of aluminum siding, but with an added touch of elegant high-tech styling. More than 20 galleries display the latest in contemporary as well as radical art. The Santa Monica Museum of Art, within the Bergamot Station, focuses on the work of contemporary artists, particularly those who are involved in performance art.

Santa Monica Pier
Colorado & Ocean Aves. ***Tel*** *(310) 458-8900, (310) 266-8744 Pacific Park information.* *daily.* **Carousel** *11am–5pm Mon–Thu, 11am–10pm Sat–Sun.* *(310) 395-4248.* **www**.santamonicapier.org

Bergamot Station
2525 Michigan Ave. ***Tel*** *(310) 829-5854.* *10am–5pm Tue–Fri, 11am–5:30pm Sat.* *Sun, public hols.*

Venice ③

Map B5. *2904 Washington Blvd, Suite 100, (310) 822-5425.* **www**.venicechamber.net

Founded by tobacco tycoon Abbot Kinney, as a US version of Venice (Italy), this lively beach town was a swampland little more than 100 years ago. Hoping to spark a cultural renaissance in California, Kinney built a system of canals, and imported gondolas to punt along the waterways. Today, only a few of the original canals remain, the rest having been filled in. The best place to see the canals is on **Dell Avenue**, where old bridges, boats, and ducks grace the waterways.

However, the town is best known for the bustling, circus atmosphere of its beach. On the boardwalk during weekends, men and women whiz past on bicycles and skates, while a zany array of jugglers, acrobats, and one-man bands captivate the crowds. Muscle Beach, where Arnold Schwarzenegger used to work out, still attracts body builders.

Man-made canal in Venice

RAYMOND CHANDLER

American novelist Raymond Chandler (1888–1959) set several of his works in Santa Monica, a city that he loathed and thinly disguised as sleazy Bay City in *Farewell, My Lovely*. Corruption, vice, and the city's offshore gambling circuit of the 1920s and 1930s are well documented in his portrayal of Santa Monica. His novels, such as *The Big Sleep*, *The High Window, and The Long Goodbye,* depicting the dark side of L.A., were made into films. A leading figure of the so-called hard-boiled school of detective writing of the period, Chandler's famous detective Philip Marlowe epitomized a tough, unsentimental point of view.

Raymond Chandler

Museum of Tolerance ④

Map C4. 9786 W Pico Blvd. ***Tel*** *(310) 772-2505.* *10am–5pm Mon–Fri, 11am–5pm Sun.* *Sat, Jan 1, Thanksgiving, Dec 25, & all major Jewish hols.* **www**.museumoftolerance.com

Dedicated to the promotion of respect and understanding among all people, this museum focuses on the history of racism and prejudice in the United States, and on the European Holocaust experience.

The museum tour begins in the **Tolerancenter**, where visitors are challenged to confront racism and bigotry through interactive exhibits. A computerized wall map locates more than 250 known racist groups in the US, while a 16-screen video wall depicts the 1960s Civil Rights struggle in the country. Interactive videos also pose questions of responsible citizenship and social justice. They offer footage and interviews of the 1992 L.A. race riots, in which 26 people were killed and 3,000 homes destroyed. In the **Whisper Gallery** visitors actually hear racial and sexual taunts so that they can experience these themselves. The Holocaust section has a re-creation of the Wannsee Conference, in which Third Reich leaders decide on the "The Final Solution of the Jewish Question," outlined right down to its harrowing implementation in a reproduced gas chamber. Some of the exhibits may not be suitable for children under the age of 10.

Entrance to UCLA at the Armand Hammer Museum of Art

Westwood & UCLA ⑤

Map B4. **UCLA Campus** *(310) 825-4321.* **www**.ucla.edu **Westwood Village** *LA Visitor Information Center, 685 Figueroa St, (213) 689-8822.*

With its wide range of academic departments and professional schools, boasting a strength of over 35,000 students, the 419-acre-(170-ha) University of California Los Angeles (UCLA) is a city within a city. The original campus was designed in 1925 to resemble the Romanesque towns of Europe. But as the university expanded, more modern architecture was favored. The disappointing mix of bland structures that resulted is redeemed by the beautiful landscaped grounds. The four red-brick buildings that make up the **Royce Quadrangle** are the oldest on UCLA's campus. Built in the Italian Romanesque style, Royce, Kinsey, and Haines Halls and Powell Library far surpass the other buildings at UCLA in beauty.

Exhibition on racial prejudice at the Museum of Tolerance

Since it was first developed in 1928, Westwood Village with its pleasant, pedestrian-friendly streets has been one of the most successful shopping districts in Southern California. It remains the most densely packed movie-theater district in the US, with some theaters offering sneak previews of the latest films. South of Westwood, the **Hammer Museum** holds the art collection of oil industry businessman Armand Hammer (1899–1990). The Hammer collection includes a variety of Impressionist and Post-Impressionist works by such artists as Claude Monet, Camille Pissarro, and Vincent Van Gogh. Southeast of the museum, the tranquil **Westwood Memorial Park** marks the final resting place of several celebrities such as Dean Martin, Peter Lorre, Natalie Wood, and most famously, Marilyn Monroe.

Tucked away in a shady canyon northeast of Westwood, the serene **Mildred E. Mathias Botanical Garden** contains a wide variety of plants in its 7 acres (3 ha), with almost 4,000 rare and native species.

Farther north, UCLA's **Fowler Museum of Cultural History** holds exhibitions that focus on the prehistoric, historic, and contemporary societies of Africa, Asia, the Americas, and Oceania. The collection has 750,000 artifacts and is one of the nation's leading university museums.

Hammer Museum
10899 Wilshire Blvd. ***Tel*** *(310) 443-7000.* *11am–7pm Tue, Wed, Fri, Sat; 11am–9pm Thu; 11am–5pm Sun.* *Jul 4, Thanksgiving, Dec 25.* *(free Thu).* **www**.hammer.ucla.edu

Fowler Museum of Cultural History
308 Charles E. Young Dr. ***Tel*** *(310) 825-4361.* *noon–5pm Wed–Sun (until 8pm Thu).* *Mon–Tue, public hols.* **www**.fowler.ucla.edu

For hotels and restaurants in this region see p722 and p726

The Golden Triangle ⑥

Map C4.

The area bordered by Santa Monica Boulevard, Wilshire Boulevard, and North Crescent Drive is the business district of Beverly Hills, known as the "Golden Triangle." The shops, restaurants, and art galleries lining the streets are some of the most luxurious in the world. Cutting through the middle is **Rodeo Drive**, one of the most celebrated shopping streets. It derives its name from El Rancho Rodeo de las Aguas ("the Ranch of the Gathering of Waters"), the name of an early Spanish land grant that included Beverly Hills. Today, Rodeo Drive's wide, tree-lined sidewalks house Italian designer boutiques and the best names in fashion, such as Gucci and Christian Dior, world-class jewelers, and many leading L.A. retailers. The place is also a prime area for celebrity-spotting.

Next to it, on Wilshire Boulevard, the cream of American department stores offer a heady mix of style and opulence. Around the corner, **2 Rodeo**, developed in 1990 as a mock-European shopping street, is one of the most expensive retail centers ever built.

At the eastern end of the Golden Triangle lies the MGM Building. Built in 1920, it was the headquarters of the newly formed Metro-Goldwyn- Mayer film studios.

Façade of the Beverly Hills Civic Center in Los Angeles

To the north are the beautifully manicured Beverly Gardens and the elegant **Beverly Hills Civic Center**, with its landmark Spanish Colonial **City Hall**. Designed in 1932 by local firm Koerner and Gage, the hall's majestic tower, capped by a tiled cupola, has now become a symbol of the European-inspired city of Beverly Hills. In 1990, architect Charles Moore linked the building to a new Civic Center by a series of pedestrianized courtyards. On the upper levels, balconies and arcaded corridors continue the Spanish Colonial theme. The modern section houses a beautiful public library as well as the local fire and police stations. Billboards are banned in the area, and a height restriction of three stories is imposed on any new buildings, leaving City Hall to dominate the skyline.

The latest addition to the Golden Triangle, the **Paley Center for Media** on North Beverly Drive, holds a collection of more than 140,000 television and radio shows and offers a comprehensive history of broadcasting. Visitors can watch and listen to news and a collection of entertainment and sports programs from the earliest days of radio and television to the present. Pop music fans can see footage of the early Beatles or of a young Elvis Presley making his television debut, while sports enthusiasts can relive classic Olympic competitions. The museum also hosts exhibitions, seminars, and screenings on specialized topics and selected actors or directors.

North of Golden Triangle, above Sunset Boulevard *(see pp664–5)*, lie the palatial estates, the famed **Hollywood Actors' Homes** that have made Beverly Hills the symbol of success for those in the entertainment industry. When, in 1920, Mary Pickford and Douglas Fairbanks Sr. built their mansion, **Pickfair**, at the top of Summit Drive, everyone else followed – and stayed. Sunset Boulevard divides the haves from the have-nots: people who live south of it may be rich, but those who live to the north of the road are considered to be the super-rich. Houses come in almost every architectural style; some are ostentatious, others surprisingly modest. They can be toured along a 5-mile (8-km) drive, maps for which are available from street vendors. Visitors must remember that film stars' homes are private residences.

Cushion on display in the Gucci boutique

Mansion on exclusive Palm Drive, Beverly Hills

Beverly Hills Civic Center
455 N Rexford Dr. ***Tel*** *(310) 285-1000.* *7:30am–5:30pm Mon–Thu, 8am–5pm Fri.* *public hols.* www.beverlyhills.org

Paley Center for Media
465 N Beverly Dr. ***Tel*** *(310) 786-1000.* *noon–5pm Wed–Sun.* *public hols.* www.paleycenter.org

2 Rodeo
268 N Rodeo Dr. ***Tel*** *(310) 247-7040.* www.2rodeo.com

Sunset Boulevard ⑦

Sunset Boulevard has been associated with the movies since the 1920s, when it was a dirt track linking the burgeoning Hollywood studios with the hillside homes of the screen stars. Its liveliest and most historically rich stretch, Sunset Strip, is filled with restaurants, luxury hotels, and nightclubs. Once a magnet for gamblers and bootleggers, this 1.5-mile (2.4-km) stretch held famous nightclubs such as Ciro's and Mocambo – where legend says Margarita Cansino met studio boss Harry Cohen, who renamed her Rita Hayworth. While the Strip continues to be the center of L.A.'s nightlife, the renaissance of old "Hollywood" is the hip happening place with lots of nightclubs, restaurants, and shops, especially at the Hollywood & Highland Center.

A view of Sunset Strip from Crescent Heights

The Roxy
This trendy club stands on the site of the old Club Largo. Many famous acts have played here, from Springsteen to Nirvana.

The Comzedy Store, *a world-famous spot for stand-up comedy, occupies the site of the 1940s nightclub Ciro's.*

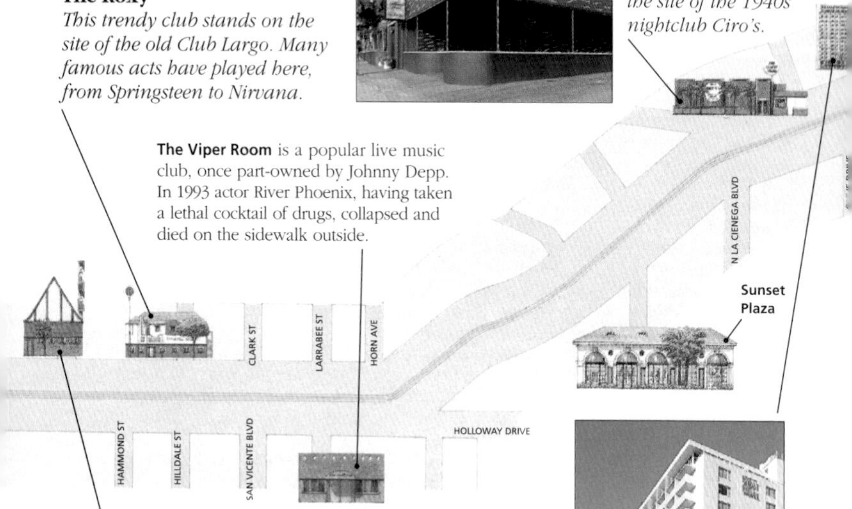

The Viper Room is a popular live music club, once part-owned by Johnny Depp. In 1993 actor River Phoenix, having taken a lethal cocktail of drugs, collapsed and died on the sidewalk outside.

The Rainbow Bar & Grill, formerly the Villa Nova, has walls lined with wine casks and gold records. Vincente Minnelli proposed to Judy Garland here and, eight years later in 1953, Marilyn Monroe met Joe DiMaggio here on a blind date.

Sunset Plaza
Lined with chic stores and cafés, this area is best explored on foot.

Hyatt West Hollywood
Visiting rock stars regularly frequent this hotel. Jim Morrison stayed here when he played with The Doors at the nearby Whisky A Go Go.

For hotels and restaurants in this region see p722 and p726

Sunset Tower Hotel
Formerly the Argyle Hotel, this Art Deco landmark was an apartment complex in Hollywood's heyday, home to stars like Clark Gable.

Chateau Marmont
The hotel was modeled on a Loire Valley château. When it opened in 1929, it attracted actors such as Errol Flynn and Greta Garbo. Among today's regulars are Leonardo DiCaprio and Jude Law.

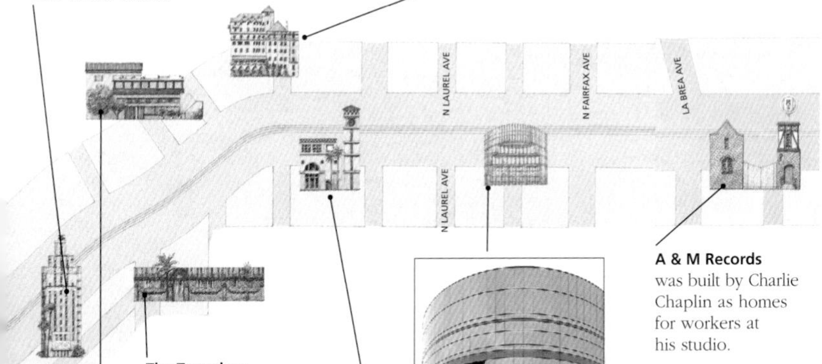

A & M Records was built by Charlie Chaplin as homes for workers at his studio.

The Trocadero nightclub had Nat "King" Cole as its pianist in its heyday. Only three steps remain of the old building.

Directors' Guild of America
This is one of the many offices on the Strip connected with the film industry.

Miyagi's, formerly the Roxbury Club, is a popular spot for sushi lovers. It stands on the site of the 1940s Players Club, owned by movie director Preston Sturges.

Schwab's Pharmacy
Now a Virgin Megastore, this former drugstore was a popular meeting place for film stars and columnists. Facing it, the legendary Garden of Allah apartment complex once held such residents as Scott Fitzgerald and Dorothy Parker.

House of Blues
This tin-roofed blues bar has been transported from Clarksdale, Mississippi. It is part-owned by the actor Dan Ackroyd, who co-starred with John Belushi in the 1980 cult movie The Blues Brothers.

Billboards
Huge billboards, handpainted by Hollywood's finest artists to promote new films or personalities, are landmark symbols of Sunset Strip.

Mulholland Drive ⑧

Map C2. Off Hwys 1 & 27, from Hollywood Fwy to Leo Carrillo State Beach.

Mulholland Drive, one of the most famous roads in Los Angeles, runs for nearly 50 miles (80 km) from north Hollywood to the Malibu Coast. As it winds along the ridge of the Santa Monica Mountains, the route offers spectacular views of Los Angeles and the San Fernando Valley.

The road was named for William Mulholland (1855–1935), who designed a series of aqueducts to channel water into Los Angeles. He oversaw the completion of Mulholland Drive in 1924.

Hollywood Boulevard ⑨

Map D3.

One of the most famous streets in the world, Hollywood Boulevard's name is still redolent with glamor. Despite its recent run-down look, many of its landmark sights retain the original appeal and charisma.

Perhaps the only pavement in the city to be cleaned six times a week, the **Walk of Fame** is set with more than 2,500 polished marble stars. Since 1960, luminaries from the worlds of film, radio, television, theater, and music have been immortalized on the boulevard and on Vine Street. However, stardom does not come easily: each personality must be sponsored and approved by the Chamber of Commerce, and pay a $7,500 installation fee.

Façade of the well-known Grauman's Chinese Theatre

The famed **Grauman's Chinese Theatre** on the north side of the boulevard has changed little since its opening in 1927, with the premiere of Cecil B. de Mille's *King of Kings*. The theater's creator, Sid Grauman, is also credited with one of Hollywood's longest-running publicity stunts: its famed autograph patio with hand- and footprints of stars. Legend has it that the custom began when silent screen star Norma Talmadge accidentally stepped on the wet cement. Grauman then invited her, along with Mary Pickford and Douglas Fairbanks Sr. to legitimately leave their imprints. Across the road stands the **Clarion Hotel Hollywood Roosevelt**, frequented by famous figures such as Marilyn Monroe, Clark Gable, and Ernest Hemingway. It was the locale of the first Academy Awards ceremony in 1929. Nearby, the restored **El Capitan Theater** was the venue for many movie openings. Neon lights draw visitors to this theater that now has premiers of Disney animations. To its west, **Ripley's Believe It or Not!** is devoted to the bizarre. Farther along, **Frederick's of Hollywood** is the flagship store of Fredrick Mellinger's famous mail-order lingerie business launched in 1946. Its Celebrity Lingerie Hall of Fame includes Marilyn Monroe's bra from the film *Let's Make Love* (1960), Tony Curtis's black lace bra from *Some Like It Hot* (1959), and Madonna's black bustier.

Star in Walk of Fame

Walk of Fame
6541 Hollywood Blvd, (323) 461-2804. (323) 469-8311.

Grauman's Chinese Theatre
6925 Hollywood Blvd. ***Tel** (323) 464-8111. daily.*
www.manntheatres.com

THE RISE OF HOLLYWOOD

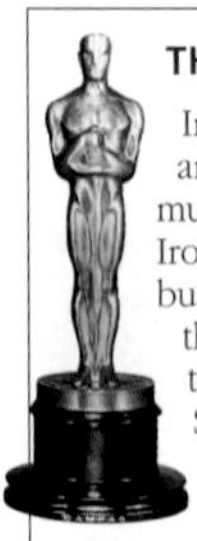
Oscar statuette

In 1887, prohibitionist Harvey Henderson Wilcox and his wife, Daeida, set up a sober, Christian community in an L.A. suburb and called it Hollywood. Ironically, over the next several decades the movie business with all its decadence came to replace their Utopia. The takeover started in 1913 with the filming of Cecil B. deMille's *The Squaw Man*. Silent film stars such as Charlie Chaplin and Mary Pickford were succeeded by icons of a more glamorous Hollywood, such as Errol Flynn and Mae West. Wall Street bankers soon realized their potential and invested heavily in the film industry.

Hollywood Bowl ⑩

Map D3. 2301 N Highland Ave. ***Tel** (323) 850-2000. late Jun–late Sep.* **Box office** *10am–6pm Tue–Sun.*
www.hollywoodbowl.com

Situated in a natural amphitheater that was once revered by the Cahuenga Pass Gabrielino Indians, the 60-acre (24-ha) Hollywood Bowl has now become sacred to Angelenos. The summer home of the L.A. Philharmonic since 1922, the site attracts thousands of people on warm evenings to listen to the orchestra.

Much altered over the years, the shell-shaped stage was first designed in 1929 by Lloyd Wright, son of architect

Frank Lloyd Wright. Rumor says that material for the building was taken from the set of Douglas Fairbanks Sr's movie *Robin Hood*.

The Edmund D. Edelman Hollywood Bowl Museum explores the site's rich history through videos, old programs and posters, and memorabilia of the artists who have come here, from violinist Jascha Heifetz to the Beatles.

Hollywood Bowl, nestling in the Hollywood Hills

Farmers Market ⑪

Map D3. 6333 W 3rd St. ***Tel*** *(323) 933-9211.* *9am–9pm Mon–Fri, 9am–8pm Sat, 10am–7pm Sun.* *Jan 1, Thanksgiving, Dec 25.* **www**.farmersmarketla.com

During the Great Depression in 1934 a group of farmers began selling their produce directly to the public in a field at the edge of town. Since then, Farmers Market has been a favorite meeting place for Angelenos. Bustling with stalls and shops selling everything from fresh produce to antiques and T-shirts, the market also has some of the best cafés and restaurants in the city.

Miracle Mile ⑫

Map D4. Wilshire Blvd between La Brea & Fairfax Aves. *685 S Figueroa St, (213) 689-8822; 6801 Hollywood Blvd, (323) 467-6412.*

Developer A.W. Ross bought 18 acres (7.2 ha) of land along Wilshire Boulevard in 1920 and built an upscale shopping district, with wide streets meant for cars and Art Deco buildings, earning it the name "Miracle Mile." Today, dotted with grocery stores, this stretch is a shadow of its former self. The western end of the Miracle Mile has fared better. With its five museums, including the **Los Angeles County Museum of Art** (LACMA), the area is now known as Museum Row.

The largest encyclopedic art museum west of Chicago, LACMA offers a comprehensive survey of the history of world art, with a collection of over 100,000 objects dating from the prehistoric to contemporary times. Collections include pre-Columbian stone objects, Islamic art, and a wide selection of European and American decorative arts, paintings, and sculpture. Especially impressive are its collection of scrolls and ceramics from the Far East.

Nearby, the **Page Museum at the La Brea Tar Pits** has over one million fossils discovered at the La Brea Tar Pits. The tar, formed some 42,000 years ago, entrapped and killed animals who came here to drink water. Their bones were then fossilized. For centuries the tar was used by the Native Americans, Mexicans, and Spanish to waterproof baskets and roofs. In 1906, geologists discovered the largest collection of fossils of mammals, birds, reptiles, plants, and insects from the Pleistocene Epoch ever found in one place. The only human skeleton found in the pits is that of the "La Brea Woman." A hologram changes her from a skeleton to a fully fleshed person and back again. The **Peterson Automative Museum** traces the evolution of the nation's car culture with detailed displays of vintage cars, old showrooms, and cars of filmstars, such as Rita Hayworth's 1953 Cadillac and Clark Gable's Mercedes-Benz. Its other exhibits include a 1920s garage; an opulent 1930s car showroom; and a 1950s drive-in restaurant. Farther along, the **Craft and Folk Art Museum**, houses more than 3,000 folk art and craft objects from around the world. These range from objects as diverse as 19th-century American quilts to contemporary furniture and African masks.

Los Angeles County Museum of Art (LACMA), Miracle Mile

African mask at the Craft Museum

LACMA
5905 Wilshire Blvd. ***Tel*** *(323) 857-6000.* *noon–8pm Mon–Tue & Thu (to 9pm Fri), 11am–8pm Sat–Sun.* *Wed, Thanksg., Dec 25.* *(free 2nd Tue of month & after 5pm).* **www**.lacma.org

Page Museum at the La Brea Tar Pits
5801 Wilshire Blvd. ***Tel*** *(323) 934-7243.* *9:30am–5pm daily.* *Jan 1, Jul 4, Thanksgiving, Dec 25.* *(free first Tue of month).* **www**.tarpits.org

Model of La Brea Tar Pits in the Page Museum

Exposition Park & University of Southern California ⑬

Map E4. *DASH Shuttle C from Business District.* *81.* **Natural History Museum of L.A. County** ***Tel*** *(213) 763-3466.* **www**.nhm.org **L.A. Memorial Coliseum** ***Tel*** *(213) 747-7111.* **www**.lacoliseum.com **University of Southern California** ***Tel*** *(213) 740-5371.* **www**.usc.edu

Located southwest of downtown, Exposition Park began life in the 1880s as an area of open-air markets, carnivals, and horse-racing. By the end of the century, the district was rife with drinking, gambling, and prostitution. When Judge William Miller Bowen's Sunday school pupils began skipping church to enjoy local temptations, he pushed for the transformation of the area into a cultural landmark that today includes three museums. The **Natural History Museum of Los Angeles County**, at the heart of the park, displays a variety of specimens and artifacts, alongside an insect zoo and a hands-on Discovery Center. A short drive southeast leads to the **California Museum of Science and Industry**, with its interactive exhibits aiming to make science accessible to all.

Farther east lies the **California African-American Museum** that is a record of Afro-American achievements in various fields. The park is also home to the **Los Angeles Memorial Coliseum**, which was the site of the 1932 and 1984 Olympics, and was also home to the University's Trojan football team. Across the street, stands the 152-acre (62-ha) **University of Southern California** that houses about 28,000 students.

Natural History Museum at Exposition Park

Rotunda of Los Angeles City Hall

Los Angeles Central Library ⑭

Map E4. 630 W 5th St. ***Tel*** *(213) 228-7000.* *10am–8pm Mon–Thu, 10am–6pm Fri–Sat, 1–5pm Sun.* *public hols.* **www**.lapl.org

Built in 1926, this civic treasure was struck by an arson attack in 1986. Seven years later, after a $213.9 million renovation program sympathetic to the original architecture, the library's capacity was doubled to more than 2.1 million books.

The original building combines Beaux Arts grandeur with Byzantine, Egyptian, and Roman architectural elements. The library also hosts prose and poetry readings, and concerts.

The **First Interstate World Center** across the street is a 73-story office block designed by I.M. Pei. At 1,017 ft (310 m), it is the tallest building in the city.

Los Angeles City Hall ⑮

Map E4. 200 N Spring St. ***Tel*** *(213) 485-2121.* *8am–5pm Mon–Fri.* *public hols.* *from Main St.* *advance reservations required.* **www**.lacity.org

When it was built in 1928, sand from every county in California and water from each of the state's 21 missions was added to the City Hall's mortar. The tower of this 28-story structure is still one of L.A.'s most familiar landmarks. It served as the Daily Planet building in the television series *Superman*. Inside, the rotunda has a inlaid-tile dome and great acoustics. The **Los Angeles Children's Museum** across the street has some 20 hands-on activities linked by a series of ramps. Called the Discovery Maze, it was designed by Frank Gehry.

Music Center ⑯

Map E4. 135 N Grand Ave. ***Tel*** *(213) 972-7211.* **Dorothy Chandler Pavilion box office** *noon–6pm Tue–Sat, noon–4pm Sun.* **Mark Taper Forum & Ahmanson Theater box offices** *noon–8pm Tue–Sun.* **www**.musiccenter.org

Music Center Plaza and Fountain

This performing arts complex is situated at the northern end of Bunker Hill. The Dorothy Chandler Pavilion is named after the wife of the former publisher of the *Los Angeles Times*. It is home to the Center theatre group, the Los Angeles Opera, the Los Angeles Master Chorale, and, from fall to spring, the Los Angeles Philharmonic. The Ahmanson Theater has movable walls to adjust the auditorium size, and it stages Broadway plays. The Mark Taper Forum has won almost every theatrical prize in the US. It presents first-class plays. The Walt Disney Concert Hall opened here in October 2003; it is the home of the L.A. Philharmonic Master Chorale.

For hotels and restaurants in this region see p722 and p726

Grand Central Market ⑰

Map E4. 317 S Broadway. ***Tel*** *(213) 624-2378.* *9am–6pm daily.* *Jan 1, Thanksgiving, Dec 25.* **www**.grandcentralsquare.com

Angelenos have been coming to this vibrant indoor bazaar since 1917. Today, over 40 stallholders operate inside the marketplace, selling fruit, vegetables, meat, and herbs. The market's Latin American clientele come here to buy exotic products from their home countries, such as fresh Nogales cacti and beans from El Salvador.

Billed as the "shortest railway in the world," the adjacent **Angels Flight** funicular transported riders between Hill Street and Bunker Hill for almost 70 years. By 1969, Bunker Hill had degenerated, and the city dismantled the funicular, promising to reinstall it once the area had been redeveloped. It fulfilled that vow in 1996, some 27 years later.

Angels Flight
Between Grand, Hill, 3rd & 4th Sts. ***Tel*** *(213) 626-1901.* *6:30am–10pm daily.* **www**.angelsflight.com

Little Tokyo ⑱

Map F4. *244 S San Pedro St, (213) 628-2725.* **www**.jaccc.org

Situated southeast of the City Hall, Little Tokyo attracts more than 200,000 visitors to its Japanese markets and temples. The first Japanese settled here in 1884. Today, the heart of the area is the Japanese American Cultural and Community Center, from which cultural activities are organized. Nearby, the Japanese Village Plaza is a lively place to shop. Housed in a former Buddhist Temple, the **Japanese American National Museum** traces the history of Japanese-American life in the US.

To its east on North Central Avenue the **Geffen Contemporary at MOCA**, once an old police garage, is used

Japanese American Art Museum, Little Tokyo

as an exhibition space for the Museum of Contemporary Art (MOCA). Redesigned by Frank Gehry, the warehouse is a permanent fixture of the L.A. arts scene, hosting exhibition highlights from MOCA.

Japanese American National Museum
369 E 1st St. ***Tel*** *(213) 625-0414.* *noon–8pm Thu, 11am–5pm Fri–Sun.* *Jan 1, Thanksgiving, Dec 25.* **www**.janm.org

Museum of Contemporary Art ⑲

Map E4. 250 S Grand Ave. ***Tel*** *(213) 621-1745.* *11am–5pm Mon, Fri, 11am–8pm Thu, 11am–6pm Sat, Sun.* *some public hols.* *(free 5–8pm Thu).* **www**.moca.org

Rated as one of the ten best works of architecture in the United States, the Museum of Contemporary Art (MOCA), designed by Japanese architect Arata Isozaki, presents an intriguing combination of pyramids, cylinders, and cubes. It holds a respectable selection of post-1940 art, including Pop Art and Abstract Expressionist works by artists as diverse as Mark Rothko, Robert Rauschenberg, and Claes Oldenburg.

El Pueblo ⑳

Map F4. Downtown L.A. between N Main St & Olvera St & N Alamenda St.

The oldest part of the city, El Pueblo de la Reina de Los Angeles was founded in 1781 by Felipe de Neve, the Spanish governor of California. Today, El Pueblo is a State Historic Monument, housing some of the city's oldest buildings, such as the Old Plaza Church and the Avila Adobe, the city's oldest existing house, furnished as it would have been in the 1840s. Olvera Street, preserved as a Mexican marketplace in the 1920s, abounds in shops selling colorful Mexican dresses, leather sandals, *piñatas* (clay or paper-mâché animals), and snacks like *churros*, a Spanish-Mexican fried bread. During festivals, such as the Blessing of the Animals, Cinco de Mayo *(see p28)*, and the Mexican Independence Day fiesta (September 13–15), El Pueblo is ablaze with color and sound.

Nearby, the 1939 grand passenger terminal, **Union Station**, is a blend of Spanish Mission, Moorish, and Streamline Moderne architectural styles. Stars of 1940s films were photographed here. Recently it has been the location for several movies, such as Sydney Pollack's *The Way We Were* (1973).

The distinctive façade of Union Station, El Pueblo

Lummis Home and Garden ㉑

Map F3. 200 E Ave 43. ***Tel*** *(323) 222-0546.* *noon–4pm Fri–Sun.* ***Donation.*** **www**.socalhistory.org

Also known as "El Alisal," Spanish for "Place of the Sycamore," this house was the home of journalist, photographer, artist, and historian Charles Fletcher Lummis (1859–1928). The structure, which Lummis built himself, displays various design elements – Native American, Mission Revival, and Arts and Crafts – revealing the influences in his life.

Today, Lummis Home is the headquarters of the Historical Society of Southern California. It exhibits Native American artifacts from the owner's collection, and its impressive interiors include a grand Art Nouveau fireplace.

The garden, originally planted with vegetables and fruit trees, now grows drought-tolerant and native southern California plant species.

Restored interior of the 19th-century Lummis Home

Southwest Museum of the American Indian ㉒

Map F3. 234 Museum Dr. ***Tel*** *(323) 221-2164.* *10am–5pm Tue–Sun.* *Jan 1, Easter Sun, Thanksgiving, Dec 25.* **www**.southwestmuseum.org

With one of the nation's richest collections of Native American art and artifacts, this museum was the brainchild of

Mission Revival-style Southwest Museum

Charles Fletcher Lummis, who donated many of his personal holdings to start the collection. During his trek from Ohio to L.A. in the late 19th century, Lummis spent a long time in the Southwest, becoming one of the first whites to appreciate the history and culture of Native Americans.

The museum displays tribal artifacts from prehistoric times to the present day, providing an excellent overview of Native American heritage. The collection of 11,000 baskets is particularly impressive.

Sequoyah Indian relief

Set atop Mount Washington, the Mission Revival building offers excellent views of downtown L.A. to the south.

The museum reopened following renovation in 2010.

Griffith Park ㉓

Map E3. *96.* *6am–10pm daily.* *4730 Crystal Springs Dr, (213) 485-5027.* **www**.laparks.org

Griffith Park is a 4,000-acre (1,600-ha) wilderness of rugged hills, forested valleys, and green meadows in the center of L.A. The land was donated to the city in 1896 by Colonel Griffith J. Griffith, a Welshman who emigrated to the US in 1865 and made a fortune speculating in mining. Today, people come to Griffith Park to escape from the city crowds, visit the sights, picnic, hike, or go horseback riding.

The **Griffith Observatory** is located on the southern slope of Mount Hollywood, and commands stunning views of the L.A. basin below. Inside, the Hall of Science explains important scientific concepts with exhibits such as the Foucault Pendulum, demonstrating the earth's rotation. Visitors are taken on a journey through space and time, as some 9,000 stars and planets are projected onto the ceiling at the Planetarium Theater. On the roof, the Zeiss Telescope is open to the public on clear nights.

Northeast of the observatory lies the **Greek Theater**. Styled after an ancient Greek amphitheater, this open-air music venue has excellent acoustics. On summer nights, more than 6,000 people sit under the stars and enjoy popular and classical music performances.

Farther north, in the hills just off Griffith Park Drive, is a 1926 merry-go-round. Adults and children can still ride on its 66 horses and listen to its giant band organ.

A short drive north leads to the 113-acre (46-ha) hilly compound of **Los Angeles Zoo**, housing more than 1,200 mammals, reptiles, and birds living in simulations of their natural habitats. Many newborn creatures can be seen in the Animal Nursery, including some from the zoo's respected breeding program for rare and endangered species. The zoo also hosts several animal shows, aimed at a young audience.

Opposite the zoo, the **Autry National Center** explores the many cultures

View of the Griffith Observatory on Mount Hollywood, Griffith Park

that have shaped the American West. Exhibits include a replica of a 19th-century Mexican-American ranch from Arizona. Founded by the film star Gene Autry, "the Singing Cowboy," the museum also houses a superb collection of movie and television memorabilia.

At the northwestern end of the park, **Travel Town** presents an outdoor collection of vintage trains and cars. Children and adults can climb aboard freight cars and railroad carriages, or ride on a small train. To its east, on Zoo Drive, miniature steam trains run at weekends.

Griffith Observatory
2800 Observatory Rd. ***Tel*** *(213) 473-0800.* *noon–10pm Tue–Fri, 10am–10pm Sat–Sun (reservations required).* *Mon, Thanksg., Dec 25.* *Planetarium.* *limited.* **www**.griffithobs.org

Hollywood Sign ㉔

Map D2. Mount Cahuenga, above Hollywood. *Hollywood Visitors Information Center, 6801 Hollywood Blvd, (323) 467-6412.*

The Hollywood Sign is an internationally recognized symbol of the movie business. Set high up in the Hollywood Hills, it is now a protected historic site. Though visible for miles from many parts of Los Angeles, it is not possible for the public to reach the sign itself, since there is no legitimate trail leading up to the tall 45-ft (13-m) letters.

Erected in 1923, it originally advertised the Hollywoodland housing development of the former *L.A. Times* publisher Harry Chandler. The "land" was removed in 1949. Nearly 30 years later, donors pledged $27,000 per letter for a new sign. It has been the scene of one suicide – that of disappointed would-be actress Peg Entwhistle, who jumped off the "H" in 1932 – and numerous prank spellings, such as "Hollyweed," acknowledging the more lenient marijuana laws of the 1970s; and "UCLA" during a football game.

Universal Studios ㉕

Map D2. 100 Universal City Plaza, Universal City. ***Tel*** *1-800-UNIVERSAL.* *424.* *Jun–Sep: 8am–10pm daily; Oct–May: 9am–7pm daily.* *Thanksgiving, Dec 25.* **www**.universalstudioshollywood.com

Spread over 415 acres (168 ha), the world's largest working movie and television studio and theme park, Universal Studios Hollywood started out as a poultry farm. In 1915, Carl Laemmle bought a chicken ranch on this site and moved his film studio here from Hollywood. He charged visitors 25 cents to see films being made, and guests could also buy fresh eggs. With the advent of the "talkies" in 1927, the sets needed quiet and the visits stopped.

Jurassic Park sign

In 1964, Universal Studios Hollywood launched its **Studio Tour** tram ride, a behind-the-scenes view of Hollywood movie making. The Studio Tour takes guests through movie sets in trams, outfitted with state-of-the-art audio and video systems. Celebrity hosts, such as actor Jason Alexander and director Ron Howard, narrate the inner workings of the real Hollywood. Passengers experience an earthquake, encounter King Kong and Jaws, and survive a collapsing bridge, a flash flood, and an avalanche. If they are lucky, visitors can even see a film being made. The popular Simpsons TV show is the theme of a motion simulator that lets you join the family on a hilarious visit to low-budget theme park Krustyland.

Another popular attraction is **CityWalk Promenade**, designed by architect Jon Jerde. With its festive assortment of façades for the shops, restaurants, bars, and theaters, Universal's CityWalk is being hailed as the entertainment mecca of Southern California. It is also one of the prime areas for visitors to buy Hollywood memorabilia.

Universal's Entertainment Center and the lower portions of the studio lots give an insight into the special effects and stunts used to make a film, and offer some of the park's most spectacular thrill rides. The audience becomes part of the wild jetskiing in the sea water spectacular, **WaterWorld**, they are terrified by monsters at the **Terminator 2:3D** show, and panicked in the heat of the blazing inferno in a re-creation of the final scene of the fire-fighting film *Backdraft*. The ride **Jurassic Park**, literally recaptures the thrill of the movie, while **Shrek 4-D**, reunites the talents of Eddie Murphy, Mike Myers, and Cameron Diaz in an all-new animated saga based on the Oscar-winning film *Shrek*. Another blockbuster ride, **Revenge of the Mummy**, takes visitors through hair-raising adventures in the labyrinth of the mummy's tomb, past Egyptian burial chambers and waterfalls of scorpions.

Terrifying the audience at the Terminator 2:3D show, Universal Studios

Greater Los Angeles

From the freeways, it is hard to appreciate the many treasures that lie within Los Angeles's sprawl. But a short drive beyond the central sights to nearby areas can be surprisingly rewarding. Upscale Pasadena with its delightful old town has some excellent museums and galleries. Farther south, Orange County offers visitors a wide range of attractions, from sandy beaches to cultural sites and museums. For visitors seeking family fun and roller-coaster thrills, there are the homey Knott's Berry Farm, and the fantasy kingdom of Disneyland.

Mausoleum at Huntington, designed by John Russell Pope

Malibu ㉖

Malibu *(310) 456-2489.* **Malibu Lagoon State Beach** ***Tel*** *(818) 880-0363.* *sunrise–sunset daily.* **www**.malibu.org
Adamson House ***Tel*** *(310) 456-8432.* *11am–3pm Wed–Sat.*
Malibu Creek State Park ***Tel*** *(818) 880-0350; for camp bookings (800) 444-7275.* *sunrise–sunset.* **www**.parks.ca.gov

Twenty miles north of Santa Monica Bay, the Rancho Topanga Malibu Sequit was bought in 1887 by Fredrick and May Rindge. The Rindge family fought with the state for many years to keep their property secluded. Eventually failing, they had to sell much of Malibu to film stars such as Bing Crosby and Gary Cooper. Today the **Malibu Colony** is a private, gated compound still favored by people from the entertainment industry.

A few miles east, the **Malibu Lagoon State Beach**, the largest village of Chumash people in the 16th century, is a natural preserve and bird refuge. To its east, Surfrider County Beach is considered by many to be the surfing capital of the world.

Nearby, the Spanish Colonial **Adamson House** with vivid tiles and opulent decor, houses a museum showcasing the history of Malibu.

To the north, the 10,000-acre (4,000-ha) **Malibu Creek State Park** features forests, meadows, waterfalls, picnic areas, and hiking trails. Much of the park was owned by 20th Century Fox until 1974. *M*A*S*H*, *Butch Cassidy and the Sundance Kid*, and *Tarzan* were all filmed here.

Pasadena ㉗

135,000. *79 from downtown.* *300 Green St, (626) 795-9311.* *Tournament of Roses Parade (Jan 1); Pasadena Spring Art Festival (mid-Apr).* **www**.visitpasadena.com

With the completion of the Santa Fe Railroad in 1887, wealthy people from the East Coast, along with artists and bohemians, settled in Pasadena to savor the warm winters of Southern California. This mix of creativity and wealth has resulted in a city with a splendid cultural legacy.

The historic district of **Old Town Pasadena**, at the heart of the city, underwent a recent face-lift ushering in a spate of upscale shops, restaurants, and cafés in restored historic buildings. The highlights of the area include the **Norton Simon Museum** featuring one of the finest collections of Old Masters and Impressionist paintings in the country.

To the north, local architects Charles and Henry Greene's sprawling **Gamble House** is considered a consummate craftsman bungalow by many.

A few miles east of Old Town, opulent San Marino is home to the **Huntington Library, Art Collections, and Botanical Gardens**. Once the estate of railroad tycoon Henry E. Huntington (1850–1927), the Beaux Arts mansion holds one of the most important libraries and collections of 18th-century British and French art in the world. Rare books in the library's collection include priceless objects such as a Gutenberg bible, a Chaucer manuscript, and Benjamin Franklin's handwritten autobiography. The botanical gardens are made up of 15 theme areas: the most popular are the Desert, Japanese, and Shakespearean Gardens.

Huntington Library, Art Collections, & Botanical Gardens
1151 Oxford Rd. ***Tel*** *(626) 405-2100.* *Jun–Aug: 10:30am–4:30pm Tue–Sun; Sep–May: noon–4:30pm Tue–Fri, 10:30am–4:30pm Sat–Sun.* *public hols.* **www**.huntington.org

Watts Towers ㉘

1761–1765 E 107th St, Watts. ***Tel*** *(213) 847-4646.* *10am–4pm Tue–Sat, noon–4pm Sun.* *(Towers).* *Arts Center only.* **www**.wattstowers.us

Watts Towers embodies the perseverance and vision of Italian folk artist Simon Rodia. Between 1921 and 1954, the tile-worker sculpted steel

View across Malibu Lagoon to the Santa Monica Mountains

For hotels and restaurants in this region see p722 and p726

rods and pipes, into a huge skeletal framework, adorning it with shells, tiles, and broken glass. He never gave a reason for building the towers and, upon finishing, deeded the land to a neighbor and left L.A. The towers, standing 100 ft (30 m) at their tallest, are now a State Historic Site. Next to the monument, the Watts Towers Arts Center holds temporary exhibitions of work by African-American artists and also hosts workshops for artists of all ages.

The *Queen Mary*, Long Beach's most famous hotel

Long Beach ㉙

Metro Blue Line from downtown Los Angeles.

With palm trees and ocean as a backdrop, downtown Long Beach is a mixture of carefully restored buildings and modern glass high-rises. At its heart, **Pine Avenue**, lined with stores, cafés, and restaurants, retains the early Midwestern charm that gave the city its nickname, "Iowa by the Sea."

Along the ocean, the restaurants and shops in Shoreline Village offer views of the ocean liner *Queen Mary (see p722)*. The Cunard flagship from 1930s to the 1960s, this luxury liner was converted into a troopship during World War II. It carried more than 80,000 soldiers during its wartime career. At the end of the war, it transported more than 22,000 war brides and children to the US during "Operation Diaper." It was permanently docked for use as a hotel and tourist attraction in 1967. Today, visitors can view part of the original Engine Room, examples of the different accommodations, and an exhibition on the war years.

Nearby, the **Aquarium of the Pacific** is one of the largest aquariums in the United States. It holds 550 species in 17 major habitats, offering visitors a fascinating exploration of marine flora and fauna from the Pacific Ocean's three distinct regions: Southern California/Baja; the Tropical Pacific, and the Northern Pacific.

Queen Mary
Pier J, 1126 Queens Hwy. ***Tel*** *(562) 435-3511.* *Mon–Sat.*
www.queenmary.com

Aquarium of the Pacific
100 Aquarium Way. ***Tel*** *(562) 590-3100.* *9am–6pm daily.*
Dec 25, weekend of the Toyota Grand Prix.
www.aquariumofpacific.org

Knott's Berry Farm ㉚

8039 Beach Blvd, Buena Park.
Tel *(714) 827-1776.* *(714) 220-5200.* *29, 38, 42.* *hours vary per season & day. Call to verify park hours.* *Dec 25.*
www.knotts.com

Located in Buena Vista in Orange County, Knott's Berry Farm has grown from a 1920s boysenberry farm to a 21st-century multi-day entertainment complex. Offering more than 165 different rides and attractions, its main charm lies in its emphasis on authenticity. The **Old West Ghost Town**, in the heart of the park, has original ghost town buildings.

America's very first theme park, Knott's offers six themed areas, dozens of live-action stages, thrill rides, shopping, and dining, as well as a full-fledged resort.

Statues of cowboys on a Ghost Town bench

Cloisters framing Mission San Juan Capistrano's central courtyard

Mission San Juan Capistrano ㉛

26801 Ortega Hwy. ***Tel*** *(949) 234-1300.* *8:30am– 5pm daily.*
Good Fri pm, Thanksg., Dec 25.
Swallow Festival (Mar). **www**.missionsjc.com

This "Jewel of the Missions" was founded in 1776, and its chapel is the only surviving building in California where Fr. Junípero Serra preached. One of the largest in the chain, the mission was built as a self-sufficient community. Its Great Stone Church was destroyed by an earthquake in 1812, leaving a rambling complex of adobe and brick buildings. A restoration of the chapel re-creates the mission's former glory.

Newport Beach ㉜

Hwy 1, S from Los Angeles.

Famous for its million-dollar homes and lifestyles to match, Newport Beach has a 3-mile (5-km) stretch of wide sand and two piers along Orange County's coast. Fresh fish, caught by the historic Dory fishing fleet, is sold beside Newport Pier at the northern end of the beach. Farther inland, the coastal wetland of **Upper Newport Bay Ecological Preserve** is a refuge for wildlife and migratory birds. It also offers a bike path, fishing, and guided tours on foot and by kayak.

Disneyland® Resort (33)

Disney's "Magic Kingdom" in Anaheim is not only the top tourist attraction in California, it is part of the American Dream. Now encompassing the original Disneyland Park, Disney's California Adventure, Downtown Disney, plus three enormous hotels, the Resort has become the model for theme parks around the globe. Visitors to "The Happiest Place on Earth" find fantasy, thrill rides, glittering shows, and shopping in a brightly orchestrated land of lines, fireworks, and Mickey Mouse, which is as American as apple pie.

Exploring the Resort

Spread over 85 acres (34 ha), the original Disneyland Park is divided into eight theme areas or "lands." Transportation around the park is provided by Disneyland Railroad and monorail. Disney's newest venture, Disney's California Adventure Park, is smaller than Disneyland Park and can easily be covered on foot. With three theme areas, it is more suited to teenagers, as the attractions may be too intense for toddlers. At the heart of the Resort, Downtown Disney is a lively area full of restaurants, shops, and entertainment venues.

It takes at least three days to explore the theme parks. Both parks stay open late during the peak seasons. The **Fireworks Show** in Disneyland and in Downtown Disney are fantastic.

DISNEYLAND PARK

Main Street USA is a colorful street lined with historic buildings. Central Plaza is the venue for the daily "Parade of the Stars," featuring Disney characters and scenes from Disney's most famous movies. Guests can meet with famous Disney characters and will find ample opportunities for photographs. City Hall offers maps, dining, and entertainment schedules, while the Main Street Cinema screens early Disney silent films. There is also a large selection of shops and eateries.

Visions of the future inspire the rides in Tomorrowland, where sights change regularly to keep one step ahead of real-life technology. One of the first attractions in 1955 was **Autopia**, that has since been updated and now takes visitors on a ride into a parallel universe. **Star Tours** was redesigned in collaboration with the *Star Wars* genius George Lucas. Its fabulous use of flight-simulator technology makes it one of the park's most realistic rides. Visitors board a StarSpeeder spaceship and are transported through outer space strewn with starships, comets, and asteroids. **Space Mountain** is a Disneyland favorite that offers a high speed roller-coaster ride, 118 ft (36 m) above the ground. Conducted almost entirely in darkness, the ride has sudden meteoric flashes and celestial showers, and is not suitable for very young children.

The colorful architecture of cartoons comes to life in Mickey's Toontown – a three-dimensional cartoon world where all Disney's favorite animated characters reside. The most popular residences are Mickey's house and Minnie's cottage. Most of the attractions are geared toward kids from age three up. **Chip 'n Dale Treehouse**, a mini-roller coaster; **Goofy's Playhouse**; and a floating bumper-boat ride offer gentle thrills. **Roger Rabbit's Car Toon Spin** is the favorite. Its spinning cars take visitors on a madcap drive through a surreal cartoon world.

Fantasyland, dominated by the pink and gold towers of **Sleeping Beauty's Castle** and a replica of the **Matterhorn**, is a shrine to children's dreams. Nursery heroes such as Peter Pan and Snow White provide the themes for gentle fairytale rides. The historic **Matterhorn Bobsleds** offers "icy" roller-coaster rides down the slopes of a replica of Switzerland's famous peak. Bobsleds climb to its summit, then drop into a high-speed descent, passing glacier caves and waterfalls as they go. **It's a Small World** creates a Utopian vision of global harmony, with almost 300 singing-and-dancing Audio-Animatronics® dolls dressed in national costumes.

The nightly **Parade of Dreams** is a family-oriented spectacle that combines music, lights, and Disney characters. The parade down Main Street, U.S.A. features the most beloved characters. And every weekend the night skies are lit up with "Dreams Come True" firework display. Thrill-seekers should not miss the **Big Thunder Mountain Railroad** roller-coaster ride, where a runaway train speeds through the cavernous interior of Big Thunder Mountain, narrowly escaping boulders and waterfalls.

Critter Country is built in a rustic style, based on the

TICKETS & TIPS

Each theme park (except for Downtown Disney) has a separate admission ticket that covers all the rides and shows, and includes a park map and schedule of events. Parking is extra, as are certain shows, food, and arcades. Multi-day tickets for three to four days and Annual Passports allow unlimited admission and access to attractions. A Fastpass lets guests obtain a voucher with a computer-assigned boarding time for specific attractions or rides. This eliminates waiting in long lines. Guests can also save time at the front gate by buying tickets in advance at any Disney store or online at www.disney.com. To help plan your day, there is updated information on showtimes, waiting times, and ride closures at the information board at the end of Main Street opposite the Plaza Pavillion.

rugged American Northwest. It is home to **Splash Mountain**, one of Disneyland's most popular attractions. This watery ride in hollowed-out logs features singing characters from the 1946 film *Song of the South* such as Brer Rabbit and Brer Fox, and ends in a plummet down a steep waterfall.

The charming New Orleans Square is modeled on the French Quarter in New Orleans as it was during the city's heyday in the 19th century. Quaint wrought-iron balconies adorn buildings housing French-style shops. One of its top attractions, **Haunted Mansion**, promises "999 ghosts and ghouls," and some visitors are so familiar with its introductory commentary that they join in as they descend into its spooky world of mischievous spirits and grave-diggers. The ethereal figures, including a talking woman's head in a crystal ball, are extremely realistic. Another favorite, **Pirates of the Caribbean** provides a floating ride through a yo-ho-ho world of ruffians who have the gifts of song, dance, and heavy drinking with the use of Audio-Animatronics®. This technique, which brings models to life using electronic impulses to control sounds and actions, was perfected at Disneyland. **The Disney Gallery** shows visitors the art behind the world of Disney, and some of the original artworks and designs for Disney's elaborate projects are on display here.

The exotic atmosphere in Adventureland offers dark, humid waterways lined with tropical plants. This is the smallest, but perhaps most adventuresome, "land" in the park. The **Enchanted Tiki Room** showcases mechanical singing birds in a zany, musical romp through the tropics. Inspired by the 1982 film trilogy, the **Indiana Jones™ Adventure** sets off on a jeep-style drive through the Temple of the Forbidden Eye. Theatrical props and scenery, a realistic soundtrack, superb film images, and the sensation of a roller coaster make this the ultimate experience in Disneyland. The safari-style **Jungle Cruise** boat ride leads visitors through a jungle full of rampant apes and bloodthirsty headhunters, accompanied by a real-life captain.

DOWNTOWN DISNEY

Located between the entrances to Disneyland Park and Disney's California Adventure, Downtown Disney® is a garden paradise, offering visitors some 300,000 sq ft (27,870 sq m) of innovative restaurants, shops, and entertainment venues. The fact that this area has no admission fee makes Downtown Disney® one of the more popular – but crowded – spaces. A 12-screen AMC Theatre®, ESPN Zone™, and a LEGO Imagination Center® are its top attractions. The snack shops, restaurants, vast range of retail and specialty shops, and a travel center create a total Disney experience.

SHOPPING

The Disneyland shops, particularly those along Main Street USA, are often busy late in the day, especially at closing time. If you can, it is worth making your purchases earlier in the day and then collecting them later from the Redemption Center. Although many of the goods on sale in the theme park bear the faces of Disney characters, each of the eight lands adds its own variations to what is available. In Adventureland, for example, you can buy Indiana Jones-style clothing, while Native American Crafts are on sale in Frontierland. The Disney Gallery in New Orleans Square sells limited-edition lithographs by the Disney cartoonists. The largest of all the shops within the Magic Kingdom is the Emporium in Main Street.

VISITORS' CHECKLIST

1313 Harbor Blvd, Anaheim. **Tel** *(714) 781-7290.* *24 hrs a day, (714) 781-4565.* *from LAX.* *435.* *Jun–Aug: 8am–midnight daily; Sep–May: 9am–6pm daily.* **www**.disneyland.com

DISNEY'S CALIFORNIA ADVENTURE

The newest star in Anaheim is Disney's California Adventure, lying adjacent to Disneyland. It is divided into three "lands," each offering themed experiences that celebrate the California dream. The emphasis is on adults and older teens, but there are still plenty of rides available for all ages.

Hollywood Pictures Backlot offers a tongue-in-cheek view of the motion picture industry. The two blocks of façades and fakery give the visitor a Disney-eye view of Hollywood. The **Hyperion Theater** features staged live musical shows, and at Jim Henson's **Muppet*Vision 3-D** visitors can see Miss Piggy, Kermit, and all the lovable Muppet characters in a tribute to movie making. Golden State features California's topography and agriculture. The star ride is **Soarin' Over California**, a simulated hang-glider ride that portrays the beauties of California's landscape on a huge wrap-around screen. Guests can feel the wind currents and smell the scent of orange blossoms as they soar 40 feet (12 m) high. **Bountiful Valley** features healthy snacks and a 3-D film starring Flik from *A Bug's Life*. Smell-o-Vision and touchy-feelies make this a completely buggy experience for all.

Considerably lower key than the thrills in the original park, Paradise Pier is the place where roller coasters, Ferris wheels, and parachute rides rule. **California Screamin'**, the giant **Sun Wheel**, and **King Triton's Carousel** are reminiscent of seaside recreation parks as they used to be years ago.

Los Angeles Practical Information

Los Angeles offers a wealth of entertainment and outdoor pleasures to its visitors. At the center of the film industry, L.A. dominated the world stage for most of the 20th century. It is therefore not surprising that L.A. sees itself as the "Entertainment Capital of the World." But the glamor of the movies is just one aspect of the city that manufactures the American Dream. This year-long vacation spot is also famous for its long beaches, mountain ranges, and some of the world's best museums.

TOURIST INFORMATION

The main branch of the **Los Angeles Convention and Visitors' Bureau** is in downtown L.A., and it offers multilingual assistance. Its visitors' guide, *LA Now*, gives listings of restaurants, coffee houses, hotels, shops, and other attractions. There are also specialty guides available from their website. The city's two other main information centers are the **Hollywood Visitors' Information Center** and the **Beverly Hills Visitors' Bureau**. Various publicationS can help sift through the city's entertainment riches. The *L.A. Weekly* – a free paper available at bars, clubs, and corner markets across Los Angeles – has the most comprehensive entertainment and arts listings.

GETTING AROUND

The sprawling 467 sq miles (1,200 sq km) city of Los Angeles may seem a bit daunting to navigate. The most cost-effective method of getting around is by car. A network of freeways provides a convenient, if crowded, means of traveling in the area. It is advisable to avoid the freeways during rush hours (8am to 9:30am and 4am to 6:30pm). Some freeways are busy regardless of the hour, and it can be less stressful to take one of the city's major streets. When parking, read the posted signs for limitations, and carry plenty of quarters for the parking meters. At nights, it is safer to valet park.

Although the city is spread out, many of its districts are pedestrian-friendly. Third Street Promenade and the beach in Santa Monica are best explored on foot. Other such areas include Old Pasadena, downtown, and the Golden Triangle in Beverly Hills. Visitors should avoid walking at night unless the street is well lit and populated.

Greater Los Angeles is served by the **Metropolitan Transportation Authority (MTA)**. Bus stops display an MTA sign, and buses run on the main thoroughfares. The **DASH** shuttle provides travel within small areas, such as downtown and Hollywood, for a quarter. Bus tickets are sold at most grocery stores.

L.A.'s growing rail subway system, the **Metro**, serves parts of the city well. It is made up of six lines, red, blue, purple, orange, gold, and green, which serve different areas. The Green Line is useful for the airport.

Other ways to get around include the somewhat expensive taxis, which have to be called by phone. Two reliable taxi companies are **Yellow Cab** and the Independent Cab Co. Visitors can also rent a limousine for a luxurious alternative. Private bus lines, such as **L.A. Tours**, offer package tours of the city.

OUTDOOR ACTIVITIES

Each year more than 30 million people visit the beaches around Los Angeles, making them the most popular vacation destinations on the West Coast. The Malibu headland, from Point Dume to Malibu Lagoon, alternates between rocky shorelines and beaches. Farther along, the shoreline becomes a long sandy strand leading to the renowned beaches of Santa Monica and Venice. Inland, the pristine and rugged terrain of the Santa Monica Mountains offer plenty of hiking trails with panoramic views of the Pacific Ocean. L.A.'s beaches are a great natural resource and offer great swimming and volleyball opportunities. The waters off the Malibu Pier and Topanga State Beach are considered to be the best for surfing.

Griffith Park offers miles of hiking trails, opportunities for horseback riding, and cycling. But the best place for cyclists is the coastal bike path that runs for 25 miles (40 km) along Santa Monica Bay (bicycles are not allowed on the freeways). Bicycles and skates can be rented from **Sea Mist Rentals** (Santa Monica Pier) and at the local pizza stands (Santa Monica Beach). Sports include baseball at the famed Dodger Stadium, and college football at Pasadena's Rose Bowl. Basketball and ice hockey, at the Great Western Forum, are popular draws, as are horse racing at the Hollywood Park Racetrack and polo at the Will Rogers State Historic Park.

ENTERTAINMENT

Los Angeles's large and successful artistic community guarantees that there is always plenty to do in the city, although only small areas tend to be lively after dark.

Most visitors don't spend a lot of time seeing movies in Los Angeles, even though all the current releases and countless classics are always being shown. The movie palaces themselves, however, draw the crowds, with Mann's Chinese and El Capitan theaters on Hollywood Boulevard being the best known. Multiplexes, such as those in **Universal City** and the Beverly Center, offer state-of-the-art facilities.

Stage productions are also plentiful and diverse, with L.A. putting up over a 1,000 professional plays each year. Pantages in Hollywood is a leading venue for touring Broadway musicals. Housed in beautiful Mediterranean-style theaters, the **Pasadena Playhouse** and the **Geffen**

Playhouse both put on new works as well as old favorites.

The city has a well-respected symphony orchestra, the L.A. Philharmonic, and an opera company, the **L.A. Opera**. In the summer there are outdoor concerts in places such as the Hollywood Bowl.

Naked ambition and unbridled youth fuel the rock clubs that line Sunset Strip. The venerable **Whiskey a Go Go** and **The Roxy** compete with relative newcomers such as the Viper Room and the Key Club. L.A.'s jazz scene is exemplified by cozy joints such as **The Baked Potato**.

Whether it's house or hiphop at The Century Club, or hipster big beats at The Garage, the L.A. club scene runs all types of dance music. With its large gay population, West Hollywood has several discos. A current favorite is **The Factory**.

Many of L.A.'s television and film studios offer behind-the-scenes tours as well as tickets to tapings of popular shows. In the high-tech **CBS-TV** studios, soap operas, such as *The Bold and the Beautiful*, and game shows are taped before live audiences. The popular **Warner Bros** tour is probably the truest look at modern-day filmmaking.

Most of the areas within L.A. have local festivals, particularly in the summer, which feature food, live music, arts, and crafts.

SHOPPING

Whatever money can buy can be found in Los Angeles, from Cartier necklaces to everyday items. While indoor shopping malls are the norm for much of the US, L.A.'s temperate climate allows for a range of pleasant outdoor alternatives. Melrose Avenue and Santa Monica's Third Street Promenade are both young, lively areas, while upscale Rodeo Drive is probably the most famous. One of the more pleasant shopping areas in L.A. is Old Pasadena, which has a range of unique shops in late 19th-century buildings.

L.A.'s favorite and best known department stores are **Bloomingdales** and **Macy's**, and **Nordstrom,** which attracts hordes of customers especially in January and June during its half-price sales.

Fashion styles are casual in L.A. but couture clothes are available in Beverly Hills. Todd Oldham and Tyler Trafficante are two of the hottest women's fashion labels in town, while Bernini and Mark Michaels have some of the best fashions for men.

Antique shops are centered around Melrose Place, close to Melrose Avenue, while some of L.A.'s leading art galleries are located at Bergamot Station.

Hollywood memorabilia is on sale as well. Two good shops are Fantasies Come True and **Larry Edmund's Cinema Bookshop**. There is a selection of Latin American arts and crafts, popular in Los Angeles, at The Folk Tree.

The California fresh produce and wines have representation in L.A. Grand Central Market, and Farmers Market overflows with a wide range of fresh fruit and vegetables. Trader Joe's, cited as one of the finest reasons to live in the city, sells a vast array of gourmet foods and wines.

DIRECTORY

TOURIST OFFICES

Hollywood
6801 Hollywood Blvd.
Tel *(323) 467-6412.*

Los Angeles Visitor Information
685 Figueroa St. ***Tel*** *(213) 689-8822.* **www.**discoverlosangeles.com

TRANSPORTATION

L.A. Tours
Tel *(323) 460-6490.*
www.latours.net

MTA
Tel *(800) 266-6883.*
www.mta.net

Yellow Cab
Tel *(800) 200-1085, (877) 733-3305.*
www.layellowcab.com

CYCLING

Sea Mist Rentals
1619 Ocean Front Walk, Santa Monica, CA 90401.
Tel *(310) 395-7076.*

CINEMAS

Cineplex Odeon Universal City Cinemas
Universal City, CA 91608.
Tel *(818) 508-0588.*
www.amctheatres.com

THEATERS

Geffen Playhouse
10886 Le Conte Ave.
Tel *(310) 208-5454.* **www.**geffenplayhouse.com

Pasadena Playhouse
39 S El Molino Ave, Pasadena, CA 91101. ***Tel*** *(626) 356-7529.* **www.**pasadenaplayhouse.org

OPERA

L.A. Opera
135 N Grand Ave.
Tel *(213) 972-8001.*
www.losangelesopera.com

ROCK, JAZZ, BLUES, & CLUBS

The Baked Potato
3787 Cahuenga Blvd W, Studio City, CA 91105.
Tel *(818) 980-1615.*

Key Club
9039 W Sunset Blvd.
Tel *(310) 274-5800.*
www.keyclub.com

The Factory
652 N La Peer Dr.
Tel *(310) 659-4551.*

The Roxy
9009 W Sunset Blvd.
Tel *(310) 278-9457.*

Whiskey a Go Go
8901 W Sunset Blvd.
Tel *(310) 652-4202.*

STUDIO TOURS

CBS-TV
7800 Beverly Blvd.
Tel *(323) 575-2624.*

Warner Bros
4000 Warner Blvd, Burbank.
Tel *(818) 977-1744.*

SHOPPING

Bloomingdales
Beverly Center, 8500 Beverly Blvd.
Tel *(310) 360-2700.*
www.bloomingdales.com

Larry Edmund's Cinema Bookshop
6644 Hollywood Blvd.
Tel *(323) 463-3273.*
www.larryedmunds.com

Macy's
8500 Beverly Blvd.
Tel *(310) 854-6655.*
www.macys.com

Nordstrom
10830 W Pico Blvd.
Tel *(310) 470-6155.*
www.nordstrom.com

San Diego County

San Diego's character has always been determined by the sea. Its magnificent natural harbor attracted the Spanish as well as gold prospectors and whalers. The US Navy arrived in 1904, and today San Diego has become one of the largest military establishments in the world. Extending to the Mexican border, its coastline has 70 miles (112 km) of stunning beaches, rocky cliffs, coves, and seaside resorts, with plentiful opportunities for leisure activities.

The Gaslamp Quarter, the star of downtown San Diego

San Diego ❷

1,500,000. 1050 Kettner Blvd. 120 W Broadway. 1040 W Broadway, (619) 236-1212. Wine & Food Festival (Nov). **www**.sandiego.org

The museums and art venues of **Balboa Park** *(see pp680–81)* are the prime cultural attractions of San Diego, California's second largest city. San Diego's growth as a modern city began with the waterfront development initiated by San Francisco businessman, Alonzo Horton, in the 1870s. He also designed the plan of the **Gaslamp Quarter**, which is now the centerpiece of downtown, and the best place to shop and dine. The wealth of period buildings ranges from a pie bakery to ornate offices and grand Victorian hotels. The district is particularly attractive at night, when it is illuminated by graceful gaslamps. Close by is **Horton Plaza**, an innovatively designed shopping center built in 1985.

At the western end of Broadway is the **Santa Fe Depot**, a Spanish Colonial-style railroad station dating from 1915. The towering America Plaza houses the **Museum of Contemporary Art**, whose galleries display work by new artists and selections from its large permanent collection.

The promenades and piers of the **Embarcadero** waterfront pathway lead to the Maritime Museum and its three historic ships. Of these, the highlight is the *Star of India*, an 1863 merchantman. To the south is Broadway Pier, where visitors can take a harbor excursion.

North of downtown is **Old Town**, site of the original Spanish settlement near the San Diego River. Today, more than 20 historic buildings have been restored to form the Old Town San Diego State Historic Park. The Plaza, at its center, was where parades and fiestas once took place. The old Spanish presido and mission is now part of Presido Park. Crowning the hill the **Junípero Serra Museum** is named after the founder of California's missions *(see p692)*. On display are archaeological finds as well as exhibits on San Diego's successive Native American, Spanish, Mexican, and American communities.

To the west of Old Town is the **Point Loma Peninsula**, at the southern tip of which is the Cabrillo National Monument, named after the city's discoverer, Juan Rodríguez Cabrillo; his statue overlooks the Bay. Between December and March, the nearby Whale Overlook is a popular spot to watch gray whales.

The peninsula of Coronado has the city's most exclusive boutiques and hotels. The **Hotel del Coronado**, or "Del," opened in 1888 and is a lovely Victorian seaside hotel *(see p722)*. Its guest list reads like a Who's Who of 20th-century US history, including Presidents Franklin D. Roosevelt and Bill Clinton, and film star Marilyn Monroe. It has been the setting for several films, including *Some Like It Hot*, the 1959 classic starring Marilyn Monroe, Jack Lemmon, and Tony Curtis. The Coronado Ferry ride is enchanting at dusk, when the sun's last rays illuminates the skyscrapers of downtown.

Junípero Serra Museum
2727 Presidio Dr. ***Tel*** *(619) 297-3258. 10am–4:30pm Tue–Sat, noon–4pm Sun. Dec 25.*

Impressive turrets and gables of the Hotel del Coronado, San Diego

SeaWorld ❸

500 Sea World Dr. ***Tel*** *(800) 380-3203.* *9 (Jun–Aug), 10 (Sep–May).* *daily.*
www.seaworld.com

San Diego's SeaWorld covers 189 acres (60 ha) of Mission Bay. The ride up the Skytower, a 320-ft (98-m) column, offers splendid views. Another fabulous ride is the 100-ft (30-m) Bayside Skyride, where gondola cars make an enormous loop over Mission Bay.

The stars of SeaWorld are the performing whales and dolphins. One performance reveals the intelligence of dolphins and pilot whales, while another demonstrates the virtuosity of killer whales. Other attractions include the shark and otter pools, and opportunities to feed killer whales and seals. Shamu's Happy Harbor is an aquatic adventure park for children.

SeaWorld's staff are devoted to animal rescue and rehabilitation, and run educational and conservation programs.

Killer whales performing acrobatic feats for the crowd at SeaWorld

La Jolla ❹

32,000. *from San Diego.* *7966 Herschel Ave, (619) 236-1212.* **www**.lajollabythesea.com

Set amid cliffs and coves, La Jolla is an elegant coastal resort. Its streets are lined with gourmet chocolatiers and jewelers, and visitors come to enjoy the art galleries and the restaurants that promise a "Mediterranean" view. The town is home to the University of California at San Diego and the **Salk Institute for Biological Studies**, founded by Dr. Jonas Salk, who developed the polio vaccine. The Scripps Institution of Oceanography has the **Birch Aquarium at Scripps Institute of Oceanography**. It provides an insight into the world of oceanography. The **San Diego Museum of Contemporary Art** occupies a prime oceanfront location. A companion to the gallery in San Diego, it displays works of post-1950 art.

Tijuana, Mexico ❺

Mexico. *San Diego Trolley to San Ysidro, then bus or walk.* **Tourist Office** *Ave Revolución and First.* ***Tel*** *(888) 775-2417, (01152664) 685-2210.* *daily.*

Thousands of Americans have traditionally visited Tijuana every year, for the inexpensive shopping and exuberant nightlife. Reports of violence between rival drug cartels in 2008 and increased border controls have, however, seen visitor numbers drastically decline. Greater services and discounts are now on offer to attract tourists back.

The futuristic **Centro Cultural Tijuana**, built on the banks of the Tijuana River, has an OMNIMAX theater, which screens films on Mexico. The open-air Mexitlán rooftop exhibition re-creates the country's architectural treasures in miniature.

The best shopping is in the quiet bazaars located on the lively Avenida Revolución. Painted pottery, leather boots, silver jewelry, and tequila are some favorite buys. Visitors rarely need to change money, as US dollars and credit cards are accepted widely.

Centro Cultural Tijuana
Paseo de los Héroes and Javier Mina Zona Rosa. ***Tel*** *(0115266) 4687.*
daily.

The beautiful rocky shoreline of La Jolla Cove

Balboa Park

Statue of El Cid in Balboa Park

Located in the heart of San Diego *(see p678)*, Balboa Park is one of the city's most popular attractions. Founded in 1868, its lush beauty owes much to the horticulturalist Kate Sessions, who planted trees throughout its 1,200 acres (485 ha). In 1915, the park was the site of the Panama-California International Exposition, which celebrated the opening of the Panama Canal. Many of the Spanish Colonial-style pavilions built in that year survive along El Prado (the park's main street); the animals gathered for the exhibition formed the nucleus of the renowned San Diego Zoo. Today, Balboa Park has one of the country's richest concentrations of museums and performance spaces.

Plaza de Panama
This plaza was at the heart of the famous 1915 Exposition.

★ San Diego Museum of Man
Housed in the historic 1915 Spanish Colonial California Building, this anthropological museum traces the early history of mankind.

Air & Space Museum
This A-12 Blackbird, built in 1962, is beside a museum devoted to flight history. Over 60 original and reconstructed aircrafts are on display here.

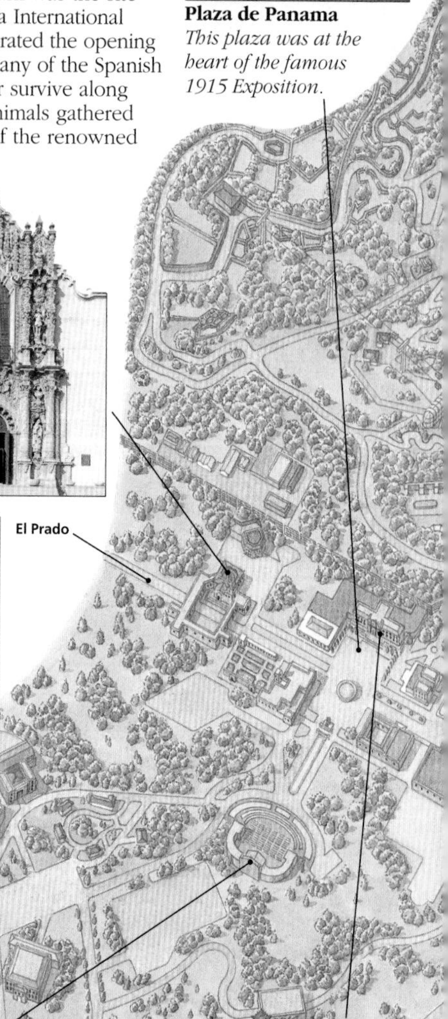

★ San Diego Museum of Art
This fine museum, displaying American and European works, is the main art museum in the park.

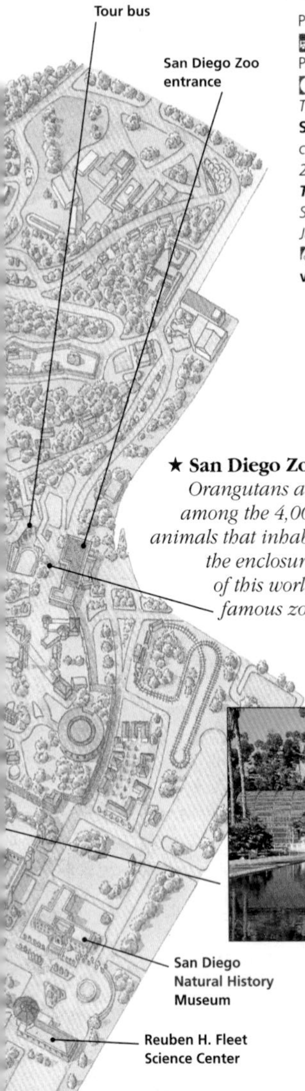

VISITORS' CHECKLIST

Park Blvd, Laurel & 6th Sts. 7. **Visitor Center** Plaza de Panama. ***Tel*** *(619) 239-0512.* *9am–4pm daily.* *Jan 1, Thanksgiving, Dec 25.* **Spreckels Organ Pavilion** *Free concerts Jun–Aug: 7:30pm Mon, 2–3pm Sun.* **San Diego Zoo** ***Tel*** *(619) 234-3153.* *early Sep–Jun: 9am–4pm daily; late Jun–early Sep: 9am–8pm daily.*
www.sandiegozoo.org

★ San Diego Zoo
Orangutans are among the 4,000 animals that inhabit the enclosures of this world-famous zoo.

Botanical Building
Constructed from thin strips of redwood, this shaded sanctuary is full of tropical and subtropical plants.

San Diego Automotive Museum
Dream cars and motorcycles from the US and Europe shine on in this nostalgic museum.

STAR SIGHTS

★ California Building/San Diego Museum of Man

★ San Diego Museum of Art

★ San Diego Zoo

Exploring Balboa Park

Most of the park's museums lie along the central El Prado, while some are located to the south. The pleasant grounds, shady picnic groves, and traffic-free promenades are usually crowded with joggers, cyclists, and street artists.

The **San Diego Museum of Man**, at the western end of El Prado, is an anthropological museum about the early history of mankind. Exhibits cover the cultures of ancient Egypt and the Mayans, and Native American crafts. Close by, the **San Diego Museum of Art's** large and varied collection is boosted by special exhibitions. It displays a vast range of European and American art from 1300 to the 20th century, as well some fine exhibits from South Asia, Japan, and China.

The **Timken Museum of Art**, lying east of the Museum of Art, displays a handful of splendid works by European masters such as Frans Hals, Rembrandt, and Paul Cézanne. It also has a collection of Russian icons.

Farther east along El Prado, the **Natural History Museum** features its own giant-screen film, *Ocean Oasis*, taking visitors on an incredible journey through Baja California and the Sea of Cortes. The main attraction at the **Reuben H. Fleet Science Center**, just across the plaza, is the IMAX® cinema in the Space Theater, where films are projected onto an enormous domed screen. Laser and planetarium shows are also staged here.

Just north of the museums, the **San Diego Zoo** is one of the best in the world and is famous for its conservation programs. Spread over 100 acres (40 ha), it houses 800 animal species in enclosures designed to closely resemble their natural habitat. A 35-minute narrated bus tour covers most of the zoo, while the aerial Skyfari ride offers an exciting trip across the south of the park in gondola cars that run 180 ft (55 m) up. There is also a Children's Zoo. The zoo is open in summer for nocturnal exploration.

The Deserts

National park sign

The searing deserts of Southern California have a haunting beauty all their own, with jagged canyons, steep hills, and carpets of wildflowers in spring. At the heart of the Low Desert is Palm Springs, the region's most sought-after resort, with hotels and golf courses. The stark Joshua Tree National Park lies to the east. Farther north, the Mojave Desert is the state's greatest secret, all too often missed by visitors. Its main draw, Death Valley National Park, has some of the highest temperatures in the Western Hemisphere.

Sculpture Garden in the Palm Springs Desert Museum

Palm Springs ❻

42,000. *Indio.* *3111 N Indian Ave.* *2901 N Palm Canyon Drive, (800) 347-7746, (760) 778-8418.* *Palm Springs International Film Festival (early–mid-Jan).*
www.palm-springs.com

The largest of the desert cities, Palm Springs was first sighted in 1853 when a survey party came across a grove of palm trees surrounding a freshwater spring pool in the Coachella Valley. The first hotel was constructed in 1886, and by the turn of the century, Palm Springs was a thriving health spa. Soon after, it became a fashionable winter resort for the rich and famous. Today, its population doubles each winter, when visitors come to enjoy the relaxing, outdoor lifestyle. First-class hotels such as the Marriot and Hyatt Regency abound, and a number of celebrities live here. The area around Palm Springs has numerous resort cities, such as Rancho Mirage, Indian Wells, and La Quinta, and more than 100 luxury golf courses.

Downtown's two main shopping streets are Palm Canyon and Indian Canyon Drives; both are lined with restaurants, boutiques, and art galleries. The **Village Green Heritage Center**, in the heart of the shopping area, has a few historic buildings, including Ruddy's 1930s General Store Museum, a replica of the original, with authentic packaged goods ranging from licorice to patent medicines. The Agua Caliente Cultural Museum displays the heritage of the area's Cahuilla people.

The state-of-the-art **Oasis Water Resort** has 13 waterslides, including a 70-ft (20-m) free-fall slide. An enormous wave-action pool creates 4-ft (1.2-m) high waves suitable for surfing and boogie boarding. The resort also has a hotel, heated spas, health clubs, and restaurants.

Oasis Water Resort in Palm Springs

The **Palm Springs Aerial Tramway** covers a 2.5-mile (4-km) trip via cable car, which ascends 5,900 ft (1,790 m) over spectacular scenery to the Mountain Station in the Mount San Jacinto Wilderness State Park. Visitors travel through five distinct ecosystems, ranging from desert to alpine forest, where the weather becomes icy cold. At the top, there are 54 miles (85 km) of hiking trails, a ski center, campsites, and a cafeteria. Observation decks offer terrific views of the Coachella Valley, Palm Springs, and the San Bernardino Mountains to the north. On a clear day, it is possible to see the Salton Sea, 50 miles (80 km) away.

The **Palm Springs Art Museum** focuses on art, natural science, and the performing arts. The galleries contain paintings from the 19th century to the present day, as well as Native American artifacts and natural history exhibits. Modern sculpture adorns the gardens.

About 5 miles (8 km) south of Palm Springs are the **Indian Canyons**, four spectacular natural palm oases, set in rocky gorges. Clustered along streams fed by mountain springs, Murray, Tahquitz, Andreas, and Palm Canyons are located on the land of the Agua Caliente Cahuilla people. Rock art and other traces of these early inhabitants can still be seen. Palm and Andreas Canyons have many popular trails.

Palm Springs Aerial Tramway
Tramway Rd. ***Tel*** *(760) 325-1391, (888) 515-8726.* *daily.*
www.pstramway.com

Anza-Borrego Desert State Park ❼

Escondido. **Visitor Center** ***Tel*** *(760) 767-5311.* *Jun–Sep: Sat & Sun; Oct–May: daily.*
www.parks.ca.gov

During the Gold Rush of 1849 *(see p654)*, tens of thousands of miners passed through the Anza-Borrego Desert. Today, this former gateway to San Diego County is a remote and pristine park, offering an insight into the unique desert environment, with its steep ravines and rocky badlands.

The visitor center is in **Borrego Springs**, the park's only significant town. Nearby, the Palm Canyon Nature Trail leads to an oasis where endangered bighorn sheep can often be seen. From the **Box Canyon Historical Monument**, lying southwest of the visitor center, there are views of the old road once used by miners en route to the goldfields, which lay 500 miles (800 km) to the north.

The desert bursts into bloom between March and May. Cacti and desert flowers such as desert poppies and dune primroses produce a riot of color.

Much of the park, including its campsites, is accessible via the 100 miles (160 km) of roads. Four-wheel drive vehicles are recommended, however, for the 500 miles (800 km) of unsurfaced roads.

Salton Sea State Recreation Area 8

Mecca. Indio. **Visitor Center** 100–225 State Park Rd, North Shore. ***Tel*** *(760) 393-3059.* *Fri–Sun (summer).* **www**.parks.ca.gov

The Salton Sea was created by accident in 1905 when the Colorado River flooded and flowed into a newly dug irrigation canal leading to the Imperial Valley. By the time the flow was stemmed two years later, a 35-mile (55-km) inland sea had formed in the Salton Sink.

Despite the high salinity, saltwater game fish live here, with 10-lb (4.5-kg) orange-mouth corvina being caught regularly. Waterskiing, wind-surfing, and boating are other popular activities. The area off Mecca Beach has the best spots for swimming. The adjoining marshlands are a refuge for migrating birds. On the eastern side, there are hiking trails and camp sites.

Spiny-leaved Joshua trees in Joshua Tree National Park's western half

Joshua Tree National Park 9

Desert Stage Lines from Palm Springs to Twenty-nine Palms. **Oasis Visitors' Center** 74485 National Park Dr, Twenty-nine Palms. ***Tel*** *(760) 367-5500.* *8am–4:30pm daily.* *Dec 25.* **www**.joshua.tree.national-park.com

The Joshua Tree National Park was established to protect the unique Joshua tree. The tree was named by early Mormon travelers, who saw the upraised arms of the biblical Joshua in its twisted branches. The species can grow up to 30 ft (9 m) and live for about 1,000 years.

The 794,000-acre (255,300-ha) park, with its formations of pink and gray rocks, abandoned mines, and oases, is a climber's and hiker's paradise. A popular trail begins close to the **Oasis Visitors' Center**. South of here, the gigantic boulders in **Hidden Valley** form corrals, which were hideouts for cattle rustlers. Farther south, **Key's View** offers sweeping vistas of the valley, desert, and mountains. Close to Key's View, the **Lost Horse Mine** was the historic mine where over $270,000 in gold was extracted in its first decade of operation.

A variety of animals, which have specially adapted to this environment, thrive here. The kangaroo rat gets its food and water from seeds alone, and the jackrabbit has a coat of muted fur to camouflage it from predators such as the coyote, bobcat, and eagle.

Mojave Desert 10

Barstow. *831 Barstow Rd, (760) 256-8619, (888) 422-7869.* **www**.barstowchamber.com

Lying at an altitude of 2,000 ft (600 m), the Mojave or High Desert was the gateway to California for traders in the 19th century. **Barstow**, the largest town, is a stop-over between L.A. and Las Vegas. In the 1870s, gold and silver were discovered and towns such as Calico sprang up. They were soon abandoned and became ghost towns when the mines became exhausted. Many of Calico's buildings are intact, and visitors can even take a ride in a mine train. To the west, Edwards Air Force Base is famous for its space shuttle landings. The **Red Rock Canyon State Park** nearby has red sandstone and pink volcanic rock, while the **Mitchell Caverns** have limestone formations. Northern Mojave is dominated by the **Death Valley National Park** *(see pp684–5)*.

Rock formations in the Mitchell Caverns, Mojave Desert

Death Valley National Park ⓫

The Native Americans called the valley Tomesha, "the land where the ground is on fire," an apt name for Death Valley, which has the highest mean temperature on earth – the highest ever recorded was 134° F (57° C) in the shade in 1913. This is a land of wrenching extremes, a sunken trough in the earth's crust that reaches the lowest point in the Western Hemisphere. The park stretches 140 miles (225 km) and is guarded on two sides by some of the highest mountains on the continent. Its unique landscape includes delicate rock formations, polished canyons, and burning salt flats. Although always inhospitable, it is one of the most popular tourist destinations in California.

Dante's View, taking in jagged peaks and the entire valley floor

Exploring Death Valley National Park

Death Valley was once an insurmountable barrier to miners and emigrants. Today, it is accessible by car, and visitors can take short walks from the roads to spectacular viewpoints. The best time to visit is between October and April, when temperatures average 65° F (18° C). Avoid the period between May and September, when the ground temperatures can exceed a searing 100° F (38° C).

There is a surprising amount of plant life, and for a few weeks each year wildflowers appear amid the rocks. An array of animals such as foxes and tortoises have evolved to survive in this harsh climate.

Furnace Creek, with its visitors' complex, is located in the heart of Death Valley. Millennia of winter floods have carved a gateway into the Valley through the eastern hills. The springs here are some of the desert's few freshwater sources and are thought to have saved the lives of hundreds of gold prospectors crossing the desert. Today, the same springs make Furnace Creek a desert oasis shaded by date palms. There are a variety of restaurants and motels, and the **Death Valley Museum and Visitor Center** has exhibits and slide shows explaining the area's natural and human history. In winter, ranger programs and guided walks are available. The world's lowest golf course, lying at 214 ft (65 m) below sea level, and the 1920s Furnace Creek Inn *(see p723)*, which runs bus tours in winter, are also located here.

On Hwy 190, close to the visitor center, the eerie ruins of the **Harmony Borax Works** can still be seen. Borax was discovered here in 1873, but mining did not begin until the 1880s, when crystallized borate compounds were taken to be purified. They were then loaded onto wagons and hauled 165 miles (265 km) to Mojave Station. Used for producing heat-resistant glass, borax is commonly used today as an ingredient in detergents. The Borax Museum has exhibits of mining tools and transport machinery used at the 19th-century refinery.

Salt Creek, lying near the Borax Museum, supports the hardy pupfish. Endemic to Death Valley, the pupfish can live in water almost four times as salty as the sea and can withstand temperatures of up to 111° F (44° C). The fish attract other wildlife, including great blue herons. Walkways allow visitors to explore this unique site.

Some of the Valley's most breathtaking natural features lie south of Furnace Creek. About 3 miles (5 km) south, on Hwy 178, a short hike leads into **Golden Canyon**. The mustard-colored walls after which the canyon was named, are best seen in the afternoon sun. Native Americans used the red clay at the mouth of the canyon for face paint. The layers of rock were originally horizontal, but geological activity has now tilted them to an angle of 45°. The roads are often in bad condition due to flash floods. **Zabriskie Point** offers great views of the mud hills of Golden Canyon. Made famous by Antonioni's eponymous 1960s film, the point was named after a general manager of the Valley's borax operations.

Dante's View lies 5, 475 ft (1,650 m) above sea level at Death Valley's southern end. Its name was inspired by Dante's *Inferno*. The best time

Multicolored hills of the Artist's Palette

For hotels and restaurants in this region see p723 and p727

Salt formations at the Devil's Golf Course

to see the view, which takes in the entire floor of Death's Valley, is in the morning.

Badwater, to the west, is the lowest point in the Western Hemisphere. It lies 282 ft (85 m) below sea level and is one of the world's hottest places. The air can reach 120° F (49° C), and as the ground temperature is 50 percent higher than the air temperature, it really is possible to fry an egg on the ground. The water here is not poisonous, but it is unpalatable, filled with sodium chloride and sulfates. In spite of the extreme conditions, Badwater is home to several species of insect and to the endangered Death Valley snail.

Devil's Golf Course is an expanse of salt pinnacles, located 12 miles (19 km) south of Furnace Creek, off Hwy 178. Until about 2,000 years ago, a succession of lakes covered the area. When the last lake evaporated, it left behind alternating layers of salt and gravel, some 1,000 ft (305 m) deep and covering 200 sq miles (520 sq km). The ground is 95 percent salt, and visitors can actually hear the salt expand and contract with the continual change of temperature. New salt crystals (identified by their whiter hue) continue to form. The multicolored hills known as the **Artist's Palette** are to the north. Created by mineral deposits and volcanic ash, their hues are at their most intense in the late afternoon.

Located northwest of the visitor center, the village of **Stovepipe Wells**, founded in 1926, was the valley's first resort. According to legend, a lumberjack traveling west struck water here and stayed on. An old stovepipe, similar to the ones that were used to form the walls of wells, marks the site, which is the Valley's second-largest outpost.

A walk along the 14 sq miles (36 sq km) of undulating **Sand Dunes**, north of Stovepipe Wells, is one of the greatest experiences of Death Valley. Shifting winds blow the sand into the classic crescent dune shape. Mesquite trees dot the lower dunes. A variety of wildlife feeds on the seeds of these trees, such as kangaroo rats and lizards. Among the region's other, mainly nocturnal, creatures are animals that are as diverse as the rattlesnake, the chuckwalla lizard, and the coyote.

Northern Death Valley has the 3,000-year-old **Ubehebe Crater**, where few tourists venture, despite the beauty of the landscape. This is only one of the dozen volcanic craters in the Mojave area; it is 900 yds (800 m) wide and 500 ft (150 m) deep).

East of the crater, lies the Moorish-style **Scotty's Castle**. It was commissioned by Albert Johnson at a cost of $2.4 million in 1922, and covers about 30,000 sq ft (2,800 sq m). "Death Valley Scotty," a friend of Johnson's, lived here until his death in 1948. In 1970 it was bought by the National Park Service which gives guided tours.

VISITORS' CHECKLIST

Death Valley Museum & Visitor Center Rte 190, Furnace Creek. ***Tel*** *(760) 786-3200.* ○ *daily.* ● *Jan 1, Thanksgiving, Dec 25.*
Emergency *For Park Rangers, call up 911.*
www.nps.gov/deva

Scotty's Castle
Hwy 267. ***Tel*** *(760) 786-2392.*
Castle ○ *daily.*
Grounds ○ *daily.*

DEATH VALLEY SCOTTY

Walter Scott, would-be miner, beloved charlatan, and sometime performer in Buffalo Bill's Wild West Show, liked to tell visitors that his wealth lay in a secret gold mine. That "mine" was, in fact, his friend Albert Johnson, a Chicago insurance executive, who paid for the castle where Scott lived and received visitors. Built in the 1920s by European craftsmen and Native American labor, the castle has a Moorish feel. Scott never owned the building, and Johnson paid all his bills. "He repays me in laughs," said Johnson. Although Johnson died in 1948, Scott was allowed to remain here until his death in 1954. The edifice is still known as Scotty's Castle.

The grandiose, Moorish-style Scotty's Castle

Central Coast

California's Spanish heritage is highly visible in this pleasant coastal area. Several of the 21 missions, established by Franciscan friars in the 18th and early 19th centuries, are located here. These, as well as the Spanish Colonial capital at Monterey, preserve vestiges of the state's rich Colonial past. Besides historic sights, the rugged shoreline along the Pacific Ocean harbors beach resorts and large areas of natural beauty.

The 1929 Spanish Colonial-style County Courthouse, Santa Barbara

Santa Barbara ⓬

90,200. 209 State St. 1020 Chapala St. 34 W Carrillo. Stearns Wharf. 1601 Anacapa St, (805) 966-9222. I Madonnari Italian Street Painting Festival (May); Old Spanish Days Fiesta (Aug). **www**.santabarbaraca.com

Santa Barbara is a Southern Californian rarity: a city with a single architectural style. Following a devastating earthquake in 1925, the entire center was rebuilt according to strict rules that dictated Mediterranean-style architecture. Santa Barbara is today a quiet administrative center with a sizable student population.

Often called the "Queen of the Missions," **Santa Barbara Mission** is the most visited in the state. The tenth mission built by the Spanish, it was founded in 1786 on the feast day of St. Barbara – four years after the colonists established a garrison here. The present structure took shape after the third adobe church on the site was destroyed by an earthquake in 1812. Its twin towers and the blend of Roman, Moorish, and Spanish styles, were the inspiration for what came to be known as Mission Style. This is the only California mission that has been in continuous use since it was founded.

The beautifully landscaped Sacred Gardens were once a working area for Native Americans. The surrounding living quarters now display a rich collection of mission artifacts. The church's Classical façade was designed by Padre Antonio Ripoll, who was influenced by the Roman architect Vitruvius Pollio (around 27 BC). Its Neo-Classical interior has imitation marble columns, while the reredos has a painted canvas backdrop and carved wooden statues. The **County Courthouse** on Figueroa Street is still in use. In the Assembly Room are murals depicting California history. The **Museum of Art**, close by, has an outstanding collection that includes Asian and American art, antiquities, and photographs. To its south is the **Lobero Theater**. This graceful 1924 structure stands on the site of the city's original theater. Farther east is the **Presidio**. Built in 1782, this was the last in a chain of four Spanish forts erected along the coast. Other sights include the **Paseo Nuevo**, a colorful outdoor shopping center, and the Historical Museum, housed in two adobe buildings. Among the many artifacts on display here is a statue of the 4th-century martyr St. Barbara.

Santa Barbara Mission
2201 Laguna St. ***Tel*** *(805) 682-4713. 22. 9am–4:30pm daily.* ***Donation.***
www.sbmission.org

Museum of Art
1130 State St. ***Tel*** *(805) 963-4364. 11am–5pm Tue–Sun. (free Sun).* **www**.sbma.net

Channel Islands National Park ⓭

Ventura. Island Packers, 1867 Spinnaker Dr, (805) 642-1393. **Visitor Center** *1901 Spinnaker Dr, (805) 658-5730. daily. Thanksgiving, Dec 25.* **www**.nps.gov/chis

The unpopulated volcanic islands of Santa Barbara, Anacapa, San Miguel, Santa Cruz, and Santa Rosa, together comprise the Channel Islands National Park. Access is strictly monitored by park rangers, who issue landing permits from the visitor center. Camping is allowed on all the islands, but visitors must book two weeks in advance. They must also bring their own food and water, since none is available on any of the five islands. Day trips to Anacapa Island, nearest the mainland, offer an insight into this unique coastal ecosystem. All the islands' rock pools are rich in marine life, and the surrounding kelp forests provide shelter for more than 1,000 plant and animal species. The islands' many sea caves make sea kayaking

Statue of the 4th-century martyr St. Barbara

an exciting experience. The snorkeling and scuba diving here are considered to be among the best on the entire Pacific Coast.

Wildlife on these islands is plentiful and includes sea lions, elephant seals, cormorants, and gulls. Depending on the time of year, visitors can spot gray whales, dolphins, and California brown pelicans on the passage across the Santa Barbara Channel.

La Purísima Concepción Mission in Lompoc Valley

Lompoc Valley ⓮

Lompoc. 111 S I St, Lompoc, (800 240-0999). www.lompoc.com

One of the world's major producers of flower seed, Lompoc Valley is surrounded by hills and flower fields, and is a blaze of color between late spring and midsummer each year. Marigolds, sweet peas, asters, lobelia, larkspur, nasturtiums, and cornflowers are just some of the varieties grown here. A map of the area's flower fields is distributed by Lompoc town's Chamber of Commerce. The Civic Center Plaza, between Ocean Avenue and C Street, has a display garden where all the varieties of flowers are labeled and identified.

California's 11th mission, **La Purísima Concepción**, located 3 miles (5 km) northeast of Lompoc, was declared a State Historic Park during the 1930s. The early 19th-century buildings have now been perfectly reconstructed, and the entire complex provides a real insight into the missionary way of life. Visitors can view the priests' living quarters, furnished with authentic pieces in the elegant residence building. The simple, narrow church is decorated with colorful stencilwork. The adjacent workshops at one time produced cloth, candles, leather goods, and furniture.

The mission's gardens also have been faithfully restored. The numerous varieties of fruit, vegetables, and herbs that are now grown here were all common in the 19th century. Visitors can also view the system that provided the mission with water.

La Purísima Concepción Mission
2295 Purísima Rd, Lompoc. *Tel (805) 733-3713.* *9am–5pm daily.* *Jan 1, Thanksgiving, Dec 25.* www.lapurisimamission.org

San Luis Obispo ⓯

43,000. *811 El Capitan Way, (800 634-1414).* www.sanluisobispocounty.com

This small city, situated in a valley in the Santa Lucia Mountains, developed around the **San Luis Obispo Mission de Tolosa**, founded on September 1, 1772, by Father Junípero Serra *(see p692)*. Fifth in the chain of 21 missions, and also one of the wealthiest, it is still in use as a parish church. Beside the church, the mission's museum displays Chumash Indian artifacts, the padre's bed, and the mission's original altar.

In front of the church is Mission Plaza, a landscaped public square bisected by the tree-lined San Luis Creek. During the 1860s, bullfights and bear-baiting took place here; today it hosts many of the city's less bloody events.

Just west of the Plaza, is the Ah Louis Store. Founded in 1874 by a Chinese cook, and railroad laborer, it became the center of a then thriving Chinatown and served as a post office, bank, and store. The property is still owned by the Louis family, but it is now a gift shop.

San Luis Obispo Mission de Tolosa
751 Palm St. *Tel (805) 781-8220.* *9am–5pm Mon–Fri.* *Jan 1, Easter, Thanksgiving, Dec 25.* www.missionsanluisobispo.org

MISSION ARCHITECTURE

Santa Barbara Mission

The 21 missions established along El Camino Real were adaptations of Mexican Baroque architecture. Designed by friars, these provincial versions were built of adobe bricks and wood by unskilled Native Americans. Over the years they decayed or were shaken by earthquakes, but many have been carefully restored. Distinctive features include massive walls covered with white lime cement, small window openings, rounded gables, and tiered bell towers. The early 20th-century Mission Revival style is a more elegant version of the original. Today, most missions offer public tours.

Hearst Castle® ⓰

Tile detail

Perched on a hill above the village of San Simeon and set in extensive grounds, Hearst Castle® was the private playground and estate of media tycoon William Randolph Hearst. One of California's top tourist attractions, its three guest houses are superb buildings in their own right, but the highlight of the tour is the twin-towered Casa Grande (the "Main House"). Designed by the Paris-trained architect Julia Morgan and built in stages from 1919 to 1947, its 165 rooms hold numerous artworks and epitomize the glamor of the 1930s and 40s.

Casa Grande®
Casa Grande's "poured concrete" façade is in the Mediterranean Revival style. It is embellished with ancient architectural fragments.

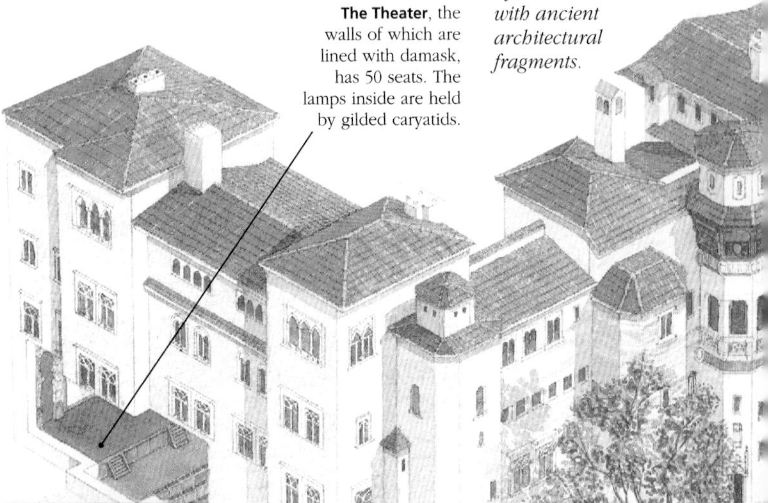

The Theater, the walls of which are lined with damask, has 50 seats. The lamps inside are held by gilded caryatids.

★ Billiard Room
This room features an early 16th-century millefleurs tapestry of a stag hunt.

STAR FEATURES

- ★ The Assembly Room
- ★ Billiard Room
- ★ Gothic Study
- ★ Refectory

WILLIAM RANDOLPH HEARST

The son of a multimillionaire, W.R. Hearst (1863–1951) was an ebullient personality who made his own fortune in magazine and newspaper publishing. He married Millicent Willson, an entertainer from New York, in 1903. On his mother's death in 1919, Hearst inherited the San Simeon property. He began to build the castle and grounds as a tribute to his mother, and then lived there with his mistress, the actress Marion Davies. The couple entertained royally at San Simeon over the next 30 years. When Hearst suffered problems with his heart in 1947, he moved to a house in Beverly Hills, where he died in 1951.

Portrait of Hearst, age 31

For hotels and restaurants in this region see p723 and pp727–8

★ Gothic Study
Hearst ran his media empire from the Gothic Study. His most prized books and manuscripts were kept behind grilles.

★ The Assembly Room features a 16th-century French fireplace. Italian choir stalls line the walls, which are hung with Flemish tapestries.

★ Refectory
Tapestries and choir stalls cover the walls of the dining hall. Its Renaissance table has cathedral seats and is decorated with silver candlesticks.

VISITORS' CHECKLIST

750 Hearst Castle Rd. ***Tel*** *(800) 444-4445.* *8am–4pm daily.* *Jan 1, Thanksgiving, Dec 25.* *call ahead.* *obligatory.*
www.hearstcastle.com

Exploring Hearst Castle®
Visitors must take one of the five guided tours. Experience Tour is best for first-timers. In spring and autumn, evening tours feature docents or "guests" in period costume.

Casa Grande® was built from reinforced concrete to withstand California's earthquakes. This gilded playhouse for Hearst's many famous guests has 38 bedrooms, an Assembly Room, a Billiard Room, two pools, and a theater, where up to 50 guests could watch film premieres. Hearst himself lived in the sumptuous, third-floor Gothic Suite. The exquisite heated indoor **Roman Pool** is entirely covered with mosaics made of colored and fused-gold glass tiles.

The magnate transformed the California hillside into a veritable Garden of Eden, laying 127 acres (51 ha) of gardens. Fan palms, Italian cypresses, and huge 200-year-old oaks were hauled up at great expense. Four greenhouses and thousands of fruit trees supplied plants and fruit. Ancient and modern statues were collected to adorn the terraces. Among the finest are four statues of Sekhmet, the Egyptian goddess of war, dating from 1560 to 1200 BC. The 104-ft (32-m) light-veined marble **Neptune Pool** is flanked by colonnades and the façade of a Greek temple.

A great lover of the outdoors, Hearst had a covered bridlepath built, so that he could ride in all weather. There was also a private zoo on Camp Hill that once had lions, bears, elephants, leopards, and pumas. Zebras, giraffes, ostriches, and even a baby elephant were free to wander the grounds. The three guesthouses – Casa del Mar, Casa del Sol, and Casa del Monte – are luxurious mansions in their own right.

Big Sur ⑰

California's wildest length of coastline was named El Pais Grande del Sur, the "Big Country to the South," by Spanish colonists at Carmel *(see p692)* in the late 18th century, and since then, Big Sur has been attracting hyperbole. The novelist Robert Louis Stevenson called Point Lobos "the greatest meeting of land and sea in the world," and the 100 miles (160 km) of breathtaking mountains, cliffs, and rocky coves still leave visitors groping for adjectives.

The scenic Highway 1 was constructed across this rugged landscape during the 1930s, but otherwise Big Sur has been preserved in its natural state. There are no large towns and very few signs of civilization in the area. Much of the shore is protected in a series of state parks that offer dense forests, scenic rivers, and crashing surf, all easily accessible within a short distance of the road.

Crashing surf and rocky cliffs, typical of the Big Sur coastline

Point Lobos State Reserve
This is the habitat of the Monterey cypress, the only tree to survive the region's mixture of fog and salt spray. Its branches are shaped by the strong sea winds.

Point Sur Lighthouse sits atop a volcanic cone. It was manned until 1974 but is now automated.

Bixby Creek Bridge
This picturesque arched bridge was built in 1932. For many years it was the world's largest single-arch span, standing 260 ft (79 m) tall and 700 ft (213 m) long. Hwy 1 was named the state's first scenic highway here in 1966.

Nepenthe is a lovely restaurant hidden from the road by oak trees. It has long been frequented by Hollywood movie stars.

KEY

- Minor road
- Scenic route
- Hiking trail
- National park boundary
- River or lake
- Camping
- Viewpoint

Andrew Molera State Park
Opened in 1972, this park includes 10 miles (16 km) of hiking trails and 2.5 miles (4 km) of quiet, sandy beach.

Julia Pfeiffer Burns State Park
A tunnel under Hwy 1, accessible only on foot, leads to a 100-ft (30-m) high bluff, from which the McWay Creek waterfall spills into the Pacific Ocean.

VISITORS' CHECKLIST

1,500. Julia Pfeiffer Burns State Park. (831) 667-2100.

Ventana Wilderness
Most of the steep ridges of this beautiful wilderness, a part of the Los Padres National Forest, are accessible only to experienced hikers. Campsites cover the lower reaches.

The Esalen Institute was set up in the 1960s to hold New Age seminars. Its hot springs were first frequented by Native Americans and still attract visitors.

Jade Cove
This beautiful cove can be reached only by way of a steep path down the cliff face. The removal of jade above the high tide level is prohibited.

Simeon Point is
atural harbor that
s used by William
ıdolph Hearst to
p in materials for
estate, Hearst
stle™, located
the inland hilltop
pp688–9).

The beautiful Gothic arch of the main altar, Carmel Mission

Carmel 18

24,000. Monterey-Salinas Transit (MST), (831) 899-2555. San Carlos between 5th & 6th, (800) 550-4333. Carmel Bach Festival, Monterey (Sep–Mar). **www**.carmelcalifornia.org

This wealthy resort, with its art galleries and shops, has one of the area's most spectacular beaches. Among the town's many cultural events is a Bach Festival.

A short drive from town is the **Carmel Mission**, founded in 1770 by the father of California's mission chain, Junípero Serra. The most important of the 21 missions, it served as the administrative center for the state's northern missions. Father Serra, who lived here until his death in 1784, is buried at the foot of the altar. The sarcophagus, one of the finest in the US, depicts Father Serra recumbent in death, surrounded by three mourning priests. Carmel Mission was abandoned in 1834, and restoration work began in 1924, following the original plans. It now functions as a Catholic church. Its beautiful altar, with a Gothic arch and ornate decoration, is the only one of its kind among the 21 missions in California. The reconstructed living quarters evoke 18th-century mission life.

Carmel Mission
3080 Rio Rd, Carmel. ***Tel*** *(831) 624-1271. 9:30am–5pm Mon–Sat. 10:30am–5pm Sun. Thanksgiving, Dec 25.*

Monterey 19

35,000. Tyler, Pearl & Munras Sts, (831) 899-2555. 150 Olivier St, (888) 221-1010. Monterey Blues Festival (Jul); Monterey Jazz Festival (Sep); Laguna Seca Races (May–Oct). **www**.montereyinfo.org

The navigator Sebastián Vizcaíno landed here in 1602 and named the bay after his patron, the Count of Monterrey. But it was not until the Spanish captain Gaspar de Portolá and Father Serra arrived in 1770, establishing a church and presidio, that Monterey grew into a pueblo. It served as the Spanish Colonial capital of California until the Gold Rush of 1848, when it lost its status to San Francisco. Monterey still retains its unique character as a fishing port and market town. Today, visitors come to tour its carefully restored historic sites and attend the famous annual jazz festival in September.

In the center of town, a cluster of old buildings form the Monterey State Historic Park. The stately **Colton Hall** was where the California State Constitution was first signed in 1849. It now houses a museum commemorating the event. A short distance to the north, **Larkin House** was built in 1837 by an East Coast merchant, Thomas Larkin. Its architectural style, with two stories of adobe brick, wooden porticoes, and symmetry of plan and elevation, has become representative of the Monterey style. Farther east, **Stevenson House** is where Robert Louis Stevenson lived in 1879. It is now a museum. The Royal Presidio Chapel on Church Street was built in 1794 and is the town's oldest building. To the north are the Old Whaling Station, where mementos of the whaling industry are displayed, and the Custom House, preserved as it was in the 1830s and '40s. Close by, **Fisherman's Wharf**, once the center of the fishing and whaling industries, is now well known for its seafood restaurants.

Street sign in Cannery Row

Cannery Row, a six-block harbor-front street celebrated by John Steinbeck in his ribald novels *Cannery Row* and *Sweet Thursday*, was once the site of more than 20 fish-packing plants that processed fresh sardines. The canneries thrived in the early 20th century. In 1945 the sardines disappeared, and the canneries were abandoned. The buildings that remain house a collection of electic restaurants and shops. One notable building, at No. 800, is the old laboratory of "Doc" Ricketts, noted marine biologist, beer drinker, and Steinbeck's best friend. It is now a private club.

The **Monterey Bay Aquarium**, at the end of

THE 17-MILE DRIVE

The Monterey Peninsula has a spectacular coastline, best explored via a toll road, the 17-Mile Drive. The road offers superb views of crashing surf, coastal flora, and the Del Monte Forest. The drive begins at Spanish Bay, a popular picnicking area at the edge of Pacific Grove. Sights include the Carmel Mission; the striking Tor House, built in rock by the poet Robinson Jeffers; Lone Cypress, perhaps the most photographed tree in the world; and Spyglass Hill, a golf course named after a site in Robert Louis Stevenson's novel, *Treasure Island*. Among the other attractions are the exculsive country clubs and championship golf courses.

Spanish Bay, a picnicking area

For hotels and restaurants in this region see p723 and pp727–8

Cannery Row, is the largest in the US. More than 570 species and 350,000 specimens portray Monterey Bay's rich marine environment. Among the exhibits are an enclosed kelp forest, a rock pool, and a display of live jellyfish. The Outer Bay Wing has a one million-gallon (4.5 million-liter) tank, which re-creates the conditions of the ocean. It contains yellowfin tuna, ocean sunfish, and barracuda. The Research Institute offers visitors a chance to watch marine scientists at work, while the Splash Zone is a hands-on aquarium for kids.

The wealthy resort of **Pacific Grove**, at the end of the peninsula, was originally founded in 1889 as a religious retreat. Today, it is best known for its quaint wooden houses, many now converted into inns, coastal parks, and the beautiful migratory monarch butterflies that arrive between October and April.

Monterey Bay Aquarium
886 Cannery Row. ***Tel*** *(831) 648-4888.* *daily.* *Dec 25.*
www.mbayaq.org

Santa Cruz ⑳

252,000. 920 Pacific Ave.
1211 Ocean St, (831) 425-1234.
Santa Cruz Fungus Fair (Jan); Clam Chowder Cook-Off (Feb).
www.santacruzca.org

Perched at the northern tip of Monterey Bay, Santa Cruz is a lively beach town, backed by densely forested mountains. Surrounded by farmland, it evokes an agricultural rather than suburban feel. The town's cosmopolitan character is due to the presence of the large University of California campus, with its students and professors from all over the world.

Much of the downtown area was badly damaged by the Loma Prieta earthquake in 1989. It has recovered since then, and many good bookstores, art galleries, and cafés now line the streets.

The town's highlight is the waterfront, particularly the **Santa Cruz Beach Boardwalk**, the last surviving old-style amusement park on the West Coast. Its main attraction is the Giant Dipper roller coaster, built by Arthur Looff in 1924 and now a National Historic Landmark. The car travels along the 1-mile (1.6-km) wooden track at 55 mph (88 km/h). The carousel nearby has horses and chariots hand-carved by Looff's father, craftsman Charles Looff, in 1911. The ride is accompanied by a 100-year-old pipe organ. The park also has 27 other modern rides and an Art Deco dance hall.

Eroded archway at the Natural Bridges State Park, Santa Cruz

The **Museum of Art and History at the McPherson Center**, on Front Street, is a 20,000 sq ft (1,858 sq m) cultural center, which opened in 1993. The Art Gallery shows works primarily by local north central artists, while the History Gallery displays various aspects of Santa Cruz County's past.

Standing on a hill to the northeast of town is a replica of the **Mission Santa Cruz**, founded in 1791. All traces of the original were destroyed by frequent earthquakes, and the present structure was built in 1931. It now houses a small museum.

The scenic Cliff Drive along the coast takes in the **Natural Bridges State Beach**, named for the archways that were carved into the cliffs by ocean waves. One of the original arches still remains, through which waves roll into a small sandy cove. The park also preserves a eucalyptus grove and a nature trail, which shows the stages in the life cycle of the monarch butterfly. Also along the coast is the Surfing Museum, housed in a lighthouse. The museum has artifacts from every era of] Santa Cruz surfing history. Surfboards range from 1930s redwood planks to today's high-tech laminates.

East of downtown, Mystery Spot is a redwood grove, which has been drawing visitors for decades due to various strange events here. Balls roll uphill, parallel lines converge, and the laws of physics seem to be suspended. Part tourist trap, part genuine oddity, this attraction has to be seen to be believed.

Santa Cruz Beach Boardwalk
400 Beach St. ***Tel*** *(831) 423-5590.*
call ahead for opening times.

SURFING IN CALIFORNIA

Surfing was originally practiced by the Hawaiian nobility as a religious ceremony; it was introduced to California by Hawaiian George Freeth in 1907. The sport evolved into a truly California pursuit with the Beach Boys' hit song "Surfin" in 1961. Films such as *Ride the Wild Surf* (1964), and *Beach Blanket Bingo* (1965) helped to establish its cultural allure, and beach parties in the style of these films were highly popular in the 1960s. Today, surf culture determines fashion as well as speech.

Surfers on fiberglass boards

San Francisco ㉑

San Francisco is, after New York, the second most densely populated city in the US, with 750,000 people crowded into 47 sq miles (122 sq km). It is located at the tip of a peninsula, with the Pacific Ocean to the west and San Francisco Bay to the east. To the north, Golden Gate Bridge links it to the Marin Headlands. The Greater San Francisco area includes the cities of Oakland and Berkeley. San Francisco is a compact city, and most of the area can be explored on foot. The estimated 43 hills give many of the streets near impossible gradients but offer superb views.

A panoramic view of San Francisco from a penthouse bar on Nob Hill

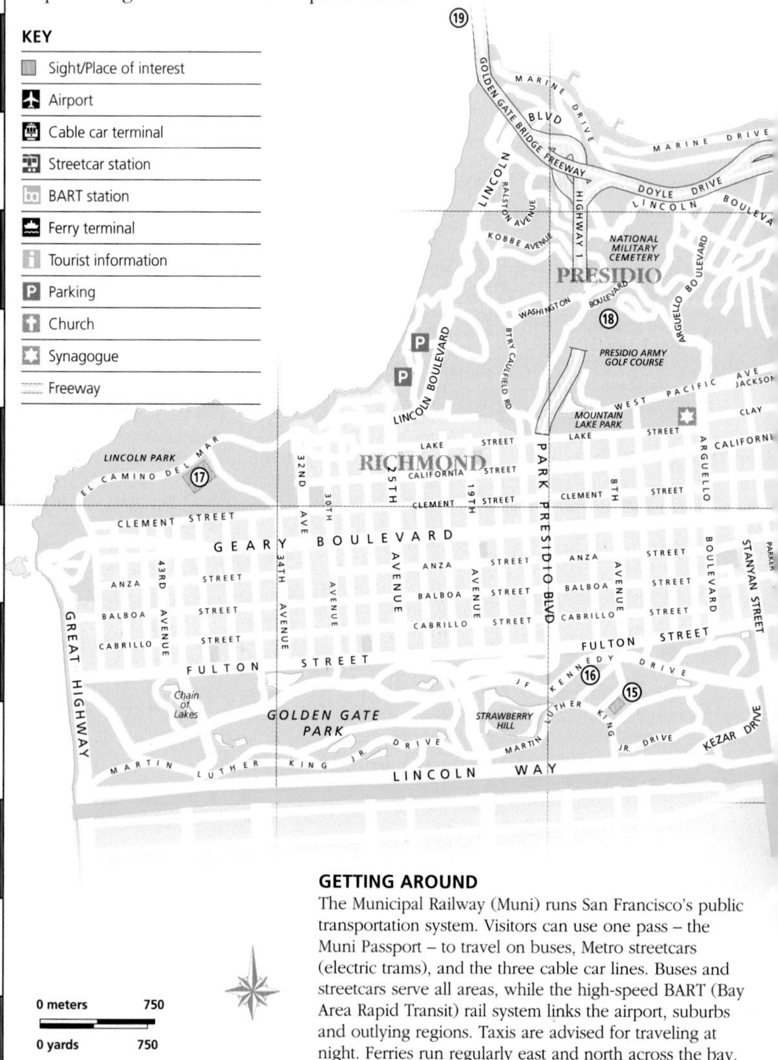

GETTING AROUND

The Municipal Railway (Muni) runs San Francisco's public transportation system. Visitors can use one pass – the Muni Passport – to travel on buses, Metro streetcars (electric trams), and the three cable car lines. Buses and streetcars serve all areas, while the high-speed BART (Bay Area Rapid Transit) rail system links the airport, suburbs and outlying regions. Taxis are advised for traveling at night. Ferries run regularly east and north across the bay.

SIGHTS AT A GLANCE

Financial District ①
Wells Fargo History Museum ②
Yerba Buena Center for the Arts ③
San Francisco Museum of Modern Art ④
Union Square ⑤
Chinatown ⑥
Nob Hill p701 ⑦
Fisherman's Wharf ⑧
North Beach ⑨
Alcatraz Island p703 ⑩

Pacific Heights ⑪
Asian Art Museum ⑫
Mission Dolores p705 ⑬
Haight Ashbury ⑭
California Academy of Sciences ⑮
de Young Museum ⑯
Legion of Honor ⑰
The Presidio ⑱
Golden Gate Bridge ⑲

Greater San Francisco
(see inset map)
San Jose ⑳
Palo Alto ㉑
Oakland ㉒
Berkeley ㉓
Sausalito ㉔
Muir Woods ㉕

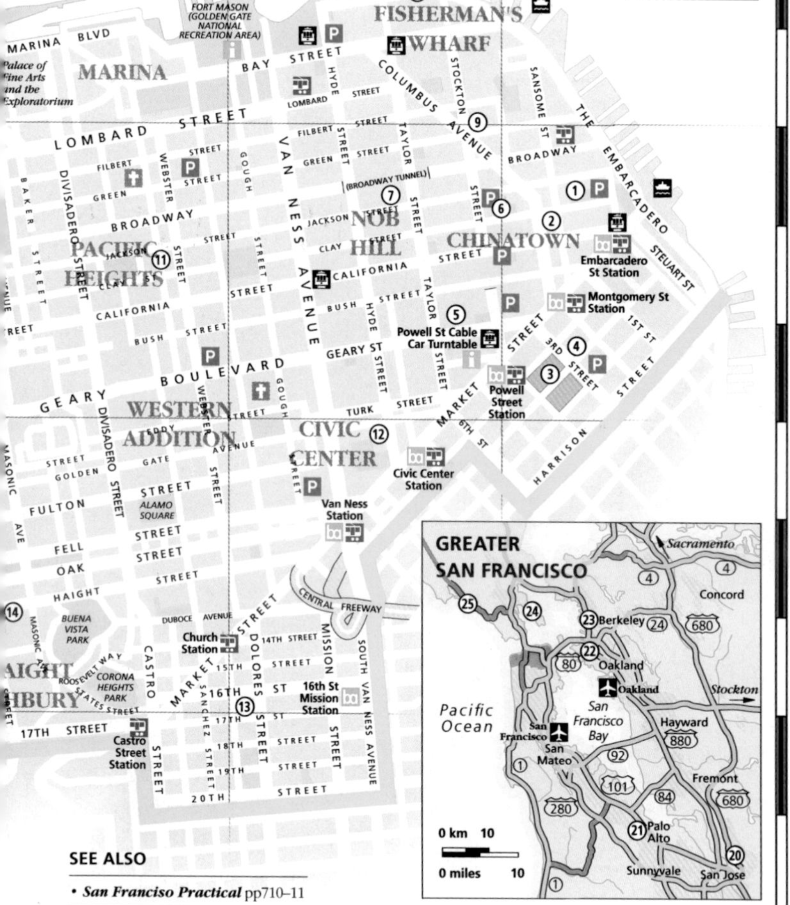

SEE ALSO
• ***San Francisco Practical*** pp710–11
• ***Where to Stay*** p724
• ***Where to Eat*** p728

KEY
Area of main map

The 49-Mile Scenic Drive

Official sign

Linking the city's most intriguing neighborhoods, fascinating sights, and spectacular views, the 49-Mile Scenic Drive (79 km) provides a splendid overview of San Francisco. Keeping to the well-marked route is easy: just follow the blue-and-white seagull signs. Some of these are hidden by overhanging vegetation, so you need to be alert. Set aside a whole day for this trip; there are plenty of places to stop to take photographs or admire the views.

The Palace of Fine Arts & the Exploratorium ㉔
The grand Neo-Classical building and its modern science museum stand near the entrance to the Presidio.

Stow Lake ⑤
There is a waterfall and a Chinese pavilion on the island in this picturesque lake, where you can also rent boats.

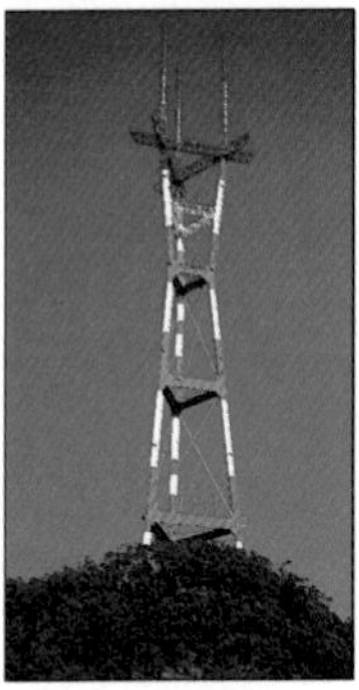

Sutro Tower ⑧
This distinctive orange-and-white tower is visible from all over the city.

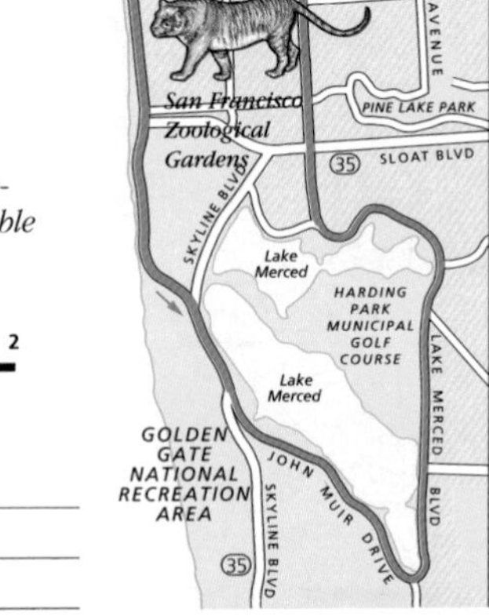

Five-tiered pagoda in Japantown

0 km 2
0 miles 1

KEY

— 49-Mile Scenic Drive

Viewpoint

Coit Tower ⑳
Overlooking North Beach, Telegraph Hill is topped by this tower, which has fine murals and an observation deck.

San Francisco National Maritime Museum ㉑
This 1939 building houses a collection of nautical bric-a-brac. It is closed for renovation until 2009.

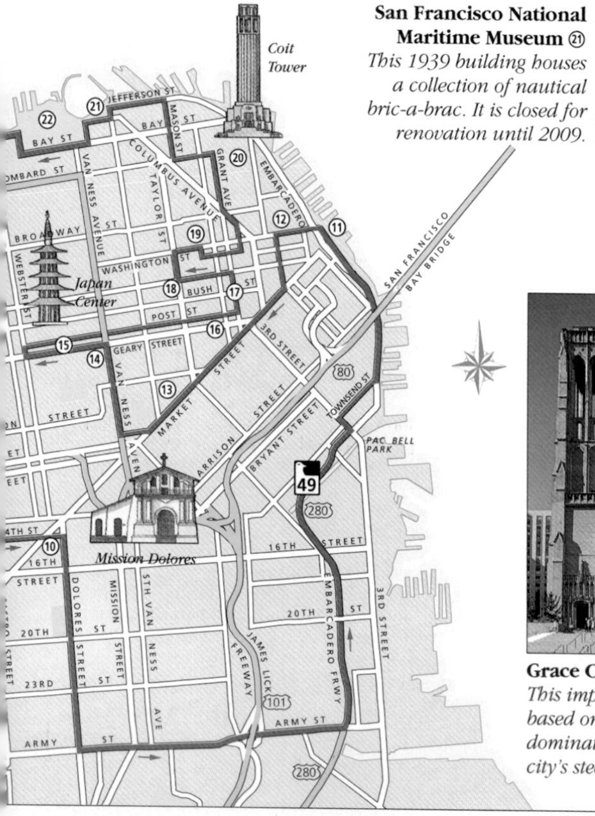

Grace Cathedral ⑱
This impressive cathedral, based on Notre Dame in Paris, dominates the summit of the city's steepest hill, Nob Hill.

TIPS FOR DRIVERS

Starting point: *Anywhere. The circuit is designed to be followed in a counterclockwise direction starting and ending at any point.*
When to go: *Avoid driving during rush hours: 7–9am, 4–7pm. Most of the views are as spectacular by night as by day.*
Parking: *Use the parking lots that are located around the Financial District, the Civic Center, Japan-town, Nob Hill, Chinatown, North Beach, and Fisherman's Wharf. Elsewhere, street parking is usually easily available.*

FINDING THE SIGHTS

① Presidio *p707*
② Fort Point *p707*
③ Legion of Honor *p706*
④ Queen Wilhelmina Tulip Garden
⑤ Stow Lake
⑥ Conservatory of Flowers
⑦ Haight Street
⑧ Sutro Tower
⑨ Twin Peaks
⑩ Mission Dolores *p705*
⑪ Ferry Building *p698*
⑫ Embarcadero Center *p698*
⑬ Civic Center
⑭ St. Mary's Cathedral
⑮ Japan Center
⑯ Union Square *p699*
⑰ Chinatown Gateway *p700*
⑱ Grace Cathedral *p701*
⑲ Cable Car Barn *p701*
⑳ Coit Tower *p702*
㉑ San Francisco National Maritime Museum *p702*
㉒ Fort Mason
㉓ Marina Green
㉔ Palace of Fine Arts and the Exploratorium *p704*

Transamerica Pyramid, the tallest building on the city's skyline

Financial District ①

Map F3. *Between Washington & Market Sts.* 1, 12, 15, 32, 42, 83. *F, J, K, L, M, N.* *California St.* **Embarcadero Center** *1, 32, 42.* *J, K, L, M, N.* *California St.*

San Francisco's economic engine is fueled by the Financial District, lying at the heart of downtown. The district stretches from the imposing skyscrapers and plazas of the **Embarcadero Center** to staid Montgomery Street, called the "Wall Street of the West." All the main banks, brokers, and law offices are located here.

Completed in 1981 after a decade of construction, the vast Embarcadero Center stretches from Justin Herman Plaza to Battery Street and houses a large number of commercial outlets and offices. A shopping arcade occupies the first three tiers of its four high-rise towers. The splendid foyer of the Hyatt Regency Hotel, located here, has a 17-story atrium.

North of Washington Street, the **Jackson Square Historical District** was once the heart of the business community. Renovated in the early 1950s, this area contains brick, cast-iron, and granite façades dating from Gold Rush days. From 1850 to 1910 it was known as the Barbary Coast, notorious for its brothels and squalor. Today, the buildings are used as showrooms, law offices, and antique shops; some of the best ones can be seen in Jackson and Montgomery Streets.

Standing adjacent is a soaring San Francisco landmark, the **Transamerica Pyramid**. Capped with a spire on top of its 48 stories, it reaches 853 ft (260 m) and is the tallest building in the city. Its 3,678 windows take cleaners an entire month to wash. Designed by William Pereira, the building stands on what was earlier the site of the historic Montgomery Block, which contained many important offices. Numerous artists and writers took up residence in the block, including the writer Mark Twain, who often visited the Exchange Saloon, located in the building's basement. Farther south, the granite **Bank of America** was originally the Bank of Italy, founded by A.P. Giannini in San Jose. Its 52 floors make it one of the city's tallest skyscrapers, with incredible views from the top. At the district's northeastern corner lies the **Ferry Building**, built in 1903. In the early 1930s, over 50 million passengers a year passed through here, to and from the transcontinental railroad in Oakland or homes across the bay. Its clock tower was inspired by the Moorish bell tower of Seville Cathedral in Spain. With the opening of the Bay Bridge in 1936, it began to deteriorate. A few ferries still cross to Tiburon, Sausalito, and Oakland. On the building's east side stands the Gandhi Monument (1988). Designed by K.B. Patel and sculpted by Z. Pounov and S. Lowe, it bears an inscription of Gandhi's words.

Transamerica Pyramid
600 Montgomery St. *8:30am–4:30pm Mon–Fri.* *public hols.*

Bank of America
555 California St. ***Tel*** *(415) 433-7500 (Carnelian Room).*
www.carnelianroom.com

A splendid old stagecoach at the Wells Fargo Museum

Wells Fargo History Museum ②

Map F3. 420 Montgomery St. ***Tel*** *(415) 396-2619.* *1, 12, 15, 42.* *Montgomery St.* *9am–5pm Mon–Fri.* *public hols.* **www**.wellsfargohistory.com

Founded in 1852, Wells Fargo & Co. became the greatest banking and transportation company in the West. The company moved people, goods, gold, and mail. The Pony Express was one of their mail ventures. The museum displays splendid stagecoaches – famous for the legendary stories of their heroic drivers and the bandits who robbed them. The best known bandit was Black Bart, who left poems at the scene of his crimes. He was later identified as the mining engineer Charles Boles. Exhibits include a simulated stagecoach ride, Pony Express mail, photographs, gold nuggets, and the imperial currency of the eccentric Joshua Norton, who proclaimed himself Emperor of the United States in 1854.

Yerba Buena Center for the Arts ③

Map F3. 3rd St, between Mission & Howard Sts. ***Tel*** *(415) 978-2700.* *9, 14, 15, 30, 45, 76.* *J, K, L, M, N.* **Center for the Arts Galleries & Forum** *noon–5pm Tue–Wed, Fri–Sun (to 8pm Thu).* *public hols.* *(free first Thu of month).* **Zeum** *221 4th St (415) 820-3320.* *1–5pm Wed–Fri, 11am–5pm Sat & Sun (in term time).* *Dec 25.* **www**.ybca.org

The construction of the underground Moscone Center, San Francisco's largest venue for conventions, heralded the beginning of ambitious plans for Yerba Buena Gardens, now the Yerba Buena Center for the Arts. New housing, hotels, museums, and shops

Esplanade Gardens in the Yerba Buena Center for the Arts

have sprung up. The center is situated at the heart of SoMa (South of Market), an area that has become the city's "artists' quarter," with its warehouses-turned-studios, bars, and avant-garde theaters. The **Esplanade Gardens** give visitors a chance to wander along paths or relax on benches. Close by, the Martin Luther King Jr. Memorial has words of peace in several languages. The adjacent **Center for the Arts Galleries and Forum** have visual arts galleries and a screening room featuring contemporary art and films. The **Center for the Arts Theater** presents performing arts that reflect the cultural diversity of the city. **Zeum**, located at the Yerba Buena Rooftop, has an ongoing program of events involving design. The **Contemporary Jewish Museum** showcases scholarly and artistic work relating to the Jewish experience. It includes film, music, and literary readings.

San Francisco Museum of Modern Art ④

Map F3. 151 Third St. ***Tel*** *(415) 357-4000.* *5, 9, 12, 14, 15, 30, 38, 45.* *J, K, L, M, N.* *11am–9pm Thu, 11am–6pm Fri–Tue. Times may change, please call to confirm.* *Wed, Jan 1, Thanksgiving, Dec 25.* *(free first Tue of month; half-price admission Thu 6–9pm).* **www**.sfmoma.org

This dramatic museum forms the nucleus of San Francisco's reputation as a leading center of modern art. Created in 1935 with the aim of displaying works by 20th-century artists, it moved into its new quarters in 1995. The focus of Swiss architect Mario Botta's Modernist building is the 125-ft (38-m) cylindrical skylight, which channels light down to the first floor atrium court. More than 17,000 works of art are housed in its 50,000 sq ft (4,600 sq m) of gallery space, and it offers a dynamic schedule of changing exhibits from around the world.

The galleries display paintings, sculptures, architecture, design, photography, and media art. Among the highlights are works by Dali, Matisse, and Picasso; Diego Rivera's mural *The Flower Carrier*, a powerful irony on the human cost of luxury, painted in oil and tempera on Masonite in 1935; and Richard Shaw's sculpted figure *Melodius Double Stop* in the California Art section.

Victory Monument in Union Square

Union Square ⑤

Map E3. *2, 3, 4, 30, 38, 45.* *J, K, L, M, N.* *Powell–Mason, Powell–Hyde.*

Union Square, lined with palm trees, is at the heart of the city's main shopping district and has a wealth of fine department stores. It was named after the pro-Union rallies held here during the Civil War of 1861–65. The original churches, gentlemen's clubs, and a synagogue were eventually overtaken by shops and offices. Some of the main stores include Macy's, Saks, and Gump's. The area also houses many antiquarian bookshops and smaller boutiques. Union Square marks the edge of the **Theater District** and is bordered on the west side by the luxurious Westin St. Francis Hotel. At the center of the square there is a bronze statue of the Goddess of Victory, sculpted by Robert Aitken in 1903 to commemorate Admiral Dewey's victory during the Spanish–American War (1898). The **Circle Gallery Building** at 140 Maiden Lane is an art gallery designed by Frank Lloyd Wright. It was the precursor to his Guggenheim Museum in New York *(see p82)*.

CALIFORNIA'S EARTHQUAKES

The San Andreas Fault extends some 600 miles (965 km) along California's coastline and is one of the few sites on Earth where an active plate boundary occurs on land. Each year, the Pacific Plate moves 1–1.6 inches (2.5–4 cm). The terrible fire of 1906 that destroyed San Francisco was caused by an earthquake estimated at 7.8 on the Richter Scale. More recently, the earthquake of October 1989, south of San Francisco, killed 62 people and caused at least $6 billion worth of damage. In 1994, the Northridge quake, magnitude 6.7, rocked Los Angeles. Scientists predict that the next major earthquake, the "Big One," will hit Southern California.

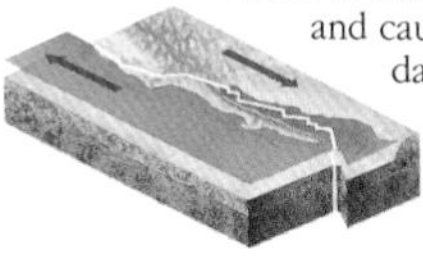
The San Andreas Fault

Colorful oriental architecture along Grant Avenue, Chinatown

Chinatown ⑥

Map F3. 1, 2, 3, 4, 15, 30, 45. *all three lines go to Chinatown.*

An estimated 25,000 Chinese migrants settled in the plaza on Stockton Street during the Gold Rush era of the 1850s *(see p654)*. Today, the district evokes the atmosphere of a bustling southern Chinese town, although the architecture and customs are distinctly American hybrids on a Cantonese theme. The sweatshops, laundries, and cramped apartment buildings that once earned this area the nickname "Golden Ghetto" have been replaced with tidy shops and refurbished residential areas. Cable cars run down two sides of the district.

The ornate Chinatown Gateway, marking the southern entrance to Chinatown, was designed by Clayton Lee as an arch over the start of the main tourist street, **Grant Avenue**. The three-arched structure was inspired by the ceremonial entrances of traditional Chinese villages. It is capped with green roof tiles and a host of propitiatory animals in glazed ceramic.

Dragon lampposts, upturned roofs, and stores selling everything from kites and cooking utensils to antiques, embroidered silks, and gems line Grant Avenue. Most of the buildings were erected after the 1906 earthquake in an Oriental Renaissance style. In the 1830s and 40s it was the main thoroughfare of Yerba Buena, the village that preceded San Francisco. A plaque at No. 823 marks the site of the first dwelling, a canvas tent that was built in 1835.

To the east of Grant Avenue is the city's original town square, **Portsmouth Plaza**, which was laid out in 1839. In 1846 marines raised the American flag above the plaza, officially seizing the port as part of the United States. Two years later, it was here that Sam Brannan announced the discovery of gold in the Sierra Nevada Mountains *(see pp718–19)*. It soon became the hub of the new booming city in the 1850s. Today, Portsmouth Plaza is the social hub of Chinatown. In the morning people practice t'ai chi, and from noon to evening gather to play cards.

Running parallel to Grant Avenue, **Stockton Street** is where locals shop. Boxes of the freshest vegetables, fish, and other produce spill over onto crowded sidewalks. The Kong Chow Temple, located here, features fine Cantonese wood carvings.

Chinatown's busy alleys, located between Grant Avenue and Stockton Street, echo with authentic sights and sounds of the Orient. The largest of the four narrow lanes is Waverly Place, also known as the "Street of Painted Balconies." Watch for the Tin How Temple, which is brightly decorated with hundreds of gold and red lanterns. Nearby, Ross Alley has the tiny Fortune Cookie Factory, where visitors can see how the famous San Francisco creation is made. The alleys have many old buildings as well as old-fashioned herbalist shops, displaying elk antlers, sea horses, snake wine, and other exotic wares. Numerous small restaurants, above and below street level, serve cheap and delicious food.

Dragon's Head at the Chinese Historical Society

The **Chinese Historical Society** has a range of fascinating exhibits including a ceremonial dragon costume and a "tiger fork," a triton that was wielded in one of the battles during the reign of terror known as the Tong Wars. The Tongs were rival Chinese clans who fought over the control of gambling and prostitution in the city in the late 19th century. Other artifacts, documents, and photographs illuminate the daily life of Chinese immigrants in San Francisco from the 1600s to the present day. Among these is a yearbook written in Chinese.

Chinese Historical Society
965 Clay St. ***Tel*** *(415) 391-1188.*
1, 30, 45. *Powell St.*
noon–5pm Tue–Fri. *public hols.* **www**.chsa.org

CABLE CARS

One of the city's cable cars

The cable car system was launched in 1873, with its inventor Andrew Hallidie riding in the first car. He was inspired to tackle the problem of transporting people up the city's steep slopes after seeing an accident, where a horse-drawn tram slipped down a hill. His system was a success, and by 1889 cable cars were running on eight lines. Before the 1906 earthquake, over 600 cars were in use. With the advent of the internal combustion engine, however, they became obsolete, and in 1947 attempts were made to replace them with buses. After a huge public outcry, the present three lines were retained.

Nob Hill ⑦

Map E3. *1, 12, 30, 45, 83.* *California St, Powell–Mason, Powell–Hyde.*

Nob Hill is the highest summit of the city itself, rising 338 ft (103 m) above the bay. It is San Francisco's most celebrated hilltop, famous for its cable cars, plush hotels, and views. The steep slopes kept prominent citizens away until the opening of the California Street cable car line in 1878. The rich then flocked to build homes here, including the "Big Four" railroad barons, who were among its richest tenants. The name "Nob Hill" is thought to come from the Indian word *nabob*, meaning chieftain. Sadly, all the grand mansions were leveled in the great earthquake and fire of 1906. The only building that survived was the home of James C. Flood, which is now the Pacific Union Club.

Nob Hill still attracts the affluent to its hotels, which recall the opulence of the Victorian era and offer fine views of the city.

Grace Cathedral is the main Episcopal church in San Francisco. Designed by Lewis P. Hobart, this building was inspired by Notre Dame in Paris. Preparatory work began in 1928, but the cathedral was not completed until 1964. Its entrance doors are cast from molds of Ghiberti's "Doors of Paradise," made for the Baptistry in Florence.

A short distance north of Nob Hill is the **Cable Car Barn**, erected in 1909, which garages cable cars at night. It is a repair shop, museum, and powerhouse of the cable car system. Anchored to the ground floor are the engines and wheels that wind the cables through the system of channels and pulleys beneath the city's streets. Visitors can observe them from the mezzanine, then walk down to look under the street. The museum also houses an early cable car and the mechanisms that control individual cars.

Grace Cathedral
1100 California St. ***Tel*** *(415) 749-6300.* *Choral evensong see website for schedule; Choral Eucharist 11am Sun.* **www**.gracecathedral.org

Cable Car Barn
1201 Mason St. ***Tel*** *(415) 474-1887.* *summer: 10am–6pm daily; winter: 10am–5pm daily.* *Jan 1, Easter, Thanksgiving, Dec 25.* *mezzanine only.* ***Video show.*** **www**.cablecarmuseum.com

GRACE CATHEDRAL

The interior of this Gothic-style cathedral is replete with marble and beautiful stained glass. The leaded windows were designed by Charles Connick, using the blue glass of Chartres as his inspiration. The rose window has thick faceted glass, which is illuminated from the inside at night. Other windows are by Henry Willet and Gabriel Loire, and include depictions of Albert Einstein and astronaut John Glenn. The cathedral also features a 13th-century Catalonian crucifix and a 16th-century Brussels tapestry, and is popular for its choral evensong; check website for schedule.

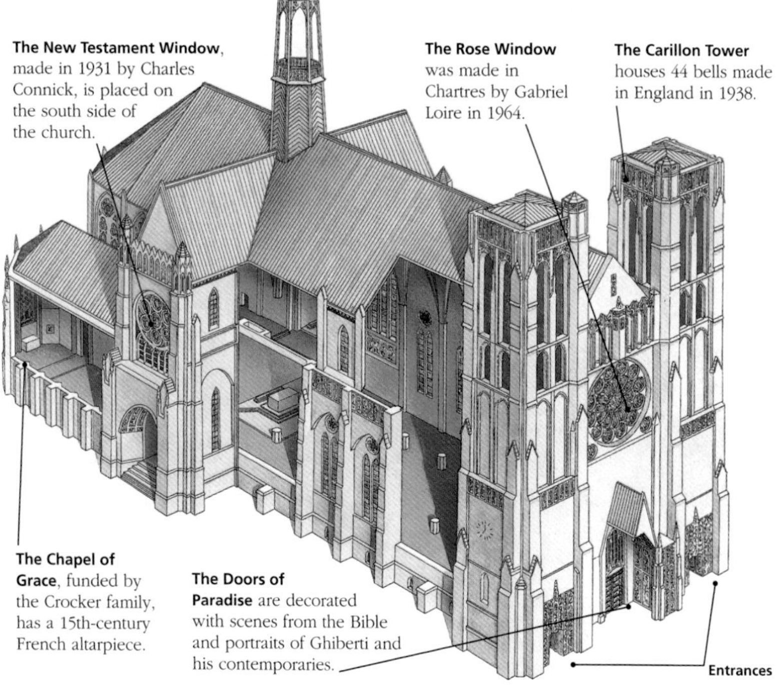

Shops and amusements at Pier 39, Fisherman's Wharf

Fisherman's Wharf ⑧

Map E2. Between the coastline & Beach St. *15, 19, 25, 30, 32, 39, 42, 45, 47.* *Powell–Mason, Powell–Hyde.*

Italian seafood restaurants have replaced fishing as the primary focus of Fisherman's Wharf. Fishermen from Genoa and Sicily first arrived here in the late 19th century and founded San Francisco's fishing industry. Since the 1950s, the area has given way to tourism, although brightly colored boats still set out to sea early each morning. The specialty here is the delicious Dungeness crab.

Pier 39 is the Wharf's hub, with restaurants, shops, and specialty stores, set against a backdrop of stunning bay views. Refurbished in 1978 to resemble a quaint wooden fishing village, the pier is also home to groups of sea lions that bask on the docks. Docked at Pier 45 is the World War II submarine **USS *Pampanito***, which fought several battles in the Pacific, sinking six enemy ships. Visitors can tour the torpedo room, galley, and officer's quarters. To its south on Jefferson Street is **Ripley's Believe It Or Not! Museum**, which displays the cartoonist's collection of curiosities – one of which is a cable car built of 275,000 matchsticks. Farther along Jefferson Street, **The Cannery**, earlier a fruit processing factory, now houses a mall with restaurants, museums, and shops. The **San Francisco Maritime National Historical Park** incorporates a museum on Beach Street, which displays various nautical objects, and hosts visiting exhibitions. The park also includes a large collection of old ships moored at the nearby **Hyde Street Pier**. Among the finest is the *C.A. Thayer*, a three-masted schooner built in 1895.

North Beach ⑨

Map E2. 15, 30, *39, 45.* *Powell–Mason, Powell–Hyde.*

South of Fisherman's Wharf is North Beach, also known as "Little Italy." Settlers from Chile, China, and Italy brought their enthusiasm for nightlife to the area, earning North Beach its vibrant reputation and attracting bohemians and writers, including the leading chronicler of the "Beat generation," Jack Kerouac. At the junction of Broadway and Columbus Avenue, the **City Lights Bookstore**, once owned by the Beat poet Lawrence Ferlinghetti, was the first bookshop in the US to sell only paperbacks. **Vesuvio**, south of City Lights, was one of the most popular Beat bars. Welsh poet Dylan Thomas was a patron here, and it is still a favorite with poets and artists. The former **Condor Club** is located on a stretch of Broadway known as The Strip, noted for its "adult entertainment." This landmark establishment was where the area's first topless show was staged in June 1964. **Caffè Trieste**, on the corner of Vallejo Street, is the oldest coffee house in San Francisco and a genuine Beat rendezvous since 1956. Very much a part of Italian-American culture, it offers live opera on Saturday afternoons.

Lombard Street, a little to the north, is renowned as "the crookedest street in the world." Banked at a natural incline of 27 degrees, this hill proved too steep for vehicles to climb. In the 1920s the section close to the summit of Russian Hill was revamped, and eight tight curves were added. There are spectacular views of San Francisco from the summit, especially at night. Close by, the **San Francisco Art Institute** is famous for its Diego Rivera Gallery, which contains an outstanding mural by the famous Mexican muralist created in 1931.

The 210-ft **Coit Tower** lies at the top of Telegraph Hill. The lobby has many Depression-era murals.

Cars negotiating Lombard St, "the crookedest street in the world"

SAN FRANCISCO'S MURALS

Coit Tower's mural of Fisherman's Wharf in the 1930s

San Francisco's cosmopolitan heritage comes alive in the bright murals that decorate walls and public places in several parts of the city. Life in the metropolis is one of the major themes. The Mission District has over 200 murals showing every aspect of daily life on the walls of restaurants, banks, and schools. Many of these were painted in the 1970s, when the city and various public bodies commissioned many public works of art. One of the best is the *Carnaval Mural* on 24th Street. The city also has three major murals by Diego Rivera, the Mexican artist who revived fresco painting in the 1930s and 40s.

For hotels and restaurants in this region see p724 and p728

Alcatraz Island ⑩

Alcatraz means "pelican" in Spanish and refers to the first inhabitants of this rocky, steep-sided island. In 1859, the US Army established a fort here that guarded San Francisco Bay until 1907, when it became a military prison. From 1934 to 1963 it served as a maximum-security federal penitentiary. Dubbed "The Rock" by prisoners, it housed an average of 264 of the country's most infamous criminals, who were transferred here for disobedience while serving time in prisons elsewhere in the US. Today, Alcatraz is part of the Golden Gate National Recreation Area.

VISITORS' CHECKLIST

Tel *(415) 981-7625 or online for tickets & schedules.* ⛴ *from Pier 33.* ◯ *daily: first ferry 9am; last ferry 2:15pm (4:15pm in summer).* ● *Jan 1, Dec 25.*
Night Tours ***Tel*** *(415) 981-7625.* ♿ *accessible in places.*
Film presentation *free with ticket.*
www.alcatrazcruises.com

The Cell Block
Prisoners spent between 16 and 23 hours every day alone in stark cells, equipped with only a toilet and bunk. Many cells measured 5 ft by 9 ft (1.5 m by 2.7 m).

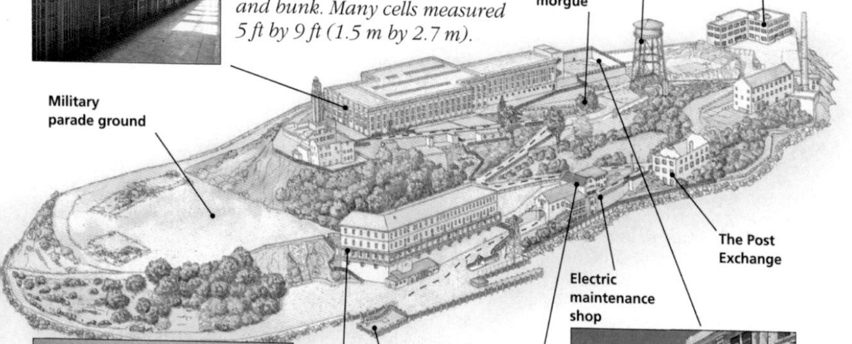

Alcatraz from the Ferry
Looming ominously out of the ocean, "The Rock" promised its inmates strict discipline and constant vigilance.

The Visitor Center is in the barracks building behind the jetty. It houses an information center, bookstore, exhibits, and a multimedia show providing a historical overview of Alcatraz.

Exercise Yard
Meals and a walk around the exercise yard were the highlights of a prisoner's day. This walled yard appeared in films that were shot here.

FAMOUS INMATES OF ALCATRAZ ISLAND

Al Capone
Al Capone was convicted in 1934 for income tax evasion and spent much of his five-year sentence at Alcatraz in an isolation cell. He left the prison mentally unstable.

Robert Stroud
Stroud spent most of his 17 years here in solitary confinement. Despite assertions to the contrary in the film *The Birdman of Alcatraz* (1962), he was forbidden from keeping birds in his cell.

Anglin Brothers
John and Clarence Anglin and Frank Morris chipped through the walls of their cells, hiding the holes with cardboard grates. They made a raft to escape and were never caught. Their story was dramatized in the film *Escape from Alcatraz* (1979).

George Kelly
George "Machine Gun" Kelly was the prison's most dangerous inmate and has the singular distinction of serving 17 years for kidnapping and extortion.

Haas-Lilienthal House in Pacific Heights, an 1886-Queen Anne mansion

Pacific Heights ⑪

Map D3. 🚌 *1, 3, 12, 19, 22, 24, 27, 28, 29, 30, 42, 43, 45, 47, 49, 83.* 🚋 *California St.*

The steep blocks between **Alta Plaza** and **Lafayette Park** are set in the heart of the exclusive Pacific Heights district. After cable cars linked it with the downtown area in the 1880s, it quickly became a desirable place to live, and many palatial Victorian houses line its quiet streets. Some date from the late 19th century, while others were built after the devastating earthquake and fire of 1906.

The **Haas-Lilienthal House**, an elaborate Queen Anne-style mansion, was built in 1886 for the merchant William Haas. Furnished in Victorian style, it is the only intact private home of the period that opens regularly as a museum. It houses the headquarters of the Architectural Heritage Foundation. The impressive **Spreckels Mansion** on Washington Street, constructed on the lines of a French Baroque palace, is now home to best-selling novelist Danielle Steele. Close by, Lafayette Park is one of San Francisco's loveliest hill-top gardens, lined with pine and eucalyptus trees. It offers excellent views of the numerous Victorian houses in the surrounding streets. Located across the street from the park, **2151 Sacramento Street** is an ornate French-style mansion, which has a plaque commemorating a visit by the famous author Sir Arthur Conan Doyle in 1923. At the center of Pacific Heights is Alta Plaza, a landscaped urban park, where the San Franciscan elite come to relax. Set up in the 1850s, this hilltop green has tennis courts and a playground. The stone steps rising from Clay Street on the south side offer views of Haight Ashbury.

North of Pacific Heights, the streets drop steeply down to the Marina District, which was created from reclaimed land for the 1915 Panama-Pacific Exposition. The Expo's only surviving monument is the grand **Palace of Fine Arts**. This Neo-Classical building has a large rotunda with allegorical paintings on its dome. It houses the entertaining Exploratorium Science Museum and hosts events such as the May Film Festival.

Haas-Lilienthal House
2007 Franklin St. ***Tel*** *(415) 441-3004.* 🕒 *noon–3pm Wed & Sat, 11am–4pm Sun.* **www**.sfheritage.org

Asian Art Museum ⑫

Map E4. 200 Larkin St. ***Tel*** *(415) 581-3500.* 🚌 *5, 8, 19, 21, 26, 42, 47, 49.* 🚋 *F, J, K, L, M, N.* 🕒 *10am–5pm Tue–Sun (until 9pm Thu).* **www**.asianart.org

The Asian Art Museum is located on Civic Center Plaza in a building that was the crown jewel of the Beaux Arts movement. The former Main Library, built in 1917, has undergone seismic strengthening and adaptive reuse of space to create the largest museum outside Asia devoted exclusively to Asian art. The museum's exhibits include 12,000 art objects spanning 6,000 years of history and representing over 40 Asian nations. There are also performance venues, education programs, and a hands-on discovery center. The terrace café overlooks the Civic Center and Fulton Street Mall.

The grand staircase at the Asian Art Museum

THE SOUNDS OF 1960S SAN FRANCISCO

During the late 1960s, and most notably during the 1967 "Summer of Love," young people from all over the country flocked to the Haight Ashbury district. They came not just to "turn on, tune in, and drop out," but also to listen to rock bands such as Janis Joplin's Big Brother and the Holding Company, Jefferson Airplane, and the Grateful Dead, all of whom emerged out of the thriving music scene. Impresario Bill Graham put unlikely pairs such as Miles Davis and the Grateful Dead on the same bill at Fillmore Auditorium. He also brought in big-name performers such as Jimi Hendrix and The Who, making "the Haight" the focus of the rock world.

A 1960s street scene in Haight Ashbury

For hotels and restaurants in this region see p724 and p728

Mission Dolores ⑬

Map E4. 3321 16th St. 22. J. (415) 621-8203. 9am–4pm daily. Jan 1, Thanksg, Dec 25. **www**.missiondolores.org

Preserved intact since it was built in 1791, Mission Dolores, after which the surrounding Mission District is named, is the oldest building in the city and an embodiment of San Francisco's Spanish Colonial roots. Founded by Father Junípero Serra as the sixth California mission, it is formally known as the Mission of San Francisco de Asis. The name Dolores reflects its proximity to Laguna de los Dolores (Lake of Our Lady of Sorrows), an ancient swamp. The building is modest by mission standards, but its 4-ft (1.2-m) thick walls have survived.

Figure of saint in the mission

Paintings by Native Americans adorn the restored ceiling. There is a fine Baroque altar and reredos, and a display of historical documents in the small museum. Most services are held in the basilica, built adjacent to the mission in 1918. The cemetery contains graves of San Franciscan pioneers, as well as a mass grave of 5,000 Native Americans, who died in the measles epidemics of 1804 and 1826.

The altarpiece of Mission Dolores, imported from Mexico in 1780

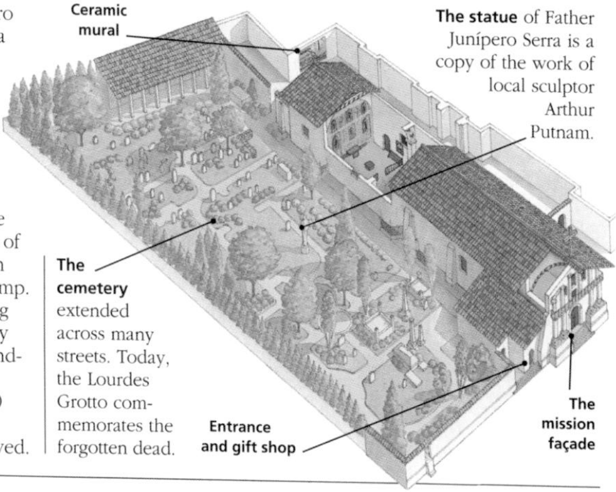

Ceramic mural

The statue of Father Junípero Serra is a copy of the work of local sculptor Arthur Putnam.

The cemetery extended across many streets. Today, the Lourdes Grotto commemorates the forgotten dead.

Entrance and gift shop

The mission façade

Haight Ashbury ⑭

Map D4. 6, 7, 33, 37, 43, 66, 71. N. **Lower Haight** 6, 7, 22, 66, 71. K, L, M.

Stretching from Buena Vista Park to Golden Gate Park, Haight Ashbury was the center of the hippie world in the 1960s. Originally a quiet, middle class suburb – hence the dozens of elaborate Queen Anne-style houses – it changed dramatically into the mecca of a free-wheeling, bohemian community that defied social norms and conventions. In 1967, the "Summer of Love," fueled by the media, brought some 75,000 young people in search of free love, music, and drugs, and it became the focus of a worldwide youth culture. Thousands lived here, and there was even a free clinic to treat hippies without medical insurance.

Today, "the Haight" retains its radical atmosphere and has settled into being one of the liveliest and most unconventional places in San Francisco, with an eclectic mix of people, second-hand clothing shops, renowned music and book stores, and a variety of excellent cafés.

Buena Vista Park on its eastern fringe has a mass of knotted trees and offers magnificent views of the city. The grand (Richard) Spreckels Mansion on Buena Vista Avenue (not to be confused with the one on Washington Street), is a typical late-Victorian home. It was once a guest house, and its visitors included writer Jack London and journalist Ambrose Bierce. The **Red Victorian Hotel**, affectionately dubbed the "Jeffrey Haight" in 1967, was a favorite among hippies. It now caters to a New Age clientele and offers rooms with transcendental themes.

The Red Victorian B&B in Haight Ashbury, a relic of the hippie era

Halfway between City Hall and Haight Ashbury, the **Lower Haight** marks the border of the predominantly African-American Fillmore District, which is one of the liveliest parts of the city. Unusual art galleries, boutiques, inexpensive cafés, and bars serve a largely bohemian clientele. It also has dozens of houses known as "Victorians," built from the 1850s to the 1900s, including cottages such as the Nightingale House at 201 Buchanan Street. Although safe during the day, the Lower Haight can be unnerving after dark.

California Academy of Sciences ⑮

Map C4. 55 Music Concourse Dr, Golden Gate Park **Tel** *(415) 379-8000.* *44.* *9:30am–5pm Mon–Sat (until 9pm Thu), 11am–5pm Sun.* *Thanksg., Dec 25.* *some areas.* **www**.calacademy.org

Founded in 1853, California Academy of Sciences is San Francisco's oldest and most popular science museum. Several years of planning and rebuilding have given the venerable museum a thoroughly modern home and added several world-class exhibits. Designed by Renzo Piano, the building is encased by glass walls that allow natural light to stream in. A planetarium, aquarium, outstanding natural history museum, anthropology section, and rainforest are worthy of more than one visit.

Tyrannosaurus rex skeleton

The **African Hall**, with its displays of realistic models of animals from Africa's jungles in lifelike dioramas, provides an opportunity to examine big game at close range. The diorama of a watering hole in the African savanna features the changing light and sounds of an African day, compressed into a 20-minute cycle. One of the museum's star exhibits, in its Earth and Space section, is **The Earth Quake!**, where visitors experience earth tremors and learn about their destructive power. The **Morrison Planetarium** has one of the world's most precise star projectors, which transforms the ceiling into the night sky. Popular shows include "The Sky Tonight" and "Worlds Unseen."

A small percentage of the museum's sizable collection relating to American Indian, Polynesian, Asian, Melanesian, and other cultures is on display at any one time. Navajo and Pueblo artworks are well represented in the superb **Elkus Collection of Native American Art**.

Evolutionary history is the subject of the **Life Through Time** section, which has life-sized models of Velociraptors and of a Quetzalcoatlus, the largest flying creature that ever lived. A popular draw is the skeleton of a *Tyrannosaurus rex*.

The enchanting **Steinhart Aquarium**, the oldest and one of the most diverse aquariums in the US, houses more than 8,000 specimens of tide-pool animals, sea mammals, and other aquatic creatures. Prime attractions here include the Giant Pacific octopus and the Sharks of the Tropics tank. The **Gem and Mineral Hall** contains more than 1,000 specimens of gemstones and minerals, including a 1,350-lb (612-kg) quartz crystal from Arkansas. In **Wild California**, naturalistic dioramas portray the landscapes and animals of California, with recorded commentaries helping to explain the scenes.

Lifelike dioramas in the African Hall of the California Academy of Sciences

de Young Museum ⑯

Map C4. 50 Hagiwara Tea Garden Dr. **Tel** *(415) 863-3330.* *44.* *9:30am–5:15pm Tue–Sun (until 8:45pm Fri).* *Mon.* *(free 1st Tue of month).* **www**.thinker.org

The de Young Museum was founded in 1895 and has been an integral part of Golden Gate Park for more than 100 years. In 1989 the building suffered irreparable damage from an earthquake and the old building closed to make way for a new, seismically stable one. The museum, which opened in 2005, has double the exhibition space of the old one, but returns nearly two acres of open space to the Park.

The de Young's permanent collection comprises American art from the 17th to the 20th centuries as well as work from nearly 30 countries. There are also special exhibitions held regularly, and outside, there's a sculpture garden and terrace, and a children's garden.

Legion of Honor ⑰

Map C4. 34th Ave & Clement, Lincoln Park. **Tel** *(415) 750-3600.* *18.* *(415) 863-3330.* *9:30am–5pm Tue–Sun.* *Mon.* *(free 1st Tue of month).* **www**.thinker.org

Inspired by the Palais de la Légion d'Honneur in Paris, Alma de Bretteville Spreckels built this museum in the 1920s to promote French art in California. Designed by the architect George Applegarth, it displays European art from the last eight centuries, with paintings by Rembrandt, Monet, and Rubens, and more than 70 sculptures by Rodin. The Achenbach Foundation, a well-known collection of graphic works, occupies a part of the gallery.

The museum's collection of European art is displayed in the galleries on the first floor. The portrait *The Impresario* (1877) by Edgar Degas emphasizes the subject's size by making him appear too large for the frame. Claude Monet's beautiful *Waterlilies* (1914–17) is one of a series depicting the lily pond in his gardens in Giverny, near Paris. The original bronze casting of Rodin's *Le Penseur* (1904), better known as *The Thinker*, is located at the center of the colonnaded Court of Honor. It is one of the 11 castings of the statue in collections around the world.

The Presidio ⑱

Map C3. **Visitor Center** *102 Montgomery St.* ***Tel*** *(415) 561-4323.* *9am–5pm daily.* *public hols.* **www**.nps.gov

To the north of Golden Gate Park, overlooking San Francisco Bay, the Presidio was established as an outpost of Spain's New World empire in 1776. For many years it was a military base but in 1994 it became a national park, with acres of woodland full of wildlife. There are also many hiking trails, bike paths, and beaches. The coastal path is very popular.

Detail, Arguello Gate

The Presidio Museum is part of the new **Mott Visitor Center** in the Main Post area. It houses artifacts relating to the Presidio's long history. Close by, the **Officers' Club** was built over the adobe remains of the original 18th-century Spanish fort, still preserved inside the building. A 19th-century cannon from the Spanish–American War lies across the adjoining parade ground.

To the north, close to the bay, is the large, grassy **Crissy Field**, that was reclaimed from marshland for the 1915 Panama-Pacific Exposition. The **Military Cemetery**, east of the visitor center, holds the remains of 15,000 US soldiers killed during various wars.

The northwestern tip of the Presidio, **Fort Point** is an impressive brick fortress that once guarded the Golden Gate during the Civil War and also survived the 1906 earthquake. The fort was built

Detail of the 19th-century cannon located on the Presidio grounds

in 1861 to protect the bay from attack, and to defend ships carrying gold from the California mines. It is a good place from which to view Golden Gate Bridge and there is also a museum displaying military uniforms and arms.

Golden Gate Bridge ⑲

Map B2. Hwy 101, Presidio. ***Tel*** *(415) 923-2000.* *2, 4, 8, 10, 18, 20, 28, 29, 50, 72, 76, 80. Pedestrians & cyclists allowed during daylight hours, east walkway only.* *observation area only.* **www**.goldengatebridge.org

Named after the part of San Francisco Bay called "Golden Gate" by John Frémont in 1844, the Golden Gate Bridge opened in 1937, connecting the city with Marin County. It took just over four years to build, at a cost of $35 million. This world-famous landmark offers breathtaking views; the bridge has six lanes for vehicles plus a free pedestrian walkway. Each year, more than 40 million vehicles cross it, averaging a daily count of about 118,000. It is the world's third largest single-span bridge, stretching 1.7 miles (2.7 km). When it was built, it was the world's longest and tallest suspension structure, rising 746 ft (227 m) above the water.

Designed by engineers Joseph Strauss and Leon Moisseiff, the mammoth structure was built to withstand 100 mph (160 km/h) winds. Its south pier was sunk 100 ft (30 m) into the seabed, while each pier supports a 44,000-ton steel tower. The original coat of paint lasted for 27 years, but since 1965 it has needed continuous painting. The two 7,650-ft (2,332-m) cables contain 80,000 miles (128,744 km) of steel wire, enough to circle the earth at the equator three times. The best views are seen from Marin County.

At the foot of the bridge, the **Bay Area Discovery Museum** is the only children's museum in the US to be located in a national park. It offers hands-on art, science, and environmental exhibitions, performances, special events, and cultural festivals for children aged from six months to 8 years.

Bay Area Discovery Museum
557 McReynolds Rd, Sausalito. ***Tel*** *(415) 339-3900.* *check for times.* **www**.baykidsmuseum.org

The Golden Gate Bridge, with a single span of 4,200 ft (1,280 m)

Greater San Francisco

Many of the settlements encircling San Francisco Bay were once summer retreats for the city's residents, but today they are sprawling suburbs or cities in their own right. Two popular destinations in the East Bay are Oakland's museum and Berkeley's famous university. The landmark San Francisco–Oakland Bay Bridge stretches 4.5 miles (7.2 km) and is crossed by 250,000 vehicles a day – even more than the Golden Gate. Farther south, San Jose combines the technology of Silicon Valley with fine museums and Spanish Colonial architecture. To the north is the rocky coastline of the Marin Headlands, with its abundant wildlife.

San Jose ⑳

846,000. 65 Cahill St. 70 Almeden Blvd. 408 Almaden Blvd, (800) 726-5673, (408) 295-9600 Festival of the Arts (Sep). **www**.sanjose.org

The only other original Spanish Colonial town in California apart from Los Angeles, San Jose was founded in 1777 by Felipe de Neve and has become the state's third largest city. It is now the commercial and cultural center of South Bay and the civic heart of Silicon Valley.

The **Mission Santa Clara de Asis**, on the campus of the Jesuit University of Santa Clara, is a modern replica of the adobe original, first built in 1777. Relics include bells given to the missionaries by the Spanish monarchy.

Organ, Winchester Mystery House

The large **Rosicrucian Egyptian Museum and Planetarium** has an extensive collection of ancient Egyptian artifacts. Displays include mummies, burial tombs, and toys, some of which date to 1500 BC. There are replicas of the sarcophagus in which Tutankhamen was discovered in 1922, and the Rosetta Stone.

At the heart of San Jose, the fascinating **Tech Museum of Innovation** is crowded with hands-on exhibits, encouraging visitors to discover how technological inventions work. Here, the focus is on understanding the workings of computer hardware and software.

The **Winchester Mystery House**, on the outskirts of town, has a remarkable history. Sarah Winchester, widow and heiress of the Winchester Rifle fortune, was told by a medium that the expansion of her farmhouse would exorcise the spirits of those killed by the rifle. She kept builders working 24 hours a day, 7 days a week, for 38 years, until her death in 1922. The result is a bizarre complex of 160 rooms, including stairs that lead nowhere and windows set into floors. The total cost amounted to $5.5 million.

The center of the computer industry, **Silicon Valley** covers about 100 sq miles (260 sq km) from Palo Alto to San Jose. The name refers to myriad businesses rather than a specific location. The seeds of the hardware and software industries were sown in the 1980s at Stanford University, at the Xerox Palo Alto Research Center, and in the garages of pioneers William Hewlett, David Packard, and later Steve Jobs and Stephen Wozniak, who invented the Apple personal computer.

Winchester Mystery House
525 S Winchester Blvd. ***Tel*** *(408) 247-2100. check for times. Dec 25. gardens only.*

The Thinker **by Auguste Rodin at the Stanford Museum of Art**

Palo Alto ㉑

Stanford University ***Tel*** *(650) 723-2560.* **Visitor Center** *11am–3:15pm except during winter break. university hols; call ahead.*

Among the most pleasant of the Bay Area suburbs, Palo Alto grew up to serve Stanford University, one of the most reputed centers of education in the US. It was founded in 1891 by the railroad tycoon Leland Stanford in honor of his son who died at the age of 16. The campus covers 8,200 acres (3,320 ha), and is larger than the downtown district of San Francisco. Designed in a mixture of Romanesque and Mission styles, its sandstone buildings are capped by red-tiled roofs. The Memorial Church is decorated with gold-leaf and tile mosaic. The **Stanford Museum of Art** holds one of the largest collections of sculptures by Auguste Rodin, including the impressive *Gates of Hell*.

Oakland ㉒

387,000. 463 11th St. (510 839-9000). Festival at the Lake (Jun). **www**.oaklandcvb.com

At one time a small, working-class suburb of San Francisco, Oakland grew into a flourishing city when it became the West Coast terminus of the transcontinental railroad. Many of the African Americans who worked on the railroad settled

For hotels and restaurants in this region see p724 and p728

here, later followed by the Hispanics, giving Oakland a multicultural atmosphere that continues to this day. Its literary associations, including Jack London and Gertrude Stein, have also enhanced the area as a cultural center.

Jack London Square on the waterfront was named after author Jack London who grew up in Oakland in the 1880s and frequently visited the area. Today, it is a bright promenade of shops, restaurants, and pleasure boats. The Jack London Museum contains books, photographs, and memorabilia. To the east is the **Oakland Museum of California**, which reopened early in 2010 following completion of a $53 million renovation program. The museum is dedicated to documenting the state's art, history, and ecology, and is famous for its early oil paintings of San Francisco and Yosemite.

To the north, the two blocks of **Old Oakland** (also known as Victorian Row) attract crowds of shoppers. Northern California's only **Mormon Temple**, situated on a hilltop on the eastern edge of the city, offers great views of the Bay Area. Its central ziggurat is surrounded by four towers, all clad with white granite and capped by golden pyramids.

Oakland Museum of California
Oak & 10th Sts. *(510) 238-2200.* *10am–5pm Wed–Sat, noon–5pm Sun.* *Jan 1, Thanksgiving, Dec 25, Mon & Tue.* *(free 2nd Sun).* **www**.museumca.org

Berkeley 23

104,900. *2160 Shattuck Ave.* *2015 Center St, (800) 847-4823* *Fourth of July Fireworks; Telegraph Ave Book Fair (Jul).* **www**.visitberkeley.com

Berkeley began to boom after the earthquake of 1906, when many San Franciscans fled their city and settled on the East Bay. It was the seat of the student uprisings against the Vietnam War in the 1960s, earning itself the nickname "Beserkeley." Many stores still hark to the hippie era with psychedelic merchandise, but in recent years Berkeley has begun to change its profile. Stylish restaurants have emerged, as well as a reputation for fine food; it was here that the popular California cuisine was born.

Model of DNA at the Lawrence Hall of Science, UC Berkeley

Berkeley is essentially a university town. The **University of California at Berkeley's** reputation for countercultural movements sometimes eclipses its academic reputation, yet with its student body of 30,000, it is one of the country's most prestigious institutions. Founded in 1868, it has at least ten Nobel laureates among its professors. There are many museums, cultural amenities, and noteworthy buildings to visit. The **University Art Museum** includes works by Piccasso and Cézanne among its exhibits. The main campus landmark, the 307-ft (94-m) **Sather Tower** and the splendid **Lawrence Hall of Science** are all outstanding.

To the south, the **Telegraph Avenue** was the center of student protest in the 1960s. Today, there is a plethora of bookstores, coffee houses, and cheap eateries. North of the University, **Shattuck Avenue**, nicknamed "Gourmet Ghetto," is known for its restaurants.

University of California at Berkeley
Tel *(510) 642-5215.* **Berkeley Art Museum & Pacific Film Archive** ***Tel*** *(510) 642-1412.* *11am–5pm Wed–Sun, until 7pm Thu.* *public hols.* **www**.berkeley.edu

Sausalito 24

7,300. *777 Bridgeway Ave, 4th floor, (415) 332-0505.* **www**.sausalito.org

In this small town, Victorian bungalows cling to hills rising from San Francisco Bay. Bridgeway Avenue along the waterfront serves as a promenade for crowds that patronize the restaurants and shops and enjoy the views. The **Bay Model Visitor Center** is a fascinating model simulating the tides in San Francisco Bay.

Bay Model Visitor Center
2100 Bridgeway Ave. ***Tel*** *(415) 332-3871.* *9am–4pm Tue–Sat.* *Sun–Mon, public hols.*

Muir Woods 25

Mill Valley. **Visitor Center** *Hwy 1, Mill Valley, (415) 388-2595.* *8am–5pm daily* **www**.visitmuirwoods.com

Nestling at the foot of Mount Tamalpais is Muir Woods National Monument, one of the few remaining stands of old-growth coastal redwoods. Before the 19th-century lumber industry boom, these tall trees (the oldest is 1,000 years old) covered the Californian coastline. The woods were named in honor of John Muir, the naturalist responsible for turning Yosemite into a national park *(see p718)*. Muir Beach nearby is a wide expanse of sand.

Muir Woods, the last remaining redwood forest in the Bay Area

San Francisco Practical Information

San Francisco occupies a compact area, making it a sightseer's dream. Its efficient transportation system has cable cars, buses, streetcars, Muni Metro, and BART lines. The city prides itself on its variety of cultural and entertainment opportunities, which make it one of the most enjoyable vacation spots in the world. The Civic Center is the main venue for classical music, opera, and ballet, while pop music – in particular jazz and blues – is where the city really excels. There are also diverse theater companies and specialty movie houses.

TOURIST INFORMATION

Visitors planning a trip will find the *San Francisco Visitors Planning Guide*, published twice yearly by the **San Francisco Convention & Visitors' Bureau**, very helpful. It is available free at the **Visitor Information Center** at Hallidie Plaza. Listings of what's on are given in the *San Francisco Chronicle* and *Examiner* newspapers. Weekly newspapers, such as the *San Francisco Weekly* or the *San Francisco Bay Guardian*, also give listings and reviews of live music, films, and nightclubs.

GETTING AROUND

The best way to explore San Francisco is on foot, although the hills can be strenuous. The city's main sights all lie within 15 to 20 minutes of each other. City taxis are licensed and operate 24 hours a day. **FogCityCab** and Yellow Cab are good bets.

The San Francisco Municipal Railway or **Muni**, runs the city's transportation system. The Muni Passport, valid for 1, 3, or 7 days can be used for unlimited travel on Muni buses, Muni Metro streetcars, as well as San Francisco's three cable car lines. These are available at the Visitor Information Center.

Buses and streetcars serve all areas. Buses stop only at designated places, every few blocks, and route numbers are printed on the buses. The **Culture Bus** makes convenient stops at major museums. Buses run every 20 minutes and for one fare you can ride all day. Muni Metro streetcars and BART trains both use the same underground terminals on Market Street. The high-speed BART trains stop at five downtown stations: Van Ness, Civic Center, Powell, Montgomery, and Embarcadero.

San Francisco's famous cable cars operate from 6:30am to 12:30am daily, at 15-minute intervals. Cars run on three routes; the popular Powell–Hyde line, the Powell–Mason line, and the California line.

Boats and passenger ferries are also a fun way to get around the city's shoreline. The Ferry Building is the terminal for the **Golden Gate Ferries**. Bay sightseeing cruises from Fisherman's Wharf are operated by the **Blue & Gold Fleet. Hornblower Dining Yachts** offer various meals on their cruises.

Other modes of travel include bicycles, which can be rented for around $25 a day or $125 a week. Details of scenic routes are available from the **Start to Finish** rental. Pedicabs and horse-drawn cabs are found on the Embarcadero. Sightseeing bus tours are also available.

SPORTS & OUTDOOR ACTIVITIES

The city has plenty of options for sports fans. The home ground of the San Francisco 49ers is Monster Park. Other football teams are supported by local colleges, UC Berkeley, and Stanford University. Two professional baseball teams play in the Bay Area, the National League San Francisco Giants (in AT&T Park) and the American League Oakland Athletics (in the McAfee Coliseum).

Golfers have a range of courses to choose from, including the municipal links in **Harding** and **Lincoln** parks. Most of the public swimming pools are located in the suburbs; for details contact the **City of San Francisco Recreation and Parks Department**. To swim in the chilly ocean, head out to China Beach. There are tennis courts in almost all the public parks, with the largest ones in Golden Gate Park. **Claremont Resort Spa and Tennis Club** in Berkeley offers fine courts with unlimited playing time. There are dozens of running clubs and events in all seasons. The **Golden Gate Running Club** is one of many.

ENTERTAINMENT

San Francisco offers visitors an unending variety of high-quality entertainment. It has an avid film-going community, and one of the best movie houses is the **Sundance Kabuki**, an eight-screen complex in the Japan Center, which also hosts the San Francisco **International Film Festival** each May. The main venue for first-run foreign films is the **Opera Plaza** on Van Ness Avenue. For theater goers, major shows are staged at Theater District venues, the two largest being the **Curran Theater** for Broadway shows and the Geary Theater, now home to the **American Conservatory Theater (ACT)**, both on Geary Street.

The **San Francisco Opera** season runs from September to December; tickets can cost over $100, but there is a summer season with less expensive tickets and many free outdoor concerts. The **Civic Center** complex on Van Ness Avenue offers opera, classical music, and dance. The **San Francisco Ballet** season runs from late June through May, while the Yerba Buena Center for the Arts is home to the **LINES Ballet**.

Two of the best rock clubs, **Slim's** and **Paradise Lounge**, are opposite one another in the SoMa district. Another popular place is the **Fillmore Auditorium** on Geary

Boulevard, the legendary birthplace of psychedelic rock during the 1960s. Places to hear live jazz include **Jazz at Pearl's**, and live blues is played in bars such as **The Saloon** on Grant Avenue. The annual **San Francisco Blues Festival** attracts blues bands from all over the country.

The **Bambuddha Lounge** has some of San Francisco's best DJs. The clientele here is mainstream, but some of the most popular clubs are primarily, though rarely exclusively, gay. These include **Rawhide II** on Seventh Street.

Piano bars all have nightly live music. One of the best is the Art Deco-style **Top of the Mark** at the top of the Mark Hopkins InterContinental Hotel on Nob Hill.

San Francisco also has a number of free concerts all over the city. Watch for the San Francisco Symphony Orchestra in late summer at Stern Grove and Yerba Buena Gardens. The San Francisco Opera performs in Golden Gate Park in the "Opera in the Park" event. The summer Shakespeare Festival is held in the Presidio.

SHOPPING

Shopping in San Francisco is a complete experience that allows a glimpse into the city's culture. The diversity of San Francisco makes buying anything here an adventure. An enormous range of goods is available, from the practical to the more eccentric, but you can take your time in choosing, since browsers are made to feel welcome, particularly in the many small specialty shops and boutiques. Guided shopping tours are available for those who want to be directed to the best shops.

For visitors who want convenience, the numerous shopping centers, such as the Embarcadero Center and Japan Center, are excellent.

Similarly, huge retail department stores such as **Macy's** and **Neiman Marcus** offer an outstanding selection of goods and services.

The city's innovative entrepreneurial spirit is evident in its specialty shops, such as the humorous art at **Smile–A Gallery with Tongue in Chic** or the unusual toys at **Ambassador Toys**.

A mecca for designer wear, the city is home to the famous **Levis Strauss & Co**, which has been making jeans since 1853 and offers factory tours on Tuesdays and Wednesdays to visitors. For discount designer wear, head to the trendy SoMa district.

Book lovers should head for **Green Apple Books**, or the famous Beat hideout **City Lights Bookstore**, which stays open late and is a famous San Francisco institution.

Art lovers will find something to their liking in the city's hundreds of galleries, featuring works by emerging and more established artists as well as expressions of Native American folk artists.

The city is also home to many dedicated "foodies," gastronomes whose liking for fine wine and gourmet meals have resulted in unusual and delicious grocery stores. Regular farmers' markets, held in the center of the city, abound in locally grown fruit and vegetables, while seafood and wines from **Napa Valley Winery Exchange** figure among the city's best buys.

DIRECTORY

TOURIST OFFICES

Visitor Information Center
900 Market St.
Tel (415) 391-2000. www.onlyinsanfrancisco.com

TRANSPORTATION

Blue & Gold Fleet
Tel (415) 205-8200.

Culture Bus
www.sfculturebus.org

FogCityCab
Tel (415) 282-8749.

Golden Gate Ferries
Tel (415) 921-5858.
www.goldengateferry.org

Muni Information
www.sfmta.com

FILM & THEATER

American Conservatory Theater (ACT)
Tel (415) 749-2228.

Sundance Kabuki
1881 Post St.
Tel (415) 346-3243.
www.sundancecinemas.com

OPERA, CLASSICAL MUSIC, & DANCE

LINES Ballet
26 Seventh St.
Tel (415) 863-3040.

San Francisco Opera
301 Van Ness Ave.
Tel (415) 864-3330.
www.sfopera.org

San Francisco Symphony
201 Van Ness Ave.
Tel (415) 864-6000.
www.sfsymphony.org

JAZZ

Jazz at Pearl's
256 Columbus Ave.
Tel (800) 838-3006.

CLUBS

Bambuddha Lounge
601 Eddy St.
Tel (415) 885-5088.

SPORTS & OUTDOOR ACTIVITIES

Golden Gate Running Club
www.goldengaterunningclub.org

Recreation & Parks Department
www.parks.sfgov.org

SHOPPING

Ambassador Toys
186 W Portal Ave.
Tel (415) 759-8697.

Bloomingdale's
845 Market St.
Tel (415) 856-5300.

City Lights Bookstore
261 Columbus Ave.
Tel (415) 362-8193.

Green Apple Books
506 Clement St.
Tel (415) 387-2272.

Levi Strauss & Co
250 Valencia St.
Tel (415) 565-9159.

Macy's
Stockton & O'Farrell Sts.
Tel (415) 954-6271.

Napa Valley Winery Exchange
415 Taylor St.
Tel (415) 771-2887.

Neiman Marcus
150 Stockton St.
Tel (415) 362-3900.

Saks Fifth Avenue
384 Post St.
Tel (415) 986-4758.

Smile–A Gallery with Tongue in Chic
500 Sutter St.
Tel (415) 362-3437.

The Wine Country

Born in the Sonoma Valley in 1823, when Franciscan priests planted grapes to make sacramental wines, California's wine industry was taken to new heights by the flamboyant Hungarian Count Agoston Haraszthy in 1857. Known as the "Father of California Wine," he planted European grapes in the state's first big vineyard at the revered Buena Vista Winery. Today, in addition to its superb wines and vineyards, the Wine Country is known for its mild climate, rocky landscapes, secluded beaches, redwood groves, and impressive architecture.

View of vineyards in the Sonoma Valley, famous for wineries

Sonoma Valley ㉒

8,600. *90 Broadway & W Napa Sts, Sonoma Plaza.* *453 1st St E, (866) 996-1090.* *Valley of the Moon Vintage Festival (late Sep).* **www**.sonomavalley.com

Nestling in the crescent-shaped Sonoma Valley are 6,000 acres (2,400 ha) of beautiful vineyards. At the foot of the valley lies the tiny town of Sonoma. This town has had a colorful past, as it was here on June 14, 1846, that about 30 American farmers captured Mexican General Mariano Vallejo and his men, to protest the fact that land ownership was reserved for Mexican citizens. They seized control of Sonoma, declared California an independent republic, and flew their own flag, with a crude drawing of a grizzly bear. Although the republic was annulled 25 days later when the United States annexed California, the Bear Flag design was adopted as the official state flag in 1911.

Sonoma's main attractions are its world-famous wineries and meticulously preserved historical sites lining the Spanish-style plaza. Many of the adobe buildings house wine shops, boutiques, and restaurants serving excellent local cuisine. East of the plaza is the restored **Mission San Francisco Solano de Sonoma**, the last of California's 21 historic Franciscan missions (founded by Father José Altimira of Spain in 1823). Today, all that survives of the original building is the corridor of his quarters. The adobe chapel was built by General Vallejo in 1840.

A short drive northward leads to the **Jack London State Historic Park**. In the early 1900S, London, the famous author of *The Call of the Wild* and *The Sea Wolf*, abandoned his hectic lifestyle to live in this tranquil 800-acre (325-ha) expanse of oaks, madrones, and redwoods. The park retains eerie ruins of London's dream home, the Wolf House, mysteriously destroyed by fire just before completion. After London's death, his widow, Charmian Kittredge, built a magnificent home on the ranch, called the House of Happy Walls. Today, the house has been made into a museum, worth a visit for its display of London memorabilia.

Mission San Francisco Solano de Sonoma
E Spain St. ***Tel*** *(707) 938-9560.* *daily.* *Jan 1, Thanksg., Dec 25.*

Jack London Historic State Park
London Ranch Rd, Glen Ellen. ***Tel*** *(707) 938-5216.* **Park & Museum** *daily.* *Jan 1, Thanksgiving, Dec 25.* *museum only.*

Napa Valley ㉓

115,000. *1310 Town Center Mall, Napa, (707) 226-7459.* *Napa Valley Mustard Festival (Feb–Apr).* **www**.napavalley.com

Lying at the heart of California's wine industry, the 35-mile (56-km) sliver of land known as Napa Valley encompasses the towns of Yountville, Oakville, St. Helena, Rutherford, and Calistoga. More than 250 wineries are scattered across its hillsides and valleys, some dating from the early 19th century. Prominent among these is the **Mumm Napa Valley** winery, partly owned by French champagne producer G.H. Mumm, where wines are made in the classic tradition. To its north, the **Rutherford Hill Winery** features caves dug into the hillsides, for aging wines. Farther north, the modern **Clos Pegase** winery is famed for its distinctive art collection and superior wines.

For a bird's-eye view of the valley, visitors can take hot-air balloon trips over the Wine Country from Yountville or a three-hour luxury tour in the Napa Valley Wine Train, enjoying gourmet cuisine. But the best way to explore the valley is along a scenic 40-mile (64-km) drive, stopping along the way at the B&B inns in the towns of St. Helena and Calistoga. The latter is popular for its spa treatments and good Wine Country

Statue at Clos Pegase

For hotels and restaurants in this region see p724 and p729

cuisine, prepared with the freshest ingredients. A few miles north of Calistoga, the Old Faithful Geyser spouts jets of boiling mineral water 60 ft (18 m) into the sky, once every 40 minutes. To the west lies the **Petrified Forest**, home of the largest petrified trees in the world – huge redwoods which were turned to stone by a volcanic eruption that took place more than three million years ago.

Petrified Forest
4100 Petrified Forest Rd. ***Tel*** *(707) 942-6667.* *daily.* *Thanksgiving, Dec 25.* *limited.*

The Clos Pegase winery designed by Michael Graves, Napa Valley

Russian River Valley 24

from Healdsburg. *16209 1st St, Guerneville, (707) 869-9000, (877) 644-9001.* **www**.russianriver.com

Bisected by the Russian River and its tributaries, this valley contains many smaller valleys, dotted with vine-yards, apple orchards, red-wood groves, family farms, and sandy river beaches. At its hub is the town of **Healdsburg**, with a splendid Spanish-style town square lined with shops, restaurants, and cafés.

Southwest of Healdsburg lies **Guerneville**, a summer haven for San Francisco's gay population. Every September, the town hosts the famous Russian River Jazz Festival at Johnson's Beach, where visitors can take a canoe or raft down the gentle Russian River. Otters and blue herons can be often be seen here.

Hikers and equestrians also flock to Guerneville to visit the 805-acre (330-ha) **Armstrong Redwoods State Reserve**, one of the few remaining old-growth redwood forests in California. Among its redwoods is a 308-ft (94-m) giant – a 1,400-year-old tree named Colonel Armstrong.

Armstrong Redwoods State Preserve
17020 Armstrong Woods Rd, Guerneville. ***Tel*** *(707) 869-2015.* *daily.*

Fort Ross State Historic Park 25

Tel *(707) 847-3286.* *from Point Arena.* *19005 Coast Hwy, Jenner.* *sunrise–sunset daily.* *Thanksgiving, Dec 25.*
www.parks.ca.gov

On a windswept headland north of Jenner stands this well-restored Russian trading outpost, founded in 1812 (the name "Ross" is a derivative of the Russian word "Rossyia," meaning Russia). The Russians were the first Europeans to visit the region, serving as representatives of a Russian-American Company, established in 1799. They never tried to expand their territory in California and abandoned the fort after 30 years of peaceful trading.

Built in 1836, the house of the fort's last manager, Alexander Rotchev, is still intact. Within the wooden palisade are several other reconstructed buildings. The most impressive is the 1824 Russian Orthodox chapel. Every July, a living history day is held with costumed actors.

Town of Mendocino perched on the rocky Mendocino headlands

Mendocino 26

1,200. *332 N Main St, Fort Bragg, (707) 961-6300.*
www.mendocinocoast.com

The founders of this fishing village came to California from New England in 1852, building their new homes to resemble those they had left behind. The Mendocino coastline is thus often referred to as "California's New England Coast." Perched on a rocky promontory above the Pacific Ocean, Mendocino retains the picturesque charm of its days as a fishing center. Its heather-covered bluffs, migrating gray whales, and stunning ocean vistas make it a popular tourist center, yet the town seems untarnished by commercialism. It is a thriving arts center with a large number of resident artists and writers. Visitors can stroll around the many exclusive boutiques, art galleries, bookshops, and cafés.

CALIFORNIA WINES

With over 327,000 acres (132,000 ha) of land under viticulture, California produces 90 percent of the nation's wine. Its latitude, proximity to the ocean, and sheltered valleys create a mild climate, ideal for growing grapes. Half the grapes grown here are harvested from the fertile stretch of land bordered by the Sacramento Valley to the north and San Joaquin Valley to the south. The north coast, home to most of the state's 800 wineries, accounts for less than a quarter of California's wine-growing acreage, but produces many of the country's best Sauvignon Blanc, Cabernet Sauvignon, Merlot, and Chardonnay grapes. Chardonnay and Pinot Noir grapes are the mainstays of the central coast region, which extends from the San Francisco Bay Area to Santa Barbara.

Sparkling Cuvee Napa by Mumm

Northern California

Rugged and sparsely populated, Northern California has a diverse landscape of dense forests, volcanic mountains, and arid plains. It also has the world's largest concentration of giant redwood trees, now protected by national parks. Scenic routes in the parks offer visitors a chance to view their awesome beauty. To experience the full immensity of the trees, however, it is best to walk around in these majestic groves.

Avenue of the Giants in the Humboldt Redwoods State Park

Humboldt Redwoods State Park 27

US Hwy 101. Garberville. **Visitor Center** Weott ***Tel*** *(707) 946-2263.* *Apr–Oct: 9am–5pm; Nov–Mar: 10am–4pm.* *Thanksg., Dec 25.* **www**.humboldtredwoods.org

This park has the world's tallest redwood trees and the most extensive primeval redwood groves. The tallest individual specimen, the 364-ft (110-m) Dyersville Giant, was blown over by a storm in 1991. Now seen lying on its side, its size appears even more astounding.

The serpentine 33-mile (53-km) **Avenue of the Giants** runs through the 52,000-acre (21,053-ha) park. The visitor center is halfway along the road.

To the north is the town of **Scotia**, built in 1887 to house the workers of the Pacific Lumber Company's massive redwood mill. Scotia is the only complete lumber community still in existence in California. Its small museum traces the history of the town, and of the lumber industry, and offers self-guided tours.

Eureka 28

27,600. *1034 2nd St, (800) 346-3482.* **www**.redwoodvisitor.org

Founded by gold miners in 1850, Eureka was named after the state's ancient Greek motto, meaning "I have found it." Today, it is the northern coast's largest industrial center, with extensive logging and fishing operations surrounding the state-protected natural harbor. Its Old Town's many restored 19th-century buildings are now fashionable cafés, bars, and restaurants.

Eureka also houses the 1885 Carson Mansion, home of the millionaire lumber baron William Carson, and now a private club. Its Gothic design is enhanced by its redwood construction, painted to resemble stone.

Redwood National Park 29

Arcata to Crescent City is 78 miles (125km). US Hwy 101 is the quickest route. *1111 Second St, Crescent City, (707) 465-7306.* **www**.nps.gov

Some of the largest original redwood forests in the world are preserved in this national park. Stretching along the coastline, the 58,000-acre (23,500-ha) park includes many smaller state parks and can be explored along a day-long drive. A two-day trip, however, allows time to walk away from the roads and experience the tranquility of the stately groves, or spot one of the world's last remaining herds of Roosevelt elk.

The park's headquarters are in **Crescent City**, a few miles north of which lies the 9,200-acre (3,720-ha) Jedediah Smith Redwoods State Park, with the most awe-inspiring coastal redwoods. Named after the fur trapper Jedediah Smith, the first white man who walked across the US, it has excellent campground facilities. South from Crescent City, the **Trees of Mystery** grove features unusual looking fiberglass statues

REDWOODS & THE LUMBER INDUSTRY

The tallest tree on earth, the coniferous coastal redwood *(Sequoia sempervirens)* is unique to the northwest coast. It can live for 2,000 years and reach 350 ft (105 m), with roots that grow up to 200 ft (60 m) horizontally but only 4–6 ft (1–2 m) deep. Its fast growth and resistance to disease makes it ideal for commercial use. By the 1920s, however, logging had destroyed 90 percent of the groves. The Save the Redwoods League was formed, buying land now under state park protection. Lumber firms still own some groves, and their future remains a major environmental issue, both locally and nationally.

Redwood lumber

For hotels and restaurants in this region see p725 and p729

of the mythical lumberjack Paul Bunyan and his faithful ox, Babe *(see p419)*. The park's main attraction is the world's tallest tree, a 368-ft (112-m) giant, standing in the **Tall Trees Grove**. Farther south is Big Lagoon, a freshwater lake stretching for 3 miles (5 km) and two other estuaries. Together, they form the **Humboldt Lagoons State Park**. The headlands at Patrick's Point State Park, at the southern end, are a good place to watch for migrating gray whales in winter.

Weaverville ㉚

3,500. *215 Main St, (800) 487-4648.* **www**.trinitycounty.com

This small rural town has changed little since it was founded by gold prospectors 150 years ago. The **Jake Jackson Museum**, in the heart of the small commercial district, traces the history of the town and its surrounding gold mining and lumber region. Next door, the **Joss House State Historic Site** is the country's oldest and best-preserved Chinese temple. Built in 1874, it is a reminder of the many Chinese immigrants who came to the US to mine gold, and stayed on as cheap labor to build the California railroads.

North of Weaverville, the Trinity Alps rise up at the center of beautiful mountain wilderness. The mountains are popular with hikers and backpackers in summer and with cross-country skiers during the winter months.

Mount Shasta ㉛

Dunsmuir. *Siskiyou.* *Shasta.* **Visitor Center** *300 Pine S.* ***Tel*** *(530) 926-4865, (800) 926-4865.* *daily.* **www**.mtshastachamber.com

At a height of 14,162 ft (4,316 m), Mount Shasta is the second highest of the Cascade Mountains, after Mount Rainier in Washington *(see pp626–7)*. Visible more than 100 miles (160 km) away and usually covered with

Mount Shasta, towering over the town of Shasta below

snow, the summit is a popular destination for adventure sports enthusiasts such as mountaineers. At its foothills lies the picturesque town of **Shasta**, which was once one of the state's largest gold mining camps. Today, Shasta makes a welcome base with plenty of good places to stay.

Lava Beds National Monument ㉜

Tel *(530) 667-2282.* *Klamath Falls.* *daily.* **www**.nps.gov

Spreading over 46,500 acres (18,800 ha) of the Modoc Plateau, this eerie landscape of lava flows has over 200 caves and lava tubes – those cylindrical tunnels created by exposed lava turning to stone. Most of the volcanic caves lie near the visitor center, where visitors can take ranger-led or self-guided tours down into the caves. To visit any of the caves, wear sturdy shoes, carry a flashlight, and check first with the visitor center.

The park is also notable as the site of the 1872–73 Modoc War, one of the many conflicts between the US and the Native Americans. For six months a group of Modoc Indians, under the command of "Captain Jack," evaded the US Cavalry from a natural fortress of passageways along the park's northern border. The captain was eventually hanged, and the rest were forced into a reservation in what is now Oklahoma.

Lassen Volcanic National Park ㉝

Chester, Red Bluff. **Visitor Center** ***Tel*** *(530) 595-4444.* *daily.* **www**.nps.gov

Before the eruption of Mount St. Helens in Washington in 1980 *(see p629)*, the 10,457-ft (3,187-m) high Lassen Peak was the last volcano to erupt on mainland US. In nearly 300 eruptions between 1914 and 1917, it laid 100,000 acres (40,500 ha) of the surrounding land to waste.

Lassen Peak is considered to be still active. Numerous areas on its flanks show clear signs of the geological processes. The boardwalk trail of Bumpass Hell (named for an early guide, who lost his leg in a boiling mudpot in 1865) leads past a series of steaming sulfurous pools of boiling water, heated by molten rock deep underground. In summer, visitors can take the winding road through the park, climbing more than 8,500 ft (2,590 m) high to Summit Lake. The road continues winding its way through the so-called Devastated Area, a bleak gray landscape, which terminates at the Manzanita Lake, and the **Loomis Museum**.

Loomis Museum
Lassen Park Rd, N Entrance.
Tel *(530) 595-4444.* *late Jun–mid-Sep: daily.*

Sulfur springs in Lassen Volcanic National Park

The Gold Country

Located at the heart of California, the Gold Country was once a real life El Dorado, where a thick vein of gold sat waiting to be discovered. Once home of the Miwok and Maidu peoples, the Gold Rush turned this quiet region into a lawless jamboree of gold miners from all over the world. But the boom went bust by 1860. A few years later, the area saw another short-lived boom, when the transcontinental railroad was constructed through the Sierra Nevada Mountains by low-paid laborers, many of whom were Chinese.

Firehouse #1 Museum, a Nevada City landmark

Nevada City 34

2,855. *132 Main St, (530) 265-2692, (800) 655-6569, 9am–5pm daily.*
www.nevadacitychamber.com

Located at the northern end of the Mother Lode gold fields, this picturesque city deserves its reputation as the "Queen of the Northern Mines." But the once thriving city faded into oblivion after the Gold Rush subsided. It was resurrected as a tourist destination a century later with galleries, restaurants, and inns re-creating Gold Rush themes. The town boasts one of the region's most photographed façades in the **Firehouse #1 Museum**, with its dainty balconies and white cupola. It is now a local history museum. Other historic buildings include the Nevada Theater, a performance venue since 1865, and the National Hotel. One of California's oldest hotels, it first opened in the mid-1850s.

Grass Valley 35

9,000. *248 Mill St, (530) 273-4667, (800) 655-4667, daily.*
www.grassvalleychamber.com

One of the largest and busiest gold mining towns, Grass Valley employed workers from the tin mines of Cornwall in England. It was their expertise that enabled local mines to stay in business long after the others had fallen quiet. At the entrance to the **Northstar Mine Powerhouse & Pelton Wheel Museum** are the giant Pelton wheel that increased production in underground mines. Also on view are a stamp mill and a Cornish pump used to filter out water.

A nugget of gold set inside quartz crystal

Grass Valley also served the nearby **Empire Mine**, the state's richest and longest surviving gold mine. Now a state park, the mine had recovered almost six million ounces of gold when it closed in 1956. Mining equipment and artifacts can be seen in the park and in the museum.

Northstar Mine Powerhouse & Pelton Wheel Museum
Mill St at McCourtney Rd. ***Tel** (530) 273-4255.* *Apr–Oct: daily.*

Empire Mine Historic State Park
10791 E Empire St. ***Tel** (530) 273-8522.* *daily.* *Jan 1, Thanksgiving, Dec 25.*

Marshall Gold Discovery State Park 36

***Tel** (530) 622-3470.* *from Placerville.* *8am–sunset daily.* *Jan 1, Thanksg, Dec 25.*
www.parks.ca.gov

This peaceful park protects the site where gold was first discovered in 1848. James Marshall spotted shiny flakes in the water channel of a sawmill he and other workers were building for the Swiss entrepreneur John Sutter. Gold miners soon took over Sutter's land leaving him penniless. Within a year, Coloma had turned into a thriving city but then declined, with news of richer deposits elsewhere.

A replica of **Sutter's Mill** stands on the original site. The park's Gold Country Museum features Native American artifacts, films, and other exhibits on the discovery of gold.

Reconstructed Sutter's Mill, Marshall Gold Discovery State Park

For hotels and restaurants in this region see p725 and p729

Sacramento 37

30, 31, 32. 1002 St, 10am–5pm daily, (916) 442-7644. www.cityofsacramento.org

Founded by John Sutter in 1839, California's capital city preserves many historic buildings along the waterfront in Old Sacramento. Most of the structures date from the 1860s, when it became the supply point for miners. Both the transcontinental railroad and Pony Express had their western terminus here, with riverboats providing passage to San Francisco. The **California State Railroad Museum**, at the northern edge of the old town, houses some restored locomotives. A little away from the old city, the State Capitol stands in a landscaped park. To its east, Sutter's Fort is a re-creation of the town's original settlement.

California State Railroad Museum
111 I St. ***Tel*** *(916) 445-6645.* *10am–5pm daily.* *Jan 1, Thanksgiving, Dec 25.*

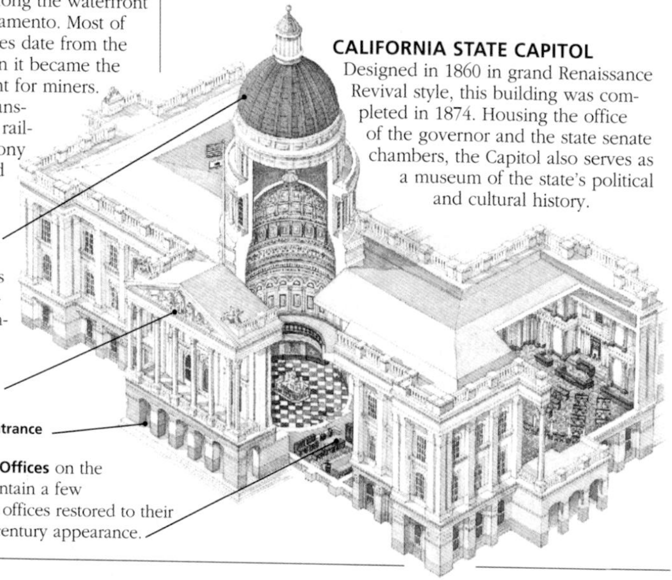

CALIFORNIA STATE CAPITOL
Designed in 1860 in grand Renaissance Revival style, this building was completed in 1874. Housing the office of the governor and the state senate chambers, the Capitol also serves as a museum of the state's political and cultural history.

Highway 49 38

542 Main St, Placerville, (530) 621-5885.

The Gold Country offers one of California's best scenic drives, through rocky ridges and flowing rivers, along Highway 49. Many of the towns it passes through, such as **Sutter Creek**, have survived unchanged since the Gold Rush. Named after John Sutter, this scenic town grew up to service the Old Eureka Mine, owned by Hetty Green, the "Richest Woman in the World." Leland Stanford, the railroad baron, made his fortune here, by investing in the town's Lincoln Mine. He used the money to become a railroad magnate and then the governor of California.

A short drive southeast leads to **Jackson**, a bustling gold mining community that has continued to thrive as a lumber mill town since 1850. The Amador County Museum, located on a hill above the town, features a range of old mining equipment.

Northward, Highway 49 passes through **Placerville**. Once a busy supply center for the area's mining camps, the town is still a major transportation center. Of interest here are the Placerville History Museum and the El Dorado County Historical Museum, which displays a replica of a 19th-century general store, artifacts from the Chinese settlement, and other local historical exhibits.

Parrots Ferry Bridge along Highway 49

Columbia State Historic Park 39

Hwy 49. *N255 Jackson St, (209) 588-9128.* www.parks.ca.gov

At the height of the Gold Rush, Columbia was one of the most important towns in the Gold Country. Most of the state's mining camps disintegrated once the gold ran out in the late 1850s. But Columbia was kept intact by its residents until 1945, when it was turned into a state historic park. Many of the town's buildings are preserved in their original state, like the **Wells Fargo Express Office**, and the restored **Columbia Schoolhouse**. Visitors can buy pans of sand to try panning gold.

Wells Fargo Express Office & Columbia Schoolhouse
10am–4pm daily, Jun–Aug: until 6pm. *Thanksgiving, Dec 25.*

The High Sierras

Forming a towering wall at the eastern side of central California, the densely forested, 14,000-ft (4,270-m) high Sierra Nevada Mountains were formed 3 million years ago. Known as the High Sierras, these rugged mountains make up one of the state's most popular recreation areas, preserved by a series of national parks.

Skiing at Lake Tahoe's Alpine Meadows Resort

Lake Tahoe 40

3066 Lake Tahoe Blvd, (530) 544-5050. **www**.visitinglaketahoe.com

The deep, emerald waters of this beautiful lake are set within an alpine valley at the highest point of the High Sierras. For over a century, Lake Tahoe has been a year-round recreational haven, offering water sports, hiking, and camping. South Lake Tahoe, the largest town here, caters to visitors headed for Nevada's casinos. To its west, the inlet of Emerald Bay State Park is the most photographed part of the lake. To the north is the D.L. Bliss State Park with its 1903 Ehrman Mansion. The surrounding peaks are also famous for their ski resorts. The world-class Alpine Meadows and Squaw Valley are well-known because the Winter Olympics were held here in 1960.

Yosemite National Park 41

from Merced. Yosemite Valley. from Merced. PO Box 577, Yosemite, (209) 372-0200. daily. **www**.nps.gov/yose

A wilderness of evergreen forests, high meadows, and sheer granite walls, the 1,170 sq mile (3,030 sq km) Yosemite National Park (established in 1890) protects some of the world's most beautiful mountain terrain. Soaring cliffs, rugged canyons, valleys, gigantic trees, and waterfalls all combine to lend Yosemite its incomparable beauty. Each season offers a different experience, from the swelling waterfalls of spring to the russet colors of fall. Numerous roads, bus tours, bike paths, and hiking trails lead visitors from one awe-inspiring panoramic view to another.

Yosemite Valley is a good base from which to explore the park. **Yosemite Museum**, in the village, displays the history of the Native Miwok and Paiute people, along with works by local artists. Nearby is the **Ahwanee Hotel** *(see p725)*. Built in 1927, this is one of the country's best-known hotels. Just to the south of the Valley Visitor Center, the tiny wooden **Yosemite Chapel** (1879) is the sole reminder of the park's Old Village, dating from the 19th century.

Standing nearly 1 mile (1.6 km) above the valley floor, the silhouette of the **Half Dome** cliff has become the symbol of Yosemite. Geologists believe that it is now three-quarters of its original size, rather than a true half. It is thought that 15,000 years ago glacial ice floes moved across the valley, scything off rock, depositing it downstream. A formidable trail leads to the 8,840-ft (2,695-m) summit, offering panoramic views of the valley. The other major cliff, **El Capitan**, standing guard at the valley's western entrance, attracts rock-climbers, who spend days on its sheer face

El Capitan, the world's largest piece of exposed granite, Yosemite NP

to reach the top. But the great Yosemite panorama is best experienced from the 3,215-ft (980-m) high **Glacier Point**. It can be reached only in summer, because snow blocks the road during winter.

Among the park's most recognizable features are the cascading Yosemite waterfalls, the highest in North America. Tumbling from a height of 2,425 ft (740 m) in two great leaps, **Upper** and **Lower Yosemite Falls** are at their peak in May and June, when the snow melts. By September, however, the falls often dry up.

In summer, when the wildflowers are in full bloom, the park's striking landscape is best explored in the subalpine **Tuolumne Meadows** along the Tuolumne River at the Yosemite's eastern edge.

A few miles past Yosemite's southern entrance, **Mariposa Grove** features over 500 giant sequoia trees *(Sequoiadendron gigantea)*, some more than 3,000 years old.

The 1879 Yosemite Chapel, Yosemite National Park

Eastern Sierras ㊷

Bodie State Historic Park *from Bridgeport.* *End of Hwy 270, (760) 647-6445.* *daily.* **Mono Lake** ***Tel*** *(760) 647-3044.* *Merced.*

High up in the foothills of the eastern Sierras lies **Bodie State Historic Park**, the largest ghost town in California. It was named after the prospector Waterman S. Bodey, who discovered surface gold here in 1859. The town thrived in the mid-1870s but declined when the gold ran out in 1882. Now protected as a state historic park, Bodie's 170 buildings have been maintained in a state of "arrested decay." The result is an experience of empty streets lined by deserted wooden buildings. The Miner's Union Hall has been converted into a visitor center and a museum.

Tufa spires rising out of Mono Lake, Eastern Sierras

Nearby **Mono Lake**, covering 60-sq miles (155-sq km), lies at the eastern foot of the Sierra Nevada Mountains and presents an eerie sight of limestone towers rising from the water. Set between two volcanic islands, the lake has no natural outlet, but evaporation and water diversion to Los Angeles, through aqueducts, have caused it to shrink to one-fifth of its size. The lake's water has turned brackish and alkaline, putting the local wildlife and ecosystem in grave danger. In recent years, Mono Lake has been the subject of much environmental debate.

Sequoia & Kings Canyon National Parks ㊸

Ash Mountain, Three Rivers. ***Tel*** *(559) 565-3135.* *daily.* *call ahead.* *summer only.* **www**.nps.gov/seki

These twin national parks preserve lush green forests, magnificent glacier-carved canyons, and granite peaks. America's deepest canyon, the south fork of the Kings River, cuts a depth of 8,200 ft (2,500 m) through Kings Canyon. Roads serve the western side of the parks; the rest is accessible only to hikers or rented pack-trains of horses or mules.

The parks embrace 34 separate groves of the sequoia tree, the earth's largest living species. **Giant Forest**, at the southern end of Sequoia National Park, is one of the world's largest groves of living sequoias. A 3-mile (5-km) trail from here leads to Moro Rock, a granite monolith affording a 360-degree view of the High Sierras and the Central Valley. To its east lies the marshy Crescent Meadow, bordered by sequoias. Another short trail leads to **Tharp's Log**, a hollowed-out sequoia, home to Hale Tharp, a 19th-century farmer who was introduced to the area by Native Americans.

North of Giant Forest is the world's largest living thing, the 275-ft (84-m) **General Sherman's Tree**. It still grows 0.4 inches (1 cm) every ten years and is rivaled by the third largest sequoia, **General Grant Tree** in Kings Canyon Park. This park also features the Big Stump Trail, lined with tall stumps, left by loggers in the 1880s.

Along the eastern boundary of Sequoia is the 14,496-ft (4,420-m) **Mount Whitney**, one of the highest peaks on the US mainland. A steep trail leads from Whitney Portal Road to the summit, offering a panorama over the High Sierras. The mountain, named in honor of geologist Josiah Whitney, was first climbed in 1873. The lovely green alpine meadows around it are ideal for backpacking in the summer months.

Practical Information

California is a vibrant and diverse vacation destination. The spirit of the state can be felt in the busy cities of San Francisco, Los Angeles, and San Diego as much as in the quiet wilderness of the Sierra Nevada Mountains. At the center of the film industry, Los Angeles prides itself as the entertainment capital of the world. All over the state visitors needs' are well tended. The state's major tourist spots see a rush of visitors from mid-April to September. But the winter months are equally popular, either for the warm climate of the south or the ski slopes of Lake Tahoe.

TOURIST INFORMATION

Advance information can be obtained from the **California Division of Tourism** or the nearest US Consulate. Local Visitors' and Convention Bureaus supply maps, guides, event listings, and discount passes for public transportation and tourist destinations.

PERSONAL SECURITY

San Francisco is one of the safest large cities in the US. Problems are more visible in Los Angeles, although the notorious gangs of the city generally do not bother visitors. Still, as in every big city, visitors can be victims of petty thefts or car crime. Although police patrol regularly in the tourist areas, it is good to be cautious. Safety rules for pedestrians are strictly observed – jay-walking, or crossing the road anywhere except at an intersection, can result in a fine.

NATURAL HAZARDS

In the event of an earthquake, it is most important not to panic. Most injuries occur from falling material. Stand in a doorway, or crouch under a table. In a car, slow down and pull over.

When hiking in the wilderness, be wary of occasionally dangerous wildlife. Also be careful of rapid climatic changes in deserts, where temperatures can drop to below freezing points at high elevations. The Pacific Ocean can often be rough, with a strong undertow.

GETTING AROUND

Although often more time-consuming, traveling by train, bus, and ferry is an inexpensive way of getting around the state. Within the major cities of San Francisco, Los Angeles, and San Diego, the public transportation network serves parts of the city very well, with shuttle buses, trams, Metro trains, ferries, taxis, and cable cars.

The network of Amtrak railroad lines and connecting bus services serves the state's populous areas. Guided bus tours are a convenient way of sightseeing. Express boat services provide a fast link from Los Angeles to Santa Catalina Island, while others sail more leisurely across San Francisco Bay. Most ferries carry foot passengers and bicycles.

DRIVING IN CALIFORNIA

Driving is the best way to travel around the state. It is best to arrange a fly-drive package before leaving for California. Find out exactly what is included and whether any extra payments may arise when the car is returned. These additions – which may include collision damage waiver, drop-off charges, and rental tax – can double the original fee. Litigation is common in California, so it is best to be fully insured.

In the US, cars are driven on the right side of the road. Seat belts are compulsory. The maximum speed limit is generally 65 mph (104 km/h) In cities, the speed limits are restricted as marked and may vary within a few miles. These controls are rigorously enforced by the Highway Patrol. Drunk driving is a serious offense and carries very heavy penalties. You can turn right on red at traffic lights if there is nothing coming the other way. The first vehicle to reach a stop-sign junction has the right of way. It is against the law to use a cell phone while driving unless it is "hands-free".

Parking in California cities is strictly controlled and can be somewhat expensive. In remote areas, drivers should be wary of wildlife that may stray onto the roads.

OUTDOOR ACTIVITIES

California is practically synonymous with the great outdoors. The deserts, redwood forests, alpine

THE CLIMATE OF CALIFORNIA

Apart from the extremes of the north and the deserts, the state's climate is neither oppressive in summer, nor too cold in winter. The Northern Coastal Range is temperate, although wet in winter. To the east, rain turns to snow on the Sierra Nevada Mountains. Central California and the Central Valley have a Mediterranean climate, characterized by seasonal changes in rainfall – a dry summer and a rainy winter – but only moderate changes in temperature. The weather becomes drier and warmer toward the south with soaring temperatures in the desert in summer.

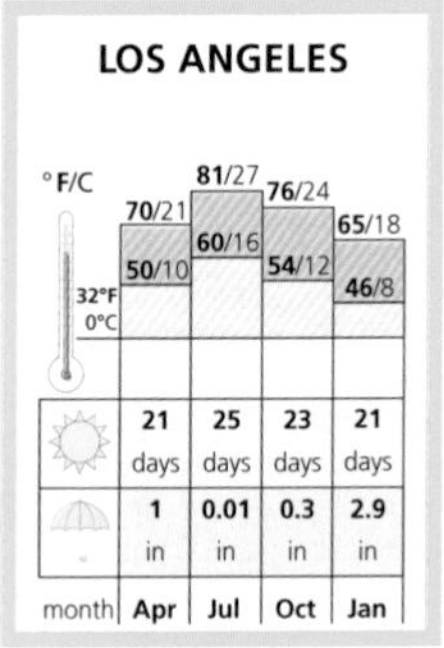

meadows, mountains, lakes, and white beaches all welcome visitors. The state has a culture rich with physical activity, and wilderness is never far from any city.

With more than 250 places classified as state parks, wilderness areas, or historic sites, California is a hikers' and campers' paradise. For camping, reserve a site with **State Park Reservations** or **Yosemite Reservations**. There are more than 1 million miles (1.6 million km) of trails in California, the longest being the Pacific Crest Trail, stretching from Canada to Mexico. The **Sierra Club** organizes guided outings and provides detailed maps. Many state parks also allow cyclists on their hiking trails. Outfitters such as **Backroads** lead groups of cyclists on tours.

Equestrians find a wide variety of riding trails here. California's 900-mile (1,450-km) coastline offers various beaches. Some have rough waves and rocky shores; others, with white sand, arching waves, and warm water, are ideal for surfing. The best beaches include the **Leo Carrillo State Beach** in Orange County, **Windansea Beach** in La Jolla, and **Corona del Mar** in Newport.

The lakes, rivers, and beaches of California offer a variety of watersports, from slow cruises on houseboats to parasailing and whitewater rafting. Most outfitters that offer river rafting also provide kayak and canoe trips. For more information, contact **American River Touring Association**. The rivers and coastline are feeding grounds for migrating birds. In autumn, ducks, geese, and other shorebirds can be spotted here. The state is also an angler's haven. The rivers and streams of the Sierra Nevada Mountains have plenty of trout. Bass fishing in California's lakes and reservoirs is plentiful throughout the year.

From December through April, gray whales travel 7,000 miles (11,260 kms) from the California coast to Mexico. Ocean cruises offer views of the impressive mammals.

California's great outdoors list also includes island hopping. Five volcanic islands off the coast of Southern California form the Channel Islands National Park, ideal for hiking, exploring rock pools, and spotting whales and dolphins. **Island Packers** is only one of the many outfits that offer island tours.

California is famed for its special interest vacations, the most popular being the tours of the state's missions along El Camino Real. Resident writers often give readings at local writers' workshops such as the **Santa Barbara Writers' Conference**. Institutes such as **Tante Marie's Cooking School** provide lodging, cooking classes, shopping tours, and visits to the Wine Country.

SHOPPING

A major player in the global economy, California is known for its casual clothing as well as the best in cutting-edge fashion. It is the largest producer of children's clothing in the US, with Sara's Prints and **Levi Strauss** being among the best. It is equally famous for its sportswear and swimwear, designed by names such as **C&C California**.

Fresh fruit, nuts, and vegetables from the San Joaquin Valley feeds the entire nation. The fine wines of Napa and Sonoma Valleys are available in wineries across the state. Some, such as **Viansa Winery** and **Sebastiani Vineyards**, also sell a wide range of wine-related products.

Aside from the shopping districts of L.A. and San Francisco, the state's smaller towns offer a wide range of merchandise and local produce in roadside food stands, wineries, antique shops, and flea markets, where prices tend to be cheaper than in cities.

DIRECTORY

TOURIST OFFICES

California Division of Tourism
Tel (877) 225-4367.
www.visitcalifornia.com

SPECIAL INTEREST VACATIONS

Santa Barbara Writers' Conference
PO Box 6627, Santa Barbara, CA 93160.
Tel (805) 964-0367.
www.sbwc.org

Tante Marie's Cooking School
271 Francsico St, S.F., CA 94133. *Tel (415) 788-6699.*
www.tantemarie.com

CAMPING

State Park Reservations
Tel (800) 444-7275.
www.parks.ca.gov

Yosemite Reservations
Tel (559) 253-5635.
www.yosemitepark.com

HIKING

Sierra Club
Tel (415) 977-5500.
www.sierraclubcalifornia.org

MOUNTAIN BIKING

Backroads
801 Cedar St, Berkeley.
Tel (800) 462-2848.
www.backroads.com

WHITEWATER RAFTING & KAYAKING

American River Touring Association
24000 Casa Loma Rd, Groveland, CA 95321.
Tel (800) 323-2782.
www.arta.org

ISLAND HOPPING

Island Packers
1867 Spinnaker Dr, Ventura, CA 93001.
Tel (805) 642-1393.
www.islandpackers.com.

SHOPPING

C&C California
www.candccalifornia.com

Original Levi Store
300 Post St, San Francisco, CA 94108.
Tel (415) 501-0100.
www.levi.com

WINERIES

Sebastiani Vineyards
389 Fourth St E, Sonoma, CA 95476.
Tel (800) 888-5532, (707) 933-3370.
www.sebastiani.com

Viansa Winery
25200 Arnold Dr, Sonoma, CA 95476.
Tel (800) 995-4740.
www.viansa.com

Choosing a Hotel

Framed by rugged coastal mountains, forested hills, sophisticated urban centers, and a long coastline, California is one of the premier vacation destinations in the world. There is a wealth of hotel options. Hotels here have been selected across a wide price range for their excellent facilities and locations.

PRICE CATEGORIES IN US DOLLARS ($)
For a standard double room per night, including breakfast, service charges, and taxes.
$ Under $100
$$ $100–$150
$$$ $150–$200
$$$$ $200–$250
$$$$$ Over $250

LOS ANGELES

BEVERLY HILLS Peninsula Beverly Hills $$$$$

9882 S Santa Monica Blvd, 90212 ***Tel*** *(310) 551-2888, (800) 462-7899* ***Fax*** *(310) 788-2319* ***Rooms*** *196*

The last word in LA luxury for the rich and the famous, this sleek, elegant hotel pays meticulous attention to detail. Rooms are equipped with every conceivable amenity, including a remote control that operates almost everything. It also has a top-rated spa and restaurant. **www.peninsula.com**

HOLLYWOOD Ramada Inn Hollywood $$

1160 N Vermont Ave, 90029 ***Tel*** *(323) 660-1788, (800) 800-9733* ***Fax*** *(323) 660-8069* ***Rooms*** *130*

This hotel has full amenities, including many family-friendly conveniences, and it offers complete conference facilities. The heart of Hollywood is a short drive from the hotel, and a shuttle service to Universal Studios is available. **www.hollywoodhotel.net**

LONG BEACH Hotel Queen Mary $$$

1126 Queen's Hwy, 90802 ***Tel*** *(562) 435-3511* ***Fax*** *(562) 437-4531* ***Rooms*** *365*

Guests booking aboard this restored historic cruise liner are afforded ship tours and treated to a bit of ocean-going history. Rooms are equipped with select modern amenities. The restaurant and spa facilities are first-rate. The Ghost Tour is a fun diversion. **www.queenmary.com**

MALIBU Casa Malibu Inn on the Beach $$$

22752 Pacific Coast Hwy, 90265 ***Tel*** *(310) 456-2219* ***Fax*** *(310) 456-5418* ***Rooms*** *21*

This small, friendly beachside inn retains some of the old coastal charm. Rooms have a private feel. A few have fireplaces, while many have been updated with tile tubs. Amenities include high-end linen, DVD players, and wireless Internet access. The hotel has a secluded sun deck and its own stretch of beach.

PASADENA Ritz Carlton Huntington Hotel $$$$$

1401 S Oak Knoll Ave, 91106 ***Tel*** *(626) 568-3900, (800) 542-8680* ***Fax*** *(626) 568-3700* ***Rooms*** *392*

With luxury and sophistication at every turn, this hotel offers exemplary service and a secluded location away from the city center. The grounds are quiet and well-manicured. The historic building boasts modern amenities in each room, including top-end linen and robes. The full-service spa is a prime attraction. **www.ritzcarlton.com**

SANTA MONICA Sheraton Delfina Santa Monica $$$$$

530 Pico Blvd, 90405 ***Tel*** *(310) 399-9344, (888) 627-8532* ***Fax*** *(310) 399-2504* ***Rooms*** *308*

This hotel offers the latest amenities in its contemporary guestrooms, including upscale linen and luxury bath soaps. Many rooms have ocean views. On-site features include a state-of-the-art fitness center and wireless Internet access in the lobby. **www.sheratonsantamonica.com**

SAN DIEGO COUNTY

CORONADO Hotel Del Coronado $$$$$

1500 Orange Ave, 92118 ***Tel*** *(619) 435-6611, (800) 468-3533* ***Fax*** *(619) 522-8262* ***Rooms*** *700*

A landmark in San Diego for more than a century, this grand Victorian building is as famous for its accommodations as for its history and hospitality. Situated on a stretch of beautiful beach, the hotel offers every amenity. The rooms are modern, comfortable, and well appointed. Fine spa and superb restaurant. **www.hoteldel.com**

LA JOLLA Embassy Suites Hotel $$

4550 La Jolla Village Dr, 92122 ***Tel*** *(858) 453-0400* ***Fax*** *(858) 453-4226* ***Rooms*** *335*

This mid-size, efficiently run hotel is convenient for families and groups. The property features two-room suites, and is close to freeway access, San Diego attractions, and the University of California San Diego campus. Full business amenities are offered, including high-speed Internet access and work desks. **www.embassysuites1.hilton.com**

Key to Symbols *see back cover flap*

SAN DIEGO US Grant Hotel $$$$$

326 Broadway, 92101 ***Tel*** *(866) 837-4270, (800) 237-5029* ***Fax*** *(619) 239-9517* ***Rooms*** *315*

In the heart of downtown, this beautiful historic property features rooms with a period feel, but equipped with modern amenities including plush bath robes and pillowtop mattresses. The lobby and public areas are opulent and regal. Within walking distance of many shops and restaurants. **www.usgrant.net**

TIJUANA Grand Hotel Tijuana $$

Blvd Agua Caliente 4500, CP, 22420 ***Tel*** *(866) 472-6385* ***Rooms*** *423*

Just south of the United States border in Mexico, this large, modern hotel is part of a complex featuring resort-style amenities, including a swimming pool and recreational facilities. The suites have kitchens and Internet access. Service is helpful and prompt. **www.grandhoteltij.com.mx**

THE DESERTS

PALM SPRINGS Spa Resort and Casino $$

100 N Indian Canyon Dr, 92262 ***Tel*** *(888) 999-1995* ***Fax*** *(760) 325-0688* ***Rooms*** *230*

Built over hot springs that gave the town its name, this hotel has a lavish spa and comfortable rooms. A variety of activities are in walking distance, including the hotel's Las Vegas-style casino with live entertainment. **www.sparesortcasino.com**

PALM SPRINGS Hilton Palm Springs $$$$$

400 E Tahquitz Canyon Dr, 92262 ***Tel*** *(760) 320-6868* ***Fax*** *(760) 320-2126* ***Rooms*** *260*

A downtown hotel, with rooms situated around a large swimming pool. The rooms are spacious and comfortably appointed; many have mountain views and balconies. Amenities include a full spa, fitness facilities, and a business center. Plaza Al Fresco is a poolside lounge, while the lovely Terrace Restaurant is an excellent dining choice. **www.hiltonpalmsprings.com**

PALM SPRINGS Parker Palm Springs $$$$$

4200 E Palm Canyon Dr, 92264 ***Tel*** *(760) 770-5000* ***Fax*** *(760) 324-2188* ***Rooms*** *144*

This sleek-looking desert classic features hotel rooms, suites, and villas, each with the latest amenities. The staff are friendly and efficient, and the service is first-rate. There is a top-of-the-line spa and fitness facility on the premises as well as indoor and outdoor pools and tennis courts. **www.theparkerpalmsprings.com**

TWENTYNINE PALMS Best Western Garden Inn & Suites $

71487 Twentynine Palms Hwy, 92277 ***Tel*** *(760) 367-9141* ***Fax*** *(760) 367-2584* ***Rooms*** *84*

Select rooms at this tidy, well-located hotel are beautifully appointed, featuring kitchenettes. Amenities include a pool, hot tub, laundry facilities, free parking, and breakfast. This is a good stop-over for Joshua Tree National Park, which is located just 5 miles (8 km) away. **www.bestwesterncalifornia.com**

CENTRAL COAST

BIG SUR Post Ranch Inn $$$$$

PO Box 219, Hwy 1, 93920 ***Tel*** *(831) 667-2200, (800) 527-2200* ***Fax*** *(831) 667-2512* ***Rooms*** *30*

Architecturally stunning, this away-from-it-all resort features sumptuously appointed rooms, with dazzling ocean views and romantic seclusion – an unforgettable experience. Morning yoga is offered. They also have a spa, pool, and fitness center. The restaurant is exceptional. **www.postranchinn.com**

MONTEREY Monterey Plaza Hotel & Spa $$$$$

400 Cannery Row, 93940 ***Tel*** *(831) 646-1700, (800) 334-3999* ***Fax*** *(831) 656-0439* ***Rooms*** *290*

One of the best-known hotels in the area, this well-run establishment has European styling and is situated centrally on the bay. Spacious rooms have all the facilities, including fantastic bath accessories and high-speed Internet connections. There is a notable restaurant on the premises. **www.montereyplazahotel.com**

SANTA BARBARA Four Seasons Biltmore $$$$$

1260 Channel Dr, 93108 ***Tel*** *(805) 969-2261* ***Fax*** *(805) 565-8323* ***Rooms*** *209*

Exquisite seaside luxury and attention to every detail make this the premier Santa Barbara indulgence. The Spanish Colonial-style property is set elegantly on sprawling grounds, across from the beach and away from town. Rooms are sumptuous and secluded, and come with every amenity. **www.fourseasons.com**

SANTA CRUZ Terrace Court Motel $$$

125 Beach St, 95060 ***Tel*** *(831) 423-3031* ***Fax*** *(831) 423-2607* ***Rooms*** *40*

A popular, great-value, motel-style hotel located within easy walking distance to the beach and Boardwalk. Terrace Court features comfortably appointed rooms and suites, ranging in size from standard to three-room family suites, many with commanding ocean views. It has an on-site surf shop, market, deli, and heated outdoor pool. **www.terracecourt.com**

SAN FRANCISCO

BERKELEY Claremont Resort & Spa $$$$$

41 Tunnel Rd, 94705 **Tel** *(510) 843-3000, (800) 551-7266* **Fax** *(510) 843-3229* **Rooms** *279*

A large, historic retreat set in the hills above Berkeley, near the border with Oakland. Facilities include comfortable guestrooms, appointed with all the modern amenities, a large spa, meeting rooms, and children's programs. There are also tennis courts and a good restaurant on the premises. **www.claremontresort.com**

CHINATOWN AND NOB HILL Hotel Triton $$

342 Grant Ave, 94108 **Tel** *(415) 394-0500, (800) 800-1299* **Fax** *(415) 394-0555* **Rooms** *140*

Design and media professionals frequent the small but stylish Triton, which has a friendly and cheerful ambience. It is just across the street from Chinatown and in the heart of San Francisco's art gallery district. For overseas travelers, foreign newspapers are normally available at the downstairs Café de la Presse. **www.hoteltriton.com**

FINANCIAL DISTRICT AND UNION SQUARE Clift $$$$$

495 Geary St, 94102 **Tel** *(415) 775-4700, (800) 652-5438* **Fax** *(415) 441-4621* **Rooms** *363*

The dramatic Clift is a striking example of modern design, with a lobby created by Phillippe Starck. Each room is elegantly furnished, with all the amenities one would expect from a hotel of this caliber. The downstairs Redwood Room and award-winning Asia de Cuba Restaurant are enchanting. **www.clifthotel.com**

FISHERMAN'S WHARF AND NORTH BEACH The Sheraton $$$$

2500 Mason St, 94133 **Tel** *(800) 325-3535, (415) 362-5500* **Fax** *(415) 956-5275* **Rooms** *529*

Primarily a family-oriented, tourist hotel, the Sheraton is housed in a large, attractive 1970s building, with all the comforts expected by regular travelers. It provides easy access to Fisherman's Wharf and the ferry that goes to Alcatraz Island. It is also popular with business travelers. **www.sheratonatthewharf.com**

HAIGHT ASHBURY AND THE MISSION Red Victorian Bed and Breakfast $$

1665 Haight St, 94117 **Tel** *(415) 864-1978* **Fax** *(415) 863-3293* **Rooms** *18*

The Red Victorian is the ubiquitous Haight Street accommodation, perfect for travelers who want to channel San Francisco in the "Summer of Love." All the rooms are individually themed, with names such as Redwood Forest and Flower Child. No radios or TVs are available, but there is a meditation room. **www.redvic.com**

PACIFIC HEIGHTS Edward II Inn & Suites $$$

3155 Scott St, 94123 **Tel** *(415) 922-3000, (800) 473-2846* **Fax** *(415) 931-5784* **Rooms** *30*

Edward II Inn and Suites is a real find for those looking for a quiet place in a convenient location. The house, built in 1914, is now a three-story inn, a few blocks from San Francisco's Yacht Harbor. Some of the suites have Jacuzzis, and there are two small meeting rooms available. Complimentary breakfast. **www.edwardii.com**

SAN JOSE San Jose Marriott $$$$

301 S Market St, 95113 **Tel** *(408) 280-1300* **Fax** *(408) 278-4444* **Rooms** *506*

This sleek business-friendly, high-rise hotel is located next to the convention center and within walking distance to downtown restaurants and attractions. The rooms are fully equipped with the latest technology, and many have excellent cityscape views. The street-level restaurant is exceptional. **www.sanjosemarriott.com**

WINE COUNTRY

MENDOCINO MacCallum House Inn $$$

45020 Albion St, 95460 **Tel** *(707) 937-0289, (800) 609-0492* **Fax** *(707) 937-2243* **Rooms** *19*

Rooms at this charming coastal inn are set in various historic structures, and range from the antiques-filled main house to private cottages with fireplaces and decks. The landscaped gardens are lovely. Within walking distance to various shops and galleries in town. **www.maccallumhouse.com**

NAPA Silverado Country Club Resort $$$$$

1600 Atlas Peak Rd, 94558 **Tel** *(707) 257-0200, (800) 532-0500* **Fax** *(707) 257-2867* **Rooms** *260*

This popular Wine Country resort is renowned for its golf course and casual sophistication. The rooms are spacious and well appointed, set in bungalows among beautiful grounds. Additional amenities include indoor and outdoor swimming pools, a top-rated spa, fitness center, tennis, and golf. **www.silveradoresort.com**

SONOMA El Pueblo Inn $$$$

896 W Napa St, 95476 **Tel** *(707) 996-3651, (800) 900-8844* **Fax** *(707) 935-5988* **Rooms** *53*

Located close to the town's plaza, this charming, family-run inn has lovely grounds and rooms appointed with modest style and casual comfort. Most rooms face the garden and offer privacy. The Sonoma rooms' facilities include DVD players and private patios. Guests can also enjoy the spa whirlpool. **www.elpuebloinn.com**

Key to Price Guide *see p722* **Key to Symbols** *see back cover flap*

NORTHERN CALIFORNIA

EUREKA Quality Inn $

1209 4th St, 95501 **Tel** *(707) 443-1601, (800) 772-1622* **Fax** *(707) 444-8365* **Rooms** *60*

A chain hotel in the heart of old town Eureka, providing basic amenities such as a swimming pool and sauna. Some rooms have whirlpool baths. The hotel offers special rates and upgrade considerations for business travelers. They also serve an elaborate Continental breakfast. **www.qualityinn.com**

MOUNT LASSEN Mineral Lodge $

PO Box 160 Mineral, 96063 **Tel** *(530) 595-4422* **Fax** *(530) 595-4452* **Rooms** *20*

A great rest stop for hikers in Lassen Volcanic National Park. This modest motel has a Western ambience, and features double and family-size rooms as well as a friendly general store and a saloon. The owners also offer rentals of outdoor recreation equipment. **www.minerallodge.com**

MOUNT SHASTA Best Western Tree House Motor Inn $$

111 Morgan Way, 96067 **Tel** *(530) 926-3101, (800) 780-7234* **Fax** *(530) 926-3542* **Rooms** *99*

Part of the Best Western chain, this comfy hotel is outfitted with redwood furniture, and has nice rooms as well as a welcoming lounge and a lobby with a fireplace. Tree House Inn has a business center, an indoor swimming pool, non-smoking rooms, and a restaurant. Also caters to disabled guests. Complimentary breakfast. **www.bestwestern.com**

WEAVERVILLE Motel Trinity $

1112 Main St, 96093 **Tel** *(530) 623-2129, (877) 623-5454* **Fax** *(530) 623-6007* **Rooms** *25*

Rooms in this mountain hotel have pine-paneled walls, and some feature whirlpool tubs and kitchenettes. There is also a heated swimming pool and a shady lawn area. The property is close to many outdoor recreational pursuits, including hiking and stream fishing. **www.moteltrinity.com/**

GOLD COUNTRY AND THE CENTRAL VALLEY

NEVADA CITY National Hotel $

211 Broad St, 95959 **Tel** *(530) 265-4551* **Fax** *(530) 265-2445* **Rooms** *38*

This Victorian-style hotel has been in operation since 1855 and still recalls the thriving Gold Rush era, from the friendly staff to the covered sidewalk. The rooms are quaint and outfitted in period decorations; most have private baths. The swimming pool is perfect for sunny afternoons. **www.thenationalhotel.com**

SACRAMENTO Hyatt Regency $$$$

1209 L St, 95814 **Tel** *(916) 443-1234* **Fax** *(916) 321-3099* **Rooms** *503*

This smoothly operated hotel is central to downtown and directly across from the Capitol building. The rooms are spacious and well appointed with cable TV, full bath amenities, and Wi-Fi access. There is a good lobby-level lounge near the pool and a fitness center. The IMAX theater is just behind the hotel. **www.sacramento.hyatt.com**

SUTTER CREEK Sutter Creek Inn $$$

75 Main St, 95685 **Tel** *(209) 267-5606* **Fax** *(209) 267-9287* **Rooms** *17*

Built in 1859, this country-style inn has private cottages with wood-burning fireplaces, and is surrounded by shady gardens laced with walkways and hammocks. Some rooms have beds that swing from the ceiling. Sutter Creek Inn is a good base for exploring the Amador County wineries and other historic sites. **www.suttercreekinn.com**

THE HIGH SIERRAS

KINGS CANYON NATIONAL PARK Montecito Sequoia Lodge $$

8000 Generals Hwy, 93633 **Tel** *(559) 335-5500, (800) 227-9900* **Fax** *(559) 565-3223* **Rooms** *52*

With ample activity options, this mountain lodge appeals to families and large groups year-round. Rooms are lodge-style or in cabins, and feature large beds, deluxe bunks, and complete bath amenities. Camp-style activities are planned regularly for guests. Meals are included in the price. **www.mslodge.com**

YOSEMITE NATIONAL PARK The Ahwahnee $$$$$

Yosemite Valley, 95389 **Tel** *(801) 559-4884* **Fax** *(209) 372-1463* **Rooms** *123*

This famed historic hotel is synonymous with the valley. Opened in 1927, it is elegant and rustic, built of stone and timber, with a Native American ambience. The lodge features a soaring lobby, well-appointed rooms, and an excellent restaurant. The solarium and winter club room are great. **www.yosemitepark.com**

Choosing a Restaurant

Of all the states in the country, California has perhaps the widest variety of places to eat. "California cuisine" – light food prepared in a range of international styles using locally grown ingredients – is now internationally recognized. The large variety of ethnic cuisines reflect the state's many cultures.

PRICE CATEGORIES
For a three-course meal for one, half a bottle of house wine, and all unavoidable extra charges such as sales tax and service.
$ Under $25
$$ $25–$35
$$$ $35–$50
$$$$ $50–$70
$$$$$ Over $70

LOS ANGELES

BEVERLY HILLS Nate'n Al $$

414 N Beverly Dr, 90210 ***Tel*** *(310) 274-0101*

It may be in one of the fanciest neighborhoods in town, but this unassuming traditional deli could just as easily be found on a Brooklyn side street – and that is the beauty of it. Homesick New Yorkers or anyone looking for simple treats such as pastrami on rye or potato knishes head to Nate'n Al, where the Beverly Hills glitz is left at the door.

DOWNTOWN Cicada $$$$

617 S Olive St, 90014 ***Tel*** *(213) 488-9488*

Possibly the grandest dining room in LA, Cicada is housed in the historic Oviatt Hotel, and its dramatic Art Deco design features soaring maple columns, lots of gold leaf, and Lalique glass. The cuisine is a blend between modern Italian and progressive American, with everything from foie gras to risotto turning up on the intriguing menu.

HOLLYWOOD The Gumbo Pot $

Farmers Market, 6333 W 3rd St, 90036 ***Tel*** *(323) 933-0358*

Finding an authentic taste of the Big Easy in LA is not a simple matter, but this little operation, hidden in the historic Farmers Market, is the genuine article. This casual, order-at-the-counter eatery is one of the few places to find authentic beignets and *muffaletta* or po-boy sandwiches, not to mention solid jambalaya and, of course, gumbo.

LONG BEACH Parkers' Lighthouse $$$

435 Shoreline Village Dr, 90802 ***Tel*** *(562) 432-6500*

With a real working lighthouse, this Long Beach landmark has great views of the harbor and the *Queen Mary*. The menu showcases mesquite-grilled seafood, including salmon, swordfish, mahi mahi, and halibut. Nothing too fancy or cutting-edge here, but a bucket of steamed clams on the patio is a great way to spend a summer evening.

MALIBU Gladstone's of Malibu $$$

17300 Pacific Coast Hwy, 90272 ***Tel*** *(310) 454-3474*

One of the top-grossing restaurants in the nation, this monster-sized beachfront seafood house is famous for its sprawling patio overlooking the Pacific. Big portions of chowder, grilled fish, lobster, *cioppino*, and Cajun-style blackened salmon may not be the world's finest, but most folks are thrilled with its quintessential LA feel.

PASADENA Yujean Kang's $$

67 N Raymond Ave, 91103 ***Tel*** *(626) 585-0855*

This is not your typical neighborhood Chinese restaurant. The dining room is elegant and tasteful, the service polished, and the menu unique. Innovative chef/owner Kang incorporates non-traditional ingredients, such as Parma ham and salmon, into unique dishes prepared with classic Chinese technique. Delicious desserts and good wines.

SANTA MONICA Broadway Deli $$

1457 Broadway, 90401 ***Tel*** *(310) 451-0616*

This massive, bustling restaurant offers a wide range of traditional deli specialties, and the menu goes way beyond corned beef or pastrami sandwiches. Here you will find everything from pizzas to ostrich burgers to duck enchiladas. There is also a wine shop on the premises and a gourmet market for picnickers.

VENICE Rose Café $

220 Rose Ave, 90291 ***Tel*** *(310) 399-0711*

Representative of the old bohemian Venice that is gradually disappearing in favor of rapid gentrification, the Rose Café has a roomy interior and a pleasant, sunny patio. An assortment of pastries, quiches, and salads are what the regulars return for. A cappuccino and a croissant, with a book on the patio, is a good way to spend time here.

WEST HOLLYWOOD The Spanish Kitchen $$$

826 N La Cienega Blvd, 90069 ***Tel*** *(310) 659-4794*

This handsome hacienda-style restaurant, inspired by the diverse cooking methods of the southern regions of Mexico (Chiapas, Yucatan, and Oaxaca), turns out many intriguing dishes. A lively cocktail bar dispensing flavored margaritas and the *mariscos y mescal* bar, are part of the festive atmosphere. Rather upscale for a Mexican eatery in LA.

SAN DIEGO COUNTY

CORONADO Azzura Point $$$$

Loews Coronado Bay Resort, 4000 Coronado Bay Rd, 92118 ***Tel*** *(619) 424-4000*

With panoramic views of the Coronado Bay bridge and the glistening city skyline, Azzura Point is a dazzling contemporary room that is not overly formal. The diverse Californian-Mediterranean menu includes foie gras, lobster risotto, and healthful ahi tuna. Linger over the view with fine wine, cheeses, and winning desserts.

LA JOLLA Tapenade $$$

7612 Fay Ave, 92037 ***Tel*** *(858) 551-7500*

A bit of Nice in the heart of La Jolla, this casually elegant restaurant derives its cuisine from the south of France. Escargots, duck, and steak *au poivre* are offered. The Maine lobster here comes in many forms, such as salad, soup, and risotto. Desserts are decadent, and a fine plate of cheeses is also available. There's a children's menu, too.

SAN DIEGO The Big Kitchen $

3003 Grape St, 92102 ***Tel*** *(619) 234-5789*

Located behind Balboa Park, this little gem of a diner, with a nice little patio, is extremely popular for its huge breakfasts. The omelets, pancakes, and *huevos rancheros* are quite good. Its owner has a strong personal following, and artistic and cultural groups often meet over coffee at this quirky, but endearing, eatery. Open 8am–2pm.

THE DESERTS

BARSTOW Idle Spurs Steak House $$$

690 Hwy 58, 92311 ***Tel*** *(760) 256-8888*

This traditional, Western-style steakhouse is a good, relaxing place to recharge after a long day of driving. The jalapeño poppers and chicken wings are popular starters, followed by tender aged steaks. The old school bar is a popular watering hole for locals. The attractive patio, dominated by a massive tree, offers a pleasant alfresco option.

DEATH VALLEY Wrangler Steakhouse $$

Furnace Creek Resort, Hwy 190, 92328 ***Tel*** *(760) 786-2345*

Not as formal as the dining room at the adjoining Furnace Creek Resort, this restaurant is housed in a former working ranch, beautifully preserved to reflect the mystique of this desert oasis. The restaurant features an all-you-can-eat buffet for breakfast and lunch. In the evening, it operates as a traditional steakhouse.

PALM DESERT Ristorante Tuscany $$$$

Marriott Desert Springs Resort & Spa, 74855 Country Club Dr, 92260 ***Tel*** *(760) 341-2211*

Better than most hotel dining rooms, this place is one of the desert's preferred northern Italian restaurants. The main room is a soaring space with floor-to-ceiling murals and elegantly appointed tables. The diverse menu features fresh seasonal ingredients and a superb selection of seafood. Tasting menu also available. Dinner only.

CENTRAL COAST

BIG SUR Nepenthe $$$

Hwy 1, 93920 ***Tel*** *(831) 667-2345*

This restaurant, with its stunning coastside setting, has a cult-like following, though the food is not quite as dazzling. The simple preparations of American fare are comforting, as are the freshly-made breads and desserts. The ambrosia burger, a ground steak sandwich with the house-made ambrosia sauce, is a favorite.

CARMEL Anton and Michel $$$

Corner of Mission Ave & 7th St, 93921 ***Tel*** *(831) 624-2406*

A Carmel landmark, this downtown restaurant is popular for its contemporary French-inspired cuisine, sophisticated ambience, and attentive service. The fare is reliably prepared using seasonal ingredients. The pan-roasted duck breast is an all-time favorite. The dining room tends to get a bit touristy. Book in advance, and request a patio seat.

MONTEREY Tarpy's Roadhouse $$

2999 Monterey-Salinas Hwy, 93940 ***Tel*** *(831) 647-1444*

Built in an old ranch house, this rustic and appealing restaurant has friendly service and a devoted following. The wide-ranging menu includes wood-fired wild game, great steaks, fresh seafood, salads, and burgers. Select a seat on the patio on warm evenings. There is a full bar and a critically-acclaimed wine list. Service is professional.

SAN LUIS OBISPO Buona Tavola $$$

1037 Monterey St, 93401 **Tel** *(805) 545-8000*

Next to the historic Fremont Theatre, this is a cosmopolitan, art-filled trattoria with a lovely garden patio that is more serene than the bustling interior. The moderately priced menu offers a wide choice of antipasti, pastas such as agnolotti stuffed with scampi in saffron sauce, steaks, and chicken. A good wine list is featured here as well.

SANTA BARBARA The Wine Cask $$$$

813 Anacapa St, 93101 **Tel** *(805) 966-9463*

With an adjoining wine shop, this restaurant features inventive California cuisine reflected by nuanced dishes such as venison rack with blueberry risotto and duck with smoked Mission fig nage. The bustling room, complete with handcrafted beamed ceilings and a stately fireplace, is casually elegant. The stellar wine list fills 53 pages.

SANTA CRUZ Crow's Nest $$

2218 E Cliff Dr, 95062 **Tel** *(831) 476-4560*

An icon of the harbor since 1969, this simple, friendly, and entertaining restaurant serves great seafood specialties as well as pasta, steaks, and chops. The upstairs bar, Breakwater, has a more casual atmosphere, serving a selection of sandwiches, burgers, and small seafood plates. There is live music on select nights.

SAN FRANCISCO

BERKELEY Chez Panisse Restaurant $$$$$

1517 Shattuck Ave, 94709 **Tel** *(510) 548-5525*

Proprietor and chef Alice Waters is famed as the innovator of California cuisine, which is on offer in this simple wood-framed restaurant where it all began. Dishes are prepared simply with the freshest ingredients. Book well in advance or opt for the more affordable café upstairs.

CHINATOWN AND NOB HILL Great Eastern $$

649 Jackson St, 94133 **Tel** *(415) 986-2500*

A longtime favorite in Chinatown, Great Eastern has a menu featuring reliable, if not inspired, Mandarin dishes. The real draw here is the fresh seafood swimming in the tanks – make sure to ask the waiter for the day's specials to sample the best that the restaurant has to offer.

DOWNTOWN Delancey Street Restaurant $$

600 Embarcadero St, 94107 **Tel** *(415) 512-5179*

A wonderful place for dining, Delancey Street Restaurant serves delicious comfort food, including the excellent meatloaf and ribs, and other American dishes. The service is beyond good. The restaurant supports a respected substance-abuse recovery program. Reservations are recommended.

DOWNTOWN Cortez $$$$

550 Geary St, 94102 **Tel** *(415) 292-6360*

In the stylish Hotel Adagio near the Theater District, this is a choice spot for the after-show crowd. Fresh, organic ingredients are used to create tapas-style small plates of Mediterranean-influenced dishes. Order several to share, with a glass of wine from the extensive list. Sautéed sea scallops, and sugar and spice beignets are favorites.

FISHERMAN'S WHARF AND NORTH BEACH Alioto's $$$

8 Fisherman's Wharf, 94133 **Tel** *(415) 673-0183*

Lit by spectacular sunsets filtered through the Golden Gate, Alioto's has been serving well-prepared Sicilian-style seafood since 1925. The food is good, especially the bountiful shrimp or crab Louies (juicy seafood on a bed of crisp romaine lettuce). The kitchen uses fresh seasonal ingredients, sourced locally.

GOLDEN GATE PARK AND THE PRESIDIO Beach Chalet Brewery $$$

1000 Great Hwy, 94122 **Tel** *(415) 386-8439*

Craft brews, big hamburgers with side dishes of crispy fries, and a spectacular view of the Pacific make Beach Chalet Brewery a promising destination after a day in Golden Gate Park. The WPA murals on the first floor and carved stone stair-rails are a must-see. An excellent brunch is served at weekends and there is live music on Tuesdays and Fridays.

HAIGHT ASHBURY AND THE MISSION DISTRICT Cha Cha Cha $

2327 Mission St, 94110 **Tel** *(415) 648-0504*

As much a lively nightlife scene as it is a restaurant, Cha Cha Cha serves small tapas plates and excellent sangria against a background of foot-tapping Latin music. Ever buzzing with an upbeat crowd, this place is not meant for a romantic dinner. Be prepared for an hour's wait, as it gets crowded on Friday and Saturday nights.

SAN JOSE Tied House Café and Brewery $$

65 N San Pedro St, 95112 **Tel** *(408) 295-2739*

Lively and sometimes raucous, this microbrewery and pub-style restaurant has an amazing selection of homemade beers on tap to complement the better-than-average seafood dishes and other American fare. The menu is extensive, ranging from Mexican-inspired to New Orleans-style and Italian classics, and is sure to please even fussy diners.

Key to Price Guide *see p726* **Key to Symbols** *see back cover flap*

WINE COUNTRY

NAPA Bistro Don Giovanni $$$$

4110 Howard Ln, 94558 ***Tel*** *(707) 224-3300*

The inviting dining room of this extremely popular Napa Valley restaurant has a large wood-burning fireplace and a lovely outdoor terrace. The menu has a delicious offering of rustic Italian fare, with French influence, and an excellent wine list. It presents striking views of magnificent mountains and extensive, well-kept gardens.

SONOMA The Swiss Hotel $$

18 W Spain St, 95476 ***Tel*** *(707) 938-2884*

One of the best meals in town can be found at this historic restaurant on the plaza, with an appetizing menu of rustic Italian classics and pizzas from a wood-burning oven. The atmosphere is convivial and welcoming, and the clientele consists of tourists and locals alike.

NORTHERN CALIFORNIA

EUREKA Lost Coast Brewery & Café $

617 4th St, 95501 ***Tel*** *(707) 445-4480*

This fun and funky brewpub, situated in an old stand-alone building, has an unassuming atmosphere and lively ambience provided by the chatting clientele at its collection of wood tables. The food is cheap, the portions are plentiful, and some selections venture well beyond the typical pub grub. The homemade beers are exceptional.

MOUNT SHASTA Michael's $$

313 N Mount Shasta Blvd, 96067 ***Tel*** *(530) 926-5288*

Quite popular among locals, this welcoming, intimate restaurant serves mostly Italian cuisine, including such staples as linguine and spaghetti. A good selection of salads and sandwiches is also available for lunch. The efficient service and relaxing ambience add to the charm. Michael's is closed on Sundays.

GOLD COUNTRY AND THE CENTRAL VALLEY

NEVADA CITY Country Rose Café $$$

300 Commercial St, 95959 ***Tel*** *(530) 265-6248*

With a bustling atmosphere and casual decor, this restaurant is among the most prolific in the area. The food is French country-inspired, skillfully prepared, and presented artistically by the inventive kitchen staff. Service is friendly and spirited. There is occasional live music played in the dining room.

SACRAMENTO Fat City Bar & Café $$$

1001 Front St, 95814 ***Tel*** *(916) 446-6768*

Built in an historic brick building in Old Sacramento, this friendly restaurant has long been a regular haunt for politicos and local families. The lively atmosphere is perfect for enjoying the hearty American- and Asian-inspired dishes. The dining room gets quite crowded on weekend nights, so book in advance.

THE HIGH SIERRAS

SOUTH LAKE TAHOE Lake Tahoe Pizza Company $

1168 Lake Tahoe Blvd, 96150 ***Tel*** *(530) 544-1919*

Well-cooked food and excellent prices are the key at this friendly, family-style pizza parlor that uses a special brick oven to make pizzas. The menu features mainly traditional Italian favorites, including barbecued chicken pizza, salads, sandwiches, and pasta. There is also a lean-calorie menu for weight-watchers and a good beer selection.

YOSEMITE NATIONAL PARK Ahwahnee Dining Room $$$$

Yosemite Valley, 95389 ***Tel*** *(559) 252-4848*

The highlight of dining here is the beautiful setting, although the food has improved recently to match the memorable atmosphere. Mostly American standards find a place on the menu; the best choices are the grilled steaks and chops. Save some room for the delectable desserts.

ALASKA & HAWAI'I

INTRODUCING ALASKA 732–735

ALASKA 736–743

INTRODUCING HAWAI'I 744–747

HAWAI'I 748–755

ALASKA

For most visitors, familiar images of Alaska include pristine waterways, towering snowcapped peaks, glaciers calving to form icebergs, and massive grizzly bears feasting on salmon. All this and much more can still be found here on North America's "Last Frontier," where less than one percent of the state's 375 million acres (150 million ha) shows any sign of human habitation.

Situated at the top of the North American continent and separated from the rest of the country by Canada, Alaska is more than twice the size of Texas, the next largest state. Alaska can be divided into three regions, both geographically and for the purpose of travel. Southeast Alaska, commonly called the Inside Passage, is a long, narrow stretch of islands and channels sandwiched between the Pacific Ocean and Canada's Coast Mountains. Picture-postcard coastal towns, including the state capital Juneau, are linked conveniently by an efficient state-run ferry system.

The bulk of Alaska's land mass, however, lies in the continent's extreme northwest corner, closer to Russia than the "Lower 48" states. The modern city of Anchorage is a good base for exploring the Kenai Peninsula and Denali National Park, or as a jumping-off point for more adventurous destinations such as Kodiak Island and the Alaska Peninsula. To the west of the mainland, the windswept volcanic archipelago of the Aleutian Islands stretches 1,200 miles (1,932 km) west into the Bering Sea

Russian doll on sale in Juneau

HISTORY

Alaska's southeast corner is 500 miles (805 km) from the rest of the US, but its farthest reaches a mere 50 miles (80 km) from Russia. As a result, the state's history reflects its role as a bridge and buffer between these two powerful nations. Human history here goes back much farther, since Alaska was the point of entry for some of the first people to set foot in North America, who crossed a land bridge over the Bering Strait 13,000 to 30,000 years ago. While some groups continued their migrations southward, a few remained for millenia, hunting and fishing until the arrival of Western Europeans. The original Alaskans' descendants today include the island-dwelling Aleut, the coastal Tlingit, the Athabascans of the interior, and the Eskimos of Arctic and western Alaska.

A panoramic view of North America's highest peak, Mount McKinley in Denali National Park

◁ **Hawai'i's Makapu'u Beach on southeast O'ahu, backed by the peaks of the Ko'olau Range**

A brown bear fishing for salmon at Brooks Camp, Katmai National Park, Alaska Peninsula

The first non-Native settlements were outposts built by Russian fur traders in the late 18th century. Although their far-flung colony stretched as far south as California, it declined as trappers decimated once-huge populations of seals and sea otters. Seen as a liability, Alaska was sold by Russia in 1867 to the US Secretary of State William Seward. The purchase was popularly considered a waste of money and dubbed "Seward's Folly"; however, doubts vanished when the first of many deposits of gold was found near Juneau. More mineral discoveries, including gold in 1898 at distant Nome, as well as vast quantities of copper, and oil at Prudhoe Bay, have all proved the wisdom of Seward's purchase.

ALASKA TODAY

Alaska is home to 685,000 people. Of the population, 16 percent are of Native descent, while the remainder come from diverse backgrounds (only 34 percent of the total are born in the state). It has a population density of just one person per square mile (compared to over 1,000 in New Jersey).

Visitors at Aialik Glacier, one of the main attractions at Kenai Fjords National Park

Alaska's economy depends upon oil from the North Slope, but government jobs, seafood processing, and tourism are also important. Anchorage is a major international hub for air cargo shipments. Over time, there has been a growing awareness to preserve and protect Alaska's unique wilderness from the commercial pressures arising from the state's natural wealth. The vast majority of Alaska is owned by the government, and much of this is protected in national parks and other undeveloped areas stretching from Glacier Bay to the Gates of the Arctic.

KEY DATES IN HISTORY

13,000–30,000 years ago Migratory peoples cross from present-day Siberia into Alaska

1741 Working for the Czar of Russia, Danish explorer Vitus Bering and his crew are the first Europeans to visit Alaska

1867 To ease an economic recession, the Czar of Russia sells Alaska to the US for $7.2 million

1880 Gold is discovered near Juneau

1897 The Klondike Gold Rush hits Skagway

1912 Alaska becomes a US Territory

1942 US Army builds the 1,442-mile (2,322-km) Alaska Highway as an overland link

1959 Alaska becomes the 49th state

1964 Good Friday earthquake destroys much of Anchorage

1968 Oil discovered at Prudhoe Bay

1977 Trans-Alaska pipeline completed

1989 *Exxon Valdez* runs aground on Bligh Reef, spilling 11 million gallons (50 million liters) of oil into Prince William Sound

2000 onwards Global warming is causing dramatic changes in Alaska, particularly in the Arctic. Climate changes will have major impacts on the state's people, animals, and plants

Exploring Alaska

A vast wilderness of virgin rivers, towering mountain peaks, abundant wildlife, and calving glaciers, Alaska is by far the largest state in the United States. Its sheer size means that travel takes up a fair proportion of a visitor's time. However, the state has an excellent transportation and tourism infrastructure, which caters to a million visitors each year, most of whom arrive during the brief summer season from late May to early September. Good roads connect Anchorage, Fairbanks, and other cities, but much of Southeast Alaska – including the capital city of Juneau – are inaccessible by road. Ferries, planes, and cruise ships connect coastal towns, while remote bush villages are accessed only by air.

King Salmon Antler's Inn, outside Katmai NP, Alaska Peninsula

SIGHTS AT A GLANCE

Ketchikan 1
Sitka 2
Juneau 3
Glacier Bay National Park 4
Skagway 5
Anchorage 6
Valdez 7
Seward 8
Homer 9
Kodiak Island 10
Alaska Peninsula 11
Aleutian Islands 12
Nome 13
Fairbanks 14
Wrangell-St. Elias National Park 15
Denali National Park pp742–3 16

SEE ALSO

• ***Practical Information*** p756
• ***Where to Stay*** pp758–9
• ***Where to Eat*** p762

KEY

Airport

Major road

International border

MILEAGE CHART

10 = Distance in miles
10 = Distance in kilometers

	SKAGWAY	ANCHORAGE	VALDEZ	SEWARD	HOMER	FAIRBANKS
ANCHORAGE	**833** 1340					
VALDEZ	**757** 1218	**307** 494				
SEWARD	**960** 1544	**127** 205	**429** 690			
HOMER	**1055** 1697	**236** 379	**531** 854	**180** 289		
FAIRBANKS	**712** 1145	**429** 690	**362** 582	**484** 779	**582** 936	
DENALI NP	**833** 1340	**237** 382	**504** 811	**364** 585	**473** 761	**121** 195

Aialik Glacier near Seward, with seals on icebergs in the foreground

Floatplanes docked on Kodiak Island, Gulf of Alaska

Ketchikan ❶

9,000. ✈ 🚢 2 miles (3 km) S of downtown. ℹ 131 Front Street, (907) 225-6166, (800) 770-3300. www.visit-ketchikan.com

Strung out along the waters of the Tongass Narrows and backed by forested hills, Ketchikan is the first stop along the Inside Passage for Alaska-bound cruise ships and ferries. All kinds of watercraft, floatplanes, and kayakers jostle for space along the crowded waterfront. Cruise ships dock outside downtown, providing passengers with easy access to local attractions such as the **Creek Street** precinct. Formerly the heart of a red-light district, the street is lined with colorfully restored wooden houses built on pilings over the water and linked by a boardwalk.

Even for those who are not planning a trip into the wilderness, the **Southeast Alaska Discovery Center** is definitely worth a visit. Exhibits here relate the human and natural history of the southeast region of Alaska, and also include a fabulous re-creation of a rainforest. Ketchikan's **Totem Heritage Center** displays an incredible collection of more than 30 original totems poles, many more than a century old.

Lying to the north of the city, Tongass Avenue runs along the waterfront all the way to the **Totem Bight State Historical Park**. From here, a trail leads past huge totem poles to a reconstruction of a Native clan house.

Southeast Alaska Discovery Center
50 Main Street. ***Tel*** *(907) 228-6220.* *May–Oct: 8am–5pm daily; Nov–Apr: 10am–4pm Thu–Sun.*

Sitka ❷

9,000. ✈ 🚢 7 miles (11 km) N of downtown. ℹ 303 Lincoln St, (907) 747-5940. Alaska Day (Oct 18). www.sitka.org

Totem pole, Sitka

Founded by Russian entrepreneur Alexander Baranof in 1799, Sitka was the capital of Russian America until Alaska was sold to the United States in 1867. Even now, a strong Russian influence survives here. The center of town is dominated by **St. Michael's Cathedral**, a Russian Orthodox cathedral that was rebuilt after the original 1848 structure burned down in 1966. It preserves many Russian artifacts, including the Sitka Madonna, supposedly blessed with healing powers. Beyond St. Michael's is **Sitka National Historical Park**, the site of a fierce week-long battle between the Russians and local Tlingit tribe in 1804. The area is sprinkled with totem poles, and its shores are gently lapped by the waters of Sitka Sound. Native workers display their craft skills at a cultural center throughout the warm summer. The park is also a good place to view the town's natural setting. Islands dot the Sound, and the snowcapped volcano Mount Edgecumbe – often compared to Japan's Mount Fuji – sits majestically on the horizon.

The Russian-style St. Michael's Cathedral, Sitka

The **Alaska Raptor Center**, across Indian River from the park, rehabilitates bald eagles, owls, and falcons. Visitors are free to walk or join a guided tour. Sitka also has a network of hiking and biking trails.

Alaska Raptor Center
1000 Raptor Way. ***Tel*** *(907) 747-8662, (800) 693-9425.* *May–Sep: 8am–5pm daily.* *Oct–Apr.*
www.alaskaraptor.org

Juneau ❸

31,000. ✈ 🚢 Auke Bay, 14 miles (22 km) NW of downtown, (907) 465-3940. ℹ Centennial Hall Visitor Center, 101 Egan Dr, (907) 586-2201, (888) 581-2201. www.traveljuneau.com

Juneau is possibly the most spectacularly located capital city in the US. It is also the most remote, with no road access to the outside world or even to the rest of Alaska. With its large resident population, as well as the 900,000 visitors who arrive during the short summer (late May–early Sep), Juneau is the busy hub of the Inside Passage. Sandwiched between steep-sided forested peaks and the Gastineau Channel, the heart of the city is an intriguing mix of modern high-rise buildings and historic gems such as the **Red Dog Saloon**, and the **Alaskan Hotel**.

Ketchikan's Creek Street, with restored buildings linked by a boardwalk

For hotels and restaurants in this region see pp758–9 and pp762–3

The best way to appreciate the town's wonderful location is by taking the tramway up **Mount Roberts**, from where the panorama extends across Gastineau Channel. The downtown **Alaska State Museum** holds a fine collection of Russian artifacts as well as Native crafts such as Eskimo masks. Its natural history section exhibits a re-creation of a bald eagle's nest. Located at the northern end of the city, 13 miles (21 km) from downtown, **Mendenhall Glacier** is an impressive attraction. A part of the massive Juneau Icefield, this slowly retreating 1.5-mile (2.4-km) wide glacier is calving icebergs into Mendenhall Lake. A lakeside visitor center offers interpretive panels describing the forces behind glacial movement. This is the starting point for hiking trails that provide close-up views of the glacier. Rafting is also offered.

Alaska State Museum
395 Whittier St. ***Tel*** *(907) 465-2901.* *mid-May–mid-Sep: daily; mid-Sep–mid-May: Tue–Sun.* *major public hols.*
www.museums.state.ak.us

Mendenhall Glacier
Off Mendenhall Loop Rd. ***Tel*** *(907) 789- 6640.* *May–Sep: 8am–7:30pm daily; Oct–Apr: 10am–4pm Thu–Sun.*

Glacier Bay National Park ❹

from Juneau. *(907) 697-2230.* **www**.nps.gov/glba
Glacier Bay Lodge & Tours
Departures: Jun–mid-Sep: daily (times vary). ***Tel*** *(907) 264-4600, (888) 229-8687.* **www**.visitglacierbay.com

The scenic White Pass & Yukon Route Railroad near Skagway

Glacier Bay has changed greatly since the British explorer Captain George Vancouver *(see p612)* found his way through Icy Strait in 1794. During the ensuing 200 years, the glaciers have retreated almost 100 miles (160 km), creating a magnificent waterway indented by long bays and protected by the 5,156-sq-mile (13,354-sq-km) national park. Six glaciers reach the sea and break up into massive chunks of ice, which float into a bay inhabited by humpback whales, porpoises, and seals.

Most visitors to Glacier Bay arrive aboard cruise ships. Travelers can also come by way of the hamlet of Gustavus from Juneau, making the short overland trip to Bartlett Cove and Glacier Bay Lodge *(see p758)* by shuttle bus. From Bartlett Cove, it is 40 miles (64 km) to the nearest glacier in a high-speed catamaran. An onboard park naturalist describes the bay's natural history.

Skagway ❺

800. *SW end of Broadway.* *Broadway at 2nd Ave, (907) 983-2854.* **www**.skagway.com

The final northbound stop for travelers on the Inside Passage is this little tourist town surrounded by towering peaks. In 1897, thousands of fortune seekers heading for the Klondike goldfields arrived here only to be faced with an almost insurmountable obstacle – the 33-mile (53 km) **Chilkoot Trail**. This trail traversed a harrowing 45-degree slope nicknamed the "Golden Staircase" over the White Pass to the headwaters of the Yukon River. In the following years, Skagway became a lawless outpost, unofficially ruled by the notorious businessman "Soapy" Smith, who died in a famous shootout with a local surveyor outside the City Hall.

Today, Skagway's fortunes rely largely on promoting its colorful history. The whole of the downtown district is protected as the **Klondike Gold Rush National Historic Park**, encompassing false-fronted buildings, old-time saloons, as well as the distinctive Arctic Brotherhood Hall, whose interesting façade is decorated with over 8,000 pieces of driftwood. The **White Pass & Yukon Route Railroad**, which was originally built over the White Pass as an alternative to the Chilkoot Trail, now operates purely for tourists on a scenic three-hour long round-trip to the pass and back.

ALASKA MARINE HIGHWAY

Logo, Alaska Marine Highway

The state-operated ferry service links towns that are inaccessible by road throughout southeast and south central Alaska, extending service as far south as Prince Rupert (British Columbia) and Bellingham (Washington). En route, visitors pass magnificent fjords, towering glaciers, and virgin forests. The comfortable and well-equipped vessels carry vehicles, and feature cabins, dining areas, and onboard naturalists. It is possible to even pitch tents on the outer deck. Bookings should be made well in advance *(see p756)*.

Clan house in the Alaska Native Heritage Center, Anchorage

Anchorage 6

280,000. 4th Ave at F St, (907) 274-3531. Alaska State Fair (late Aug). **www**.anchorage.net

Lying between Cook Inlet and the Chugach Mountains, Anchorage is Alaska's largest city. Although this coastal urban sprawl is often described as being un-Alaskan, it is still worth spending a little time in this northern metropolis. It also serves as Alaska's financial and transportation hub. Most of downtown was destroyed by the 1964 Good Friday earthquake *(see p733)*, when the north side of 4th Avenue sank 10 ft (3 m). Interpretive displays at **Earthquake Park**, west of downtown toward the airport, tell the story of the Big One.

One of Alaska's finest museums, the **Anchorage Museum at Rasmuson Center** displays an impressive collection of Alaska-themed paintings, and an Alaska Gallery with creative dioramas that chronicle prehistoric times through the present day. At the **Alaska Native Heritage Center**, costumed actors provide visitors with a glimpse of Native culture through dance. An entire section has been dedicated to a re-created Native village set beside a pond. Located 50 miles (80 km) southeast of the city, **Portage Glacier** is steadily retreating and is now out of sight from the visitor center. A tour boat plies the lake close to the glacier. The **Iditarod Trail Sled Dog Race** takes place in March.

Anchorage Museum at Rasmuson Center
121 W 7th Ave. ***Tel*** *(907) 343-6173. mid-May– mid-Sep: 9am–6pm daily; mid-Sep–mid-May: 10am–6pm Tue–Sat, noon– 5pm Sun.* **www**.anchoragemuseum.org

Alaska Native Heritage Center
8800 Heritage Center Dr. ***Tel*** *(907) 330-8000, (800) 315-6608. mid-May–mid-Sep: 9am–5pm daily. mid-Sep–mid-May.* **www**.alaskanative.net

Valdez 7

4,000. downtown. 200 Chenega St, (907) 835-2984. **www**.valdezalaska.org

Stan Stephens Glacier & Wildlife Cruises *Departures: late Jun–early Sep: daily, (907) 835-4731, (866) 867-1297. limited.* **www**.stanstephenscruises.com

The picturesque town of Valdez nestles below snow-capped peaks along an arm of Prince William Sound, a vast bay encompassing islands, glaciers, and icy waters teeming with wildlife. This is North America's northernmost ice-free port. The **Trans-Alaska Pipeline**, which runs above ground for 800 miles (1,288 km) across the state from Prudhoe Bay on the Arctic Ocean, ends here, from where it is transferred to oil tankers. The *Exxon Valdez* ran aground in 1989, spilling millions of gallons of oil into the Sound. A huge cleanup effort has attempted to restore the Sound, and although there are no obvious signs of the spill today, its adverse effect on birds, fish, and marine mammals persists. A cruise of the Sound passes the **Columbia Glacier**, which is more than 3 miles (4.8 km) wide at its 250-ft (75-m) high face, and continuously calves icebergs into the sea. Check with the vistor center for summer tours. The town's **Valdez Museum** explores the Native culture, the importance of oil for the local economy, the *Exxon Valdez* oil spill, and the 1964 Good Friday earthquake, whose epicenter lay less than 60 miles (97 km) from Valdez.

Bronze sculpture, Valdez Museum

Valdez Museum
217 Egan Dr. ***Tel*** *(907) 835-2764. mid-May–Sep: 9am–6pm daily; Oct–mid-May: 1pm–5pm Mon–Fri, noon–4pm Sat.* **www**.valdezmuseum.org

Re-creation of a traditional miner's cabin, Valdez Museum

The magnificent Exit Glacier in the Kenai Fjords National Park, north of Seward

Seward 8

4,000. downtown. 3rd St, (907) 224-8051.
www.sewardak.org

One of the only large towns on the Kenai Peninsula, Seward is a charming fishing port at the head of Resurrection Bay, surrounded by the snow-capped Kenai Mountains. One of its main attractions is the **Alaska SeaLife Center**, which exhibits the marine life of the surrounding ocean. The centerpiece is a string of three huge aquariums holding colorful puffins, seals, and sea lions. Smaller tanks provide a home for crabs and octopuses, while a "touch tank" encourages a hands-on approach to exploring sessile life along the tidal zone.

Seward is encircled by the **Kenai Fjords National Park**, a 906-sq-mile (2,347-sq-km) glaciated coastal wilderness. From the gigantic Hardy Icefield, glaciers radiate in all directions, eight of which are "tidewater glaciers," which extend to sea level. Seward's downtown dock is the departure point for boat trips along the park's coastline. These day cruises also provide excellent opportunities for viewing whales, seals, sea lions, porpoises, and large concentrations of photogenic puffins perched on rocky outcrops. The park's most accessible glacier is Exit Glacier, located off the highway, 4 miles (6.4 km) north of Seward. From the end of the access road, a short trail leads through a forest of stunted trees, emerging at a deep-blue river of ice running through the trees.

Alaska SeaLife Center
Railway Ave. ***Tel*** *(907) 224-6300, (800) 224-2525. May–mid-Sep: 9am–6:30pm Mon–Thu, 8am–6:30pm Fri–Sun; mid-Sep–May: 10am–5pm daily. Thanksg., Dec 25.* **www**.alaskasealife.org

Kenai Fjords National Park
Park Visitor Center *Tel* *(907) 224-7500. May–Sep: daily.*
www.nps.gov/kefj

Homer 9

6,000. Homer Spit. *201 Sterling Hwy, (907) 235-7740.*
www.homeralaska.org
Islands and Ocean Center *95 Sterling Hwy, (907) 235-6961.*

At the end of the Sterling Highway lies Homer, a delightful little hamlet by the water. It was discovered by Homer Pennock, a gold-prospector who arrived here in 1896. Today, this town has become a popular destination for visitors. Its main focus is **Homer Spit**, a 4-mile (6.4-km) finger of land that juts into Kachemak Bay, with the rugged Kenai Mountains glistening across the water. A busy road traverses the entire Spit, passing beaches, a colorful collection of fishing boats, fishing-supply stores, and lively restaurants. Known as the "Halibut Capital of the World," fishing is its main attraction. Charter operators and their boats line the Spit; day trips include tackle and bait as well as instruction. Those who manage to hook a 200-lb (90-kg) halibut can arrange to have it frozen and shipped home. The **Fishing Hole** on the Spit is a man-made waterhole stocked with salmon for an easy catch.

The magnificent wilderness of the **Kachemak Bay State Park**, on the bay's opposite shore, can be explored through a number of hiking trails. The best-known of these leads the visitor to the Grewingk Glacier.

Fishermen with a halibut "weigh-in" on Homer Spit

The northern end of Kodiak Island, covered with thick spruce forests

Kodiak Island ⑩

14,000. downtown. 100 Marine Way, (800) 789-4782, (907) 486-4782. www.kodiak.org

The second-largest island in the United States, Kodiak extends for 100 miles (160 km) across the Gulf of Alaska. Most of the island is an inaccessible stretch of wilderness protected by the 2,969-sq-mile (7,690-sq-km) **Kodiak National Wildlife Refuge**. Kodiak Island is famous as the habitat of about 2,500 Kodiak bears – the world's largest brown bear – some of which stand 10 ft (3 m) tall and weigh up to 1,500 lb (675 kg). The visitor center provides details on charter flights to the best viewing spots.

Most of the island's residents live in the town of Kodiak, home of the country's largest Coast Guard station and its third-largest fishing fleet. North America's oldest Russian building, a storehouse dating to 1808, is now the excellent **Baranov Museum**. A repository of Kodiak's history, the museum's highlights include a superb samovar (urn) collection, Aleut kayaks, and photographs of the town after it was hit by a *tsunami* (massive tidal wave), triggered by the 1964 Good Friday earthquake *(see p733)*. To explore the local fishing industry, follow Shelikof Street past the harbor to the canneries.

Baranov Museum
101 Marine Way. ***Tel** (907) 486-5920.*
Jun–Aug: 10am–4pm Mon–Sat; noon–4pm Sun; Sep–May: 10am–3pm Tue–Sat. *Feb.*

Alaska Peninsula ⑪

King Salmon Airport, (907) 246-4250.

Samovar, Baranov Museum

Dominated by the Alaska Range, this remote part of the state attracts visitors for its intriguing wilderness and wildlife viewing opportunities. In 1912, the second-largest blast in recorded history occurred when the peninsula's Mount Novarupta erupted, covering a 400-sq-mile (1,036-sq-km) area with ash and pumice up to a height of 700 ft (210 m). The blast was heard as far away as Seattle, and the ash that erupted stayed in the atmosphere for an entire year.

The 6,250-sq-mile (16,187-sq-km) **Katmai National Park** encompasses the area where the volcano was most active. A remnant is the Valley of 10,000 Smokes, where gases and ash continue to spew across a lunar-like landscape.

Adjacent to Katmai, photographers from around the world gather at the **McNeil River State Game Sanctuary** to photograph brown bears catching salmon as they struggle up to McNeil River Falls. Access to the falls is by air taxi from King Salmon or Homer *(see p739)*.

Katmai National Park
(907) 246-3305.
www.nps.gov/katm

McNeil River State Game Sanctuary
Best viewing: Jul–mid-Aug. ***Permit required** from Department of Fish & Game, (907) 267-2253.*
www.wildlife.alaska.gov

A brown bear at Katmai National Park, Alaska Peninsula

Aleutian Islands 12

14,000. Unalaska. Unalaska Dutch Harbor Convention and Visitors' Bureau, (907) 581-2612, (877) 581-2612. **www**.unalaska.info

Beyond the Alaska Peninsula, the summits of the Aleutian Range have created a string of islands that extend 1,200 miles (1,932 km) into the Pacific Ocean. Originally settled by hardy Aleut seal hunters, the islands were occupied for more than a year by the Japanese during World War II. Today, over half the archipelago's population live in the town of **Unalaska**, set around a picturesque Dutch Harbor. This town is North America's number one seafood producer. The catch includes crab, halibut, cod, and pollock. Its harbor is lined with fishing boats, container cranes, and processing plants, all catering to this industry. The **Russian Orthodox Church of the Holy Ascension**, built in 1827, dominates the foreshore.

Nome 13

3,500. 301 Front St, (907) 443-6624, (800) 478-1901. **www**.nomealaska.org/vc

Few would argue with the local catchphrase that "there's no place like Nome." Perched on the edge of the Bering Sea, closer to Russia than to Anchorage, the town was named after an early cartographer marked this location as "Name?" on a map. Later another mapmaker misread the annotation as "Nome."

Although Nome is now a shadow of its former self, it is still a fascinating and popular destination. Friendly staff at the tourist information office obligingly indicate historic relics such as the **Last Train to Nowhere**, and the rusting hulks of dredges that have long since been abandoned. There are many hiking trails stretching across the treeless tundra. Panning for gold along the beach is another unique activity.

Fairbanks 14

35,000. 101 Dunkel St, (907) 456-5774, (800) 327-5774. **www**.explorefairbanks.com

Surrounded by sub-arctic wilderness, Fairbanks is Alaska's second-largest city and has one of the largest populations at this latitude anywhere in the world.

Located just 150 miles (241 km) south of the Arctic Circle, the sun barely dips below the horizon at the time of the summer solstice (Jun 21). The long hours of darkness through winter make it a good place to view the aurora borealis, or northern lights, a phenomenon of dazzling sheets of light produced in the sky by electron and proton particles of the solar wind. Fairbanks is also known for its extremes in temperature, which often soar well above 90° F (32° C) in summer, but dip below -60° F (-15° C) in winter. The city's many unique attractions include the **Ice Museum**, where a huge walk-in freezer holds impressive ice sculptures. Another museum on the University of Alaska grounds provides a home for a 36,000-year-old mummified bison. At **Pioneer Park**, historic buildings collected from around the state help to re-create a Gold Rush-era town on the banks of the Chena River. Each summer evening, Pioneer Park plays host to a musical revue, with dancers who are dressed in period costume.

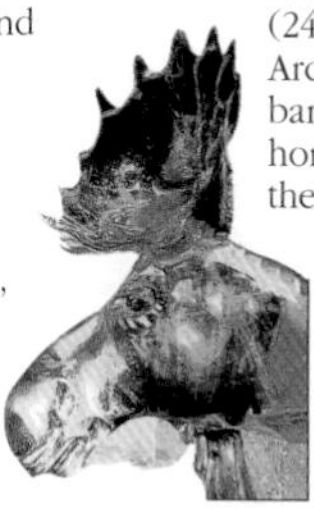

Caribou at the Ice Museum, Fairbanks

View of the aurora borealis, or northern lights, Alaska

The old mining town of McCarthy in Wrangell-St. Elias National Park

Pioneer Park
Airport Way. ***Tel*** *(907) 459-1087.* *daily.* **Gold Rush Town** *Memorial Day–Labor Day: noon–8pm daily.*

Wrangell-St. Elias National Park 15

McCarthy. to McCarthy. Wrangell-St. Elias National Park Visitors' Center, Mile 106.5 Richardson Highway; (907) 822-5234. Ranger stations at Chitina and Slana. **www**.nps.gov/wrst

The largest National Park in the US – six times the size of Yellowstone. Wrangell-St. Elias National Park is a 20,000-sq mile (52,500-sq km) wilderness sprawling across the southeast corner of the Alaskan mainland. Dominated by the volcanic Wrangell Mountains and the glaciated St. Elias Range, the park has nine of the 16 highest mountains in the US. Designated a UNESCO World Heritage Site in 1992, the park contains historic mining sites, such as the town of McCarthy.

Denali National Park 16

Alaska's top attraction, Denali National Park encompasses 9,375 sq miles (24,281 sq km). The 20,320-ft (6,194-m) high Mount McKinley, North America's highest peak, dominates the landscape, rising 10,000 ft (3,048 m) above the surrounding peaks. The park is home to abundant wildlife, including grizzly bears, moose, and caribou, and wildflowers explode with color across the tundra in July. Only one road penetrates Denali, traversing varied landscapes that include lowlands and high mountain passes. Several hiking trails can be enjoyed in the vicinity of the visitor center. Other activities include sled dog demonstrations, rafting on the Nenana River, and flight-seeing around Mount McKinley.

The Alaska Railroad
Many travelers opt for rail travel when it comes to visiting Denali.

★ Wonder Lake
On a clear day, Mount McKinley is visible from various locations within Denali National Park.

★ Mount McKinley
View of the snow clad Mount McKinley from Park Road, en route to Wonder Lake. Originally called Denali, "the Great One," by Athabascan Natives, many Alaskans still continue to refer to Mount McKinley by its old name.

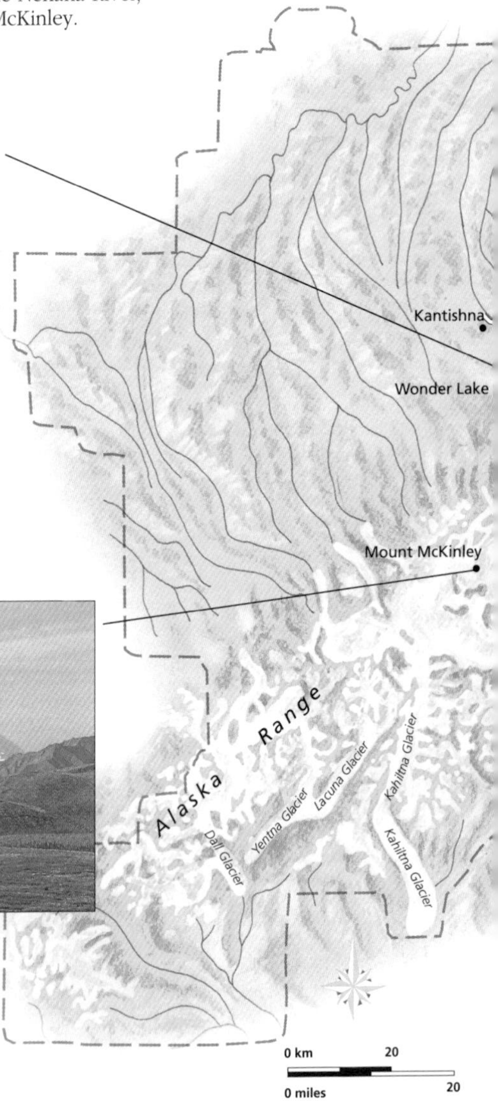

★ **Whitewater Rafting**
Thrills and spills abound on the Nenana River, which flows along the eastern boundary of the national park.

VISITORS' CHECKLIST

Park ◯ *daily.* **Visitor Center** ◯ *mid-May–mid-Sep: 8am–6pm daily.* ***Tel*** *(907) 683-2294.* **www**.nps.gov/dena **Park shuttle buses:** *Reserve seats in advance. Some buses return from the Eielson Visitor Center, which has great views of Mount McKinley; others continue to Wonder Lake 25 miles (40 km) from the peak. The 90-m/150-km round trip takes 13 hours.* **Departures:** *mid-May–mid-Sep: daily from 6am to 2pm at regular intervals. Check website for schedule.* ***Tel*** *(907) 272-7275, (800) 622-7275.* **www**.reservedenali.com

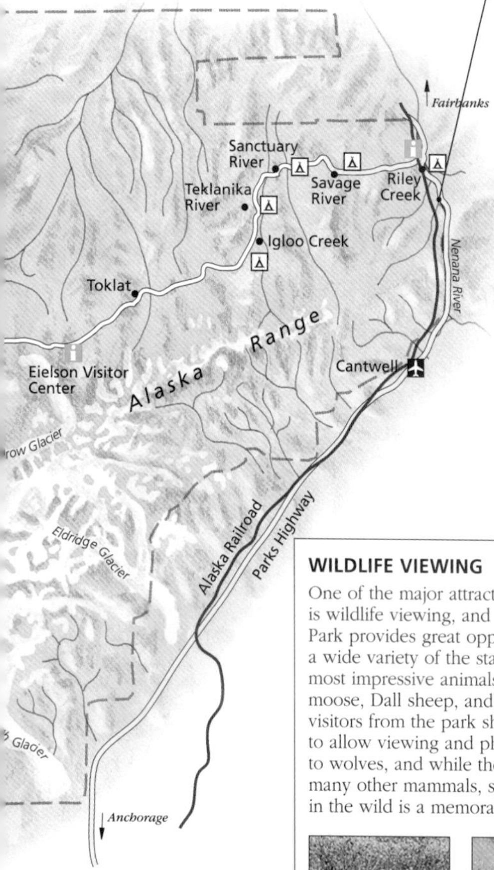

Tourists on a park shuttle bus trip

KEY

- - Park boundary
Camping
Alaska railroad
Major road
Unpaved road

WILDLIFE VIEWING

Mountain goat

One of the major attractions in Alaska is wildlife viewing, and Denali National Park provides great opportunities to see a wide variety of the state's largest and most impressive animals. Grizzly bears, moose, Dall sheep, and caribou are routinely sighted by visitors from the park shuttle buses, with drivers stopping to allow viewing and photography. The park is also home to wolves, and while they are not as commonly sighted as many other mammals, spotting these magnificent creatures in the wild is a memorable experience for visitors.

Grizzly bear feeding on berries

Moose wading in water

Caribou are a common sight

STAR SIGHTS

★ Mount McKinley
★ Whitewater Rafting
★ Wonder Lake

HAWAI'I

A tropical island paradise of golden sand beaches, waterfalls, and lush forests, the Aloha State attracts more than 6 million visitors a year. An isolated archipelago in the middle of the Pacific Ocean, the islands' exotic landscape and luxurious hospitality offer a wealth of experiences from volcanic eruptions and world-class surfing to glimpses of the fascinating cultural heritage of Polynesia.

Located in the middle of the Pacific Ocean, 2,500 miles (4,000 km) southwest of Los Angeles, the Hawaiian Islands are volcanic in origin. In fact, the islands are still evolving, as is evident from the lava flows on the slopes of 13,796-ft (4,205-m) Mount Kīlauea on the island of Hawai'i or the "Big Island."

Polynesian dancer, a popular attraction

The next largest island, Maui, was formed by the dormant volcano Haleakalā. This, the fastest-growing of the islands, still retains some significant history, especially in the former whaling port of Lahaina. The next island along in the chain, Moloka'i, is well off the tourist trail. Formerly a pineapple ranching center, Moloka'i is famous for the towering cliffs that line its northern coast. Lāna'i, another small island, is also offshore from Maui.

The most popular and developed island is O'ahu, where three-quarters of the population lives and most of the visitors congregate. The center of O'ahu is Honolulu, the state capital and only big city. Across the ocean from O'ahu sits magical Kaua'i, known as the "Garden Isle" for its verdant rainforests, kept moist by more than 400 inches (10 m) of annual rainfall.

The summit of Maui's Mount Haleakalā

HISTORY

Hawai'i's historical connections to the US mainland are both distant and contentious. Originally colonized by Polynesians, Hawai'i was a group of independent kingdoms when it was discovered by English sailor Captain James Cook in 1778. Initially welcomed by the natives, Cook was killed by them a year later. Other explorers followed, bringing new, often fatal diseases. By the end of the 18th century, however, the islands had been united into a respected monarchy under the revered monarch, King Kamehameha the Great (ruled 1795–1819).

During the early 19th century, European traders introduced fundamental changes. Christianity was introduced by Puritan missionaries from Boston in 1820, while economically, forestry and whaling gained importance. These proved destabilizing to Native culture, and by the 1880s, white American entrepreneurs, mainly sugar cane and pineapple farmers, acquired control, and the monarchy was overthrown in 1893. After a series of highly complicated political maneuvers, Hawai'i became part of the US in 1898. Much later, in 1993, the US issued a formal apology to the people of Hawai'i for its leading role in the "illegal overthrow of the Kingdom of Hawai'i."

Canoeing and swimming, some of the most popular water activities in Hawai'i

Powerful American plantation owners dominated the first half of the 1900s, and all attempts to unionize the low-paid, mostly Japanese labor force were fi rmly squelched. Ironically, it took the threat of invasion to make the feudal institutions democratic. On December 7, 1941, Japan attacked Pearl Harbor, instigating America's entry into World War II, and changing Hawai'i forever.

HAWAI'I TODAY

Located midway between mainland US and the Far East, Hawai'i has a diverse population. Of its 1.1 million residents, roughly one-third are non-Asian, one-third are of Japanese descent, and the rest a wide-ranging mix of Filipinos, Chinese, Koreans, and Samoans. Only a few thousand full-blooded indigenous Hawaiians survive today, but the native spirit of "Aloha," a Hawaiian word that simultaneously means hello, goodbye, welcome, and love, is still alive.

The introduction of air travel in 1959 brought Hawai'i within easy reach of the West Coast. As tourism became the chief industry, resort developments proliferated, signaling a new era for island economy. At the same time, a resurgence in Native culture, language, and crafts has softened the harsher edges of the commercial development, so that no matter where you go in the islands, Polynesian roots grow very close to the surface.

Cyclist on a scenic bike ride, away from the crowded beach Waikīkī

KEY DATES IN HISTORY

AD 400 Polynesians migrate to the Hawaiian Islands from the Marquesas Islands

1778 James Cook is the first European to the islands, which he names the Sandwich Islands after his benefactor, the Earl of Sandwich

1795 Reign of Kamehameha begins

1893 With the support of the US Navy, American businessmen overthrow the Kingdom of Hawai'i, declaring an independent republic

1898 Hawai'i is annexed as a US Territory

1941 Japanese bombers attack Pearl Harbor on December 7

1959 Hawai'i becomes the 50th state

1983 Mount Kīlauea begins its present eruption

1993 US government issues a formal apology on the 100th anniversary of the overthrow of the Kingdom of Hawai'i

1996 Citizens vote to convene on the issue of sovereignty

Exploring Hawai'i

The world's most isolated archipelago, Hawai'i lies 2,500 miles (4,000 km) from the West Coast. The five main islands – O'ahu, Moloka'i, Maui, Hawai'i, and Kaua'i – stretch across over 500 miles (805 km) of the Pacific Ocean. Although most of its six million annual visitors arrive by air in Honolulu, the state capital, travel from one island to another is mainly by inter-island flights. A handful of ferry services and some luxury cruises also link the islands. The most reliable way to explore individual islands is by car, as public transportation is minimal, except on O'ahu.

A secluded swimming spot on the rocky coast of the Ke'anae Peninsula

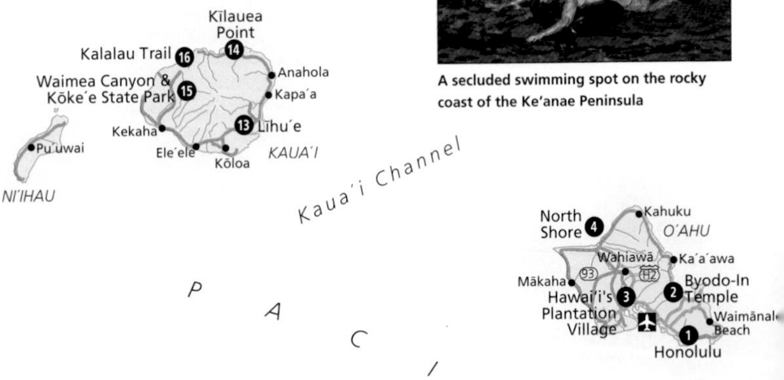

SIGHTS AT A GLANCE

O'ahu
Honolulu 1
Byodo-In Temple 2
Hawai'i's Plantation Village 3
North Shore 4

Moloka'i & Maui
Kaunakakai 5
Kalaupapa National Historical Park 6
Lahaina 7
Haleakalā National Park 8
Hāna 9

Hawai'i Island
Hawai'i Volcanoes National Park p752 10
Hilo 11
Pu'uhonua O Hōnaunau National Historical Park 12

Kaua'i
Līhu'e 13
Kīlauea Point 14
Waimea Canyon & Kōke'e State Park 15
Kalalau Trail 16

Windsurfers in action at Ho'okipa Beach County Park, near the beach town of Pā'ia on Maui's north shore

Dramatic Honomanū Bay with its clear blue waters, surrounded by lushly forested cliffs

SEE ALSO

- ***Practical Information*** p757
- ***Where to Stay*** pp760–61
- ***Where to Eat*** p763

KEY

- Airport
- Ferry port
- Highway
- Major roar
- Ferry route

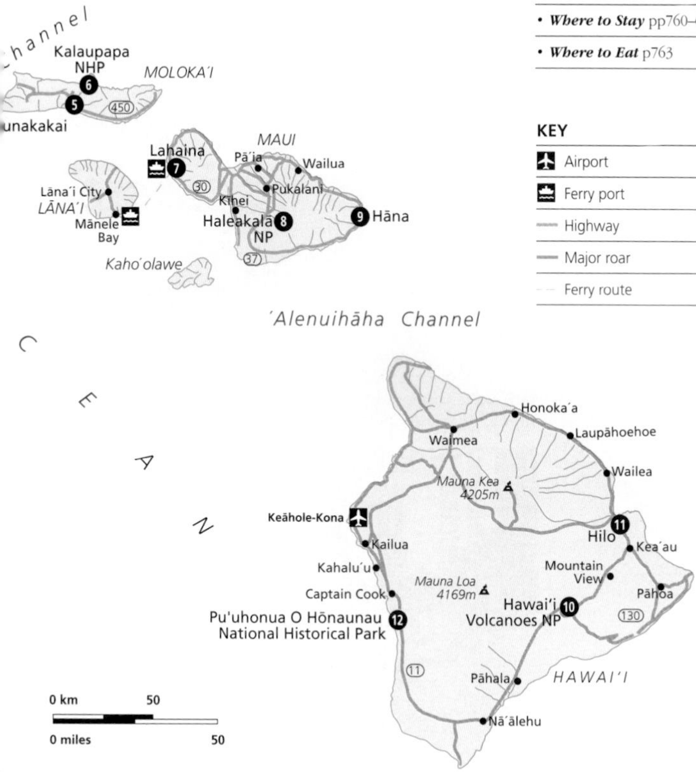

O'ahu

The third largest island in the archipelago, with an area of 600 sq miles (1,550 sq km), O'ahu is Hawai'i's most visited and most populous island. Three-quarters of the state's 1.275 million residents live here, most of them in the Greater Honolulu area. Outside the urban areas, with their cultural attractions, O'ahu offers spectacular scenery, with lush plantations, tropical beaches, and a surfers' paradise on the North Shore.

Statue of King Kamehameha, his hand extended in welcome

Honolulu ❶

905,000. O'ahu VB, (808) 524-0722. **www**.visit-oahu.com; *HVCB (Hawai'i Visitors and Convention Bureau), (808) 923-1811, (800) 464-2924.* **www**.gohawaii.com

Hawai'i's capital city has two focal points – the historic and business district of downtown Honolulu, and the world famous resort of Waikīkī, 3 miles (5 km) to its east. The downtown area, which first gained prominence as a trading port in the early 19th century, today manages to squeeze together towering skyscrapers, a royal palace, Japanese shrines, New England-style missionary houses, a bustling Chinatown, strip joints, and fish markets in a relatively small and compact area.

'Iolani Palace crest

Dominating downtown's Capitol District is the magnificent Victorian-style **'Iolani Palace**, completed in 1882. The only royal palace in the US, it was designed and first lived in by King David Kalākaua, followed by his sister Queen Lili'uokalani, who reigned for only two years before the monarchy was overthrown in 1893 *(see p744)*. Recently used as a movie set, the palace has luxurious interiors and a *koa*-wood staircase.

To its south is the New England-style **Kawaiaha'o Church**, constructed of coral blocks. It was built in 1842, by which time American missionaries had gained many influential local converts to Christianity. The upper gallery has portraits of Hawaiian monarchs, most of whom were baptized, married, and crowned here. Adjacent to the church is the **Mission Houses Museum**, which contains the oldest timber frame house in Hawai'i, built in 1821 by the New England missionary Reverend Hiram Bingham. Housed in three buildings, the museum has a printing house and lovingly preserved interiors.

Nearby is the bronze **Statue of King Kamehameha**, Hawai'i's most revered monarch, who ruled from 1795 to 1819 *(see p744)*. The statue, with its feathered cloak and an arm extended in a welcome, is one of Hawai'i's most famous sights.

North of the Capitol District is **Chinatown**, with two marble lions guarding its entrance. The area is an exotic neighborhood of open-air markets, *lei* (flower garland) stands, eateries, and herbal medicine shops. Hawai'i's first Chinese arrived on merchant ships in 1789, followed in 1852 by larger numbers who came to work on O'ahu's sugar plantations. Chinatown's buildings include the Art Deco **Hawai'i Theatre** and the state's oldest Japanese Shinto shrine, the **Izumo Taisha Shrine**, built in 1923. At Honolulu Harbor, the fascinating **Hawai'i Maritime Center** displays antique canoes and exhibits tracing the exploits of Polynesian navigators. Moored next to it are the *Hōkūle'a*, a modern replica of an ancient Polynesian canoe with sails, and the restored 1878 *Falls of Clyde*, the world's last surviving full-rigged four-masted sailing ship.

Waikīkī, originally a place of taro patches and fish ponds, now has one of the world's famous beaches – a sliver of people-packed sand against the backdrop of **Diamond Head** crater. Waikīkī bustles with some 65,000 tourists a day who flock here to sunbathe on the golden sand, swim in the sheltered water, and surf the gentle waves. The sandy beach stretches for 2.5 miles (4 km), from the Hilton Hawaiian Village to Diamond Head. The streets and shopping malls are packed with beachwear vendors, honeymooners, Japanese matrons, and boys carrying surfboards. Conspicuous amid the glass and concrete skyscrapers are two stately old hotels – the

The Waikīkī Beach front, lined with high-rise hotels

coral pink **Royal Hawaiian Hotel** and the Colonial-style **Moana Hotel**, Waikīkī's oldest.

Several interesting sights are also located in Greater Honolulu. Considered the world's finest museum of Polynesian culture, **Bishop Museum** was created by American businessman Charles Bishop to preserve royal heirlooms left by his wife, a Hawaiian princess. Its priceless exhibits include fabulous ceremonial feather standards, rare *tamate* costumes made of shredded fiber, sacred images, and a *hale* (traditional house) thatched with *pili* grass.

The **National Memorial Cemetery of the Pacific**, located in Punchbowl, the crater of an extinct volcano, has over 33,000 graves. Among those buried here are victims of Pearl Harbor and those killed in the Korean and Vietnam wars.

Pearl Harbor, a place of pilgrimage for many visitors, houses warships, military museums, and memorials. Most significant among these is the **USS *Arizona* Memorial**, which stands perched above the ship of the same name that was sunk during the Japanese bombing on December 7, 1941. Some of the volunteer guides that you will meet here happen to be survivors of that fateful attack, which killed more than 2,000 US officers and men, and destroyed 18 battleships, bringing the United States into World War II *(see p745)*.

Hawai'i Maritime Center
Pier 7, Honolulu Harbor. ***Tel** (808) 599-3810.* *19, 20.* *9am–5pm daily.* *Dec 25.* **www**.holoholo.org/maritime

Bishop Museum
1525 Bernice St. ***Tel** (808) 847-3511.* *2.* *9am–5pm daily.* *Dec 25.* *Craft demonstrations, music & dance recitals: daily.* **www**.bishopmuseum.org

Pearl Harbor
7 miles (11 km) NW of downtown Honolulu. *20, 42.* **USS *Arizona* Memorial** 1 Arizona Memorial Drive. ***Tel** (808) 422-0561.* *7:30am–5pm daily.* *Jan 1, Thanksgiving, Dec 25.* **www**.nps.gov/usar

Byodo-In Temple ❷

47-200 Kahekili Hwy (Hwy 83), Kāne'ohe. ***Tel** (808) 239-8811.* *on Kahekili Hwy (Hwy 83), then 10-min walk.* *8:30am–4:30pm daily.* *Dec 25.*

This replica of a 900-year-old Japanese temple in a tranquil and secluded spot is O'ahu's hidden treasure, its bright red walls framed against the backdrop of fluted green cliffs. A curved vermilion footbridge and a three-ton bell lead to the Byodo-In Temple, which houses a beautiful 9-ft (3-m) Buddha. Sunset here is a magical experience, with the cliffs giving off pink and mauve hues.

Sign for Hale'iwa, O'ahu's surf town

Hawai'i's Plantation Village ❸

94-695 Waipahu St, Waipahu. ***Tel** (808) 677-0110.* *43.* *10am–4:30pm Mon–Sat.* *public hols.* **www**.hawaiiplantationvillage.org

This three-million dollar restored village portrays a hundred years of sugar plantation culture, from 1840 to 1943. It also contains various re-created buildings from the major ethnic groups that worked in the plantations – Korean, Puerto Rican, and Japanese homes – as well as a Shinto shrine. Personal objects placed in the houses give the impression that the occupants have just left, soon to return. The small on-site museum runs informative walking tours for visitors.

North Shore ❹

2,500. *HVCB, Waikīkī, (808) 924-0266.* *O-Bon Buddhist Festival (Jul or Aug).* **www**.northshoreoahu.org

The hub for the North Shore surfing community is **Hale'iwa**. The town's picturesque harbor is flanked by well-appointed public beaches. **Ali'i Beach** is famous for big waves and surfing contests. The adjacent **Hale'iwa Beach Park** is one of the few North Shore spots where it is usually quite safe to swim in winter. At the enchanting annual O-Bon Festival, thousands of floating lanterns are released into the ocean here.

Another popular North Shore spot is **Waimea Valley**. The valley is a botanical paradise, with 36 gardens, thousands of rare tropical plants, and 30 species of birds. There are no longer the commercial shows that Waimea Valley was once famous for, such as hula, and cliff-diving. Instead, the center provides an important educational resource and is a beautiful and unspoilt environment. Visitors can tour the valley, but bring binoculars as the park has great opportunities for bird watchers. Afterwards, swim or snorkel at the Waimea Beach Park across the street from the center.

Waimea Valley
59-864 Kamehameha Hwy (Hwy 83), Waimea. ***Tel** (808) 638-7766.* *9am–5pm Mon–Fri.* *Jan 1, Thanksgiving, Dec 25.*

The enchanting Byodo-In Temple, a Buddhist shrine

Moloka'i & Maui

The small island of Moloka'i, between O'ahu and Maui, is much less developed for tourism than its neighbors. The gentle pace of life, and the spectacular scenery of its flower-decked south coast and of the Kalaupapa National Historical Park, backed by the world's highest sea cliffs, enchant most visitors. Maui, Hawai'i's second largest island, offers lively resorts with a range of water sports, as well as lush plantations and the awesome grandeur of the Haleakalā Volcano.

Moloka'i's isolated Kalaupapa Peninsula, backed by towering cliffs

Kaunakakai ❺

2,700. *Ala Malama St & Kamehameha V Hwy (Hwy 450), (808) 553-3876. Ka Moloka'i Makahiki (cultural festival, late Jan).* **www**.molokai-hawaii.com

Moloka'i's main town, Kaunakakai, was built in the 19th century as a port for the local sugar and pineapple plantations. Today, commercial agriculture has all but disappeared from the island, and Kaunakakai looks its age. The main street, with its wooden boardwalk, is lined with false-fronted stores. A short distance from the town center, local fishermen throng **Kaunakakai Harbor**, its long stone jetty jutting out into the ocean. About 2 miles (3 km) west of town is the **Kapuāiwa Coconut Grove**, whose 1,000 soaring trees are a majestic sight, silhouetted against the setting sun.

Environs

East of Kaunakakai begins the **Kamehameha V Highway**, which is among the most beautiful coastal drives in Hawai'i. The 27-mile (44-km) highway takes in ancient sites, picturesque churches, pristine beaches, and sleepy villages tucked away amid tropical flowers and luxuriant rainforests. The road finally twists to a halt at the stunningly beautiful **Hālawa Valley** which, with its soaring walls, lush vegetation, idyllic beaches, and shimmering waterfalls, is Moloka'i's most scenic spot.

Kalaupapa National Historical Park ❻

Reached by foot or mule on Kalaupapa Trail: trailhead on Hwy 470, 3 miles (5 km) N of Kualapu'u, between the mule stables & Kalaupapa Overlook. *compulsory. Father Damien Tours, (808) 567-6171. Book well in advance. Visitors must be 16 years of age or older. For Moloka'i Mule Ride, (808) 567-6088, book in advance.* **www**.muleride.com

The isolated Kalaupapa Peninsula, sealed off from the rest of Moloka'i by a mighty wall of cliffs, is home to the **Kalaupapa National Historical Park**. In 1865, when the imported disease of leprosy seemed to threaten the survival of the Hawaiian people, the peninsula was designated a leper colony, and those afflicted were exiled here. The park now serves as a memorial. The main settlement was at the village of Kalaupapa, on the western side of the peninsula. The last patients arrived in 1969, when the policy of enforced isolation ended. Kalaupapa's small population today includes a few aging patients who chose to live out their lives here.

South of the village is the **Kalaupapa Trail**, a favorite with hikers and mule riders who enjoy stupendous views during the 2-mile (3-km) trip. At the center of the peninsula is the **Kauhakō Crater**, with an 800-ft (245-m) deep lake.

On the peninsula's eastern shore is **St. Philomena Church**, in the original leprosy settlement of Kalawao. Shipped out from Honolulu in 1872, the church was later modified by the Belgian priest Father Damien (1840–89), who dedicated his life to caring for the leprosy patients. Father Damien succumbed to leprosy in 1889 and has been beatified by the Pope. His right hand is interred in the church. From the peninsula's eastern side, small islands poke out of the waters of the ocean, next to staggering 2000-ft (600-m) cliffs – the tallest sea cliffs in the world.

St. Philomena Church, where Father Damien's hand is buried

For hotels and restaurants in this region see pp760–61 and p763

Locals demonstrating their courage at Keka'a Point, Kā'anapali

Lahaina 7

9,100. Lahaina Harbor. 648 Wharf St, (808) 667-9175. A Taste of Lahaina (food festival, mid-Sep); Halloween Mardi Gras of the Pacific (Oct 31). **www**.visitlahaina.com

One of Maui's most popular attractions, this small harbor town was the capital of the Kingdom of Hawai'i until 1845 and a major center of the whaling trade. The area around Front Street has a wealth of well-restored historic sites, evocative of Lahaina's past. Among them is the **Baldwin Home**, Maui's oldest Western-style dwelling, dating from the 1830s, with original furnishings and artifacts. Nearby is the **Chinese Wo Hing Temple**, built in 1912. A favorite landmark is Lahaina's first hotel, the charming 1901 **Pioneer Inn**, still a tourist mecca and hotel.

Docked in the harbor, beside the lighthouse, is the *Carthaginian II*, a 1920s German schooner transformed to look like the kind of small freighter that brought cargo and people to the islands in the 1800s. It has a fascinating museum in the hold, devoted to whales and the whale trade.

Just 6 miles (10 km) north of Lahaina is Maui's biggest resort, **Kā'anapali**, its long white beach lined with hotels. **Pu'u Keka'a**, better known as Black Rock, towers above the beach and overlooks one of Maui's best snorkeling spots. Vintage steam locomotives make the short and scenic trip here from Lahaina.

A 20-minute drive north of Kā'anapali is Maui's other major resort, **Kapalua**, with its exquisite crescent bays, blue waters, luxury hotels, golf courses, and beautiful pineapple plantations.

Haleakalā National Park 8

Haleakalā Crater Road (Hwy 378). *24 hrs daily.*
Park Headquarters ***Tel*** *(808) 572-4400. 8am–4pm daily.*
Visitor Center *6:30am–3:30pm daily.* **www**.nps.gov/hale
Cabins www.fhnp.org/wcr *(for reservations).*

The land mass of East Maui is really the top of an enormous volcano that begins more than 3 miles (5 km) below sea level. Haleakalā last spewed molten lava some 200 years ago and is still considered to be active, although not currently erupting. Its summit depression is 7.5 miles (12 km) long and 2.5 miles (4 km) wide. This natural wonder is preserved as part of the national park. The 2-hour drive to the 10,023-ft (3,055-m) **Pu'u 'Ula'ula Summit**, the highest point in Maui, offers a breathtaking view of the entire volcano, with its cinder cones and brightly colored ashes.

The best way to appreciate Haleakalā's scale and varied terrain is to descend 3,000 ft (900 m) into the volcano. The 10-mile (16-km) **Sliding Sands Trail** takes you from the visitor center through scenery that ranges from barren cinder desert to alpine shrubland. Also worth exploring is the **Silversword Loop** where one of the world's rarest plants, the Haleakalā Silversword, thrives. It takes up to 50 years to flower, when it raises a spectacular spike of purplish flowers.

Hāna 9

700. MVB, Wailuku, (808) 244-3530. East Maui Taro Festival (Mar/Apr). **www**.hanamaui.com

Often called Hawai'i's most Hawaiian town, Hāna continues to lag lazily behind modernity. Its perfect round bay and dreamy climate have made it a prized settlement since ancient times. **Ka'uiki Head**, the large cinder cone on the right flank of the bay, served as a natural fortification.

The **Hāna Cultural Center** presents a *kauhale* (residential compound) in the precontact style once unique to this area and exhibits artifacts that give a sense of local history. **Wānanalua Church**, constructed from blocks of coral in 1838, was built by missionaries on top of an existing *heiau* (temple), thus symbolizing the triumph of Christianity over paganism.

The scenic **Hāna Belt Road** twists along the coast to Pā'ia, with views of waterfalls, gulches choked with vegetation, taro fields, botanical gardens, rocky cliffs, and the dramatic Honomanū Bay with its black sand beach.

Pu'u 'Ula'ula Summit in Haleakalā National Park, Maui's highest point

Hawai'i Island

Spreading over 4,035 sq miles (10,450 sq km), Hawai'i Island, also known as the Big Island, is more than twice the size of all the other islands combined. Its natural wonders include the earth's most massive mountain, Mauna Loa, which rises over 30,000 ft (9,150 m) from the ocean floor, and Kīlauea, the most active volcano on earth, both of which form part of the Hawai'i Volcanoes National Park. Equally fascinating are the island's well-preserved cultural sites within the Pu'uhonua O Hōnaunau National Historical Park.

Hawai'i Volcanoes National Park ⑩

Hawai'i Belt Road (Hwy 11). *24 hours daily.* **Kīlauea Visitor Center *Tel*** *(808) 985-6000.* *7:45am–5pm daily.* **Jaggar Museum *Tel*** *(808) 985-6049.* *8:30am–8pm daily.* **Volcano Art Center *Tel*** *(808) 967-7565, (866) 967-7565.* *9am–5pm daily.* *Dec 25.* **Volcano House Hotel *Tel*** *(808) 967-7321.* **www**.nps.gov/havo

Encompassing about a quarter of a million acres, this national park includes the 13,677-ft (4,169-m) summit of Mauna Loa, 150 miles (240 km) of hiking trails, and vast tracts of wilderness that preserve some of the world's rarest species of flora and fauna. But it is Kīlauea Caldera and the lava flows of its furious East Rift Zone that draw most visitors. Two roads – **Crater Rim Drive**, which loops around the caldera, and **Chain of Craters Road**, which descends through the recent outpourings – form a gigantic drive-through museum. The present eruption started in 1983 and produces slow-moving lava, which poses no threat to visitors. However, you should stay out of closed areas; no one knows how long the flow will continue or where it will next erupt.

East of the park, the **Kīlauea Iki Overlook** gives a view of the crater, which in 1959 filled with bubbling lava,

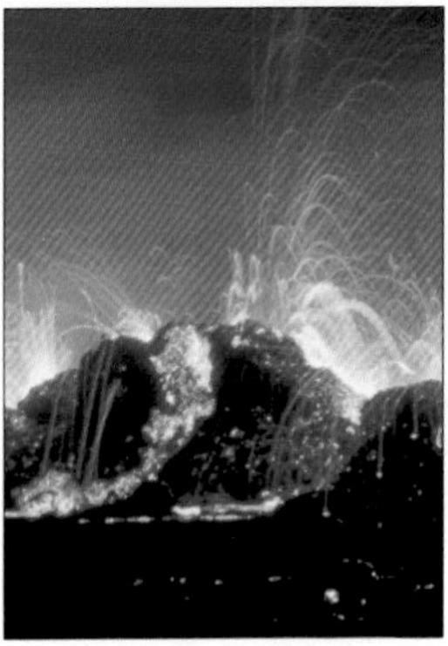

Lava fountains spewing from Kīlauea during the 1983 eruption

KEY

- Major road
- Minor road
- Hiking trail
- Vista

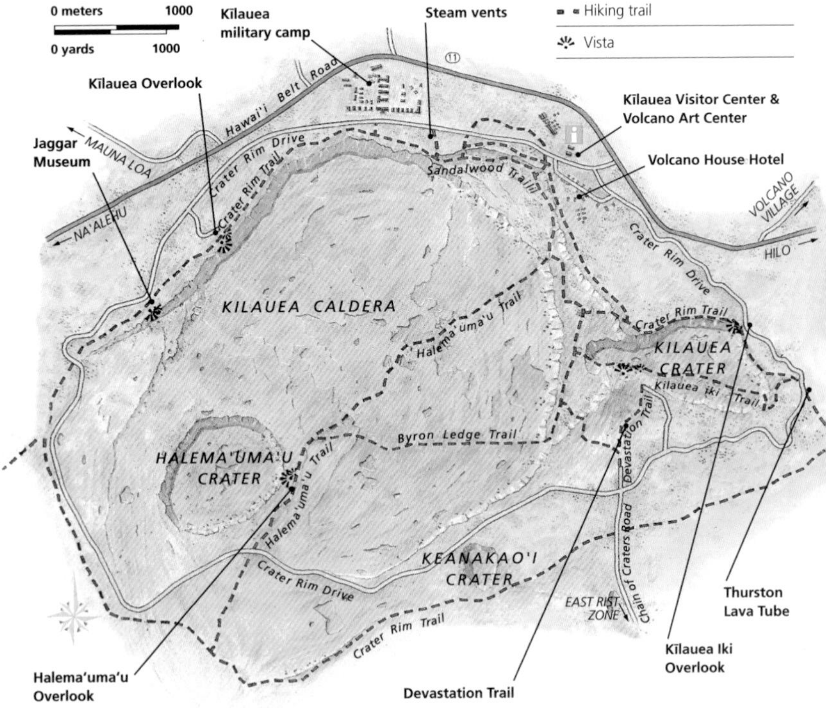

For hotels and restaurants in this region see pp760–61 and p763

Thurston Lava Tube, formed by the hardening of a lava stream

shooting fire fountains 1,900 ft (580 m) into the air. Across the road from the crater, at the eastern edge of the park, lies the Thurston Lava Tube. This huge tunnel was left behind when a subterranean river of lava drained away. An easy trail runs through the tube and a grove of giant ferns. Nearby, the short Devastation Trail features ghostly remains of a rainforest, wiped out by ash falling from Kīlauea Iki's 1959 eruption. Farther west, the Halema'uma'u Overlook affords views of the once boiling lake of lava. The crater below still steams with sulfurous fumes. This is the home of Pele, the fiery-tempered volcano goddess, who migrated from Kahiki (Tahiti) seeking a dry place for her eternal fires.

Hilo ⓫

45,000. *Kamehameha Ave, near Mamo St, (808) 961-8744.* *BIVB, 250 Keawe St, (808) 961-5797.* *Merrie Monarch Festival (Mar or Apr).* **www**.bigisland.org

Although it is the state's second city, "rainy old Hilo" is a contrast to sunny, urban Honolulu. The city's progress has been checked by nature – rain falls 278 days of the year, and two destructive *tsunamis* pounded Hilo in 1946 and 1960. The city has since retreated from the sea, turning the waterfront area into enormous parks, while the rain has made it a natural garden, full of orchids and anthuriums. Hilo's population is largely Japanese and Filipino in ancestry.

The downtown business district, with its restored buildings, is worth exploring on foot. The **Lyman Museum and Mission House** vividly evokes a bygone era – it is preserved as it was in the 1830s, with Victorian furnishings and artifacts.

On the Waiākea Peninsula, jutting into Hilo Bay, is the 30-acre (12-ha) **Lili'uokalani Gardens**, landscaped in Japanese style, while east of downtown are the 80-ft (24-m) high **Rainbow Falls**. The morning sun, filtering through the mist of the waterfall, often creates beautiful rainbows.

The east side of Hilo Bay offers fine snorkeling and swimming at the **James Kealoha Beach Park**; and at the **Richardson Ocean Park**.

Pu'uhonua O Hōnaunau National Historical Park ⓬

Hwy 160, off Hawai'i Belt Rd (Hwy 11). ***Tel*** *(808) 328-2326.* *7am–8pm daily.* **Visitor Center** *8am–5pm. Daily orientation talks.* **www**.nps.gov/puho

From the 11th century on, social interactions were regulated by the *kapu* (taboo) system, and even minor infractions, such as stepping on a chief's shadow, were punished by violent death. Lawbreakers could, however, escape punishment by reaching a *pu'uhonua* (place of refuge). The greatest of these was at **Hōnaunau**, a 6-acre (2-ha) temple compound dating from the 16th century, which offered absolution to all those who could swim or run past the chief's warriors. The sanctuary was stripped of power in 1819, after the fall of the *kapu* system. Now partly restored, it provides a glimpse into precontact Hawai'i.

Located on a peninsula of black lava, whose jagged shoreline made it difficult for *kapu*-breakers to approach from the sea, the *pu'uhonua's* focal point is the 1650 **Hale O Keawe Heiau**, the temple that once held the bones and therefore the *mana* (sacred power) of great chiefs. Outside it stand Ki'i – wooden images of gods. As impressive is the great drystone wall, 10 ft (3 m) high and 17 ft (5 m) wide. Built around 1550, it separated the *pu'uhonua* from the palace area inland.

The Hale O Keawe Heiau, a place of spiritual power

PROFESSOR JAGGAR (1871–1953)

Thomas A. Jaggar was a pioneer in the young science of volcanology. A professor of geology at Massachusetts Institute of Technology, he founded the Hawaiian Volcano Observatory at Kīlauea Caldera in 1912. Four years later, he and Honolulu publisher Lorrin Thurston persuaded Congress to preserve the area as a national park. Professor Jaggar developed techniques for collecting volcanic gases and measuring ground tilt, seismic activity, and lava temperatures. The work he initiated has made Kīlauea one of the world's best understood volcanoes.

Professor Jaggar on a boat trip

Kaua'i

Wind and water have had six million years to transform Kaua'i, the oldest of the major Hawaiian islands, into a stunning array of pleated cliffs and yawning chasms, cloaked with a mantle of emerald green vegetation. Also known as the "Garden Island," Kaua'i is Hawai'i's most beautiful and irresistible destination. Its highlights include Kīlauea Point's glorious beaches, the dramatic Waimea Canyon, and the soaring cliffs of the Kalalau Trail on the Nā Pali Coast. You can drive anywhere in Kaua'i in three hours or less.

The shady *koa*-wood veranda at Grove Farm Homestead

Līhu'e ⓭

5,900. Rice St, (808) 241-6410. KVB, 4334 Rice St, Suite 101, (800) 262-1400, (808) 245-3971. Kaua'i-Tahiti Fete (mid-Aug). **www**.kauaidiscovery.com

Although Līhu'e happens to be the administrative and business center of Kaua'i, it is actually little more than a plantation village. It was built in the 19th century to serve the Līhu'e Sugar Mill, whose rusting machinery still dominates the downtown area. Līhu'e's oceanfront district, with the beautiful Kalapakī Beach, is especially appealing, and the outskirts of town offer such delights as grand plantation mansions and a stunning waterfall.

Within the town, **Kaua'i Museum** displays a splendid collection of traditional artifacts, including huge *koa*-wood bowls, royal feather standards, and old weapons. It also has exhibits on the island's history and geology. The imposing **Grove Farm Homestead** on Nāwiliwili Road is an early 20th-century mansion, paneled in dark, heavy *koa* wood. A guided tour, which must be reserved in advance, covers the rather formal house, the cramped servants' quarters, and the beautifully scented orchard.

Kalapakī Beach, with gently sloping beautiful white sands and sheltered inshore waters, is the safest beach in the area and especially suitable for families with small children. On its far side, the scenic palm-fringed **Nāwiliwili Beach County Park** is ideal for picnics.

The grand 1930s house known as **Kilohana Plantation**, 1.5 miles (2.5 km) west of Līhu'e, resembles an English country estate. Visitors can tour the house, which has a restaurant and some shops, and explore the cane fields in old-fashioned horse-drawn carriages. The mansion commands superb views of the Kilohana mountain inland.

Environs

Just 5 miles (8 km) north of Līhu'e, a winding road through cane fields leads to the twin cascades of the 80-ft (24-m) **Wailua Falls**. They are best viewed from the roadside parking lot, as the path down the hillside can be slippery. **Menehune Fish Pond** 1.5 miles (2.5 km) south, is located in idyllic pastoral landscape. With its ancient stonemasonry, the pond was used to fatten mullet for the royal table.

Kīlauea Point ⓮

Kīlauea Road, off Kūhiō Hwy (Hwy 56), 10 miles (16 km) NW of Anahola. *Kīlauea. KVB, Līhu'e, (808) 245-3971.* **www**.kauaidiscovery.com

The northernmost spot on the Hawaiian archipelago, Kīlauea Point is a rocky promontory pounded by mighty waves. The windswept clifftop has been set aside as the **Kīlauea Point National Wildlife Refuge**, where bird-watchers can spot frigatebirds, Laysan albatrosses, and many other species. A short walk beyond the visitor center leads to the red and white **Kīlauea Lighthouse**, erected in 1913. Approaching the tip of the headland, there are splendid views westward to the fabled **Nā Pali** cliffs. Half a mile (800 m) west of the Kīlauea turn-off on Kalihiwai Road, a red dirt track leads to

The twin cascades of Wailua Falls near Līhu'e

For hotels and restaurants in this region see pp760–61 and p763

The Pu'u O Kila Lookout, with views of the Kalalau Valley

the vast but little-visited shelf of glorious yellow sand known as **Secret Beach**. The ocean can be rough for swimming here, but it is a beautiful place to walk, with its dramatic views of the lighthouse and a glorious waterfall at the far end.

Kīlauea Point National Wildlife Refuge
Kīlauea Point. ***Tel*** *(808) 828-1413. 10am–4pm Mon–Fri. Jan 1, Thnksg., Dec 25.*

Official marker

Waimea Canyon & Kōke'e State Park ⓯

Kōke'e Road (Hwy 550). ***Tel*** *Kaua'i Division of State Parks, (808) 587-0400.* **Kōke'e State Park** *daily.* **Kōke'e Museum** ***Tel*** *(808) 335-9975. Donation. 10am–4pm daily.* **www**.kokee.org **Kōke'e Lodge** ***Tel*** *(808) 335-6061. Cabins available for rent.*
www.waimea-plantation.com

No visitor should leave Kaua'i without taking in the rugged grandeur of Waimea Canyon and the breathtaking views from Kōke'e State Park. Waimea Canyon, known as the "Grand Canyon of the Pacific," was created by an earthquake that almost split Kaua'i in two. The gorge, now 3,000 ft (915 m) deep, is still eroding as landslides and the Waimea River continue to carry away tons of soil. Of the several lookouts dotted along the rim, the **Waimea Canyon Lookout**, despite being the lowest of the lookouts, offers the best canyon views. The more adventurous can take hiking trails to explore in greater depth. The **Kukui Trail** heads sharply down into the canyon as far as the Waimea River – a relatively easy and rewarding trip. At the North End of Waimea Canyon is **Kōke'e State Park**, laced through with more hiking trails. From the park's **Pu'u O Kila Lookout**, the majestic amphitheater of the Kalalau Valley opens out; another view is from the nearby **Kalalau Lookout**. A highlight of the park is the **Alaka'i Swamp**, a bowl-like depression drenched by nearly 42 ft (13 m) of rain every year. Part rainforest, part bog, the area boasts some of Hawai'i's rarest birds, such as the *'i'iwi* or honeycreeper, and the tiny yellow *'anianiau*. Information, hiking advice, and maps are all available at the Kōke'e State Park headquarters.

Kalalau Trail ⓰

Visitors must obtain permission in advance from the State Parks office.
Na Pali Coast State Parks office
3060 'Eīwa St, Līhu'e, HI 96766, (808) 274-3444.
www.hawaiistateparks.org

The precipitous cliffs of the Nā Pali Coast make it impossible for the road to continue west of Kē'ē Beach on Kauai's north shore. But hardy hikers can follow the narrow Kalalau Trail for another 11 miles (18 km) to isolated Kalalau Valley. One of the most dramatic hikes in the world, it covers a landscape of almost primeval vastness and splendor. While this is not an expedition to undertake lightly, a half-day round trip to Hanakāpī'ai Valley is within most capabilities and is an unforgettable experience.

The trail begins at the end of **Kūhiō Highway**, climbing steeply to **Makana Peak** and affording spectacular views of the rugged coastline. It continues on to **Ke Ahu A Laka**, which was once Hawai'i's most celebrated school for *hula* dancing. The next stop is **Hanakāpī'ai Valley** where in summer a pristine sandy beach replaces the pebbles found at the valley mouth in winter. Wading and swimming here are unsafe, due to dangerous rip currents.

The more challenging part of the trail continues through an abandoned coffee plantation to the **Hanakāpī'ai Falls**, and then to **Pā Ma Wa'a**, an 800-ft (240-m) cliff, which is the highest point on the trail. The trail then dips into several hanging valleys where the streams have still to cut their way down to sea level, before reaching the beautiful campsite at **Hanakoa Valley**, set amid the ruins of ancient taro terraces. For the last 5 miles (8 km), the trail clings perilously to a sandstone cliff. The magical view of **Kalalau Valley** is the trail's reward. Note that there is no food or safe drinking water en route.

The soaring, pleated cliffs of the Nā Pali Coast, Kalalau Trail

Alaska Practical Information

Traveling around the largest state in the US requires a great deal of advance planning. From endless snowfields, towering mountains, majestic rainforests, sweeping tundra, active volcanoes, and the spectacular "northern lights" to some of the world's most abundant wildlife preserves, Alaska has much to offer its visitors. Although traveling in Alaska is more expensive than in other parts of the country, visitors on a small budget can also have a memorable trip.

TOURIST INFORMATION

The best source of travel information is the very comprehensive Alaska Vacation Planner, published by the **Alaska Travel Industry Association** (ATIA). The ATIA is run jointly by the state and various travel businesses. Many regional tourism councils also publish brochures on travel in their areas.

GETTING AROUND

Visitors have a number of transportation options. **Alaska Airlines** flights link larger cities and towns, while smaller "bush" planes take visitors to more remote areas. The state-run **Alaska Railroad** connects Fairbanks, Anchorage, Seward, and Denali National Park. The main intercity bus service, **Alaska Direct Bus Line**, has year-round service.

A government-operated ferry service, the **Alaska Marine Highway System** links towns throughout southeast and south central Alaska, with service extending as far south as Prince Rupert in British Columbia and Bellingham, Washington. The large, comfortable, and well-equipped ships carry hundreds of vehicles and feature cabins, multiple dining areas, and onboard naturalists. The pace is relaxed and the atmosphere is very casual; some travelers even sleep under the stars on the outer deck. Book well in advance for this popular ferry service. However, driving within Alaska involves long distances; be especially careful of collisions with Alaska's wildlife.

NATURAL HAZARDS

Most travelers visit Alaska in the milder summer season between late May and early-September. Even so, bring a jacket and warm clothes for chilly nights. Summer also brings the worst of Alaska's insects, mainly mosquitoes and blackflies. Backcountry travelers also need to take precautions in bear country. **Park Service** or **Forest Service** rangers can provide safety tips.

THE CLIMATE OF ALASKA

Although situated near the Arctic Circle, weather patterns vary a great deal in Alaska. Winters are cold and dark, but summer with its warm weather and long days is the prime season for visitors. In the state's northern tier, the sun does not set for two months of the year, and there is daylight for as many as 22 hours each day in June at Fairbanks. July is the rainiest month. Most coastal cruises take place in the summer.

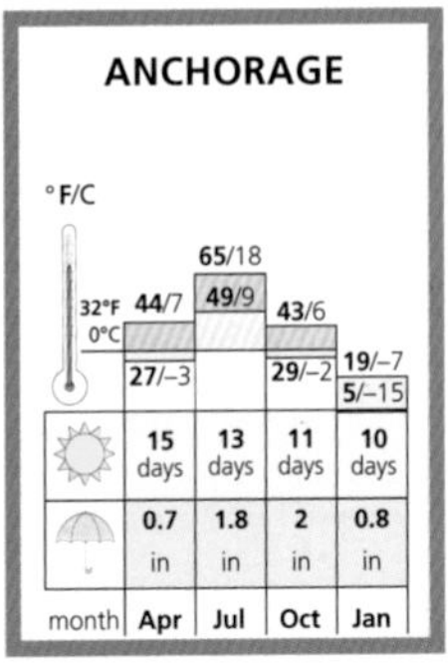

DIRECTORY

TOURIST INFORMATION

Alaska Travel Industry Association (ATIA)
Tel (907) 929-2200, (800) 862-5275.
www.travelalaska.com

TRAVEL

Alaska Airlines
Tel (206) 433-3100, (800) 426-0333.
www.alaskaair.com

Alaska Direct Bus Line
Tel (907) 277-6652, (800) 770-6652.

Alaska Marine Highway System
Tel (907) 465-3941.
www.ferryalaska.com

Alaska Railroad
Tel (907) 265-2494, (800) 544-0522.
www.alaskarailroad.com

FESTIVALS

There are a number of special events taking place in Alaska at different times of the year. Starting in spring, the famous **Iditarod Trail Sled Dog Race** runs between Anchorage and Nome. April sees the **Alaska Folk Festival** held in Juneau. The **Alaska State Fair** (August) in Palmer is famous for its pumpkins and cabbages, which grow to world-record sizes under the state's 24-hour sunshine. On October 18th, the **Alaska Day Celebration**, the day Alaska was bought from Russia by the US, livens up the Colonial town of Sitka.

OUTDOOR ACTIVITIES

The vast majority of Alaska is set aside as public land, making the state a paradise for hikers, fishermen, and other outdoor enthusiasts. Trekking, mountain climbing, skiing, rafting, kayaking, and whale-watching are some of the activities that visitors can enjoy here. Most tourist offices provide information and details of outdoor pursuits that Alaska has to offer.

Hawai'i Practical Information

Tourism is Hawai'i's most important industry. From the bright lights of Waikīkī and Honolulu to the remote waterfalls of Maui's Hāna district, the islands offer something to suit all budgets. The cost of living in Hawai'i is about 40 percent higher than that in the rest of the US; even so, Hawai'i is a year-round destination. However, visitors will enjoy better prices in the off-season, between April and December.

TOURIST INFORMATION

Visitor information desks at all airports provide maps and guides, and all major hotels have a guest services desk. All islands have a branch of the **Hawai'i Visitors' and Convention Bureau** (HVCB), or some other visitors' bureau.

GETTING AROUND

Driving is the best way to get around, since public transportation is limited. Seat belts are mandatory, and children under three must sit in approved car seats. Distances between gas stations can be long, so keep the tank at least half full. Always check the weather – many roads wash out during or after heavy rains.

Allow plenty of time for any trip. The locals move at a leisurely pace, seldom using horns. On narrow roads, pull over to let cars pass.

NATURAL HAZARDS

Visitors should be aware of certain potential dangers that the sun and the ocean pose to health. Thus, wear a hat and sunglasses, use sunblock cream, and drink plenty of fluids as a protection against the harsh sun.

Ask the lifeguard about ocean conditions, as some beaches can be safe in summer but very dangerous in winter. Swim facing away from the beach, as sudden rogue waves can sweep you out to sea. If you get carried out by a rip current, try to swim with it until it dissipates. Always check for rocks and corals below the surface, and wear protective foot gear. If you cut yourself on coral, clean the cut thoroughly with antiseptic. If you step on a sea urchin, or are stung by a jellyfish, apply a paste of vinegar and meat tenderizer. Although shark encounters are rare, it's best that you check with the lifeguard before swimming.

OUTDOOR ACTIVITIES

Hawai'i offers a plethora of outdoor activities, many focused on the ocean, such as surfing, swimming, fishing, scuba diving, and snorkeling. In addition, sports enthusiasts have a variety of opportunities such as horseback riding, hiking, and playing golf on some of the world's best courses.

THE CLIMATE OF HAWAI'I

Hawai'i has two distinct seasons, summer and winter. May to October is hot and dry, while November through April is cooler and wetter. Happily for visitors, there are very few days when Hawai'i's beaches do not beckon. Sudden rains or storms mean the onset of winter, as do the big waves that surfers eagerly await. However, Hawai'i is not all sunshine, and residents in the cooler upcountry areas spend Christmas Eve gathered around the fireplace.

HONOLULU

°F/C				
high	78/25	82/28	82/28	76/24
low	68/20	73/22	73/22	68/20
sunshine	21 days	24 days	22 days	20 days
rainfall	1.5 in	0.6 in	2.3 in	3.5 in
month	Apr	Jul	Oct	Jan

DIRECTORY

TOURIST INFORMATION

Hawai'i Visitors & Convention Bureau
Tel *(800) 464-2924.*
www.gohawaii.com

SNORKELING

Snorkel Bob's
700 Kapahulu Ave, Honolulu, O'ahu. **Tel** *(800) 262-7725.*
www.snorkelbob.com

SCUBA DIVING

Bubbles Below
PO Box 157, Eleele, Kaua'i.
Tel *(808) 332-7333.*
www.bubblesbelowkauai.com

ENTERTAINMENT

Music and dance are as important to Hawaiians as the air they breathe. Most islands offer extravagant Polynesian shows, with *lū'au*-style meals, and music and dance from other Pacific islands such as Tahiti and Fiji. You can dance the night away in nightclubs in Honolulu and Maui, but also be prepared for earlier nights in other parts of the state.

FESTIVALS

A diverse range of festivals and events take place all through the year. The onset of summer sees **Lei Day** with everyone donning flowered garlands. The **King Kamehameha Day** honors the chief who united the islands. All summer long, there are cultural, music, and food festivals, as well as sports events, from rodeos to canoe races and the grueling **Ironman Triathlon**. Summer draws to a close with the grand **Aloha Week Festivals**.

Winters offer sports and cultural events such as the **Triple Crown of Surfing**, and the **Merrie Monarch Festival** which culminates with the "Olympics" of *hula*.

Choosing a Hotel

These hotels have been selected across a wide price range for their excellent facilities and locations. While Hawai'i is a year-round destination, Alaska's accommodations fill fast during the short and busy summer. This chart lists hotels by region and within this by price category.

PRICE CATEGORIES
For a standard double room per night, including service charges and any additional taxes.

$ Under $100
$$ $100–$200
$$$ $200–$300
$$$$ $300–$450
$$$$$ Over $450

ALASKA

ANCHORAGE Spenard Hostel International $

2845 W 42nd Ave, 99517 ***Tel*** *(907) 248-5036* ***Fax*** *(907) 248-5036* ***Rooms*** *8*

Located about a mile (2 km) away from the international airport on a main bus route, this friendly hostel with laundry and cooking facilities is the best low-budget accommodation in Anchorage. There are bike trails nearby and bicycles are available to rent for a small daily charge. The hostel has no lockout. **www.alaskahostel.org**

ANCHORAGE Dimond Center Hotel $$$$

700 E Dimond Blvd, 99515 ***Tel*** *(907) 770-5000, (866) 770-5002* ***Fax*** *(907) 770-5001* ***Rooms*** *109*

Despite its location adjacent to a south-side shopping mall, this hotel owned by an Alaska Native corporation is one of the most pleasant lodging choices in Anchorage. There's a spacious lobby and guests appreciate deluxe beds, large bathrooms with jetted tubs, free airport shuttle, and filling hot breakfasts. **www.dimondcenterhotel.com**

ANCHORAGE Inlet Tower Hotel and Suites $$$

1200 L St, 99501 ***Tel*** *(907) 276-0110, (800) 544-0786* ***Fax*** *(907) 258-4914* ***Rooms*** *180*

Rooms at this hotel boast wonderful views – the Chugach Range to the east, Mount Susitna and Cook Inlet to the west, and Mount McKinley to the north. The restaurant, Mixx Grill, is well-known for its game meat and seafood dishes. The hotel is a short walk from the Tony Knowles Coastal Trail. **www.inlettower.com**

DENALI (MCKINLEY) VILLAGE Denali Mountain Morning Hostel $

Mile 224.5 Parks Hwy, PO Box 208, 99755 ***Tel*** *(907) 683-7503* ***Rooms*** *12*

In a quiet location on the banks of Carlo Creek, just south of Denali National Park, this is a good budget choice. Guests sleep in dorms and cabins of varying prices. The hostel rents backpacking gear and has free luggage storage. A free shuttle operates to and from the National Park Visitors' Center. Open May–mid-Sep. **www.hostelalaska.com**

DENALI (MCKINLEY) VILLAGE Denali Crow's Nest $$$

Mile 238.5 Parks Hwy, 99755 ***Tel*** *(907) 683-2723, (888) 917-8130* ***Fax*** *(907) 683-2323* ***Rooms*** *39*

Offering a spectacular view, this collection of cozy log cabins clings to the hillside above Glitter Gulch. In the evening guests can relax in the soothing outdoor hot tub farther up the hill or in the precariously perched bar and restaurant, which enjoys an excellent reputation. **www.denalicrowsnest.com**

FAIRBANKS RV Park – River's Edge Resort $

4140 Boat St, 99709 ***Tel*** *(907) 474-0286, (800) 770-3343* ***Fax*** *(907) 474-3665* ***Rooms*** *180 sites and 94 cottages*

Situated beside the Chena River, this RV park and resort offers sites with full hook-ups and tent camping, as well as fully-equipped cottages and lodge-style accommodation. The RV park and the executive suites offer Internet access. Extras include a restaurant, laundry, and tour-booking services. **www.riversedge.net**

FAIRBANKS Minnie Street B&B $$

345 Minnie St, 99701 ***Tel*** *(907) 456-1802, (888) 456-1849* ***Fax*** *(907) 451-1751* ***Rooms*** *13*

Centrally located and just a short walk from the Chena River, this attractive bed and breakfast provides a variety of upscale suites. Some units have fitted kitchens and jetted baths. Guests have use of an outdoor hot tub and a flower-filled courtyard. Substantial breakfasts. Massage and spa services are available. **www.minniestreetbanb.com**

GLACIER BAY NATIONAL PARK Glacier Bay Lodge $$

199 Bartlett Cove Rd, 99826 ***Tel*** *(907) 264-4600, (888) 229-8687* ***Fax*** *(907) 258-3668* ***Rooms*** *55*

Surrounded by large rainforest trees on the shores of Bartlett Cove, Glacier Bay Lodge offers the only accommodation located within Glacier Bay National Park. The lodge's sitting area, with a roaring fire in the large stone fireplace, is inviting after a day of cruising past glaciers. Basic, small rooms. **www.visitglacierbay.com**

HOMER Land's End Resort $$

4786 Homer Spit Rd, 99603 ***Tel*** *(907) 235-0400, (800) 478-0400* ***Fax*** *(907) 235-0420* ***Rooms*** *89*

Located at the end of Homer Spit, this lodge is surrounded on three sides by the waters of Kachemak Bay. In addition to the excellent views of the bay and the Kenai Mountains, the resort offers an indoor lap pool, a sauna, and an outdoor hot tub. **www.lands-end-resort.com**

Key to Symbols *see back cover flap*

HOMER Old Town Bed and Breakfast $$

106 W Bunnell St, 99603 ***Tel*** *(907) 235-7758* ***Rooms*** *3*

First opened as part of a 1940s-era trading post, this cozy bed and breakfast is a step back in time. The three rooms contain period furnishings such as four-poster beds and quilts, along with curiously sloping floors. Breakfast is served downstairs in Maura's Café. The building also houses the Bunnell Arts Center. **www.oldtownbedandbreakfast.com**

JUNEAU Juneau International Hostel $

614 Harris St, 99801 ***Tel*** *(907) 586-9559* ***Rooms*** *46 dorm beds, 1 room*

This hostel, high on the hill above downtown Juneau, provides friendly and very inexpensive dormitory accommodation with the use of cooking and laundry facilities as well as free Internet access. There is limited parking on the steep street outside. The only notable drawback is the daytime lockout. **www.juneauhostel.org**

JUNEAU Historic Silverbow Inn $$

120 2nd St, 99801 ***Tel*** *(907) 586-4146, (800) 586-4146* ***Fax*** *(907) 586-4242* ***Rooms*** *6*

Right in the heart of historic downtown Juneau, this friendly little boutique hotel also operates the adjacent bakery, reputedly haunted by the benign ghost of the original owner, Austrian baker Gus Messerschmitt. Guests can relax in the lounge or try the games and puzzles on offer. Breakfast is included in the room rate. **www.silverbowinn.com**

JUNEAU Alaska's Capital Inn $$$

113 W 5th St, 99801 ***Tel*** *(907) 586-6507, (888) 588-6507* ***Fax*** *(907) 588-6508* ***Rooms*** *7*

Located right next to the State Capitol, this 1906 hotel has a friendly, casual ambience and period furnishings. Some rooms feature lovely stained-glass windows. In the evening guests can relax in the outdoor hot tub in a pleasant leafy setting. Breakfast is included in the room rate. **www.alaskacapitalinn.com**

KETCHIKAN Gilmore Hotel $$

326 Front St, 99901 ***Tel*** *(907) 225-9423, (800) 275-9423* ***Fax*** *(907) 275-7442* ***Rooms*** *38*

The historic Gilmore Hotel, built in 1927, rounds out its retro ambience with puffy feather beds and pillows. It has pleasant views of Tongass Narrows and the attached restaurant, Annabelle's, is a Ketchikan favorite. There is free wireless Internet access. Drivers must secure an on-street parking permit. **www.gilmorehotel.com**

KETCHIKAN New York Hotel $$

207 Stedman St, 99901 ***Tel*** *(907) 225-0246, (866) 225-0246* ***Fax*** *(907) 225-1803* ***Rooms*** *14*

This scenic corner of Ketchikan enjoys pleasant harbor views and is walking distance to the town center. In addition to the standard rooms, suites on nearby Creek Street offer Jacuzzi tubs and views of spawning salmon in Ketchikan Creek. The lively café serves coffees and light meals. Internet access available. **www.thenewyorkhotel.com**

KODIAK A Smiling Bear B&B $$

2046 Three Sisters Way, 99615 ***Tel*** *(907) 481-6390* ***Fax*** *(907) 486-6390* ***Rooms*** *2*

With a Kodiak bear theme and a fabulous garden, this lovely place near the Monashka Bay shore offers personable home accommodation and attention to detail. Breakfast, which is included in the room rate, often consists of items grown in the extensive attached forest garden. **www.asmilingbear.com**

KODIAK Best Western Kodiak Inn $$

236 W Rezanof Dr, 99615 ***Tel*** *(907) 486-5712, (888) 563-4254* ***Fax*** *(907) 486-3430* ***Rooms*** *80*

Part of the Best Western chain, this centrally-located hotel caters largely to business travelers and anglers. The vaulted lobby displays a stuffed mountain goat and an enormous Kodiak bear. Freezers are available for visitors' fish catches, and the hotel also provides shuttle services from the ferry dock and airport. **www.kodiakinn.com**

SEWARD Seward Windsong Lodge $$$

Mile 0.5 Herman Leirer/Exit Glacier Rd, 99664 ***Tel*** *(907) 224-7116, (877) 777-4079* ***Fax*** *(907) 224-711* ***Rooms*** *108*

Surrounded by high peaks in the Resurrection River Valley, this beautifully situated and well-appointed lodge caters especially to package visitors heading for Kenai Fjords National Park. It is several miles from the town center, but is very well-placed for visits to Exit Glacier. **www.sewardwindsong.com**

SITKA Sitka Hotel $

118 Lincoln St, 99835 ***Tel*** *(907) 747-3288* ***Fax*** *(907) 747-8499* ***Rooms*** *60*

Located in the heart of town, this historic hotel offers a variety of well-maintained rooms, including budget options with down-the-hall bathrooms. Victoria's Restaurant offers fresh local seafood, as well as soups, salads, and sandwiches. **www.sitkahotel.net**

SKAGWAY Skagway Inn $$

7th & Broadway, 99840 ***Tel*** *(907) 983-2289, (888) 752-4929* ***Fax*** *(907) 983-2713* ***Rooms*** *10*

Built in 1897, the Skagway Inn was first a brothel, then a residence, and later a boarding house. The Victorian-style inn now features period furnishings and a fabulous garden, which supplies the house restaurant (open for cooking tours only) with organic produce. Breakfast is included in the room rate. **www.skagwayinn.com**

VALDEZ Valdez Harbor Inn $$

100 Fidalgo Dr, 99686 ***Tel*** *(907) 835-3434, (888) 222-3440* ***Fax*** *(907) 835-2308* ***Rooms*** *88*

The finest hotel in town, the Valdez Harbor Inn does everything possible to accommodate business travelers. Amenities include a business center and fitness room, and some rooms have hot tubs. Rooms with views of the harbor cost extra. **www.valdezharborinn.com**

HAWAI'I

GREATER HONOLULU Doubletree Alana Hotel-Waikīkī $$

1956 Ala Moana Blvd, 96815 ***Tel*** *(808) 941-7275, (800) 222-8733* ***Fax*** *(808) 949-0996* ***Rooms*** *268*

This small boutique hotel has a reputation for hospitality and offers the amenities of a luxury hotel at affordable prices. These include a poolside fitness center, a business center, room service, and in-room massage. Freshly baked cookies are provided at check-in. Guest rooms are compact, but well equipped. **www.alana-doubletree.com**

GREATER HONOLULU The Ilikai Hotel $$

1777 Ala Moana Blvd, 96815 ***Tel*** *(808) 949-3811, (800) 245-4524* ***Fax*** *(808) 947-4523* ***Rooms*** *267*

This hotel is convenient for Waikīkī beaches, the Ala Moana Shopping Center, and Beach Park. Its main attractions are Sarento's Restaurant, a fitness center, a tennis court, and pool. Most of the 267 rooms have *lānai* (verandas). All have kitchens, televisions with on-demand movies, and Internet access. **www.ilikaihotel.com**

HĀNA Josie's Hāna Hideaway $$

PO Box 265, 96713 ***Tel*** *(808) 248-7727* ***Fax*** *(808) 248-8418* ***Rooms*** *12*

Close to the peaceful village of Hāna, Josie offers 12 vacation houses, each with its own special charm. Ranging from one-bed studios to large homes, some have ocean views and others are surrounded by coconut, banana, and papaya groves. All have baths, televisions, washer-dryers, telephones, ceiling fans, and barbecues. **www.hanahideaways.com**

HĀNA 'Ekena $$$

Kalo Road, PO Box 728, 96713 ***Tel*** *(808) 248-7047* ***Fax*** *(808) 248-7047* ***Rooms*** *2*

Perfect for visitors seeking total peace, this beautiful hillside home has two master bedroom suites, each with an over-sized tub, and is equipped with all necessities. Wrap-around balconies offer fabulous 360-degree views of the ocean, sky, coast, and lush green hills of Hāna. There is also a one-bedroom, one-bath home available. **www.maui.net/~ekena**

HILO Uncle Billy's Hilo Bay Hotel $

87 Banyan Dr, 96720 ***Tel*** *(808) 935-0861* ***Fax*** *(808) 935-7903* ***Rooms*** *144*

Uncle Billy's is the least expensive place to stay on Hilo Bay. The rooms have televisions and air conditioning; some have kitchenettes. The on-site general store offers deli-style food, souvenirs, sundries, and resort apparel. There is a hula show nightly in the restaurant. This is the place for a fun, island-style experience. **www.unclebilly.com**

HILO Naniloa Volcanoes Resort $$

93 Banyan Dr, 96720 ***Tel*** *(808) 969-3333* ***Fax*** *(808) 969-6622* ***Rooms*** *135*

Formerly the Hawai'i Naniloa Hotel, this affordable place remains a Hilo landmark. Rooms are air-conditioned and have tvs and refrigerators. Amenities include an oceanfront pool, wireless Internet, and a restaurant. Right on Hilo Bay, it is well placed for a trip to Hawai'i Volcanoes National Park. **www.hottours.us**

KĀ'ANAPALI Ka'anapali Beach Hotel $$$

2525 Kā'anapali Pkwy, 96761 ***Tel*** *(808) 661-0011, (866) 716-8109* ***Fax*** *(808) 667-5978* ***Rooms*** *430*

Right on the beach in the Kā'anapali Resort, this is known as Maui's most Hawaiian hotel. Rooms and suites are furnished island-style and have *lānai* (verandas) looking onto a lush tropical garden. The six-story Maui, Lāna'i, and Kaua'i wings have elevators; the three-story Moloka'i does not. Hawaiian cultural activities abound. **www.kbhmaui.com**

KĀ'ANAPALI Royal Lahaina Resort $$$

2780 Keka'a Dr, 96761 ***Tel*** *(808) 661-3611, (800) 222-5642* ***Fax*** *(808) 661-6150* ***Rooms*** *516*

This well-established beachfront property has hotel rooms and suites, cottages, and cottage suites. Its recreational facilities include three swimming pools and The Royal Lahaina Tennis Ranch, with 22 courts and a tennis stadium. Complimentary Hawaiiana program for guests and an award-winning lu'au nightly. **www.hawaiihotels.com**

KAUNAKAKAI (MOLOKA'I) Dunbar Beachfront Cottages $$

Kamehameha V Hwy, just past Mile Marker 18, 96748 ***Tel*** *(808) 558-8153* ***Fax*** *(808) 558-8153* ***Rooms*** *4*

The two green-and-white plantation-style cottages sit right at the water's edge on their own secluded beach. Each has two bedrooms, a kitchen, television with VCR, and ceiling fans. Their large decks have views of the nearby islands of Maui, Lānai, and Kaho'olawe. They are truly idyllic and peaceful. **www.molokai-beachfront-cottages.com**

KAUNAKAKAI (MOLOKA'I) Hotel Moloka'i $$

Kamehameha V Hwy, 96748 ***Tel*** *(808) 553-5347, (800) 535-0085* ***Fax*** *(808) 553-5047* ***Rooms*** *45*

Not fancy, but right on the water and affordable, this is the only centrally located hotel on the island. The ocean-front dining room, Hula Shores, provides a gathering place for local residents on Friday nights, when everyone brings their ukuleles and joins in a Hawaiian jam session by the pool. **www.hotelmolokai.com**

LAHAINA Best Western Pioneer Inn $$

658 Wharf St, 96761 ***Tel*** *(808) 667-5708, (800) 457-5457* ***Fax*** *(808) 661-3636* ***Rooms*** *34*

The Pioneer Inn's colorful history dates back to 1910, when a Canadian Mountie came to Maui to catch his man. Now managed by Best Western, its rooms are not deluxe but the location is: right at the water's edge in scenic Lahaina Harbor. Rooms are on the second floor. There is a pool, a rowdy bar, and a restaurant. **www.pioneerinnmaui.com**

LAHAINA Lahaina Inn $$

127 Lahainaluna Rd, 96761 ***Tel*** *(808) 661-0577, (800) 669-3444* ***Fax*** *(808) 667-9480* ***Rooms*** *12*

This small boutique hotel in the heart of Lahaina has nine rooms and three parlor suites lovingly decorated with authentic Victorian furnishings. Continental breakfast is included. Lahaina Grill & Maui Restaurant is on the first floor and the ocean is half a block away. **www.lahainainn.com**

LAHAINA Lahaina Shores Beach Resort $$$

475 Front St, 96761 ***Tel*** *(808) 661-4835, (800) 642-6284* ***Fax*** *(808) 661-4696* ***Rooms*** *200*

The only hotel in Lahaina that is right on the beach also offers great value. Accommodations include studios, one-bedroom, and penthouse suites with full kitchens, *lānai* (verandas), and ocean or mountain views. The location is right next to the 505 Front Street shopping village, with its restaurants and boutiques. **www.lahainashores.com**

LAHAINA Sheraton Maui $$$

2605 Kā'anapali Pkwy, 96761 ***Tel*** *(808) 661-0031, (866) 716-8109* ***Fax*** *(808) 661-0458* ***Rooms*** *508*

Kā'anapali's first luxury resort hotel sits above Black Rock, but the original 1950s-style decor is gone. Now the furnishings are reminiscent of Hawai'i's plantation era, using natural materials and pastel shades. Almost all guest rooms face the ocean and have air conditioning, a *lānai* (veranda), and small refrigerator. **www.sheraton-maui.com**

LĪHU'E Kaua'i Marriott Resort & Beach Club $$$

3610 Rice St, 96766 ***Tel*** *(808) 245-5050* ***Fax*** *(808) 245-5049, (800) 220-2925* ***Rooms*** *345*

This resort stretches along a white sand beach, just a mile (1.6 km) from Līhue Airport. A spectacular pool, two Jack Nicklaus-designed golf courses, and several restaurants, including the casual Duke's Canoe Club, are available to guests. In-room amenities include a mini-refrigerator and cable television. **www.marriott.com**

PRINCEVILLE Hanalei Bay Resort & Suites $$

5380 Honoiki Rd, 76722 ***Tel*** *(808) 826-6522, (800) 827-4427* ***Fax*** *(808) 826-6680* ***Rooms*** *182*

Perched above Hanalei Bay, this resort has all the tropical amenities one would want, including fabulous views, lagoon pools with waterfalls, open-air restaurants, tennis courts, and superb golf. The rooms are light and airy, with tropical furnishings, *lānai* (verandas), air conditioning, telephones, and daily maid service. **www.hanaleibayresort.com**

VOLCANO VILLAGE Chalet Kīlauea – The Inn at Volcano $$$

Wright Rd & Laukapu Rd, 96785 ***Tel*** *(808) 967-7786, (800) 937-7786* ***Fax*** *(808) 967-8660* ***Rooms*** *6*

The rooms at this charming, affordable place are individually decorated and have names such as "Jade Room" or "Treehouse Suite". They are adorned with art and memorabilia from the travels of the owners. The day begins with a three-course candlelit gourmet breakfast and there's afternoon tea in the living room. **www.volcano-hawaii.com**

VOLCANO VILLAGE Kīlauea Lodge $$$

Old Volcano Rd, 96785 ***Tel*** *(808) 967-7366* ***Fax*** *(808) 967-7367* ***Rooms*** *17*

Built as a YMCA camp in 1938, this refurbished lodge is just a mile (1.6 km) from Hawai'i Volcanoes National Park. There are 12 rooms and three vacation cottages. Some rooms have fireplaces or wood-burning stoves; stained-glass windows feature throughout. Cottages have a kitchen and two bedrooms. **www.kilauealodge.com**

WAIKĪKĪ J&B's Haven B&B $$

Kahena St at Ainapo St, off Hawaii Kai Drive, 96825 ***Tel*** *(808) 396-9462* ***Rooms*** *2*

Located in a quiet residential area, J&B's is a spotless, homey place away from hectic Waikīkī Beach. The rooms have private baths and floor-to-ceiling windows. The B&B is operated by an accommodating mother and daughter team, originally from England but both very knowledgeable about Hawaii. Fine breakfasts. Three-night minimum stay.

WAIKĪKĪ Royal Garden at Waikīkī $$

440 Olohana St, 96815 ***Tel*** *(808) 943-0202, (800) 438-6493* ***Fax*** *(808) 945-7407* ***Rooms*** *208*

This boutique hotel is a luxurious breath of fresh air. Located on a peaceful, tree-lined street, a half block from the Ala Wai Canal, it is quiet and beautifully appointed. Rooms have one king, one queen, or two twin beds, a small refrigerator, and Internet access. There is a pool, a sauna, and a restaurant. **www.extraholidays.com**

WAIKĪKĪ Westin Moana Surfrider $$$

2365 Kalākaua Ave, 96815 ***Tel*** *(808) 922-3111, (866) 716-8109* ***Fax*** *(808) 923-0308* ***Rooms*** *791*

This stunning "First Lady of Waikīkī," whose central section was built in 1901, combines modern comforts with high elegance. The hotel has retained many of its Victorian features, such as the porte-cochère, or replicated them, as in the case of the ornate plasterwork. On-site acitivites include a children's program. **www.moana-surfrider.com**

WAIKĪKĪ The Royal Hawaiian $$$$$

2259 Kalākaua Ave, 96815 ***Tel*** *(808) 923-7311, (866) 716-8109* ***Fax*** *(808) 931-7098* ***Rooms*** *528*

This elegant Waikīkī hotel is affectionately known as the "Pink Palace of the Pacific": its stucco exterior, furnishings, towels, and even the beer, are pink. Right on the beach and surrounded by lush tropical gardens, the hotel has been a Waikīkī landmark since 1927, hosting movie stars and heads of state. **www.royal-hawaiian.com**

WAIMEA Aston Waimea Plantation Cottages $$$

9400 Kaumuali'i Hwy, 96796 ***Tel*** *(808) 338-1625, (877) 997-6667* ***Fax*** *(808) 338-2338* ***Rooms*** *47*

Step back into old Hawai'i at these wonderful seaside plantation cottages, set in a coconut grove at the gateway to Waimea Canyon. Situated on the western coast of Kauai, these cottages have all been individually restored, with period-inspired furnishings, kitchens, and a front porch overlooking the grassy lawn. **www.astonhotels.com**

Choosing a Restaurant

Both Alaska and Hawai'i offer an enormous choice of places to eat. Restaurants in this chart have been selected across a wide range of price categories for their good value, excellent food, atmosphere, and location. Restaurants are listed by area, and within the area by price.

PRICE CATEGORIES
For a three-course meal for one, including a glass of house wine (where served), and all other unavoidable charges such as sales tax.

($) Under $15
($)($) $15–$30
($)($)($) $30–$55
($)($)($)($) $55–$80
($)($)($)($)($) Over $80

ALASKA

ANCHORAGE Corsair Restaurant ($)($)($)($)

944 W 5th Ave, 99502 ***Tel** (907) 278-4502*

Founded in 1979 with a sailing vessel theme, this fine-dining restaurant is one of Anchorage's best options for an elegant night out. The renowned bouillabaisse is made from Alaskan seafood. The Corsair boasts the state's largest wine list. Closed Sunday.

DENALI VILLAGE Overlook Bar and Grill ($)($)($)

Mile 224 Parks Hwy, 99755 ***Tel** (907) 683-2723, (888) 917-8130*

Meals in the acclaimed bar and grill of the Denali Crow's Nest are enhanced by spectacular panoramic views over the village. In addition to the excellent salmon, halibut, and steak, the menu includes pasta, fresh bread, and imaginative salads, sandwiches, and burgers. Open in the summer only.

FAIRBANKS The Pump House ($)($)($)

Mile 1.3 Chena Pump Rd, 99708 ***Tel** (907) 479-8452*

On perpetually daylit summer evenings this sprawling place, which hugs the banks of the Chena River, is probably the busiest venue in town. Diners can enjoy well-prepared Alaskan seafood, steaks, chicken, and even reindeer or elk meat. Sunday brunches are especially popular. Bookings are recommended.

HAINES Mountain Market and Café ($)

151 3rd Ave, 99827 ***Tel** (907) 766-3340*

An excellent option for a healthy breakfast or light lunch, the Mountain Market and Café offers up a dozen excellent wraps, as well as croissants, deli sandwiches, home-made soups, and a variety of seasonal specialties. Behind the café is a complete healthfood shop.

HOMER Fresh Sourdough Express ($)($)

1316 Ocean Dr, 99603 ***Tel** (907) 235-7571*

Originally housed in a bakery wagon parked on Homer Spit, this popular little place has expanded and now serves three healthy, organic meals every day. In addition to excellent breakfasts, fresh salmon and halibut, steak, pasta, and organic chicken dishes are served.

JUNEAU Hangar at the Wharf ($)

2 Marine Way, 99801 ***Tel** (907) 586-5018*

With its waterside location in the heart of downtown Juneau, this noisy restaurant is a favorite of both tourists and locals. The wide-ranging pub menu includes shareable appetizers, along with salads, wraps, fish and chips, steaks, burgers, and Alaskan seafood. Window seats fill quickly, and on rare sunny days diners can sit on the deck.

KETCHIKAN Steamers at the Dock ($)($)($)

76 Front St, 99901 ***Tel** (907) 225-1600*

On the cruise ship dock with a lovely water view, this seafood restaurant has a long wooden bar and a raucous atmosphere. The restaurant gets its name from its signature dish – steamer clams in butter sauce. It also dishes up excellent local oysters and other fresh seafood. Closed October to mid-April.

KODIAK The Old Power House Restaurant ($)($)

516 E Marine Way, 99615 ***Tel** (907) 481-1088*

Under the bridge on the waterfront, this place offers the best dining in Kodiak. With a sushi bar and various other Japanese choices, there's also fish, pork, beef, chicken, pasta, and vegetarian dishes with an Oriental twist. It is open from Tuesday to Saturday for lunch and dinner. No lunch service on Sunday.

SEWARD Yoly's Bistro ($)($)($)

220 4th Ave, 99664 ***Tel** (907) 224-3295*

Seward's most distinctive restaurant is a great downtown discovery, with an open kitchen and Southwest-meets-Alaska decor. Yolanda Iflander's creations include an unusual fusion that stars Alaskan seafood with Asian influences. Vegetarian options too. Open Sunday to Thursday and, in summer, Friday and Saturday. Closed January to March.

Key to Symbols *see back cover flap*

SITKA Ludvig's $$$

256 Katlian St, 99835 ***Tel*** *(907) 966-3663*

Named for the owner's dog, this cozy bistro is well-regarded for its superb Spanish *tapas*, served in the afternoon. The dinner menu includes Spanish and Cuban specialties, seafood, unique home-baked breads, and gourmet desserts. Open Sunday for tapas only. Reservations are recommended. Closed January to March.

SKAGWAY Red Onion Saloon $

2nd & Broadway, 99840 ***Tel*** *(907) 983-2222*

Once Skagway's exclusive bordello, this historic site is a lively drinking establishment serving bar meals. In addition to snacks, the menu includes excellent salads, a range of fresh sandwiches, and creative pizzas. There is great locally brewed beer on tap and live entertainment when cruise ships are in port. Closed November to March.

HAWAI'I

HALE'IWA Coffee Gallery $

66-250 Kamehameha V Hwy, North Shore Marketplace, 96712 ***Tel*** *(808) 637-5355*

This North Shore eatery has a classic surf-beach atmosphere. Popular with surfers and local residents, its breakfasts are legendary. The huge omelets have surf-lingo names such as "Off the Wall" and "Off the Lip". There is also an espresso bar featuring a large selection of fresh roasted gourmet coffee, including Kona and organically grown beans.

HĀNA Hotel Hāna-Maui Dining Room $$$$

5031 Hāna Hwy, 96713 ***Tel*** *(808) 270-5285*

Here you can enjoy exquisite Pacific Rim cuisine created with organic fruits and vegetables from a nearby farm and the freshest fish available. The beautiful tropical setting overlooks the hotel's gardens. Informal hula performances by local dancers take place in the dining room on Friday evenings. The experience is a little pricey, but worth it.

HILO Café Pesto $$$

308 Kamehameha Ave, 96721 ***Tel*** *(808) 969-6640*

Occupying a 1910 building that has survived more than one tsunami, this causal café is in a lovely setting near Hilo Bay. Hawai'i regional cuisine is featured here, including island fish prepared in a variety of ways, fresh organic salads, innovative pastas, and creative pizzas. This restaurant has a reputation for quality food and good service.

HONOLULU Ono Hawaiian Foods $

726 Kapahulu Ave, 96816 ***Tel*** *(808) 737-2275*

This eatery is always busy, serving delicious Hawaiian dishes such as *poi* (taro paste), *laulau* (leaf-wrapped meat or fish bundles), and *lomi-lomi* salmon. You know it is genuinely Hawaiian because the combo plates come with a small cup of raw onion and Hawaiian 'alaea salt. This restaurant is clean, basic, and inexpensive. It is closed on Sundays.

KAUNAKAKAI Kanemitsu Bakery $

79 Ala Malama St, 96748 ***Tel*** *(808) 553-5855*

Famous for its Molokai sweet bread, this bakery offers an array of fresh-baked goods, snacks, and beverages. In the adjoining coffee shop, local-style breakfasts and lunches are served. You can take out, or eat in at a 1950s booth table. On Friday nights a line forms for the hot French bread stuffed with cream cheese, jam, and cinnamon butter.

LAHAINA Longhi's $$$$

888 Front St, 96761 ***Tel*** *(808) 667-2288*

Longhi's is famous. In business at the same location for over 30 years, it is still an "in" spot. The food is Italian, well-prepared, and pricey. Most tables are next to a window, so you can enjoy the hustle and bustle of Maui's busiest town along with your food. There is a good wine list and an espresso bar. The valet parking is a plus.

LĪHU'E Tip Top Café $

3173 Akahi St, 96766 ***Tel*** *(808) 245-2333*

This spotlessly clean, large dining room has 1950s-style booths and orchids on every table. Breakfasts and lunches are hearty. The macadamia pancakes are legendary at breakfast, while the oxtail soup is the highlight at lunch. This café-bakery has been in business since 1916 and is still a local favorite. It is closed on Mondays.

WAIKĪKĪ Duke's Canoe Club $$$

2335 Kalākaua Ave, 96815 ***Tel*** *(808) 922-2268*

Named after famed Hawaiian surfing champion Duke Kahanamoku, this is a good spot for live Hawaiian music and spirited crowds at sunset. Located on the beach at the Outrigger Waikīkī, it is a steak-and-seafood restaurant, but offers breakfast as well as lunch and dinner, and a light, inexpensive menu at its Barefoot Bar.

WAIKĪKĪ La Mer at Halekulani $$$$$

2199 Kālia Rd, 96815 ***Tel*** *(808) 923-2311*

Choose this elegant, romantic, and expensive French restaurant when you are in the mood to savor each exquisite bite. Dishes are impeccably prepared. On the second floor of the Halekulani, it has a magnificent ocean view and is one of the best places in Waikīkī for watching the sun set. Gentlemen are required to wear jackets.

General Index

Page numbers in **bold** type refer to main entries.

A

Aaron, Hank 258
Abilene (TX) **493**
Abolitionists 135, 220, 221, 458
  Brown, John 220, 221, 458
  Garrison, William Lloyd 128
Academy Awards 28
Acadia National Park (ME) 35, **172**
Acadians 357
  see also Cajun
Accommodation **18–19**
Ackroyd, Dan 665
Adams, John 52, 206
Adams, John Quincy 52
Adams, Samuel 139
Adirondack Mountains (NY) **93**
Adler Planetarium & Astronomy Museum (Chicago) 393
Adoration of the Magi (Andrea Mantegna) 660
Aerial Lift Bridge (Duluth, MN) 419
African Americans 61, 135, 341, 346, 361, 395, 708
  Gullah heritage & culture 255
African Meeting House *see* Museum of African American History
Aialik Glacier (AK) 735
AIDS, museum & exhibit on (Chicago) 394
Aitken, Robert 699
Air travel **20–21**
  Alaska 756
  Boston & New England 174
  California 720
  Deep South 366
  domestic airlines 21
  Great Plains 462
  Hawai'i 757
  Rockies 598
  Texas 494
Airline Carriers, directory **21**
Alabama **364–5**, 335
  hotels 371,
  restaurants 375
Alamitos Bay (Los Angeles) 658
Alaska **732–43**
  Alaska Marine Highway **737**
  Alaska Railroad 742
  aurora borealis 741
  climate 32, 756
  Denali National Park **742–3**
  directory 756
  earthquake 738
  festivals 756
  getting around 756
  history 732–3
  hotels **758–9**
  Iditarod Trail Sled Dog Race **738**
  map 734–5
  mileage chart 735
  natives 736, 742
  natural hazards 756
  outdoor activities 756
  population 733
  practical information 756–7
Alaska (cont.)
  restaurants 762–3
  sled dog race 741
  transportation 734
Alaska Marine Highway **737**
Alaska Native Heritage Center (Anchorage) 738
Alaska Peninsula **740**
Alaska Raptor Center (Sitka) 736
Alaska SeaLife Center (Seward) 739
Alaska State Museum (Juneau) 737
Alba Madonna (Raphael) 200
Albany (NY) **92**
Albright-Knox Art Gallery (Buffalo, NY) 95
Albuquerque (NM) **548–50**
  map 548–9
Albuquerque Museum of Art & History 549
Alcatraz Island (San Francisco) **703**
Aldrich, Thomas Bailey 169
Aldrin, Buzz 201
Aleutian Islands (Alaska) 732, **741**
Alexandria (VA) **212–13**
Alexander, Jason 671
Alferez, Enrique 353
Allen, Woody 87
Allman Brothers 258
Alta Plaza (San Francisco) 704
Amana Colonies (IA) **452**
Amarillo (TX) **493**
Amelia Island Museum of History (Fernandina Beach, FL) 315
American Express Credit Card 17
American flag 12, 101
American Folk Art Museum (NYC) 83
American Immigrant Wall of Honor (NYC) 67
American International Rattlesnake Museum (Albuquerque, NM) 549
American Jews 69
American Museum of Natural History (NYC) **83**
American Presidents **52–3**
  Adams, John 52, 206
  Adams, John Quincy 52
  Arthur, Chester A. 52
  Buchanan, James 52
  Buren, Martin Van 52
  Bush, George 53
  Bush, George W. 53
  Carter, Jimmy 53, 244, 258
  Cleveland, Grover 52, 53
  Clinton, William J. 53, 336, 358, 359, 678
  Coolidge, Calvin 53, 464
  Eisenhower, Dwight D. 53, 91, 208
  Fillimore, Millard 52
  Ford, Gerald 53, 209,
  Harrison, Benjamin 52
  Harrison, W.H. 52
  Harding, Warren 53
  Hayes, Rutherford B. 52
  Hoover, Herbert 53, 219, 453, 514
  Garfield, James A. 52
  Grant, Ulysses, S. 52, 91, 398
  Jackson, Andrew 52, 265, 286, 347, 362
  Jefferson, Thomas 52, 74, 192, 198,
American Presidents (cont.)
  204–5, 217
  Johnson, Andrew 52
  Johnson, Lyndon B. 53, 475, 482
  Kennedy, John, F. 53, 208, 478
  Lincoln, Abraham 52, 71, 154, 162, 205, 207, 222, 270, 271, 399
  Madison, James 52, 217
  McKinley, William 53
  Monroe, James 52, 216
  Nixon, Richard 53, 209
  Obama, Barack 53, 386
  Pierce, Franklin 52
  Polk, James K. 52
  Reagan, Ronald 53
  Roosevelt, Franklin D. 53, 91, 173, 205, 678
  Roosevelt, Theodore 52, 72, 206
  Taft, William, H. 53
  Truman, Harry S. 53, 457
  Tyler, John 53, 216
  Washington, George 52
  Wilson, Woodrow 53
American Revolution 44, 136, 149, 171
Americus (GA) **258**
Amerind Foundation (AZ) **533**
Amicalola Falls State Park (GA) 259
Amish, the 106, **109**, 401, 405
Ancestral Puebloans 506, 542, 553, 544
Anchorage (AK) 732, **738**
  climate 756
Anchorage Museum at Rasmuson Center (AK) 738
Ancient civilizations
  Pueblo Indians 570
  Ancestral Puebloan 553
  Hohokam 553
  Mimbres Mogollon 553
  Mississippian 357
Ancient Spanish Monastery (Miami) **298**
Anderson, Sherwood 383
Anheuser-Busch Brewery (St. Louis, MO) 455
Ann Arbor (MI) **410**
Annapolis (MD) **223**
Antietam National Battlefield (MD) **222**
Anza-Borrego Desert State Park (CA) **682–3**
Apache, Indian 506
Apalachicola (FL) **317**
Apostle Islands (WI) **415**
  Apostle Islands National Lakeshore
Appalachian Trail 175, 221, 262
Appellate Court (NYC) 72
Appomattox Court House and National Historical Park (VA) **218**
Aquarium of the Pacific (Los Angeles) 673
Aransas National Wildlife Refuge (TX) **488–9**
Arches National Park (UT) 503, **520–21**
  map 520
Architectural styles
  American Creole-style 350
  antebellum architecture 363

Architectural styles (cont.)
Art Deco 140, 292, 665
Beaux Arts 74, 75, 668
Byzantine 668
cast-iron 70
Chicago **388–9**
Contemporary/modern 669
Creole 350, 357
Egyptian 668
Federal-style 134, 352
see also Davenport House
French Colonial 346
French Empire 208
French Renaissance 392
Georgian 85
German-style 483
Gilded Age 156
Gothic 211, 692, 701
Gothic Revival 66, 77, **388**
Greek Revival-style 141, 346, 403
high-rise/modern 673, 698
International Style **389**
Italianate design **388**
Mediterranean 686
Mediterranean Revival 292, 688
Mission 686, 687, 708
Mission Revival 670
modern 403
modernist 699
Monterey Style 692
Moorish 669, 685
Native American 670
Neo-Classical 202, **389**, 696, 704
Ocean Drive: Deco Style, Miami **292–3**
Oriental Renaissance 700
palazzo-style 75
Post-Modern **389**
Prairie School 388, 395, 399, 415
Queen Anne **389**, 704, 705
Renaissance 85
Renaissance Revival 717
Richardsonian Romanesque **388**
Roman 668
Romanesque 708
Southwest Architecture **532–3**
Spanish Colonial 663, 672
Spanish Mission 669
Streamline Moderne 292, 669
Tropical Deco 292
Victorian 591, 621, 704, 705
Architecture in Chicago **388–9**
Arizona **528–43**
Canyon de Chelly National Monument **542–3**
Grand Canyon 536–9
Heart of Arizona Tour **529**
hotels 557–9
Monument Valley **540–41**
Phoenix **530–31**
restaurants 561–3
Southwest Architecture **532–3**
Wild West, the **541**
Arkansas 335, **358–9**
hotels 370
restaurants 374
Arlington National Cemetery (Washington, DC) **211**
Armand Hammer Museum of Art & Culture (Los Angeles) 662
Armstrong Redwoods State Preserve (CA) 713
Armstrong, Louis 346, 349
Armstrong, Neil 201
Arnaud's (New Orleans) 350
Art Institute of Chicago 390
Art museums & galleries
Albright-Knox Art Gallery (Buffalo, NY) 95
Albuquerque Museum of Art & History (NM) 549
American Visionary Art Museum (Baltimore, MD) 222
Armand Hammer Museum of Art (Los Angeles) 662
Art Institute of Chicago 390
Arthur M. Sackler Gallery (Washington, DC) 200
Asian Art Museum (San Francisco) 704
Baltimore Museum of Art (MD) 222
Bass Museum of Art (Miami) **293**
Birmingham Museum of Art (AL) 365
Blanton Museum of Art (Austin, TX) 482
Boca Raton Museum of Art (FL) 300
Brooklyn Museum of Art (NYC) 87
Carnegie Institute's Museum of Art (Pittsburgh, PA) 108
Cedar Rapids Museum of Art (IA) 453
Charles Hosmer Morse Museum of American Art (Orlando, FL) 312
Cincinnati Art Museum (OH) 404
Cleveland Museum of Art (OH) 406
Cornell Fine Arts Museum (Orlando, FL) 312
Currier Gallery of Art (Manchester, NH) 169
Dallas Museum of Art (TX) 478
Dayton Art Institute (OH) 404
Delaware Art Museum (Wilmington, DE) 226
Denver Art Museum (CO) 588
Des Moines Art Center (IA) 452
Detroit Institute of Arts (MI) 408
Farnsworth Art Museum (ME) 171
Fenimore Art Museum (Cooperstown, NY) 93
Figge Art Museum (IA) 453
Fogg Art Museum (Cambridge, MA) 148
Freer Gallery of Art (Washington, DC) 200
Hallie Ford Museum of Art (Salem, OR) 634
Henry Art Gallery (Seattle, WA) 619
Indiana University Art Center (Bloomington) 400
Indianapolis Museum of Art (IA) 402
J.B. Speed Art Museum (Louisville, KY) 271
Japanese American Art Museum (Los Angeles) 669
Joslyn Art Museum (Omaha, NE) 451
Art museums & galleries (cont.)
Los Angeles County Museum of Art 667
Lyndon House Arts Center (Athens, GA) 258
Maryhill Museum of Art (WA) 625
Metropolitan Museum of Art (NYC) 80–81
Milwaukee Art Museum (WI) 413
Minneapolis Institute of Arts (MN) 416
Museum of Contemporary Art (Los Angeles) **669**
Museum of Modern Art (NYC) **77**
Museum of Art & History at the McPherson Center (Los Angeles) 693
Museum of Contemporary Art (San Diego, CA) 678
Museum of Early Southern Decorative Arts (Winston-Salem, NC) 248
Museum of Fine Arts (Boston) 146–7
National Gallery of Art (Washington, DC) 201
National Museum of African Art (Washington, DC) 200
Nelson-Atkins Art Museum (Kansas City, MO) 457
New Orleans Museum of Art (LA) 353
North Carolina Museum of Art (Raleigh) 248
North Dakota Museum of Art (Grand Forks) 442
Northwest Museum of Arts & Culture (Spokane, WA) 625
Orlando Museum of Art (FL) 312
Philadelphia Museum of Art (PA) **105**
Plains Art Museum (Fargo, ND) 443
Portland Art Museum (OR) 630
Portland Museum of Art (ME) 170
RISD Museum of Art (Providence) 154
San Diego Museum of Art (CA) 681
Santa Monica Museum of Art (Los Angeles) 661
Seattle Art Museum (WA) 617
Spencer Museum of Art (Lawrence, KS) 458
St. Louis Art Museum (MO) 455
Stanford Museum of Art (San Francisco) 708
Tacoma Art Museum (WA) 628
Tampa Museum of Art (FL) 318
Terra Museum of American Art (Chicago) 389
Thomas Gilcrease Institute (Tulsa, OK) 460
Toledo Museum of Art (OH) 407
Ulrich Architecture & Design Gallery (Minneapolis, MN) 416
Virginia Museum of Fine Arts (Richmond) 216
Walker Art Center (Minneapolis, MN) 416
Walters Art Gallery (Baltimore, MD) 223

Art museums & galleries (cont.)
Ward Museum of Wildfowl Art (Salisbury, MD) 225
Wadsworth Atheneum (Hartford, CT) 158
Yellowstone Art Gallery (Billings, MT) 581
Arthur, Chester A. 52
Asheville (NC) **249**
Ashland (OR) **637**
Asian Art Museum (San Francisco) **704**
Asimov, Isaac 84
Aspen (CO) 594
Astoria (OR) **632**
Astronaut Hall of Fame (Titusville, FL) 303
Athens (GA) **258**
Atlanta (GA) 240, **260–61**
climate 272
Atlantic City (NJ) **96–7**
ATMs **14**
Atwood, Charles B. 394
Austin (TX) 473, **482**
Audubon Nature Institute (New Orleans, LA) **352**
Australian Embassy 17
Autry, Gene 671
Avalanche Creek (MT) 579
Avenue of the Giants (CA) 714

B

Babe Ruth 93
Babe the Blue Ox 419
Bacon, Henry 205
Badlands National Park (SD) 34, **444–5**
Balboa Park (San Diego, LA) **680–81**
Bald eagles 269, 315, 320, 415, 418, 574, 624, 736
Ballard (Seattle, WA) 619
Baltimore (MD) 189, **222–3**
Bancroft, Jr, Samuel 226
Bank notes 15
Banking **14–15**
Banner, Peter 139
Baraboo (WI) **414**
Baranov Museum (Kodiak Island, AK) 740
Bardstown (KY) **271**
Barker, Blue Lu 349
Barnes, Albert C. 105
Barnes Foundation (Philadelphia, PA) **105**
Barosaurus 83
Bartholdi, Frédéric-Auguste 67, 145
Bartlesville (OK) **460**
Baseball **93**
Bash Bish Falls (MA) 153
Bass Museum of Art (Miami) **293**
Baton Rouge (LA) **355**
Battery Park City (NYC) **67**
Battles
Battle Above the Clouds 263
Battle of Bloody Marsh 257
Battle of Bunker Hill 135, 149
Battle of Concord 150
Battle of Gettysburg 106
Battle of Fallen Timbers 407
Battle of Lake Erie 407
Battles (cont.)
Battle of Little Bighorn 443
Battle of New Orleans 347
Battle of Saratoga 61, 92
Blackhawk War 398
Battle of Bunker Hill (John Trumbull) 127
Battle of New Orleans, The (Dennis Malone Carter) 340
Bay Bridge (San Francisco) 698
Bayou Teche (LA) **356–7**
Beach Boys 693
Beaches of the Panhandle (FL) **316–17**
Beacon Hill (Boston) **134–5**
Bears 585
Bear's Lodge (WY) 586
Beaufort (NC) **251**
Bed-&-Breakfast Inns 18
Beer, *see* Breweries
Beinecke Rare Book & Manuscript Libraries (New Haven, CT) 160
Bell, Alexander Graham 140
Belle Meade Plantation (Nashville, TN) 265
Bellingham (WA) **621**
Belltown (Seattle, WA) 617
Bellow, Saul 129
Belushi, John 665
Beman, Solon S. 391
Bennington (VT) 162
Belvedere Castle (NYC) 79
Ben & Jerry's Ice Cream Factory (VT) **165**
Bend (OR) **635**
Bennett, H.H. 414
Bennington Museum & Grandma Moses Gallery (VT) 162
Benton, Thomas Hart 203, 400
Berea (KY) **268**
Bergamot Station (Los Angeles) 661
Berkeley (San Francisco) **709**
Berlin (OH) **405**
Berkshires (MA) **153**
Bernstein, Carl 209
Berry, Chuck 406
Best Scenic Routes 27, **40–41**
Blue Ridge Parkway 41
Columbia River Scenic Highway 40
Going-to-the-Sun Road 40
Great River Road 41
Natchez Trace Parkway 41
Pacific Coast Highway (Hwy-1) 40
Route (100) 41
Route (66) 40
Best time to visit 12
Bethel (ME) **173**
Bethesda Fountain (NYC) 78
Beverly Hills (Los Angeles) 663
Bezos, Jeff 613
Bicycles 24
Bierce, Ambrose 705
Big Bend National Park (TX) **490–91**
Big Cypress National Preserve (FL) 320
Big Cypress Swamp (FL) **320**
Big Hole National Battlefield (MT) **578**
Big Hole Valley (MT) 578
Big Sur (CA) 650, **690–91**
Big Thicket National Preserve (TX) **488**
Bighorn Mountains (WY) **586**
Billings (MT) 567, **581**
Billings Farm & Museum (Woodstock, VT) 163
Billy Bob's Texas Nightclub (Dallas) 481
Biltmore Hotel (Miami) **296**
Biltmore Estate (Asheville, NC) 249
Bird-watching 79, 173, 303, 315, 321, 400–401, 449, 633
Birmingham (AL) **365**
Bisbee (AZ) **533**
Biscayne Bay Boat Trips (FL) **294**
Biscayne National Park (FL) **322**
Bischoff, Elmer 655
Bismarck & Mandan (ND) **443**
Bison 585
mummified 741
Bitterroot Mountains (MT) 578
Bixby Creek Bridge (Big Sur, CA) 690
Black Bart 698
Black Canyon of the Gunnison National Park (CO) **597**
Black Heritage Trail (MA) **135**
Black Hills (SD) 434, **446–7**
"Black ivory" 350
Blanchard Springs Caverns (AR) 359
Block Island (RI) 124, **157**
Bloomington (IN) **400**
Blue Ridge Mountains (VA) 219
Blue Ridge Parkway 41, 188, **218**, 249
Bluegrass music 341
Blues music 336, 341, **361**
Boca Raton (FL) **300**
Bodmer, Karl 438, 451
Boise (ID) **575**
Boles, Charles 698
Boone, Daniel 268
Borglum, Gutzon 259, 447
Borrego Springs (CA) 683
Boston (MA) 123, **132–49**
Beacon Hill **134–5**
climate 174
hotels 176–8
Greater Boston **146-9**
map 132–3
Massachusetts State House **138–9**
restaurants 182
The Freedom Trail **136–7**
Trinity Church **144**
Boston Athenaeum 135
Boston Brahmins 129
Boston Common & Public Garden **135**
Boston Massacre 44
Boston Public Library 145
Boston Tea Party **128**, 140, 141, 143
Boulder (CO) **590**
Boulder City (Las Vegas) 514–15
Boundary Waters Canoe Area Wilderness (MN) **420**
Bourbon Street (New Orleans) **350**
Bourne, George 171
Box Canyon Historical Monument (CA) 683
Bozeman (MT) **581**
Brainerd Lakes Area (MN) **419**
Brancusi, Constantin 105
Brand, William 350
Brannan, Sam 700
Branson (MO) **456**

Breakers, The (Newport, RI) 156
Breckenridge (CO) 595
Bretton Woods (VT) **166**
Breweries 412–13
Brick Store Museum (The Kennebunks) 171
Bronx (NYC) **87**
Brooklyn (NYC) **87**
Brooklyn Botanic Gardens (NYC) 87
Brooklyn Bridge (NYC) **68**
Brooks, Mel 87
Brown University (Providence) 154
Brown, John 220, 221, 458
Brown, Margaret Tobin
see Brown, Molly
Brown, Molly 588
Brule, Etienne 382, 411
Brumidi, Constantino 198, 199
Bruneau Dunes State Park (ID) **576**
Bryce Canyon National Park (UT) **526–7**
Buchanan, James 52
Buckhorn Saloon & Museum (San Antonio) 485
Buddha, statue of 749
Buddy Guy 392
Buddy Holly **492**
Buffalo (NY) **94–5**
Buffalo Bill 438, 449, 451, 481, 590
Buffalo Bill Historical Center (Cody) 582
Buffalo Bill Ranch State Historical Park (North Platte) 449
Buffalo Gap Historical Village (Abilene) 493
Buffalo Gap National Grassland (Badlands NP) 445
Bulfinch, Charles 134, 135, 138
Bunker Hill Monument (Charlestown, Boston) 137, 149
Bunyan, Paul 419, 715
Buren, Martin Van 52
Burlington (VT) **164**
Burne-Jones 144
Burnham, Daniel 424
Burnham, David 72
Bus travel **25**
Alaska 756
California 720
Deep South 366
Hawai'i 757
Los Angeles 676
Rockies 598
San Francisco 710
Southeast 272
Southwest 554
Texas 494
Washington, DC & Capital Region 228
Busch-Reisinger Museum (Boston) 149
Bush, Barbara 53
Bush, George 53
Bush, George W. 53, 475
Business Travelers **18**
Butte (MT) **580**
Butterfield Trail (TX) 492
Byodo-In Temple (O'ahu, HI) **749**

C

Cable Cars (San Francisco) **700**
Cabrillo, Juan Rodríguez 678
Cadillac Mountain (ME) 172
Café du Monde (New Orleans) **347**
Cagney, James 84
Cahokia Mounds State Historic & World Heritage Site (IL) 399
Cajuns 341, 356, 357
Cajun Country
see Lafayette
Calamity Jane 446
Calder, Alexander 202
Calendar Islands (Portland, ME) 170
California **648–729**
17-Mile Drive (CA) **692**
Alcatraz Island **703**
Big Sur **690–91**
Cable Cars **700**
Central Coast **686–93**
climate 32
culture & the arts 655
Deserts, The **682–5**
directory 721
driving 720
earthquakes **699**
getting around 720
Gold Country **716–17**
Greater San Francisco **708–709**
Hearst Castle **688–9**
High Sierras **718–19**
history 653–4
hotels 722–5
Los Angeles **658–77**
map 656–7
mileage chart 657
natural hazards 720
Northern California **714–15**
outdoor activities 720–21
personal security 720
restaurants 726–9
San Diego County **678–81**
San Francisco **694–711**
San Francisco's Murals **702**
shopping 721
society & politics 654–5
Sunset Boulevard **664–5**
surfing 693
vineyards 712–13
Wine Country **712–13**
California Academy of Sciences (San Francisco) **706**
California State Capitol (Sacramento) 650, 717
California State Railroad Museum (Sacramento) 717
California Wines **713**
California's Earthquakes **699**
Cambridge (Boston, MA) **148–9**
Camden (Penobscot Bay, ME) 171
Camp Verde (AZ) 529
Campgrounds **19**
Campobello Island (ME) **173**
Canadian Embassy 17
Canaveral National Seashore (FL) 303
Canaveral National Seashore & Merritt Island (FL) **303**
Cañon City (CO) **593**
Cansino, Margarita 664
Canterbury Shaker Village (NH) 124, **168**
Canton (OH) 406
Canyon (TX) **492–3**
Canyon de Chelly National Monument (AZ) **542–3**
Canyonlands National Park (UT) **522**
Cape Cod (MA) 125, **152**
Cape Hatteras Lighthouse (Outer Banks, NC) 250
Cape Hatteras National Seashore (Outer Banks, NC) 250
Cape May (NJ) **97**
Capital Reef National Park (UT) **524**
Capitol Hill (Seattle, WA) 618
Capone, Al 104, 294, 296, 703
Car rental agencies, directory 23
Car travel **22–3**
Boston & New England 174
California 720
Florida 324
Great Lakes 422
Great Plains 462
Los Angeles 676
NYC & the Mid-Atlantic Region 110
Rockies 598
San Francisco 710
Southeast 272
Southwest 554
Texas 494
Washington, DC & Capital Region 228
Caribou 35
Carlsbad Caverns National Park (NM) **552**
Carlyle House (Alexandria, VA) 212
Carmel (CA) **692**
Carmel Mission
Carnegie, Andrew 108
Carson City (NV) **516**
Carson, Kit 542, 544
Carson, William 714
Carter, Jimmy 53, 244, 258
Carter, Rosalynn 53, 203
Cartier (NYC) 77
Carver, George Washington 365
Cascade Mountains (WA) 624, 632, 715
Casinos 96, 97, **510–15**
first 512
Casper (WY) **586**
Cassatt, Mary 103
Cassidy, Butch 480, 586, 587
Castro, Fidel 295
Cathedral of St. John the Baptist (Lafayette, LA) 356
Cathedral of St. John the Divine (NYC) 84
Catlett, Elizabeth 85
Catlin, George 418
Cattle drives 475, 480
Cave of the Winds (Manitou Springs, CO) 592
Cedar City (UT) **524**
Cedar Point Amusement Park (Sandusky, OH) 407
Cedar Rapids (IA) **453**
Celestin, Oscar "Papa" 349
Centennial Olympic Park (Atlanta, GA) 260

Central Coast (CA) **686–93**
  Big Sur **690–91**
  Hearst Castle **688–9**
  hotels 723
  restaurants 727–8
  Hearst, William Randolph 686, **689**
  Mission Architecture 687
  Surfing in California 686, **693**
  17-Mile Drive 686, **692**
Central Park (NYC) **78–9**
Central Park West (NYC) 83
Centro Cultural Tijuana (Mexico) 679
Cézanne, Paul 82, 105, 391
Chaco Culture National Historical Park (NM) **544**
Chadron (NE) **448**
Chamizal National Memorial (El Paso) 491
Chandler, Dorothy 668
Chandler, Joel 354
Chandler, Raymond 661
Channel Islands National Park (CA) **686–7**
Chaplin, Charlie 665, 666
Charles Street (Boston) 134
Charles Street Meeting House (Boston) 134
Charleston (SC) **252–3**
Charlestown (Boston, MA) **149**
Charlottesville (VA) **217**
Chatham (Cape Cod) 152
Chattanooga (TN) **263**
Chattanooga & Chickamauga National Military Park (TN) 263
Chautauqua (NY) **94**
Cherokee 249, 263, 340, 364, 438, 460
  Heritage Center 461
  museum 461
  Trail of Tears 263, 438, 461
Cherokee Heritage Center (Tahlequah) 460
Cheyenne (WY) **587**
Chicago (IL) **386–97**
  Architecture in Chicago 377, **388–9**
  climate 422
  From Plaster to Stone (Museum of Science & Industry) **394**
  getting around 386
  Greater Chicago **396-397**
  hotels 424
  map 386–7
  Old money **393**
  restaurants 428
  The Loop **390–91**
Chicago Children's Museum **389**
Chicago History Museum **388**
Chicago Public Library, Harold Washington Library Center 392
Chicago theater 387
Chicago Tribune 389
Chief Blackhawk 398
Chief Sitting Bull 581
Chihuly, Dale 613, 628
Children's Museum of Maine (Portland) 170
Children's Museum of New Hampshire 169
Chimney Rock (Scottsbluff, NE) 450
Chinatown (San Francisco) **700**
Chinatown (Boston) **139**
Chincoteague (VA) **217**
Chinese immigrants 139, 631, 715, 716
Chinese Historical Society (San Francisco) 700
Chisholm Trail 480
Chopin, Kate 357
Christ Church (Boston) 148
Christ Episcopal Church
  see Old North Church
Christ of the Ozarks (Eureka Springs, AR) 359
Chrysler Building (NYC) 75
Church of the Covenant (Boston) 145
Churchill Weavers 268
Churchill, Winston 166, 209
Cincinnati (OH) **404**
Ciro's (Los Angeles) 664
City Hall (NYC) 69
City Park (New Orleans) **353**
Civic Center (NYC) **69**
Civil Rights Movement 51, 255, 364, 662
Civil War **46–7**, 91, 138, 192–3, 218, 222, 268, 361
Clear Creek History Park (Golden) 590
Cleaveland, Moses 406
Cleopatra (Romanelli) 314
Cleveland (OH) **406**
Cleveland, Grover 52, 53, 67
Climate **12**, **32–3**
  Alaska 756
  Anchorage 756
  Atlanta 272
  Boston 174
  Chicago 422
  Dallas 494
  Deep South 366
  Denver 598
  Florida 324
  Great Lakes 422
  Great Plains 462
  Hawai'i 757
  Honolulu 757
  Kansas City 462
  Las Vegas 554
  Los Angeles 720
  Miami 324
  Mid-Atlantic Region 110
  New England 174
  New Orleans 366
  New York City 110
  Pacific Northwest 642
  Rockies 598
  Seattle 642
  Southeast 272
  Southwest 554
  Texas 494
  Washington, DC 228
Clingman's Dome (Great Smoky Mountains NP) 247
Clinton, Bill 53, 336, 358, 359, 678
  William J. Clinton Presidential Center (Little Rock, AR) 358
Clinton, Hillary 53
Cloisters, the (NYC) 8, **86**
Cloud Peak (Bighorn Mountains, WY) 586
CNN Studio (Atlanta, GA) 260
Coastal Islands (SC) **255**
Cobb, Henry Ives 388, 395
Coca-Cola 240, 260
Cocoa Beach (FL) **302**
Coconut Grove Village (Miami) **297**
Cody (WY) **582**
  Cody Night Rodeo
Cody, William Frederick
  see Buffalo Bill
Coeur d'Alene (ID) 566, **574**
Coffee 347
Cohen, Ben 165
Cohen, Harry 664
Coins **15**
Coit Tower (San Francisco) **697**, 702
Cole, Nat King 365, 665
Cold War 50
College of Physicians of Philadelphia/ Mutter Museum (PA) **104**
Collins, Michael 201
Colonial National Historical Park (Yorktown) 216
Colonial Theater (Boston) 139
Colonoial Williamsburg (VA) 214–15
Colorado 565, 588–97
  Colorado Ski Resorts **594–5**
  hotels 603
  restaurants 606–607
  Whitewater Rafting in Colorado **593**
Colorado National Monument **597**
Colorado Plateau 536
Colorado River 536
Colorado Ski Resorts **594–5**
Colorado Springs (TX) **592**
Colter, Mary E.J. 538
Columbia (SC) **254**
Columbia River Gorge (OR) **632**
Columbia State Historic Park (CA) **717**
Columbia University (NYC) **84**
Columbus (IN) **403**
Columbus (OH) **405**
Commonwealth Avenue (Boston) **145**
Communications **14–15**
  ATMs 14
  banking 14
  financial services directory 14
  foreign exchange 15
  postal services 14
  telephones 14
  traveler's checks 15
Concord (MA) **150–1**
Concord (NH) **168**
Coney Island (NYC) 87
Congaree Swamp National Park (SC) 254
Connecticut 124, **158–161**
  hotels 179
  restaurants 184
Connecticut Coast 161
Connecticut River Valley **159**
Connick, Charles 701
Conrad, Paul 660
Constitution, USS (Charlestown, MA) 137, 149
Conversion chart **13**
Cook, Captain James 612, 745
Coolidge, Calvin 53, 464
Cooper, Gary 672

Cooperstown (NY) **93**
Copley Square (Boston) **145**
Copley, John Singleton 145, 147, 149
Copp's Hill Burying Ground (Boston) **142**
Coral Gables (Miami) **296**
Coral Reef (FL) **323**
Corbin (KY) 269
Corcoran Gallery of Art (Washington, DC) **208**
Corcoran, William Wilson 208
Corn Palace (Mitchell, SD) 444
Cornwell, Dean 140
Coronation of the Virgin (Domenico Ghirlandaio) 293
Corot, Jean-Baptist Camille 208
Corpus Christi (TX) **489**
Cosby, Bill 235
Costner, Kevin 468
Cotton Bowl 479
Cotton Trail (FL) 316
Country & Bluegrass Music (KY) **269**
Country Music Hall of Fame & Museum (Nashville, TN) 264
Country Music Highway (KY) 268, 269
Coward, Noël 83
Cowboys (TX) 459, 639, **481**
Cracker farmers 286
Cradle of Liberty (Boston) 136
Craggy Bass Harbor Head (Acadia NP, ME) 127
Craters of the Moon National Monument (ID) **577**
Crater Lake National Park (OR) **636–7**
Crater Lake
Crazy Horse, Oglala Sioux chief 446, 448
Creation, The (Frederick Hart) 210, 211
Credit cards **14**
Cripple Creek (CO) **593**
Crisfield (MD) **225**
Crosby, Bing 392, 672
Crow Indian Reservation (MT) 581
Cubans 295
Cumberland Falls State Resort Park (KY) 269
Cumberland Gap National Historic Park (KY) **268**
cummings, e e 71
Currency **15**
Currier Gallery of Art (Manchester, NH) 168
Curtis, Tony 678
Custom House (New Orleans) **352**
Customs **12–13**
see also Passports & visas
Custer, Colonel George Armstrong 446
Cypresses (Van Gogh) 81

D

Daguerre, Louis-Jacques-Mande 660
Dahlonega (GA) **259**
Dairy, the (NYC) 78
Dakota Sioux Indians 418
Dali, Salvador 318
Dallas (TX) 38, 473, **478–9**
climate 494
Daniel Boone National Forest (KY) **269**
Davenport House (Savannah, GA) 256
Davidson, Arthur 107
Davies, Marion 688
Davis, Jefferson 259, 364
Davis, Miles 704
Davis Mountains (TX) 491
Dayton (OH) **404**
Daytona Beach (FL) **314**
deMille, Cecil B. 666
de Niro, Robert 70
de Young Museum (San Francisco) **706**
Deacon John Grave House (CT) 161
Dead, Grateful 704
Deadwood Stage 587
Death Valley National Park (CA) 34, 651, **684–5**
Death Valley Scotty **685**
Declaration of Independence 39, 98, 100, 101, **139**, 141
handwritten copy 74
Dee Wright Observatory (OR) 635
Deep South **334–75**
Alabama 335, **364–5**
Arkansas 335, **358–9**
climate 366
culture & arts 341
directory 367
entertainment 367
etiquette 366
festivals 367–¶
getting around 366
history 339–41
hotels **368–71**
Louisiana 335, **354–57**
maps 336–7, 342–3
Mardi Gras **353**
mileage chart 343
Mississippi 335, **360–63**
natural hazards 366
New Orleans 335, **344–53**
New Orleans Ironwork **347**
New Orleans Jazz **349**
people & the economy 341
restaurants **372–5**
sports & outdoors 367
Voodoo Worship **348**
Deering, James 297
Degas 223
Delaware 187, **226–7**
hotels 233
restaurants 237
Delgado, Isaac 353
Denali National Park (AK) 35, **742–3**
Denver (CO) 567, **588–9**
climate 598
Depp, Johnny 664
Des Moines (IA) 435, **452**
Deserts
flora & fauna 683
Painted Desert (AZ) 534
springs 684
wildlife 684, 685
Deserts, The (CA) **682–5**
Death Valley National Park 682, **684–5**
hotels 723
restaurants 727
Destin (FL) 317
Detroit (MI) 379, **408–409**
Devils Lake (ND) **442**
Devil's Tower National Monument (WY) **586**
Diebenkorn, Richard 103
Disabled Travelers **13**, 19
Discovery Cove (FL) 311
Disney Wilderness Preserve (Orlando, Florida) 313
Disneyland Resort (Los Angeles) **674–5**
Disney's California Adventure 675
Disneyland Park 674
Downtown Disney 675
shopping 675
tickets & tips 674
D.L. Bliss State Park (CA) 718
Doc Holliday 446
Doc Rickett 692
Dodge City (KS) **459**
Dodger Stadium (Los Angeles) 677
Dog mushers 741
Domestic airlines **21**
Door County (WI) **413**
Downtown Atlanta, map (GA) 261
Downtown Charleston, map (SC) 253
Downtown Crossing (Boston) **139**
Downtown Dallas, map (TX) 479
Downtown Denver, map (CO) 589
Downtown Detroit, map (MI) 409
Downtown Memphis, map (TN) 267
Downtown (Miami) **294–5**
Downtown Minneapolis & St. Paul, map (MN) 416
Downtown Nashville, map (TN) 265
Downtown Seattle, map (WA) 617
Doyle, Sir Arthur Conan 704
Drake, Sir Francis 612
du Pont, Alfred I. 227
du Pont, Eleuthere 226
du Pont, Henry 226
Dubuque (IA) **453**
Duke Ellington 49, 365
Duluth (MN) **419**
Dumbarton Oaks Conference 209
Dunaway, Faye 663
Duncan, Isadora 83
Durango (CO) **596**
Durango & Silverton Narrow Gauge Railroad 596
DuSable Museum of African American History (Chicago) **395**
Dyersville Giant 714
Dylan, Bob 70

E

Eagle Bluff Lighthouse (WI) 413
Earhart, Amelia 201
Early feminists 93
Earp, Wyatt 446, 459, 533, 736
Earthquakes (CA) 693, **699**
Eastwood, Clint 481
East Village (NYC) **71**
Easter 28
Eastern Sierras (CA) **719**
Eastern State Penitentiary (Philadelphia) **104**
Eastern States Buddhist Temple (NYC) 69

Easton (MD) **224–5**
Edison, Thomas Alva 320
Einstein, Albert 96
Eisenhower, Dwight D. 53, 91
Eiteljorg, Harrison 403
Eiteljorg Museum of American Indian & Western Art (Indianapolis, IN) 402–403
El Pais Grande del Sur
  see Big Sur
El Paso (TX) **491**
El Pueblo (Los Angeles) **669**
Eldridge Street Synagogue (NYC) **69**
Eleutherian Mills/Hagley Museum (DE) **226**
Eliot, T.S. 74
Ellis Island (NYC) **67**
Elks 583
Ely, Joe 492
Emancipation Proclamation 222
Embarcadero Center (San Francisco) 698
Embassies 17
Emergency services 17
Emerson, Ralph Waldo 150
Empire Arts Center (Grand Forks, ND) 442
Empire State Building (NYC) **73**
Engine, Cummins 403
Entertainment
  Boston & New England 175
  Deep South 367
  Florida 325
  Great Lakes 423
  Great Plains 463
  Hawai'i 757
  Los Angeles 676
  New York City 88–9
  NYC & the Mid-Atlantic Region 111
  Pacific Northwest 642
  Rockies 599
  San Francisco 710
  Southeast 273
  Southwest 555
  Texas 495
  Washington, DC & Capital Region 228–9
Erie Canal (NY) 61, 92
Erie Canal Museum (Syracuse, NY) 94
Estefan, Gloria 294, 295
Ethnic minorities 61, 69, 346, 716
Etiquette
  Deep South 366
  Florida 324
  Great Lakes 422
  Great Plains 462
  Pacific Northwest 643
  Rockies 598
  Southeast 272
  Southwest 554
  Washington, DC & Capital Region 228
Eugene (OR) **634**
Eureka (CA) **714**
Eureka Springs (AR) **359**
Everglades & the Keys (FL) **320–23**
  Florida's Coral Reef **323**
  hotels **329**
  restaurants **333**
Everglades National Park (FL) 35, **321**
Exit Glacier (AK) 739
Experience Music Project (Seattle, WA) 618
Exposition Park & University of Southern California (Los Angeles) **668**
Exxon Valdez 738

F

Fabergé, Peter Carl 216, 223
Fairbanks (AK) **741**
Fairbanks, Douglas Sr. 663, 666, 667
Fairchild Tropical Garden (Miami) **299**
Fairmount Park (PA) **104–105**
Fair Park (Dallas, TX) 479
Fall Foliage in New England **166**
Famous inmates of Alcatraz 703
Fargo (ND) **443**
Farmers Market (Los Angeles) **667**
F.A.O. Schwarz (NYC) 77
Ferlinghetti, Lawrence 702
Faulkner, William 341, 360
Fermi, Enrico 395
Fernandina Beach (FL) **315**
Ferry to Algiers & Mardi Gras World (New Orleans) **352**
Festivals **28–31**
  Alaska 756
  Deep South 366–7
  Great Lakes 423
  Great Plains 462
  Hawai'i 757
  NYC & the Mid-Atlantic Region 110
  Rockies 598–9
  Southeast 272–3
  Texas 494
Field, Sabra 129
Fifth Avenue (NYC) 77
Figge Art Museum (IA) 453
Financial District (San Francisco) **698**
Financial services **14**
Finger Lakes (NY) **93**
Firehole Lake Drive (Yellowstone NP) 569
First Baptist Church (Boston) 145
First Baptist Church in America (Providence, RI) 154
First Church of Christ (New Haven, CT) 160
First Congregational Church (Bennington, VT) 162
First Lady, the **53**, 203
First Unitarian Church (Burlington, VA) 164
First Unitarian Church (Providence, RI) 154
Fisher, Carl 402
Fisher, Mel 323
Fisherman's Wharf (San Francisco) **702**
Fishing in the Florida Keys **322**
Fitzgerald, F. Scott 365, 383, 665
Fitzgerald, Zelda 365
Flagler Museum (Palm Beach, FL) 301
Flagler, Henry 286, 301, 322
Flagstaff (AZ) **528**
Flathead Valley (MT) **578**
Flatiron Building (NYC) **72**
Flint Hills (KS) **458–9**
Flood, James C. 701
Flora of the Great Smoky Mountains (TN) **262**
Florence Griswold Museum (Old Lyme, CT) 159
Florida **282–333**
  climate 33, 324
  culture 286–7
  directory 325
  driving 324
  economics & tourism 287
  entertainment 325
  etiquette 324
  Everglades & the Keys 283, **320–23**
  Florida's Coral Reef **323**
  Gold & Treasure Coasts 283, **300–301**
  Gulf Coast 283, **318–19**
  health 324
  history 285–6
  hotels 326–9
  map 288–9
  Miami 283, **290–99**
  mileage chart 288
  natural hazards 324
  Northeast 283, **314–15**
  Orlando & the Space Coast 283, **302–313**
  outdoor activities 325
  Panhandle 283, **316–17**
  restaurants 330–33
  SeaWorld & Discovery Coast **310–11**
  security 324
  shopping 325
  society 286–7
  Universal Orlando **308–309**
  Walt Disney World® Resort **304–307**
Florida's Coral Reef **323**
Flynn, Errol 665, 666
Fogg Art Museum (Cambridge, MA) 148
Ford, Gerald R. 53, 209, 410
Ford, Henry 320, 382, 408
Ford, Justina 589
Foreign exchange 15
Fort Abraham Lincoln State Park (Mandan) 443
Fort Adams State Park (Newport) 157
Fort Conde (Mobile) 364
Fort Davis (TX) **491**
Fort George (ME) 171
Fort Knox (KY) 271
Fort Larned National Historic Site (Dodge City) 459
Fort Lauderdale (FL) **300**
Fort Mackinac (Mackinac Island, MI) 411
Fort Massachusetts (MS) 363
Fort Myers (FL) 320
Fort Robinson State Park (NE) 448
Fort Ross State Historic Park (CA) **713**
Fort Totten State Historic Site (ND) 442
Fort Vancouver (WA) **629**
Fort Walton Beach (FL) 317
Fort Wayne (IN) **401**
  Fort Wayne Children's Zoo (IN) 401
Fort Worth (TX) 473, **480–81**

Fortune Cookie Factory (San Francisco) 700
Fossils, prehistoric 638–9
Foster, Stephen 271
Founding Fathers 192
see also Pilgrims
Foxhunt, The (Winslow Homer) 103
Franconia Notch (VT) **166**
Franklin D. Roosevelt Memorial (Washington, DC) **205**
Franklin, Benjamin 60, 100, 101
Franklin Park Conservatory & Botanical Garden (Columbus) 405
Frederick (MD) **222**
Fredericksburg (VA) **213**
Fredericksburg (TX) **482–3**
Frederik Meijer Gardens and Sculpture Park (MI) 410
Freedom Trail (Boston) **136–7**
Freeman, Morgan 375
Fremont (Seattle, WA) 618
Frémont, John 707
French, Daniel Chester 205
French Market (New Orleans) **346**
Freeth, George 693
Frick Collection (NYC) **80**
Frick, Henry Clay 80
Frost, Charles S. 389
Frost, Robert 162, 167, 323
Fuente, Larry 208
Full Gospel Tabernacle Church (Memphis, TN) 267
Furnace Creek (CA) 684

G

Gable, Clark 665, 666, 667
Galena (IL) **398**
Gallagher, Percival 402
Galveston (TX) **488**
Gandhi Monument (San Francisco) 698
Garbo, Greta 665
Garden District (New Orleans) **353**
Garden Island (Kaua'i, HI) **754–5**
Garden of the Gods (Colorado Springs) 592
Garfield, James A. 52
Garland, Hamlin 383
Garland, Judy 664
Garrison, William Lloyd 139
Gaslamp Quarter (San Diego, CA) 678
Gates, Bill 613, 628
Gateway Arch (St. Louis, MO) 435, 454
Gauguin, Paul 82, 402
Gaye, Marvin 409
Gay 70–71, 293, 323, 350
Gehry, Frank 407, 668, 669
General Benjamin "Beast" Butler 347
General Sherman's Tree (CA) 719
General Tilghman 343
George Washington (Gilbert Stuart) 203
George Washington Carver Museum (Tuskegee, AL) 365
Georgetown (Washington, DC) **209**
Georgetown (SC) **254–5**
Georgia 239, **256–61**
hotels 275–6
restaurants 279–80
Geronimo 506
The Getty Center (Los Angeles) **660**
Getty, J. Paul 660
Gettysburg (PA) **106**
Gettysburg National Military Park (PA) 106
Geysers 584–5
Ghirlandaio, Domenico 293
Giant Dipper Roller Coaster (Santa Cruz, CA) 693
Giannini, A.P. 698
Gila Cliff Dwellings National Monument (NM) **553**
Gilbert, Cass 72, 199, 417
Gilded Ghetto (San Francisco) 700
Gillette Castle (CT) 159
Girard, Alexander 403
Glacial Grooves (OH) 407
Glacier Bay National Park (AK) **737**
Glacier National Park (MT) **579**
Glaciers
Aialik Glacier (AK) 733, 735
Columbia Glacier (AK) 738
Emmons Glacier (WA) 627
Exit Glacier (AK) 739
Mendenhall Glacier (AK) 737
Nisqually Glacier (WA) 626
Portage Glacier (AK) 738
Glenn, John 701
Gold 590, 684, 700
mines 683, 715, 716–17
prospectors 741
Gold Country **716–17**
hotels 725
restaurants 729
Gold Rush 616, 653, 654, 682, 692, 698, 700, 716–17
see also Gold
Golden (CO) **590**
Golden Gate Bridge (San Francisco) 650, **707**
Golden Isles (GA) **257**
Gold & Treasure Coast (FL) **300–301**
hotels 327
restaurants 331
Golden Triangle (Los Angeles) **663**
Goodnight, Charles 492–3
Gordon, Ruth 393
Gordy Jr, Berry 409
Gortner, Mollie Kathleen 593
Grace Cathedral (San Francisco) **697**, 701
Graceland (Memphis, TN) 267
Graham, Bill 704
Graham, Bruce 389, 391
Grand Canyon (AZ) 502, **536–9**, 585
Grand Canyon National Park (AZ) 34, **538–9**
Grand Canyon of Texas 493
Grand Central Market (LA) **669**
Grand Central Terminal (NYC) **75**
Grand Forks (ND) **442**
Grand Hotel (MI) 411
Grand Loop Road (WY) 584
Grand Ole Opry House (Nashville) 265
Grand Prismatic Spring (Yellowstone NP) 584
Grand Rapids (MI) **410**
Grand Staircase-Escalante National Monument (UT) **524**
Grand Teton Mountains 577
Grand Teton National Park (WY) 34, **583**
Granite Mountain Mine Memorial (Butte) 580
"Grandma" Moses, Anna Mary 162
Grant, Cary 660
Grant, Ulysses S. 52, 91, 398
Grass Valley (CA) **716**
Grauman, Sid 666
Grayton (FL) 317
Great American Cities 27, **38–9**
Boston 132–49
Chicago 386–97
Dallas 478–9
Los Angeles 658–77
Miami 290–99
New Orleans 344–53
New York 64–89
Philadelphia 98–105
San Francisco 694–711
Seattle 616–9
Washington, DC 196–211
Great Basin National Park (NV) **517**
Great Depression 49, 150, 667
Great Falls (MT) **580**
Great Fire of 1871 (Chicago) 388
Great Lakes **376–431**
climate 33, 422
Chicago 377, **386–97**
culture 383
Detroit 408–409
directory 423
distance chart 385
entertainment 423
etiquette 422
festivals 422
getting around 422
history 381–2
hotels 424–7
Illinois 377, **386–99**
immigrants 382–3
Indiana 377, **400–403**
industry 382–3
maps 378–9, 384–5
Michigan 377, **408–411**
Minneapolis & St. Paul 416–17
Minnesota 377, **416–21**
natural hazards 422
Ohio 377, **404–407**
outdoor activities 422–3
politics 383
restaurants 428–31
shopping 423
sports 423
The Loop **390–91**
Wisconsin 377, **412–15**
Great Plains **432–71**
Black Hills **446–7**
climate 33, 439, 462
culture 439
directory 463
distance chart 441
driving 462
entertainment 463
etiquette 462
festivals 463
geology 439
getting around 462

Great Plains (cont.)
history 437–9
hotels 464–7
Iowa 433, **452–3**
Kansas 433, **458–9**
map 434–5, 440–41
Missouri 433, **454–7**
natural hazards 462
Nebraska 433, **448–51**
North Dakota 433, **442–3**
Oregon Trail **450**
outdoor activities 463
people 439
restaurants 468–71
shopping 463
sports 462–3
South Dakota 433, **444–7**
St. Louis 454–5
The Oregon Trail 450
Great Lakes Aquarium & Freshwater Discovery Center (Duluth, MN) 419
Great River Bluffs State Park (MN) 418
Great Salt Lake (UT) **518**
Great Sand Dunes National Monument & Preserve (CO) **596**
Great Smoky Mountains National Park (TN) 35, 247, **262**
Green Mountain National Forest (VT) **162**
Green, Hetty 717
Green River (UT) **523**
Greenfield, Jerry 165
Greenwich (CT) 161
Greenwich Village (NYC) **70–71**
Griffith, Colonel Griffith J. 670
Griffith Observatory (Los Angeles) 671
Griffith Park (Los Angeles) **670–71**
Grima, Judge Felix 350
Groening, Matt 613
Grunsfeld, Ernest 393
Guadalupe Mountains National Park (TX) **492**
Gucci (Los Angeles) 663
Guernsey (WY) **587**
Guggenheim SoHo (NYC) 82
Guggenheim, Solomon 82
Gulf Coast (MS) **363**
Gulf Coast (FL) **318–19**
climate 33
hotels 329
restaurants 333
Gulf of Alaska (AK) 735
Guy, Buddy 392

H

Haas, William 704
Habitat for Humanity (GA) 258
Hagley Museum/Eleutherian Mills (DE) **226**
Haight Ashbury (San Francisco) 704, **705**
Haleakalā National Park (Maui, HI) **751**
Haleakalā Silversword
Hallidie, Andrew 700
Hamill House Museum (CO) 591
Hammer, Armand 662
Hammonasset Beach State Park (CT) 161
Hampton, James 203
Hamptons & Montauk (NY) **90**
Hāna (HI) **751**
Hancock, John 136, 139
Handy, W.C. 361, 365
Haraszthy, Count Agoston 712
Harding, Warren 53
Harlem (NYC) 85
Harley, William 107
Harley-Davidson (PA) **107**
Harlow, Jean 665
Harper, Robert 221
Harpers Ferry (WV) **221**
Harpist, The (Florence Griswold Museum, CT) 159
Harris, Joel Chandler 354
Harrison, Benjamin 52
Harrison, Peter 148
Harrodsburg (KY) **270**
Hart, Thomas 479
Hartford (CT) **158–9**
Harvard Museum of Natural History (Cambridge, MA) 149
Harvard University (Cambridge, MA) 148
Hastings 74
Hawai'i 731, **744–63**
climate 32, 757
directory 757
entertainment 757
festivals 757
getting around 757
Hawai'i Island 752–3
Hawai'i Volcanoes NP 752–3
history 744
hotels 760–61
Kaua'i 754–5
map 746–7
Maui 750
Moloka'i 751
monarchy 748
natural hazards 757
O'ahu 748–9
outdoor activities 757
Professor Jaggar 753
restaurants 763
royal palace 748
today 745
Hawai'i Maritime Center (O'ahu, HI) 748
Hawai'i's Plantation Village (O'ahu, HI) **749**
Hawai'i Volcanoes National Park (Hawai'i, HI) **752–3**
Professor Jaggar 753
Hawthorne, Nathaniel 140
Hayes, Rutherford B. 52
Haystack Rock (OR) 633
Hayworth, Rita 664, 667
Health & Security **16–17**
directory 17
insurance 17
medical 17
police 17
safety 16
Heap of Birds, Cheyenne artist 392
Hearst Castle (CA) **688–9**
Hearst, William Randolph 298, **688**, 691
Helena (MT) **580**
Hells Canyon National Recreation Area Tour (OR) **640–41**
Hells Canyon National Recreation Area (ID) **574**
Hell's Half Acre (WY) 586
Hemingway House (Key West, FL) 323
Hemingway, Ernest 323, **397**, 666
Hendrix, Jimi 613, 704
Hennepin, Louis 95
Hepzibah Swan Houses (Boston) 135
Herald Square (NYC) **73**
Herbert Hoover National Historic Site (IA) 453
Heritage Museums & Gardens (Sandwich, MA) 152
Hermann-Grima Historic House (New Orleans, LA) **350**
Hershey (PA) **106–107**
Hewlett, William 708
Hickock, Wild Bill 446
Hermitage (Nashville, TN) 265
High Sierras **718–19**
hotels 725
restaurants 729
Highway (49) **717**
Hill, Abram 85
Hillbillies 341
Hilo (Hawai'i, HI) **753**
Hippies 71, 297, 705, 709
Hispanics 287, 551, 612, 613, 709
Historic railroads 25
History of the USA **42–53**
American Presidents 52–3
American Revolution 44
Birth of a Nation 45
Boom & Bust 49
Civil Rights Movement 51
Civil War 46–7, 192–3
Cold War 50
Competing Colonies 43
Destruction of the Indians 46
Early European Explorers 43
Great Depression & the New Deal 49
Immigration, Urbanization, & Industrialization 48–9
Independence 192–3
Manifest Destiny 45
Modern Era 51
Postwar Prosperity 50–51
Territorial Conflict 46
Wild West 48
Ho'okipa Beach County Park (Maui, HI) 746
Hoban, James 206
Hobart, Lewis P. 701
Hockney, David 655
Hodgenville (KY) **270–71**
Hoffman, Dustin 83
Hoh Rainforest (WA) 620
Hohauser, Henry 292
Hohokam 506
Holabird, William 390

Holley, Charles Hardin,
see Buddy Holly
Hollywood (Los Angeles) 671
behind-the-scenes 671
rise of 666
sign 671
Studio Tour 671
Hollywood Actors' Homes (Los Angeles) 663
Hollywood Boulevard (Los Angeles) **666**
Hollywood Sign (Los Angeles) **671**
Hollywood Bowl (Los Angeles) **666–7**
Holocaust Memorial (FL) **293**
Holocaust, survivors of the memorial
Homer (AK) **739**
Homer, Winslow 226, 402
Honolulu (O'ahu, HI) **748–9**
climate 757
Honomanū Bay (HI) 747
Hoodoos (Bryce Canyon NP, UT) 526
Hoover Dam (Las Vegas, NV) 514
Hoover, Herbert 53, 219, 453, 514
Hope Diamond 202
Hopewell Culture National Historic Park (OH) **405**
Hopi Indians 502
handicrafts
Reservation **534–5**
Hopi Indian Reservation (AZ) **534–5**
Hopkins, Stephen 151, 154
Hopper, Edward 81, 402, 405, 416
Hostels **18**
Hot Springs National Park (AR) **358–9**
Hot Springs 336, 358–9, 584–5
Hotels & Resorts **18**
Alabama 371
Alaska 758–9
Arizona 557–9
Arkansas 370
Boston 176–8
California 722–5
Central Coast (CA) 723
Central Valley (CA) 725
Chicago 424
Colorado 603
Connecticut 179
Deep South 368–71
Delaware 233
Deserts, The (CA) 723
Everglades & the Keys (FL) 329
Florida 326–9
Georgia 275–6
Gold Country (CA) 725
Gold & Treasure Coasts (FL) 327
Great Lakes 424–7
Great Plains 464–7
Gulf Coast (FL) 329
Hawai'i 760–61
High Sierras (CA) 725
Idaho 600
Illinois 424
Indiana 425
Iowa 465–6
Kansas 466–7
Kentucky 277
Los Angeles (CA) 722
Louisiana 368–9
Hotels & Resorts (cont.)
Maryland 232
Massachusetts 178
Miami (FL) 326
Michigan 425–6
Minnesota 426
Mississipi 370–71
Missouri 466
Montana 601
Nebraska 465
Nevada 556
New England 176–81
New Jersey 116
New Mexico 559
New York City (NY) 112–15
NY & the Mid-Atlantic Region 112–17
New York State 115–16
North California 725
North Carolina 274
North Dakota 464
Northeast Florida 328
Ohio 426–7
Oklahoma 467
Oregon 645
Orlando & the Space Coast (FL) 327–8
Pacific Northwest 644–5
Panhandle (FL) 328–9
Pennsylvania 117
Rhode Island 179
Rockies 600–603
San Diego County (CA) 722–3
San Francisco (CA) 724
South Carolina 275
South Dakota 464–5
Southeast 274–7
Southwest 556–9
Tennessee 276–7
Texas 496–7
Utah 557
Vermont 180
Virginia 232–3
Washington 644–5
Washington, DC 230–31
Washington, DC & Capital Region 230–33
West Virginia 233
Wine Country (CA) 724
Wisconsin 427
Wyoming 602
House on the Rock (WI) 415
Houston (TX) 473, **486–7**
Hovenweep National Monument (UT) **523**
Howard, Robert 706
Howard, Ron 671
Hudson River Valley (NY) **91**
Hudson, Henry 60, 92
Hughes, Archbishop John 77
Humboldt Redwoods State Park (CA) **714**
Huntington Library, Art Collections, & Botanical Gardens (Los Angeles) 672
Huntington, Henry E. 672
Huntsville (AL) **365**
Hutchings, Dr. William D. 403
Hutterite 401
Hyannis (Cape Cod, MA) 152
Hyde Street Pier (San Francisco) 702

I

Idaho 565, **574–7**
hotels 600
restaurants 604
Idaho Falls (ID) **577**
Idaho Springs & Georgetown (CO) **591**
Iditarod Trail Sled Dog Race (AK) 738
Iglesias, Julio 294, 295
Illinois 377, **386–99**
Chicago 386–97
hotels 424
restaurants 428
Immigrants **382–3**
Asians 631
Czechoslovaks 453
Chinese 139, 631, 716
French 357
French Canadian (Cajun) 336
Germans 106, 412, 419, 439, 482 483
Icelandic 413
Moravian 248
Scandinavians 419, 619
Immigration & Naturalization Services 17
Independence Hall (Philadelphia, PA) 101, **102**
Independence National Historic Park (Philadelphia, PA) **100–101**
Independence Day 29
Independence Mall
see Independence National Historic Park
Independence Seaport Museum (Philadelphia, PA) **102–103**
Indian Peaks Wilderness Area (CO) 590
Indiana 377, **400–403**
hotels 425
restaurants 429
Indiana Dunes National Lakeshore (IN) **400–401**
Indianapolis (IN) 379, **402–403**
Indianapolis 500 auto race
Indianapolis Motor Speedway
International Bridge (TX) 491
International Drive (FL) **313**
International dialing code 14
International UFO Museum & Research Center (Roswell, NM) 552
Internet Cafés 14
Inuit 732
'Iolani Palace (Honolulu) 748
Iowa 433, **452–3**
hotels 465–6
restaurants 469–70
Iowa City (IA) **453**
Iron Range (MN) **420**
Irving, Washington 91
Isabella Stewart Gardner Museum (Boston) **146**

J

Jackson Hole (Grand Teton NP, WY) 583
Jackson (MS) **362**

Jackson (WY) **582**
Jackson Square (New Orleans, LA) **347**
Jackson, Andrew 52, 265, 286, 347, 362
Jackson, Stonewall 259
Jaggar, Professor Thomas A. **753**
James, Henry 134
James, Jesse 457
Jamestown & Yorktown (VA) **216**
Jazz 336, 341, 346
  Jazz Age 49
  jazz artists 349, 365
  Riverboat Jazz Bands 349
Jean Lafitte National Historic Park (LA) 356
Jedediah Smith Redwoods State Park (Redwood NP, CA) 714
Jefferson City (MS) **456**
  Jefferson Landing State Historic Site
Jefferson Memorial (Washington, DC) **204–205**
Jefferson, Thomas 52, 74, 192, 198, 204, 217
Jemison, Mae 408
Jennings, Waylon 492
Jenny Lake (Grand Teton NP, WY) 583
Jerde, Jon 671
Jerome (AZ) 529
Jimmy Carter National Historic Site (Plains, GA) 258
JN "Ding" Darling National Wildlife Refuge (FL) 320
Jobs, Steve 708
John Brown House (Providence, RI) 155
John Brown's Fort (Harpers Ferry NP, WV) 194
John Day Fossil Beds National Monument (OR) 615, **638–9**
John F. Kennedy Library & Museum (Boston) **146**
John G. Shedd Aquarium (Chicago) 393
John Hancock Center (Chicago) **389**
John Hancock Tower (Boston) 145
Johns, Jasper 203
Johnson, Albert 685
Johnson, Andrew 52
Johnson, Lyndon B. 53, 475, 482
Johnson, Philip 294, 390, 480
Jolliet, Louis 382
Jones Beach State Park (NY) **90**
Jones, Jasper 80
Jones, John Paul 169
Jones, Robert Trent 403
Jongers, Alphonse 159
Joplin, Janis 482, 704
Jordan, Alex 415
Joshua Tree National Park (CA) **683**
Joss House State Historic Site (Weaverville, CA) 715
Judd, Donald 416
Juneau (AK) **736–7**

K

Kahn, Louis 481
Kalalau Trail (Kaua'i, HI) **755**
Kalapakī Beach (Līhu'e, HI) 754
Kalaupapa National Historical Park (Moloka'i, HI) **750**
Kansas City (MS) **456–7**
  climate 462
Kansas 433, **458–9**
  hotels 466–7
  restaurants 471
Katmai National Park (AK) 733
Kaua'i (HI) **754–5**
Kaunakakai (Moloka'i, HI) **750**
Kawaiaha'o Church (Honolulu, HI) 748
Ke'anae Peninsula (HI) 746
Keaton, Diane 83
Keillor, Garrison 423
Kelleys Island State Park (Lake Erie Islands, OH) 407
Kelly, George 703
Kemp's Ridley sea turtle 489
Kenai Fjords National Park (AK) 733, 739
Kennebunks (ME) **171**
  Kennebunkport
Kennedy Space Center (FL) **302–303**
Kennedy Center (Washington, DC) **208**
Kennedy, Jacqueline 53, 203, 208, 209
Kennedy, John F. 53, 208, 294, 302, 475, 478, 482
  burial place 211
Kennedys, the 152
  summer home 152
Kentucky 239, **268–71**
  Country & Bluegrass Music **269**
  hotels 277
  restaurants 281
Kentucky Derby 268, 271
Kentucky Fried Chicken 269
Kentucky Guild of Artists & Craftmen's Fair 268
Kerouac, Jack 655, 702
Kerrville (TX) **483**
Ketchikan (AK) **736**
Ketchum Sun Valley Heritage & Ski Museum (ID) 576
Key Biscayne (FL) **299**
Key Largo (FL) 322
Key West (FL) **323**
Key, Francis Scott 193, 203, 222
Keys, The (FL) **322–3**
Khan, Fazlur R. 389, 391
Kīlauea Point (Kaua'i, HI)) **754–5**
Killington (VT) **163**
King Jr, Martin Luther 205, 255, 260, 409, 364, 365
  burial place 245
  memorial 699
King Kamehameha 748
King, Stephen 129
King Tutankhamen 394
King's Chapel (Boston) 136, **140**
King, B.B. 360
Kinney, Abbot 661
Kissimmee (FL) **313**
Kissing Camels (CO) 592
Knievel, Evel 577
Knife River Indian Village National Historic Site (ND) 442
Knott's Berry Farm (Los Angeles) **673**
Kodiak Island (AK) 732, 735, **740**
Kong Chow Temple (San Francisco) 700
Konza Prairie (KS) 458
Krewes 353
Kīlauea Caldera (Hawai'i Volcanoes NP, HI) 752
Kīlauea Point (Kaua'i, HI) **754–5**
  Kīlauea Point National Wildlife Refuge 754, 755
Kushner, Tony 668

L

La Crosse (WI) **415**
La Jolla (San Diego, CA) **679**
La Purísima Concepción Mission, (CA) 687
LaBranche, Jean Baptiste 351
Lady Meux (James Whistler) 80
Labino, Dominick 407
Laemmle, Carl 671
Lafayette (LA) 336, **356**
Lafayette Park (San Francisco) 704
Lafitte's Blacksmith Shop (New Orleans, LA) 351
Lafitte's in Exile (New Orleans) 350
Lafitte, Jean & Pierre 350, 488
Lahaina (Maui, HI) **751**
Lake Champlain (VT) **164–5**
  Maritime Museum
Lake Chelan (WA) **624**
Lake Erie Islands (OH) **407**
Lake Havasu City (AZ) **528**
Lake McConaughy State Recreation Area (NE) 448
Lake Mead National Recreation Area (Las Vegas) 515
Lake Michigan Shore (MI) **411**
Lake Powell & Glen Canyon National Recreation Area (UT) **523**
Lake Tahoe (CA) **718**
Lake Winnipesaukee (NH) **167**
Lakes
  Burnstide Lake (MN) 426
  Crater Lake (OR) 636
  Flathead Lake (MT) 578
  Great Salt Lake (UT) 518
  Jenny Lake (WY) 583
  Lake Champlain (VT) 164–5
  Lake Chelan (WA) 624
  Lake Coeur d'Alene (ID) 566, 574
  Lake Erie Islands (OH) 407
  Lake Havasu (AZ) 528
  Lake Josephine (MT) 566
  Lake Martin (LA) 356
  Lake McConaughy (NE) 448, 463
  Lake McDonald (MT) 579
  Lake Mead (Las Vegas) 515
  Lake Mendota (WI) 414
  Lake Michigan (MI) 411
  Lake Monona (WI) 414
  Lake Pepin (MN) 418
  Lake Placid (NY) 93
  Lake Powell (UT) 523
  Lake Superior (MN) 419
  Lake Tahoe (CA) 517, 718
  Lake Winnipesaukee (NH) 167
  Locator Lake (MN) 421

Lakes (cont.)
Mendenhall Lake (AK) 737
Mille Lacs Lake (MN) 419
Mono Lake (CA) 719
Profile Lake (NH) 166
Rainy Lake (MN) 421
Redfish Lake (ID) 575
Shagawa Lake (MN) 426
Stow Lake (CA) 696
Swiftcurrent Lake (MT) 579
Wonder Lake (AK) 742
Lancaster (PA) **106**
Lanier, James 403
Lansing (MI) **410**
Lapidus, Morris 293
Laramie (WY) **587**
Laredo (TX) **490**
Larkin, Thomas 692
Las Vegas (NV) 502, **510–15**
casinos & hotels 510–13
climate 554
Hoover Dam 514
hotels 556
Lake Mead 515
museums 514
neon signs 513
restaurants 560
"the Strip" 510–13
Lassen Volcanic National Park (CA) **715**
Lassen Peak
Last Train to Nowhere (Nome, AK) 741
Laura Plantation (LA) 354
Laurel Highlands (PA) **109**
Lava Beds National Monument (CA) **715**
Laveau, Marie 348
Lawrence (KS) **458**
Laws
New England 174
Pacific Northwest 643
Le Corbusier 148
Leavenworth (WA) **624**
Lee, Clayton 700
Lee Island Coast (FL) **320**
Lee, General Robert E. 91, 106, 193, 211, 212, 218, 259
Legal assistance 17
Léger, Fernand 293
Legion of Honor (San Francisco) **706**
Lemmon, Jack 678
Lennon, John 78
León, Juan Ponce de 285, 292
Lesbian & Gay Pride Day 29
Lewes (DE) **227**
Lewis & Clark 438, 442, 570, 574, 580
Lewis, George 346
Lewis, Sinclair 383
Lexington (Boston) 149
Lexington (KY) 240, **270**
L'Enfant, Pierre 211
Libbey, Edward Drummond 407
Liberace Museum (Las Vegas) 514
Liberty Bell (Philadelphia, PA) 100, 102
Libraries
Asher Library (Chicago) 392
Butler Library (NYC) 84
Libraries (cont.)
Cleo Rodgers Memorial Library (Columbus, IN) 403
Family History Library (Salt Lake City, UT) 518
Harold Washington Library Center (Chicago) 389
Huntington Library (Los Angeles) 672
Library of Congress (Washington, DC) 198
Low Library (NYC) 84
Morgan Library (NYC) 85
New York Public Library (NYC) 74
Newbury Library (Chicago) 388
Widener library (Cambridge, MA) 148
Library of Congress (Washington, DC) **198**
Lichtenstein, Roy 80
Lied Discovery Children's Museum (Las Vegas, NV) 514
Lighthouses
Bodie Island Lighthouse (NC) 250
Cape Hatteras Lighthouse (NC) 250
Cape Henry Lighthouse (VA) 216
Concord Point Lighthouse (MD) 224
Eagle Bluff Lighthouse (WI) 413
Fenwick Island Lighthouse (DE) 227
Hooper Strait Lighthouse (MD) 224
Kilauea Lighthouse (HI) 754
Marblehead Lighthouse (OH) 407
Montauk Point Lighthouse (NY) 90
Old Mission Lighthouse (MI) 384, 411
Point Sur Lighthouse (CA) 690
Point Wilson Lighthouse (WA) 621
Portland Headlight (ME) 170
Sand Island Light (WI) 415
St. Simons Lighthouse (GA) 257
Līhu'e (Kaua'i, HI) **754**
Lilly Jr, J.K. 402
Lin, Maya 205
Lincoln/Woodstock (NH) 167
Lincoln (NE) **449**
Lincoln Center (NYC) **83**
Lincoln Center for the Performing Arts
Lincoln County Historical Museum (North Platte, NE) 449
Lincoln Highway 570
Lincoln Home National Historic Site (Springfield, IL) 399
Lincoln Memorial (Washington, DC) **205**
Lincoln Park Zoo (Chicago) **396**
Lincoln, Abraham 52, 205, 207, 222, 399
birthplace 271
memorabilia 154
son of 162
speech 71
wife of 270
Lindbergh, Charles 201
Litchfield (CT) **159**
Little Bighorn Battlefield National Monument (MT) **581**
Little Blue Nude (Renoir) 94
Little Havana (Miami) **295**
Little Italy (NYC) **69**
Little Italy (San Francisco) 702
Little Richard 258
Little Rock (AR) **358**
Little Tokyo (Los Angeles) **669**
Locator Lake (Voyageurs NP, MN) 421
Log cabins 164, 262
Loire, Gabriel 701
Lombard Street (San Francisco) 702
Lompoc Valley (CA) **687**
London, Jack 709, 712
Long Beach (Los Angeles) **673**
Long Island (NY) 90
Long Wharf (Boston) 143
Long, Huey 355
Longfellow, Henry Wadsworth 142, 148, 356
Longwood Gardens (PA) **107**
Loneliest Road 517
Looff, Charles 693
Lookout Mountain (TN) 263
Loon Mountain (NH) 167
Loop Road 35
Loop, The (Chicago) **390–91**
Lorre, Peter 662
Los Angeles (CA) **658–77**
Chandler, Raymond **661**
climate 720
directory 677
Disneyland Resort **674–5**
entertainment 676
getting around 659, 676
Greater Los Angeles **672–3**
hotels 722
map 658–9
outdoor activities 676–7
restaurants 726
shopping 677
Sunset Boulevard **664–5**
The Rise of Hollywood **666**
20th Century Fox 672
Los Angeles City Hall (CA) **668**
Los Angeles Central Library (CA) **668**
Los Angeles County Museum of Art (CA) 667
Lost Horse Mine (Joshua Tree NP, CA) 683
Louis, Joe 365, 408
Louisburg Square (Boston) 134
Louisiana 335, **344–57**
Baton Rouge 355
history 354
hotels 368–9
New Orleans **344–53**
plantations 354–5
restaurants 372–4
The Acadians – Cajun Country 357
Louisiana Old State Capitol (Baton Rouge, LA) 355
Louisiana Plantations 354–5
Louisville (KY) **271**
Lowell (MA) **150**
Loxahatchee National Wildlife Refuge (FL) **300–301**
Lubbock (TX) **492**
Lucy, the Margate Elephant (Atlantic City, NJ) 97
Lummis Home and Garden (LA) **670**

Lummis, Charles Fletcher 670
Luncheon of the Boating Party, The (Renoir) 210

M

MacArthur, Douglas 91
Mackinac Island (MI) **411**
Macon (GA) **258**
Macy's (NYC) 73, 699
Macy, Rowland Hussey 73
Madame Tussaud's Wax Museum (Las Vegas, NV) 512
Madison (CT) 161
Madison (IN) 403
Madison (WI) **414**
Madison County (IO) 452
Madison Square (NYC) **72**
Madison, Dolley 53
Madison, James 52, 192
Madonna 666
Madras & Warm Springs (OR) **634**
Magna Carta 271
Magnificent Mile (Chicago) **388–9**
Maher, George W. 397
Maine 123, 125, **170–73**
  hotels 181
  Portland **170**
  restaurants 185
Malheur National Wildlife Refuge (OR) **638**
Malibu (Los Angeles) **672**
Mall, The (Washington, DC) **200–201**
Mammoth Cave National Park (KY) **268**
Mammoth Hot Springs (Yellowstone NP, WY) 584
Mammoth Site (Black Hills, SD) 447
Man With Arms Crossed (Cézanne) 82
Manatees 319
Manchester (NH) **168–9**
Manchester (VT) 162
Manitou Springs (CO) **592**
  Manitou Springs Cliff Dwellings
Mann's Chinese Theatre (Los Angeles) 666
Mantenga, Andrea 660
Maps
  Alaska 734–5
  Arches National Park (UT) 520
  Arizona, The Heart of 529
  Baton Rouge Center (LA) 355
  Beacon Hill (Boston) 134–5
  Best Scenic Routes 40–41
  Big Sur (CA) 690–91
  Black Hills (SD) 446–7
  Boston (MA) 132–3
  Bryce Canyon National Park (UT) 526–7
  California 650–51, 656–7
  Canyonlands National Park (UT) 522
  Chicago (IL) 386–7
  Colonial Williamsburg (VA) 214–15
  Colorado Ski Resorts 594–5
  Crater Lake National Park (OR) 636–7
  Deep South 336–7, 342–3
  Downtown Albuquerque (NM) 548–9
  Downtown Atlanta (GA) 261
Maps (cont.)
  Downtown Charleston (SC) 253
  Downtown Dallas (TX) 479
  Downtown Denver (CO) 589
  Downtown Detroit (MI) 409
  Downtown Hartford (CT) 158
  Downtown Memphis (TN) 267
  Downtown Minneapolis & St. Paul (MN) 416–17
  Downtown Nashville (TN) 265
  Downtown Portland (ME) 170
  Downtown Phoenix (AZ) 530–31
  Downtown Providence (RI) 155
  Downtown Seattle (WA) 617
  Downtown St. Louis (MO) 455
  Florida 288–9
  49-Mile Scenic Drive (CA) 696–7
  Freedom Trail (Boston) 136–7
  Glacier National Park (MT) 579
  Great American Cities 38–9
  Great Lakes 378–9, 384–5
  Great Plains 434–5, 440–41
  Greater Boston (MA) 133
  Greater Chicago (IL) 387
  Greater Los Angeles (CA) 659
  Greater Miami (FL) 291
  Greater New Orleans (LA) 345
  Greater New York (NY) 65
  Greater Philadelphia (PA) 99
  Greater San Francisco (CA) 695
  Greater Washington, DC 197
  Hells Canyon National Recreation Area Tour (OR) 640–41
  Independence Hall National Historic Park (Philadelphia, PA) 100–101
  Los Angeles (CA) 658–9
  Miami (FL) 290–91
  Monument Valley (AZ) 540–1
  Mount Rainier National Park (WA) 626–7
  National Parks 34–5
  New England 124–5, 130–31
  New Orleans (LA) 344–5
  New York (NY) 64–5
  New York City & the Mid-Atlantic Region 62–3
  Northern Pueblos Tour (NM) 545
  Oak Park (Chicago) 397
  Pacific Northwest 614–15
  Putting USA on the Map 10
  Rockies 566–7, 572–3
  San Antonio (TX) 484–5
  San Francisco (CA) 694–5
  San Juan Islands (WA) 622–3
  Santa Fe (NM) 546–7
  Southeast 240–41, 246–7
  Southwest 502–503, 508–509
  Strip, The (Las Vegas, NV) 510–11, 512–13
  Texas 476–7
  Walt Disney World® Resort (FL) 304
  Washington, DC 196–7
  Washington, DC Mall 200–201
  Washington, DC & Capital Region 188–9, 194–5
  Yellowstone National Park (WY) 584–5
  Zion Canyon (UT) 525
Mardi Gras 352, **353**
Mardi Gras Museum (New Orleans, LA) 348, 364
Marine life 321, 322, 633, 693, 739
  coral reef 322
  dolphins 322
  manatees 319, 321
Mark Twain House and Museum (Hartford, CT) 158
Marlowe, Philip 661
Marquette Building (Chicago) 390
Marquette, Jacques 382
Marshall Gold Discovery State Park (CA) **716**
Marshall, Thurgood 193
Martha's Vineyard (MA) 153
Martin, Dean 662
Martinez, Maria 544
Mary Todd Lincoln House (Lexington, KY) 270
Maryhill (WA) **625**
Maryland 187, **222–5**
  hotels 232
  restaurants 236
Masefield, John 71
Mason-Dixon Line 61
Masonic Temple (Philadelphia, PA) **103**
Massachusetts 123, **150–53**
  Beacon Hill (Boston) 134–5
  Boston **132–49**
  hotels 178
  restaurants 183
  Salem Witch Trials **150**
Massachusetts Institute of Technology (Cambridge, MA) 148
Massachusetts State House (Boston) **138**
Massasoit 151
Mastercard 17
Masterson, Bat 459
Matisse, Henri 105
Mayflower 127, 151
Mayflower II 151
Mayo, Will & Charles 418
McAuliffe, Christa 168
  McAuliffe-Shepherd Discovery Center (Concord, NH) 168
McDonald Observatory (Fort Davis, TX) 491
McKinley, William 53
McKittrick Canyon (Guadalupe Mountains NP, TX) 492
McLaughlin, John 655
McNeil River State Game Sanctuary (AK) 740
McVeigh, Timothy 438
Medicine Wheel (WY) 586
Meier, Richard 403
Mellinger, Fredrick 666
Mellon, Andrew 202
Melrose Plantation (Natchez, MS) 363
Melville, Herman 153
Memphis (TN) **266–7**
Mencken, H.L. 103
Mendenhall Glacier (AK) 737
Mendocino (CA) **713**
Menno-Hof Mennonite Anabaptist Interpretive Center (Shipshewana, IN) 401

Mennonites 401, 439
Merritt Island National Wildlife Refuge (FL) 303
Mesa Verde National Park (CO) 34, 567, **596–7**
Messiah 139
Metro-Goldwyn-Mayer (Los Angeles) 663
Metropolitan Museum of Art (NYC) **80–81**
Mexico 491, 546
culture 669
independence 546
Mexican War, the 474
Meyer, Danny 118
MGM Grand Hotel (Las Vegas, NV) 510
Miami (FL) 39, **290–99**, 326, 330
getting around 291
Greater Miami 291, **298–9**
hotels 326
map 290–91
Ocean Drive **292–3**
restaurants 330
Miami-Dade Cultural Center (FL) **294**
Miami Metrozoo (FL) **299**
Michener, James 482
Michigan 377, **408–411**
hotels 425–6
restaurants 429–30
Mickey Mouse 305
Microsoft 616
Midtown Manhattan (NYC) **74–5**
Mildred E. Mathias Botanical Garden (Los Angeles) 662
Millay, Edna St. Vincent 171
Mille Lacs Lake (MN) 419
Mille Lacs Band of Ojibwe tribal reservation (MN)
Millennium Park (Chicago) 390
Miller, Frederick 413
Milwaukee (MN) **412–13**
Mingus, Charles 533
Minneapolis & St. Paul (MN) **416–17**
Minnelli, Vincente 664
Minnesota 377, **416–21**
hotels 426
Minneapolis & St. Paul (MN) **416–17**
restaurants 430
Wolves **421**
Minutemen 149, 150
Minute Man National Historic Park (Concord, MA) 150
Miracle Mile (Los Angeles) **667**
Miracle Rock (Colorado National Monument, CO) 597
Mission Architecture (CA) **687**
Mission Dolores (CA) **705**
Mission San Juan Capistrano (Los Angeles) **673**
Missions National Historical Park (TX) **484**
Mississippi 335, **360–63**
Blues Music **361**
hotels 370–71
restaurants 375
Mississippi Delta (MS) **360**, 361
Mississippi Delta Blues Festival
Mississippi River 418
Mississippi River Towns (MN) **418**
Missoula (MT) **578**
Missouri 433, **454–7**
hotels 466
restaurants 470
Missouri River Valley (ND) 442
Mitchell (SD) **444**
Mitchell Caverns (CA) 683
Mizner, Addison 301
Moab (UT) **521**
Mobile (AL) **364**
Moby Dick (Herman Melville) 128, 153
Modoc War 715
Mogollon 506
Mohegan Bluffs (Block Island, RI) 157
Moisseiff, Leon 707
Mojave Desert (CA) **683**
Mollie Kathleen Gold Mine (Cripple Creek, CO) 593
Moloka'i & Maui (HI) **750–51**
Mondrian, Piet 479
Mono Lake (CA) 719
Monona Terrace Community & Convention Center (Madison, WI) 414
Monongahela National Forest (WV) **220**
Monroe, James 52, 216
Monroe, Marilyn 662, 664, 666, 678
Montana 565, **578–81**
hotels 601
restaurants 605
Montauk Point Lighthouse (Montauk, NY) 90
Monterey (CA) **692–3**
Monterey State Historic Park
Montezuma Castle National Monument (AZ) 529
Montgomery (AL) **364–5**
Monticello (VA) **217**
Monument Valley (AZ) **540–41**
Moody Gardens (Galveston, TX) 488
Moore, Charles 663
Moore, Henry 76, 395
Moore, Marianne 71
Moran, Thomas 203
Morgan, Charles W. 161
Morgan, Julia 688
Morgan, J.P. 118
Morgan Library & Museum (NYC) **75**
Mormons **519**, 523
church 518
founder 519
Joshua tree 683
temple 709
trail center 451
Mormon Tabernacle (Salt Lake City, UT) 518
Mormon Trail Center (Omaha, NE) 451
Morris, William 144
Morrison, Jim 406, 664
Morse, Reynolds 318
Morton, Jelly Roll 349
Motels **18**
Motorcycle rentals & tours 24
Mount Constitution (San Juan Islands, WA) 622
Mount Crested Butte (CO) 573
Mount Hood (OR) 613, **632**
Mount Locke (TX) 491
Mount Mansfield (VT) 165
Mount Marcy (NY) 93
Mount Mazama (OR) 636
Mount McKinley (AK) 732, 742
Mount Mitchell (NC) 249
Mount Novarupta (AK) 740
Mount Olympus (WA) 620
Mount Rainier National Park (WA) **626–7**
Mount Rushmore (SD) 434
Mount Rushmore National Memorial (Black Hills, SD) 447
Mount Shasta (CA) **715**
Mount Shuksan (WA) 624
Mount St. Helens National Volcanic Monument (WA) **629**
Mount Vernon (VA) **212–13**
Mount Vernon Street (Boston) 134
Mount Washington (NH) 166
Mount Whitney (CA) 719
Mountain View (AR) **359**
Mud Island (Memphis, TN) 266
Muddy Waters 361
Muir Woods (CA) **709**
Muir Woods National Monument
Muir, John 709
Mulholland Drive (Los Angeles) **666**
Mulholland Point (Campobello Island, ME) 173
Mulholland, William 666
Multnomah Falls (OR) 632
Museum Campus (Chicago) **393**
Museum of African American History (Boston) 135
Museum of Broadcast Communications (Chicago) **390**
Museum of Contemporary Art (Los Angeles) **669**
Museum of Fine Arts (Boston) **146–7**
Museum of Modern Art (NYC) **77**
Museum of Science & Industry (Chicago) **394**
From Plaster to Stone
Museum of Television & Radio (Los Angeles) 663
Museum of Tolerance (LA) **662**
Museums
Abbe Museum (Bar Harbor, ME) 172
Abraham Lincoln Presidential Library and Museum (Springfield, IL) 399
Adler Planetarium & Astronomy Museum (Chicago) 393
Aerospace Museum (San Diego, CA) 680
African-American Museum (Philadelphia, PA) 100
Alaska State Museum (Juneau) 737
Amelia Island Museum of History (Fernandina Beach, FL) 315
American Folk Art Museum (NYC) 83
American International Rattlesnake Museum (Albuquerque, NM) 549
American Jazz Museum (Kansas City, MO) 457
American Saddlebred Museum (Lexington, KY) 270
Amon Carter Museum (Fort Worth, TX) 481
Anchorage Museum at Rasmuson Center (AK) 738
Andy Warhol Museum (Pittsburgh, PA) 108

Museums (cont.)
Argo Gold Mine, Mill & Museum (Idaho Springs, CO) 591
Arizona-Sonora Desert Museum (Tucson, AZ) 532
Armand Hammer Museum of Art & Culture (Los Angeles) 662
Asian Art Museum (San Francisco) 704
Astor House Museum (Golden, CO) 590
Atwater-Kent Museum (Philadelphia, PA) 100
Autry National Center (Los Angeles) 670
Baranof Museum (Kodiak Island, AK) 740
Basque Museum & Cultural Center (Boise, ID) 575
Battles for Chattanooga Electric Map (Chattanooga, TN) 263
Bennington Museum & Grandma Moses Gallery (VT) 162
Bible Museum (Eureka Springs, AR) 359
Billings Farm & Museum (Woodstock, VT) 163
Bishop Museum (Honolulu, HI) 749
Black American West Museum & Heritage Center (Denver, CO) 589
Boca Raton Museum of Art (FL) 300
Boot Hill Museum (Dodge City, KS) 459
Brick Store Museum (Kennebunk, ME) 171
Brooklyn Children's Museum (NYC) 87
Burke Museum of Natural History & Culture (Seattle, WA) 619
C&D Canal Museum (Chesapeake, MD) 224
California African American Museum (Los Angeles) 668
California Heritage Museum (Los Angeles) 661
California Museum of Science & Industry (Los Angeles) 668
California State Railroad Museum (Sacramento, CA) 717
Campbell House (Spokane, WA) 625
Captain George Flavel House Museum (Astoria, OR) 632
Central High Museum & Visitor Center (Little Rock, AR) 358
Chapin Mesa Archaeological Museum (Mesa Verde NP, CO) 596
Charles H. Wright Museum of African American History (Detroit, MI) 408–409
Charles M. Russell Museum (Great Falls, MT)) 580
Charleston Museum (SC) 253
Chattanooga Regional History Museum (TN) 263
Chesapeake Bay Maritime Museum (MD) 224

Museums (cont.)
Chicago Children's Museum (IL) 389
Chicago History Museum (IL) 388
Children's Museum of Indianapolis (IN) 402
Children's Museum of Maine (Portland, ME) 170
Chrysler Museum (Norfolk, VA) 216
Cincinnati History Museum (OH) 404
Circus World Museum (Baraboo, WI) 414
Colorado History Museum (Denver, CO) 588
Colorado Springs Pioneer Museum (Colorado Springs, CO) 592
Columbia River Maritime Museum (Astoria, OR) 632
Cottonlandia Museum (Greenwood, MS) 360
Craft & Folk Art Museum (Los Angeles) 667
Crisfield/Tawes Historical Museum (Crisfield) MD 225
de Young Museum (San Francisco) 706
Delta Blues Museum (Clarksdale, MS) 360
Denver Museum of Nature & Science (CO) 589
Detroit Historical Museum (MI) 408
Door County Maritime Museum (Sturgeon Bay, WI) 413
Dorothy Molter Museum (Ely, MN) 420
Durango & Silverton Narrow Gauge Railroad & Museum (CO) 596
Durham-Western Heritage Museum (Omaha, NE) 451
DuSable Museum of African American History (Chicago) **395**
The Eisner: American Museum of Advertising and Design (Milwaukee, 412)
Eiteljorg Museum of American Indian & Western Art (Indianapolis, IN) 402–403
Ellis Island Immigration Museum (NYC) 67
Erie Canal Museum (Syracuse, NY) 94
Fernbank Natural History Museum (Atlanta, GA) 261
Field Museum (Chicago) 393
Firehouse #1 Museum (Nevada City, CA) 716
Flagler Museum (Palm Beach, FL) 301
Flying Tigers Warbird Restoration Museum (Kissimmee, FL) 313
Figge Art Museum (IA) 453
Fogg Art & Busch-Reisinger Museums (Cambridge, MA) 149
Fort Caspar Museum (Casper, WY) 586
Fort Myers Historical Museum (FL) 320
Fort Walla Walla Museum (Walla Walla, WA) 625
Fowler Museum of Cultural History (Los Angeles) 662

Museums (cont.)
Frontier Days Old West Museum (Laramie, WY) 587
Galena/Jo Daviess County History Museum (Galena, IL) 398
Gallatin Pioneer Museum (Bozeman, MT) 581
Gerald R. Ford Museum (Grand Rapids, MI) 410
The Getty Center (Los Angeles) 660
Gold Museum (Dahlonega, GA) 259
Great Plains Black History Museum (Omaha, NE) 451
Hagley Museum (DE) 226
Halifax Historical Society Museum (Daytona Beach, FL) 14
Hamill House Museum (CO) 591
Harvard Art Museum (Cambridge, MA) 148
Harvard Museum of Natural History (Cambridge, MA) 149
Havre de Grace Decoy Museum (MD) 224
Hay House Museum (Macon, GA) 258
The Henry Ford (Detroit, MI) 409
High Desert Museum (Bend, OR) 635
High Museum of Art (Atlanta, GA) 261
Hirshhorn Museum (Washington, DC) 201
Historic Fort Wayne & Tuskegee Airmen Museum (Detroit, MI) 408
Historic New Orleans Collection (LA) 351
Historical Museum of Southern Florida (Miami) 294
Home Sweet Home Museum (The Hamptons, NY) 90
Ice Museum (Fairbanks, AK) 741
Indiana State Museum (Indianapolis, IN) 402
Indianapolis Museum of Art (IN) 402
International Museum of Photography (Rochester, NY) 94
International Museum of the Horse (Lexington, KY) 270
Isabella Stewart Gardner Museum (Boston) 146
Japanese American National Museum (Los Angeles) 669
Jimmy Carter Library & Museum (Atlanta, GA) 261
John F. Kennedy Library & Museum (Boston) 146
John Gorrie State Museum (Apalachicola, FL) 317
Junípero Serra Museum (San Diego, CA) 678
Kansas City Museum (MO) 456
Kaua'i Museum (Līhu'e, HI) 754
Kelsey Museum of Archaeology (Ann Arbor, MI) 410
Kentucky Derby Museum (Louisville) 271

Museums (cont.)
Ketchum Sun Valley Heritage & Ski Museum (ID) 576
Kimbell Museum (Fort Worth, TX) 481
Lake Champlain Maritime Museum (Basin Harbor, VT) 165
Landis Valley Museum (Lancaster, PA) 106
Las Vegas Natural History Museum (NV) 514
Leavenworth Nutcracker Museum (WA) 624
Legion of Honor (San Francisco) 706
Lewis & Clark National Historic Trail Interpretive Center (Great Falls, MT) 580
Lied Discovery Children's Museum (Las Vegas, NV) 514
Lincoln County Historical Museum (North Platte, NE) 449
Loomis Museum (Lassen Volcanic NP, CA) 715
Los Angeles Children's Museum (CA) 668
Los Angeles County Museum of Art (CA) 667
Lost City Museum of Archaeology (Las Vegas, NV) 515
Louisiana State Museum (Shreveport, LA) 357
LSU Rural Life Museum (Baton Rouge, LA) 355
Louisville Slugger Museum (KY) 271
Lowe Art Museum (Miami) 296
Lyman Museum & Mission House (Hilo, HI) 753
Madame Tussaud's Wax Museum (Las Vegas, NV) 512
Maine Narrow Gauge Railroad Co. & Museum (Portland, ME) 170
Margaret Mitchell House & Museum (Atlanta, GA) 260–61
Maritime & Seafood Industry Museum (Biloxi, MS) 363
Memphis Rock-N-Soul Museum (TN) 266
Merchant's House Museum (NYC) 71
Miami Art Museum of Dade County (FL) 294
Miami-Dade Cultural Center (FL) 294
Michigan Historical Museum (Lansing) 410
Michigan Maritime Museum (South Haven) 411
Mid-America All-Indian Center (Wichita, KS) 459
Mille Lacs Indian Museum (MN) 419
Milwaukee County Historical Center (WI) 412
Mission Houses Museum (Honolulu, HI) 748
Mission Mill Museum (Salem, OR) 634

Museums (cont.)
Mississippi Agriculture & Forestry Museum (Jackson) 362
Mississippi River Museum (Dubuque) 453
Morgan Library & Museum **75**
Motown Historical Museum (Detroit, MI) 409
Museo de las Americas (Denver, CO) 589
Museum at Warm Springs (OR) 634
Museum Campus (Chicago) **393**
Museum of African Art (NYC) 70
Museum of African American History (Boston) 135
Museum of Colorado Prisons (Cañon City) 593
Museum of Contemporary Art (Los Angeles) **669**
Museum of Contemporary Photography (Chicago) 392
Museum of Fine Arts (Boston) **146–7**
Museum of Fine Arts (Santa Fe, NM) 546
Museum of Flight (Seattle) 617-18
Museum of Florida History (Tallahassee) 316
Museum of Idaho (Idaho Falls) 577
Museum of International Folk Art (Santa Fe, NM) 547
Museum of Modern Art (NYC) **77**
Museum of Natural History of the Florida Keys (Marathon Key) 322
Museum of Nebraska History (Lincoln) 449
Museum of Northern Arizona (Flagstaff) 528
Museum of Science & Industry (Chicago) **394**
Museum of Tolerance (Los Angeles) **662**
Museum of the Confederacy (Richmond, VA) 216
Museum of the Fur Trade (Chadron, NE) 448
Museum of the Rockies (Bozeman, MT) 581
Museum of Western Art (Kerriville, TX) 483
Museum of Westward Expansion (St. Louis, MO) 454
Mutter Museum (Philadelphia, PA) 104
National Air & Space Museum (Washington, DC) 201
National Automobile Museum (Reno, NV) 517
National Baseball Hall of Fame (Cooperstown, NY) 93
National Civil Rights Museum (Memphis, TN) 266
National Cowboy Museum (Oklahoma City, OK) 461
National Czech & Slovak Museum (Cedar Rapids, IA) 453
National Frontier Trails Center (Independence, MO) 457

Museums (cont.)
National Museum of American History (Washington, DC) 200
National Museum of Jewish History (Philadelphia, PA) 100
National Museum of Natural History (Washington, DC) 200
National Museum of Nuclear Science & History (Albuquerque, NM) 550
National Museum of the Pacific War (Fredericksburg, TX) 482
National Prisoner of War (POW) Museum (Andersonville, GA) 258
National Route 66 Museum (Elk City, OK) 461
National Voting Rights Museum (Selma, AL) 364
Natural History Museum of Los Angeles County (CA) 668
Negro Leagues Baseball Museum (Kansas City, MO) 457
Nelson-Atkins Art Museum (Kansas City, MO) 457
Nevada State Museum (Carson City) 516
Nevada State Railroad Museum (Carson City) 516
New Mexico Museum of Natural History & Science (Albuquerque) 549
New Orleans Jazz Collection (LA) 346
New Orleans Museum of Art (LA) 353
New York State Museum (Albany, NY) 92
Nichols House Museum (Boston) 135
Nordic Heritage Museum (Seattle, WA) 619
Norman Rockwell Museum (Stockbridge, MA) 153
North Carolina Maritime Museum (Beaufort) 251
North Carolina Museum of History (Raleigh) 248
North Star Mining Museum (Grass Valley, CA) 716
Northwest Museum of Arts & Culture (Spokane, WA) 625
Norton Simon Museum (Los Angeles) 672
Oakland Museum of California (San Francisco, CA) 709
Ocean City Life-Saving Station Museum (MD) 225
Oklahoma History Center (Oklahoma City) 461
Old Capital Museum of Mississippi History (Jackson, MS) 362
Old Courthouse Museum (LA) 357
Old Cowtown Museum (Wichita, KS) 459
Old State House State History Museum (Little Rock, AR) 358
Oregon Museum of Science & Industry (Portland) 631

Museums (cont.)
Oriental Institute Museum (Chicago) 395
Page Museum at the La Brea Tar Pits (Los Angeles) 667
Paley Center for Media (Los Angeles, CA) 663
Palm Springs Art Museum (CA) 682
Panhandle-Plains Historical Museum (Canyon, TX) 492
Peabody Essex Museum (Salem, MA) 150
Peabody Museum of Archaeology & Ethnology (Cambridge, MA) 149
Peabody Museum of Natural History (New Haven, CT) 160
Peterson Automative Museum (Los Angeles) 667
Pilgrim Hall Museum (Plymouth, MA) 151
Pony Express Museum (Kansas City, MO) 457
R.E. Olds Transportation Museum (Lansing, MI) 410
Ralph Mark Gilbert Civil Rights Museum (Savannah, GA) 256
Republic of the Rio Grande Museum (Laredo, TX) 490
Rice Museum (Georgetown, SC) 254–5
Ringling Museum Complex (Sarasota, FL) 319
Rio Grande Valley Museum (TX) 490
Robert Hull Fleming Museum (Burlington, VT) 164
Rock & Roll Hall of Fame & Museum (Cleveland, OH) 406
Roger Maris Baseball Museum (Fargo, ND) 443
Rosicrucian Egyptian Museum & Planetarium (San Jose, CA) 708
Salem Witch Museum (Salem, MA) 150
Salvador Dali Museum (St. Petersburg, FL) 318
San Diego Museum of Man (CA) 680
San Diego Automotive Museum (CA) 681
San Diego Museum of Art (CA) 680
San Diego Natural History Museum (CA) 681
San Francisco Maritime National Historical Park (CA) 697, 702
Science Museum of Virginia (Richmond) 216
Seashore Trolley Museum (Kennebunkport, ME) 171
Shelburne Museum (VT) 163
Ships of the Sea Maritime Museum (Savannah, GA) 256
Sophienburg-New Braunsells Archives & Museum of History (New Braunfels, TX) 483
South Carolina Confederate Relic Room & Museum (Columbia) 254
South Carolina State Museum (Columbia) 254

Museums (cont.)
Southwest Museum of the American Indian (Los Angeles) 670
Spertus Museum (Chicago) 392
SS *William A. Irwin* (Duluth, MN) 419
St. Petersburg Museum of History (FL) 318
Strong National Museum of Play (Rochester, NY) 94
Studebaker National Museum (South Bend, IN) 401
Surfing Museum (Santa Cruz, CA) 693
Tacoma Museum of Glass (WA) 628
Tech Museum of Innovation (San Jose, CA) 708
Tennessee State Museum (Nashville) 264
TT Wentworth, Jr., Florida State Museum (Pensacola) 317
Turquoise Museum (Albuquerque, NM) 548
United States Air Force Museum (Dayton, OH) 404
University of Nebraska State Museum (Lincoln) 449
University of Oregon Museum of Natural History (Eugene) 634
US Naval Academy Museum (Annapolis, MD) 223
Vermilionville (Lafayette, LA) 356
Voigt House Victorian Museum (Grand Rapids, MI) 410
Wallowa County Museum (Joseph, OR) 639
Washington Park Arboretum (Seattle, WA) 619
Washington State History Museum (Tacoma, WA) 628
Western Washington University (Bellingham, WA) 621
Whale Museum (Friday Harbor, WA) 622
Whatcom Museum of History & Art (Bellingham, WA) 621
Wings Over Miami (FL) 299
Woolaroc Ranch Museum (OK) 460
World Museum of Mining (Butte, MT) 580
Zwaanendael Museum (Lewes, DE) 227
Music Center (Los Angeles) **668**
Mutter Museum (Philadelphia, PA) **104**
My Old Kentucky Home State Park (Bardstown) 271
Myrtle Beach (SC) 241, **254**
Mystic Seaport (CT) 161

N

Nags Head Woods Preserve (NC) 250
Nanocole 129
Nantucket Island (MA) 153
Napa Valley (CA) 650, **712–13**
NASA (FL) 286, 302
NASA-Marshall Space Flight Center (Huntsville, AL) 365
Nasher Sculpture Center (Dallas, TX) 479
Nashville (TN) 240, **264–5**
Natchez (MS) **363**
Natchez, steamboat (New Orleans) 351
Natchez Trace Parkway (MS) 41, 265, **362–3**
Natchitoches (LA) **357**
National Aeronautics & Space Administration
see NASA
National Air & Space Museum (Washington, DC) **201**
National Center for Atmospheric Research (Boulder, CO) 590
National Elk Reserve (Jackson, WY) 582
National Forests
Apalachicola National Forest (FL) 317
Bighorn National Forest (WY) 586
Daniel Boone National Forest (KY) 269
Gila National Forest (NM) 553
Green Mountain National Forest (VT) 162
Los Padres National Forest (CA) 691
Monongahela National Forest (WV) 220
Nebraska National Forest (NE) 448
Ocala National Forest (FL) 315
Pike National Forest (CO) 91
Prescott National Forest (AZ) 529
San Juan National Forest (CO) 596
Shawnee National Forest (IL) 399
Superior National Forest (MN) 420, 421
White Mountain National Forest (NH) 167
National Gallery of Art (Washington, DC) 201, **202**
National Historic Districts
Fort Worth Stockyards National Historic District (TX) 480–81
Manitou (CO) 592
Martin Luther King Jr. National Historic District (Atlanta, GA) 260
Pioneer Square (Seattle, WA) 616
Printing House Row Historic District (Chicago) 392
National Historic Landmark Districts
Bathhouse Row (Hot Springs, AR) 358
Mount Rainer National Park (WA) 626–7
Strand National Historic Landmark District (Galveston, TX) 488
National Historic Landmarks
Adler Planetarium & Astronomy Museum (Chicago) 393
Chinatown (NYC) **69**
Eldridge Street Synagogue (NYC) 69
Giant Dipper roller coaster (Santa Cruz, CA) 693
Old Town & Chinatown (Portland, OR) 631

National Historic Landmarks (cont.)
Ozark Folk Center State Park (Mountain View, AR) 359
Port Townsend (WA) **621**
Rockefeller Center (NYC) 76
San Francisco Plantation (LA) 354
Sloss Furnaces National Historic Landmark (Birmingham, AL) 365
Virginia City (NV) **516**
National Historic Parks
Appomattox Court House (VA) 218
Chaco Culture National Historical Park (NM) 544
Cumberland Gap National Historic Park (KY) 268
Harpers Ferry National Historic Park (Harpers Ferry, WV) 221
Hopewell Culture National Historic Park (OH) 405
Independence National Historic Park (Philadelphia, PA) 101
Jean Lafitte National Historic Park (Lafayette, LA) 356
Kalaupapa National Historic Park (Moloka'i, HI) 750
Klondike Gold Rush National Historical Park (Seattle, WA) 616
Lyndon B. Johnson National Historical Park (TX) 482–3
Minute Man National Historic Park (Concord, MA) 150
Missions National Historical Park (San Antonio, TX) **484**
Saratoga National Historical Park, (NY) 92
National Historic Sites
Abraham Lincoln Birthplace National Historic Site (Hodgenville, KY) 270
Central High School (Little Rock, AR) 358
Fort Davis National Historic Site (TX) 491
Fort Laramie National Historic Site (Guernsey, WY) 587
Fort Larned National Historic Site (Dodge City, KS) 459
Fort Raleigh National Historic Site (Roanoke Island, NC) 251
Fort Vancouver (WA) 629
Herbert Hoover National Historic Site (Iowa City, IA) 453
Home of Franklin D. Roosevelt National Historic Site (NY) 91
Jimmy Carter National Historic Site (Plains, GA) 258
John F. Kennedy National Historic Site (Boston) 146
Knife River Indian Village National Historic Site (Washburn, ND) 442
Lincoln Home National Historic Site (Springfield, IL) 399
Longfellow National Historic Site (Cambridge, MA) 148
Salem Maritime National Historic Site (MA) 150
Tuskegee Institute National Historic Site (AL) 365
National Historic Sites (cont.)
Whitman Mission National Historic Site (WA) 625
National Hurricane Center (Miami) 366, 367
National Lakeshores 415
Apostle Islands National Lakeshore (WI) 415
Indiana Dunes National Lakeshore (IN) 400–401
Pictured Rocks National Lakeshore (MI) 411
Sleeping Bear Dunes National Lakeshore (MI) 411
National Memorial Cemetery of the Pacific (O'ahu, HI) 749
National World War II Memorial 204
National Monuments
Cabrillo National Monument (San Diego, CA) 678
Canyon de Chelly National Monument (AZ) 542–3
Cedar Breaks National Monument (UT) 524
Colorado National Monument 597
Craters of the Moon National Monument (ID) 577
Devil's Tower National Monument (WY) 86
Federal National Monument (NYC) 66
Fort Frederica National Monument (Golden Isles, GA) 257
Fort Pulaski National Monument (GA) 256
Fort Sumter (SC) 252–3
Gateway Arch-Jefferson National Expansion Monument (St. Louis, MO) 454
Gila Cliff Dwellings National Monument (NM) 553
Grand Staircase-Escalante National Monument (UT) 524
Great Sand Dunes National Monument & Preserve (CO) 596
Hovenweep National Monument (UT) 523
Jewel Cave National Monument (Black Hills, SD) 446
John Day Fossil Beds National Monument (OR) 638–9
Lava Beds National Monument (CA) 715
Little Bighorn Battlefield National Monument (MT) 581
Mount St. Helens National Volcanic Monument (WA) 629
Montezuma Castle National Monument (AZ) 529
Muir Woods National Monument (CA) 709
Navajo National Monument (AZ) 535
Newberry National Volcanic Monument (OR) 635
Ocmulgee National Monument (Macon, GA) 258
Oregon Caves National Monument (OR) 637
Petroglyph National Monument (Albuquerque, NM) 550
National Monuments (cont.)
Pipestone National Monument (MN) 418
Poverty Point National Monument (LA) 357
Rainbow Bridge National Monument (UT) 523
Scotts Bluff National Monument (OR) 450
Timpanogos Cave National Monument (UT) 519
Tuzigoot National Monument (AZ) 529
White Sands National Monument (NM) 552–3
National Museum of African Art (Washington, DC) 200, **202–203**
National Museum of American History (Washington, DC) 200, **203**
National Museum of Natural History (Washington, DC) 200, **202**
National Museums & Galleries
National Air & Space Museum (Washington, DC) 201
National Automobile Museum (Reno, NV) 517
National Atomic Museum (Albuquerque, NM) 550
National Baseball Hall of Fame (Cooperstown, NY) 93
National Civil Rights Museum (Memphis, TN) 266
National Cowboy & Western Heritage Museum (Oklahoma City, OK) 461
National Czech & Slovak Museum (Cedar Rapids, IA) 453
National Frontier Trails Center (Independence, MO) 457
National Gallery of Art (Washington, DC) 202
National Museum of African Art (Washington, DC) 202–203
National Museum of American History (Washington, DC) 200
National Museum of Natural History (Washington, DC) 200, 202
National Museum of the Pacific War (Fredericksburg, TX) 482
National Portrait Gallery (Washington, DC) 203
National Prisoner of War (POW) Museum (Americus, GA) 258
National Route 66 Museum (Elk City, OK) 461
National Voting Rights Museum (Selma, AL) 364
National Parks 27, **34–7**
Acadia National Park (ME) 172
accomodation 37
Arches National Park (UT) 520–21
background 36
Badlands National Park (SD) 444–5
Big Bend National Park (TX) 490–91
Biscayne National Park (FL) 322
Black Canyon of the Gunnison National Park (CO) 597
Bryce Canyon National Park (UT) 526–7

National Parks (cont.)
Canyonlands National Park (UT) 522
Capitol Reef National Park (UT) 524
Carlsbad Caverns National Park (NM) 552
Channel Islands National Park (CA) 686–7
Congaree Swamp National Park (Columbia, SC) 254
Crater Lake National Park (OR) 636–7
Death Valley National Park (CA) 684–5
Denali National Park (AK) 732, **742–3**
directory 37
Everglades National Park (FL) 321
Glacier Bay National Park (AK) 737
Glacier National Park (MT) 579
Grand Canyon National Park (AZ) 536–9
Grand Teton National Park (WY) 583
Great Basin National Park (NV) 517
Great Sand Dunes National Monument & Preserve (CO) 596
Great Smoky Mountains National Park (TN) 262
Guadalupe Mountains National Park (TX) 492
Haleakalā National Park (HI) 751
Hawai'i Volcanoes National Park (HI) 752
Hot Springs National Park (AR) 358–9
Joshua Tree National Park (CA) 683
Kalaupapa National Historic Park (HI) 750
Katmai National Park (AK) 733, 740
Kenai Fjords National Park (AK) 733, 739
Lassen Volcanic National Park (CA) 715
ark (KY) 268
Mesa Verde National Park (CO) 596–7
Missions National Historical Park (TX) 484
Mount Rainier National Park (WA) 626
North Cascades National Park (WA) 624
Olympic National Park (WA) 624
passports, fees & permits 36–7
Petrified Forest National Park (AZ) 534
practical tips 37
Pu'uhonua O Hōnaunau National Historical Park (HI) 752, 753
Rocky Mountain National Park (CO) 591
Sequoia & Kings Canyon National Park (CA) 719
Sitka National Historical Park (AK) 736
Skyline Drive (VA) 219
The Presidio (San Francisco) 707
Theodore Roosevelt National Park (ND) 443

National Parks (cont.)
Voyageurs National Park (MN) 421
Wind Cave National Park (SD) 447
Wrangell-St. Elias National Park **741**
Yosemite National Park (CA) 718–19
Zion National Park (UT) 525
National Park Service 36
National Seashores
Canaveral National Seashore (FL) 303
Cape Cod National Seashore (MA) 152
Cape Hatteras National Seashore (NC) 250
Cape Lookout National Seashore (NC) 251
Gulf Islands National Seashore (MS) 363
Padre Island National Seashore (TX) 489
National Wildlife Refuges
Aransas National Wildlife Refuge (TX) 488–9
Blackwater National Wildlife Refuge (MD) 224
Chincoteague National Wildlife Refuge (VA) 217
JN "Ding" Darling National Wildlife Refuge (FL) 320
Kīlauea Point National Wildlife Refuge (HI) 754
Kodiak National Wildlife Reserve (AK) 740
Malheur National Wildlife Refuge (WA) 638
Merritt Island National Wildlife Refuge (FL) 303
Nimigret National Wildlife Refuge (RI) 157
Okefenokee Swamp National Wildlife Refuge (GA) 257
National Zoological Park (Washington, DC) **210**
Native Americans
Abbe Museum 172
Adena people 405
Algonquian Indians 59
Apache 506–507
Arapahoe 570
Arikara tribe 442
Blackhawk War 398
burial mounds 405
Caddo 437
Cahokia mounds 399
Cahuenga Pass Gabrielino Indians 666
Cayugas 60
ceremonial mounds 362
Cherokee 249, 263, 340, 364, 438, 460
Cheyenne 570, 581
Chickasaws 340
Chief Joseph 640
Choctaw 340, 364
Chumash Indians 687
Comanche 437
Crazy Horse 446, 448
Creek 340, 364
Crow 570
Dakota 444

Native Americans (cont.)
Dakota Sioux Indians 418
destruction of 46
Erie Indian tribes 407
Eiteljorg Museum 402–403
Fox 382
Ghost Dance, ceremony 445
Havasupai Indians 536
heritage centers 460
Hidatsa tribe 442
hogan 543
Hopewell people 405
Hopi 506
Huron 382
Huron Indian tribes 407
Iroquois Indians 59, 60, 91
Kansa tribes 458
Kootenai tribes 578
Lakota 444, 445
Mandan 437, 442, 443
Menominee 382
Mille Lacs Indian Museum 419
Miwok & Paiute people 718
Modoc Indians 715
Mohawks 60
Nakota Sioux 444
Nanticoke tribe 227
Navajo 506, 541, 542, 543
Nez Perce 570, 639, 640, 578
Oglala Sioux 445
Ojibwe 382, 420
Oneidas 60
Onondagas 60
Osage 437, 458
Ottawa Indian tribes 407
Paiute tribe 634
Paleo-Indians 493
Pawnee 437
Pend D'Oreille Indian tribes 578
Pine Ridge Indian Reservation 445
Potawatomi Indians 413
prehistoric city 399
Quapaw 340
Sac Indians 398
Salish tribes 578
Seminole Indians 286, 321
Senecas 60
Shawnee 382
Shoshone 570
Sioux 438, 444, 570, 581
Sitting Bull, Chief 581
Walla Walla tribe 634
Wasco tribe 634
Natural Disasters
earthquakes 693, 738, 740, 755
fire 616, 699
hurricane 298, 488
Hurricane Andrew 298
Hurricane Camille 363
largest avalanche 629
tsunamis 740, 753
volcanic eruption 629
Natural hazards
Alaska 756
Boston & New England 174
California 720
Deep South 366
Florida 324
Great Lakes 422

Natural hazards (cont.)
Hawaii 757
NYC & the Mid-Atlantic Region 110
Rockies 598
Southeast 272
Texas 494
Nauticus, The National Maritime Center (Norfolk, VA) 216
Navajo 506, 542
crafts 541, 551
homes 541, 543
massacre of 543
national monument 535
Navajo National Monument (AZ) **535**
Navarre Beach (FL) **316**
Navy Pier (Chicago) **389**
Nebraska 433, **448–51**
hotels 465
restaurants 469
The Oregon Trail **450**
Nebraska City (NE) **451**
Nelson, Willie 482
Nemours Mansion & Gardens (DE) **227**
Nevada **516–17**
hotels 556
Lake Tahoe 517
restaurants 560
Nevada City (CA) **716**
Neve, Felipe de 669, 708
New Braunfels (TX) **483**
New Castle (DE) **227**
New Deal 49
New England **124–85**
Beacon Hill **134–5**
Boston **132–49**
climate 33, 174
Connecticut 158–61
directory 175
entertainment 175
Fall Foliage in New England **166**
Freedom Trail **136–7**
getting around 174
Greater Boston **146–9**
Hartford 158–9
history of 127–8
laws 174
map 124–5, 130–31
Maine **170–73**
Massachusetts **150–53**
Massachusetts State House **138–9**
mileage chart 131
natural hazards 174
New Hampshire **166-9**
outdoor activities 174–5
people 128–9
personal security 174
Portland **170**
Providence **154–5**
Rhode Island **154–7**
safety for drivers 174
Salem Witch Trials **150**
shopping 175
Skiing 123, **165**
sports 174–5
Trinity Church 123, **144**
Vermont **162–5**
New England Anti-Slavery Society 135
New England Aquarium (Boston) 143
New Hampshire **166–9**
hotels 180–81
restaurants 185
New Harmony (IN) **400**
New Harmony State Historic Site
New Haven (CT) **160**
New Jersey **96–7**
hotels 116
restaurants 121
New Mexico 503, 506, **544–53**
Albuquerque **548–50**
desert flora & fauna 552–3
Hispanic culture 551
hotels 559
northern pueblos 545
restaurants 563
Santa Fe **546–7**
New Orleans (LA) 335, **344–53**
climate 366
getting around 345
map 344
Mardi Gras **353**
New Orleans Ironwork **347**
New Orleans Jazz **349**
Royal Street **350–51**
Voodoo Worship **348**
New Orleans Ironwork (LA) **347**
New Orleans Jazz (LA) **349**
New River Gorge National River 188, (WV) **220–21**
New York Botanical Garden (NYC) 87
New York City (NY) 39, **64–89**
Central Park 78–9
climate 110
directory 89
entertainment 88–9
etiquette 88
getting around 65, 88
hotels 112–15
map 64–5
Midtown Manhattan **74–5**
personal security 88
restaurants 118–19
shopping 89
Works of Art at the UN **76**
New York City & the Mid-Atlantic Region **54–121**
annual events & festivals 110
Central Park 78–9
climate 110
culture 61
directory 111
entertainment 111
events & festivals 110
getting around 110
Harley-Davidson 107
history 59–60
hotels 112–17
independence 60–61
industry 60–61
outdoor activities 111
people 61
map 56–7, 62–3
mileage chart 63
natural hazards 110
New Jersey 96–7
New York City 64–89
New York City & the Mid-Atlantic Region (cont.)
New York State 90–95
Pennsylvania 98–109
Philadelphia 98–105
restaurants 118–21
shopping 111
sports 110
New York Philharmonic (NYC) 83
New York Public Library (NYC) **74**
New York State **90–95**
hotels 115–16
restaurants 120
New York State Capitol (Albany, NY) 92
New York Stock Exchange (NYC) 66
New York Times 74
New Zealand Embassy 17
Newberry Library (Chicago) **388**
Newberry, Walter 388
Newberry National Volcanic Monument (OR) **635**
Newbury Street (Boston) **145**
Newman, Paul 661
Newport (RI) **156–7**
Newport Beach (Los Angeles) **673**
Newton, Robert 142
Niagara Falls (NY) 59, 61, **95**
Niagara Falls State Park
Nichols House Museum (Boston) 135
Nichols, Rose 135
Nimitz, Admiral Chester 482
Nixon, Richard 53, 209
Nob Hill (San Francisco) 697, **701**
Nogales (AZ) **533**
Nome (AK) **741**
Norfolk (VA) **216**
Noriega, Manuel 295
North Bay (MD) **224**
North Beach (San Francisco) **702**
North Beaches (Miami) **298**
North Carolina 239, **248–51**
hotels 274
restaurants 278
North Cascades Highway (WA) **624**
North Dakota 433, **442–3**
hotels 464
restaurants 468
North Dakota Heritage Center (Bismarck, ND) 443
North Platte (NE) **449**
North Shore (O'ahu, HI) **749**
Northeast, The (FL) **314–15**
hotels 328
restaurants 332
Northern California (FL) **714–15**
hotels 725
restaurants 729
Northern Pueblos Tour (NM) **545**
Norton, Joshua 698
Nottoway Plantation (LA) 354
Nurse, Rebecca 150

O

O'Keeffe, Georgia 80, 168, 402, 403, 507, 545, 547
O'Neill, Eugene 71
Oak Park (Chicago) **396–7**
map 397

Oakland (San Francisco) **708–709**
Oberlin (OH) 406
Ocala National Forest (FL) **315**
Ocean City (MD) **225**
Ocean Drive: Deco Style (Miami) **292–3**
Ogallala (NE) **448–9**
Oglethorpe, General James 256, 257
Ohio 377, 379, **404–407**
hotels 426–7
restaurants 430–31
Ohio River Valley **403**
OK Corral, gunfight at (Tombstone, AZ) 533
Okefenokee Swamp National Wildlife Refuge (GA) **257**
Oklahoma 433, 435, **460–61**
hotels 467
Old Route 66: "The Historic Mother Road" **461**
restaurants 471
Oklahoma City (OK) **461**
Old Faithful Geyser (Yellowstone NP) 566, 584
Old Faithful Geyser (Napa Valley, CA) 713
Old Granary Burying Ground (Boston) 139
Old Idaho Penitentiary (Boise) 575
Old Ironsides (Boston) 137, 149
Old Man of the Mountain 166
Old Money (Chicago) **393**
Old North Church (Boston) **142**
Old Salem (NC) 249
Old South Meeting House (Boston) **140**
Old St. Patrick's Cathedral (NYC) 69
Old State House (Boston) **141**
Old Stone House (Georgetown, Washington, DC) 209
Old Ursuline Convent (New Orleans) **346**
Old US Mint (New Orleans) **346**
Old West Ghost Town (Los Angeles) 673
Oldenburg, Claes 669
Olds, Ransom E. 410
Oliver, King 349
Olmsted, Frederick Law 104, 210, 249
Olympia (WA) **628–9**
Olympic Peninsula (WA) **620**
Olympic Mountains (WA) 620, 629
Olympic National Park (WA) 34, 620
Omaha (NE) **451**
Onate, Juan de 491
Ono, Yoko 78
Oregon **630–41**
Crater Lake National Park 630, 636–7
Hells Canyon National Recreation Area Tour 630, 640–41
hotels 645
Portland **630–31**
restaurants 647
Oregon Caves National Monument **637**
Oregon Coast **633**
Oregon Dunes National Recreation Area (OR) 633
Oregon Shakespeare Festival (Ashland) 637
Oregon Trail, The (NE) 612, **450**
Orlando (FL) **312**
Orlando & the Space Coast (FL) **302–313**
hotels 327–8
restaurants 331–2
SeaWorld & Discovery Cove **310–11**
Timeline of Space Exploration 302
Universal Orlando **308–309**
Walt Disney World® Resort **304–307**
Ory, Edward "Kid" 349
Oswald, Lee Harvey 478
Ouray (CO) **597**
Outdoor activities
Alaska 756
Boston & New England 174–5
California 720–21
Deep South 367
Florida 325
Great Lakes 423
Great Plains 463
Hawai'i 757
Los Angeles 676–7
NYC & the Mid-Atlantic Region 111
Pacific Northwest 643
Rockies 599
San Francisco 710
Southeast 273
Southwest 555
Texas 495
Washington, DC & Capital Region 228
Outer Banks (NC) **250**
Oval Office (Washington, DC) 195
Owens, Jesse 365
Owyhee Mountains (ID) 576
Oxford (MS) **360–61**
Oyster Bar (NYC) 75
O'ahu (HI) **748–9**

P

Pabst, Captain Frederick 412
Paca, William 223
Packard, David 708
Pacific Heights (San Francisco) **704**
Pacific Northwest **608–647**
climate 642
Crater Lake National Park 609, **636–7**
directory 643
distance chart 615
economy & industry 613
etiquette 643
getting around 642–3
Hells Canyon National Recreation Area Tour **640–41**
history 611–12
hotels 644–5
laws 643
map 614–15
Mount Rainier National Park **626–7**
natural hazards 642
Oregon **630–41**
outdoor activities 643
people & politics 612–13
restaurants 646–7
San Juan Islands **622–3**
Seattle 616–9
Pacific Northwest (cont.)
shopping 643
sports 643
Washington **616–29**
Padre Island National Seashore (TX) **489**
Pain, Elizabeth 140
Paine, Robert 139
Painted Canyon (Theodore Roosevelt NP, ND) 443
Painted Wall (Black Canyon of the Gunnison NP, CO) 597
Palace of Fine Arts & the Exploratorium (San Francisco) **696**
Palisades Park (Los Angeles) 660
Palm Beach (Miami) **301**
Palm Springs (CA) **682**
Palm Springs Aerial Tramway 682
Palmer, Potter 393
Palo Alto (San Francisco) **708**
Palo Duro Canyon State Park (TX) 493
Panama City Beach (FL) 317
Panhandle, The (FL) **316–17**
beaches 316–17
hotels 328–9
restaurants 332–3
Parks
Acadia National Park (ME) 35, 172
Amicalola Falls State Park (GA) 259
Anza-Borrego Desert State Park (CA) 682–3
Badlands National Park (SD) 34, 444–5
Balboa Park (CA) 680–81
Big Bend National Park (TX) 490–91
Biscayne National Park (FL) 322
Black Canyon of the Gunnison National Park (CO) 597
Bodie State Historic Park (CA) 719
Bruneau Dunes State Park (ID) 576
Bryce Canyon National Park (UT) 526–7
Buffalo Bill Ranch State Historical Park (North Platte, NE) 449
Canyonlands National Park (UT) 522
Capital Reef National Park (UT) 524
Carlsbad Caverns National Park (NM) 552
Cedar Point Amusement Park (Sandusky, OH) 407
Centennial Olympic Park (Atlanta, GA) 260
Central Park (NYC) 78–9
Central Park West (NYC) 83
Chaco Culture National Historical Park (NM) 544
Channel Islands National Park (CA) 686–7
Chattanooga & Chickamauga National Military Park (TN) 263
Chesapeake & Ohio Canal (Washington, DC) 209
City Park (New Orleans) 353
Clear Creek History Park (Golden, CO) 590
Colonial National Historical Park (VA) 216
Columbia State Historic Park (CA) 717

Parks (cont.)
Crater Lake Nat'l Park (OR) 636–7
Cumberland Falls State Resort Park (KY) 269
Cumberland Gap National Historic Park (KY) 268
D.L. Bliss State Park (CA) 718
Death Valley National Park 34, 651, 684–5
Denali National Park (AK) 5, 742–3
Disneyland Park (CA) 674
Everglades National Park (FL) 35, 321
Exposition Park & University of Southern California (CA) 668
Fair Park (Dallas, TX) 479
Fairmount Park (Philadelphia, PA) 104–105
Fort Abraham Lincoln State Park (Mandan, ND) 443
Fort Adams State Park (Newport, RI) 157
Fort Robinson State Park (NE) 448
Fort Ross State Historic Park (CA) 713
Franklin Park Conservatory & Botanical Garden (Columbus, OH) 405
Gettysburg National Military Park (PA) 106
Glacier Bay National Park (AK) 737
Glacier National Park (MT) 579
Grafton Notch State Park (ME) 173
Grand Canyon National Park (AZ) 34, 536–9
Grand Teton National Park (WY) 34, 583
Great Basin National Park (NV) 517
Great River Bluffs State Park (MN) 418
Great Smoky Mountains National Park (TN) 35, 247, 262
Griffith Park (Los Angeles) 670
Guadalupe Mountains National Park (TX) 492
Haleakalā National Park (Maui, HI) 751
Hammonasset Beach State Park (Madison, CT) 161
Hampton Plantation State Park (SC) 255
Harpers Ferry National Historic Park (WV) 221
Hawai'i Volcanoes National Park (Hawai'i Island) 752–3
Ho'okipa Beach County Park (Maui, HI) 746
Hopewell Culture National Historic Park (OH) 405
Hot Springs National Park (AR) 358–9
Humboldt Redwoods State Park (CA) 714
Independence National Historic Park (Philadelphia, PA) 100–101
Jean Lafitte National Historic Park (Lafayette, LA) 356
Jedediah Smith Redwoods State Park (CA) 714

Parks (cont.)
Jones Beach State Park (NY) 90
Joshua Tree National Park (CA) 683
Kalaupapa National Historic Park (Moloka'i, HI) 750
Katmai National Park (AK) 733
Kelleys Island State Park (Lake Erie Islands, OH) 407
Kenai Fjords National Park (AK) 733, 739
Lafayette Park (San Francisco) 704
Lassen Volcanic National Park (CA) 715
Lincoln Park Zoo (Chicago) 396
Lyndon B. Johnson National Historical Park (TX) 482–3
Mammoth Cave National Park (KY) 268
Marshall Gold Discovery State Park (CA) 716
Mesa Verde National Park (CO) 34, 567, 596–7
Millennium Park (Chicago, IL) 390
Minute Man National Historic Park (Concord, MA) 150
Missions National Historical Park (San Antonio, TX) 484
Monterey State Historic Park (CA) 692
Mount Rainer National Park (WA) 626–7
My Old Kentucky Home State Park (Bardstown) 271
Natural Bridges State Park (Santa Cruz, CA) 693
Niagara Falls State Park (NY) 95
North Cascades National Park (WA) 624
Oak Park (Chicago) 396–7
Olympic National Park (WA) 624
Ozark Folk Center State Park (AR) 359
Palisades Park (Los Angeles) 660
Peninsula State Park (WI) 413
Perrot State Park (WI) 415
Petrified Forest National Park (AZ) 534
Point Defiance Park (Tacoma, WA) 628
Pu'uhonua O Hōnaunau National Historical Park (Hawai'i Island, HI) 753
Redwood National Park (CA) 714–15
Rocky Mountain National Park (CO) 591
Royal Gorge Bridge & Park (CO) 593
Saratoga National Historical Park (NY) 93
Sequoia & Kings Canyon National Park (CA) 719
Sitka National Historic Park (AK) 736
Stone Mountain Park (GA) 259
Taughannock Falls State Park (NY) 93
Theodore Roosevelt National Park (ND) 434, 437

Parks (cont.)
Three Island Crossing State Park (ID) 576
Tubbs Hill Park (Coeur d'Alene, ID) 574
Vicksburg National Military Park (MS) 361
Voyageurs National Park (MN) 35, 378, 421
Waimea Canyon & Kōke'e State Park (Kaua'i, HI) 755
Waimea Valley Audubon Center (O'ahu, HI) 749
Wakulla Springs State Park, Tallahassee (FL) 316
Westwood Memorial Park (Los Angeles) 662
Will Rogers State Historic Park (Los Angeles) 677
Wind Cave National Park (Black Hills, SD) 447
Wrangell-St. Elias National Park **741**
Wyoming Territorial Park (Laramie) 587
Yellowstone National Park (WY) 584–5
Yosemite National Park (CA) 718–19
Zion National Park (UT) 525
Parks, Rosa 364
Park City (UT) **519**
Park Street Church (Boston) **139**
Parker, Dorothy 665
Parrish, Maxfield 226
Pasadena (Los Angeles) **672**
Passports & Visas **12–13**
Pat O'Brien's 350
Patel, K.B. 698
Paul Revere House (Boston) **142**
Paul Revere Mall (Boston) **142**
Pauling, Linus 613
Peabody Essex Museum (Salem, MA) 150
Peabody Museum of Archaeology & Ethnology (Cambridge, MA) 149
Peabody Museum of Natural History (New Haven, CT) 160
Peale, Rembrandt 43
Pearl Harbor (O'ahu, HI) 749
Pei, I.M. 147, 400, 403, 406, 668
Pendleton (OR) **639**
Peninsula State Park (WI) 413
Penn Center (St. Helena Island, SC) 255
Penn's Treaty with the Indians (Benjamin West) 60
Penn, William 60, 98, 227
Pennsylvania **106–109**
Harley-Davidson **107**
hotels 117
restaurants 121
The Amish 109
Pennsylvania Academy of Fine Arts **103**
Penobscot Bay (ME) **171**
Pensacola (FL) **316–17**
Pensacola Beach (FL) 316
Pentagon (Washington, DC) **211**
Perdido Key (FL) 316
Peregrine Funds World Center for Birds of Prey (Boise, ID) 575

Perrot State Park (WI) 415
Perry, Commodore Oliver Hazard 407
Petrified Forest National Park (AZ) **534**
Petrified Forest (CA) 713
Philadelphia (PA) 39, 101, **98–105**
  getting around 98
  Independence National Historic Park 100–101
  map 98–9
Philadelphia Museum of Art (PA) **105**
Philadelphia Quakers 104
Philadelphia Zoo (PA) **104**
Phillips Collection (Washington, DC) **210**
Phoenix (AZ) **530–31**
Phoenix, River 664
Picasso, Pablo 77, 81, 82, 95, 223, 353
Pike, Zebulon 570
Pikes Peak Cog Railway 592
Pickfair (Los Angeles) 663
Picket's Charge 106
Pickford, Mary 660, 663, 666
Pier 39 (San Francisco) 702
Pierce, Franklin 52
Pierre (SD) **444**
Pike Place Market (WA) 616
Pilgrim Hall Museum (Plymouth, MA) 151
Pilgrims, the 151, 152
Pine Ridge Indian Reservation (SD) **445**
Pioneer Square (Seattle, WA) 616
Pipestone National Monument (MN) **418**
Pittsburgh (PA) **108**
Plant, Henry 286, 318
Plantation Alley (LA) **354**
Plantations
  Ashley River Plantations (SC) 253
  Belle Meade Plantation (Nashville) 265
  Destrehan Plantation (LA) 354
  Hampton Plantation State Park (SC) 255
  Kenmore Plantation (Fredericksburg, VA) 213
  Laura Plantation (LA) 354
  Louisiana plantations 354–5
  Magnolia Plantation (SC) 253
  Magnolia Mound Plantation (Baton Rouge, LA) 355
  Melrose Plantation (Cane River Country, LA) 357
  Nottoway Mansion (LA) 354
  Oak Alley (Vacherie, LA) 335, 354
  Plimoth Plantation (Plymouth, MA) 151
  San Francisco Plantation (LA) 354
Plymouth (MA) **151**
Pocahontas 216
Point Defiance Park (Tacoma, WA) 628
Police 17
Poe, Edgar Allen 193
Polk, James K. 52
Pollack, Sydney 669
Pollock, Jackson 81, 95, 152
Polynesian dancer 741
Pont, Henry du 226
Pont, Pierre du 107
Pontalba, Baroness Micaela **347**
Pontaut Chapter House (NYC) 86
Pony Express 457, 698
Population **10**
Port Townsend (WA) **621**
Portland, (ME) **170**
  town map 170
Portland (OR) 613, **630–31**
Portsmouth (NH) **169**
Portsmouth Plaza (San Francisco) 700
Postal services 14
Poverty Point National Monument (LA) 357
Practical Information **12–19**
Prairies 458, 459, 460
Prescott 529
Preservation Hall (New Orleans) 350
Presidio (San Francisco) **707**
Presley, Elvis 267, 360, 361, 461, 511
Pretty Boy Floyd 456
Prince Maximilian 438, 451
Princeton (NJ) **96**
  Princeton University
Printing House Row Historic District (Chicago) 392
Professor Jaggar **753**
Profile Lake (Franconia Notch, NH) 166
Prospectors 684, 715, 719
  also see Gold
Providence (RI) **154–5**
  town map 155
Providence Atheneum (RI) 154
Providence City Center, map of (RI) 155
Provincetown (Cape Cod, MA) 152
Pu'u 'Ula'ula Summit (Haleakalā NP, HI) 751
Pu'uhonua O Hōnaunau National Historical Park (Hawai'i Island, HI) **753**
Public Holidays **13**
Public Jewish Library (Chicago) 392
Puck, Wolfgang 655, 664
Puebloans 523, 596
  architecture 550
  Indian Pueblo Cultural Center 550
  revolt 546
Pulitzer, Joseph 84
Punk rock 71
Puritans 127
Pyle, Howard 226

Q

Quad Cities (IA) **453**
Quakers 168, 625
Quechee Gorge 163
Queen Mary 673
Quietwater Beach (FL) 316
Quincy Market (Boston) **141**

R

Race riots 662
Radio City Music Hall (NYC) 76
Rainforests (WA) 620
Rainy Lake (MN) 421
Raleigh, Sir Walter 251
Randolph, Peyton 192
Rankin, Jeanette 580
Rauschenberg, Robert 203, 669
Reading (PA) **107**
  Reading Pagoda
Reading Terminal Market (Philadelhia, PA) **103**
Reagan, Nancy 53, 203
Reagan, Ronald 53
Reclining Figure (Henry Moore) 76
Recreational cycling 24
Recreational vehicles 23
Red Cloud, Oglala Sioux chief 445, 448
Red Earth Native American Festival 29
Redding, Otis 258, 414
Redfish Lake (ID) 575
Redford, Robert 519
Redwood National Park (CA) **714–15**
  Redwoods & the Lumber Industry
  Redwood trees 713
Rehoboth Beach (DE) 189, **227**
Rembrandt 146
Remington, Frederic 403
Reno (NV) **516–17**
Renoir, August 94, 105, 210, 406
Rental cars 23
Renwick Gallery (Washington, DC) **208**
  Renwick, James
Research Triangle Region (NC) **248**
Restaurants
  Alabama 375
  Alaska 762–3
  Arizona 561–3
  Arkansas 374
  Boston 182
  Boston & New England 182–5
  California 726–9
  Central Coast (CA) 727–8
  Central Valley (CA) 729
  Chicago 428
  Colorado 606–607
  Connecticut 184
  Deep South 372–5
  Delaware 237
  Deserts, The (CA) 727
  Everglades & the Keys (FL) 333
  Florida 330–33
  Georgia 279–80
  Gold Country (CA) 729
  Gold & Treasure Coasts (FL) 331
  Great Lakes 428–31
  Great Plains 468–71
  Gulf Coast (FL) 333
  Hawai'i 763
  High Sierras (CA) 729
  Idaho 604
  Illinois 428
  Indiana 429
  Iowa 469–70
  Kansas 471
  Kentucky 281
  Las Vegas 560
  Los Angeles 726
  Louisiana 372–4
  Maine 185
  Maryland 236
  Massachusetts 183
  Miami 330

Restaurants (cont.)
Michigan 429–30
Minnesota 430
Mississippi 375
Missouri 470
Montana 605
Nebraska 469
Nevada 560
New Hampshire 185
New Jersey 121
New Mexico 563
New Orleans 372–4
New York City 118–19
NYC & the Mid-Atlantic Region 118–21
New York State 120
North California 729
North Carolina 278
North Dakota 468
Northeast Florida 332
Ohio 430–31
Oklahoma 471
Oregon 647
Orlando & the Space Coast (FL) 331–2
Pacific Northwest 646–7
Panhandle (FL) 332–3
Pennsylvania 121
Philadelphia (PA) 121
Rhode Island 184
Rockies 604–607
San Diego County (CA) 727
San Francisco 728
Seattle (WA) 646
South Carolina 279
South Dakota 468–9
Southeast 278–81
Southwest 560–63
Tennessee 280–81
Texas 498–9
Utah 561
Vermont 185
Virginia 237
Washington, DC 234–6
Washington, DC & Capital Region 234–7
Washington State 646–7
West Virginia 237
Wine Country (CA) 729
Wisconsin 431
Wyoming 606
Reunion Tower (Dallas, TX) 478
Revere, Paul 136, 137, 140, 154
bell 168
burial place 139
legendary ride 142
statue of 142
Rhode Island 123, **154–7**
hotels 179
Providence 154–5
restaurants 184
Rhode Island State House 155
Rialto Beach (WA) 620
Richardson, Henry Hobson 144
Richmond (VA) **216**
Riley, James Whitcomb 402
Rimrocks (Billings, MT) 581
Ringling Museum Complex (Sarasota, FL) **319**
Ringling Museum Complex (cont.)
Ringling, John
Rio Grande Valley (TX) **490**
Ripley's Believe It Or Not! Museum (San Francisco) 702
Ripley's Believe It or Not!® (Los Angeles) 666
RISD Museum of Art (Providence, RI) 154
Rivera, Diego 383, 408, 528
Riverside Church (NYC) **84–5**
Riverwalk Marketplace (New Orleans, LA) **352**
Roanoke Island (NC) **251**
Robert Hull Fleming Museum (Burlington, VT) 164
Robie House (Chicago) 395
Robie, Frederick 395
Robinson, Smokey 409
Roche, Martin 390
Rochester (NY) **94**, 418
Rock 'n' roll 341, 361
Rockefeller Center (NYC) **76**
Rockefeller Memorial Chapel (Chicago) 395
Rockefeller, John D. 214, 394, 583
Rockefeller, Jr, John D. 76
Rockefellers, the 163
Rockford (IL) **398**
Rockies, The **564–607**
Buffalo Bill **582**
Climate 598
Colorado 588–97
Colorado Ski Resorts **594–5**
Denver (CO) 588–9
directory 599
entertainment 599
etiquette 598
festivals 598–9
getting around 598
Grand Teton National Park **583**
Idaho 574–7
history 569–70
hotels 600–603
maps 566–7, 572–3
mileage chart 573
Montana 578–81
natural hazards 598
outdoor activities 599
progress & development 571
restaurants 604–607
sports 599
tourism & the economy 571
Wyoming 582–7
Yellowstone National Park **584–5**
Rockwell, Norman 83, 153
Rocky Mountain National Park (CO) **591**
Rodeo Drive (Los Angeles) 663
Rodia, Simon 672
Rodin, Auguste 400, 625, 706, 708
Rodriguez, Juan 612
Roebling, John A. 68, 404
Roger Maris Baseball Museum (Fargo, ND) 443
Rogers, Will 461
Rolfe, John 216
Roosevelt, Eleanor 53, 91, 207
Roosevelt, Franklin D. 53, 91, 173, 205, 678
Roosevelt, Theodore 72, 206
Rosenwald, Julius 394
Ross, Betsy 101
Ross, Diana 409
Ross, John 263
Roswell (NM) **552**
Rothko, Mark 152, 669
Rowes Wharf (Boston) 143
Royal Gorge Bridge & Park (CO) 593
Royal Street (New Orleans, LA) **350–51**
Rules of the road **22**
Russell, Charles M. 403, 580
Russian River Valley (CA) **713**
Ryder, Winona 665

S

Saarinen, Eliel 403
Sabal Palm Audubon Sanctuary (TX) 490
Sacagawea, Indian woman 570
Sacagawea Center (Salmon, ID) 574
Sackler Museum (Cambridge, MA) 149
Sacramento (CA) **717**, 650
Safety 16
Saint Patrick's Cathedral (NYC) **77**
Saks 77, 699
Salem (MA) **150**
Salem Witch Trials
Salem (OR) **634**
Salinger, J.D. 84
Salisbury (MD) **225**
Salk, Dr. Jonas 679
Salmon (ID) **574**
Salt Lake City (UT) **518**
Salton Sea State Recreation Area (CA) **683**
Salvador Dali Museum (St. Petersburg, FL) 318
San Andreas Fault (CA) 699
San Antonio (TX) 473, **484–5**
Missions National Historical Park 484
San Diego (CA) 651, **678**
San Diego Bay (CA) 656
San Diego County (CA) **678–81**
Balboa Park 678, 680–81
hotels 722–3
restaurants 727
San Francisco (CA) **694–711**
Alcatraz Island 703
Cable Cars **700**
California's Earthquakes **699**
directory 711
entertainment 710–11
Famous Inmates of Alcatraz **703**
fire 699
getting around 694, 710
Grace Cathedral 701
Greater San Francisco **708–709**
hotels 724
map 694–5
newspapers 710
outdoor activities 710
restaurants 728
San Francisco's Murals **702**
shopping 711

San Francisco (cont.)
The Sounds of 1960s San Francisco **704**
spectator sports 710
49-Mile Scenic Drive 696–7
San Francisco Maritime National Historical Park (CA) **697**, 702
San Francisco Museum of Modern Art (CA) **699**
San Jose (CA) **708**
San Juan Islands (WA) **622–3**
San Juan Mountains (CO) 596
San Luis Obispo (CA) **687**
San Luis Obispo Mission de Tolosa
San Simeon Point (Big Sur, CA) 691
San Xavier del Bac Mission (Tucson, AZ) 532
Sand Island Light Station (Apostle Islands, WI) 415
Sandusky (OH) **407**
Sandwich (MA) 152
Santa Barbara (CA) 650, **686**
Santa Cruz (CA) **693**
Santa Cruz Beach Boardwalk
Santa Fe (NM) **546–7**
Loretto Chapel 547
Museum of Fine Arts **546**
Palace of Governors **546**
Saint Francis Cathedral 547
Santa Fe Railroad 672
Santa Monica (CA) **660–61**
Santa Monica Pier
Santa Rosa Beach (FL) 317
Sarasota (FL) **319**
Saratoga Springs (NY) **92**
Saratoga National Historical Park
Saratoga Spa State Park
Sargent, John Singer 146, 147
Sausalito (CA) **709**
Savannah (GA) **256**
Sawtooth Mountain Range 381
Sawtooth National Recreation Area (ID) **575**
Sawtooth Mountains
Scarlet Letter, The (Nathaniel Hawthorne) 140
Schrock's Amish Farm (Berlin, OH) 405
Schwarzenegger, Arnold 661
Scotia (Humboldt Redwoods State Park, CA) 714
Scott, Walter 685
Scotts Bluff National Monument (NE) 434, **450**
Scottsdale (Phoenix, AZ) 530
Screw Auger Falls (Bethel, ME) 173
Sea cows, *see* manatees
Sea World (San Diego, CA) **679**
Seafood, main producer (AK) 741
Sears Tower (Chicago) **391**
Seashore Trolley Museum (Kennebunkport, ME) 171
Seattle (WA) 38, 613, **616–19**
climate 642
restaurants 646
Seattle Aquarium (WA) 616
Seattle Art Museum (WA) 617
Seattle Center (WA) 618
Seattle Monorail (WA) 618
SeaWorld & Discovery Cove (FL) **310–11**
exhibits & rides 310
SeaWorld 310
shows & tours 310–11
tips for guests 310
Second Bank of the United States (Philadelphia, PA) **102**
Security **16–17**
Boston & New England 174
California 720
Florida 324
Southwest 554
Washington, DC & Capital Region 228
Sedona (AZ) 529
Seigel, Bugsy 505, 511
Selma (AL) 337, **364**
Seminole Indians 321
Sequoia & Kings Canyon National Parks (CA) **719**
Sequoia trees
Serpent Mound (OH) 379, **405**
Serra, Fr. Junípero 673, 687, 692
Sessions, Kate 680
Seward (AK) **739**
Shadows-on-the-Teche (LA) 356
Shaker Village of Pleasant Hill (Harrodsburg, KY) 270
Shakers 168, 270
Shamu's Happy Harbor (Sea World, CA) 679
Shaw, Robert 699
memorial of 135
Shawnee National Forest (IL) 399
Shelburne Museum & Farms (VA) **163**
Shenandoah River (WV) 221
Shepard, Alan 223
Sherman, General 218, 254, 256, 260, 362
Shipshewana (IN) **401**
Shopping
Boston & New England 175
California 721
Florida 325
Great Lakes 423
Great Plains 463
Los Angeles 677
New York City 89
NYC & the Mid-Atlantic Region 111
Rockies 599
San Francisco 711
Southwest 555
Texas 495
Washington, DC & Capital Region 229
Shreveport (LA) **357**
Sierra Nevada Mountains *see* High Sierras
Sierra Silver Mine Tour (Wallace, ID) 574
Silicon Valley (CA) 708
Silver Springs (FL) 315
Simon, Neil 87
Simon, Paul 83
Sinatra, Frank 294
Sioux City (IA) **452**
Sisters (OR) **635**
Sitka (AK) **736**
Skagway (AK) **737**
Ski resorts (CO) 165, **594–5**
Aspen (CO) 594
Blackwater Falls State Park (WV) 220
Breckenridge (CO) 595
Canaan Valley Resort State Park (WV) 220
Catamount Trail (VA) 165
Cedar City (UT) 524
Copper Mountain (CO) 595
Crested Butte (CO) 594
directory 595
Keystone (CO) 595
Killington (VT) 163
Leadville (CO) 595
Snowshoe Mountain Resort (WV) 220
Snowmass (CO) 594
Steamboat Springs (CO) 594
Sugarloaf (ME) 173
Telluride (CO) 594
Trapp Family Lodge Ski Center (VA) 165
Vail (CO) 595
Skiing in New England **165**
Ski Resorts & Companies 595
Skyline Drive (VA) **219**
Slave traffickers 350
Smith, Captain John 225
Smith, Jedediah 714
Smith, John 127
Smithsonian American Art Museum & National Portrait Gallery (Washington, DC) **203**
Smokejumpers Base (Missoula, MT) 578
Snake River (OR) 640, 641
Snake River Gorge (ID) 577
SoBe, *see* South Beach
SoHo Historic District (NYC) **70**
Solomon R. Guggenheim Museum (NYC) **82**
Song of Hiawatha, The (Henry Wadsworth Longfellow) 148
Sonoma Valley (CA) **712**
Sonoran Desert (AZ) 528
Sorin, Edward Father 401
Soto, Hernando de 340
Sounds of 1960s San Francisco (CA) **704**
Soul Food 341
South African Embassy 17
South Beach (Miami) **292–3**
South Bend (IN) **401**
South Carolina 239, **252–5**
Charleston **252–3**
hotels 275
restaurants 279
South County Beaches (RI) **157**
South Dakota 433, **444–7**
hotels 464–5
restaurants 468–9
Southeast, The **238–81**
Atlanta **260–61**
climate 272
Charleston **252–3**
Country & Bluegrass Music **269**
directory 273
entertainment 273
etiquette 272
festivals 272–3

Southeast, The (cont.)
- Georgia **256–61**
- getting around 272
- history 243–5
- hotels 274–7
- Kentucky **268–71**
- map 240–1, 246–7
- mileage chart 247
- Memphis **266–7**
- Nashville **264–5**
- natural hazards 272
- North Carolina **248–51**
- restaurants 278–81
- society, culture, & the arts 245
- South Carolina **252–5**
- sports & outdoors 273
- Tennessee **262–7**
- tourism 245

South Loop (Chicago) **392**
South Rim Road (Black Canyon of the Gunnison NP, CO) 597
South Street Seaport (NYC) **68**
Southwest, The **500–563**
- Albuquerque 548–50
- Arches National Park 520–21
- Arizona **528–43**
- Bryce Canyon National Park 526–7
- Canyon de Chelly National Monument 542–3
- Canyonlands National Park 522
- climate 32, 505
- culture 506–507
- Desert Flora & Fauna 552–3
- directory 554
- distance chart 508
- entertainment 555
- etiquette 554
- getting around 554
- Grand Canyon 536–9
- Heart of Arizona Tour 528
- Hispanic Culture 551
- history 505–506
- hotels 556–9
- Las Vegas **510–15**
- maps 502–503, 508–509
- Massacre Cave 543
- Monument Valley 540–41
- Mormons, the 519
- Nevada **516–27**
- New Mexico **544–53**
- Northern Pueblos Tour 545
- outdoor activities 519, 525, 543, 544, 555
- Phoenix **530–31**
- restaurants 560–63
- Santa Fe **546–7**
- shopping 555
- Southwest Architecture 532–3
- Utah **518–27**
- Wild West, the 541
- Zion National Park 525

Southern Illinois (IL) **399**
Southwest Museum (Los Angeles) **670**
Space Needle (Seattle, WA) 614, 618
Spanish influence 551
Spanish–American War 699
Splash Zone (Monterey, CA) 693
Spokane (WA) **625**
Spoonbridge and Cherry (Walker Art Center, Minneapolis, MN) 416
Sports
- Boston & New England 174–5
- Deep South 367
- Great Lakes 422–3
- Great Plains 462–3
- Los Angeles 677
- NYC & the Mid-Atlantic Region 110–11
- Rockies 599
- San Francisco 710
- Southeast 273
- Texas 495
- Washington, DC & Capital Region 228

Spring Green (WI) **415**
Springfield (IL) 378, **399**
SS *Ticonderoga* (Shelburne Museum, VA) 163
St. Andrews (FL) 317
St. Augustine (FL) **314**
St. Charles Avenue Streetcar (New Orleans, LA) 353
St. Joseph (MO) **457**
St. Louis Cemetery # 1 (New Orleans, LA) **348**
St. Louis (MO) 435, **454–5**
St. Louis Cathedral, Cabildo, & Presbytère (New Orleans, LA) **348**
St. Louis City Center, map (MO) 455
St. Louis County Heritage & Arts Center (Duluth, MN) 419
St. Mark's Episcopal Cathedral (Seattle, WA) 618
St. Mark's-in-the-Bowery (NYC) 71
St. Michael's Cathedral (Sitka, AK) 736
St. Michaels (MD) **224**
St. Nicholas Historic District (NYC) **85**
St. Paul's Chapel (NYC) 84
St. Petersburg (FL) **318–19**
St. Philomena Church (Kalaupapa National Historical Park, HI) 750
Stanford, Leland 708, 717
Stanford University (Palo Alto, CA) 708
"Star-Spangled Banner," The 193
Starbucks (Seattle, WA) 613
State Beaches
- East Matunuck State Beach (RI) 157
- Malibu Lagoon State Beach (CA) 672
- Misquamicut State Beach (RI) 157
- Scarborough State Beach (RI) 157

State Capitols
- Colorado State Capitol (Denver) 588
- Connecticut State Capitol (Hartford) 158
- New Capitol Building (Tallahassee, FL) 316
- Idaho State Capitol (Boise) 575
- Iowa State Capitol (Des Moines) 452
- Louisiana State Capitol (Baton Rouge) 355
- Maryland State House (Annapolis) 223
- Minnesota State Capitol (St. Paul) 417
- Mississippi State Capitol (Jackson) 362
- Missouri State Capitol (Jefferson City) 456

State Capitols (cont.)
- Montana State Capitol (Helena) 580
- Nebraska State Capitol (Lincoln) 449
- New York State Capitol (Albany) 92
- North Dakota State Capitol (Bismarck) 443
- Oregon State Capitol (Salem) 634
- South Dakota State Capitol (Pierre) 444
- State Capitol (Carson City, NV) 516
- State Capitol Campus (Olympia, WA) 629
- State Capitol (Raleigh, NC) 248
- Texas State Capitol (Austin) 482
- United States Capitol (Washington, DC) 198–9
- Utah State Capitol (Salt Lake City) 518
- Wisconsin State Capitol (Madison) 414

State Forests
- Mount Everett State Forest (MA) 153
- Mount Washington State Forest (MA) 153

State Game Sanctuary
- McNeil River State Game Sanctuary (AK) 740

State Historic Monuments
- El Pueblo (Los Angeles) 669

State Historic Parks
- Bodie State Historic Park (CA) 719
- Columbia State Historic Park (CA) **717**
- La Purísima Concepción (CA) 687

State Historic Sites
- Fort Totten State Historic Site (Devil's Lake, ND) 442
- Jefferson Landing State Historic Site (Jefferson City, MO) 456
- Joss House State Historic Site (Weaverville, CA) 715
- Kaw Mission School (Flint Hills, KS) 458
- Lanier Mansion State Historic Site (Madison, IN) 403
- Longfellow-Evangeline State Historic Site (St. Martinville, LA) 356
- New Harmony State Historic Site (New Harmony, IN) 400
- Oregon Trail Ruts State Historic Site (Guernsey, WY) 587
- Thomas Wolfe State Historic Site (Asheville, NC) 249
- Watts Towers (Los Angeles) 672–3

State Historical Parks
- Monterey State Historic Park (CA) 692
- Totem Bight State Historical Park (Ketchikan, AK) 736

State Parks
- Amicalola Falls State Park (GA) 259
- Andrew Molera State Park (Big Sur, CA) 690
- Antelope Island State Park (Great Salt Lake, UT) 518
- Anza-Borrego Desert State Park (CA) **682–3**
- Arbor Lodge State Historical Park (Nebraska City, NE) 451

State Parks (cont.)
Bahia Honda State Park (FL) 322
Blackwater Falls State Park (Monongahela National Forest, WV) 220
Bruneau Dunes State Park (ID) **576**
Buffalo Bill Ranch State Historical Park (North Platte, NE) 449
Bullards Beach State Park (OR) 633
Camden Hills State Park (Camden, ME) 171
Canaan Valley Resort State Park (WV) 220
Cape Henlopen State Park (Lewes, DE) 227
Cape Lookout State Park (OR) 633
Cass Scenic Railroad State Park (WV) 220
Chadron State Park (NE) 448
Cove Palisades State Park (OR) 634
Crow Wing State Park (MN) 419
Cumberland Falls State Resort Park (Daniel Boone Natl' Forest, KY) 269
Custer State Park (Black Hills, SD) 447
Delaware Seashore State Park (Rehoboth Beach, DE) 227
D.L. Bliss State Park (Lake Tahoe, CA) 718
Ecola State Park (OR) 633
Elk Neck State Park (MD) 224
Fort Abraham Lincoln State Park (Bismarck, ND) 443
Fort Adams State Park (RI) 157
Fort Clinch State Park (FL) 315
Fort Robinson State Park (Chadron, NE) 448
Franconia Notch State Park (Franconia Notch, NH) 166
Frontenac State Park (MN) 418
Grafton Notch State Park (ME) 173
Great River Bluffs State Park 418
Great Salt Lake State Park (MN) 418
Hampton Plantation State Park (Georgetown, SC) 255
Hawk's Nest State Park (WV) 221
Heceta Head State Park (OR) 633
Humboldt Lagoons State Park (Redwood NP, CA) 715
Humboldt Redwoods State Park (CA) **714**
Hunting Island State Park (Hunting Island, SC) 255
Huntington Beach State Park (Myrtle Beach, SC) 254
Jedediah Smith Redwoods State Park (Redwood NP, CA) 714
Jockey Ridge State Park (NC) 250
John Pennekamp Coral Reef State Park (Key Largo, FL) 322
Jones Beach State Park (NY) **90**
Julia Pfeiffer Burns State Park (Big Sur, CA) 691
Kachemak Bay State Park (AK) 739
Kelleys Island State Park (OH) 407
Kōke'e State Park (Kaua'i, HI) **755**
Laurel Ridge State Park (PA) 109
Lime Kiln Point State Park (San Juan Islands, WA) 622

State Parks (cont.)
Mackinac Island State Park (MI) 411
Malibu Creek State Park (Malibu, CA) 672
Marshall Gold Discovery State Park (CA) **716**
McConnell's Mill State Park (PA) 109
Moraine State Park (PA) 109
Mount San Jacinto Wilderness State Park (CA) 682
Mount Tom State Park (Litchfield, CT) 159
Mustang Island State Park (Corpus Christi, TX) 489
My Old Kentucky Home State Park (Bardstown, KY) 271
Natural Bridge State Resort Park (Daniel Boone Natl' Forest, KY) 269
Niagara Falls State Park (Niagara Falls, NY) 95
Ohiopyle State Park (Laurel Highlands, PA) 109
Ozark Folk Center State Park (Mountain View, AR) 359
Palo Duro Canyon State Park (TX) 493
Patrick's Point State Park (Redwood NP, CA) 715
Peninsula State Park (WI) 413
Perrot State Park (WI) 415
Porcupine Mountains Wilderness State Park (MI) 411
Red Rock Canyon State Park (Mojave Desert, CA) 683
Riverside State Park (WA) 625
Saratoga Spa State Park (Saratoga Springs, NY) 92
Silver River State Park (Silver Springs, FL) 315
Stephen C. Foster State Park (Okefenokee Swamp, GA) 257
Taughannock Falls State Park (NY) 93
Three Island Crossing State Park (ID) **576**
Valley of Fire State Park (NV) 515
Wakulla Springs State Park (FL) 316
State Reserves
Point Lobos State Reserve (Big Sur, CA) 690
Statue of Liberty (NYC) **67**, 72, 145
sculptor 145
Steamboat *Natchez* (New Orleans, LA) **351**
Steamboat Springs (CO) 569, 594
Steele, Danielle 704
Steens Mountain (OR) **638**
Stein, Gertrude 709
Steinbeck, John 435, 439, 461, 692
Stevenson, Robert Louis 690, 692
Stewart, Paul 589
Stone Mountain Park (GA) **259**
Storyville Jazz Salon (New Orleans, LA) 349
Stow Lake (San Francisco) **696**
Stowe (VA) **165**
Stowe, Harriet Beecher 159, 404
Strauss, Joseph 707
Strawberry Fields (NYC) 78

Strawbery Banke (Portsmouth, NH) 169
Street of Painted Balconies (San Francisco) 700
Strickland, William 346
Stroud, Robert 703
Stuart, Gilbert 155, 203
Studio Museum in Harlem (NYC) **85**
Sturbridge (MA) **153**
Sublette, William 450
Suffrage Movement, beginnings of 93
Sugarloaf (ME) **173**
Sunflower River Blues & Gospel Festival (Greenville, MS) 360
Sulfur springs (Lassen Volcanic NP, CA) 715
Sun Studio (Memphis, TN) 267
Sun Valley (ID) 566, **576**
Sundance Film Festival (Park City, UT) 519
Sundance Kid 480
Sunset Boulevard (Los Angeles) 663, **664–5**
Sunset Plaza (Los Angeles) 664
Superdome (New Orleans, LA) 367
Surfing in California **693**
Sutro Tower (San Francisco) **696**
Sutter, John 717
Swiftcurrent Lake (Glacier NP, MT) 579
Switzerland of America (Ouray, CO) 597
Synagogue, oldest (Newport, RI) 156
Syracuse (NY) **94**

T

Tacoma (WA) **628**
Taft, William H. 53
Tahlequah (OK) **460–61**
Talbott, William Henry Fox 660
Taliesin (Spring Green, WI) 415
Tallahassee (FL) **316**
Tallgrass Prairie National Preserve (Bartlesville, KS) 459
Talmadge, Norma 666
Tampa (FL) **318**
Taos (NM) **544**
Tarzan 315
Taughannock Falls (NY) 62
Taughannock Falls State Park (NY) 93
Taylor, Zachary 52
Teach, Edward "Blackbeard" 251
Telegraph Hill (San Francisco) 697
Telephone Men & Women at Work (Dean Cornwell) 140
Telephones 14
Telluride (CO) 594
Tennessee 239, **262–7**
Flora of the Great Smoky Mountains **262**
hotels 276–7
Memphis **266–7**
Nashville **264–5**
restaurants 280–81
Tennessee Aquarium (Chattanooga) 263
Tepees 570
Terrorist attack 66, 67, 211
Texas 473, **472–99**
annual events & festivals 494

Texas (cont.)
Buddy Holly **492**
climate 494
Cowboys **481**
Dallas 473, **478–9**
directory 495
distance chart 477
economy & culture 475
Fort Worth 473, **480–81**
getting around 494
history 474–5
hotels 496–7
Houston 473, **486–7**
map 476–7
natural hazards 494
outdoor activities 495
restaurants 498–9
San Antonio 473, **484–5**
shopping 495
sports 495
Visiting Mexico **491**
Texas State Aquarium (Corpus Christi) 489
Texas State Capitol (Austin, TX) 482
Thanks-giving Square (Dallas, TX) 479
Tharp, Hale 719
Theater District (Boston) **139**
Theodore Roosevelt National Park (ND) 434, 437, **443**
Thinker, The (Rodin) 708
Thomas, Dylan 702
Thoreau, Henry David 150
Three Island Crossing State Park (ID) **576**
Three Sisters (Monument Valley, AZ) 540
Three Sisters Mountain (OR) 635
Thurston Lava Tube (Hawai'i Volcanoes NP, HI) 753
Tiffany's (NYC) 77
Tiffany, Louis Comfort 312
Tijuana, Mexico **679**
Time zones **20**
Timeline of Space Exploration (FL) **302**
Times Square (NYC) **74**
Timpanogos Cave National Monument (UT) **519**
Tin How Temple (San Francisco) 700
Titanic 588
Todd, Mary 270
Toledo (OH) **407**
Tombstone (Bisbee, AZ) 533
Tomesha (Death Valley NP, CA) 684–5
Tongs 69, 700
Topeka (KS) **458**
Tor House (CA) 692
Tourist information
Alaska 756
Boston & New England 174
California 720
Deep South 366
Florida 324
Great Lakes 422
Great Plains 462
Hawai'i 757
Los Angeles 676
NYC & the Mid-Atlantic Region 110
Pacific Northwest 642
Tourist information (cont.)
Rockies 598
San Francisco 710
Southeast 272
Southwest 554
Texas 494
Washington, DC & Capital Region 228
Touro Synagogue (Newport, RI) 156
Trail of Tears 438
Trail Ridge Road (Rocky Mountain NP, CO) 591
Train travel **25**
Alaska 756
California 720
Deep South 366
Great Lakes 422
Hawai'i 757
NYC & the Mid-Atlantic Region 110
Rockies 598
San Francisco 710
Southeast 272
Southwest 554
Washington, DC & Capital Region 228
Trans-Alaska Pipeline 738
Transamerica Pyramid (San Francisco) 698
Transcontinental railroad 654
Trapp Family Lodge (Stowe, VA) 165
Travel by air **20–21**
Travel by bike **24**
Travel by motorcycle **24**
Travel by road **22–3**
Travel information **20–25**
Travel insurance 17
Traveler's checks 15
Treaty of Paris 223
Treister, Kenneth 293
Tribal Reservations
Mille Lacs Band of Ojibwe Tribal Reservation (MN) 419
TriBeCa (NYC) **70**
Trinity Alps (CA) 715
Trinity Church (NYC) 66
Trinity Church (Boston) 133, **144**
Truman, Harry S. 53, 457
Trumbull, John 127
Trump, Donald 78
tsunamis 740
Tuba City (AZ) **535**
Tubbs Hill Park (Coeur d'Alene, ID) 574
Tucker, Tanya 492
Tucson (AZ) **532**
Tulsa (OK) **460**
Tupelo (MS) **361**
Turnbull, Swan 417
Tuskegee (AL) **365**
Tuzigoot National Monument (AZ) 529
Twain, Mark 71, 158–9, 340, 698
Twin Falls (ID) **577**
Tyler, Ann 193
Tyler, John 52, 216
Tyrannosaurus Rex, skeleton of 393, 706

U

Uncle Tom's Cabin (Harriet Beecher Stowe) 159
Uncle Tom's Trail (Yellowstone NP, WY) 585
Union Square (NYC) **72**, 699
United Kingdom Embassy 17
United Nations (NYC) 74, **76**
United States Capitol (Washington, DC) **198–9**
United States Holocaust Memorial Museum (Washington, DC) **204**
US Military Academy (NY) 91
Universal Studios (Los Angeles) **671**
Universal Orlando (FL) **308–309**
eating & shopping 308
The Islands of Adventure 309
Universal Studios Florida 308
Universal CityWalk 309
University of Arizona (Tucson, AZ) 532
University of California Los Angeles (UCLA) 662
University of California at Berkeley (CA) 709
University of Chicago (IL) **394–5**
University of Colorado (Boulder) 590
University of Michigan (Ann Arbor) 410
University of North Carolina (Chapel Hill) 248
University of Southern California (Los Angeles) 668
University of Texas (Austin) 482
Updike, John 129
Upper Newport Bay Ecological Preserve (CA) 673
Upper Peninsula (MI) **411**
US (61) 418
US (93), highway 574
US Embassy 17
US Mint (Philadelphia, PA) **102**
US Space & Rocket Center (Huntsville, AL) 365
US Supreme Court (Washington, DC) **199**
USA, map **10–11**
Utah **518–27**
Arches National Park **520–21**
Bryce Canyon National Park **526–7**
Canyonlands National Park **522**
hotels 557
Mormons, The 519
restaurants 561
Zion National Park 525
Utopian communities/sects 400
Harmonists, the 400
Harmony Society 400

V

Vail (CO) 595
Valdez (AK) **738**
Valdez Museum (AK) 738
Vallejo, General Mariano 712
Valley of 10,000 Smokes (Katmai NP, AK) 740
Van Gogh, Vincent 77, 81, 82, 223, 406, 660
Vancouver, Captain George 626, 737
Vanderbilt II, Cornelius 156
Vanderbilt Mansion (Hyde Park, NY) 91

Vanderbilt, Cornelius 75
Vanderbilt, Frederick W. 91
Venetian Pool (Miami, FL) **296**
Venice (CA) **661**
Ventura, Jesse 382
Venturi, Robert 403
Vermont 124, **162–5**
  hotels 180
  restaurants 185
Vermont Institute of Natural Science (Woodstock, VA) 163
Verrazano, Giovanni da 60
Vespucci, Amerigo 43
Vicksburg National Military Park (MS) **361**
Vietnam Veterans Memorial (Washington, DC) **205**
Vietnam War 709
Village, the (NYC) 70–71
  see also Greenwich Village
Village, the (FL) 297
  see also Coconut Grove Village
Vineyards, California
  see Wine Country
Virginia **212–19**
  Colonial Williamsburg **214–15**
  hotels 232–3
  restaurants 237
  Skyline Drive 219
Virginia City (NV) **516**
Vizcaya (Miami, FL) **297**
Vizcaíno, Sebastián 692
Volcanos
  Haleakalā Volcano (HI) 744, 751
  Lassen Peak (CA) 715
  Mount Edgecumbe (AK) 736
  Mount Kīlauea (HI) 744, 745
Voodoo Worship (New Orleans) **348**
Voyageurs National Park (MN) 35, 378, **421**

W

Wadsworth Atheneum (Hartford, CT) 158
Waikīkī (Oʻahu, HI) **748–9**
Wailua Falls (Kauaʻi, HI) 754
Waimea Canyon & Kōkeʻe State Park (Kauaʻi, HI) **755**
Waimea Valley Center (Oʻahu, HI) 749
Wakulla Springs State Park (FL) 316
Walden Pond (Concord, MA) 150
  Walden Pond State Reservation
Waldorf-Astoria (NYC) 75
Walk of Fame (Los Angeles) 666
Walken, Christopher 665
Wall (SD) **445**
Wall Street of the West (San Francisco) 698
Wall Street (NYC) **66**
Walla Walla (WA) **625**
Waller, Robert 452
Wallowa Mountains (OR) **639**
Wallowa-Whitman National Forest (Hells Canyon Natl' Recreation Area, OR) 640
Walt Disney World® Resort (FL) **304–307**
Walt Disney World® Resort (cont.)
  Animal Kingdom 307
  disabled travelers 304
  Disney's Hollywood Studios 307
  Eating & Drinking 306
  Epcot 306–307
  Experimental Prototype Community of Tomorrow *see* EPCOT
  getting around 304
  length of visit 304
  Magic Kingdom 306
  map 304
  parking 305
  safety 305
  staying in the resort 305
  tickets & passes 305
  useful numbers 304
  very young children 304
  when to visit 304
Warhol, Andy 108, 203, 223, 404
Warm Springs Reservation (OR) 634
Washburn (ND) **442**
Washington Artillery Park and Moonwalk (New Orleans) 348
Washington, Booker T. 365
Washington Crossing the Delaware (Delaware Art Museum, Wilmington) 226
Washington, DC **196–211**
  climate 228
  getting around 196
  hotels 230–31
  map 196–7
  restaurants 234–6
  The Mall **200–201**
  The White House **206–207**
  United States Capitol **198–9**
Washington, DC & the Capital Region **186–237**
  Civil War 192–3
  Colonial Williamsburg **214–15**
  Delaware **226–7**
  directory 229
  entertainment 229
  etiquette 228
  getting around 228
  history 191–2
  hotels 230–33
  independence 192–3
  people & culture 193
  maps 188–9, 194–5
  mileage chart 195
  Maryland **222–5**
  Mount Vernon 212–3
  outdoor activities 228
  personal security 228
  restaurants 234–7
  shopping 229
  Skyline Drive **219**
  The Mall **200–201**
  The White House **206–207**
  United States Capitol **198–9**
  Virginia **212–19**
  Washington, DC **196–211**
  West Virginia **220–21**
Washington, George 52, 148, 155, 192
  burial place 100
  bust of 142
Washington, George (cont.)
  home & tomb 212–13
  inauguration 70
  library of 135
  portrait 81
  statue of 135
Washington, Harold 395
Washington Island (WI) 413
Washington Monument (Washington, DC) **204**
Washington National Cathedral (Washington, DC) **210–11**
Washington Square (NYC) **70**
Washington, state of **616–29**
  hotels 644–5
  Mount Rainier National Park **626–7**
  restaurants 646–7
  San Juan Islands **622–3**
  Seattle **616–19**
WASPS 129
Waterfront (Boston) **143**
  Children's Museum
Watergate Complex (Washington, DC) **209**
Water sports 316, 317
Waters, Alice 655
Watts Towers (Los Angeles) **672–3**
Wayne, John 438, 452, 481
Weather
  Alaska 756
  Anchorage (AK) 756
  Atlanta (GA) 272
  Boston (MA) 174
  Chicago (IL) 422
  Dallas (TX) 494
  Deep South 366
  Denver (CO) 598
  Florida 324
  Great Lakes 422
  Great Plains 462
  Hawaiʻi 757
  Honolulu (Oʻahu, HI) 757
  Kansas City (MO) 462
  Las Vegas (NV) 554
  Los Angeles (CA) 720
  Miami (FL) 324
  Mid-Atlantic Region 110
  New England 174
  New Orleans (LA) 366
  New York City (NY) 110
  Pacific Northwest 642
  Rockies 598
  Seattle (WA) 642
  Southeast 272
  Southwest 554
  Texas 494
  Washington, DC 228
Weaverville (CA) **715**
Weber, Roland 394
Wedding Cake House (Kennebunk, ME) 171
Weismuller, Johnny 296, 315
Wells Fargo History Museum (San Francisco) **698**
Welty, Eudora 362
West End (Dallas, TX) 478
West Virginia 187, **220–21**
  hotels 233
  restaurants 237

West, Benjamin 103
West, Mae 666
Western Amish Country (PA) **109**
Westwood Memorial Park (Los Angeles) 662
Westwood & UCLA (Los Angeles) **662**
Whales 152
Wharton, Edith 72
Whiskey distilleries (KY) 271
Whistler, James 80, 146, 224
White House (Washington, DC) 189, **206–207**
  White House Visitor Center
White House Tavern (Newport, RI) 156
White Mountain National Forest (NH) **167**
  White Mountains Trail
White Pass & Yukon Route Railroad (Skagway, AK) 737
White Sands National Monument (NM) **552–3**
Whitewater Rafting in Colorado **593**
Whitman, Walt 87
Whitney, Josiah 719
Whitney Museum of American Art (NYC) **80**
Wilcox, Harvey Henderson 666
Whooping cranes 488–9
Wichita (KS) 435, **459**
Widener Library, Harvard (Cambridge, MA) 148
Wild Bill Hickock 446
Wild West 48, 683
Wilder, L. Douglas 192
Wildlife
  alligators 35, 321, 353
  bears 740
  caribou 743
  crocodiles 321
  Dall sheep 743
  Florida black bear 315
  Grizzly bears 743
  manatees 319, 321
  moose 743
  panthers 320
  red foxes 172
  white-tailed deer 172
  wolves **421**, 743
  woodchucks 172
Will Rogers State Historic Park (Los Angeles) 677
Willet, Henry 701
William Paca House (Annapolis, MD) 223
Williams, Hank 264, 365
Williams, Roger 154
Williams, Tennessee 139, 347, 353, 360
Wilmington (DE) **226**
Wilson, Woodrow 53
Wilshire Boulevard (Los Angeles) 663
Winchester Mystery House (San Jose, CA) 708
Winchester, Sarah 708
Window Rock (AZ) **535**
Wines **712–13**
  Blanc 713
  Cabernet 713
  Chardonnay 713
  Merlot 713
  Pinot Noir 713
  Sauvignon 713
Wineries (CA) **712–13**
  Clos Pegase Winery 713
  Mumm Napa Valley 712–13
  Rutherford Hill Winery 712
  Sebastiani Vineyards 721
  Viansa Winery 721
Wine Country (CA) **712–13**
  hotels 724
  restaurants 729
Winfrey, Oprah 360
Wings Over Miami (FL) **299**
Winston-Salem (NC) **248–9**
Winter Park (CO) 595
Winter Park (FL) **312**
Winterthur (DE) **226**
Wisconsin 378, **412–15**
  hotels 427
  restaurants 431
Wisconsin Dells (WI) **414**
Wisconsin State Capitol (Madison, WI) 414
Wolfe, Thomas 249
Wolves **421**, 743
Wonder, Stevie 409
Wood, Grant 224, 453
Wood, Natalie 662
Woods Hole Oceanographic Institute (Cape Cod, MA) 152
Woodstock (VA) **163**
Woodward, Bob 209
Woolaroc Ranch (Bartlesville, OK) 460
Woolworth Building (NYC) 69
Works of Art at the UN (NYC) **76**
World Financial Center (NYC) 67
World of Coca-Cola (Atlanta, GA) 260
World Trade Center Site (NYC) **66**
World War II 166
Worth Avenue (Palm Beach, FL) 301
Wozniak, Stephen 708
Wrangell-St. Elias National Park **741**
Wren, Sir Christopher 139, 142
Wright Brothers National Memorial (Kill Devil Hills, NC) 250
Wright, Frank Lloyd 82, 109, 169, 391, 395, 396, 399, 410, 413, 415, 667, 699
Wright, Orville & Wilbur 250, 404
Wyeth, Andrew 168, 171
Wyeth, N.C. 72, 226
Wyoming **582–7**
  Buffalo Bill **582**
  Grand Teton National Park **583**
  hotels 602
  restaurants 606
  Yellowstone National Park **584–5**
Wyoming Territorial Park (Laramie, WY) 587

Y

Yakima Valley (WA) **625**
Yale University (New Haven, CT) 160
  Yale Center for British Art
  Yale University Art Gallery
Yankee Stadium (NYC) 87
Yellowstone National Park (WY) 34, 566, **584–5**
Yerba Buena Center for the Arts (San Francisco) **698–9**
York (PA) **107**
Yosemite National Park 34, 651, (CA) **718–19**
Young, Andrew 245

Z

Zoos
  Acadia Zoo (Acadia NP, ME) 172
  Audubon Zoo (New Orleans, LA) 353
  Bronx Zoo (NYC) 87
  Cape May County Park & Zoo (NJ) 97
  Denver Zoo (CO) 589
  Fort Wayne Children's Zoo (IN) 401
  Insect Zoo (Washington, DC) 202
  Lincoln Park Zoo (Chicago, IL) 396
  Los Angeles Zoo (CA) 670
  Miami Metrozoo (FL) 299
  National Zoological Park (Washington, DC) 210
  Oregon Zoo (Portland) 631
  Philadelphia Zoo (PA) 104
  Point Defiance Zoo & Aquarium (Tacoma, WA) 628
  Rio Grande Zoological Park (Albuquerque, NM) 549
  Roger Williams Park & Zoo (Providence, RI) 154
  San Diego Zoo (CA) 681
  Woodland Park Zoo (Seattle, WA) 619
Zion National Park (UT) **525**

Acknowledgements

Proof Reader & Indexer

Glenda Fernandes.

DK London

Editorial & Design Assistance

Emma Anacootee, Emily Anderson, Brigitte Arora, Lydia Baillie, Sherry Collins, Jo Cowen, Caroline Elliker, Nicola Erdpresser, Caroline Evans, Madeline Farbman, Rhiannon Furbear, Jacky Jackson, Maite Lantaron, Pamela Marmito, Alison McGill, Sam Merrell, Catherine Palmi, Rada Radojicic, Ros Walford.

Factcheckers

Mary Bergin, D. Clancy, Jerry Dean, Paul Franklin, Lyn Kidder, Jill Metzler, Carolyn Patten, Don Pitcher, Mike Rogers.

Senior DTP Designer

Jason Little.

Senior Cartographic Editor

Casper Morris.

DK Picture Library

Mark Dennis.

Production Controllers

Sarah Dodd, Melanie Dowland.

Managing Art Editor

Jane Ewart.

Publishing Manager

Helen Townsend.

Publisher

Douglas Amrine.

Dorling Kindersley would like to thank the following people whose contributions and assistance have made the preparation of this book possible.

Additional Contributors

Ruth & Eric Bailey, Jyl Benson, Eleanor Berman, Jeremy Black, Lester Brooks, Patricia Brooks, Tom Bross, Susan Burke, Rebecca Carman, Richard Cawthorne, Brett Cook, Donna Dailey, Jackie Finch, Bonita Halm, Michelle de Larrabeiti, David Dick, Susan Farewell, Rebecca Poole Forée, Paul Franklin, Donald S. Frazier, Bonnie Friedman, Rita Goldman, Patricia Harris, Ross Hassig, Carolyn Heller, Pierre Home-Douglas, Lorraine Johnson, Penney Kome, Esther Labi, Philip Lee, Helga Loverseed, David Lyon, Clemence McLaren, Guy Mansell, Fred Mawer, Nancy Mikula, Melissa Miller, Kendrick Oliver, Barry Parr, Ellen Payne, J. Kingston Pierce, Alice L. Powers, Jennifer Quasha, George Raudzens, Juliette Rogers, John Ryan, Alex Salkever, Litta W. Sanderson, Kem Sawyer, AnneLise Sorenson, Emma Stanford, Brett Steel, Arvin Steinberg, Phyllis Steinberg, Nigel Tisdall, Brian Ward, Greg Ward, John Wilcock, Ian Williams, Marilyn Wood, Paul Wood, Stanley Young.

Additional Illustrators

Ricardo Almazan, Ricardo Almazan Jr, Arcana Studios, Robert Ashby, William Band, Gilles Beauchemin, Richard Bonson, Joanne Cameron, Stephen Conlin, Gary Cross, Richard Draper, Dean Entwhistle, Eugene Fleurey, Chris Forsey, Martin Gagnon, Vincent Gagnon, Stephen Gyapay, Stéphane Jorisch, Patrick Jougla, Nick Lipscombe, Claire Littlejohn, Luc Normandin, Lee Peters, Mel Pickering, Robbie Polley, Kevin Robinson, Hamish Simpson, Mike Taylor, Pat Thorne, Chris Orr & Associates, Jean-François Vachon, John Woodcock.

Additional Photographers

Max Alexander, Peter Anderson, Jaime Baldovinos, Alan Briere, Demetrio Carrasco, Philippe Dewet, Philip Dowell, Neil Fletcher, Bruce Forster, John Heseltine, Ed Homonylo, Philip C. Jackson, Eliot Kaufman, Alan Keohane, Dave King, Andrew Leyerle, Neil Lukas, David Lyons, Norman McGrath, Andrew McKinney, Tim Mann, Gunter Marx, Neil Mersh, Howard Millard, Michael Moran, Sue Oldfield, Scot Pitts, Rob Reichenfeld, Julio Rochon, Kim Sayer, Neil Setchfield, Mike Severns, Chris Stevens, Clive Streeter, Giles Stokoe, Scott Suchman, Matthew Ward, Stephen Whitehorne, Linda Whitwam, Francesca Yorke.

Sheridan; National Park Service: Tom Patterson; Philadelphia Convention & Visitors Bureau: Danielle Cohn, Ellen Kornfield, Marissa Philip, San Antonio Convention & Visitors Bureau: Angela McClendon; M&A Design: Ajay Sethi, Mugdha Sethi; AirPhoto USA: Brian Garcia, Shannon Kelley.

Photography Permissions

Dorling Kindersley would like to thank the following for their assistance and kind permission to photograph at their establishments (the establishments are listed in chapter order):

Old Merchant's House, East Village, NY; American Museum of Natural History, NY; Museum of American Folk Art, NY; Studio Museum in Harlem, NY; The Cloisters, NY; Columbia University, NY; Rockefeller Group, NY; Massachusetts State House, Boston; Nichols House Museum, Boston; Trinity Church, Boston; Museum of Fine Arts, Boston; Sackler Museum, Boston; New England Aquarium, Boston; Salem Witch Museum, MS; Plimoth Plantation, MS; Mark Twain House, CT; Florence Griswold Museum, CT; Currier Gallery of Art, Manchester; National Air and Space Museum, Washington, DC; National Museum of Natural History, Washington, DC; National Museum of African Art, Washington, DC; National Museum of American History, Washington, DC; Kenmore House, VA; Library of Congress, Washington, DC; South Carolina State Museum, SC; Stone Mountain Park, GA; Shaker Village of Pleasant Hill, Harrodsburg, KY; Graceland, TN; Historic New Orleans Voodoo Museum, New Orleans, LA; Nottoway Plantation, LA; National Voting Rights Museum and Institute, Selma, AL; Elvis Presley Park, Tupelo CVB; Spertus Museum of Jewish Studies, Chicago; Field Museum, Chicago; Oriental Institute Museum, Chicago; Museum of Broadcast Communications, Chicago; University of Notre Dame, IN; Eiteljorg Museum, IN; Franklin Park Conservatory and Botanical Gardens, OH; Detroit Metro CVB, MI; The Detroit Institute of Arts, MI; Circus World Museum, Baraboo, WI; Walker Art Center, MN; The Mammoth Site of Hot Springs, South Dakota Inc., SD; The Nelson Atkins Museum of Art, MO; City Manager, Vince Capell, St. Joseph, MO; Woolaroc Ranch Museum, OK; Oral Roberts University, OK; Cowboy Artists of America Museum, Kerville,TX; Museum of Indian Arts and Culture, Santa Fe; Millicent Rogers Museum, Taos, NM; Las Vegas Natural History Museum; Cedar City Museum, UT; Museum of Northern Arizona, Flagstaff, AZ; Phoenix Museum of History, Phoenix, AZ; Hopi Learning Center, AZ; New Mexico Museum of Natural History and Science, Albuquerque, NM; Albuquerque Museum of Art and History, Albuquerque; Maxwell Museum of Anthropology, Albuquerque, NM; Hubbell Trading Post, NM; Odyssey Maritime Discovery Center, WA; Seattle Art Museum, WA; National Park Service, OR; Museum of Tolerance, Los Angeles, CA; Balboa Park, San Diego; Hearst Castle, San Simeon; Huntington Library, San Marino; Knotts Berry Farm, Buena Park; Museum of Contemporary Art, LA; *Queen Mary,* Long Beach; Sacramento State Capitol; San Diego Aerospace Museum; San Diego Automotive Museum; San Diego Museum of Art; San Diego Zoological Society; Santa Barbara Mission, CA; Wells Fargo History Museum, San Francisco, CA; San Francisco History Center, San Francisco Public Library, CA; University of California, Berkeley; University of California, LA; Winchester Mystery House, San Jose; Valdez Museum, Valdez, AK; Baranof Museum, Kodiak Island, AK; Ice Museum, Fairbanks, AK; as well as all the other churches, museums, hotels, restaurants, shops, galleries and sights too numerous to thank individually.

Picture Credits

t = top; tl = top left; tlc = top left centre; tc = top centre; tr = top right; cla = centre left above; ca = centre above; cra = centre right above; cl = centre left; c = centre; cr = centre right; clb = centre left below; cb = centre below; crb = centre right below; bl = bottom left; b = bottom; bc = bottom centre; bcl = bottom centre left; br = bottom right.

left; b = bottom; bc = bottom centre; bcl = bottom centre left; br = bottom right.
Every effort has been made to trace the copyright holders and we apologize in advance for any unintentional omissions. We would be pleased to insert the appropriate acknowledgements in any subsequent edition of this publication.

Works of art have been reproduced with the permission of the following copyright holders:

© Albuquerque Museum of Art and History: Museum Purchase, 1993 General Obligation Bond Estella Loretto *Earth Mother, Offerings for a Good Life (No Wa Mu Stio)*, 1994, 548tl; Bell Atlantic Building: *Telephone Men & Women at Work* by Dean Cornwell, 140tl; Columbia University: 84cla; Courtesy Commonwealth of Massachusetts Art Commission: *Civil War Army Nurses Memorial* Bela Pratt, 1911, 138tr; Stained-glass window, Main Stair Hall, 1900/details: *Magna Carta seal 43, Seal of the Commonwealth* (pre-1898) 138cl; *Return of the Colours to the Custody of the Commonwealth*, December 22, 1986, mural by Edward Simmons 1902: 139cbl. © Denman Fink: Detail from *Law Guides Florida's Progress*, 1940, 287tl; Historic New Orleans Voodoo Museum: *Marie Laveau* by Charles M. Gandolfo, 348br; Courtesy Florence Griswold Museum: *The Harpist, A Portrait of Miss Florence Griswold*, by Alphonse Jongers, 1903, 159br; © Georg John Lober: *Hans Christian Anderson*, 1956, 78br. Millicent Rogers Museum: 507tl; Henry Moore Foundation: *Reclining Figure: Hand* (1979), the work illustrated on page 76bl has been reproduced by permission of the Henry Moore Foundation; Sackler Museum, Cambridge, Boston: 149tc; Courtesy Kenneth Treister Holocaust Memorial: © Kenneth Treister, *A Sculpture of Love and Anguish*, 1990, 293cl. Courtesy The Seattle Arts Commission © Jonathan Borofsky: *Hammering Man*, 1988, 617tr. © Victor Arnautoff, *City Life*, Coit Tower, 1934, 702bl. Collection of Spertus Museum: *Flame of Hope* by Leonardo Nierman, 1995, 392crb.

The publisher would like to thank the following individuals, companies and picture libraries for permission to reproduce their photographs:

Alamy Images: Patrick Eden 513tl; Joseph Sohm 652; The African American Museum in Philadelphia: 100cla; Atlanta–Fulton Public Library Foundation, Inc. Courtesy The Atlanta History Center: 260cr;

© Richard Beyer: *People Waiting for the Interurban* 619tl; The Brooklyn Museum of Art: 87bc; Caesars Entertainment: 511br; Bruce Coleman Inc., New York: Jeff Foott 122-123; Bruce Coleman, London: Raimund Cramm GDT 303br; Colorado Historical Society: William Henry Jackson Collection: *Westward HO!* 1904, 612bl; Convention and Visitors Association of Lane County, OR: 634tl; Corbis: 32br, 34br, 38tr, 38cl, 39br, 47b, 49t, 53ca, 95tl, 95b, 127b, 166br, 189tl, 335 (inset), 376-377, 394bl, 433 (inset), 565 (inset), 688br, 730 (inset), 741tr; 752cra, 753bl; AFP 53br; James L. Amos 57tl; Craig Aurness 204bl, 688tr (Hearst Castle, CA Park Service), 692tl; Dave Bartruff 101br, 450tc; Tom Bean 35tl, 41br, 527br, 741bc; Nathan Benn 56cl; Corbis-Bettman 28br, 43b, 44br, 45t, 46tl, 50tl, 50br, 53tl, 53tc, 53tr, 60cl, 90bl, 94bl, 187 (inset), 193bl, 225cl, 225bc, 226cla, 349br, 393crb, 421cla, 450cla, 511bl, 655ca, 661br; Richard Bickel 108cr; Kristi J. Black 689tl; © Carnegie Museum of Art, Pittsburgh, photo by W. Cody 108bc; Steve Chenn 102bl; L. Clarke 54-55; Jerry Cooke 92cr, 243b; Richard A. Cooke 109b, 188bl, 221b; Lake County Museum 9 (inset), 519br; Richard Cummins 30bc, 103tc, 107tr, 338, 339b, 485tc; Jeff Curtes 595bl; Corcoran Gallery of Art, Washington, D.C.; 2003: *Washington Before Yorktown*, 1824-25, by Rembrandt Peale, 42; *George Washington*, 1796, by Gilbert Stuart, 52clb; Dennis Degnan 105tl; Hulton–Deutsch Collection 140 cr; Jay Dickman 219br; Henry Dittz 665br; Duomo 29br; Sandy Felsenthal 484tr; Peter Finger 90tr, 91tr; Kevin Fleming 189cr, 192t, 225tr, 226br, 227br,

238-239, 407br; Owen Franken 29cl; Michael Freeman 198cl; Raymond Gehman 527tc; Mark E. Gibson 194br; Tod A. Gipstein 189br; Farell Grehan 97br, 165bl; Bob Gomes 29tr; The Solomon R. Guggenheim Foundation, NY: (*Man with Arms Crossed*, 1895-1900, by Cézanne, photo by Francis G. Mayer) 82tr; Liz Haymans 593br; Robert Holmes 104bc, 334-335; Dave G. Houser 712cla; George H. H. Huey 503ca; Swim Ink 48ca; Woolfgang Kaehler 34cl; Catherine Karnow 101tc, 512crb; Steve Kaufman 579tr; Layne Kennedy 109tr, 380, 421tr; Dave King 552clb; Bob Krist 61bl, 98tr, 103cl, 352bl, 688clb, 689bl; Owaki-Kulla 242, 353bl; Robert Landau 93tl; Larry Lee 32tr; Danny Lehman 35tr; George D. Lepp 39tr; Craig Lovell 32cl; Georgia Lowell 706bl; James Marshall 517bc; Francis G. Mayer 44tl, 60tr, 81tl, 94crb; Buddy Mays 91cr, 475br; Joe McDonald 65b; Louis K. Meisel Gallery 8-9; Kelly-Mooney Photography 31tr, 96br, 97tl, 199cr; David Muench 33tl, 56bl, 64, 92bc, 106cla, 126, 188tr, 218br, 219cla, 220cla, 224tr, 436, 527cbr, 755tl; Marc Muench 594tr, 595tl, 595crb; Walley McNamee 53crb; © National Portrait Gallery, Smithsonian Institution, Washington, DC, acquired as a gift to the nation through the generosity of the Donald W. Reynolds Foundation, 2003; 203br (*Lansdowne portrait of George Washington*, 1796, by Gilbert Stuart, photo by Archivo Iconografico, S. A.); Richard T. Nowitz 104tl, 191b, 220br, 221tl; Pat O'Hara 610; Douglas Peebles 33bl, 594cl; The Phillips Collection, Washington, D.C.: (*The Luncheon of the Boating Party*, 1881, by Pierre Auguste Renoir (1841-1919), photo by Francis G. Mayer) 210tl; Charles Philip 35bl; Philadelphia Museum of Arts: 105crb; Neil Preston 269bl; Greg Probst 564-565; Carl & Ann Purcell 94tc; Roger Ressmeyer 286br, 608-609, 629tr; Jim Richardson 33cr; Bill Ross 38bl, 63br; Ron Sanford 437b; Paul A. Souders 224b; Kevin Schafer 56tr; Alan Schein 57br, 92tl, 108tl; Phil Schermeister 378cb, 516bc; Flip Schulke 51tr; Michael T. Sedam 34tr, 611b, 750cla; Leif Skoogfors 102cla, 107clb; Lee Snider 61ca, 91bl, 96clb, 100tr, 101cr, 101cb, 106br, 198tr, 218tl, 227tl; Joseph Sohm; ChromoSohm Inc. 39tl, 41tl, 57cra, 217cra; 486b; Ted Spiegel 57crb; Mark L Stephenson 31crb, 755br; David Stoecklein 500-501; Bequest of Mrs. Benjamin Ogle Tayloe, Collection of the Corcoran Art Gallery: 52ctl; Underwood & Underwood 93bl, 264cla, 381b; Ron Watts 32bl, 33tr, 62tr, 93br; David H. Wells 105b; Nick Wheeler 669bcl; Oscar White 53cb; Michael S. Yamashita 96cla, 421b; Bo Zaunders 472-473, 481tl; CURRIER MUSEUM OF ART: 168crb; PAUL FRANKLIN: 539tr; THE FRICK COLLECTION: *Lady Meux* by James Abbot McNeill Whistler, 1881, 80bl;

GETTY IMAGES: Jack Dykinga 26-27; Robert Glusic 648-649; Chris Noble 568; © J PAUL GETTY TRUST: *Adoration of the Magi*, 1495-1505, by Andrea Mantegna, 660tl; GRANGER COLLECTION, NEW YORK: 52tc, 52clb, 52bl, 52bc, 52br, 53bl, 501 (inset); Obama Transition Office/Pete Souza 53cr;

Courtesy of HARLEY DAVIDSON MOTOR COMPANY: 107bl; HELLS CANYON ADVENTURES: 641crb, 641bl; HISTORIC NEW ORLEANS COLLECTION: 351cb; HISTORIC NEW ORLEANS VOODOO MUSEUM: *Portrait of Marie Laveau* 348br; LINCOLN PARK ZOO, Chicago: 396cl;

MARY EVANS PICTURE LIBRARY: 27 (inset), 55 (inset), 123 (inset), 239 (inset), 283 (inset), 377 (inset), 473 (inset), 481bl; 609 (inset); 649 (inset); MASTERFILE: Garry Black 432-433; Bill Brooks 40tr; Gail Mooney 35crb; Randy Lincks 41cr; MGM MIRAGE: 512c; MUSEUM OF FINE ARTS, BOSTON: HU–MFA Expedition *Shawabtis of Taharka* 147tl; Egypt Exploration Fund *Inner Coffin of Nes-mut-aat-neru* 147cl; Ruth & Carl J. Shapiro Colonnade and Vault *John Singer Sargent Murals* 147br; MUSEUM OF INTERNATIONAL FOLK ART, A UNIT OF THE MUSEUM OF NEW MEXICO: Girard Foundation Collection, Photo Michel Monteaux *Toy Horse* Bangladesh, Indian. C. 1960. 547cb;

© 2003 Board of Trustees, National Gallery of Art, Washington, DC: *The Alba Madonna*, 1510, by Raphael (Raffaello Sanzio of Urbino, 1483–1520), Andrew W. Melon Collection: 201tl; NHPA: David Middleton 553 br; NATIONAL MUSEUM OF AMERICAN JEWISH HISTORY: Collection of Congregation Mikveh Israel: 100clb;

NATIONAL MUSEUM OF NATURAL HISTORY, WASHINGTON/© SMITHSONIAN INSTITUTION: Dane Penland 202cr; NATIONAL PARK SERVICE, OR: 637tr; THE NATURE CONSERVANCY: Rich Franco Photography 313b; NELSON-ATKINS MUSEUM OF ART, KANSAS CITY, MISSOURI: *Shuttlecocks* by Claes Oldenburg and Coosje van Bruggen, 1994: 457tl; NEW ORLEANS METROPOLITAN CONVENTION & VISITORS BUREAU: Ann Purcell 344bl; Carl Purcell 346tl;

PEDRO E. GUERRERO © 2002, Talesin Preservation Inc.: 415tl; © COURTESY OF THE PENNSYLVANIA ACADEMY OF FINE ARTS; PHILADELPHIA: Joseph E. Temple Fund, 2003: *The Fox Hunt,* 1893, by Winslow Homer 103br;

REDFERNS MUSIC PICTURE LIBRARY: 49bc; RIVIERA HOTEL & CASINO: 513cr; THE RONALD GRANT ARCHIVE: 666bl; MAE SCANLAN: 202tl; JOHN G. SHEDD AQUARIUM, Chicago: © Edward G. Lines 393tr; SUPERSTOCK: 174tl;

TERRA GALLERIA PHOTOGRAPHY: 624tl;

Courtesy of UNIVERSAL ORLANDO RESORT: 308tl; © 2002 UNIVERSAL STUDIOS, INC.: 308br, 309tl, 309br; VENTANA WILDLIFE SOCIETY: 691cra; VIEWFINDERS: Bruce Forster 623cra, 637ca, 637bl, 639bc; Trevor Graves 613tl; Rich Iwasaki 620tc; Pefley 622tr; Bob Poole 632br; Greg Vaughn 620b, 623tl, 628br, 632cra, 633t, 633crb, 635br, 636cla, 636 br, 638b, 640bl, 641tl; WALLA WALLA CHAMBER OF COMMERCE: 625bl; WALKER ART CENTER, MINNEAPOLIS: *Spoonbridge and Cherry* by Claes Oldenburg and Coosje van Bruggen, 1987-1988, Gift of Frederick R. Weisman in honor of his parents, William and Mary Weisman, 1988: 416tr; © WHITE HOUSE HISTORICAL ASSOCIATION (WHITE HOUSE COLLECTION): 206cla, 206bc, 207tc, 207cr, 207bl (653, 579, 656, 140, 663) Bruce White 195tr (3074); WORDS AND PICTURES: 334bl, 346tl; WORLD PICTURES: 653b, 730-731.

Back Endpaper: CORBIS: Tom Bean, Jan Butchofsky-Houser, Charles Krebs, Owaki-Kulla, Robert Landau, Lester Lefkowitz.

JACKET
Front - DK IMAGES: Kim Sayer clb; HEMISPHERES IMAGES: John Frumm main image. Back - ALAMY IMAGES: Ambient Images Inc. Scott Murphy/cla; DK IMAGES: Demetrio Carrasco tl; Jon Spaul clb; Stephen Whitehorn bl. Spine - ALAMY IMAGES: Ian Dagnall b; HEMISPHERES IMAGES: John Frumm t.

All other images © Dorling Kindersley. For further information see **www.dkimages.com**

Further Reading

Fiction

Winesburg, Ohio Anderson, Sherwood, Random House, 1995.
I Know Why the Caged Bird Sings Angelou, Maya, Random House, 1983.
Midnight in the Garden of Good and Evil Berendt, John, Random House, 1994.
Dandelion Wine Bradbury, Ray, Random House, 1985.
A Walk in the Woods Bryson, Bill, Random House, 1999.
Breakfast at Tiffany's Capote, Truman, Penguin, 1988.
The Awakening Chopin, Kate, Random House, 1985.
The Last of the Mohicans Cooper, James Fenimore, Penguin, 1984.
The Red Badge of Courage Crane, Stephen, Penguin, 1994.
Time and Again Finney. Jack, Simon & Schuster, 1995.
The Great Gatsby Fitzgerald, F. Scott, Penguin, 1994.
The Little Shepherd of Kingdom Come Fox, Jr, John, University Press of Kentucky, 1987.
The Scarlet Letter Hawthorne, Nathaniel, Penguin, 1994.
Farewell to Arms Hemingway, Ernest, Simon & Schuster, 1995.
The Legend of Sleepy Hollow Irving, Washington, Penguin, 1999.
On the Road Kerouac, Jack, Penguin, 1998.
To Kill a Mockingbird Lee, Harper, Warner Books, 1988.
Call of the Wild and Other Stories London, Jack, Penguin, 1995.
A River Runs Through It and Other Stories Maclean, Norman, University of Chicago Press, 2001.
Lonesome Dove McMurtry, Larry, Simon & Schuster, 1986.
Gone With the Wind Mitchell, Margaret, Warner Books, 1993.
Beloved Morrison, Toni, Penguin, 1998.
The Octopus Norris, Frank, Penguin, 1994.
Catcher in the Rye Salinger, JD, Penguin, 1994.
The Jungle Sinclair, Upton, Penguin, 1985.
Uncle Tom's Cabin Stowe, Harriet Beecher, Penguin, 1981.
The Grapes of Wrath Steinbeck, John, Penguin, 2001.
The Adventures of Tom Sawyer, Twain, Mark, Penguin, 1986.
The Color Purple Walker, Alice, Pocket Books, 1990.
Our Town and Other Plays Wilder, Thornton, Penguin, 2000.
A Streetcar Named Desire Williams, Tennessee, Signet, 1989.
Look Homeward Angel Wolfe, Thomas, Simon & Schuster, 1995.

History & Politics

One Nation: America Remembers September 11, 2001 Life Magazine/ Giuliani, Rudolph W, Little Brown & Company, 2001.
The Penguin History of the USA Brogan, Hugh, Penguin, 2001.
An Hour Before Daylight Carter, Jimmy, Simon & Schuster, 2001.
The Civil War: A Narrative Foote, Shelby, Vintage, 1986.
1939: The Lost World of the Fair Gelertner, David, Free Press, 1999.
Dispatches Herr, Michael, Vintage, 1991.
Benjamin Franklin: An American Life Isaacson, Walter, Simon & Schuster, 2003.
Writings Jefferson, Thomas, Library of America, 1984.
Profiles in Courage Kennedy, John F, Perennial Press, 2000.
Profiles in Courage for Our Time Kennedy, Caroline, Hyperion, 2003.
The Columbia Historical Portrait of New York Kouwenhoven, John, Icon, 1972.
John Adams McCollough, David, Simon & Schuster, 2002.
Collected Writings Paine, Thomas, Library of America, 1995.
American Colonies Taylor, Alan, Penguin, 2002.
Civil Disobedience Thoreau, Henry David, Dover, 1993.
Democracy in America Tocqueville, Alexis de, Alfred A. Knopf, 1994.
Writings from The New Yorker White, E.B., Perennial Press, 1991.
All the President's Men Woodward, Bob, and Bernstein, Carl, Simon & Schuster, 1994.

Natural History & Travel

National Audubon Society Field Guide to North American Mammals Whitaker Jr, John O, Alfred A. Knopf, 1996.
North American Wildlife: Wildflowers Reader's Digest Association, 1998.
North American Wildlife: Trees & Non-Flowering Plants Reader's Digest Association, 1998.
America's National Parks Tehabi Books/ Dorling Kindersley, 2001.
National Geographic on Assignment USA National Geographic, 1997.
The Mississippi and the Making of a Nation National Geographic, 2002.
Route 66 Main Street USA Freeth, Nick, Taylor, Paul, Motorbooks Intl, 2001.
Bayou Farewell Tidwell, Mike, Pantheon, 2003.

Art

Twentieth Century American Art Lee Doss, Erika, Oxford University Press, 2002.
Framing America: A Social History of American Art Pohl, Frances K., Thames & Hudson, 2002.

DK publishes an extensive range of guides to the US cities, states, and regions

Our guides are available at all good bookstores, or directly online from us at www.dk.com

DK EYEWITNESS TRAVEL GUIDES

ALASKA

ARIZONA & THE GRAND CANYON

BOSTON

CALIFORNIA

CHICAGO

FLORIDA

HAWAII

LAS VEGAS

NEW ENGLAND

NEW ORLEANS

NEW YORK

PACIFIC NORTHWEST

PHILADELPHIA & THE PENNSYLVANIA DUTCH COUNTRY

SAN FRANCISCO

SOUTHWEST USA & LAS VEGAS

WALT DISNEY WORLD RESORT & ORLANDO

WASHINGTON, DC

DK TOP 10 GUIDES

BOSTON

CHICAGO

HONOLULU & O'AHU

LOS ANGELES

LAS VEGAS

MAUI, MOLOKA'I & LANA'I

MIAMI & THE KEYS

NEW YORK

ORLANDO

SAN ANTONIO & AUSTIN

SAN DIEGO

SAN FRANCISCO

SANTA FE

SEATTLE

VIRGIN ISLANDS

WASHINGTON, DC

DK

LONDON, NEW YORK,
MELBOURNE, MUNICH AND DELHI
www.dk.com